Windows® 98 Secrets®

Windows® 98 Secrets®

Brian Livingston and Davis Straub

IDG Books Worldwide, Inc.
An International Data Group Company

Foster City, CA ♦ Chicago, IL ♦ Indianapolis, IN ♦ Southlake, TX

Windows® 98 Secrets®

Published by
IDG Books Worldwide, Inc.
An International Data Group Company
919 E. Hillsdale Blvd., Suite 400
Foster City, CA 94404
www.idgbooks.com (IDG Books Worldwide Web site)

Library of Congress Catalog Card No.: 97-78218

ISBN: 0-7645-3186-7

Printed in the United States of America

10 9 8 7 6 5 4 3 2

1E/SU/QT/ZY/FC

Distributed in the United States by IDG Books Worldwide, Inc.

Distributed by Macmillan Canada for Canada; by Transworld Publishers Limited in the United Kingdom; by IDG Norge Books for Norway; by IDG Sweden Books for Sweden; by Woodslane Pty. Ltd. for Australia; by Woodslane New Zealand Ltd. for New Zealand; by Longman Singapore Publishers Ltd. for Singapore, Malaysia, Thailand, and Indonesia; by Simron/Intersoft for South Africa; by Toppan Company Ltd. for Japan; by Distribuidora Cuspide for Argentina; by Livraria Cultura for Brazil; by Ediciencia S.A. for Ecuador; by Addison-Wesley Publishing Company for Korea; by Ediciones ZETA S.C.R. Ltda. for Peru; by WS Computer Publishing Corporation, Inc., for the Philippines; by Unalis Corporation for Taiwan; by Contemporanea de Ediciones for Venezuela; by Computer Book & Magazine Store for Puerto Rico; by Express Computer Distributors for the Caribbean and West Indies. Authorized Sales Agent: Anthony Rudkin Associates for the Middle East and North Africa.

For general information on IDG Books Worldwide's books in the U.S., please call our Consumer Customer Service department at 800-762-2974. For reseller information, including discounts and premium sales, please call our Reseller Customer Service department at 800-434-3422.

For information on where to purchase IDG Books Worldwide's books outside the U.S., please contact our International Sales department at 650-655-3200 or fax 650-655-3295.

For information on foreign language translations, please contact our Foreign & Subsidiary Rights department at 650-655-3021 or fax 650-655-3281.

For sales inquiries and special prices for bulk quantities, please contact our Sales department at 650-655-3200 or write to the address above.

For information on using IDG Books Worldwide's books in the classroom or for ordering examination copies, please contact our Educational Sales department at 800-434-2086 or fax 817-421-5012.

For press review copies, author interviews, or other publicity information, please contact our Public Relations department at 650-655-3000 or fax 650-655-3299.

For authorization to photocopy items for corporate, personal, or educational use, please contact Copyright Clearance Center, 222 Rosewood Drive, Danvers, MA 01923, or fax 978-750-4470.

 is a trademark under exclusive license to IDG Books Worldwide, Inc., from International Data Group, Inc.

ABOUT IDG BOOKS WORLDWIDE

Welcome to the world of IDG Books Worldwide.

IDG Books Worldwide, Inc., is a subsidiary of International Data Group, the world's largest publisher of computer-related information and the leading global provider of information services on information technology. IDG was founded more than 25 years ago and now employs more than 8,500 people worldwide. IDG publishes more than 275 computer publications in over 75 countries (see listing below). More than 60 million people read one or more IDG publications each month.

Launched in 1990, IDG Books Worldwide is today the #1 publisher of best-selling computer books in the United States. We are proud to have received eight awards from the Computer Press Association in recognition of editorial excellence and three from *Computer Currents'* First Annual Readers' Choice Awards. Our best-selling *...For Dummies®* series has more than 30 million copies in print with translations in 30 languages. IDG Books Worldwide, through a joint venture with IDG's Hi-Tech Beijing, became the first U.S. publisher to publish a computer book in the People's Republic of China. In record time, IDG Books Worldwide has become the first choice for millions of readers around the world who want to learn how to better manage their businesses.

Our mission is simple: Every one of our books is designed to bring extra value and skill-building instructions to the reader. Our books are written by experts who understand and care about our readers. The knowledge base of our editorial staff comes from years of experience in publishing, education, and journalism — experience we use to produce books for the '90s. In short, we care about books, so we attract the best people. We devote special attention to details such as audience, interior design, use of icons, and illustrations. And because we use an efficient process of authoring, editing, and desktop publishing our books electronically, we can spend more time ensuring superior content and spend less time on the technicalities of making books.

You can count on our commitment to deliver high-quality books at competitive prices on topics you want to read about. At IDG Books Worldwide, we continue in the IDG tradition of delivering quality for more than 25 years. You'll find no better book on a subject than one from IDG Books Worldwide.

John Kilcullen
CEO
IDG Books Worldwide, Inc.

Steven Berkowitz
President and Publisher
IDG Books Worldwide, Inc.

Eighth Annual
Computer Press
Awards ≥1992

Ninth Annual
Computer Press
Awards ≥1993

Tenth Annual
Computer Press
Awards ≥1994

Eleventh Annual
Computer Press
Awards ≥1995

IDG Books Worldwide, Inc., is a subsidiary of International Data Group, the world's largest publisher of computer-related information and the leading global provider of information services on information technology. International Data Group publishes over 275 computer publications in over 75 countries. Sixty million people read one or more International Data Group publications each month. International Data Group's publications include: **ARGENTINA:** Buyer's Guide, Computerworld Argentina, PC World Argentina; **AUSTRALIA:** Australian Macworld, Australian PC World, Australian Reseller News, Computerworld, IT Casebook, Network World, Publish, Webmaster; **AUSTRIA:** Computerwelt Osterreich, Networks Austria, PC Tip Austria; **BANGLADESH:** PC World Bangladesh; **BELARUS:** PC World Belarus; **BELGIUM:** Data News; **BRAZIL:** Annuario de Informatica, Computerworld, Connections, Macworld, PC Player, PC World, Publish, Reseller News, Supergamepower; **BULGARIA:** Computerworld Bulgaria, Network World Bulgaria, PC & MacWorld Bulgaria; **CANADA:** CIO Canada, Client/Server World, ComputerWorld Canada, InfoWorld Canada, NetworkWorld Canada, WebWorld; **CHILE:** Computerworld Chile, PC World Chile; **COLOMBIA:** Computerworld Colombia, PC World Colombia; **COSTA RICA:** PC World Centro America; **THE CZECH AND SLOVAK REPUBLICS:** Computerworld Czechoslovakia, Macworld Czech Republic, PC World Czechoslovakia; **DENMARK:** Communications World Danmark, Computerworld Danmark, Macworld Danmark, PC World Danmark, Techworld Denmark; **DOMINICAN REPUBLIC:** PC World Republica Dominicana; **ECUADOR:** PC World Ecuador; **EGYPT:** Computerworld Middle East, PC World Middle East; **EL SALVADOR:** PC World Centro America; **FINLAND:** MikroPC, Tietoverkko, Tietoviikko; **FRANCE:** Distributique, Hebdo, Info PC, Le Monde Informatique, Macworld, Reseaux & Telecoms, WebMaster France; **GERMANY:** Computer Partner, Computerwoche, Computerwoche Extra, Computerwoche FOCUS, Global Online, Macwelt, PC Welt; **GREECE:** Amiga Computing, GamePro Greece, Multimedia World; **GUATEMALA:** PC World Centro America; **HONDURAS:** PC World Centro America; **HONG KONG:** Computerworld Hong Kong, PC World Hong Kong, Publish in Asia; **HUNGARY:** ABCD CD-ROM, Computerworld Szamitastechnika, Internetto online Magazine, PC World Hungary, PC-X Magazin Hungary; **ICELAND:** Tolvuheimur PC World Island; **INDIA:** Information Communications World, Information Systems Computerworld, PC World India, Publish in Asia; **INDONESIA:** InfoKomputer PC World, Komputek Computerworld, Publish in Asia; **IRELAND:** ComputerScope, PC Live!; **ISRAEL:** Macworld Israel, People & Computers/Computerworld; **ITALY:** Computerworld Italia, Macworld Italia, Networking Italia, PC World Italia; **JAPAN:** DTP World, Macworld Japan, Nikkei Personal Computing, OS/2 World Japan, SunWorld Japan, Windows NT World, Windows World Japan; **KENYA:** PC World East African; **KOREA:** Hi-Tech Information, Macworld Korea, PC World Korea; **MACEDONIA:** PC World Macedonia; **MALAYSIA:** Computerworld Malaysia, PC World Malaysia, Publish in Asia; **MALTA:** PC World Malta; **MEXICO:** Computerworld Mexico, PC World Mexico; **MYANMAR:** PC World Myanmar; **NETHERLANDS:** Computer! Totaal, LAN Internetworking Magazine, LAN World Buyers Guide, Macworld Netherlands, Net, WebWereld; **NEW ZEALAND:** Absolute Beginners Guide and Plain & Simple Series, Computer Buyer, Computer Industry Directory, Computerworld New Zealand, MTB, Network World, PC World New Zealand; **NICARAGUA:** PC World Centro America; **NORWAY:** Computerworld Norge, CW Rapport, Datamagasinet, Financial Rapport, Kursguide Norge, Macworld Norge, Multimediaworld Norge, PC World Ekspress Norge, PC World Nettverk, PC World Norge, PC World ProduktGuide Norge; **PAKISTAN:** Computerworld Pakistan; **PANAMA:** PC World Panama; **PEOPLE'S REPUBLIC OF CHINA:** China Computer Users, China Computerworld, China InfoWorld, China Telecom World Weekly, Computer & Communication, Electronic Design China, Electronics Today, Electronics Weekly, Game Software, PC World China, Popular Computer Week, Software Weekly, Software World, Telecom World; **PERU:** Computerworld Peru, PC World Profesional Peru, PC World SoHo Peru; **PHILIPPINES:** Click!, Computerworld Philippines, PC World Philippines, Publish in Asia; **POLAND:** Computerworld Poland, Computerworld Special Report Poland, Cyber, Macworld Poland, Networld Poland, PC World Komputer; **PORTUGAL:** Cerebro/PC World, Computerworld/Correio Informático, Dealer World Portugal, Mac*In/PC*In Portugal, Multimedia World; **PUERTO RICO:** PC World Puerto Rico; **ROMANIA:** Computerworld Romania, PC World Romania, Telecom Romania; **RUSSIA:** Computerworld Russia, Mir PK, Publish, Seti; **SINGAPORE:** Computerworld Singapore, PC World Singapore, Publish in Asia; **SLOVENIA:** Monitor; **SOUTH AFRICA:** Computing SA, Network World SA, Software World SA; **SPAIN:** Communicaciones World España, Computerworld España, Dealer World España, Macworld España, PC World España; **SRI LANKA:** Infolink PC World; **SWEDEN:** CAP&Design, Computer Sweden, Corporate Computing Sweden, Internetworld Sweden, it.branschen, Macworld Sweden, MaxiData Sweden, MikroDatorn, Nätverk & Kommunikation, PC World Sweden, PCaktiv, Windows World Sweden; **SWITZERLAND:** Computerworld Schweiz, Macworld Schweiz, PCtip; **TAIWAN:** Computerworld Taiwan, Macworld Taiwan, NEW ViSiON/Publish, PC World Taiwan, Windows World Taiwan; **THAILAND:** Publish in Asia, Thai Computerworld; **TURKEY:** Computerworld Turkiye, Macworld Turkiye, Network World Turkiye, PC World Turkiye; **UKRAINE:** Computerworld Kiev, Multimedia World Ukraine, PC World Ukraine; **UNITED KINGDOM:** Acorn User UK, Amiga Action UK, Amiga Computing UK, Apple Talk UK, Computing, Macworld, Parents and Computers UK, PC Advisor, PC Home, PSX Pro, The WEB; **UNITED STATES:** Cable in the Classroom, CIO Magazine, Computerworld, DOS World, Federal Computer Week, GamePro Magazine, InfoWorld, I-Way, Macworld, Network World, PC Games, PC World, Publish, Video Event, THE WEB Magazine, and WebMaster; online webzines: JavaWorld, NetscapeWorld, and SunWorld Online; **URUGUAY:** InfoWorld Uruguay; **VENEZUELA:** Computerworld Venezuela, PC World Venezuela; and **VIETNAM:** PC World Vietnam. 3/24/97

Credits

Acquisitions Editor
Nancy Stevenson

Development Editors
Heidi Steele
Ron Hull

Technical Editor
Greg Guntle

Copy Editor
Tracy Brown

Production Coordinator
Susan Parini

Cover Photo
Images © 1998 PhotoDisc, Inc.
Myrleen Cate/Tony Stone Images

Graphics and Production Specialists
Mario F. Amador
Renée Dunn
Linda J. Marousek
Hector Mendoza
Elsie Yim

Quality Control Specialists
Mick Arellano
Mark Schumann

Proofreader
Arielle Carole Mennelle

Indexer
Nancy Anderman Guenther

About the Authors

Brian Livingston is the author of IDG Books Worldwide's best-selling *Windows 3 Secrets*; *Windows 3.1 Secrets*, 2nd Edition; *More Windows 3.1 Secrets*; and coauthor of *Windows Gizmos*, a collection of shareware and freeware tools and games, and *Windows 95 Secrets*. His books are printed in more than 20 languages. In addition to writing books, Mr. Livingston is a contributing editor of *InfoWorld* magazine, and has been a contributing editor of *PC/Computing*, *PC World*, *Windows Sources*, and other magazines. He was a recipient of the 1991 Award for Technical Excellence from the National Microcomputer Managers Association.

Davis Straub is the coauthor of *Windows 95 Secrets* and technical editor for *Windows Gizmos*. He previously worked as a Windows multimedia software and content developer. He is the former president of Generic Software (a successful CAD software company) and Personal Workstations, Inc. (a successful CAD VAR). When not furiously digging for Windows secrets, he spends his time hang gliding.

This book is dedicated to Margie Livingston and Belinda Boulter.

Acknowledgments

No book is the sole work of its authors. While we focused our efforts on writing and researching this work, many others provided the help we needed to complete it. Belinda Boulter added to many of the chapters, particularly in the "Plug and Play" and "Connectivity" sections. Without her efforts, this book would have been too difficult to write.

We would have been lost and our readers wouldn't have had a readable book, if it weren't for our editor, Heidi Steele. An accomplished author in her own right, Heidi checked everything we wrote and made us rewrite until it was understandable. We can't thank her enough.

We spent a considerable amount of time on the Microsoft Windows 98 beta news groups. Our fellow Windows 98 and Internet Explorer beta testers provided us with crucial assistance and guidance. The beta support people at Microsoft were top notch and deserve great praise from everyone in the industry for their commitment to quality and their willingness to help make Windows 98 a better product.

Throughout this book we have mentioned various beta testers, news group participants, and support personnel who were especially helpful and insightful. Without their assistance *Windows 98 Secrets* would not be nearly as useful.

Contents at a Glance

Acknowledgments ix

Part I: Introduction, Installation, and Startup 1
Chapter 1: Read This First 3
Chapter 2: Installing and Setting Up Windows 98 15
Chapter 3: A Quick Look at Windows 98..69
Chapter 4: A Tutorial for Windows 98..79
Chapter 5: Customizing Your Windows 98 Startup 89

Part II: Interface to the Desktop and the Internet 119
Chapter 6: The Desktop and the Taskbar 121
Chapter 7: My Computer—Folders and Windows 157
Chapter 8: The Explorer 189
Chapter 9: Internet Explorer 225
Chapter 10: Shortcuts at Home and Abroad 261
Chapter 11: The Start Button and Finding 295
Chapter 12: Desktop Strategies—Making Windows 98 Your Own 325
Chapter 13: Documents First 349
Chapter 14: The Recycle Bin: Going Through the Trash 377
Chapter 15: The Registry: The Real User Interface 391
Chapter 16: The Control Panel and Properties 419

Part III: Internet Applications 449
Chapter 17: Dial-Up Networking 451
Chapter 18: Connecting to the Internet..481
Chapter 19: Outlook Express 517
Chapter 20: Windows Messaging 563

Part IV: Connectivity 621
Chapter 21: Calling the Bulletin Boards 623
Chapter 22: Laptop to Desktop 637
Chapter 23: Synchronized Filing—The Briefcase 659
Chapter 24: Networking..675

Part V: Plug and Play 719
Chapter 25: Plug and Play: Device Management 721
Chapter 26: Fonts 751
Chapter 27: Keyboards and Characters 795
Chapter 28: Displays 833
Chapter 29: Printer Drivers...869

Chapter 30: The Mighty Mouse (Other Pointing Devices, Too)..909
Chapter 31: Modems, Serial Ports, and Parallel Ports 943
Chapter 32: Telephony...979
Chapter 33: Disk Tools and File Systems 997

Part VI: DOS Secrets **1051**

Chapter 34: Meet the New DOS . . . Same As the Old DOS 1053
Chapter 35: Configuring Windows 98 Memory...1123

Part VII: Shareware **1151**

Chapter 36: The Best in Windows Shareware..1153

Index **1161**

IDG Books Worldwide, Inc.
End-User License Agreement.......................................**1208**

CD-ROM Installation Instructions **1212**

Contents

Acknowledgments ix

Part I: Introduction, Installation, and Startup 1

Chapter 1: Read This First 3
Why Windows 98 Secrets 3
How to Use This Book 3
This Book's Overall Structure..4
    Part I: Introduction, Installation, and Startup................................4
    Part II: Interface to the Desktop and the Internet 5
    Part III: Internet Applications 5
    Part IV: Connectivity...5
    Part V: Plug and Play 6
    Part VI: DOS Secrets 6
    Part VII: Windows 98 Shareware 6
Getting Commands Right the First Time..6
Finding the Good Parts 7
Getting Technical Support for Windows 98 8
    Online News about Windows 98 9
    Accessing Microsoft Support Newsgroups 10
    Accessing Technical Support on CompuServe.....................................10
    Technical Support for the CD-ROM 11
What Are Windows 98 Secrets? 12

Chapter 2: Installing and Setting Up Windows 98 15
Take a Moment to Reflect 15
    Requirements..16
    Unsupported hardware 17
    Making room for Windows 98 17
    Upgrading DOS to Windows 98 19
    Upgrading from Windows 3.1x...20
Upgrading Windows 95 to Windows 98..26
    Loading the source files...26
    Installing over a network or from a CD-ROM 28
Getting Ready to Start Windows 98 Setup 29
    Back up some files 29
    Changes will be made...30
    Running Setup from DOS or Windows 30
    Setup switches 30
The Setup Process 32
    Starting Setup 32
    Copy files 53
    Finishing Setup 54

Installing Windows 98 Over a Copy of Windows 3.1*x* 54
Adding and Removing Parts of Windows 98 57
Copying All Your Windows 98 Files to a New Hard Disk 58
Installing Windows 98 With Other Operating Systems 60
    DR DOS 60
    Windows NT 61
    OS/2 61
    Uninstalling Windows 98 62
    Back to DOS 7.1 62
    Back to an earlier version of MS-DOS 64
    Back to Windows NT 66

Chapter 3: A Quick Look at Windows 98 ....**69**
    The Desktop 69
    Active Desktop 71
    Single-Click Icons 72
    Finding Stuff the Web Way 73
    The Start Button 73
    What's on the Desktop? 74
    Tune in the Channels 75
    What's in the My Computer Window? 76
    Disk Drives, Folders, and Files 77
    Special Folder Windows 77
    Quitting 77

Chapter 4: A Tutorial for Windows 98 ....**79**
    Starting 79
    Switching Views 79
    Using the Explorer 81
    Creating a Folder or Two 83
    Creating a File 83
    Moving a File 84
    Creating a Shortcut 85
    Deleting a Shortcut 86
    Deleting a File 86
    So What Was the Point? 87

Chapter 5: Customizing Your Windows 98 Startup **89**
    Do I Need to Do This? 89
    How Windows 98 Starts Up 90
    First, the BIOS 90
    Then, DOS 90
    Finally, Windows 98 91
    Msdos.sys 91
    Editing Msdos.sys 92
    Msdos.sys file contents 93
    Msdos.sys options 94
    The Windows 98 Startup Menu 101
    Normal 101
    Logged 101

Safe mode 101
Safe mode with network support 101
Step-by-step confirmation 101
Command prompt only 102
Safe mode command prompt only 102
Previous version of MS-DOS 102
Startup Keys 102
What Gets Loaded When 103
Config.sys 104
Config.sys variables 105
Memory Management 105
Autoexec.bat 106
Multiple Configurations 107
Config.sys 107
Autoexec.bat 108
Multiple Hardware Configurations 108
Changing the Startup Graphic 111
Dual-Boot Configuration 112
The StartUp Folder 113
Temporarily turn off Startup 114
Windows 98 Troubleshooting 115
System configuration utility 116

Part II: Interface to the Desktop and the Internet 119

Chapter 6: The Desktop and the Taskbar 121

What You See Is a Mess 121
First, Your Password 122
The Desktop 124
The invisible grid 125
Changing the font and size of icon title text 128
Changing other properties of the Desktop 130
Putting new items on the Desktop 130
Pasting and undoing actions 130
The Active Desktop 131
The Icons and Items on the Desktop 134
New icons for Desktop items 135
Make your own icons 137
High Color icons 138
Corrupted Desktop icons 139
Scraps 139
The Taskbar and Its Toolbars 140
The Taskbar buttons 140
Drag and wait to a Taskbar button 141
Hiding the Taskbar 142
Sizing the Taskbar 144
Moving the Taskbar 144
Which Desktop edge is best for the Taskbar? 145
Resizing and moving windows on the Desktop 146
The Start button 147

Toolbars 147
The Tray on the Taskbar 149
The clock 150
Sliding windows 153
Task Switching with the Keyboard...154
The Task Manager 155

Chapter 7: My Computer—Folders and Windows...................157

Viewing Your Computer...157
Once is enough 158
My Computer, your computer...158
Changing My Computer to Fred 159
The My Computer Window 159
Folders 161
The special folders in the My Computer window 162
My Computer window properties...162
Drive properties 163
Opening a new window 164
One window or many?...164
Switch to a single window view on the fly 165
Open a window in the Explorer view 166
Closing a folder window..166
Change Your Window View 166
Order the icons 167
Line up your icons 167
Changing the columns in Details view 168
Freshening up the folder window 169
Windows toolbars 169
The Explorer bar 171
Customizing this folder 171
New, Copy, Cut, Paste, Rename, and Delete 173
Creating a folder 173
Moving a file or folder 173
Copying a file or folder...178
Copy with Copy and Paste...179
Cut or Copy now, Paste later...181
Renaming files and folders 181
Deleting files and folders 182
The Undo command 182
Selecting Items in a Window 183
Selecting multiple files and folders 183
Selecting a group of files and/or folders 184
Lasso those icons, cowboys and cowgirls 185
Select everything 186
Select everything but 186
Deselect with Ctrl+hover 186
Select a few bunches of icons 187
Grabbing the icon group 187
Dragging multiple icons 187
Press Esc to cancel...188

Chapter 8: The Explorer **189**

Explorer Basics 189
    The Explorer views a web page 191
    Finding the Explorer 193
    The Windows Explorer and the Start button 194
    Putting the Explorer on the Desktop 194
    Turning My Computer into the Explorer 194
Getting an Overview of Your Computer 196
    Special folders 199
    Two panes — connected and yet independent 200
    Thumbnails 200
Folder Options 201
    Sticky view settings 202
    Seeing all the files on your computer 202
    Seeing hidden folders 203
    Single-click or double-click 204
Navigating with the Explorer 204
    Highlighting a folder icon 205
    Folder icons in the Explorer 206
Two versions of the Standard Buttons toolbar 206
    Making the left pane bigger 206
    Full-screen Explorer 206
    The Network Neighborhood 207
    Using the keyboard with the folder tree 208
Creating New Folders 208
Copying and Moving Files and Folders 209
Creating Two Explorer Windows 210
Explorer (and My Computer) Keyboard Shortcuts 211
Explorer Command Line Parameters 213
Going from the Windows 3.1*x* File Manager to the Explorer 216
    Open, Copy, Move, Delete 217
    Rename 217
    Run 217
    File association 218
    Open an unassociated file 218
    Create directory 218
    Create file 219
    Search or File Find 219
    File view filters 219
    Copy, Label, Format, make a system disk 219
    Change the font used 220
    Print a directory listing 220
    Put two directory listings side-by-side 221
    Sort files by name, date, file type, size 221
    View file contents 222
    Undo and Delete 222
    Share a disk drive or folder 223
    Customize the toolbar 223
    See hidden files 223
    See free disk space 223

File attributes 223
File size..224
Additional File Manager strengths 224
Additional Explorer strengths...224

Chapter 9: Internet Explorer 225

The Windows 98 User/Browser Interface 225
Starting the Internet Explorer 226
New link, new window 227
Channels...227
ActiveX documents..228
Internet Explorer PowerToys 229
Connecting to the Internet with the Internet Explorer 230
Internet Explorer, the 128-bit version 231
Commands to connect to the Internet...232
Managing downloads from the Internet......................................233
Finding web sites 233
Customizing the Internet Explorer Address field.....................233
Creating custom versions of the Internet Explorer 234
Underlining hyperlinks..235
Edit on the Internet Explorer toolbar 236
Make history a quick link 236
Stop dialing up my Internet service provider............................237
Favorites and URL Shortcuts 238
Organizing your favorites 239
URL shortcuts 240
Capturing URLs in a frame..241
Deleting typed URLs in the Address field 242
Converting Netscape Navigator bookmarks to favorites 242
Saving Web Pages on Your Hard Disk 243
Internet Explorer drag and drop links 244
Drag and drop images 245
Saving graphics off the Internet 245
Internet Security..245
Internet Explorer's security options 246
Beneath your level 247
Where are the cookies? 249
Corrupted Files in the Internet Cache Folder...............................250
Corrupt History folder 251
Defrag hangs 252
Filling in forms gives me an error..253
Slow browsing 253
Err Msg: MPREXE caused an invalid page fault in Kernel32.dll ...253
The trouble with web sites 253
Can't find an Internet site 253
File Download dialog box..254
Browse in a new process 255
Browser Wars 255
Keyboard Shortcuts for Internet Explorer 256
Where Does the Search Start? 257
Windows 98 Home Pages..257
Internet Explorer's Easter Egg 259

Chapter 10: Shortcuts at Home and Abroad 261

What's a Shortcut? 261
Shortcuts Are Great 263
    Put your favorite files and programs on the Desktop 263
    Automatically start programs when Windows starts 264
    The Start button is full of shortcuts - add more 265
    Shortcuts in toolbars 266
    Move, copy, print, and view files and folders easily 266
    Start DOS programs by clicking icons 266
    Use a shortcut to do more than one thing at a time 267
    Modify how a Windows program operates 267
    Use a different program to open a document..267
    Put shortcuts to parts of documents on the Desktop..................................268
    Shortcuts to web pages and through the mail 268
    Shortcuts to e-mail recipients and newsgroups 269
Creating Shortcuts 272
    Drag and drop to create a shortcut 272
    Name that shortcut...272
    Get rid of "Shortcut to" 273
    Cut and paste a shortcut 273
    Create a new "unattached" shortcut, then create the link 273
Shortcuts on the Desktop 274
Creating a Shortcut to a Folder of Shortcuts 275
Shortcuts to Folders, Disks, Computers, Printers, and More 276
    Folders 276
    Disk drives 276
    Audio CD 276
    Computers 278
    Printers...279
    Control Panel icons..279
    HyperTerminal connections 280
    Shortcuts to files far, far away 280
    Mail out shortcuts 281
    Paste shortcuts into documents...281
    And on and on..281
Right-Click to a Powerhouse...282
    Send to a Printer 283
    Send to a menu of printers 284
    Send to a computer on the network 284
    Send to SendTo 285
    Send to the Desktop 285
Create Shortcuts to DOS Programs 285
What's Behind the Shortcut? 286
    The Target field 287
    The Start In field 288
    Hot keys 288
    Run in which size window? 289
    Change the shortcut's icon 289
    Find that target 290
    DOS shortcut properties 290
Shortcuts on the Start Button 291
A Shortcut to a Shortcut 291

What Happens If I Move or Delete the Linked File?..291
Shortcuts in the Help Files 292
Creating Application-Specific Paths..293
Disabling Link Tracking 294

Chapter 11: The Start Button and Finding..............................295

Starting...295
Stopping..296
    Shut down 296
    Restart 297
    Restart in MS-DOS mode 297
    Stand by 298
The Start Menu 298
    Programs 299
    Documents 301
    Settings 303
    Find 308
    Help 308
    Run 309
    Log on as a different user 310
Right-Click the Start Button 310
Drop It on the Start Button 311
    The Desktop on the Start menu 312
    Folders in the Start menu folder...312
    Control Panel on a Start menu 313
Keyboard Control of the Start Menus 314
Long Start Menus 315
The Find Function 315
    Finding files or folders 316
    What you can do with Find 321
    Finding a computer on your network 322
    Searching the Internet 322

Chapter 12: Desktop Strategies—Making Windows 98 Your Own 325

It Comes with a Start Button 325
A Desktop Strategy...326
Whose Desktop Is This Anyway? 326
    Setting up Windows 98 for multiple users..328
    Setting up your network logon option 331
    Securing the Windows 98 Desktop 333
    Dealing with a corrupted password file..333
Dealing with the Start Button 334
    The Start button itself 335
    The menus on the Programs menu 336
    Multiple toolbars..336
Pile It on the Desktop 337
Massage the Context Menu..339
The Active Desktop 339
Turn a Folder Window into the Program Manager 340
    The Program Manager window...341

The Explorer as File Manager 343
Use the Real Program and File Managers 345
Making Windows 98 a Complete Operating System 346

Chapter 13: Documents First 349

Document-Centric?..349
Associating Actions with File Extensions 350
Where Are These Actions? 351
Creating and Editing File Types and Actions 351
    Creating a new file type 352
    Editing an existing file type 357
    One application associated with two file extensions 358
    File associations via the Registry...358
    Change the edit application for batch files..360
    Multiple extensions-one application..360
    Editing (not merging) exported Registry files 362
    Re-associating RTF files with WordPad 362
    Associating more than one program with a given file type 363
Opening Unregistered File Types 363
    Opening a registered file type with another application......................364
    Create a default file opener 365
    General actions on any file type 366
    Printing files using other applications..367
Changing BMP Icons to Show Thumbnail 368
Viewing a File Without Starting an Application 369
Easiest Way to View/Open an Unregistered File 371
Documents on the Start Menu 372
New Blank Documents...373
Adding Items to the New Menu 373
    Immediately invoke an application with a new file 375
    Taking items off the New menu...375

Chapter 14: The Recycle Bin: Going Through the Trash 377

What's Recyclable about the Recycle Bin?...377
The Recycled Folders 378
The Recycle Receptacle Icons 379
What Does the Recycle Bin Do? 380
    Delete files from common file dialog boxes 381
    Deleted, what does that mean?..382
    Deleting shortcuts 383
    Right- or left-drag to the Recycle Bin 383
    Shift+Delete 384
Don't Delete Your Hard Disk..384
You Can't Delete My Computer or Other Key Components 384
You *Can* Delete a Floppy Disk...384
Going Through the Trash—Retrieving Deleted Files 385
Emptying the Recycle Bin 386
Remove Files Immediately When Deleted..386
The Recycle Bin and Networks...387
Undelete and Unerase 388

Chapter 15: The Registry: The Real User Interface 391

Ini Files, Forever 391
The Registry Keys and Structure 392
    HKEY_CLASSES_ROOT 393
    HKEY_USERS 394
    HKEY_CURRENT_USER 394
    HKEY_LOCAL_MACHINE 394
    HKEY_CURRENT_CONFIGURATION 395
    HKEY_DYN_DATA 395
    Registry Monitor 395
The Registry Files...397
    What if bad things happen?..398
The Registry Editor 405
    Starting the Registry editor 406
    Editing with the Registry editor 406
    Exporting and importing the Registry 409
    Changing the Registered Owner 413
    Your own tips 414
    Editing the Most Recently Used list 414
    Editing other people's Registries 416
The DOS Version of the Registry Editor 417

Chapter 16: The Control Panel and Properties.....................419

What Will You Find Where?...419
Getting to the Control Panel 420
Shortcuts to the Control Panel..421
    Fine-tuning your Control Panel shortcuts 422
    Assigning hot keys to Control Panel shortcuts 425
Control Panel Settings 426
    Missing files 426
    Add/Remove Programs 428
    Make Compatible 437
    Multimedia 440
    Regional settings 441
    Sounds 441
    TweakUI 446
Properties 447

Part III: Internet Applications 449

Chapter 17: Dial-Up Networking......................................451

Networking? Over a Modem? 451
Dial-Up Networking 453
    DUN version 1.2..453
    Dial-up servers 453
    Network protocols 454
    Dial-up protocols...454
Setting Up Your Windows 98 Computer at Work As a Host 455
    Running fax software and DUN Server together.......................458

Disallowing dial-in access 459
Security...460
Setting Up Your Computer at Home As a Guest...460
General connectoid settings 463
Preparing for server dial-back 464
Dialing into another operating system 465
Copying your DUN connectoids to another computer 466
SLIP server type 467
Setting up your basic telephone information 468
Your modem 468
The Dial-Up Adapter 468
Dialing into the Office 470
Dialing in manually 471
DUN command line parameters 472
Networking over a modem 472
Monitoring your calls 474
Getting your e-mail when you're on the road 476
Printing on the printer at work from home...476
Faxing from work while on the road 477
Play DOS multiuser games over the network 477
Connecting to a Personal Web Server...477
DUN Troubles 479
Compatible protocols...479

Chapter 18: Connecting to the Internet **481**

Your First Point of Internet Attachment 481
Microsoft's TCP/IP Stack 482
Installing an Internet dial-up connection...483
Installing and configuring your modem...483
An Internet service provider account 483
Service provider account information 484
The Internet Connection Wizard..487
Dial-Up Networking...488
Bind TCP/IP to your Dial-Up Adapter...489
Configuring the TCP/IP stack 490
Speeding up file transfers 490
Multiple TCP/IP settings for multiple connections 492
Dial-up connection to your service provider 492
Calling Your Service Provider...497
Automating your DUN logon 500
Making sure you have a good connection..501
Connecting to CompuServe..503
Creating a DUN connectoid for your Netcom account 505
Internet Through Your LAN 506
Configuring the TCP/IP stack for a network adapter.................................506
Connecting a Windows 98 network to the Internet 510
Microsoft Network (not MSN) over the Internet 511
TCP/IP Utilities 511
Displaying your TCP/IP settings 513
Telnet 514
Network file system 514

Chapter 19: Outlook Express..517

Outlook Express Is Configurable 517
Configuring Outlook Express...518
Changing Outlook Express options right away........................519
More Outlook Express changes 522
Shortcuts to Outlook Express 524
POP3, SMTP, and XOVER required 525
Where is everything stored? 525
Transferring Inbox Assistant rules and newsgroup filters to a new computer 526
Connecting with the DUNs..527
Multiple accounts for the same server 529
Corrupted passwords...530
Different service providers for Internet Explorer and Outlook Express 530
Sending messages now or later 531
Outlook Express security...532
Spell checking 532
More than meets the eye 532
Adding Outlook Express messages to the New menu 533
Saving attachments..534
Dragging and dropping messages 535
Sending web addresses 535
UUENCODE or MIME..536
Multiple users and user profiles...537
Where to find more help 538
Messages Formatted in HTML 538
Editing HTML messages 539
Stationery...540
Fancy signatures 542
Pictures and text..543
Outlook Express Mail...544
Multiple e-mail accounts 544
Choose which account to send your messages through 545
Duplicate messages downloaded from the mail server 545
Outlook Express as the default mail program 546
Sending messages to a group 546
Undeleting deleted messages 547
Corrupted folders 548
Waving when the mail arrives..548
Leaving mail on the server 549
Converting the mail 549
Importing and exporting addresses with the Windows Address Book.......................549
Merging Windows Address Books 551
Outlook Express News..551
Anti-SPAM...552
Corrupted newsgroups 553
Beware of cross posters...554
Reading the news offline 555
Keeping newsgroup messages 557
Catching up with the news 557
ROT 13 in the news..558
Multi-part files 558
Connecting to a news server..558

Getting rid of old newsgroup files 559
Windows 98 newsgroups 560
Access to public news servers 561

Chapter 20: Windows Messaging 563

Windows Messaging/Fax Is on the Windows 98 CD-ROM 563
  A little history 564
Quickly Setting Up Windows Messaging to Send a Fax.................................565
Windows Messaging Features 567
Or Lack Thereof 568
Installing Windows Messaging 569
  The Inbox Setup Wizard..569
  Windows Messaging command line parameters 570
Changing the Windows Messaging User Interface 571
Windows Messaging Profiles...571
  Personal Information Store 573
  Address books..574
  Mail delivery services 575
Creating Windows Messaging Profiles...577
  Windows Messaging profiles for multiple users...579
  Editing Windows Messaging profiles 579
  Opening Windows Messaging with a specific profile...................................583
  Choosing mail delivery services..583
  Internet mail properties 584
  CompuServe properties 587
Message Stores 587
  Adding a message store to a profile..588
  Changing a message store's name 589
  Which message store? 590
  Sorting message headers 590
  Messages outside message stores 591
Importing Other Messages 591
Address Book 592
  Changing the name of the address book..593
  The address book's big problem 594
  Opening the address book from the Desktop...595
Creating and Sending Mail 595
  Sending mail 596
  Receiving mail 598
  Using Word to create e-mail messages 599
  Internet Explorer and Windows Messaging...599
  Signatures and ">" indents 600
  Sending mail without using an address book 601
  It's more than e-mail...602
  Sending pointers to attachments 603
Microsoft Mail Workgroup Postoffice 604
  Upgrading your Microsoft Mail message store..605
  Remote access to a Microsoft Mail postoffice 605
Troubleshooting Windows Messaging..609
Microsoft Fax 609
  Faxing from the Start button 610
  Receiving faxes 612

Fax type 613
Sharing a fax/modem on a network 614
Connecting to a shared fax/modem server....................................616
Troubleshooting Microsoft Fax 617

Part IV: Connectivity...621

Chapter 21: Calling the Bulletin Boards 623

A Flash from the Past..623
Creating Connections (Connectoids) 624
Making a Connection 627
Typing on the Terminal 628
Downloading a File..628
Changing the Properties of a Connectoid....................................630
Changing the phone number and modem properties 630
Setting terminal emulation and buffer size 631
ASCII text handling 632
Capturing Incoming Text to a File 633
Answering Incoming Data Calls 634
HyperTerminal vs. Terminal 635

Chapter 22: Laptop to Desktop 637

Connecting Two Computers 637
LapLink for DOS—a history 637
Interlnk—Microsoft's cable network...638
Direct Cable Connection 639
Speed 640
Setup..641
Configuration..642
Network configuration 643
Connected to what? 647
Running Direct Cable Connection...648
Accessing the host 649
Serial ports...650
Parallel ports and cables—one-third the speed of 10Mb Ethernet 650
More on speed...652
Watch the interrupts 653
Using the infrared communications driver 654
Troubleshooting DCC 654
DCC to Windows NT...655
DCC to Windows 3.11..656
Administering the Host Computer's Print Queue 656
So What About LapLink for Windows 98?.....................................657

Chapter 23: Synchronized Filing—The Briefcase 659

Why a Briefcase? 659
Scenario 1..660
Scenario 2..660
Scenario 3..661

What Does a Briefcase Do? 661
Creating a Briefcase 662
Copying Files or Folders into a Briefcase 664
Moving a Briefcase 664
   Moving a Briefcase to a floppy disk 665
   Moving a Briefcase over a network 666
   Moving a Briefcase to a portable computer 667
Opening a Briefcase 667
Copying Files or Folders from a Briefcase 667
Determining the Status of Files or Folders in Your Briefcase 668
Updating Files and Folders 670
   Multiple syncs 671
   Both the original and the Briefcase copy have been modified 672
Breaking the Sync Link 673
Data Files 673

Chapter 24: Networking 675

Basic Network Support 675
What Windows 98 Networking Buys You 677
Quick and Dirty Networking 678
Network Installation 681
   Choosing a client 683
   Choosing an adapter 684
   Configuring resources for the adapter driver 685
   Choosing a networking protocol 688
   Choosing network services 690
   Sharing your resources 691
   Primary Network Logon 693
   File and Print Sharing 693
   Name that computer 693
Microsoft Networks 694
   Configuring your computer as Client for Microsoft Networks 695
   Configuring a Microsoft Networking protocol 697
   Diagnosing Microsoft Networking problems 698
   Putting your DOS machine on your Windows network 698
Novell NetWare Networks 699
   Configuring your computer as Client for NetWare Networks 700
   Using a Windows 98 computer as a NetWare file and print server 701
   Configuring the IPX/SPX-compatible protocol 701
   Configuring the adapter driver 701
Logging onto the Network 702
The Network Neighborhood 704
The Universal Naming Convention (UNC) 704
Resource Sharing 705
Network Security 705
   Choosing between two kinds of security 706
   Setting the type of security 707
Network Administration 708
   Enable remote administration 709
   Install Remote Registry services 711
   Net Watcher 711

System Policy Editor 715
Registry editor..717
System Monitor 717
Network Applications 717

Part V: Plug and Play 719

Chapter 25: Plug and Play: Device Management 721

Peace Among the Pieces 721
32-bit Drivers...722
16-bit Drivers...723
Plug and Play BIOS and Devices...723
Hardware Detection 724
   Detection after Setup 726
   The Registry of hardware 726
Adding New Hardware Drivers 727
Getting the Settings Right 728
The Device Manager 730
   IRQs, I/O, memory addresses, DMA channels 732
   Specific device drivers 733
   Changing device driver settings 733
   PC Cards 739
   Updating device drivers 739
   Resolving resource conflicts the easy way 741
Hardware Profiles 741
   LCDs and external monitors 743
   Hot swapping and hot docking 748
Autorun 748
   AutoEject 749
Sound Cards, CD-ROMs, and LPT Ports 749
Detlog.txt, Setuplog.txt, and Ios.log...750

Chapter 26: Fonts 751

What Are Fonts? 751
Using Fonts in an Application..752
Where Are the Fonts Installed? 752
Installing Fonts 754
   Limits on the number of fonts installed 756
   Where are the missing True Type fonts?...757
   Uninstalling fonts 757
   Viewing fonts 758
   Extended font properties...759
The Kinds and Types of Fonts 760
   Bitmapped fonts 760
   Scaleable fonts 761
   Screen fonts 762
   Printer fonts...763
   Scaleable fonts that work with both the printer and the screen 764

Proportional and fixed-pitch fonts 764
DOS fonts 764
Font Sizes 765
The logical inch 765
The magnifier...768
Can you comfortably read the text?..768
Can you see enough text? 769
Screen Fonts in Detail 769
Font point sizes 772
Fixed-pitch screen fonts...772
Proportional screen fonts 778
Screen Fonts Turn to Flakes 782
TrueType Fonts..782
Freedom from screen fonts and printer fonts.....................................783
The TrueType fonts that come with Windows 98 783
Marlett 789
Send your favorite typeface 789
PostScript 790
OpenType 791
Font Cataloging...792
Sources of TrueType Fonts 793

Chapter 27: Keyboards and Characters...............................795

Fonts and Characters...795
Windows Character Sets 796
The Windows ANSI character set 797
The DOS/OEM character set 800
Easily Typing the Less-Used Characters 802
The U.S.-International keyboard layout 803
Switching between keyboard layouts in one language 808
Accessing unusual characters in Word for Windows 95 and 97............808
Accessing more hidden characters 811
Using Multiple Languages 812
Setting up and using multilingual identifiers 814
Multilingual documents 815
Multilingual proofing tools 817
The web is multilingual 817
Multilingual e-mail...819
Using Keyboard Shortcuts 821
The most important (and poorly documented) shortcuts...................821
Alt+Tab+Tab — the task switcher 825
Using the humble Shift key 825
Caps Lock Notification 827
Keyboard Remap 827
Turning Num Lock On or Off at Boot Time...828
DOS National Language Support 828
Making the Keys Repeat Faster 829
If You Get a New and Different Keyboard 830
Behind the Keyboard Properties 831

Chapter 28: Displays **833**

Getting the Picture 833
Installing a New Video Driver 834
   Installing Windows 3.1 drivers 838
Performance Graphics 839
Setting Windows Magnification 842
   The displayed inch 845
Changing the Size, Color, and Font of Objects on the Desktop 846
   The schemes 847
   The items 848
   Changing the color of Explorer items 850
   Color 851
   Fonts on the Desktop 857
   Size 859
   Registry values 859
   Themes 860
   Smoothing edges in bitmap files 861
The Desktop Wallpaper 861
   Two-color patterned wallpaper 862
   Repeated picture element wallpaper 862
   Big-picture wallpaper 863
   Using RLE files as graphic backgrounds 863
Choosing a Screen Saver 864
   A hot key and Desktop shortcut for screen savers 865
Non-Plug and Play Monitors and Cards 866
LCD Displays and External Monitors 867

Chapter 29: Printer Drivers **869**

Printing Features 869
   32-bit printer driver 869
   Image Color Management 870
   Universal print driver 870
   Unified printer control interface 871
   Spooling EMF, not RAW printer codes 871
   DOS and Windows printing work together 871
   Offline printing 872
   Bidirectional communications 872
   Support for enhanced parallel port 872
   PostScript 872
   Printer shortcuts 873
   Print without installing printer drivers first 873
   Network printer management 874
   NetWare print services 874
   No need for logical port redirection 874
The Printers Folder 874
Drag and Drop to a Printer Icon 876
Installing a Printer Driver 877
Printer Driver Properties 879
   Getting to a printer's properties 880
   Basic printer properties 880
   Separator page 881
   Details 882

Fonts 884
Sharing 886
PostScript properties 887
Defining your own printer 888
Managing Print Queues 888
Deferred Printing 888
Printing with the Task Scheduler 889
Printing to a file..892
Printing to an offline PostScript printer 893
Printing PostScript files 893
Troubleshooting with Windows 98 Help...895
Other troubleshooting strategies 896
Windows Printing System 897
Sharing a Printer..898
Enabling print sharing 898
Actually sharing your printer 899
A shortcut to a shared printer 901
Monitoring shared printer use 901
Slow network printing with MS-DOS programs....................................902
Microsoft Print Server for NetWare 902
Point and Print 903
Automated printer driver installation 904
Point and print to a NetWare server 906

Chapter 30: The Mighty Mouse (Other Pointing Devices, Too) 909

Mouse Basics 909
Double-Clicking Versus Single-Clicking 910
Clicking to open 910
Hovering to select...911
Other places where single-clicking works 912
The Right Mouse Button Stuff 912
Right-clicking My Computer 913
Right-clicking the Start button 913
Right-clicking the Taskbar 913
Right-clicking the time 914
Right-clicking a file icon 914
Shift+right-clicking a file icon 914
Right-clicking a folder icon 914
Right-clicking a shortcut 914
Right-clicking the Desktop 915
Right-clicking the client area of a folder window................................915
Right-clicking the title bar of the active application 915
Right-clicking in a dialog box 916
Right-clicking in the client area of an active application 917
Disabling the right mouse button...917
Driving Your Mouse 917
Setting Up Your Mouse Driver 918
Changing the driver for an existing mouse...918
Adding a driver for a new mouse 922
Configuring Your Mouse Driver Properties 923
Changing the handedness of the mouse buttons..................................924
Changing the double-click speed 925

Changing the double-click height and width 925
Desensitizing dragging 926
Changing mouse menu speed 927
Using different mouse pointers...927
Changing mouse pointer speed 931
Changing mouse speed values in the Registry 932
Changing the pointer trails 934
Creating Your Own Mouse Pointers...935
What Is Missing in Mouse Configuration?...935
Built-in Trackballs and Mice 936
The Mouse in a DOS Box...936
Double-Clicking with the Middle Mouse Button 937
Placing the Mouse Icon on the Desktop 939
Your Mouse in the Device Manager 940
Whipping Your Mouse Clicks into Shape 940

Chapter 31: Modems, Serial Ports, and Parallel Ports 943

Hello, World..943
Windows 98 Communications 944
One modem for all communications software 944
Windows 3.1x communications support 945
DOS communications support 945
Configuring Your Modem 947
Testing your modem configuration 950
Changing basic global modem settings 951
Changing the basic modem connection properties......................................952
Changing more advanced connection settings...955
Changing 16550A UART settings...957
Changing any modem settings 958
Test and Interrogate Your Modem 959
Modem speed 961
Using a modem with DOS programs 964
Two modems 964
Serial and Parallel Ports as Modems 965
Cable Modems 966
Configuring Serial Ports..967
Changing serial port settings 967
Serial port address and interrupt values...968
Changing serial port addresses and interrupts 969
Infrared communications...972
Better Serial Ports 973
Testing Your Internal Modem for a 16550A UART 973
Configuring Parallel Ports..974
Configuring ECP and EPP Ports 975
How Many Serial and Parallel Ports?..976
Port Values Stored in Win.ini 976
Null Modem Cables 977

Chapter 32: Telephony 979

Where Am I Calling From?..979
Preliminary Location Information 980

Dialing Properties...980
    Setting up a new location 982
    Defining how to dial out..983
    Credit card calls 983
    Adding a long-distance carrier/method to your list 984
    The dialing rules 985
Format for the Numbers That You Dial Out 988
    Which local prefixes require long-distance dialing 989
    10-digit phone numbers 989
    Using a prefix other than 1 to dial long distance 990
Phone Dialer 991
    Setting up speed-dial numbers 992
    One click speed dialing 992
    Telephony Location Manager 993
Telephon.ini...993
    Locations section 994
    Cards section..994
    Changes in international dialing access codes...995

Chapter 33: Disk Tools and File Systems 997

The Real Changes...997
    Moving from Windows 3.1*x* to Windows 98 997
    Moving from Windows 95 to Windows 98 1000
Finding Your Disks and the Disk Tools 1002
    The Start button 1002
    A drive icon 1002
    Using help 1003
    In a DOS window 1003
    Device Manager...1003
    File system performance 1004
    Virtual memory performance 1005
    System Monitor 1006
    SuperMonitor...1008
    WinTop 1008
Disk Tools 1009
    ScanDisk...1009
    Defrag, the disk defragmenter..1013
Disk-Related Functions 1016
    Disk space 1016
    Disk Cleanup 1018
    File size and attributes...1018
    Format 1019
    Diskcopy...1019
    Sharing 1020
    Recycle Bin size...1020
    Chkdsk /f 1021
    Troubleshooting disk access...1021
Disk Compression...1022
    Compressed disk size...1023
    Creating a compressed drive 1024
    Changing the size of the compressed drive 1027
    Estimated compression ratio 1028

Other DriveSpace options 1030
Compressing a diskette 1030
The amount of file compression 1031
Compression safety 1031
Dblspace.ini 1031
DriveSpace speed 1032
DriveSpace command line parameters 1032
Upgrading to DriveSpace 3 1033
Compression Agent...1034
Moving to FAT 32 1037
Disk Caching 1039
Setting disk cache parameters 1039
Managing Your Swap Space 1040
Swap space on a compressed drive 1042
Windows 3.1x permanent swap file 1042
Virtual File System 1043
Lock and unlock 1043
Real-mode disk drivers...1043
Long Filenames 1044
Valid filenames 1044
DOS commands and long filenames 1045
Long filenames across the network 1045
Turning off long filename support 1046
Changing Drive Letters for Removable Media 1047
Disk Drive Partitioning...1047
DMF Diskettes 1048
Booting from a Zip Drive 1049

Part VI: DOS Secrets
....**1051**

Chapter 34: Meet the New DOS . . . Same As the Old DOS
..............**1053**

DOS Lives On 1053
DOS and Windows, Together 1053
It Sure Looks Like DOS...1054
A Thing on a Thing...1055
The Real DOS Concerns of Windows 98 Users 1056
What's Left of DOS? 1057
The remaining DOS commands...1058
DOS commands that are no longer around 1060
Cautions about some DOS commands 1061
Wonderful DOS commands 1061
Modifying DOS commands...1062
Shortcuts to DOS commands 1062
DOS commands you shouldn't run...1063
The path and Windows 98 applications 1064
Running DOS Programs 1065
DOS before Windows 1065
DOS in Windows 1066
DOS in MS-DOS mode without a reboot.................................1067
DOS in MS-DOS mode with a reboot.................................1069

DOS in a Box 1069

    DOS window vs. DOS screen 1070

    Sizing and locating the DOS window 1071

    Choosing the DOS display fonts 1072

    Mark, copy, and paste text or graphics to and from the DOS window and the Clipboard....1075

    Changing directories in a DOS window 1075

    Connecting a DOS window to the Explorer 1076

    Expand the DOS window to full screen 1077

    Change the properties of the shortcut to the DOS application 1077

    Background button 1077

    Closing a DOS application 1077

Creating a Virtual Machine for DOS Programs 1078

    Creating multiple shortcuts 1079

    Opening Program Information Files (pifs) 1080

Editing Shortcut Properties 1081

    Program properties 1081

    Font properties 1089

    Memory properties 1089

    Screen properties 1093

    Misc properties 1095

MS-DOS Mode 1099

    Creating an MS-DOS mode shortcut 1099

    Private Autoexec.bat and Config.sys files 1100

    Problems in MS-DOS mode 1105

Creating a Distinct Prompt for DOS 1106

    DOS prompt for Windows DOS sessions 1107

    DOS prompt for MS-DOS mode sessions 1107

A Way Cool DOS Banner Instead 1107

    A banner for MS-DOS mode 1110

    Making your own prompt using Ansi.sys 1110

Windows/DOS Batch Files 1113

    Commands you can use in batch files 1113

    Launching batch files from macro languages 1114

    Finding the Windows folder..1114

Using the Clipboard in DOS Sessions 1116

    DOS applications recognize the Clipboard/Clipbook 1116

    End runs around the Clipboard 1117

    Can't start a DOS app? Delete stuff in the Clipboard..1117

Using the Print Screen Key in DOS Sessions 1118

Getting a Directory Listing 1118

Increasing Files in Config.sys vs. System.ini..1120

Chapter 35: Configuring Windows 98 Memory **1123**

Why Worry About Memory? 1123

No More Real-Mode Drivers 1124

When to Worry About Memory 1125

    Hard disk space for virtual memory 1125

    Windows 98 resources 1126

    Windows 3.1*x* programs spring memory leaks 1127

    Piggy Windows programs 1128

    Memory conflicts 1129

    Fatal exception errors 1129

The Short of It — More Conventional Memory 1129
 DOS programs in Windows DOS sessions 1130
 DOS programs in MS-DOS mode 1130
The PC Memory Map 1132
 UMBs from A to F 1135
Windows Memory Management 1136
 Himem.sys 1136
 Emm386.exe 1137
 Loading drivers in UMBs 1138
 Stack pages 1138
 How Windows uses upper memory 1140
Memory for DOS Programs 1140
 Examples of available memory for DOS programs..............................1141
 More Memory for DOS Programs 1142
Troubleshooting Memory Conflicts 1147
Using Mem to Determine Available Memory 1147
Windows 98 and DOS Games 1149

Part VII: Shareware **1151**

Chapter 36: The Best in Windows Shareware **1153**

What Is Shareware? 1153
What Is Freeware? 1153
The CD-ROM and Software are Copyrighted 1154
How Do I Get Technical Support? 1154
What Do I Get if I Register? 1155
Shareware Registration from Outside the U.S. 1155
Why Have Shareware Registration Notices? 1156
What is the Association of Shareware Professionals? 1156
 The ASP Ombudsman program 1156
 General ASP license agreement..1157
Tips for New Windows Users 1158
 How to add a program to a new directory or folder 1158
 How to add an application to your path 1158
 How to make an application run when you start Windows 98...............1159
The Best Is Yet to Come 1159

Index **1161**

IDG Books Worldwide, Inc. End-User License Agreement **1208**

CD-ROM Installation Instructions **1212**

Part I

Introduction, Installation, and Startup

Chapter 1

Read This First

In This Chapter

▶ Why you need a book like *Windows 98 Secrets*

▶ Finding the section with the answers to your questions

▶ Brief descriptions of what you will find in each section of the book

▶ How to correctly type Windows 98 commands as used in this book

▶ Where to get the best technical support

Why Windows 98 Secrets

Windows 98 is a large and complicated piece — actually many pieces — of software with thousands of features and capabilities. Microsoft focused on writing the code for the operating system as its primary task. Documentation was a secondary consideration.

Windows 98 is open to a great deal of customization. You have the opportunity to turn it into your personal operating system. *Windows 98 Secrets* provides you with the (often secret) knowledge that you need to take charge of Windows 98 and make it behave properly.

Windows 98 isn't that great the way it comes out of the box, or on your new computer. If you don't change it to respond to how you work with your computer, you just aren't going to be that happy with it. Microsoft has provided many ways to change it. Other programmers have developed tools based on the Windows Explorer extensions that add great functionality. We show you how to find these tools and use them.

How to Use This Book

If you haven't yet installed Windows 98 on your existing computer, turn to "The Setup Process" in Chapter 2.

If you want a feel for Windows 98 (assuming that it is already installed) turn to Chapters 3 and 4. These chapters provide a quick look at Windows 98 and a basic tutorial to get you familiar with the Windows 98 Desktop.

More detailed information on all aspects of the Windows 95 user interface, including using the Internet Explorer, is provided in Part II. Go to the chapter that addresses the part of the Windows interface that you are most interested in.

If you want to connect to the Internet and send e-mail, turn to Part III. We discuss how to create a Dial-Up Networking connectoid, hook up with an Internet service provider, and send e-mail using Outlook Express or Windows Messaging.

You can use Windows 98 to communicate with bulletin board operators, between your laptop and desktop computer, and over your local area network. Turn to Part IV for details on how to configure and use these communications options.

Windows 98 comes with routines to automatically detect the hardware in your computer. This doesn't mean that you won't need to or want to make some changes in how that hardware is configured. Part V covers the most common hardware types that are found in computers today. Turn to the chapter that covers the hardware that interests you.

If you have DOS programs that you continue to use, you will be happy to know that Windows 98 provides a robust DOS environment and lots of services to help you better use these older applications. Turn to the two chapters in Part VI to learn (among other secrets) how to customize the DOS environment for each of your DOS applications.

Finally, Part VII provides you with some software help and fun to go with your new operating system.

This Book's Overall Structure

Windows 98 Secrets is organized into seven parts:

Part I: Introduction, Installation, and Startup

Part II: Interface to the Desktop and the Internet

Part III: Internet Applications

Part IV: Connectivity

Part V: Plug and Play

Part VI: DOS Secrets

Part VII: Windows 98 Shareware

Part I: Introduction, Installation, and Startup

This part summarizes the features of Windows 98 and explains how Windows 98 differs from previous versions of Windows. It also details the installation procedures required to get Windows 98 up and working on your computer. If you already have Windows 98 installed, you can go on to the next chapters.

In addition, Chapters 3 and 4 will familiarize you with the underlying logic of the Windows 98 user interface. If you read and carry out the procedures in these two chapters, it will be that much easier for you to become proficient at using Windows 98.

In Chapter 5 we get into the messy details about how Windows 98 starts up and how to change that behavior.

Part II: Interface to the Desktop and the Internet

Most of us think of the user interface as Windows 98, forgetting all that is going on in the background. This part goes into detail about every aspect of the Windows 98 user interface. We discuss the Windows 98 Explorer, the Internet Explorer, and the Active Desktop, providing you with the knowledge you need to use and control Windows 98 and its applications.

We discuss the Desktop, the My Computer and Explorer windows, how to manipulate files, and how to access the Internet. If you want to see how to use shortcuts, check out Chapter 10. In Chapter 12, we show you some major strategies for dealing with your Desktop.

Part III: Internet Applications

Windows 98 provides a wealth of tools to facilitate communication. Dial-Up Networking gives you a way to hook up two computers or connect your computer to the Internet. Once you've connected to the Internet, you'll want to send and receive e-mail.

Microsoft first released Windows Messaging (as Exchange 4.0) with Windows 95, and it hasn't updated it for Windows 98. You have to download Windows Messaging yourself from Microsoft's web site if you want to install it on a new computer. Outlook Express comes with Windows 98 and works well as an Internet/Intranet e-mail client.

Part IV: Connectivity

You can connect to bulletin boards using HyperTerminal, connect your portable to your office network using Direct Cable Connection, and send e-mail through your local area network or over the Internet. Using Windows 95's advanced networking clients, you can connect your computer to any of the popular local area networks.

The Windows 98 Briefcase helps you make sure that both of your computers have the latest copies of your files and documents.

Part V: Plug and Play

This part tells you how to make changes in the Windows 98 configuration of your hardware. We introduce you to the Device Manager, the Fonts and Printers folders, and new characters sets, and we tell you how to set up your display and change your Desktop. Windows 98 comes with some powerful disk and file management tools that you'll want to learn about so you can protect your data.

Modems, ports, and the operating system's phone-management capabilities are all covered in this section.

Part VI: DOS Secrets

This part gives you the complete story on how to continue running DOS applications and take advantage of the DOS services provided by Windows 98. You can run DOS programs in a sizable window using TrueType fonts, or you can run them full screen. You can tailor each DOS virtual machine (the environment surrounding your DOS application) to provide just the right amount of memory and other resources.

Part VII: Windows 98 Shareware

Shareware authors have been busy creating Windows 98-specific software to give you added features, more functionality, and more control. We provide you with the best Windows 98 shareware and freeware available.

Getting Commands Right the First Time

You'll be able to use the secrets in this book faster if you know exactly how to type the many Windows commands shown in the text.

Throughout this book, we've indicated many commands like this:

```
WORDPAD {/p} filename
```

or

```
Wordpad {/p} filename
```

In this command, *filename* is shown in *italics* to indicate that you should change *filename* to the actual name of the file you want to open in the WordPad text editor. The command /p is shown in curly braces {like this} to indicate that this *command line parameter* is optional. You should *not* type the curly braces if you decide to add /p to this command. Because Windows often uses square brackets [like this] to indicate the beginning of sections in initialization *(ini)* files and in the text version of the Registry, we do not use square brackets to indicate optional parameters. If you see a line that contains square brackets, you must type the square brackets along with the rest of the line.

If you want to print the Readme.txt file using WordPad, for example, you could click the Start button on the Taskbar, click Run, and then type this line followed by Enter:

```
Wordpad /p Readme.txt
```

When a command that you should type appears within a paragraph, it is shown in **boldface**. Often, you can enter commands in any combination of upper- and lowercase — in all lowercase, ALL UPPERCASE, or A mixture Of both. However, some command line parameters, such as /p, are case sensitive. When something you need to type is case sensitive, we let you know.

Whenever you see the term *filename* in italics, you can change it to any form of a valid filename that DOS or Windows will recognize, including drive letters and directory names. For example, if C:\Windows\Command is your current folder, any of the following names for the Readme.txt file are valid in this WordPad command:

```
WORDPAD README.TXT
Wordpad Readme.txt
WORDPAD C:\WINDOWS\COMMAND\README.TXT
WORDPAD \WINDOWS\COMMAND\README.TXT
```

We denote special keys on your keyboard with an initial capital letter, like this: Enter, Tab, Backspace, Shift, Alt (Alternate), Ctrl (Control), and Esc (Escape). When you see a phrase such as *press Enter*, you know not to type the keys *e*, *n*, *t*, *e*, and *r*, but to press the Enter key.

If one of the shift keys (Shift, Alt, or Ctrl) should be *held down* at the same time that you also press another key, the two keys are written with a plus sign between them. For example, *press Ctrl+A* means *hold down the Ctrl key, then press the A key, then release both keys.*

If you are supposed to *let up* on a key *before* pressing another one, those keys are separated by commas. If we say *press Alt, F, O,* this means *press and release Alt, then F, then O.* This sequence activates the menu bar of a Windows application, then pulls down the File menu, then executes the Open command. This is the same as saying *click File, Open.*

In this book, we do not indicate a keyboard-only procedure every time we describe how to do something with your mouse. The phrase *click File, Open* always means *click the File menu and then click the Open command,* but it can also mean *press the keys on your keyboard to issue the File, Open command.*

Finding the Good Parts

Each chapter begins with an introduction that gives you a quick idea of the neat tricks in store in that chapter. The summary at the end of each chapter provides a more detailed look at what you can expect to learn in the chapter.

When we discuss a secret, an undocumented feature, a tip, or a set of steps to carry out a specific task, you'll see an icon in the margin of the page. If you want to just hit the high points of this book, you can go from icon to icon, reading the surrounding paragraphs for helpful supporting material.

Secret

The secret icon indicates some useful information that Microsoft would rather that the end user not be aware of. Microsoft feels that the rest of us need to be protected from ourselves, so it would prefer that you didn't mess with the Registry, for example.

Undocumented

An undocumented feature is an aspect of Windows 98 that really should be explained, but for some reason got left out of the manual. Windows 98 is filled with helpful features that the programmers put in but the documenters didn't have an opportunity to tell you about.

Tip

Tips are just that — little explanations about how to do a certain task in a particularly nifty manner. Windows 98 gives you lots of ways to do various things, and the documentation from Microsoft misses quite a few of them.

STEPS

We often give you step-by-step instructions on how to carry out a specific task. One of our goals in creating these steps is to make sure that nobody gets lost. So even if you're unfamiliar with the theory, we include enough details in the steps for you to complete specific tasks. You can breeze through some of the steps as you learn more about Windows 98.

Getting Technical Support for Windows 98

All Windows programs (and books about Windows programs) have bugs. This includes all retail Windows software and all shareware featured in *Windows 98 Secrets*. Every program, no matter how simple, has some unexpected behavior. This is the nature of software, and existing bugs are usually fixed and new ones introduced with the release of a newer version.

It is not possible for the coauthors or IDG Books Worldwide to provide technical support for Windows 98 or for the many DOS and Windows applications that may cause conflicts in your system. For technical support for the shareware on the CD-ROM, see the section "Technical Support for the CD-ROM" later in this chapter, and the discussion of this topic in Chapter 36.

For technical support for Windows 98, you will be better off contacting Microsoft directly — or using electronic support (which we describe in a moment).

Microsoft provides telephone technical support for its DOS and Windows products through these numbers:

Type of Support	*Number to Call at Microsoft*
Microsoft Windows 98 Support 90 days of free support starting with your first phone call	425-635-7000 905-568-4494 (Canada)
Microsoft Pay-Per-Call Support ($35/incident)	900-555-2000 (U.S.) or 800-936-5700 (U.S.) 800-668-7975 (Canada)
Microsoft Foreign Pay-Per-Call Support	425-635-3909
Microsoft International Support (for referral to a non-U.S. office)	425-882-8080
Microsoft Windows Environment	425-637-7098
Microsoft Download Service (BBS)	425-936-6735
Microsoft Fast Tips — automated touch tone	800-936-4200 (U.S.)

Secret

The best technical support (in our humble opinion) has *never* been provided on phone lines — it has always been provided (this is the secret) on Microsoft's newsgroup server (see the "Accessing Microsoft Support Newsgroups" section). This server replaces Microsoft's technical support forums on CompuServe (although you can still get help on CompuServe in the same forums, which are now managed by Wugnet).

Online News about Windows 98

If you don't already have a modem, we encourage you to buy the fastest modem available — 56Kbps — and start taking advantage of online services, newsgroups, and web sites for the excellent technical support and news they provide.

Here are some good places to seek technical support and read the latest news about Windows 98:

Where to Get Help	*How to Get There*
WWW	http://www.microsoft.com/supportnet
MSKB	http://premium.microsoft.com/support/
CompuServe	Type **GO WINNEWS**
AOL	Go to the keyword Winnews
Prodigy	Type **Jump Winnews**
FTP	ftp://ftp.microsoft.com/PerOpSys/Win_News

In "Windows 98 Home Pages" in Chapter 9 we provide a number of web addresses for Windows 95 and 98 support.

Accessing Microsoft Support Newsgroups

The best place to get Microsoft support is from the Microsoft support newsgroups. These newsgroups combine peer support (for the most part), support from Microsoft volunteers (MVPs, ClubWin, and ClubIE members), and every now and then (depending on the newsgroup), actual support engineers from Microsoft.

Microsoft hosts the newsgroups on its news server, msnews.microsoft.com. While some Internet service providers carry the newsgroups, they aren't generally available to other news servers at Internet service providers. To access the newsgroups, choose msnews.microsoft.com as your news server (or as one of a number of news servers) in your newsgroup reader. Outlook Express, the mail and news reader that comes with Windows 98, allows you to subscribe to multiple news servers.

Log on to the Microsoft news server after logging on to your Internet service provider. Choose from the long list of product and interest area-specific newsgroups hosted by Microsoft and be prepared for a lot of reading. You can start here: http://support.microsoft.com/support/news/. Turn to "Windows 98 Newsgroups" in Chapter 19 for a list of Microsoft Windows 98 support newsgroups.

If you want actual one-on-one contact with Microsoft support engineers, you are pretty much going to have to pay for it on a per-contact or contract basis. You get support for the first ninety days, but after that it's pay as you go.

Accessing Technical Support on CompuServe

The CompuServe Information Service (CIS) is a worldwide computer service (one of many). Many vendors of Windows products maintain forums on CompuServe. A *forum* is a message area that technical support people may monitor, answering questions and comments left by users of each vendor's products.

To get electronic technical support from Wugnet on CompuServe, for example, you call a CompuServe local number with your modem, and then type **GO MICROSOFT** at any CompuServe prompt to get to the Microsoft Connection. You will see a list of services, including several Microsoft Connection forums. You can also go to the Microsoft Knowledge Base from this area.

You can type **GO WINNEWS** to go to the WinNews forum and get the latest information about Windows 98. The Microsoft Knowledge Base is available at **GO MSKB**. For Windows 98 shareware, type **GO WINSHARE** or **GO WUGNET**. To get to the Windows 98 help switchboard, type **GO WIN98**.

If you need support from someone other than Wugnet, type **GO SOFTWARE** or **GO HARDWARE**. You will see a listing of scores of companies, each with its own forum or forums filled with technical messages posted by company technicians and users.

Once you're in the forum for your particular vendor, choose the menu option Announcements from Sysop. This displays a listing of system operators (sysops), along with the latest news about the forum, such as new program enhancement files you can copy (download) to your computer, for example. Write down the name and CompuServe number that corresponds to the sysop in your particular area of interest. Then switch to the Messages section of the forum, compose a detailed message about your problem, and address it to the number of the sysop you wrote down.

When you *post* a message in this way, it is seen not only by the sysop you addressed it to, but also by anyone else who reads the messages for that forum. Check the Messages section 24 to 48 hours later, and you'll probably find several responses. Some of them will likely be from people who are not employees of the vendor, but are more expert users of the company's products than many employees!

To gain access to CompuServe, call the Customer Service Dept. at 800-848-8990. Customer service is available 8 a.m. to 1 a.m., Eastern Time, Monday through Friday, and 10 a.m. to 10 p.m. Saturday, Sunday, and holidays. CIS will send you a packet of information on how to find the closest local number in your area, and how to use the service.

Many Windows programs include a coupon good for a free trial membership on CompuServe as well as information on how to reach that vendor's forum. You should look for these valuable free offers when you open the box of software.

Technical Support for the CD-ROM

If the CD-ROM disc that comes with this book is damaged, you should of course contact IDG Books Worldwide, which is committed to providing you with a CD-ROM disc in perfect condition.

However, the coauthors of this book and IDG Books Worldwide are not familiar with the details of every program on the CD-ROM and do not provide any technical support for the programs on the CD-ROM. The programs are supplied as-is. Most shareware authors, but not all, provide technical support to users after they register. Some shareware authors provide limited technical support to unregistered users if they have problems installing the software. In either case, the best way to get technical support is to look in the text file or help file that accompanies each program and send e-mail to the address listed there. Some shareware authors also provide technical support by fax or by U.S. mail.

Shareware authors do not usually have a technical support telephone line, although some do for registered users. If a program is freeware, it probably has no technical support. In this case, if a program does not work on your particular PC configuration, you probably will not be able to obtain technical support for it. See Chapter 36 for further information on the CD-ROM and its contents. See the complete text of the IDG Books Worldwide License Agreement at the back of this book for a thorough discussion of the uses and limitations of the CD-ROM and its contents.

What Are Windows 98 Secrets?

Where do secrets come from? And what makes something a secret or an undocumented feature?

All the people presently working at Microsoft who have worked on Windows 98 taken together do not know everything about Windows 98. Windows 98 is too complex to be completely understood. Windows 98 is a very big piece of software. In fact, there is no way you can really call it a *piece* of software. A typical setup includes more than 10,000 files — and many more that are on the Windows 98 CD-ROM are not copied to your hard disk.

Many different programmers have worked to create Windows 98 — it's an evolving operating system. Much of its core functionality is found in Windows 386 version 2.0 and later versions of Windows. Because it has been created over time, because so many people have been involved in it, and because it is so multifaceted, no one person can document or even be aware of it all.

Windows 98 resembles an organism in its complexity. In the same manner that there isn't a book that completely describes a dog, there isn't a manual that completely describes Windows 98. We have to make do with books that help us understand dogs and operating systems. (No implication here that this operating system is a dog.)

As we wrote this book, we had to rely on our own experience of Windows 98 as the rock bottom guide to what Windows 98 truly was. It didn't matter to us what was written about how it was supposed to work. What mattered was how it, in fact, did work. It is our experience that we have written about in this book.

We had plenty of help from the many participants on the Microsoft support newsgroups. These newsgroups weren't available when we first wrote *Windows 95 Secrets*. While there is much that is of little interest discussed in these newsgroups, once every 1,000 messages or so, a real nugget of clear thinking arrives. We thank those newsgroup participants who made an effort to help their fellow man at no evident reward to themselves. Wherever we use one of their generously and freely provided secrets, we give them their much due credit.

Web sites devoted to Windows 95 and Windows 98 have proliferated, and a number of them are quite good. We have learned a great deal from several of them. Throughout the book, we provide web addresses for the most technically adept sites.

Microsoft has significantly expanded access to its Knowledge Base through its web site. It has also added links from Windows 98 online help to the Knowledge Base. We found the knowledge links to be less than helpful (as they restate the obvious), but we assume that they will improve with time. There are more substantial Knowledge Base articles that are well worth the effort we expended in finding them, and we have mentioned their URLs throughout the book.

The people responsible for the documentation of Windows 98 at Microsoft are under the impression that you don't read the documentation. Maybe you just don't read *their* documentation. We feel that Microsoft is justified in its cynicism, whatever the cause, and it really makes little sense for the company to write something that you won't read.

The documentation writers at Microsoft can't write a book about Windows 98 secrets, because they are obliged to maintain that there aren't any. They can't poke at the rough edges of the operating system and give you workarounds, because they need to put the operating system in the best light. Some areas just don't get mentioned.

We are not so constrained. So when we see something that definitely shows that an operating system is the handiwork of human beings, we point out how to get around its shortcomings.

The "secrets" and "undocumented features" were there waiting for us and others to find and document. The official documenters had their hands full with other issues. All of us taken together still haven't gotten it all down on paper.

Something is a "secret" or an "undocumented feature" if it is useful and isn't found in the documentation (either in the "manual" or in the online help) that you get when you purchase Windows.

This book is meant to be a reference work. It doesn't read like a novel (well, actually some reviewers have said that our previous book did, so just maybe . . .). If you want to know more about an area, you should follow along on the computer as you read through the steps that we detail.

We feel that if you find just one really clever trick that helps you use Windows 98, then your purchase of this book will be worth it. We have striven to provide you many more than one really neat insight into how to effectively master this operating system.

Because the world of computers is increasingly online and wired together, this book is just one way of obtaining the information you need to better use Windows 98.

At press time for this book, the U.S. Dept. of Justice was considering an injunction against Microsoft to prevent the company from including its Internet Explorer browser in Windows 98. This book assumes that Internet Explorer is installed as part of Windows 98. If you do not have access to a copy of Internet Explorer, you can download it from Microsoft's website at http://www.microsoft.com.

We hope you enjoy this book.

Summary

- ▶ Because plenty is missing from Microsoft's documentation of Windows 98, it's difficult to find out how to access all its power.

- ▶ If you have a question about Windows 98, use this chapter to find out where you can turn in this book to find the answer.

- ▶ We tell you how to recognize commands that you need to type from your keyboard.

- ▶ We describe icons, step-by-step lists, and other shortcuts that will help you find the best parts of the book.

- ▶ We tell you how to get the best technical support for Windows 98, by phone from Microsoft and electronically through the Microsoft support newsgroups.

Chapter 2

Installing and Setting Up Windows 98

In This Chapter

We discuss how to install and set up Windows 98 on your hard disk on a single computer. You can start from a computer with only DOS, a computer with Windows 3.1*x*, or a Windows 95 computer.

▶ The minimum requirements for installing and running Windows 98

▶ How to get enough free hard disk space to run Windows 98

▶ Protecting your DOS files from being erased by Windows 98 Setup

▶ Applets that Windows 98 forgot

▶ Problems setting up Windows 98 from a network server or CD-ROM drive

▶ A guided tour through the setup process

▶ Installing Windows 98 on Windows NT and OS/2 computers

▶ Uninstalling Windows 98

Take a Moment to Reflect

In this chapter we discuss how to install and set up Windows 98 on a single standalone computer. By *standalone* we mean the computer can (and will) boot Windows 98 from its local hard disk without requiring any connection to a network. The standalone computer can be attached to a network and operate as a server on a peer-to-peer network. A standalone computer can stand alone but is not necessarily unconnected.

Windows 98 can also be installed on a network server, allowing network client computers to use and share this single copy of Windows 98. While we don't discuss this type of installation here, you can turn to Chapter 24 for a discussion of networking.

Requirements

Before you install Windows 98, you'll want to take stock of your situation. If you have just bought a new computer and Windows 98 is already installed, all you need to do is click the Start button, Settings, Control Panel, Add/Remove Programs icon, and Windows Setup tab to add or remove optional components of Windows 98. If you have an older computer, you need to be sure that it meets the requirements for Windows 98 shown in Table 2-1.

Table 2-1	Hardware Requirements for Installing and Running Windows 98
Component	**Requirements**
Processor	486/66 or greater
Memory	8MB of RAM is required for Windows 98. If you want the Internet Explorer/Windows 98 interface to seem responsive or if you use Windows Messaging, 16MB is much better. If you keep a few applications open at once, 32MB and beyond is even nicer.
Video	VGA is the minimum, with SVGA recommended by Microsoft. Larger monitors and higher resolution give you more real estate for multiple applications or larger areas for more text, numbers, and so on. Accelerated display cards make a real difference. We recommend at least 800×600 and 256 colors. Almost all new video cards surpass these minimum standards.
Disks	A 200MB hard disk partition is about the minimum you can get away with and still install some Windows applications. Windows 98 in its stripped-down configuration requires 135MB, and in this state it is missing a lot of functionality. You need at least 147MB of free disk space to install Windows 98 in its most stripped-down state (additional hard disk space is required for temporary files during the install process). You need less free disk space if you are installing Windows 98 into an existing Windows directory. 190MB or more of free disk space is required for a full install. You must have a file allocation table (FAT or FAT-32) disk partition (required if you are running DOS and/or Windows 3.1x). Computers that run Windows NT or OS/2 do not necessarily have FAT partitions on their hard disks.
Others	Windows 98 takes advantage of modems, CD-ROM drives, sound cards, midi add-on cards, accelerated video, network cards, joy sticks, and so on.

Whether you will be happy upgrading an existing computer to Windows 98 is heavily dependent on the whether your hardware is up to the task. As you can see, there are significant hard disk and memory requirements. If you can't come close to meeting them, you might want to leave well enough alone. If this is the case, but you want the power of Windows 98, consider purchasing a new computer.

Unsupported hardware

The Windows 98 CD-ROM comes with a very long list of hardware drivers, but it doesn't come with drivers for everything. There may not be any specific drivers for your particular piece of hardware, so you may need to use your real-mode drivers (those that work with DOS or Windows 3.1*x*). Otherwise, you will need to get new Windows 98-specific drivers from your hardware manufacturer or from the Windows Update site on the Microsoft web site (click Start, Settings, Windows Update).

Windows 98 doesn't support some older CD-ROM drives with 32-bit drivers and requires that you keep calls to their existing real-mode drivers in your Autoexec.bat and Config.sys files. If you remove these drivers, you will not be able to access your CD-ROM. To see which CD-ROM drives are not supported, check out the Microsoft Knowledge Base article at http://premium.microsoft.com/support/kb/articles/q131/4/99.asp.

If your CD-ROM drive doesn't have a 32-bit driver, Windows 98 won't cache the drive. During Windows 98 Setup, if Windows 98 recognizes that you have a 16-bit driver, it will automatically run SmartDrive (smartdrv.exe in the \Win98 folder of the Windows 98 CD-ROM) to speed up access to data on your CD-ROM during the setup process. Setup will also automatically install SmartDrive on your system and put a call to SmartDrive in your Autoexec.bat file.

16-bit CD-ROM drivers are also required in MS-DOS mode. If you exit Windows 98 to MS-DOS mode, or boot your computer to the command prompt instead of into Windows 98, you won't have access to your CD-ROM unless you have loaded the real-mode drivers.

You are most likely going to be setting up Windows 98 off your CD-ROM drive. Unless you are upgrading from Windows 95, you'll want to be sure that you can access your CD-ROM using the real-mode drivers. Check your Config.sys and Autoexec.bat files to be sure they contain these drivers. Turn to "Emergency Startup disk" for more on how to do this.

Making room for Windows 98

Before you install Windows 98, again carefully consider its hard disk space requirements. If you have a computer with only a 200MB hard drive, Windows 98 is going to eat up a big chunk of your hard disk space. You might want to consider a new hard disk or a new computer. The bare bones Windows 98 configuration takes up a great deal more hard disk space than Windows 95 (or Windows 3.1*x*).

The amount of free hard disk space required to install Windows 98 is greater than the amount required to run it. About 11MB of temporary files are installed on your hard disk during the installation process, so you need more room during installation than is required later. In Table 2-2, we lay out the additional hard disk space needed to run Windows 98 on top of the amount already used by the existing operating system.

Table 2-2   Additional Disk Space Requirements

	Installation Type	
	Typical	*Compact*
New or over DOS	155MB	140MB
Over Windows 3.1	145MB	130MB
Over Windows 95	130MB	115MB

If you are installing Windows 98 in a new directory and not over an existing Windows directory, you will need at least 140MB (compact), and in some cases 190MB (full), of free hard disk space during the installation process. 11MB of this is for temporary files. You can subtract about 10MB from your free hard disk requirements needed for installation if you are installing over a Windows 3.1x folder and about 25MB if you are installing over Windows 95.

If you install more than the bare minimum, you'll need up to 190MB of free hard disk space in order to install Windows 98. The Windows 98 Setup dialog boxes will display the free hard disk space requirements needed during the installation process and warn you if you do not meet them. If you don't have enough room, you have the option of going back and making different choices about how many Windows 98 optional components to install. You can always quit, delete some older files and applications, and then restart the Windows 98 installation process.

If you don't have enough room to install everything at once, you can install a minimal amount and then later add optional components of Windows 98 one at a time.

When you install Windows 98, you can choose to save your previous operating system, so that you have the option of uninstalling Windows 98. You can then go back to DOS, Windows 3.1x, or Windows 95. If you do this, your hard disk requirements (for both installation and later) will increase from anywhere from 2MB (DOS) up to 16MB (Windows 95).

Just because you can meet the hard disk space requirements detailed in Table 2-2 doesn't mean you have enough hard disk space to have a viable system. You'll need additional space for your Windows 98 applications, as well as 20 to 40MB for a dynamically sized swap file.

If you are installing on a computer with compressed drives, you'll need at least 3MB of free uncompressed hard disk space during installation. This uncompressed disk space must be on your host drive (the physical drive or partition that "hosts" the compressed logical drive).

Where to put the Windows folder

You can install the Windows 98 folder (and all of its subfolders) on any hard drive (or logical drive partition or volume) as long as the disk partition is a FAT or FAT-32 partition. A few Windows 98 files must be installed on your boot drive, and the setup routines will place them there.

If your boot drive is compressed, its host drive must have at least 3MB of free space in order for Windows 98 to install. If your compressed drive uses all of the space on your host drive, you must uncompress enough of it to get 3MB of uncompressed space on the host drive. This may require you to move some files out of either logical drive.

One of the files that Windows 98 installs on the boot drive, Io.sys, will reside in the boot tracks. After you install Windows 98, it takes over the startup process for your computer. In addition, Windows 98 has its own Command.com file and can have Autoexec.bat and Config.sys files that reside in the root directory of the boot drive. Windows 98 keeps other files on the boot drive as well. These are detailed in "What Gets Loaded When" in Chapter 5.

The total size of the Windows 98-related files that will, of necessity, be installed on the boot drive is less than 2MB. You can place the rest of Windows 98 in another volume.

Compressed drives

Compressed drives are actually large files, called *compressed volume files* (CVFs), on a physical drive (the host drive) that are treated as (and named as) separate logical drives. You can install Windows 98 on a compressed drive.

The capacity of a compressed drive is estimated by the Windows 95 and Windows 98 compression algorithms assuming average file compression rates. Unfortunately, the Windows 98 operating system files are not very compressible. This means the actual size of an empty compressed drive is much less than its estimated and reported size would be if you installed Windows 98 on it. You should double the additional hard disk requirements shown in Table 2-2 if you are installing Windows 98 on a compressed drive.

Windows 98 manages a dynamically sized swap file. This swap file can be stored on the compressed drive that stores the bulk of the Windows 98 files, or it can be on an uncompressed drive. To prevent file compression from slowing the swap file, Windows 98 places the swap file at the end of the CVF and doesn't compress it. The issues of file compression and the swap file are discussed in detail in "Disk Compression" in Chapter 33.

Upgrading DOS to Windows 98

You can upgrade a computer running just the DOS operating system (version 3.2 or later) to Windows 98, if it meets the hardware requirements detailed previously.

You must also have a copy of Windows 95 or 3.1*x* installed, although not necessarily running, on your hard disk, or a handy Windows 95 or 3.1*x* setup diskette.

Undocumented

There is a way to fool the upgrade Windows 98 installation routines into installing Windows 98 if you don't have Windows 3.1*x* installed and you don't have your Windows 3.1*x* setup diskette handy. We assume that you have a license for Windows 3.1*x*. Create a text file in the root directory of your hard disk. Rename it Ntldr with no file extension. Type one line in the file: **Rem**. Then save the file. Now when you install Windows 98 you won't be asked to insert a Windows 3.1 diskette.

If you have an OEM version of the Windows 98 CD-ROM, you can use it to update a DOS computer. This version of the Windows 98 CD-ROM doesn't look for your existing Windows files.

Upgrading from Windows 3.1x

If you install Windows 98 in your existing Windows 3.1*x* directory, you carry the past forward with you—all of the past. The up side is that you don't have to reconfigure or reinstall any of your applications. During the setup process, Windows 98 reads your Windows 3.1*x* Win.ini, System.ini, and Protocol.ini files to find out what applications you have installed, and then it updates your Registry accordingly. (The *Registry* is a database that stores information about Windows and your Windows applications.)

In short, here are the advantages of installing Windows 98 in your existing Windows 3.1*x* directory:

- The values stored in System.ini, Win.ini, and Protocol.ini are now stored in your Windows 98 Registry.

- The values stored in these files that refer to other applications are stored in the Registry, maintaining existing file/application associations and fonts.

- Existing 16-bit network client software is automatically updated for a number of networks, including those from Microsoft, Novell, Digital Equipment Corporation, Sun, and Banyan.

- Existing Windows 3.1*x* Program Manager groups are converted to menus on your Start button.

If you install to a new folder or delete your old Windows 3.1*x* directory and install to an empty Windows folder, you will need to reinstall some to most of your Windows applications. You have to do this because many Windows applications:

- Install portions of themselves in the Windows folder, and that folder is either wiped out or no longer on the path (the DLLs won't be found when the executable is called).

- Need to be registered in the Registry if they use OLE or create file associations.

■ Install configuration files (*ini* files) in the Windows directory that need to be moved to the new Windows folders and, perhaps, re-edited.

Installing Windows 98 in a new folder makes a clean break with the past. You have to deliberately reinstall the applications that you use (or get new ones built for Windows 95 or 98). You have to configure all the settings in your applications to match your preferences. You have to remember (or relearn) where all those special program settings were hidden. You have to go find all the diskettes or CD-ROMs for the applications you have to reinstall.

If you install over Windows 3.1*x*, you might first want to use an uninstall program and get rid of unused files. You can manually edit Win.ini and System.ini (using Sysedit.exe in the \Windows\System directory) to clean up references to the unused past. If you have a lot of fonts that you don't use, you can uninstall and delete them from your hard disk.

Another route you could take is to install Windows 98 over a *copy* of your Windows 3.1*x* directory. With this method, the Windows 98 Registry is updated with all the information about your installed Windows applications, your program groups, and so on. However, you would also have an intact installation of Windows 3.1*x* to switch (dual-boot) to if need be.

We give a complete step-by-step method of installing over a copy of your existing Windows directory, while keeping your Windows 3.1*x* directory intact so that you can dual-boot back to Windows 3.1*x* during the transition period. See the section later in this chapter entitled "Installing Windows 98 Over a Copy of Windows 3.1*x*."

If you choose to install over Windows 3.1*x*, you do have the option of saving enough information to uninstall Windows 98 and to get back to Windows 3.1*x*. We'll show you when to do that in the section entitled "The Setup Process" later in this chapter.

Alternatively, you can keep your Windows 3.1*x* directory intact, not make a copy of it, and install Windows 98 in its own new empty folder. This will allow you to dual-boot between these two operating systems. You just want to make sure you have enough disk space for both (no small accomplishment on an older computer). Of course, you'll still have to reinstall most of your applications after you boot up Windows 98. The dynamic link library files that these applications store in the Windows folder will then be installed in both the Windows 3.1*x* directory and the Windows 98 folder.

Secret

If you install Windows 98 in its own folder, a temporary way to get around reinstalling all these Windows 3.1*x* programs under Windows 98 is to include references in your path statement to the old Windows directory and System directory at the *end* of your Path *after* all other directories. This may let your old Windows applications find their DLLs. It doesn't update their file associations or register them for OLE.

Disk space requirements upgrading from Windows 3.1x

About 10MB of Windows 3.1x files are deleted and replaced by Windows 98 files if you install it in your Windows 3.1x folder. To install Windows 98 over Windows 3.1x requires 145MB of free hard disk space for a typical installation.

If you find that you have almost enough space to install Windows 98, but not quite, you can get rid of the permanent swap file that you may have previously designated under Windows 3.1x. This will give the Windows 98 Setup program more free hard disk space.

To get rid of the Windows 3.1x permanent swap file, at least temporarily, take the following steps:

STEPS

Getting Rid of the Windows 3.1x Permanent Swap File

Step 1.   Run Windows 3.1x.

Step 2.   Double-click the Control Panel icon in your Program Manager. Double-click the Enhanced icon in the Control Panel.

Step 3.   Click the Virtual Memory button, and then click Change.

Step 4.   From the drop-down list in the Type field, choose Temporary. Click the OK buttons to exit from the Control Panel.

Step 5.   Exit Windows 3.1x to DOS.

Step 6.   At the DOS command prompt, change directories to the root directory of the boot drive (**cd **).

Step 7.   Type **attrib 386spart.par** and press Enter.

Step 8.   If the result of step 7 is a listing for this file, type **del 386spart.par** and press Enter.

You do not need a permanent swap file to run Windows 98. (It automatically creates a *dynamic* swap file, as described in the "Managing Your Swap Space" section of Chapter 33.) If you need a permanent swap file to continue running programs under Windows 3.1x, you can re-create it using the Windows 3.1x Control Panel.

Protecting your DOS files

Windows 98 installs its own DOS 7.1 files in its Command folder (\Windows\Command). These files are updated versions of some of the DOS files that you can find in your DOS (version 5.x or 6.x) directory. Not all files that come with DOS 6.2*x* come with Windows 98. DOS 6.22 Help, for example, is available on the Windows 98 CD-ROM, but doesn't get loaded onto your hard disk, and it isn't updated to DOS 7.1.

Some of the utilities that came with earlier versions of DOS will cause problems if you run them after you install Windows 98. DOS 6.*x* versions of the disk utilities Scandisk.exe and Defrag.exe break the link between short filenames and long filenames maintained by Windows 98. You should not run these versions of these programs after you install Windows 98.

Some newer DOS programs that come with Windows 98 are really only slightly different than their older DOS versions. Microsoft updated all the DOS 7.1 programs that require disk access to handle FAT-32 volumes.

When you install Windows 98, the setup procedures rename the older DOS programs that cause problems with long filenames. For example, Scandisk.exe becomes Scandisk.ex~. In addition, a batch file is created, Scandisk.bat, which is invoked when you type **Scandisk** at the DOS prompt (if you boot to the old operating system). This batch file essentially tells you to use the ScanDisk program in Windows 98. (You can do this by clicking Scandisk.exe in the \Windows\Command folder or by right-clicking a hard disk icon, clicking Properties, Tools, and then clicking the Check Now button.)

Secret

If you install Windows 98 in an existing Windows 3.1*x* directory, about 2MB worth of DOS files will be deleted from your existing DOS directory, including the DOS 6.*x* version of Scandisk.exe. These files are not needed (as far as Microsoft is concerned), are replaced by files installed in the Command folder, or are too dangerous to use with Windows 98.

If you install Windows 98 to a new folder, the DOS files are not deleted. This allows you to have full DOS functionality when you dual-boot to the previous DOS version instead of into Windows 98. Even if you boot to the previous DOS version, you don't want to use the previous version's disk tools that cause problems with long filenames. That is why Setup renames these previous disk utilities, no matter where you put Windows 98.

Microsoft decided to delete these older DOS programs because it replaced them in the new Command folder and saw a way to reclaim 2MB of disk space for you automatically. As long as you are overwriting Windows 3.1*x* and changing your path to include the Command folder, Microsoft feels that the right thing to do is to get rid of replicated DOS programs.

Tip

If you want to make sure that the Windows 98 installation procedures don't change or delete any existing DOS programs, copy them to another directory that is not on your path, or create a zipped file that includes a copy of all of them. Just changing their file attribute to Read-Only won't do any good. Check the section entitled "BootMulti" in Chapter 5 for more details.

After you have installed Windows 98, you can copy the files back from the other folder, or unzip the zipped files. Just be sure not to use the older disk utilities ScanDisk, Defrag, DoubleSpace, and DriveSpace.

Saving some Windows 3.1*x* applets

Some applets that Microsoft included with Windows 3.1*x* have not been upgraded or even made available with Windows 98. If you like using these applets, you'll need to make them available under Windows 98. If you installed Windows 98 in a new folder, you can create shortcut icons on the Desktop or add items to the Start menu that refer to these applets in the Windows 3.1*x* directory.

Windows Write

Windows Write is not saved. If you install Windows 98 in your Windows 3.1*x* directory, then the Write executable file (Write.exe) is written over by an executable stub (Write.exe) that merely calls Wordpad.exe. If you install Windows 98 to a new folder, this same stub executable is installed. WordPad will now open all your Windows Write files.

Secret

To keep this from happening, make sure you save a copy of the original Write.exe and Write.hlp files. If you are going to install Windows 98 in the Windows 3.1*x* directory, copy these files to a temporary directory before you install Windows 98. After installing Windows 98, you can copy these files back into the Windows 98 folder.

Secret

It does no good to just write-protect Write.exe because Windows 98 Setup ignores the Read-Only attribute and writes right over it.

Even after you restore Windows Write, you won't be able to invoke it by clicking files with the *wri* extension. You'll need to change the file extension association in the File Types tab of the View, Folder Options dialog box in your Explorer or My Computer window. For step-by-step instructions on how to do this, turn to "Associating Actions with File Extensions" in Chapter 13.

When Windows 95 came out, we recommended that you save Windows Write, because WordPad took so long to load. The Windows 98 version of WordPad is reasonably fast. You might just try it and see if you feel comfortable using it instead of Windows Write to edit small files.

Tip

It's a good idea to create a folder that contains all your own system files, such as Write.exe and Write.hlp. That way, they will be protected when you update Windows 98 in the future. You might want to name the new system folder \My System.

The Recorder

The least-appreciated of Windows tools, the macro recorder, is not included with Windows 98 and doesn't work well with the 32-bit applets. If you install Windows 98 over Windows 3.1*x*, however, Windows 98 doesn't overwrite Recorder as it does Write.

While many sophisticated Windows applications have their own macro recorders, it is still great to have a general-purpose version that can help automate repetitive tasks. If you purchased Windows 98 without ever installing Windows 3.1*x*, your system doesn't have a copy of Recorder.exe. We have featured some shareware on the *Windows 98 Secrets* CD-ROM that gives you some general macro capabilities with Windows 98.

Clipbook

You can find Clipbook, which comes with Windows for Workgroups 3.11, on the Windows 98 CD-ROM, but Windows 98 Setup doesn't necessarily install it. (Unlike Clipbook, you can easily install Clipboard or add it later. To add Clipboard after you install Windows 98, click the Start button, Settings, Control Panel. Click the Add/Remove Programs icon, click the Windows Setup tab, highlight System Tools, click the Details button, and mark the Clipboard Viewer check box. You can also choose Clipboard during Setup in the Select Components dialog box under System Tools.)

You will need to extract the Clipbook from the Windows 98 cabinet files after you install Windows 98, if you are not installing over WFWG 3.11.

STEPS

Adding the Clipbook

Step 1. Click the Start button, Programs, MS-DOS Prompt. Change directories to the \win98 folder on your Windows 98 CD-ROM.

Step 2. At the DOS prompt, type **extract /a /d Win98_23.cab Clipbook.* | more** and press Enter.

Step 3. Write down the names of the cabinet files that store the Clipbook.* files.

Step 4. Using your Explorer, click the cabinet files that contain the Clipbook files.

Step 5. Drag and drop the Clipbook.exe file to your \Windows folder. Drag and drop the rest of the Clipbook files to your \Windows\Help folder.

Step 6. Drag and drop Clipbook.exe to the Desktop. This will create a shortcut to the Clipbook on your Desktop. You can later move this shortcut to wherever you like.

Secret

If you have any problems using the sharing facilities of Clipbook, put NetDDE.exe in your StartUp folder (and start it up). Windows for Workgroups 3.11 automatically starts NetDDE; Windows 98 doesn't.

Dual-booting

Do you want to be able to boot your computer to your previous version of DOS (6.22 and earlier) and/or Windows 3.1*x*? You should answer this question before you install Windows 98 on a computer with only DOS or Windows 3.1*x*.

If you are upgrading Windows 95 to Windows 98, you don't need to worry about this question. If you can dual-boot your computer with Windows 95 installed, you'll be able to dual-boot it after you install Windows 98, unless you convert your boot drive to FAT 32.

If you are unsure whether some of your Windows 3.1x applications will work with Windows 98 and you have the necessary hard disk space, you can install Windows 98 in a separate folder. You can then migrate your Windows applications over one at a time to make sure that everything is working. If Windows 98 doesn't work out for you, you can then uninstall it and go back to your previous version of Windows.

In order to dual-boot, you'll need to install Windows 98 in a new folder and not in your existing Windows 3.1x directory. If you are installing Windows 98 on a DOS computer, you will automatically have dual-boot capability (unless it is DOS 7.x).

Clean up your Startup folder

If you install Windows 98 over your existing Windows 3.1x directory, the applications in your Startup group will migrate to your new StartUp folder. When you start Windows 98, these programs will also be started.

Some of these programs may not be applicable to Windows 98. For example, the Windows 3.1x version of Plug-In, a wonderful add-on to the Program Manager, will not work with Windows 98. Windows 98 Setup will find Plug-In and take references to it out of Win.ini.

You should remove all programs from your Windows 3.1x Startup group before you install Windows 98.

Upgrading Windows 95 to Windows 98

Windows 98 Setup finds your Windows 95 folder and, with very few questions, replaces your existing Windows 95 system components with their Windows 98 counterparts.

Microsoft has incrementally updated Windows 95 ever since it was first unveiled. It has released new Windows CD-ROMs and multiple Internet Explorer versions. Over the last few years, it has made available new versions of the various components of Windows 95 for download from the Microsoft web site. There is no way the Windows 98 Setup can know in advance just what your Windows 95 installation consists of.

The Windows 98 CD-ROM updates all of your existing Windows 95 components. If you have a basic Windows 95 installation, the setup routines delete and replace about 25MB of files. Windows 98 adds about 110MB over a basic Windows 95 installation.

Loading the source files

Installing Windows 98 from an older CD-ROM drive can be quite slow. If you have a fast CD-ROM drive, things are quite a bit brighter.

Tip

If you have the spare hard disk space, consider copying the CD-ROM to a hard disk directory, and then installing Windows 98 from your hard disk. This is the way that computer manufacturers do it. If you do this, the original source files will always be available locally off a high-speed device (your hard disk). If you make changes to your Windows 98 setup, the reconfiguration routines point back to the source files on your hard disk and allow you to quickly update Windows 98. You don't have to go searching for your Windows 98 CD-ROM.

The problem, of course, is that you just used up 116MB of hard disk space that you might actually need. You can erase these source files after you have successfully installed Windows 98, but another problem arises. Any subsequent updates will point back to the now-erased source files, expecting to find them on your hard disk, so you will need to point the update routines toward your Windows 98 CD-ROM when prompted to do so. See the next section for instructions on how to do this.

Most of the source files are in a compressed format and have the extension *cab*, which stands for *cabinet*. The setup routines extract the files from the file cabinets. You can use the File Manager, the Explorer, or the DOS Copy command to copy the cabinet files from a CD-ROM.

You can view the contents of the cabinet files in two ways. If you are upgrading from Windows 95 and have installed the Cabinet Viewer (Cabview.inf and Cabview.dll), which comes with the Microsoft Windows 95 PowerToys (http://www.microsoft.com/windows/software/powertoy.htm), you can click a cabinet file to view its contents. Windows 98 installs the cabinet-viewer extension automatically.

You can also use the Extract command in real-mode DOS or in a DOS window. You'll find Extract.exe in the \Win98 folder on the Windows 98 CD-ROM. You can copy it into your \Windows\Command or \DOS folder if you haven't done so previously. At a DOS prompt, type **extract /?** to view the online documentation for the Extract command.

Tip

You can get listings of all the files in the Windows 98 source cabinets by using a variation of the Extract command and piping the results to a new file. At the DOS prompt (while in the Windows 98 source directory) issue the command:

Extract /d /a win98_23.cab > \temp\ListWin98.txt

This command extracts all the names of the files stored in the set of cabinet files starting with win98_23.cab. You can create similar lists for all the other sets of cabinet files by replacing win98_23.cab with the first cabinet filename in each of the sets.

You can read more about the Extract command in the Microsoft Knowledge Base. Use your Internet Explorer to find http://premium.microsoft.com/support/kb/articles/q129/6/05.asp.

Installing over a network or from a CD-ROM

If your computer is connected to a network and the source files are stored on a server, either on a hard disk or a CD-ROM, you can install Windows 98 from the server. Unless your system administrator has custom-designed the installation procedures, it is no different than installing Windows 98 from a local diskette drive, CD-ROM, or hard disk—with one exception.

Secret

Near the end of the Windows 98 installation, Windows 98 reboots your computer and grabs further files from the source cabinets. It reboots your computer under Windows 98. If, using the Windows 98 network or CD-ROM drivers, it is unable to make the connection to your network server or to your local CD-ROM drive, Windows 98 can't continue configuring itself.

If you're upgrading over a Windows 3.1*x* directory, it may be difficult to get back to your previous connections to the server or the CD-ROM. There is obviously a bug if Windows 98 can't access your network or CD-ROM. But the bug shows up at an inopportune time.

While you won't be able to completely install Windows 98 because you don't have access to some files, in particular the printer files, you will have a semi-working version of Windows 98 at the end of your setup process. You will need to make some changes in your configuration to regain access to the network or your CD-ROM, perhaps using your previously working 16-bit drivers.

Windows 98 keeps track of the location of its source installation files. In most cases, this location will be the \win98 folder in your CD-ROM drive.

When you make certain changes to your Windows 98 configuration, Windows 98 searches for the files that it needs in the original location. If it doesn't find these files there, it will ask you where it can find them. If you've installed from the Windows 98 CD-ROM, you'll just put it in your CD-ROM drive and continue. If the source files are stored somewhere other than their original location, you can type in this new location when asked.

Windows 98 stores the source file location and the source file type (cabinet files or expanded files) in the Registry. You can edit your Registry, once you've installed Windows 98, to specify a new file location and to change the source file type. (Refer to Chapter 15 to see learn more about the Registry editor.)

STEPS

Changing the Source File Location and Type

Step 1.   After you install Windows 98, click Regedit.exe in your \Windows folder.

Step 2.   Navigate in your Registry to HKEY_LOCAL_MACHINE\ SOFTWARE\Microsoft\Windows\CurrentVersion\SETUP. Highlight SETUP.

Step 3.   Double-click SourcePath in the right pane of your Registry editor. Type a new path for the location of your source files. Click OK.

Step 4.   Double-click SourcePathType. To change it from the expanded NETSETUP value to the cabinet value, type **05 00 00 00**. Click OK, and exit the Registry editor.

Step 5.   If you are changing SourcePathType to the cabinet value, you'll also need to extract the Layout.inf file from the cabinet files and place it in your \Windows\Inf folder. Follow the instructions in the "Loading the source files" section to do this. Backup your current Layout.inf file first.

Getting Ready to Start Windows 98 Setup

Your installation of Windows 98 may choke if you have loaded DOS TSRs into memory or are running Windows utilities, including virus checkers or other add-ons. Microsoft provides a list of TSRs known to cause problems in the file setup.txt, which you will find on the Windows 98 CD-ROM in the \Win98 folder. It is a good idea to read this file before starting to install Windows 98.

So many combinations of TSRs and Windows utilities could cause problems that Microsoft would prefer you eliminate as many variables as possible. Most of the support calls that Microsoft receives concern setup issues.

Just before you install Windows 98, you should remark out as many of the calls to TSRs in Config.sys and Autoexec.bat as you can live without during the installation. You should also close any programs that are started by your Windows Startup group and eliminate unnecessary programs from the Startup group before installing Windows 98.

If your computer BIOS includes a virus-checking option, you'll need to turn off this function. Otherwise, Windows 98 Setup will freeze. The most common way to access this function is to press a key (usually Delete, F2, or Escape) during your computer's power-on self test to bring up the built-in BIOS editor.

Back up some files

Changes are going to be made to a number of your existing files. If you want to play it safe, you can back them up and edit the newer versions later.

If you are updating your Windows 3.1*x* directory, you may want to back up all configuration *(ini)* files, Registry *(dat)* files, and password *(pwl)* files. No matter how you install Windows 98, you'll want to back up Autoexec.bat and Config.sys and any network configuration files and logon scripts.

Changes will be made

You don't want to remark out the real-mode drivers in Autoexec.bat and Config.sys before you start installation. The hardware-detection procedures in Windows 98 Setup use these calls to help configure Windows 98.

Changes will be made to your Autoexec.bat and Config.sys files. Lines will be remarked out that are no longer needed. You will undoubtedly want to edit Autoexec.bat and Config.sys further or even remove these files.

If you have a Config.sys file with different sections for multiconfiguration, only the currently active portion of the Config.sys file is used by Windows 98 Setup when configuring Windows 98. All other sections of Config.sys (and Autoexec.bat) are remarked out. If you want to use a multiconfiguration version of Config.sys and Autoexec.bat with Windows 98, you will need to edit these files after the Windows 98 installation is complete.

Setup creates a new file called Dosstart.bat, which it places in the Windows 98 folder. Lines remarked out of your Autoexec.bat file are placed in this file. Dosstart is run when you start an MS-DOS mode session under Windows 98 (under some circumstances). Turn to "MS-DOS Mode" in Chapter 34 for more details.

Running Setup from DOS or Windows

You can run Windows 98 Setup from your previous version of DOS (version 3.2 or higher), from Windows 3.1*x*, or from Windows 95. (You can't run it from Windows 3.0.) If you have only DOS on your computer, you can run Setup from DOS.

When you start Windows 98 Setup from DOS, it loads a mini version of Windows 3.1 from your Windows 98 CD-ROM and then runs Setup from this version of Windows. It will run a DOS 7.1 version of ScanDisk before it loads this mini version of Windows. If you start from Windows, the DOS 7.1 version of ScanDisk will be run behind the scenes.

It is best to run Windows 98 Setup from your previous operating system, either Windows 3.1*x* or Windows 95.

Setup switches

The easiest way to run Windows 98 Setup is to start your Windows 3.1*x* File Manager or your Windows 95 Explorer and then double-click the setup.exe file in the root directory of the Windows 98 CD-ROM. However, if you run Setup from the DOS prompt, or if you choose File, Run in the Windows 3.1*x* File Manager or Start, Run in Windows 95, you can add some command line parameters, as shown in Table 2-3.

Table 2-3   Command Line Parameters for Setup

Switch	*Resulting Action*
setup /?	Lists some of the setup switches. You get different results depending on whether you do this in a Windows DOS session or in MS-DOS mode. Different switches work when starting in real-mode DOS than when starting in Windows.
setup /T:tmp	You can name a directory that will store the temporary files that are created and destroyed during the Windows 98 Setup. If you specify a different disk drive for this directory, you can reduce by 11MB the amount of hard disk space needed on the original drive for installing Windows 98.
setup *script-file*	If you have a batch file that automates the setup process, this is how you run it. The batch file will likely be on a network server, which you will need to log into before you begin setting up.
setup /iq	Doesn't check for cross-linked files.
setup /im	Skips the memory (RAM) check.
setup /id	Skips the disk space check. Our tests indicate that it still checks for disk space even with this switch.
setup /in	Setup won't ask about or install network software. If you want to install Direct Cable Connection or Dial-Up Networking (for your Internet connection, for example), don't use this switch.
setup /is	Runs Setup without first running ScanDisk. We recommend that you run ScanDisk first. If you get a message that there is not enough free conventional memory to run ScanDisk, and you have freed up as much conventional memory as possible, you can run Setup with this switch. This setting is also required if Windows 98 Setup persists in believing that there are errors on your hard drive, when this is not the case.
setup /C	Doesn't load the SmartDrive disk cache. If you don't use this switch, SmartDrive will be loaded to speed the Windows 98 Setup over DOS or Windows 3.1*x*, or off a CD-ROM with 16-bit drivers.
setup /ie	Creates an Emergency Startup disk.
setup /ih	Runs Registry consistency checks.
setup /d	Doesn't use the existing version of Windows to run Windows 98 Setup. Use this switch only when running Setup from real-mode DOS.
setup /IW	Bypasses the licensing screen (use uppercase letters).
setup /iv	Doesn't show the Microsoft advertisement graphics as Setup proceeds.
setup /nostart	Copies from the Windows 98 source files the minimum Windows 3.1*x* DLLs required to run Windows 98 Setup and then exit to DOS.

The Setup Process

You might be getting the idea that setting up Windows 98 is no simple matter. Developing the setup software was almost as complicated for Microsoft as creating the core of Windows 98 itself. According to Microsoft, it delayed the release of Windows 98 because corporate customers wanted setup procedures that would handle Windows 3.1*x* upgrades in a very robust manner.

Running Windows 98 Setup is not that difficult because Microsoft has done so much to make it do the work for you. While we can't cover every step, we do point out some key areas and give you extra guidance about how to proceed.

Most of the dialog boxes that you'll see while Setup runs have Next and Back buttons. You get to choose when you go forward. If you want to go back and make a choice over again, you often have that option.

You can cancel Windows 98 Setup at any time, and not disturb your existing Windows or DOS computer. No new files (other than Setuplog.txt and a few small hidden files in the root directory) will be installed, and no files will be changed until you click the Next button in the Start Copying Files dialog box at the end of the setup process.

Starting Setup

You can start Windows 98 Setup using any one of the three methods described earlier in the section entitled "Setup switches." The setup routines create a full-screen display with a welcome dialog box, as shown in Figure 2-1. Click Continue to continue.

If you are running Setup from the DOS prompt, you won't see this screen first. Instead, you will see the DOS 7.1 version of ScanDisk.

Running ScanDisk

As soon as Setup starts, it calls ScanDisk from the Windows 98 CD-ROM to check your hard disk. If you start Windows 98 Setup from the DOS prompt, this DOS 7.1 version of ScanDisk will run in the foreground. If you start Setup from Windows, the DOS 7.1 version of ScanDisk runs in background while Setup tells you in a Windows message box that it is performing a routine check of your system, as shown in Figure 2-2.

If, while running Windows 98 Setup, ScanDisk reports a lack of conventional memory, quit Setup. You can then edit your existing Autoexec.bat and Config.sys files to remove unneeded calls to various applets, and so on. Restart your computer to see if you have freed up more conventional memory. This may allow the DOS 7.1 ScanDisk program to work correctly.

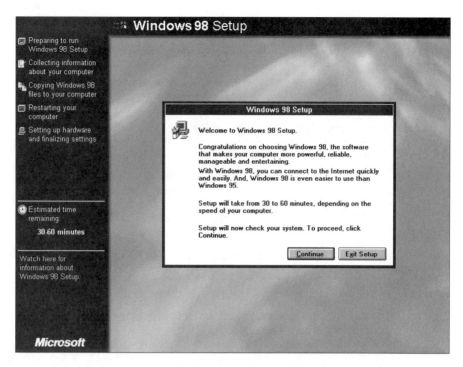

Figure 2-1: The Windows 98 Setup opening screen. If you decide that you really aren't ready to start, you can exit Setup now. There will be plenty of other opportunities throughout the setup sequence to quit or go back a step without suffering any untold consequences.

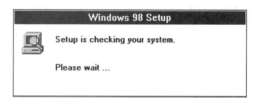

Figure 2-2: If you start Windows 98 Setup from Windows (3.1x or 95), this message box appears while the DOS 7.1 version of ScanDisk (not the Windows 98 version) is running in the background.

Undocumented

If Windows 98 Setup has trouble running the DOS 7.1 version of ScanDisk, you can run an earlier DOS 6.2x version of ScanDisk (if you are installing Windows 98 over DOS or Window 3.1x) before you run Setup again. You can also run Defrag if you have DOS 6.x. *Don't run these older versions of ScanDisk or Defrag after you have installed either Windows 95 or Windows 98.*

You can, alternately, run the DOS 7.1 version of ScanDisk that comes on the Windows 98 CD-ROM yourself (although you are using an earlier version of DOS). You can run this version of ScanDisk from the DOS prompt before you start Windows 98 Setup again.

If you get an error message that says you must run ScanDisk to fix some problems encountered on your hard disk, you'll want to run the DOS 7.1 version of ScanDisk. To do so, take the following steps:

STEPS

Running DOS 7.1 ScanDisk to Correct Hard Disk Problems

Step 1. Quit Windows 98 Setup (and Windows 3.1*x*).

Step 2. Make sure that your Windows 98 CD-ROM is in its drive, or that the Windows 98 source files are on your hard disk.

Step 3. At the DOS command prompt, type:

d:\win98\Scandisk.exe /all

where *d* is the drive designator for the location of the Windows 98 CD-ROM.

Step 4. Follow the directions on the screen.

Step 5. Start your earlier version of Windows again and run Windows 98 Setup again.

If you were originally running Windows 98 Setup from DOS, the DOS 7.1 ScanDisk will run and you'll be able to fix most disk problems without having to get out of Setup. Once you are sure that there are no problems with your hard disk—that is, you have been able to run some version of ScanDisk— you can start Windows 98 Setup with the /is switch (see "Setup switches" earlier in this chapter).

After ScanDisk runs successfully under Setup, you are asked if you wish to continue running Setup, as shown in Figure 2-3. You can exit without any consequences at this point.

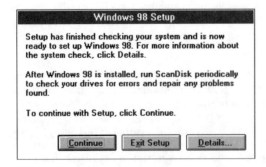

Figure 2-3: ScanDisk has tested your system and Windows 98 Setup is ready to continue. If you would like to know what ScanDisk found, click the Details button.

If you click Continue, the Windows 98 setup routines load the Windows 98 Setup Wizard, as shown in Figure 2-4. This Wizard will take over the setup process.

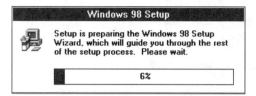

Figure 2-4: The I'm-loading-the-Wizard box, so please bear with me — a little feedback to tell you that something useful is going on and to please be patient as it will take a while.

Warning about open programs

If Setup detects that some Windows programs are running, you will get the message shown in Figure 2-5. Press Alt+Tab to switch to those programs, close them, and then continue setup by clicking OK.

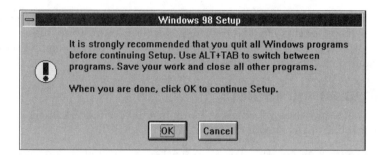

Figure 2-5: Windows 98 Setup detects running Windows programs. Press Alt+Tab to switch to other programs, which you can then close. Click OK to continue Setup, or click Cancel to stop Setup.

Windows 98 Setup detects all running Windows programs, the vast majority of which will cause no problems. Microsoft just doesn't want any problems here, so it asks you to close all Windows programs. We have never had a problem with just proceeding, but for safety's sake, you might want to take the time to close your applications at this point.

Safe recovery

Setup will display the Safe Recovery dialog box, shown in Figure 2-6, if you previously tried to install Windows 98. Choose Use Safe Recovery if there was a problem with your last attempt to run Setup and you want to skip over that problem.

Figure 2-6: The Safe Recovery dialog box. The Use Safe Recovery option is the default. Click Next to use this option if there was a problem with your last attempt to run Setup.

The setup process creates a log file, Setuplog.txt. When you run Setup again, it searches for this file, and determines where Setup stopped the last time. Setup won't need to reinstall various Windows 98 components if they were installed on the previous attempt.

License agreement

You have another opportunity to stop installing Windows 98 by clicking the Cancel button, as shown in Figure 2-7.

The License Agreement dialog box marks the division in Windows 98 Setup between upgrading Windows 95 and upgrading DOS or Windows 3.1x. If you are upgrading from DOS or Windows 3.1x, Setup gives you the option of selecting a directory within which to install Windows 98. When you install Windows 98 over Windows 95, it updates your existing Windows 95 directory.

If you are installing Windows 98 over Windows 95, you can jump to "Checking for free hard disk space" later in this chapter.

The Windows 98 directory

Windows 98 Setup will, by default, attempt to install Windows 98 in your existing Windows 3.1x directory. If you are upgrading over a DOS computer, it defaults to installing it in a new \Windows directory. If you have an existing Windows 3.1x directory, you have to tell it *twice* if you want to install Windows 98 in a new directory. You can choose the current Windows directory or another directory, as shown in Figure 2-8.

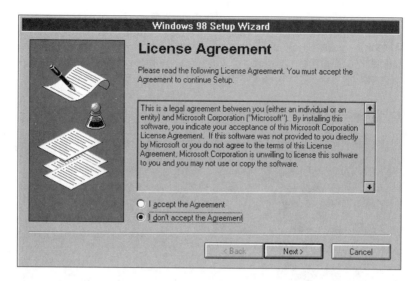

Figure 2-7: If you mark the I Don't Accept The Agreement option button and then click Next, you are just asked if you want to review the agreement or quit Setup.

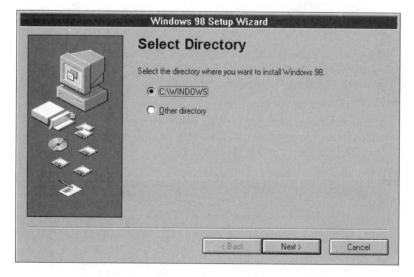

Figure 2-8: The Select Directory dialog box. The default choice is to upgrade your existing Windows 3.1x directory with Windows 98. Choose Other Directory to install Windows 98 in a new directory.

If you choose to install Windows 98 into your existing Windows 3.1x directory, you do have the option, a bit later, of saving your Windows 3.1x software and configuration. If you do this, you will be able to uninstall Windows 98 and go back to Windows 3.1x. You will see how to do this in "Save system files" later in this chapter.

If you choose Other Directory and click Next, you can type in the name of a new Windows directory (see Figure 2-9). Again, Setup wants to put Windows 98 into your current Windows 3.1*x* directory. You have to type the volume, path, and directory name of your new Windows 98 directory if you want to install it in a directory other than your existing Windows 3.1*x* directory.

Figure 2-9: The Change Directory dialog box. The default is the current Windows 3.1*x* directory — not much of a change. Type the name of a new directory if you want to install Windows 98 in a new separate directory.

If you choose to install Windows 98 into a new directory, Setup warns you that you will need to reinstall all your Windows applications to update the Windows 98 Registry (see Figure 2-10).

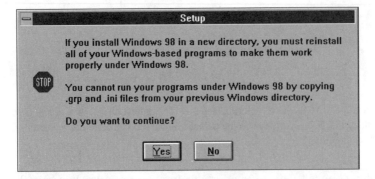

Figure 2-10: Setup displays a little warning to remind you that you will probably have to reinstall all your Windows applications so that they can update the Windows 98 Registry, install their DLLs in the new Windows directory, and place their icons on the Start menu.

The Select Directory dialog box marks another fork in the road for Windows 98 Setup. If you choose to update your existing Windows 3.1x directory, you don't see either the Setup Options dialog box (Figure 2-15) or the Select Components dialog box (Figure 2-19). Setup chooses which Windows 98 components to install based on your current Windows 3.1x configuration. You can go back later and install or remove additional components.

Checking for free hard disk space

Windows 98 Setup now checks your computer. If you are installing over Windows 95, you'll see the Checking Your System screen shown in Figure 2-11.

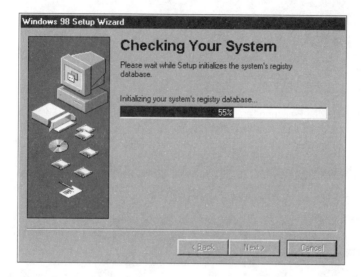

Figure 2-11: The Checking Your System dialog box. Windows 98 Setup is searching through your existing Windows 95 Registry to figure out what Windows 98 should install and how your computer is configured.

Windows 98 Setup also checks whether your computer meets the minimum requirements, including sufficient available disk space, as shown in Figure 2-12.

Save system files

If you install Windows 98 in an existing Windows (3.1x or 95) directory or on a DOS-only computer, you will be given the option of saving your previous Windows and/or DOS system files, as shown in Figure 2-13. If you choose to save these files, you can uninstall Windows 98 later if you decide that you want to go back to your previous configuration.

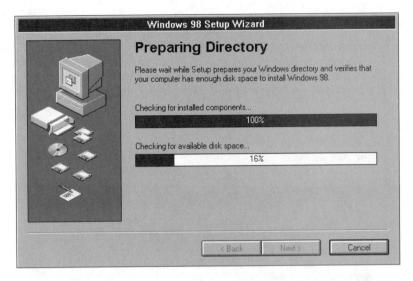

Figure 2-12: The Preparing Directory dialog box. You can cancel Setup while it is checking your computer for sufficient hard disk space.

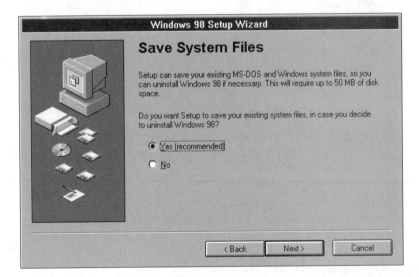

Figure 2-13: The Save System Files dialog box. Saving your previous operating-system files takes up disk space. You may not have enough.

If you choose to save your system files, Setup displays the progress of that process, as shown in Figure 2-14.

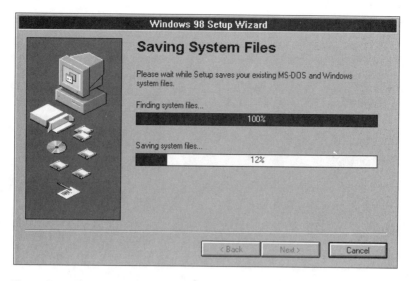

Figure 2-14: The Saving System Files dialog box. Click Cancel to stop saving these files.

If you are installing over Windows 95, the next sections don't apply to you. You can skip down to "Emergency Startup disk."

Setup options

Windows 98 comes with a core set of components and a number of optional components. If you are installing Windows 98 on a new computer, or on a computer that only has DOS installed, or in a new directory on a computer with Windows 3.1*x* installed, you can choose from among four basic sets of options: Typical, Portable, Compact, and Custom. While it is not obvious at first just what each option represents, as you can see in Figure 2-15, Setup gives you an opportunity to further refine and understand these choices later (see "Select components" below).

If you do not have enough space to install the set of optional Windows 98 components that you have chosen in the Setup Options dialog box, Setup will display the Caution: Low Disk Space dialog box shown in Figure 2-16.

If you have less than 147MB of free hard disk space, you get a Not Enough Disk Space dialog box. No cautions here. The only options are to go back or to cancel Windows 98 Setup.

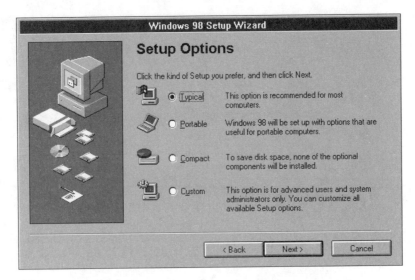

Figure 2-15: The Setup Options dialog box. If you are in a hurry, pick the choice that roughly meets your needs. Setup gives you an opportunity to modify your choice.

Figure 2-16: The Caution: Low Disk Space dialog box. You can proceed by clicking the Next button, but you will have to install other Windows 98 optional components later, because none will get installed now.

User information

If you are installing Windows 98 on a DOS computer or in a new directory, Setup asks you to supply user information, as shown in Figure 2-17.

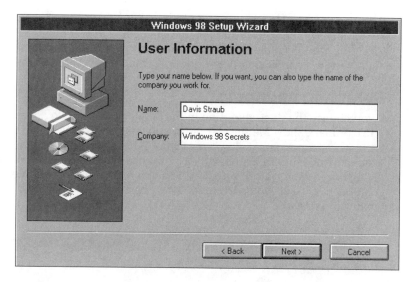

Figure 2-17: The User Information dialog box. The user name and company name show up in the Help, About Windows dialog box and as the default user information in Microsoft Fax if you install it separately.

Windows components

If you choose Typical, Portable, or Compact in the Setup Options dialog box (see Figure 2-15 earlier in the chapter), you get the option of refining the set of components that are installed, as you can see in Figure 2-18.

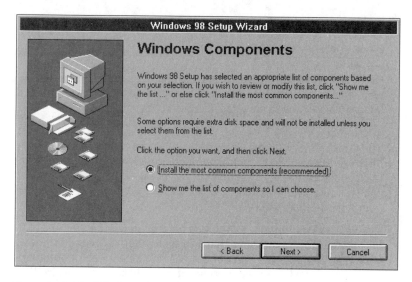

Figure 2-18: The Windows Components dialog box. You can choose whether to modify the list of components that Setup will install.

If you mark Show Me the List of Components So I Can Choose and click Next, Setup displays the Select Components dialog box. If you choose Custom in the Setup Options dialog box, you go directly to the Select Components dialog box without seeing the Windows Components dialog box.

Select components

If you choose the Custom option in the Setup Options dialog box (Figure 2-15), or mark Show Me the List of Components So I Can Choose in the Windows Components dialog box (Figure 2-18), you can specify exactly which components to install with Windows 98. The Select Components dialog box, as shown in Figure 2-19, lets you mark which components, or component classes, you wish to include or exclude. *Read the text in this dialog box carefully.*

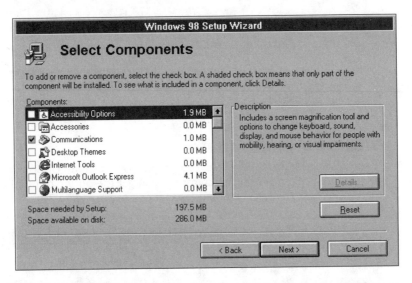

Figure 2-19: The Select Components dialog box. Use it to determine what features you want installed with Windows 98. Select an item in the list box, and click the Details button to see what components are part of that class of components.

The Select Components dialog box is the top of a hierarchy. Each item displayed in the Components list leads to a list of individual components. Double-click an item in the list (or highlight an item and click Details) to bring up an additional dialog box that lets you choose which specific components to install.

The Select Components dialog box also displays the amount of free hard disk space and the amount that will be needed to install Windows 98 and whatever components you choose. As you select each component for installation, the increased amount of hard disk space required to install Windows 98 is displayed under the Components list box.

If you wish to reset the list of components that Setup will install back to your original choice in the Setup Options dialog box, click the Reset button. Also, you can easily go back to the Setup Options dialog box by clicking the Back button.

If you choose too many components, that is, they take up more space than is needed to successfully complete the Windows 98 installation, you will be asked to uncheck some of your choices, as shown in Figure 2-20.

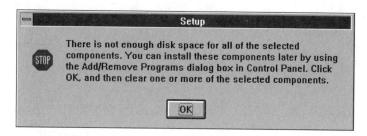

Figure 2-20: A warning that you don't have enough disk space.

In order to make wise choices about what components to install, you need to know:

- What benefits/features the component offers
- How much hard disk space it costs

You can easily add or delete any of these components anytime after you have installed Windows 98, so you can wait to make choices later if you so desire. See "Adding and Removing Parts of Windows 98" later in this chapter or turn to "Add/Remove programs" in Chapter 16 for more details.

Accessories

Highlight Accessories in the Select Components dialog box and click the Details button. You will see a dialog box that lists the individual accessories you can install with Windows 98, as shown in Figure 2-21.

When you highlight an individual accessory in this list, details about that accessory are shown in the Description area. The hard disk size requirements are shown to the right of each accessory named in the list box. To add an accessory to the list of components to be installed, click the check box to the left of the accessory name. When you are finished choosing accessories, click OK.

Communications

If you want to connect two computers together using a parallel or serial cable to easily transfer files, select Dial-Up Networking and Direct Cable Connection from the Communications dialog box shown in Figure 2-22. If you want to dial into an Internet service provider or call your computer at work from your computer at home, you should also install Dial-Up Networking.

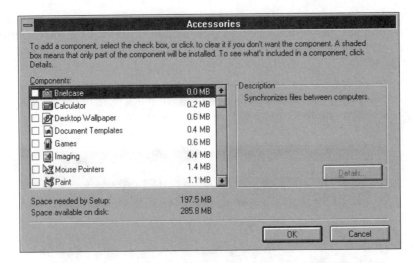

Figure 2-21: The Accessories dialog box. Scroll through this list to see all the possible accessory choices.

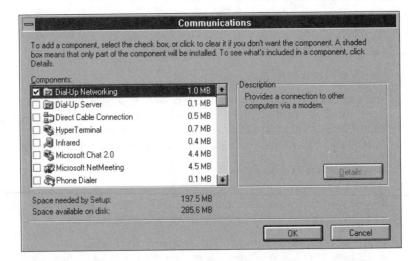

Figure 2-22: The Communications dialog box. The first and third choices allow you to connect two computers.

If you have a modem, you might want to choose HyperTerminal to dial into bulletin boards and/or the applet Phone Dialer, which remembers a few phone numbers and can dial your phone for you. Windows 98 comes with a number of optional Internet applications, such as MS Chat and NetMeeting. If you have Internet or Intranet access, you'll want to install these.

System tools

The System Tools component includes hard disk backup, compression, a Drive converter and other system components, as shown in Figure 2-23. Backup is not chosen by default. You might want it if you have a device that works with it. You need compression only if you have compressed hard drives and/or want to add compressed volumes later. The Drive converter allows you to convert existing FAT volumes to FAT-32 volumes.

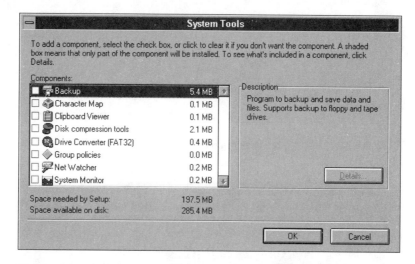

Figure 2-23: The System Tools dialog box. ScanDisk and Defrag are installed in the core components. You get to choose whether to install these three optional components.

Multimedia

The list of multimedia optional components has growth substantially since Windows 95, as shown in Figure 2-24. If you have a sound card, and perhaps a video input source, you can take advantage of these features.

Identification

In order to keep track of who is who on a network (which could consist only of Direct Cable Connection), Windows 98 needs a unique identifier for your computer. You enter this information, plus the name of your workgroup, in the dialog box shown in Figure 2-25.

The computer must be unique on your network. The name cannot be longer than 15 characters. The name should contain alphanumeric characters, and it can include the following special characters:

! @ # $ % ^ & ( ) - _ ' { } . ~

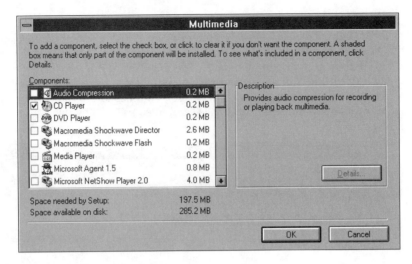

Figure 2-24: The Multimedia dialog box.

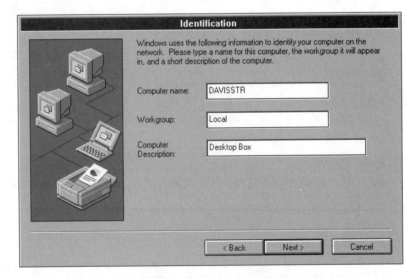

Figure 2-25: The Identification dialog box. Enter a unique computer name, the name of the workgroup to which you wish to be attached, and, if you like, a description to help others identify your computer.

Your workgroup name uses these same naming conventions. A workgroup name is shared among members of the workgroup. If you are connecting to an existing one, get the name from a network administrator or your fellow networkees. The name can contain spaces, but because it's easy to mistake two spaces for one and a common name is needed to identify members of a workgroup, you might shy away from using them.

Windows 98 displays the content of the Computer Description field as a comment to the right of your computer name when other users on the Microsoft Windows network search for your computer.

Network information required

Unless your network card is plug and play compatible, Setup may not be able to correctly configure its driver to match the card's setup. If this is the case, you will see the dialog box shown in Figure 2-26. If you know the network card's settings, you can enter them. If you want to wait until later to correctly configure this card, choose the first option in this dialog box.

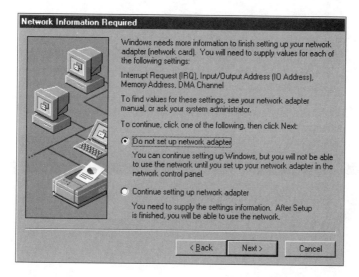

Figure 2-26: The Network Information Required dialog box. You'll need to know how your network card is configured to use it with Windows 98. With non-plug and play cards, you have to set hardware jumpers on the board or use a DOS or Windows 3.1x program. You may have to take your computer apart to find the values, or run the program that came with the card.

If you are able to remember or find the values for your network card, click the second option button in the Network Information Required dialog box and click Next. You can set these values in the Network Resources dialog box shown in Figure 2-27.

Emergency Startup disk

If there is a problem with booting your computer under Windows 98 from the hard disk, you have to be able to boot from a diskette. Setup displays the Emergency Startup Disk dialog box (see Figure 2-28) to give you the opportunity to create such a diskette.

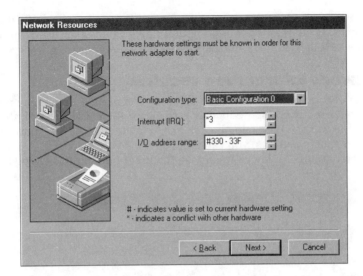

Figure 2-27: The Network Resources dialog box. Enter the interrupt and I/O address range for your network card.

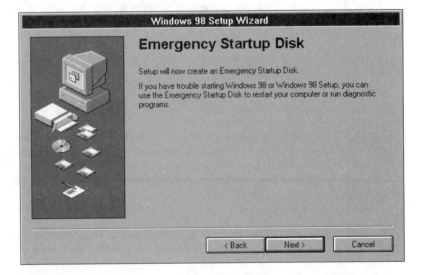

Figure 2-28: The Emergency Startup Disk dialog box. Click Next prepare Setup to create an emergency Startup diskette. If you have a bad floppy drive and might have trouble creating such a diskette, you will be able to cancel later.

You can always create a bootable emergency Startup diskette later by clicking the Start button, Settings, Control Panel, Add/Remove Programs, the Startup Disk tab, and then the Create Disk button. If you want to postpone creating the Startup disk, click Next to continue Setup, and then click Cancel in the Insert Disk dialog box. Clicking Cancel in the Emergency Startup Disk dialog box will stop the entire setup process.

Click Next to have the Windows 98 Setup collect the files that it needs to store on the diskette. Setup will ask you to insert a diskette when this process is complete, as shown in Figure 2-29.

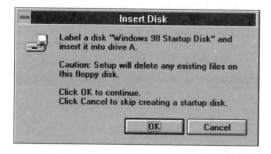

Figure 2-29: The Insert Disk dialog box. Click OK to create a Startup diskette. Click Cancel to go on to the next dialog box.

When you boot the computer using the Emergency Startup diskette, a boot menu appears which let's you load real-mode drivers for the most common CD-ROM drives. Config.sys loads the CD-ROM driver and then creates a 1MB RAMDrive.

Setup places a generic CD-ROM driver on the diskette and a call to it in the Config.sys file. If you have your own 16-bit CD-ROM driver, copy it to the diskette and edit Config.sys to call it instead. Place this call after the call to Himem.sys. Use the following syntax for the call to your 16-bit CD-ROM driver, replacing *yourCD-ROMdriver* with the actual name of your driver:

Device=*yourCD-ROMdriver*.SYS /D:mscd0001 /i:0

The Startup diskette will not be able to connect you to your network. It will contain the files listed in Table 2-4.

Table 2-4   Files on the Startup Diskette

Files	Function
Aspi2dos.sys	Real-mode Adaptec CD-ROM driver
Aspi4dos.sys	Real-mode Adaptec CD-ROM driver
Aspi8dos.sys	Real-mode Adaptec CD-ROM driver
Aspicd.sys	Real-mode Adaptec CD-ROM driver
Autoexec.bat	Startup batch file
Btcdrom.sys	Mylex/BusLogic CD-ROM driver
Btdosm.sys	Mylex/BusLogic CD-ROM driver
Command.com	DOS command interpreter

(continued)

Table 2-4   *(Continued)*

Files	*Function*
Config.sys	Loads the device drivers
Drvspace.bin	DriveSpace compression driver
Ebd.cab	Cab file containing extract utilities
Ebd.sys	File identifying the ESD
Extract.exe	File to expand the Ebd.cab file
Fdisk.exe	Disk partition tool
Findramd.exe	Utility to find the RAMDrive during startup
Flashpt.sys	Mylex/BusLogic CD-ROM driver
Himem.sys	XMS Memory Manager
Io.sys	System boot file
Msdos.sys	Boot option information
Oakcdrom.sys	Generic device driver for ATAPI CD-ROM drives
Ramdrive.sys	Creates a RAMDrive during startup
Readme.txt	Explains how the Startup diskette works
Setramd.bat	Searches for first available drive to be a RAMDrive
Io.sys	Boot DOS
Ebd.cab contains:	
Attrib.exe	Adds or removes file attributes
Chkdsk.exe	Check disk tool
Debug.exe	Debugging utility
Edit.com	DOS real-mode text editor
Extwrap.exe	New file extract utility
Format.com	Disk format tool
Mscdex.exe	CD-ROM file extension for MS-DOS
Scandisk.exe	Disk status tool
Scandisk.ini	Disk status tool configuration file
Sys.com	Transfers system files and make disk bootable
Uninstal.exe	Removes Windows 98 from the system

Files	Function
You might want to add the following files after Setup is complete (you'll find them all in the \Windows\Command folder):	
YourCD-ROMdriver.sys	16-bit real-mode driver from your CD-ROM manufacturer
Edit.hlp	Help file for Edit.com
Fc.exe	File compare utility
Mem.exe	Display memory status
More.com	Display one page at a time
Msd.exe	System diagnostics
Setver.exe	Utility to set DOS versions for some programs
Xcopy.exe	Extended copy utility

Copy files

Once Setup has gathered the information it needs from you and your computer to successfully configure and install Windows 98, it copies the files that it needs from the Windows 98 cabinet source files. You initiate this process by clicking Next in the Start Copying Files dialog box, shown in Figure 2-30.

Figure 2-30: The Start Copying Files dialog box. You can go back, cancel Setup, or go forward with Setup by clicking Next.

Finishing Setup

Copying files proceeds automatically, and at the end Setup will reboot your computer and start up in Windows 98. Unlike the Windows 95 Setup, Windows 98 waits until after rebooting your computer before it runs hardware detection. After that, it takes a while for Setup to configure the Windows 98 files. If you didn't correctly configure your network card, you will receive a message to that effect, and Setup will tell you that you can make the required changes later.

Next, Windows 98 will set up your Control Panel, configure your Start menus, and set up your help files. It will also ask you to choose your time zone setting. In addition, Windows 98 will prompt you to set up your printer and your pre-plug and play modem, if you have one.

If you like, you can ignore these setup dialog boxes and simply click the Cancel button. Later, you can use the Control Panel to set up your time zone and other devices.

If VGA was chosen for your display adapter during Setup, you can change it after Windows 98 starts by clicking the Start button, Settings, Control Panel, Display, Settings, Advanced, Adapter, Change and choosing a new video adapter. See "Installing a New Video Driver" in Chapter 28 for more details.

Installing Windows 98 Over a Copy of Windows 3.1x

You have the option, when installing Windows 98 over Windows 95 or Windows 3.1x, of saving the previous operating system files. If your install of Windows 98 is successful, but you decide to remove it later, you can always get back to your previous version of Windows, if you have chosen to save these files.

If you install Windows 98 into your Windows 3.1x directory, it will be impossible to dual-boot between the two versions of Windows (although you can manually configure your computer to dual-boot between your older version of DOS and Windows 98). Installing Windows 98 in its own directory also has drawbacks: Windows 98 won't inherit your Win 3.1x preferences, nor will it inherit your application settings in Win.ini and System.ini. (To re-establish these settings, you'll have to reinstall your applications.)

Secret

For the best of both worlds, you can copy your Windows 3.1x directory and install Windows 98 over the copy of Windows 3.1x. This not only saves your Windows 3.1x settings, but it also lets you dual-boot. Here's how to do it.

STEPS

Installing Windows 98 in a Copy of the Windows 3.1*x* Directory

Step 1. Exit Windows 3.1*x* and return to the C:\prompt.

Step 2. At the C:\prompt, type **Xcopy C:\Windows*.* C:\Win98*.* /s /e /v**.

This command duplicates your Windows 3.1*x* files. Substitute the name of the directory in which your Windows 3.1*x* files reside. Then name the directory where you want to place your Win98 files. The /e switch copies all subdirectories, including empty ones (handy when programs create directories that aren't used initially, such as Tmp directories). When you install Windows 98 in its new directory, it replaces most of the files there but still needs an extra 11MB to fully install. If the setup routine issues a message that there's not enough disk space, it will not be considering the space it recovers by overwriting files. So if Setup complains that you don't have the space available when in fact you do, you can ignore the message.

Step 3. You should still be at the C:\prompt. Type **Xcopy C:\DOS*.* C:\DOSSave*.*. /e /v**.

This command saves your DOS files. When you install Windows 98 into a directory containing Windows 3.1*x*, Windows 98 deletes older DOS files that aren't compatible with such Windows 98 features as long filenames. But you'll need these files later to dual-boot.

Step 4. At the C:\prompt, type **Edit C:\Autoexec.bat**. In your Autoexec.bat file, replace references to C:\Windows with C:\Win98. Save the file and exit. Also change Config.sys in the same way.

Next, type **Edit C:\Win98\Progman.ini** and change references to C:\Windows to C:\Win98. Unfortunately, some Windows applications (including Word) reference C:\Windows in their *ini* files. To ensure that these applications work in Windows 98, you'll have to edit every single *ini* file in the C:\Win98 directory. The best command to do this is:

```
For %f in (C:\Win98\*.ini) Do Edit %f
```

This loads, in turn, each *ini* file. Save each file and exit. Now reboot. Windows 3.1*x* should start normally in the renamed directory (C:\Win98).

If you have Tessler's Nifty Tools batch file creator (Dir2Bat), you can make this process easier using the following command:

```
Dir2Bat /F /X C:\Windows C:\Win98\*.ini "edit !"
```

(continued)

STEPS *(continued)*

Installing Windows 98 in a Copy of the Windows 3.1*x* Directory

This creates a batch file that edits only the *ini* files that contain the string "C:\Windows."

You can download this utility from http://ourworld.compuserve. com:/homepages/NIFTY_TOOLS/tnt.htm.

Edit any Program Manager icons that mention C:\Windows by right-clicking each icon in each Program Manager group and changing any references to C:\Windows to C:\Win98.

Again, this process will be easier if you use two Tessler's Nifty Tools applets. We refer you to his site at http://ourworld. compuserve.com:/homepages/NIFTY_TOOLS/tnt.htm for further instructions.

Step 5.   Now you're in Windows 3.1*x*. Choose File, Run and then type **regedit/v**. In the Registry editor, search for all instances of C:\Windows and change them to C:\Win98. Exit the Registry editor. Now run Windows 98 Setup from inside your altered copy of Windows 3.1*x*.

Setup will see a copy of Windows 3.1*x* in C:\Win98, and it will install there by default. (You've now preserved your Windows 3.1*x* preferences under Windows 98, and you still have a stored copy of your Windows 3.1*x* configuration.)

Step 6.   Delete your old C:\DOS directory using the Windows 98 Explorer.

Then rename C:\DOSSave to C:\DOS. (You've just restored your old DOS utilities.)

Remember: When running Windows 98, your new DOS 7.1 utilities will be in C:\Win98\Command. But when you dual-boot to Windows 3.1*x*, your DOS 5 or 6 files are in C:\DOS. Either way, Windows 98 automatically switches between two sets of Autoexec.bat files to set the correct path statement.

Step 7.   When you boot to Windows 98, your edited Config.sys and Autoexec.bat files for Windows 3.1*x* are renamed Config.dos and Autoexec.dos. Open these files with a text editor and change the references to C:\Win98 back to C:\Windows (or whatever folder holds your original Windows 3.1*x* installation). The Window 98 Setup created new Autoexec.bat and Config.sys files from the old ones. You may wish to delete these old files, or edit them. See "Cleaning up Config.sys and Autoexec.bat" in Chapter 35 for guidance.

Step 8.   Exit to DOS and change the properties of Msdos.sys (a hidden file in the root directory) so it is not read-only, hidden, or system. Do this by changing to the C:\Windows\Command directory, and then typing **Attrib -r -h -s C: \Msdos.sys**. Now, open Msdos.sys with a text editor.

In the [options] section, add this line, and then save the file:

```
BootMulti=1
```

You can also use the batch file EditMSDOSSys.bat to help edit this file—see "Editing Msdos.sys" in Chapter 5.

Step 9.   Reboot your PC. Press and hold the Ctrl key during the power-on self test. You'll be presented with a series of options, the last one of which is Previous Version of MS-DOS. Choose this option and your system will boot to Windows 3.1*x*.

After you install Windows 98 over your Windows 3.1*x* directory, you can delete your old Win32s directory or back it up to removable media. You'll find it under the \Windows\System directory. This directory contains the 32-bit code needed to run 32-bit apps under Windows 3.1*x*. If you're not going back to Windows 3.1*x*, you won't need it anymore. Be sure to edit your System.ini file to remove any references to it.

Adding and Removing Parts of Windows 98

You can revisit the list of Windows 98 components you saw in the Select Components dialog box during Setup, and then add or remove parts of Windows 98. Here's how to make changes:

STEPS

Adding or Removing Parts of Windows 98

Step 1.   Click the Start button, Settings, and then Control Panel.

Step 2.   Click the Add/Remove Programs icon.

Step 3.   Click the Windows Setup tab. Highlight a category of components and click Details.

Step 4.   You can clear installed components that you want removed, and mark uninstalled components that you want installed.

A subfolder of Windows 98, named \Windows\Inf, contains the setup-information files that guide the installation and removal of Windows 98 components (as well as Windows 98 Setup). These files have an *inf* extension.

You can view and edit these files by clicking them. They are all fairly short, so you can edit them with Notepad. If you want to do away with your (or someone else's) ability to easily add or remove Windows 98 components, you can delete this folder.

Copying All Your Windows 98 Files to a New Hard Disk

You can make a copy of your Windows 98 hard disk installation, including all the applications that you have installed, on a new hard disk. This makes the transition to a bigger hard disk a lot easier. Errol Nielson provided the original methods.

STEPS

Copying All Your Windows 98 Files

Step 1. If you are moving to a hard disk that is bigger than your BIOS can handle, you are going to have to use the manufacturer's setup instructions before you follow these steps. You'll either have to upgrade your BIOS, or use a program in the boot tracks of the new hard disk that supersedes your BIOS settings.

Step 2. Physically install your new hard disk as a slave (setting the correct jumper position) and using your BIOS settings to tell the computer to see it as the secondary drive. We'll refer to the first drive as C and the new one as D.

Step 3. Make sure you have a Windows 98 Emergency Startup diskette. If you haven't already created one, click the Start button, Settings, Control Panel, and click the Add/Remove Programs icon. Click the Startup Disk tab, and then the Create Disk button.

Step 4. Start Windows 98 and click the Start button, Programs, Windows Explorer. Right-click each of the two hard disk icons, and click Properties. Label the C drive *Old Disk* and the D drive *New Disk*.

Step 5. Click the Start button, Programs, MS-DOS Prompt. Type **fdisk**, press Enter, and select Change Current Fixed Disk Drive. Select the number that stands for your new drive, usually 2.

Step 6. In Fdisk, select Create DOS Partition or Logical DOS Drive, and then select and create a primary DOS partition. Exit Fdisk and restart the computer.

Step 7. Click the Start button, Programs, Windows Explorer. Right-click the D drive (the New Disk drive). Select Format, Full, and Copy System Files.

Step 8. In the Windows Explorer, choose View, Folder Options, click the View tab, and select Show All Files.

Step 9. You are now going to copy everything from C to D. The one file you don't want to copy is WIN386.swp (located in your \Windows folder on drive C). You can right-drag all the files and folders from C to D, but don't drag the Windows folder because that will copy this file also.

You can also get rid of WIN386.swp by turning off virtual memory and rebooting your computer. If you do this, you can just copy everything from C to D without worrying about working around this file. Click the Start button, Settings, Control Panel, click the System icon, click the Performance tab, click the Virtual Memory button, and mark Let Me Set My Own Virtual Memory Settings, and Disable Virtual Memory. Click OK and OK. Reboot.

If you don't disable virtual memory, you'll need to create a new \Windows folder on drive D and right-drag all the files (except WIN386.swp) and folders in the \Windows folder on C to the \Windows folder on D. Turn to "Copying a file or folder" in Chapter 7 to see how to copy files using the Explorer.

Be sure to use the right mouse button to drag and drop because if you drag with the left mouse button, Windows 98 won't actually copy the executable files. Rather, it will create shortcuts to them on the destination drive. When you right-drag and choose Copy Here from the context menu, Windows 98 copies the files themselves.

Step 9a. There is an alternative to right drag and drop copying. You can click the Start button, click Run, and then type:

```
XCOPY C:\ D:\ /c /e /f /h /r /s
```

Do not use XCopy in MS-DOS mode because it will destroy long filenames.

Step 10. Right-click your D drive hard disk icon. Choose Properties, and then click the Tools tab. Click the Check Now button and click the Thorough option button in the ScanDisk dialog box. Click the Start button.

Step 11. When error checking is complete, exit Windows 98 and turn off your computer. Unplug or remove the old drive (the C drive). Reset the jumpers on the slave to turn it into the master.

Step 12. Place your Windows 98 Startup diskette in the A drive. Restart your computer, press the key that gets you into your BIOS editor, change the drive table settings to reflect the changes in the hard disk configuration. Continue the boot process, saving your new BIOS settings to boot off your floppy drive.

Step 13. Type **fdisk** and press Enter. Select Set Active Partition. Exit Fdisk, remove the Windows 98 Startup diskette from the floppy drive. Restart your computer. You should be running Windows 98 off your new hard disk.

(continued)

STEPS *(continued)*

Copying All Your Windows 98 Files

Step 14. If everything is working, you can reinstall your original hard disk as your D drive. Set the jumpers on it to be the slave, exit Windows 98 and turn off the computer. Re-plug in your old drive. Restart your computer and go to your BIOS settings. Edit the BIOS table to match your current hard disk configuration.

Some computers won't boot with a bootable drive set up as a slave drive. If you find this to be the case, place your Windows 98 Startup diskette in your floppy drive, boot to it and use Fdisk to Delete Partition of Logical Disk Drive on drive D. Don't do this until you are sure that your new disk drive is working.

There are more automated ways of accomplishing this task. You can find a program designed for system administrators at http://www.ghostsoft.com (it costs $250). Another option is the wonderful program Partition Magic 3.0. This program lets you resize your hard disk partitions without losing all your files and data. It also lets you move all of Windows 98 to a new disk. Check it out at http://www.powerquest.com/partitionmagic.

Windows 98 comes with a new facility to allow you to make multiple clones of a given installation. You'll find the program on your Windows 98 CD-ROM.

Installing Windows 98 With Other Operating Systems

If your computer has OS/2, Windows NT, or DR DOS installed as its operating system, you can still install Windows 98 on it and have both operating systems living in harmony. There are a few basic requirements.

DR DOS

Installing Windows 98 on a computer with DR DOS version 3.x through 7.x is similar to installing it on a computer with MS-DOS. None of the DR DOS files are erased. Certain DR DOS programs will cause a conflict with Setup. Setup checks to see if these programs are running. Remark them out of Autoexec.bat and Config.sys if there is a problem with Setup.

When Setup creates new Autoexec.bat and Config.sys files at the end of Setup, it comments out the command lines that start DR DOS utilities that cause problems for Io.sys.

Remove password protection for your volumes before you start Windows 98 Setup.

Windows NT

Windows NT has its own multi-boot capability, the Windows NT Boot Loader. This is not true of MS-DOS, DR DOS, or Windows 3.1x.

On a computer that will have both Windows NT and Windows 98 installed, you want the Windows NT Boot Loader to be in charge. The Windows NT Boot Loader will be in the boot tracks of the boot device, your bootable hard disk.

When you boot your computer, the Windows NT Boot Loader will appear first and let you choose between NT and DOS. Windows 98 Setup doesn't change this arrangement. To run Setup, you need to choose MS-DOS.

Once Setup has run and rebooted your computer, you must choose MS-DOS again to let Windows 98 Setup configure all the files that it needs to continue successfully. Choosing MS-DOS from the Windows NT Boot Loader will allow your computer to load Windows 98.

It is possible that the copy of Windows NT on your computer was installed in your Windows 3.1x directory. Both Windows NT and Windows 3.1x can successfully run from the same directory. This is not true of Windows NT and Windows 98. You will need to install Windows 98 in a different directory than your Windows NT directory.

After installing Windows 98 on a Windows NT computer, you can boot to Windows 98 by booting to MS-DOS at the Windows NT Boot Loader. The Windows 98 file Io.sys will actually be started if you make this choice at boot time. Io.sys reads Msdos.sys to determine whether it should boot into Windows 98, DOS 7.1, your previous version of DOS, or Windows 3.1x, if Windows 3.1x is installed on your computer.

You can edit Msdos.sys to specify which way your Windows NT computer will boot if you choose MS-DOS. See "Editing Msdos.sys" in Chapter 5 for guidelines on editing this file. The same guidelines apply whether you have a Windows NT or a Windows 98 computer.

You can only set up dual-booting on a disk partition that is formatted for the FAT file system. This is the file system that works with DOS. Windows NT can manage this kind of disk partition as well as NTFS driver partitions. Windows 98 won't even see these NTFS partitions.

Secret

You can install Windows NT on a Windows 98 computer. Io.sys will be moved out of the boot tracks by the Windows NT setup, just as though it were the DOS version of Io.sys. The Windows NT Boot Loader will be placed there instead.

You should install Windows NT from the DOS 7.1 prompt.

OS/2

Like Windows NT, you let the OS/2 Boot Manager have the first crack at deciding which operating system is going to be loaded. Like Windows NT, OS/2 has its own file system (HPFS) that it manages along with any FAT drive partitions on your computer. Windows 98 must be installed in a FAT partition. It cannot see the HPFS partitions.

You have to run Windows 98 Setup from MS-DOS. Be sure that your OS/2 system is configured to dual-boot to MS-DOS. You may need to reconfigure OS/2 before you run Windows 98 Setup.

The OS/2 Boot Manager is disabled by Windows 98 Setup. You'll want to re-enable it by running the OS/2 Fdisk utility from your OS/2 boot diskette after Windows 98 is completely installed.

An OS/2 computer will most likely have Windows 3.1x installed also. You need to install Windows 98 in a new directory. This will give you the option of booting to OS/2, DOS, Windows 3.1x, or Windows 98.

Secret

You can install OS/2 after you have installed Windows 98. Like Windows NT, the OS/2 installation thinks that the Windows 98 Io.sys file in the boot tracks is the DOS version.

Uninstalling Windows 98

You can uninstall Windows 98, and there are various levels of uninstall. If you chose to save your existing Windows 3.1x installation when you installed Windows 98, you can uninstall Windows 98 by just going to the Add/Remove Programs icon in the Control Panel and choosing to uninstall Windows 98. If you didn't do this, you can use the following procedures.

You can uninstall just the Windows portion of Windows 98 and keep the DOS 7.1 portions. You can remove the DOS 7.1 portions and go back to booting your computer to an earlier version of DOS. It helps if you have protected your previous DOS files, although you can also restore them from your DOS diskettes.

If you installed Windows 98 to a directory other than your Windows 3.1x directory, you can go back to your earlier version of Windows. If you installed Windows 98 in your Windows 3.1x directory and didn't save the information necessary to uninstall Windows 98, you'll need to reinstall Windows 3.1x (as well as nearly all of your Windows programs).

Most of Windows 98 is installed in the Windows 98 folder. This folder may be named Windows, Win98, or whatever other name you chose when you installed Windows 98.

Back to DOS 7.1

Secret

You can remove Windows 98 and still boot to its DOS 7.1 portions. You can run Windows 3.1x from DOS 7.1 (although you may have to reinstall Windows 3.1x if you installed Windows 98 over it). You can use the DOS 7.1 that comes with Windows 98 just like an upgraded version of DOS, which it is (although not completely).

STEPS

Deleting Windows 98 Back to DOS 7.1

Step 1. Turn on your computer. Press and hold the Ctrl key during the power-on self test. Choose Command Prompt Only.

Step 2. Create a DOS 7.1 folder and copy the DOS 7.1 files into this folder. At the DOS 7.1 command prompt, type:

```
c:
cd\
md\DOS71
cd\DOS71
xcopy \Win98\Command\*.*
xcopy \Win98\Emm386.exe
xcopy \Win98\Smartdrv.exe
xcopy \Win98\Command.com
xcopy \Win98\Setver.exe
```

(\Win98 is your Windows 98 folder.)

Step 3. Delete most of the Windows 98 files. At the DOS 7.1 command prompt type:

```
path c:\DOS71
deltree c:\WIN98
```

Step 4. Edit your Autoexec.bat and Config.sys files to refer to the \DOS71 directory instead of the \Win98 or \Win98\Command directory. You may want to put Smartdrv back into your Autoexec.bat file to get disk caching. You can add Emm386.exe to Config.sys to get memory management. Turn to Chapter 35 for more details on DOS.

Step 5. Edit Msdos.sys to start at the DOS 7.1 command prompt. At the DOS 7.1 command prompt type:

```
attrib -r -h -s Msdos.sys
edit Msdos.sys
```

Add the following lines to the [options] section of Msdos.sys:

```
BootGUI=0
BootWin=1
```

When you are finished editing Msdos.sys, save it and type the following at the command prompt:

```
attrib +r +h +s Msdos.sys
```

Step 6. You can delete some extraneous files from your root directory. Some of these files may be hidden, so you can't see them unless you type **dir /a** and press Enter while at the DOS prompt at the root directory.

(continued)

STEPS *(continued)*

Deleting Windows 98 Back to DOS 7.1

```
del setuplog.*
del Bootlog.*
del Setlog.*
del Sudhlog.*
del Netlog.*
del System.1st
```

Back to an earlier version of MS-DOS

You can remove Windows 98 completely and revert to your earlier DOS and perhaps Windows 3.1*x* operating system.

You remove Windows 98 from the DOS command line prompt (as only seems fitting). You can do this from either the DOS 7.1 command line prompt or the command prompt of your earlier version of DOS (if you have dual-boot capability).

STEPS

Removing Windows 98 Completely

Step 1.   Make sure you have a DOS diskette that will boot your computer to your previous version of DOS. This diskette must contain the file Sys.com. If you have deleted your earlier version of DOS from your hard disk, you also need diskettes containing all your earlier DOS files. The number 1 diskette in the DOS 6.*x* set is bootable. This is not true of earlier versions of MS-DOS, and you may need to create such a bootable diskette, perhaps using another DOS computer.

Step 2.   Turn on your computer. Press and hold the Ctrl key during the power-on self test. Choose Command Prompt Only or Previous Version of MS-DOS. Choosing Command Prompt Only boots your computer to DOS 7.1. Choosing Previous Version of MS-DOS boots it to your older DOS (if you have dual-boot capability).

Step 3.   Copy the Windows 98 versions of Deltree.exe and Scandisk.exe to the root directory. At the command prompt type:

```
c:
cd\
copy \Win98\Command\Deltree.exe
copy \Win98\Scandisk.*
copy \Win98\Attrib.exe
```

(We assume that \Win98 is your Windows 98 folder.)

Step 4.   Edit your Scandisk.ini file so ScanDisk can clean up your long filenames. At the command prompt type:

```
edit scandisk.ini
```

Set labelcheck=on and spacecheck=on so ScanDisk will check for invalid characters and spaces in volume labels and filenames.

Step 5.   Run ScanDisk to remove these bad filenames (long names that are proper under Windows 98). At the command prompt type:

```
Scandisk c:
```

You can scan all your volumes from inside ScanDisk.

Step 6.   Delete most of your Windows 98 files. At the command prompt type:

```
deltree c:\Win98
```

Step 7.   You can now delete files in the root directory that are associated with Windows 98. If you chose menu item 6 in step 2, at the command prompt type:

```
del Autoexec.bat
del Config.sys
ren Autoexec.w40 Autoexec.bat
ren Config.w40 Config.sys
```

If you chose menu item 8 in step 2, at the command prompt type:

```
del Autoexec.w40
del Config.w40
del Winboot.sys
```

Step 8.   Delete additional files in the root directory associated with Windows 98. Some of these files may be hidden, so you can't see them unless you type **dir /a** and press Enter while at the DOS prompt at the root directory. At the command prompt type:

```
del Setlog.*
del Detlog.*
del Bootlog.*
del Sudhlog.*
del netlog.*
del System.1st
del *.---
```

Step 9.   Delete the real-mode DOS files associated with Windows 98. If you chose menu item 6 in step 2, at the command prompt type:

```
del Command.com
```

If you chose menu item 8 in step 2, at the command prompt type:

```
del Winboot.sys
del Msdos.w40
del Command.w40
```

(continued)

If your boot drive is compressed, you need to erase these files from the root directory of your host drive.

Step 10. If you were using DoubleSpace or DriveSpace compression under Windows 98, you can also delete the compression drivers. Don't do this if you are using Stacker version 3.1. At the command prompt type:

```
del D??space.*
```

If your boot drive is compressed, you need to erase these files from the root directory of your host drive.

Step 11. Put your bootable DOS diskette into drive A and reboot your computer.

Step 12. Place the boot portion of your earlier version of DOS in the boot tracks of your bootable hard disk by typing at the command prompt (after your computer starts):

```
sys c:
```

Step 13. You may need to copy Command.com from your boot diskette to the root directory of your hard disk. Also, you may need to edit Autoexec.bat and Config.sys.

Step 14. If you have MS-DOS version 6.*x* and you are using disk compression, you'll want to place the real-mode DOS 6.*x* version of the DoubleSpace or DriveSpace compression driver in the root directory.

Step 15. Remove the bootable floppy from drive A and restart your computer.

Back to Windows NT

If you have installed Windows 98 on a computer that has Windows NT with its Boot Loader managing the bootup process, you can erase Windows 98 and restore your computer to its previous configuration.

STEPS

Removing Windows 98 from a Computer with Windows NT

Step 1. Follow all the steps used in the previous section to get back to your previous version of MS-DOS.

Step 2. Reboot your computer with the first Windows NT setup diskette in drive A.

Step 3. Choose the Repair option after you boot off this diskette.

Step 4. When you are prompted to do so, put your Windows NT emergency repair diskette in drive A and choose the option to repair the boot files.

Step 5. You may need to edit your MS-DOS Autoexec.bat and Config.sys files and reinstall Windows 3.1x if it is in a separate directory from Windows NT and you installed Windows 98 in that directory.

Summary

Lots of little wrinkles come with installing and setting up Windows 98.

▶ Follow our guidelines to determine if your computer can run Windows 98.

▶ We show you how to free hard disk space so that you can have enough room to install Windows 98.

▶ If you want to maintain your old DOS setup, we show you how to protect your existing DOS files.

▶ Did you like Windows Write? We get it back for you.

▶ The Windows 98 Setup is slow. We show you how to speed it up.

▶ You can run into problems setting up Windows 98 from a CD-ROM or a network server. We show you how to avoid these problems.

▶ Windows 98 Setup goes on and on. We help you each step of the way.

▶ Want to inhabit a multioperating system environment? We show you how Windows 98 can coexist with OS/2 and Windows NT.

▶ If you want to revert to an earlier operating system, you can uninstall Windows 98.

Chapter 3

A Quick Look at Windows 98

In This Chapter

This chapter is an introduction to the workings of Windows 98. Follow along and in a few minutes you will have a good grasp of the basic notions that underlie Windows 98.

- What are those icons doing on my Desktop?
- Where do I start?
- How do I run a program?
- Where do I find help?
- What is the Active Desktop?
- What are channels?
- What is the My Computer icon?
- What happens when I click the My Computer icon, a drive icon, a folder icon?
- How do I see what is on My Computer?
- How do I quit Windows 98?

The Desktop

We assume that you have been able to install and set up Windows 98 correctly (or that it was already installed on your computer), and that the Windows 98 Desktop is now displayed on your screen. Your screen should look something like Figure 3-1. If this is not the case, first check Figure 3-2 in the next section to see if you are viewing the Active Desktop. If your screen doesn't resemble that figure either, then you should go back to "Starting Setup" in Chapter 2 to get Windows 98 installed properly.

On the left side of the Desktop you'll find five or more icons, depending on the options you chose during installation. You use these icons to find and view the files and folders that are stored on your computer (and, if you are connected to other computers, on the network of computers). At the bottom of the Desktop is the Taskbar with its Start button and clock. The Taskbar is a switcher — it lets you easily move between open documents and active applications.

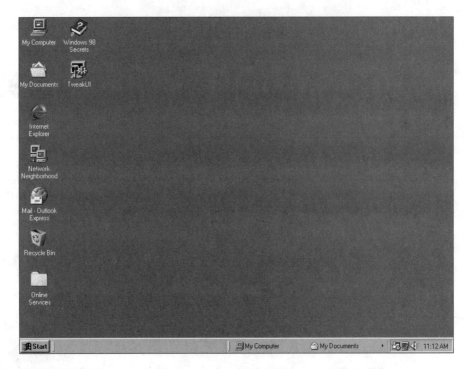

Figure 3-1: The Windows 98 Desktop. Click the Start button or any of the icons on the Desktop.

Tip

If you don't see your Taskbar at all, slide your mouse pointer to the bottom of your screen. The Taskbar should jump into view. Right-click a part of the Taskbar without buttons or icons, and choose Properties. In the Taskbar Options tab, clear the Auto Hide check box and click OK.

For a little fun, try moving the Taskbar around the edges of the Desktop. Take the following steps:

STEPS
Moving the Taskbar

Step 1.   Position your mouse pointer over the Taskbar, but not over the clock or the Start button (or any other buttons representing applications that are currently open).

Step 2.   Press and hold the left mouse button.

Step 3.   Holding the left mouse button down, move the mouse pointer to a side or the top of the Desktop.

Step 4. When an outline of the Taskbar appears on a side or the top of the Desktop, release the mouse button.

Step 5. Repeat steps 1 through 4 to move the Taskbar around the Desktop.

Active Desktop

Windows 98 combines the interface of the Internet Explorer web browser with the Windows 95 user interface. This combined interface mixes two metaphors: the Desktop, with its files and folders, and *Web style*, with its hyperlinks between documents. Web style is intended to make folders and icons behave as they would if they were part of a web page. (The way they used to behave in Windows 95 is now called *Classic style*.) Carry this concept through to viewing the Desktop as a web page, and you get the *Active Desktop*.

The Active Desktop allows you to have live open documents on your Desktop, regardless of whether they reside on your hard disk, on your local network, or on the Internet (see Figure 3-2). These documents may be continuously updated, if you have a continuous Internet or Intranet connection, or periodically updated if you don't. If the documents contain graphical elements, they may even be animated.

To turn your Desktop into the Active Desktop, click Start, Settings, Active Desktop, View As Web Page.

You can add an object to the Active Desktop by picking one from the Microsoft Active Desktop gallery (a Microsoft web site) or from any other web site or a channel.

STEPS

Adding an Active Item to the Desktop

Step 1. Click Start, Settings, Active Desktop, Customize My Desktop.

Step 2. Click the Web tab, and make sure that View My Active Desktop As a Web Page is marked.

Step 3. Click the New button, and then click Yes in the New Active Desktop Item dialog box. If you have an Internet connection, you will soon be connected to the Microsoft Active Desktop gallery.

Step 4. Click an object in the gallery of possible objects.

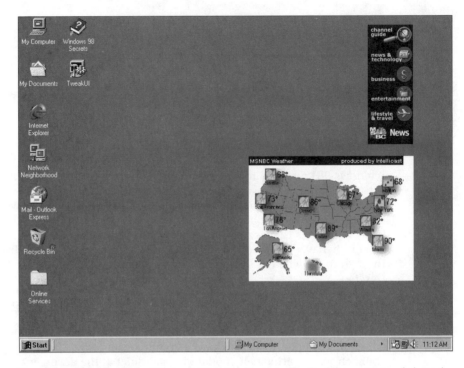

Figure 3-2: An example of a Windows 98 Active Desktop. The Desktop content and channels have been customized for this user. Use the channels or add items from the web to create your own live information connections.

You can also add an object by right-dragging any link on a web page onto your Desktop, and then selecting Create Active Desktop Item(s) Here. If you want to add the current page to your Desktop, drag the icon from the left end of the Address bar in the Internet Explorer to your Desktop. Once it's on your Desktop, you can drag the object around and resize it using its title bar. Try adding a page with stock market results or a weather map, for starters.

If you don't have a continuous connection to the Internet, you can update your active content whenever you like by right-clicking the Desktop, and selecting Active Desktop, Update Now. You can set up your computer to connect to the Internet and update an item on a schedule by right-clicking the item, clicking Properties, and then clicking the Schedule tab. To learn more about working with the Active Desktop, turn to "The Active Desktop" in Chapter 6.

Single-Click Icons

With Windows 98 you can just single-click Desktop icons to open the associated program or window instead of double-clicking them as you had to in the past. Although Windows 98 comes with double-clicking set as the default, we feel so strongly about the ease of single-clicking that we've made it the default throughout this book. Whenever you see instructions to *click* an icon on the Desktop or in the Explorer, keep in mind that you still have the option of double-clicking if you prefer.

Although single-clicking is associated with Web style and double-clicking is associated with Classic style, you can use the Custom option to pick your favorite features of both styles.

To enable single-clicking if you haven't already, click the Start button, Settings, Folders & Icons. Either mark the Web style option button — or mark the Custom option button, click the Settings button, and mark the Single-Click to Open an Item (Point to Select) option button. You can still easily select icons (by hovering your mouse pointer over them) or groups of icons (by using the Shift or Ctrl key in combination with hovering). See the "Single-click or double-click" section of Chapter 8 for more about single-clicking.

Finding Stuff the Web Way

Desktop, *folders*, *files*, *documents* — the Windows 98 Desktop view is based on these office-related metaphors.

In contrast, the Active Desktop and Web style are based on the metaphor of linked objects. When you point to an icon, the mouse pointer becomes a pointing hand, and clicking once takes you to the object represented by the icon, be it on your local hard disk, your network, or the Internet. When you're using Web style, items on your screen are often *active*, meaning that they incorporate multimedia effects such as movies, sound, and 3D images. If you prefer to stick to the office metaphor, you can still use Classic style — or you can use Custom to select which features of each style you want to use.

The standard Desktop view emphasizes where things are stored. The Active Desktop concentrates on showing you what content is available (regardless of where it is stored) and how you can interact with it.

The Start Button

Click the Start button. Among the commands on the menu is Help. Click Help to launch general help for Windows 98. You can learn a lot here — take a look at the genuinely useful Troubleshooting section, for example.

The Start menu also contains several menu names (Programs, Documents, and so on). Note that menu names all have small black triangles to their right. To display a menu, simply point to its name. Point to Programs, then to Accessories, then to Games (if you installed games during the setup process), and then click FreeCell. This is an example of how you run programs from the Start button in Windows 98.

What's on the Desktop?

There are a number of icons on the Windows 98 Desktop. Unlike the icons on the Windows 3.1x Desktop, these icons do not represent active programs or "tasks," which is why we are emphasizing this point.

The icons represent *capabilities* sitting there waiting for you to do something. Nothing happens or is happening until you click one of the icons. When you click one of these icons, you open a *window*.

The My Computer icon looks like a computer, and it represents your computer. Click this icon and see what you get. Then right-click the My Computer window again, point to View, and choose one of the following: Large Icons, Small Icons, List, or Details.

You can also view your My Computer window as a web page (see Figure 3-3). This option gives you additional information about each icon as you highlight it. To change views, right-click the My Computer window, point to View, and then choose As Web Page.

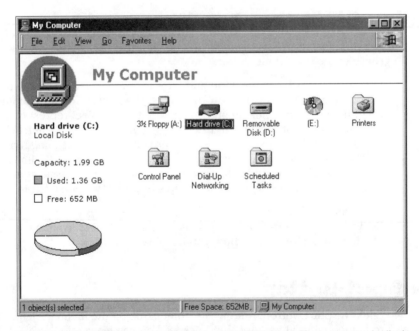

Figure 3-3: The My Computer window viewed in Web style. Your computer is displayed in the My Computer window. The computer shown has one hard drive volume, one floppy diskette drive, a CD-ROM drive, a removable hard drive, and four folders — Control Panel, Printers, Dial-Up Networking, and Scheduled Tasks. Note the additional information (on the left) about the highlighted hard drive.

Other icons you may see include the Recycle Bin, Network Neighborhood, My Documents, My Briefcase, and Internet Explorer. The exact number and type of icons you see depends on your installation. You can add and change the icons on your Desktop; we show you how throughout this book.

Tune in the Channels

An unmistakable new feature of your Desktop is the Channel Bar, appearing as a column of bright buttons down the right portion of your display (shown in Figure 3-2 earlier in the chapter). If you don't see the Channel Bar at first, right-click the Desktop, click Properties, click the Web tab, mark the View My Active Desktop As a Web Page and Internet Explorer Channel Bar check boxes, and then click OK.

In some ways, a channel is a lot like a shortcut to a web site. However, for web content that changes frequently—such as news, finance, and sports—it can be a lot more. You can subscribe to a channel so that its content is updated either automatically throughout the day, or whenever you choose to update it. To *subscribe* to a channel just means that you choose an update schedule (which may mean that updates happen automatically in the background). You can view a channel in an Internet Explorer window—either displayed at standard size or in full-screen mode—or as continually or periodically updated wallpaper.

The Channel Bar contains buttons for individual channels—such as PointCast, MS-NBC, and MSN—and categories of channels, such as Entertainment, Business, and Sports. When you click a button in the Channel Bar, Internet Explorer opens in full-screen mode (it fills the entire screen and its title bar is hidden), starts a connection to the Internet (dialing up through your modem if necessary), and displays the channel or category you chose.

The column of buttons that appears on the left side of the Internet Explorer window when you're viewing a channel is the Channel Explorer Bar. (All of the buttons in the Channel Bar on the Desktop are also displayed in the Channel Explorer Bar.) Microsoft starts you off with its favored channels, but you can remove any you don't care for and add your own. To remove a channel, just right-click it and click Delete.

The Channel Explorer Bar goes away as soon as you move your mouse pointer off of it. To make it stay put, slide your mouse pointer all the way to the left of the screen to bring it into view, and then click the push-pin icon in the upper-right corner of the bar. To get out of full-screen mode, click the Fullscreen button in the toolbar at the top of the screen (it looks like a small window superimposed on a larger window). To get back to full-screen mode if the Fullscreen button isn't visible, hold down the Ctrl key while you click the Maximize button at the right end of the Internet Explorer title bar.

Click the Channel Guide button in the Channel Bar (or the Channel Explorer Bar) to go to Microsoft's Active Channel Guide web site and browse through Microsoft's most recent selection of channels. You can search for a channel by clicking a category heading and then entering a keyword in the search field, or you can just scroll through the selections. If you find a channel that you want to add to your Channel Bar, click the Add Active Channel button on the web site's preview window. Once you've added a channel, you can subscribe to it by clicking another button on its home page.

There are more channels than those listed on the Active Channel Guide web site. If you visit a web site and see the Add Active Channel button, all you have to do is click it to add that site to your Channel Bar.

Look in the "Channels" section of Chapter 9 for more on channels, including how to use them as wallpaper.

What's in the My Computer Window?

In the My Computer window, you'll find icons that look like disk drives and, in fact, represent the disk drives connected to your computer. (The drives may be connected directly to your computer or to other computers on your local area network.) These drive icons act just like icons on the Desktop. That is, you can click them to view their contents.

You also see four folder icons labeled Control Panel, Printers, Dial-Up Networking, and Scheduled Tasks. You can click these icons as well to see what's in the folders.

Click the C: drive icon in the My Computer window. (In Figure 3-3, the C: volume is named Hard Drive.) The C: drive window appears on your Desktop, as shown in Figure 3-4.

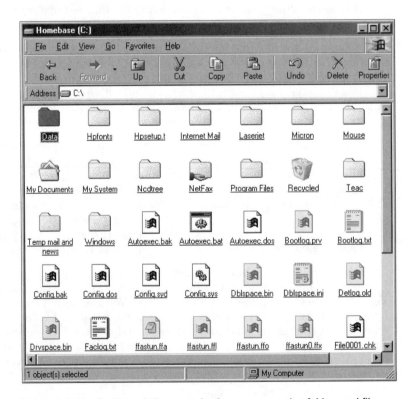

Figure 3-4: The C: drive window contains icons representing folders and files.

The My Computer icon on the Desktop and the drive icons in the My Computer window respond in the same manner. Click them to open a window.

Disk Drives, Folders, and Files

The C: drive window contains icons that look like manila folders with tabs on the left side. These folder icons represent folders. Folders can contain files and other folders.

The other icons in the C: drive window represent different kinds of files. One icon that's present in the drive windows of local hard disks is the Recycled icon, which vaguely looks like a recycle receptacle. This icon is equivalent to the Recycle Bin icon on the Desktop. (You'll learn about the Recycle Bin in Chapter 14.)

You started with the My Computer icon, which looks like a computer. When you opened My Computer, you found that it contained drive icons and some folder icons. When you opened a drive icon, you saw that it contained icons representing folders and files, including one that displays the Recycle Bin. Clicking a folder icon in turn displays the folders and/or files it contains.

All of the icons that are on your Desktop the first time you start Windows 98 represent containers. They can contain disk drives, folders, and/or files.

Special Folder Windows

Everything on your computer is displayed within a window. You open a window by clicking an icon that represents the Internet, a network, a computer, a drive, a folder, a document, or an application. Some icons, such as the Recycle Bin and the My Briefcase icons (if you installed the Briefcase) represent special kinds of folders. These special folders are *objects* that can have properties beyond merely containing files and folders.

For example, when you delete files from your local hard disks, Windows 98 stores them in the Recycle Bin. A property of the Recycle Bin is that you can *restore* files within it back to their previous locations (until you issue the File, Empty the Recycle Bin command). A property of My Briefcase is that you can change files you've copied into this folder, and then use them to "update" the original files on your hard disk.

Windows 98 knows the properties that special folders support, and it automatically takes advantage of them when acting on files within these folders.

Quitting

If this is enough and you want to quit now—after all, this is just a first look— click the Start button at the left end of the Taskbar, and then click Shut Down.

In the Shut Down Windows dialog box, choose Shut Down, and click the OK button. After a moment, if you have a newer computer with advanced power management capability, your computer turns off. Otherwise, Windows 98 displays a message stating "It's now safe to turn off your computer." At this point, you can safely turn off your machine.

You will find a great deal of discussion about the Desktop, the Start button, folders, and windows in Part II.

Summary

We provide a quick look at the Windows 98 user interface. If you followed the steps in this chapter, you should now have a good grasp of the most basic structure of Windows 98.

▶ Explore what's on the Desktop.

▶ Move the Taskbar around the Desktop.

▶ Switch between the standard Desktop and the Active Desktop.

▶ Investigate what the Channel Bar has to offer.

▶ Switch between Classic style and Web style.

▶ Use the Start button to start a program and find help.

▶ See what is in the My Computer window.

▶ Open a drive or folder window.

▶ Quit Windows 98.

Chapter 4

A Tutorial for Windows 98

In This Chapter

We provide a step-by step tutorial that introduces the basic features of the Windows 98 user interface. You will learn about:

▶ Switching views in windows and on the Desktop

▶ Creating files and folders

▶ Moving a file between folders

▶ Creating a shortcut to the file and putting it on the Desktop

▶ Deleting the shortcut and the file

▶ Restoring the file and shortcut

Starting

Complete this tutorial and within a few minutes you'll be familiar with the main concepts underlying Windows 98. Grasp these concepts and the logic of Windows 98 is revealed. Using this logic, you can explore on your own.

Before continuing, be sure to go over the steps in Chapter 3 so that you are familiar with the concepts we use in this chapter.

Switching Views

Windows 98 lets you choose between two different styles for how windows and their contents will behave. You can either have them appear and behave more as they would if you were viewing them on the web (this is called *Web style*), or you can have them look and behave more as they did in Windows 95 (this is called *Classic style*). You can also pick and choose among the features that make up these two styles. For example, you can choose the Windows 95 look for your Desktop (part of the Classic style) but still enable single-clicking to open a window (part of the Web style).

STEPS

Switching Between Classic Style and Web Style

Step 1. Click the Start button, Settings, Folders & Icons to display the Folder Options dialog box.

Step 2. If you want to use the default settings for Web style or Classic style, just mark either one of these option buttons and click OK. If, instead, you want to pick and choose among the options contained in these two styles, mark Custom, Based On Settings You Choose, click the Settings button, and continue with the remaining steps.

Step 3. In the Custom Settings dialog box, notice the various options for changing how folders and other objects are treated.

Step 4. While you're here, enable single-clicking (if you haven't done so already) by marking the Single-Click to Open an Item (Point to Select) option button. In this tutorial (and throughout this book) we assume that you have single-clicking enabled.

Step 5. When you have finished selecting any options you'd like to try, click OK twice to close the Custom Settings dialog box and the Folder Options dialog box.

Your changes will take effect immediately. If you've chosen single-clicking, remember that you now select an item by hovering instead of clicking.

You can view your My Computer and Explorer windows as if they were web pages. (You'll learn about Explorer windows in the next section.) Regardless of whether you have chosen Web style or Classic style, you can set this viewing option independently for individual windows. When you first open a window, the web page view may not be turned on. To turn on web page view for the My Computer window, take the following steps:

STEPS

Viewing a Window as a Web Page

Step 1. Click the My Computer icon.

Step 2. Right-click an empty part of the My Computer window. Point to View, and then mark or clear As Web Page.

Step 3. Highlight different disk drives and folders in the My Computer window. Notice the additional information you see on the left side of the window when you're using this view.

Step 4. Click View, Explorer Bar, and then try out the different options in this menu to see how they work. If you haven't connected to the Internet yet, you probably won't see much under Favorites or History.

Step 5. Click the Close button (the X) in the upper-right corner of the window to close My Computer.

If you enable the Active Desktop, your Desktop can become a connection to the Internet, containing "live" objects that are periodically updated.

STEPS

Changing to the Active Desktop

Step 1. Right-click the Desktop, steering clear of your icons.

Step 2. Point to Active Desktop at the top of the context menu, and then mark View As Web Page to see your Desktop transformed.

The Active Desktop will contain at least the Channel Bar, and may contain other windows that represent Active Desktop components. If you don't see the Channel Bar, refer to "Tune in the Channels" in Chapter 3 to see how to bring it back.

Step 3. Right-click the Desktop again, point to Active Desktop, and this time clear the check mark next to View As Web Page to switch back to the standard Desktop view. Switch back and forth a few times until you are comfortable with it.

Using the Explorer

Another tool that you can use in addition to My Computer to see what's in your computer is the Windows Explorer. The two tools are very much alike, with one significant difference: You can turn the Explorer window into a My Computer window, but not vice versa.

STEPS

Comparing the Explorer to My Computer

Step 1.   Right-click your My Computer icon and click Explore in the context menu to start the Explorer. (You can also start the Explorer by clicking the Start button, pointing to Programs, and clicking Windows Explorer.) Notice the similarities to My Computer. The Explorer is sort of a My Computer with two panes.

Step 2.   In the Explorer window, choose View, Explorer Bar, and notice that the All Folders command is marked by default. Click None. The Explorer window changes to a single-pane window much like the My Computer window. Now choose View, Explorer Bar, and click All Folders to go back to a dual-pane window.

If you start with the Explorer window, you have the option of turning off the All Folders pane, which in essence lets you turn the Explorer into My Computer. Click the Close button (the X) in the upper-right corner of the window to close the Explorer. (This is the same as choosing File, Close.)

Step 3.   Now click the My Computer icon to open the My Computer window, and choose View, Explorer Bar. Notice that there is no All Folders choice. You can't go from a My Computer window to an Explorer window. Click the Close button to close My Computer.

The Explorer and My Computer give you four different options for viewing their contents:

STEPS

Changing How Icons Are Displayed

Step 1.   Right-click the My Computer icon, and choose Explore.

Step 2.   Click View, and choose Large Icons, Small Icons, List, or Details from the menu that appears.

Step 3.   Try all four views to see which one you prefer.

Step 4.   When you're finished, close the Explorer window.

In Chapter 7 and Chapter 8, you will learn a lot more about both My Computer and the Windows Explorer.

Creating a Folder or Two

The first thing you need to do is create some folders to store files. You can easily delete these folders later if you choose.

STEPS

Creating a Folder

Step 1. Click My Computer (the My Computer icon on the Desktop).

Step 2. Click the C: drive icon in the My Computer window.

Step 3. Right-click in an empty area of the C: drive window, away from any icons.

Step 4. Point to New in the context menu.

Step 5. Click Folder in the submenu that appears. A new folder icon appears in the client area of the C: drive window, and the name of the folder (New Folder) is highlighted.

Step 6. Type **Temporary** as the name of the folder and press Enter. (The text you type replaces the original folder name.)

Step 7. Right-click the client area of the C: drive window (away from any icons) to display the context menu, and this time point to Arrange Icons, and then click Auto Arrange. (This command is not available if you are using List or Details view. See step 2 under Changing How Icons Are Displayed in the previous section.)

Step 8. Repeat steps 3 through 6, but this time type **Temporary 2** as the folder name.

You have just created two folders in the root directory of the C drive. They are named *Temporary* and *Temporary 2* so you'll know you can delete them later with no negative consequences.

Creating a File

Now, you are going to create a file and edit it a bit. Windows 98 lets you create a document first before opening an application. It also associates the appropriate application with that document.

STEPS

Creating a File

Step 1.   Click the Temporary folder in the C: drive window. Click View, Folder Options, click the View tab, and clear the Hide File Extensions for Known File Types check box. Click OK. You want to be able to see the file extension of the file you are about to create.

Step 2.   Right-click the client area of the Temporary folder window.

Step 3.   Point to New in the context menu.

Step 4.   Click Text Document in the submenu. A file icon with the name New Text Document.txt appears in the Temporary folder. The name is highlighted.

Step 5.   Type **Temporary File.txt** as the new name for the document and press Enter.

Step 6.   Click the Temporary File.txt icon. The Notepad application starts and gives you a blank client area in which to type some text. When you have a bit of text in the file, click File and then Save in the Notepad menu.

Step 7.   Click the Close button (the X) in the upper-right corner of the Notepad window to quit the application.

You have created a new file, added some text to it, and saved the edited file in the Temporary folder.

Moving a File

Next, you will move Temporary File.txt from the Temporary folder to the Temporary 2 folder. You'll find that the Windows 98 user interface makes it easy to move, copy, and delete files.

STEPS

Moving a File

Step 1.   Right-click the Temporary File.txt icon in the Temporary window.

Step 2.   Click Cut in the context menu. The icon for Temporary File.txt is now grayed out to show that the file will be moved from this location.

Step 3.   On the Taskbar, click the button with the drive icon, which should represent your C drive.

Step 4. Right-click the Temporary 2 folder icon in the C: drive window. You may have to scroll the client area of the window by using the scroll bars (if any) on the right and bottom edges of the window.

Step 5. Click Paste in the context menu. The Temporary File.txt document disappears from the Temporary folder window. If you can't see the Temporary folder window, click its button in the Taskbar.

Step 6. Click the Temporary 2 folder icon in the C: drive window. If this folder icon is obscured by the Temporary folder window, click the title bar of the C: drive window to bring it to the top.

Step 7. Notice that Temporary File.txt is now in the Temporary 2 folder.

You have just moved a file from one folder to another using the Cut and Paste commands. You could have also used *drag and drop* to drag Temporary File.txt from the Temporary folder and drop it in the Temporary 2 folder. You'll learn more about this technique in "Moving a file or folder" in Chapter 7.

If you want to copy a file instead of moving it, you can use the steps above, but click Copy instead of Cut in step 2.

Creating a Shortcut

Temporary File.txt is now in the Temporary 2 folder. If you are going to work on this file a bit, it is not a bad idea to put a shortcut icon for it on your Desktop. A *shortcut icon* is simply a pointer to an object (such as a document, folder, or application). When you click a shortcut icon, Windows 98 opens the associated object for you. Here are the steps to create a shortcut for Temporary File.txt:

STEPS

Creating a Shortcut to a File

Step 1. Click the Temporary 2 folder icon in the C: drive window.

Step 2. Point to the Temporary File.txt icon and press and hold down the right mouse button.

Step 3. Drag the icon over to a clear space on your Desktop.

Step 4. Release the right mouse button.

Step 5. Click Create Shortcut(s) Here in the context menu.

Step 6. Press F2, and then type a new name for the shortcut, something like **Temporary File**. Press Enter.

(continued)

STEPS *(continued)*

Creating a Shortcut to a File

Step 7.   Notice the little curved arrow in the lower-left corner of the file icon. This indicates that this icon is a shortcut (and not the file itself).

Step 8.   Click the button for the Temporary 2 folder on the Taskbar and notice that the Temporary File.txt icon is still there. Putting a shortcut to a file onto the Desktop (or anywhere else) doesn't move the file.

Step 9.   Click the Temporary File shortcut icon on the Desktop. Windows 98 launches Notepad and opens Temporary File.txt for you.

Step 10. Click the Close button in the upper-right corner of the Notepad window to close it.

Deleting a Shortcut

You can delete a shortcut to a file, folder, or application without affecting the object itself. Here's how:

STEPS

Deleting a Shortcut

Step 1.   Right-click the Temporary File shortcut icon on the Desktop.

Step 2.   Click Delete in the context menu.

Step 3.   A message box appears asking if you are sure you want to delete the shortcut to Temporary File.txt.

Step 4.   Click Yes.

Step 5.   Click the button for the Temporary 2 folder on the Taskbar. Notice that Temporary File.txt is still there.

Deleting a File

Deleting a shortcut doesn't affect the associated file. Now you will delete (and restore) the actual file.

STEPS

Deleting a File

Step 1.   Hover your mouse pointer over the Temporary File.txt icon in the Temporary 2 folder to select it.

Step 2.   Press the Delete key on your keyboard. You will be asked if you want to delete the Temporary File.txt file.

Step 3.   Click Yes.

Step 4.   Notice that the Temporary File.txt icon has disappeared from the Temporary 2 folder window.

Step 5.   Click the Recycle Bin icon on the Desktop. Notice that both Temporary File.txt and the Temporary File shortcut are stored in the Recycle Bin.

Step 6.   To restore Temporary File.txt to the Temporary 2 folder, right-click the Temporary File.txt icon in the Recycle Bin window and click Restore.

Step 7.   Notice that Temporary File.txt is back in the Temporary 2 folder window.

Step 8.   Click the Close button in the upper-right corner of the Recycle Bin window.

You can also restore the Temporary File shortcut to the Desktop. Note that it doesn't do much good to restore a shortcut if you've deleted (or moved) the object to which it points. If you like, delete Temporary File.txt again, and then restore only the Temporary File shortcut from the Recycle Bin. Try clicking the shortcut (which now points to a file that you've deleted) and see what happens.

So What Was the Point?

You can choose to make Windows 98 behave more like the web with Web style, or more like Windows 95 with Classic style. If you prefer, you can pick and choose features of each style with the Custom option. You can use the View, As Web Page command to set whether or not an individual My Computer or Explorer window displays as a web page.

My Computer contains icons representing each of your drives, which in turn contain folders. The Explorer is similar to My Computer, but it lets you view your folders and files in a dual-pane window that can be helpful in navigating.

In this tutorial, you opened your C drive and created two new folders in it. A folder can contain other folders, files, and shortcuts to folders and/or files stored elsewhere.

The Desktop is actually a folder. You will learn more about this in "Put your favorite files and programs on the Desktop" in Chapter 10.

You can start an application by clicking a file icon. When you do this, Windows 98 starts the application used to create the file, and then opens the file in the application for you.

Shortcuts don't move the associated object (a document, folder, or application), they just give you quick access to it.

Deleting a shortcut doesn't delete the associated document, folder, or application. Deleted shortcuts and files reside in the Recycle Bin until you either restore them or empty the Recycle Bin.

Summary

In this chapter we provide a hands-on, step-by-step tutorial to familiarize you with some of the basic concepts of working with the Windows 98 user interface.

▶ You switch views and display a window as a web page.

▶ You explore ways of viewing folders and icons.

▶ You create folders and create and store files in those folders.

▶ You move a file between folders.

▶ You create a shortcut to a file on the Desktop.

▶ You delete a shortcut and a file.

Chapter 5

Customizing Your Windows 98 Startup

In This Chapter

Your computer can start up in all sorts of different configurations. We show you how to set the options for how Windows 98 starts. We discuss:

▶ Getting rid of the Windows 98 startup logo

▶ Booting your computer to a DOS 7.1 prompt instead of to the Windows 98 graphical user interface

▶ Using a hot key to start Windows in Safe mode if there is a problem with your hardware

▶ Booting to your previous version of DOS or Windows

▶ Choosing a startup hardware profile depending on your computer's hardware configuration

▶ Using multiconfiguration Config.sys and Autoexec.bat files to control startup

Do I Need to Do This?

Do you need to customize your Windows 98 startup? No. Not if all the defaults are just right for you. The Windows 98 Setup program creates all the necessary files and sets up everything invisibly and automatically, so you may not need to worry about anything.

But if you installed Windows 98 in a separate directory from your earlier Windows 3.1x directory and you want to be able to switch between operating systems, you'll find the tricks provided here useful. If you want to know the sequence of commands and actions that occur when your computer starts up, you'll find them here. If you want to load DOS real-mode drivers, or work easily with multiple hardware configurations on pre-plug and play computers, we'll show you how.

This chapter also explains what basic changes you might want to make to your Autoexec.bat and Config.sys files for Windows 98, and it outlines the function of the files in your root directory.

How Windows 98 Starts Up

A lot happens between the time you turn on your computer and when the Windows 98 Desktop appears on your screen. The bootup process goes through three phases: power-on self test, DOS, and Windows.

First, the BIOS

When you first turn on your computer, it goes through its power-on self test. The commands stored in your computer's BIOS (and your video card's ROM) chips are carried out. These commands provide low-level drivers for some of your basic hardware (disk drives, ports, video cards, and so on). The last command found in your BIOS is to execute the program that resides in the boot tracks of the boot device (most likely your hard disk).

If you want to learn more about your particular BIOS, check out the following web sites: http://www.award.com, http://www.phoenix.com, and http://www.ami.com.

The BIOS will find Io.sys (the route to Windows 98) in the boot tracks unless you have Windows NT or OS/2 installed. In these cases, their boot program will be found in the boot tracks. The boot managers that come with these operating systems allow you to go to the Windows 98 Io.sys next, if you desire.

Often, some BIOS settings are displayed on your screen during the power-on self test. Right after these BIOS settings are displayed, the DOS bootup process begins, and on some computers you see the text message "Starting Windows 98." Not all computers display this message.

Windows 95 allowed you two seconds to press a Startup key at this point to alter the way Windows 95 started up. Microsoft removed this two-second delay in order to allow Windows 98 to start up more quickly.

In its place, Windows 98 allows you to press and hold the Ctrl key during the power-on self test. If you hold down this key until you see "Starting Windows 98," the startup process will bring up the Startup menu. (If your computer doesn't display the "Starting Windows 98" message, just hold down the Ctrl key for a few seconds during the power-on self test.) For more information, see the section later in this chapter entitled "Startup Keys."

Then, DOS

Io.sys is DOS. Just as in DOS 4, 5, and so on, Io.sys is a hidden file in the root directory of your boot drive. Io.sys starts your processor in real mode, sets up the DOS data structures in conventional memory, and initializes the low-level DOS functions. DOS starts before Windows 98 starts. DOS starts Windows 98. Your processor is set to real mode and runs DOS before Windows 98 gets going.

Io.sys also calls some DOS real-mode programs, carries out the commands in Config.sys, and loads the command interpreter for Autoexec.bat, if these files exist. Depending on what it finds in Config.sys and Autoexec.bat, it may carry out a number of DOS real-mode commands.

Before Io.sys reads Config.sys and Autoexec.bat (if they exist), it reads Msdos.sys, which is a text file that determines the startup configuration for Windows 98. Msdos.sys may tell Io.sys to ignore your Config.sys and Autoexec.bat files.

If you want to display the Windows Startup menu, you should hold down the Ctrl key before Io.sys takes over the bootup process.

Finally, Windows 98

Io.sys reads Config.sys and Autoexec.bat next, in that order, unless you have asked (perhaps through pressing a Startup key or through the parameters of Msdos.sys) that the contents of these files be ignored. (If you press and hold down the Shift key just before and during the DOS phase of your startup, Io.sys ignores Config.sys and Autoexec.bat.) If Msdos.sys is configured so Windows is set to start, Io.sys loads Windows 98. If Winstart.bat exists, Io.sys reads it and carries out the commands in it. After all this, your computer is finally under the control of the Windows 98 operating system, unless you have configured Msdos.sys to leave you at real-mode MS-DOS.

You can change the DOS and Windows 98 startup sequence in a number of ways:

■ Press and hold the Ctrl key during the power-on self test.

■ Repeatedly press a Startup key to get it read between the power-on self test and the DOS bootup phase. (This includes the Shift key.)

■ Edit your Autoexec.bat, Config.sys, and Winstart.bat (if it exists) files.

■ Use the system configuration utility to determine which files are processed during startup.

■ Edit the Msdos.sys file to set startup parameters.

Msdos.sys

Undocumented

Msdos.sys is a very important configuration file. Io.sys reads this file early on. You can use it to determine whether you will start in real-mode DOS 7.1 or in Windows 98. It determines whether you will boot to a previous version of DOS or not, whether you see the Windows 98 startup logo or not, and whether you can use the startup function keys.

You will find Msdos.sys in the root directory (folder) of your boot hard disk, most likely the C drive. In spite of its *sys* extension, it is a text file like Config.sys. You can edit it with Notepad or Microsoft Edit (Edit.com in the \Windows\Command folder).

Msdos.sys is a hidden, read-only system file. To find and check out the attributes of this file, take the following steps:

STEPS

Viewing the Attributes of Msdos.sys

Step 1. Right-click My Computer on your Desktop and then click Explore.

Step 2. Click View, Folder Options. Click the View tab, and then mark the Show All Files option button. Click OK.

Step 3. Click the hard disk icon in the left pane of the Explorer that represents your boot drive, most likely C. Scroll the right pane until you see Msdos.sys.

Step 4. Right-click Msdos.sys, and then choose Properties.

You can change the attributes of Msdos.sys by marking or clearing the check boxes in its Properties dialog box. However, you can't change the System property (unless you use the Attrib command in a DOS window). If you want to edit Msdos.sys, clear the Read-Only check box.

Editing Msdos.sys

We have created a batch file that you can use to edit Msdos.sys. The batch file changes the attributes of Msdos.sys, opens Microsoft Edit, allows you to make changes to the file, and then resets the attributes of the file back to their original values.

To use this batch file to edit your Msdos.sys file, take the following steps:

STEPS

Using a Batch File to Edit Msdos.sys

Step 1. Using the Explorer, copy the file Msdossys.bat from the \Registry folder of the *Windows 98 Secrets* CD-ROM to an appropriate folder on your hard disk. You might have a folder where you store batch files, but you can use any folder. We suggest creating a folder called My System and storing it there.

Step 2. Right-drag Msdossys.bat from this folder to the Desktop. Click Create Shortcut(s) Here in the context menu. Press F2 and edit the shortcut's name to **Edit Msdos.sys**.

Step 3. Right-click the Edit Msdos.sys icon on your Desktop and choose Properties. Click the Program tab. Click the Change Icon button.

Step 4. You will be presented with icons from the Pifmgr.dll file. Pick one that reminds you that you are editing the Msdos.sys file.

Step 5. Click OK in the Change Icon dialog box, and OK in the Properties dialog box.

Step 6. Click the Edit Msdos.sys icon on your Desktop to begin editing Msdos.sys.

Msdos.sys file contents

Your Msdos.sys file may look something like this:

```
[Paths]
WinDir=C:\WINDOWS
WinBootDir=C:\WINDOWS
HostWinBootDrv=C
UninstallDir=C:\
[Options]
BootGUI=1
Network=1
;
;The following lines are required for compatibility with other
programs.
;Do not remove them (MSDOS.SYS needs to be >1024 bytes).
;xxxxxxxxxxxxxxxxxxxxxxxxxxxxxxxxxxxxxxxxxxxxxxxxxxxxxxxxxxxxxxxa
;xxxxxxxxxxxxxxxxxxxxxxxxxxxxxxxxxxxxxxxxxxxxxxxxxxxxxxxxxxxxxxxb
;xxxxxxxxxxxxxxxxxxxxxxxxxxxxxxxxxxxxxxxxxxxxxxxxxxxxxxxxxxxxxxxc
;xxxxxxxxxxxxxxxxxxxxxxxxxxxxxxxxxxxxxxxxxxxxxxxxxxxxxxxxxxxxxxxd
;xxxxxxxxxxxxxxxxxxxxxxxxxxxxxxxxxxxxxxxxxxxxxxxxxxxxxxxxxxxxxxxe
;xxxxxxxxxxxxxxxxxxxxxxxxxxxxxxxxxxxxxxxxxxxxxxxxxxxxxxxxxxxxxxxf
;xxxxxxxxxxxxxxxxxxxxxxxxxxxxxxxxxxxxxxxxxxxxxxxxxxxxxxxxxxxxxxxg
;xxxxxxxxxxxxxxxxxxxxxxxxxxxxxxxxxxxxxxxxxxxxxxxxxxxxxxxxxxxxxxxh
;xxxxxxxxxxxxxxxxxxxxxxxxxxxxxxxxxxxxxxxxxxxxxxxxxxxxxxxxxxxxxxxi
;xxxxxxxxxxxxxxxxxxxxxxxxxxxxxxxxxxxxxxxxxxxxxxxxxxxxxxxxxxxxxxxj
;xxxxxxxxxxxxxxxxxxxxxxxxxxxxxxxxxxxxxxxxxxxxxxxxxxxxxxxxxxxxxxxk
;xxxxxxxxxxxxxxxxxxxxxxxxxxxxxxxxxxxxxxxxxxxxxxxxxxxxxxxxxxxxxxxl
;xxxxxxxxxxxxxxxxxxxxxxxxxxxxxxxxxxxxxxxxxxxxxxxxxxxxxxxxxxxxxxxm
;xxxxxxxxxxxxxxxxxxxxxxxxxxxxxxxxxxxxxxxxxxxxxxxxxxxxxxxxxxxxxxxn
;xxxxxxxxxxxxxxxxxxxxxxxxxxxxxxxxxxxxxxxxxxxxxxxxxxxxxxxxxxxxxxxo
;xxxxxxxxxxxxxxxxxxxxxxxxxxxxxxxxxxxxxxxxxxxxxxxxxxxxxxxxxxxxxxxp
;xxxxxxxxxxxxxxxxxxxxxxxxxxxxxxxxxxxxxxxxxxxxxxxxxxxxxxxxxxxxxxxq
;xxxxxxxxxxxxxxxxxxxxxxxxxxxxxxxxxxxxxxxxxxxxxxxxxxxxxxxxxxxxxxxr
;xxxxxxxxxxxxxxxxxxxxxxxxxxxxxxxxxxxxxxxxxxxxxxxxxxxxxxxxxxxxxxxs
AutoScan=1
WinVer=4.10.xxxx
```

While only three options are listed in this sample file, you can add numerous options to change how your computer starts up. Note that if you have installed Windows 98 onto another hard drive volume or in a different directory, the WinDir folder in your copy of Msdos.sys may in fact be named something other than C:\Windows.

Msdos.sys options

The options you can specify in Msdos.sys are listed in Table 5-1. If an option is not listed in the Msdos.sys file, Io.sys uses its default value. The default value varies depending on the option. Most of the options' default values are 1. The default value for each option is the first value listed after the equal sign.

Table 5-1   Options for Msdos.sys
BootMulti=0 or 1
BootWin=1 or 0
BootGUI=1 or 0
BootMenu=0 or 1
BootMenuDefault=n (default is either 1 or 3)
BootMenuDelay=n (default is 30 seconds)
BootKeys=1 or 0
Logo=1 or 0
DrvSpace=1 or 0
DblSpace=1 or 0
DoubleBuffer=1 or 0
Network=1 or 0
BootFailSafe=0 or 1
AutoScan=1, 0, or 2
BootWarn=1 or 0
LoadTop=1 or 0

BootMulti

If you recently purchased your computer, the manufacturer may have installed Windows 98 and configured the boot drive on your hard disk as a FAT-32 volume. If this is indeed the case, you won't be able to boot between a previous version of DOS or Windows 3.1x and Windows 98. DOS and earlier versions of Windows don't work with the 32-bit file system, FAT 32.

Windows 98 can configure and read/write to FAT-16 hard disk volumes, and you can use these volumes with previous versions of DOS and Windows 3.1*x*. To multi-boot to these other operating systems, you'll need to have your boot or C drive configured with FAT 16, regardless of where the operating systems reside. Volumes that are configured with FAT 32 will not be readable while you are using previous versions of DOS and Windows.

BootMulti=1: You can boot to a previous version of DOS and/or Windows 3.1*x* using the Ctrl, F4, or F8 keys.

BootMulti=0: This is the default. You can start only Windows 98 (or DOS 7.1). If no reference to BootMulti is found in Msdos.sys, you will not be able to boot to your previous version of DOS or Windows.

If you do not have this option in Msdos.sys and if Io.sys is in the boot tracks of your hard disk, you will not be able to start previous versions of DOS or Windows 3.1*x*. If either the Boot Manager for OS/2 or the Windows NT Boot Loader is in the boot tracks, then these programs control whether you are able to multi-boot or not.

DOS by itself doesn't have a multi-boot capability. You will not have a multi-boot capability if you set up Windows 98 over your existing Windows 3.1*x* directory (you updated Windows 3.1*x*). You cannot multi-boot between Windows 95 and Windows 98. If you installed Windows 98 in a directory separate from your Windows 3.1*x* directory, you will have the ability to start your previous version of DOS.

Undocumented

You must be careful when setting up Windows 98 because the setup routines automatically delete a number of DOS files without telling you. These DOS files have almost exact DOS 7.1 equivalents, but these new files will be stored in the C:\Win98\Command directory and not in your old DOS directory. If your path statements vary depending on which operating system you start up (very likely), you may not have access to your previous DOS functions.

If you want to save existing DOS programs that would otherwise be erased, you need to take some steps before you set up Windows 98.

Copy all your DOS files to a separate directory that is not found in your path statement. The Windows 98 Setup program looks for a set of files and uses the path statement to help it find them. Once it finds them it erases them. For an extra margin of comfort you might compress this backup copy of your DOS directory.

After Windows 98 is set up, you can copy all your DOS files back to your regular DOS directory and erase the temporary directory.

If Windows NT or OS/2 controls the boot tracks, and you indicate when prompted by one of their multi-boot dialog boxes that you want to boot to DOS and BootMulti=1, you will then have the option of booting to your previous version of DOS or Windows 98 (or DOS 7.1).

If BootMulti is not found in Msdos.sys, the F4 function key will not do anything at startup.

The program System Commander from V Communications lets you boot to any operating system set up on your computer and works great with Windows 98. You can also boot any other PC-compatible OS. Call V Communications for more information at 408-296-4224 or 800-648-8266, or go to http://www.v-com.com.

BootWin

BootWin=1: The default value. Boot to Windows 98 (or DOS 7.1). BootWin means to boot to Windows 98, which includes DOS 7.1.

BootWin=0: Without any intervention by the user, boot automatically to the previous DOS version. BootWin=0 means to boot to DOS 5 or 6, or Windows 3.1x, instead of Windows 98.

If the value is 1, then Windows 98 (or DOS 7.1) is started by default — without any action required by you.

If the value is 0, then your previous version of DOS is started by default. Autoexec.dos and Config.dos are renamed Autoexec.bat and Config.sys, and the commands in them are executed.

The BootWin setting determines the effect of the F4 Startup key. After Msdos.sys is read, a startup message appears (on most computers). If BootWin=1, then this message will say that Windows 98 is starting. If you press F4 immediately at this point (start repeatedly pressing it before the message appears), a new message appears, saying that MS-DOS is starting.

If BootWin=0, then the initial message states that MSDOS is starting. You'll need to press F4 before this message appears to get the message that Windows 98 is starting.

If the boot programs for OS/2 or Windows NT are in the boot sectors of your boot device (your hard disk), they determine first if you can boot to another operating system. If you choose to boot to DOS from their boot programs, you then have the choice of booting to Windows 98 or to your previous version of DOS.

If BootWin=0, using MS-DOS mode automatically restarts your computer using your previous version of DOS. You must press F4 to avoid this. See Chapter 34 for details on MS-DOS mode.

BootGUI

BootGUI=1: The default value. If BootWin=1 (or BootWin is not in the Msdos.sys file), start Windows 98.

BootGUI=0: If BootWin=1, don't start Windows 98 after starting DOS 7.1.

If BootWin=0, and you do not press F4, the value of BootGUI is ignored.

If BootWin=1 and BootGUI=1, the WIN command is issued automatically after your Autoexec.bat file (if any) is processed. If BootWin=1 and BootGUI=0, no WIN command is given and you will be presented with the DOS 7.1 prompt after the Autoexec.bat file is processed.

Whether BootGUI=1 or BootGUI=0, all the commands in Config.sys and Autoexec.bat will be carried out. All the default commands, including the loading of Himem.sys, will also occur.

If BootGUI=0, your computer starts up DOS 7.1 and you are presented with the DOS prompt. Your computer is now running real-mode DOS. You can run Windows 98 by typing **win** at the command prompt and pressing Enter.

Tip

You can also create a Win.bat file in the root directory. If this file is empty, Windows 98 boots to the command prompt. This is the same as setting BootGUI=0 in the Msdos.sys file.

You can use TweakUI to set BootGUI to 0 and boot to the command prompt. Just clear the Start GUI Automatically check box in the Boot tab. (If you don't see TweakUI in your Control Panel, you can install it from the \tools\ResKit\Powertoy folder on your Windows 98 CD-ROM.)

BootMenu

BootMenu=1: Display the Startup menu.

BootMenu=0: The default value. Don't display the Startup menu.

The default is to require that you press and hold the Ctrl key during the power-on self test or press F8 between the power-on self test and the DOS bootup phase to display the Startup menu. Setting BootMenu=1 forces the menu to appear each time you start up or reboot your computer.

The Startup menu (shown in Figure 5-1) provides you with a number of different ways to start up your computer. Some of these mirror the values that you can set in the Msdos.sys file.

```
Microsoft Windows 98 Startup Menu
===================================
    1.    Normal
    2.    Logged (\BOOTLOG.TXT)
    3.    Safe mode
    4.    Safe mode with network support
    5.    Step-by-Step confirmation
    6.    Command prompt only
    7.    Safe mode command prompt only
    8.    Previous version of MS-DOS
Enter a Choice: 1          Time Remaining: 30

 F5=Safe mode   Shift+F5=Command Prompt   Shift+F8=Step-by-Step Confirmation [N]
```

Figure 5-1: The Startup menu. Choose whether your computer starts in Windows 98 or your previous version of DOS, whether your computer starts in Safe mode, and whether Autoexec.bat and Config.sys are read.

You can use TweakUI to set BootMenu to 1. Just mark the Always Show Boot Menu check box in the Boot tab.

Undocumented

You should only include BootGUI in the Msdos.sys file if it is set to 1. If you include it set to 0, you won't be able to boot to the Windows 98 Desktop even if you choose 1 (Normal) from the Startup menu. The BootMenuDefault and BootMenuDelay values work with the BootMenu value. If you want to be able to boot to your previous DOS, BootMulti must be equal to 1.

BootMenuDefault

BootMenuDefault=*n*: The default value is 1 if the last time you ran Windows 98 you exited normally, 3 if you exited abnormally and don't have a network connection, and 4 if you exited abnormally and do have a network connection. Set the value you want the BootMenu to use without user input.

The Startup menu is not static. Whether certain values appear in this menu depends on the values you set in Msdos.sys and Config.sys. You may want to choose which value in your menu is the default choice.

BootMenuDelay

BootMenuDelay=*n*: The default value is 30 seconds. This option sets the number of seconds the Startup menu is displayed before the default menu item is acted upon. You can also use TweakUI to set the BootMenuDelay value. You'll find it in the Boot tab.

BootKeys

BootKeys=1: This is the default. The function keys that work during the boot process (F4, F5, F6, F8, Shift+F5, Ctrl+F5, Shift+F8) are enabled.

BootKeys=0: These function keys don't work.

If you, as a system administrator, want to disallow certain actions, you can disable the actions taken by these function keys. These function keys are described in detail in the section later in this chapter entitled "Startup Keys." This does nothing to make a PC "more secure," because anyone can change Msdos.sys from within Windows or DOS.

Windows 98 doesn't allow you much time to press these keys during the bootup process. Press the key as soon as you see "Starting Windows 98." (If you don't see this message, press the key repeatedly during the power-on self test.) In Windows 95, there was a two-second delay, but this delay was removed in Windows 98. The time interval that is available is between the end of the power-on self test and the start of the DOS startup (which precedes the Windows startup).

You can use TweakUI to determine whether these function keys are available or not. Just mark or clear the Function Keys Available check box in the Boot tab.

Logo

Logo=1: The default value. Display the Windows 98 logo screen as Windows 98 boots up.

Logo=0: Leave the screen in text mode.

Some third-party memory managers have trouble when this logo is displayed. Also, it can be annoying in general, and it can prevent you from seeing important messages from real-mode drivers. You can replace Logo.sys with another *bmp* file. See the section later in the chapter entitled "Changing the Startup Graphic."

You can use TweakUI to set this value. Mark or clear the Display Splash Screen While Booting check box in the Boot tab.

Drvspace

Drvspace=1: The default value. Load Drvspace.bin if it is there.

Drvspace=0: Don't load Drvspace.bin even if it is there.

If you have a drive that is compressed with Drvspace, you most likely will want to have it mounted and available. If not, you can disable this action.

Dblspace

Same as Drvspace, except for the spelling. DoubleSpace and DriveSpace drives are now handled by one 32-bit driver, Drvspace.bin.

DoubleBuffer

DoubleBuffer=1: The default value.

The Windows 98 Setup program adds this line to your Msdos.sys file if you have one of these controllers:

- A SCSI controller

- A controller that incorrectly assumes that your computer can only have a maximum total physical memory of 16 megabytes

- A controller that uses its own DMA controller (as opposed to the one of the pre-defined DMA channels on the system board) or whose BIOS lacks support for Virtual DMA Services (VDS)

Secret

Double buffering is used only during the Windows 98 bootup process (or if your hard disk requires 16-bit drivers — compatibility mode). Once the protected mode IDE driver loads, it takes over and handles the DMA buffers directly, with full performance. To see if your hard disk requires 16-bit drivers, turn to the "Real-mode disk drivers" section in Chapter 33.

Setting DoubleBuffer to 1 adds about 1/2 second to your boot time. There is no other performance degradation.

DoubleBuffer=0: You can set the DoubleBuffer value to 0 if you are convinced that it won't corrupt data on your computer. This value is set to 1 in many cases where it is not necessary (because there is so little penalty). If your disk hardware configuration is fast enough to handle the hard disk throughput, you can set this value to 0. You save about 2K of memory space.

Network

Network=1: The default value if network components are installed. Enables the Startup menu item Safe Mode with Network Support.

Network=0: Either the network isn't installed or you don't want the option of booting in safe mode with network support. If Network=0, then menu item 4 will not appear in the Startup menu, and the items below it will be renumbered.

BootFailSafe

BootFailSafe=0: The default value. Windows 98 doesn't boot into Safe mode automatically.

BootFailSafe=1: Forces your computer to start in Safe mode.

AutoScan

While all the rest of these Msdos.sys options were available with Windows 95, this one is new to Windows 98. The default is to present you with a prompt to run ScanDisk from the DOS screen that comes up before the Windows 98 startup logo. The ScanDisk version that is invoked is \Windows\ Scanregw.exe /autorun. (See "ScanDisk" in Chapter 33 for more on details.)

You are prompted to run ScanDisk if you turned off your computer without going through the standard shut down procedure, or if Windows 98 doesn't shut itself down properly. While the errors ScanDisk would find are very often not the culprits, Microsoft hopes that a little of this and a little of that will cut down on its support calls.

AutoScan=1: The default. Prompts you to run ScanDisk and does it itself if you don't press Enter.

AutoScan=0: Don't run ScanDisk and don't prompt either.

AutoScan=2: Run ScanDisk on Windows restart and don't prompt.

You can use TweakUI to set this value. Just go to the Boot tab and choose a setting from the Autorun Scandisk drop-down list.

Just because you have set AutoScan to 1 or 2 doesn't mean that you have to let ScanDisk run. Just press the X key when it starts to exit from ScanDisk.

BootWarn

BootWarn=1: The default value. When BootWarn=1, you see a warning message box when you boot in Safe mode.

BootWarn=0: Don't show the Safe warning message box.

LoadTop

LoadTop=1: The default value. Command.com and Drvspace.bin or Dblspace.bin can be loaded at the top of conventional memory. This is standard.

LoadTop=0: If there is a problem with NetWare or other software, forces these programs not to load at the top of conventional memory.

The Windows 98 Startup Menu

The Windows 98 Startup menu (shown earlier in Figure 5-1) gives you a set of choices regarding how your computer starts before Io.sys carries out its default commands and before it reads Autoexec.bat and Config.sys. Io.sys reads Msdos.sys before the Startup menu appears.

Normal

If BootGUI=1, start Windows 98; otherwise go to DOS 7.1 prompt. Carry out the commands in the Autoexec.bat and Config.sys files. Hangs if BootWin=0.

Logged

Same as Normal but writes out the file Bootlog.txt, which tracks the load and startup sequence. Hangs if BootWin=0.

Safe mode

If BootGUI=1 and BootWin=1, start Windows 98 in Safe mode. Safe mode is a generic Windows 98 startup with VGA graphics, but no networking. It doesn't read or carry out the commands in Config.sys or Autoexec.bat, and it boots to DOS 7.1 or Windows 98 (depending on BootGUI) even if BootWin=0.

Safe mode with network support

Same as Safe mode but also loads the network drivers. You would want to do this if you are loading Windows 98 off the network or need network resources when trying to change your incorrect drivers.

Step-by-step confirmation

Same as Shift+F8. Ask for confirmation before carrying out each command from Io.sys, Config.sys, and Autoexec.bat. Helps to isolate trouble. Boots to DOS 7.1 or Windows 98 (depending on BootGUI) even if BootWin=0.

Command prompt only

Carry out a normal boot sequence but don't start Windows 98. If BootWin=0, starts previous DOS version.

Safe mode command prompt only

Same as Safe mode but don't start Windows 98. Autoexec.bat and Config.sys are not read; nor are their commands carried out.

Previous version of MS-DOS

Same as F4. Load the previous version of DOS. If BootWin=0, restart Windows 98 Startup menu, and if chosen again load previous version of DOS.

Startup Keys

Table 5-2 shows which keys are read just after the power-on self test ends and before the DOS bootup phase begins. If your fingers are very quick, you can use the keys to modify how Windows 98 starts. If BootKeys=0 in Msdos.sys, the keys won't work.

Windows 98 doesn't allow you any time to press these Startup keys. Windows 95 allowed two seconds. You have to press the key repeatedly just as the power-on self test stops.

Table 5-2	Keys That Modify How Windows 98 Starts
Key	**Result**
F4	If BootWin=1, starts the previous version of DOS. If Windows 98 has been installed in its own directory on a computer that has MS-DOS 6.x or a previous DOS operating system, then this key will start that version of DOS instead of Windows 98. This also works if Windows 98 has been installed on a computer that already has OS/2 and Windows NT installed after you use their multi-boot menus. If BootWin=0, pressing F4 boots up Windows 98. Only works if BootMulti=1. Same as menu item 8 on the Windows 98 Startup menu.
F5	Safe startup of Windows 98. This allows Windows 98 to start with its most basic configuration, bypassing your Autoexec.bat and Config.sys files, using the VGA driver for video, and not loading any networking drivers. You can use Safe startup if there are any problems starting Windows 98. Same as menu item 3 on the Windows 98 Startup menu.
Shift+F5	Command line start. Boots to real-mode DOS 7.1. MS-DOS, Command.com, and Dblspace.bin (or Drvspace.bin) are loaded in low memory, taking up valuable conventional memory space. Bypasses Config.sys and Autoexec.bat. Same as menu item 7 on the Windows 98 Startup menu.

Key	Result
Ctrl+F5	Command line start without compressed drives. The Dblspace.bin and Drvspace.bin files are ignored and DoubleSpace and DriveSpace drives are not mounted.
F6	Safe startup (like F5) but with the addition of the network. Same as menu item 4 on the Windows 98 Startup menu.
Ctrl or F8	Starts the Windows 98 Startup menu. You need to hold down the Ctrl key before the DOS bootup process begins. If you have quick fingers, you can press the F8 key in between the end of the power-on self test and the beginning of the DOS bootup phase.
Shift+F8	Interactive start that goes through Config.sys and Autoexec.bat one line at a time and lets you decide if you want that line read and acted upon. Also goes through each command that Io.sys initiates before it carries out the commands in Config.sys. (This is interesting to watch in itself.) Same as menu item 5 on the Windows 98 Startup menu.

What Gets Loaded When

Undocumented

Io.sys carries out a default sequence of commands. These commands can be overridden or modified by entries in Config.sys. You can easily see just what commands Io.sys carries out if you don't have a Config.sys or an Autoexec.bat file (rename your existing files) or if these files are empty. You can also just instruct your interactive startup (Shift+F8) to ignore these files.

The easiest way to get to interactive startup is to hold down the Ctrl key during the power-on self test, and when the Startup menu appears, choose item 5. You will be asked to confirm if you want various actions to be carried out. Here's how to interpret the questions:

```
Load DoubleSpace driver [Enter=Y, Esc=N]?
Process the system registry [Enter=Y, Esc=N]?
```

If you are actually going to start Windows 98, you want the Registry to be processed.

```
Create a startup log file (BOOTLOG.TXT) [Enter=Y, Esc=N]?
```

The file Bootlog.txt is created and a backup of the previous Bootlog.txt is written to Bootlog.prv.

```
Process your startup device drivers (CONFIG.SYS) [Enter=Y, Esc=N]?
```

If you have a Config.sys file, Io.sys will read and carry out the commands within it. Answer no to this question to see the bare commands that Io.sys carries out.

```
DEVICE=C:\WINDOWS\HIMEM.SYS [Enter=Y, Esc=N]?
```

Windows can't start unless Himem.sys is loaded first. Your Windows directory may be C:\Win98, or some other name and drive letter.

```
DEVICEHIGH=C:\WINDOWS\IFSHLP.SYS [Enter=Y, Esc=N]?
```

This is the helper file for the installable file system. This is needed for the Virtual File Allocation Table (VFAT) file system that Windows 98 uses to imitate the standard DOS and Windows FAT file system and still store long filenames.

Notice that the last command asked to be loaded high. It is, in fact, loaded in conventional memory as long as you haven't loaded Emm386.exe.

```
Process your startup command file (AUTOEXEC.BAT) [Enter=Y, Esc=N]?
```

Answer no to this request.

```
Load the Windows graphical user interface [Enter=Y, Esc=N]?
```

If you say no to this question, you are left at a command line prompt with the Windows 98 version of DOS loaded. Windows hasn't been loaded. This is the same as choosing Shift+F5 or putting the line BootGUI=0 in Msdos.sys.

```
Load all Windows drivers [Enter=Y, Esc=N]?
```

If you answer yes, you have the option of not loading some drivers, mostly network drivers. If you answer no, you'll start Windows 98 in Safe mode. You may choose not to load some drivers in order to troubleshoot Windows 98 networking problems.

This default load sequence gives you an idea why Config.sys and Autoexec.bat are not needed. Many of the functions that would be carried out by Config.sys are carried out by Io.sys, if you let it. In the next sections, you will see that Io.sys sets values that are normally set in Config.sys. You also will see that Io.sys sets parameter values normally set in Autoexec.bat.

Undocumented

You can suppress the commands loaded by Io.sys by putting the following line in your Config.sys file:

```
DOS=NOAUTO
```

Config.sys

There is a great deal more, hardware-wise, to the standard personal computer than was the case when MS-DOS was designed. Config.sys files before the advent of Windows 95 reflected that growth. This file was filled with calls to software drivers that support additional hardware.

Mice, sound cards, CD-ROM drives, and network cards are among the hardware components that didn't have built-in support in the original MS-DOS operating system. Memory management, including the ability to load programs in high memory and provide expanded memory for DOS programs that required it, also necessitated software drivers that were called by references to them in Config.sys.

Since the advent of Windows 95, a mostly 32-bit operating system, these software drivers have been called *real-mode* or *16-bit* drivers. Under MS-DOS or Windows 3.1*x*, these drivers had to be loaded either in conventional memory (below the 640K line) or in upper memory between the 640K line and the 1MB line.

Both Windows 95 and 98 incorporate the functionality of the real-mode drivers into the operating system. In other words, they are part of Windows. No longer are drivers stored in conventional or upper memory blocks. This frees up a significant amount of conventional memory that can be used for DOS programs that require it.

The new drivers are called *32-bit* or *protected-mode* drivers. They are loaded above the 1MB boundary. Information about them is stored in the Registry. When Windows 98 starts, it reads the Registry files and loads the appropriate protected-mode drivers.

You do not need a Config.sys file unless you have to use real-mode drivers for a piece of hardware that is not supported by 32-bit drivers or you want to support hardware with 16-bit drivers when you run in MS-DOS mode. Windows 98 includes 32-bit mouse drivers that provide full mouse functionality to DOS programs in a Windows DOS session, so you don't need a 16-bit mouse driver unless you use the mouse in MS-DOS mode.

If you want to access your CD-ROM drive when running programs in MS-DOS mode, you'll definitely need to have your CD-ROM driver in your Config.sys file and a call to your Mscdex.exe file in your Autoexec.bat file. More information about this can be found in "DOS in MS-DOS mode without a reboot" in Chapter 34.

Config.sys variables

Various values that were previously set in Config.sys, such as Files= or Fcbs=, are now set at values higher than the previous defaults. You may or may not need to set higher values for some of these variables.

Here are the new default values:

```
files=30
fcbs=4
buffers=11
stacks=9,256
lastdrive=Z
```

Memory Management

If you have real-mode drivers (say you have a CD-ROM drive that isn't supported with 32-bit drivers) and want to load them in upper memory, you need to use the expanded memory manager (with perhaps the expanded memory option turned off) to access the memory between 640K and 1MB. Loading these drivers into upper memory gives you more conventional memory for DOS programs. If you are not running DOS programs that require a lot of memory, then there is no point in doing this.

Put the following lines in Config.sys before any lines that load real-mode drivers:

```
DEVICE=C:\WINDOWS\HIMEM.SYS /TESTMEM:OFF
DEVICE=C:\WINDOWS\EMM386.EXE NOEMS
DOS=HIGH,UMB
```

You should put calls to the real-mode drivers after these lines, and start the lines that load the real-mode drivers with Devicehigh=.

For a more thorough discussion of memory management, see Chapter 35.

Autoexec.bat

Much of the functionality that was found in Autoexec.bat and Config.sys is now incorporated into the Registry or into Windows 98 defaults, so these files can be much shorter or even eliminated altogether.

Tip

For example, the default DOS prompt is now the equivalent to that created by the PROMPT pg line in Autoexec.bat. This prompt command creates a DOS command prompt that includes the volume and directory name and the greater-than symbol (C:\Windows>). If you want a different DOS prompt, you still need to create an Autoexec.bat file and put in your own prompt statement.

The Windows 98 default path is C:\Windows;C:\Windows\Command. If your programs require additional directories in the path, you need to create a path statement in your Autoexec.bat. There is no reason why a Windows program should require a path value, but a lot of Windows 3.1x programs do. DOS programs use them extensively.

If you have a DOS program that requires a path, you can create a batch file that runs before the program starts and sets the path for the program in a Windows DOS session. You don't have to mangle the global path statement to accommodate these DOS programs. You can name the batch file by creating a specific shortcut (actually a *pif*) to the DOS program. See "Batch file" in Chapter 34 for more details.

It is a good idea not to store the temporary files that are created by Windows 98 and various application programs in the extensive \Windows folder. Windows 98 automatically sets the environment variables Tmp and Temp to C:\Windows\Temp. This makes it convenient to browse this folder and erase old temporary files.

You should have your Autoexec.bat file load any program whose capabilities you need when you open any DOS window on the Windows 98 Desktop. For example, if you want to keep a history of DOS commands in your DOS window so you can easily go back to previous ones and edit or run them again, you should put the statement Doskey in Autoexec.bat.

Multiple Configurations

In previous versions of DOS, you could create a menu of configuration choices to be displayed when you first started your computer. You used special commands in Config.sys and Autoexec.bat to create the menus and respond to your choices.

Windows 98 also accommodates multiple configurations. The menu of configuration choices is displayed after a normal startup (after Config.sys and Autoexec.bat files have been read) but before Windows 98 itself is started. (See Figure 5-2.)

```
Microsoft Windows 98 Startup Menu
=================================
    1.    Normal
    2.    Logged (\BOOTLOG.TXT)
    3.    Safe mode
    4.    Safe mode with network support
    5.    Step-by-Step confirmation
    6.    Command prompt only
    7.    Safe mode command prompt only
    8.    Previous version of MS-DOS
Enter a Choice: 1          Time Remaining: 30

F5=Safe mode  Shift+F5=Command Prompt  Shift+F8=Step-by-Step Confirmation [N]
```

Figure 5-2: If you have BootMenu=1 in your Msdos.sys file, press F8 during Windows 98 startup, or press and hold the Ctrl key during the power-on self test, this Startup menu is displayed.

Here are example Config.sys and Autoexec.bat files that illustrate how to create a multiple configuration menu.

Config.sys

```
;config.sys, Config.w40 when booted to DOS 6.2x
[menu]
Menuitem=windows,Load Windows for Workgroups 3.11
Menuitem=win98,Load Windows 98
Menudefault=win98,7
[global]
DEVICE=C:\WIN98\himem.sys /testmem:off /v
DEVICE=C:\WIN98\EMM386.EXE NOEMS /V
dos=UMB,High
[windows]
include=global
BUFFERS=20,0
FILES=99
LASTDRIVE=H
FCBS=16,0
```

```
BREAK=ON
STACKS=9,256
DEVICEHIGH=C:\WIN98\SETVER.EXE
DEVICEHIGH=C:\UTIL\SFXCD\DEV\MTMCDE.SYS /D:MSCD001 /P:310 /A:0 M:64
/T:S /I:5 /X
DEVICEHIGH=c:\windows\IFSHLP.SYS
DEVICEHIGH=C:\WIN98\COMMAND\DRVSPACE.SYS /MOVE
shell=C:\WIN98\COMMAND.COM c:\WIN98 /e:512 /p
[win98]
include=global
shell=C:\WIN98\COMMAND.COM c:\WIN98 /e:512 /p
```

Autoexec.bat

```
@rem autoexec.bat, autoexec.w40 when booted to DOS 6.2x
@echo off
goto %config%
:windows
PROMPT $P$G
PATH;
PATH C:\WINDOWS;C:\WIN98\COMMAND;C:\UTIL\BATCH
SET TEMP=C:\UTIL\TEMP
SET LMOUSE=C:\UTIL\LOGITECH
LH C:\UTIL\LOGITECH\MOUSE
LH C:\WINDOWS\SMARTDRV.EXE /X 2048 128
LH C:\WINDOWS\MSCDEX.EXE /S /D:MSCD001 /M:10
LH C:\WIN98\COMMAND\doskey
WIN
GOTO END
:win98
PATH;
PATH C:\WIN98;C:\WIN98\COMMAND;C:\UTIL\BATCH
LH C:\WIN98\COMMAND\doskey
:END
```

Both of these files assume you want to start in DOS 7.1. They allow you to choose between running Windows for Workgroups 3.11 or Windows 98. If you want to boot to Windows 98 and not to DOS 7.1, set BootGUI to 1 in Msdos.sys. If BootWin=0, these files will not be read and their associated configuration menu will not be displayed.

These files create the Startup menu shown in Figure 5-3.

Multiple Hardware Configurations

You can create multiple hardware configurations for one computer. For example, if you have a non-plug and play portable computer that is sometimes connected to a docking station, you might want to create a hardware configuration that includes the cards in the docking station and the network connected to the docking station.

```
Microsoft Windows 98 Startup Menu
==================================
   1.    Load Windows for Workgroups 3.11
   2.    Load Windows 98

Enter a Choice: 2        Time Remaining: 07

F5=Safe mode  Shift+F5=Command Prompt  Shift+F8=Step-by-Step Confirmation [N]
```

Figure 5-3: The multiple configuration menu. In spite of the heading for this menu, it is not the same as the Windows 98 Startup menu. You can display that menu before this menu appears. Shift+F8 won't work. Shift+F5 will.

The startup sequence for a computer with multiple hardware configurations includes a menu that allows you to choose which hardware configuration you want to use. A sample hardware configuration startup menu is shown in Figure 5-4.

```
Windows cannot determine what configuration your computer is in:
Select one of the following:

   1.    Docking Station with Network
   2.    Disconnected Portable
   3.    None of the Above

Enter your choice:
```

Figure 5-4: The multiple hardware configuration menu. This text menu appears after the Windows 98 logo is displayed.

To create multiple hardware configurations, take the following steps:

STEPS

Creating Multiple Hardware Configurations

Step 1.   Click the Start button, point to Settings, and then click Control Panel.

Step 2.   Click the System icon, and then click the Hardware Profiles tab to display the Hardware Profiles list, as shown in Figure 5-5.

(continued)

STEPS *(continued)*

Creating Multiple Hardware Configurations

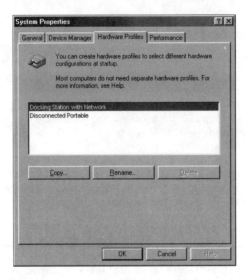

Figure 5-5: The Hardware Profiles list. You can copy, remove, and rename hardware profiles. You define hardware profiles in the Device Manager.

Step 3.   Click the Rename button to rename your current profile to something that appropriately describes your current hardware configuration.

Step 4.   Click the Copy button, highlight the new hardware profile, and click Rename to rename the new hardware profile.

Step 5.   Click the Device Manager tab. Click the plus sign next to the device types that will vary between hardware profiles.

Step 6.   Double-click a device that will be found in one hardware profile but not in the other. Clear the check box next to the name of the hardware profile that will not use this device, as shown in Figure 5-6.

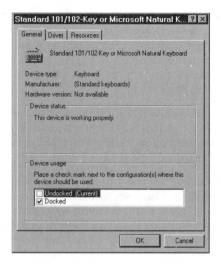

Figure 5-6: Choose which devices go with which hardware configuration.

Your Device Manager may not list all the devices that are available among your various hardware configurations. You have to install device drivers for these devices before you can assign them to your different hardware profiles.

To learn how to add hardware device drivers, turn to Chapter 25.

Changing the Startup Graphic

Before your computer displays the Windows 98 Desktop, you're treated to an animated (640 × 400) Microsoft Windows 98 advertisement. This graphic is embedded in the Io.sys file in your root directory.

Undocumented

If you have installed Windows 98 over Windows 95 and Microsoft Plus!, there is an additional file in your root directory, Logo.sys, which contains a slightly edited version of the original advertisement. In spite of its *sys* extension, it is a *bmp* file and can be edited by MS Paint.

You can create your own animated Logo.sys file and replace Microsoft's billboard with your own. You don't have to animate the graphic, but you can if you want to. Logo.sys is an animated bitmapped file, so if you edit it with MS Paint, you'll lose the animation.

If you decide that you want a new Logo.sys, the first step is to save the original Logo.sys (assuming you have one), perhaps as Oldlogo.sys. Next, if you view Logo.sys in MS Paint, you'll notice that it is sized 320 pixels wide by 400 pixels high. The Windows 98 startup routines stretch it out to 640 × 400 when it's displayed. You can create a new graphic at 640 × 400 — or at 533 × 400 if you want to maintain the 4:3 ratio (width to height) that is the standard for video monitors — and then use MS Paint or Paint Shop Pro to shrink the graphic to 320 × 400.

Your logo.sys file must have a color depth of 256 colors (8 bit), and its file size must be 127K. If it is 320 pixels × 400 pixels × 256 colors, it will be 127K in size. The Windows 98 startup routine will reject a Logo.sys file that doesn't meet these criteria.

There are lots of animated Logo.sys replacements available online. We suggest that you point your browser at http://www.nucleus.com/ ~kmcmurdo/win95logo.html. Karl McMurdo, who maintains this site, has collected more animated logos than you'll ever need. You will also find a tool called XrX Animated Logo Utility at the site. This program will help you animate your *bmp* files. The site has complete directions for creating more animated logos.

Secret

If you delete Logo.sys, the graphic embedded in Io.sys will be used instead. Getting rid of Logo.sys doesn't make the graphic go away. But if you set Logo=0 in your Msdos.sys file, no graphic will be displayed before the Windows 98 Desktop appears.

You can use the Boot tab of TweakUI to set Logo=0 in Msdos.sys so that the startup graphic is not displayed.

Your \Windows folder contains two additional graphics files named Logos.sys and Logow.sys. These are the two screens you see when you exit Windows 98. Just as with Logo.sys, you can edit these two files or create replacements for them.

Dual-Boot Configuration

You can have multiple operating systems running on your computer. DOS 6.2*x* combined with Windows 3.1*x*, Windows 98, OS/2, and Windows NT can all coexist on the C drive (or on multiple drives) of your computer as long as you have the room for them (and you use the FAT-16 file system).

You can put almost all of DOS 6.2*x*, Windows 3.1*x*, and Windows 98 on a non-bootable hard disk, even a compressed hard disk. The only files you need to leave on the boot drive are the bootup files (Io.sys, Msdos.sys, Config.sys, and Autoexec.bat) and the files that work with a compressed drive.

When you first install Windows 98 over an existing DOS/Windows system, you have the option of installing over an existing Windows 3.1*x* directory or in a new directory. Windows 98 uses the existing DOS file structure, so there is no need to start by reformatting your hard disk, unless you want to use the FAT-32 file structure for large drives. If you install Windows 98 to a new directory, then you have the option of booting either DOS (which can get you to Windows 3.1*x*) or Windows 98.

Remember that dual-booting will not work if your C drive is formatted with FAT 32, or if the non-Windows 98 operating system resides on a FAT-32 partition.

If you have a computer that dual-boots between DOS and Windows 98, the files in the root directory will be renamed depending on whether you have booted into DOS or booted into Windows 98. Assuming that you previously booted into Windows 98, the renaming shown in Table 5-3 will take place if you boot into DOS.

Table 5-3   Files Renamed in Dual Boots from Windows 98 to DOS

From	To
Io.sys	Jo.sys
Msdos.sys	Msdos.w40
Command.com	Command.w40
Autoexec.bat	Autoexec.w40
Config.sys	Config.w40
Io.dos	Io.sys
Msdos.dos	Msdos.sys
Command.dos	Command.com
Config.dos	Config.sys
Autoexec.dos	Autoexec.bat

The StartUp Folder

When Windows 98 starts, it runs the programs in the Startup folder. Windows 98 knows which folder is the Startup folder because there is an entry in the Registry specifying a particular folder, usually \Windows\Start Menu\Programs\StartUp. You can change which folder is used as the Startup folder, as well as which folders are used for other special functions, by editing the entries found in the Registry under the following branch:

HKEY_CURRENT_USER\Software\Microsoft\Windows\CurrentVersion\ Explorer\shellfolders

Even better, use TweakUI to designate which folders are used for special functions. Click the General tab in TweakUI, choose the folder, and then choose the location.

You may want to load a file and execute it when Windows 98 starts up, but you don't want to place the file (or a shortcut to it) in the Startup folder. You could put it on the load or run line in Win.ini. But there is a special set of branches in the Registry where calls can be made to start programs without those programs showing up in the Startup folder.

Undocumented

If you want to know why you can't find the call to Task Scheduler, or if you're curious about other programs that start up without you knowing about it, get out your Registry editor and check this out:

STEPS

Seeing and Creating Hidden Startup Programs

Step 1.   Click Regedit.exe in your \Windows folder.

Step 2.   Navigate to either HKEY_LOCAL_MACHINE\SOFTWARE\Microsoft\ Windows\CurrentVersion\Run or HKEY_LOCAL_MACHINE\ SOFTWARE\Microsoft\Windows\CurrentVersion\RunOnce. You can also check the RunServices or RunServicesOnce keys.

Step 3.   Highlight Run in the left pane. You'll see which programs are currently running when you start up.

Step 4.   To enter a call to a new program to run at startup time (once or always), right-click in the right pane with either Run or RunOnce highlighted. Click New, String Value.

Step 5.   Type any name you want to identify the application that is going to be run at startup.

Step 6.   Double-click this new name. Type the complete path and filename for the application. Click OK.

Step 7.   Exit the Registry editor.

For more information about editing your Registry, turn to Chapter 15.

Temporarily turn off Startup

You may have some programs that you'd sometimes like to run as part of your Startup group, but not always. A handy solution is to put the shortcuts to these programs in a separate StartUp.Not folder beneath the C:\Windows\ Start Menu\Programs folder (see Figure 5-7). You can then easily drag the shortcuts from the StartUp.Not subfolder to the regular Startup folder when you want to re-commence running the applications at startup time.

You can keep Windows 98 from loading the entire Startup group by holding down the Shift key during the Windows phase of the bootup process.

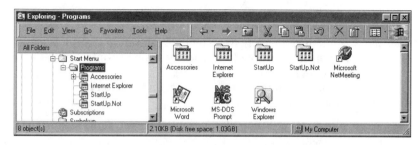

Figure 5-7: The StartUp and StartUp.Not folders in the Explorer.

Windows 98 Troubleshooting

If you press and hold the Ctrl key during the power-on self test, and then choose to go to the command prompt at the Windows Startup menu, you can start Windows 98 with the debug switch. Here's the debug syntax:

```
WIN {/D:{F} {M} {N} {S} {V} {X}}
```

/D:	Used for troubleshooting when Windows does not start correctly.
F	Turns off 32-bit disk access. Equivalent to SYSTEM.INI file setting: 32BitDiskAccess=FALSE.
M	Enables Safe mode. This is automatically enabled during Safe startup (function key F5).
N	Enables Safe mode with networking. This is automatically enabled during Safe startup (function key F6).
S	Specifies that Windows should not use ROM address space between F000:0000 and 1MB for a break point. Equivalent to SYSTEM.INI file setting: SystemROMBreakPoint=FALSE.
V	Specifies that the ROM routine will handle interrupts from the hard disk controller. Equivalent to SYSTEM.INI file setting: VirtualHDIRQ=FALSE.
X	Excludes all of the adapter area from the range of memory that Windows scans to find unused space. Equivalent to SYSTEM.INI file setting: EMMExclude=A000-FFFF

Microsoft provides troubleshooting guidelines to help you determine what is causing a problem when you can't start Windows 98 in the normal fashion. To access those guidelines, connect to Microsoft's Knowledge Base on its web site at http://premium.microsoft.com/support/kb/articles/q136/3/37.asp.

System configuration utility

Windows 98 includes a new system configuration utility (Msconfig.exe) that gives you much easier and more finely grained control of the Windows 98 startup process. To find it, click Start, Programs, Accessories, System Tools, and System Information. In the System Information menu, click Tools, System Configuration Utility.

You can use this utility to choose which files to process during startup, as shown in Figure 5-8.

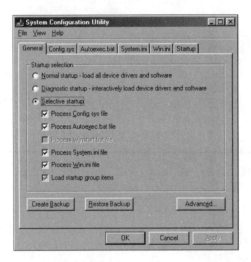

Figure 5-8: The system configuration utility.

Other dialog boxes within this utility allow you to choose which lines of which files to process. You can also use it to edit all of the files indicated on the tabs, and to enable and disable items in the Startup folder.

Summary

Windows 98 gives you a great deal of control over how your computer starts up. By editing a few files you can control the startup process.

▶ Boot your computer to a DOS 7.1 prompt either by creating an empty Win.bat file or by editing Msdos.sys.

▶ Start up in your previous version of DOS or Windows either by pressing a function key or by default.

▶ Edit Msdos.sys in order to get rid of the Windows 98 logo.

▶ Use function keys to go step-by-step through the startup process, start Windows 98 in Safe mode if there is a problem with your hardware, or bring up the Startup menu.

▶ Create different hardware profiles and choose between them at startup depending on your current hardware setup.

▶ Develop multiconfiguration Config.sys and Autoexec.bat files to design your own Windows 98 Startup menu.

Part II

Interface to the Desktop and the Internet

Chapter 6

The Desktop and the Taskbar

In This Chapter

Windows 98 looks like an Internet browser as well as a Desktop with stuff just piled on top of it. It's two, two, two interfaces in one. You get to pick which to use. Here, we discuss:

▶ Turning your regular old Desktop into the Active Desktop

▶ Arranging the icons on your Desktop the way you want them

▶ Replacing existing icons with new ones and fixing corrupted icons

▶ Changing the invisible grid that determines icon spacing

▶ Changing the font and font sizes used for icon titles

▶ Placing new blank documents on your Desktop ready to be opened by an application with a click

▶ Putting the Taskbar where it will do you the most good

▶ Adding a Desktop toolbar

▶ Getting rid of "sliding" windows

▶ Task switching between applications and folders using the keyboard

What You See Is a Mess

The Windows 98 user interface is a mess — a jumble of metaphors and layers that go in every direction at once. For those of you who don't spend all your working hours researching and writing about this stuff, we wonder how Microsoft expects you to keep up. We know that it will get even more complex (and powerful) as Windows continues to evolve.

Fortunately, you really can get it under control if you're willing to follow along with us through the next few chapters. Then, as Microsoft moves to the next metaphor, perhaps once again pulled by something as powerful as the World Wide Web, you'll be ready to roll.

For those of you moving up from Windows 3.1x, the first step is to notice that the wallpaper is alive. No longer is it just the place behind the Program Manager where the minimized application icons go when they are at rest.

Now you can arrange the application and document icons on the wallpaper to be ready for you to activate them. Active windows display updated information. The wallpaper itself can display the latest news.

Your wallpaper is the Desktop with stuff on it. The icons on your Desktop represent different applications and documents, sort of like a regular desktop. The Taskbar keeps track of whatever you are currently working on (the icons for active applications now live there whether the application is minimized or not). The Start button cascades to multiple menus that organize and reveal your applications and documents. The toolbars give you ready access to your favorite documents and applications. The clock . . . well, you can figure that out for yourself.

Windows 98 integrates the Internet Explorer web browser into the Windows 95 Desktop. You can open web documents in little windows on your Desktop and have the windows' contents updated automagically. You can single-click Desktop icons to open the associated application or document, just as you single-click links in web pages.

We discuss the Desktop, the Active Desktop, and the Taskbar and its toolbars in this chapter. We also discuss some aspects of the Start button, but leave deeper details to "The Start Menu" in Chapter 11. Each of the icons on the Desktop has its own chapter — see "The Icons and Items on the Desktop" later in this chapter for more information.

First, Your Password

Before you can use Windows 98 for the very first time, it prompts you to enter your name and password as shown in Figure 6-1. Windows 98 uses this information to differentiate you from other people who may share your computer and, most importantly, to remember all the other passwords that you will undoubtedly collect as you use this computer. Windows stores all your other passwords in an encrypted file that your other applications can access after you log on to Windows 98 under your name and password. For example, because you log on as you, Outlook Express remembers your e-mail user name and password.

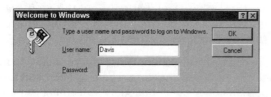

Figure 6-1: The user logon box.

If you configure Windows 98 for multiple users, it can remember different profiles for each person, and it uses each person's name and password to determine which configuration to display. If you are on a network, your name and password let you log on to network servers.

If you have multiple users on your computer, perhaps other family members, you can configure Windows 98 to present you with a pick box when it first starts up. To log on you can pick from among the designated users. We discuss the Windows family logon in "Logging onto the Network" in Chapter 24.

If you type a name and a nonblank password, this logon box will appear every time you start up Windows 98. You can make this logon box go away and not reappear the next time you start your computer by typing your name and then clicking the OK button without entering a password. You will be asked to confirm that you want a blank password. Click OK.

Tip

TweakUI lets you bypass the logon box, and still enter a nonblank password. The logon box still appears when you first start Windows 98, but it goes away quickly. The first time you start Windows 98, enter a user name and a password. Then start TweakUI, click the Network tab, mark Log On Automatically at System Startup, and enter your user name and password. (If you don't see TweakUI in your Control Panel, you can install it from the \Tools\ResKit\Powertoy folder on the Windows 98 CD-ROM.)

While Windows 98 lets you use user names and passwords, it is not a secure system. Other users can get into your computer by simply pressing the Esc key when asked for their name and password. You can, however, use the System Policy Editor (see "The Icons and Items on the Desktop") and third-party software (see "Securing the Windows 98 Desktop" in Chapter 12) to improve the security of Windows 98 computers. Passwords, multiple users, and multiple Windows 98 configurations are discussed in "Whose Desktop Is This Anyway?" in Chapter 12.

After you've closed the logon box, the Windows 98 user interface appears, the plain-vanilla version of which is shown in Figure 6-2. The background used for the Desktop can vary (based on how you set it up) from one solid color, to a photographic image, to an HTML document. If you have just installed Windows 98 over Windows 3.1x or if you got Windows 98 on a new computer, you'll find just a few icons in the upper-left corner of the Desktop. On the bottom edge is the Taskbar, a rectangular bar with a Start button on the left-hand side, the Quick Launch toolbar next to it, and a digital clock on the right.

Figure 6-2: The Windows 98 plain-vanilla user interface. It will soon look different as you change it to suit your preferences. If you have set it up to use the Active Desktop, you'll have the opportunity to mix little windows in with your icons on the Desktop.

The Desktop

Part of the Windows 98 user interface is based on the *desktop* metaphor. Your screen is turned into a graphical desktop with lots of little items on the desktop for you to work with.

In fact, the Windows 98 Desktop doesn't look much like a real desktop, although it doesn't really matter whether it looks like one or not. The primary purpose of the Desktop is to provide a background on which to display graphical objects such as icons and windows. Your open applications and documents appear in separate windows on top of the Desktop.

With the advent of the World Wide Web, the computing world quickly adopted a new *hyperlink* metaphor, which was popularized by the browser software you use to navigate the web. This metaphor emphasizes the connections (hyperlinks) between documents, both locally and globally.

Even before it released Windows 95, Microsoft realized that it was in its best interest to incorporate this approach into the part of the computer that it owns almost completely, the operating system. Microsoft's Internet Explorer browser is completely integrated into the Windows 98 user interface. The new *Web style* view and the Active Desktop have expanded and morphed the Windows interface so that it takes on many browser-like characteristics.

For example, many of the same icons that are found in Windows 95 are there, but you can now single-click them instead of double-clicking. As you move your mouse pointer over an icon, it becomes a pointing hand, a familiar shape to anyone who has used a web browser.

If you right-click an empty part of the Desktop, a context menu appears that lets you control the Desktop. This basic menu — it does change — is shown in Figure 6-3.

Figure 6-3: The Desktop context menu. Right-click anywhere on the Desktop to bring up the menu.

Click Properties (or Active Desktop, and then Customize My Desktop) to change many aspects of the Desktop. Move the icons around with Arrange Icons and Line Up Icons. Click Active Desktop, View As Web Page to switch between the standard Desktop and the new Active Desktop.

Undocumented

When the context menu is showing, you can only carry out the actions listed on that menu until you left-click (a right-click won't work) the Desktop or click (either left or right) in a window or someplace other than the Desktop. If your Taskbar is hidden, it will not pop up as long as the Desktop context menu appears on the Desktop.

The invisible grid

There is an invisible grid on your Desktop. The icons on the Desktop are centered in the cells defined by this grid and placed on the left side of the Desktop, starting at the top of the screen. You can place the icons in other locations, although most are not as convenient as this default top/left positioning. You can also determine the size of the grid cells.

Arranging the icons

To align your icons in the center of the grid cells, right-click the Desktop and then click Line Up Icons. Because you can line them up afterwards, you can drag icons to different parts of the Desktop and still have them look orderly when you are finished.

To arrange the icons in one of four predefined orders, right-click the Desktop, point to Arrange Icons, and then choose By Name, By Type, By Size, or By Date. The icons will arrange themselves starting in the upper-left corner and proceeding down to the next cell in the sort order specified. Additional columns of icons will be added to the right if there are more icons than can fit in the first column.

If you want the icons to always place themselves in columns starting at the left-hand side of the Desktop, right-click the Desktop, point to Arrange Icons, and then click Auto Arrange. Auto Arrange is a toggle switch; when it's active, you see a check mark next to the command. If Auto Arrange is checked, the icons always move back into the columnar arrangement no matter where you move them or where you originally place them.

Undocumented

Auto Arrange does not sort the icons. When Auto Arrange is checked, you can specify the order for the icons by simply dragging them to new positions in the columns. If you move an icon to the right of the column(s) of icons, it gets placed at the bottom of the right-most column.

If you turn Auto Arrange off (clear it), you can place icons wherever you like and in any order. If you don't want to be restricted to placing your icons in a particular order or location on the Desktop, don't use the Line Up Icons, Arrange Icons, or Auto Arrange commands. If you don't use these commands, you can drag and drop your icons wherever you like and space them as close together or as far apart as you want.

Changing the size of the grid

The grid starts in the upper-left corner of the Desktop. The vertical line that marks the right-hand edge of the first cell is so many pixels to the right of the left edge of the Desktop. The horizontal line that marks the bottom edge of the first cell is so many pixels below the top edge of the Desktop. The invisible grid is revealed in Figure 6-4.

Secret

The size of the cells depends on the icon pixel size, icon spacing (both horizontal and vertical), and display magnification (Small Fonts, Large Fonts, or Other), as discussed in "Changing the Size, Color, and Font of Objects on the Desktop" in Chapter 28. The default cell size (for Small Fonts) is 75 × 75 pixels with a default icon size of 32 pixels and default icon spacing of 43 pixels (32+43 = 75). The grid in Figure 6-4 is set at 75 pixels high by 75 pixels wide.

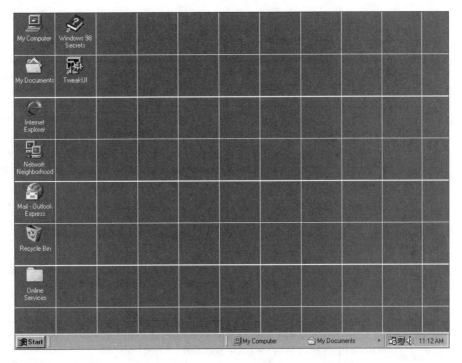

Figure 6-4: A faux icon spacing grid. The size of each cell in the default grid spacing in pixels (assuming a display magnification set at Small Fonts) is 75 pixels high and 75 pixels wide.

You can change the size of the icon spacing grid by editing the vertical and horizontal icon spacing values. To do this, take the following steps:

STEPS

Editing Icon Spacing

Step 1. Right-click the Desktop. Click Properties. Click the Appearance tab.

Step 2. Click the drop-down arrow in the Item field to open up the drop-down list of Desktop items.

Step 3. Click, one at a time, Icon Spacing (Horizontal) and Icon Spacing (Vertical).

(continued)

STEPS *(continued)*

Editing Icon Spacing

Step 4.   Adjust the size of each — in pixels — using the spin controls in the Size field to the right of the Item field. (Click the up and down arrows or enter a new number value to change the size.) The total vertical size of the cell will be the sum of the icon size plus the vertical spacing. Horizontal size is calculated similarly.

Step 5.   To see what the effect is on icon spacing, click the Apply button when both sizes are adjusted. Keep adjusting icon spacing until you are pleased with the results.

Step 6.   Click OK.

If an icon's title text doesn't fit within the boundaries of the cell, Windows 98 truncates the text and adds ellipses. If you make the vertical or horizontal spacing too small, the icons will overlap — not a good idea.

Undocumented

If you make the horizontal spacing of the cells too large, you may receive an "Explorer Caused a Divide error in Module Shell32.dll" error message. You'll know then that you've gone too far.

While the Desktop icons are created on a 32 × 32-pixel grid, you can blow them up to a bigger size. This may be useful if you have a high-resolution screen that displays 32 pixels as a very small physical size. Right-click the Desktop, click Properties, click the Effects tab, and mark the Use Large Icons check box. Click OK.

Changing the font and size of icon title text

By default, the icon titles use the MS Sans Serif 8-point font (at 800 × 600 display resolution — higher resolution displays default to a 10-point font). You have the option of changing the font used to display the icon titles. You can also change the font's point size and make it boldface and/or italic. You can't change the text color to something other than black unless you set your Desktop to a dark color, in which case Windows 98 automatically sets the text color to white.

Tip

MS Sans Serif is a *screen* font, which means that it has been designed to be readable at 96 or 120 pixels per logical inch. You can use any font that you want, including Arial, which looks a lot like MS Sans Serif but is a TrueType font. Check out the various fonts and choose one that you find easy to read.

If you increase the font point size, icon titles get bigger and may not fit in the grid cells.

To change the font used for the icon titles, take the following steps:

STEPS
Changing Icon Title Fonts

Step 1.   Right-click the Desktop. Click Properties. Click the Appearance tab.

Step 2.   Display the Item drop-down list.

Step 3.   Click Icon. You can change the Font and Size fields. You can also use the Bold and Italic buttons (see Figure 6-5).

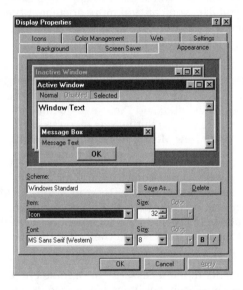

Figure 6-5: The Appearance tab of the Display Properties dialog box. Display the Item drop-down list and then choose Icon. Pick a font style from the Font drop-down list and a point size from the Size field. The B and I buttons stand for bold and italics.

Step 4.   Click the Apply button when you have chosen a font, point size, and so on, to see the effect of the choices. Keep adjusting these values until you are pleased with the results.

Step 5.   When you are done, click OK.

Changing other properties of the Desktop

You can change the background graphics, the colors used on the Desktop, the size of the icons, as well as many other properties of the Desktop. All of these changes are described in "The Desktop Wallpaper" in Chapter 28.

Putting new items on the Desktop

It is easy to put new items, represented by icons, on the Desktop. You can place new (empty) folders, new shortcuts, or new (blank) documents on the Desktop. By default, you can create new documents of these types: Internet Document (HTML), Text, WordPad, Bitmap Image, Briefcase, and Wave Sound. And if you like, you can add more document types to the list, or remove document types from the list. (You learn how to do this in "Adding Items to the New Menu" in Chapter 13.)

When you create a new shortcut (right-click the Desktop, point to New on the context menu, click Shortcut), a Wizard starts that guides you through the process of linking your new shortcut to an application. When you install new applications, they often add their own document type to the New menu. You can edit the list of types in the New menu using the steps detailed in the "Adding Items to the New Menu" section in Chapter 13.

Tip

Placing new blank documents on the Desktop is a pretty nifty feature and contributes to the document-centric character of Windows 98. When you click a new document icon on your Desktop, Windows 98 brings up the appropriate application and opens the blank document within it so that you can edit the document. To add new document icons to the Desktop, right-click the Desktop, point to New, and then click the document type that you want to add.

The new documents don't necessarily have to be empty or unformatted. You can create forms or certain subtypes of documents, such as "my standard format letter," and use them as a basis for creating new documents.

Pasting and undoing actions

The Paste command on the Desktop context menu lets you copy (or move) a file (or application, folder, or shortcut) to the Desktop. For example, if you want to copy a file to the Desktop, you first select a file in a folder window or in the Explorer. Then you right-click the file and choose Copy, which means "copy this file to someplace as soon as I tell you where." Finally, you right-click the Desktop and choose Paste to tell Windows 98, "this is where I want you to copy the file." (We discuss folder windows, the Explorer, and shortcuts in "Copying a file or a folder" in Chapter 8, "Copying and Moving Files and Folders" in Chapter 9, and "Cut and paste a shortcut" in Chapter 10, respectively.)

Windows 98 includes the Paste command in context menus for a variety of other (yet to be investigated) Desktop icons. As you can see, the Cut, Copy and Paste commands (and functionality) have made their way out of the word processor and into the operating system.

Your Desktop context menu might include an Undo command below the Paste command. The specific Undo command that appears depends on what actions you have taken in folder windows. If you have just renamed a file, for example, you will see the Undo Rename command. If you have just deleted a file, you will see the Undo Delete command.

The Undo command shows up in the Desktop context menu (and in most context menus) whenever you have taken an action that can be undone. If you remember what it was that you did and you want to undo it (as long as you haven't quit and restarted Windows 98), here's your chance. For additional details, see the section entitled "The Undo command" in Chapter 7.

The Active Desktop

The Active Desktop lets you place HTML-based windows/objects/ components/items on your Desktop, as shown in Figure 6-6. You can get "live" continuously or periodically updated information from the Internet.

While Microsoft really hypes the Active Desktop, it will be of more interest to people with large monitors and continuous fast connections to the Internet or a company Intranet. The fact that the Desktop (and all folders for that matter) can contain and display HTML documents is neat, but not necessarily always that useful. As more HTML content is added to folder views, however, you will see significant changes in how files are displayed in folder windows.

To switch between the standard Desktop and the Active Desktop, right-click the Desktop, click Active Desktop, and mark or clear View As Web Page.

The components on the Desktop are HTML files and may include ActiveX objects, JavaScript, and anything else that can go into an HTML document. The MSNEWS Weather Map shown in Figure 6-6 is simply a reference to a URL at the MSNBC web server. You can view the source code for the HTML document just by right-clicking the component (in the MSNEWS Weather Map, this is the black area near the top of the window) and choosing View Source.

Microsoft makes it easy to download its Active Desktop components. Right-click the Desktop, point to Active Desktop, and choose Customize My Desktop. Click the Web tab, click the New button, and then click Yes in the New Active Desktop Item dialog box. This opens your Explorer focused on Microsoft's Active Desktop Gallery.

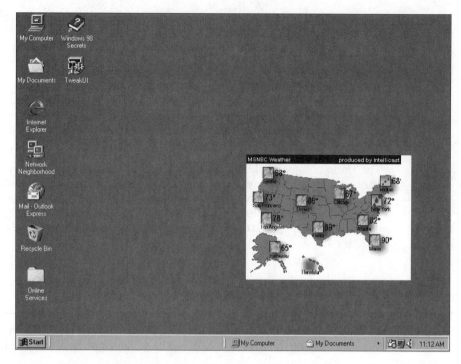

Figure 6-6: The Active Desktop with the MSNEWS Weather Map.

Tip

If you want to get components from other sources, follow the steps in the previous paragraph, except click No in the last step. This displays the New Active Desktop Item Wizard. You can type a URL in the Location field or browse to one in your Favorites. Additional components are available at ActiveIE at http://www.activeie.com/ie4.html, IE Gallery at http://www.iegallery.com/, or the Site Builder Network at http://www.gpick.net/sbr/asp/default.asp.

The New Active Desktop Item dialog box, which opens the first time you click the New button, gives you the option of not displaying the dialog box again. If you mark this option, you lose your quick access to Microsoft's Active Desktop Gallery. If you have done this, you can still get to Microsoft's site by typing http://www.microsoft.com/ie/ie40/gallery/ in the Location field of the New Active Desktop Item Wizard, which appears when you click the New button.

Secret

If you want the New Active Desktop Item dialog box back, use your Registry editor to navigate to HKEY_CURRENT_USER\Software\Microsoft\Internet Explorer\Desktop\General. Change VisitGallery in the right pane from no to yes. Turn to "The Registry Editor" in Chapter 15 to see how to use the Registry editor.

You can create your own Active Desktop items and put them on your Desktop. For example, you might want to create items that gather updated information from the specific sites that you are interested in, and forget about the limited options provided by the entertainment giants. Using the New Active Desktop Item Wizard, you can browse to a folder on your hard disk, pick out one of your own web documents, and place it on the Desktop. Or, you can just right-drag an HTML document onto the Desktop and click Create Active Desktop Item(s) Here. You'll want to create an HTML document that is small enough (using a *gif* file as an image map perhaps) to fit in a restricted area on your Desktop.

The Active Desktop can use any HTML-formatted document as wallpaper. The default HTML background for the Active Desktop is found at \Windows\Web\Wallpaper\wallpapr.htm. You can create your own web pages using FrontPage Express or any other web editor, and use them as background for your Active Desktop.

To turn one of your own web pages into your Desktop background, right-click the Desktop, click Properties, click the Background tab, click the Browse button, and navigate to the folder that holds the HTML document. To make it fit properly on your screen, you'll want to only make the document as long as the screen is high. All the links in the web page will be active after it becomes the background image. In Figure 6-7, the Windows 98 Secrets web page is set as the background for the Active Desktop.

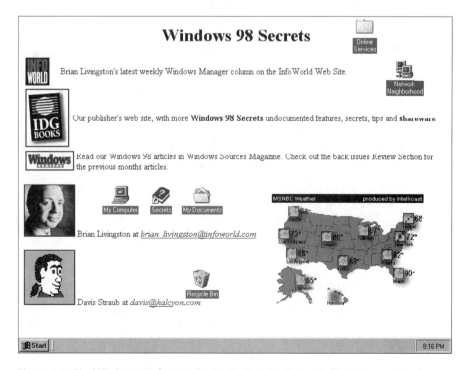

Figure 6-7: The Windows 98 Secrets Active Desktop background. The icons on the left-hand side are active links to web sites and e-mail addresses.

You don't have to use an HTML document as your background/wallpaper. You can continue to use *bmp* files, or capture *gif* files off the Internet and have them automatically converted into bitmaps and placed as wallpaper. While viewing a web page, right-click a graphic on the web page, and click Set As Wallpaper. You'll find the latest picture you have downloaded in \Windows\Internet Explorer Wallpaper.bmp.

You can't use an HTML page as wallpaper and your Active Desktop components won't show up unless you activate the Active Desktop (right-click the Desktop, point to Active Desktop, and click View As Web Page).

The Icons and Items on the Desktop

The icons that first appear on the Desktop stand for powerful Windows functions. They are discussed in later chapters. The My Computer icon is discussed in Chapter 7. The Recycle Bin is covered in Chapter 14. The My Briefcase icon is discussed in Chapter 23. The Internet Explorer icon is covered in Chapter 9.

The great thing about the Desktop is that there are icons on it. If you're upgrading from Windows 3.1*x*, you'll notice that the Desktop takes over much of the function of the Windows 3.1*x* Program Manager. Put up a digitized photograph as your background and the icons hang there in space on your Desktop. In contrast, the Windows 3.1*x* Program Manager presented a rather boring background for your program groups (unless you had a specialized wallpaper application).

The Active Desktop goes a step further and let's you put active connections to web-based information right on your Desktop. You can schedule these components to update on regular intervals with the latest information from their web source.

You can put any icon on the Desktop that you want. It is much more natural to put your stuff on the Desktop than it is to be constrained to the confines of the Program Manager. We discuss this in a lot more detail in "Put your favorite files and programs on the Desktop" in Chapter 10.

You can use the System Policy Editor to get rid of all the icons on your Desktop or to just get rid of the Network Neighborhood icon. (Turn to "System Policy Editor" in Chapter 24 to see how to install the System Policy Editor.) To use the System Policy Editor, take the following steps:

STEPS
Getting Rid of All the Icons on the Desktop

Step 1.   Install the System Policy Editor from the Windows 98 CD-ROM. You'll find it in the \tools\apptools\poledit folder.

Step 2. Click the Start button, point to Programs, Accessories, System Tools, and then click System Policy Editor.

Step 3. Double-click the Local User icon in the System Policy Editor window. Choose File, Open Registry.

Step 4. Click the plus sign next to the word *Shell*, and then click the plus sign next to the word *Restrictions*.

Step 5. Click the Hide All Items On Desktop or Hide Network Neighborhood check box.

Step 6. Click OK. Choose File, Save from the System Policy Editor's menu bar. Then choose File, Exit.

Step 7. Restart Windows 98.

If you want to selectively choose which icons to display on the Desktop, use TweakUI instead of the System Policy Editor. This is a much-preferred method because it allows you to quickly change your mind about which icons you want to display. Click your TweakUI shortcut on your Desktop (or click the TweakUI icon in the Control Panel), click the Desktop tab, and then mark or clear any of the check boxes.

You can quickly get the icons off your Active Desktop by right-clicking the Desktop, clicking Properties, clicking the Effects tab, and then marking the Hide Icons When the Desktop Is Viewed As a Web Page check box.

New icons for Desktop items

You can choose new icons to replace the default ones that come with your Desktop. The Windows 98 CD-ROM comes with all the themes that were first released on the Microsoft Plus! CD-ROM. Each theme includes different icons for the Desktop items in keeping with the theme. For example, the Mystery theme uses a deer stalker cap to represent My Computer. There are also many themes available for downloading on the Internet (lots with copyright infringement written all over them). See http://www.windows98.com.

If you want to choose your own new icons instead of using the default Windows 98 icons, you need to do manually what the themes application does automatically: You have to edit the Registry. Of course, to do this you also have to find a source of new icons.

Icons are stored in some executable files (files with *exe* extensions), in some dynamic link libraries (files with *dll* extensions), in icon files (files with *ico* extensions), and in icon libraries. By far the easiest way to find the icons that are already stored on your hard disk is to use one of the shareware icon search and library manager programs found on the *Windows 98 Secrets* CD-ROM.

You can change four of the Desktop icons by right-clicking your Desktop, clicking Properties, clicking the Effects tab, highlighting My Computer, My Documents, Network Neighborhood, or Recycle Bin (full or empty), clicking the Change Icon button, and browsing for icons.

You can also use the File Types tab of the Folder Options dialog box to search an individual file for icons:

STEPS

Looking at Icons

Step 1. Click My Computer. Choose View, Folder Options, and then click the File Types tab.

Step 2. Click any file type in the Registered File Types list. Click the Edit button.

Step 3. Click the Change Icon button. The icons you see under Current Icon are contained in the file listed in the File Name field. To see icons in other files, click the Browse button. You can now search for another file that contains icons. (For more on searching for a file, turn to "Creating and Editing File Types and Actions" in Chapter 13.)

Step 4. Be sure to click the Cancel buttons when you are done looking at icons.

Secret

To replace the Desktop icons, you can edit your Registry as follows:

STEPS

New Icons for Old

Step 1. Click My Computer. Click the drive icon for your hard disk. Click your Windows folder icon. Click Regedit.exe in the \Windows folder. (To find out more about the Registry, turn to "The Registry Editor" in Chapter 15.)

Step 2. Using the Registry editor, click the plus signs in the left pane to navigate to HKEY_CLASSES_ROOT\CLSID. Click the plus sign next to CLSID.

Step 3. To change the My Computer icon, scroll down the left pane of the Registry editor to {20D04FE0-3AEA-1069-A2D8-08002B30309D}. This is the Class ID for the My Computer object. Click the plus sign next to it and highlight DefaultIcon in the left pane.

Step 4.   Double-click Default in the right pane. Type the name of the file that contains the icon you want to use instead of the existing icon. Follow the complete path and filename with a comma and then a number representing the icon's position in the file. (You can determine an icon's position using the Looking at Icons steps above. In step 3, the icons in the Current Icon box are numbered from left to right, top to bottom, beginning with 0 for the upper-left icon.)

Step 5.   Click OK, and then exit the Registry editor.

Undocumented

You can change the icons of the other Desktop items by going to the following Class IDs in step 3 of New Icons for Old steps:

Network Neighborhood	{208D2C60-3AEA-1069-A2D7-08002B30309D}
Dial-Up Networking	{992CFFA0-F557-101A-88EC-00DD010CCC48}
Printers	{2227A280-3AEA-1069-A2DE-08002B30309D}
Briefcase	{85BBD920-42A0-1069-A2E4-08002B30309D}
Control Panel	{21EC2020-3AEA-1069-A2DD-08002B30309D}
Internet Explorer	{FBF23B42-E3F0-101B-8488-00AA003E56F8}
Outlook Express	{DACF95B0-0A3F-11D1-9389-006097D503D9}
Microsoft Network	{00028B00-0000-0000-C000-0000000000046}
Recycle Bin	{645FF040-5081-101B-9F08-00AA002F954E}
Inbox (Windows Messaging)	{00020D75-0000-0000-C000-000000000046}

The Recycle Bin has two icons, one for empty and one for full. Double-click *empty* and *full* in the right pane of the Registry editor to assign new icons to each of them.

Make your own icons

You can easily make your own icons, just by using MS Paint. Here's how:

STEPS

Making Your Own Icons

Step 1.   Click the Start button, Program, Accessories, and then Paint.

(continued)

STEPS *(continued)*

Making Your Own Icons

Step 2.   In the Paint window, choose Image, Attributes. Make the Height and Width 32 pixels, and click OK.

Step 3.   Click View, Zoom, and then Show Grid.

Step 4.   Click View, Zoom, Custom. Choose 800% and click OK.

Step 5.   Create your new icon. Save it as a *bmp* file.

Step 6.   You can now treat this file as a regular icon file. Following the New Icons for Old steps in the previous section, you can point to it and use it on your Desktop.

When you replace a Desktop icon with one you made yourself, you don't need to refer to it by anything other than its filename (see step 4 under New Icons for Old). You don't need to use an index number (in this case 0) because there is only one icon in the file.

High Color icons

While icons were originally limited to 16 colors, you can now have 16-bit (High Color, or 64 thousand colors) or 24-bit (True Color, or 16 million colors) color icons. If you create your own icons with MS Paint, you can choose the color depth.

To display High Color or True Color icons, you need a video card with enough memory at a given resolution. Right-click the Desktop, click Properties, and then click the Settings tab. Check the Color drop-down list to find out what your color depth is. If you have enough memory, you'll see High Color (16 bit) and/or True Color (24 bit) in the list. If you don't see these values, reduce your screen resolution using the Screen Area slider. Then choose either High Color or True Color from the drop-down list, and click OK.

Once you've set your color depth to High Color or True Color, you can enable your Desktop to display High Color or True Color icons. Right-click your Desktop, click Properties, click the Effects tab, and mark Show Icons Using All Possible Colors.

If you choose High Color or True Color, you also get gradient fills in the title bars of your dialog boxes. For details on how to set the colors used for these gradient fills, turn to "Changing the Size, Color, and Font of Objects on the Desktop" in Chapter 28.

Corrupted Desktop icons

If your Desktop icons get sick, you can refresh them. Windows 98 stores all the icons on the Desktop in a file named ShellIconCache, which is stored in the \Windows folder. It is a hidden file, so be sure to choose View, Folder Options in your Explorer or My Computer window, click the View tab, and mark Show All Files if you want to see the file listing. Windows 98 caches the shell icons in this file so that it can access them quickly instead of having to search through all the files that hold these icons every time it starts up.

Secret

You can refresh the icon cache by deleting ShellIconCache from your \Windows folder. To do this, first restart your computer in MS-DOS mode or exit to MS-DOS mode. Then type **del ShellIconCache**. (If you type **dir sh*.* /a** at the DOS prompt while in the \Windows folder, ShellIconCache will show up as Shelli~1.) Exit MS-DOS mode and restart Windows 98. The ShellIconCache file is automatically rebuilt from the original icons in their source files.

It's even easier to rebuild your icons using TweakUI. Just click the Repair tab, highlight Rebuild Icons in the drop-down list, and then click the Rebuild Now button.

Scraps

Some Windows 98-aware applications can place *scraps* on the Desktop (or in any folder window). You can try this out using WordPad. Open up a WordPad document. Select some text. Drag and drop it onto the Desktop.

An icon with the name Scrap appears on the Desktop. This is a document that can be read by WordPad. It is made up solely of the text that you dropped on the Desktop. Click its icon on the Desktop, and WordPad launches.

Scraps give you an easy way to pile up a bunch of notes or graphics on your Desktop (or in any other folder) and then make something of them later. For example, you might want to put a scrap containing your company logo on the Desktop, and then paste it into documents as you edit them. Scraps give you an alternative to the Clipboard, and the advantage of using them is that you can keep multiple pieces available at one time.

It is also possible to store a bit of boilerplate text in your Tray on the Taskbar. (See the section entitled "The Tray on the Taskbar" later in the chapter.) You'll need to download a small shareware application to be able to do this. You'll find TrayText at http://ourworld.compuserve.com/homepages/MJM_Software/traytext.htm.

The Taskbar and Its Toolbars

The first time you start up Windows 98, the Taskbar displays little more than the Start button, the Quick Launch toolbar, and a digital clock in the Tray. The Taskbar is the home of the *active* applications — those applications that you started by clicking a file or an application icon. There is a button on the Taskbar (or an icon in the Tray) for every major active application or window (it is possible for applications to hide their Taskbar icons).

An application or a document needs to be read into memory from the hard disk before it can act or be acted upon. We refer to an application that has been loaded into memory as an *active* application. Applications that are stored on your computer's hard disk but haven't been loaded into memory are *inactive*. A document is loaded into memory with its application. There aren't any stray documents out there in memory without their associated applications.

Some applications don't put buttons on the Taskbar or icons in the Tray. These "hidden" applications run in the background and aren't looking for any user input. You can hide the Taskbar buttons of whatever applications you choose. You can also move Taskbar buttons over to the Tray, where they are displayed as small icons. To make these changes, you need to use shareware apps that are included on the *Windows 98 Secrets* CD-ROM. (See "The Tray on the Taskbar" later in this chapter for more information.)

The Windows 98 comes with a set of default toolbars. These toolbars resemble the Taskbar and are connected to it. Right-click your Taskbar, point to Toolbars, and click Address, Links, Desktop, or Quick Launch to display one of the default toolbars, or click New Toolbar to define your own (see the "Toolbars" section later in this chapter). If you want to hide a toolbar, clear the check mark next to its name in the Toolbars submenu. (You can't temporarily hide a user-defined toolbar. When you clear its check mark, the toolbar is removed.)

The Taskbar buttons

Each Taskbar button includes the application's or window's icon and name. If there is an associated document or file with the application, its name is supposed to appear first on the button (according to the Windows 98 software design guidelines). The icons on the Taskbar button are smaller versions of the icons you see on the Desktop. They are 16×16 pixels instead of 32×32 pixels.

Windows 3.1*x* or multidocument applications place the name of the application first on the Taskbar button. For example, if you open a copy of Microsoft Word, you'll see a button labeled Microsoft Word on the Taskbar, and you will be hard pressed to see the name of the open document. If you open the Windows 98 Notepad without a document, Untitled appears as the first name on the Taskbar button.

Tip

Every user-interactive active application or window is represented on the Taskbar, regardless of whether the application is currently minimized, restored, or maximized. (The only exceptions are applications that run behind the scenes, which don't need Taskbar buttons, and those that have icons in the Tray instead of Taskbar buttons.) *This means that the Taskbar is a task switcher.* No matter if the active application has been minimized or is now buried under other application windows on the Desktop, you can bring it to the top by clicking its button (a single click at that) on the Taskbar.

The Taskbar is one of Window 98's most fundamental "ease of use" improvements over Windows 3.1x. It is also an advantage that Windows 98 has over the Apple Macintosh. This feature makes it almost impossible to lose track of which documents and programs are open, even when they are stacked on top of each other.

The Taskbar takes the place of the minimized active application and window icons that by default were displayed at the bottom of your Windows 3.1x Desktop. Because it has a button for every major active application, whether the application is minimized or not, the Taskbar has much of the task-switching functionality of the Windows 3.1x Task Manager.

Tip

The single-click operation of the Taskbar makes it easy to switch between *tasks* — which are simply active applications or windows. Combine this with Windows 98's enhanced resource management, and it is easy to find yourself using multiple active applications and opening multiple instances of your Explorer or My Computer windows. Windows 98 makes multitasking (defined from the user's perspective as quickly jumping among active applications and windows) easy enough to be useful.

To toggle between minimizing and restoring an application window, just click the application's Taskbar button, and then click again. This functionality was added with Internet Explorer 4.0. Therefore, it is available to Windows 98 users and to Windows 95 users who installed Internet Explorer 4.0 and chose the integrated mode.

Drag and wait to a Taskbar button

You can drag a file to a Taskbar button and continue to hold down the mouse button after you reach the Taskbar button. As you hold the file over the Taskbar button, the application associated with that button will spring to life. If it was minimized, it will open into a window on the Desktop. If it was buried under other windows, it will come to the top.

Tip

Once the application window has appeared, you can drop the file icon on it. The application determines what happens next. If the application is a Windows editor or word processor, it will open or insert the dropped file, depending on where you drop it. Drop it on the title bar and the document opens. Drop it in the client window, and the document may be inserted into an existing document.

If the program is a DOS editor, dropping a file will put the name of the dropped file at the insertion point in a DOS file. This behavior isn't all that useful unless you want to build a text document full of file names.

Specialized Windows 3.1*x* applications that are meant only to be displayed as icons and never expanded into windows do not work with Windows 98.

Hiding the Taskbar

The Taskbar has two mode switches: Always on Top and Auto Hide.

Always on Top means always on top of other windows on the Desktop (not exactly *always*, but often enough anyway). Turn on this feature and other windows do their best to stay out of the way of the Taskbar. Turn off this feature and other windows don't know that the Taskbar is there.

If you turn on Auto Hide, the Taskbar disappears (except for a thin line) unless it is the last thing you clicked on. An Auto-Hidden Taskbar doesn't take up Desktop real estate except when you want to do something with it, such as switch to another task.

When Auto Hide is on, the Taskbar hides itself as soon as you click on another application. To get the Taskbar to display itself, move the mouse pointer to the edge of the screen on which you've docked the Taskbar. You'll see a 2-pixel-wide line along the edge that is a remnant of the Taskbar. When your mouse pointer hot spot gets within 2 pixels of the edge of the Desktop, the pointer becomes a resize arrow, and the Taskbar pops up. The mouse pointer then changes back to a normal selection arrow.

Undocumented

If you move your mouse pointer more than 10 pixels away from the Taskbar without clicking it (or one of the Taskbar buttons) first, the Taskbar disappears. It doesn't disappear instantly. Depending on what is beneath the Taskbar, the screen usually takes longer to repaint the Desktop to show what was obscured by the Taskbar than it took to pop up the Taskbar in the first place. This can be quite a bother.

If you click the Taskbar after it pops up, it gains the focus. You can then move the mouse pointer around the Desktop and the Taskbar doesn't disappear until you click another window or the Desktop. You have to click directly on the Taskbar and not on any of the buttons. Sometimes this is a little difficult, because much of the Taskbar itself might be covered by buttons.

If Auto Hide is on and Always on Top is off, when the Taskbar pops up, it will pop up behind any window that it might have otherwise obscured. You may still be able to have a partial view of the Taskbar and be able to switch tasks, and so on.

If Auto Hide is off and Always on Top is on, the Taskbar sits on top of your Desktop and other windows try to get out of its way. When you maximize a window, it does not cover up the Taskbar. The application calculates the maximum window size as the actual screen resolution minus the number of pixels in the Taskbar.

If Always on Top is on, this doesn't mean necessarily that the Taskbar will always be on top. Other windows can have this same property. If two windows have this "always on top" property, whichever window has the focus will be on top.

To change the Auto Hide and Always on Top modes, take the following steps:

STEPS

Changing Taskbar Modes

Step 1. Right-click the Taskbar and click Properties to display the Taskbar Properties dialog box, as shown in Figure 6-8. (You can also get to this dialog box by clicking the Start button, pointing to Settings, and clicking Taskbar & Start Menu.)

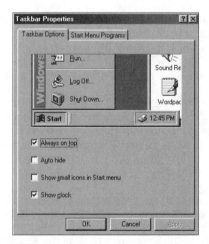

Figure 6-8: The Taskbar Options tab of the Taskbar Properties dialog box. Check the Auto Hide and/or Always on Top check boxes to change these Taskbar modes.

Step 2. Click Auto Hide and/or Always on Top to change the Taskbar modes. Click the Apply button to see the effect of these modes.

Step 3. When you are done, click OK.

One utility that is absolutely essential if you have your Taskbar set to be on the top edge of the Desktop with Always on Top turned on and Auto Hide turned off is Shoveit. Shoveit moves misbehaving application windows out from under the Taskbar. We discuss it further in the "Which Desktop edge is best for the Taskbar?" section later in this chapter.

Sizing the Taskbar

The Taskbar starts out thin, but you can make it bigger. In fact, you can make it large as one-half of the Desktop.

Move your mouse pointer to the top edge of the Taskbar so that the mouse pointer turns into a resize arrow. Hold down the left mouse button and drag the Taskbar's edge upward. The Taskbar increases in height in button-height increments.

Windows 98 sizes the buttons on the Taskbar automatically. All the buttons are the same size, no matter how long the names of the application and its associated document are. If the names are too long to fit in the button, Windows 98 truncates them and places an ellipses after them, if there is room.

You can see the full name of the application and document associated with a given button by placing your mouse pointer over the button and waiting for less than a second. A ToolTip (a small pop-up box with text) appears next to your mouse pointer. This happens only if the full name of the application and its associated document can't fit on the button face.

Undocumented

As you open additional applications, the Taskbar buttons shrink, unless you increase the size of the Taskbar. When the buttons become so small that they are just big enough to contain the 16×16 pixel icons within them, they get no smaller. If you add more active applications at that point, all the icons will not be displayed at the same time on the Taskbar. In this situation, a *spin control* appears on the Taskbar. You can spin the control to see icons that are not currently in view.

The Taskbar is attached to an edge of the Desktop. If it is on the bottom, you can't narrow it by detaching it from the right or left edge. The resize arrow appears only when the mouse pointer is near the top of the Taskbar.

Tip

The icons on the Desktop move to avoid the Taskbar when you resize it (as long as it isn't in Auto Hide mode, as explained in the "Which Desktop edge is best for the Taskbar?" section that follows). You have to have quite a few icons on the Desktop to see this effect.

Moving the Taskbar

The Taskbar doesn't have to be on the bottom of your Desktop. You can move it to any other edge (the top, bottom, left, or right side of the screen).

To move the Taskbar, position the mouse pointer over it, but not over any of the buttons on the Taskbar, nor over the line at the left (or top) end of the Taskbar button area. Press down the left mouse button and drag toward one of the other Desktop edges. Release the mouse button when the outline of the Taskbar is positioned on the desired edge.

Which Desktop edge is best for the Taskbar?

In application windows, the menu bar is at the top of the window, and a scroll bar is often at the right. No doubt you use menus and scroll bars quite often. You are probably used to moving your mouse to the right, top, and bottom of a Windows application client area, in that order of frequency. The left and bottom edges of the screen are the least "natural" areas to point to. You may find yourself doing a lot of extra mousing around if you place the Taskbar in these "unnatural" areas.

Tip

If you dock your Taskbar on the right side, you can get to the buttons on the Taskbar with an easy movement of the mouse. If the Taskbar is hidden, however, it may be too easy and quite a bother. If your document is anywhere near the right edge of your screen and you move the mouse quickly to the right to scroll, you are likely to overshoot the scroll bar and move to the Desktop edge. Up pops the Taskbar, which you didn't want. Now you have to move the mouse at least 10 pixels to the left of the Taskbar to get it to disappear — a waste of time.

The advantage of placing the Taskbar on the right is that it is easy and natural for you to get to it. And if Auto Hide is off, the Taskbar stays in view so you don't have to worry about making it pop up accidentally. However, there are disadvantages to placing the Taskbar on the right as well. If Auto Hide is turned on, you have to be accurate with your mouse to avoid inadvertently displaying the Taskbar. Furthermore, a vertical Taskbar with horizontal buttons is most likely fatter than a horizontal Taskbar with horizontal buttons, because the buttons have to be wide enough to display the names (although this is only an issue if Auto Hide is off).

One advantage of leaving the Taskbar on the bottom or moving it to the left is that you can have Auto Hide on and still not accidentally pop up the Taskbar so often that it becomes annoying. And if you are left-handed, it might feel natural to attach the Taskbar to the left edge of the Desktop. However, docking the Taskbar on the left side will probably be a difficult adjustment for most people, and if you place it on the bottom, the Start menu on the Taskbar pops up instead of dropping down.

Placing the Taskbar on the top edge of the Desktop will make it feel like a menu bar or a toolbar, and moving the mouse to the top of your screen is a "natural" movement for Windows users. The Start menu also drops down from the Start button in a familiar manner. If you have the real estate, put the

Taskbar on the top edge and keep Always on Top turned on and Auto Hide turned off. This option will probably feel comfortable to you. (Just remember that if you turn on Auto Hide, you'll have the problem of mouse overshoot when you choose menu items, although it won't be nearly as bad as if the Taskbar is at the right.)

Test out each location to figure out which one works the best for you. Be sure to give yourself a reasonable amount of time to try each one — a couple of days is about right.

Secret

Windows applications may get partially covered by the Taskbar if they are at their restored size and the Taskbar is attached to the top edge of the Desktop with Always on Top turned on and Auto Hide turned off. When Windows applications are maximized, they do not get obscured by the Taskbar.

The fact that Windows applications can't seem to find the Taskbar when they are at their restored size can be quite annoying. If a window's title bar is covered by the Taskbar, you have to use the keyboard to lower the window enough to bring the title bar into view. (Press Alt+Spacebar, M, press the down arrow repeatedly to move the window down, and then click once.) You could also just maximize the application's window by pressing Alt+Spacebar, X.

A little donation-ware application, ShoveIt, solves this problem very elegantly. Install it from the *Windows 98 Secrets* CD-ROM. You can choose whether to have it move the application window down from the top of the Desktop (you'd do this if you have the Taskbar attached at the top) or from any of the other edges. We find this applet to be absolutely indispensable.

Resizing and moving windows on the Desktop

Using the Taskbar, you can cascade, tile, or minimize all the sizable windows on the Desktop. Right-click the Taskbar and choose one of these sizing options.

Minimize All Windows is a very powerful function, because it is paired with Undo Minimize All. (When you right-click the Taskbar after choosing Minimize All Windows, the context menu contains an Undo Minimize All command.) You can clear your Desktop with one command, and then place everything back where it came from with the opposite command. This is a very handy feature if you want to get to some icons on your Desktop that are covered up by your application windows.

It is even easier to use the Show Desktop button on the Quick Launch toolbar. This button is also a toggle switch. Click it once to clear your Desktop of all open windows. Click it again to restore them.

The Start button

We discuss many of the Start button's interesting secrets in "Drop It on the Start Button" in Chapter 11, but here are a few of the high points.

The Start button contains the Stop button, in the form of the Shut Down command. Click the Start button and then click Shut Down to get out of Windows 98.

Clicking the Start button displays the Start menu. This menu provides a series of cascading menu choices that give you access to much of the functionality of Windows 98. You can easily change all of the menus that are attached to the Programs menu item to include the menus, folders, files, and applications that you want displayed.

Right-clicking the Start button lets you open and explore your computer and easily change items in the Start menus. You can add items to the Start menu by dragging them over and dropping them on the Start button.

You can rearrange some icons on the Start menus by using drag and drop and well as by right-clicking them. The Start menu is just a special version of a window.

Ctrl+Esc displays the Start menu, as does the Win key on Windows keyboards.

Toolbars

Toolbars are another way to get at your documents, web pages, and applications. Applications don't have to be active to be on a toolbar (unlike the Taskbar). You can think of toolbars as folder windows with special properties. For the most part, they just contain shortcuts to documents, URLs, and applications. You can leave the toolbars connected to the Taskbar, or move them to any location on your Desktop. To display a toolbar, right-click an empty part of the Taskbar, click Toolbars, and then click the toolbar.

One of the four default toolbars is the Address toolbar. If you type a URL or a folder name in the Address field of the Address toolbar and press Enter, a window appears on the Desktop displaying the contents of that folder or the web page associated with the URL.

You can move a toolbar by dragging and dropping it. To do this, move your mouse pointer over the line at the far left (or top) edge of the toolbar. When you see the resize arrow, drag the toolbar to one of the edges of the screen to dock it on that side, or drag it into the middle of the Desktop to make it float. This technique also works to adjust the relative positions of the Taskbar and the toolbars if they are sharing the same edge of the screen.

You can create a new toolbar that contains the contents of a folder. One way to do this is to just drag the folder icon (or a shortcut to the folder icon) to the very edge of your Desktop and drop it there. You can do this with My Computer, My Documents, and Network Neighborhood, as well as any icons that represent folders containing documents and/or applications.

Another way to create a toolbar for the contents of a folder is to use the New Toolbar dialog box. To see an example of this, take the following steps:

STEPS

Creating a New Toolbar

Step 1. Click the Start button, Programs, Windows Explorer.

Step 2. Click one of your hard disk icons in the left pane of your Explorer. Right-click in a clear area in the right pane of the Explorer.

Step 3. Click New, Folder, and type **My System**. Press Enter.

Step 4. Double-click the My System folder icon in the right pane of the Explorer.

Step 5. Right-click the right pane of the Explorer, click New, Folder, type **Test**, and press Enter.

Step 6. Right-click the Taskbar, click Toolbars, and then click New Toolbar.

Step 7. In the New Toolbar dialog box, click the plus sign next to the hard disk icon, click the plus sign next to My System, highlight the Test folder icon, and click OK. Your new (as yet empty) toolbar appears at the bottom of the Desktop.

Of course, even though you can create toolbar out of any existing folder, it is best to use folders that only contain shortcuts. If you want to add shortcuts to the toolbar that you just created (and its corresponding folder), just drag and drop them to the toolbar.

You can also drag and drop shortcuts to the Links toolbar and the Quick Launch toolbar. The Links toolbar appears both on your Desktop and in your Explorer window. Any shortcuts you drag and drop onto it show up on the toolbar in both places.

If you want to remove the toolbar you created in the Creating a New Toolbar steps, right-click the Taskbar, click Toolbars, and clear the check mark next to the toolbar (or right-click the toolbar and click Close). You can't temporarily hide toolbars that you create, unlike the four pre-existing toolbars.

Using a toolbar to make the Desktop always available

The default Windows 98 configuration displays a single toolbar (the Quick Launch toolbar) attached to the Taskbar. However, you can display multiple toolbars and place them on any edge of the Desktop (or in the middle of it, if you like).

Tip

For example, you might want to place the Desktop toolbar on the side of your Desktop so that your Desktop icons are always accessible. To do this, take the following steps:

STEPS
Making the Desktop Always Accessible

Step 1. Right-click the Taskbar, point to Toolbars, and click Desktop.

Step 2. Point to the vertical bar at the far left edge of the Desktop toolbar (which is now partially covering your Taskbar), and drag and drop the toolbar to the left or right edge of your Desktop.

Step 3. Right-click the Desktop toolbar and choose View, Small.

Step 4. Right-click the toolbar again, and clear Show Text (make sure that you have distinctive icons for every icon on your Desktop).

Step 5. Right-click it again and clear Show Title.

Step 6. Right-click it again and mark Auto Hide. Move your mouse pointer to the edge of the Desktop until the Desktop toolbar appears.

Step 7. Right-click once more, and mark Always on Top.

Step 8. Resize the Desktop toolbar to show all your Desktop icons.

Now you have a pop-up Desktop toolbar that gives you immediate access to all your Desktop icons. Of course, you can also use the Deskmenu applet from Power Toys set to put a Deskmenu icon in your Tray. When you download Power Toys, be sure to put it in a folder with no more than eight letters because its installer can't handle long path or folder names. You'll find Power Toys at http://www.microsoft.com/windows/software.htm.

The Tray on the Taskbar

The little indented area on the right edge of the Taskbar is called the *Tray*. Some applets that start up when Windows 98 starts up put their icons in here. The idea is that by putting small icons in the Tray, applets that are always running don't take up as much space on the Taskbar as bigger applications, which run only when you choose to start them.

G.L. Liadis Software, publisher of numerous shareware applications for Windows 98, has come out with WinTray. If you put this 249K application in your Startup folder, you gain the ability to store up to eight icons of your choice in the Tray.

Once you've used WinTray's dialog box to select the applications you want in the Tray, their icons automatically show up in the Tray every time you start Windows. You can configure the icons to launch your favorite apps with a double-click or a single-click (your choice). You can keep WinTray's dialog box open during your Windows session or instruct it to hide. Right-clicking any icon you placed in the Tray brings up the WinTray window again so you can reconfigure the program, adding or removing icons from the Tray.

The Tray is usually used for small system utilities, such as resource monitors and diagnostic tools that you want to frequently check on with a click. For example, the Windows 98 Resource Meter (C:\Windows\Rsrcmtr.exe) automatically places itself in the Tray when you run it. WinTray lets you store other utilities in the Tray as well.

There's no particular reason, however, that you should be limited to putting utilities in the Tray. Any major application that you use frequently could be a candidate — your word processor, say, or a favorite game.

You can download an unregistered shareware version of WinTray from the Internet by setting Internet Explorer to http://members.aol.com/glliadis/index.htm. Click the Utilities keyword to download Win Tray or see a listing of many other programs from this prolific shareware author.

Another shareware application, Icon Corral, not only lets you place application icons in the Tray, it allows you to remove the space-wasting buttons for these applications from the Taskbar itself while they're running. You can download a fully-functional version from http://www.armadillobrothers.com/download.htm.

Tray Shortcuts is a free program that doesn't remove apps from the Taskbar, but does place icons in the Tray like WinTray does. You can find Tscuts.zip at http://www.cybermad.com/best/tools.html.

You'll find a couple of additional applets on our *Windows 98 Secrets* CD-ROM that help you manage the Tray. If you want your own applications to put their icons in the Tray, then install the applet named Tray. If you want to be able to hide the Tray, install TrayHide.

The clock

The Taskbar has a digital clock. If you rest your mouse pointer over the time, you'll see the date in a ToolTip. If you right-click the time, you can choose

Adjust Date/Time in the context menu to display the Date/Time Properties dialog box, as shown in Figure 6-9.

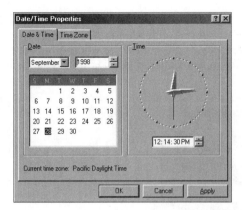

Figure 6-9: The Date/Time Properties dialog box. You can set the date and time by typing new values or clicking the spin controls in the date and time fields.

You can change the date by choosing the month from the drop-down list, spinning the year field, and clicking on a day. You can change the time by typing a new time or by using the spin control. To change the clock to a 24-hour display (instead of AM and PM), take the following steps:

STEPS

Changing the Time Format Display

Step 1. Click the Start button, point to Settings, and then click Control Panel.

Step 2. Click the Regional Settings icon.

Step 3. Click the Time tab.

Step 4. Display the Time Style drop-down list and choose a style with an uppercase H.

Step 5. Click the OK button in the Regional Settings Properties dialog box.

If you want to change the date format, click the Date tab in step 3 instead of the Time tab.

If you change the Short Date style, the new style won't be used until you restart Windows 98.

You can also set your time zone by clicking the Time Zone tab, as shown in Figure 6-10. Check out the world map. This map used to be pretty cool, because you could click an area to illuminate the whole time zone/daylight savings zone. No longer. Too many political entities with disagreements about borders.

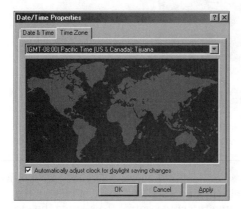

Figure 6-10: The Time Zone map. Click the drop-down list above the map to pick a time zone.

Undocumented

There are 63 separate entries in the list of time zones (in the original version of Windows 95 there were 51) even though you might assume that there are only 24 unique time zones. Windows 98 keeps track of the daylight savings time rules for various locations, so, for example, there is a unique entry for Arizona (USA) that doesn't honor daylight savings time. There are also separate entries for Darwin and Adelaide (Australia), both of which are plus 9½ hours from Greenwich Mean Time.

When the first day of daylight savings time arrives, you get a message asking if you want to have your computer's clock moved an hour ahead.

The time zone value does have something of a practical value. If you are on a network that crosses time zones, say, your own company's WAN, your computers will use this time zone value to get everyone's time synched to a universal standard such as Zulu, Greenwich Mean Time, or whatever arbitrary one you choose. Your computers can correctly compare files that are time-stamped on the West Coast with files that are time-stamped on the East Coast.

The Windows 98 Time Zone Editor is a customization tool for those with an abiding interest in the start and end dates of daylight savings time and other time-related policies. You can edit the start and end dates of daylight savings time, create new time zones, and so on. Download Microsoft's Kernel Toys from http://www.microsoft.com/windows95/info/kerneltoys.htm. Inside Kernel Toys, you'll find the Time Zone Editor. You will also find it on the Windows 98 CD-ROM, in \tools\apptools\tzedit.

You can add a date display to the Tray. This lets you see the date without having to place your mouse pointer over the time display. You can download TrayDay from http://www.mjmsoft.com.

Sliding windows

You'll notice as you click application buttons on the Taskbar that the title bar of the application is displayed first in a shrunken form and then expanded until the complete application is displayed in a window on the Desktop. This is called *sliding* or *zooming* windows, and it occurs only if the application has been minimized first.

If you minimize an application on the Desktop, the opposite effect occurs. The window's title shrinks, and then the application's window disappears. Windows 98 is trying to show you that your application has now gone to the Taskbar and to get it back you need to click its button there.

Secret

If you don't like this effect, you can turn if off. Here's how:

STEPS

Turning Off Sliding Windows

Step 1. Click Regedit.exe (the Registry editor) in the \Windows folder. See Chapters 7 and 8 for more on viewing the \Windows folder in the Explorer or a folder window.

Step 2. Click the plus sign to the left of HKEY_CURRENT_USER. (This will make the change for the current user only. Often the current user is the only user.)

Step 3. Click the plus sign to the left of Control Panel and then Desktop. Highlight WindowMetrics.

Step 4. Right click the right pane, and choose New, String Value. Type **MinAnimate** as the new name for the string value.

Step 5. Double-click MinAnimate in the right pane. Type the value **0**. Click OK.

Step 6. Exit the Registry editor and restart Windows 98.

If you want the sliding windows effect to reappear, you can always change this value back to 1. If you find that someone has already created MinAnimate, you can change its value by double-clicking it.

TweakUI makes it easier to get rid of the zooming windows effect. Just click the General tab in TweakUI and clear the Window Animation check box.

Task Switching with the Keyboard

Three keyboard combinations let you switch among active applications and folders.

Hold down Alt and press the Tab key. A window that contains the icons of the active applications and folders appears on the Desktop. By pressing and releasing the Tab key you can switch between the active applications and folder windows.

If you want to get back to the Start button, press Ctrl+Esc. This displays the Taskbar and the Start menu. You can get to the menu items on the Start menu by pressing the letter key corresponding to the underlined letter in the menu item, or by pressing the up and down arrow keys to highlight the item and then pressing Enter. Menu items in the other menus (ones that cascade off the Start menu) don't have unique assigned letters. However, you can still choose them by pressing the letter key that corresponds to the first letter in the item's name, or by highlighting the item with the up and down arrow keys and then pressing Enter.

Undocumented

You can get to the icons on the Taskbar or the icons on the Desktop with the keyboard. Press Ctrl+Esc to get to the Start menu. Press Esc to put the focus on the Start button and hide the Start menu. Press Tab to put the focus on the Taskbar. You can now use the arrows keys to move among the Taskbar icons.

Press a second Tab after the first to shift the focus to the icons on the Desktop. You can then use the arrow keys to highlight one icon after another. The Tab key (or the F6 key) toggles the focus between the Start button, the Taskbar, any toolbars, and the icons on the Desktop. (The focus must first be on one of these items for this to work.) The Start button doesn't open the Start menu until you focus on it and press the Enter key. If the Taskbar is in Auto Hide mode, it appears when the focus shifts to the Start button or the Taskbar and disappears when the focus shifts to the Desktop.

Undocumented

If you are in a full-screen DOS Windows session, you can return to the Desktop by holding down Alt, pressing the Tab key, and clicking the pop-up window that is displayed when you press Alt+Tab.

You can also switch between tasks by holding down Alt and pressing the Esc key. If the task you switch to is minimized, the only action you will notice is that the task's button on the Taskbar is depressed and the title bar of the previously active application changes to its inactive color.

The Task Manager

The old Windows 3.1*x* Task Manager is still here, although in a new suit of clothes. Many of its functions have been taken over by the Taskbar, but that doesn't mean it isn't useful. It might be just the right tool for you.

The nice thing about the Windows 3.1*x* Task Manager was that it was always right there, a double-click away on the Desktop. You always had the option of bringing up the Task Manager and using it to switch to another task, no matter how deeply it was buried in the pile on your Desktop. Short of minimizing all the covering windows, this was often the only way to switch to a non-minimized task.

Third-party vendors had a field day with the Windows 3.1*x* Task Manager, finding lots of ways that they could improve upon it. They turned their Task Manager replacements into shells that replaced the Windows 3.1*x* Program Manager.

The Task Manager in Windows 98 is a floating Taskbar without the Start button or the clock.

Undocumented

The Task Manager is Taskman.exe in the \Windows folder. You can always click it in a folder window or the Explorer. Bring it up and you get a button for every active task, as shown in Figure 6-11.

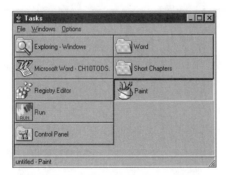

Figure 6-11: The Task Manager. Click a button to switch to that task.

You can change the size of the buttons and choose whether or not you want text in them by clicking Options in the menu bar. One nice thing about the Task Manager is that it has buttons that display the big icons.

Unfortunately, the Windows 98 Task Manager does not appear when you double-click the Desktop, as the Windows 3.1*x* Task Manager did. If you'd like to use the Task Manager, you should create a shortcut for it and assign a hot key to it so that you can get to it when you need it. To do this, follow the steps detailed in "Creating Shortcuts" in Chapter 10. You can put a shortcut to the Task Manager in your Startup folder so that it is available to you when you start Windows.

Summary

The Desktop, the Active Desktop, the Taskbar, and the toolbars form the core of the Windows 98 user interface. In this chapter (and Chapter 28) we show you how to set them up your way.

▶ We show you how to arrange the icons on your Desktop and change the underlying invisible grid that determines their placement.

▶ It is easy to place empty documents on the Desktop and then click them to bring up applications to edit these documents.

▶ The Taskbar can be transformed into a useful tool if you take the time to move and size it for your needs. We show you what kind of problems you will run into using it in certain configurations and how to find the right edge of the Desktop to use.

▶ Use shareware applets to put Taskbar buttons in the Tray.

▶ Create toolbars from folder shortcuts by dragging the shortcuts to the edge of the Desktop.

▶ You can use Alt+Tab, Alt+Esc, and Ctrl+Esc to choose among active applications and folders.

▶ The Task Manager is still with us. You can use it as a floating task switcher.

Chapter 7

My Computer—Folders and Windows

In This Chapter

We discuss My Computer, the other major part of the Windows 98 user interface besides the Desktop. With its single-pane view, My Computer is the window to your computer and the Internet. It is transformed from just a file-management tool in the earlier versions of Windows 95 into a flexible viewer.

▶ Turning My Computer into Your Computer

▶ Quickly viewing the disk drives, folders, and files on your computer

▶ Ordering and placing your icons in a folder window just the way you want them

▶ Closing multiple folder windows with one click

▶ Quickly moving, copying, renaming, or deleting folders and files

▶ Using special key and mouse-click combinations to speed the selection of files and folders

Viewing Your Computer

You need a window, or several windows, to see what is on your computer, your network, or the Internet. This chapter focuses on how to use folder windows (or *single-pane* windows). In Chapter 8, we discuss the Windows Explorer, a *dual-pane* window.

Frankly, we almost never use a single-pane window to view the contents of our computers. It is just too painful. The Windows Explorer, with its hierarchical view of folders, is much more powerful as a navigation device. On the other hand, the single-pane view is just fine for viewing web documents and navigating with hyperlinks.

We suggest that you use this chapter to become familiar with how window views work with your computer. You can use almost everything that we discuss here with the Windows Explorer. Later, in "Turning My Computer into the Explorer" in Chapter 8, we'll show you how to turn My Computer into My Explorer.

Once is enough

If you use the new Windows 98 interface, you can open an application or document with a single-click (although you can change this setting to require a double-click if you prefer). To choose the new way, click the Start button, Settings, Folder Options. Mark the Web Style option button and click OK. You can also mark Custom, Based on Settings You Choose, click the Settings button, mark Single-Click to Open an Item (Point to Select), and click OK twice.

If you choose Web style, Windows 98 sets your Desktop to the Active Desktop. You can single-click items on the Desktop, whether it is active or not.

In this chapter and others, we use the term *click* as a stand-in for both methods. When we refer to a click in this book, keep in mind that you can use a double-click instead if you have configured your computer to use the *Classic style* interface (this is the Windows 95 interface). We also state that you can rest your mouse pointer over an icon to select it. If you have chosen the Classic style interface, you'll need to click the icon to select it.

Hovering (resting the mouse pointer over an icon to select it) and single-clicking represent the triumph of the web browser interface over the previous Windows interface. Microsoft was forced to adopt these options because they are so popular among web enthusiasts. We applaud anything that reduces the wear on our fingers.

You can also choose between single-clicking or double-clicking in the My Computer window, by choosing View, Folder Options, and marking either Web style or Classic style. If you mark Custom, you can click the Settings button, and choose Single-Click.

My Computer, your computer

There it is in the upper-left corner of your display—My Computer. Wait a minute, it's *your* computer. *My* computer is here. As far as you are concerned it's *your* computer, but then you would tell us that "It's *My* Computer."

Microsoft was well aware of this "Who's on first, What's on second, and I don't know who's on third" problem but went ahead and called it My Computer anyway. You can imagine some computer instructor saying to his or her students, "Click My Computer," and then having to say, "No, I mean click the My Computer icon on the screen of *your* computer."

Not only that, My Computer is just an icon on your computer's screen. It's not your computer. It's a computer within a computer. Microsoft hopes that this doesn't confuse you.

As you shall see, this is not just a semantic issue. When something has a representation of itself within itself, the representation has to be distorted so as not to go on endlessly. After all, My Computer is on the Desktop, but the Desktop is both in My Computer and is displayed on your computer.

Changing My Computer to Fred

Tip

Fortunately, you can change the name of the My Computer icon to something else, like Your Computer. Highlight the My Computer icon, press F2, type a new name, and press Enter.

You can also change the Network Neighborhood to something like Network Neighbourhood if you are in England. Furthermore, if you use the Registry editor, you can change the name of the Recycle Bin (see "What's Recyclable about the Recycle Bin?" in Chapter 14).

The My Computer Window

When you first set up Windows 98, you will see a few icons on the left side of your Desktop. How many you see depends on which options you chose during the Windows 98 setup process, and whether you are updating a Windows 95 computer or have purchased a new computer with Windows 98 already installed.

The My Computer icon (and a rather generic-looking computer icon it is) is the first icon on the Desktop — an indication of its importance (as far as Microsoft is concerned) in the hierarchy of items on the Desktop. You can place it somewhere else, if you want. If you arrange the Desktop icons in any of the predetermined sort orders (by right-clicking the Desktop, pointing to Arrange Icons, and choosing any of the sort orders from the submenu), it will again appear in the upper-left corner.

When you click My Computer, a single-pane window much like the one shown in Figure 7-1 appears on your Desktop. In the figure, it's displayed in Large Icons view with the menu bar and the Standard Buttons toolbar showing. The Address bar is turned on, and View, As Web Page is not checked.

Figure 7-1: The My Computer window. Click the My Computer icon on the Desktop to open it.

Tip

You can also right-click the My Computer icon and then click Open from the context menu. The Open command is at the top of this menu. You can left- or right-click the context menu item — it doesn't care which mouse button you use.

Clicking My Computer opens a window that displays the contents of My Computer. *Open* means to display in a window. If you open an application, it will be displayed in a window. If you open a document, it will also be displayed in a window. Opening an icon such as the My Computer icon means to display its contents within a window.

You don't find windows on real-world desktops — so much for desktop metaphors. You might think of a window as the thing itself plus its edges. A window displays a document on the Desktop, and the edges of the document contain commands that determine how the document is displayed.

The contents that are displayed are not the physical contents of the computer — what you would normally expect to see when you "opened" up your computer — but its logical contents. The My Computer window contains icons that look like physical items: your floppy drive(s) and your hard disk drive(s). The window also has some manila folder icons with graphics on them (*special folders*).

The diskette and hard disk drive icons represent the logical contents — the files, folders, documents, and applications — that are stored on these devices. The special folder icons give you quick access to certain useful functions. For example, the Printers folder (see "The Printers Folder" in Chapter 29) contains the printer drivers. We discuss these particular special folders in much more detail in other chapters. To open and display the contents of any drive or folder icon, click it.

You can also display the contents of My Computer as a web page (right-click the My Computer window and choose View, As Web Page). In this view, you see something like the My Computer window shown in Figure 7-2.

Secret

Microsoft allows you to create your own web page view for most folders. You do this by right-clicking the client area of the folder window and choosing Customize This Folder, which launches the Customize This Folder Wizard. However, the Customize This Folder command is not available in the My Computer window because Microsoft has already defined My Computer's web page view. The HTML template file it uses to define this view and its capabilities is \Windows\Web\mycomp.htt.

The Customize This Folder Wizard works for most folders, but it doesn't work on most system or special folders such as Control Panel, Printers, Downloaded Program Files, Subscriptions, and Tasks. The Wizard creates a hidden Desktop.ini file in the folder, and this *ini* file contains pointers to the resources that are used to create the new web page (HTML) view of the folder. The Wizard uses the HTML template \Windows\Web\folder.htt as its starting point. We discuss this further in the "Customizing this folder" section later in this chapter.

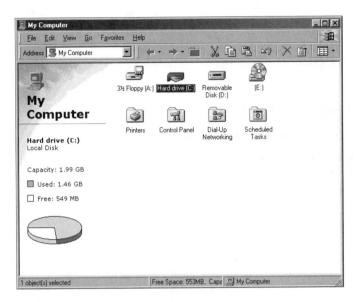

Figure 7-2: The My Computer window displayed as a web page. Position your mouse pointer over a hard drive icon in this view to display its capacity and free space.

Folders

Windows 98 has replaced the term *directory* (from DOS, Windows 3.1x, and many operating systems before DOS) with *folder*—a more office-oriented name. Also, folders can do much more than DOS directories. Some special folders, such as the folders in the My Computer window, have additional capabilities. You can place folders (or better yet, shortcuts to folders) on the Desktop, and they can contain folder windows of their own.

You can place a folder icon (or a shortcut to a folder icon) on the Desktop or in a folder window. Folders can contain other folders, just as DOS directories can contain subdirectories. To locate your files, you click a folder icon to display a window containing other folder icons.

If you are moving up from Windows 3.1x, you'll remember that in the File Manager, the hard disk and floppy disk drive icons sat on a special bar above the client area of the window. In Windows 95 and 98, they have come down to join the folders and files in the client area of the My Computer window.

If you display the My Computer window as a web page (right-click the window, and click View, As Web Page), you will still see folder icons in the window. Although web pages out on the World Wide Web could conceivably have folder icons in them, they rarely do. Microsoft is clearly stretching it a bit in its efforts to get the two metaphors (desktop and World Wide Web) to work together.

Viewing My Computer as a web page provides more information about the contents of My Computer. For example, if you place your mouse pointer over the Control Panel icon, an explanation about what the Control Panel is appears on the left side of the window. See Figure 7-2 for another example.

The special folders in the My Computer window

Undocumented

The four folders in the My Computer window are unlike most other folders on your hard disk. They have special functions, and their contents are not stored within the folder. For example, the contents of the Control Panel folder are stored in the \Windows\System folder in files with the *cpl* extension. The other folders are just front ends to information stored only in the Registry.

Microsoft made an arbitrary design decision to put these special folder icons in the My Computer window and to put little graphics on the folder icons to remind us that they are special. It placed the special folder icons in the My Computer window because this provides an easy way for you to get to folders that contain useful Windows 98 functions. We have devoted a chapter each to three of these folders.

The Printers folder is introduced in "The Printers Folder" in Chapter 29, the Control Panel folder in "Getting to the Control Panel" in Chapter 16, and the Dial-Up Networking folder in "Dial-Up Networking" in Chapter 17.

You can use the Scheduled Tasks folder to create a list of actions that Windows 98 will perform at a certain time without further input from you. Examples include running ScanDisk, running Defrag, and so on.

My Computer window properties

If you right-click an empty area in the My Computer window, a context menu like the one shown in Figure 7-3 appears. This menu is similar to the one you get when you right-click the Desktop, except that it has a View menu item instead of Active Desktop. When you point to View, a submenu appears that lets you change how the icons in the window are displayed. Your choices are As Web Page, Large Icons, Small Icons, List, and Details. Icons on the Desktop are always displayed as large icons.

Tip

The Properties command displays the System Properties dialog box, which functions as the Windows 98 hardware interface. You can also right-click the My Computer icon on your Desktop and click Properties to get to this dialog box. Turn to "The Device Manager" in Chapter 25 for details on setting system-wide properties.

Figure 7-3: The context menu for the My Computer window with the View options showing.

Drive properties

When you place your mouse pointer over a drive icon in the My Computer window, a report of its free space and disk capacity appears in the status bar. If you are viewing My Computer as a web page, this information also appears on the left side of the client window.

To view or change the properties of a drive, right-click the drive icon and click Properties. You can change the drive's volume label, as shown in Figure 7-4. You can also check the drive for errors, back it up, or defragment it by clicking the Tools tab. Check out "A drive icon" in Chapter 33 for details.

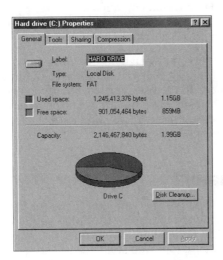

Figure 7-4: The General tab of the Properties dialog box for a disk drive. Type a new volume label for your drive. If you want to check for errors, click the Tools tab. You can share your drive with others on your network by setting your share configuration in the Sharing tab. To compress or decompress your drive or to change its compression ratio, click the Compression tab. You can also remove files you may not need by clicking the Disk Cleanup button and choosing what to remove.

You can use TweakUI to decide which hard drives are displayed in your My Computer or Explorer window. This is one way to make sure that others don't have the opportunity to see what is on your drives. This is a per-user setting, so if you have multiple users with multiple user profiles on your computer, you can hide different drives for each user. Click the TweakUI icon in your Control Panel, click the My Computer tab, and choose which disk drives to hide. (If you don't have the TweakUI icon, you can install the utility from the \tools\ResKit\Powertoy folder of your Windows 98 CD-ROM.)

Opening a new window

Click a drive icon in the My Computer window to open a window that displays the contents of the drive. The contents will consist of folder and file icons.

Each icon has an associated window. If you are using the "classic" Windows 95 settings (see the next section, "One window or many?"), when you click an icon in one of these windows, you will open yet another window. My Computer has its own window, and all your disk drives have their own windows.

You can continue to click folder icons to move hierarchically through the folders stored on your drive. Folders can contain subfolders, which in turn can contain more subfolders. You can move sideways by returning to a parent folder and then moving to a different subfolder.

If you view your computer's contents through one window, you can also go backward and forward along the path that you have traveled. Click the Back (left-pointing) button to go back to the previous view that you chose. If you've gone back, click the Forward (right-pointing) button to move forward to where you were before you went back. (If you don't see the toolbar, choose View, Toolbars, Standard Buttons.)

One window or many?

Choose View, Folder Options from the My Computer menu (or from the menu of any drive or folder window) to display the Folder Options dialog box, as shown in Figure 7-5. The General tab gives you three major options for viewing windows and your Desktop: Web style, Classic style, or Custom.

If you choose Classic style, Windows 98 opens a separate window each time you double-click an icon within the My Computer window, a drive window, or a folder window. If you choose Web style, Windows 98 reuses and renames the My Computer window each time you single-click an icon within the window.

If you choose Custom, you can set whether to use single or multiple windows independently of the other settings in the Classic and Web styles. Choose Custom, click the Settings button to display the Custom Settings dialog box, and then mark Open Each Folder in the Same Window or Open

Each Folder in Its Own Window. The Custom Settings dialog box also allows you to choose between single-click and double-click without changing your other Classic or Web style settings.

Figure 7-5: The General tab of the Folder Options dialog box. You can choose to browse folders in separate windows (Classic style) or in a single window (Web style).

Your Desktop can fill up pretty quickly if you choose to open a new window every time you double-click a drive or folder icon. (See "Closing a folder window" later in the chapter to learn how to close folder windows.) However, opening multiple windows does let you see the contents of several windows at one time. It also makes it easier to move items from one folder to another. When you open a new window, a button for it appears on the Taskbar, so you can simply click Taskbar buttons to switch among multiple open windows.

Switch to a single window view on the fly

Secret

If you have chosen the Classic style, which means you use double-click and open each folder in its own window, you can still choose to open the next folder in the current window. Rather than double-clicking a folder icon, which would display the new folder in its own window, hold down the Ctrl key as you double-click the icon. The existing window will now display the contents of the double-clicked folder.

Undocumented

This trick doesn't work with the middle mouse button if you have defined the button to be a double-click. You actually have to double-click with the left mouse button. See "Double Clicking with the Middle Mouse Button" in Chapter 30 for details on how to define the middle mouse button as a double-click.

If you are using the Custom style and have chosen to single-click and to open each folder in its own window, holding down the Ctrl key will also work with a single click.

Open a window in the Explorer view

Secret

If you are using the Classic style, you can hold down the Shift key as you double-click a folder icon to open the new window as an Explorer window (see Chapter 8). You need to make sure that the focus is on the folder icon you want to open before you hold down the Shift key and double-click. Otherwise, you could easily open a few more Explorer windows than you had planned. The reason for this is that you also use the Shift key with the mouse to select multiple items (see "Selecting a group of files and/or folders" later in this chapter).

Undocumented

This option, unlike the one described in "Switch to a single window view on the fly," does work with the middle mouse button defined as a double-click.

If you are using the Custom style and have chosen to single-click and open each folder in its own window, holding down the Shift key will also work with a single click.

Closing a folder window

The three buttons in the upper-right corner of a window allow you to minimize, maximize or restore, and close a folder window, respectively from left to right. The Close button was new with Windows 95.

Undocumented

Hold down the Shift key as you click the Close button to close not only the window with the focus, but all its parent windows as well. If you opened a number of windows to get to the current one, this method gives you an easy way to get rid of all the preceding windows.

Change Your Window View

The big jump from Windows 95 to Windows 98 is quite evident when you consider the different options available under the View menu item. You now have multiple toolbars, an Explorer bar, and the ability to view your window as a web page (View, As Web Page).

You can choose how the drive icons, folder icons, and other icons are displayed in a window by choosing among four views: Large Icons, Small Icons (rows), List (columns), and Details. You can cycle from one view to the next by repeatedly clicking the Views button at the right end of the Standard Buttons toolbar. To switch directly to a particular view, click the down arrow next to the Views button and then click the desired view in the menu. To see how to order your icons, refer to the next section, "Order the icons."

Unlike Windows 95, Windows 98 allows you to set and maintain unique window display preferences (although not toolbar settings) for every window and every folder. On the other hand, you can force every folder view to be the same. We discuss how to do this in the "Sticky view settings" section of the next chapter.

Order the icons

You can specify the order in which your icons are displayed in a window. Choose View, Arrange Icons, and then click the desired option in the submenu that appears.

If you are viewing the top-level My Computer window (you have just clicked the My Computer icon on the Desktop), your choices are By Drive Letter, By Type, By Size, and By Free Space. If you are viewing other drive and folder windows, the choices are usually By Name, By Type, By Size, and By Date. However, the exact set of options you see in the Arrange Icons submenu depends on what kind of folder you are currently viewing.

If you are using Details view, you can also choose which variable to sort on by clicking the heading buttons (Name, Size, Type, and Modified) located at the top of the columns. If you want to toggle between ascending and descending order, click the heading button a second time. You also have the option of displaying an Attributes column to list file or folder attributes, as shown in Figure 7-6. To display this column, choose View, Folder Options, click the View tab, and mark Show File Attributes in Detail View.

Line up your icons

Secret

If you are not viewing your folder window as a web page, and if you use the Large Icons or Small Icons view of a window, you can place the icons where you like. They will stay where you put them, even if you switch views, resize the window, or close the window and go back to it. The Large Icons view will mirror the Small Icons view, and vice versa.

As with the Desktop, every folder window contains an invisible grid, although Windows 98 only uses the grid in the Large Icons and Small Icons views. The size of the grid depends on the size of the icons, the font size (magnification), and the display resolution. You can snap your icons to the center of the cells in the grid by right-clicking the client area of the folder window and choosing Line Up Icons.

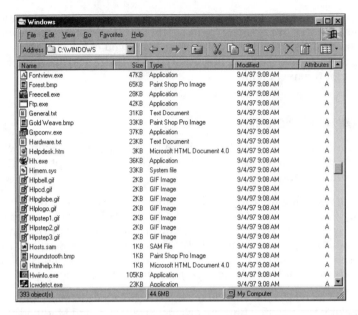

Figure 7-6: A folder window in Details view. Click one of the column heading buttons (Name, Size, Type, Modified, or Attributes) at the top of the client area to order the icons by that variable.

Changing the columns in Details view

When you choose the Details view of a folder window (View, Details), heading buttons appear above each column. At the edge of each of these buttons is a black spacer line. When you rest your mouse over the line, the mouse pointer becomes a vertical line with two horizontal arrows.

You can change the order of the columns by dragging a column header to the left or right. Just place your mouse pointer over a heading button, press and hold down the left mouse button, and drag the button to the desired position. We often find ourselves moving the Modified column and putting it just to the right of the Name column.

You can change a column's width by dragging the spacer line on the right edge of the column's heading button to the left or right. If you drag the spacer line for the Name button to the right, for example, the Name column widens, and the remaining columns shift over to the right.

Tip

If you want to temporarily hide a column in Details view for a given folder window, drag the spacer line on the right edge of the heading button all the way to the left edge of the column. You can redisplay the column — even though you can't see it — by dragging the now-invisible heading button's edge to the right.

Each folder window has its own properties. Before you adjust the width of the columns in a window, they have the default properties. After you change the column widths, Windows 98 retains the new settings and uses them the next time you open that particular folder. This is true even if you open the folder window through My Computer and make changes to it, and then open the same folder in Explorer view (see the next chapter).

Secret

Do you want to adjust a column's width in Details view so that none of the entries in the column are truncated? Rest your mouse pointer over the spacer line, and double-click. Windows 98 widens (or narrows) the column just enough to fit the widest entry. This is the same method you use to "AutoFit" columns in Excel and Access.

Freshening up the folder window

Tip

A folder window may not always accurately display the actual contents of the folder. You might have copied files in and out of the folder without the window noticing and updating itself. Files may also have changed in size, content, or name. You can update the display of a window by pressing the F5 key, by choosing View, Refresh, or by right-clicking the client area of the My Computer window and clicking Refresh.

Windows toolbars

In Windows 95, the My Computer window and Explorer window only came with one toolbar. In Windows 98 these windows come with three toolbars, Standard Buttons, Address Bar, and Links. The Standard Buttons toolbar has a standard version and an Internet Explorer version (which we often refer to as the *Internet toolbar*). You can decide which toolbars to display (if any), how they should be positioned, how wide they should be, and whether text will accompany their icons — in short, you have lots of flexibility.

Windows 98 combines the Internet Explorer browser window with the regular Windows 95 windows such as My Computer. Therefore, Microsoft had to come up with a way to combine the toolbars applicable to each window.

If you are moving up from Windows 95, this plethora of toolbars can be a bit confusing. If you have a small screen (like that on a portable), they can hog a bunch of precious real estate. Thankfully, they are flexible enough that you can decide just how much space to allot to them and how many to use.

To get back to the Windows 95 look, take the following steps:

STEPS

Getting Back to the Windows 95 Look

Step 1.   Click the My Computer icon on your Desktop.

Step 2.   In the View, Toolbars menu, mark Standard Buttons and Address Bar, and clear Links and Text Labels.

Step 3.   Point to the vertical line at the left end of the Address bar and drag it to the left edge of the window, directly under the menu bar.

Step 4.   Drag the Standard Buttons toolbar to the right of the Address bar. You should have something that looks like Figure 7-7.

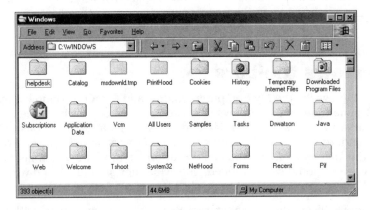

Figure 7-7: A Windows 98 folder window made up to look like a Windows 95 folder window.

The Address bar lets you navigate to Internet URLs or to folders on your own computer. For example, you could enter http:\\www.halcyon.com\ davis\secrets.htm or C:\Windows in this field.

If you want more space and fewer toolbars, right-click a blank area of the Standard Buttons toolbar, and clear the Address bar. Then drag the Standard Buttons toolbar to the right of the menu bar.

Secret

Windows 98 retains the toolbar settings for your My Computer window, so the next time that you open a folder window, you'll see the same toolbars in the same positions. The Windows Explorer and the Internet Explorer windows also retain their own toolbar settings. You can use these three windows interchangeably to perform similar functions, but establish unique toolbar settings in each one.

The Explorer bar

They call it the Explorer bar, but it doesn't really turn a My Computer window into an Explorer window. Choose View, Explorer Bar in a My Computer window, and you'll see a submenu of essentially Internet-type functions. When you mark one of these options, a new pane appears in the My Computer client area. The content of the pane varies depending on which option you choose (Search, Favorites, History, and so on). Figure 7-8 shows what the My Computer window looks like if you choose View, Explorer Bar, History.

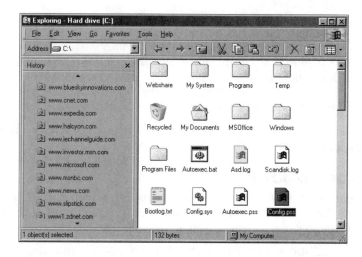

Figure 7-8: A Windows 98 folder window with the History Explorer bar.

What is missing in My Computer's Explorer Bar submenu is the All Folders option, which gives you a folder tree pane. To get this option to appear in the Explorer Bar submenu, you have to open an Explorer window. To do this, right-click the My Computer icon on your Desktop and choose Explore.

While you can't turn My Computer into the Explorer, it's simple to go in reverse. In the Explorer, just choose View, Explorer Bar, None. This turns the Explorer into a single-pane window that is almost, but not exactly, like the My Computer window.

Customizing this folder

Windows 98 gives you the option of adding background graphics to your folder and Explorer windows. You can also modify a copy of the HTML template for folders, \Windows\Web\folder.htt, to change the web page view of a given folder. To make either type of change, choose View, Customize This Folder in the folder whose view you want to modify. In the Wizard that appears, mark Choose a Background Picture to add a background graphic, or Create Or Edit an HTML Document to modify a copy of the HTML template file, and then continue with the remaining steps in the Wizard.

If you select a background graphic, you don't have to view the folder as a web page in order to see the background. If you modify a copy of the folder template file, Windows 98 places both an edited copy of folder.htt and a hidden Desktop.ini file in your folder. The Desktop.ini file references this copy of folder.htt.

Windows 98 places a hidden Desktop.ini file in the folder whether you choose a background graphic or a customized web page view. You can easily get rid of the customization by clicking View, Customize This Folder, Remove Customization. This erases the Desktop.ini file, and the graphic file and/or the folder.htt file (if present).

Undocumented

If you customize a folder that already has a Desktop.ini file, Windows 98 updates this file to include the pointers to the new resources. If you remove this customization, your file reverts to its previous version (almost). The changes that were made in this file during the customization and removal process don't affect its operation. However, the Desktop.ini file is no longer hidden, and if the folder had been given the System attribute, the attribute is removed by the customization process.

In the next section, we discuss one reason why you might have a Desktop.ini file in a folder that you haven't yet customized.

Custom folder icons

Secret

You can change the little manila folder icons into something a bit more pleasing. You do this by adding a little Desktop.ini file to the folder and marking the folder's System attribute.

You won't be able to use these methods to change the little graphics on the manila folder icons of special folders. You can, however, change those folder icons using the steps detailed in the "New icons for Desktop items" section of the previous chapter.

A little freeware program called Icon Wizard adds the Desktop.ini file, marks the System attribute for the folder, and lets you easily choose from its library of folder-like icons. Download the file icw1inst.exe from http://wildsau.idv.uni-linz.ac.at/~cfe/iconwiz/.

The Desktop.ini file that Icon Wizard creates just includes an icon filename and an index to the icon in the file. If there is only one icon in the icon file, the index is zero. If you browse to a file with multiple icons, the index will reflect which icon you choose. You can also manually edit the Desktop.ini file to change the icon yourself.

If you use the Customize This Folder Wizard (see the previous section) to customize a folder whose icon you've changed, you will lose your System attribute and your icon won't display anymore. You'll need to run the Icon Wizard again to restore the System attribute. When you do this, the changes that you made with the Customizing This Folder Wizard will be preserved.

After you use Icon Wizard to change a folder icon, the icon won't be updated in all of the windows in which it's displayed. To get it to update in every window, use TweakUI. Click the Repair tab, choose Rebuild Icons in the drop-down list, and click Repair Now.

New, Copy, Cut, Paste, Rename, and Delete

You can use folder windows for file maintenance, including creating, copying, moving, renaming, and deleting files and folders.

Creating a folder

It's easy to create a new folder. All you have to do is right-click in the folder window within which you want to place your new folder. Follow these steps:

STEPS

Creating a New Folder

Step 1. Click the My Computer icon on the Desktop.

Step 2. Decide which drive you want to store your folder in, and click the appropriate drive icon to open the drive window.

Step 3. If you want to store your folder in the root — in other words, at the top of the hierarchy of folders on that disk drive — go to step 5. If you want to store your folder within another folder on the drive, click that folder icon in the drive window.

Step 4. Continue clicking folder icons until you get to the folder window that you want to contain your new folder.

Step 5. Right-click the client area of the window (or choose File, New, Folder). In the context menu, point to New, and then click Folder. A new folder icon appears in the window.

Step 6. To replace the temporary name *New Folder* with a name of your choosing, simply type over it with the new name and press Enter.

Moving a file or folder

There are numerous ways to move a file or folder from one folder to another. As a general suggestion, you'll have an easier time accomplishing this task and learning how it's done if you have both the source folder window and the destination folder window open on your Desktop and fully visible.

Move with Cut and Paste

For those of you moving up from Windows 3.1*x*, you may be surprised to see that the Cut and Paste commands have moved out of your word processor and have taken an honorable position in the operating system. The Cut and Paste commands allow you to cut (or copy) a file from one location and then navigate around until you get to the target location before pasting it. These commands are easier to use than drag and drop when the source and target aren't both visible at the same time.

Follow these steps to move a file or folder with the Cut and Paste commands.

STEPS

Moving a File or Folder with Cut and Paste

Step 1. Click the My Computer icon. If you haven't already done so, Choose View, Folder Options, choose Custom, click the Settings button, and mark Open Each Folder in Its Own Window. Click OK, and then click OK again.

Step 2. Click the drive icon that contains the file or folder you want to move. If the file or folder is in a subfolder, continue clicking folder icons until you open the folder window that contains the item you want to move. (This is the source folder.)

Step 3. If the destination folder window — the folder to which you want to move the item — is already open, click its title bar (or its Taskbar button) to bring it to the front, and go on to the next step. If it isn't open yet, first open the window of its parent folder (or an ancestor folder), and then continue clicking folder icons until you open the destination folder window.

Step 4. Make sure that you can see both the source and the destination folder windows. They don't have to be fully visible.

Step 5. Right-click the folder or file you want to move, and click Cut in the context menu. (Or select the folder or file, and then choose Edit, Cut.)

Step 6. Right-click an empty part of the destination folder window, and click Paste (or choose Edit, Paste).

Move with right drag and drop

You can also drag and drop the file or folder to the destination folder window. As you drag the file or folder icon, it looks semi-transparent.

STEPS

Moving a File or Folder with Right Drag and Drop

Step 1. Carry out the first four steps in the "Move with Cut and Paste" section above.

Step 2. Position the mouse pointer over the file or folder to be moved. Press the right mouse button and, while holding it, pull the file or folder over to the destination folder window.

Step 3. Release the right mouse button when the mouse pointer is over the destination folder window. You can drop the file or folder when you're pointing to the title bar, the menu bar, the toolbar, or the client area. Just make sure you don't point to an icon.

Step 4. Click Move Here in the context menu.

Move with left drag and drop

If you use the left mouse button to drag and drop, you don't have to deal with a context menu. But it helps to know what kind of file you are moving and where you are moving it to.

STEPS

Moving a File or Folder with Left Drag and Drop

Step 1. Carry out the first four steps in the "Move with Cut and Paste" section earlier in this chapter.

Step 2. Position the mouse pointer over the file or folder to be moved. Press the left mouse button and, while holding it, drag the file or folder over to the destination folder window.

Step 3. Release the left mouse button when the mouse pointer is over the destination folder window. You can drop the file or folder on the title bar, the menu bar, the toolbar, or the client area, but not on any icons in the folder.

Secret

If you have followed the steps in this section, you've taken the steps required to open two windows. You therefore know which drives the destination and source folders are stored on. When you drag and drop a file or folder, Windows 98 only *moves* the item out of the source folder and into the destination folder *if both folders are on the same drive*.

If you drag and drop a file or folder from a folder on one drive to a folder on another drive, then Window 98 *copies* the file instead of moving it.

In both cases, this is *not* true if you are dragging a file that isn't a document or a data file, but rather an application. When you drag and drop an application file, Windows 98 creates a *shortcut* to the application in the destination folder. What is an *application file*? You can identify application files by their extensions if you have cleared the box labeled Hide File Extensions for Known File Types. (In the My Computer window, choose View, Folder Options, and click the View tab; see the "Seeing all the files on your computer" section in Chapter 8 for more information.) Application files have extensions such as *exe* or *com*. There is an even easier way to tell, as you'll see if you keep reading.

You can force a *move* by holding down the Shift key after you have selected the file or folder to move. Don't press Shift until you have selected the file or folder. If you do, you may instead change which icons are selected because the Shift key is also used to select.

Tip

If you drag and drop an executable file (an application file), Windows 98 creates a shortcut to the application when you release the mouse button. You can tell before you actually release the mouse button if Windows 98 intends to create a shortcut. As you drag the file over the destination folder window, you'll see a black curved arrow in a white box in the lower-right corner of the semi-transparent file icon. Press and hold the Shift key and the arrow disappears, indicating that Windows 98 will *move* the file or folder instead. This is one way to tell that Windows 98 thinks you are dragging an application file.

Windows 98 treats the Desktop like a folder. Like all folders, it is located on a disk drive, most likely your C drive. You may have thought about *moving* something to the Desktop, which is actually not a good idea unless it is a shortcut. If the Desktop is on a drive other than the one that contains the file or folder you are dragging, Windows 98 will, by default, *copy* the file or folder instead (unless you hold down the Shift key).

Tip

You can tell if a file or folder is going to be copied because a plus sign appears in the lower-right corner of the semi-transparent icon representing the file or folder icon as you drag it over the destination folder window (or Desktop). If you see this black plus sign in a white box, you know a *copy* will occur if you release the left mouse button. Press and hold the Shift key to force a *move*.

If you decide not to move the icon, just put it back where you got it — in the same window. If you were using a left drag and drop, then nothing will happen. If you were using a right drag and drop, a context menu will appear. Click Cancel.

Secret

If you don't want to continue with your drag and drop, press Esc while holding down the mouse button. We love this secret because it makes Windows 98 just that much more user friendly. You don't have to worry that you will do something wrong. If it looks wrong, just press Esc. Later, you will see how you can undo by releasing the mouse button.

There is an even trickier way to cancel a drag and drop. Click the other (in most cases, the right) mouse button before you release the primary mouse button.

Tip

You can drop your file or folder on a folder icon to move it into that folder. You don't have to open the destination folder window. If the destination folder icon is visible in its parent folder window, you can drop the file or folder icon on it to move it to that folder.

You can't move a drive icon. The disk drive is fixed in place. You can't move the total contents of the disk by dragging the drive icon. If you try to move the disk drive, you will be given the option of creating a shortcut to the drive. You have to select the contents of the disk if you want to move them.

You can't move any of the icons in the My Computer window. You can only create shortcuts to them.

Secret

If you point to a file or folder icon in a window that has the focus (its title bar is highlighted) and press and hold down either mouse button, the name of the icon becomes highlighted. This makes it obvious that the icon is selected and ready to be moved. If you do the same thing to an icon in a window that does not have the focus, the icon will not become highlighted (nor will the window gain the focus). However, the icon is still selected and ready to be moved.

If the destination folder window happens to have the focus and is partially obscuring the source folder window, as shown in Figure 7-9, you can still left or right drag a file or folder icon from the source folder window and drop it into the destination folder window. The source folder window won't gain the focus when you select the icon and drag, so it won't cover up the destination folder window.

If you download the Microsoft PowerToys (http://www.microsoft.com/windows/software/powertoy.htm), you can completely change this mouse behavior using X Mouse. The focus will stay with the mouse pointer and shift from window to window as you move the pointer. X Mouse does cause some incompatibilities with some programs, so you'll need to test it if you want your mouse to behave this way.

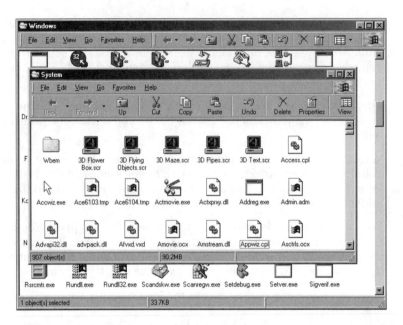

Figure 7-9: The destination folder window is on top of and partially obscuring the source folder window. When you drag a file or folder icon from the source window into the destination window, the source window doesn't gain the focus and cover the destination window.

Move with Send To Any Folder

You'll need to download the PowerToys utilities from the Microsoft web site (http://www.microsoft.com/windows/software/powertoy.htm) before you can use Send To Any Folder.

Once you install SendToX (part of PowerToys), you'll be able to move or copy files or folders to other folders by right-clicking a file or folder name, clicking Sent To in the context menu, and then clicking Any Folder. SendToX maintains a history of previous destination folders so you can easily send files to a common folder.

You can also add a common destination folder or two to the Send To folder to allow you to move files or folders to a folder just using the Send To option on the context menu. Turn to the "Right-Click to a Powerhouse" section of Chapter 10 for instructions on how to set this up.

Copying a file or folder

You copy a file or folder to a new folder or disk drive using pretty much the same methods that you use to move a file or folder, but with a slight variation—just enough of a variation to perform a copy rather than a move. Therefore, much of the information in "Moving a file or folder" applies to the

Copy command. This is your clue to look there for further help with the copy methods, and pay special attention to the tips and secrets.

Copy with Copy and Paste

Follow these steps to copy a file or folder with Copy and Paste:

STEPS

Copying a File or Folder with Copy and Paste

Step 1. Click the My Computer icon. Click View, Folder Options, and if you haven't already done so, choose Custom, click the Settings button, and mark Open Each Folder in Its Own Window. Click OK, and then click OK again.

Step 2. Click the drive icon that contains the file or folder you want to copy. If the file or folder is in a subfolder, continue clicking folder icons until you open the folder window that contains the item you want to copy. (This is the source folder.)

Step 3. If the destination folder window — the folder to which you want to copy the item — is already open, click its title bar (or its Taskbar button) to bring it to the front, and go on to the next step. If it isn't open yet, first open the window of its parent folder (or an ancestor folder), and then continue clicking folder icons until you open the destination folder window.

Step 4. Make sure you can see both the source and the destination folder's windows. They don't have to be fully visible.

Step 5. Right-click the source folder or file you want to copy, and click Copy in the context menu. (Or select the file or folder, and then choose Edit, Copy.)

Step 6. Right-click an empty part of the destination folder window, and click Paste (or choose Edit, Paste).

Copy with right drag and drop

Follow the instructions in the steps in the "Move with right drag and drop" section, but with the following exception: Choose Copy Here instead of Move Here from the context menu.

You can also use this method to create a copy of a file in the same folder as the original file. After you drop the file in the same folder and choose Copy Here, Windows 98 creates a duplicate file with the prefix "Copy of." It is easy to rename this file later.

Copy with left drag and drop

Follow these steps to copy with left drag and drop:

STEPS

Copying a File or Folder with Left Drag and Drop

Step 1.   Carry out the first four steps in the "Copy with Copy and Paste" section.

Step 2.   Position the mouse pointer over the file or folder to be copied. Press the left mouse button and, keeping it held down, drag the file or folder over to the destination folder window.

Step 3.   Press and hold the Ctrl key.

Step 4.   Release the left mouse button when the mouse pointer is over the destination folder window, and then release the Ctrl key. You can drop the file or folder on the title bar, the menu bar, the toolbar, or the client area, but not on any icons in the folder.

Notice that step 3 says to press the Ctrl key, which forces a copy operation. If you are copying from a folder on one drive to a folder on another drive, you don't have to use the Ctrl key. When you drag and drop between volumes (between local disk drives or over a network) Windows 98 assumes you want to copy instead of move.

Remember that if you are *copying* a file or folder, a small black plus sign in a white box will appear on the icon when you drag it over the destination folder window. If you don't see the plus sign, press and hold the Ctrl key.

Tip

You can't copy a drive icon. Instead, click the drive icon to display its contents in a drive window, and then copy the contents of the drive. You can't copy any of the icons in the My Computer window.

Secret

You can make a copy of a file in the same folder as the original by holding down the Ctrl key while you left drag and drop the file in the same folder window. Windows creates a new file with the prefix "Copy of." To do this using the Explorer, see the "Copying and Moving Files and Folders" section of Chapter 8.

If you drag and drop a file onto an icon that represents an executable file, Windows 98 will start the application. If the application can read and use the file you dropped, it will do so. For example, if you drop a file icon with the extension *doc*, *rtf*, or *txt* onto the WordPad icon, WordPad will start and open the file.

Cut or Copy now, Paste later

While it's easy to see what you're doing if you have both the source and the destination folder windows on the Desktop, you don't have to do it this way. You can first cut or copy a file or folder, and then paste it to its new location when you get to it later. As long as you don't do another cut or copy, the files or folders remain on the Clipboard waiting to be pasted.

Renaming files and folders

You can rename a file or folder (but not a disk drive) by selecting it with the mouse and then pressing the F2 key. You can also right-click the icon and choose Rename from the context menu, or select the item and then choose File, Rename. Once you've issued the Rename command using one of these three methods, you just type the new name right over the existing one and press Enter.

If you have double-clicking enabled, you can rename a file or folder (but not a disk drive) by clicking the name once, and then clicking it again to select it. The clicks have to be far enough apart that they qualify as separate clicks and not a double-click.

Tip

After you issue the Rename command, a dotted line appears around the name, and the name becomes highlighted, ready to be wiped out as soon as you type a letter. If you want to edit the existing name instead of typing a new one, press an arrow key or click the name. The highlighting goes away and you get an insertion point. You can now edit the name using the arrow keys to move the insertion point, and Backspace and Delete to delete individual characters. Press the Home or End key instead of the arrow keys to move quickly to the beginning or end of the name.

If you are displaying file extensions (check out the "Seeing all the files on your computer" section of Chapter 8) and you change an extension, Windows 98 displays a message box when you finish editing the name asking if you are sure you want to change the extension. In the few hundred times we have done this, neither of us has ever said no.

Change File Type, a freeware application, lets you change a file extension without having to reassure Windows 98 that it's really what you mean to do. It's available at http://www.windows98.com.

This renaming process can get quite tedious if you are renaming a lot of files, for example, all your *.*w4w* files to *.*doc* files. If you want to do group renames, you must use the File Manager (which doesn't support long filenames) or the DOS command line. The standard commands you can use in folder windows aren't quite strong enough. Turn to the "Going from the Windows 3.1x File Manager to the Explorer" section in Chapter 8 to learn more about the File Manager or to the "Wonderful DOS commands" section of Chapter 34 to learn more about DOS.

Microsoft would rather that we not discuss file extensions. They want file extensions to go away and for Windows users to quit seeing them in their windows. We feel it is a much better idea to display file extensions because Windows (and DOS) use them so heavily. In fact, it is easier and more reliable to change file extensions when they are displayed than when they are not. Check out "Creating and Editing File Types and Actions" in Chapter 13 for more details.

Valid file and folder names are discussed in the "Valid filenames" section of Chapter 33.

Deleting files and folders

To get rid of a file or folder, highlight its icon and press the Delete key. You can also right-click an icon and choose Delete in the context menu or choose File, Delete. If the file or folder is on a local nonremovable drive, it gets sent to the Recycle Bin.

Dragging and dropping an icon from a folder window to the Recycle Bin on the Desktop also works. The benefit of this method is that Windows 98 does not ask you to confirm the delete. (You can configure the Recycle Bin to not require a confirmation for a file delete.) Note that your files and folders aren't necessarily deleted just yet. The Recycle Bin provides a safety net for us careless users. We tell you more about deleting in the "Deleted, what does that mean?" section of Chapter 14.

Tip

To delete a file or folder without sending it to the Recycle Bin, hold down the Shift key while you press the Delete key. Windows 98 will delete the highlighted file or folder, and won't put it in the Recycle Bin.

The Undo command

Undocumented

Every time you perform an action such as renaming, copying, moving, or deleting, you have a chance to undo it (in the same Windows 98 session). Not just now, but later as well. Windows 98 builds an undo stack as you do things, adding new actions to the top of the stack. You can only undo multiple actions in the reverse order that you did them.

The Undo command and an associated action verb—Rename, Copy, Move, or Delete—appears in the context menu that appears when you right-click a window or the Desktop (but only if you have performed an undoable action). For example, if you just renamed a file, Undo Rename will appear on the context menu when you right-click the client area of a window.

This undo business is global. It doesn't matter if you renamed a file in one window and deleted a file in another, they both show up (actually you see only the last action) on the context menu in any window. After you issue the Undo command once to undo the most recent action, choosing Undo a second time undoes the previous action, and so forth.

This can get kind of confusing. You may not remember in which window you renamed or deleted or copied a file or folder. But when you right-click any window, the reference to that previous action shows up.

It's best to undo something within the window that you did it in. This way, you can see the action get undone—for example, the file takes back its old name. If the action you're undoing is a few actions down the stack, it might be hard to remember which window you did what in. Unless you are working in just one or two windows, it's all too complicated.

Undo is a great confidence builder. You just can't mess up too badly because you can undo the damage that you did. This gives you a little leeway to experiment with Windows 98.

Tip

The keyboard shortcut to undo your most recent action is Ctrl+Z.

Selecting Items in a Window

You place your mouse pointer over an icon to select it, and then choose an action—such as Move, Copy, Delete, or Rename—to do something to the icon. This is an illustration of the Windows syntax: first a noun (the object), then a verb. You can also right-click an icon in a window to select it. When you right-click, a convenient context menu appears with a series of verbs—actions—you can take.

Undocumented

If you select an icon in a window, the window is automatically highlighted and given the focus. If you simply drag an icon from a window, the window doesn't get the focus. The icon isn't highlighted either. This comes in handy when you're copying or moving files or folders between windows. See the "Move with left drag and drop" section earlier in this chapter.

Selecting multiple files and folders

If you want to move, copy, or delete (but not rename) more than one file or folder, you can select all of the items first, before issuing the command. That way, you only have to issue the command once instead of numerous times. To select multiple files and/or folders, rest your mouse pointer over the first icon (this is called *hovering*), and then hold down the Ctrl key while hovering over the additional icons (no need to click). The Ctrl key is just a continue-selection key.

Tip

You can't rename more than one file or folder at a time. It just won't work. If you have multiple files and/or folders selected when you choose Rename, Windows 98 automatically deselects all the icons but the one you most recently selected.

Selecting a group of files and/or folders

You can select a group of adjacent icons with the Shift key. Select the first icon in the group by resting your mouse pointer over it (this is called *hovering*). Then hold down the Shift key as you hover over the last icon in the group (no need to click). Windows 98 will select all the icons in between the two you hovered over.

When you display your icons in Details view, it is pretty clear what *in between* means. You hover over one file or folder and then you Shift+hover over a second one located either above or below the first. All the icons in between these two icons get selected.

Undocumented

In other views, *in between* means different things. For example, in Large Icons or Small Icons view, *in between* means all the icons that fit in a rectangle formed when you take the diagonal corners of the rectangle as the two selected icons. To select the group of large icons shown in Figure 7-10 using the Shift key method, you would select the icon in the second row, fifth column, and then hold down the Shift key as you select the icon in the fourth row, seventh column.

Figure 7-10: The Large Icons view of a window. The icons were selected by hovering over an icon in one corner of a rectangle and then Shift+hovering over the icon in the opposite corner.

In the Large Icons or Small Icons view, if both the icons you select with the "hover, Shift-hover" method are in the same row or column, all the icons between the two selected icons in the same row or column will get selected.

Undocumented

The List view orders icons by columns — sort of like wrapping columns of text in a word processor. You can't select rectangular groups of icons in this view as you can in Large Icons or Small Icons view. If you hover over an icon in one column and then Shift+hover over an icon in another column, all the icons below the selected icon in the first column get selected, along with all the icons above the Shift-selected icon in the second column, as shown in Figure 7-11.

Figure 7-11: Selecting icons in List view. List view arranges icons by column. In this example, all the icons below the selected icon in the second column and above the Shift+selected icon in the third column are selected.

Lasso those icons, cowboys and cowgirls

You can draw your own rectangle (or *lasso*) around or through the icons that you want to select. You don't have to completely enclose an icon to get it lassoed.

Undocumented

To drag a rectangle around the icons that you want to select, move the mouse pointer to an area near the icons. Press and hold down the left mouse button. Drag the mouse pointer over the additional icons that you want to select. The icons are highlighted as you lasso them. Release the mouse button when you have highlighted all the icons. A group of icons selected with a lasso is shown in Figure 7-12.

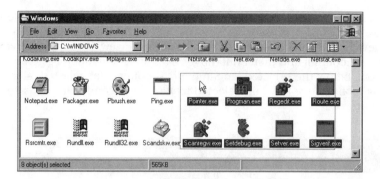

Figure 7-12: Lassoing the icons. Drag a rectangle around a group of icons to select them. Use either the left or right mouse button.

Secret

You can lasso with the right mouse button. When you release the right button, a context menu appears. You can select an action from the context menu to perform on all the icons you have rounded up. Exactly which context menu appears depends on what kind of icons you have rounded up. Windows 98 displays a menu containing actions that can be used on almost all the selected files and/or folders. Some of the actions may not be applicable to some of the icons.

You can use the lasso on the Desktop just as you use it in a folder window.

Select everything

If you want to select everything in a folder window, choose Edit, Select All, just as you would to select all the text in a document. See, you already knew how to do this.

Tip

To select all the icons in a folder window with the keyboard, highlight the window (make sure the window's title bar shows that it has the focus) and press Ctrl+A.

Select everything but

Select, by whatever means you want (except, of course, Select All) everything that you *don't* want to select. Then choose Edit, Invert Selection. This selects everything in the folder window that you didn't select the first time. This is a great way to select everything but a few things.

Deselect with Ctrl+hover

After you've selected everything in a window or selected a bunch of icons with the lasso or Shift+hover, you might want to remove a few icons from the selection. To do this, Ctrl+hover over each icon you want to deselect. This is an easy way to select a bunch of icons, and then pull out a few that you don't want selected. You can then right-click one of the selected icons if you want to display a context menu.

Select a few bunches of icons

Combine hover and Ctrl+hover with Shift+hover and Ctrl+Shift+hover to select bunches of icons. Ctrl+Shift+hover (that is, holding down Ctrl and Shift keys while resting your mouse pointer over something) works the same as Shift+hover, but it doesn't wipe out previous selections. The Ctrl key continues to be the continue-selection key.

Choose some icons with hover, Ctrl+hover, and/or Shift+hover. Choose another bunch of icons with a Ctrl+hover and then a Ctrl+Shift+hover. By mixing and matching these selection methods, you can grab little grouplets of icons in the folder window. There are many variations on how this works (we'll let you experiment rather than go through them all) but the behavior of the Shift and Ctrl keys is consistent — trust us on that.

Grabbing the icon group

If you have selected a group of icons and want to move or copy them with drag and drop, you need to drag all of them together. To left or right drag the group, point to one of the selected items and start dragging — you'll bring the whole group with you. If you start dragging when the mouse pointer is between the selected icons, you end up deselecting the icons.

Dragging multiple icons

Here is where it gets ugly, literally. When you drag a single icon (and its name), you get an aesthetically pleasing half-transparent version of the icon and its name. You can tell right away what you're dragging around. In contrast, when you drag a group of icons, you get a group of box outlines that stand for the icons and lines that stand for the icon names, as shown in Figure 7-13.

When these icon ghosts first appeared in Windows 95, we found them quite displeasing. We thought that Microsoft couldn't be too happy about them either. But they are still with us in Windows 98.

Why aren't all the icons in the group half-transparent? On slow computers with unaccelerated video cards, the repaint time required to show multiple half-transparent images is too long.

Not only are the ghosted icons ugly, they are hard to manage because they are so spread out. Your mouse pointer still tells you where the hot spot is, but you can easily get confused as to where the icons are if you drag them to another folder window or onto the Desktop. It feels like you're dragging around this big blob of stuff, which is no fun at all. Nonetheless, it looks like we're stuck with them.

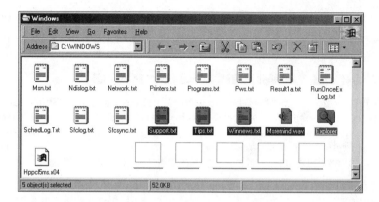

Figure 7-13: Dragging multiple files and folders in a folder window. The icons in Large Icons view are portrayed as box outlines and the icon names are portrayed as lines.

Normally, when you select and then drag an executable file, Windows 98 creates a shortcut to the executable in the destination folder and leaves the executable itself in its original folder. If you select a group of files that includes executable files (but includes other file types as well), Windows 98 moves (or copies) *all* the files instead. This is dangerous, because it can make some programs cease to work.

Press Esc to cancel

We mentioned this earlier in the "Moving a file or folder" section, but we want to emphasize it again here. If there is a problem while you're dragging an icon or a group of icons around, just press Esc. This aborts the drag operation, but leaves the icons selected.

You can also just click the other (usually, the right) mouse button.

Summary

If you want to know how to manage your computer most efficiently, this chapter and the next chapter are the places to look.

▶ We show you how to change the name of My Computer.

▶ The folder window views let you look at your computer in many different ways, and we show you how to change these views to suit your needs.

▶ We provide a number of methods you can use to quickly select files and folders in a folder window.

▶ Afraid of drag and drop? Don't be. We show you how to use this powerful technique with all the safety built in.

Chapter 8

The Explorer

In This Chapter

The Windows 98 Explorer has come a long way since its lowly days as the Windows 95 version of the File Manager. Leaving behind the not-so-friendly confines of your computer, it has merged with the Internet Explorer to become a tool that lets you venture far beyond your own hard disk and local network. We discuss:

▶ Modifying the Explorer on the Start button to act the way you want it to

▶ Putting the Explorer on the Desktop

▶ Using the Explorer to quickly copy and move files and folders

▶ Using keyboard shortcuts to reduce mouse clicking in the Explorer and My Computer windows

▶ Controlling multiple Explorer windows on your Desktop

▶ Learning to use the Explorer for just about everything you did with the File Manager, and much more

Explorer Basics

To the user, the Windows 98 Explorer first appears as a hierarchical file cabinet or outline view of My Computer — actually *your* computer. It lets you easily understand the file and folder structure of your computer. It is a replacement for the Windows 3.1*x* File Manager. You can use the Explorer to move, copy, rename, view, and delete files and folders on your computer and on the network. You can also run programs or access documents by clicking files displayed in the Explorer. It gives you a dual-pane view of a folder window.

After Windows 98 is installed, you'll find files and folders have already been stored on your disk drives in a hierarchical structure. Folders divide up your hard drive(s), subfolders divide up folders, and sub-subfolders divide up subfolders. The Explorer makes this upside-down tree organization evident to you, as shown in Figure 8-1.

Figure 8-1: An Explorer view of the organization of My Computer. Notice that the hard disk (C:) is connected to and to the right of My Computer. This indicates that it is a part of My Computer. The folder labeled Windows is a part of C:, and Command is a subfolder of the Windows folder.

Like the Windows 3.1*x* File Manager, the Explorer shows both a tree view and a folder (directory) view. The left pane gives you a hierarchical view of your computer, disk drives, and folders. It also gives you quick access, through special folder icons, to a number of functional areas. The right pane displays the contents of the folder, disk drive, computer, or networked server computer currently selected in the left pane.

Unlike the Windows 3.1*x* File Manager, you can view each branch of the tree in the Explorer by single-clicking the small plus signs to the left of the folder and drive icons. Gone is the need to double-click the icon to expand the branch. A click on the plus sign does not highlight the folder or display its contents in the right pane. This ability to navigate the tree without displaying the contents of folders makes the Explorer easier to use and more versatile than the File Manager.

Tip

You can quickly navigate through your folders and subfolders by clicking the plus signs next to folder names. The Explorer won't try to read the filenames in a folder until you actually select a folder name; therefore, it is much faster than the File Manager.

Almost everything that we said in Chapter 7 regarding My Computer is applicable to the Explorer. All the various ways of copying, moving, renaming, and deleting files and folders are exactly the same for the Explorer.

The Explorer is just a dual-pane version of the single-pane windows that we examined in Chapter 7. The left pane provides an additional navigation tool that makes some operations easier.

The Explorer views a web page

Windows 98 adds an Internet Explorer icon to the second-level icons displayed in the left-hand pane of your Explorer window. Click the Internet Explorer icon in the left pane of the Explorer, and the right pane displays your home page. Right-click the Internet Explorer icon in the left pane of the Explorer, and click Open. This time, your home page gets displayed in a new single-pane window.

The Explorer can display web pages, as can the My Computer window. When you visit a web page using the Explorer, the web page's title is shown in the left pane of the Explorer window attached to the Internet Explorer icon, as shown in Figure 8-2.

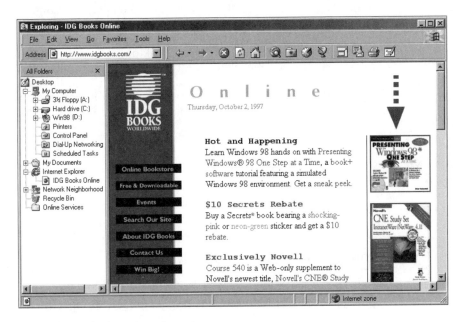

Figure 8-2: An Explorer view of a web page.

The integration of the Internet Explorer with the Windows Explorer means that the Explorer is no longer only capable of displaying folders, filenames, and icons. The Explorer can now display HTML documents because it has gained an integrated HTML-viewing engine.

The Explorer is a dual-pane version of the Internet Explorer. The left pane of the Explorer is called the *Explorer bar.* By default, the Explorer bar appears with the All Folders option turned on (View, Explorer Bar, All Folders). This option gives you the folder tree. Click the little X in the upper-right corner of the Explorer's left pane to close the Explorer bar, and the Explorer becomes the Internet Explorer (almost).

The only difference between the single-pane window you get when you close the Explorer bar in Explorer and when you click the Internet Explorer icon on your Desktop is that with the second method, you don't have the option of opening a folder tree view in the left pane (the All Folders option is not present in the Internet Explorer's View, Explorer Bar submenu).

Given that the Explorer can view HTML documents, it was an easy step for Microsoft to define a way to view folders as HTML documents. It defined a standard HTML template file (\Windows\Web\Folder.htt) for viewing folders, and it used HTML programming in this file to display the folder icons.

Microsoft also created HTML template files to display the Control Panel (\Windows\Web\Controlp.htt), My Computer (\Windows\Web\Mycomp.htt), Recycle Bin, and Dial-Up Networking in new ways. To see an example of this, click the My Computer icon under the Desktop icon in the left pane of an Explorer window. Right-click the right pane, and choose View, As Web Page. Place your mouse pointer over a hard disk icon. This HTML view gives you a graphical display of the hard disk size, and the amount of used and unused space on the disk. This is a very similar view to the one shown in Figure 7-2 in the previous chapter.

Secret

You can edit the HTML template files to display different features. For example, you can change the name displayed in the My Computer window by taking the following steps:

STEPS

Changing the Name in the My Computer Window

Step 1.   Open \Windows\Web\Mycomp.htt in Notepad.

Step 2.   Find %THISDIRNAME%. Comment out this entry by replacing it with

`<!-%THISDIRNAME%->.`

Step 3.   Type a new name right after this entry.

Step 4.   Choose File, Save.

Step 5.   Click the My Computer icon on the Desktop. You'll see your new name in the window if you have View, As Web Page marked.

The Explorer, My Computer, and the Internet Explorer are just slight variations on the same thing. All of them give you single- or dual-pane windows through which you view the contents of your computer or the Internet. And all of them can display a web page or the contents of your computer through the filter of an HTML template file.

Finding the Explorer

Let's check out the Desktop. There's a My Computer icon and an Internet Explorer icon, but there doesn't seem to be an Explorer icon. Could Microsoft have misplaced one of the most important windows of its Windows 98 interface?

Actually, Microsoft is still afraid that you will find the Explorer too difficult, so it gave the Explorer a less prominent place. You'll find it under the Programs menu on the Start button. Hiding the Explorer is Microsoft's way of saying that it's for experts only.

There is a file named Explorer.exe in your \Windows folder, and if you click it, Explorer appears on your Desktop. But surely this isn't how it was meant to be. After all, My Computer sits there in all its glory as the first among icons on the Desktop. Doesn't the Explorer rate something better than a convoluted pathway to Explorer.exe?

If you right-click My Computer, the context menu invites you to Explore. Click Explore and My Computer turns into a dual-pane window view of your computer. The title bar says it all: Exploring - My Computer.

Tip

You can also explore by holding down the Shift key while you double-click the My Computer icon. Just be sure that My Computer is the only icon on your Desktop that is highlighted. Otherwise, you will inadvertently open all the highlighted applications on your Desktop. This happens because Windows 98 interprets the Shift key to mean "select all the icons between the last one highlighted and the My Computer icon." You have to double-click whether you have set single-click or double-click to open an item (View, Folder Options, Custom, Settings).

The Explore menu option is available when you right-click the Network Neighborhood icon, the Recycle Bin, the Internet Explorer icon, the Start button, or any folder or disk drive icon. You can view the contents of any of these items in the Explorer view.

You can change My Computer into My Explorer. We discuss ways to do this in the "Turning My Computer into the Explorer" section later in this chapter.

The Windows Explorer and the Start button

The Explorer has its own icon in the Programs submenu of the Start menu.

Click the Start button, point to Programs, and click Windows Explorer in the Programs menu. You can determine just how the Explorer starts up (when you start it from the Programs menu) by editing the properties of this menu item. See the section later in this chapter entitled "Explorer Command Line Parameters."

Putting the Explorer on the Desktop

My Computer is on the Desktop. You can put the Explorer on the Desktop, too. By doing this you are saying that the Explorer view is just as important as the My Computer view of your computer. The easiest way to do this is to put a shortcut to the Explorer on the Desktop. To create a shortcut to Explorer, take the following steps:

STEPS

Putting the Explorer on the Desktop

Step 1.   Click Start, point to Programs, and right-click the Windows Explorer icon.

Step 2.   Click Create Shortcut. A new Windows Explorer icon will be added to the menu. Click the down arrow at the bottom of the menu to see it.

Step 3.   Drag the new Windows Explorer shortcut to the Desktop and drop it there.

Step 4.   Right-click the new Windows Explorer icon on the Desktop and click Rename to get rid of the (2) in the name or change the name to Explorer (or whatever you like). Press Enter.

Turning My Computer into the Explorer

If you want to change how the My Computer icon responds when you click it, you've got a couple of options. The first requires editing your Registry, but to your advantage, it only affects the My Computer icon. The second changes the default action that takes place when you click My Computer from Open to Explore. Unfortunately, it also makes the same change for other Desktop objects (such as Network Neighborhood, the Recycle Bin, Internet Explorer, and so on).

Secret

Thanks to Dan Norton for pointing out this first method:

STEPS

Changing My Computer to My Explorer

Step 1. Click Regedit.exe in your \Windows folder.

Step 2. Click the plus sign next to HKEY_CLASSES_ROOT. Scroll down the left pane of the Registry editor to CLSID. Click the plus sign next to CLSID.

Step 3. Scroll down the left pane of the Registry editor to {20D04FE0-3AEA-1069-A2D8-080022B30309D}. Click the plus sign next to this identifier.

Step 4. Highlight *shell* in the left pane. Right-click the right pane, and then choose New, Key. Type **Open** as the name for the new key.

Step 5. Highlight the Open key in the left pane, right-click the right pane, choose New, Key, and create a key called Command.

Step 6. Highlight the new Command key, right-click the Default key, choose Modify, and set the default value of Command to Explorer.exe. You can use any of the parameters detailed in "Explorer Command Line Parameters" later in this chapter to modify this command.

Step 7. Exit the Registry editor. These changes take effect immediately.

Step 8. Highlight the My Computer icon on your Desktop, press the F2 key, and change the name from My Computer to My Explorer, or whatever you like. Press Enter.

If you right-click My Explorer, you'll notice that the context menu now contains two different Open commands. The second Open command is the one you just created. It's displayed in boldface to indicate that it's the default action Windows 98 takes when you click My Explorer. This bold Open command is not going to open My Computer, but rather it opens the Explorer, or, one could say, opens My Computer in explore mode.

The first Open command is an action associated with the general class of objects of which My Explorer is a member. Clicking it opens a My Computer window. Both Open commands work without interfering with each other.

In step 8 above, you may not want to change the name of the My Computer icon to My Explorer. Windows uses the name of this icon throughout its interface. It will seem a bit weird to have your drives displayed as entities subordinate to My Explorer instead of to My Computer.

It does make a lot of sense to rename your computer from My Computer to an actual unique name for that computer, Fred, for example. Just because the default action is to open in explore mode instead of in a single-pane window doesn't mean you have to use the name My Explorer to remind you of this fact.

Secret

If you would rather not edit your Registry, you can simply change the default action associated with My Computer's file type from Open to Explore:

STEPS

Opening My Computer with Explore

Step 1.   In the Explorer, choose View, Folder Options, and then click the File Types tab.

Step 2.   Select the Folder entry in the Registered File Types list. Click the Edit button to display the Edit File Type dialog box.

Step 3.   Click Explore in the Actions box, click the Set Default button, and then click OK.

Step 4.   Click the OK button to exit the Folder Options dialog box.

Step 5.   If you wish, you can also change the name of My Computer to My Explorer or something else.

Changing the default action for the Folder file type to Explore not only affects My Computer, it also affects every other object on the Desktop that normally opens in a folder window. For example, if you click the Recycle Bin icon, it now opens in Explorer view. If you ever want to see My Computer, the Recycle Bin, and so on, in the old folder windows, simply right-click the icon and select Open. To reverse the whole change, follow the steps above and make Open instead of Explore the default action.

Getting an Overview of Your Computer

The Explorer displays icons arranged hierarchically in its left pane, as shown in Figure 8-3. The topmost icon is the Desktop. At the second level you'll find My Computer, the Internet Explorer, the Network Neighborhood, and some additional icons. Floppy-disk drive icons, hard disk drive icons, and folder icons (some with little graphics on them) are attached to My Computer.

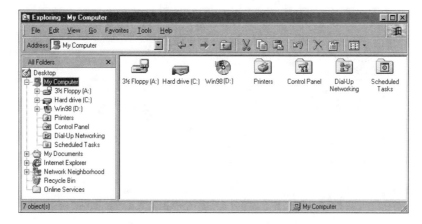

Figure 8-3: The Explorer view. The left pane shows the Desktop and the items that are attached to it.

The view of your computer in the left pane of the Explorer is somewhat strange. It states that everything is part of and contained within the Desktop. But it is clear if we view the contents of the \Windows folder (after marking Show All Files, as described in the "Seeing all the files on your computer" section later in this chapter) that the Desktop is a subfolder of your \Windows folder. The \Windows folder is contained within a disk drive that is contained within My Computer. In addition, the Explorer (remember it is Explorer.exe) resides in the \Windows folder.

The Desktop appears at the top and the Desktop appears as a sub-sub-sub-folder of itself, as shown in Figure 8-4. The Explorer appears as a window on top of the Desktop, and at the same time it displays the Desktop (as a folder and as the Desktop) within the Explorer, which is itself a member of the Desktop.

So making a conceptual leap, you see that My Computer is connected to the Desktop, and that the disk drives, hard and floppy, are connected to My Computer.

The dotted lines are your guides. If a vertical dotted line comes out of the bottom of an icon, the icons connected to that line by horizontal dotted lines are contained within the top icon. My Computer, My Documents, Network Neighborhood, Internet Explorer, Online Services, and Recycle Bin are all contained within the Desktop. The disk drives are contained within My Computer.

So why did Microsoft give the Online Services folder, as plain-Jane as it is, such high status? It gave several companies, including AOL, AT&T, and CompuServe, this juicy piece of Explorer real estate in exchange for making the Internet Explorer their default browser. This makes sense to the marketing department if not to the user interface design team. It's easy to delete the Online Services folder; just right-click it and choose Delete.

Figure 8-4: Viewing the Desktop as both the icon at the top of the hierarchy and as a folder in the \Windows folder.

The My Documents icon is just a shortcut to your My Documents folder. You can rename this icon and the My Documents folder anything you like and/or change the shortcut to point to any folder. (Right-click the icon, choose Properties, and change the contents of the Target field in the Shortcut tab.) Microsoft is just providing an easy way for you to get to the general area, the folder, that you use to store all your documents. Presumably, you'll divide the My Documents folder into subfolders.

The My Documents folder has a different folder icon. Since you can name this folder anything you like, you might as well use this folder to store all your documents and data.

The Network Neighborhood icon represents all the computers connected to yours over a LAN. You won't have a Network Neighborhood icon on your Desktop unless you have installed a network or set up Dial-Up Networking or Direct Cable Connection. You shouldn't remove it from the Desktop (and therefore from the Explorer) with TweakUI unless you are not using DCC or any other networking function, including dialing into the Internet.

Network Neighborhood and Recycle Bin are displayed on the same level as My Computer. Microsoft wants you to think of the network in the same way as you think of your computer. The Recycle Bin spans local hard disk drives (but not floppy drives). In this way, it is indeed equal to My Computer. Also, Microsoft wanted the Recycle Bin on the Desktop permanently.

The Internet Explorer icon also appears in the left pane of your Explorer. Of course, the Internet Explorer icon is right there on your Desktop as well. Microsoft wants to be sure that you know how easy it is to get connected to the Internet, so it placed this icon near the top of the hierarchy.

Shortcuts that you have placed on your Desktop don't appear in the left pane of the Explorer — too much clutter. They do, however, appear in the right pane if you highlight the Desktop icon in the left pane. The Outlook Express, Microsoft Network, and the Inbox icons, even though they are on the Desktop, don't show in the left pane. File icons on the Desktop don't show either. If you place folders on the Desktop, they do show up in the left pane.

Some special folders, such as Control Panel, Dial-Up Networking, Scheduled Tasks, and Printers, are displayed on the same level as the disk drives. Microsoft doesn't want you to have to go searching for them through the hierarchy of folders. Like cream, they have risen to the top.

Ordinary folders are stored in the disk drives, and the folder icons are connected to the drive icons. Figure 8-3 doesn't show any folder icons attached to the drive icons because the view in the left pane hasn't been expanded to include them. You can see them in Figure 8-4. File icons never show up in the left pane of the Explorer window.

Special folders

When you install Windows 98, it sets up a number of preconfigured folders that have special characteristics. These include \My Documents, \Recycled, \Program Files, \Windows\Recent, \Windows\SendTo, and \Windows\Fonts. In order to work with the Internet Explorer, Windows 98 also creates a \Windows\Favorites folder for Internet web pages, and a \Windows\History folder to keep track of the URLs for previously visited web sites. There are numerous other special or system folders as well.

Some of these folders contain a hidden file called Desktop.ini. This file may have a reference to a dynamic link library (*dll*) file that defines a particular set of behaviors for the folder. Windows 98 gives these folders the System attribute. Others are just regular folders that Windows 98 uses as default storage locations for certain kinds of files. For example, the default storage location for new applications is \Program Files.

Windows 98 keeps track of some of these folders in the Registry. You can edit their entries to point to other locations. This can be useful if you want to move one of these folders to another drive. This doesn't work for the Fonts folder, however.

You can use your Registry editor (see Chapter 15) to review the settings in HKEY_CURRENT_USER\Software\Microsoft\Windows\CurrentVersion\Explorer\shellfolders. Better still, use TweakUI to make the necessary Registry changes. Click the General tab, choose the folder you want to move in the Folder drop-down list, and click the Change Location button.

We suggest that you create another folder under the root directory named \My System. You can use this folder to store files and applications that modify the behavior of your computer, but are specific to your computer alone. We have included a number of batch files and *reg* files on the *Windows 98 Secrets* CD-ROM that you might want to place in this folder. Then, no matter how often you update your \Windows or \Windows\System folders, your still have your original files in \My System.

Two panes — connected and yet independent

The two panes of the Explorer window are connected. You click an icon in the left pane, and the contents of that drive or folder appear in the right pane.

Much of the power of the Explorer comes from the fact that the two panes, although connected, are also independent of each other. You can view the contents of one folder in the right pane and, without disturbing that view, expand the tree in the left pane to find another folder. This makes it easy to copy or move files and folders from one folder to another.

Think of the right pane of the Explorer window as a folder window. It acts just like a folder window, except that the default action when you click a folder icon in the right pane is to open the folder in the existing Explorer window, rather to open a folder window.

Notice that you do have to click an icon in the left pane to select it. In the right pane, you can hover to select an icon.

The left pane of the Explorer window is now called the Explorer bar (click View, Explorer Bar). If you've used Windows 95, you'll notice that Windows 98 adds four new Internet-oriented left panes — Search, Favorites, History, and Channels. Microsoft designated the folder tree version of the Explorer bar as All Folders.

Choose View, Explorer Bar, None (or click the little X in the upper-right corner of the Explorer bar) and the Explorer turns into a folder window. You can go from the Explorer to a folder window, but not the other way around unless you started with the Explorer. You don't get the All Folders option if you click the My Computer or the Internet Explorer icon.

Thumbnails

If you display a folder or Explorer window as a web page, you can display thumbnail views of some of the files in the folder. Right-click the right pane of the Explorer window and choose View, As Web Page. Place your mouse pointer over a *gif* file and a thumbnail view of it appears in the window. Thumbnail views of quite a few different types of files are available, including graphics files in *bmp, gif, jpg,* and *tif* formats, HTML files (*htm* or *html*), and PowerPoint files (*ppt*).

Costas Andriotis has developed a sophisticated web page view that lets you display thumbnails of more file types. For example, you can preview videos in *mpg* and *avi* format, *wav* sound files, and text files (see Figure 8-5). You can find his site at http://www.biznet.com.gr/sail/isa/index.htm. Click the Windows button at the top of his home page.

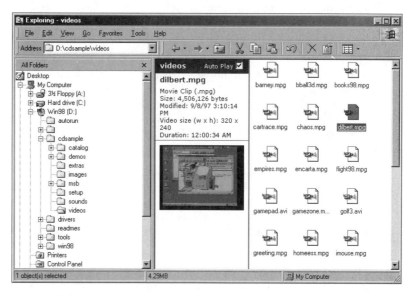

Figure 8-5: Previewing a movie in the Explorer.

Folder Options

Choosing View, Folder Options in any Explorer or My Computer window lets you set a number of Desktop, Explorer, My Computer, and Internet Explorer options.

If you click the Internet Explorer icon in the left pane of an Explorer window, view a web page in the Explorer, or click the Internet Explorer icon on the Desktop, the Folder Options command in the View menu becomes Internet Options. This command is not the same deal at all—it displays a completely different set of choices. Whether you see Folder Options or Internet Options depends on what you are viewing. View a web page, and you have Internet Options. View a hard disk or folder (even if you have clicked View, As Web Page), and you get Folder Options.

Windows 98 settings are spread all over the place; Folder Options is just one location of many. This is the dialog box you use to make the basic choice between Web style and Classic style. Web style lets you single-click to open and hover to select, and it displays all folders as web pages. Classic style requires that you double-click to open and single-click to select, and it doesn't display folders as web pages unless you choose View, As Web Page for a particular folder.

Sticky view settings

For some users, the improvement to the interface in Windows 98 that they appreciate the most is the fact that each folder can now maintain its own settings. Now you can design each folder window to be the way you like it.

If you want to associate a specific view with each folder, you have to open a new window for each folder. To do this, choose View, Folder Options. In the General tab, either choose Classic style or choose Custom, click the Settings button, and mark Open Each Folder in Its Own Window.

The view settings that you have control over are the icon views in a folder window (Large Icons, Small Icons, List, or Details), the icon order (By Name, By Type, By Size, and By Date), and the widths and order of the columns in Details view. You can also choose the Web style or Classic style view (mark or clear View, As Web Page). In addition, Windows 98 remembers the size and location of each folder window.

Now you can display each folder in a manner that is best suited for the contents of that folder. You might display a folder full of shortcuts to applications in Large Icons view sorted by name. If a folder contains pictures, you might choose web page view so that you can see thumbnails of the files. And if a folder contains documents, you might display it in Details view sorted by date.

To modify how Windows 98 handles view settings, choose View, Folder Options, and click the View tab. If you want each folder to remember its view settings, mark Remember Each Folder's View Settings. To force the view settings for all folders to be same as the current folder, mark the Like Current Folder button. To force all folders back to the default view settings, click the Reset All Folders button. This process is much easier than it was with Windows 95, when you had to change existing views one at a time.

Seeing all the files on your computer

Microsoft is somewhat ashamed of the three-letter file extensions it uses to define file types. It is also a bit embarrassed by its 8-character followed by 3-character filenames. It has created a way of doing long filenames (255 characters long) without upsetting its existing disk file structure (FAT, for file allocation table). It wants Windows 98 users to forget about file extensions.

When you first install Windows 98, it doesn't show files with certain extensions in folder windows or in Explorer windows. And it doesn't show the three-letter extensions for files of registered file types. You can tell Windows 98 to display these missing files and extensions. Here's how:

STEPS

Viewing All Files and File Extensions

Step 1. Click your My Computer icon.

Step 2. Choose View, Folder Options, and click the View tab, as shown in Figure 8-6.

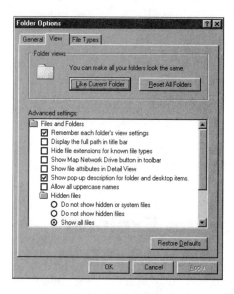

Figure 8-6: The View tab of the Folder Options dialog box.

Step 3. Mark the Show All Files option button and clear the check box labeled Hide File Extensions for Known File Types.

Step 4. Click OK.

Seeing hidden folders

Secret

If you mark the Show All Files option button, you also get to see more folders contained in the \Windows folder. Microsoft appears to think that less "advanced" users will have a problem with these folders showing up in their folder windows, so it hides them from the view of users who choose to hide files of certain types.

You can see which folders get hidden by opening an Explorer window and expanding the branch connected to your \Windows folder icon in the folder tree. Watch the list of folders change as you switch back and forth between Show All Files, Do Not Show Hidden Files, and Do Not Show Hidden Or System Files, clicking the Apply button after each change.

Single-click or double-click

The General tab of the View, Folder Options dialog box lets you choose between Web style, Classic style, or Custom. *Web style* and *Classic style* are just names for two specific constellations of options. To see which options are contained in each style, choose one of them, click Apply, and then choose Custom and click the Settings button. The options selected for you in the Custom Settings dialog box are the ones contained in the style you chose. If you don't like one of them, you can change it in the Custom Settings dialog box.

The options contained in the Web style let you single-click to open file, folder, or application icons, and open each folder in the same window. When single-clicking is enabled, you can select icons by hovering your mouse pointer over them. The Classic style contains options that require a double-click to open file, folder, and application icons, and open each folder in a separate window. When double-clicking is enabled, you have to click to select icons.

Throughout this book, we assume that you have selected the single-click option.

Navigating with the Explorer

The Explorer is your navigator. It guides you to the files and folders on your computer's disk drives or, if you are connected to a network, on other computers. The Explorer displays, in an expandable tree, your computer's drives and the drives of other computers to which you are networked. You search through the drives by clicking the Explorer tree to expand it. The Explorer also gives you an easy way to copy, move, and link files or folders across disk drives, folders, or the network.

Because the Explorer gives you an overview and a road map of your computer and the server computers you are connected to, you can use it to find your way around computer space. The key to navigating is using the little plus signs to the left of the icons in the folder tree. Clicking a plus sign expands that branch of the tree. For example, clicking the plus sign next to your C: drive icon expands the tree to allow you to see all the folders attached to the root directory of the C drive.

Click the plus sign next to any of the folders on the C drive, and you'll see the folders contained within that folder. Each branch of the folder tree gets expanded as you climb out the branches. To collapse a branch, click the minus sign to the left of an icon. The minus sign appears as soon as you expand a branch.

Tip

The folder tree appears in the left pane of the Explorer, which is called the Explorer bar. The version of the Explorer bar that shows you the folder tree is called All Folders. (This is the default setting.) You can display other versions of the Explorer bar by choosing View, Explorer Bar, and clicking Search, Favorites, History, or Channels. These versions let you navigate the

Internet in the left pane of the Explorer window. However, most of the time you will probably find it more convenient to navigate the Internet by clicking hyperlinks in a single-pane window (such as a folder window or the Internet Explorer).

You can also navigate by clicking the Back and Forward buttons on the Standard Buttons toolbar. These buttons let you move back to a previously viewed web page or folder, and then move forward again to the web page or folder you viewed most recently.

Highlighting a folder icon

If you click a folder icon in the left pane, you see the contents of that folder in the right pane. If the contents of the right pane include folder icons, you can expand a branch by clicking one of them. The folder tree in the left pane of the Explorer also expands when you do this.

The default action of clicking a folder icon in the left pane is to display the contents of the folder in the right pane. If you instead right-click a folder icon and choose Open in the context menu, Windows 98 opens a new folder window on the Desktop with the contents of the folder.

Tip

If you click a folder icon in the tree, you both expand the branch at that node and display the contents of the folder in the right pane.

Secret

If you click a folder icon in the right pane of the Explorer, the Explorer view expands to display the contents of that folder in the right pane. By making a change to the Folder definition in your Registry, you can have this action display the contents of the folder in a new window instead of in the Explorer.

STEPS

Making Single-Pane Views from the Explorer

Step 1.   Click Regedit.exe in the \Windows folder. Click the plus sign next to the HKEY_CLASSES_ROOT key. Scroll down to the Folder key.

Step 2.   Click the plus sign next to the Folder key, and highlight the *shell* key.

Step 3.   Double-click Default in the right pane to display the Edit String dialog box. Type **Open** in the Value Data field and click OK.

Step 4.   Click a folder icon in the right pane of the Explorer and notice this action now opens a new window. If you click a folder icon in the left pane in the Explorer, the right pane still displays the contents of that folder.

Folder icons in the Explorer

Double-click a folder icon in the left pane of the Explorer. If this folder has subfolders, clicking it will display them in the folder tree. The double-click is a toggle. If you double-click the folder icon again, the folder tree collapses to hide the subfolders. You have to double-click even if you are using Web style.

Undocumented

Try this: Drag and hold a file or folder icon from the right pane over a folder icon in the left pane. If the folder in the left pane has subfolders that were previously not displayed (the folder had a plus sign next to it), they are now displayed. This allows you to navigate down the folder tree and find the target subfolder as you are dragging.

Two versions of the Standard Buttons toolbar

As we saw in Chapter 7, Windows 98 provides two versions of the Standard Buttons toolbar. One version looks something like the toolbar in Windows 95, and the other contains Internet-related buttons. We often refer to this version as the *Internet toolbar*. The Explorer automatically switches to the Internet toolbar if you are using the Explorer to view a web page.

The Internet toolbar first appeared in earlier versions of the Internet Explorer. Now this toolbar shows up wherever you view web pages, even in My Computer and Explorer windows. We discuss this aspect of the Windows 98 user interface in more detail in Chapter 9.

You can increase the height of the Standard Buttons toolbar by pulling down on its bottom edge. If you do this, the toolbar will include text names as well as icons. You can also right-click a blank part of any of the toolbars and mark or clear Text Labels.

Making the left pane bigger

The two panes of the Explorer window are divided by a vertical bar. You can increase the width of the left pane so that you can see more of its contents as you expand branches of the folder tree. To do this, rest your mouse pointer over the vertical bar. When the mouse pointer turns into a vertical line with two arrows, drag the bar to the right.

Full-screen Explorer

Windows 98 comes with a full-screen version of the Explorer. (It also has full-screen versions of folder windows and the Internet Explorer.)

To open a full-screen window, hold down the Ctrl key and click the Maximize button at the right end of the Explorer title bar. Your Explorer window will enlarge to cover the Desktop (see Figure 8-7).

You can turn this view into a dual-pane view by moving your mouse pointer to the left. The All Folders pane slides into view. Move your mouse pointer back to the right side of this Desktop-sized window, and the All Folders pane disappears.

If you want your Taskbar to appear over this window, move your mouse pointer to the edge of the screen to which the Taskbar is attached.

There is no way to make the Explorer window shrink back to maximized or restored size from full-screen view (unless you're viewing a web page). You can minimize the window, but clicking its Taskbar button brings it back to full-screen view. To get back to a maximized or restored view, you have to close the full-screen Explorer window and open another. If you view a web page in full-screen mode, you can click the Fullscreen button (a toggle) in the Internet toolbar to maximize or restore the window.

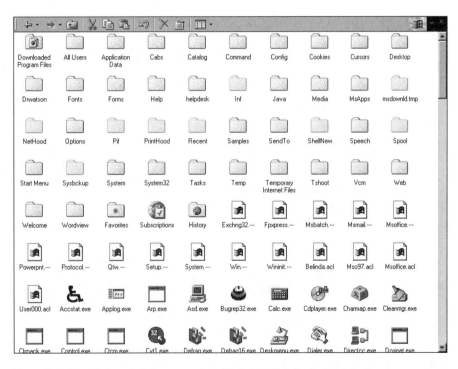

Figure 8-7: The Explorer in full-screen view. Click the Minimize button to get your Desktop back.

The Network Neighborhood

The Network Neighborhood icon contains the shared resources of the computers to which your computer is connected. Click this icon to see the disk drives, folders, and printers that are available (shared) to you.

You can expand branches of the folder trees found on other computers just as easily as you can on your computer. Windows 98 treats the networked computers just like My Computer to encourage you to do likewise. You can use the Explorer window to browse networked computers just as you do your own computer.

If you like, you can map a shared folder or disk drive to a drive letter, thereby making it appear as though it is part of My Computer. To do this, choose Tools, Map Network Drive in the Explorer window.

If you want to connect to a shared printer, use the Printers folder (located in the My Computer window).

You can put buttons for the Map Network Drive and Disconnect Network Drive commands on your Standard Buttons toolbar. Choose View, Folder Options, click the View tab, and mark the Show Map Network Drive Button in Toolbar check box.

Using the keyboard with the folder tree

Secret

You can, if you like, expand all the branches of the folder tree at once. To do this, hold down the Alt key and press the asterisk (*) above the number pad. We don't really recommend expanding all branches at once because it can take a long time.

To expand or collapse branches with your mouse, you click the plus and minus signs next to the branches. If you want to use the keyboard instead, press Tab a few times if necessary to bring the focus to the left pane of the Explorer window, use the arrow keys to highlight the branch you want to expand or collapse (or type the first few letters of the folder or drive name), and then press the plus key to expand the branch or the minus key to collapse it.

Secret

Normally, if you collapse a high-level branch when branches underneath it are displayed, the next time you expand the branch, all the branches within it are redisplayed as well. If you want to only see the first level of folders under the branch the next time you expand it, press F5 after you collapse it. Windows 98 "invisibly" collapses the branches under the high-level branch so that they won't show the next time you expand it.

Creating New Folders

Windows 98 and your applications create the folders they need during installation. If you want additional folders for your own work, you need to create them yourself. To create folders using the Explorer, take the following steps:

STEPS

Creating a Folder

Step 1. Right-click the My Computer icon on the Desktop. Choose Explore in the context menu.

Step 2. Expand the folder tree in the left pane of the Explorer window until you see the folder in which you want to place your new folder. Click this folder icon to select it. Make sure that the folder name is highlighted and that its name is in the Explorer window title bar.

Step 3. Right-click a blank part of right pane to display a context menu. Point to New, and then click Folder.

Step 4. A new folder icon appears in the right pane, and its name is highlighted. Type an appropriate name for the folder and press Enter.

It would seem natural to right-click a folder or drive icon in the left pane of the Explorer and choose New from a context menu to create a new folder, shortcut, or whatever within the selected folder (or root directory if you right-click a drive icon). Unfortunately, there is no New option on the context menu that appears when you right-click items in the folder tree.

Copying and Moving Files and Folders

You can move and copy files a lot more easily with the Explorer dual-pane window than with a single-pane folder window. You just have to be willing to put up with this dual-pane hierarchical view.

You can view the contents of the source folder in the right pane and independently find the destination folder in the left pane. Once you see both the source and destination, you can copy or move the files and/or folders from the right pane to the left.

Almost all the copying and moving techniques detailed in Chapter 7 work the same with the Explorer. Instead of dragging and dropping between folder windows, you select icons in the Explorer window's right pane and drop them on folder icons in the left pane.

Secret

You can copy a file into the same folder that contains the original file by pressing the Ctrl key as you drag and drop the file in the right pane of the Explorer.

If you want to move or copy files or folders in the Explorer with Cut and Copy, first select the icons in the right pane with any of the techniques detailed in "Selecting Items in a Window" in Chapter 7. Issue the Cut or Copy command, display the contents of the destination folder in the right pane, and issue the Paste command to move or copy the selected files and/or folders to the new folder.

If you have downloaded Microsoft's PowerToys utility (http://www.microsoft. com/windows/software/powertoy.htm), you can use Send To Any Folder to move or copy a file or folder to another folder (see the "Right-click to a Powerhouse" section in Chapter 10).

Creating Two Explorer Windows

Using the Windows 3.1x File Manager, it was much easier to manage files if you had two child windows open at the same time. Each window had two panes (the directory tree on the left and the directory contents on the right), so when two child windows were open, the File Manager contained a total of four panes.

You could use one child window to display the source directory and the other window to display the destination directory. This made it much easier to copy and move files, or to simply compare the contents of two directories.

Using the File Manager, you couldn't expand the directory tree while maintaining the same contents in the right pane. In contrast, the tree and folder panes in the Explorer are more independent, which allows you to manage files with just two panes.

The File Manager does have an advantage over the Explorer. The File Manager has a multidocument interface. It can contain two child windows within its window border. Microsoft (at least the part of it that isn't producing the Office applications) has decided to drop this interface and have the operating system, not the applications, control the window borders.

As a result of this decision, the Explorer does not have a multidocument interface. So if you want to reduce the amount of scrolling required to find the source and then go to the destination folder when you're moving and copying files, you might find it easier to open two Explorer windows at the same time on the Desktop. This is quite easy to do, because Windows 98 opens a new copy of the Explorer each time you right-click My Computer and click Explore, or each time you click an Explorer shortcut on the Desktop (see "Putting the Explorer on the Desktop" earlier in this chapter).

Undocumented

You can open another copy of the Explorer that's already focused on a particular folder by following these steps:

STEPS

Opening a Second Copy of the Explorer

Step 1. In the left pane of an Explorer window, right-click the folder icon you want to Explore. This could be either the source or destination folder.

Step 2. Click Open in the context menu.

Step 3. Right-click the system menu icon (at the left end of the title bar) of the newly opened folder window.

Step 4. Select Explore in the context menu.

Step 5. Click the Close button in the upper-right corner of the folder window you created in step 2.

This will open a new copy of the Explorer with the focus on the selected folder. Once you have two Explorer windows, you can display the contents of the destination folder in one and the source folder in the other.

Tip

You can arrange the Explorer windows like the child windows in the File Manager by right-clicking the Taskbar and choosing Cascade, Tile Windows Horizontally, or Tile Windows Vertically. (Before you issue one of these commands, make sure all your other open windows are minimized.) When tiled, the two Explorer windows cover your Desktop completely and look like the two child windows in the Windows 3.1x File Manager when it was maximized.

Undocumented

If you leave two tiled Explorer windows open when you shut down your computer, they will be ready to go when you start it again. Unfortunately, the two windows won't stay tiled, but will instead be stacked on top of each other. (This is because Window 98 erroneously saves the position of only one Explorer window.) You'll need to right-click the Taskbar and choose Tile Windows Horizontally or Tile Windows Vertically to separate the windows again.

Explorer (and My Computer) Keyboard Shortcuts

The Explorer and the My Computer folder windows share a common set of keyboard shortcuts. They are listed in Table 8-1.

Table 8-1   Explorer and Folder Window Keyboard Shortcuts

Key	Action
F1	Help
F2	Rename the highlighted file or folder.
F3	Bring up the Find dialog box.
F4	Display down the list in the Address bar (if any). This is a toggle switch.
F5	Refresh the windows. You saw one use for this command in "Using the keyboard with the folder tree" earlier in this chapter. If the files or folders in a window have changed and have not yet been updated, this will update the display.
F6	Move the focus from left pane, to the Address bar (if you have one), to the right pane, and back to the left pane again. In a folder window there is only one pane.
F10	Put the focus on the File menu.
Alt+*	Expand all the branches in the folder tree.
*	Expand all branches below the focused node (folder or drive icon).
Backspace	Move up one level in the folder hierarchy.
Tab	Same as F6; shift the focus between the two panes and the Address bar. This is very useful for navigating the folder tree or picking out files and folders in the right pane.
Arrow keys	Move up and down the folder tree in the left pane or the list of files and folders in the right pane. If you move quickly enough in the left pane, the highlighted folder's contents do not show in the right pane. If you leave the focus on one icon for more than a second, its contents are displayed in the right pane.
Right arrow	Expand the highlighted folder if it isn't expanded already. If it is, go to the subfolder.
Left arrow	Collapse the highlighted folder if is it expanded. If not, go to the parent folder.
Ctrl+Arrow keys	Scroll the left or right pane, depending on which pane has the focus. You can use PgUp and PgDn keys also. The focus isn't changed.
Enter	Does nothing in the folder tree. In the right pane, pressing Enter runs the selected file or opens the selected folder, just as clicking would.
Shift+F10	Display the context menu. Same as right-click. Throughout the Windows interface, pressing Shift+F10 is equivalent to clicking the right mouse button.
+	The keypad plus sign. When a folder name is highlighted and the branch below it is collapsed, expand the branch.

Key	Action
–	The keypad minus sign. When a folder name is highlighted and the branch below it is expanded, collapse the branch. When combined with F5, collapse all the branches below.
Alt+Spacebar	Open the system menu. This menu allows you to move, minimize, maximize, size, or close the folder or Explorer window.
Alt+Enter	Display the folder's properties.
Ctrl+G	Open the Go To Folder dialog box. This allows you to enter the name of a folder or computer to go to.
Ctrl+X	Cut highlighted item.
Ctrl+C	Copy highlighted item.
Ctrl+V	Paste copied or cut item.
Ctrl+Z	Undo a previous action.
Letter(s)	Jump to the first folder whose name starts with that letter(s). If you type the same letter(s) again, jump to the next folder whose name starts with those letters. You need to type multiple letters quickly or Windows 98 will interpret the second letter as a new first letter.
Alt+F4	Close the application window. Throughout the Windows interface, Alt+F4 closes all applications.

Explorer Command Line Parameters

Take a moment to look at how the Explorer command line parameters work:

STEPS

Viewing the Windows Explorer Command Line Parameters

Step 1. Click the Start button, point to Programs, right-click Windows Explorer, and click Properties.

Step 2. Look at the Target field in the Shortcut tab.

The target for the Windows Explorer shortcut is:

```
C:\WINDOWS\EXPLORER.SCF
```

Change it to:

```
C:\WINDOWS\EXPLORER.EXE /n,/e,C:\
```

With the command line parameters /n,/e,C:\, an Explorer window you open by clicking Windows Explorer in the Start menu looks like Figure 8-8.

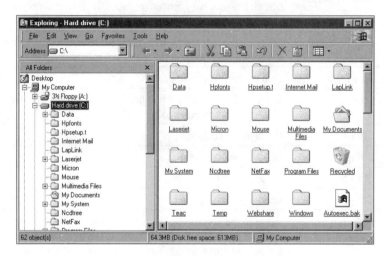

Figure 8-8: An Explorer window focused on the C drive.

The syntax for the Explorer command line is:

```
C:\Windows\Explorer.exe {/n,}{/e,}{options,}{folder}
```

The parameters have the following meanings:

/n,	Opens a *new* Explorer window — by itself, this commands opens a window in folder view
/e,	Opens an *expanded* folder with its contents displayed in Explorer view
options	May be either one of the following: /root, Selects a folder as the *root* of a folder tree or /select, Highlights a folder's parent and displays parent folder's content
folder	May be any folder name or path, such as: C:\ or C:\Windows

Note that you have to use commas between switches on the Explorer command line.

Undocumented

If there were no command line parameters after Explorer.exe, clicking Windows Explorer in the Start menu would bring up an Explorer window focused on the C drive (where the Explorer.exe file is most likely stored).

If you add C:\Windows or any other folder name to the Explorer command line, clicking Windows Explorer in the Start menu displays a folder window containing the contents of that folder. Adding a folder name to the Explorer command line turns the Explorer into My Computer.

Undocumented

If you insert /e, (the comma is required) in front of the folder name, clicking Windows Explorer in the Start menu displays an Explorer window focused on the specified folder with the folder expanded and the contents of the folder displayed in the right pane. Putting a folder name in the Target field (command line) takes Explorer out of its default behavior. Using /e, restores some of that default behavior; /e, means Explorer view.

If instead of clicking Windows Explorer in the Start menu, you open an Explorer window and click the shortcut to Windows Explorer found in the C:\Windows\Start Menu\Program folder, Windows 98 does not display another Explorer window. Instead, it refocuses your existing Explorer window on the folder in the Target field. To force Windows 98 to create a new Explorer window, you need to add the /n, command line parameter. Adding /n, restores the rest of the Explorer's default behavior (except for its focus); /n, means *new*.

Undocumented

When you click Windows Explorer in the Start menu, you get another Explorer window even if you don't use the /n, command parameter. The only situation in which you need the /n, parameter to get another Explorer window is if you launch the Explorer by clicking the Windows Explorer shortcut within an Explorer window.

You can't replace C:\Windows with My Computer or Network Neighborhood. Desktop will work, but it doesn't get you to the top of the hierarchical view of your computer. You might try it to see what we mean.

Undocumented

The normal topmost icon in the Explorer is the Desktop. This is referred to as the root of the folder tree. You can specify a different root if you want. Add /root, to the command line and follow it with your new root. The new root could be My Computer, or C:\Windows, or whatever you like. Here's an example:

```
C:\WINDOWS\EXPLORER.EXE /n,/e,/root,C:\
```

This example produces an Explorer window that looks like Figure 8-9.

You can use the /select, parameter to open a given folder and highlight the folder's parent. Here's an example (see Figure 8-10):

```
C:\WINDOWS\EXPLORER.EXE /n,/e,/select,C:\
```

Notice the differences that these command line parameters produce by comparing Figures 8-9 and 8-10 with Figure 8-8.

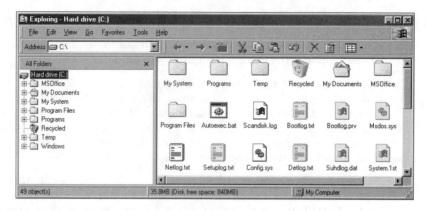

Figure 8-9: An Explorer window with the C drive as its root (/root,).

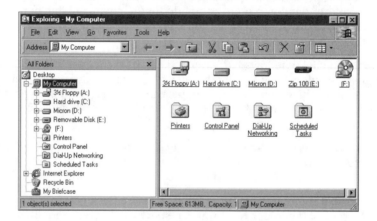

Figure 8-10: An Explorer window focused on the parent of the C drive, My Computer (/select,).

Going from the Windows 3.1x File Manager to the Explorer

If you are moving up from Windows 3.1x, how do you go from using the File Manager to using the Explorer? In this section, we review almost all the things you can do with the File Manager and show you how to do them better with the Explorer or another part of the Windows 98 interface. Much of what we say here about the Explorer is also true of the My Computer folder windows. Where it isn't true, and isn't obviously *not* true, we point it out.

Open, Copy, Move, Delete

The File Manager's File menu offers these choices: Open, Copy, Move, and Delete.

The Explorer accomplishes those same tasks with the context menu, substituting the Cut and Paste commands for Move, and the Copy and Paste commands for Copy. Because the Explorer can use the right mouse button, it can use right drag and drop, which allows for easier-to-understand copy and move operations. The Explorer also supports the Windows 3.1*x* conventions of copying a file by selecting it and holding down the Ctrl key as you drag it to a new folder, and moving a file by selecting it and holding down the Alt key as you drag it to a new folder.

In Windows 3.1*x*, you could drag a file from the File Manager to the Program Manager to create a shortcut. However, the Explorer is much better at creating shortcuts, mainly because it makes full use of drag and drop and the context menu.

Rename

File Manager lets you use wild cards when you're renaming files. This makes it easy to rename a group of files, or to change a bunch of file extensions. Explorer only lets you rename one file at a time.

If you are set to single-click (see "Single-click or double-click" earlier in this chapter), hover over a filename to select it, press F2, type a new name or edit the existing one, and press Enter. If you are set to double-click, click a filename to select it and press F2 (or click the filename twice slowly), and then rename the file and press Enter. Regardless of whether you are set to single- or double-click, you can rename a file by right-clicking it and choosing Rename in the context menu.

You can also rename files in the common file dialog box (used by many applications for the Open and Save As dialog boxes). Even if you are set to single-click, you can't hover to select a file in a common file dialog box, so use the renaming methods that work if you're set to double-click.

The File Manager doesn't work with long filenames. It is possible to upgrade the File Manager to handle long filenames using a shareware application, File Manager Long File Name Support for Windows 95. You can download this application from http://ourworld.compuserve.com/homepages/sweckman/winfilee.htm.

Run

File Manager lets you run an executable file by choosing File, Run to display the Run dialog box, typing the filename, and adding command line parameters. If you are focused in the File Manager on a particular directory, it puts the directory's pathname in the command line.

In Windows 98, Run is on the Start menu in the Taskbar. It doesn't know which folder you have highlighted, so it doesn't put your current path in the Run dialog box's command line. Run keeps a history from session to session of past command lines.

File association

File Manager can create an *association* with an application to open and print associated documents.

The Explorer has a similar easy-to-use file association feature, but one that is much more powerful. You can create many more commands than opening and printing. Just click an unregistered file type, enter an optional name for the file type, and pick an application to open it.

In the Explorer, the Print command only appears in the context menu for files of registered types. The File Manager doesn't dim the File, Print command even when you highlight a file that it doesn't know how to print.

With the Explorer, you can add other commands or change an existing association by choosing View, Folder Options, and changing settings in the File Types tab. Check out "Creating and Editing File Types and Actions" in Chapter 13 for details.

Open an unassociated file

With the File Manager, you can drag a file to an open application or a minimized icon on the Desktop to view or open it.

With the Explorer, you can put a shortcut in the Send To folder that points to a default file opener (or two). Then you can right-click a file in the Explorer, and use the Send To command to send the file to the default file opener. (See "Create a default file opener" in Chapter 13 for details.) You can drag a file to a minimized application button on the Taskbar, or to an application window that is open on the Desktop.

You can also right-click a file, choose Open, and pick which application you want to open the file with.

Create directory

One of the main reasons you use the File Manager or the Explorer is to create new directories (or, in Windows 98 terminology, new folders). You can use both the File Manager and the Explorer to build hierarchical folder structures.

To create a folder in the Explorer, highlight the folder icon in the left pane that will contain the new folder. Right-click the right pane, point to New in the context menu, and click Folder. Rename the folder from New Folder to whatever you like and press Enter.

Create file

You can't create a new, empty file in the File Manager.

You can in the Explorer. Right-click in the right pane and choose New. Then click the desired document type in the New menu.

Search or File Find

You can use the File Manager to find a file using wild cards, and you can tell it what directory (and subdirectories) to search.

The Explorer has a much more powerful Find capability. It remembers your past searches, so you can edit them and use them again. The Find feature allows you to use a greater number of search criteria, and you can search for files by looking for text within them. There is no comparison. Check out "The Find Function" in Chapter 11 for details.

You initiate a Find with the Explorer by choosing Tools, Find, Files or Folders or by pressing F3 if your focus is on the Desktop, a folder window, or an Explorer window. You can also search for computers on your local network, or for documents on the Microsoft Network (if you have signed up for MSN) or on the Internet.

File view filters

If you choose View, By File Type and type an extension or filename, the File Manager restricts the files it displays to ones that have the extension or filename you specify.

The Explorer lets you do this with Find. You can display in the Find window only files that have a given name or extension. This is slower than the File Manager's way of doing it, but less prone to error.

Copy, Label, Format, make a system disk

The File Manager lets you do a disk copy. You can also change the label of a disk drive, including a hard disk drive. And you can format a diskette (or a hard drive) and create a system diskette.

To disk-copy a diskette in the Explorer, right-click the floppy icon and select Copy Disk from the context menu.

To label a hard disk drive or a diskette, right-click the drive icon, click Properties, and then type the new label.

To format a drive, right-click the drive icon, and click Format.

To make a system disk or diskette, right-click the drive icon and choose Format. If you want to format the diskette and make it bootable, select the Full option button, and mark the Copy System Files check box under Other options (see Figure 8-11). If the disk is already formatted, select the Copy System Files Only option button, and click Start.

Figure 8-11: The Format dialog box. Mark the Copy System Files Only option button to make a system diskette of a formatted diskette. Select Full and Copy System Files to format a bootable diskette.

To create an emergency boot diskette, click the Control Panel icon in the left pane of the Explorer window, click the Add/Remove Programs icon, click the Startup Disk tab, and then click the Create Disk button.

Change the font used

In the File Manager, you can choose what font you want to use to display files, and so on.

The font that the Explorer uses is determined by the Icon font setting in the Appearance tab of the Display Properties dialog box. Right-click the Desktop and click Properties. Click the Appearance tab, and then select Icon in the Item drop-down list. Choose the desired font and size, and click OK.

Print a directory listing

Tip

You can't print a directory listing in either the File Manager or the Explorer. In the File Manager, choose File, Run (or in the Explorer, click the Start button and click Run) and then type:

```
COMMAND/c DIR *.* >LPT1
```

This command prints a directory listing. You need to manually eject the last page on a laser printer. See "Getting a Directory Listing" in Chapter 34 for more details on how to do this.

Put two directory listings side-by-side

The File Manager has a multidocument interface, which lets you compare two directories side-by-side, or show a source and destination directory within one window controlled by the File Manager.

The Explorer has a single-document interface. To get two copies of a folder or two different folders on the Desktop, you need to open two Explorers. If you want to arrange them next to each other, you need to minimize all other applications, and then right-click the Taskbar and choose Tile Windows Vertically or Tile Windows Horizontally from the context menu.

The Explorer has a stronger mechanism for expanding the folder tree, which allows you to copy and move files and folders between folders without needing two separate windows, as you do with the File Manager.

Click the plus and minus signs next to folder names in the Explorer to expand and collapse branches of the folder tree. This doesn't affect the contents of the right pane.

The Explorer shows all your disk drives in one folder tree; you don't need two windows to see more than one disk drive's folders.

Sort files by name, date, file type, size

The File Manager lets you click a toolbar button or choose a menu item to sort your files. The order is fixed for each variable: ascending for name, descending for date, and so on.

The Explorer lets you sort on name, date, file type, or size in all four icon views (the File Manager has only two icon views). It also lets you order your files and folders by ascending or descending order. If you sort by type, the Explorer sorts on the description of each file type (if you don't like this, see the next section), while the File Manager sorts alphabetically by extension.

Tip

If you're using Details view in the Explorer (View, Details), you can sort files or folders by clicking any of the gray header buttons at the top of the right pane. Click twice to reverse the sort order.

Sorting by extension in Explorer

One of the annoying features of the Explorer is that it sorts filenames by file types (View, Arrange Icons, By Type), but not by the literal extensions of those filenames. This means you can sort by the description of each file type, such as AmiPro Document or Configuration Settings, but you can't sort files by extension—in this case, *sam* and *ini*. Sorting filenames by description doesn't make it easy to find particular extensions that have meaning to you. For example, AmiPro Document sorts near the top of any list, but the actual filenames mostly end with *sam*, so you would normally think to look for them near the end of the list.

The fix that lets you sort by actual extensions involves a bit of extra keyboarding on your part:

Sorting Files by Extension

Step 1. In the Explorer, choose View, Folder Options, and then click the File Types tab. Select each file type in turn, click the Edit button, and add the document's typical extension to the *beginning* of the entry in the Description of Type field. In this way, the file type Microsoft Word Document, say, would become DOC Microsoft Word Document.

Step 2. After you have added the file extension to the beginning of the Description of Type field for each file type, Explorer will sort your filenames by the actual extension when you choose View, Arrange Icons, By Type. Of course, there are some file types that have two or more different extensions associated with them, such as BMP and PCX for bitmaps graphics files. In that case, you'll need to choose the extension most commonly used by your files and give your Description of Type that prefix.

If, on the other hand, you find the Type column in Explorer to be useless anyway, you can eliminate it from your Explorer windows. To do this, drag the right edge of the Type heading button to the left until the column consumes no space. If you ever want the Type column back, you can easily restore it by dragging the left edge of what was the Type column back to the right.

View file contents

The File Manager doesn't have a set of file viewers that let you see the file without launching the program that created the file.

The Explorer comes with a raft of file viewers that Microsoft calls *Quick Viewers*. You can access them by right-clicking a file. You can put the Quick View manager in the SendTo folder. (Quick View is actually a stripped-down version of the popular Outside In program for Windows from Inso Corp., which also markets additional Quick Viewers.)

The Windows 98 Explorer window can display web pages at full size and thumbnail versions of many other file types.

Undo and Delete

Undo is not available in the File Manager. The Explorer has an Undo command on the context menu that lets you undo rename, copy, move, and delete operations. You can also recover a previously deleted file from the Recycle Bin.

When you delete a file using the File Manager, you have to confirm that you want to delete the file. If you do, it's gone (unless you use the DOS program Unerase). If you delete a file using the Explorer, it goes to the Recycle Bin, and you can recover the file later if you realize you acted in haste (unless you turned off this capability or you deleted the file from a removable or network drive).

Share a disk drive or folder

In the Explorer, right-click the folder or drive icon and choose Sharing. This option isn't available in the File Manager.

Customize the toolbar

The File Manager lets you customize the toolbar. Just double-click it.

You are limited in what you can do with the Explorer toolbars. You can decide which toolbars to use and whether to display the Map Network Drive buttons or not. And you can also customize context menus, although it is somewhat difficult (see "Creating and Editing File Types and Actions" in Chapter 13).

See hidden files

In the File Manager, you can see a file that has the Hidden or System attribute turned on if you choose View, By File Type, Show Hidden/System Files.

The Explorer automatically hides files with certain extensions unless you choose View, Folder Options, click the View tab, and mark Show All Files. If you do this, Explorer indicates hidden files and folders by making them "ghosted" so that they appear half hidden. It's kind of cute.

See free disk space

Both the Explorer and the File Manager show the available disk space in the status bar. The Explorer also displays these values in a web page view of the hard drives in My Computer. To see this, click the My Computer icon in the left pane of the Explorer, right-click the right pane, and choose View, As Web Page. Then select a hard disk icon in the right pane.

File attributes

The File Manager displays file attributes in All File Details view.

The Windows 98 Explorer displays file attributes in Details view. To see them, choose View, Folder Options, click the View tab, and mark Show File Attributes in Detail View. If you select multiple files and then right-click any of the selected files and choose Properties, Windows 98 shows you the common file attributes for the selected files.

File size

The File Manager displays a greater degree of precision than the Explorer when giving the file size. The Explorer only shows the number of bytes to the nearest 1K.

Additional File Manager strengths

The File Manager is very fast. You can ask the File Manager to minimize itself after you start a file by double-clicking it in the File Manager.

Additional Explorer strengths

The Explorer gives you immediate access to the Control Panel, Network Neighborhood, the Printers folder, Dial-Up Networking, Scheduled Tasks, and so on.

You can use the universal naming convention (UNC) to access a network drive without having to map it to a drive letter.

Summary

The Explorer is the most powerful tool that Windows 98 provides to manage your computer. Unfortunately, much of its power is hidden.

▶ Use the Explorer to navigate throughout your computer and the network connected to your computer.

▶ We reveal the hidden command line parameters that determine how the Explorer behaves.

▶ We show you how to put the Explorer on the Desktop, or just about anywhere that makes sense to you.

▶ If you know how to use the Explorer, you can quickly copy and move files and folders around on your computer.

▶ The Explorer and My Computer come with keyboard shortcuts, and we show you what they are.

▶ We show you how to size and display the Explorer or multiple Explorers on your Desktop.

▶ We compare what the Windows 3.1*x* File Manager does with how the Explorer handles the same tasks.

Chapter 9

Internet Explorer

In This Chapter

Windows 98 integrates the Internet Explorer with the Windows Desktop and the Explorer. Using the Explorer to access the Internet as well as to view the contents of your computer can get a bit confusing.

▶ Starting the Internet Explorer

▶ If you want 128-bit encryption, Internet Explorer comes in a special U.S.- and Canada-only version

▶ Organizing and moving your Favorites folder

▶ Converting Netscape Navigator bookmarks

▶ Finding a URL, even in a frame

▶ Adding the Edit button to the Internet toolbar

▶ Filling in forms causes an error

▶ Cool Windows 98-related web sites

The Windows 98 User/Browser Interface

Soon after the August 24, 1995 release of Windows 95, much of the Windows development team became the Internet products development team under Brad Silverberg, who had headed up the Windows 95 effort. Future Windows 95 work was split between the user interface and Internet applications, and the underlying operating system and its utilities. These were separate development paths, and one could occur without the other.

Part of the Internet development team worked on improving the then rudimentary Internet Explorer browser that came with Microsoft Plus!. They both added functionality and made the browser work with other operating systems.

Given the mass acceptance of the browser idiom as the user interface to the World Wide Web, Microsoft saw that it was in its best interest both to develop a strong browser and to integrate it with its existing Windows 95 user interface. Now we all know why Microsoft did this: They want to preserve their monopoly position in personal-computer operating systems. The Netscape Navigator browser has threatened to turn Windows into the equivalent of your computer's BIOS—a necessary component, but hardly sufficient for getting your work done, and getting less necessary by the minute.

Microsoft released Internet Explorer 4.0 in late 1997. This version of the Internet Explorer integrated the browser with the Windows 95 Desktop and Explorer. Until the release of Windows 98, however, users still had to buy separate products or download the Internet Explorer to get the new combined Windows 95/Internet Explorer interface.

Windows 98 combines Internet Explorer with an upgraded Windows 95 operating system foundation. Microsoft has to have a single product that it can sell to its OEMs (computer manufacturers) and to the public as a shrink-wrapped item. Even though much of the functionality of Windows 98 (although not all) is available to Windows 95 users, Microsoft still needed to produce a single product to go with new computers.

So as far as this chapter is concerned, it doesn't matter whether you have Windows 95 and the latest version of Internet Explorer, or Windows 98. Windows 98 has additional functionality that we discuss in other chapters, but the user interfaces for Windows 98 and Windows 95 plus Internet Explorer 4.0 are the same.

As it did in Windows 95, the Internet Explorer icon sits on the Desktop and in the Control Panel. However, now a browser-friendly toolbar appears in any Windows 98 Explorer or My Computer window as soon as it's needed. For example, it appears as soon as you type a URL in the Address bar and press Enter. Any Explorer or My Computer window can now look like what Internet Explorer used to look like when it was a stand-alone application.

Microsoft will continue to develop Internet Explorer. You will undoubtedly be able to upgrade your Windows 98 Explorer and Desktop by downloading a newer version from the Microsoft web site. Microsoft will also continue developing Internet Explorer for other operating systems such as the Mac and Windows 3.1.

You can download the latest version of the Internet Explorer/Windows 98 Desktop from http://www.microsoft.com/ie.

Starting the Internet Explorer

Click the Internet Explorer icon on your Desktop to start the Internet Explorer. You can also start the Internet Explorer by clicking the Start button, pointing to Favorites, and then clicking a favorite web site.

In a My Computer window, click Favorites in the menu bar, and choose a favorite web site. You can also do this in an Explorer window. Both windows will turn into the Internet Explorer, and the Standard Buttons toolbar will change into its Internet version, which we refer to as the *Internet toolbar*.

Type a web address (a URL) in the Address bar in an Explorer window. The Explorer becomes the Internet Explorer.

Click a Channel button on the Channel Bar. Click a web URL in a Word document or an Outlook or Outlook Express e-mail message. A new Internet Explorer window opens up.

Click a file on your local hard disk that has an *htm* or *html* extension. The file is displayed in an Internet Explorer window. Click the Internet Explorer icon on the right end of the menu bar in an Explorer or My Computer window. This transforms the window into an Internet Explorer window and connects you to http://home.microsoft.com.

If you take any of these actions, you'll open up an Internet Explorer window. If the Standard Buttons toolbar is displayed, it will become the Internet toolbar to give you easy access to a number of Internet functions.

When you open up the Internet Explorer, display the View menu. Notice that the Internet Explorer window doesn't have a Folder Options command; it has an Internet Options command. The Internet Options dialog box allows you to set a number of Internet Explorer parameters.

You can take the Internet Explorer icon off of your Desktop. Right-click the Internet Explorer icon on your Desktop, click Properties, and click the Advanced tab. Clear the Show Internet Explorer Icon on the Desktop check box. Click OK. Click Start, Shut Down. Choose Restart, and then press and hold your Shift key as you click OK.

The Internet Explorer is a version of (or an extension of) the Explorer/My Computer window. You can transform either the Explorer or a My Computer window into the Internet Explorer. You can also transform the Internet Explorer into either the Explorer or a My Computer window.

New link, new window

If you want to open a new window when you jump to a new site, hold down the Shift key when you click the link. You'll then be able to see both the target site and the source page in different Internet Explorer windows.

You can also right-click a link and choose Open in New Window.

Channels

In earlier versions of the Internet Explorer, Microsoft proposed using the left pane as a *site map*. If Microsoft had pursued this idea, it would have asked Web site developers to create a special file that contained the structure of their web site, and Internet Explorer would have displayed this structure in the left pane.

As it turns out, the site map was superceded by the Channel Definition Format (CDF). Webmasters can easily designate which pages on their site are part of a channel, and they can add this information to existing sites. More information on CDF can be found at http://www.microsoft.com/standards/cdf-f.htm and http://www.microsoft.com/sitebuilder/workshop/prog/ie4/channels/cdf1-f.htm, or better still, at http://www.datachannel.com/channelworld/.

The Channel Bar, which is on your Active Desktop by default, gives you a quick way to get to web sites that conform to the CDF. Many of these sites provide time-sensitive information. When you click a Channel Bar button, the Internet Explorer opens in full-screen mode. The channel provider wants your complete attention. If the Internet Explorer doesn't open full-screen and you like this mode, click the Fullscreen button on the Internet Explorer toolbar.

If you want to find out what sites are available in addition to those so favored by Microsoft that they are on the Channel Bar, click the Channel Guide button in the Channel Bar. This opens an Internet Explorer window focused on the Microsoft Channel Guide web site. Once there, you can click any channel listed to go to it.

To get a channel working (to get information downloaded from it periodically), you first need to click one of the channel buttons. You have the option of pulling the channel's initial screen from your Windows 98 CD-ROM (if it is one of the favored channels), or from the channel's web site on the Internet. If you pull it off the CD-ROM, click the Add Active Channel button on the first web page to go to the channel's web site.

Clicking the Add Active Channel button brings up a dialog box that let's you subscribe to the channel. The term *subscribe* just means to download information periodically. You get to decide how often it is downloaded and at what time during the day, week, month, or whatever.

ActiveX documents

Drag and drop a Word document, Excel spreadsheet, or any other OLE 2-enabled document onto the Internet Explorer Address bar or menu bar.

The document is displayed in an Internet Explorer window. It looks just as it would appear inside the associated application (see Figure 9-1), toolbars and all. You can edit the document in the Internet Explorer just as you would in the application itself.

Using Internet Explorer, type the full path and filename of an OLE 2 document in the Internet Explorer's Address bar. Again, the document is displayed in the Internet Explorer window. To display or hide the Word toolbars, choose View, Toolbars.

If you are an Intranet webmaster, you don't have to convert all the documents you want to put up on the Intranet into HTML. People will be able to view the original documents quite easily in the Internet Explorer window. To view them, they'll need the OLE 2 application or a viewer such as Microsoft Word Viewer installed on their computer.

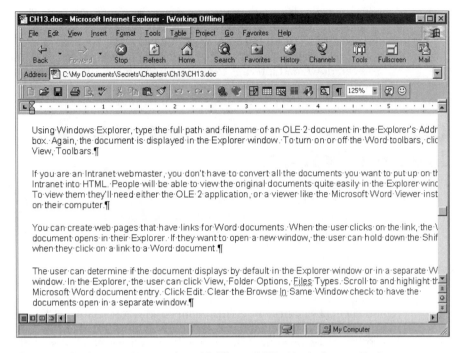

Figure 9-1: In-place word processing with Microsoft Word in the Internet Explorer.

You can create web pages that have links to Word documents. When you click this type of link, the Word document opens in your Internet Explorer. If you want to open the Word document in a new window, hold down the Shift key when you click the link.

You can also change the default so that Word documents automatically appear in a separate Word window instead of in the Internet Explorer window. To do this, click Start, Settings, Folder Options, and click the Files Types tab. Scroll to and highlight Microsoft Word Document in the Registered File Types list. Click the Edit button, and clear the Browse in Same Window check box.

Internet Explorer PowerToys

Microsoft programmers write a few little programs to help out as they create the big applications. The Windows project managers have been willing to round up these little gems and put them in a downloadable package of unsupported applets. Not everyone needs all their functionality, but if one of these little applets works to solve your problem, hey that's what it's all about.

To give you two examples of the applets in PowerToys, the Image Toggler is a button that appears on your Links toolbar. You click the button to quickly turn Web graphics on or off—great when you want to switch frequently between "fast" text-only mode and slower graphics-and-text. The QuickSearch feature lets you type a line in your Address bar to launch a particular search engine with a specific keyword. For example, typing **av software** launches the AltaVista search engine with *software* as the keyword. You can download Internet Explorer 4.0 PowerToys from http://www.microsoft.com/ie/ie40/?/ie/ie4/powertoys/main.htm.

Connecting to the Internet with the Internet Explorer

The Windows 98 Internet Explorer comes with the Internet Connection Wizard, which automates many of the steps required to create an Internet connection (as explained in "The Internet Connection Wizard" in Chapter 18). You can use the Wizard to create a connection, and then go back and manually check what the Wizard did by following the steps we detail in Chapter 18.

The Internet Connection Wizard creates a Dial-Up Networking connectoid for you if you connect to the Internet through a dial-up connection to an Internet service provider. This connectoid is automatically associated with the Internet Explorer, and it is called every time you click the Internet Explorer icon on your Desktop, or place an Internet address in the Address bar of an Explorer window.

The Wizard also installs and configures the Internet icon in your Control Panel. Clicking this icon displays the Internet Properties dialog box. The Dial-Up Networking connectoid that the Internet Connection Wizard created for you is specified in the Connection tab of this dialog box. If you have another connectoid that you want to use to call another Internet service provider instead of the one you originally created using the Internet Connection Wizard, you can specify it in this dialog box by clicking the Settings button.

You can also right-click the Internet Explorer icon on your Desktop and click Properties to display the Internet Properties dialog box. Then click the Connection tab, click the Settings button, and choose another DUN connectoid. To start the Internet Connection Wizard from the Internet Properties dialog box, click Connect instead of Settings.

If you set up your computer at work and find that when you take it home you can't browse the Internet, this may be because your computer is still trying to use the domain name server located at work. This domain name server is unavailable to you at home when you call through a dial-up Internet service provider.

To allow your Internet Explorer to find sites on the Internet while you are at home, you will want to disable the connection to the domain name server at work. Follow these steps:

STEPS

Disabling a Domain Name Server

Step 1. Click the Start button, point to Settings, and click Control Panel.

Step 2. Click the Network icon. Scroll down to TCP/IP -> Dial-Up Adapter. Click Properties.

Step 3. Click the DNS Configuration tab. Mark the Disable DNS option button, and click OK twice.

Step 4. You will be asked to restart Windows. Click OK.

We assume that you have correctly created a Dial-Up Networking connectoid for your local Internet service provider. The TCP/IP settings associated with this connectoid include a DNS setting, as detailed in "Service provider account information" in Chapter 18.

Internet Explorer, the 128-bit version

Internet Explorer comes in two flavors. One supports 40-bit (or weaker) encryption, and the other supports 128-bit (very strong) encryption. Because of federal government regulations restricting the export of products that incorporate 128-bit encryption, Microsoft normally ships the 40-bit version. You can, however, download the 128-bit version from the Microsoft web site (http://www.microsoft.com/ie/download/) if your IP address indicates that you live in the United States or Canada.

If you want to find out more about 40-bit versus 128-bit encryption, check out http://wellsfargo.com/per/services/security/encryption/.

In June of 1997, Microsoft obtained U.S. government (Department of the Interior) permission to incorporate, in a limited fashion, 128-bit encryption into the versions of its products that it ships overseas, including Internet Explorer. 128-bit encryption is enabled (switched on) in the Internet Explorer when you connect to a bank's web site, if the bank has a digital certificate on its server. Banks obtain their digital certificates through a third-party organization.

Only transactions with certified banks will be protected with 128-bit encryption if you are using the standard version of the Internet Explorer. If your bank isn't certified, your transactions will be encrypted using the 40-bit method. Again, this is because the U.S. government restricts the export of products with higher levels of encryption.

Can't download the 128-bit version?

The Microsoft web server checks to see if you have a valid IP address (that is, one in Canada or the U.S.) before it will ship the 128-bit version of the Internet Explorer. If it does not get a valid DNS address return from its query of your Internet service provider, it won't let you download this version. You know that this is the case if the DNS entry on the query form is blank.

Secret

Many Internet service providers keep their domain name servers behind firewalls for security reasons. The service provider's domain name server may not send your IP address to Microsoft's web server when requested. If you have this problem, contact your service provider and ask them to reconfigure their firewall to permit DNS address queries without compromising security.

Commands to connect to the Internet

Undocumented

You can start the Internet Explorer and connect to the Internet just by typing the address of the place you want to go in the Run dialog box. Click the Start button, and then click Run. Type a location such as the following:

ftp://ftp.microsoft.com

or

http://www.windows98.com

Secret

You don't need to type the http:// or the ftp://. If the resource is stored in your cache, an Internet Explorer window will open and you can cancel your dial-up Internet connection and display the resource from the cache.

Undocumented

If you want to log in to an FTP site with your username and password, type:

ftp://*username:password@address*/

For example, you could type ftp://davis:straub@coho.halcyon.com.

Tip

Want to send e-mail while you're using the Internet Explorer? Click in the Address bar (or click the Start button and then click Run). Type the following:

mailto:brian_livingston@infoworld.com

Then press Enter.

This will start Outlook Express, Windows Messaging, or whatever your default e-mail program is and open a New Message window addressed to the person whose e-mail address you typed after mailto:.

You can send a friend a document that contains the shortcuts to your favorite places on the Internet. You can put shortcuts in Word or WordPad documents, and you can send these documents as e-mail attachments. You can also put URL shortcuts in Windows Messaging or Outlook Express e-mail messages. Just copy and paste or drag and drop them from your Favorites folder.

Managing downloads from the Internet

The Windows 98 Internet Explorer provides only basic functions for downloading files from Internet servers. Internet Explorer for the Mac comes with a slick download-management system. You can add a download manager for your Windows 98 version by going to any one of the following sites:

Find FileHound at http://www.nexi.com/albinofrog or Getright at http://www.headlightsw.com/ or check out the download manager at http://www.download.com.

Secret

Want to find out where the Internet Explorer will download files from the Internet? Open RegEdit and go to HKEY_CURRENT_USER\Software\Microsoft\Internet Explorer. Double-click Download Directory in the right-pane. Change it to a new folder name.

You can also just download a new file from the Internet and save it to a new location. This will update the Download Directory value.

Finding web sites

Do you want to find a specific web site?

In an Internet Explorer window, click in the Address bar, type **find**, **search**, or **?**, type a space, and then type the name of the company or organization whose site you want to find. If the name has a space in it, forget typing the **find**, **search**, or **?**, and just put double quote marks around the name.

This will automatically start a search for the company or organization on Yahoo. You can set which search site is accessed using TweakUI. You'll find the option in the General tab.

Tip

What Internet Explorer won't do is go to a web site when you just type the web site's name without the *www* and the *com,* unless you press Ctrl+Enter after you enter the name.

Customizing the Internet Explorer Address field

The Internet Explorer, by default, tries to complete the name that you type in the Address bar. There are a number of settings that determine how it guesses at the names, and these can set the Internet Explorer up to make the wrong guesses, so you might have to ask them to back off a bit.

The Internet Explorer completes an address if you start from the first letters of an address and you have previously visited the site. For example, you type *w* and the Internet Explorer finishes (as you are about to type the next *w*) with the last web site that you visited. You keep typing and the completed address changes to match and complete what you have typed with its best guess. You can set whether the Internet Explorer will try to complete your address or not by choosing View, Internet Options, clicking the Advanced tab, and marking or clearing the Use AutoComplete check box.

The Internet Explorer will also search the Internet domain name servers using the common root domain names (com, org, edu, gov) when it fails to find a specified site. For example, if you type www.netscape.org, the search will fail, and the Internet Explorer will then look for http://www.netscape.com, which it will find.

The Internet Explorer may run into trouble out on the Internet looking for these other root domain names. It may appear to hang as it searches. If you want to stop it from searching, choose View, Internet Options, click the Advanced tab, and clear the Autoscan Common Root Domains check box under Searching.

If you find that the Internet Explorer is adding parts of names that it shouldn't, you can ask it not to by choosing View, Internet Options, clicking the Advanced tab, and marking the Never Search option button under Searching.

Tip

If you type the main name of a web site in the Internet Explorer Address bar — *Netscape,* for example — and then press Ctrl+Enter, the Internet Explorer adds *www.* before the name and *.com* after it.

Creating custom versions of the Internet Explorer

Microsoft makes its version of the Windows 98 Internet Explorer. You can make your own version. Download the Internet Explorer Administration Kit (IEAK). With this program, you can set up the default start and search pages, the pages for the Quick Links in the Links toolbar, the logos and title bars, and so on. How about your own animated icon in the upper-right corner? To apply for the IEAK CD-ROM, sign up at https://ieak.microsoft.com/release2/ default.asp.

You can customize your links and your home page without having to use the IEAK. By making these adjustments, you can actually make these links useful and not just ways for Microsoft to draw you into its fold.

To change your links, open your Windows Explorer to \Windows\Favorites\ Links. Drag and drop shortcuts to URLs from your other Favorites folders into the Links folder. Delete any shortcuts in the Links folder that you no longer want to use as links.

To replace the globe icon, you'll need to add two strings to your Registry. Navigate to HKEY_CURRENT_USER\Software\Microsoft\Internet Explorer\ Toolbar, and add the string values BrandBitmap and SmBrandBitmap to this key. Give these two values the path and filenames of the *bmp* files that contain the replacement graphics.

Underlining hyperlinks

By default, hyperlinks on web pages are displayed as underlined in most web browsers. And if you have chosen single-clicking (Start, Settings, Folder Options), you will notice that as you move your mouse pointer over the icons on your Desktop, they also are underlined, mimicking hyperlinks in web pages.

You can determine when file and folder names, shortcuts, and so on are underlined in the right pane of the Explorer, in a My Computer window, and on the Desktop. To get this to work, you need to make changes in two separate dialog boxes — another triumph of user-interface engineering.

STEPS

Setting Up Underlining

Step 1. Click the Internet Explorer icon on the Desktop, choose View, Internet Options, and click the Advanced tab. Scroll down to Underline Links.

Step 2. Mark the option button for the type of underlining that you want for web pages. Click OK.

Step 3. Click your My Computer icon on the Desktop.

Step 4. Choose View, Folder Options, mark the Custom, Based on Settings That You Choose option button, and then click the Settings button.

Step 5. In the Custom Settings dialog box, mark Single-Click to Open an Item (Point to Select) and either Underline Icon Titles Consistent with My Browser Settings, or Underline Icon Titles Only When I Point at Them. Click OK.

Because underlining Desktop items can depend on how you view hyperlinks in Internet Explorer, you'll first want to set how underlining will work when you are using Internet Explorer to view a web page or an HTML document. In Internet Explorer, you can choose to have hyperlinks always underlined, never underlined, or underlined only when you rest your mouse pointer over them. (This last option is called *hover*.)

If you choose Single-Click to Open an Item (Point to Select) and Underline Icon Titles Only When I Point at Them, it doesn't matter what your browser settings are. You can have no underlining on a web page, but you'll have hover underlining on the Desktop and in the right-pane of the Explorer when viewing files and folders. This is true even if you are viewing your files and folders as a web page (in an Explorer or My Computer window, click View, As Web Page).

If you choose Underline Icon Titles Consistent with My Browser Settings, and you have chosen to always underline hyperlinks in the Internet Explorer, all your file and folder names will always be underlined. You might think this over a bit.

Edit on the Internet Explorer toolbar

You get the Internet toolbar when you start the Internet Explorer. See "Starting the Internet Explorer."

Undocumented

If you have installed FrontPage or other Microsoft HTML editors, you'll notice that the Internet toolbar has an additional button—the Edit button. If you click this button, you can edit the page that you are currently viewing in the Internet Explorer.

If you don't have the Edit button and wish you did, here's how to get it:

STEPS

Putting the Edit Button on the Internet Toolbar

Step 1. Click My Computer on the Desktop. Choose View, Folder Options, and click the File Types tab.

Step 2. Scroll down to Microsoft MHTML Document 4.0. Click the Edit button, and then click the New button.

Step 3. In the Action field, type **&Edit**. In the Application Used to Perform Action field, either click the Browse button or type the path to your HTML editor. If you don't have one, type **C:\Windows\Notepad.exe**.

Step 4. Click the Internet Explorer icon on the Desktop. You'll see the Edit button in the Internet toolbar.

If you are using Notepad to edit HTML documents and you install FrontPage or FrontPage Express, it will change the action associated with the Edit button. You can switch it back to Notepad using the steps above.

If you install Netscape Communicator, you may lose your Edit button. You can get it back using these steps.

Make history a quick link

Microsoft includes a few of its web sites as Quick Links, that is, buttons on the Links toolbar. You can display the Links toolbar in the Internet Explorer window or on the Desktop. Right-click any of the toolbars (including the menu) in an Explorer, Internet Explorer, or My Computer window. Click Links.

If you display the Links toolbar on the Desktop, you can connect it to the Taskbar or let it stand alone as a floating toolbar. If the Links toolbar isn't already displayed, right-click the Taskbar, click Toolbars, and click Links. To move it away from the Taskbar, place your mouse pointer at the left edge of the Links toolbar, and drag the toolbar to anywhere on your Desktop.

You can decide what buttons go on the Links toolbar. They can be links to Internet URLs or to local files or folders. You can drag and drop shortcuts to the Links toolbar or right-click existing items to delete or cut them.

One quick way to get to your History folder is to put it on the Links toolbar. To do so, take the following steps:

STEPS
Putting History on the Links Toolbar

Step 1.   Click the Internet Explorer icon on your Desktop.

Step 2.   Type **c:\windows\history** in the Address bar and press Enter.

Step 3.   Right-click the Taskbar and click Toolbars (or right-click the Internet Explorer menu or toolbar), and click Links if it isn't already checked.

Step 4.   Drag the history folder icon at the left edge of the Address bar to the Links toolbar, and drop it there.

If you haven't used TweakUI to turn off "Shortcut to . . ." you'll find this prefix in your new History button on the Links toolbar. To keep this from happening in the future, click your TweakUI shortcut on your Desktop (or in the Control Panel), click the Explorer tab, and clear the Prefix "Shortcut to" on New Shortcuts check box. You'll have to rename the History button in the \Windows\Favorites\Links folder.

You'll find the shortcuts on the Links toolbar at \Windows\Favorites\Links. You can use the Explorer to move any shortcut into and out of this folder. (In general, toolbars should just contain shortcuts. You could put anything you like in the Links toolbar, but it's really designed to store shortcuts to documents, folders, and web sites.)

Stop dialing up my Internet service provider

If you connect to the Internet through one of your Dial-Up Networking connectoids, you automatically start up the connectoid that is connected to your Internet Explorer whenever you choose to browse the Internet. This happens when you click the Internet Explorer icon on your Desktop or click the Start button and choose any of the Internet web pages in the Favorites submenu.

You can turn off this capability if you'd rather connect to the Internet manually by clicking the appropriate connectoid when you want to connect. To disconnect the connectoid from the Internet Explorer, take the following steps:

STEPS

Disconnecting the Connectoid from the Internet Explorer

Step 1.   Right-click the Internet Explorer icon on the Desktop, click Properties, and then click the Connection tab.

Step 2.   Mark the check box labeled Connect to the Internet Using a Local Area Network (even if you aren't connected to a local area network).

Step 3.   Click the OK button.

Now when you want to connect to the Internet, do so by clicking your DUN connectoid. Once you are connected, you can use your Internet Explorer to browse the Internet.

Favorites and URL Shortcuts

A URL (Uniform Resource Locator) is a unique identifier for a web page or other resource on the Internet. Windows 98 maintains a list of the URLs for your favorite sites. Your *favorites* are actually shortcuts stored in the \Windows\Favorites folder.

You can store whatever you like in the Favorites subfolders, but we suggest limiting what you put in these folders to shortcuts (either to URLs or to other folders or documents). You can put copies of URL shortcuts on your Desktop and start your Internet Explorer by clicking the shortcut's icon. You can also create shortcuts to URLs on the fly as you're browsing. See "URL shortcuts" later in this chapter for more information.

Secret

You can drag and drop (move) your Favorites folder wherever you like (say, on a drive other than the drive that contains the \Windows folder), and the Internet Explorer will track its location. The current Favorites folder location is stored in the Registry at HKEY_CURRENT_USER\Software\ Microsoft\Windows\CurrentVersion\Explorer\Shell Folders and at HKEY_CURRENT_USER\Software\Microsoft\Windows\CurrentVersion\ Explorer\User Shell Folders, if you move it.

You can use TweakUI to see how the Registry keeps track of the Favorites folder location. Drag and drop the \Windows\Favorites folder to a new location. Click your TweakUI icon in the Control Panel, and click the General tab. Choose Favorites in the Folders drop-down list. Notice that the new location is displayed in the Location field. You can also use TweakUI to switch from one folder of favorites to another. See how in the next section.

To create a shortcut to your favorites, open an Explorer window and navigate to \Windows\Favorites. Right-drag and drop your Favorites folder onto your Desktop. Choose Create Shortcut(s) Here.

You can get to your favorites from the Start menu, the My Computer menu, the Internet Explorer menu, and the Explorer menu. You'll also find a Favorites button in the Internet toolbar. This button opens a Favorites pane on the left side of the client area of the Internet Explorer. If you click View, Explorer Bar, Favorites, this same Favorites pane appears. You can right-click the favorites in this pane to open their associated context menus.

Organizing your favorites

You can divide your Favorites folder into subfolders organized around common topics, and then place shortcuts to your favorite sites in these subfolders. To create Favorites subfolders, choose Favorites, Organize Favorites in an Explorer window. Right-click an empty part of the Organize Favorites window, and then choose New, Folder from the context menu. (You can also click the Create New Folder button on the Organize Favorites toolbar.)

Tip

You can also open a window to display the contents of your Favorites folder by holding down the Shift key when you click the Organize Favorites command. Unlike the Organize Favorites window, this is a regular folder window focused on one of the favorites subfolders.

You can create subfolders for your Favorites folder in any Explorer window. You can move these folders around (after all, they are just folders containing shortcuts), but if you want them to show up under the Favorites menu item, you need to leave them stored under the Favorites folder. You can subdivide the Favorites folder's subfolders, and you can drag shortcuts from folder to folder. You can also rename shortcuts. This is helpful because the default name of a shortcut is often not that meaningful. (The default name is whatever the webmaster came up with for the document at the specific URL to which the shortcut is linked.)

Undocumented

What you can't do from an Explorer window is drag and drop a file or folder into the Favorites folder itself. (To move a file or folder to the Favorites folder, you need to use the Organize Favorites window.) But you can create new Favorites subfolders in an Explorer window, and then drag and drop files or folders into these subfolders.

Tip

You'll notice that your Favorites list contains a shortcut to your My Documents folder. This shortcut gives you a way to use the Favorites menu item to navigate to your My Documents folder. Of course, you can add other shortcuts to local files or folders to your Favorites folder as well. Just open an Explorer window, navigate to the file or folder that you want to create a shortcut for, and choose Favorites, Add to Favorites.

You can have multiple lists of favorites. One way to do this is to drag and drop a copy of your \Windows\Favorites to the new location. Rename the new folder, and then edit the contents of both folders. You can then use TweakUI to switch back and forth between folders, first designating one as your Favorites folder, and then the other. To switch the favorites folder, click the TweakUI icon, click the General tab, and choose Favorites in the Folder drop-down list. Click the Change Location button, and then browse to the new favorites folder.

URL shortcuts

The Internet Explorer keeps track of web sites using shortcuts to URLs. These shortcuts have an extension of *url* instead of the standard *lnk* extension for Windows shortcuts.

URL shortcuts store more information about the URLs than just their values. (See Figure 9-2.) Internet Explorer uses this additional information to help you manage your shortcuts as well as to let you view web sites offline.

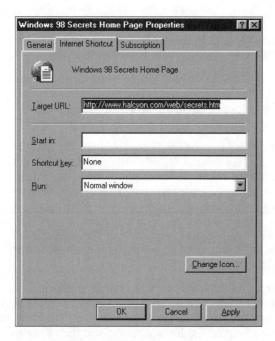

Figure 9-2: The Properties dialog box for a URL shortcut. Notice the tabs for additional properties.

You can create a URL shortcut to a web site just by displaying the site in an Internet Explorer window, and choosing Favorites, Add to Favorites. If you want to place the shortcut in an existing or new subfolder of the Favorites folder, click the Create In button. To use an existing subfolder, just select it and then click OK. To create a new subfolder, click the New Folder button.

If you would rather put the shortcut directly on the Desktop, right-click an area on the web page that doesn't include a graphic or a link to another location, and choose Create Shortcut from the context menu. Or, click File, Send, Shortcut To Desktop.

You can also drag the icon at the left end of the Address bar to the Desktop to create a shortcut to the web page. If you right-drag this icon, you have the choice of creating a shortcut or an Active Desktop item.

Tip

To create a shortcut to a link (a jump to another URL) in a web page, drag the link to the Desktop. You can later click this shortcut to open an Internet Explorer window and go to the indicated location on the Web.

Tip

You don't have to put URL shortcuts in the Favorites folder or one of its subfolders. If you do, then the shortcuts are accessible from the Favorites toolbar button or menu item in an Explorer window. But you are free to put them wherever you like. You can create many folders of URL shortcuts, and place shortcuts to these folders on your Desktop.

Capturing URLs in a frame

Normally when you display a web page or site, its URL appears in the Address bar. However, if you open a web page that uses frames (panes within the Internet Explorer client window), and then navigate within the main, or largest, frame to a page on another site, the Address bar will not update to show you the URL for the page you're currently viewing. This happens because web designers often use frames as a way to let you view other people's pages without leaving their own site. This allows them to keep their text, logos, navigational buttons, and graphics in view (in smaller frames around the main frame) even as you're viewing pages at other locations.

Undocumented

You may want to know the new URL for a page you're viewing in a frame, if for no other reason than to get out of the frame at the original site and onto the new site of the page you're viewing. Here's how to capture the URL:

STEPS

Finding the URL for a Site That's Been "Framed"

Step 1. Right-click an open spot in the frame that contains the web page whose URL you want to know. Select Properties.

Step 2. You'll now see the URL. If you want to jump to the site, highlight the URL, and press Ctrl+C to copy it.

Step 3. Click in Internet Explorer's Address field, press Ctrl+V to paste the URL, and then press Enter.

Deleting typed URLs in the Address field

If you type a URL in the Address field in Internet Explorer, you can go back later and choose that URL from a drop-down list attached to the Address field. This list lets you scroll through previously typed URLs to pick the one you want. (Sometimes URLs are put on this list that you didn't type—they get "typed in" automatically.)

Undocumented

You can edit this list or delete it using your Registry editor. Just navigate to HKEY_CURRENT_USER\Software\Microsoft\Internet Explorer\TypedURLs. You'll notice a list of URLs in the right pane of the Registry editor. To delete an entry, select it (click its url*x* name in the Name column) and press Delete. To edit an entry, double-click its url*x* name.

Converting Netscape Navigator bookmarks to favorites

If you install a version of Internet Explorer on Windows 95, it looks to see that you have Netscape Navigator installed. If you do, it shaves 5 percent off the speed of your processor. No, no, just joking. It automatically converts the Netscape Navigator bookmarks to Internet Explorer favorites.

If you have installed Netscape Navigator on a Windows 98 computer and you want to convert your Netscape bookmarks to Internet Explorer favorites, you can do it either one step at a time or in batch mode.

STEPS

Converting Navigator Bookmarks—the Manual Method

Step 1.   In the Explorer, navigate to your Netscape folder (in the Program Files folder) and find the file Bookmark.htm.

Step 2.   Click this file to open it.

Step 3.   Right-click a bookmark in the Bookmark file, and then click Add To Favorites on the menu that appears.

Step 4.   Repeat step 3 for each bookmark you want to convert.

Undocumented

If you want to convert all your Netscape Navigator bookmarks at once, you can download the applet that automatically converts them when Windows 95 users install Internet Explorer 4.0 on their computers from ftp://ftp.microsoft.com/Softlib/Mslfiles/WINBM2FV.EXE.

You can also use a shareware package called Bookmark Importer at http://www.webobj.com/bookmark, and one called Bookmark Manager at http://ourworld.compuserve.com/homepages/Edgar_Hofer/BookMM.htm.

Saving Web Pages on Your Hard Disk

You can save a web page just by navigating to it and then choosing File, Save As on the menu. You can also save a target page by right-clicking its link in the source page and choosing Save Target As.

Tip

If you would prefer to name a web page you're saving with its title (likely a name that appears at the top of the document) instead of its filename, first highlight the title and press Ctrl+C to copy it to the Clipboard. Then issue the File, Save As command, click in the File Name text box, and press Ctrl+V to paste in the title.

You create web pages using a markup language called HTML (Hypertext Markup Language). It's called a *markup language* because you use it to mark up the plain text of a web page with *tags* that tell web browsers such as Windows 98 Internet Explorer how to format the page and what links to include where. The term *HTML document* (or *HTML page*) refers to the file that contains the plain text and HTML tags (or *source code*) required to display a web page. These files have an extension of *htm* or *html*. You place a graphic image in a web page by inserting a tag in the underlying HTML document that tells the browser the name of the graphics file to display, and its location on the web server.

Unfortunately, when you save a web page with File, Save As, the Internet Explorer saves the text in the page (the HTML document itself), but not the graphic images displayed in the page, because these are actually separate files. You can save the individual graphics files one at a time by right-clicking the graphic and then choosing Save Picture As. This can get tiresome, however, and even if you save all the graphics in a web page this way, you probably still won't be able to open the saved HMTL document at a later date and see both its text and graphics.

The reason for this is that graphic images are usually stored in a subdirectory of the directory on the web server that originally stored the HTML page, and the graphics tags in the HTML page usually (although not always) contain relative pointers to that subdirectory (which is often called Images).

Undocumented

If you have saved the graphics from a web page in the same folder as the HTML page itself on your hard disk, Internet Explorer probably won't be able to find the graphics when you open the HTML page because the graphics tags in the page most likely contain pointers to a subdirectory on the web server that doesn't exist on your computer. If you are familiar with HTML, you could use an HTML editor (or a plain text editor such as Notepad) to view the HMTL source code for the page. If you see relative references to a particular directory, move the graphics files to a subfolder of the same name on your own hard disk. This would be quite a pain, however. It sure would be great if you could just grab a site and have it display correctly after you store it on your hard disk.

There are numerous third-party applications that get around this problem by saving the contents of web pages outside of the Internet temporary file cache, and letting you redisplay them later in their entirety (both text and graphics) without having to connect to the Internet (see http://www.

windows98.com). These applications allow you to store the saved web pages outside of the Internet Explorer cache folders. This means they won't disappear as the cache grows past its limits and Windows deletes older cached web pages and graphics.

Internet Explorer does a good job of displaying a previously cached web site as long as it's still there in the cache. If the web site is on your list of favorites, your history list, or your subscribed list, you can click its name when you are offline, and remain offline while you view the page. Internet Explorer displays the site for you by retrieving the last downloaded instance of this site from the cache.

The problem with letting Internet Explorer display previous web pages it that it relies on the cache to continue to store the web pages locally until you want to view them again. It may be a while before you get back to one of your saved web sites, so your \Windows\Temporary Internet Files folder may no longer contain the pages that you want to see.

One way to give the page a better chance of still being there when you come back to it is to increase the maximize size of the Internet cache folder. Right-click your Internet Explorer icon on your Desktop, click Properties, and click the Settings button in the General tab. Move the slider to the right to increase the amount of disk space allocated to the cache.

Secret

One truly tricky way to save web pages in all their glory is to mail them to yourself using Outlook Express as your default mailer. Outlook Express uses Microsoft's version of HTML (MHTML) to store all the files that make up a web page in one *eml* file. The text, graphics, and sound files that make up a web page are all there. Tom Koch, who answers lots of questions on the Microsoft Outlook Express newsgroup, let us on to this neat little secret.

You'll have to use Outlook Express to view the web page if it is stored as an *eml* file, but you can store it either in your Outlook Express mail folders or in your Explorer folders. Once you have received the web page through e-mail, you can choose File, Save As and save it wherever you like on your hard disk.

To send a complete web page to yourself, open the web page in the Internet Explorer, and choose File, Send, Page By E-Mail. If Outlook Express is your default e-mail program, a New Message window will appear on your Desktop. Be sure to address the web page to yourself.

Secret

Now for the real trick. You can rename the web page with a new extension after you have received it in Outlook Express. Click File, Save As and save the web page with the *htm* extension. Now you can view this web page with the Internet Explorer; just click it. The always-clever Costa Costas at http://www.biznet.com.gr/ sail/ isa/ index.htm taught us this one.

Internet Explorer drag and drop links

It's easy to save links and graphics files as you browse the web if you open up Internet Explorer with two panes. You can do this by right-clicking the Internet Explorer icon on your Desktop, and choosing Explore. Starting

Internet Explorer this way adds the All Folders option to the View, Explorer Bar submenu and automatically selects it, so you see your folders listed in the left pane.

As you browse web sites in the right pane, you can drag and drop links — either to web pages or to files you want to download — and graphics into appropriate folders in the left pane. Links are stored as URL shortcuts. If you later click a shortcut for a link to a web page, Internet Explorer takes you to the linked web site. If you click a shortcut for a link to a file you want to download, you start the download process. Graphics files are copied from your cache and stored in the folder into which you drag them.

Drag and drop images

If you are displaying a web site or HTML document in your Internet Explorer, you can drag an image on the web page to the title bar or Address bar to display the image by itself. This is not the same as a web page *thumbnail*, which is a small version of an image that leads to a larger, more detailed version when you click it.

Undocumented

This doesn't work if you are viewing a page constructed using the Microsoft HTML format (MHTML), which includes graphics in the same file as the text file that makes up the web page. These files have the *mht* extension and are discussed in "Saving web pages on your hard disk" later in this chapter.

You'll can also drag links or mail addresses from the displayed page onto the title bar or Address bar as a way to command Internet Explorer to go to the linked page or to open your default e-mail client. Of course, you can also just do this by clicking the links on the web page.

Saving graphics off the Internet

Do you want to save a web-based graphic that you are viewing in Internet Explorer? Right-click it, choose Save Picture As, and then give it a path and a name. If you don't save a graphics file as you're viewing it, you can save it later from the cache. When Internet Explorer first downloads a graphics file, it automatically caches (saves) it in the \Windows\Temporary Internet Files folder. You can find the file in this folder and save it permanently by copying it to another location.

If you want to turn a graphic in a web page into wallpaper on your Desktop, right-click the graphic and choose Set As Wallpaper.

Internet Security

Windows 98 Internet Explorer's "security levels" — designed by Microsoft to protect you from the Internet as you surf the World Wide Web — have caused consternation among some Windows users. There are ways to keep Internet Explorer's warning messages from popping up every time you move from one web site to another. If you know where you're going on the Internet—and you don't need a 'Net nanny—follow the advice in the next three sections and you'll see far fewer dialog boxes interrupting your journeys.

If you see a little padlock on the right side of your status bar, you know that you are on a site that has some sort of security. If you want to know just what sort, right-click in a clear area of the page you are viewing, choose Properties, and then click the Security tab.

You can get Microsoft's latest word on security at http://www.microsoft.com/ie/security/?/ie/ security/ie4security.htm. However, you might also try the Unofficial Microsoft Internet Explorer Security FAQ at http://www.nwnetworks.com/iesf.html.

If you've looked at the \Windows\Temporary Internet Files folder, you'll notice the random names for the four subfolders. This is a security feature you're seeing. It's theoretically possible for someone to embed a destructive program in a web page and then run it from the cache, but only if he or she has the exact pathname. This is not as easy with four random subfolder names.

Internet Explorer's security options

In the Internet Explorer, choose View, Internet Options, and click the Security tab. Select Internet Zone in the Zone drop-down list, click the Custom option button, and then click the Settings button to display the Security Settings dialog box, as shown in Figure 9-3.

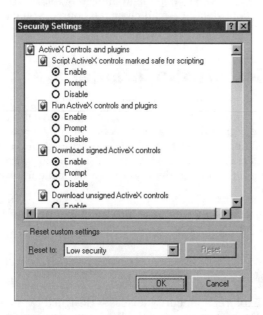

Figure 9-3: Security settings for the Internet Explorer.

In this dialog box, you can see some of the assumptions Microsoft has built into Windows 98. If you select the Low default settings, these are the values you get. All types of data are acceptable to Internet Explorer under these defaults, except ActiveX controls that are not "signed" or are not marked "safe."

Microsoft's security model divides Internet sites into four different types, or *zones*:

1. Local Intranet Zone — Web sites within your own company

2. Trusted Sites Zone — Sites you expect won't contain a computer virus or harmful code

3. Restricted Sites Zone — Sites that *do* contain the potential risk of viruses and antisocial behaviors

4. Internet Zone — Everything else

The View, Internet Options dialog box allows you to set a different level of security for each zone: High, Medium, Low, or Custom. You will need to add the web sites by name in the first three zones for this security system to work.

You may find it easier to simply pick the set of security rules you think you can live with, and configure the Internet Zone accordingly. All of the sites you visit will be subject to those rules — unless you go out of your way to list particular sites in the Trusted or Restricted category.

Beneath your level

Choosing the security level you're comfortable with isn't too hard. Table 9-1 shows the choices you're making when you adopt a High, Medium, or Low security setting:

Table 9-1   Internet Explorer's Security Settings

	High	*Medium*	*Low*
Run ActiveX controls and plug-ins	Disable	Enable	Enable
Download signed ActiveX controls	Disable	Prompt	Enable
Download unsigned ActiveX controls	Disable	Prompt	Prompt
Script ActiveX controls not "safe"	Disable	Prompt	Prompt
Java permissions (security level)	High	Medium	Low
Active scripting	Enable	Enable	Enable
Scripting of Java applets	Disable	Enable	Enable
File downloads	Disable	Enable	Enable

(continued)

Table 9-1 *(Continued)*

	High	*Medium*	*Low*
Font downloads	Disable	Prompt	Enable
Submit non-encrypted form data	Prompt	Prompt	Enable
Launching applications and files	Disable	Prompt	Enable
Installation of desktop items	Disable	Prompt	Enable
Drag and drop or copy and paste files	Prompt	Enable	Enable

If you feel fairly confident about your ability to notice when a rogue web site is messing around in files it should not be getting into, you may want to set your security level to Low. This enables all behaviors of web sites, except that Internet Explorer will still prompt you with a dialog box prior to acting on ActiveX controls and scripts that are unsigned or not marked as safe — in other words, the ones that do not carry an "electronic certificate" acting as a kind of Good Housekeeping seal.

You can even turn off the warnings for suspect ActiveX controls by resetting all defaults to Low. To do this, click the Custom option button, click the Settings button, choose Low Security in the Reset To drop-down list, click the Reset button, and then choose Enable under Download Unsigned ActiveX Controls and Initialize and Script ActiveX Controls Not Marked As Safe. But with these two cases, it probably makes sense to remain on the Prompt security level, since the whole premise of electronic certificates is to distinguish between ActiveX controls developed by reputable sources and those that might not be so reputable.

In addition to the security settings in the Security tab of the View, Internet Options dialog box, there are others to be found in the Advanced tab of the same dialog box. Scroll down to the Security heading to display the choices shown in Figure 9-4.

PCT and SSL refer to Private Communications Technology and Secure Sockets Layer. These are two encryption standards that let you enter sensitive information such as credit card numbers in web page forms. There's little reason to turn these settings off, unless you want to send out your credit card numbers as plain text.

Do Not Save Encrypted Pages to Disk turns off some of Windows 98's caching, which could hurt your Internet browsing performance.

We recommend clearing Warn If Changing Between Secure and Not Secure Mode, unless you've turned off PCT or SSL for some reason. We suggest that you keep Check for Certificate Revocation turned off, and keep Warn About Invalid Site Certificates turned on.

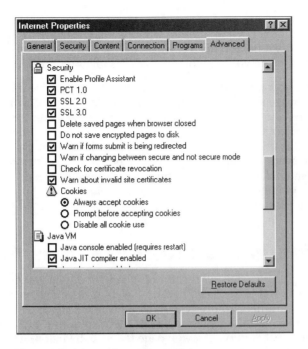

Figure 9-4: Advanced security settings.

Where are the cookies?

The companies that webmasters work for want to keep track of who visits their sites and just what it is that they looked at or did there. One way webmasters can do this is to store a little bit of information on your hard disk that is accessible to them the next time you come around. If you fill out a form when you are at a site, the information goes into the company's transaction-processing database, but some or all of it might also get placed back on your computer, in the form of a *cookie*.

Tasty bits of data, or cookies, are stored on your computer, ready and able to be used by the companies and individuals that own the web sites you visit. Microsoft likes to cite its MSN web site as an example of a web page that is customizable. It can present you with the types of information you have selected (from a rather anemic menu) the next time you go to the site. MSN does this by storing your preferences on your computer as a nice big cookie.

Where's the cookie jar? \Windows\Cookies. The cookie filenames are usually your host name followed by an @ symbol, and then the name of the web site. The files have a *txt* extension and they are readable, but they don't make much sense.

If you have your Internet Explorer set to warn you about incoming cookies, you'll get a cookie alert message. You can choose whether to take the cookie or not. If you want to just take the cookies, you can turn off this warning mechanism by choosing View, Internet Options, and clicking the Advanced tab. Under Security, Cookies, mark Always Accept Cookies. If you don't want to have any cookies on your computer, mark Disable All Cookie Use.

If you want more cookie control, check out Anonymous Cookie from Luckman Interactive at http://www.luckman.com. Another utility that deals with cookies and allows you to accept or reject them on a site-specific basis (instead of all or nothing) is Cookie Pal, available from http://www.kburra. com. Cookie Pal is free for 30 days, after which it's $15. The controversy over cookies has spawned a number of web pages, one of which, http://www. illuminatus.com/cookie.fcgi, tells you how many times you've visited the site (using cookies, of course). A more thorough description is at http://www.cdt. org; click Privacy Issues.

Corrupted Files in the Internet Cache Folder

Tip

The Internet Explorer caches quite a bit of the material you gather off the Internet. This makes it faster to go back to a web page you've recently visited, because Internet Explorer can open it from your disk instead of retrieving it from the Internet again. The Internet Explorer always checks to see if it has the latest version of a web page in its cache before it opens it. If it discovers that the page has been updated on the web site since it was cached, it retrieves the updated version instead of using the cached copy. To make sure that you have the latest information from a site, you can force the Internet Explorer to retrieve a new copy of a web page instead of using a copy from the cache. Just choose View, Refresh or press the F5 key.

You can determine whether Internet Explorer refreshes a web page every time you view it, just when you start the Internet Explorer, or not until you press F5. In an Internet Explorer window, choose View, Internet Options, click the General tab, click the Settings button, and choose the desired option at the top of the Settings dialog box.

You can also set the size of the Internet cache folder (\Windows\Temporary Internet Files) in the Settings dialog box. Slide the slider under Amount of Disk Space to Use to a percentage of the hard disk that you are willing to use for caching these Internet files.

Want to view what is in your cache? Click the View Files button in the Settings dialog box. If you order the files by Internet address, all the files from the same site will show up next to each other.

If some of the files in your Internet cache are corrupt, this can lead to a number of different error messages and Internet Explorer crashes. These include errors indicating cross-linked files and Kernel32.dll errors. If the errors are not so bad that you can't start your Internet Explorer, click the Internet Explorer icon, choose View, Internet Options, and click the Delete Files button in the General tab. You should also click the Clear History button.

If you still have similar error messages, take the following steps:

STEPS

Deleting the Internet Cache files

Step 1.   Click the Start button, choose Shut Down, select Restart in MS-DOS Mode, and click OK.

Step 2.   At the DOS prompt, type **Attrib -s c:\Windows\Tempor~1** and press Enter.

Step 3.   At the DOS prompt type **Deltree \Windows\Tempor~1** and press Enter.

Step 4.   Type **exit** and press Enter.

This will delete the cache files folder. This folder will be recreated when you restart Windows 98.

You can tell Internet Explorer to store its cached files in a different folder. This might be a good idea if you have limited space on the drive that contains the \Windows folder.

To specify a different folder for your cached web pages, right-click the Internet Explorer icon on your Desktop, choose Properties, click the General tab, click the Settings button, and then click the Move Folder button. In the Browse for Folder dialog box, highlight the desired folder and click OK. You have to restart Windows for the change to take effect. Note that when you specify a new cache folder, the Internet Explorer deletes all the cached files from the original folder.

Corrupt History folder

Undocumented

If you open your History folder (click the History button on the Internet toolbar) and find that there are no URLs listed, you have a corrupt History folder (unless you haven't yet started exploring the Internet with the Internet Explorer). To solve this problem, click the Start button, click Run, type **Regsvr32.exe/u C:\Windows\System\cachevu.dll**, and click OK. Next, click the Start button, click Run, type **Regsvr32.exe C:\Windows\System\cachevu.dll**, and click OK.

Undocumented

If you get error messages stating that there is not enough memory when you try to view the History folder, you might have too many entries for the Internet Explorer to handle correctly. If clicking your Clear History button (View, Internet Options, General, Clear History) doesn't get rid of these error messages, take the following steps:

STEPS

Fixing a History Folder That Is Too Big

Step 1.   Click the Start button, choose Shut Down, select Restart in MS-DOS Mode, and click OK.

Step 2.   At the DOS prompt, type **Attrib -s c:\Windows\Tempor~1** and press Enter.

Step 3.   Type **Deltree \Windows\Tempor~1** and press Enter.

Step 4.   Type **Attrib -s c:\Windows\History** and press Enter.

Step 5.   Type **Deltree \Windows\History** and press Enter.

Step 6.   Type **exit** and press Enter.

Step 7.   Click the Start button, click Run, type **Regsvr32.exe/u C:\Windows\System\cachevu.dll** and click OK.

Step 8.   Click the Start button, click Run, type **Regsvr32.exe C:\Windows\System\cachevu.dll** and click OK.

Regsvr32 registers applications in your Registry. It finds the target code in Cachevu.dll. It creates the History and Temporary Internet Files folders if they are not present, and then initializes them by creating a copy of Desktop.ini with the proper pointer to the registered objects. It also creates the history index files (Mm*.dat).

After you run Regsvr32, you might discover that the Desktop.ini file in your History folder has been deleted. As a precaution, you might want to put a copy of it in your personal \My System folder (see "Special folders" in Chapter 8) before you run Regsvr32. To create a copy of the Desktop.ini file that's stored in the History folder, use Notepad to create a text file with the following contents:

```
[.ShellClassInfo]
UICLSID={FF393560-C2A7-11CF-BFF4-444553540000}
CLSID={FF393560-C2A7-11CF-BFF4-444553540000}
```

Save this file as History Desktop.ini. When and if you need to put it back in your History folder, copy it there, rename it as Desktop.ini, and set its attribute to Hidden.

Defrag hangs

Undocumented

If you have URLs in your History folder whose names are longer than 256 characters, Defrag may choke. ScanDisk won't find any problems. You can get around this problem by deleting the History folder, as detailed in the previous section.

Filling in forms gives me an error

If you get an error message when you click the Submit button on a simple web-based form, you've run into an incompatibility between Netscape Navigator's extensions and those used by Internet Explorer. The web site author used a Netscape Navigator extension that allows Netscape Navigator to send e-mail disguised as a form.

Presently, there isn't a way around this other than to tell the web site designer to quit using this extension. Of course, it's tough to tell the author unless he or she gives you an e-mail address, which is specifically what the author is trying to hide with the use of this extension. You can find more information on this problem at http://support.microsoft.com/support/kb/articles/Q154/8/64.asp.

Slow browsing

If you have enabled the Content Advisor rating system, you may find that your Internet Explorer is taking its own sweet time downloading web sites. Check to see if you can speed up your browsing by disabling ratings.

In the Internet Explorer, choose View, Internet Options, click the Content tab, and click the Disable button.

Err Msg: MPREXE caused an invalid page fault in Kernel32.dll

Numerous problems with the Windows 98 interface can be traced to a corrupt password file. If this happens, you may get this error message: "MPREXE caused an invalid page fault in module Kernel32.dll." If you get this message, delete or rename the files in the \Windows folder with the extension *pwl*. You can find out more about this problem in the "Dealing with a corrupted password file" section in Chapter 12.

The trouble with web sites

The Internet Explorer will give you an idea if there is something amiss on the other end of the line. To see the kind of information that Internet Explorer can supply, go to a site that has a web page with misplaced tags, such as http://logan.creek.net/ie/index.html. With this particular page, you'll notice that nothing shows up. Click View, Source, and you'll see Internet Explorer's explanation of the problem.

Can't find an Internet site

If you are trying to view your own start page, and you get an error message stating that Internet Explorer can't find the site, you may have an old, missing, or corrupt Url.dll file. One source of the problem: If you uninstalled earlier beta versions of Netscape Navigator, they didn't restore the original Url.dll file.

STEPS

Fixing Url.dll

Step 1. If you can find Url.dll file in the \Windows\System folder, remove or rename it.

Step 2. Type the following command at a DOS prompt, and then press Enter:

```
copy C:\Windows\Sysbckup\Url.dll C:\Windows\System
```

Step 3. Click the Start button, choose Shut Down, choose Restart, and then click OK.

File Download dialog box

By default, the Internet Explorer displays the File Download dialog box when you access a file on the Internet. This dialog box gives you the option of opening the file or saving it to your hard disk to be opened later. If the file is a graphics file, to open it is to view it. If it is an executable file, to open it is to run the program.

For every file type, the Windows 98 Registry keeps track of whether it should display the File Download dialog box when you start to download a file of that type from the Internet.

The first time you download an executable file, Internet Explorer displays the File Download dialog box with the Always Ask Before Opening This Type of File check box marked. If you clear this check box, you will not be asked whether you want to save or open executable files in the future. They will automatically be opened.

Secret

If executable files (files with *exe* extensions) are opening automatically and you want to regain the option to save them instead, use the Registry editor to navigate to exefile in HKEY_CLASSES_ROOT. Highlight *exefile* in the left pane, and double-click EditFlags in the right pane. Change **d8 07 01 00** to **d8 07 00 00**. Click OK. The File Download dialog box will now display when you begin to download an executable file.

To turn off the File Download dialog box for file types other than executable files, take the following steps:

STEPS

Turning Off the File Download Dialog Box

Step 1.   Click Start, Settings, Folder Options, and the Files Types tab.

Step 2.   Scroll down to and highlight the file type that you want to change.

Step 3.   Click the Edit button. Clear the Confirm Open After Download check box to eliminate the File Download dialog box for this file type. Mark it to display this dialog box.

Step 4.   Click OK twice.

Tip

One way to download a file that always lets you choose whether to open or save is to right-click the filename, and then click Open or Save Target As in the context menu.

Browse in a new process

Windows 98 picks up a little of the ability of Windows NT to separate processes into their own memory space. If the Internet Explorer crashes while browsing or viewing web documents, you can set it up so that at least your Desktop and Tray don't go down with it.

You can set the Internet Explorer to open up in its own memory space each time it is invoked. It will take a bit longer to start (because it has to read the executable code again instead of using the code that is already in memory) and use a little more memory. You set the Internet Explorer to use a new process by choosing View, Internet Options, clicking the Advanced tab, and marking the Browse in a New Process check box.

Browser Wars

Netscape would like you to set its browser as the default browser. Microsoft wants you to choose its browser. At least they both give you a choice.

In the Internet Explorer, choose View, Internet Options, and click the Programs tab. If you mark the Internet Explorer Should Check to See Whether It Is The Default Browser check box at the bottom of this dialog box, the Internet Explorer will check to make sure that it is the default browser every time you start it up. If you have installed Netscape Navigator and made it the default, the Internet Explorer will ask if you want to set Internet Explorer as the default browser.

If you don't mark this check box and Netscape Navigator is your default browser, it will open when you click an HTML page. Windows 98 does all of this through file type associations in the Registry. Click Start, Settings, Folder

Options, and the File Types tab. Scroll down to and highlight Internet Document (HTML) or Microsoft MHTML Document 4.0 to see which browser is associated with HTML files.

You can make changes in the File Types tab if you like, but to make them permanent, you need to issue commands in Netscape to tell it whether it is the default browser and whether it should check if it's the default, just as you do in the Internet Explorer.

Keyboard Shortcuts for Internet Explorer

You can use the keyboard shortcuts listed in Table 9-2 to navigate with Internet Explorer:

Table 9-2   Keyboard Shortcuts for the Internet Explorer

Key or Combination	Effect
Enter	Goes to the highlighted link
Backspace and Shift+Backspace,	Same as Back and Forward arrow buttons on the Internet toolbar
Alt+Left Arrow and Alt+Right Arrow	Same as Back and Forward arrow buttons on the Internet toolbar
Shift+F10	Displays a context menu for a link
F5	Reloads the current page from the server
Esc	Stops downloading a page
Ctrl+O or Ctrl+L	Goes to a new location (URL)
Ctrl+N	Opens a new window
Ctrl+S	Saves the current page
Ctrl+Shift+Tab	Cycles between frames
Tab and Shift+Tab	Cycles between links on a page
Ctrl+B	Opens the Organize Favorites window
Ctrl+D	Adds current web page to Favorites (immediately and silently)
Ctrl+R	Reloads the current page (F5)
Ctrl+W	Closes the active Internet Explorer window

Tip

One thing that is cool about Tab and Shift+Tab is that they highlight the active areas on an image map. An *image map* is a (usually large) graphic on a web page. The graphic is generally divided into active areas that point to different URLs. When you press Tab or Shift+Tab, you can see an outline around each active area.

Where Does the Search Start?

The Internet toolbar contains a Search button. It connects to http://home.microsoft.com/search/search.asp. This is a search page at Microsoft's web site. You can set up your version of Microsoft's search page for a specific search engine or change it every time you access this URL.

You can change what URL the Search button connects to by specifying where the Search button begins the search.

STEPS

Specifying a URL for the Search Button

Step 1.   Open RegEdit.

Step 2.   Go to HKEY_LOCAL_MACHINE\SOFTWARE\Microsoft\Internet Explorer\Main.

Step 3.   Double-click Search Bar in the right pane of RegEdit.

Step 4.   Type the URL for your favored search engine, click OK, and then close RegEdit.

If you want to change where the menu item Go, Search the Web takes you (instead of http://home.microsoft.com/access/allinone.asp), use these steps, but go to Search Page instead of Search Bar.

Here are some URLs for search sites:

Site	Address
AltaVista	http://www.altavista.digital.com/cgi-bin/query?pg=q&q=%s
Excite	http://www.excite.com/search.gw?search=%s
InfoSeek	http://guide-p.infoseek.com/Titles?qt=%s
Lycos	http://www.lycos.com/cgi-bin/pursuit?query=%s
Magellan	http://searcher.mckinley.com/searcher.cgi?query=%s
Yahoo (plain search)	http://search.yahoo.com/bin/search?p=%s
Yahoo (IE autosearch)	http://msie.yahoo.com/autosearch?p=%s

Windows 98 Home Pages

Table 9-3 lists some interesting Windows-related sites you can visit on the web:

Table 9-3 Windows Related Web Sites

Site	Address
Windows 98 Secrets	http://www.halcyon.com/davis/secrets.htm
IDG Books	http://www.idgbooks.com
Brian's InfoWorld Column	http://www.infoworld.com/cgi-bin/displayNew.pl?/livingst/livingst.htm
Microsoft Downloads	http://support.microsoft.com/support/downloads/default.asp
Microsoft FAQs	http://support.microsoft.com/support/default-faq.asp
MS Internet Explorer Start page	http://home.microsoft.com/
Microsoft Knowledge Base	http://support.microsoft.com/support/
Microsoft Known Problems	http://support.microsoft.com/support/problems/ default.asp
Microsoft Newsgroups	http://support.microsoft.com/support/news/default.asp
Outlook Express	http://www.microsoft.com/products/prodref/578_ov.htm
Troubleshooting wizards	http://support.microsoft.com/support/
Windows Sources	http://www.zdnet.com/~wsources/
Windows98.com	http://www.windows98.com
Windows Annoyances	http://www.creativelement.com/win95ann/index.html
The Microsoft Exchange Center	http://www.slipstick.com/exchange/
Bob Cerelli's Windows Page	http://www.halcyon.com/cerelli/
Gordon Carter's Exchange help site	http://ourworld.compuserve.com/homepages/G_Carter/default.htm
The Internet Starting Point for Windows	http://www.orbit.org/win/
Animated Cursor Schemes	http://www.islandnet.com/~wwseb/cursors.htm
Stroud's Windows Applications	http://www.stroud.com/
Ed Tiley's Windows Home Page	http://www.supernet.net/~edtiley/win95/
Eric Miller's Outlook Express help	http://www.activeie.com/oe/

(continued)

Table 9-3 *(Continued)*

Site	Address
Outlook Expressions	http://www.barkers.org/ie/oe/
Dale's Windows Themes Page	http://209.8.76.171/index.htm/
Windows Startup Logos	http://www.nucleus.com/~kmcmurdo/win95logo.html
Download.com	http://www.download.com/PC/Win95/
Windows FAQ	http://www.orca.bc.ca/win95/
Software for the Internet	http://tucows.tierranet.com/window95.html
Microsoft's Windows Games Pages	http://www.microsoft.com/windows/games/
Windows Tip Sheet	http://www.cs.umb.edu/~alilley/win.html
Club Internet Explore	http://www.clubie.com/
Costa's Tips for Windows	http://www-na.biznet.com.gr/sail/isa/tipfrm.html
WindoWatch Magazine	http://www.windowatch.com/
The 32-bit Software Archive	http://www.32bit.com/software/index.phtml
Windows & IE Resource Page	http://www.raton.com/~chip/reskit.htm
Windows Help Desk	http://www.southwind.net/faq/help/win95/
The Computer Paper	http://www.tcp.ca/

Internet Explorer's Easter Egg

The people who created the Windows 98 Internet Explorer would like you to know who they are. You can find out by clicking Help, About Internet Explorer on the Explorer toolbar.

Hold down the Ctrl key and click the IE logo in the upper-right corner of the dialog box. Holding the Ctrl key down, drag the IE logo to the globe and then quickly to the right of the globe, so that it hits the "Microsoft Internet Explorer 4.0" text. The text will fly off the right side of the dialog box, revealing an Unlock button.

Drop the IE logo on the globe, and then click the Unlock button. The globe will expand. A new window opens and a scrolling list of credits appears.

Summary

Internet Explorer is now integrated into the Windows 98 Desktop. This chapter is devoted to helping you make this integration work for you.

▶ With the Internet Explorer Administration Kit, you can create your own Internet Explorer browser.

▶ There are plenty of web sites devoted to Windows 98.

▶ You can start the Internet Explorer in lots of different ways.

▶ You have plenty of options for organizing your favorite web sites.

▶ You don't have to translate your documents into HTML to view them over an Intranet.

▶ The Internet Explorer has lots of keyboard shortcuts.

Chapter 10

Shortcuts at Home and Abroad

In This Chapter

If it weren't for shortcuts, we wouldn't get anywhere fast. They are an essential means of turning this sow's ear of an operating system into something a bit more personal and friendly. Shortcuts get us around our computers and around the Internet. We discuss:

▶ Putting shortcuts to anything in your computer on your Desktop

▶ Viewing any document with a shortcut to the Quick View file viewers built into Windows 98

▶ Starting any program when Windows 98 starts

▶ Copying, moving, opening, and viewing files easily with Send To

▶ Opening a New Message window in Outlook Express without opening Outlook Express

▶ Starting DOS programs and DOS/Windows batch files from icons

▶ Starting different versions of your applications with different icons

▶ Printing files by dragging and dropping them to an icon on the Desktop

▶ Making the full power of your computer visible

▶ Making sure your applications can find all their accessory files without having to add folder names to your Path statement in your Autoexec.bat file

What's a Shortcut?

We want to clear up something right away. We use the word *shortcut* to mean two very different things in this book. When we say something like *keyboard shortcut*, we mean a keystroke that does something that otherwise would have taken a bunch of keystrokes or a lot of mousing around. The *shortcuts* we talk about in this chapter refer to icons that represent, and are linked to, applications, documents, folders, and Internet addresses.

This kind of shortcut is a shortcut in the sense that you don't have to use the Explorer or My Computer windows to find your application, document, folder, or web page. You can just put a shortcut (a link) to it in a convenient place. Clicking the shortcut is the same as — and sometimes even better than — clicking the original file.

You can create three types of shortcuts:

- Windows shortcut — links to a Windows application, folder, or document
- URL shortcut — links to an Internet address
- DOS shortcut — links to a DOS window, application, or file (also called a *pif*)

Depending on the type of target, Windows 98 gives you different ways of modifying the shortcut once you've created it.

If you are moving up from Windows 3.1*x*, you'll probably remember that it had something like shortcuts. The Program Manager was full of them. You could drag a file from the File Manager and drop it on the Program Manager to create a new program item within a program group. Double-clicking the program item started the application or opened a file with its associated application (if its file type was registered).

Shortcuts make your information much more accessible. Microsoft has made shortcuts flexible and powerful. It isn't obvious at first, but you will soon discover that Windows 98 shortcuts are a huge improvement over the Windows 3.1*x* interface.

Shortcuts are easily recognizable because the lower-left corner of a shortcut icon has a curved black arrow in a little white box. This "icon on an icon" shows up automatically when you create a shortcut. Take a look at the example in Figure 10-1.

Figure 10-1: A shortcut icon. All shortcut icons have a black arrow in a little white box in the lower-left corner.

You can use TweakUI to change this dark black arrow into a light arrow that is somewhat difficult to see, or even into no arrow at all. Start TweakUI by clicking its shortcut on your Desktop if you have placed one there — we heartily recommend that you do this. (If you don't have a shortcut, click the TweakUI icon in your Control Panel. If you don't have the icon, you can install TweakUI from the \tools\ResKit\Powertoy folder of your Windows 98 CD-ROM.) Click the Explorer tab. Under Shortcut Overlay at the top of the dialog box, mark the option you want to use. If you have changed the shortcut overlay from the black arrow, you may not be able to tell if an icon represents a shortcut, or the actual application, document, folder, or address.

An important fact to remember is that if you delete a shortcut icon from the Desktop (or anywhere else, for that matter) you have deleted only the shortcut, not the item to which the shortcut points. But if you move an actual file to the Desktop and then delete that file's icon, you have deleted the file.

If you attempt to delete the icon of a program on your computer, you receive this warning from Windows 98: "The file *appname.exe* is a program. If you remove it, you will no longer be able to run this program or edit some documents. Are you sure you want to delete it?" If you answer yes, Windows 98 sends the program file to the Recycle Bin, unless you held down the Shift key when you pressed Delete or you have configured the Recycle Bin to purge deleted files. In all these cases, the program will no longer be available. So be careful out there.

Shortcuts Are Great

If it weren't for shortcuts, Windows 98 wouldn't have much to say for itself in the user-friendly interface department. Shortcuts are a powerful means of user customization—a way to fight back against the Microsoft corporate vision. If you use Windows 98 the way it came out of the box, you are not going to be very happy.

Just because a folder is a good place to store something doesn't mean that it's a convenient place to go when you want to get the item you stored. You probably have really good reasons for putting some files or applications in a particular folder, but it also makes perfect sense to give yourself a way to get at them quickly.

Fixed disk drives on new computers have immense storage capacity. The amount of information that can be stored on one can quickly overwhelm the most meticulous person. If you stack a lot of boxes in a room, you're going to have a hard time getting around in it.

Our computers are being hooked up ever more tightly to other people's computers, both on local area networks and around the world via the Internet. We're looking for stuff on these other machines and other people on our local area network may be searching for files on ours. A gigabyte here, a gigabyte there, and pretty soon it adds up to real chaos.

Click a shortcut to a web page, and the Internet Explorer will start, dial up your Internet service provider (if that is how you are connected to the Internet) and take you to the target web page. The same thing is true if you are on a local area network and want to get to a page on your Intranet web server. You can use shortcuts in the Favorites list to quickly get to your favorite web sites. Shortcuts not only open up your computer and your network, they open up the Internet.

Put your favorite files and programs on the Desktop

Your Desktop is an icon container, and the perfect spot for shortcuts. You don't really want to put your documents or applications on your Desktop. Keep them in the folders that they share with other similar applications and files. For example, keep all your game applications in subfolders of the Games folder, but put shortcuts to your favorite games on the Desktop.

Tip

Put shortcuts to documents on the Desktop — just the ones that you are currently working on. Working on a set of similar documents? Create a shortcut to the folder that holds them. If the documents themselves are stored in separate folders, place shortcuts to them in a folder, and place a shortcut to that folder on the Desktop.

You can make a group of similar applications available on the Desktop, without letting their icons cover the Desktop. Place a shortcut to a folder on the Desktop and put shortcuts to the applications in the folder.

Want the Explorer on the Desktop? Put a shortcut to Explorer.exe on the Desktop, but leave the file Explorer.exe where it belongs, in the \Windows folder.

Tip

Wouldn't it be convenient to drag and drop files to the Quick Viewer so you could take a peek at their content? Put a shortcut to \Windows\System\ Viewers\Quickview.exe on the Desktop and rename it Quick Viewer.

If you put a shortcut to your printer on your Desktop, you can drag and drop a document to your printer.

Remember — the Desktop is itself a subfolder of the \Windows folder. Its full pathname is C:\Windows\Desktop. You usually don't want to *move* files to the Desktop folder. Instead, you want to create *shortcuts* in the Desktop folder, and these shortcuts will appear on your Desktop.

Microsoft has made the fact that the Desktop is a wonderful place for shortcuts less than obvious by placing a bunch of icons on the Desktop that aren't shortcuts and aren't stored in the \Windows\Desktop folder. My Computer, Recycle Bin, and Internet Explorer are prime examples. You have to use TweakUI if you want to get these off the Desktop.

You'll have to ignore the fact that Microsoft puts these application icons on the Desktop. Instead of following Microsoft's example and placing your own applications on the Desktop, just put shortcuts to them there.

Automatically start programs when Windows starts

You no doubt have some programs that you want to start when you start Windows. You can put shortcuts to these programs into the StartUp folder, and leave the programs where they are.

Undocumented

Want to make sure that the programs start in the order that you want them to? It's easy. Create a DOS batch file that is nothing but a series of calls to the programs you want to start, in the order that you want. For example:

```
Winapp1.exe
Winapp2.exe
Winapp3.exe
```

Create a shortcut to this batch file in the StartUp folder, and then delete the shortcuts to the programs themselves.

You can control some aspects of how these Windows programs are displayed by adding the Start command in front of the Windows program names in the batch file and then using one of the Start command's switches. To see how the switches work, click Start, Programs, MS-DOS Prompt, and type **Start /?** at the DOS prompt. The DOS Start command is not related to the Windows 98 Start button.

The Start button is full of shortcuts—add more

The Start menus cascading across the Desktop are filled with shortcuts. If you install a Windows 3.1x application under Windows 98, its setup program thinks it is creating a program group. In fact, it is creating a folder full of shortcuts to the application and its companion files. Shortcuts in the Start menu make it easy to get to applications. Click the Start button and follow the menus out to the shortcut to the application you want.

The Start menu items under Programs, Favorites, and Documents are shortcuts, and the cascading submenus under these items are just special windows full of shortcuts.

Tip

You can put a shortcut on the Desktop (or in any folder) to a folder that holds the shortcuts to a set of documents or applications — shortcuts within a shortcut to a folder. One way to do this is to copy to the Desktop an icon on the Start menu that represents a set of application icons. Here are the steps:

STEPS
Putting a Shortcut to a Start Menu Folder on the Desktop

Step 1. Click the Start button, point to Programs, and point to Accessories. Accessories is just an example of one folder/menu item you might want to choose; you can pick others.

Step 2. Right-click the Accessories icon in the Start menu, and click Copy in the context menu.

Step 3. Click the Desktop and click Paste Shortcut.

You now have a copy of part of your Start menu on your Desktop. You can add or remove shortcuts from this folder with ease just by dragging and dropping. Adding and removing shortcuts from this folder adds and removes the same shortcuts in the associated Start menu.

Shortcuts in toolbars

Like the Start menu, toolbars are full of shortcuts. To see an example, right-click the Taskbar, and choose Toolbars, Quick Launch. The Quick Launch toolbar contains shortcuts to the Internet Explorer and Outlook Express (as well as two or more additional icons). The folder that holds these shortcuts is \Windows\Application Data\Microsoft\Internet Explorer\Quick Launch.

Toolbars make excellent locations for shortcuts. They provide another quick way to get to applications, documents, and web pages. The Desktop toolbar contains both the shortcuts on your Desktop and the icons that Microsoft placed there.

You can create a folder full of shortcuts, and then drag the folder icon from your Explorer or Desktop to the edge of your Desktop to create a new toolbar containing all of the shortcuts in the folder.

Move, copy, print, and view files and folders easily

Put shortcuts to the Briefcase, default file opener, Quick Viewer, printer, file compression program, or whatever into your SendTo folder. Then, whenever you right-click a file or folder, you can choose Send To and click one of these destinations to send it there.

Send a file to the shortcut for your default file opener, and the application opens it. Send a file of an unregistered type to the shortcut for Quick Viewer, and the viewer does its best to display the file.

We use the ability to send a file to Notepad all the time. Right-click a file, click Send To, click Notepad, and it opens, ready for editing. To do this, you must first add a shortcut to Notepad in your Send To menu: Right-drag the Notepad icon from the \Windows folder to the \Windows\Send To folder, and click Create Shortcut(s) Here. See "Right-Click to a Powerhouse" below for more on the Send To menu.

Start DOS programs by clicking icons

Put a shortcut to DOS on your Desktop. There's already one in your Start menu, but it's that much closer if it is on the Desktop (at least when the Desktop isn't covered up).

You can create shortcuts to all your DOS programs. You can use icons from any icon library or from the files that come with Windows 98. You can treat your DOS programs just like Windows programs. Why not? Most DOS programs run fine in a window.

To see how to create DOS shortcuts, turn to "DOS in Windows" in Chapter 34.

Use a shortcut to do more than one thing at a time

You can create a shortcut to a DOS batch file that calls a Windows program in addition to calling some DOS functions. If you combine DOS and Windows programs in the batch file, they can all do more together. Here's an example that uses encom and modem, two proprietary DOS utilities that are often provided by portable computer manufacturers:

```
echo off
:: The next line switches COM2 from modem to port
c:\util\encom
:: The next line runs the Direct Cable Connection
:: Start /w is used to suspend the batch file processing
start /w c:\Windows\Directcc.exe
:: This utility switches COM2 back to the internal modem
c:\util\modem
```

The Start command is described in "Windows DOS Batch Files" in Chapter 34.

Modify how a Windows program operates

A shortcut allows you to combine the call to your Windows application with some of its command line parameters. The Windows Explorer shortcut on the Start, Programs menu is a good example of this (see "The Windows Explorer and the Start button") in Chapter 8.

If your program has the ability to take command line parameters, you can create different versions of the command line in different shortcuts to the same program. Who cares if it is just one program behind the scenes (behind the shortcut)? If it acts differently when you call it with one shortcut than with another shortcut, it might as well be a different program.

Use a different program to open a document

If you have a shortcut to a document, you can change the application that opens or acts on that document. The default shortcut just names the document and its path. Insert the name of the application that you want to act on the document into the definition of this shortcut (in the Target field) to override the file/application association found in the Registry.

The properties for such a shortcut are displayed in Figure 10-2. (To display a shortcut's properties, right-click the shortcut and click Properties.) The name of the application and any command line parameters precede the name of the file. If the pathname to the application includes a space, surround the pathname and filename with double quotes.

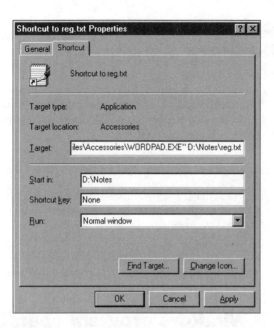

Figure 10-2: The properties for a shortcut to a file ending in the *txt* extension. By default, Windows associates *txt* files with Notepad. To override this file association, we have specified that the WordPad application open this file. The file is too big for Notepad.

Put shortcuts to parts of documents on the Desktop

You can copy a paragraph from a document and paste a shortcut to it on the Desktop. Just highlight the paragraph, issue the Copy command, right-click the Desktop, and click Paste Shortcut.

The "scrap" on the Desktop is now a piece of data or text that you can insert into another document. If you click it, Windows 98 invokes the application that created it, and the scrap is displayed in the application's window. The application that opens the document must be OLE-enabled.

Shortcuts to web pages and through the mail

You can mail a shortcut by dragging and dropping it into an e-mail message. When the recipient receives the message, he or she can access the file or folder that is linked to the shortcut by clicking the shortcut in the mail message. This works with Microsoft Mail on your local area network, with the Microsoft Network (MSN), and with web pages on the Internet.

You can put shortcuts to Internet addresses in your \Windows\Favorites folder, on your Desktop, or wherever. If you put them in your Favorites folder, they are displayed when you click Favorites in the Explorer menu bar or on the Start menu. If you put them in your \Windows\Favorites\Links folder, they appear on the Links toolbar.

If you want to change the destination that a URL shortcut points to, right-click the shortcut, choose Properties, and edit the contents of the Target URL field in the Internet Shortcut tab. You can use any legitimate URL format in this field, including http://, ftp://, news://, and mailto://.

You can create URL shortcuts in several ways. If you drag and drop the icon at the left end of the Address bar in Internet Explorer to the Desktop, a URL shortcut for the currently displayed web page is automatically created. If you right-drag and drop a hyperlink in a web page to the Desktop and choose Create Shortcut(s) Here, a shortcut to the target of the hyperlink appears on the Desktop.

One other way to easily create a shortcut to a web page is to open the web page using your Internet Explorer, and choose File, Send, Shortcut To Desktop. And you can e-mail the URL shortcut to this web page by choosing File, Send, Link By E-mail.

Shortcuts to e-mail recipients and newsgroups

Secret

You can easily create a shortcut to a newsgroup or a news server. The shortcut will open Outlook Express (or whatever your default newsgroup reader is) and focus on the newsgroup or news server.

Tom Koch, who provided a lot of help to Outlook Express beta testers, came up with the steps needed to create such a shortcut:

STEPS
Creating a Shortcut to a Newsgroup or News Server

Step 1. Click the Outlook Express icon on your Desktop.

Step 2. In the Outlook Express window, click Outlook Express in the Folder List pane to display the top-level of Outlook Express in the right pane. (If you don't see the Folder List, choose View, Layout, and mark the Folder List check box.)

Step 3. Drag and drop any one of the six icons in the right pane to your Desktop.

Step 4. Right-click the new shortcut icon on your Desktop, and click Properties.

(continued)

STEPS *(continued)*

Creating a Shortcut to a Newsgroup or News Server

Step 5.   In the Target URL field, type **news://**, followed by the name of the news server and the newsgroup (for example, news://msnews. microsoft.com/microsoft.public.inetexplorer.ie4.outlookexpress).

Step 6.   Click OK.

Step 7.   Click anywhere on the Desktop. Press F5 to refresh the Desktop icons and change the shortcut's icon to the newspaper-like icon.

Step 8.   Click your new icon to make sure that Outlook Express opens and focuses on your newsgroup. You may want to rename your shortcut with the name of the newsgroup it targets, for example Outlook Express News.

If you want your shortcut to connect to the news server as a whole (and not to a particular newsgroup on that server), don't include the name of the newsgroup. The news server name that you type in the Target URL field must be exactly as you have defined it in the News Account field in Outlook Express (choose Tools, Accounts, click the News tab, highlight the account, and click the Properties button). The name of the news account may differ from the name of the actual news server, so you have to be careful. Use the name in the News Account field (in the General tab), not the name in the Server Name field (in the Server tab).

Secret

The shortcut may have difficulty parsing the news account name. It turns uppercase letters to lowercase. If you have uppercase letters in your news account name, the shortcut will just create a new news account name and not focus on your existing one. You can avoid this problem by changing the account name to all lowercase before creating a shortcut.

You can also create a shortcut that displays a New Message window. To do this, follow the steps above, but in step 5, type **mailto:** instead the name of a news server or newsgroup. The new shortcut icon on your Desktop will have a mail icon. Clicking it opens a New Message window without starting Outlook Express. Don't forget to rename your shortcut icon something like Compose New Message so that you remember what it is.

You can also create a New Messages toolbar that gives you easy access to either a new e-mail message or a new newsgroup posting without opening Outlook Express. Take the following steps:

STEPS

Creating a New Messages Toolbar

Step 1. Right-click your My Computer icon, click Explore, and navigate to your \My System folder. If you don't have one, focus your Explorer on your bootable drive, right-click in the right pane, choose New, Folder and rename the folder **My System**.

Step 2. Click the \My System folder icon in the left pane, right-click the right pane, choose New, Folder, and rename the folder **New Messages**.

Step 3. Click your Outlook Express icon on your Desktop. Click the Inbox icon in your Folder List pane, click the Compose Message toolbar button, choose File, Save As in the New Message window, and save the new empty message to the New Messages folder created in the previous step. Name it something like Mail Message (the exact name is not critical). Then close the message.

Step 4. Click a newsgroup in the Folder List pane of Outlook Express. Click the Compose Message toolbar button, choose File, Save As in the New Message window, and save this message to the New Messages folder with a name that corresponds to the newsgroup you chose (again, the name is not critical). Close your message. Repeat this step for every newsgroup you normally send messages to.

Step 5. Drag and drop the New Messages folder icon from your Explorer to any edge of the Desktop or onto the Taskbar.

You have just created a New Messages toolbar. If you want to make it take up less space, right-click it and clear Show Title. (If you only have one shortcut to a newsgroup, you can also clear Show Text — but if you have more than one, you'll need the text to distinguish among them.) To make the icons smaller, right-click the toolbar again and choose View, Small.

You can use this toolbar anytime that you want to send a new message. For example, if you are in the midst of reading a newsgroup and decide to send an e-mail message (as opposed to a post to the newsgroup), you don't have to switch to one of the mail folders in Outlook Express to compose your message, and thus lose your place in the newsgroup. Instead, you can just click the e-mail icon in the New Messages toolbar.

The New Message window for newsgroup messages now contains the name of the newsgroup that was highlighted when you created it. You need to change this name if you want to send a posting to another newsgroup.

Creating Shortcuts

The whole point of shortcuts is to put them in convenient places. These include the Desktop, the Start menu, the toolbars, the SendTo folder, folders on the Desktop, and whatever windows you regularly have open on the Desktop. You can put shortcuts wherever you want, but then, what's the point of some of the possible locations?

Drag and drop to create a shortcut

Undocumented

If you drag and drop a binary executable file to a folder or to the Desktop, Windows 98 automatically creates a shortcut to the file. Executable files have *exe*, *com*, or *bat* extensions. However, *bat* files are a major exception to this rule. If you drag a *bat* file to the Desktop, it gets *moved*—a shortcut is *not* created. (Files that end with the *pif* extension were executable files under Windows 3.1x. They are now shortcuts.)

If you left-drag a binary executable file icon from a folder or Explorer window into another window or onto the Desktop, you will see a black curved arrow in the lower-left corner of the transparent file icon. This tells you that Windows 98 will create a shortcut if you release the left mouse button.

Undocumented

You can choose to create a shortcut when you drag and drop an icon by holding down the Ctrl and Shift keys. You can also do this by right-dragging the icon. In both cases, you will get a context menu asking if you want to Move Here, Copy Here, Create Shortcut(s) Here, or Cancel the operation. To explicitly create a shortcut with drag and drop, choose Create Shortcut(s) Here.

Name that shortcut

Tip

You can change the name of a shortcut. It is a good idea to change the name to something meaningful, rather than a short filename. Don't hold back; make the names work for you.

If a shortcut icon is already highlighted, press F2 to invoke the rename function. If it isn't highlighted, right-click the icon and then click Rename on the context menu. When you see a black box around the name, type the new name, and then press Enter.

Give your shortcuts names that are long enough to be meaningful, but not so long that they fill up the Desktop. Windows 98 wraps names to fit in the icon grid on the Desktop. It shortens single words with ellipses.

You can't use these symbols in a shortcut name:

/ * ? .< > |

Get rid of "Shortcut to"

Do you get tired of seeing "Shortcut to" as the first part of your shortcut's name? TweakUI lets you defeat this behavior. Click the TweakUI shortcut on your Desktop (if you don't have one, click the TweakUI icon in the Control Panel), click the Explorer tab, and clear the Prefix "Shortcut to" on New Shortcuts check box.

Cut and paste a shortcut

You can create a shortcut whose first location is the same folder as the application or document itself and then move it to the folder that you want. Right-click an icon in a folder window or the Explorer and click Create Shortcut. A shortcut to the file that you right-clicked will appear.

You can then move the shortcut out of this folder to your desired destination by using the Cut and Paste commands (see "Move with Cut and Paste" in Chapter 7). This combined method avoids dragging and dropping.

Create a new "unattached" shortcut, then create the link

You can create a new shortcut first, and link it to an application or document second. (You can't use this method to create a shortcut to a folder.) To do this, take the following steps:

STEPS
Creating a New Shortcut

Step 1. Right-click the Desktop, a folder window, or the right pane of an Explorer window. Point to New, and click Shortcut. This launches the Create Shortcut Wizard, as shown in Figure 10-3.

Step 2. Type the complete path and filename of the program or document that you want to create the shortcut to. Click the Browse button if you would rather find the file instead of typing in the name.

Step 3. Click the Next button. You can type a new name for the shortcut or leave the default name (the name of the file you linked to).

Step 4. Click the Finish button.

(continued)

STEPS *(continued)*
Creating a New Shortcut

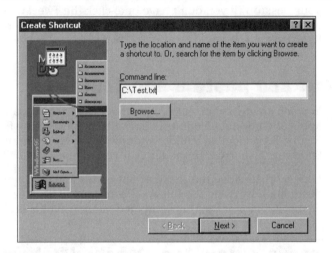

Figure 10-3: The Create Shortcut Wizard. You can type the path and filename of the application, document, or file that you want to create a shortcut to, or you can click the Browse button to look for the file.

Shortcuts on the Desktop

The Desktop is like any other folder, except that it is always open on the Desktop, so to speak. Drag an application icon from a folder or Explorer window and drop it on the Desktop and you automatically create a shortcut. Right-click the Desktop, point to New, and click Shortcut to create a new shortcut on the Desktop.

Tip

You can create folders on the Desktop and put shortcuts in them. This is a handy way to put a lot of stuff on the Desktop without cluttering it up. To do this, right-click the Desktop, and choose New, Folder. You can change the folder name at any time.

The new folder is now a subfolder of the C:\Windows\Desktop folder. You can use the Explorer to find the Desktop folder. Click the plus sign next to the Windows folder icon in the folder tree and you will see it (if you have configured the Explorer to show all files with View, Folder Options, View).

Tip

You can drag and drop shortcuts to the new folder on your Desktop. To do this, click the new folder to open its folder window. Then right-drag icons from other folder windows, drop them onto the new folder window, and click Create Shortcut(s) Here.

Creating a Shortcut to a Folder of Shortcuts

Tip

You don't have to put a folder of shortcuts on the Desktop. Instead, you can put a shortcut to a folder on the Desktop. To do this, use the Explorer to find an appropriate location for a folder that will contain shortcuts. You might, for example, create a Two Person Games subfolder under your Games folder. Or, as the steps below illustrate, you might create a folder called Desktop Folders, and create subfolders of shortcuts within it. You can then put shortcuts to these subfolders on your Desktop. If you click one of the shortcuts on the Desktop, you'll see the contents of the associated subfolder. You can add shortcuts to the subfolders by dragging and dropping icons to the appropriate Desktop shortcut.

STEPS

Creating a Shortcut to a Folder of Shortcuts

Step 1. In the Explorer, navigate to your **\My System** folder. If you don't have one, highlight the drive icon of your boot drive in the left pane. Then right-click the right pane, and choose New, Folder. Type **My System** as the name for the folder, and press Enter. You can use this folder to store files that are particular to your Windows 98 setup.

Step 2. Highlight the \My System folder icon in the left pane of the Explorer, right-click the right pane, and choose New, Folder. Type **Desktop Folders** as the name for the new folder, and press Enter.

Step 3. Highlight Desktop Folders in the left pane of the Explorer, right-click the right pane of the Explorer window, and choose New, Folder. Type the name of a folder that will hold shortcuts to documents or applications of a certain type. For example, **Graphics**. Press Enter

Step 4. Right-drag the Graphics folder icon to the Desktop and click Create Shortcut(s) Here.

Step 5. You can now drag and drop shortcuts to graphics files and/or graphics applications to this Graphics folder shortcut on the Desktop. These shortcuts will actually be stored in the \My System\Desktop Folders\Graphics folder, but they will be visible and available via the shortcut to the Graphics folder sitting on your Desktop.

Since you've placed a *shortcut* to the Graphics folder on your Desktop, instead of the Graphics folder itself, you can easily change the icon that represents this folder. Just right-click the Graphics folder shortcut, click Properties, and then click the Change Icon button. You can browse to find new icons.

Shortcuts to Folders, Disks, Computers, Printers, and More

You can have shortcuts to items other than files, documents, applications, or URLs. The following sections describe some suggested shortcut opportunities.

Folders

Let's say that you are working on documents you have placed in the C:\JonesAccount\BillsIssues folder. You can right-drag this folder from a folder window or the Explorer onto the Desktop, and then choose Create Shortcut(s) Here in the context menu. Clicking the shortcut to the BillsIssues folder quickly displays the contents of the folder in a folder window.

Disk drives

Tip

Right-drag a drive icon from the Explorer and drop it on the Desktop. The context menu will let you choose only between Create Shortcut(s) Here and Cancel. You'll find it particularly useful to create shortcuts to mapped drives representing shared resources (folders or drives) located on other peer computers or server computers.

Do you want to know the properties of a hard disk or get quickly to the ScanDisk, Backup, and Defrag disk tools? Put a shortcut to the hard disk on your Desktop. Right-click the shortcut, click Properties, click the Shortcut tab, click the Find Target button, right-click the target drive icon in the folder window, and click Properties. (You can access the disk tools in the Tools tab.)

Even better, install Target.dll. This utility comes with PowerToys. After you've installed it, right-click the hard disk shortcut icon on your Desktop, and choose Target, Properties to display the Properties dialog box for the target of the shortcut (in this case, your hard disk), not the shortcut itself. The disk tools will be on the Tools tab. Download PowerToys from http:// www.microsoft.com/windows/software/powertoy.htm.

Audio CD

Windows 98 comes with an applet called CD Player that lets you play audio CDs (see Figure 10-4). You should be able to find it by clicking Start,

Programs, Accessories, Entertainment, CD Player. The file Cdplayer.exe is normally located in your \Windows folder.

Figure 10-4: Controls for CD Player.

CD Player lets you play tracks on audio CDs. If you place an audio CD in your CD-ROM drive and switch to that drive with the Windows Explorer, you'll find a list of files with names like Track01.cda, Track02.cda, and so on. The *cda* extension stands for *CD Audio*, and indicates a track on a playable compact disk. You can drag one or more of these *cda* files to your Desktop or Start button, change the shortcut's name to the name of the song or artist, and so on. You can even create hot keys that start and stop your favorite recorded tracks.

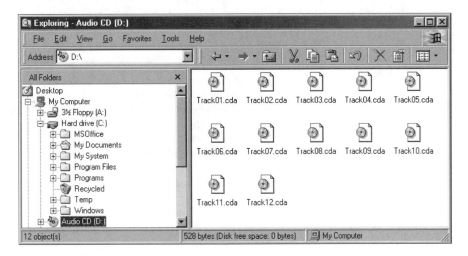

Figure 10-5: CD Player displays tracks as files in an Explorer window.

To set up hot keys, you need to create a shortcut that launches CD Player with a particular track.

STEPS

Making a Shortcut to an Audio CD

Step 1.   Right-click the Start button, and choose Explore. Right-click in the right pane of the Explorer window, and choose New, Shortcut. This will create a shortcut in the \Windows\Start Menu folder, so it will appear as a menu item in the Start menu itself.

Step 2.   In the first dialog box of the Create Shortcut Wizard, type a line such the following in the Command Line field:

```
c:\windows\cdplayer.exe /play f:\track01.cda
```

Replace c: and f: with the drive letters for your hard disk and CD-ROM drive, and replace track01.cda with the filename of the track you want to play. The /play switch is an undocumented feature of CD Player that also works with several other versions of CD Player-like software that are available. For example, the FlexiCD applet that Microsoft distributes with its PowerToys freeware supports the same switch. (You can download PowerToys from http://www.microsoft.com/windows/software/powertoy.htm.)

Click the Next button. In the dialog box that appears, type a name for this shortcut, such as the name of the song represented by the filename. Click Finish.

Step 3.   Click the Start button. A shortcut for your song title should appear in the menu. If you already have too many items crowding your Start menu, go back to the Explorer window and drag your shortcut from the \Windows\Start Menu folder into another folder. For example, you might want to move it to the \Start Menu\Programs\Accessories folder. If you do this, the shortcut will appear in the Start, Programs, Accessories menu.

Step 4.   To give your new shortcut a hot key (such as Ctrl+Alt+Z, if no application is using that key combination), right-click the shortcut in the Explorer window, and choose Properties. In the Shortcut tab, click in the Shortcut Key field, and then press the key combination you want to use. You should see this combination in the Shortcut Key field. Click OK. (If you later want to remove the key combination, click in the Shortcut Key field, press Backspace, and click OK.) You can now press Ctrl+Alt+Z to start your CD track.

Computers

You can put a shortcut to an entire computer on the Desktop (or anywhere you like). Right-click the My Computer icon on the Desktop and click Create Shortcut. You've got yourself a shortcut on the Desktop to something already on the Desktop (not a very practical idea, but definitely doable).

A far more useful application of this idea is to create shortcuts to networked computers, even computers that you remotely dial into. Just right-drag them out of Network Neighborhood and onto the Desktop (or another folder window), and choose Create Shortcut(s) Here. If you are dialing into the computer through remote access, you can put a shortcut to the computer on your Desktop and initiate the call by clicking the computer's shortcut icon. However, if you're using Direct Cable Connection (DCC) you'll have to make the connection first.

Printers

Right-drag a printer icon out of your Printers folder and drop it on the Desktop. Click Create Shortcut(s) Here. Now you can drag and drop files to the printer.

Control Panel icons

Open the Control Panel (Start, Settings, Control Panel). Right-drag one of the icons from the Control Panel to the Desktop, to a folder on the Desktop, or to a shortcut on the Desktop that points to a folder. Click Create Shortcut(s) Here. Now you have immediate access to whatever that icon does. Want to keep changing your mouse properties? You got it.

We would like to thank Matthias Koenig for his great investigative work in finding the following undocumented features.

To display the Device Manager the "long way," you right-click My Computer, click Properties, and then click the Device Manager tab of the System Properties dialog box. Want to put a shortcut to the Device Manager on your Desktop? Take the following steps:

STEPS

Creating a Shortcut to the Device Manager

Step 1. Right-click the Desktop, point to New, and then click Shortcut.

Step 2. In the Command Line field, type

```
C:\Windows\Control.exe Sysdm.cpl, System,1
```

Step 3. Click Next.

Step 4. Type **Device Manager** in the Name field. Click Finish.

You normally display the Settings tab of the Display Properties dialog box by right-clicking the Desktop and choosing Properties (or clicking the Display icon in the Control Panel), and then clicking the Settings tab. How about a shortcut to these properties?

STEPS

Creating a Shortcut to the Display Control Panel

Step 1.   Right-click the Desktop, point to New, and then click Shortcut.

Step 2.   In the Command Line field, type

```
C:\Windows\Control.exe Desk.cpl, Display,3
```

Step 3.   Click Next.

Step 4.   Type **Display Settings** in the Name field. Click Finish.

The format of the above examples is

```
Control.exe {cpl filename} {,applet name} {,tab#}
```

You can find the *cpl filename* of any of the Control Panel icons by searching (using Find as detailed in Chapter 11) for files with the *cpl* extension in the \Windows\System folder. The *applet name* you can find by looking in the Control Panel. Click any of the Control Panel icons to figure out the applet's tab number (if any). In the dialog box that appears, count the tabs, starting with 0 for the first tab on the left.

HyperTerminal connections

Right-drag the desired connection icon out of the HyperTerminal folder (open it from Start, Programs, Accessories, Communications, HyperTerminal). Drop it on the Desktop and click Create Shortcut(s) Here. Now when you want to call, click the connection's shortcut icon on the Desktop.

Shortcuts to files far, far away

You can create a shortcut to a document that resides on a computer that you have to dial into with Dial-Up Networking. When you click the shortcut for the file, your modem automatically dials the phone number and makes the connection to the other computer. Once it gets into the other computer, the linked document is displayed on your Desktop. This works for web pages and for other documents that you access through Dial-Up Networking.

Tip

If you use Direct Cable Connection, you can place shortcuts on the guest's Desktop to resources on the host computer. This is a quick way to navigate to those resources (perhaps a folder that you copy files back and forth from). However, the connection is not automatic — you must start DCC first before the shortcut will work.

Mail out shortcuts

You can paste a shortcut to a document into an e-mail message, and send the message over Microsoft Mail on your local area network. The recipient can open the document by clicking the shortcut icon if the document is stored in a shared folder or disk drive. All you have to send by mail is the shortcut, not the document itself. One advantage of e-mailing shortcuts is that you don't overburden the e-mail post office with numerous documents.

You can e-mail shortcuts to other Microsoft Network users by sending shortcuts to Microsoft Network bulletin boards, chat areas, documents, and so on. Users can click the shortcut and go to the targeted area or document.

You can e-mail URL addresses as shortcuts to people over the Internet as long as their mail clients can handle attachments in MIME or UUENCODE format (as Outlook Express can). When the recipient clicks a URL shortcut, it launches his or her browser, which then jumps to the targeted web page.

(If you have Outlook Express or Office 97, you'll notice that e-mail and Internet addresses in documents are automatically live. You can click on them and immediately call up your e-mail client or web browser to send e-mail or go to the web site.)

Paste shortcuts into documents

Microsoft has attempted to blur the line between the shell (the Desktop or user interface) and the Windows applications that you use while in Windows 98. The fact that Cut and Paste are part of the Windows user interface is one example of this.

Another is the fact that you can place shortcuts — which you store in folders for the most part — in documents and e-mail messages. To paste a shortcut into your document, right-click a shortcut in a folder, click Copy, right-click the client window area in your word processor, and then click Paste.

As an example of when this would be useful, you can give someone a document that contains shortcuts to other documents on the Internet. The recipient can then click the shortcuts to access to the latest versions of all the targeted documents. When you click a shortcut in a document, Windows 98 takes the appropriate actions to retrieve that document from wherever it is.

And on and on

Create shortcuts for Direct Cable Connection, Dial-Up Networking, Phone Dialer — whatever you want or need on the Desktop. The idea is to not hold back. Make your computer convenient; put the shortcuts where they do the most good. You should always see if you can make a shortcut to help accomplish a task. It may not work every time, but it's certainly worth trying.

Don't hide your computer under a bushel or in the Explorer. The Explorer is obviously well named: You use it when you have to go exploring for the functionality that you want. Shortcuts can help you reduce this work to a minimum.

Right-Click to a Powerhouse

Secret

Placing shortcuts in the SendTo folder can turn your context menu into a powerhouse. The Send To command is on almost all context menus. And it doesn't really mean *send to*. It means *drop this file on this application or folder*.

However the recipient application or folder deals with drag and drop is how the application reacts when something is sent to it. You can modify the application's behavior using command line parameters. (See the section later in this chapter entitled "The Target field.")

Applications in the Send To menu are like commands on the context menu. You can do such things as send files to be compressed in the background, print files, view files, or open files with a particular editor. The difference is that with the Send To menu items, you don't have to associate a file type with an action as you would to create a context menu item. You can just send any file to an application in the Send To menu and let it take the action.

Tip

Use the Explorer to expand your folder tree so you can see the \Windows\SendTo folder. To see how Send To works, right drag and drop a printer icon from your Printers folder to the SendTo folder to create a shortcut to the printer. Now when you want to send a file to the printer, you can right-click the file, point to Send To in the context menu, and click the shortcut to your printer in the Send To submenu.

If you haven't turned off (using TweakUI) the "Shortcut to" text that gets added when you create shortcuts, you'll probably want to edit the names of these shortcuts to get rid of this extraneous text.

You can place other items in the SendTo folder: a shortcut to a folder on a server computer perhaps; a shortcut to an application that you want to use to open files of unregistered types (see "Easiest Way to View/Open an Unregistered File" in Chapter 13), or a shortcut to the Quick Viewer (Quickview.exe in the \Windows\System\Viewers folder).

Undocumented

When you use Send To, Windows 98 acts as though you used your left mouse button and dragged the file or folder you right-clicked to the application, folder, or object in the Send To menu. For example, say you are using the Send To command to send a file to a folder. If the file is on the same disk drive (or volume) as the folder, it gets moved. If it is on another disk drive, it gets copied.

PowerToys, Microsoft's little user interface fixer-upper, contains a pair of SendtoX files that add four new destinations to your Send To menu: Any

Folder, Clipboard As Contents, Clipboard As Name, and Command Line. If you don't like any of these destinations, you can delete them from the SendTo folder. You can download Powertoys.exe from http://www.microsoft.com/windows/software/powertoy.htm.

The Send To Any Folder command allows you to copy or move a file from one folder to any other folder. The Other Folder dialog box, which appears when you choose Send To, Any Folder, lets you browse to find the target folder, or find it in a drop-down list if it's a previous target.

Send to a Printer

If you have access to two or more printers — whether they are attached to your PC or to your network — you can Send To any of your printers. This is a lot faster than manually changing your current printer every time you want to print a document to one or the other.

One way to get a printer onto your Send To menu is to right-drag its icon from the Printers folder (in the Control Panel) to the C:\Windows\SendTo folder.

You can even have the same printer show up twice on the Send To menu with different settings — for instance, draft versus presentation quality. To do this, click the Add Printer icon in the Printers window, then select a printer model you already have installed. When Windows asks if you want to "replace" or "keep" the existing driver, reply "keep" (unless you really do possess an updated driver).

After you finish installing this "new" printer driver, you should have a "Copy 2" icon in your Printers folder. Right-click this icon, click Properties, and configure this copy of your printer driver any way you like. Then right-drag it into the SendTo folder to create a shortcut to it. Your new alternate printer settings will appear on your Send To menu the next time you right-click a file icon.

Other things you may want to add to your Send To menu are the Desktop, the Start menu, and the StartUp folder. To get these in the menu, right-drag the subfolders named Desktop, Start Menu, and Start Menu\Programs\StartUp from your \Windows folder to the \Windows\SendTo folder. When you find a file that you want to put on your Desktop, in your Start menu, or in your StartUp folder, right-click the file, point to Send To, and click the desired option.

There are some caveats. Remember that when you drag a file to a folder in the Explorer, the file is *moved* if the folder is on the same drive, but *copied* if the folder is on a different drive. It works the same way if you send a file to a folder in the Send To menu. Also, if you send an executable file to the Desktop or to any part of the Start menu via the Send To command, the file doesn't get moved. Instead, Windows 98 creates a shortcut to the file (which is actually what you want).

Send to a menu of printers

Instead of creating individual shortcuts to each of your printers, you can create a live cascading menu of printers in your Send To menu. This is especially helpful if you have a lot of printer drivers installed, or if you often add or remove printer drivers.

To create the cascading menu, you add the resource ID for the Printers window to your Send To menu. A *resource ID* is a unique, hexadecimal identifier that Windows 98 uses to keep track of each of the many resources available on your computer. The resource IDs are stored in the Registry. (We saw a different example of using resource IDs in the section on "New icons for Desktop items" in Chapter 6.) Because you refer to the resource ID in the shortcut (as opposed to the object itself), every time you make a change in the Printers window, the cascading menu will update automatically.

To add the resource ID for Printers to your Send To list, select the \Windows\ SendTo folder in Explorer. Right-click an unoccupied space in Explorer's right pane, and choose New, Folder. In the space where you would name the folder, type the following resource ID — including the period, the two curly braces, the four hyphens, and the hexadecimal codes — and press Enter:

```
Printers.{2227A280-3AEA-1069-A2DE-08002B30309D}
```

Now when you right-click a document and choose Send To, Printers, you will see the entire contents of your Printers folder. And no matter how often you add or remove printer drivers, this menu will always be up to date.

Send to a computer on the network

You can also use the Send To menu on your network. This is especially helpful for your associates who may not be "into" computers, don't know how to open shortcuts in their mail clients to see embedded documents, or don't want to figure out how to access files across a network. Since it requires that you have access to your co-worker's \Windows folder, it is probably most appropriate for smaller networks and workgroups. Thanks to Paul Howell for this idea.

To place a shortcut in your Send To folder that points to your co-worker George's personal Desktop, sharing must first be enabled for George's C drive, and you must have access to George's \Windows folder. Then, on your own computer, open Network Neighborhood, click George's computer, click his C drive, and click his \Windows folder to display its contents. Right-click the Desktop folder and select Copy. Now, in your Explorer, navigate to your own \Windows\Send To folder, right-click in the right pane, and choose Paste Shortcut. You should see a new shortcut named Desktop in the right pane. Press F2 and rename this shortcut George's Desktop, or whatever you like.

Now when you select a document in your Explorer, right-click it, and choose Send To, George's Desktop, a copy of that document is created on, you guessed it, George's Desktop. All George does is click the icon to view the document.

Send to SendTo

You can put a shortcut to the SendTo folder in the SendTo folder.

If you want to browse for executables that you want to put in the SendTo folder as targets, you can send them there easily by right-clicking them, pointing to Sent To, and then clicking Shortcut to Send To. A message box appears telling you that you cannot move or copy the executable to this location, and it asks if you want to create a shortcut instead, which you do.

Attempting to right-drag the SendTo folder from the left pane of the Explorer into the SendTo folder in the right pane doesn't work. All you get is Open and Cancel in the context menu that appears — not Create Shortcut(s) Here.

What you need to do instead is right-drag the SendTo folder from the right pane of the Explorer to the SendTo folder in the left pane.

Now browse through your whole system, looking for executable files that would be great targets for sending documents to. When you find one, right-click it and choose Send To, Shortcut to Send To.

Send to the Desktop

You can create a shortcut to the Desktop folder, which is a subfolder of your \Windows folder. You can even create the shortcut on your Desktop. Then drag this shortcut to the SendTo folder, which is also a subfolder of your \Windows folder. This makes for an easy way to send stuff to the Desktop when it's not visible.

Create Shortcuts to DOS Programs

You can drag and drop a DOS application file to the Desktop or to a folder window just as easily as you can a Windows executable file. You automatically create a shortcut when you drop the file.

You'll probably want to make some changes to a DOS program's shortcut. You might want a different icon than the default MS-DOS icon that you get, and you may need to change some other properties as well. (All shortcuts have properties, which we'll get to in the next section.)

You can create a folder to store the shortcuts to your DOS programs, or you can mix these DOS program shortcuts with your Windows shortcuts. It's up to you.

If you have DOS files, such as files that you edit with the DOS Edit program, you can create shortcuts to these and store them on the Desktop or in a folder. The DOS programs and files can fit right in with the Windows programs and files, as long as they can run in a Windows DOS session.

Tip

You can run a mixture of DOS and Windows programs from a DOS batch file. Windows programs will run from the DOS prompt of a DOS virtual machine, so you can combine commands to run these programs with DOS programs.

You can call a DOS batch file with a shortcut, and the batch file can contain lines that start Windows programs. If you include the following command in a batch file, you can have a DOS batch file run a Windows program and wait for you to quit the Windows program to continue processing the commands in the batch file:

```
Start /w {Windows program}
```

We discuss many aspects of running DOS programs in "DOS in Windows" in Chapter 34.

What's Behind the Shortcut?

To see what's behind a shortcut, right-click it and choose Properties. The tabs and options in the resulting Properties dialog box differ depending on the type of shortcut that you right-clicked. If you are examining a shortcut to a Windows application, folder, or document, you will see a dialog box similar to the one shown in Figure 10-6.

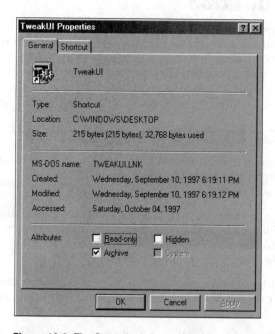

Figure 10-6: The General tab for a Windows shortcut. You can change the file attributes if you like.

The Properties dialog box for a Windows shortcut has two tabs: General and Shortcut. The filename of the shortcut (after all, it is a file) has a *lnk* extension. A shortcut is a link (or *lnk*) to another file. The only things you can change on the General tab are the file attributes of the shortcut file.

Click the Shortcut tab for a Windows shortcut to view the set of options shown in Figure 10-7.

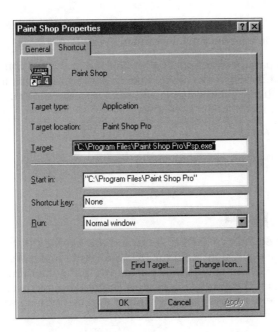

Figure 10-7: The Shortcut tab for a Windows shortcut. The Target field contains the name of the target file. You can change this field in numerous ways. The Change Icon button lets you change the shortcut's icon.

The properties of URL shortcuts are similar to those of Windows shortcuts, so most of the content in the next six sections regarding Windows shortcuts applies to them as well. Where there are differences, we point them out.

We discuss the properties of DOS (*pif*) shortcuts in detail in "Editing Shortcut Properties" in Chapter 34 and "DOS shortcut properties" later in this chapter.

The Target field

The Target field in the Shortcut tab lists the file that is linked to the shortcut. (The equivalent field for a URL shortcut is the Target URL field in the Internet Shortcut tab.) You can modify this field in many ways. If the target file is an application that accepts command line parameters, you can include them after the application name.

Tip

If you want to view the document or data file in the Target field with an application other than the one assigned to this file's file type in the Registry, you can type the path and filename of the desired application in front of the file's path and filename. In addition, you can add command line parameters after the application's name to alter its behavior. For example, if you type this entry in the Target field:

```
"C:\Program Files\Accessories\Wordpad.exe" /p
D:\Myfolder\Thisfile.txt.
```

The shortcut will print the file Thisfile.txt using WordPad.

Secret

The command line parameters in the Target field won't work if you drag a file to a shortcut. This is also true if you place a shortcut like this in the SendTo folder and then right-click a file and send it to the shortcut. Windows 98 acts as if the command line is as follows:

```
"C:\Program Files\Accessories\Wordpad.exe" %1
```

In this command line, %1 is the name of the dragged or sent file. The /p parameter is ignored.

The Start In field

The field now labeled *Start In* used to be called the Working Directory in Windows 3.1*x*. (The equivalent field for DOS shortcuts is the Working field in the Program tab.) This field is blank unless you put something in it. You may need to do this if the application in the Target field needs to find some application helper files in another folder and can't do so without help from you.

If the application doesn't require assistance in finding any helper files, you can make the Start In folder the folder that you want to contain the documents that use the application.

Hot keys

A *hot key*, which we also refer to as a *shortcut key* or an *accelerator key*, is a key combination that runs a shortcut. For example, press Ctrl+Alt+F and up pops FreeCell. Well, not actually, but it could if you defined the hot key for FreeCell. (If you're in Word, it opens the footnote pane.) Hot keys give you a keyboard method of quickly getting to the applications and files you use most often.

Secret

The problem with hot keys is that you have to remember which keyboard combination does what. (You also have to make sure you are not in a program that uses that hot key for another function.) When you use the mouse, the visual user interface gives you feedback that you are headed in the right direction. In contrast, you have to rely exclusively on your finger memory if you want to use hot keys. But then, to each his or her own.

To define a hot key, type the letter in the Shortcut Key field. Crtl+Alt will automatically be added to and precede the letter, making the hot key Ctrl+Alt+*letter*. If you want to use Ctrl+Shift+*letter* instead, then hold down the Ctrl key and the Shift key as you press the letter.

You can also define hot keys for shortcuts to DOS programs. The Shortcut Key field in a *pif* (the shortcut file to a DOS program) operates somewhat differently than it does in a shortcut to a Windows file. See "Hot Keys" in Chapter 34 for more details.

Undocumented

If you have just created a shortcut, you have to restart Windows to have the hot key take effect.

Tip

Want to create a hot key to call the Task Manager? Why not create one that resembles the Windows 3.1 keystrokes that called it? How about Ctrl+Alt+~ (Ctrl+Alt+tilde)?

Just define a shortcut to the Task Manager, which you'll find in the \Windows folder, and put the shortcut in one of the Start menus or on the Desktop. Define the hot key for this shortcut and you're in business.

Run in which size window?

Most of the time you want a shortcut to display the application or document in its normal (restored) window, in other words, a window that is bigger than the button on the Taskbar, but smaller than the whole Desktop (minus the Taskbar). The Run field lets you choose among these three alternatives.

If the shortcut just prints a document, for example, you might as well leave it minimized. If you want the application or document to fill the whole Desktop, then choose Maximized. There isn't an option for full-screen view.

Change the shortcut's icon

When you create a shortcut to an application, Windows 98 uses the first icon referenced in the application's executable file. Often this is adequate. If you have different shortcuts to the same application, though, you might want to distinguish them with different icons. You can choose among the icons that may be stored in the application's executable file (not all executable files have icons).

If your shortcut is to a document, Windows 98 chooses the first icon in the associated application's executable file. If a document doesn't have an associated application, then Windows 98 chooses the blank document icon. Just how documents get associated with applications is discussed in "Associating Actions with File Extensions" in Chapter 13.

To browse for icons, click the Change Icon button. In addition to looking for icons in the application's executable file, you can look in many other executable files as well. Three files that contain icons are \Windows\Explorer.exe, \Windows\Moricons.dll, and \Windows\System\Shell32.dll.

Tip

Lots of icons are available to use with your shortcuts. You can pick icons from icon libraries distributed as shareware, or from other executable files. The shareware on the *Windows 98 Secrets* CD-ROM features numerous icon editors and managers. These applications search through your files and automatically create icon libraries. This cuts down on the time it takes to choose new icons.

Find that target

Tip

If you have a shortcut, you can get back to the file linked to the shortcut by clicking the Find Target button. This is helpful if you want to run the application without any of the command line switches you may have put in the Target field.

When you click the Find Target button, Windows 98 opens a folder window that contains the target. If the Target field contains an application, Windows 98 opens the folder that contains the application, even if the field also contains a document. If the Target field only contains a document, the folder window containing the document opens.

This doesn't apply to URL shortcuts; in fact, the Internet Shortcut tab of the Properties dialog box for a URL shortcut doesn't even have a Find Target button.

DOS shortcut properties

If the shortcut targets a DOS window, application, or file (a file whose file type is associated with a DOS application), you'll get a different set of shortcut properties than the ones you get with Windows shortcuts. These properties are so extensive and so interwoven with the workings of DOS programs under Windows 98 that we devote an entire chapter to them. Turn to "Editing Shortcut Properties" in Chapter 34 for further details.

Undocumented

A DOS shortcut's properties are stored in a file that used to be called a Program Information File, or *pif*. The shortcuts that link to Windows files use the *lnk* extension. The shortcuts that link to DOS files use the *pif* extension. You can see these extensions if you use the File Manager or a DOS window. The *pif* extension isn't visible in the Explorer or in a folder window.

There is a folder named \Windows\Pif. This folder can contain the *pif*s that are associated with DOS programs. Anytime you click a DOS program name in the Explorer, you create a default *pif* for it in the same folder as the DOS program, unless it can't be created there, in which case Windows 98 places it in the \Windows\Pif folder. For example, if the DOS program is in a folder on a CD-ROM, Windows 98 won't be able to place the *pif* file on the CD-ROM (when you click the DOS program) so it will put the *pif* in the \Windows\Pif folder. If you drag a shortcut to a DOS file or DOS application onto your Desktop, the *pif* is stored in \Windows\Desktop.

All *pif*s are shortcuts. You can open an Explorer window and focus on a folder that contains a *pif* to see that it has the little black arrow in the white box in the lower-left corner of the MS-DOS icon.

Secret

Let's say that you create a shortcut to a Windows file or application. Later you decide to change this shortcut and have it link to a DOS batch file that calls your Windows application after running some other functions. What happens to your shortcut? Windows 98 automatically changes the *lnk* file to a *pif*. Easy as can be.

This doesn't work the other way. If you edit the Target field in a *pif* so that it refers to a Windows file, the *pif* does not automatically change to a *lnk* file.

Shortcuts on the Start Button

We discuss how to put shortcuts on the Start button and in the Start menus in "Drop It on the Start Button" in Chapter 11.

A Shortcut to a Shortcut

In "Creating a Shortcut to a Folder of Shortcuts" earlier in this chapter, we showed you how to make a shortcut to a folder that contains shortcuts. Can you create a shortcut to a shortcut? After all, a shortcut is a file, and if we can have shortcuts to files, why not a shortcut to a shortcut file?

Right-drag one of the shortcut icons that you have created from its source folder and drop it on the Desktop. Click Create Shortcut(s) Here. Now, right-click the shortcut on the Desktop and click Properties. If this is a Windows file shortcut, click the Shortcut tab and examine the Target field. If it's a DOS shortcut, or *pif*, click the Program tab and look at the Cmd Line field. If it's a URL shortcut, look at the Target URL field in the Internet Shortcut tab.

Notice that the name in the Cmd Line, Target, or Target URL field is not the name of the shortcut in the source folder, but rather the name of the file that the original shortcut is linked to. A shortcut to a shortcut isn't really a shortcut to a shortcut; it is a shortcut to the original file.

What Happens If I Move or Delete the Linked File?

Shortcuts are linked to a specific item — a file, a folder, and so on. If you move or delete that item, what happens when you click the shortcut?

If you have moved the item, Windows 98 tries to find it the next time you open its shortcut. While Windows 98 is searching, it displays the Missing Shortcut dialog box, as shown in Figure 10-8.

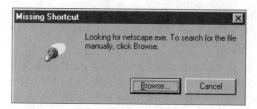

Figure 10-8: The Missing Shortcut dialog box. If you know where you moved the target, you can help out by clicking the Browse button.

When Windows 98 creates a shortcut, it records the creation time and date of the linked file or folder down to a fraction of a second and stores this information in the shortcut file. It is extremely unlikely that any two files or folders would be created at the same time and date to this level of precision.

Using a built-in function, Windows 98 begins searching for the lost file, folder, or object starting at its original location. You may have edited the file or changed its name—Windows 98 doesn't care, because it is searching on the file or folder's creation time/date.

The search method is not foolproof. If you move the target object (say a linked file) from one volume (say the D drive) to another volume (say the C drive), it won't find it. If your shortcut is to a file on a mapped networked drive, and the mapping of that drive changes (say from D to F), the link to the target is lost.

If you delete the file or folder, then of course Windows 98 won't find it. As it's looking, Windows 98 does keep track of the file or folder that is nearest in time/date to the actual linked item. If it can't find what it is looking for, it gives you the option of choosing the item closest in time, which can provide some weird "matches." You don't have to accept the file that Windows 98 suggests.

Shortcuts to URLs come up short all the time because the webmasters on Internet are always moving their web pages around. No big deal—you just get an error message in the Internet Explorer stating that the page can't be found. You'll have to look around for it, or whatever replaces it. You might try clicking in the Address bar, pressing the End key, and erasing the last part of the URL up to the previous forward slash (/). If this shortened URL takes you to the web page above the one you are looking for, you may be able to travel a link from there to the page you "lost."

Shortcuts in the Help Files

The Windows 98 help files, which you access by clicking the Start button and choosing Help, are filled with shortcuts that take you to the item that you have a question about. Of course, you may already be there.

The shortcut icon in the help file is a little like the black arrow used to indicate shortcut icons. It is a purple arrow curving to the upper-left corner instead of a black arrow curving to the upper-right corner.

Click the shortcut arrows in the help files to take the action that is explained in the sentence surrounding the arrow icon.

Creating Application-Specific Paths

If you start an application from a shortcut, you may find that it won't work because you haven't correctly identified the location of necessary accessory files in the Start In or Working directory (see "Working directory" in Chapter 34). You might also want to be able to run an application from the Run dialog box (Start, Run) without specifying the path to the executable file.

Secret

By editing the Registry, you can associate a set of folders that house the accessory files an application needs to work correctly. In addition, you can specify the complete pathname to the application. Michael Giroux gave us the basis for these steps:

STEPS

Specifying Paths to Applications in the Registry

Step 1. Click Regedit.exe in your \Windows folder.

Step 2. Click the plus signs in the left pane of the Registry to drill down to the following branch:

```
HKEY_LOCAL_MACHINE\SOFTWARE\Microsoft\Windows\
CurrentVersion\App Paths
```

Step 3. Right-click the App Paths icon in the left pane, point to New, and then click Key. A new key folder appears in the left pane of the Registry editor. Type the name of the executable file, including the *exe* extension.

Step 4. Double-click Default in the right pane while the new folder is highlighted in the left pane. Type the full path to the executable file in the Edit String dialog box. Click OK.

Step 5. You will now be able to type the name of the executable file in the Run dialog box without the pathname and have the application actually run.

Step 6. Define the path to the executable file's associated files by right-clicking the right pane of the Registry editor while the focus is on the new folder.

Step 7. Point to New, and then click String Value. Enter the name **Path** in the highlighted name field in the right pane of the Registry Editor.

Step 8. Double-click Path in the right pane. In the Edit String dialog box, enter the complete path to the folders that contain the associated files. If there is more than one folder, separate the pathnames with semicolons. Click OK.

(continued)

Step 9.   If you have any trouble with these steps, look at the other examples under the App Paths folder. When you are done, exit the Registry.

The paths that you entered in step 8 will be added temporarily to your path statement when you invoke the executable file, whether by clicking a shortcut to it, by entering its name in the Run dialog box, or by clicking it in the Explorer or a folder window.

Disabling Link Tracking

Windows 98 comes with a little utility that you can use to disable the link-tracking feature for a shortcut. This comes in handy if your shortcut links to a resource on a network server and that resource is moved around by the network administrator.

You can also use it to specify a new target for a shortcut. Network administrators can use this tool to help users stay connected to networked resources. Of course, if your resources are managed through an Intranet web server, many of these problems go away.

You can find shortcut.exe on your Windows 98 CD-ROM in the \tools\apptools\envvars folder. To see what you can do with it, open a DOS window and type **shortcut /?**.

Summary

Windows lets you put links to your applications and files on your Desktop and anywhere you find useful. Shortcuts are an incredibly powerful and convenient means of accessing resources on your computer.

▶ We show you how to use the power of shortcuts to put your most important applications and documents within easy reach.

▶ We guide you through the many ways of creating shortcuts.

▶ We show you how you can drag and drop files to a Desktop file viewer, a Desktop printer, or a default file opener.

▶ DOS and Windows applications can get along much better under Windows 98, and you can even make them appear to like each other.

▶ If you add application-specific paths to your Registry, you can run applications from the Run dialog box without specifying their paths.

Chapter 11

The Start Button and Finding

In This Chapter

Microsoft paid millions to the Rolling Stones to let them use their song *Start Me Up* for the rollout of Windows 95. The Start button has met with mixed success ever since. At least with Windows 98, it has gained a bit of badly needed flexibility. We discuss:

▶ Shutting down Windows 98

▶ Optimizing your Start and Programs menus

▶ Deleting unwanted shortcuts to recent documents from your Documents menu

▶ Adding and removing items from your Start menus

▶ Putting the Desktop on the Start button

▶ Running the Start menus from the keyboard

▶ Creating and saving complex file searches

▶ Using Find to build Start menus and get rid of unwanted files

Starting

In "The Taskbar and its Toolbars" in Chapter 6, we looked at the Desktop and the Taskbar. The Start button is attached to the Taskbar, but there is enough going on with it that it gets its own chapter. It is a primary entry point into Windows 98. As you change your Desktop to match your needs, the Start button continues to provide useful services.

The Start button is the Windows 95 and 98 replacement for the Windows 3.1*x* Program Manager. And like the Program Manager, the Start button gives you a way to quit Windows. The Start button inherits all the program groups and program items when you convert from Windows 3.1*x* to Windows 98.

Secret

If you want, you can change the name on the Start button to something like Panic. The new name has to be five letters to exactly replace Start. You can use a hex editor (see the *Windows 98 Secrets* CD-ROM) or WinHacker to edit the Explorer.exe file. To change the name, replace all instances of *Start* in Explorer.exe with your new five letters (after you save a copy of your original Explorer.exe).

WinHacker saves a good copy of Explorer.exe as Explorer.old in your \Windows folder before it makes the change, so you can recover by booting to the DOS prompt and copying the "old" Explorer over the hacked version. You can find it at http://www.albert.com/authorpage/000103280/wh95-11r.htm.

Stopping

We start our discussion of the Start button by talking about the Stop button. The most important function you can find on a computer is how to stop it, how to get it ultimately under your control so that if you have any problems you can just stop the whole thing.

Click the Start button. Click Shut Down, and mark the Shut Down option button. We're outta here. We know it seems funny that the Start button is also the Stop button, but there it is.

Clicking Shut Down presents you with the dialog box shown in Figure 11-1. This dialog box gives you four choices. If your computer's BIOS has a Windows-compatible Automated Power Management (APM) facility, and you haven't disabled it, the default option (the first time you start the computer) is Stand By. Your other choices are Shut Down, Restart, and Restart in MS-DOS Mode.

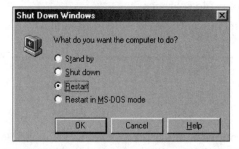

Figure 11-1: The Shut Down Windows dialog box. Make one of four choices.

Windows 98 defaults to the option you chose the last time you made a selection in this dialog box.

You can use the System Policy Editor (see "System Policy Editor" in Chapter 24) to disable the shut down function.

Shut down

Shut down actually means to shut down Windows 98. If you have the Windows 98 Advanced Power Management capabilities, and most new computers do, your computer turns off as soon as you choose Shut Down and click OK.

To keep your computer running after you choose Shut Down, you need to disable APM in your computer's BIOS setup. If you do this, you have to turn off the computer yourself after shutting it down. If you have disabled APM and want to restart Windows after issuing the Shut Down command, wait until you see the "It's now safe to turn off your computer" screen and then press Ctrl+Alt+Delete.

Undocumented

The Windows 98 shut down screens are Windows bitmap (*bmp*) files. Microsoft gave them *sys* extensions just to keep your prying eyes out of them. If you want to change them, you can edit them with MS Paint. Their names are Logos.sys and Logow.sys. You'll find them in the \Windows folder.

Undocumented

Using a shareware utility called Shutdown95 and Task Scheduler, you can automatically close down Windows 98 at a pre-arranged time. You'll find Shutdown95 and a Task Scheduler replacement, ClockMan95, on the Windows 98 Secrets CD-ROM. You can find also find Shutdown95 at http://www.windows98.com.

Troubleshooting Windows 98 shut down problems

If your computer hangs when you shut it down, you may have an incompatible device driver, incorrectly configured hardware, or other problems. Microsoft provides a detailed troubleshooting guide. You can find it in the Knowledge Base at http://premium.microsoft.com/support/kb/articles/q145/9/26.asp.

Restart

If you have had a problem with Windows 98 and just want to start over again, you can choose Restart in the Shut Down Windows dialog box. This option works just like Shut Down does, but it doesn't require that you press Ctrl+Alt+Delete to restart Windows 98. It restarts Windows 98 with a warm boot.

Undocumented

To restart Windows 98 quickly without going through the warm reboot process, mark Restart, and then hold down your Shift key while clicking the OK button in the Shut Down Windows dialog box.

Restart in MS-DOS mode

Choosing Restart in MS-DOS Mode means closing down Windows 98 and going to the DOS command prompt. Your computer isn't rebooted, so when DOS starts, it doesn't read a special Config.sys or Autoexec.bat file. Instead, it reads the file DOSstart.bat, which is located in your \Windows folder. You can get out of MS-DOS mode and back to Windows 98 by typing **Exit** or **Win** at the DOS prompt and pressing Enter.

To get the full details on how to use this option to run recalcitrant DOS programs, turn to the "DOS in MS-DOS mode without a reboot" section of Chapter 34.

When you exit Windows 98 in this manner for the first time, you automatically create an Exit to Dos.pif file in your \Windows folder. You can edit this file so that it will in fact reboot the computer before going to MS-DOS mode (real-mode DOS). We discuss this in great detail in "DOS in MS-DOS mode with a reboot" in Chapter 34.

Stand by

Windows 95 displayed a Suspend option in the Start menu on computers that supported APM, as long as APM hadn't been disabled in the BIOS setup. Windows 98 does not have this option; Microsoft wants to encourage you to use Stand by mode, so they've now made that the first choice in the Shut Down Windows dialog box. (You won't see this option if you've disabled APM.)

If you put your computer in Stand by mode, its power usage is reduced and you can restart it quickly without having to reload all your applications. This would be great if everything worked after your computer spent a night in Stand by mode. Maybe this will be the case, maybe not. Microsoft wants computers to be perceived as ready to go at a moment's notice. Perhaps most will be someday.

The Start Menu

Click the Start button and up pops the Start menu, as shown in Figure 11-2. This is the first of the cascading menus. The nice thing about the Start button is that it is a starting point. There never was much of a starting focus with the Windows 3.1x Program Manager.

What is not so great about the Start button is that it takes a lot of mousing to get to where you want to be. One way to cut down on extra mousing is to drag an icon for an application, folder, or document and drop it on the Start button to create a shortcut to the item in the main Start menu. We discuss Start menu shortcuts in more detail later in this chapter.

In programmer-speak, the Start menu is a specialized window object. It has specific methods not found in most windows, but it has inherited many of the basic window methods. What this means for you as a user is that you can right-click the items in the Programs, Favorites, and Documents menus and get an appropriate context menu.

Because all of the submenus under the Programs and Favorites menu items are folders (all subfolders of \Windows\Start Menu), their context menus are the same ones that you find when you right-click a folder icon in an Explorer or folder window. By the same token, when you right-click an application or document shortcut in the Start menu, you get the same context menu as you get when you open an Explorer or folder window and right-click the same shortcut in the \Windows\Start Menu folder or one of its subfolders.

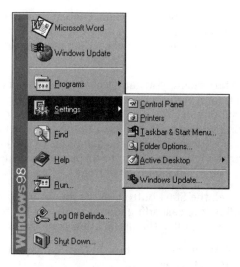

Figure 11-2: The Start menu — your window into the world of Windows 98.

You can drag and drop submenu items from the Programs and Favorites menus onto other submenus to rearrange your Start menu. To move items up and down in a menu, just drag and drop them to the desired location.

You can use TweakUI to name other folders as the Start Menu folder, the Programs folder, and the StartUp folder. You should do all three if you want to completely move the Start Menu folder. You might want to make a copy of the Start Menu folder (and all its subfolders) in its new location first, edit it, and then use TweakUI to designate this new folder as the Start Menu folder. Once all that is working, you can delete the original Start Menu folder or switch back and forth between multiple Start Menu folders. We provide more details in the next section.

Programs

Look closely at the Programs icon in the Start menu. It looks like a folder window to remind you that the Programs menu is like a folder window that contains applications. Windows 98 comes with a collection of shortcuts to applications and accessory programs, which it stores in the \Windows\Start Menu\Programs folder.

If you installed Windows 98 in an existing Windows 3.1*x* directory, all the previous program groups are converted to folders and placed in the Programs folder as well. What you see in the Programs menu is the contents of the Programs folder. You aren't restricted to putting just applications in the Programs folder. You can put documents in it too, just as you could with the program groups in the Windows 3.1*x* Program Manager.

The Programs menu can have multiple submenus. Each submenu can have its own submenus. The submenus are displayed as a separate cascading menus in the Programs menu. Of course, the cascading menus can get pretty complicated after a while.

Using tools built into the Start menu, you can easily organize everything in the Programs menu to suit your preferences. You can create a flat or hierarchical structure of submenus. You can rename the application or document icons to anything you want. If you want to move items in the Programs menu, just drag and drop them to new locations in the menu hierarchy. You can also right-click menu items to display a context menu that lets you create new menu items, among other options.

To get to an application, click the Start button, move the mouse pointer over the Programs icon, and follow the cascading menus until you get to the application that you want to run. Click the application once to run it.

Can't find your application? We'll show you how in the "What you can do with Find" section later in this chapter.

The \Windows\Start Menu\Programs folder is a special folder. Your Registry keeps track of it. Using TweakUI, you can designate another folder as the Programs folder.

STEPS

Naming a New Folder As the Programs Folder

Step 1. Click your TweakUI shortcut on your Desktop (or click the TweakUI icon in the Control Panel), and click the General tab.

Step 2. In the Folder drop-down list, select Programs, and click the Change Location button.

Step 3. In the Browse for Folder dialog box, highlight the desired folder, click OK, and then click OK again.

Step 4. You'll have to restart Windows. Click the Start button, choose Shut Down, mark Restart, and then hold down the Shift key as you click OK to restart Windows without going through a warm reboot.

The new Programs folder (whatever its actual name) won't have very useful menu items in it unless you have carefully constructed it. You can make a copy of your previous Programs folder (\Windows\Start Menu\Programs), edit it, and then use TweakUI to designate this new edited folder as your Programs folder.

You can also use a slight variation of these steps to designate a different folder as the Start Menu folder, and another folder as the StartUp folder. If you paste a copy of your Start Menu folder into a new location (not under \Windows), you can edit it to create the basis for your three new menus.

StartUp menu

If you have applications that you want to start when Windows 98 starts, you can put shortcuts to them in this menu (which corresponds to the \Windows\Start Menu\Programs\StartUp folder). You can close a program that started when Windows started any time you choose. If you then decide you want to start the program again, click the application in the StartUp menu.

We show you how to put shortcuts in the StartUp folder/menu later in this chapter.

You can use TweakUI to change which folder acts as your StartUp folder; just follow the Naming a New Folder As the Programs Folder steps in the previous section and substitute *Startup* for *Programs* in step 2.

Documents

The last 15 documents that you started by clicking an icon in an Explorer or My Computer window are displayed in this menu. You can restart a document and its associated application by clicking it once in the Documents menu.

For Windows 98 to add a document to this list, you have to have started it from an Explorer or folder window. That way, Windows 98 can grab the document name. If you open a document from inside your application, Windows 98 doesn't know how to put it on the list. However, applications written specifically for Windows 95 or 98 can also place their newly opened documents on the menu.

The list contains shortcuts to the documents. You can delete all the shortcuts at once (without affecting the documents themselves). Right-click the Taskbar, click Properties, click the Start Menu Programs tab, and click the Clear button. All the shortcuts in the Documents menu are gone.

Undocumented

You can also remove shortcuts individually. Windows 98 puts the shortcuts to your recently opened documents in the \Windows\Recent folder. You can edit these shortcuts or delete them as you like. You need to be sure that the Show All Files option button is marked in the View tab of the Folder Options dialog box (choose View, Folder Options in any folder or Explorer window). Otherwise, the Recent folder will be hidden from view.

Cleaning Up the Documents Menu

Step 1. Open an Explorer window.

Step 2. Click the plus sign next to the \Windows folder. Highlight the Recent subfolder under the \Windows folder.

Step 3. The shortcuts to the documents are displayed in the right pane. You can delete them in any manner you choose.

Clearing the Documents menu

You can use TweakUI to clear the Documents menu every time you restart Windows. Just click the Paranoia tab, and then mark Clear Document History at Logon. (The TweakUI icon is in your Control Panel. If you don't have it, you can install TweakUI from the \tools\ResKit\Powertoy folder of your Windows 98 CD-ROM.)

To keep recent document shortcuts from ever appearing in the Documents menu (or in the \Windows\Recent folder), click the IE4 tab in TweakUI and clear the Add New Documents to Documents on Start Menu check box. You'll have to restart Windows to have this change take effect.

If you'd like to see the inner workings of a trick like this, you can make the contents of the Documents menu go away without using any utilities:

Making the Documents Go Away

Step 1. This trick requires that you turn off the Recycle Bin's habit of saving deleted files. To do this, right-click the Recycle Bin icon on your Desktop, choose Properties, and click the Global tab. Mark the Use One Setting for All Drives option button and the Do Not Move Files to the Recycle Bin check box. Then click OK.

Step 2. Click Regedit.exe in your \Windows folder to run the Registry editor. Click the plus sign to the left of HKEY_CURRENT_USER, and continue opening subfolders until you display this key:

```
HKEY_CURRENT_USER\Software\Microsoft\Windows\Current
Version\Explorer\Shell Folders
```

Step 3. Highlight the Shell Folders folder, and look in the right pane for an object named Recent. If this object doesn't exist, create one now by right-clicking a blank space in the right pane, clicking New, String Value, typing **Recent**, and pressing Enter.

Step 4. Double-click the Recent object. In the Edit String dialog box that appears, replace the value C:\Windows\Recent with the value C:\Recycled. From now on, Windows 98 will immediately send all additions to your Documents menu to the Recycle Bin instead, so they will not appear on the Documents menu. The actual file you accessed will not be affected.

Step 5. Close the Registry editor.

No Documents or Favorites on the Start menu

You can use TweakUI to remove the Favorites and Documents menu items from the Start menu. Click your TweakUI shortcut on your Desktop (or click the TweakUI icon in the Control Panel), click the IE4 tab, and clear the Show Documents on Start Menu and Show Favorites on Start Menu check boxes. You'll have to restart Windows to have this change reflected in the Start menu.

Furthermore, you can use TweakUI to change which folder acts as the Documents folder. Follow the Naming a New Folder As the Programs Folder steps in the "Programs" section earlier in this chapter, and substitute *Recent Documents for Programs* in step 2.

Put a shortcut to your recent documents folder on the Desktop

Tip

If you want to be able to quickly edit the contents of your recent documents folder, put a shortcut to it on the Desktop. Open the Explorer and focus on the \Windows\Recent folder. Right-drag the Recent folder to the Desktop and drop it there. Click Create Shortcut(s) Here. Edit the name of the shortcut folder icon to Recent Docs or whatever.

Now you can quickly get to the folder of recent documents and remove the documents that you don't care to have there.

Settings

The Settings menu provides access to the folders and dialog boxes that you use to change most of the Windows 98 parameter values. Because there are many different values, and they are spread all over the place, this is a convenient starting point.

The Settings menu contains shortcuts (although not actual Windows shortcuts as described in the previous chapter) to the Control Panel and the Printers folder. It also contains the Taskbar & Start Menu command, which leads to the Taskbar Properties dialog box; the Folders & Icons command, which displays the Folder Options dialog box; and the Active Desktop, Customize My Desktop command, which brings up the Display Properties dialog box.

The Control Panel

The Control Panel doesn't exist as an actual folder, so if you use the Explorer to look for a subfolder called Control Panel under your hard disk drive, you won't find one. You will see it in the Explorer in the left pane, on the same level as the local hard drives and the Printers folder, Dial-Up Networking folder, and Scheduled Tasks folder. We discuss the Control Panel in "Getting to the Control Panel" in Chapter 16.

You can use the System Policy Editor to keep users out of the Control Panel. (See "System Policy Editor" in Chapter 24.)

The Printers folder

All the hardware drivers for your currently installed printers are stored in the Printers folder. This folder also contains the Add Printer icon, which lets you add new printers. You can reach the Printers folder through the Control Panel and the My Computer window as well as the Settings menu. The Printers folder isn't an actual folder, so it only shows up in the left pane of the Explorer window. There are no files associated with the Printers folder (other than printer driver files) — just Registry settings. As you add new printers, their properties are stored in the Registry.

We cover the Printers folder in Chapter 29.

Taskbar and Start menu properties

Clicking the Taskbar & Start Menu item in the Settings menu brings up the Taskbar Properties dialog box. You can display the same dialog box by right-clicking the Taskbar and choosing Properties. The first tab in the dialog box is Taskbar Options.

We describe the first two check boxes in the Taskbar Options tab in "Hiding the Taskbar" in Chapter 6. The Show Small Icons in Start Menu check box lets you change how the Start menu looks. Mark and clear this box to see which look you prefer. The Show Clock check box lets you choose whether or not to display the clock at the right end of the Taskbar.

The Start Menu Programs tab is where you will find much of the power to add, remove, clean up, and move menu items (which are just shortcuts) in the various Start menus. This tab is shown in Figure 11-3.

Windows 98 has modified the Start menu to let you move some menu items from one part of the Start menu to another without invoking the Start Menu Wizard. Just drag a Start menu item from its present location to a new location on the Start menu. This trick also works on the Favorites menu, both the one displayed on the Start menu and the one in the My Computer and Explorer windows.

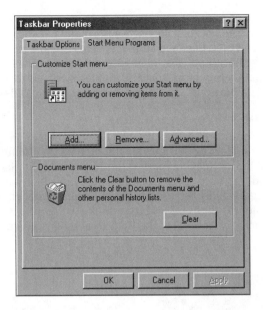

Figure 11-3: The Start Menu Programs tab of the Taskbar Properties dialog box.

Add Start menu items

You can use the Start Menu Programs tab of the Taskbar Properties dialog box to create shortcuts for applications and then place them on the Desktop or add them to the Start menu, the Programs menu, or the submenus of the Programs menu. Click the Add button to start the Create Shortcut Wizard, as shown in Figure 11-4. This Wizard lets you browse for an application, select the menu folder that you want to place the shortcut in (\Windows\Desktop, \Windows\Start Menu, \Windows\Start Menu\Programs, or one of the Programs subfolders), and change the shortcut's name.

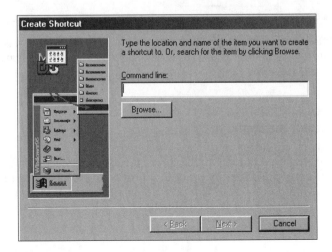

Figure 11-4: The Create Shortcut Wizard.

The menu items, which are really shortcuts, don't display the little black arrow in the lower-left corner of their icons. We normally expect to see this black arrow on shortcut icons. Because all menu items are shortcuts, the Microsoft designers felt that there was no need to add the arrow to the icons displayed in the menus. Keep in mind that the menus themselves are not shortcuts, but rather subfolders of the \Windows\Start Menu folder.

Remove Start menu items

To remove menu items or entire menus, use the Remove button in the Start Menu Programs tab of the Taskbar Properties dialog box. Be careful—these removals aren't stored in the Recycle Bin for you to put back in place. The Remove Shortcuts/Folders dialog box, which is displayed when you click the Remove button (see Figure 11-5), lets you navigate among the menus/folders to find the items (or folders) that you wish to remove. Of course, the quickest method is to simply right-click the item directly in the Start menu and choose Delete.

Figure 11-5: The Remove Shortcuts/Folders dialog box. You can highlight the menu item or menu folder that you want to remove. If you remove a menu folder, you also remove (delete) all the shortcuts in that menu.

Edit, move, add, delete Start menu items—the Advanced button

Click the Advanced button in the Start Menu Programs tab of the Taskbar Properties dialog box to open an Explorer view of your Start Menu. This clipped Explorer works like any other Explorer window. (The Start Menu folder is set as the root—see "Explorer Command Line Parameters" in Chapter 8 to learn how this is accomplished.)

You get all the capability you need to move menu items throughout the Programs menu and in and out of the Start menu. You can right-drag menu items (shortcuts) from another Explorer window and drop them in any menu folder that you like. You can create new menu folders in the Start menu or in any submenu folder.

The Start Menu Explorer, as shown in Figure 11-6, demonstrates very clearly that the Start menu is really a series of folders — special folders, but folders nonetheless. You can manipulate them as you would any other folders.

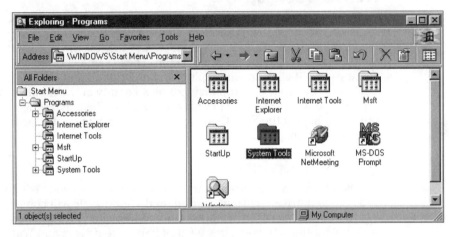

Figure 11-6: The Start Menu Explorer. If you highlight a menu folder icon name in the left pane, the contents of that menu folder appear in the right pane.

The menu folders are meant to hold shortcuts. If you want to add a shortcut to a menu folder, the best way to do it is to right-drag an application icon from another Explorer window to the Start Menu Explorer, drop it in the menu folder that you want, and choose Create Shortcut(s) Here.

You can copy or move application icons (and document or folder icons) to the menu folders in the Start menu if you wish, but the menu folders are really intended to hold shortcuts to applications.

The Start Menu Explorer is especially useful for moving menus about. You can't move menus using the Add and Remove buttons.

Windows 98 has added the capability of dragging and dropping the Programs, Favorites, and Documents menu items around (although you cannot drag items *into* the Documents menu, only out of it). You can also use drag and drop to move items that you've dropped on the Start button. Windows 98 added the drag and drop capability because users wanted a quick and dirty way to change their Start menus without having to use the "advanced" Start Menu Explorer.

Folder Options

The Start button provides another way to reach the Folder Options dialog box. This is the same dialog box that you see when you are focused on a drive, folder, or file in the Explorer and click View, Folder Options. Since the Start button is always easily accessible, this is a quick way to get to these settings. For more on how the Folder Options dialog box works, see "Folder Options" in Chapter 8.

Active Desktop

To turn your Active Desktop on or off, click the Start button, click Settings, Active Desktop, and mark or clear View As Web Page. To update your Active Desktop, do the same and click Update. And to view the Display Properties dialog box, click Customize My Desktop. These same choices are available when you right-click an empty part of your Desktop and choose Active Desktop—but your Desktop may not be so empty at the moment. We discuss the Active Desktop in Chapter 6, and the Display Properties dialog box in "Changing the Size, Color, and Font of Objects on the Desktop" and elsewhere in Chapter 28.

Windows Update

The Windows Update setting is there to help you keep your Windows 98 software and drivers current. Click it, and Windows 98 will connect via the Internet to the Microsoft Windows Update web site. After asking your permission, this site compares a list of hardware drivers and Windows applications generated on your computer by a Windows 98 applet against a Microsoft list of the latest versions of these drivers and applets. If there are updates available from Microsoft for your software and hardware drivers, you will be notified and you can choose to download any of them. We suggest you use Windows Update periodically to make sure you receive the latest Windows 98 updates.

Find

The Find command is on the Start menu, it's located in the Tools menu in the Explorer window menu, and it's available by pressing the F3 key. We discuss the Find capability later in this chapter.

You can eliminate Find (although not the F3 key version) using the System Policy Editor. (See "System Policy Editor" in Chapter 24.)

Help

The Start menu Help command gets you to the unified help for all of Windows 98. Click Help and you get the Windows 98 Help window, as shown in Figure 11-7.

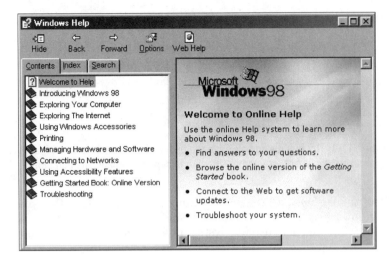

Figure 11-7: The Windows 98 Help window.

Because Windows 98 help is a unified help system, you don't have to search a lot of separate help files to learn about Windows 98. Windows help files are stored in the \Windows\Help folder.

The Windows help engine has been greatly updated since the August 24, 1995 roll out of Windows 95. For example, if you click the Web Help button on the Help toolbar, you can connect to the Windows Update web site on a Microsoft server. This site is also accessible more directly in the Start menu by clicking Settings, Windows Update.

Run

This is a command line interface. If you want to run a program by typing its path and name and perhaps some command line parameters, then this is the place for you. This is like calling a program from the DOS command line, especially now that you can run Windows programs from the DOS command line.

The Run dialog box (shown in Figure 11-8) keeps a little history in the Open drop-down list. You can bring up previous commands, edit them, and run them again.

You can type the name of a document that has an associated application (as defined in the Registry) and run it. For example, you can type the name and path of an *ini* file. When you click OK, Notepad is invoked, and it displays the *ini* file in its client window area.

Undocumented

Want to quickly open a window that displays the files and folders in the root directory of your boot drive? Click the Start button, and then click Run. Type a backslash (\ ) in the Run dialog box, and then click OK.

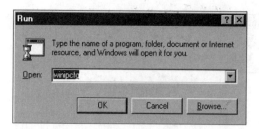

Figure 11-8: The Run dialog box. Type the path and filename of your DOS or Windows application, document, or Internet URL. Put in some command line parameters, if you like.

You can use TweakUI to clear the Run history every time that you start Windows 98. Click the Paranoia tab, and then mark Clear Run History at Logon. You can also use the System Policy Editor to hide the Run command.

Log on as a different user

The option to Log Off (and thereby log on as a different user) appears in the Start menu if you have a network, have installed or used Direct Cable Connection, or have enabled user profiles. If you haven't done any of these things, you won't see it.

Log Off allows you to get out of the current user's setup and into a new user's configuration. Turn to "Whose Desktop Is This Anyway?" in Chapter 12 for more details.

Right-Click the Start Button

You can right-click the Start button and choose Open, Explore, or Find. Depending on what software you have installed, you may see another option here (such as Add to Zip). Choose Open to display a folder window focused on the Start Menu folder, which is a subfolder of the \Windows folder.

The Start Menu folder contains an icon for the Programs folder. Notice that the icon is the same as the one displayed next to Programs in the Start menu. Clicking the Programs folder icon opens a folder window containing the Accessories folder, the StartUp folder, and other folders and applications. The hierarchy of folders and subfolders in the Start Menu folder corresponds to the cascading menus and submenus within the Start menu.

The Start Menu folder gives you a way of traversing the menus using folders, a different style for those who wish to use it. Because the Start menu is also a folder, you can drag shortcuts into it and its subfolders. You can click icons in the Start Menu folder window to open up other folder windows, and then navigate back up to the parent folders.

When you right-click the Start button and click Explore, Windows 98 displays an Explorer window focused on the Start Menu folder. Unlike the Explorer window that's displayed when you click the Advanced button in the Start Menu Programs tab of the Taskbar Properties dialog box, this is a full Explorer. The folder tree in the left pane will take you anywhere you want to go; it's not restricted to the Start Menu folder and its subfolders.

Finally, right-clicking the Start button and choosing Find opens the Find dialog box. We describe this dialog box in the section entitled "The Find Function" later in this chapter.

Drop It on the Start Button

There is an easy way to add menu items to the Start menu. Drag and drop icons from the Desktop or from a folder or Explorer window to the Start button. When you drag an icon to the Start button, Windows 98 automatically adds a shortcut to it in the Start menu. When you click the Start button to display the main Start menu, any icons you've added in this way appear in their own little section above the Programs command, as shown in Figure 11-9. Better yet, drag and hover over the Start button, and the Start menu opens up; you can now drop your icon onto the Programs or Favorites menu, or one of their cascading submenus.

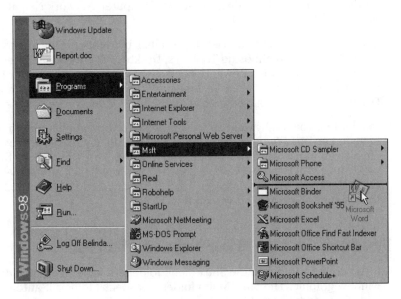

Figure 11-9: The Start menu opens to let you drop an icon into one of the Programs submenus. The icon is translucent while it's being dragged. Notice that, as with other menu items, the shortcuts that were added at the top of the Start menu don't have the little black arrow in the lower-left corner.

These menu items are shortcuts just like the other menu items. The nice thing about them is that the icons are full size, so you can see them more easily. These shortcuts are stored in the Start Menu folder. You can place them in any order that you like. Just drag and drop them to the appropriate location. The shortcuts that originally came on the Start menu can't be moved.

The Desktop on the Start menu

Undocumented

A neat trick is to put parts of the Desktop itself on your Start button. Since the Desktop is also a folder, you can drag it from the Explorer onto the Start button. The Desktop folder is located under the \Windows folder.

When you click the Desktop icon on the Start menu, you open a window to your Desktop (minus some crucial pieces). You now have a Desktop window on your Desktop. All the shortcuts that you placed on the Desktop are in the window, along with any documents or folders that you put on the Desktop. This is very handy if the icons on your Desktop are covered with other windows. You just place a window to your Desktop over them.

This trick also comes in handy when you use the keyboard to get to the Start menu. Press Ctrl+Esc to get to the Start menu from anywhere — even full-screen DOS sessions. After the Start menu pops up, you can use your arrow keys to get to the Desktop icon. This gives you a quick way to switch to an inactive application that has a shortcut on the Desktop. The Desktop folder on the Start menu does not contain My Computer, Network Neighborhood, or Recycle Bin.

You can display a separate Desktop toolbar by right-clicking an empty part of the Taskbar and choosing Toolbars, Desktop. The Deskmenu item that comes with Microsoft's PowerToys also lets you easily get to your Desktop. It creates a Tray icon called Deskmenu. When you click the icon, a menu of Desktop items is displayed on top of all the windows on your Desktop.

In addition, you might want to try a little shareware application that we have included on our *Windows 98 Secrets* CD-ROM called Tab2Desk. This program allows you to use Alt+Tab to get to the Desktop. Tab2Desk works the same as Minimize All Windows (available when you right-click an uncovered part of the Taskbar). When you press Alt+Tab, you can choose the Tab2Desk icon to minimize all open windows on the Desktop.

Folders in the Start menu folder

If you create a folder in the Start Menu folder, its folder icon includes a little window graphic. The Start Menu folder is a special folder; it automatically adds this window graphic to the icon of any folder stored within it. You can see this by navigating in your Explorer to your \Windows\Start Menu folder. You'll notice that all the subfolders of the Start Menu folder have icons that include this graphic.

At times, it may be more convenient for you to create a new folder in the Start Menu folder than to add a shortcut to a folder. When you click an item in the Start menu for a *shortcut* to a folder, Windows 98 just opens the folder window for you. In contrast, if you add an *actual* folder to the Start Menu folder and then put shortcuts inside the folder (to documents, executables, or other folders), then when you point to the menu item for the folder in the Start Menu, a cascading menu appears with all the shortcuts you placed in the folder.

To do this while in the Explorer view of the Start Menu folder, right-click a blank area of the right pane. Then point to New, and click Folder. Type a name for your folder, press Enter, and it's ready to go. You can now right-drag executables, documents, and so on into this new subfolder of the Start Menu folder to create shortcuts. Once you've done this, you can easily pick them from the Start menu.

One other difference between creating a folder in the Start Menu folder versus creating a shortcut to a folder is that a folder containing shortcuts does not change when you add or subtract items in the actual folder. In contrast, a shortcut to a folder is dynamic and always remains up-to-date with the contents of that folder.

Control Panel on a Start menu

Secret

You normally get to the Control Panel by clicking the Start button, pointing to Settings, and finally clicking Control Panel. The Control Panel is usually displayed in a folder window. However, you can make the Control Panel a menu item in any of the Start menus, and you can display it as a menu and not as a window. To do so, take the following steps:

STEPS

The Control Panel as a Menu

Step 1. Right-click the Start button, and click Open. If you want to place the Control Panel on the main Start menu, stop here. Otherwise, continue to open up windows of menu items until you open the menu folder that you want to contain the Control Panel.

Step 2. Right-click an open area of the window. Point to New in the context menu, and then click Folder.

Step 3. The temporary name New Folder is highlighted so that you can type over it with a new name. Type the following text exactly as we have printed it here:

```
Control Panel.{21EC2020-3AEA-1069-A2DD-08002B30309D}
```

Step 4. Press Enter, and the New Folder icon is replaced with the Control Panel icon.

Step 5. Click the Start button. The Control Panel icon appears as a menu item, and all the Control Panel icons are listed in a cascading menu attached to it.

The resource ID given in step 3 is unique to the Control Panel. You can find it by using your Registry editor and searching for Control Panel. We discuss some additional ways that you can put Control Panel applets on your Start menu in the "Shortcuts to the Control Panel" section of Chapter 16.

You can use the same trick for the Printers folder and/or the Recycle Bin folder; their resource IDs are as follows:

```
Printers       Printers.{2227A280-3AEA-1069-A2DE-08002B30309D}
Recycle Bin    Recycle Bin.{645FF040-5081-101B-9F08-00AA002F954E}
```

Use these resource IDs in step 3 of the Control Panel As a Menu steps to put these folders on the Start menu.

Keyboard Control of the Start Menus

You can run the Start menus with your keyboard. The most important keyboard combination is Ctrl+Esc, which displays the main Start menu. The Windows key on Windows keyboards also displays the Start menu.

Tip

If you press the Ctrl button while you click the Maximize button in the upper-right corner of a folder or Explorer window, the window expands to full screen and the Taskbar disappears. When you have opened a window in full-screen mode, pressing Ctrl+Esc or the Windows key still displays the Start menu.

You can choose menu items on the Start menu by pressing the letter key that corresponds to the underlined letter in the name. If you have added items to the Start menu that begin with the same letter, the letter key will take you to these items first. The letter keys operate in round-robin fashion, going to the first item that starts with that letter, and then the next, until it starts over at the top again.

The letter keys work in all the submenus also. There is no underlined letter in the shortcut names under the Programs menu, so you type the first letter of the item.

The arrow keys can also move you through the menus. The up and down arrow keys move you within a menu. When you get to the bottom of a menu, pressing the down arrow again takes you up to the top. (By the same token, pressing the up arrow when you're at the top of a menu takes you to the bottom.) The right and left arrow keys move you forward and back between the cascading menus. When you reach a menu item that you want to run, press Enter.

Undocumented

If you press Ctrl+Esc and then Esc, the Start menu disappears, but the focus stays on the Start button. When the Start button has the focus, you'll see the focus rectangle on it. You can confirm the Start button still has the focus by pressing Enter after you've pressed Ctrl+Esc, Esc. The Start menu will reappear.

Once the Start button has the focus, you can press Tab repeatedly to change the focus clockwise from the Start button to other objects on your display. If you have a toolbar immediately to the right of the Start button, the focus will shift there, then to the Taskbar, then to any other toolbars, then to the Desktop, then to any of Active Desktop items, and then back to the Start button. If the Taskbar is immediately to the right of the Start button, the focus will shift there first.

If the focus is on the Taskbar, you can use the arrow keys to move the focus from button to button. To restore an application or bring it to the top of the windows on the Desktop, move the focus to the Taskbar button for that application, and press Enter.

If the focus is on an icon on the Desktop, you can use your arrow keys to move among the Desktop icons to focus on the application, folder, or file you want to open. Press Enter when the focus is on the desired icon.

Undocumented

It's hard to see whether the focus is on the Start button, the Taskbar, or the Desktop, and using the Windows default color scheme (called the Windows Standard scheme) makes this even more difficult. If the Start button has the focus, you'll see the typical dotted rectangle around the word Start. If the Taskbar or the Start button has the focus, and if your color scheme has an Active Window Border color that differs from the 3D Object color (something that is not true of the Windows Standard scheme), you will see a border line around the Taskbar.

If the Desktop has the focus, the Taskbar border will display the Inactive Window Border color, and an icon on the Desktop will be highlighted. See "Changing the Size, Color, and Font of Objects on the Desktop" in Chapter 28 for details on how to change these colors.

If you have defined hot keys for the shortcuts on the Start menus, you can start an application immediately without going through the Start button, just by pressing its hot key combination. We describe how to create hot keys in "Hot keys" in Chapter 10 and Chapter 34.

Long Start Menus

Windows 95 menus that were too long to fit on the screen produced a second column of menu items. Windows 98 does away with double columns in favor of scroll arrows at the bottom and top of the single menu column. When you point to the scroll arrows, the menu items that are currently hidden scroll into view. The best way to get rid of these long menu columns is to hierarchically divide your menu items.

Secret

You can speed up the display of the hidden menu items by clicking the scroll arrows instead of pointing to them. To further speed the scrolling, hold down the Ctrl key as you point to the arrows or, faster still, hold down the Ctrl key while you click the arrows.

The Find Function

Windows 98 includes a real search capability.

You can get to this Find function in a number of ways. If you want to search for files or folders, right-click the Start button, the My Computer icon, or any folder icon, and then click Find in the context menu. You can also choose Tools, Find, Files or Folders in any Explorer or folder window.

The option of searching for computers is available if you have installed any form of networking, including just Direct Cable Connection. Click the Start button and choose Find, Computer in the Start menu or choose Tools, Find, Computer in any folder or Explorer window. You can also right-click the Network Neighborhood icon and click Find Computer in the context menu.

Windows 98 expands the capability of the Find option from what was originally available in Windows 95. You can now search for people using directory services on the Internet or your Windows Address Book. You can also connect to Internet search engines to search for topics, words, or phrases found on web sites or in newsgroups.

Tip

The easiest way to find a file or folder? Press the F3 key when the focus is on the Desktop, a folder window, an Explorer window, or the Taskbar.

Tip

Just because the command is called Find doesn't necessarily mean the usefulness of this function is limited to finding things. For example, you can use Find as a filter to list all the executables in a folder or in a set of folders in one window.

Finding files or folders

You can find files and/or folders that match the criteria you set in the Find dialog box (right-click the Start button and click Find). Windows 98 gives you a significant number of options to define your search strategy.

File or folder name

Undocumented

If you are looking for a specific file or folder and you know its name, type the name in the Named field, as shown in Figure 11-10. You can search for multiple folders, files, or file types. Just separate their names by commas, as in:

```
*.bat, *.sys, *.txt, bill?.*
```

Secret

You can type a partial name with wild cards. The wild cards are ? and *. The question mark stands for one letter and the asterisk for one or more letters. Table 11-1 shows these and other options.

Notice that unlike searching in DOS for filenames, you can have an asterisk or question mark in front and still get meaningful results. In fact, the search algorithm is much more flexible and powerful than what was available with DOS or Windows 3.1*x*.

In the Look In field, enter the general location for the file or folder. If you know a file or folder is on a certain disk drive, choose that drive letter. If you want to narrow it down further, use the Browse button to choose a folder, or include a pathname in the Named field.

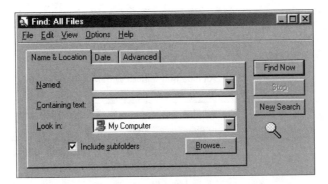

Figure 11-10: The Name & Location tab of the Find dialog box. Type a file or folder name or partial name. If you know the general area (folder or drive) where the file or folder is located, choose a drive from the Look In drop-down list, and/or type the pathname to a folder in the Named field.

By default, Windows 98 includes subfolders in the search. You probably want to do a top-down search, so leave the Include Subfolders check box marked unless you know what folder the file is in.

Table 11-1   Find Options

Entered in Named Field	Search Location
*	All files and folders.
.	All files and folders.
*.	All files.
.	No files or folders.
.exe	No files or folders (because a filename cannot start with a period).
abc	All files and folders with *abc* in name (including extensions).
exe	All files and folders with exe in name or extension. Most likely executable files.
*.exe	All files with exe in extension only.
abc	All files and folders with *abc* in name.
*abc	All files with *abc* as last letters in name (not including extension).
*abc?	All files with *abc* as second to last letters in name (not including extension).
?abc	All files and folders with *abc* as at least second letters in name if not later.

(continued)

Table 11-1 *(Continued)*

Entered in Named Field	Search Location
?abc*	All files and folders with *abc* as the second through fourth letters in name.
??abc	All files and folders with *abc* as at least the third letters in name if not later.
?abc?	All files and folders with at least one letter in front of *abc* and at least one behind in name.
?a?.*	Three-letter file name with middle letter of name given and extension unknown.

Secret

Find will search for your files in hidden subfolders if you have marked the Show All Files option button in the View tab of the Folder Options dialog box (click View, Folder Options in an Explorer or folder window). Find will not find your fonts in the Fonts folder (which has the System attribute set, but is not hidden) if the Look In field in your Find dialog box is set to \Windows and not to Windows\Fonts. The hidden subfolders under the \Windows folder are NetHood, Recent, Pif, Sysbckup, ShellNew, Spool, and Inf.

You may find it convenient to "root" two or more searches at different starting points. In the Look In dialog box, just separate multiple roots with semicolons. For example, you could type **C:\Windows; D:\Temp** to start searching at two folders on separate drives. (See Figure 11-11.)

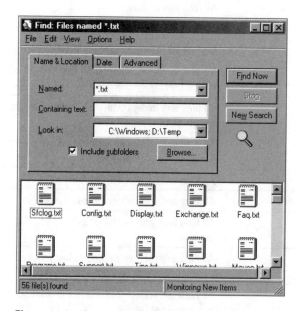

Figure 11-11: Separate drive letters with semicolons to search multiple drives. By indicating the folder to start in, you can make one search start at several different points.

Text string

You can search for files that contain a given text string by typing it in the Containing Text field. However, Windows 98 doesn't index your computer files, so it will take a while to search through all your files (if that is what you choose) to find instances of the text string. The search method has to open and search through each file to find out if it contains the string.

Microsoft Office contains its own indexer, called Find Fast, which lets you use the File Open dialog box of any Office application to quickly search for documents based on a text string. If you have installed Microsoft Office, you may want to use this method of searching for text strings in documents instead. Other document indexers are available, such as AltaVista Personal Search 97, which provides a very powerful means of indexing and thereby quickly finding documents that pertain to your text search criteria. Personal Search 97 recognizes over 200 file formats, including Outlook Express and Windows Messaging, and presents the list of matching files in seconds. It's available for free at http://altavista.digital.com/av/content/searchpx.htm.

If you leave the Named field blank, Find searches through all the files that match the criteria you set in the Look In and Containing Text fields.

Date

Windows 98 lets you limit your searches based on dates. You can restrict a search to a particular time frame, and you can further restrict the search by specifying whether you're looking for files/folders that were modified during that period. You can also restrict the search to a time period during which the files or folders were created or last accessed.

To set search criteria based on the date, click the Date tab (shown in Figure 11-12) .

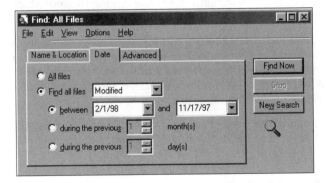

Figure 11-12: The Date tab of the Find dialog box. You can limit the search for files and folders based on the time/date they were modified, created, or last accessed. If you're looking for a recently changed file, search for files that have been modified in the last few days.

File type and file size

You can search for files that are of a certain file type, or are at least as big as or greater than a certain size. Click the Advanced tab in the Find dialog box, as shown in Figure 11-13.

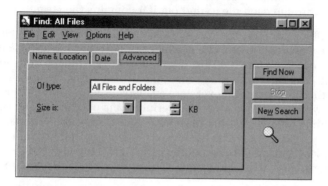

Figure 11-13: The Advanced tab of the Find dialog box.

You use the Advanced tab to limit the search to files of a certain type — for example, all text files, all Microsoft Word files, or all Quattro Pro files. Moreover, if you have some idea of how large the files you're looking for are, you can use size as a search criterion.

Starting the search

After you have entered all the criteria in the various tabs of the Find dialog box, click Find Now. Windows 98 expands the Find dialog box and displays the search results in the pane below the search criteria, as shown in Figure 11-14. You can use the View menu to choose among the four standard views (Large Icons, Small Icons, List, and Details).

The results pane looks like a folder window with one exception: When you view the results in Details view, Windows 98 adds a column named In Folder that lists the folder in which each item was found. You can sort the found files and folders by filename, folder name, size, file type, or date modified, in either ascending or descending order.

If you want to go to the folder that contains a file or folder listed in the results pane, select the file or folder and choose File, Open Containing Folder.

Saving the search

Windows 98 retains your search criteria after you've performed the search. If you don't like the results of a search, you can modify the criteria and do another one. If you want to use a particular set of search criteria as the basis of future searches, you can save it as an icon on your Desktop. To do this, make sure the criteria you want to save is specified in the Find dialog box, and choose File, Save Search.

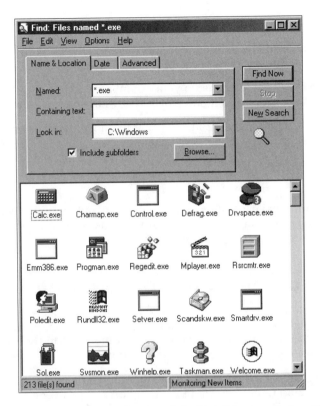

Figure 11-14: The results pane of the Find dialog box displayed in Large Icons view. If you use Details view (the default), you can sort the results in ascending or descending order by filename, folder name, size, file type, or date modified.

Tip

The saved search will end up as an icon on your Desktop, which is not the best of locations. You might want to create a folder under your \My System folder called Find. You can drag these icons off the Desktop and into this folder, and then create a shortcut to the Find folder on the Desktop.

When you want to perform a search that you've saved as an icon, click the icon (or a shortcut to it). Windows 98 displays the Find dialog box with all the search criteria specified. Optionally modify the criteria, and then click Find Now to perform the search.

What you can do with Find

Tip

You can use Find to locate all the executable files in your games folder and then drag shortcuts to all these games to a newly created games submenu on your Start menu. It is great to be able to see all the executables within the subfolders of a folder that defines a general class of applications. This is especially true if you use Large Icons view in the results pane.

This is a good way to create menus under the Start menu. You can search for all executables on your hard disk and then drag them in groups to new menu folders. You can also create folders or shortcuts to folders on the Desktop, and then drag documents or executables over to these folders.

The Find command really opens up your computer and lets you see what is hiding under the covers. You'll be surprised at what you have ignored.

Tip

Use Find for file management. You can use it to find all the files on your entire hard disk so that you can order them by size or age or file type. You can get rid of all the *tmp* (temporary) files, or all the really old text files. If you have over 10,000 files on your hard disk, you'll have to break this search up by folders.

If you want additional capabilities (such as search and replace) check out http://home.sprynet.com/sprynet/funduc/ for a complete search-and-replace program that supports regular expressions.

Finding a computer on your network

You can use a completely different Find function to find a server or computer on your local network, as long as you know its unique name. Click the Start button, point to Find, and then click Computer. This option won't appear unless you have installed the network options on your computer.

You can also right-click the Network Neighborhood icon on your Desktop and then click Find Computer. Or, in your Explorer, choose Tools, Find, Computer.

You have to know the exact name of the computer; you can't use wild cards. Needless to say, a find utility isn't worth much if you have to know exactly what it is you are looking for.

If you do use this feature, you need to preface the name of the computer you are looking for with two back slashes (\\ ). This is the universal naming convention for a server — and therefore a computer — name.

Searching the Internet

You can also click the Start button, point to Find, and then click On the Internet. This starts the Dial-Up Networking connectoid that connects to your Internet service provider (if this is how you connect to the Internet). After you connect, the Internet Explorer starts up and displays your default search page.

You can configure which search service you want to use to find things on the Internet. The default service is Microsoft's search page. If you are using the Internet Explorer, you can change the default search page. Follow the steps in "Where Does the Search Start?" in Chapter 9.

You can also search for people's e-mail addresses (found by web crawlers). Just choose Find, People. This command also lets you search your local store of e-mail addresses in your Windows Address Book.

Summary

You can use the Start button and the Find function to make your work easier and increase your efficiency.

▶ We show you how to create and modify Start menus to match the way that you work.

▶ We provide a means to trim the unnecessary files from the recently used files list.

▶ If you find that Desktop icons are often covered up, you'll appreciate being able to put the Desktop on the Start menu.

▶ Windows 98 has a very powerful search engine. You can define intricate searches that are quite useful in file management, and you can use searches to build Start menus and create Desktop folders.

Chapter 12

Desktop Strategies — Making Windows 98 Your Own

In This Chapter

Windows 98 is a set of tools waiting for an artist. This is a chance to let your creativity shine. We discuss:

▶ Cleaning up the clutter in your Start menus

▶ Putting the Start button to work with your heavily used applications

▶ Letting loose and just piling it on the Desktop

▶ Putting folders on the Desktop to hold your shortcuts

▶ Letting out the TV lurking inside your computer

▶ Turning a folder window into your Program Manager and using the Explorer as your File Manager

▶ Using the real Program Manager and File Manager as your user interface without giving up of the power of the new interface

---

It Comes with a Start Button

"But, I don't know where to start."

Microsoft went for the uncluttered look in Windows 95. Many of its customers thought the Windows 3.1x Program Manager was ugly. In a reaction to this criticism, Microsoft reduced the Desktop to a Taskbar, a Start button, and a few icons.

Along comes Windows 98 and your Desktop is suddenly quite cluttered. Microsoft apparently saw all that unused space and decided to fill some of it up. As a result, it designed the Active Desktop to let you display *active windows,* which are narrowly defined applets that can be updated frequently, and *channels,* which you can set up to download specific information off the Internet as it is updated. You can set Internet Explorer to full-screen mode so that the channels provide the working background for all your other application windows.

The addition of these Active Desktop elements, however, does nothing to change a basic reality: You have to build your own virtual computer — which, after all, is the real computer — for yourself. Windows 98 provides the tools, but leaves the design up to you.

Windows 98 gives you shortcuts, cascading menus off the Start button, a Desktop that can contain icons as well as "live" channels, folders with properties, a powerful browser in the Internet Explorer, a configurable context menu, a SendTo folder, a configurable connection to the Internet, and a moveable/hideable Taskbar with toolbars. We provide a collection of add-on utilities to increase your computer's functionality still further.

A Desktop Strategy

Every one of you would like to set up the Windows Desktop to match your own preferences. In most cases, you can. However, you'll be prevented from making the changes that make your computer your own if a network administrator or system information manager has set up your computer over the network — and enforced a mandatory style (stored on a secure server).

Windows 98 provides a great deal of flexibility — although, of course, there will never be enough to completely please any of us. In this chapter, we present five major strategies for designing a Windows Desktop. You can ignore all our hard work here and go off on your own, or you can start with one of our approaches that closely matches your own style, and then build on it.

The major considerations in developing a Desktop strategy are getting the tools and putting them close at hand. Windows 98 doesn't include everything that you need in the user interface, so you are going to have to add a number of utilities to make it work for you. We have some, and we point out areas where you'll need to get more.

Don't hide the power of Windows 98 under a bushel. Bring it out, make it accessible, make it easy. Take advantage of additional utilities and make them accessible, too.

Whose Desktop Is This Anyway?

When you start Windows 98 for the very first time, you get a logon box similar to the one shown in Figure 12-1. The point of the logon box is to let the computer know who you are and whether you really are who you say you are. Windows 98, in turn, will let you configure your own Desktop, so even if other people use the computer they won't mess with your Desktop settings.

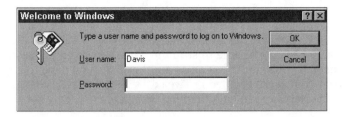

Figure 12-1: The Windows 98 logon box. Type your user name and password to protect your Desktop configuration.

You can configure Windows 98 to make the logon box go away and not come back. If you do this, you are telling Windows 98 that either you are the only user of this computer or that everyone should be treated the same and should get the same Desktop with this computer. You are also saying that you do not want to log on to a local area network at Windows 98 startup.

You must satisfy these three conditions to make the logon box go away:

1. You must have a blank password.

2. You must disable user profiles.

3. You must have Windows configured so that your primary network logon is Windows Logon.

If you meet these conditions (described in the next two sections), Windows 98 won't display the logon box the next time it loads because it won't have any need for your user name and password.

You could also make the logon box go away by simply clicking the Cancel button or pressing the Escape key. However, if you use this method, you only cancel the logon process this one time. The next time Windows 98 starts, it will display the logon box again. Furthermore, if you cancel the logon process and then try to use Windows 98 features that require your account name and password, such as Dial-Up Networking, you'll find that Windows 98 won't remember this information, and you won't be able to save any passwords.

It is possible to log on onto your computer and onto a network without typing your user name and password. If you use this method, you don't need to make your password blank, you don't need to disable user profiles, and you can log onto your local area network. To do this, you need to use TweakUI to send your name and password to the logon box.

Click the TweakUI icon in the Control Panel, click the Network tab, fill in your name and password, and mark Log On Automatically At System Startup. You'll see the logon box flash briefly on your Desktop. You don't need to click OK.

If you use this logon method, you won't be able to set Windows 98 to clear the last user's name from the logon box. (You normally set this option by marking the Clear Last User At Logon check box in TweakUI's Paranoia tab.) In addition, you won't be able to stop the logon box to enter the name of another user. If you want to log on as another user, you have to log on as the default user (the user specified in TweakUI's Network tab), change the values in the Network tab, and then log on again.

Setting up Windows 98 for multiple users

You can easily configure Windows 98 to allow for multiple users on one computer. Each user can have his or her own settings, including the Desktop, Start menu, Favorites, and so on. Individual settings are determined by *user profiles* (see the steps below) and by *user policies*. We discuss how to set user policies in "System Policy Editor" in Chapter 24.

Windows 98 comes with a Wizard that makes it easy to set up new user profiles:

STEPS

Configuring User Profiles

Step 1. Start your computer after installing Windows 98.

Step 2. When the logon box appears, type a user name and click OK. You have to enter a user name, but you can omit the password. This enters your password as blank.

If you have installed Windows 98 over Windows 3.1*x*, you won't necessarily have a logon box. If not, go to step 3 and finish the rest of the steps. This will configure Windows 98 to call up a logon box the next time you start.

Step 3. Click the Start button, point to Settings, and then click Control Panel.

Step 4. Click the Users icon in the Control Panel to initiate the Multi-User Wizard, as shown in Figure 12-2, and then click Next.

Step 5. Enter a user name and password in the next two dialog boxes. You don't have to enter a password for a given user. No password just means it is easier to log on as that user; it doesn't get rid of the logon box because you have still enabled user profiles.

Step 6. Next, choose among the options shown in the Personalized Items Settings dialog box, as shown in Figure 12-3.

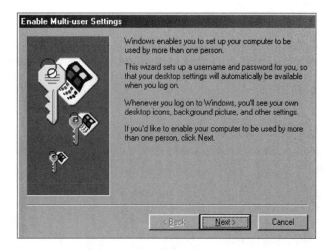

Figure 12-2: The Multi-User Wizard helps you create user profiles for each user name and password.

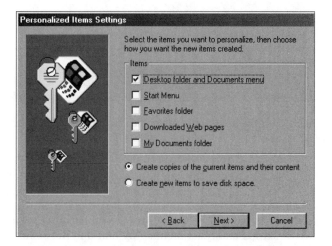

Figure 12-3: Each user can have his or her own Start menu, Favorites folder, temporary Internet cache folder, Internet Explorer history folder, recent documents folder, Desktop, and so on.

Step 7. Choose whether to create these individual settings from existing folders, or start anew with blank folders. Click Finish.

As soon as you create one new user, Windows 98 enables user profiles and updates the parameters in the User Profiles tab of the Passwords Properties dialog box to the values shown in Figure 12-4. (To display this dialog box, click the Passwords icon in the Control Panel.) The new user's settings, as well as the settings for all the original users, are stored in separate subfolders (one for each user) under \Windows\Profiles.

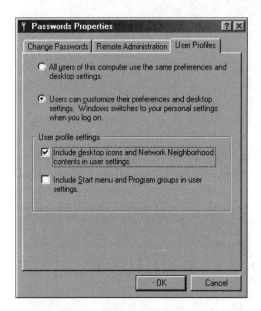

Figure 12-4: The User Profiles tab of the Passwords Properties dialog box. User profiles are enabled as soon as you set up a new user.

If you choose to use the same Desktop for all users (by marking the first option button in the User Profiles tab), any changes you make to the current user in the Registry and any changes you make on the Desktop or in the Start menus will apply to all users. If you let different users customize their own Desktops and Start menus (by marking the second option button), their changes will apply only to their configuration.

Once you set up one additional user, clicking the Users icon in the Control Panel displays the User Settings dialog box (see Figure 12-5). You can add new user profiles, delete existing ones, and change the passwords or settings for a given user. Of course, any user can change his or her own settings or those of any other user. Only by implementing user policies can you restrict users from altering these settings.

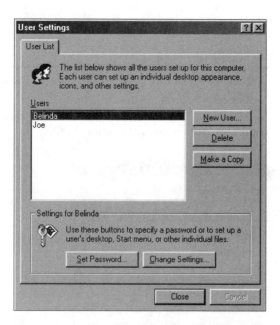

Figure 12-5: The User Settings dialog box. You can add or remove users and change all their settings.

You can also use the Passwords icon in the Control Panel to change your password. In the Passwords Properties dialog box, click the Change Passwords tab, and make the desired changes. You can even change your password to blank if you have previously put in another password.

Some settings on your computer apply to all users, and some can be individually determined. Using TweakUI, the System Policy Editor, and user profiles, you can configure individual user settings to some degree, but not completely. Clicking the question mark the upper-right corner of the TweakUI dialog box and then clicking a setting will tell you if the setting is determined on a per-user or global basis.

Setting up your network logon option

To log onto the network when you first start Windows 98, you have to enter your user name in the logon box. If you want to just get into Windows 98 locally, you don't need to log onto a network, and you can forego the logon box at startup time. To set up your logon options, follow these steps:

STEPS

Configuring Logon Options

Step 1. Click the Start button, point to Settings, and then click Control Panel.

Step 2. Click the Network icon in the Control Panel. Display the Primary Network Logon drop-down list (see Figure 12-6).

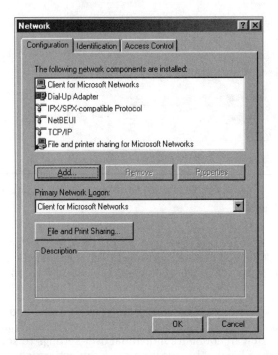

Figure 12-6: The Network dialog box. If you click the Primary Network Logon field, the Description field tells you about the field. To get more detailed information, right-click the field and choose What's This?.

Step 3. Choose Windows Logon, Client for Microsoft Networks, Client for NetWare Networks, or other possible choices.

Step 4. Click OK. Restart Windows to have your changes take effect.

If you choose Windows Logon in step 3, you are saying you don't want to log onto the network, whatever network that might be. If you choose Windows Logon and you've met the first two conditions described in "Whose Desktop Is This Anyway?" earlier in this chapter, the logon box won't appear the next time you start Windows 98.

You can choose Client for Microsoft Networks in step 3, and as long as you aren't logging on when you start up Windows 98, you can still make the logon box disappear. If your network connection is through Dial-Up Networking, for example, and not through a local area network, you won't have to see the logon box or actively log onto your Windows 98 computer.

Even though you can set up Windows 98 so that you don't see the logon box, this doesn't mean that you haven't logged onto your own computer. If you have a user name and a blank password, you are logged on as your user name when you start Windows 98, and all your other passwords (for example, your DUN passwords) are stored in your password file.

Securing the Windows 98 Desktop

Windows 98 is designed to be user-friendly, not secure. Your Windows 98 computer is not protected from unauthorized use, even if you set up a name and password to protect (sort of) your Desktop configuration. Anyone with physical access to your computer can just log on under a new name and password or press Escape when the logon box appears.

If you want a higher level of access restrictions, you'll need add-on utilities. Passwords and security features are not "friendly," but neither is the experience of discovering that someone has tampered with your computer.

We have included shareware utilities on our *Windows 98 Secrets* CD-ROM. You can find more utilities that provide an additional measure of safety at http://www.windows98.com. If you don't control physical access to your computer, you might consider using them. In addition, if you have enabled user profiles, you can modify Windows 98 to be more secure. Details are available at http://www.conitech.com/windows/secure.html.

You can also download Clasp97 from http://www.cyberenet.net/~ryan/ or the killer security application StopLight 95 ELS at http://www.safe.net/stoplite.htm/.

Dealing with a corrupted password file

If you have logged onto a Windows 98 computer, Windows 98 creates a password file and saves all your other passwords in this file. You gain access to the additional passwords in this password file by logging onto your computer with your user name and password (which may be blank). Windows 98 will not create and save a password file for you if you have not logged on under your user name (at least once), and it will not let you access that password file unless you are logged on under that user name. If you canceled the logon box, then you aren't logged on, so you won't have access to any passwords and you won't be able to save any passwords.

If you have never seen the Windows 98 logon box, check to see if you have any password (*pwl*) files stored in your \Windows folder. If not, you can either configure user profiles for multiple users as described in the "Whose Desktop Is This Anyway?" section or install Dial-Up Networking. Either of these actions will let you log in anew.

If you find that other applications are unable to remember their passwords, but their Save Password check boxes are not grayed out and are checkable, your password file might be corrupted. You will need to either delete or rename it.

If you find that your DUN connectoids no longer have attached passwords, your password file might be corrupted. See "Saving your DUN connectoid passwords" in Chapter 18.

Undocumented

If you get the error message "MPREXE Caused an Invalid Page Fault in Kernel32.dll" while you're trying to access your Internet service provider or when you're using Dial-Up Networking, you most likely have a corrupted password file.

If you suspect that your password file is corrupted, delete or rename your *pwl* files in your \Windows folder. Restart Windows and let Windows rebuild them. You'll have to enter all new passwords, but now they can at least be saved.

You can look at a number of Microsoft Knowledge Base articles that deal with password issues. Go to http://premium.microsoft.com/support/kb/articles/Q135/1/97.asp or http://premium.microsoft.com/support/kb/articles/Q137/3/61.asp or http://premium.microsoft.com/support/kb/articles/Q148/9/25.asp.

Dealing with the Start Button

If you installed Windows 98 over your existing Windows 3.1*x* directory, you will likely find a large number of submenus attached to the Programs menu on your Start button. Windows 98 transforms all your program groups into menus (and their corresponding subfolders in the \Windows\Start Menu\Programs folder), and it turns your program items into shortcuts. All these menus add up to a big mess.

Windows 98 has its own collection of menus and shortcuts on the Programs menu as well, and these only add to the clutter. You'll probably want to reorganize things soon after you set up Windows 98. You may wonder if you can get rid of some of the menus. You also may not remember the functions of the applications that now have shortcuts in your various new menus.

Tip

One way to deal with all this clutter and still have a manageable set of Start menus is to drag the menu folders out of the \Windows\Start Menu\Programs folder into a temporary holding folder. Take the following steps to clean up your Start menus:

STEPS

Uncluttering Your Start Menus

Step 1. Right-click the My Computer icon on your Desktop. Click Explore to display the Explorer window.

Step 2. Make sure that Show All Files is turned on (choose View, Folder Options, and click the View tab).

Step 3. In the left pane of the Explorer window, highlight the drive or folder in which you want to put a folder that will temporarily store some Start menu items.

Step 4. In the right pane, right-click, point to New, click Folder, and then type a name for the folder such as **TempStart**.

Step 5. Navigate to the \Windows\Start Menu folder in the left pane.

Step 6. Highlight the Programs folder, find the menu folders in Programs that you want to temporarily move out of the Start menus, and drag (move, not copy) them from the Programs folder over to the TempStart folder.

You can also temporarily move shortcuts out of the menus; you might want to drag them to a subfolder of the TempStart folder.

You can use the Explorer to rearrange the menu folders under the \Start Menu\Programs folder so that they make more sense to you. Unlike the Windows 3.1x Program Manager, the Start menus are hierarchical. The hierarchy of folders and subfolders under the Programs menu corresponds directly to the hierarchy of menus and submenus in the Start menu.

You can continue to move folders and subfolders back and forth between TempStart and your \Windows\Start Menu\Programs folder, rearranging their order, pulling shortcuts from one folder to another, and so on. TempStart gives you a place to store all the extra folders from your Windows 3.1x configuration until you decide what to do with your new configuration.

The Start button itself

You can place shortcuts right on the main Start menu by dragging folder, application, or document icons over to the Start button and dropping them on it. You should only put your most heavily used applications (or folders or documents) on the main Start menu. To start an application that you've dropped on the Start button, all you have to do is click the Start button and then click the application icon (or press Ctrl+Esc, use the down arrow key to highlight the application icon, and press Enter). This level of convenience demands that you list just the applications (or folders) that deserve it.

There is a cost to this strategy. As the main Start menu gets bigger, it takes longer to draw, and the shortcuts you add make it hard to get to the other items on the Start menus. The icons on the main Start menu are full-size (unless you right-click the Taskbar, click Properties, and then mark Show Small Icons in Start Menu), which means they take up a considerable amount of room. You should restrict the number of icons you place on the main Start menu so that they don't bog you down.

You aren't restricted to placing your shortcuts on the main Start menu. If you drag a shortcut to the Start button and wait until the menu pops up, you can then drag the shortcut up the menu and out onto one of the submenus. (Not all submenus allow you to add shortcuts in this way; two that do are the Favorites and Programs submenus.)

The menus on the Programs menu

The Programs menu is the replacement for the Windows 3.1*x* Program Manager. It can contain submenus as well as icons for applications or documents. You can choose how to mix these different elements. If you are moving up from Windows 3.1*x*, you can create a Programs menu that duplicates the program groups you had in your Program Manager. You just configure it to have only submenus, and you configure the submenus to correspond to your program groups.

Tip

If you have just one level of submenus in your Programs menu, these submenus will contain the shortcuts to your applications. If you prefer, you can create a hierarchy of two or more levels of submenus. With this type of setup, you could group similar submenus together (for example, all editing and word processing submenus), and then put them under a more general submenu (say, editors), which would be located directly under Programs.

You can use the Programs menu as often or as infrequently as you like. It can take a fair amount of mousing to get to applications in your Programs menu because you may have to navigate through several cascading menus. You might want to use the Programs menu for applications that you use only once in a while. Another idea is to place the applications you use the least out in the most far-flung submenus, and put the programs you use all the time in the main Programs menu.

Multiple toolbars

Windows 98 (and Internet Explorer 4.0) adds toolbars to the Taskbar. (To display/hide them, right-click an empty area on the Taskbar, point to Toolbars, and mark/clear the check marks next to the toolbars in the submenu.) These toolbars don't have to stick with the Taskbar. They can either connect to the edges of the screen or float freely on the Desktop. To move a toolbar, point to the line at the left (or upper) edge of the toolbar. When the mouse pointer becomes a double-headed arrow, drag the toolbar to an edge of the screen and drop it there, or drop it over the Desktop.

A toolbar can function as a window full of shortcuts to applications and documents. The advantage of a toolbar over a folder window is that you can keep it hidden until you move your mouse pointer to the edge of your screen where it is docked, at which point it slides into view. (To do this, right-click an empty area on the toolbar and mark Auto Hide.) In addition, you can force it to display even if you are working in another application in a maximized window. (Right-click the toolbar and choose Always on Top.)

You can turn off text labels for the toolbar buttons by right-clicking the toolbar and choosing Show Text. If you also right-click the toolbar and choose View, Small, you can make the toolbar available but unobtrusive, as shown in Figure 12-7.

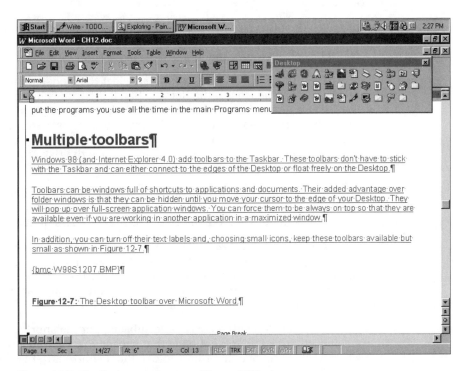

Figure 12-7: The Desktop toolbar over Microsoft Word.

Pile It on the Desktop

Your computer Desktop can take it, so why not pile it on? You can throw just about anything that you want on the Desktop, but the best idea is to put shortcuts to applications, folders, and documents there. There is little need to hold back; if you have something that you are dealing with right now, put a shortcut to it on the Desktop.

The Desktop is often easy to get to (especially if you have a large high-resolution monitor) so you may want to put shortcuts to your most heavily used applications on the Desktop. However, just because shortcuts to your most important applications (in terms of use) end up on the Desktop doesn't mean you should reserve the Desktop for only these high-priority items. You can put just about anything there.

The Desktop is a very convenient temporary storage area. You can right-drag files out of a folder window or the Explorer and drop them there (creating shortcuts when the context menu appears) without having to open another folder window. You can go back later and drag these shortcuts to new locations. Alternatively, you can drop the actual files on the Desktop, and move them later.

You can even drag text selections out onto the Desktop from documents created in WordPad or other Windows 98-aware word processors. When you use the Desktop this way, it functions like a permanent Clipboard.

It's easy to get things off your Desktop. Just select the icon and press the Delete key, or drag the icon to the Recycle Bin. If the icon is just a shortcut, then no harm is done. You've just removed a link to your application or document. If the icon represents a file, however, you've deleted the whole file. That's why it's a good idea to not put important files and applications on the Desktop, but only shortcuts to them. You reduce the risk of deleting something that you wanted.

Tip You can use the Explorer or My Computer to create folders in your \My System folder (if you don't have this folder, you can create it now), and then put shortcuts in them. Then put shortcuts to these folders on the Desktop.

Tip Putting shortcuts to folders on the Desktop is particularly convenient when you're working on a project with many different files in many different folders. You can create a folder to store shortcuts to the files in the project. Put a shortcut to this folder on the Desktop (or on the main Start menu). Now you have a quick way to access all the files in the project.

If the project is divided into recognizable subsets, put the shortcuts to files in each subset into a folder identifying that subset. Put shortcuts to the subset folders into an overall project folder. Put a shortcut to the project folder on the Desktop.

If you have a document that you are working on, drag a shortcut to it onto the Desktop. Click the shortcut, and the document opens in the application you used to create it.

Sometimes you might find it inconvenient to reach the Desktop, especially if you don't have much real estate. For example, you might be running at 640×480 on a 14-inch monitor, or maybe you're running your applications in maximized windows. In these situations, you can still use your Desktop. In "The Desktop on the Start menu" in Chapter 11, we show you how to put the Desktop (the \Windows\Desktop folder) on the main Start menu so that you can always access it, even if it is covered up.

Of course, it's easy to add a Desktop toolbar to your Taskbar. Just right-click the Taskbar, click Toolbars, and then click Desktop.

Massage the Context Menu

Both the Explorer and My Computer provide navigational windows that give you a view of your computer. Because the Explorer has a folder tree view in the left pane, it has greater navigational abilities, but both can display folders, applications, documents, and web pages.

If you right-click any of the icons displayed in these views, you get a context menu. You can modify the context menu to make it significantly easier to use. In "Send To Send To" in Chapter 10 and "Creating and Editing File Types and Actions" in Chapter 13, we discuss how to modify the context menu and add destinations—such as a default file opener for all files of unregistered types, Quick View, a file compression program, and your printer—to the Send To menu item. Some of these changes are very easy to make, while others require that you edit the Registry a bit.

The Active Desktop

In "Turn a Folder Window into the Program Manager . . ." and "Use the Real Program and File Managers" later in this chapter, we show you how to connect the Windows 98 Desktop to the rapidly fading Windows 3.1x past. Here, we talk about the present and future incarnations of the Desktop.

By default, Windows 98 displays the Active Desktop and the Channel Bar, but it also makes it easy to switch back to the Classic style Windows 95 Desktop. Microsoft did this is on purpose, because it is moving toward fully integrating the Internet/Intranet into your computer, and it wants to make this transition as painless as possible.

Channels are actually pretty cool, given that just about anyone can turn his or her web site into a channel. Of course, it is a slow moving channel if you don't have a legion of writers and artists behind the scenes updating the material that you're pushing. Turn to "Channels" in Chapter 9 for more details.

If you want to view a channel and nothing else, you can hide all your Desktop icons and turn your Desktop into a slow-mo TV set. Hold down the Ctrl key and click the Maximize button in the Internet Explorer window that is displayed when you click a button in the Channel Bar (see Live Wired in Figure 12-8). To get back to the Start button and the Taskbar, press Ctrl+Esc or the Windows key.

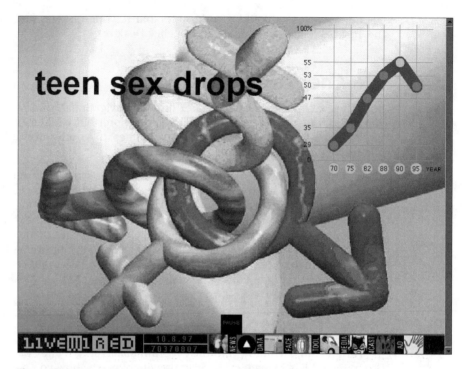

Figure 12-8: Wired Magazine takes over the Desktop.

You can also turn an HTML page into your Desktop and get rid of all the icons on your Desktop. Code the HTML page to include hyperlinks that replace your icons. When you have it working, click My Computer, choose View, Folder Options, click the View tab, and mark Hide Icons When Desktop Is Viewed As Web Page. Right-click the Desktop, click Properties, click the Background tab, click the Browse button, and navigate to the folder that holds the HTML document.

Turn a Folder Window into the Program Manager . . .

. . . and turn the Explorer into the File Manager.

Windows 98 integrates the Windows 3.1x File Manager and Program Manager functions (and a lot more) into the Explorer window and My Computer folder windows, respectively. You can think of the Explorer as just a window with two panes. My Computer gives you access to single-pane folder windows. Shortcuts, which are similar to program icons in Windows 3.1x, are now stored in folders. You can view shortcuts in both the Explorer and My Computer windows. If you use Large Icons view (choose View, Large Icons in the Explorer or any folder window), your shortcuts will look something like your program icons did in the Windows 3.1x Program Manager.

The Program Manager window

Undocumented

You can set up your Desktop so it resembles the Windows 3.1*x* interface. You can use a Windows 98 folder window to function as the Program Manager.

STEPS

Creating a Program Manager-Like Folder

Step 1. Right-click My Computer on your Desktop and click Explore. If you already have a \My System folder, select it in the left pane of the Explorer. If you don't have one yet, you should create it now. To do so, click your hard drive icon in the left pane of the Explorer. Then right-click the right pane of the Explorer, choose New, Folder, and type the name **My System**.

Step 2. Create a subfolder of \My System called PMShortcuts. Do this by right-clicking in the right pane of the Explorer when the \My System folder is selected in the left pane. Choose New, Folder, and type the name **PMShortcuts**.

Step 3. Highlight the new PMShortcuts folder in the left pane of the Explorer. Right-click the right pane, choose New, Folder, and type the name **Program Manager**.

Step 4. Continue to right-click the client area of the PMShortcuts folder, adding new folders that are the equivalent of program groups. You will place shortcuts to them in the Program Manager folder (see Figure 12-9).

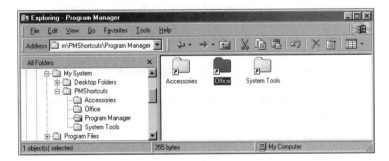

Figure 12-9: The Program Manager as a folder under the \My System folder.

(continued)

Give each program group-like folder a name that represents all the shortcuts to applications that you will store in it. For example, you could create a folder named Microsoft Office that will store all of your shortcuts to Microsoft Office applications.

Step 5. After you have created all the program group-like folders, right-drag the Program Manager folder icon to the Desktop. Click Create Shortcut(s) Here after you drop it there, and change the name of the new shortcut to **Program Manager**.

Step 6. Click the Program Manager icon and it opens up a Program Manager window. Right-drag the other folders you created from the PMShortcuts folder, drop them on the Program Manager folder window, and choose Create Shortcut(s) Here to create shortcuts to them.

Step 7. Now you can right-drag shortcuts or application icons from the Explorer, or maybe from a Find window, to any of the shortcuts to folders within the Program Manager folder window.

Step 8. In the Program Manager folder window, choose View, Folder Options, mark the Custom option button in the General tab, and click the Settings button. Mark the Open Each Folder in Its Own Window option button, and click OK twice.

Step 9. Click each of the folder icons in the Program Manager folder window. Right-click the Taskbar, and choose Tile Windows Horizontally to display all the program-group folder windows, as shown in Figure 12-10.

You now have a Program Manager folder window that resembles the Program Manager in Windows 3.1*x*. You also have a shortcut to it on the Desktop; any time you want to open the Program Manager window, just click this icon. You can also drag this shortcut icon to the Start button to place it on the main Start menu. This is very similar to placing a shortcut to the \Windows\Desktop folder on the main Start menu.

Because you put a shortcut to the Program Manager folder on the Desktop instead of the folder itself, you won't accidentally delete the folder. The same is true of all the folders displayed within the Program Manager window. All the icons within these folders are also just shortcuts.

You can leave the program group folder windows open on your Desktop, just as you could with the Windows 3.1*x* Program Manager.

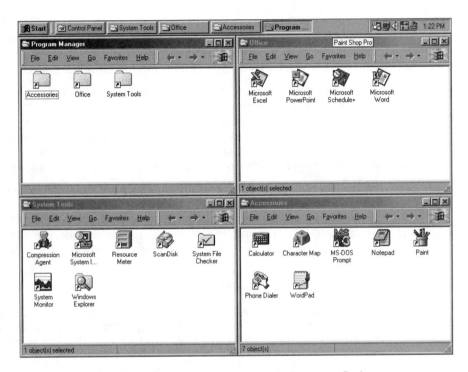

Figure 12-10: Your Program Manager folder windows tiled over your Desktop.

The Explorer as File Manager

If you use Details view (View, Details), the Explorer looks a lot like the Windows 3.1*x* File Manager. It can accomplish many, but not all, of the functions that the File Manager can and quite a few that the File Manager can't. You can certainly use it as a replacement for the File Manager. For a comparison of the two, see "Going from the Windows 3.1*x* File Manager to the Explorer" in Chapter 8.

Secret

You can't place a shortcut to Explorer.exe in the StartUp folder without making any modifications to the shortcut. Explorer.exe contains the complete user interface (Desktop, Taskbar, and so on), so it causes a problem to have the Explorer (the user interface) call itself when it starts up. You can, however, put a shortcut to Explorer.exe in the StartUp folder if you modify the Target field of the shortcut (right-click the shortcut, click Properties, and click the Shortcut tab) to C:\WINDOWS\EXPLORER.EXE /n,/e, {*pathname and filename*}. (Yes, the commas are necessary in that command line.) The command line parameters that follow Explorer.exe modify this command to start the Explorer and not the complete user interface.

You don't have to put a call to the Explorer in the StartUp folder to keep the Explorer close at hand. When you quit Windows 98, just be sure that the Explorer icon is on a Taskbar button; that is, that the Explorer is active. The next time you start Windows 98, the Explorer is one click away.

You can also place a shortcut to the Explorer on the Desktop so you can click it to start the Explorer. Right-drag Explorer.exe from the \Windows folder. Drop Explorer.exe on the Desktop and click Create Shortcut(s) Here. Alternatively, you could drag Explorer.exe to the Start button to put a shortcut to the Explorer in the main Start menu. By default, the Programs menu contains a shortcut to the Explorer, called Windows Explorer.

The Explorer isn't the File Manager. It doesn't have a multidocument interface, so you can't display two folder trees next to each other within the Explorer window. Microsoft wants to get away from the multidocument interface and let the operating system manage multiple documents and applications. However, you can run more than one copy of the Explorer by clicking its shortcut on the Desktop twice.

Want to put up two Explorer windows side by side? Here's how.

Tip

Minimize all active windows. If you have created a shortcut to the Explorer on your Desktop, click it twice, and then right-click the Taskbar and click Tile Windows Vertically. You now have two Explorer windows side-by-side, as shown in Figure 12-11.

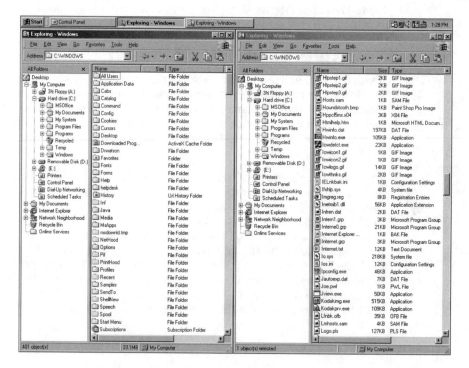

Figure 12-11: Windows 98 as a multidocument interface showing two Explorers side by side.

Use the Real Program and File Managers

Program Manager and File Manager are still there (\Windows\Progman.exe and \Windows\Winfile.exe) and you can use them. No shame in that. You can place shortcuts to the Program Manager and File Manager in the StartUp folder, so that they come up every time you start Windows 98. You can choose (by right-clicking the shortcut, choosing Properties, and clicking the Shortcut tab) whether they will start up restored, maximized, or minimized on the Taskbar.

Program Manager (as shown in Figure 12-12) and File Manager act the same as they did in Windows for Workgroups 3.1*x*. That is their charm. You don't have to learn something new, and you get all the advantages of these applications.

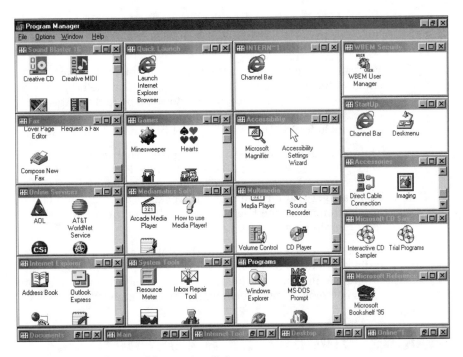

Figure 12-12: The Program Manager is still there.

The File Manager is quicker than the Explorer. For one thing, it doesn't have to display all the file icons. For another, it doesn't have to go looking for long filenames. Of course, you can't use the File Manager to display long filenames, because it knows nothing about them.

You can use the File Manager to rename groups of files (as long as the filenames are less than nine characters), which is something you can't do with the Explorer or My Computer. You can configure the Program Manager to minimize itself after you launch an application, and you can't do this with the Explorer or My Computer either.

Even if you don't use File Manager or Program Manager as your primary interface, you can place shortcuts to them in your other interface areas and call them when you want to use their power.

If you leave the Program and File Manager active (on the Taskbar) when you quit Windows 98, you won't have to worry about putting them in the StartUp folder. They will return to their positions the next time you start up Windows. You might also want to put shortcuts to them on the Desktop, the main Start menu, or the Programs menu, so that you can start them quickly if you need to.

You can think about ways to combine the use of the Desktop, Start menus, and the Program Manager and File Manager. Some applications, perhaps less-used ones, could go on the Start menus. Applications you use the most frequently could go in the Program Manager.

Some of you may have used the File Manager as your primary shell or user interface. The Start menu mimics the File Manager with its hierarchical structure. You might mix and match these two means of getting to your files.

You can change the shell setting in System.ini. For example, you can set shell=Winfile.exe to make the File Manager your shell (or user interface) in Windows 98. You can then quit Windows 98 by quitting the File Manager. (The default shell is, of course, the standard Windows 98 Explorer shell, which includes the Desktop, the Start button, and the Taskbar.)

There are some problems with using the Program Manager and the File Manager as the Windows 98 user interface. Right-clicking doesn't work in the Program Manager or the File Manager. You can't drag things out of the File Manager and put them on the Desktop, although you can drag applications from the File Manager and drop them into a program group in the Program Manager.

In addition, Ctrl+Esc gets you to the Start menu, not to the Task Manager as it did in Windows 3.1x. Also, you won't find program group icons in your Program Manager. Instead you see the rather ugly minimized application icons common to multidocument interfaces under Windows 98.

Making Windows 98 a Complete Operating System

Microsoft's strategy, because it owns the operating system, is to include within the operating system increasing levels of basic functionality that appeal to a broad market. That's why it built the Internet Explorer into the user interface.

No matter how good Windows 98 is, however, it is never going to be good enough. With time, it will age and your needs will change as you see other possibilities.

Microsoft can't provide everything (neither can we), and Windows 98 needs some improvements. That's why we provide shareware on the *Windows 98 Secrets* CD-ROM. Programs on the CD-ROM can add to the basic Windows 98 software set to make a system that you can use every day.

The *Windows 98 Secrets* CD-ROM includes lots of shareware and freeware applications, many of which have been designed to extend the Windows 98 operating system. We suggest that you look through the categories of shareware on the CD-ROM and see for yourself how you might want to enhance the power of the basic system.

Summary

Windows 98 is still in the box and waiting for you to assemble it. You might want to add some batteries.

▶ We show you how to dredge up the good stuff and put it where the sun does shine.

▶ We give you a way to clean up the clutter Windows 98 created in your Start menus when you set it up over your Windows 3.1*x* directory.

▶ We encourage you to use the Desktop as you would any horizontal surface in your office — pile it on. We also show you how you can keep it neat with shortcuts to folders.

▶ Want the Windows 3.1*x* retro look? Turn a folder window into the Program Manager.

▶ We show you that you can still use the real Program Manager and File Manager as your user interface.

Chapter 13

Documents First

In This Chapter

Why have an application in the way of getting to your documents? We show you what you need to know about:

▶ Opening, printing, or taking other useful actions on a file with two clicks

▶ Opening Word files that don't have *doc* extensions without opening another copy of Word

▶ Creating your own file types and defining convenient actions to take on them without having to first open the application

▶ Using right-click to do what you want with your documents

▶ Making Notepad instead of the slower WordPad the program of choice to edit batch files

▶ Creating shortcuts to view and open files without knowing their file type

▶ Clearing the Documents list on the Start menu

▶ Opening new blank documents on your Desktop

Document-Centric?

When Windows 95 was about to be released, Microsoft touted it as a "document-centric" operating system. With Windows 98, they've taken the next step. To understand what they're hyping, shift your focus to a non-computer-mediated way of dealing with a document.

If you were going to write a personal letter, perhaps to your mother, you might decide to take out a nice piece of stationery, retrieve a serviceable pen from your desk drawer, and begin the letter. Your attention would be on the letter first, the paper second, and the writing implement third.

If you want to write the letter on a computer, you have to start a letter-writing application before you start writing the letter. The letter-writing software package is the container for the letter. It's as though the pen contains the paper and the letter.

Windows 98 lets the letter-writing application take its more "natural" place as the means (perhaps one of many) of getting the words (and numbers, pictures, and sounds) into the document. The document has gained a measure of independence from the application.

This document-centric approach is reflected in a number of Windows 98 features. For example, you can place new blank documents on the Desktop or in any folder window. You can access documents via the Documents menu on the Start menu. You can click a file icon and have its associated application open it, and you can define actions to be taken on a file and display those actions as options in the context menu.

Because Windows 98 integrates the Internet Explorer into the Windows 98 user interface, this document-centric orientation is extended to include documents on the Internet as well as on your own computer or network. You experience the World Wide Web as a web of interconnected documents. The Explorer or your Desktop is just a viewing area. The documents can be active—for example, they may be forms that let you purchase something—but they still look like documents and not like applications.

The Windows 98 Explorer and Desktop can display HTML documents, including ones that contain GIF and JPEG files, ActiveX objects, Java applets, and anything else that you can view in a web browser.

You can access HTML documents from the Windows 98 Desktop with a single click if you use the Web style with the Desktop. (In the Explorer, choose View, Folder Options, and mark the Web Style option button in the General tab.) If you right-click an HTML document icon in the Explorer and choose Open in Same Window, the document appears in an Internet Explorer window. Do this for another HTML document, and it will open in the same Internet Explorer window. To traverse from one HTML document to another in the Explorer, you can click hyperlinks embedded in the text.

Associating Actions with File Extensions

Like Windows 3.1*x*, both Windows 98 and 95 use file extensions to designate file type. A file with the extension *txt* can be, and is by default, designated as having the file type of *text*. Your computer can take certain *actions* on files depending on their file type. For example, sound cards can play music files.

Usually, applications perform the actions. For example, a file with the extension *cda* contains information necessary to successfully play an audio track, but it needs CD Player (or any other application that can read *cda* files) to perform the action—to actually play the song.

You can choose (and modify) the actions that will be taken on a file from among all the possible actions that are open to you. The available actions depend on what Windows 98 provides and which other applications you have installed on your computer.

File types and their associated actions are defined (registered) in the Registry files. Windows 98 defines more than 100 file types (and their associated actions) before you get a chance to define your own.

Where Are These Actions?

If you right-click a file of a registered (defined) file type, a context menu appears. In the top section of the context menu are the actions defined for this file type, including any actions you have added. The action listed in boldface (usually the first choice) is the default action. If you click the file, this action occurs.

It is quite possible for an application to be able to take literally thousands of different actions on a file. Just think of the many different ways that a word processor (with your help) acts on a document. Not all the actions that an application can undertake need to or should be defined in the Registry.

It only makes sense to define certain kinds of actions in the Registry. Actions that can be taken without significant additional user input come to mind, such as opening, printing, translating the file from one format to another, playing (musically speaking), and updating.

Creating and Editing File Types and Actions

The file type/action association is fundamental to the document-centric character of Windows 98. Without it, you could not click a filename or file icon on the Desktop or in a window and have it and its application open in a window. You would always have to start an application first, and then search for the document in the application's File Open dialog box.

One of the main purposes of the Windows 98 Desktop metaphor is to make applications subservient to the data or document. This metaphor falls down when you can't get to your data without going through an application. If you can right-click a file and choose among associated actions in the context menu, it feels like the file is in charge.

You can change which file extensions are associated with which actions. You can add (or register) new extensions. When you install Windows 98 over your existing Windows 3.1x or Windows 95 directory, the Setup program reads your existing Win.ini and Registry files and places all your existing file types and their associated actions in the Windows 98 Registry files.

When you install a new application under Windows 98, the application stores all its defined file types and their associated action(s) in the Registry. The associated action may simply be opening a file.

You can edit or add new file type/action associations in either a My Computer window or an Explorer window. To do so, take the following steps:

STEPS

Viewing File Types

Step 1. Right-click My Computer and choose either Open or Explore.

Step 2. Choose View, Folder Options to display the Folder Options dialog box, and click the File Types tab (see Figure 13-1).

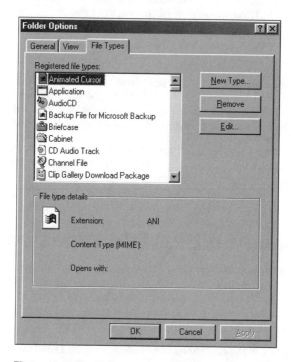

Figure 13-1: The File Types tab of the Folder Options dialog box. Scroll the Registered File Types list to view all registered file types.

Step 3. You can use the New Type, Remove, and Edit buttons to create a new registration for an extension, remove an existing registered extension, or edit the description and associated actions for an existing file type.

Creating a new file type

New file types are usually created when you install a new application. The application developers designate a set of file extensions that are associated with their application, and they include code in the application setup routine that edits your Registry to register their file types and associated application actions.

You can also create your own file types and application actions. While you can do this by editing the Registry directly (see "File associations via the Registry" later in this chapter), you can accomplish the same thing by using dialog boxes. If you only want to define the Open action for the new file type, it's fastest to use the Open With dialog box (see "Multiple extensions — one application" later in this chapter). If you want to define actions other than Open, you need to use the Add New File Type dialog box, as described here.

STEPS

Creating a New File Type

Step 1. If you haven't already done so, follow the Viewing File Types steps in the previous section to display the File Types tab of the Folder Options dialog box.

Step 2. Click the New Type button to display the Add New File Type dialog box (see Figure 13-2).

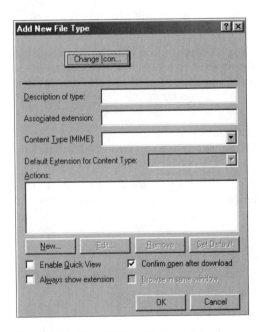

Figure 13-2: The Add New File Type dialog box.

Step 3. Press Tab once. Enter a description of the file type in the Description of Type field. The new file type will be listed in the File Types tab of the Folder Options dialog box in alphabetical order by the first letter of this description. Any name that is relevant to you is okay.

(continued)

STEPS *(continued)*

Creating a New File Type

Tip

Windows 98 also uses this field to sort files in folder and Explorer windows when you use Details view and order by type. When you order by type, Windows 98 doesn't sort files by their extension, as was true under Windows 3.1*x*. Rather, it sorts them in alphabetical order by the contents of the Description of Type field.

Step 4. Enter the file extension in the Associated Extension field. The extension should be no longer than three letters if the application can't handle long filenames — that is, a Win-16 application or one written for Windows 3.1*x*. You don't have to type the period.

You won't be allowed to enter an extension that is already registered. This prevents Windows 98 from having to choose between applications when you click a file.

Step 5. If your file type has a defined content type (such as HTML, GIF, JPF, AVI, or MPEG), select it from the Content Type (MIME) drop-down list. The Default Extension for Content Type field will display the default extension as soon as you choose the content type.

Step 6. Click the New button. The New Action dialog box is displayed, as shown in Figure 13-3. In the Action field, enter an action that you want an application to perform on files of this file type. You might want to begin by defining the default action that an application performs on the file when you click it.

You can use any action name you like. You will associate your action name with an action that you define. You can define a number of different actions, and name each one.

For example, Open and Print are possible action names. Windows 98 will use the action names you choose to describe the associated actions, so you should make them understandable.

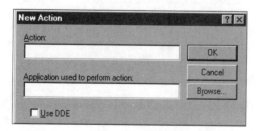

Figure 13-3: The New Action dialog box.

Put an ampersand (&) in front of the letter that you want to use to select the action from a context menu with the keyboard. For example, &Open underlines the letter O, so you can press the O key and then Enter to execute this action from the keyboard. Capitalize the first letter of the action.

Step 7. In the Application Used to Perform Action field, enter the name of an application that will perform the named action and that is associated with the file type. Type the complete pathname and the application filename. Add to the application name the command line parameters that will instruct the application to perform the action.

For example, if you want a text file to be printed, you might define the action named Print as **C:\Windows\Notepad.exe /p.** If the application is in a folder with a space in its name, you need to surround the application and its pathname with double quote marks:

```
"C:\Programs Files\Accessories\MSPaint.exe" "%1"
```

This action will open a file (referenced by the parameter %1) using Microsoft Paint.

The possible actions that an application can take on files of this type and the macro language of the application program determine which action names make sense. The default action for most applications is Open. If you put the filename of the application in the Application Used to Perform Action field without any command line parameters, the action it will most likely carry out is to open the file that you right-clicked.

If you put in command line parameters, don't put double quote marks around them. For example:

```
"C:\Program Files\Accessories\MSPaint.exe" /p "%1"
```

Step 8. You can also use Dynamic Data Exchange (DDE) to modify the behavior of the application by passing it a message. If the application has a macro language, you can use that macro language to make the application behave in all sorts of different ways when you choose some action on the context menu. If you want to use DDE to define an action, mark the Use DDE check box. Windows 98 expands the dialog box to display additional fields that let you specify how you want to use DDE.

Undocumented

Figure 13-4 shows a way to modify how files with extensions other than *doc* can be opened by Word for Windows without opening a new copy of Word when it is already active. If you don't use DDE to send a message to Word, another copy of Word is opened when you click a file with an extension other than *doc*.

(continued)

STEPS *(continued)*

Creating a New File Type

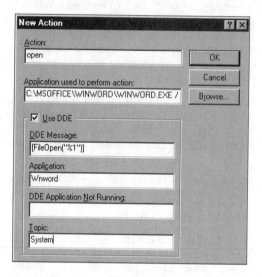

Figure 13-4: Using DDE to modify how a file is opened by Word for Windows.

Step 9. Click OK when you have finished defining the application's action to return to the Add New File Type dialog box. You can continue defining new actions for a given file type by repeating steps 6 and 7. The actions you define will be listed in the Actions box in the middle of the Add New File Type dialog box. When you've finished defining actions, select one of the actions in the Actions box, and click the Set Default button. This will define the selected action as the action that occurs when you click the file.

Step 10. If you want to change the icon that will represent the new file type, you can do so by clicking the Change Icon button in the Add New File Type dialog box. Optionally mark one or more of the check boxes at the bottom of the dialog box (see the next four sections for descriptions of these options), and then click OK, and click OK again to close the Folder Options dialog box.

You now have a new file type — a new file extension that is associated with a given set of actions, which most likely originate in one or more applications. All of the actions appear on the context menu that is displayed when you right-click a file of this type.

Confirm open after download

If the Confirm Open after Download check box at the bottom of the Add New File Type (or Edit File Type) dialog box is marked—the default choice—Windows 98 will ask whether you want to open files of this type after you download them from an Internet site. This is a safety measure to guard against viruses that could be hiding in executable or document files.

Enable Quick View

If you mark the Enable Quick View check box at the bottom of the Add New File Type (or Edit File Type) dialog box, you can use Quick Viewers to see files on the Desktop without having to open (or even own) an application that is normally used to open them. Windows 98 ships with more than 20 viewers for some common file types. Application developers can ship their own Quick Viewers with their applications. In addition, Inso Corporation, the maker of Outside In and the Quick View technology, ships Quick View Plus, which contains many more viewers.

Quick View is not installed during the typical Windows 98 setup. If you used our guidelines to "Select components" in Chapter 2 and did a custom setup, you had the opportunity to install Quick View then. If you want to install it now, click the Start button, point to Settings, and click Control Panel. Click the Add/Remove Programs icon, click the Windows Setup tab, click Accessories, and then click the Details button. Scroll down to the Quick View check box. Mark it and then click OK twice. You may be asked for your Windows 98 CD-ROM.

You can implement this feature for a file type that has an associated Quick Viewer by marking this check box. If you installed the application, it should have marked this check box during setup.

Always show extension

If you mark the Always Show Extension check box in the Add New File Type (or Edit File Type) dialog box, Windows 98 will show the extension for this file type even if the Hide File Extensions for Known File Types option is checked in the View tab of the Folder Options dialog box (choose View, Folder Options in any Explorer or folder window).

Browse in same window

ActiveX (or OLE 2) applications such as Microsoft Word can pop up in the Internet Explorer window. If you click a link in a web page that points to a Word document, for example, you can decide whether the Word document is displayed in the Internet Explorer window or in a separate Word window. Clear this check box if you want it to be displayed in a separate window.

Editing an existing file type

To edit an existing file type, choose View, Folder Options (in any Explorer or folder window) and click the File Types tab. Select the file type whose actions, icons, or associated application(s) you want to change, and click the Edit button. You will be presented with the Edit File Type dialog box, which, with the exception of the name, looks just like the Add New File Type dialog box.

You can use the Edit File Type dialog box to add new actions, edit or remove existing ones, or declare a different action as the default. You can also change the icon associated with the file type if you like. The steps for editing a file type are very similar to the ones detailed in the "Creating a new file type" section earlier in the chapter.

One application associated with two file extensions

Secret

If you scroll carefully through the list of registered file types in the File Types tab of the Folder Options dialog box, you will find some file types that show two file extensions. If you use the New Type button on the File Types tab of the Folder Options dialog box, you will find that you can't create a new file type with two extensions. You also can't add extensions to an existing file type. You can, however, do this using the Registry editor or the Open With dialog box. (See the section entitled "Multiple extensions — one application" later in this chapter.)

File associations via the Registry

Undocumented

The File Types tab of the Folder Options dialog box is a front end to the Registry — but then so are most of the dialog boxes that you deal with in Windows 98. You can edit the Registry entries for your file types directly, if you like, using the Registry editor.

STEPS

Editing File Types in the Registry

Step 1. Go to "The Registry Keys and Structure" in Chapter 15 if you need to learn more about the Registry. If you have put a shortcut to the Registry editor on your Desktop, click it. Otherwise, find Regedit.exe in the \Windows folder using the Explorer or My Computer, and click it.

Step 2. Click the plus sign next to HKEY_CLASSES_ROOT to expand this branch of the Registry. The first keys shown are the file extensions. They all start with a period. There should be at least 100 keys, all marked with folder icons, as shown in Figure 13-5.

Step 3. Click any of the keys that are file extensions. A file type name will be associated with each one (listed in the right pane). Look at a few of these names to get an idea of how they are associated with the extension.

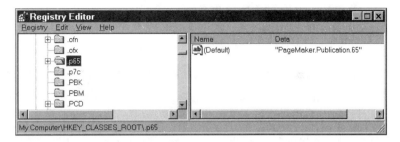

Figure 13-5: The Registry listing of file extensions. The selected file extension is associated with Adobe PageMaker.

Step 4.   Scroll down the HKEY_CLASSES_ROOT branch until you pass the extension keys and get to the file type names. Click the plus sign next to a file type name that corresponds to a file type or extension that you previously viewed in step 3.

Step 5.   Click the plus sign next to *shell* under the file type name. Notice that the action names associated with that file type are displayed. Click the plus signs by those action names and then click the *command* key, as shown in Figure 13-6.

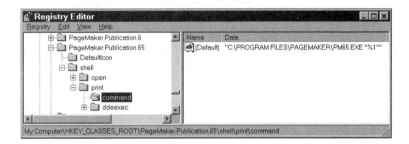

Figure 13-6: The file type names are displayed in the Registry, along with the commands required to carry out assigned actions. This is the command key for printing a PageMaker publication.

Step 6.   Notice that the action defined in the New Action (or Editing Action) dialog box is defined here. If DDE is used, you will find references to it under whichever action it was defined for.

Step 7.   Use the Registry editor's New, Delete, and Rename commands (in the Edit menu) to create new file types or edit existing ones, using the models you explored in steps 1 through 6. You may need to turn to "Editing with the Registry editor" in Chapter 15 for more information on how to edit these values. When you are done, exit the Registry.

You may find old file types and file type names that no longer apply. You can prune them out of the Registry if you like.

Change the edit application for batch files

Tip

If you right-click an MS-DOS batch file (a file with the *bat* extension) while it is displayed in a folder window, and then click Edit, you will notice that Notepad is used to edit the file. To use WordPad instead of Notepad as the editor for *bat* files, take the following steps:

STEPS

Editing the Action Associated with *bat* Files

Step 1.   Right-click My Computer and choose either Open or Explore.

Step 2.   Choose View, Folder Options, and click the File Types tab.

Step 3.   Select MS-DOS Batch File in the Registered File Types box. Click the Edit button.

Step 4.   Highlight Edit in the Actions field and notice that the Edit button is grayed out. You can't change the application associated with editing a batch file this way. This is why you need access to the Registry.

Step 5.   If you have a shortcut to the Registry editor on your Desktop, click it. Otherwise, find Regedit.exe in the \Windows folder using the Explorer or My Computer, and click it.

Step 6.   Click the plus sign next to HKEY_CLASSES_ROOT. Scroll down to *batfile*. Click the plus sign next to *batfile*. Click the plus signs next to *shell*, and then *edit*.

Step 7.   Select *command*. Click Default in the right pane of the Registry editor.

Step 8.   Type **"C:\Program Files\Accessories\Wordpad.exe" %1**.

Step 9.   Exit the Registry editor.

Multiple extensions — one application

Secret

Using the Registry editor you can create multiple extensions, and associate them with one application. If you have Microsoft Word installed, you will notice that the extensions *.dot* and *.doc* in the Registry (under HKEY_CLASSES_ROOT) both refer to Word Document. This is how multiple extensions are associated with one application.

Using the Registry editor, you can edit an entry for an extension to change the application that the extension is associated with. Highlight an extension entry in the Registry editor, click Default in the right pane of the Registry editor, and type a new file type name or the name of an existing file type.

If you created a new file type name, you will then need to create a new key value in HKEY_CLASSES_ROOT by that name. In addition, you will need to define some actions that are associated with that file type. Use the existing keys in this section of the Registry as examples.

You can also use the Open With dialog box to associate a new file type with the Open action for an existing application. Unfortunately, when using Open With, the only action you can associate with this new file type and extension is the Open action. Other actions may be associated with the file types that were created when the application was first installed, and you can't use the Open With dialog box to associate these actions with the new file type and extension. However, once you've used Open With to associate a file type with an application, you can edit the file type to associate it with other actions.

To see how the Registry is changed when you use the Open With dialog box, take the following steps:

STEPS

New File Types with Open With

Step 1. Right-click the Desktop, point to New, and click Text Document.

Step 2. Rename the document **Test.tst**. Click Yes when warned about changing the extension. (Be sure that you are showing your MS-DOS extensions. To do this in the Explorer, choose View, Folder Options, click the View tab, clear the Hide File Extensions for Known File Types check box, and click OK.)

Step 3. Right-click Test.tst. Choose Open With on the context menu. Choose some existing registered application, or click Other to specify any other application. Exit the application after Test.tst has been opened.

Step 4. Now open up your Registry editor, scroll down HKEY_CLASSES_ROOT to .*tst*, and find the application name associated with this extension. Scroll further down and find this application name. Notice the associated command for opening a file in the application. Close the Registry editor.

Editing (not merging) exported Registry files

Tip

Exporting your Registry or a branch of your Registry creates a file with a *reg* extension. The default action for this file type is Merge, as in merge this file back into the Registry. We find this a bit dangerous. Fortunately, you can easily change the default action for this file type.

STEPS

Changing the Default Action for an Exported Registry File

Step 1.   Open a folder or Explorer window. Choose View, Folder Options, and click the File Types tab.

Step 2.   Scroll through the Registered File Types list and select Registration Entries.

Step 3.   Click the Edit button.

Step 4.   Select Edit in the list of actions. Click the Set Default button.

Step 5.   Click the Close button twice to close the Edit File Type and Folder Options dialog boxes.

Re-associating RTF files with WordPad

Tip

If you install Word for Windows after you install Windows 98, the Open action for Rich Text Format (RTF) files is associated with Word and not WordPad. If you want to open this type of file with WordPad, edit the Open action associated with *rtf* files so it points to \Program Files\Accessories\ Wordpad.exe instead.

Secret

If you find that your new associations are reverting to their previous association (for example, if after changing the *rtf* association to WordPad, it goes back to Word), you are the victim of Microsoft's not-too-smart Registry association update routines. These go in after you install a new program and update the Registry based on what is in the [Extensions] section of the Win.ini file.

If you have an old association of *rtf* with Word in the Win.ini file, Windows 98 might use it to "update" your Registry and wipe out your new change. A way to get around this is to erase this association in the [Extensions] section of Win.ini. Unless you are using cc:Mail, you can erase this whole section. You might want to make a copy first, just in case.

Associating more than one program with a given file type

You can define many actions for a given file type. And you can associate each of these actions with a different application. Each action has to have a unique name. The following example describes one situation in which you might want to associate multiple programs with a single file type.

Tip

Files of the file type screen saver have a *scr* extension. Script files used by many different programs (although not by Windows 98 Dial-Up Networking) also use the *scr* extension. You can create an action, which we call Edit Scripts, that is associated with script files. To do so, take the following steps:

STEPS

Associating an Edit Action with the Script File Type

Step 1. Open a folder or Explorer window. Choose View, Folder Options, and click the File Types tab.

Step 2. Scroll through the Registered File Types list and select Screen Saver.

Step 3. Click the Edit button, and then click the New button.

Step 4. Type **Edit Scripts** in the Action field. Browse to \Windows\ Notepad.exe in the Application Used to Perform Action field.

Step 5. Click OK, then Close, and then Close again.

Opening Unregistered File Types

If you click a file that has an extension that is not registered, Windows 98 will not try to open the file. Instead, it will display the Open With dialog box, as shown in Figure 13-7. This dialog box lists all the programs associated through actions to registered file types.

The Always Use This Program to Open This File check box is marked by default. If, in general, you want files with this extension to be opened by the application that you are about to choose, then leave this box checked. You can also type a description of the file type in the Description of *'.XXX'* Files field. Choose a program to open this file by clicking the program name in the list box or by clicking the Other button to find the program that you want.

If you just want to open this file now and not worry about establishing an association between its file type and an application, clear the Always Use This Program to Open This File check box and click an appropriate program to open the file.

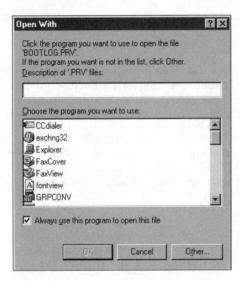

Figure 13-7: The Open With dialog box.

This method of opening files of an unregistered type gives you a great deal of flexibility, at a cost of having to scroll to find an appropriate application. It also lets you create new file types and associate them with applications without using the File Types tab of the Folder Options dialog box.

Opening a registered file type with another application

Sometimes, you might want to open a file whose file type is already registered and whose Open action is already associated with an application that you would rather not use this time. If you click the file in the Explorer or a folder window (or right-click the file and choose Open from the context menu), the associated application will open it.

Tip

Hold down the Shift key and right-click the file in an Explorer or folder window. An Open With command is added to the context menu, allowing you to choose an application other than the one already associated with this file type.

When you choose Open With, the Open With dialog box (refer to Figure 13-7) appears, but the Always Use This Program to Open This File check box is not marked. If you want to change the associated Open action for this file type to the new application, mark this box. (If you only want to use the new application this one time, leave it blank.)

This is a quick way of changing the associated Open action for a given file type. You don't have to go to the File Types tab in the Folder Options dialog box and edit the reference to the application associated with the Open action. When you use the Shift+right-click method, you just change the default Open action, and leave the other actions as they are.

Create a default file opener

Secret

You can define a default program that will always open a file of an unregistered type when you right-click the file and choose OpenNote (or a different name of your choosing) from the context menu. This lets you avoid going through the rigmarole of the Open With dialog box. A variation on this method lets you open the file with a click.

STEPS

Defining a Default File Opener

Step 1. If you have a shortcut to the Registry editor on your Desktop, click it. Otherwise, find Regedit.exe in the \Windows folder using the Explorer or My Computer, and click it.

Step 2. Click the plus sign next to HKEY_CLASSES_ROOT. Scroll down the left pane until you find Unknown. Click the plus sign next to the Unknown folder icon. Click *shell*.

Step 3. Choose Edit, New, Key. Type **OpenNote**, and then select OpenNote.

You don't have to name the command OpenNote. You can type any name that will make sense to you as a menu item in the context menu, and that corresponds with the action or command that you are about to define.

Step 4. Choose Edit, New, Key. Type **command**. Highlight the *command* folder icon.

Step 5. Click Default in the right pane of the Registry editor. Enter the filename and path to the application that you want to use as the default file opener. For example, type **C:\Windows\Notepad.exe %1**.

Step 6. Click OK, and exit the Registry editor.

A variation on these steps lets you click to open a file of an unregistered file type with the default file-open application. You need to first examine the *openas* key under the *shell* key described in step 2 above because you are going to delete it (and the *command* key under it) and then put it back in.

The steps required to do this are the same as the ones given above — but before you take step 3, examine *openas*, write down the command data, and then delete the *openas* key. After step 5, use Edit, New, Key to put the *openas* key and its *command* key back in as before, but now under OpenNote (or whatever name you chose).

Now when you click a file of an unregistered type in Explorer, it will open the file in the specified program. Both OpenNote and Open With will now be in the context menu when you right-click an unregistered file. You can still use Open With if you want to choose a different program to open the file.

You can substitute other applications instead of Notepad for your default file opener. You might try WordPad. Unlike Notepad, which chokes on non-text files, WordPad can open files of almost any format except executables. If you have a hex editor, use that in this example instead.

General actions on any file type

Secret

You can define a set of actions that will apply to any file type or to any unregistered file type. These actions will then appear in the context menu when you right-click any file or when you right-click any file of an unregistered file type. Matthias Koenig showed us this little gem.

In the earlier section entitled "Create a default file opener," we showed you how to use the Registry editor to create OpenNote, an action that would open unknown file types with Notepad.exe. You had to use the Registry editor to create this action because the "file types" Unknown and All are not displayed in the File Types tab of the Folder Options dialog box.

You can, if you like, display these two "file types" in the File Types tab of the Folder Options dialog box. Once they are there, you can define any actions you care to for them.

STEPS

Defining Actions for Any File Type

Step 1. Right-click the Desktop, point to New, and then click Text Document.

Step 2. Rename the text document **All.reg**. Click Yes when asked about the extension change. (Be sure that you are showing your MS-DOS extensions. To do this in the Explorer, choose View, Folder Options, click the View tab, clear the Hide File Extensions for Known File Types check box, and click OK.)

Step 3. Right-click the new document icon that you have just created, and choose Edit. Type the following text into the document, save, and close it when you are done:

```
REGEDIT4
[HKEY_CLASSES_ROOT\Unknown]
"EditFlags"=hex:02,00,00,00
[HKEY_CLASSES_ROOT\*]
"EditFlags"=hex:02,00,00,00
```

Step 4.   Right-click the All.reg document icon, and then click Merge.

Step 5.   Open an Explorer or folder window. Choose View, Folder Options, and then click the File Types tab.

Step 6.   The first entry should now be an asterisk (*), which stands for All file types. Scroll down the file types list to find the Unknown file type. You can use the methods described in this chapter to add new actions to these "file types."

Printing files using other applications

One of the biggest limitations of the Send To menu item is that you cannot configure a Send To command line with parameters. Say you have *txt* files associated with Notepad, but you frequently want to print *txt* files with WordPad because you like the fact that WordPad doesn't automatically add headers and footers to the output, as Notepad does. You could try adding /p as a parameter to Wordpad.exe's command line in a Send To shortcut, but it doesn't work. Windows ignores any parameters that follow the executable name in the shortcut. (To see the command line underlying a Send To shortcut, right-click the shortcut in the C:\Windows\SendTo folder, click Properties, and then click the Shortcut tab.)

The best way to get around this limitation is to define a shortcut that will appear on your context menus and do anything you desire. This will let you use your right mouse button to select a file and launch almost any action you can think of.

It's easy to define a new action for all files with a particular extension. Here's how to create a new context menu item that appears when you right-click a *txt* file in the Explorer or a folder window, and automatically prints text files through WordPad instead of Notepad:

STEPS

Printing a Text File Using WordPad

Step 1.   In the Explorer, choose View, Folder Options, and click the File Types tab.

Step 2.   In the Registered File Types list, scroll down and select Text Document, click the Edit button, and then click the New button.

Step 3.   In the New Action dialog box that appears, type **Print Using WordPad** as the Action. In the Application Used to Perform Action box, type the following:

```
"C:\Program Files\Accessories\WordPad.exe" /p
```

(continued)

STEPS *(continued)*

Printing a Text File Using WordPad

In this example, the quotes are necessary because one of the folder names contains a space. The parameter /p (which must be lowercase) causes Wordpad.exe to print the *txt* file.

Step 4.   Click OK, and then click Close twice to exit the dialog boxes.

Back in the Explorer window, find a *txt* file and right-click it. You should see a new Print Using WordPad command on the context menu. Click this choice. You should see WordPad flash for a moment as it reads the file and automatically sends it to the printer.

You can create all kinds of commands for all types of files. Many applications support a variety of command line parameters that launch different kinds of behaviors on files you open. Word for Windows, for example, supports the parameter /m followed by a Word command. For example, if you use /mFilePrintPreview with *doc* files, you can open documents in Print Preview mode, rather than in Normal view. (In Word, choose Tools, Customize, Commands, All Commands to see other possible commands you can use.)

Changing BMP Icons to Show Thumbnail

Secret

Each file type displays its associated icon in the Explorer, on the Desktop, or in folder windows. Instead of using a single uniform icon for all your *bmp* files, you can display a crude thumbnail sketch of each file. If you use this trick, you will know in advance what you're going to see when you click a *bmp* file icon:

STEPS

Thumbnails for *bmp* Files

Step 1.   Click Regedit.exe in your \Windows folder.

Step 2.   Click the plus sign next to HKEY_CLASSES_ROOT. Scroll down the left pane of the Registry editor to Paint.Picture.

If you have installed another bitmap editor that has supplanted the default action for *bmp* files, which is to open them with MS Paint, you have to scroll down to the file type name for that application instead. To find out the file type name, highlight *.bmp* under HKEY_CLASSES_ROOT in the left pane of your Registry editor.

Step 3.   Click the plus sign next to Paint.Picture, and select DefaultIcon in the left pane of the Registry editor.

Step 4.   Double-click Default in the right pane.

Step 5.   In the Edit String dialog box, delete the existing value in the Value Data field, and type **%1** instead. Click OK, and then close the Registry.

Go to an Explorer or folder window and focus on a folder that contains *bmp* files. Choose View, Large Icons, and check out the new thumbnails. The file icons should be tiny thumbnails of the bitmaps, not the generic MS Paint icon.

Viewing a File Without Starting an Application

If you right-click a file icon in the Explorer, you may see Quick View in the context menu (if you don't, see the "Enable Quick View" section earlier in this chapter). You have this option if the file that you right-click is of a registered file type and Windows 98 has a file viewer for that type.

Windows 98 ships with more than 20 file viewers. These viewers know about the file format of the documents of a given file type. They can load quickly, read the document, and display it on your Desktop.

Microsoft encourages application developers to ship file viewers with their applications, so you may have additional viewers stored in the \Windows\System\Viewers folder. Windows 98 ships with Quick Viewers for the file types shown in Table 13-1.

Tip

Many of the applications that Quick View can display are either rarely used or not the latest versions. You can download free quick viewers for Word 97 and Excel 97 from the Inso web site (see last paragraph in this section).

All you have to do is right-click a file of one of the above file types (or with one of the above file extensions) and choose Quick View in the context menu. Quick View will display the file in a view window. If you want to edit the file and you have the associated application, click the Edit button in the view window, and Quick View will load that application for you.

Undocumented

You can create a shortcut on the Desktop for the Quick Viewer, and then drag and drop files to the Quick Viewer from the Explorer or a folder window. If you drag a file to the Quick Viewer that is not associated with any viewer, Quick View will ask if you want to view it with the default viewer.

Table 13-1   Files Windows 98 Recognizes

File Extension	File Type
asc	ASCII
bmp	Windows bitmapped graphics
cdr	Corel Draw versions 4 and 5
dib	Windows bitmapped graphics
dll	Dynamic link libraries (application extensions)
doc	Microsoft Word 2.0, 6.0, and 7.0, WordPad, others
drw	Micrographic draw
exe	Executable format
inf	Windows setup files (text)
ini	Windows configuration files (text)
mod	Multiplan versions 3, 4, 4.1
ppt	PowerPoint version 4
pre	Freelance Graphics for Windows
rle	Bitmapped graphics (Run Length Encoded)
rtf	Rich Text Format
sam	Ami, Ami Pro
wb1	Quattro Pro for Windows
wdb	MS Works Database
wk1	Lotus 1-2-3 versions 1 and 2
wk3	Lotus 1-2-3 version 3
wk4	Lotus 1-2-3 version 4
wks	Lotus 1-2-3 or MS Works version 3
wmf	Windows Meta File
wp5	WordPerfect 5
wp6	WordPerfect 6
wpd	WordPerfect demo
wps	MS Works word processing
wq1	Quattro Pro for MS-DOS
wq2	Quattro Pro for MS-DOS version 5
wri	Windows Write
xlc	MS Excel Chart
xls	MS Excel versions 4 and 5

STEPS

Putting the Quick Viewer on Your Desktop

Step 1. Use My Computer or the Explorer to view the \Windows\System\ Viewers folder.

Step 2. Right-drag Quickview.exe to the Desktop and drop it there.

Step 3. Change the icon name to **Quick Viewer**.

For an even easier and quicker way to view files without a specific viewer, see the next section.

Inso, the manufacturer of Quick View, also offers Quick View Plus, which contains approximately 200 file viewers. Inso's latest version works with the Windows 98 Explorer and Netscape Navigator (as an ActiveX component or as a Netscape Plug-In, respectively) to allow you to view other types of documents while online. You can find Inso at http://www.inso.com.

Easiest Way to View/Open an Unregistered File

If you right-click a file in the Explorer or in a folder window, you will see the Send To command in the context menu. When you point to it, a submenu appears, as shown in Figure 13-8. When you first set up Windows 98, this submenu should contain such items as 3½ Floppy, Desktop as Shortcut, Fax Recipient, Mail Recipient, My Briefcase, and My Documents.

Figure 13-8: The Send To menu.

The Send To list contains your common destinations.

Undocumented

You can add shortcuts to the Quick Viewer and your text file opener. Then when you want to view or open a file of an unregistered type, you can right-click it, point to Send To, and then click either the Quick Viewer or the application you use as your text file opener. Here's how to set up Notepad as a text file-open application:

STEPS

Sending a File to Notepad

Step 1.   Open an Explorer window. Make sure you can see all file extensions. If you can't, choose View, Folder Options, click the View tab, and clear the Hide File Extensions for Known File Types check box.

Step 2.   Navigate to the \Windows folder in the left pane, and click the plus sign next to it. Then select the Windows folder icon.

Step 3.   Scroll down the right pane until Notepad.exe is visible. Right-drag Notepad.exe to the SendTo folder icon in the left pane and drop it there. Click Create Shortcut(s) Here.

Step 4.   Select the SendTo folder icon in the left pane of the Explorer. Select the Shortcut to Notepad.exe icon in the right pane, and then press F2. Rename this icon **Notepad** and press Enter.

Step 5.   Notepad will now be a choice in your Send To menu. You can place a shortcut to Quickview.exe in the SendTo folder in a similar manner. (See "Viewing a File Without Starting an Application" earlier in this chapter for more information about Quick View.)

Of course, you don't have to choose Notepad as your text file opener. You can also put numerous other shortcuts in the SendTo folder.

Documents on the Start Menu

If you open a file by clicking it (or by right-clicking it and then choosing Open) in a folder window or an Explorer window, a reference to it will show up in the Documents submenu of the Start menu. The last 15 documents you open this way appear on this list. If you want to work with one of these documents, simply click its name in the Documents submenu. Windows 98 will start the application you used to create the document, and then open the document inside it.

If you open a document within a Windows 3.1x application — using the File, Open command, for example — it does not show up on the Documents list.

Undocumented

To clear the Documents list, right-click the Taskbar, click Properties, click the Start Menu Programs tab, and then click Clear. To clear just the documents that you want cleared, open the \Windows\Recent folder in the Explorer or a folder window and delete the undesired documents. (Make sure you have Windows 98 set to show all files; otherwise, you won't see the Recent folder. To check, choose View, Folder Options, View in any Explorer or folder window.)

You can put a shortcut to \Windows\Recent on your Desktop. This is another way to get to these recently opened documents, and it also lets you easily edit the list.

You can clean out the contents of the Recent folder every time that you start up Windows 98 using a setting found in TweakUI. Just click the Paranoia tab and then select Clear Document History at Logon.

New Blank Documents

You can create blank documents by right-clicking the Desktop (or an empty part of a folder or Explorer window), pointing to New, and then clicking the desired document type.

If your desired file type isn't on the New menu, don't worry. Click any file type. When the new blank document icon appears, its name is selected. Type a new name with an extension of the registered file type you want. You will get a dialog box asking if you are sure you want to change the extension. You do.

The new file will contain the data associated with the file type you just chose (but not the file type associated with the new extension). If you chose to create a new document of the Text Document file type, but later change the file extension to *doc,* the file will still contain plain text until you save it in Word for Windows or another word-processing document format.

Adding Items to the New Menu

You can use TweakUI to add items to the New menu (or remove them from the menu). It's a simple matter of dragging and dropping a blank document or file of the correct file type onto TweakUI's New tab. The document you drag needs to be associated with an application.

You might have installed an application, but an association with the file extension you want to use for the new blank document has not been created. You can easily create an association by first creating a new blank document in your application. Rename the document with the new extension that you want to associate with this application. Then Shift+right-click the new document in an Explorer or folder window, and choose Open With. Make sure the Always Use This Program to Open This Type of File check box is marked. Click the Other button in the Open With dialog box, and browse to your application.

Once you have created an association between the document and an application, you can create a New menu item by dragging the blank document onto TweakUI's New tab.

Secret

You can also edit your Registry to manually create the New menu item. This gives you complete control over the process.

If you are going to manually create a New menu item, the first step is to make sure you have registered the document type in the Registry. Do this by following the steps in the section entitled "Creating a new file type" earlier in this chapter.

Next, you need to edit the new file type's entry in the Registry. The following steps show you how to do this:

STEPS

Creating an Item on the New Menu

Step 1.   Go to "The Registry Keys and Structure" in Chapter 15 if you need to learn more about the Registry. If you have put a shortcut to the Registry editor on your Desktop, click it. Otherwise, find Regedit.exe in the \Windows folder using the Explorer or My Computer, and click it.

Step 2.   Click the plus sign next to HKEY_CLASSES_ROOT to expand this branch of the Registry. The first keys shown are the file extensions. They all start with a period. There should be at least 100 keys, all marked with folder icons.

Step 3.   Click the file extension key that matches the file type you just created.

Step 4.   Right-click the right pane of the Registry editor. Choose New, Key. Change the name of the key to **ShellNew** and press Enter.

Step 5.   Click the new ShellNew key in the left panel of the Registry. Right-click the right panel. Choose New, String Value. Type the name **NullFile** and press Enter.

Step 6.   Exit the Registry editor when you are done.

The file type description for a file with this extension is now added to the New menu. When you select this file type from the New menu, Windows 98 will create a text file, but it will have the extension you just picked in the Registry.

Immediately invoke an application with a new file

If you want to have an application called immediately when you create a new blank file using the New menu, you can add a command string value to the ShellNew key. To do so, take the following steps:

STEPS

Invoking an Application When You Create a New File

Step 1. Follow the first five steps in the previous section.

Step 2. If it is not highlighted, click the ShellNew key in the left pane of the Registry. Right-click the right pane. Click New, String Value. Type the name **command** and press Enter.

Step 3. Double-click *command*. In the Value Data field, type the path and filename of the application that will be invoked. Include a space and then a **%1** after the filename to allow the new file to be opened by the application. If the application is stored in a folder with a pathname that includes a space, put double quote marks around the combined path and filename of the application, and put double quote marks around the %1.

Step 4. Click OK, and then exit the Registry editor.

Taking items off the New menu

Install a bunch of applications and pretty soon your New menu gets unwieldy. You can take document types off the menu and put them back on when you need to. Again, TweakUI comes to the rescue. Just click the New tab and choose which items to keep on the menu.

TweakUI accomplishes its New menu management task by placing a minus sign as the last character in the ShellNew key name associated with the file type extension in the HKEY_CLASSES_ROOT section of the Registry. You can use your Registry editor to examine some of the file extensions listed and see how this works.

Summary

We describe how to make it easy to get to your documents without having to go through your applications first.

▶ The Desktop and folder windows can give you a view of your documents. It is such a bother to have to open an application first to see these documents and work on them. We show you how to get right to the document and let the application take care of itself.

▶ We show you how to create new file types and define actions that can be taken on files of those types — actions that can automate your work.

▶ We use the Registry editor to change the assigned edit application for MS-DOS batch files from WordPad to Notepad.

▶ We show you how to create new menu choices for the right mouse button so that you can right-click (or click) your files and have something useful happen.

▶ We give you a couple of ways to create shortcuts for opening and viewing files of unknown file types.

▶ We describe how to clear the Documents list on the Start menu and open new blank documents on your Desktop.

Chapter 14

The Recycle Bin:
Going Through the Trash

In This Chapter

We reveal the secrets and subtleties of deleting files, folders, and shortcuts, including:

▶ Using the Recycle Bin to store your deleted files and shortcuts until you are sure that you want to get rid of them

▶ Seeing how files are stored in these hidden folders

▶ Deleting (and copying, moving, and renaming) files in the common file dialog boxes

▶ Restoring deleted files and folders or moving the files to new locations out of the Recycle Bin

What's Recyclable about the Recycle Bin?

The Recycle Bin doesn't recycle anything but your disk space. If you want to stretch the analogy a bit, you could say that if you delete unused files, you won't have to go out and buy new hard disks, but that is stretching it.

Our take on the use of this symbol for the trash can is that Microsoft realized people would rather have a Recycle basket on their Desktop than a trash can. It is cooler. Right?

So why the Bin part of Recycle Bin? During the early stages of the Windows 95 (then code-named Chicago) beta testing, its name was Recycle.bin. This is a pun. In a Unix file system, *bin* is a standard subdirectory where the *binary* files (executable programs) are stored. Combine the trash-receptacle meaning of the word *bin* with its Unix-world meaning, and the nerds at Microsoft got *.bin* on the Chicago Desktop. An art designer or somebody in marketing made them get rid of the period and capitalize the *b*.

 Secret

Want to change the name of the Recycle Bin to Trash Can? All you need to do is search your Registry for all occurrences of the name *Recycle Bin* and change each one to *Trash Can*. You can also open the Registry editor and navigate to HKEY_CLASSES_ROOT\CLSID\{645FF040-5081-101B-9F08-00AA002F954E}, double-click Default in the right pane, and type the new name. Searching and editing the Registry is discussed in Chapter 15.

The Recycled Folders

The Recycle Bin is an alias (a stand-in) for the special folders labeled Recycled. You can use the Explorer to see these folders — you'll find one on every hard disk and every logical drive on the hard disk. (If you have divided the hard disk into multiple drives, such as C, D, and so on, you will see a Recycled folder on each logical drive.) The Recycle Bin icon is displayed on the Desktop, and it's attached to the Desktop icon in the Explorer, on the same level as the My Computer and Network Neighborhood icons. The Recycled folder icons are attached to the hard disk drive icons along with your other folders. (The Recycled folders are indeed folders, even though they don't have the standard folder icons.) They are designated as file type Recycle Bin.

If you click the Recycle Bin icon or any of the Recycled folder icons, you will find that they all display the same contents. Opening the Recycled folder icon attached to one hard disk will show the files deleted from your other local hard disks as well.

Microsoft made it a point to put the Recycle Bin on the Desktop and make it hard to remove. The Recycle Bin stores all the files that have been deleted from your hard disks. You have to go to only one place to find all your deleted files.

Want to get the Recycle Bin icon off the Desktop? Use TweakUI to clear it. Don't worry, you can still get to the Recycle Bin by going to the Recycled folders.

Secret

You can change the name of the Recycled folders; it just doesn't do any good. If you change the name *Recycled* to *Wasted*, the next time you start Windows 98, it creates a new Recycled folder. You end up with two recycle receptacle icons, both of which display the same list of deleted files when you click them.

If you were following along and really created a Wasted folder, now we have to bail you out. You have a Recycled folder and a Wasted folder. How do you erase or get rid of the Wasted folder? It's not so easy.

STEPS

Getting Rid of the Wasted Folder

Step 1.   Click the Start button, point to Programs, and click MS-DOS Prompt to open a DOS window.

Step 2.   Change directories to the \Wasted directory. (You'll find it in the root directory.)

Step 3. Type **dir /a** to see if any files are stored in the Wasted directory. You are going to purge these files, so be sure to restore any that you might want to keep before you take the next step. To restore any of these files, right-click the Wasted folder, click Open, right-click any file that you want to restore, and click Restore.

Step 4. Type **Attrib -r -s -h Desktop.ini**.

Step 5. Type **del *.*** and press the Enter key.

Step 6. Change directories to the root directory of the hard disk partition that contains the Wasted directory (**cd **).

Step 7. Remove the Wasted directory by typing **rd Wasted** at the DOS prompt.

The Recycled folders are system resources. Windows 98 regenerates them if you change the name of a Recycled folder. It doesn't want you to mess with these resources because it needs them to manage deleted files.

Secret

The Recycled folders are indeed folders, but they are special ones. When you display the contents of a Recycled folder in Details view, you'll see an additional column named Original Location. And Recycled folders don't use the folder icon. Furthermore, the Recycled folders are hidden so that you can't see them if you go to DOS and type **dir** (although you can see them if you type **dir /a**).

Windows 98 puts the deleted files in these folders, but it stores them under new names (although you don't see this). Each Recycled folder contains an additional file named Info. Again, you don't see this file (unless you type **dir /a** at the DOS prompt). Windows 98 combines the deleted files and the Info file to create entries that look like the original deleted filenames with the addition of a column that lists their original location.

What is really unusual about these Recycled folders is that their folder windows display the names and icons of all the deleted files, not just the ones stored in that particular folder or deleted from that particular logical disk drive. The files deleted from a particular drive, however, are actually stored in the Recycled folder on that drive. You can see this for yourself by going to the DOS prompt, changing directories to the Recycled folder on a particular drive, and typing **dir /a**.

The code that makes the Recycled folders special is stored in a dynamic link library named Shell32.dll. This file is referenced in the Desktop.ini file.

The Recycle Receptacle Icons

Both the Recycle Bin and the Recycled folders use a recycle bin as their icon. If there are no files in the Recycle Bin, the icon shows an empty bin. If there are any deleted files in the Recycle Bin, the icon displays white paper stuffed into the bin. This bin is for paper recycling only — no cans or bottles.

If you delete a file and the Recycle Bin was previously empty, the Recycle Bin icon on the Desktop changes to its "stuffed with white paper" state. If you click the Recycle Bin icon to open it and then drag a file to the Recycle Bin folder window, the recycle bin icon in the title bar changes from the empty state to the "stuffed with white paper" state.

If the Recycle Bin properties have been set to remove files immediately when deleted, a message box with a shredding paper icon (as shown in Figure 14-1) will appear when you issue the Delete command. You will be asked for confirmation before the file is purged from the file system. (To check your Recycle Bin's properties, right-click the Recycle Bin icon and choose Properties.)

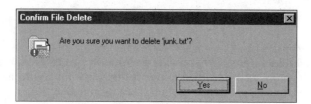

Figure 14-1: The Confirm File Delete message box. If you click Yes, the file is "deleted," in the sense that it is lost to the file management system and its space on the hard disk is free to be written over.

Secret

You can change the icons that represent an empty or a full Recycle Bin. Use your Registry editor to navigate to HKEY_CLASSES_ROOT\CLSID\{645FF040-5081-101B-9F08-00AA002F954E}. Highlight DefaultIcon in the left pane. Double-click first on *empty* and later on *full* in the right pane. Type the path and filename for the files that contain the icons you want to use to represent the Recycle Bin in both states. See "New icons for Desktop" in Chapter 7 for more on this subject.

What Does the Recycle Bin Do?

Unless you have configured the Recycle Bin to remove files immediately on delete, the Recycle Bin stores the files (and shortcuts, which are stored as files) that you have deleted from your local hard disks using the Explorer or a folder window.

The deleted files remain in the Recycle Bin until you issue the Empty Recycle Bin command (by right-clicking the Recycle Bin icon and choosing Empty Recycle Bin, or by choosing File, Empty Recycle Bin in the Recycle Bin window). If you want to restore a file (or files) in the Recycle Bin, you can select it, and then choose File, Restore (or right-click the file and choose Restore). The selected file is returned to its original folder, even if the folder has been deleted. Windows 98 restores the folder simultaneously.

You'll also see deleted folders in the Recycle Bin. You can restore a folder (and any subfolders it contains) by right-clicking the folder icon in the

Recycle Bin and choosing Restore from the context menu. And unlike the pre-Internet Explorer 4.0 version of Windows 95, Windows 98 lets you restore empty folders. This is useful, since some transaction software uses empty folders as temporary storage and requires that these folders be always available.

You can send files or folders to the Recycle Bin in several ways. You can select a file/folder in a folder window or the Explorer and press Delete. You can right-click a file/folder and click Delete on the context menu. You can also drag and drop a file/folder to the Recycle Bin icon on the Desktop or in the Explorer, or to the Recycled folder icons in the Explorer and folder windows.

Delete files from common file dialog boxes

You can delete files from the common file dialog boxes that are used by Windows 98-aware applications. If you choose File, Open (or File, Save As) to display the Open (or Save As) dialog box, you can right-click a file and choose Delete from the context menu, or select the file and press Delete. The deleted file is stored in the Recycle Bin.

WordPad, Notepad, and MS Paint use these dialog boxes. 32-bit versions of Word, Excel, and Access don't use these common dialog boxes, but use similar ones that don't have all their functionality. An example of the common file dialog box is shown in Figure 14-2.

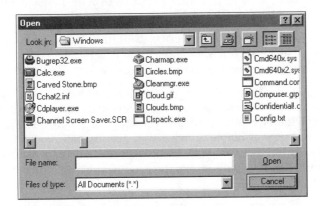

Figure 14-2: The Windows 98 common file dialog box. You can highlight a file listed in this box and delete it by pressing the Delete key. You can also drag and drop files to and from this dialog box.

The Windows 98 common file dialog boxes work a lot like folder windows. You can drag and drop files to and from them. You can rename files. You can create new folders or files. You can't, however, select multiple files or folders.

You can't delete files in the older common file dialog boxes, such as those used by Windows 3.1*x* Write. Microsoft now refers to these as *Win-16* common dialog boxes.

Deleted, what does that mean?

To *delete* a file means to move it to the Recycle Bin.

The fact that deleted files are stored in the Recycle Bin means that they aren't "really" deleted. They are still taking up space on your hard disk. If you don't get around to emptying the Recycle Bin until your disk is full, you will experience performance slowdowns or problems with other applications as your free disk space shrinks.

What is great about the Recycle Bin is that it allows you to organize and clean up your file system without having to make a decision that you may regret a few minutes later. If you delete something and then realize it's more important than you had thought, you can restore it easily.

The Recycle Bin provides a trade-off between the safety and convenience of not deleting the file until later and the valuable disk space taken up by these deleted items. It is up to you to decide when to empty it.

Secret

Files that you delete in a DOS session are not sent to the Recycle Bin. Likewise, if an application deletes files without using an Explorer window, folder window, or the new common file dialog boxes, these files are not sent to the Recycle Bin. As far as the Windows 98 or DOS file management system is concerned, the files are deleted.

Do you want the files you delete in a DOS window to go to the Recycle Bin? You can if you use a little freeware application called Delete.exe. You'll find it at http://ourworld.compuserve.com/homepages/vrangan/.

When you empty the Recycle Bin or delete files in a DOS session, the names of the deleted files are altered so that they don't show up in the file listings in the Explorer, folder windows, or DOS directory lists. The disk space taken up by the files is now available to be written over by new files. If they haven't been written over yet, you can recover these files by using low-level tools. For additional information, see the section entitled "Undelete and Unerase" later in this chapter.

To summarize, there are three levels of delete. If you delete a file in a folder or Explorer window, it is stored in the Recycle Bin. If you delete it from the Recycle Bin or delete it in a DOS window, it is deleted from the file management system. If you use low-level tools to wipe the space on the hard disk that it occupied, it can't be recovered. Still, a slightly earlier version of the file may be intact on the hard disk in some other location—in which case it would be recoverable.

Deleting shortcuts

If you delete a shortcut, only the shortcut goes to the Recycle Bin, not the target (whether it be a file, application, or folder). The original item stays right where it was and continues to work fine. You are only deleting the shortcut file itself — which has an extension of *lnk, pif* or *url* — not the target of the shortcut.

Right- or left-drag to the Recycle Bin

There are many ways to delete a file. You can drag the file to the Recycle Bin icon, to a Recycled folder icon, or to an open Recycle Bin or Recycled folder window. If you left-drag the file icon, it is moved to the Recycle Bin. If you right-drag it, you are given the choice to move the file or cancel the move.

You can drag files back out of the Recycle Bin and place them in any folder, not just in their original location. If you right-drag a file out of the Recycle Bin to a folder window, you will be given the chance to move the file or cancel the move.

If you right-click a file icon and click Delete in the context menu, or if you highlight a file icon and press the Delete key, you will be asked to confirm your deletion. It doesn't matter if the Recycle Bin has been set to remove files immediately when deleted or not; you will still be asked for confirmation of the deletion.

If you drag a file (either left- or right-drag) to the Recycle Bin, you will not be asked for confirmation unless you've set the Remove Files Immediately When Deleted option. The Windows 98 designers assumed that if you were willing to go to all the trouble of dragging a file to the Recycle Bin, you meant it.

You can turn off the delete confirmation message by following these steps:

STEPS

Turning Off Delete Confirmation

Step 1. Right-click the Recycle Bin icon on your Desktop.

Step 2. Click Properties in the context menu.

Step 3. Click the Global tab (if necessary).

Step 4. Clear the Display Delete Confirmation Dialog Box check box.

Shift+Delete

You can delete files without sending them to the Recycle Bin — in other words, purge them — by highlighting their filenames, holding down the Shift key, and pressing the Delete key. (You can also hold down Shift while clicking Delete in a context menu.) The files won't be sent to the Recycle Bin because by deliberately holding down the Shift key, you are telling Windows 98 that you want these files purged. Don't confuse this use of Shift+Delete with the use of Shift+Delete in word processors to send selected text to the Clipboard. Most word processors also support Ctrl+X to cut to the Clipboard, so if you use this key combination, you won't mix up the meaning of Shift+Delete.

Don't Delete Your Hard Disk

If you right-click a hard disk drive icon in the Explorer or in a folder window, you won't find Delete on the context menu. It's not a good idea to delete a hard disk. You can't. But you can delete — or move to the Recycle Bin — all the files on the hard disk by dragging the drive icon to the Recycle Bin.

We don't suggest you do this, especially if the space taken up by the current files on the hard disk is greater than the space set aside for deleted files in the Recycle Bin. If you delete a hard disk, you are moving all the files on the hard disk to the Recycle Bin. This is not possible if there isn't room for them there.

All this can get quite confusing. The Recycled folders are attached to a hard disk, but they show all the files that have been deleted or moved to the Recycle Bin, no matter which hard disk (or disk partition) they were deleted from. If you drag a hard disk drive icon to the Recycle Bin, are you also deleting the files stored in the Recycled folder? The next section addresses this question.

You Can't Delete My Computer or Other Key Components

You can drag My Computer, Network Neighborhood, and the Recycle Bin and drop them on the Recycle Bin folder window. But when you do, you will just get a beep. Windows 98 won't let you delete these things, thankfully.

The same is true of the Printers folder, the Control Panel, the Fonts folder, and the Dial-Up Networking folder. You just get a beep. You can try deleting one of these folders with a right-drag, which feels safer because right-dragging normally gives you a context menu confirming the move.

You *Can* Delete a Floppy Disk

Files on a floppy disk are not moved to the Recycle Bin when you delete them. (In fact, files you delete from any removable media are not sent to the

Recycle Bin.) You can drag the floppy drive icon to the Recycle Bin (icon or folder window), and all the files will be purged after you are first advised of that fact and allowed to change your mind. The message box that appears displays an icon of a file being shredded as a way of indicating that your files will be very difficult to recover if you continue.

If you highlight a file that is stored on a floppy disk and press the Delete key, you will get the same notification. Windows 98 just doesn't provide as much safety for files on floppy disks as it does for files on your local hard disks, although it does ask every time for confirmation of the deletion (purge).

Going Through the Trash — Retrieving Deleted Files

It is easy to get files back from the Recycle Bin. Just click the Recycle Bin icon on the Desktop to open the Recycle Bin folder window, as shown in Figure 14-3. Right-click the item that you want to restore, and then click Restore. The file is restored to its original location. If the folder that it was stored in has been deleted, it is restored also.

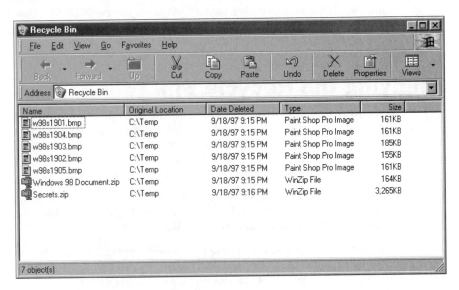

Figure 14-3: The Recycle Bin window. The second column lists the original location (folder) of the deleted file. To restore a file, right-click it and click Restore in the context menu.

You can also just drag the files out of the Recycle Bin and move them to wherever you want. Dragging only moves files in and out of the Recycle Bin, no matter whether you right-drag or left-drag. If you right-drag, you won't see options for Copy, Create Shortcut(s) Here, or any other command you usually see in a context menu when you right drag and drop.

Tip

You can use any of the selection techniques discussed in Chapter 8 to choose which files you want to move or restore to their original location. If deleting a file was the last file management action you carried out, you can choose Edit, Undo Delete in the Recycle Bin window, or right-click the window, and choose Undo Delete from the context menu.

Undocumented

Do you want to check out a graphic or text file that you have already put in the Recycle Bin? Maybe you want to edit it after you deleted it. As long as you haven't emptied your Recycle Bin, you can drag and drop the file from the Recycle Bin onto your application icon. After you're done viewing the file you don't have to worry about deleting it, because it wasn't undeleted in the first place.

If you edited a file that's currently in the Recycle Bin and want to save its new version, save it to another folder. The name of the file in the Save As dialog box will default to its Recycle Bin name, which is not its original name (even though the original name is shown in the Recycle Bin window). This name is used internally by the Recycle Bin to track the deleted files. You may want to change it if you save the edited file to a new folder.

Tip

Unlike moving, copying, or deleting a file, emptying the Recycle Bin is not a recoverable action. You won't find Unempty the Recycle Bin on the context menu. (If the emptied files haven't yet been overwritten by other files, however, you may still be able to get them back with an Undelete utility, as we discuss later in this chapter.)

Emptying the Recycle Bin

As you have seen, dropping a file into the Recycle Bin or pressing the Delete key after selecting an icon does nothing more than move the file to the Recycle Bin. It certainly doesn't delete it — unless you chose the Remove Files Immediately When Deleted option in the Recycle Bin Properties dialog box (right-click the Recycle Bin icon and choose Properties).

To delete the items in the Recycle Bin, click the Recycle Bin icon on the Desktop, and then choose File, Empty Recycle Bin in the Recycle Bin window. All the files in the Recycle Bin are purged.

If you want to purge only some of the items in the Recycle Bin, select those items first and then choose File, Delete. Or, you can right-click the items that you want purged and click Delete in the context menu.

Remove Files Immediately When Deleted

You can set a Recycle Bin property to remove files immediately when deleted. When you delete a file, it is not moved to the Recycle Bin but is immediately purged from the file system.

When this option is set, if you drag files to the Recycle Bin or highlight them and press the Delete key, Windows 98 confirms the file deletion because now they will be purged. This is also true if you right-click a file and choose Delete.

To set the properties of the Recycle Bin, right-click the Recycle Bin icon or the Recycle Bin folder window and choose Properties. The Recycle Bin Properties dialog box, as shown in Figure 14-4, appears on the Desktop.

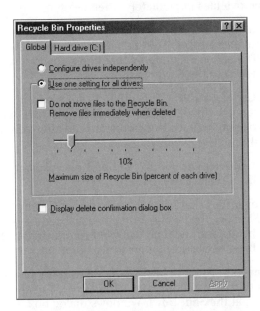

Figure 14-4: The Recycle Bin Properties dialog box. You can choose whether to remove files immediately on delete or not. You can choose the maximum size of the Recycled folders on each hard disk, and you can choose whether to configure the hard disks separately.

In the Recycle Bin Properties dialog box, choose whether you want the files to be removed immediately when deleted or not. You can set the maximum size of the Recycled folder on all or any of the hard disks.

The Recycle Bin and Networks

If the Recycle Bin shows you all the deleted files, what if you are connected to a local or wide area network? Are you going to see all the deleted files on all the servers in your Recycle Bin? Nope.

Undocumented

You see only the files that you deleted from your local hard disks. It doesn't matter if the server resources (a hard disk or folder) are mapped to a local drive letter or not. You can click a Recycled folder on the host or server computer and you still will see only the files that you deleted from your local hard disks.

If you delete a file on the host, it is the same as if you deleted a file from a floppy disk — it is purged. The deleted file is not saved to the Recycle Bin.

Undelete and Unerase

If a file is purged, it is no longer recognized by the Windows 98 file management system. Files are purged when you choose Empty Recycle Bin, when you hold down the Shift key and press the Delete key to delete a selected file, or when you delete a file and the Recycle Bin Properties dialog box has been set to remove files immediately when deleted.

When a file is purged, all that happens is that the first letter of its filename is changed so that it is no longer recognized as a legitimate filename by the file management system. The space taken up by that file is now available for use when other files are written to the hard disk.

DOS 6.x came with an Undelete utility. This utility is not available with Windows 98. But you can use the old DOS 6.x Undelete utility to unpurge files. You just need to be sure to keep this utility around after you upgrade to Windows 98. You'll find Undelete.exe in your old DOS directory.

You can also download Undelete from http://support.microsoft.com/download/support/mslfiles/pd0646.exe.

Undelete works to recover files that haven't been overwritten by new files. It doesn't do much good if more than a short time has elapsed between the time that you purged the file and the time you want to undelete it. The probability that it has been overwritten increases as time passes.

Undocumented

To use Undelete, you need to run it in MS-DOS mode with the file system locked. One way to do this is to choose Start, Shut Down, and choose Restart in MS-DOS Mode in the Shut Down Windows dialog box. At the DOS prompt, type **Lock**, and then **Undelete**. When you are done, type **Unlock** and then **Exit** to relaunch Windows 98. Be sure to copy Undelete.exe to your \Windows\Command directory before you do this, so that you can find it when you type Undelete at the DOS prompt.

If you want to be even safer, you can run Undelete's deletion sentry to store deleted files for seven days before really deleting them. This works whether you delete files at the DOS command prompt or by emptying the Recycle Bin. After you copy Undelete to your \Windows\Command folder, type **Undelete /?** at a DOS prompt to see how to use this feature.

Symantec provides Norton Utilities for Windows 98. These utilities are integrated with the Windows 98 Desktop and user interface, and they include an unerase capability. If you have installed Norton Utilities for Windows 98, when you right-click the Recycle Bin icon, you'll see some new commands in the context menu. Norton Utilities provides additional backup for deleted files by taking over the functions of the Recycle Bin.

Norton Utilities let you unerase files that have been purged without having to use the Undelete utility in MS-DOS mode. Unerase has to deal with the same issues as Undelete: The deleted file's name has been altered, so although the hard disk space may still contain the purged file's contents, the space has been marked available. Use Norton Utilities' Unerase as soon as you can after you inadvertently purge a file to increase your chances of recovering it.

Summary

There are three layers of delete. We show you how the Recycle Bin helps you delete files without undue worry.

▶ You can access and manage the Recycle Bin with minimal effort. It is right there on the Desktop.

▶ We show you how deleted files are stored in a special hidden system folder that displays their properties in the Recycle Bin manner.

▶ The common file dialog boxes are like mini folder windows. We show you how to use them to delete files listed in them. You can also copy, move, and rename files listed in these common dialog boxes.

▶ You can move files into and out of the Recycle Bin to or from any location that you please. You can drag with either the right or left mouse button.

▶ If you delete files on a floppy or over a network, they really do go away without going to the Recycle Bin first.

Chapter 15

The Registry: The Real User Interface

In This Chapter

Microsoft stores all the goodies in the Registry. The Registry takes over many of the functions of the *ini* configuration files found in previous versions of DOS and Windows. If you discover the secrets of the Registry, you have almost complete control over Windows. While in other chapters we discuss specific Registry edits, here we concentrate on the structure of the Registry, how to recover from a corrupt Registry, and how to use the Registry editor. We discuss:

▶ Recovering your Registry from a failed startup

▶ Monitoring changes in your Registry as they happen

▶ Creating shortcuts to your Registry editor

▶ Expanding and collapsing your entire Registry

▶ Stuffing data values into a Registry entry using the Registry export and import functions

▶ Finding values in the Registry using an exported Registry file

▶ Editing other people's Registries

▶ Getting to the Registry from DOS

Ini Files, Forever

In our previous books on Windows 95, we wrongly assumed that Microsoft wanted to do away with *ini* files and move all user, hardware, and application parameters to the Registry. This turns out to be only half true.

There are certainly good reasons for wanting to dispense with *ini* files. Problems caused by relying on these files became apparent with Windows 3.1*x*. Directories throughout the world were filling up with *ini* files. Win.ini and System.ini, the two files that represent Microsoft's main contribution to this blight under Windows 3.1*x*, became quite large as some developers took the easy route and used them to store their applications' vital parameters.

This led to a number of difficulties when users and system administrators tried to access configuration information. There were so many different files that no one could keep track of what was where. In addition, there was no systematic distinction between values that are user-specific and those that are machine/software-specific.

In response to these problems, Microsoft introduced the Registry (Reg.dat) in Windows 3.1 to store file associations and OLE information, and it greatly expanded the Registry in Windows NT, Windows 95, and Windows 98. The Registry is (for the most part) the central repository of user, application, and system configuration data.

Despite the advantages of maintaining one central location for configuration data, however, Microsoft programmers still use *ini* files. Indeed, these files are necessary for Windows 98 to operate properly. Just to mention a few *ini* files that are still with us: Telephon.ini is maintained in order to retain backward compatibility with 16-bit TAPI applications (the values stored in Telephon.ini are also kept in the Registry). A hidden Desktop.ini file is stored in any folder whose web view has been customized. DOS real-mode versions of ScanDisk and ScanReg use *ini* files to guide their behavior. Protocol.ini is used to store information about the network configuration. And Microsoft retained the Win.ini and System.ini files to maintain compatibility with Windows 3.1*x* applications and other previous methods of storing information about system and user configuration. The list could go on.

The *ini* files will continue to be useful in some respects, providing application-specific data that doesn't really need to be in the Registry and would just slow startup times. Unfortunately, they will also continue to cause headaches for system administrators who must search for files that users have inadvertently erased.

The Registry Keys and Structure

The Registry is a storehouse for configuration values and settings that are used to determine how Windows 98 and Windows applications operate. Of course, for the Registry to serve its full purpose, software developers must use it to store their program parameters.

The Registry also keeps track of a list of hardware and hardware configurations that the Windows 98 setup and hardware-detection routines have discovered. If you change your hardware configuration, the Registry is updated.

The *keys* in the Registry are similar to the bracketed headings in the Win.ini or System.ini files. Registry keys, unlike *ini* file headings, can and do contain subkeys. While only text strings are allowed in *ini* files, values in the Registry can consist of executable code.

The Registry is a database divided into six main branches, as can be seen in Figure 15-1. Each branch is a *handle* to a different set of key values, hence the names HKEY_CLASSES_ROOT, HKEY_CURRENT_USER, and so on.

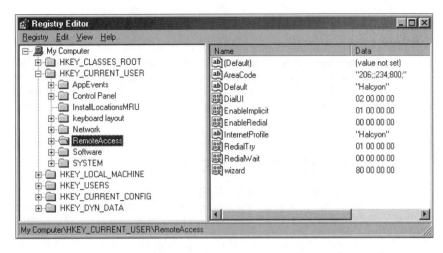

Figure 15-1: The Registry editor. Click a plus sign to open a branch of the Registry.

Each of the six main branches is divided into further branches. Each node is a key. You can follow any of the branches out until you run out of keys and have only data.

Secret

To expand all branches below a node, highlight the node and press Alt+*. (that is, press Alt plus the numeric keyboard asterisk). To collapse all the branches below a node, click its minus sign, highlight the node, and press F5.

Much of the Registry is not that useful to a user or system administrator. It is maintained by the operating system, configured when you install new software, and often better edited through dialog boxes that you access in the Control Panel and in various other elements of Windows 98. These dialog boxes serve as front ends to the Registry. In addition to using them, you can also customize Windows 98 by using TweakUI. This utility, which we refer to throughout the book, is one of the most powerful Registry front ends available. TweakUI dramatically reduces the amount of direct Registry editing work required to customize Windows 98, and we trust that you'll use it as often as we do. (The TweakUI icon is in the Control Panel. If you don't have it, you can install the application from the \tools\ResKit\Powertoy folder of your Windows 98 CD-ROM.)

We have, however, found wide applicability for directly editing the HKEY_CLASSES_ROOT branch and the HKEY_CURRENT_USER branch of the Registry. You may find that the other branches also provide useful areas for individual customization.

HKEY_CLASSES_ROOT

This branch contains the file extensions and file/application associations as well as OLE data. This branch is an *alias* for HKEY_LOCAL_MACHINE\ SOFTWARE\ Classes. Changes in this area of the Registry are discussed in *Creating and Editing File Types and Actions* in Chapter 13.

HKEY_USERS

The information displayed under this key is stored in the User.dat file. This includes user-specific Desktop configurations, network connections, and the Start menu. If your computer is configured using user profiles, a separate User.dat file is created for each user. When a user logs on to the computer, Windows 98 reads that person's User.dat file and integrates it into the Registry in memory.

HKEY_CURRENT_USER

This is the portion of HKEY_USERS that is applicable to the current user. If there is only one user, the default user, then HKEY_USERS\.Default and HKEY_CURRENT_USER are different views of the same information.

Many of the examples of editing the Registry used in this book make the assumption that you are editing the values only for the current user or for the default user. Therefore, many of those changes take place along this branch of the Registry.

If you want to make the indicated changes for other users with different login names, you need to track down the appropriate locations in the HKEY_USERS branch.

There are similar values in this branch and in the next one, HKEY_LOCAL_MACHINE. The values in this branch take precedence over the values found in HKEY_LOCAL_MACHINE.

Software developers can store user-specific information in this branch. If they do, their programs will be customized for each individual user. It doesn't matter that one user changes his or her settings. As long as those values are stored here, other users keep their settings. It's up to the software developers to put all their user-specific values in this branch. You'll find this user and application information by looking at:

HKEY_CURRENT_USER\Software*Company Name**App Name**Version*

Check out the values under HKEY_CURRENT_USER\Software\id\Doom95 (if you've installed Doom95).

HKEY_LOCAL_MACHINE

This is the branch for computer hardware and its installed software. If the computer can have multiple hardware configurations — such as hooked up to the network or not, or docked or not — the information on each configuration is stored here.

Look down the HKEY_LOCAL_MACHINE branch under SOFTWARE, and you'll find the names of the companies that make the software that you have installed. This branch is meant to be a convenient location for machine-specific information about each company's products. Application programmers don't have to use this area to store various settings, but it sure makes it easy if they do.

This is where you'll find application names, version numbers, application pathnames, and hardware settings — settings that apply to all users. Of course, Microsoft uses this branch to register its software.

Application programmers are also encouraged to store their Windows 98-compatible uninstall information under this key. You'll find it in:

HKEY_LOCAL_MACHINE\SOFTWARE\Microsoft\Windows\CurrentVersion\ Uninstall.

HKEY_CURRENT_CONFIGURATION

The display settings and the available printers are here.

HKEY_DYN_DATA

The Registry keeps data on Windows performance parameters, and these values are stored here. This information is kept in RAM after Windows 98 loads, and it is updated on an ongoing basis. You can view these statistics using the System Monitor. Plug and play devices and the software that monitors these devices make use of the information stored here.

Registry Monitor

Not only do the operating system and major applications write information to the Registry on startup, but there are many instances in which Windows 98 (or a Windows application) reads the Registry during the normal functioning of your system — to look up the value of a setting you've made in the Control Panel, for example. Registry Monitor (Regmon.exe) is a free utility that monitors the Registry's keys and the occasions when Windows and Windows applications access them. You can learn many things from watching the use of these keys.

As one example of how you might use RegMon, you can run it while you are installing an application so that you can watch the application's setup routines create keys and fill them with data. RegMon keeps a running list of the changes an application makes to the Registry during installation. You can save the output to a disk file and then later open it in WordPad or another text editor to review it more closely.

You can also use RegMon to hunt down program settings in the Registry that control important features of the user interface but are not documented in the program's Help file or manual. For example, Bill Engles, who first suggested this use of the Registry Monitor, used it to find the cause of a feature that appeared and disappeared from Windows 95 systems at his company. For no apparent reason, the Explorer would suddenly gain the ability to expand folders with a "smooth scrolling" motion instead of expanding them abruptly, which was the Explorer's default behavior. Just as suddenly, Explorer would lose this ability.

Engles finally traced this feature to the installation of beta versions of Internet Explorer 4.0. He tracked down the setting for smooth scrolling by watching RegMon while opening the Windows Explorer. What he found was that the Explorer was looking for a SmoothScroll setting in the Registry that didn't exist. By inserting SmoothScroll into the Registry and setting it to 1, Engels found he could make the behavior permanent.

Windows itself uses the Registry in a variety of different ways. When you make a change in a Control Panel applet or a dialog box, you may be able to locate where such a setting is stored in the Registry. This, in turn, may lead you to other settings in the same general area that you want to investigate.

When you start RegMon, it immediately begins displaying accesses to the Registry. Figure 15-2 shows a few lines of RegMon output. In the example shown in the figure, a fax job using Symantec's WinFax Pro software was running in the background. When it began a fax transmission, the program queried the Registry for all installed printer drivers. The RegMon output displayed these queries in its Request column.

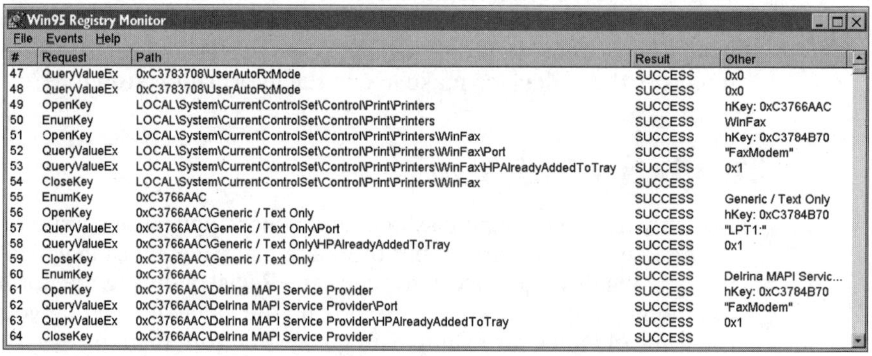

#	Request	Path	Result	Other
47	QueryValueEx	0xC3783708\UserAutoRxMode	SUCCESS	0x0
48	QueryValueEx	0xC3783708\UserAutoRxMode	SUCCESS	0x0
49	OpenKey	LOCAL\System\CurrentControlSet\Control\Print\Printers	SUCCESS	hKey: 0xC3766AAC
50	EnumKey	LOCAL\System\CurrentControlSet\Control\Print\Printers	SUCCESS	WinFax
51	OpenKey	LOCAL\System\CurrentControlSet\Control\Print\Printers\WinFax	SUCCESS	hKey: 0xC3784B70
52	QueryValueEx	LOCAL\System\CurrentControlSet\Control\Print\Printers\WinFax\Port	SUCCESS	"FaxModem"
53	QueryValueEx	LOCAL\System\CurrentControlSet\Control\Print\Printers\WinFax\HPAlreadyAddedToTray	SUCCESS	0x1
54	CloseKey	LOCAL\System\CurrentControlSet\Control\Print\Printers\WinFax	SUCCESS	
55	EnumKey	0xC3766AAC	SUCCESS	Generic / Text Only
56	OpenKey	0xC3766AAC\Generic / Text Only	SUCCESS	hKey: 0xC3784B70
57	QueryValueEx	0xC3766AAC\Generic / Text Only\Port	SUCCESS	"LPT1:"
58	QueryValueEx	0xC3766AAC\Generic / Text Only\HPAlreadyAddedToTray	SUCCESS	0x1
59	CloseKey	0xC3766AAC\Generic / Text Only	SUCCESS	
60	EnumKey	0xC3766AAC	SUCCESS	Delrina MAPI Servic...
61	OpenKey	0xC3766AAC\Delrina MAPI Service Provider	SUCCESS	hKey: 0xC3784B70
62	QueryValueEx	0xC3766AAC\Delrina MAPI Service Provider\Port	SUCCESS	"FaxModem"
63	QueryValueEx	0xC3766AAC\Delrina MAPI Service Provider\HPAlreadyAddedToTray	SUCCESS	0x1
64	CloseKey	0xC3766AAC\Delrina MAPI Service Provider	SUCCESS	

Figure 15-2: The Windows 98 Registry Monitor, a freeware program, shows requests by programs for information from the Registry, and the results of those requests.

Looking more closely at Figure 15-2, we can see how the request from the program to EnumKey (or *enumerate key*) results in Windows listing the values underneath a significant key. In the example, the program next sends an OpenKey request, and then queries the value of each item. The program may store the results of these queries in memory for later use.

The names of the keys monitored by RegMon and the abbreviations RegMon uses are listed in Table 15-1.

RegMon displays the name of a Registry key, such as HKLM\System\ CurrentControlSet\Control\Print\Printers, unless a request involves a key that was first opened before RegMon was started. In that case, RegMon displays the hexadecimal value of the key.

Table 15-1   Key Abbreviations in Registry Monitor

Key	Abbreviation
HKEY_CLASSES_ROOT	HKCR
HKEY_CURRENT_USER	HKCU
HKEY_LOCAL_MACHINE	HKLM
HKEY_USERS	HKU
HKEY_CURRENT_CONFIG	HKCC
HKEY_DYN_DATA	HKDD

If you want to see how some of your other programs access the Registry, add Regmon.exe to your StartUp folder so it will load every time Windows starts. If the display scrolls too fast for you to follow the accesses that programs are making to the Registry, choose Events, Auto Scroll and clear the check mark from this feature. You can then use the scroll bar to scroll at your own pace.

You can download RegMon for Windows 98 or Windows NT from the authors' web site, http://www.ntinternals.com/regmon.htm.

The Registry Files

System.dat and User.dat are the two hidden, read-only files that make up the Registry. Unlike the *ini* files, they are binary files that can't be read easily with an ASCII file editor. You need the Registry editor to examine the variables and values stored in the Registry.

Actually, you can use WordPad to read the Registry, but you need to export it to a text file first. This is an option in the Registry editor. The resulting file (if you export the whole thing instead of just a branch) is too big to be read by Notepad. You can make changes to the exported Registry file and import the altered file back into the Registry database, updating the previous Registry entries. We discuss this more in the later section entitled "The Registry Editor."

There is only one Registry on your computer, but it is made up of two files — System.dat and User.dat. If there is a policy file (a file with the *pol* extension), it is also part of the Registry. We discuss policy files and their implications for the Registry in the "System Policy Editor" section of Chapter 24. When you invoke the Registry editor, it displays and treats System.dat and User.dat as one Registry.

The Registry files have the DOS file attributes of Hidden and Read-Only. This doesn't prevent you from displaying them in the Explorer or a folder window, as long as you have the Show All Files option turned on. (In any Explorer or folder window, choose View, Folder Options, click the View tab, and mark the Show All Files option button.) System.dat and User.dat are by default stored in the \Windows folder. (Remember that while we call our folder *Windows*, you may have named yours something else, such as Win98 or Win.) If your \Windows folder is on a compressed drive, these files (and their backups) are stored on the boot drive. Other variations are possible with networked computers.

System.dat stores information specific to a computer and to the software on that computer. System.dat tracks the detected hardware and its configuration as well as Windows and other installed programs that put their information in the Registry.

User.dat stores user-specific information, including mouse speed, color scheme, cursor scheme, wallpaper, accessibility settings, icon spacing, fonts, keyboard layout, keyboard delay and speed, regional settings, Explorer settings, and passwords. A user's Desktop icons and network connections are stored in User.dat. If you make the appropriate choice in the User Profiles tab of the Passwords Properties dialog box (click the Passwords icon in the Control Panel), each individual user can have his or her own Start menu and Desktop settings. You can also use the Users icon in the Control Panel to set up new users and their parameters.

What if bad things happen?

Because almost all the vital information about Windows 98 and the Windows applications that you have installed is stored in the Registry, it would be a real shame if somehow the files that make up the Registry got corrupted. If you edit the Registry, you may insert values that later prove to be quite wrong, but you may be unable to determine which values those were. In both of these cases, it would be good to have a copy of the Registry files as they existed before things went awry.

If you get an error message when you start Windows 98 stating that there is not enough memory to load the Registry or that Windows has encountered an error accessing the System Registry, you have a corrupted Registry.

It is not that hard to end up with a corrupted Registry. Windows 98 reads the Registry files off a hard disk, and the disk can have weak areas that weren't marked as such before the files were stored there. Also, the Registry is stored in RAM after it is read during Windows startup, and it is often written back to the hard disk as you use Windows. Any memory errors can corrupt the Registry, and that corruption is then preserved in the Registry files when they are overwritten.

Placing everything in one file and making Windows so dependent on that file means that of course it is going to fail. Windows 95 didn't do enough to help you recover your Registry when the inevitable happened. We provided some additional means of backing up and recovering your Registry files in our previous *Windows 95 Secrets* books, but even those weren't nearly enough.

Windows 95 automatically created backups of your System.dat and User.dat files with the extension *da0*. These files were created each time Windows successfully started. Windows 98 does not create these files. As a consequence, one of our Registry recovery utilities from our previous *Windows 95 Secrets* books, Regrecov.bat, won't do anything useful because there are no files for it to operate on.

Windows 98 automatically backs up your Registry (and your Win.ini and System.ini files) every day. By default, it keeps five days worth of these backups in your \Windows\Sysbckup folder. It lets you easily create a backup at any time, as described in the next section, "Registry backup," and it allows you to boot your computer to real-mode DOS and roll back your computer to an earlier Registry (and Win.ini and System.ini files), as described in "Registry recovery" later in this chapter.

The fact that Windows 98 automatically backs up these files every day is the key. Any changes made in your Registry during the day are lost if you go back to a previous version of the Registry. If you install new software during the day and then roll back to an earlier Registry, you will need to reinstall the software. Frankly, this is a small price to pay compared to what you'd have to shell out if you hadn't been making regular backups manually.

Because you most likely won't be able to boot your computer into Windows 98 if you have a corrupted Registry, you have to be able to create new Registry files from real-mode DOS. Windows 98 provides both Windows and DOS versions of its backup and restore tool, so you can access it both to back up while you're using Windows, and to restore from DOS.

If more than just your Registry has gone bad, you may need to boot to DOS from a floppy disk and then gain access to your hard disk. You'll need to create a bootable diskette under Windows 98 to allow this to happen. We discuss this further in the "Emergency Startup disk" section later in this chapter.

Registry backup

Windows 98 automatically backs up your Registry files, Win.ini, and System.ini every day. It does this by calling the backup and restore program ScanReg (Scanregw.exe /autorun) as part of startup. ScanReg compacts these files and then stores them in your \Windows\Sysbckup folder as cabinet files with the names rb001.cab, rb002.cab, and so on. You can also use Scanreg.exe, a separate DOS real-mode program, to restore a backup after you boot to DOS (see the next section).

If you want to create a backup of the Registry yourself while you're using Windows, run ScanReg. Click the Start button and choose Programs, Accessories, System Tools, System Information, Tools, then click Registry Checker. ScanReg does indeed scan the Registry for problems, which is why Microsoft called it ScanReg instead of BackReg. If it doesn't find any errors, it tells you that it has already backed up the Registry for the day and asks if you want to back up now.

You have the option of determining whether Windows 98 calls ScanReg at all, how many days worth of backups are stored, where the backups are stored, and what other files are stored with them. You set these parameters in an *ini* file, Scanreg.ini, which is stored in your \Windows folder.

Scanreg.ini is self-documented. Start the program and follow the instructions it provides for changing how Scanregw.exe and Scanreg.exe work when they create backups. For example, you may want to include other files in your backup, such as Protocol.ini, Autoexec.bat, and Config.sys. You can do this by adding these filenames to Scanreg.ini in the required format. Files you list here will be included in backups made by both Scanregw.exe and Scanreg.exe. Of course, one of the reasons for having a Registry is that you shouldn't have to remember just which *ini* files you need to back up. Oh well.

By modifying Scanreg.ini, you can direct ScanReg to store the backup cabinet file in another folder or on another device. If you direct the backup to a floppy drive, it will be slower than storing the backup file on the hard disk. Even if you store the backups on your hard disk, you can copy them onto removable media on a regular basis. The files are compacted, so they have a chance of fitting on a floppy diskette. Of course, copying the files to another disk isn't automatic, as it is when ScanReg creates them in the first place. And, while having a copy of the backup files on a floppy could be useful if you damage those files, it really won't protect you if your hard disk dies. In that case, you will have to reinstall everything on a new drive anyway. Therefore, it is not such a bad thing if the backup file is only on the hard disk.

Use your Explorer to right-drag Scanreg.ini and Scanregw.exe from the \Windows folder to your Desktop and create shortcuts to them there. These shortcuts will let you quickly make a backup whenever you like and easily change the values in Scanreg.ini.

Scanreg.exe and Scanregw.exe replace Cfback.exe, the Windows 95 Registry backup and restore utility. This utility is no longer shipped on the Windows CD-ROM. In addition, because you can configure Scanreg.ini so that ScanReg will back up all your configuration files, there is no need to use the Emergency Recovery Utility, Eru.exe.

Registry recovery

If your Registry goes bad, or if you just want to get back to where you were before you installed some software, you will have to go into real-mode DOS to run Scanreg.exe. You can reboot your computer, press and hold the Ctrl key during your computer's power-on self test, and choose the Command Prompt Only option at the Windows Startup menu. If you type **Scanreg /?** at the DOS prompt, you'll get a listing of options (*switches*) that work with this command, though not all the options are documented there.

You can use the /fix switch to scan and fix an existing Registry. Just type **Scanreg /fix**. If you would rather restore a backup of a previous version of the Registry, type **Scanreg /restore**. A list of the backup files appears along with their dates, and you can choose which file you want to restore.

You can use the /backup switch to back up your Registry at the DOS prompt. Of course, you shouldn't do this if you've just experienced a corrupt Registry and that's why you are at the DOS prompt.

You can get rid of unused branches and parameters from your Registry files. Use the /opt switch to scan your Registry while you are in real-mode DOS and let it remove unneeded portions of your Registry. Cutting down on your Registry file size will let Windows boot up more quickly because less information will have to be read into memory.

ScanReg will automatically trim some empty branches in your Registry if it finds over 500K of empty data structures. Since ScanReg is called by Windows 98 as part of startup, it gets a chance to scan for empty data structures whenever you do a warm boot. However, this is a minor amount of optimization compared to using Scanreg.exe with first the /fix switch and then the /opt switch (the order for optimal trimming).

Emergency startup disk

You may discover that you can't boot your computer even to DOS from your hard disk. This is not a problem of a corrupt Registry, or at least not just a corrupt Registry. If you have created a Startup disk, otherwise known as an *Emergency Startup disk* (ESD), you'll be able to boot your computer and perhaps get back to your hard disk.

To create an Emergency Startup disk, click the Start button, point to Settings, click Control Panel, and click Add/Remove Programs. Then click the Startup Disk tab, click the Create Disk button, and follow the prompts. Of course, you have to do this before disaster strikes.

If you can't boot your computer from your hard disk, place an ESD in your boot floppy drive and restart your computer. If you can then access your hard disk, you can gain access to the Registry backup files and restore the Registry if necessary.

Emergency Recover Utility

Microsoft provides another backup and disaster-recovery utility called ERU (Emergency Recovery Utility), which copies the major user-configuration files, including a compressed version of User.dat, to a boot diskette. We recommend using ScanDisk instead of ERU, since it is run automatically every day—however, since ERU is there on your Windows 98 CD-ROM in the \Other\Misc\Eru folder, we have included information here for using it.

If you can't start Windows, you can reboot your PC with a bootable floppy disk containing files that ERU placed there. ERU will automatically restore these important files for you.

STEPS

Creating a Bootable Diskette and Adding the Emergency Recovery Utility

Step 1.   You need to create a bootable diskette in order to use ERU. You can do this by right-clicking your A drive in Explorer, clicking Format, and then selecting Copy System Files Only. (This performs the same function as typing **FORMAT A: /S** at your command prompt.) The resulting bootable diskette contains only four files: the two "hidden" files, Io.sys and Msdos.sys, along with Command.com (to process commands) and Drvspace.bin (to access your hard drive if it is compressed).

A Startup diskette is also bootable, but you create it through the Control Panel, and it contains many more files. To create a Startup diskette, click Start, Settings, Control Panel, Add/Remove Programs, Startup Disk, Create Disk. This results in a diskette that contains 16 files. In addition to the four files that comprise a vanilla bootable diskette, it also contains tools such as ScanDisk (to repair hard drive sectors), RegEdit (to update the Registry), Debug (to examine your hard disk at a technical level), and DOS Edit (to update text files such as Msdos.sys), as well as Fdisk, Format, and Uninstall.

Creating a standard bootable diskette leaves about 1MB free on a 1.4MB diskette. This provides ample space for the backup files ERU will place on the diskette. A Startup diskette, in contrast, leaves less than 0.5MB free, and therefore can store fewer ERU files.

If you create a Startup diskette, you can add to it as many other crucial files as ERU can pack into it (see step 3). Copy any other necessary files to a second floppy, and store both diskettes in a safe place, hoping they'll never be needed.

Step 2.   Copy ERU's files from your Windows 98 CD-ROM to your hard disk. You'll find four files in the folder D:\Tools\Misc\Eru (assuming your CD-ROM drive is named D). Copy these files into your \Windows folder. Then drag Eru.exe from your \Windows folder to your Desktop to create a shortcut to it.

Step 3.   Click the Eru.exe icon on your Desktop to copy your configuration files to your bootable diskette. When instructed to do so by ERU, insert the bootable diskette you made in step 1 into your A drive. You have some control over the files ERU copies if you click its Custom button. If you do this, you'll see a dialog box like the one in Figure 15-3.

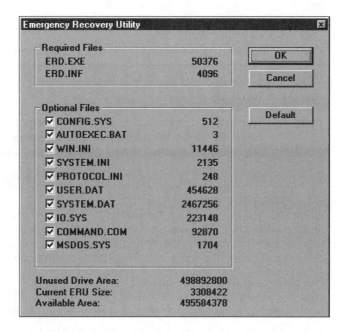

Figure 15-3: The Emergency Recovery Utility's custom dialog box.

While you're in the D:\Other\Misc\Eru folder, you may notice some odd files. One is Eru.txt, a short text file that describes some of ERU's functions.

Another is a file with the weird name of Erd.e_e. The underscore in the extension doesn't indicate that the file is compressed, as with some Microsoft distribution files. Instead, it means that you shouldn't try to run ERD under Windows. It is intended to be run only from a Safe mode command prompt, which is the mode Windows is in when you boot from an emergency disk prepared by ERU.

When you run into problems with a corrupted Registry, take these steps:

STEPS

Rebooting with the Emergency Recovery Utility

Step 1. If you find that you have a corrupted Registry and you have run ERU recently, reboot your computer with the ERU diskette in drive A. Press F8 when you see the message "Starting Windows 98." (If you don't see this message, press the Ctrl key during the power-on self test.)

(continued)

STEPS *(continued)*

Rebooting with the Emergency Recovery Utility

Step 2. At the menu, choose Safe Mode Command Prompt Only.

Step 3. Type **erd** at the command prompt.

Step 4. When the process started in step 3 is complete, restart your computer in the normal fashion. If you haven't run ERU lately, you may have to reinstall some applications you installed recently.

When ERU writes files to your diskette, it copies Erd.e_e to the disk and renames it Erd.exe. This allows the program to run when you boot your system with this diskette. There's no point in renaming the file yourself, since the file should only be run from ERU's emergency diskette.

The really useful file in the quartet you find in the D:\Tools\Misc\Eru folder, however, is Eru.inf. This file controls ERU's default behavior, much in the same way that a few Win.ini settings control Windows 98.

A sample Eru.inf file is shown in Figure 15-4. In this sample, we've removed a few lines of comment you'll find in the actual file (including one line in which Eru.inf is mistakenly spelled Err.inf).

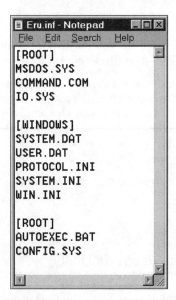

Figure 15-4: The sample Eru.inf file.

Eru.inf controls which files are copied from your hard disk to your emergency disk, and in which order. Files are copied in the order they are listed in the Eru.inf file, until ERU runs out of diskette space.

This text file is a place for you to add any drivers or other files that may be necessary for your system to boot up. For example, if you have real-mode drivers listed in a Config.sys file, you should add those to the list in Eru.inf.

You'll notice in the Eru.inf file that the section entitled [ROOT] is listed twice. This is deliberate. If ERU runs out of diskette space, it will skip the files at the end of the Eru.inf listing — in this case, Autoexec.bat and Config.sys. Listing the [ROOT] folder twice lets you put the less-critical files last.

The Registry Editor

Microsoft has created numerous user interface elements — including the Control Panel, dialog boxes, and TweakUI — that are designed to let you change the values stored in the Registry without having to edit it directly. You can find most of these elements by clicking the Start button and pointing to Settings.

If you can make the changes you need without using the Registry editor, by all means do so. That way the changes you make are reflected immediately as changes in the behavior of that portion of the operating system affected by the values stored in the Registry.

Microsoft hopes that these user interface elements are enough. They aren't.

In many of the chapters in this book, we reveal how to use the Registry editor to change a value or add a key. Changes you make using the Registry editor are often not used until the next time you start Windows (when the Registry values are read and stored in memory). We have indicated throughout the text when the changes you make take effect immediately versus when you need to restart Windows.

Secret

There is a way to make the changes that you've made to the Registry take effect quickly, if not immediately. Click the Start button, click Shut Down, choose Restart, and hold down the Shift key as you click OK. Your computer will restart Windows 98 without rebooting.

Making changes to Registry values using the Windows 98 user interface elements is the safest means of changing these values. If you use the Registry editor, it is quite possible to delete or alter vital elements of the Registry. Some changes may prevent Windows 98 from operating correctly.

One precaution that you can take to recover from such an unfortunate editing session is to make a backup of the Registry files before you edit them. The Registry scanning utility (Scanregw.exe), detailed in the "Registry backup" section earlier in this chapter, lets you easily and quickly make a backup before you begin editing.

If you engage in a course of action that damages the Registry, you still have your automatic backups. If you restart Windows after an editing session that has gotten out of hand, and Windows can't start successfully, you can always go to the backups.

On the other hand, you may have done some damage during your editing session — perhaps made some inadvertent changes that you don't remember and certainly didn't want to make — but the damage is not great enough to prevent Windows 98 from starting the next time. If you have started Windows after one of these rash editing sessions, an intentional backup you did right before your last editing session would be very handy.

We have included additional Registry editors and Registry editor extensions on the *Windows 98 Secrets* CD-ROM. One freeware extension, appropriately named Registry Editor Extensions, saves the paths within the Registry that you have visited, allowing you to get back to them quickly. You can download the latest version at http://www.dcsoft.com/ftp/regeditx.zip.

Registry Editor Extensions also adds some nice user-interface touches. You can display the drop-down list of visited keys by Shift+clicking anywhere in the list box, and you can type or cut and paste a key into the list and instantly navigate there.

Starting the Registry editor

You'll find the Registry editor in the \Windows folder. Windows 98 Setup does not place it on any of the Start menus. Microsoft is not that eager for the uninitiated to use this tool. The application filename is Regedit.exe. Your system administrator may have removed it from your computer.

If you are going to use the editor, it is a good idea to create a shortcut to access it. Place the shortcut on the Desktop or in the Start menus. If you don't know how to create shortcuts, you shouldn't be messing around with the Registry editor (unless you are following our explicit step-by-step instructions).

Editing with the Registry editor

Chapters throughout this book contain discussions that point to areas of the Registry to be edited. Let's take a minute to see what the editing commands are and how to use them.

To learn how to edit the Registry, it helps to get to a location that has some useful keys, constants, and values. We'll use the current Desktop in the following steps as an example of a very fruitful location.

STEPS

Editing the Registry

Step 1.   Click the plus sign to the left of HKEY_CURRENT_USER. Click the plus sign to the left of Control Panel, and then the one next to *desktop*. (The name HKEY refers to the fact that this is a handle to a key. The Registry is filled with keys that eventually have data attached to them.)

Step 2.   Highlight the WindowMetrics name next to its folder icon. Notice that the right pane is now filled with constant names (Name) and values (Data).

Step 3.   In the "Sliding windows" section of Chapter 6, we showed you how to create a new constant (MinAnimate) to turn off the sliding windows effect. If you haven't created this constant, you can do so now. (You can easily get rid of it or change its value so that your current configuration remains the same.)

Step 4.   Right-click in the right pane of the Registry editor (but not on a constant name or value). A New button, as shown in Figure 15-5, appears. Point to the New button, and a menu appears. You can choose to create a key, a string value, a binary value, or a DWORD value. The key and/or any of the constants will be attached to the WindowMetrics key.

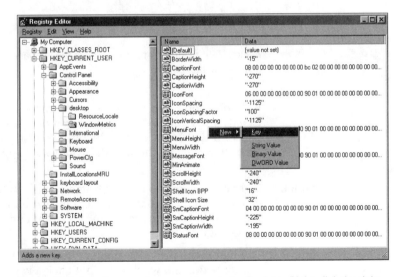

Figure 15-5: Inserting new keys or values in the Registry. Right-click the right pane of the Registry editor to insert new keys or constants.

(continued)

STEPS *(continued)*

Editing the Registry

Step 5.   Right-click the *desktop* key in the left pane of the Registry editor. As shown in Figure 15-6, the context menu will give you the choice of collapsing this expanded branch of the Registry; creating a new key, string value, or binary value; finding a text or numerical string in the local branch; or deleting or renaming the key.

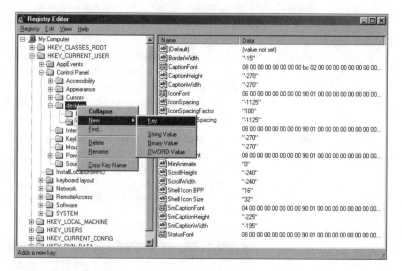

Figure 15-6: Right-click next to a key in the left pane of the Registry editor to access a context menu.

It is not a good idea to delete or rename a key unless you know exactly what you are doing. Adding a new key or value (actually a constant that has a value, which the Registry editor refers to as *Data*) may change the way the Windows 98 operates, but it won't do any damage.

Step 6.   Right-click a constant in the Name column in the right pane of the Registry editor. A context menu appears, allowing you to modify the constant's value, delete the constant and its value, or rename the constant.

Step 7.   The Edit menu provides similar choices to those that appear on the context menu when you right-click a key or a constant. The Edit menu changes depending on whether you have highlighted a key or a constant. You can't highlight a value (or Data).

Editing the Registry consists of adding or deleting keys, adding new constants and their values to be associated with the keys, and modifying those constants and their values—pretty straightforward. It's knowing what keys, constants, and values to add, rename, or delete that's the trick.

Exporting and importing the Registry

You can export the Registry to an ASCII file with the *reg* extension. If you do this, Windows 98 writes the keys, constants, and values stored in System.dat and User.dat to an ASCII text file that can be read by WordPad.

You can export the whole Registry or just a branch of the Registry. To export either, choose Registry, Export Registry File in the Registry editor. To export a branch, highlight the branch in the left pane of the Registry before you choose to export it.

Choosing Registry, Export Registry File displays the common file dialog box with an added modifier extension attached at the bottom, as shown in Figure 15-7. You can choose to export the whole Registry or just a branch by clicking one of the two option buttons at the bottom of the dialog box.

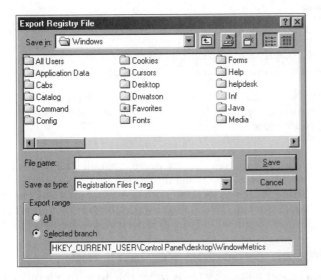

Figure 15-7: The Export Registry File dialog box. You can determine how much of the Registry is exported (the highlighted branch or the entire Registry) by clicking one of the two option buttons at the bottom of this dialog box.

You should export the Registry or a branch of the Registry into a file with a *reg* extension (the default choice in the Export Registry File dialog box). The *reg* extension will be added automatically if you type a filename. The exported Registry is a text file. Using the *reg* extension makes it easy to merge (import) the Registry or its branch later if you edit the exported file.

The exported Registry file can be read easily by WordPad. Right-click the exported file and choose Edit on the context menu. Don't click the file, because the default action for a file of this file type is to merge it back into the Registry. Figure 15-8 shows how part of an exported Registry file looks in WordPad.

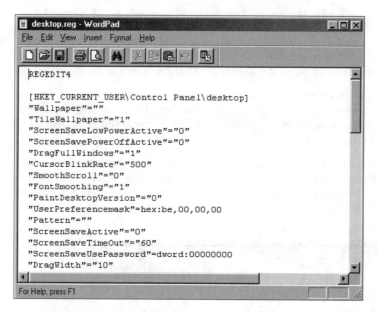

```
REGEDIT4

[HKEY_CURRENT_USER\Control Panel\desktop]
"Wallpaper"=""
"TileWallpaper"="1"
"ScreenSaveLowPowerActive"="0"
"ScreenSavePowerOffActive"="0"
"DragFullWindows"="1"
"CursorBlinkRate"="500"
"SmoothScroll"="0"
"FontSmoothing"="1"
"PaintDesktopVersion"="0"
"UserPreferencemask"=hex:be,00,00,00
"Pattern"=""
"ScreenSaveActive"="0"
"ScreenSaveTimeOut"="60"
"ScreenSaveUsePassword"=dword:00000000
"DragWidth"="10"
```

Figure 15-8: The Control Panel\Desktop key area in the Registry exported to a text file. The key values are surrounded by square brackets. The constants and their string values are surrounded by double quotes.

Tip

The exported text file encloses the key name, including all preceding key names, in square brackets. The constant names are enclosed in double quote marks. String values associated with the constant names are also enclosed in double quotes. DWORD values (double word in either decimal or hexadecimal format) begin with dword:. Binary values begin with hex:.

Searching an exported Registry file

One reason to export a Registry file is to be able to search it quickly. The Registry editor has a find facility, but it is slow. You can bring the exported Registry text file into WordPad and use its Find toolbar button (the binoculars) to find a text or numeric string much more quickly than you could if you searched in the Registry.

This can be quite useful when you're investigating the structure of the Registry or trying to find the constant name whose value you want to change. You can have the Registry editor open on your Desktop, and at the same time have the exported Registry file open in WordPad. Search for the constant name in WordPad. Then, in the Registry editor, click the plus signs next to the Registry keys to expand the branch of the Registry that contains the constant you are looking for.

We have included an additional Registry search-and-replace utility on our *Windows 98 Secrets* CD-ROM, called RegSrch.exe. This utility will automatically search for a given string and replace it with a new string. This is much quicker than editing a repeated string one instance at a time.

Editing an exported Registry file

Of course, you can edit the Registry directly, so why would you export it (or a branch of it) to edit? If you want to make a lot of changes, the editing capabilities of WordPad are much more powerful than those provided by the Registry editor.

The Registry editor allows only certain kinds of values to be typed into the fields for keys, constant names, or values. This prevents many of the errors you might make if you edit the exported Registry file.

You edit an exported Registry file so that you can import (or merge) it back into the Registry. If you are not comfortable doing this, then make all of your Registry changes either though the Windows 98 user interface elements or directly in the Registry editor.

Importing or merging a text file into the Registry

Once you have exported a branch or all of the Registry and edited it, you can put it back in. Now might be a good time to back up the Registry using the procedure outlined in the "Registry backup" section of this chapter.

Merging and importing are the same thing. Click an exported Registry file (a file with a *reg* extension), and it is imported (or merged) into the Registry. Right-click an exported file, and you will see that the first choice on the context menu is Merge. The values of the keys, constants, and data in the exported text file overwrite or are added to the values stored in the Registry.

Of course, you can create a text file with the correctly formatted key, constant name, and data values from scratch and import it into the Registry. You will need to review exported files until you understand the format.

You can also import a Registry file (actually a text file that has been correctly formatted) by choosing Registry, Import Registry File in the Registry editor.

Tip

If you are just importing a branch, then the branch is added to the Registry. If the branch is a new version of an existing branch, the values and keys in the imported branch are added to the existing branch. All of the values with the same name (and location) in the existing branch are overwritten by values in the imported branch. No existing keys or values are deleted by the imported branch.

Click to edit a Registry file

We would rather change the default behavior for exported Registry files, so that clicking a Registry file chooses the Edit command instead of the Merge command. This way, you don't run the risk of accidentally clicking a *reg* file and merging it into the existing Registry when you didn't intend to do so.

Once you change the default behavior, you have to deliberately right-click a *reg* file and choose Merge from the context menu if you want to perform a merge. This is safer and more in line with the rest of the Windows 98 interface. To make this change, take the following steps:

STEPS

Making Editing the Default Behavior for Registry files

Step 1. Open an Explorer window. Choose View, Folder Options. Click the File Types tab.

Step 2. Scroll down the Registered File Types list box to Registration Entries. Highlight Registration Entries, and click the Edit button.

Step 3. Highlight Edit in the Actions box. Click the Set Default button.

Step 4. Click Close in the Edit File Type dialog box, and then click Close again in the Folder Options dialog box.

Auto-inserting into your Registry at startup

You can insert the data from a *reg* file into your Registry when you start Windows 98. For example, if you want to stop Windows 98 from putting "Shortcut to" at the start of every *lnk* file name, you can create a *reg* file, and then put it (or a shortcut to it) in your \Windows\Start Menu\Programs\ StartUp folder.

This file would contain the following text:

```
REGEDIT4
[HKEY_CURRENT_USER\Software\Microsoft\Windows\CurrentVersion\Explorer]
"link"=hex:00,00,00,00
```

This will only work if Merge is the default action for *reg* files. If Edit is the default action, but you actually want to merge the file, edit the Target field of the shortcut file to include *regedit.exe* followed by the *reg* file's name and extension.

Of course, it is easier to use TweakUI to turn off this particularly obnoxious Windows 98 behavior, but you may think of other reasons why you want to write into the Registry at startup.

After Windows 98 runs a *reg* file, it displays a dialog box saying the merge was successful. You can get rid of this dialog box with the RtvReco utility (http://www.windows98.com). Actually, there's a free and easy way around this. The trick is an undocumented switch to RegEdit that J.T. Anderson of Los Angeles was kind enough to point out to us.

RegEdit supports an /s switch, which stands for *silent*. When you add this to a RegEdit command line, the switch suppresses the usual "merge was successful" dialog box that you would otherwise have to click OK in to get rid of.

Therefore, if you have a reason to create a shortcut to a *reg* file that you commonly want to merge into the Registry, use the /s switch on the command line. Instead of creating a shortcut to Filename.reg, for example, you would use the following command line in the Target field of the shortcut:

```
Regedit.exe /s filename.reg
```

If you like the way this eliminates the annoying "merge is successful" dialog box, you don't have to limit yourself to eradicating it for a single shortcut. You can suppress this dialog box every time you run RegEdit by editing the default action for RegEdit.

STEPS

Silencing RegEdit

Step 1.   In the Explorer, click View, Folder Options, File Types.

Step 2.   In the Registered File Types list, select Registration Entries, and then click the Edit button.

Step 3.   In the Actions box, select Merge, and then click the Edit button.

Step 4.   In the Application Used to Perform Action box, change regedit.exe to regedit.exe /s. Click OK, and then click Close twice to exit.

This changes the default command line for RegEdit. Of course, changing the command line globally in this way does mean you see no confirmation box when you merge a *reg* file. For this reason, you might want to stick with editing only those shortcuts where you really need the silent treatment.

Changing the Registered Owner

Windows 98 tracks your name and the name of your company. To see this information, choose Help, About in almost any application.

Secret

You can change your name and company settings, which are stored in your Registry, using the Registry editor:

STEPS

A New User

Step 1.   Click Regedit.exe in your \Windows folder.

Step 2.   Navigate to HKEY_LOCAL_MACHINE\SOFTWARE\Microsoft\ Windows\CurrentVersion.

Step 3.   Double-click RegisteredOwner and/or RegisteredOrganization in the right pane and change the names.

Step 4.   Exit the Registry editor.

Your own tips

Windows 98 provides a few tips for the first time user. You can turn the display of these tips on or off with TweakUI. (To do this, mark or clear the Tip of the Day check box in the Explorer tab.) You can also edit the tips that come from Microsoft and create your own new tips for another user. Here's how:

STEPS

Creating New Tips

Step 1.   In your Registry editor, navigate to

HKEY_LOCAL_MACHINE\SOFTWARE\Microsoft\Windows\ CurrentVersion\explorer\Tips

Step 2.   Right-click the right pane of the Registry editor. Choose New and then String Value.

Step 3.   Type a number one greater than the highest number of the existing tip number. For example, the last tip from Microsoft is number 47, so type **48**. Press Enter.

Step 4.   Double-click the number you just typed. Type a new tip. Click OK.

Step 5.   You can also edit an existing tip by double-clicking its associated number. When you are done, exit the Registry editor.

Editing the Most Recently Used list

Windows 98 uses the Registry to keep track of the devices and folders you use the most frequently to install software. For example, if you install most of your software from your CD-ROM drive, which happens to be drive D, Windows will default to looking on D for files that it needs during an installation. If your computer manufacturer has installed the Windows 98 source cabinet files on your hard disk (in \Windows\Options\Cabs), Windows will look there when you make a change to your Windows installation.

If you install software using the Add/Remove Programs icon in the Control Panel, you'll notice that when an installation routine can't find a needed file, a dialog box appears that asks you to browse to a new location or choose from a list. Windows 98 stores this list, called the Most Recently Used (MRU) list, in the Registry. It lists the most recent locations you used during an installation, regardless of what you were installing.

You can edit the MRU list to get rid of an incorrect listing. In particular, it is a good idea to get rid of A:\ if you don't install from floppy disks. Clicking the Browse button when A:\ is the first default installation location listed slows the search process substantially. Windows 98 will look in the first location listed, but it doesn't search beyond that location — so the order of the remaining locations in the list is not that important.

STEPS

Changing the MRU list

Step 1. In your Registry editor, navigate to

HKEY_CURRENT_USER\InstallLocationsMRU

Step 2. Double-click any of the letters in the right pane of the Explorer, as shown in Figure 15-9.

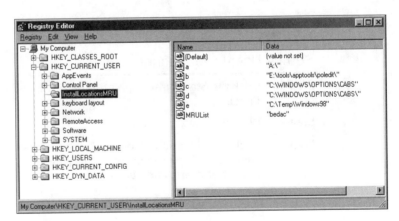

Figure 15-9: There are five locations in the MRU list.

Step 3. Type a new drive letter and path. Click OK. Repeat this process for any other location you want to change.

(continued)

STEPS *(continued)*

Changing the MRU list

Step 4.   If you want to modify the order in which the locations are presented, double-click MRUList in the right pane and type a new order. Click OK.

Step 5.   Exit the Registry editor.

Editing other people's Registries

The Registry editor gives you the option of editing Registries on other computers that you are networked to over a dial-up line, Direct Cable Connection, or LAN. This feature requires a Windows NT server on your network to provide user-level (as opposed to share-level) network security. In addition, if you are going to let your Registry be edited by someone else on your network, you must configure your networking options on your computer to add the Remote Registry Service. Only other users who have user-level access to your computer will be able to edit (or use their Registry editor to view) your Registry.

Setting user-level security

If you have a Windows NT server on your network, set your computer to use user-level security by taking the following steps:

STEPS

Setting User-Level Security

Step 1.   Click the Start button, point to Settings, and then click Control Panel.

Step 2.   Click the Network icon.

Step 3.   Click the Access Control tab. Mark the User-Level Access Control check box. Type the name of the Windows NT server that keeps the list of users, and click OK.

Setting up a computer to allow its Registry to be edited

You can set up your computer to be a Registry server. That is, you allow people at other computers to edit or view your Registry. To do this, take the following steps:

STEPS

Configuring Your Computer as a Registry Server

Step 1. Click the Start button, point to Settings, and then click Control Panel.

Step 2. Click the Network icon.

Step 3. Click the Add button. Double-click the Service icon in the Select Network Component Type dialog box.

Step 4. Click the Have Disk button. Click the Browse button, and browse to the \tools\nettools\remotreg folder on your Windows 98 CD-ROM.

Step 5. Click regsrv.inf, and then click the OK button.

Step 6. Click OK and then OK again. You will have to restart your computer for this change to take effect.

Using the Registry editor to edit someone else's Registry

If another computer user on your network has set up his or her computer as a Registry server and you have user-level access to that user's computer through a list kept on a Windows NT server, you can edit that user's Registry. You'll first need to add regsrv.inf to your computer, by following the steps above in "Setting up a computer to allow its Registry to be edited." Then start your Registry editor, and choose Registry, Connect Network Registry. Type the name of the computer containing the Registry you are going to edit. When you are done, choose Registry, Disconnect Network Registry. You can find further details on editing other people's Registries at http://premium.microsoft.com/support/kb/articles/q141/4/60.asp.

The DOS Version of the Registry Editor

You can edit the Registry from the DOS prompt. This is useful if you are having difficulties starting Windows 98. To go to the DOS prompt without starting Windows, reboot your computer and press and hold the Ctrl key during your computer's power-on self test. Choose the Command Prompt Only option in the Startup menu.

Regedit.exe is a program that runs both in real-mode DOS and in Windows, with different behavior. In MS-DOS mode, you use command line parameters to import and export the contents of the Registry files to and from text files. You can also import and export just selected branches or delete a branch from the Registry.

Earlier versions of RegEdit had trouble with particularly lengthy branches when running in real-mode DOS. This problem was fixed beginning with the OSR2 version of Windows 95.

If you type **Regedit /?** at the DOS prompt, you will get a little help on how to import and export the Registry. You'll need to use the program Edit.com to edit the exported Registry. Use RegEdit to import the edited Registry file back into the Registry.

The DOS RegEdit syntax is as follows:

```
REGEDIT    {/L:system}    {/R:user}    filename1
REGEDIT    {/L:system}    {/R:user}    /C filename2
REGEDIT    {/L:system}    {/R:user}    /E filename3 {regpath1}
REGEDIT    {/L:system}    {/R:user}    /D regpath2
/L:system        Specifies the location of the System.dat file
/R:user          Specifies the location of the User.dat file
filename1        Specifies the file(s) to import into the Registry
/C filename2     Specifies the file to create the Registry from
/E filename3     Specifies the file to export the Registry to
regpath1         Specifies the starting Registry key to export from
                 (Defaults to exporting the entire Registry)
/D regpath2      Specifies the Registry key to delete
```

You can export and edit the whole Registry or just a branch of it. Don't import a branch back into the Registry with the /C (create) option. This will create a Registry with only one branch.

Summary

If you can edit the Registry, you have complete control of Windows 98.

▶ We explain how to recover from fatal conditions in the Registry.

▶ We show you how to get that extra margin of safety by backing up your Registry with ScanReg before you edit.

▶ We describe a number of keystroke shortcuts to help you edit and display the Registry more quickly.

▶ We introduce you to editing Registries across a LAN.

▶ If there is a real problem starting Windows 98, we tell you how to edit the Registry in DOS.

Chapter 16

The Control Panel and Properties

In This Chapter

We cover the Control Panel and general features of properties.

▶ Getting to the Control Panel settings quickly

▶ Installing and removing Windows applications

▶ Creating a bootable Startup disk

▶ Controlling your multimedia hardware and drivers

▶ Configuring Windows 98 for your local currency, time, and dates

▶ Associating sounds with Windows 98 events

▶ Locating those missing parameters in Properties dialog boxes

What Will You Find Where?

Windows 98 has to keep track of itself and the computer it is running on. You need a way to see (and change) your Windows 98 configurations. Thousands of little pieces of information running around in your computer need to be right for everything to work.

In the Control Panel, you'll get a handle on most of your computer's hardware and the software drivers that work with it. In addition, you'll find the Fonts folder (it's also in your Explorer under \Windows\Fonts) and the settings for currency, dates, time, and other location-specific information.

Properties, an innovation with Windows 95, provide another means to get at the parameters that define your files, and in some cases, your hardware.

Many of the specific Control Panel settings are described in the chapters in Part IV. In this chapter, we discuss the Control Panel settings that aren't described there.

Getting to the Control Panel

It's easy to get to the Control Panel (see Figure 16-1). Just click the Start button, point to Settings, and then click Control Panel. But this isn't the only way to get to the Control Panel, nor is it necessarily the most convenient.

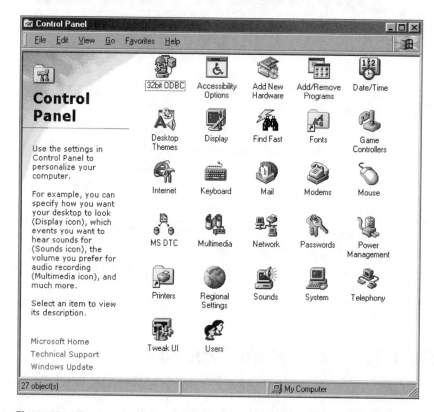

Figure 16-1: The Control Panel. Click any icon to change the settings associated with that icon.

Here are some other ways to get to the items in the Control Panel:

- If you want to use the Display control panel (the Display icon in the Control Panel), right-click the Desktop and click Properties.

- You can get to the Date/Time control panel by double-clicking the clock on the Taskbar.

- The Fonts and Printers folders are accessible through the Explorer. (The Fonts folder is under your C:\Windows folder, and the Printers folder is under My Computer).

- You can get to the System control panel by right-clicking My Computer and clicking Properties.

- Access the control panel for a specific modem by clicking HyperTerminal in your Start, Programs, Accessories, Communications menu (if you installed it), and then clicking the HyperTerminal application icon (hypertrm.exe) in the HyperTerminal folder. Choose File, Properties in the HyperTerminal window, and then click the Configure button in the New Connection Properties dialog box.

- Another way to a particular modem is through a Dial-Up Networking connectoid. Right-click a DUN connectoid (not a shortcut to one), click Properties, and then click Configure.

- You can also get to a modem by right-clicking My Computer, clicking Properties, choosing the Device Manager tab, selecting Modem, and then double-clicking the desired modem. This method gives you access to additional properties not available through the other methods — for updating the modem driver, for example, and for checking the I/O resources.

- To get the Network control panel, right-click the Network Neighborhood icon on the Desktop and choose Properties.

Shortcuts to the Control Panel

If you want a shortcut to an icon in the Control Panel, open the Control Panel, right-click an icon, and click Create Shortcut. You'll see a dialog box saying you can't create a shortcut in the Control Panel and asking whether you want to place the shortcut on the Desktop instead. You can certainly make that choice.

Shortcuts to Control Panel icons make it easy to get at the specific settings that you want changed. While the Control Panel is a reasonable organizing folder for these items, you may have one or two that you change a lot. Bring them out to the Desktop.

Tip

You can place shortcuts to Control Panel applets on your main Start menu. Even better, create a folder, perhaps under your My System folder (which we suggested you create in Chapter 6), and then drag the folder icon and drop it on the Start button. You can then put all your shortcuts to the Control Panel applets in the new folder. That way, you can determine just which applets you want on the main Start menu, and you can put all the shortcuts in one place. You can name the shortcuts anything you like, and they can point to a certain tab within an applet, such as the Device Manager tab in the System control panel (as described in the next section, "Fine-tuning your Control Panel shortcuts").

Microsoft made the Control Panel much slower in Windows 98 and Windows 3.1 than it was in the bad old days of Windows 3.0. Starting with Windows 3.1, opening the Control Panel causes Windows to read through every file in your System folder, looking for files with a *cpl* extension. These *cpl* files are, of course, Control Panel applets.Making the Control Panel read through all these files enables third-party vendors to add their own applets to the Windows interface, so this delay does have some merit. Independent developers can now install Control Panel applets for multimedia devices, tape drives, and other peripherals.

But sometimes you *don't* want to wait for the Control Panel to assemble its little list of applets. You want fast access to the *one* applet that you use all the time. Perhaps you frequently need to change a setting for your mouse or your keyboard. Or you like to change your Desktop colors or fonts every day. Or you need quick access to the handy Device Manager buried within the System applet. The next two sections teach you how to customize your Control Panel shortcuts to display the exact components you want to access.

Fine-tuning your Control Panel shortcuts

The Control Panel occupies a special place in the Desktop hierarchy. If you look for Control Panel in the Explorer, it doesn't appear as an icon under the \Windows\Start Menu folder, as you might expect. Instead, it appears in the left pane of the Explorer *after* all your floppy drives and hard drives. This implies that Control Panel isn't on any of your disks at all.

This isn't the case, of course. Control Panel is, in reality, a normal executable file stored in your \Windows folder. You can see this by clicking the Start button, clicking Run, and then typing the following command:

```
C:\Windows\Control.exe
```

When you click OK, you see the same Control Panel window appear as you do when you run Control Panel directly from the Start menu (Start, Settings, Control Panel).

If you've visited the Control Panel before, you know it includes icons for changing your keyboard, mouse, and modem settings, and for many other functions of your system. The exact complement of Control Panel applets in your Control Panel window depends on the hardware and software you've installed. But the Control Panel holds a lot of secrets beneath its humble exterior. Control.exe supports a number of parameters that can dramatically speed up your access to the settings in its applets.

For example, let's say you want to change your dialing properties frequently, perhaps because you travel a lot. You could click Start, Run and type the following:

```
C:\Windows\Control.exe Modem.cpl
```

Even better, you can create a command that displays an individual tab of an applet, rather than having to start out at the first one and click your way across to the tab you really want.

For example, you can create a command that takes you directly to the Device Manager, a tab in the System applet. That command should look as follows:

```
C:\Windows\Control.exe Sysdm.cpl, System,1
```

This command causes Control Panel to open Sysdm.cpl, the System applet, and jump to the second available tab. (In programmer-speak, the first tab is numbered 0, the second is 1, and so forth.) You need to specify the applet name in this command line because some applets contain more than one function within them.

What the three examples above have in common is the Control Panel's built-in command syntax. Stripped down to skeletal form, the syntax goes like this:

```
Control.exe {filename.cpl} {,applet-name} {,tab#}
```

If you run Control.exe with no parameters, only the Control Panel window is displayed. If you add the correct *filename.cpl*, the first tab of that applet's dialog box is displayed. And if you tack on the correct applet name and tab number, then *that* tab is displayed.

In actual practice (as opposed to theory), there seem to be some quirks in the way Windows processes the tab number for an applet. Some Control Panel applets, particularly Display, dutifully jump to the correct tab when you specify a number in the command line, such as 1, 2, or 3. Other applets refuse to display any tab but the first (tab 0) even if you've used the "correct" syntax. Apparently, some of the programmers at Microsoft didn't know they were supposed to build in this feature, so they didn't. If a particular tab doesn't seem to want to let you "jump to it," the tab simply may not be programmed to do so.

You can place commands like these on the Start menu, on your Desktop, or elsewhere, and access them with a mouse click or a hot key.

Table 16-1 shows some of the *cpl* files available in most Windows systems, and the applet name you'll need in order to jump to a particular tab. (Some applets, such as Main.cpl, contain more than one function; these are listed separately below.)

Table 16-1   Control Panel File and Applet Names

Filename	*Applet Name*
Main.cpl	Fonts
Main.cpl	Keyboard
Main.cpl	Mouse
Main.cpl	Printers
Access.cpl	Accessibility Options
Appwiz.cpl	Add/Remove Programs
Desk.cpl	Display
Dtccfg.cpl	MS DTC

(continued)

Table 16-1 *(Continued)*

Filename	Applet Name
FindFast.cpl	Find Fast*
Inetcpl.cpl	Internet
Infrared.cpl	Infrared
Intl.cpl	Regional Settings
Joy.cpl	Game Controllers
Mlcfg32.cpl	Mail
Mmsys.cpl	Multimedia
Mmsys.cpl	Sounds
Modem.cpl	Modems
Netcpl.cpl	Network
Odbccp32.cpl	32bit ODBC*
Password.cpl	Passwords
Powercfg.cpl	Power Management
Sticpl.cpl	Scanners and Cameras
Sysdm.cpl	System
Sysdm.cpl	Add New Hardware
Telephon.cpl	Telephony
Themes.cpl	Desktop Themes
Timedate.cpl	Date/Time
TweakUI.cpl	Tweak UI
Wbemcpl.cpl	WBEM
Wgpocpl.cpl	Microsoft Mail Postoffice

*These applets are only available if you have installed Microsoft Office 97.

Now that you know the filenames and applet names to use, let's make sure you never have to type these lines more than once. It's easy to create a shortcut icon on your Desktop that takes you directly to the tab of your choice in a Control Panel applet's dialog box. Here's how:

STEPS

Control Panel Shortcut Icons on the Desktop

Step 1. Right-click an unoccupied spot on your Desktop.

Step 2. On the context menu that appears, point to New, and then click Shortcut.

Step 3. In the Create Shortcut Wizard, type a command line such as the following:

```
C:\Windows\Control.exe Desk.cpl, Display,2
```

Step 4. Click the Next button. Type a name for your new shortcut, such as Display Appearance, and then click the Finish button. You're done!

You should see a new icon on your Desktop. Click it, and you will be almost instantly transported to (in this case) the Appearance tab of the Display Properties dialog box.

You'll probably want to change the icon for the shortcut, because this method produces one that looks pretty boring. Check out how to do this in the "Change the shortcut's icon" section of Chapter 10. You might also want to edit the shortcut's Target field to change the command line parameters. To do so, right-click the shortcut, click Properties, and then click the Shortcut tab.

Assigning hot keys to Control Panel shortcuts

Once you've put a command for a Control Panel applet in a shortcut and placed the shortcut icon where you want it on the Desktop or your Start menu, you can assign it a hot key combination. This lets you open the dialog box at almost any time by pressing a key combination such as Ctrl+Alt+A.

To assign a hot key to a shortcut icon, right-click the icon (you can right-click the icon on the Desktop or in the Start menu), and then click Properties. Click the Shortcut tab, click in the Shortcut Key field, and then press a letter key on your keyboard. Windows automatically adds Ctrl+Alt to the key you press. For example, pressing the letter *a* assigns the hot key Ctrl+Alt+A to that shortcut. To assign a Ctrl+Shift or Shift+Alt combination, hold down those keys while you press the letter key.

We provide some additional examples of how to make shortcuts to the Control Panel icons in the "Control Panel icons" section of Chapter 10. You can find further details on how to put the Control Panel on the Start menu in the "Control Panel on a Start menu" section of Chapter 11.

Control Panel Settings

Most of the Control Panel settings are discussed in other chapters, as outlined in Table 16-2. In this chapter, we discuss those that aren't covered elsewhere.

Table 16-2   Settings Covered in Other Chapters

Control Panel Icon	Chapter
Add New Hardware	25
Date and Time	6
Display	28
Fonts	26
Internet	9
Keyboard	27
Mail (or Mail and Fax)	20
Microsoft Mail Postoffice	20
Modems	31
Mouse	30
Network	24
Passwords	20 and 24
PC Cards	25
Printers	29
System	25
Telephony	32
Desktop Themes	28

Missing files

Accidents do happen, and it's possible for a *cpl* or *dll* file to become corrupted. A sign that this might have happened is the following error message, which appears when you exit the Control Panel:

```
FATAL EXCEPTION 0E HAS OCCURRED AT 0028:C07A2B0 IN VXD
IFSMGR(03)+000CF7C.
Run policy editor and restrict Control panel.
```

If this happens, you'll first need to start the Explorer, choose Tools, Find, Files or Folders, and search for *.cpl files in your \Windows\System folder. Open each *cpl* file individually. At some point, one of them will probably give you an error message. This is the damaged file. Rename it, and then open the

Control Panel to see if that fixes the problem. To replace a Windows *cpl* file, you'll need to extract it from the Windows 98 CD-ROM; continue reading to find out how. If the *cpl* file came from a third party, try reinstalling whatever program put it in the Control Panel.

If you find that the Windows Setup and Startup Disk tabs are missing from the Add/Remove Programs tool in the Control Panel, the cause is most likely a missing or damaged Setupx.dll file. This file should be located in your \Windows\System folder. If you find it there, compare it with the same file on your Windows 98 CD-ROM (in \win98\Precopy2.cab). The dates and sizes of the two files should match.

If the two files don't match, or if yours is missing, first rename the Setupx.dll file (if it exists) in your \Windows\System folder, and then extract a new copy of it from your Windows 98 CD-ROM. After copying it to your \Windows\System folder, you need to restart your computer.

The *cpl* and *dll* files are stored in compressed form in cabinet (*cab*) files on your Windows 98 CD-ROM. A new built-in feature of Windows 98 makes it easy to view the contents of *cab* files and extract the files you need. Click a *cab* file (or right-click it and click View) to display its contents in a folder window, and then drag and drop the file you need into your Explorer.

Almost all the Windows 98 *cpl* files are stored in the cabinet file Win98_27.cab, which is located in the \win98 folder of your Windows 98 CD-ROM. One exception is Infrared.cpl, which is stored in Driver14.cab in the \win98 folder.

If for some reason you need to work in MS-DOS mode, you can use the Extract program (Extract.exe), which runs from the command line, to extract the file you need. Copy Extract.exe from the \win98 folder of your Windows 98 CD-ROM into the root level of your C drive if it's not there already. To get help with the Extract tool, type **extract /?** at the DOS prompt or read the Microsoft Knowledge Base article about using Extract (http://premium. microsoft.com/support/kb/articles/Q129/6/05.asp).

In most cases, you shouldn't need the cumbersome Extract utility. One situation in which it is useful, however, is if you don't know which *cab* file contains the file you need. You can tell Extract to examine all the *cab* files in order and show you the file you're looking for. To do this, click the Start button, choose Programs, and click MS-DOS Prompt. At the prompt, type:

```
extract /A /D {drive}:\win98\{first cab file} {file you need} | more
```

For example, if your CD-ROM is drive E, the first *cab* file in the sequence is win98_23.cab, and you're looking for modem.cpl, type the following:

```
extract /A /D E:\win98\win98_23.cab modem.cpl | more
```

You will see one screenful of files at a time; to display the next one, press Enter. When you see the file you need, write down the name of the *cab* file listed above it, type **exit**, and press Enter to return to your Desktop. The easiest way to do the actual extraction is to drag and drop the file from the *cab* file folder window to your Explorer.

Add/Remove Programs

The Add/Remove Programs control panel lets you perform three tasks:

- Install and remove programs that use the Windows 98 version of Install Shield

- Install and remove programs that are covered by the Windows 98 setup routines or that have *inf* files consistent with the Microsoft standard for install files

- Create a bootable Startup disk, as described in "Emergency Startup disk" in Chapter 2

These functions are described in the next three sections.

Install/Uninstall

Microsoft has attempted to provide a standard Windows application installation-and-setup procedure, so you don't have to fathom a new set of steps every time you install a new piece of software. By licensing portions of the Install Shield software and integrating it into Windows 98, Microsoft provides application developers with a tool that will help you install and uninstall their programs.

To install a piece of compatible software, click the Install button, as shown in Figure 16-2.

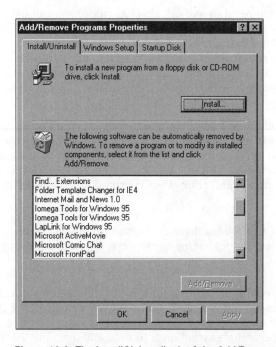

Figure 16-2: The Install/Uninstall tab of the Add/Remove Programs Properties dialog box. Use this tab to install software that uses the built-in Install Shield procedures. Developers of small shareware applications may opt not to use these.

If you install software using the Install/Uninstall tab, the Registry gets updated correctly and Windows retains enough information about the setup so that you can uninstall the software if you choose to later.

If you want to uninstall a program, it is best to use the Install/Uninstall tab so that you can remove most (if not all) of the bits and pieces of an application that are stored in various parts of your computer. If the application's programmers have written a proper uninstall routine, it will also remove references to the program in the Registry.

Microsoft will list a program in the Install/Uninstall tab if that program correctly installs itself *and* if it includes an uninstall routine. (Such programs receive the *Compatible with Windows 98* logo, which manufacturers display on the box.) The uninstall routine is a small executable file that lies dormant on your hard disk until you're ready to remove the application.

When you select a file from the list and click the Add/Remove button, Windows 98 uses the application's uninstall routine to remove the application files without affecting other programs on your system. That's an important consideration, because removing one program's files may prevent another program from launching. This can occur when applications share files. Common extensions of shared files include *dll*, *vbx*, and *ocx*.

When you install an application, it copies any shared files it needs into your \Windows or \Windows\System folder. It's almost impossible to know whether other applications depend on these files, so it's hard to know whether you can safely delete them. If you delete a shared file that another application needs, when you next try to open that application, you might see an error message such as "Can't find *Shared*.dll." It's also possible that you'll receive a more cryptic error message, or none at all. If you delete a shared *vxd* (virtual device driver) file, you may get an error message such as "Cannot find a device file that may be needed to run Windows or a Windows application" when you next start Windows 98.

Before a logo-compliant application installs a shared file, it first checks to see whether a copy of that file is already present on your hard disk. If the file already exists on your system, the application can't copy an *older* version of that file over a newer version (it makes sure this doesn't occur by checking the internal version number stored within the shared file). When an application attempts to install a shared file, a counter kept for that file in the Registry is increased by one.

When you uninstall a logo-compliant application, one is subtracted from the value of the counter for each shared file that the application used. A shared file is only deleted when its counter has a value of zero. In other words, if three applications use a shared file, the file won't be deleted it until you have uninstalled all three applications.

Commercial uninstall packages have found a niche because computer users are unsure how to safely delete software themselves. Retail uninstallers claim that they let you remove your old software painlessly, simply by clicking a button. The reality is a different story. Most retail uninstallers come with a database of all the files contained in the most popular applications (such as word processors and spreadsheets), along with the most likely locations for the files. The uninstaller program uses its database to make an educated guess about where to look for the files to be removed. And when a commercial uninstaller encounters a shared file, your guess about how to handle it might be more educated than the uninstaller's. Several programs simply display a dialog box that asks, "Safe to delete this file?"

Commercial uninstaller programs may not contain information about the application you want to remove, and some applications may contain unusual files, such as Control Panel applets, that the unininstaller will not find. If a program comes with its own uninstaller, that's usually the best method to use. An uninstall program, if there is one, is usually located in the application's parent folder (see the next section).

Manual uninstalling

If you need to uninstall an application that doesn't support the Add/Remove Programs applet, you can safely delete most, if not all of it, manually — with plenty of time and patience. But only use this method as a last resort. To ensure a clean and *total* uninstall, it's best to buy logo-compliant Windows 98 or Windows 95 software.

It's not really true, as many retail uninstall packages claim, that new programs install files at random on your disk. Most software actually installs itself into a single new set of folders under one parent folder. Let's call this C:\Program Files\Myfolder. In addition, a new program may copy one or more shared files into your C:\Windows or C:\Windows\System folder.

Beyond this, a Windows 98 application may add a few program-specific lines to the Registry.

The truth is, leaving a few leftover files in your System folder or a few unnecessary lines in your Registry rarely does your system any harm. You do, however, want to remove the bulk of files located in a program's parent folder and its subfolders, and this you *can* do manually.

Here's how to safely delete an application's files:

STEPS

Manually Uninstalling an Application

Step 1.   Before you delete anything, make an emergency Startup disk from the Startup Disk tab of the Add/Remove Programs Properties dialog box, and then make sure the Startup disk boots up to a C prompt.

Step 2.   Next, open an Explorer window and navigate to C:\Windows\Start Menu\Programs in the left pane. Select the folder under the Programs folder that contains the application you want to remove. In the right pane, right-click a few of the shortcut icons stored in this folder, choosing Properties each time. In the

Properties dialog box for each shortcut, click the Shortcut tab if necessary, and check the Target field to locate the application's parent folder — C:\Program Files\Myfolder, for example (see Figure 16-3).

Figure 16-3: The Properties dialog box for a shortcut in a program's Start Menu subfolder may indicate the folder in which that program is stored. This dialog box shows the properties for a shortcut to the executable file for Delrina WinFax 7.0. Deleting the C:\Winfax folder (and its subfolders) will remove all of WinFax's files except the printer driver, which is harmless.

Step 3. Once you've identified the folder in which the program resides, use WinZip, PKZip, or another compression program to compress all the files in that folder into a single zip file, and then delete the original files. Next, boot up your system and test your other programs. If everything still works, delete the zip file, or transfer it to a backup disk for later use.

Remember, don't delete an application folder as your first step. Instead, zip its contents first, and then test your system before going any further. Don't try anything you can't undo.

Secret

If you delete an application manually or find that you can't remove an uninstalled program's name from the list in the Install/Uninstall tab, you can use the Add/Remove tab of TweakUI to remove these superfluous entries. (If you don't have a TweakUI icon in your Control Panel, you can install it from your Windows 98 CD-ROM. See the "TweakUI" section later in this chapter.)

You can also remove these entries manually using the Registry editor:

STEPS

Removing Program Names from the Install/Uninstall List

Step 1. Click Regedit.exe in your \Windows folder.

Step 2. In the left pane of the Registry editor, navigate to this key:

HKEY_LOCAL_MACHINE\SOFTWARE\Microsoft\Windows\
CurrentVersion\Uninstall.

Step 3. In the left pane, highlight the name of the application whose name you want to remove from the Install/Uninstall list. Choose Edit, Delete.

Step 4. Close the Registry editor.

If you uninstall too much

After uninstalling an application, you might receive this error message the next time you start Windows 98:

Cannot find a device file that may be needed to run Windows or a Windows application.

The Windows registry or SYSTEM.INI file refers to this device file, but the device file no longer exists. If you deleted this file on purpose, try uninstalling the associated application using its uninstall program or setup program.

If you still want to use the application associated with this device file, try reinstalling that application to replace the missing file.

filename.vxd

The name shown in place of *filename* could be any of a number of files (Enable.vxd for example), or the filename may not be specified. When you press any key, Windows 98 may seem to run normally.

This is usually a symptom of a damaged or missing virtual device driver (*vxd*), or of an invalid or blank value for the driver in the Registry. Virtual device drivers are files required by various programs to communicate with your computer's hardware.

You'll need to reinstall the program, and then run the program's uninstall tool if it has one. If it doesn't, and if the program isn't listed in the Control Panel's Add/Remove Programs Properties dialog box, contact the software manufacturer to find out how to properly uninstall the product. As a last resort, you'll have to remove it by following the advice in the previous section, "Manual uninstalling."

If the missing file has a *386* extension instead of *vxd*, open your System.ini file, locate the line that refers to this device driver, and disable the driver by placing a semicolon (;) at the beginning of the line. For example, if the line referencing the missing device driver reads

```
device=Example.386
```

change the line to read

```
;device=Example.386
```

If the driver is not specifically named in the error message, the problem is probably one of the StaticVXD values in the Registry. Use the following steps to locate and delete the value in the Registry that refers to the missing device driver. (Be sure to back up your Registry before doing this; refer to "Registry backup" in Chapter 15 for details.)

STEPS

Troubleshooting a Missing StaticVXD Value

Step 1.   Click Regedit.exe in your \Windows folder to start the Registry editor, and navigate to the following key:

```
HKEY_LOCAL_MACHINE\System\CurrentControlSet\Services\VXD
```

Click the plus sign next to this key to display the subkeys under it.

Step 2.   In the left pane, click each subkey listed under VXD in turn. For each subkey, look for a StaticVXD value in the right pane. See if there is data listed for that value. (The data should be the name of a *vxd* file and should correspond to the subkey.) If you find a StaticVXD value that is blank, contains only spaces, or has odd characters instead of the name of the key, that value is most likely the problem.

Step 3.   Determine whether the *vxd* file in question is still on your computer. To do this, open the Explorer and use the Tools, Find, Files or Folders command to search for the file. For example, if the StaticVXD value for the PAGESWAP key is empty, search for Pageswap.vxd.

Step 4.   If you find that the *vxd* file is on your hard disk, you should be able to fix the problem by editing the file's value in the Registry. In the Registry editor, double-click the value with the missing data. In the Value Data field, type an asterisk followed by the name of the *vxd* file in capital letters (in most cases this will be identical to the name of the subkey). For instance, in the example above, you would type ***PAGESWAP**. Then exit the Registry editor.

(continued)

STEPS *(continued)*

Troubleshooting a Missing StaticVXD Value

Step 5. If you cannot find the *vxd* file on your hard disk, you should extract the original file from your Windows 98 CD-ROM and copy it to the \Windows\System folder on your computer. For more on extracting, refer to "Missing files" earlier in this chapter.

Network Install

If you commonly install software to several PCs in your company, save yourself some shoe leather. You can add a Network Install tab to the Add/Remove Programs Properties dialog box that lets you or individual users easily install new applications across a network at the click of a mouse.

Let's assume you have a site license to distribute software within your company to all users, or a license to distribute it to a certain number of users. The Network Install tab allows you to install an entire application from another PC — without diskettes or a CD-ROM. (The other PC is usually a network server, but it could be any other PC in a peer-to-peer network.)

To make the Network Install tab appear, you must create the two short text files shown here:

```
Example Contents of Netinst.reg:
REGEDIT4
HKEY_LOCAL_MACHINE\SOFTWARE\Microsoft\Windows\CurrentVersion
AppInstallPath=\\\\Server1\\Windows\\Apps.ini

Example Contents of Apps.ini:
[AppInstallList]
Microsoft Internet Explorer=\\Server1\Apps\Msie40.exe
Mapped Application=*\\Server1\Dummy\Dumsetup.exe
```

In Netinst.reg, you specify an AppInstallPath. This pinpoints the location of a text file called Apps.ini. In this example, the location is \\Server1\Windows\ Apps.ini. Notice that you must use *two* backslashes in the AppInstallPath line for every real one in the filename.

You must merge Netinst.reg into the Windows 98 Registry. To do this, right-click your Netinst.reg file, and then click Merge. This adds to the Registry the two lines below the REGEDIT4 heading.

The Apps.ini file is a plain-text file that points to the setup routines for any applications you want to appear on the Network Install tab (what we've shown is only an example). You should put it in a read-only directory on a network server.

The example Apps.ini shows lines for the Microsoft Internet Explorer and a "mapped" dummy application. Notice that the "mapped" application,

Dumsetup.exe, has an asterisk (*) before the double backslash in \\Server1. This indicates that Dumsetup.exe cannot handle the universal naming convention (UNC) for server names. The setup routine requires a drive letter such as F: instead of \\Server1. Because of the asterisk, Windows 98 will "map" a drive letter for this server and replace \\Server1 with F: when it runs Dumsetup.exe.

Once you have these two files in place and restart Windows, you will see a new Network Install tab in the Add/Remove Programs Properties dialog box.

If Apps.ini is later moved or deleted, you'll have trouble opening the Add/Remove Programs icon in the Control Panel. If this happens, use the Find tool in the Explorer to find the folder where Apps.ini is stored. Then start the Registry editor and navigate to this key:

HKEY_LOCAL_MACHINE\SOFTWARE\Microsoft\Windows\CurrentVersion\

Verify that the value for AppInstallPath in this key matches the folder in which Apps.ini is stored. You can either edit the path or move Apps.ini. If the value points to some place on a network, make sure you can connect to that network location.

Windows Setup

You can install and remove applications that have accompanying *inf* files (control files that install the application without user input) through the Windows Setup tab of the Add/Remove Programs Properties dialog box, as shown in Figure 16-4. Click the Have Disk button to install an application that has an accompanying *inf* file. This is an easy way for a developer to provide for a quick and dirty installation procedure.

You can use the Windows Setup tab to uninstall the optional applications that were installed when you first installed Windows 98. For example, you might want to uninstall games, mouse pointers, and wallpaper, which collectively take up about 3MB of disk space. Or, if you didn't install something when you installed Windows 98 the first time, you can use this tab to install it now. For descriptions of the various Windows 98 components, select the appropriate category in the Components list, and then click the Details button.

The Windows Setup tab displays the amount of disk space required for the selected category or component, and the space you have available on your hard disk. However, these values are often inaccurate. In fact, as you highlight the different components, the values may not change at all. Microsoft has acknowledged this error. It won't affect your ability to use Add/Remove Programs, but you shouldn't rely on the numbers as an indicator of whether you have room to do the installation.

If you are using multiple user profiles on a computer, the Windows Setup tab will show all the components installed for all users, regardless of whether they are available to the current user. For example, the Microsoft Network check box may be marked, even though the current user does not have access to MSN.

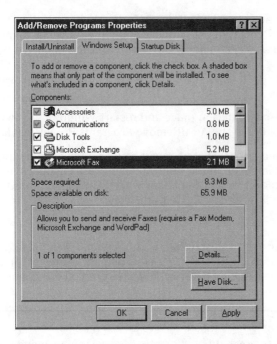

Figure 16-4: The Windows Setup tab of the Add/Remove Programs Properties dialog box. Click the Have Disk button if your diskette contains an *inf* file.

When you set up a user profile, you can avoid this problem. In the Passwords Properties dialog box, mark Include Desktop Icons and Network Neighborhood Contents in User Settings and/or Include Start Menu and Program Groups in User Settings. See "Whose Desktop Is This Anyway?" in Chapter 12 for more on user profiles.

If you already have a user profile set up without these options, it is not immediately apparent how to make an installed component available to that user, since the component's check box is already marked on the Windows Setup tab. To make a Windows 98 component that was installed by another user available to the current user, follow these steps:

STEPS

Making an Installed Component Available to the Current User

Step 1.   Clear the component's check box in the Windows Setup tab of the Add/Remove Programs Properties dialog box.

Step 2.   Click the Apply button. If you are prompted to restart the computer, click Yes. After the computer restarts, go back to the Windows Setup tab.

Step 3. Mark the component's check box.

Step 4. Click the Apply button. If you are prompted to restart your computer, click Yes.

Startup Disk

The Startup Disk tab provides an easy way to make an emergency disk that boots up your system if your hard drive fails. It also gives you a way to recover from problems that can occur when you uninstall applications or they uninstall themselves. We recommend you make a Startup disk if you haven't done so already. Insert a blank diskette in drive A and click the Create Disk button. Windows 98 will copy essential startup files, such as the DOS 7.1 hidden files, to your diskette. You should test the Startup disk to ensure that it actually will boot up your PC successfully. You may need to add some support files, such as any 16-bit drivers listed in your Config.sys or Autoexec.bat files that your system still relies upon.

Make Compatible

A small, undocumented Windows 98 utility called Make Compatible (Mkcompat.exe) can be a lifesaver for anyone who has to work with less-than-perfect Windows software. It can even make some programs work that ordinarily wouldn't work at all. It's not a Control Panel applet; you'll find it in your \Windows\System folder.

Make Compatible lets you modify Windows 98's behavior when it is running a Windows application that has a slight compatibility problem. You select a filename in Make Compatible and then specify what Windows 98 behavior you want to change. Windows 98 makes the change for that filename only; no other Windows or DOS filenames are affected.

One way Make Compatible can be useful is when Windows 3.1x programs won't install properly under Windows 98. For example, when you're installing a Windows 3.1x program by running Install.exe or Setup.exe, you might see an error message that reports, "This program requires Windows 3.1 or higher."

What's happening is that the program you're trying to install is checking the version number of Windows incorrectly. The program is checking to see if the version is 3.1 and displaying an error message if it isn't. Of course, what the application should be doing is checking whether the version number is 3.1 *or higher*. Microsoft has published a method to do this for years. But that doesn't help you if you're in this situation.

Microsoft says it knows that programs such as Outpost 1.0, 1.0a, and 1.0b by Sierra On-line and Passport 1.2 by Advantis exhibit this behavior. To resolve this type of incompatibility problem or to fix other similar problems, take these steps:

STEPS

Running Make Compatible

Step 1. Start Make Compatible by clicking Start, Run, typing **mkcompat**, and clicking OK. (You can also run Make Compatible from the Windows Explorer by clicking Mcompat.exe in your \Windows\ System folder.)

Step 2. Select File, Choose Program. In the Choose Program dialog box, select the file that you want to Windows 98 to treat differently. If you're trying to fix a Windows 3.1x program that won't install under Windows 98, select the installation file for that program (it's probably called Install.exe or Setup.exe). Click Open.

Step 3. In the Make Compatible window, mark one or more of the check boxes in the list. Then choose File, Save, and then File, Exit. Changes you have made for a 16-bit application will be written into the [Compatibility] section of Win.ini. Changes for 32-bit applications will be written into the [Compatibility32] section.

If you're fixing the installation problem we discussed above, mark Lie About Window's Version Number (see Figure 16-5). This option will let you install the affected program because Windows 98 will report to the program that it is running under Windows 3.1.

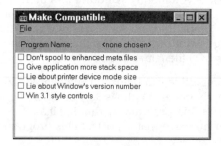

Figure 16-5: To install Windows 3.1 software that looks for the wrong version number, mark the Lie About Window's Version Number check box.

Step 4. Unfortunately, Make Compatible applies the changed behavior to all files that have the same filename as the one you selected in step 2. Therefore, if you chose Install.exe or Setup.exe, Make Compatible will affect the setup routine of any other program whose installation file has the same name. To keep this from happening, run Make Compatible again after you've installed your application. This time, clear the Lie About Window's Version Number option. Then choose File, Save, and then File, Exit.

Lying about Windows 98's version can interfere with the setup routines of programs that are fully compatible with Windows 98, which is why you want to reverse this behavior.

Step 5. If the program name you selected was the main executable of an application (not the installation file) and you marked Lie About Window's Version Number, don't clear this option until the application comes out with a new version that is Windows 98-friendly.

You may notice that the Make Compatible menu has no Help item. That's because there *isn't* any online help, nor is there any printed documentation. Make Compatible is the essence of simplicity. Its File menu contains only four commands: Choose Program, Advanced Options, Save, and Exit.

To use Make Compatible on a program that's already installed, select File, Choose Program, and then type the name of the executable file for the program, or click Browse and browse to the file. If you choose a 32-bit Windows program that is not fully compatible with Windows 98 (such as a custom program that uses Microsoft's older Win32s programming libraries), Make Compatible displays a list of options appropriate for 32-bit applications. If you choose a 16-bit application, you'll see a list appropriate for 16-bit applications. These are the five basic options:

- **Don't spool to enhanced meta files:** Some applications cannot print properly when Windows 98 uses a form of data called *enhanced meta files*. This option turns off this performance enhancement and spools data to the printer using a slower method.

- **Give application more stack space:** This option allocates more memory to an application for its program stack. This assures compatibility with older applications that expect this memory to be available.

- **Lie about printer device mode size:** Older applications may not print correctly if they cannot accommodate newer printer drivers. This option forces Windows to provide information to an application in an older format for compatibility's sake.

- **Lie about Window's version number:** Applications that request the Windows version number are given the answer *3.1*. This corrects some applications that won't run or install unless they see this version number.

- **Win 3.1-style controls:** This option makes the title bar at the top of an application's window, and some other features of the user interface, conform to Windows 3.1 standards. Some applications need this option enabled to display their window correctly.

You can switch to a larger set of options by choosing File, Advanced Options (see Figure 16-6). Issue the same command again to return to the five basic options.

Figure 16-6: Most users will never encounter an application that requires Make Compatible's advanced options. But they're there just in case you do need them some day.

Fortunately, you won't need to use Make Compatible every day. Microsoft has already inserted what it calls *AppHacks* or *Compatibility Hacks* into Win.ini to take care of tested cases it's found where Windows 98's behavior needs to be modified for a specific application to work smoothly. The [Compatibility32] section of Win.ini lists eleven applications that benefit from these hacks, while the 16-bit [Compatibility] section lists well over a hundred such applications (see Figure 16-7).

The Make Compatible applet is included with Windows 98 just in case you *do* find an application with slightly weird behavior that Microsoft didn't catch. If you find such a case, first try to resolve it using Make Compatible. If that doesn't work, check with the distributor of the application or with Microsoft Product Support Services at 206-637-7098 to see if a new AppHack that can help you has become available.

Multimedia

Audio, video, MIDI, CD music, and advanced settings — the Multimedia control panel gives you some control over very basic multimedia parameters, such as volume, size of video playback, MIDI scheme, volume of CD headphone playback, and installed multimedia drivers.

Figure 16-7: The [Compatibility] section of Win.ini lists the names of older Windows application modules that require some modification of Windows 98's behavior to work smoothly.

Most of the action with multimedia is in the Entertainment submenu of the Start menu (Start, Programs, Accessories) or comes from third-party applications that you probably received with your multimedia hardware. Microsoft provides only a basic mechanism for integrating multimedia into Windows 98. It depends on other developers to produce the really cool stuff.

Lots of multimedia software or content titles have multimedia applets that control how to play their video clips and listen to their sounds. Most of your interaction with multimedia will take place through the interfaces defined by these applications.

Regional settings

Where are you and where is your computer?

Regional settings have to do with how date, time, money, and numbers are sorted and displayed. Windows 98 keeps track of which country has which customs regarding these most core symbols of civilization. If the application you are using is smart enough to ask in advance, it can display these values correctly.

You can use the Regional Settings control panel to set the particular configuration yourself (from among many options) if you need to make adjustments.

Sounds

The Sounds control panel lets you associate a given sound with a given Windows event. Windows 98 stores the sounds it uses in files with the *wav* extension. Windows 98 understands *wav* files and can "play" them through your sound card.

Windows 98 comes with lots of sounds that you can associate with Windows events (if you installed the sound files). You can also purchase CD-ROMs full of *wav* files, download sound files from online services or bulletin boards, or get them over the Internet.

The sounds that come with Windows 98 are arranged as "sound schemes," so you can apply them all at once to the designated Windows events. This makes it a lot easier to apply sounds. You can even create your own sound schemes by choosing from among the *wav* files that are installed on your computer.

You can test the sounds by selecting an event, choosing a sound from the Name drop-down list or browsing for it, and clicking the triangular play button to the right of Preview, as shown in Figure 16-8. If you prefer that an event takes place in silence, you can choose (None) instead of a sound from the Name drop-down list.

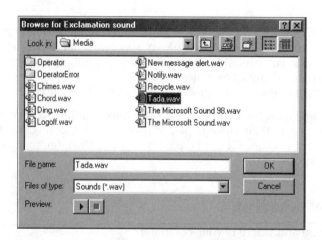

Figure 16-8: The Sounds control panel. Highlight a Windows 98 event, select or browse for a sound, and then click the triangular play button next to Preview.

If you didn't install the sound schemes when you installed Windows 98, there won't be any listed in the Schemes drop-down list. To install the sound schemes that come with Windows 98, click the Add/Remove Programs icon in your Control Panel, click the Windows Setup tab, highlight Multimedia, and then click the Details button. Mark Multimedia Sound Schemes, click OK twice, and insert your Windows 98 CD-ROM when prompted.

Undocumented

Desktop themes, which include unnamed sound schemes as well as many other Desktop elements, are available from a variety of sources, including the Internet. The sounds within the themes are associated with Windows events, but no name appears in the Schemes field. If you like, you can name and save a theme's sound scheme. First click the Desktop Themes icon in the Control Panel, choose a theme, and click OK or Apply. Second, open the Sounds applet, click the Save As button, type a name for the new scheme, and click OK.

You've now associated the sounds that came from the Desktop theme that you chose with a sound scheme name. Later, if you choose a new Desktop theme, or no theme, you can still use the sounds associated with the previous theme by applying the sound scheme that you just named.

Applying sounds to application events

Windows comes with sounds and sound schemes that you can apply to various Windows events. Application programmers can also add sounds to events that are specific to their application. If an application doesn't have a sound associated with a particular event, Windows uses the Windows sound that is associated with that event. For example, Windows uses the sound associated with its own Open Program event when you open an application, unless the application has a different sound (or no sound) associated with that event.

Events are organized by application. The first application is Windows. Scroll down the Events list in the Sounds Properties dialog box to see other applications and events.

Secret

Windows users can add sounds to specific applications and specific application events, even if the application programmers neglected to do so. This means that each application can have its own unique sounds for similar types of (or different) events. This requires editing the Registry. Here's how:

STEPS

Adding Sounds to Application Events

Step 1. Click Regedit.exe in your \Windows folder.

Step 2. Navigate to this key:

HKEY_CURRENT_USER\AppEvents\Schemes\Apps

Step 3. Highlight Apps in the left pane. Right-click the right pane, and choose New, Key. Type the name of the application's executable file. For example, type **Write** for Windows Write. Press Enter. (If your application is already listed under the Apps key, you can skip this step.)

Step 4. Highlight the key that you just created (or the existing key if your application was already listed) in the left pane of the Registry editor, right-click the right pane, and choose New, Key. Type one of the following event names:

AppGPFault

Close

(continued)

STEPS *(continued)*

Adding Sounds to Application Events

> MailBeep
>
> Maximize
>
> MenuCommand
>
> MenuPopup
>
> Minimize
>
> Open
>
> RestoreDown
>
> RestoreUp
>
> SystemAsterisk
>
> SystemExclamation
>
> SystemQuestion
>
> SystemHand
>
> You can see more about what these event names mean by navigating to:
>
> HKEY_CURRENT_USER\AppEvents\EventLabels
>
> and then clicking any one of the event names.

Step 5. Highlight the new key that you just created in the left pane of the Registry editor, right-click the right pane, and choose New, Key. Type **.current**.

Step 6. Repeat steps 4 and 5 to name events associated with your application until you have named all the events that you care to. Exit the Registry.

Step 7. Click the Sounds applet in the Control Panel. Scroll down the Events list until you find the name of the application that you just named sound events for in the Registry. Click a sound event, and select a *wav* file to associate with that event by selecting it from the Name list or browsing for it with the Browse button.

You can make this all a little easier by exporting the HKEY_CURRENT_USER\ AppEvents\Schemes\Apps key from the Registry using the Registry editor. You can use this text file as a basis for creating a *reg* file that you can merge into the Registry. Edit this *reg* file to duplicate the steps above for each application whose events you want to add sounds to.

To learn more about *reg* files, turn to the "Exporting and importing the Registry" section of Chapter 15.

Missing audio components

Sounds (*wav* files) in Windows 98 are played through the Microsoft Audio Compression Manager (MSACM), which is also known as *Wavemapper*. Windows 98 comes with a number of Audio Compression components, called *codecs*; you can see a list of them by clicking the Multimedia icon in the Control Panel, clicking the Devices tab, and clicking the plus sign next to the Audio Compression Codecs icon. Windows 98 reads each *wav* file and determines the best codec with which to play it.

If you do not have all of the Audio Compression components of Windows 98 installed (or if one becomes damaged), you may see one of the following error messages when you try to play sounds in Windows 98:

- `Your audio hardware cannot play files like the current file.`

- `Mmsystem326`
  `No wave device that can play files in the current format is`
  `installed.`

- `Mmsystem296`
  `The file cannot be played on the specified MCI device. The file`
  `may be corrupt, or not in the correct format.`

Although the last message appears when you try to play an *avi* file (video clip), the problem is with the file's Audio Compression.

The first thing to do is make sure you have installed the optional Audio Compression components of Windows 98. Open the Control Panel, click Add/Remove Programs, go to the Windows Setup tab, and double-click the Multimedia icon. If Audio Compression is not marked, do so and click OK twice.

If the Audio Compression option is marked, it may not be installed properly. To remove it, clear the Audio Compression check box, and click OK twice to complete the removal. Now follow the directions in the previous paragraph to re-install Audio Compression. Compressed sound should now play without errors.

The situation is similar with the Volume Control tool, located in the Multimedia section of the Windows Setup tab. If Volume Control is not available after you install Windows 98, you need to follow the same procedures for it as you would for Audio Compression.

Windows 98 decides whether to install tools such as Volume Control depending on the hardware that it detects during Setup. If your computer contains an ISA plug and play device that is not turned on by the BIOS, Windows 98 won't detect it until after Setup, so it won't install the related tools.

Keep video clips from disappearing

Perhaps you've been surfing the Web and downloading and playing multimedia files. Perhaps you hate the way these multimedia selections play and then disappear. Thanks to Bart Austin, here's a way to keep those clips open so you can play them again as often as you need.

STEPS

Setting Video Clips to Stay Visible

Step 1. Start the Explorer, and then choose View, Folder Options, and click the File Types tab.

Step 2. Scroll down the Registered File Types list until you get to Video Clip, and select this entry. If you have more than one Video Clip entry, select the one with *avi* as its extension (you can change the other ones later if you wish). The application used to open files of this type is ActiveMovie. (Don't worry if you see RUNDLL32 listed to the right of Open With in the File Types tab — that's just the first part of the path to ActiveMovie.) Click the Edit button.

Step 3. In the Edit File Type dialog box, click Play in the Actions box, and then click the Edit button.

Step 4. In the Application Used to Perform This Action field, delete the /close switch at the end of the command, including the space just before it (since the command will probably be longer than the field, use the End key to make sure you are at the end of the command line). The /play switch should now be the last switch on the command line.

Step 5. Click the OK button, and then click Close twice.

You should now be able to download and run *avi* files without having them vanish as soon as they reach the end of their recorded span.

TweakUI

Of course, we mention TweakUI continually throughout this book. It used to be part of Microsoft's PowerToys, but it now comes on the Windows 98 CD-ROM. Nevertheless, it is not a supported part of Windows 98.

To install TweakUI, open the Explorer, right-click tweakui.inf in the \tools\ ResKit\Powertoy folder of your Windows 98 CD-ROM, and select Install from the context menu. Once it is installed, you can open TweakUI by clicking its icon in your Control Panel.

You can use TweakUI to "tweak" all sorts of user interface settings. Play with it for a while to see what it can do. (See Figure 16-9.)

TweakUI's Control Panel tab lets you choose which applets are available in the Control Panel. Hiding applets in this way does not uninstall them, but simply protects them from tampering. Similarly, you can use the My Computer tab to hide disk drives from users.

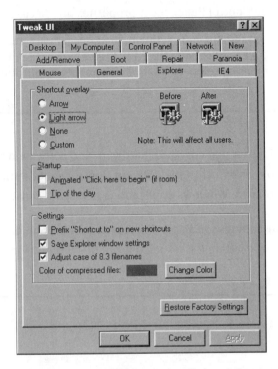

Figure 16-9: TweakUI. Click a tab to find a whole new set of "tweaks."

The Repair tab lets you fix all kinds of problems. Among others, you can rebuild icons that have gotten lost or corrupted, repair file associations, repair the Fonts folder, and repair the Registry editor.

You can also use the Desktop tab to remove or rename special icons such as the Recycle Bin. It's worth exploring TweakUI in advance, so you'll remember it's there when you need it.

Properties

Right-click an object and click Properties. The object's properties are displayed.

Tip

An even quicker way of displaying an object's properties is to hold down the Alt key and click the object's icon. You can also highlight an object, hold down the Alt key and press Enter.

Pretty much anything you see on your Desktop has properties, except, interestingly enough, the Control Panel icons, which are often properties themselves. For example, the Display icon contains the Desktop's properties.

Every file has properties. Every shortcut to a Windows program has properties, as does every shortcut to a DOS program.

Like the settings in the Control Panel, most properties are discussed in the relevant chapter. We mention properties here because we want to point out that they are a general phenomenon. While they aren't universal—you may run lots of Windows 3.1*x* applications that don't use them—they will become more common as developers integrate them into applications.

Summary

The Control Panel settings let you configure hardware and software drivers.

▶ We show you how to quickly get to the different Control Panel settings.

▶ You can install and remove Windows applications through a consistent interface.

▶ You can choose your settings for displaying currency, time, and date.

▶ The Control Panel has a setting for associating sounds with Windows 98 events.

Part III

Internet Applications

Chapter 17

Dial-Up Networking

In This Chapter

Windows 98 includes the capability to dial up another computer. This computer can be your Internet service provider's server, or any computer running Windows 95 or 98, Windows NT, LAN Manager, NetWare, or Unix. In the next chapter, we discuss using Dial-Up Networking to connect to the Internet. Here we discuss:

▶ Calling and connecting over a modem to a computer running Windows 98, Windows 95, Windows NT, Unix, or NetWare

▶ Setting up a Windows 98 computer to receive modem phone calls from another Windows 98, Windows 3.1, Windows NT, or other computer

▶ Setting up your Windows 98 computer as a guest and calling into other computers

▶ Configuring the Windows 98 Dial-Up Adapter for the correct protocols

▶ Checking the state of your communication using System Monitor

▶ Printing on a printer at work and faxing from a fax/modem at work while directing these operations from your computer at home

Networking? Over a Modem?

Those of you who can remember back to the days before the World Wide Web was the next big thing, can probably picture this typical scenario: You started some communications software, perhaps the Terminal emulator software that comes with Windows 3.1. You used it to dial into a bulletin board, a commercial online service such as CompuServe, or an Internet service provider (using a dial-up shell account). Once connected, you downloaded files, used a Unix server-based e-mail package, cruised the forums, or looked at the newsgroups. This terminal-based way of interacting with remote computer is still with us in Windows 98, as you can see in "A Flash from the Past" in Chapter 21.

Many of you have also used software that allows you to connect two computers in close proximity, either through a serial or parallel cable. You run software such as LapLink on both computers, which facilitates file transfer between the computers using a point and click interface. (See "LapLink for DOS – a history" in Chapter 22 for more about this.)

And if your computer is connected to a local area network, you have experienced high-speed communications with other computers located in your general vicinity. Clicking the Network Neighborhood icon in Windows 98 gets you quickly to the shared resources available to you on the network. You can print your files on printers connected to other computers or servers on the network. You can quickly copy files, send e-mail, chat, and so on over the LAN. (Turn to "Basic Network Support" in Chapter 24 for more details.)

Dial-Up Networking (DUN) is a mixture of all three of these communications modes — using a modem to dial into another computer, network, or Internet service provider, connecting two computers in close proximity (through Direct Cable Connection, which uses DUN), and sharing resources with other computers as though you were networked to them.

DUN lets your computer at home or on the road use a modem to access the resources of a computer at work and/or the resources of the network connected to a computer at work, including shared disk drives, folders, printers, NetWare servers, NT servers, and much more. You can also use DUN to connect your home computer to the Internet and the World Wide Web through an Internet service provider.

DUN allows your computer to communicate with a network (or a computer on a network) as if it were on the network directly, even if it's in fact only connected to the network through a modem and another computer (or modem server) on the network. The one difference is that a DUN connection is slower than a direct network connection through a dedicated network card or port.

Undocumented

You can use DUN in a whole host of ways. You can get your e-mail from work. You can send a file from your computer at home to a printer at work. You can send out fax files from your computer at home using the fax/modem on the computer at work. You can run programs that are stored on the computer at work on your computer at home. You can copy and update files between computers. You can copy programs from work. You can be a client of a client/server application running on a computer at work.

With DUN, you get what the computer business calls *remote access*. In other words, you have access to the resources on the remote, or dialed-up, computer or network. You don't have *remote control*, which is the ability to run your computer at the office as though you were typing on its keyboard while you are sitting in front of your computer at home.

Once you get everything set up (which is somewhat tricky), DUN is actually easy to use. It's easy because it uses standard Windows 98 user interface objects such as Explorer and folder windows.

In this chapter, we'll use *computer at work* and *computer at home* to cut down on the level of abstraction that you have to deal with. By *computer at work*, we mean any computer that you dial into, and by *computer at home* we mean the computer that does the dialing. You can, of course, substitute anything that makes more sense to you — computer A and computer B, computer connected to a network and remote computer, desktop computer and portable computer, host and guest, server and client, remote and mobile, or Internet service provider and user.

Dial-Up Networking

In order to dial into another computer, you need to configure your Windows 98 computer at home as the Dial-Up Networking *client*. You learn how to do this in the "Setting Up Your Computer at Home As a Guest" section later in the chapter.

If you are calling into a Windows 98 computer at work, you need to configure that computer as a Dial-Up Networking *host*. We show you how in "Setting Up Your Windows 98 Computer at Work As a Host."

To make the connection between the two computers you need:

1. Properly configured computers at home and work

2. A shared dial-up protocol (to establish the connection)

3. A shared network protocol (to allow communication between the two computers)

DUN version 1.2

Windows 98 comes with DUN version 1.2. This version includes Winsock 2.2 and ISDN version 1.1.

Microsoft made DUN 1.2 available on the Microsoft web site in July of 1997, and Windows 95 users could download and install it to upgrade their existing DUN facilities without having to redo their DUN connectoids.

DUN 1.2 features include: multilinking to allow you to link two communication ports, essentially ISDN ports, to get 128 Kbps bandwidth; integrated scripting (the original version of DUN had a stand-alone script interpreter); PPTP (Point-to-Point Tunneling Protocol) tunneling support, which allows for the creation of virtual private secure networks over the Internet; and improved DNS routing and name resolution.

The new version of Winsock is a great improvement over the early Windows 95 versions. With its multi-homing feature, you can now connect to local TCP/IP-based networks and dial into the Internet at the same time.

Dial-up servers

You can connect your Windows 98 computer at home over the phone lines to another computer or server running:

- Windows 95 or 98 Dial-Up Networking Server

- Windows NT Remote Access Server (RAS) or PPP

- Windows for Workgroups 3.11 RAS

- Microsoft LAN Manager

- NetWare Connect

- Unix with SLIP or PPP protocols
- TCP/IP with PPP protocol (especially for connections to the Internet)

You can also connect to a dedicated modem server such as the Shiva LanRover or a compatible device, or to an Internet service provider (if you have a SLIP or PPP account).

Network protocols

Windows 98 supports in native 32-bit mode the following network protocols:

- NetBEUI (Microsoft's networking protocol)
- IPX/SPX (Novell's NetWare protocol)
- TCP/IP (the Unix, Internet, and Intranet standard protocol)

Dial-up protocols

To connect to the computer at work, the Windows 98 DUN client can use any one of the following dial-up protocols:

- PPP (Point-to-Point Protocol)
- NRN (Novell NetWare Connect)
- RAS (Windows NT and Windows for Workgroups 3.11 Remote Access Server using Asynchronous NetBEUI)
- SLIP (Serial Line Internet Protocol)
- CSLIP (SLIP with IP header compression)

Point-to-Point Protocol is the default dial-up protocol used by Windows 95, 98, and NT computers. You can use PPP to connect to a network or computer running any one of the three network protocols included with Windows 98. Many Internet service providers also use PPP. You can also use PPP to call into Unix, Windows 98, or Windows NT servers.

Novell NetWare Connect allows you to dial into a NetWare Connect server.

RAS allows a Windows 98 computer to call into a Windows NT computer running RAS or into a computer running Windows for Workgroups 3.11, and vice versa.

SLIP is an older dial-up protocol, but it is still used by some Internet service providers, and it is used on some Unix servers as well.

Setting Up Your Windows 98 Computer at Work As a Host

If you have a significant network at work, you will want to provide dial-up services through a Windows NT server, which can handle up to 256 dial-up connections, a LAN modem server, a NetWare Connect server, or perhaps a Unix computer. Another option is the Shiva LanRover, which is built for handling large-scale dial-in communications in conjunction with a corporate-sized NetWare, NetBEUI, or TCP/IP local area network.

If your network isn't that big (maybe it just consists of your desktop computer) and only a few people need dial-up access, then calling into a Windows 98 computer at work may fit the bill. The Windows 98 Dial-Up Networking Server (DUN Server) can take calls from and connect to Windows 98 or Windows 95 clients, computers running RAS on Windows for Workgroups or Windows 3.1, and other computers running the PPP dial-up protocol. The Windows 98 DUN Server can't act as an IP router. That is, you can't call into a Windows 98 computer using only the TCP/IP networking protocol, and access a TCP/IP network through that Windows 98 server.

Secret

The Windows 98 Dial-Up Networking Server can handle (and route) NetBEUI and IPX/SPX network protocols and allow you to connect to network resources (other computers, for example) using these protocols. If your network at the office uses both TCP/IP and NetBEUI, you'll be able to connect and see other servers on the network. You need to be sure that the DUN connectoid on your computer at home has NetBEUI and TCP/IP checked for allowed network protocols. To do this, right-click the connectoid, choose Properties, click the Server Types tab, and mark the NetBEUI and TCP/IP check boxes. You should also make sure that NetBEUI and TCP/IP are bound to its Dial-Up Adapter. For details, turn to "Configuring the adapter driver" in Chapter 24.

Secret

You can set up your Windows 98 computer at work as a web server using Microsoft's Personal Web Server. You can connect to this web server from home using Dial-Up Networking and Internet Explorer. You can also connect to it directly with a serial or parallel cable using Direct Cable Connection (which relies on DUN).

Undocumented

You can call out with other TAPI-aware programs, such as DUN, while DUN Server is running. No one can call in while you are using the line, but once you have completed your call, DUN Server will pick up incoming calls.

We are going to assume that you want to call in from home — or from a hotel when you are on the road — to your Windows 98 computer (and your network) at work. You must do three things to set up your Windows 98 computer at work as a host:

1. Install a modem driver (this may have occurred if you had your modem installed when you set up Windows 98).

2. Install the Microsoft Dial-Up Adapter and the accompanying network software/drivers (this may also have occurred during Setup).

3. Set the Windows 98 Dial-Up Networking Server to allow caller access.

Undocumented

The Dial-Up Adapter will be automatically installed (if it is not already) the first time you choose Connections, Dial-Up Server from the menu bar of the Dial-Up Networking folder window. If you do this and you haven't yet installed your modem, you will be prompted to do so. You can separately install the Dial-Up Adapter (see the section entitled "The Dial-Up Adapter" later in this chapter) and the modem before you install the Dial-Up Networking Server.

STEPS

Setting Up a Windows 98 Computer As a Host for Dial-Up Networking

Step 1.   If your modem isn't already set up, do so now using the Modems icon in the Control Panel. Click the Add button in the Modems Properties dialog box, and then follow the steps in the Install New Modem Wizard. (See "Configuring Your Modem" in Chapter 31 if you need additional instructions.) You will be prompted to set up your modem if you take steps 4 and 5 first.

Step 2.   If you haven't yet installed Dial-Up Networking, click the Add/Remove Programs icon in your Control Panel, and click the Windows Setup tab. Select the Communications component, click the Details button, mark the Dial-Up Networking check box, and click OK twice.

Step 3.   If you haven't already done so, set up the Dial-Up Adapter by clicking the Network icon in the Control Panel. Click the Add button, highlight Adapter in the Select Network Component Type dialog box, and click the Add button. For details, see the steps in the section entitled "The Dial-Up Adapter" later in this chapter. This will happen automatically if you take steps 4 and 5.

Step 4.   Click the Dial-Up Networking folder icon in the Explorer, or choose Dial-Up Networking from the Start, Programs, Accessories, Communications menu.

Step 5.   Choose Connections, Dial-Up Server on the menu of the Dial-Up Networking folder window. The Dial-Up Server dialog box will pop up, as shown in Figure 17-1.

If you don't have Dial-Up Server on your Connections menu, click the Add/Remove Programs icon in your Control Panel, click the Windows Setup tab, highlight Communications, click the Details button, mark the Dial-Up Server check box, and click OK.

Figure 17-1: The dial-in options in the Dial-Up Server dialog box. You need to allow caller access.

Step 6.   Mark the Allow Caller Access option button. You want people (perhaps just yourself) using other computers to be able to call into your host computer (the Windows 98 computer at work).

Step 7.   To require a password to access your computer at work, click the Change Password button.

Step 8.   Click the Server Type button if you want to change the dial-up protocol used when the server answers the phone. We suggest that you leave it on Default, which starts with PPP and switches to RAS if PPP fails. This makes it easy for computers with Windows 98, Windows 95, Windows for Workgroups, Windows 3.1 RAS, Windows NT, as well other operating systems that support PPP to call into your server.

Step 9.   Click Apply or OK to begin monitoring for phone calls. (Apply leaves the dialog box on the Desktop. OK minimizes the dialog box.) The computer at the office will now pick up the phone line attached to its modem when that line is called. You don't have a way of telling it how many rings to wait until it picks up the line.

You now have a computer at work that will respond to calls from your computer at home. You need to set the computer at work into this answer mode before you can call into it. You will normally want to leave it in this mode when you are away from the office.

Remember to share some resources (disk drives, folders, printers) if you want to be able to access these resources on your computer at work when you call in. See the "Sharing your resources" section in Chapter 24.

As you can see from the steps above, it requires a few steps to activate the DUN Server. Once you set it though, it will stay set. If you shut down your computer and restart, the DUN Server reloads.

A little freeware application, RunServe, will let you easily start and stop the DUN Server. You can place a shortcut to it on your Desktop. You'll find it at it http://www.frontiernet.net/~enderw.

Running fax software and DUN Server together

Secret

Under most circumstances, the DUN Server computer can't act as a fax machine at the same time. That is, you can't set up Windows Messaging on the computer at work to automatically answer the phone and receive faxes (as discussed in "Microsoft Fax" in Chapter 20) if it is operating as a DUN Server.

Microsoft released the Unimodem V driver and a program called Operator Agent in November 1995. The driver is supposed to allow simultaneous voice and data communications when you use it with modems that have this capability. Operator Agent, when you use it with Unimodem V, can distinguish between a fax call, a voice call, and a data call. It has a bug that allows it to work only if you have a voice program such as Microsoft Phone active. Microsoft Phone and Operator Agent are only available when you purchase a new computer or a new voice/data/fax modem that supports its capabilities.

If you use Microsoft Phone, Operator Agent, a voice/data/fax modem that can use the Unimodem V driver, and the DUN Server, you can configure a server that answers both your modem calls and your fax calls. Nathan A. Curtis told us how.

If the Dial-Up Networking Server is running, it has control of your phone line until you load Operator Agent. As soon as you do, Operator Agent takes over from all other running TAPI applications that are monitoring the line. Of course, if any of these applications is connected, Operator Agent waits.

Undocumented

Once Operator Agent starts monitoring your line and provides an initial spoken greeting, it routes incoming calls to your other TAPI applications properly unless you make one of the following false moves:

- Turn off your voice software (Microsoft Phone, for example) or worse, you don't have any. A bug in Operator Agent will not allow it to answer the phone if you aren't running TAPI voice software.

- Turn off Operator Agent's initial greeting, and configure Operator Agent to answer the call and route it to some TAPI software other than voice. If you do this, your fax or data (DUN) program (depending on which application has the priority) will attempt to connect, and it will not release the line until the connection times out (usually in about 60 seconds). By then, the calling party will have hung up, and Operator Agent will not be able to route the call to the next software.

■ Turn off the initial greeting and set Operator Agent to route to voice first. Microsoft Phone (or other 32-bit TAPI voice software) takes over the line, but it doesn't know about the DUN Server. It can answer a fax call without Operator Agent's help, but not a data call.

To correctly configure your TAPI software, take the following steps:

STEPS

Setting Up Dun Server, Operator Agent, and Microsoft Phone

Step 1. Load Microsoft Phone (with fax receive enabled), the DUN Server, and Operator Agent.

Step 2. Set Operator Agent to answer on one ring, set Microsoft Phone to answer on two rings, and set your fax software (such as Windows Messaging configured to use the Microsoft Fax service) to answer on three rings. You can't set the DUN Server.

Step 3. Set Operator Agent to answer with the following order for call routing: voice, fax, and then data.

Step 4. Record Operator Agent's initial greeting with instructions in the same order given in step 3: "Press one for voice, two for fax, or three to make a DUN connection."

Step 5. Enable Operator Agent's initial greeting (which gives Operator Agent time to determine what type of call is coming in).

A better way to do this is to order distinctive ring service from your local phone company, and purchase a modem that supports it. If you use a modem that can handle distinctive ring service and you use different phone numbers for each service, the modem can route the incoming calls to the correct service without using Operator Agent.

Disallowing dial-in access

You (or your system administrator) can determine whether a Windows 98 computer has the capability of serving as a host. You can use the System Policy Editor (turn to "System Policy Editor" in Chapter 24) to permanently disable dial-in to Dial-Up Networking. If you do this, the Allow Caller Access option button in the Dial-Up Server dialog box will be grayed out. Obviously, if you only want to temporarily prohibit people from calling in, you can just choose the No Caller Access option button.

Security

Security is an issue because anyone with the right password (if even that is required) can gain access to a company's network by calling into its Windows 98 DUN Server. System administrators are justifiably wary of allowing users to configure their computers as servers because it leaves the whole network vulnerable.

If the Windows 98 DUN Server is on a network that includes NetWare or Windows NT servers, the system administrator can use (and may already be using) the NetWare or Windows NT servers to provide user-level, centrally controlled password protection.

Setting Up Your Computer at Home As a Guest

If you want to set up your computer at home to make the phone call and initiate the modem communications, you need to make sure that:

1. Your modem driver is configured.

2. You have set up your Dial-Up Adapter.

3. You have set up a specific dial-in connection (or *connectoid*) for your computer at work.

Undocumented

You don't have to set up the modem driver first. If it is not set up yet, a Wizard will guide you through the setup process.

STEPS

Setting Up Your Computer at Home

Step 1.   Click the Dial-Up Networking folder icon in the Explorer, or choose Dial-Up Networking from the Start, Programs, Accessories, Communications menu.

If you haven't installed Dial-Up Networking, you need to do so now. Click the Add/Remove Programs icon in your Control Panel, click the Windows Setup tab, highlight Communications, click the Details button, and mark Dial-Up Networking. Click OK twice.

Step 2.   Click the Make New Connection icon in the Dial-Up Networking folder window.

Step 3.   The Make New Connection Wizard will start. If you have not set up your modem driver yet, the Install New Modem Wizard will pop up on top of the Make New Connection Wizard and ask that you do this first. Follow the steps in the Install New Modem Wizard on your own, or turn to "Configuring Your Modem" in Chapter 31 for more information.

Step 4.   In the first Make New Connection Wizard dialog box, enter a name for the computer that you will be dialing into, such as **Computer at Work**. Click Next.

Step 5.   Type the area code and number for the computer at work. Click Next.

Step 6.   Click Finish.

Step 7.   If you do not have a Dial-Up Adapter set up in your network configuration (or you have no network configured), you will be asked to install it now.

Step 8.   The Dial-Up Adapter will now be installed, along with the network protocols NetBEUI, TCP/IP and IPX/SPX, and network support software, if they have not already been installed.

You should leave at least NetBEUI and IPX/SPX protocols bound to your Dial-Up Adapter if you are going to use Direct Cable Connection, as discussed in "Direct Cable Connection" in Chapter 22, or if you will connect to a Windows network or a NetWare network. If you are going to connect to an Intranet at work or the Internet, you should be sure to include the Microsoft TCP/IP protocol. This is discussed in "Bind TCP/IP to your Dial Up Adapter" in Chapter 18. The TCP/IP protocol should also be bound to the Dial-Up Adapter on your computer at work if you are going access the Personal Web Server on it. If you are dialing into a stand-alone DUN Server, NetBEUI, and IPX/SPX are sufficient.

An icon for the new connectoid will appear in the Dial-Up Networking folder window with the name you entered in step 4 above. It represents your connection to the computer at the office. When you click the connectoid, the Connect To dialog box (shown in Figure 17-2) appears to let you initiate the phone call.

If you have changed your general Dial-Up Networking settings to not prompt for information before dialing (Click Connections, Settings in the Dial-Up Networking folder window), you will not see this Connect To dialog box and you will not have to click the Connect button.

To end the connection, right-click the Modem Status icon in the Tray and click Disconnect.

Secret

If your Save Password check box is grayed out in the Connect To dialog box for your Dial-Up Networking connectoid, check to make sure that you have installed Client for Microsoft Networks. You can use the instructions provided in "Network Installation" in Chapter 24. There are also other reasons why the Save Password check box might be dim. Refer to "Saving your DUN connectoid passwords" in Chapter 18 for more details.

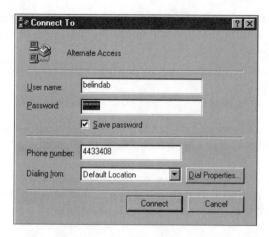

Figure 17-2: The Connect To dialog box for your Dial-Up Networking connectoid. To initiate the phone call, type your password if necessary, and then click the Connect button.

To change the server type and other properties associated with this connectoid, right-click it in the Dial-Up Networking folder window, select Properties, and click the Server Types tab. The Server Types tab (shown in Figure 17-3) allows you to determine, among other things, whether you will log onto the network when you dial into the server. If you don't log onto the network, you won't have access to the resources shared by other servers on the network.

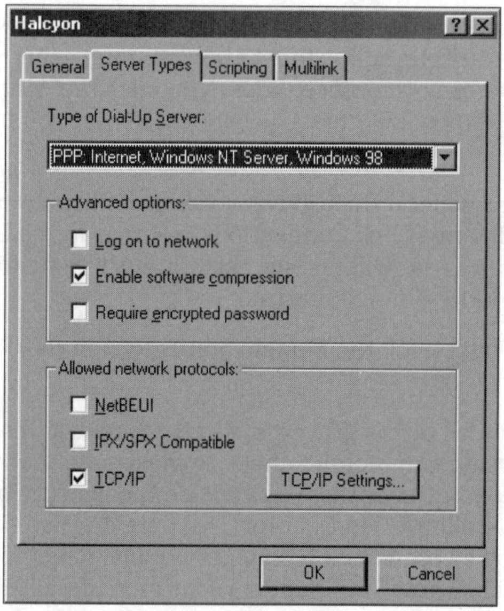

Figure 17-3: The Server Types tab.

PPP is the default dial-up protocol, and if you set your Windows 98 host computer at work to use this protocol, both computers will be in sync. In the Allowed Network Protocols area of the dialog box, you can clear any of the protocol check boxes for protocols that you don't use. See "Dialing into another operating system" later in this chapter for further guidance.

Your Window 98 client computer uses your modem as a network interface card. You have to bind the proper networking protocols to the Dial-Up Adapter. If you are calling into a Unix or Windows NT TCP/IP server, you need to be sure that the TCP/IP protocol is bound to the Dial-Up Adapter. To see how to do this, check out "Bind TCP/IP to your Dial-Up Adapter" in Chapter 18.

If you have any problems with these instructions, you can find additional help in the Microsoft Knowledge Base (of course, that assumes that you can connect to it, which is likely the problem to begin with). If you can connect to the Internet, find "How to Connect to a Remote Server" at http://premium.microsoft.com/support/kb/articles/q145/8/43.

General connectoid settings

You can set your connectoids to redial automatically if they don't make a connection on the first try. In the Dial-Up Networking folder window, choose Connections, Settings to display the General tab of the Dial-Up Networking dialog box, as shown in Figure 17-4. This dialog box lets you choose how often to try and how long to wait between tries.

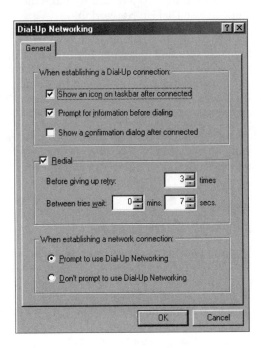

Figure 17-4: The General tab of the Dial-Up Networking dialog box.

Secret

DUN doesn't use these redial settings if you start Internet Explorer first and it uses a DUN connectoid to connect to an Internet service provider. Internet Explorer stores its own redial settings in the Registry and uses these instead. (You change these settings by choosing View, Internet Options in Internet Explorer, clicking the Connections tab, and clicking the Settings button.) If you want to use the DUN redial settings, you need to connect to your Internet service provider by first clicking your DUN connectoid and later starting Internet Explorer.

To eliminate the need to click the Connect button in the Connect To dialog box, clear the Prompt for Information Before Dialing check box. You can also get rid of the connection confirmation dialog box and the Modem Status icon in the Tray. If you do not ask DUN to show the Modem Status icon in the Tray after connecting, you won't be able to disconnect by right-clicking this icon and clicking Disconnect.

Tip

Other applications that call and use the DUN connectoid (Internet applications, for example), may have their own buttons or icons that can accomplish the disconnect function. If you want to call DUN only through these applications, you can dispense with putting the Modem Status icon in the Tray.

Mark the Prompt to Use Dial-Up Networking option button if you want a network connection to be reestablished through Dial-Up Networking. For example, assume you have a shortcut icon on your Desktop that links to a folder on another computer. You normally connect to this computer over your modem using Dial-Up Networking. If you click this icon you will be asked (the first time) which DUN connectoid to use to make the connection (if you have marked Prompt to Use Dial-Up Networking).

Secret

Once you have chosen a DUN connectoid, the next time you click this icon, the DUN connectoid is invoked and dialing begins. If you mark Don't Prompt to Use Dial-Up Networking, you won't be prompted, and a DUN connectoid will not be associated with this shortcut. You will need to connect to the computer at work first before you can click this icon and access the folder.

Undocumented

Direct Cable Connection, which uses Dial-Up Networking, but without a DUN connectoid, cannot use this capability. You have to start DCC on both computers first before you can click the icon on the guest's Desktop to successfully access resources on the host. (See "Accessing the Host" in Chapter 22).

Preparing for server dial-back

The server that you are dialing into may need to call you back before you can properly connect to it. This is a security feature. If server dial-back is implemented, each user has an assigned phone number (his or her home phone, for example). The server dials the phone number of the person who supposedly just tried to log in. If someone else is using your name and password, you still get the phone call at home, not the other person. Of course, this does make things difficult if you are in a hotel.

Secret

Windows 98 Dial-Up Networking wasn't built with the server dial-back feature in mind, but you can kludge it in if you are using the PPP protocol to communicate with the server. You'll need to create an additional modem string to properly set the state of your modem when making the connection.

STEPS

Configuring DUN for Dial-Back Servers

Step 1. Click the Start button, point to Settings, and click Control Panel. Click the Modems icon.

Step 2. Highlight your modem and click the Properties button.

Step 3. Click the Connection tab, and then click the Advanced button.

Step 4. In the Extra Settings field, enter **&C0 S0=1**. Click OK twice, and then click Close.

If there are already settings in the Extra Settings field, just add the new string to the end of the existing ones.

The &C0 setting keeps the PPP client active. The S0=1 setting sets your modem to auto-answer after one ring.

Dialing into another operating system

Dial-Up Networking lets you connect over the phone to a whole variety of networks, including the Internet. You can call into a computer running Windows NT Advanced Server, which allows up to 256 connections and supports IPX/SPX, NetBEUI, and TCP/IP protocols. You can also call into computers running Unix and the SLIP or PPP protocols.

If you are calling into a Windows NT, NetWare, Shiva Netmodem/LanRover, Windows for Workgroups, LAN Manager, or Unix server instead of a Windows 98 or Windows 95 computer, you may need to change the server type associated with your DUN connectoid. Right-click the new DUN connectoid icon in the Dial-Up Networking folder window, click Properties, and then click the Server Types tab.

You get to choose from these options:

- CSLIP: Unix Connection with IP Header Compression
- NRN: NetWare Connect Version 1.0 and 1.1
- PPP: Internet, Windows NT Server, Windows 98
- SLIP: Unix Connection
- Windows for Workgroups and Windows NT 3.1

Your Unix computer server (in some cases a remote Unix server at an Internet service provider) will use either PPP or SLIP. You need to find out which protocol it uses from your computer support staff (or ISP).

You can use Dial-Up Networking to connect to the Internet if you are calling into a dial-up Internet service provider. See "Dial-Up Networking to the Internet" in Chapter 18 for more details.

If you want to just connect to the computer that you are calling into and not to a network that the computer may be connected to, clear the Log on to Network check box in the Server Types dialog box. This goes for Internet servers also.

Few servers required encrypted passwords, so you can clear this check box also unless you know that the computer you are dialing into requires one.

A given connection may require only one or two networking protocols. Clear the check boxes for the unnecessary protocols. If you are dialing into an Internet service provider, clear the NetBEUI and IPX/SPX check boxes. If you are dialing into a NetWare server, clear NetBEUI and TCP/IP.

Copying your DUN connectoids to another computer

You'll notice that there is nothing behind the curtain when you look for your DUN connectoids on your hard disk. The Dial-Up Networking folder window looks a lot like a regular folder window, but there are no files there. This makes it a bit difficult to copy all the connectoid properties to another computer. There is no *there* there.

Undocumented

The connectoid values are stored in your Registry. You'll find them under HKEY_CURRENT_USER\RemoteAccess. You can export this whole branch of the Registry and take it with you to a new computer, or you can just take the parts that you need under Addresses and Profiles.

Unfortunately, this won't quite do it, because these values are associated with modem and COM port settings that are stored not in the User.dat but in the System.dat part of the Registry. The modem and COM port settings on one computer are not necessarily the same as those on another.

Tip

A shareware utility called Dial-Up Magic lets you export and import DUN values from one computer to another. You can also use Dial-Up Magic to clone a DUN connectoid and use it to create another. You'll find this shareware utility at http://ourworld.compuserve.com/homepages/techmagic/.

A new feature of Windows 98 is the ability to drag and drop DUN connectoids between computers. Your logon name and password aren't copied, but the other parameters are. If the two computers are connected over a network, or using Direct Cable Connection, this is easy to do.

SLIP server type

To connect to a server using the SLIP dial-up protocol, you need to be sure that the TCP/IP protocol is bound to your Dial-Up Adapter. To do so, take the steps in the "Bind TCP/IP to your Dial-Up Adapter" section of Chapter 18.

After you have checked to make sure that the TCP/IP protocol is bound to your Dial-Up Adapter, you need to create a SLIP connection. Here's how:

STEPS

Creating a SLIP Connectoid

Step 1. Click the Dial-Up Networking folder icon in the Explorer, or choose Dial-Up Networking from the Start, Programs, Accessories, Communications menu.

Step 2. Click the Make New Connection icon in the Dial-Up Networking folder window.

Step 3. The Make New Connection Wizard starts. Give the computer that you will be dialing into a name, perhaps something like **Internet**. Click Next.

Step 4. Type the area code and phone number for the SLIP computer. Click Next.

Step 5. Click Finish.

Step 6. Right-click the new connectoid, and select Properties. Click the Configure button to display the Properties dialog box for your modem, and then click the Options tab.

Step 7. Mark the Bring Up Terminal Window After Dialing check box. This allows you to log onto your SLIP account. You will need to type your name and password when you log on. (You can avoid having to enter your name and password if you use Windows 98's scripting facility, as described in "Automating your DUN logon" in Chapter 18.) Click OK.

Step 8. Click the Server Types tab and display the Type of Dial-Up Server drop-down list.

Step 9. Highlight either SLIP or CSLIP depending on the capabilities of your Internet service provider or Unix server.

Step 10. If you want to change the static IP address of your computer (or change how it is obtained), click the TCP/IP Settings button. See "Multiple TCP/IP settings for multiple connections" in Chapter 18 for more details.

Step 11. Click the OK buttons until you are back to the Dial-Up Networking folder window.

Refer to "Installing an Internet Dial-Up Connection" in Chapter 18 to learn more about the properties of TCP/IP and connectoids to the Internet. You need to bind to the Dial-Up Adapter the protocol appropriate to the network that you are dialing into. If you are dialing into different networks, you may need to bind all three protocols — IPX/SPX, NetBEUI, and TCP/IP.

Setting up your basic telephone information

Windows 98 can keep track of telephone information for multiple locations. For example, for each location you dial from, it can remember whether you have to dial an access number to get an outside line, whether your phone has call waiting, and whether the connection is local or long distance.

To edit this location-specific information, click the Modems icon in the Control Panel, and click the Dialing Properties button to display the Dialing Properties dialog box. Turn to "Dialing Properties" in Chapter 32 for a discussion of the options in this dialog box.

Your modem

Your modem was originally set up by the Install New Modem Wizard. This most likely happened automatically when you first set up Windows 98, when you set up your computer at home as a guest, or when you clicked the Modems icon in the Control Panel, but if you need to, you can change the properties for your modem now.

Right-click your connectoid icon in the Dial-Up Networking folder window, and choose Properties. Click the Configure button to display the Properties dialog box for your modem. Turn to "Changing the basic modem connection properties" in Chapter 25 for details about what changes to make.

The Dial-Up Adapter

To call into your computer at work over your modem, you need to have the Dial-Up Adapter set up on both computers. It is automatically set up on your home computer when you create a new connection. It is also automatically set up on your Windows 98 computer at work when you configure it as a host. However, you can set it up directly by following these steps:

STEPS

Setting Up the Dial-Up Adapter

Step 1. Click the Start button, point to Settings, and then click Control Panel. Click the Network icon.

Step 2. If you don't see Adapter in the list of network components in the Network dialog box, click the Add button.

Step 3. In the Select Network Component Type dialog box, click Adapter, and then click the Add button.

Step 4. In the Select Device dialog box, select Microsoft in the manufacturer list.

Step 5. Select Dial-Up Adapter in the Network Adapters list. Click OK twice.

The Microsoft Dial-Up Adapter and the network software component necessary to carry out remote communications are now installed. You will be asked to reboot your computer.

After you have rebooted you computer, go back to the Control Panel and click the Network icon. Highlight the Dial-Up Adapter and click the Properties button. You'll see the Dial-Up Adapter Properties dialog box, as shown in Figure 17-5.

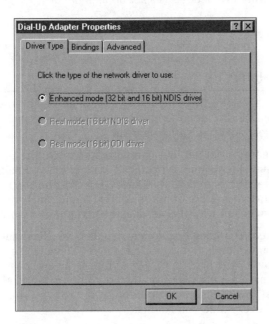

Figure 17-5: The Dial-Up Adapter Properties dialog box.

Undocumented

Microsoft has written an NDIS (Network Driver Interface Specification) 5 level driver for the modem/serial port. This is a low-level driver most often associated with network cards. The Dial-Up Adapter treats the modem as though it were a network card using this driver. NDIS 5 allows multiple protocols to run on a network interface card (or, in this case, a modem) simultaneously.

The default protocol of the Dial-Up Networking communication between two Windows 98 computers is either NetBEUI, IPX/SPX, or TCP/IP. All three protocols were installed when you set up the Dial-Up Adapter and are bound to it. *Bound* means that they are used to carry out the communication between the two computers. You can find out whether one or more of the protocols are bound by clicking the Bindings tab. Which protocol is actually used depends on the configuration of the computer at work.

If you don't find a protocol or find that it isn't bound to the Dial-Up Adapter, you can add it. To see how, turn to "Configuring the adapter driver" in Chapter 24.

Dialing into the Office

After you have connected your home computer's modem to your phone line, you can dial into the computer at work. Of course, the computer at work could actually be a networked modem server that acts like a Windows 98, Windows NT, or NetWare Connect server set up as a host.

STEPS
Dialing In from Home

Step 1.   Click the Dial-Up Networking folder icon in an Explorer window, or choose Dial-Up Networking from the Start, Programs, Accessories, Communications menu.

Step 2.   Click the connectoid for your computer at work in the Dial-Up Networking folder window. If you call work often, you might want to right-drag this icon onto the Desktop or Start button and choose Create Shortcut(s) Here from the context menu. That way, you will have a convenient way of accessing the computer at work.

Step 3.   The Connect To dialog box appears (unless you have turned off this option, which is not a good idea if you're making a connection for the first time). Type your name and password if you have set up a password on the computer at work. Mark the Save Password check box if you don't want to type your password every time you connect.

  If you are unable to make a successful connection, your password will not be saved. This can be a bit annoying. You just have to keep trying until the first successful connection.

Step 4.   If necessary, you can click the Dial Properties button to edit your (at home) location information at this point. There are other entry points for editing this information, but this is as good as any. See the previous section entitled "Setting up your basic telephone information" for more on this.

Step 5. Click the Connect button.

Your computer will dial your modem and attempt to make a network connection across the phone lines to your computer at work. If all goes well, you will be networked to your work computer.

If you have chosen the Log on to Network option (right-click the connectoid for your computer at work, choose Properties, and click the Server Types tab), you will also be logged onto the network that is connected to the server you dialed into. In this case, you can access other servers on the network by following the steps in the "Accessing shared resources" section later in this chapter.

Dialing in manually

You can dial into the host computer manually. Once you make the connection, perhaps through an operator or using your credit card, you turn over the phone line to your computer. You might want to do this if you are having trouble defining an automated dialing procedure in a new location. For this to work, the phone must be connected to the same line as your computer.

STEPS

Dialing In Manually

Step 1. Click the Dial-Up Networking folder icon in the Explorer, or choose Dial-Up Networking from the Start, Programs, Accessories, Communications menu.

Step 2. Right-click the connectoid for your computer at work in the Dial-Up Networking folder window. Click Properties.

Step 3. Click the Configure button, and then click the Options tab.

Step 4. Mark the Operator Assisted Or Manual Dial check box. Click OK twice.

Step 5. Click the connectoid. You will be prompted to pick up the receiver and dial the number.

Step 6. When you hear the tone from the computer, click Connect, and then hang up the phone.

DUN command line parameters

The easiest way to start a DUN connection is to click a shortcut of a DUN connectoid that you have placed on your Desktop. You can also invoke a DUN connectoid by using the following command line parameters:

```
rundll rnaui.dll,RnaDial My Connection
```

Replace *My Connection* with the name of one of your connectoids. You can create a shortcut and place the above syntax in the Target field (right-click the shortcut and choose Properties). Furthermore, you can type this syntax in the Run dialog box (Start, Run) to start the connectoid.

Networking over a modem

Once you have made the connection, you are another node (albeit a slow one) on the network at work. If you are just hooking two computers together, then they are networking over the modem, and that is the only network.

Undocumented

If you are calling into a Windows 98 computer acting as the host, you won't see the shared resources in your Network Neighborhood. In order to reduce the overhead on a slow link such as a modem connection, Windows 98 by default turns off the ability to browse the host computer. We show you how to turn this back on in the section entitled "Seeing shared resources."

Accessing shared resources

You access the shared resources of the computer at work (folders, printers, and drives on the host computer) by explicitly naming the resource. Once you're connected, click the Start button, and then click Run. Type the name of the computer at work followed by the shared resource name, using the universal naming convention (UNC) — \\WorkComputer\C, for example. (When you attempt to access a shared resource, you might be required to enter a password if it is not already stored in the user-password cache on your computer, or if this is the first time you have accessed a resource that is protected by a password.)

If you want to find the name of a computer, you'll need to click the Start button, Settings, Control Panel, Network, Identification tab. You have to do this on the computer whose name you need to check.

For this method (or any method) of accessing a shared resource to work, you first need to share your resources on the host computer. See "Sharing your resources" in Chapter 24.

The UNC allows you to access resources by name, without having to map them to a drive letter on your computer. It uses two backslashes before the name of the server, host, or computer at work, and a single backslash before the resource name.

A folder window containing the resource you specified will open up on the Desktop of your home computer. You can then browse the resource to find the files or programs that you are interested in. To access other computers connected by a network to your computer at work, you can type their UNC names in the Run dialog box.

You can create shortcuts on your computer at home to these shared resources on your computer at work. For example, create a shortcut to a folder on the computer at work by dragging to your Desktop a folder from an open folder window that is displaying the folder icon. The UNC name is captured in the shortcut.

You can map a networked resource (a folder or a drive) to a drive letter by clicking Tools, Map Network Drive in the Explorer menu on your computer at home. You normally map a networked resource to a drive letter, not a Dial-Up Networked resource. Unless you have a very fast dial-up connection, accessing this resource through your Explorer could make it repaint quite slowly.

In the Path field of the Map Network Drive dialog box, you just type two back slashes, followed by the name of the networked computer, followed by a single back slash and the name of the shared resource. You can also map a network drive if you are using Direct Cable Connection, which uses DUN.

Seeing shared resources

You can configure the computer at work so that its shared resources are automatically visible to your computer at home through the Network Neighborhood. (To enable file and printer sharing, you need to take the steps in "Choosing network services" in Chapter 24.)

You also need to make sure that both computers have the same workgroup name. Click the Network icon in the Control Panel on your computer at home, and click the Identification tab. Check the Workgroup field to verify that it is the same as the workgroup name of the computer at work.

Because the DUN connection can be slow, enabling the Browse Master will slow the display of resources on your Explorer at home. You can also make the resources of the computer at work automatically visible on your computer at home with Direct Cable Connection, which is usually much faster.

STEPS

Turning on the Browse Master

Step 1. On the computer at work, click the Start button, point to Settings, and then click Control Panel. Click the Network icon.

(continued)

STEPS *(continued)*

Turning on the Browse Master

Step 2. Click File and Printer Sharing for Microsoft Networks in the network components list. Click the Properties button.

Step 3. Browse Master should be the first item in the Properties dialog box. Its default value in the Value drop-down list is Automatic. Change this to Enabled.

Step 4. Click OK.

Step 5. Restart Windows 98.

Step 6. On the computer at home, click the connectoid for the computer at work.

Step 7. When you're connected, click the Network Neighborhood icon. You'll see the shared resources of the computer at work.

It may take a couple of minutes for the shared resources to show up. This is the reason that Microsoft disabled Browse Master on dial-up connections. Just be patient and they will appear.

Monitoring your calls

Undocumented

DUN 1.2 works with System Monitor to let you see the speed of your uploads and downloads. If you've been using System Monitor in early versions of Windows 95, you'll notice that the list of categories in the Add Item dialog box contains a new item, Dial-Up Adapter.

The System Monitor is a great place to display incoming and outgoing data transfer rates. If it's already installed, you'll find it under Start, Programs, Accessories, System Tools, System Monitor. If you haven't installed it yet, you should do so now. Click the Add/Remove Programs icon in your Control Panel, click the Windows Setup tab, highlight System Tools, click the Details button, and mark the System Monitor check box. It's a good idea to place a shortcut to the System Monitor on your Desktop.

To monitor your data transfer rates, choose Edit, Add Item in the System Monitor window, and select Dial-Up Adapter in the Add Item dialog box. Choose Bytes Received/Second and Bytes Transmitted/Second (see Figure 17-6).

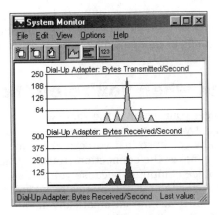

Figure 17-6: Monitoring bytes transmitted and received in System Monitor.

As you can see in the list on the right side of the Add Item dialog box, the System Monitor lets you monitor additional parameters for Dial-Up Adapter. Here is a quick run down of what they mean:

- Frames Received/Second and Frames Transmitted/Second measure *frames*, which are packets of many bytes. These two technical measurements will probably not be as useful to you as Bytes Received/Second and Bytes Transmitted/Second.

- Framing Errors and Incomplete Frames indicate frames that arrive with a smaller or larger number of bytes than expected. These errors can impede the throughput of your modem. They can be caused by incompatibilities between your modem and the modem of the computer at work, which may not be reliably capable of sending data as fast as it appears to be.

- CRC Errors indicate that something, probably line noise, has corrupted a few bits as they were being transmitted. The acronym stands for *cyclical redundancy check*. This means that a CRC code at the end of several bytes no longer matches the data received. In this case, the modems usually re-transmit and re-receive the data so that good data is ensured. But these errors can slow down your throughput. If you see CRC errors, it may be best to hang up and call again to see if a faulty line in the telephone company was causing too much noise for reliable communications.

- Timeout Errors occur when no data has been transmitted during a normal waiting period for your end of the communications. This is the opposite of Overrun Errors or Buffer Overruns, which occur when more data has been sent than your modem can process. Modems are supposed to let each other know how fast to send data, so overruns may indicate an incompatibility between your modem and the modem of the computer at work (or your Internet service provider).

- Alignment Errors indicate possible incompatibilities among the hardware and software used by both ends of the communications link. Trying different speed settings or modems may isolate this problem.

Getting your e-mail when you're on the road

Using Windows Messaging to get your e-mail is the same whether you are away from the office or sitting at your desk. You can set up your portable or home computer to automatically call in so that you can check for new messages. Windows Messaging makes the connection. You don't have to click the connectoid to your office computer, because you can configure Windows Messaging to use this connectoid automatically. (Windows Messaging is a Windows 95 product. It's not automatically installed with Windows 98, but it is on the Windows 98 CD-ROM. See Chapter 20 for more information.)

You need to create a Windows Messaging profile on your computer at home. If your office computer is on a network that uses Microsoft Mail, this profile should use Microsoft Mail to connect to a workgroup postoffice at work. See "Remote Access to a Microsoft Mail Postoffice" in Chapter 20 for details.

Even if you have only one computer at work, you can configure it and the computer at home (no doubt someone else's computer) to use Microsoft Mail as your mail delivery system. The person who calls into your office computer picks up his or her e-mail from the Microsoft Mail postoffice on your computer at work.

Printing on the printer at work from home

You can print a document on a printer at work while calling in from your computer at home or on the road. The printer at work must be shared and you need to have it in your Printers folder on your home computer.

The first step is to share the printer at work. If the printer is on a Windows 98 computer, you share it by clicking the Start button, pointing to Settings, and clicking Printers to display the Printers folder window. Right-click the printer that you want to share, and click Sharing. Click the Shared As option button, and type a name for the shared printer in the Share Name field. (If the Sharing command doesn't appear, see "Enabling print sharing" in Chapter 29.)

You also need to put the printer at work in the Printers folder on the computer at home. Click the Add Printer icon in the Printers folder on the computer at home. Tell the Add Printer Wizard that the printer is a network printer, and give it the pathname to the printer using a UNC name such as \\server\HP. Windows 98 will semi-automatically install the printer driver (if you have access to your Windows 98 CD-ROM). See "Point and Print" in Chapter 29 for more information.

Once the printer at work is shared and you have it in your Printers folder on your computer at home, then you can simply print to it.

Faxing from work while on the road

You can use Windows Messaging to send a document from your computer at home over your modem to a shared fax/modem on your network (or computer) at work, and have that document faxed out from work. You might do this if your modem doesn't have a fax capability, if your fax/modem on your computer at home isn't compatible with Microsoft Fax, or perhaps if the company is paying the bill for faxes you send from work. (Like Windows Messaging, Microsoft Fax is not automatically installed with Windows 98, but it is on the Windows 98 CD-ROM. See Chapter 20 for more information.)

The first task is to share the fax/modem at work. The second is to configure a Windows Messaging profile on your computer at home that uses the shared fax/modem at work. For details on how to do this, turn to "Sharing a fax/modem on a network" in Chapter 20.

Play DOS multiuser games over the network

Most DOS multiuser games use the IPX networking protocol. If you have configured your computer at home and the one at work to use this protocol, you can just connect to your computer at work and begin playing. You'll need to run the DOS game in a DOS window (and not in MS-DOS mode), unless you run DOS software that will make the IPX connection for you.

Connecting to a Personal Web Server

Your Windows 98 computer at work can serve as a web server if it is running the Microsoft Personal Web Server software. You can then call in from your computer at home and access the web pages on your computer at work. This also works with Direct Cable Connection.

We discuss the issues related to connecting to web servers on the Internet in "Installing an Internet dial-up connection" in the next chapter.

To connect to your own web server directly (and not necessarily through the Internet), you need to configure both computers to allow the computer at work to serve up web pages to the computer at home. Take the following steps:

STEPS

Serving Personal Web Pages

Step 1. Install Personal Web Server. To do this, use your Explorer to navigate to \add-ons\pws on your Windows 98 CD-ROM. Click setup.exe. Once you have installed the Personal Web Server, you will find the Publish shortcut on your Desktop.

Step 2. Be sure the TCP/IP protocol is bound to the Dial-Up Adapters in both your computer at work and your computer at home (see "Bind TCP/IP to your Dial Up Adapter" in Chapter 18).

Step 3. On your computer at home, create a DUN connectoid that connects to your computer at work. Be sure to include the TCP/IP protocol. You won't need NetBEUI or IPX if you are using this DUN connectoid just to connect to the web server running on the computer at work.

Step 4. Start the DUN Server on the computer at work.

Step 5. Click Start, Run, type **winipcfg**, and click OK. This starts the Windows IP Configuration utility, which lets you monitor your IP address. You'll need this address later. You can drag a shortcut to Winipcfg.exe from your \Windows folder onto your Desktop.

Step 6. Click your DUN connectoid for the computer at work on your computer at home and establish a connection. Click the Renew All button in your IP Configuration window on your computer at work. Note the IP address (for your computer at work).

Step 7. Start Personal Web Server on the computer at work. Start Internet Explorer on the computer at home.

Step 8. In the Address bar of Internet Explorer, type **http://**, followed by the IP address that you noted in the IP Configuration window on your computer at work, followed by **/homepage.htm**.

Step 9. On the computer at work, click the Network icon in the Control Panel, click the Identification tab, and note the value in the Computer Name field.

Step 10. On the computer at home, navigate with the Explorer to the \Windows folder. Right-click the right pane of the Explorer and choose New, Text Document.

Step 11. In the first line of the blank text file, enter the value from the Computer Name field from step 9, press the Tab key, enter the IP address from step 6, press the Tab key, and type **#PRE**.

Step 12. Save and close the text file. Rename it Lmhosts with no extension. You will now be able to access the Personal Web Server on your Windows 98 computer at work using its name instead of its IP address.

Step 13. In the Internet Explorer window on your computer at home, choose File, Send, Shortcut To Desktop. This creates a shortcut to the web page on your computer at work. You can edit this shortcut (right-click it and click Properties) to change the address in the target field from the IP address to the computer name.

Personal Web Server is the same web server that runs on Windows NT with a few limitations. You can access its web pages on a network, over DUN, or using Direct Cable Connection. If the Windows 98 computer is connected to a LAN at work using the TCP/IP protocol, the address assigned to this computer may be determined by a WINS or DNS server. If you call into the network instead of directly into the Windows 98 computer, you'll use these services to resolve the name of the computer at work instead of the Lmhosts file.

DUN Troubles

Dial-Up Networking is not bullet proof. There are a few areas that require your attention if you run into problems.

If you clear the Use Area Code and Dialing Properties check box in one DUN connectoid, it may force you to enter the phone number to dial in other DUN connectoids. The solution is to not clear this check box to begin with. If you do clear the check box, you'll lose the dialer's ability to set call waiting and to use area codes when needed.

When you invoke a DUN connectoid, you also load Rnaapp.exe (Remote Network Access Application). If you click a DUN connectoid and it is unable to connect to the remote computer, you may find that you aren't able to immediately try again. You can wait for a few more seconds, or you can press Ctrl+Alt+Del, highlight Rnaapp, and click End Task to clear Rnaapp out of memory. You'll then be able to start your DUN connectoid again.

Clearing Rnaapp out of memory can make little communication problems go away. It is designed to hang around for a little while so that you don't have to load it every time you start a new communications application. Unfortunately, this behavior seems to cause more problems than it is worth.

Compatible protocols

You may find that you are receiving the error message "Dial-up Networking cannot negotiate a compatible set of protocols. Please check your network settings...." You know that you do have a compatible set of protocols because your DUN connectoid works just fine most of the time. This error message is obviously wrong, but DUN doesn't know any better. Not exactly a smart system.

The problems that generated this error message have apparently been varied and widespread enough to generate significant difficulties. Microsoft acknowledged one source of the problems in late 1997 when it stated, "This problem can occur when Rasapi32.dll is unable to unload the session management module (SMM) if it returns an error during the early phase of the authentication process."

Microsoft has stated that this problem is addressed in the Windows 98 version of DUN.

Summary

You can call into a server computer over a modem from your computer at home or on the road. The server can be a Windows 98 computer, a Windows 95 computer, a Windows NT computer, a LAN Manager server, a NetWare server, a Unix computer, an Internet service provider, or a dedicated networked modem server. We show you:

▶ How to set up a Windows 98 computer as a host at work so you can call into it from home.

▶ How to set up your computer at home so you can call into various servers, including your Windows 98 computer at work.

▶ How to access and use shared resources on the network with Dial-Up Networking.

▶ How to configure a web page server and connect to it directly using DUN Server and a DUN connectoid

▶ How to use your computer at home to print on your printer at work and fax via your fax/modem at work.

Chapter 18

Connecting to the Internet

In This Chapter

Want to get on the Internet? We show you how to do it using the tools built into Windows 98. Windows 98 comes with a TCP/IP stack and a dialer to connect your computer to an Internet service provider (ISP).

▶ Getting the right kind of account (PPP, SLIP, or TIA) from your Internet service provider

▶ Asking your service provider for the right information about your account

▶ Setting up Dial-Up Networking (DUN) to make the connection to your service provider

▶ Getting your TCP/IP stack and your Dial-Up Adapter to work together

▶ Connecting to your service provider

▶ Verifying that you've got a good connection

Your First Point of Internet Attachment

There are two fundamentally different ways to gain access to the Internet from your computer — retail and wholesale. You can call through the modem connected to your computer to a local or national Internet service provider. Or you can communicate over your local area network (LAN) to a server that is connected by a phone line to an Internet service provider. The connection can vary from a dial-up 28.8 Kbps service to a fast, dedicated leased-T1 line.

Service providers that offer call-in modem access to the general public are a relatively new phenomenon. Before 1994, most users accessed the Internet through their Unix workstations on campus or on the job at defense contractors. They didn't have to worry about how to get access. The system administrator took care of those details. Once the rest of us were allowed to join the party, *we* became the system administrators for our own computers.

CompuServe, America Online, Prodigy, and other online services have turned themselves into Internet service providers (although not completely) while maintaining some or all of their online services. These national online services have offered connections to Internet mail (although not connections to Internet mail POP3 and SMTP servers) since 1993, and in

1997 they began providing almost full Internet access, like their Internet service provider competitors.

When Microsoft offered MSN with Windows 95 in 1995, it also purchased partial interest in a nationwide service provider named UUNET. MSN provides a connection to Internet mail (but it didn't install a direct connection to POP3 and SMTP Internet e-mail servers until late in 1997) and full access to Internet newsgroups with an NNTP news server (although it didn't provide access to Internet news servers outside of MSN until early 1997). As a nationwide service provider, MSN provides dial-up access that supports both the Internet TCP/IP protocol and the MSN networking protocol.

Tip

You should look for a service provider that has enough phone lines so you won't get a busy signal too often. The Internet works best at the highest speed you can afford. If the service provider has 56 Kbps modems and so do you, great. Some service providers are very small and may not have adequate technical support to keep their lines up and functioning. Move on to another one if this is the case.

Some service providers let you connect with ISDN. This will give you 56 or 128 Kbps bi-directional transfer rates. See if your telephone company will install an ISDN line to your home or business. If so, purchase an ISDN card with a Windows 98-compatible driver for your computer (now available from Microsoft), and you are ready to really cruise the Internet.

Microsoft's TCP/IP Stack

Windows 98 comes with tools that allow you to access the Internet either over a modem or through a network. At the lowest level, Microsoft provides a TCP/IP stack. TCP/IP (Transfer Control Protocol/Internet Protocol) is the Internet protocol (or language). It can be spoken over your modem, network card, or through Windows 98's Direct Cable Connection (see Chapter 22 for more on DCC).

You can associate (bind) the TCP/IP stack to your Dial-Up Adapter and/or your network card. If you bind it to your Dial-Up Adapter, you can use Windows 98's Dial-Up Networking to call your service provider and connect to the Internet using TCP/IP.

If you bind the TCP/IP stack to your network card, and your network is connected to a Unix server or Windows NT server, or to a Windows 98 computer, you can communicate with that server using Internet (or Internet-related) applications compatible with Winsock. The server can provide the gateway to the Internet. (The Windows 98 computer requires a third-party program to act as a gateway to the Internet for other computers on a LAN.)

If you use the TCP/IP protocol on your local area network, your network becomes an Intranet. (An *Intranet* is a local area network that uses Internet standards.) If you do this, you can configure Windows 98, Windows 95, Windows NT, NetWare, and, of course, Unix servers as web servers and POP3 and SMTP e-mail servers.

Installing an Internet dial-up connection

To gain Internet access through your modem, you need to carry out the following tasks:

- Install and configure your modem.

- Sign up for an Internet account with your service provider or online service.

- Obtain from the service provider the information you need to successfully connect your computer to their computer.

- Install Dial-Up Networking on your Windows 98 computer.

- Check to see that the Windows 98 TCP/IP stack is bound to the Dial-Up Adapter (your modem).

- Define and configure a Dial-Up Networking connection for your service provider.

- Configure the TCP/IP settings specific to your service provider using the information they provide.

- Write a connection script if your Internet service provider doesn't provide PPP with CHAP or PAP.

Windows 98 includes the Internet Connection Wizard, which can help you create a dial-up connection to your Internet service provider. We discuss how to use this Wizard a little later in this chapter.

Installing and configuring your modem

We discuss how to install and configure your modem in "Configuring Your Modem" in Chapter 31. The Windows 98 Setup program's hardware detection routines may already have correctly identified your modem and installed the appropriate driver for it. Even if you installed your modem after you installed Windows 98, similar hardware detection routines may have correctly detected it and installed the right driver.

To check if your modem has been detected, click the Modems icon in your Control Panel to display the Modems Properties dialog box. If your modem has been detected, it will be listed in the General tab of the dialog box. You can also click the Dialing Properties button to review or edit the properties that characterize your calling location. If your modem driver isn't yet installed, you can do so at this point by clicking the Add button.

An Internet service provider account

To connect to the Internet, you need an account with an Internet service provider. Service providers give you access to the Internet through their computers, which are connected to fast, dedicated telephone lines. The service provider maintains a bundle of dial-in phone lines attached to racks of modems, which are in turn attached to the service provider's computer(s).

Tip

If you are opening a new account, you should obtain a PPP (Point-to-Point Protocol) account from the service provider. If you already have a different type of account, you should change it to a PPP account. In addition, you should find a service provider that provides either PAP (Password Authentication Protocol) or CHAP (Challenge-Handshake Authentication Protocol), if possible. If your account supports PAP or CHAP, you don't have to type your logon name and password after you connect to the service provider. If your PPP account doesn't have one of these types of authentication, you have to either type your logon name and password each time you connect or create a script file (using a scripting utility that comes with Windows 98) that enters this information for you.

When you connect to the Internet, your computer is assigned an IP address to identify it to other computers. Most Internet service providers assign IP addresses dynamically, that is, at logon time. In some cases you can obtain a static IP address. If you have a SLIP (Serial Line/Internet Protocol) account instead of a PPP account, and you have a dynamically assigned IP address, your SLIP script will need to capture the dynamically assigned IP address and send it back to the service provider.

Some service providers don't offer PPP or SLIP accounts directly, but require that you first connect to a shell account, and then send a message once you're online to switch to a PPP or SLIP connection. A *shell account* is the most basic account type available from a service provider. It treats your expensive computer as a dumb terminal and requires that you run Unix software on the service provider's computer to do anything on the Internet. You can use your script to send a command to switch from the shell to SLIP or PPP.

Tip

If you just want to maintain a low-level shell account, you can use HyperTerminal (see "Creating Connection Connectoids" in Chapter 21) to call into your service provider. HyperTerminal doesn't come with scripting to automate the logon process, but it will still work fine as a tool for connecting to a Unix computer.

Tip

Your service provider may offer a TIA (The Internet Adapter) account, which allows you to switch to a SLIP-type account after you log on in your shell account. The Windows 98 scripting utility works with TIA accounts to switch to SLIP.

Service provider account information

The first step, of course, is to find a service provider. If you live in a metropolitan area, you should be able to find a free local computer newspaper at computer stores that lists service providers.

A local service provider will have a local number and perhaps an 800 number. A national service provider will provide local numbers, an 800 number, or a number in the closest town. You can find ads for national service providers in national computer magazines or in national newspapers such as the *New York Times* (especially the Tuesday *Science Times* section). If you have access to a friend's Internet account, you can check out online databases of service providers such as http://www.thelist.com to find ISPs in your area. Go to their home pages and check them out. You should be able to sign up with a service provider online by filling out a sign-up form on their web site.

You need some specific information from your service provider. The staff at local service providers much prefer to talk to other people (sometimes known as customers) by way of their computers. This can be quite difficult when you don't have an e-mail account (which is one of the reasons that you're trying to contact the service provider to begin with). If you already have an e-mail account with a national online service such as AOL or CompuServe, you can use that account to send e-mail to a local service provider, assuming you can find their e-mail address.

You can always just call an ISP on a voice line, but it is often difficult to reach anyone. You can fax them your questions, and hope that they fax you back the answers. This poor "out-of-the-box" experience with some service providers has been a major bottleneck in their growth. Many are very small companies run by one or two technically minded people; no glad-handing sales types are allowed. On the other hand, ISPs are independent businesses with a self interest in serving their local customers, so some do indeed make every effort to give you the assistance you need.

The major online services and the Microsoft Network are attempting to simplify the process of getting online. Microsoft is very smart to make it so easy to connect to MSN (although some would say it is unfairly using its monopoly position).

You need the following information from your service provider to configure your Windows 98 TCP/IP stack:

- Dial-in phone number you'll use to connect to the service provider's modems

- Account type

- If it is a SLIP account, whether it is compressed SLIP (CSLIP) or not

- If it is a PPP account, whether it has either PAP or CHAP

- If it is a PPP account without PAP or CHAP, whether it supports software compression and encrypted passwords

- User name (or *logon name*), for example, something like *billsmith* or *nancyf*

- Password

- Your host name (which can be the same as your user name)

  You can think of your host name as your computer's name, or as your name on the Internet. It will be appended to the service provider's domain name to become your address on the Internet. Since this will become your address, you should tell the service provider what you want as a host name, and see if they can swing it without any conflicts.

■ The service provider's domain name (for example, *netters.com*)

Your Internet address will be a combination of your host name and the service provider's domain name, as in *billsmith.netters.com*. Your e-mail address will be *billsmith@netters.com*. You can have as many different e-mail addresses on the Internet as you have accounts.

■ Domain Name System (DNS) server's IP (Internet Protocol) address

DNS servers translate (from a lookup table) the somewhat user-friendly domain names into the underlying IP addresses (for example, 207.182.15.50). Get the IP address of the DNS server that you'll be automatically accessing when you use your service provider's services. Your service provider may automatically assign the IP address of the DNS server, in which case you won't have to get this address.

You can also register your own domain name and have it translated by a DNS server. You'll need to set up a web server (or rent a spot on a virtual server at an Internet service provider) to take advantage of the name. The address for your web site will be something like www.yourname.com, and people will be able to send you e-mail at yourname@yourname.com. Talk to your service provider about registration and costs.

In most cases, your service provider will assign a different IP address to your computer every time you log on. When other people use your Internet address to contact your computer, your service provider will automatically translate your Internet address into this dynamic IP address.

If your service provider doesn't automatically assign you an IP address, you'll need to get:

■ Your own IP address (a fixed IP address)

■ An IP subnet mask

■ A gateway IP address

It can be quite useful to have a fixed IP address. It's almost like having your own domain name. Internet routers can find your computer using your IP address, so you can give out your IP address to all your "friends," and they can contact you there whenever you are connected to the Internet. Also, if you have a fixed IP address, you can publish web pages from your own Windows 98 computer, using Personal Web Server. People will be able to access your pages when you're connected to your service provider over your 28.8 modem.

Of course, the Internet routers won't have a way of finding your computer by looking for a domain name such as www.yourcomputer.com (instead of your fixed IP address) if you haven't registered one. And if you aren't online pretty much all the time, putting a web site on your own computer, while technically feasible, wouldn't be that useful. It's a better idea to put your web site on the service provider's computers because they are online 24 hours a day, they have a fast connection to the Internet, and you won't be bothered with people connecting to your computer while you're using it.

Windows 98 includes the Personal Web Server, which allows you to publish HTML pages and make them available to others on your local area network or over the Internet. If you want to publish them over the Internet, you'll have to establish an Internet connection. (See "Connecting to a Personal Web Server" in Chapter 17.)

The above information is all you need to be able to connect to your service provider. To be able to access e-mail and newsgroups, you'll need the following information:

- Your e-mail address (most likely the combination of your host name and the service provider's domain name)
- POP3 mail server's address
- SMTP mail server's address
- News server's address
- Mail gateway's address (needed only for some mail readers)

Your service provider should have no problem giving you this information (assuming you can actually talk to someone). In fact, many service providers have all of the information compiled into one document, which they can fax or mail to you. Alternatively, if you have access to a computer connected to the Internet, they can send it in an e-mail message or you can download it from their web site.

Some Internet service providers will tell you that you have to use their custom software to configure your connection and access the Internet. This is absolutely not the case. We strongly suggest that you do not use the software provided by the Internet service provider, but instead use the capabilities built into Windows 98, as described in this chapter. Politely and firmly tell the Internet service provider that you don't need their software, you just need the pieces of information listed in this section. Sooner or later, you will find someone who is willing to give you the information that you need.

The Internet Connection Wizard

The Internet Connection Wizard can help you set up an account with an Internet service provider. And for select providers, it can actually set you up with an account automatically. As you step through the Wizard, it asks you a series of questions. You can find all of the information you need to answer these questions by reading the relevant topics in this chapter.

Microsoft allows other Internet service providers a place in a folder called Online Services on the Desktop in exchange for their commitment to promoting Internet Explorer as their preferred Internet user interface. You can sign up automatically for AOL, AT&T World Net, Prodigy, or CompuServe, as well as the Microsoft Network.

The Internet Connection Wizard will also call into Microsoft's Internet Referral Server and download the latest information about Internet service providers that offer service in the area defined by your area code and the first three numbers in your phone number. This list is limited to those service providers who have agreements with Microsoft to provide Internet Explorer as their preferred browser.

If you want to sign up with another national or local Internet service provider, you have to manually provide to the Internet Connection Wizard the information that the Wizard supplies automatically for the favored service providers. In addition, if you connect to your service provider using a SLIP account, you may have to manually edit a script file.

We give you all the information that you need to create a connectoid to your service provider either manually or by using the Internet Connection Wizard in this chapter and in "Setting Up Your Computer at Home As a Guest" in Chapter 17.

The Internet Connection Wizard automatically starts the first time you run Internet Explorer. If you want to run it again, you'll find it in your Start menu, under Programs, Internet Explorer, Connection Wizard. The executable file for the Internet Connection Wizard is icwconn1.exe, and it's stored in the \Program Files\Internet Explorer\Connection Wizard folder. You can also right-click the Internet Explorer icon on your Desktop, click Properties, click the Connection tab, and then click the Connect button.

Dial-Up Networking

If you installed Direct Cable Connection (DCC) during Windows 98 Setup, Dial-Up Networking (DUN) is already installed. You may also have chosen to install DUN if you ran a Custom setup.

To find out if DUN is installed, click the Start button, point to Settings, and then click Control Panel. Click the Network icon in the Control Panel and see whether Dial-Up Adapter is listed in the Configuration tab of your Network dialog box.

If it isn't, you can install DUN by taking these steps:

STEPS

Installing Dial-Up Networking

Step 1.   Click the Start button, point to Settings, and then click Control Panel.

Step 2.   Click the Add/Remove Programs icon. Click the Windows Setup tab.

Step 3.   Highlight Communications, and then click the Details button.

Step 4. Mark the Dial-Up Networking check box, and click the OK button in the Communications dialog box.

Step 5. Click the OK button in the Add/Remove Programs Properties dialog box. You may be asked to insert your Windows 98 CD-ROM. DUN is now installed.

Bind TCP/IP to your Dial-Up Adapter

Adding Dial-Up Networking to your Windows 98 configuration may not add the TCP/IP stack to the list of protocols bound to the Dial-Up Adapter. This is especially true if you are upgrading over a Windows 95 configuration that doesn't include TCP/IP. If you don't find TCP/IP listed in the Configuration tab of your Network Configuration dialog box, take the following steps:

STEPS

Binding Your TCP/IP Stack to Dial-Up Adapter

Step 1. Click the Start button, point to Settings, and then click Control Panel.

Step 2. Click the Network icon. Click the Add button.

Step 3. Highlight Protocol in the Select Network Component Type dialog box and click the Add button.

Step 4. In the Select Network Protocol dialog box, highlight Microsoft in the Manufacturers list, and highlight TCP/IP in the Network Protocols list. Click the OK button.

Step 5. Click OK in the Network dialog box. You may be asked to insert your Windows 98 CD-ROM.

You now have a TCP/IP stack and a dialer, both of which will be encompassed in your DUN connectoid. After you configure your connectoid for your service provider account, you will be able to make an Internet connection. The default TCP/IP settings are described in the next section.

Tip

If you click the Network icon in your Control Panel, you will notice that other protocols have been installed and bound to your Dial-Up Adapter by default. You can remove these other protocols, such as NetBUEI, if you like. However, you shouldn't remove them if you are going to use Direct Cable Connection, connect to a local area network, or connect to Windows NT servers running Microsoft Networks over the Internet.

You can choose which networking protocols work with a given DUN connectoid, so there is no need to uninstall them or unbind them from the Dial-Up Adapter.

Configuring the TCP/IP stack

These are the default settings for the TCP/IP stack:

- Obtain an IP address automatically
- Use DHCP for WINS resolution
- No gateways
- NetBIOS over TCP/IP
- Disable DNS

You shouldn't change these settings if you are going to connect to the Internet only through a dial-up Internet service provider and you don't use TCP/IP on a local area network. You should set the TCP/IP settings that are specific to your service provider when you create a DUN connectoid, as shown in the "Dial-up connection to your service provider" section later in this chapter.

You might need to change the TCP/IP settings if you connect to a LAN using the TCP/IP protocol bound to a network card. If you have a LAN network adapter and a Dial-Up Adapter displayed in the Configuration tab of your Network dialog box along with the TCP/IP protocol, you will see separate entries for TCP/IP -> LAN and TCP/IP -> Dial-Up Adapter. This makes it appear as though there are two separately configurable TCP/IP stacks. Not so.

In spite of the fact that the Network dialog box shows two different TCP/IP components, setting values in the TCP/IP -> LAN card component sets those same values in the TCP/IP -> Dial-Up Adapter component. If you try to set the TCP/IP values in the TCP/IP -> Dial-Up Adapter component, you will be warned that you should set these values in the DUN connectoid. You won't get a similar warning if you try to set the TCP/IP values in the TCP/IP -> LAN card component, although you should.

For instructions on setting up TCP/IP for your network adapter, turn to "Configuring the TCP/IP stack for a network adapter" later in this chapter.

If you have both a LAN TCP/IP connection and a DUN TCP/IP connection, you need to make other provisions to deal correctly with routing. Turn to "Setting up your own routes" later in the chapter.

Speeding up file transfers

If your file transfer rates are in the neighborhood of 1000 to 1500 bytes per second on a 28.8 Kbps modem, you might be able to speed things up by adding the MaxMTU value to your Registry. One way to check out your file transfer rates is to use the System Monitor and display the bytes written to your hard disk per second as you download a large file. You should expect file transfer rates of around 3000 bytes per second on 28.8 Kbps modems.

STEPS

Setting a MaxMTU Value

Step 1. Click Regedit.exe in your \Windows folder. Navigate down to HKEY_LOCAL_MACHINE\Enum\Root\Net.

Step 2. Net will have one or more subkeys numbered 0000, 0001, and so on. Highlight each subkey until you find the one that has DeviceDesc set to "Dial-Up Adapter".

Step 3. In the left pane, highlight the subkey Bindings under the subkey you found in step 2. In the right pane, note the four-digit number immediately to the right of MSTCP\.

Step 4. Navigate to HKEY_LOCAL_MACHINE\Enum\NetWork\MSTCP. Highlight the four digit number subkey under MSTCP that corresponds to the one you found in step 3.

Step 5. In the right pane there will be a string named Driver with a four-digit number to the right of NetTrans\. Note this number.

Step 6. Navigate to HKEY_LOCAL_MACHINE\System\CurrentControlSet\Services\Class\NetTrans\.

Step 7. Under NetTrans, highlight the key whose value matches the one you found in step 5.

Step 8. Right-click the right pane. Choose New, String Value. Type the string name **MaxMTU**.

Step 9 Double-click the string name MaxMTU in the right pane. Enter the value **576**. Click OK, and exit the Registry.

Step 10. Restart Windows 98.

Undocumented

The default value for MaxMTU is 1500. John Navas, at the Navas Group, recommends setting the MaxMTU parameter to a value of 576 for PPP connections. You can check out his site, which specializes in information about modems at http://www.aimnet.com/~jnavas/modem/faq.html.

Undocumented

You can also set the value of RWIN to further speed up transfer rates under some circumstances. Take the following steps:

STEPS

Setting RWIN

Step 1. Click Regedit.exe in your \Windows folder. Navigate down to HKEY_LOCAL_MACHINE\System\CurrentControlSet\Services\ VXD\MSTCP\.

Step 2. Right-click the right pane. Choose New, String Value. Type the string name **DefaultRcvWindow**.

Step 3 Double-click the string name DefaultRcvWindow in the right pane. Enter a value. 2144 is the default value. Click OK, and exit the Registry.

If you want further information about how to set RWIN and other parameters for speeding up file transfers, visit http://www.cerberus-sys.com/~belleisl/ mtu_mss_rwin.html.

There are also little freeware and shareware packages that let you tune these values. Check out TweakDUN at http://www.sns-access.com/~netpro/ maxmtu.htm and MTU-Speed 3.08 at http://www.mjs.u-net.com.

Multiple TCP/IP settings for multiple connections

You can provide different TCP/IP settings for different connections if you have multiple Internet service providers.

These are the only TCP/IP settings that can be specific to a given connection to an Internet service provider:

■ Your IP address (fixed or dynamically assigned)

■ IP address for DNS or WINS server (fixed or dynamically assigned)

■ Use IP header compression or not

■ Use default gateway at Internet service provider or not

Follow the steps in the next section, "Dial-up connection to your service provider," to set these TCP/IP settings for each of your connections.

Dial-up connection to your service provider

Now that you have installed DUN and bound the TCP/IP stack to the Dial-Up Adapter, you are ready to create a DUN connection (a connectoid) that will call your service provider and establish the connection to your account. To do this, take the following steps:

STEPS

Creating a Service Provider Connection

Step 1. Click the Start button, point to Programs, Accessories, Communications, and then click Dial-Up Networking. (You can place a shortcut to DUN on your Desktop or in any other folder if you like. For details on creating and using shortcuts, see "Creating Shortcuts" in Chapter 10.)

Step 2. Click the Make New Connection icon in the Dial-Up Networking folder window. Enter the name of your service provider in the first dialog box of the Make New Connection Wizard. If you want to change the modem-specific characteristics for this connection, click the Configure button to display the Properties dialog box for the selected modem, make the desired changes, and click OK. Click the Next button, and enter the phone number your modem will dial to connect to the ISP. Click Next again, and then click Finish.

Step 3. Right-click the new connectoid in the DUN folder window. Click Properties to display the Properties dialog box for your connection to this service provider.

Step 4. Click the Server Types tab, as shown in Figure 18-1.

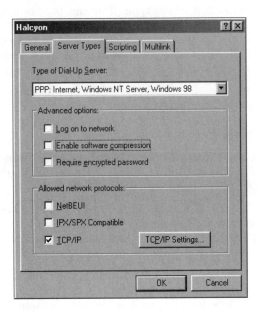

Figure 18-1: The Server Types tab of the Properties dialog box for your connection to the service provider.

(continued)

STEPS *(continued)*

Creating a Service Provider Connection

You don't need to mark the Log on to Network check box in a connectoid for an Internet service provider unless you are logging onto a Windows network over the Internet. Otherwise, it just slows things down.

Checking Enable Software Compression tells your connection software to negotiate compression with the remote computer. If your modem already handles hardware compression, then you don't really want to do this. Your modem may have already negotiated hardware compression with the server's modem (most do), so adding software compression slows things down.

If you mark the Require Encrypted Password check box, your computer sends an encrypted password directly to your server provider's computer. The ISP has to be able to decode the password before you can connect, and your password doesn't go out on the Net (where passwords can be stolen).

Require Encrypted Password only works with PPP. Many service providers can't deal with encrypted passwords, so check with yours before you mark this check box.

Step 5.   Choose the server type (from the Type of Dial-Up Server drop-down list at the top of the dialog box) that describes your account. If you have a SLIP account, you need to select either CSLIP: Unix Connection with IP Header Compression or SLIP: Unix Connection, depending on which type of SLIP account you have.

Step 6.   Clear the NetBEUI and IPX/SPX Compatible check boxes under Allowed Network Protocols. You only need TCP/IP to connect with your service provider, and clearing these boxes will speed things up a bit at connect time.

If you choose SLIP or CSLIP, these check boxes will be grayed out. You only use the TCP/IP protocol to communicate to a Unix server.

Step 7.   Click the TCP/IP Settings button to set the specific TCP/IP settings for this connection. The values that you enter in the TCP/IP Settings dialog box (see Figure 18-2) are those that you received from your Internet service provider.

Step 8.   If your computer's IP address is fixed, mark the Specify an IP Address option button, and then type your IP address in the IP Address field. If your IP address is dynamically assigned, mark the Server Assigned IP Address option button. (If you have a TIA account, your IP address will be fixed. If you have a PPP account, it will be dynamically assigned. If you have a SLIP account, it could be either fixed or dynamically assigned.)

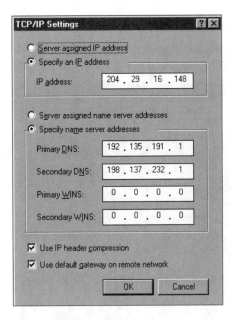

Figure 18-2: The TCP/IP Settings dialog box. These settings are specific to this connection to an individual Internet service provider.

Step 9. If your service provider gave you one or more IP addresses for their DNS or WINS server(s), mark the Specify Name Server Addresses option button, and enter the IP addresses in the four fields in the middle of the dialog box. If your service provider dynamically assigns the IP addresses of their servers, mark the Server Assigned Name Server Addresses option button.

Step 10. If you have a TIA account, clear the Use IP Header Compression check box. Click OK in the TCP/IP Settings dialog box. Click OK again in the Properties dialog box.

Step 11. Click the Configure button in the General tab of the Properties dialog box for your service provider. This brings up the Properties dialog box associated with your modem and this connection. Click the Options tab, as shown in Figure 18-3.

Step 12. If your service provider requires that you manually log in before you start your session, you will need to check Bring Up Terminal Window After Dialing. This will be the case if you have a SLIP account or a PPP account without PAP or CHAP and you are not using the scripting utility.

(continued)

STEPS *(continued)*

Creating a Service Provider Connection

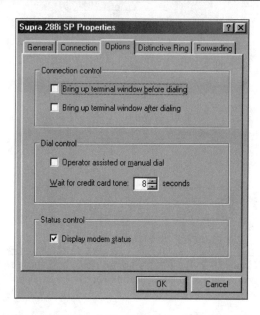

Figure 18-3: The Options tab of the Properties dialog box for your modem and connection.

If you are going to use the scripting utility, you normally want to leave this check box cleared because the scripting utility doesn't need the terminal window opened by this setting. However, when you are opening a new account at a service provider that requires a manual log on, you might want to mark this check box temporarily. That way, you can make sure that the commands that you enter are correct before you try using the script that you have edited to contain these commands.

Step 13. Make any other changes you think are necessary in the Properties dialog box associated with the modem and this connection. Then click the OK button, and click OK again to close the Properties dialog box for the service provider connection.

You are now ready to connect to your service provider. If you have a SLIP account or a PPP account without PAP or CHAP and you want to automate the connection with the scripting utility, you still have a little bit of work to do. See the section entitled "Automating your DUN logon" later in this chapter.

Saving your DUN connectoid passwords

You may find that the Save Password check box is grayed out when you click a DUN connectoid. This means that you can't save your password for this service provider connection, so you have to type your password every time you call them up. This can be quite irritating.

Undocumented

There are four possible causes for this problem:

1. You haven't installed either Client for Microsoft Networks or Client for NetWare Networks.

2. Your Windows startup is configured to ask you for a password (to identify you to the computer), and you clicked Cancel or pressed the Esc key when the logon box was displayed.

3. You have a corrupted password file.

4. You haven't enabled share-level access.

The cure to the first problem is easy. Install one of the above-named clients using the Network icon in your Control Panel. (Click the Network icon, and click the Add button. In the Select Network Component Type dialog box, highlight Client and click the Add button. In the Select Network Client dialog box, highlight Microsoft on the left side of the dialog box, highlight Client for Microsoft Networks or Client for NetWare Networks on the right, click OK, and then click OK again.)

Regarding the second problem, Windows 98 won't save your DUN passwords unless it knows who you are. If you log on with a Cancel, it won't save your passwords. You should log on as yourself, that is, type a user name in the logon box.

The solution to the third problem is more complicated. If you think your password file is corrupted, rename the *pwl* files in your \Windows folder, and then shut down and restart Windows 98. You will have to build your list of passwords from scratch. The earliest version of the Windows 95 Service Pack 1 corrupted password files. You can also check Don Lebow's Generic DUN Password Saving Advice web page at http://www.maui.net/~dml/dunpass.html for the latest approach to the problem.

To fix the fourth problem, click the Network icon in the Control Panel, click the Access Control tab, and mark the Share-Level Access Control option button.

Calling Your Service Provider

Now that you have created a connection to your service provider, you are ready to make the connection.

STEPS

Connecting to Your Service Provider

Step 1. Click the new connectoid in your DUN folder window. The Connect To dialog box appears on your Desktop, as shown in Figure 18-4. If you like, you can make this dialog box disappear by choosing Connections, Settings in the Dial-Up Networking folder window and clearing the Prompt for Information Before Dialing check box.

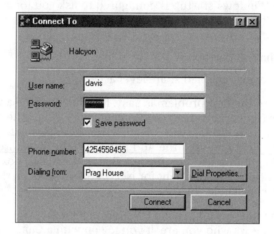

Figure 18-4: The Connect To dialog box. You don't need to use the User Name and Password fields unless you have a PPP account with PAP or CHAP. Click the Connect button to have the modem start dialing up your service provider.

Step 2. Enter your logon name and password and click the Save Password check box if you would rather not type your password every time. User names and passwords are case sensitive. Be sure you type them correctly.

Step 3. Click the Connect button to direct your modem to dial into your service provider and make a connection. Once the connection is made, you are on the Internet and ready to run Winsock-compatible Internet applications. If your account requires that you manually log in, a terminal window will be displayed first, as shown in Figure 18-5.

Step 4. If you need to specify your account type to your service provider, type **PPP** or **SLIP** and press Enter. When prompted by your service provider's computer, type your logon name and password. Again, your logon name and password are case sensitive. If you have a TIA account, you will log on first and then type **TIA** at the shell prompt.

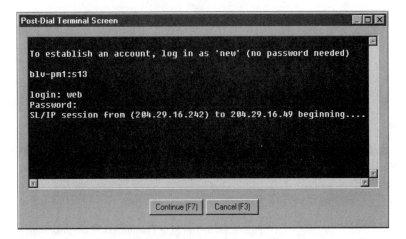

Figure 18-5: The Post-Dial Terminal Screen. Type **PPP** or **SLIP** and press Enter if your service provider requires that you first specify your account type. Type your logon name and password when prompted. If you have a SLIP account, wait for your dynamically assigned IP address to be displayed and write it down so that you can remember it for a few seconds.

Step 5. If you have a SLIP account with dynamically assigned IP addresses, your IP address will appear. Write it down; you will need it in the next step, and this terminal window is going to disappear. Click the Continue button or press F7.

(If you configured your TCP/IP stack for a fixed IP address that matches the first two or three numbers of your dynamically assigned one, you will only have to worry about typing the last number or two in the next step.)

Step 6. If you have a SLIP account, the dialog box shown in Figure 18-6 will be displayed after step 5 to let you enter your IP address. Make sure you type your IP address exactly as it was displayed in the terminal window. If you get it wrong, your Winsock-compatible Internet applications will not work.

Step 7. If you have a TIA account, you will see the dialog box shown in Figure 18-6. If you earlier specified a fixed IP address in the TCP/IP Settings dialog box, this address will be displayed here. You need to change this IP address if you were prompted to do so after you typed **TIA** in the terminal window.

(continued)

Connecting to Your Service Provider

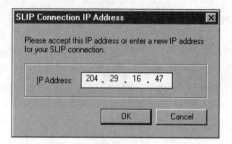

Figure 18-6: The SLIP Connection IP Address dialog box. Type your dynamically assigned IP address exactly as displayed in your terminal window.

If you are using the scripting utility, you can omit steps 4 through 7.

If you are using Windows Messaging, you can make the connection with your service provider just by clicking the Inbox icon on your Desktop (if you have configured the mode for transferring Internet messages as Automatic — see "Internet mail properties" in Chapter 20). If you have configured Windows Messaging for Remote Mail, you need to click the Inbox icon, and then choose Tools, Deliver Now.

You can configure Microsoft's Internet Explorer, Netscape's Network Navigator, Microsoft's Outlook Express, NetMeeting, and other Internet-specific applications to automatically call your service provider by invoking your DUN connectoid. To do this, click the Internet icon in the Control Panel, and click the Connection tab in the Internet Properties dialog box. Mark the Connect to the Internet Using a Modem option button, and then click the Settings button. Select the connection you want to use in the drop-down list at the top of the Dial-Up Settings dialog box, and then click OK twice.

Notice in step 3 above that you had to click the Connect button. Once you have everything set up, you can eliminate this box altogether. In the Dial-Up Networking folder window, choose Connections, Settings to display the General tab of the Dial-Up Networking dialog box and clear the Prompt for Information Before Dialing check box.

Automating your DUN logon

The Windows 98 scripting facility can run a script that you create for a specific connection. This script can send your logon name, password, and account type. It can also capture a dynamically assigned IP address and send it back to your Internet service provider.

To edit a script, right-click a DUN connectoid, click Properties, click the Scripting tab, and then browse to find the script file. Sample script files are stored in your \Program Files\Accessories folder. You can edit a copy of one of these script files (they have an extension of *scp*) to meet the requirements of your Internet service provider. Just click the Edit button in the Scripting tab after you have chosen a script file.

Undocumented

Notice that Microsoft doesn't use the *scr* extension for its script files, as everyone else in the world does. This is because it already uses this extension for its screen saver files. Windows 98 creates an association with the *scr* extension and the screen saver tester. Click a script file with an *scr* extension, and Windows 98 will try to play it as a screen saver. (In "Creating and Editing File Types and Actions" in Chapter 13, we show you how to solve this problem for any script file you have that ends in *scr*.)

Making sure you have a good connection

It's easy to check out your DUN connection to your service provider (just click its DUN connectoid). If you are having connection problems, you can try a few things in the Server Types tab of its Properties dialog box (right-click the connectoid and click Properties). Make sure you have the correct account type specified in the drop-down list, disable software compression, and, if you have a SLIP account, switch from CSLIP to SLIP or vice versa.

You can also try using the ping command. Ping sends out a request to see if a certain computer at a given address is indeed there. After you have dialed up your server provider, open a Windows DOS session. Type **ping 198.105.232.1.** This is the IP address for ftp.microsoft.com (the FTP server at Microsoft). If ping works, your TCP/IP stack and connection to the Internet is working.

Tip

You can also use ping to test your DNS server connection. To do this, try to ping to an IP address, and then ping the name that goes with that IP address. For example, type **ping 198.105.232.1** and, if that works, type **ping ftp.microsoft.com**. If both pings work, you know that you are correctly connected to a DNS server.

If the first case works but the second doesn't, then your DNS is set up wrong. If the first fails, either you are not talking to the network or the network doesn't know who you are.

Creating a connection log file

You can generate a log file that will record the progress of your attempt to connect to your service provider. This file can help pinpoint problems. To generate a log file, take the following steps:

STEPS

Creating a Connection Log File

Step 1. Click the Start button, point to Settings, and then click Control Panel.

Step 2. Click the Network icon. Highlight Dial-Up Adapter, and click the Properties button.

Step 3. Click the Advanced tab, highlight Record a Log File in the Property list, and choose Yes in the Value field.

Step 4. Click OK in both the Dial-Up Adapter Properties dialog box and the Network dialog box.

Step 5. Click your connectoid in the Dial-Up Networking folder window.

A file named Ppplog.txt will be created in your \Windows folder when you take step 5. You can review this file after you attempt to make your connection. Place a shortcut to this file on your Desktop so that you can get to it easily.

Disabling IP header compression

If you have a PPP account, you might experience connection problems that you can cure by disabling IP header compression. To do this, take the following steps:

STEPS

Disabling IP Header Compression

Step 1. Click the Start button, point to Settings, and then click Control Panel.

Step 2. Click the Network icon. Highlight Dial-Up Adapter, and click the Properties button.

Step 3. Highlight Use IP Header Compression in the Property list. Choose No in the Value field.

Step 4. Click both OK buttons.

Other problems with DUN TCP/IP connections

In the "Compatible protocols" section of Chapter 17, we spoke about one problem that causes you to receive the error message "Dial-up Networking cannot negotiate a compatible set of protocols. Please check your network settings. . ." Other sources of this problem still exist. Michael Santovec, a regular contributor to the Microsoft Windows newsgroups, created this list of possible causes for the problem and recommended actions:

1. Your Internet service provider may be experiencing temporary problems. You should try again later.

2. Some Internet service providers can't handle software compression. Right-click your connectoid in the Dial-Up Networking folder window. Click Properties, click the Server Types tab, and clear the Enable Software Compression check box.

3. Make sure that your connectoid only uses TCP/IP to connect to your Internet service provider. Right-click your connectoid in the Dial-Up Networking folder window. Click Properties, click the Server Types tab, and make sure that only the TCP/IP check box is marked under Allowed Network Protocols.

4. Make sure that your modem uses hardware flow control rather than software flow control. Right-click your connectoid in the Dial-Up Networking folder window, click Properties, and then click the Configure button in the General tab. Click the Connection tab, click the Advanced button, and mark the Hardware (RTS/CTS) option button.

5. If you have an external modem and don't have a 16550 UART chip in the COM port that the modem connects to, then you should not use FIFO. (This doesn't apply to internal modems, since they have the 16550 UART built in.) Also, if you do have a 16550 UART and have FIFO enabled, adjusting the buffer sizes may help. To disable FIFO or adjust the buffer sizes, right-click your connectoid in the Dial-Up Networking folder window, click Properties, and then click the Configure button in the General tab. Click the Connection tab, and then click the Port Settings button. In the Advanced Port Settings dialog box, clear the check box to disable FIFO, or drag the sliders to adjust the buffers.

Check out Michael's Windows help web site at http://pages.prodigy.net/michael_santovec/techhelp.htm for links to other helpful web pages.

If you want keep abreast of the latest problems and fixes for Microsoft TCP/IP connections to the Internet, check out http://www.technotronic.com/windows.shtml.

Connecting to CompuServe

CompuServe used to use a version of Air Mosaic that comes with its own Winsock.dll file. If you have installed Air Mosaic, make sure that its accompanying Winsock.dll hasn't overwritten the one that comes with Windows 98. You can look in the \Windows folder and check the file dates to be sure you have the right one.

The problem of incompatible Winsock.dll files used to be quite common, and you want to be sure your Winsock-compatible Internet applications are not using the wrong Winsock.dll. You only want one Winsock.dll on your computer, and you can search your hard disks with Find to make sure this is the case.

CompuServe's software comes with Windows 98, and all you have to do to connect is click its icon in the Online Services folder on your Desktop. However, you may want to ignore all of that and treat CompuServe as just another Internet service provider (with a worldwide selection of local phone numbers).

If you want to use CompuServe as a regular ISP without all of their client software, take the following steps:

STEPS

Connecting to CompuServe with Internet Explorer

Step 1.   Click the Start button, point to Programs, Accessories, Communications, and then click Dial-Up Networking.

Step 2.   Click the Make New Connection icon to start the Make New Connection Wizard.

Step 3.   Type **CompuServe** as the name of the connectoid, and click the Next button.

Step 4.   Type your regular local CompuServe connection number. CompuServe has added 56 Kbps lines, so if you have a 56 Kbps modem, you might try that number. Click Next. Click Finish.

Step 5.   Right-click your new CompuServe connectoid in the Dial-Up Networking folder window, and click Properties.

Step 6.   Click the Configure button, and then click the Connection tab. Under Connection Preferences, make sure the communication parameters are the default choices — 8, None, 1. Click OK.

Step 7.   Click the Server Types tab, and then click the TCP/IP Settings button.

Step 8.   Choose the following parameters in the TCP/IP Settings dialog box:

Server Assigned IP Address

Specify Name Server Addresses

Primary DNS - 149.174.211.5

Secondary DNS - 149.174.213.5

Use IP Header Compression

Use Default Gateway on Remote Network

Click OK

Step 9.   In the Server Types tab, make sure the server type is PPP (the default). Under Advanced Options, clear all three check boxes:

Log On to Network, Enable Software Compression, and Require Encrypted Password. Under Allowed Network Protocols, mark TCP/IP, and clear NetBEUI and IPX/SPX Compatible. Click OK.

Step 10. Click the Scripting tab, click the Browse button, browse to Cis.scp in the \Program Files\Accessories folder, and click OK.

Step 11. Click the Edit button in the Scripting tab to open Cis.scp in Notepad, and edit the file to make any changes necessary for your connection to CompuServe. Save the file and close Notepad. Click OK.

Step 12. Click the Internet icon in the Control Panel. Click the Connection tab, and then select CompuServe in the drop-down list. Click OK. This connects the Internet Explorer to the CompuServe connectoid.

Step 13. Click your CompuServe connectoid in the Dial-Up Networking folder window to display the Connect To dialog box. Enter your CompuServe account number in the User Name field, and your CompuServe password in the Password field. Mark the Save Password check box.

You have created a connectoid that logs you into CompuServe as an Internet service provider. You can click the connectoid to make the connection, or you can click the Internet Explorer icon on your Desktop to make the connection and start the Internet Explorer.

The CompuServe connection is similar to other Internet service provider connections, except that it lacked POP3 and SMTP mail servers until late in 1997. You can run other Internet application software on it using the Windows 98 Winsock.dll. And you can run Netscape Navigator if you like; you don't have to run Internet Explorer.

Creating a DUN connectoid for your Netcom account

You can use the instructions in the "Dial-up connection to your service provider" section earlier in this chapter to create a new DUN connectoid with the name Netcom. To make it specific to your Netcom account, you'll need to set the following properties:

Server type is PPP (the default)

IP address is dynamically assigned (as is true of all PPP accounts)

Assign the primary DNS server address as 199.182.120.203

Assign the secondary DNS server address as 199.182.120.202

Put a pound sign (#) before your user name

Internet Through Your LAN

As we mentioned at the beginning of this chapter, you can also access the Internet through your local area network. In fact, you can have Unix, NetWare, Windows 98, Windows 95, and Windows NT servers on your LAN and access them through your TCP/IP stack—no need to dial them up. Your LAN becomes an Intranet.

Tip

You can place a World Wide Web server on a local server and publish your own home pages internally. Computer users throughout your business can surf the local net, using copies of Internet Explorer or Netscape Communicator to access local home pages that are updated to provide corporate information. If you install a POP3 and SMTP mail server, you can handle e-mail as though it were any other Internet mail.

Of course, your system administrator can provide access to the Internet (in addition to the Intranet) through a server over any level of telephone access to some type of Internet service provider. (When companies do this, they often set up a firewall to keep overly inquisitive outsiders from accessing internal corporate information.)

You or your system administrator will configure your computer in a manner similar to that described earlier in this chapter in the section entitled "Installing an Internet dial-up connection." If you have a LAN connection, your TCP/IP stack is bound to your local area network card. Your system administrator can set up a local DHCP server to resolve addresses. You won't need a Dial-Up Adapter, except for Direct Cable Connection.

If you have TCP/IP bound to your Dial-Up Adapter and your network card and there is no DHCP server in your local area, your computer will pause every now and then when it's trying to find something or somebody. If this gets annoying, you will need to unbind TCP/IP from your network card (or get a DHCP server locally).

Tip

A Windows 98 computer set up as a Dial-Up Networking server can't route TCP/IP. So you can't call in from home (to this computer) by using the TCP/IP protocol bound to your Dial-Up Adapter at your home computer and expect to be able to connect over TCP/IP to your Intranet on your LAN at work.

A Windows NT server set up as a RAS (or DUN) server can take your TCP/IP call and connect you to your company's Intranet, and, through one of your company's servers, to its Internet service provider.

Configuring the TCP/IP stack for a network adapter

If you have a LAN connection over a network card to a TCP/IP network, you should turn to "Choosing a networking protocol" in Chapter 24 for additional information on local area networks.

You can configure the TCP/IP stack for a LAN connection using the following steps:

STEPS

Setting the Default TCP/IP Properties for a LAN Connection

Step 1.   Click the Start button, point to Settings, and then click Control Panel.

Step 2.   Click the Network icon. Highlight TCP/IP in the Network dialog box and click the Properties button.

Step 3.   Click the DNS Configuration tab (shown in Figure 18-7). If your LAN has a DHCP server that dynamically supplies the DNS IP addresses, don't change anything under this tab. Otherwise, mark the Enable DNS option button, and then type your host name, your service provider's domain name, and the IP address of the DNS server you will use. Click the Add button to put the DNS server's IP address in the list. If you have multiple addresses, enter them in the order that you want them searched. Be sure to click the Add button after you type each one.

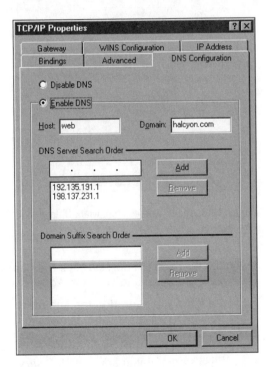

Figure 18-7: The DNS Configuration tab. Fill in the fields for your host name, your service provider's domain name, and the DNS server's IP address.

(continued)

STEPS *(continued)*

Setting the Default TCP/IP Properties for a LAN Connection

Step 4. Click the IP Address tab (shown in Figure 18-8). Mark the Obtain an IP Address Automatically option button if your network has a DHCP server that provides you with a dynamic IP address. If you have a fixed IP address, mark the Specify an IP Address option button, and enter the IP address and the subnet mask.

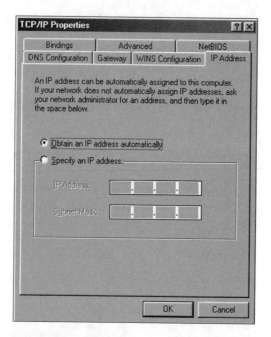

Figure 18-8: The IP Address tab. Mark Obtain an IP Address Automatically if your network has a DHCP server.

Step 5. If you have a fixed IP address, click the Gateway tab, enter your Gateway IP address, and click the Add button.

Step 6. Click the WINS Configuration tab and make sure that the Disable WINS Resolution option button is marked unless your network has a WINS server. If you have a WINS server, but not a DHCP server, mark Enable WINS Resolution and type the IP address for your WINS server. If you have a DHCP server, mark the Use DHCP for WINS Resolution option button.

Step 7. Click OK to close the TCP/IP Properties dialog box.

Step 8. Restart your computer.

If your local area network uses a DHCP server to assign IP addresses for your DNS server and for users, you really don't have to make any changes in the TCP/IP settings. This gives you the most flexibility, because addresses can by dynamically assigned regardless of how your computer connects to the Internet or Intranet.

Windows 98 will automatically and by default assign an IP address to the network card in your computer. This allows you to connect to your Intranet when you first plug in the cable to the network card. You don't need an assigned static IP address, or a DHCP server to provide a dynamically assigned one.

TCP/IP will automatically assign an IP address unless you reconfigure its settings. (Click the Network icon in your Control Panel, select TCP/IP, click the Properties button, and click the IP Address tab.) The way it does this is to first search for a DHCP server on your network. If it doesn't find one, it assigns an IP address and then checks for conflicts, changing the address if it finds any. This allows you to get up on the network without having to assign IP addresses first. If your computer later finds a DHCP server, it will use the dynamically assigned IP address.

TCP/IP conflicts between the LAN card and the Dial-Up Adapter

If you normally connect your portable to your TCP/IP LAN at your office and then you take your portable home and call in to your office network, your computer at home may try to send the network traffic out the network card and not over the modem. This occurs if you have configured your TCP/IP settings to use the DHCP server at the office to resolve IP addresses.

To solve this problem, you can run Winipcfg (see "Displaying your TCP/IP settings" later in this chapter) after you have made the connection with your office network, and click the Release All button to release assigned IP addresses. If this doesn't work and your network adapter is a PC Card, pull it out of its slot on the side of the portable.

If you have an internal network card, you'll need to disable the network card by marking the Disable in This Hardware Profile check box in the General tab of the Properties dialog box for your network adapter. (To display this dialog box, right-click your My Computer icon and click Properties. Click the Device Manager tab, click the plus sign next to Network Adapters, and double-click your network adapter card icon.)

If you do this, you will have to enable the network card the next time you connect to the network. A way around this is to set up two hardware profiles (one for home and one for the office). You can then disable the network card in the home profile.

Hardware profiles are not supposed to be necessary if you have plug and play hardware (both cards and the system board). In this case, it doesn't quite work out. To see how to set up multiple hardware profiles, turn to "Hardware Profiles" in Chapter 25.

Setting up your own routes

If you connect to a TCP/IP network locally through a network card, and at the same time you call out through a modem to an Internet service provider, you now have two routes and Microsoft's TCP/IP stack can only handle one at a time. The route assigned to the last connection made is the active route.

If your LAN network resources are behind a firewall, you lose the ability to see them if you make a connection with a service provider after connecting to the LAN. You can use the *route add* command (discussed in "TCP/IP Utilities" later in this chapter) to create a table of resources locations (IP addresses) that are associated with the IP address of the LAN gateway. If you do this, you'll still be able to access your LAN resources.

STEPS

Associating a Resource Address with a Gateway Address

Step 1. Connect your computer to your Intranet. Choose Start, Run, type **Winipcfg** (see "Displaying your TCP/IP settings" later in this chapter), and click OK. Read the Default Gateway value, and leave the IP Configuration dialog box open.

Step 2. Open up a new text file and add the following line to it:

```
Route add gateway-IP-address DNS-IP-address
```

The *gateway-IP-address* is the value that you read in step 1, and the *DNS-IP-address* is the address of the DNS service on your local area network. If you don't have a DNS server, use a DHCP server IP address instead.

Step 3. Save the file, and then rename it with a *bat* extension. Click it to run it.

Step 4. Dial into an Internet service provider on the same computer. Click the Renew All button in the IP Configuration dialog box to confirm that your IP address and gateway IP address have changed and are now the same value.

Step 5. Open a DOS window and use the ping command to access a LAN resource. For example:

```
ping www.localintranetserver.com
```

Connecting a Windows 98 network to the Internet

You can configure a peer-to-peer network of Windows 98 computers to connect to the Internet without using a Windows NT, Unix, or other type of server. One of the Windows 98 computers acts as the Internet connection server.

Qbik Software's WinGate (available at http://www.deerfield.com/wingate/) provides the gateway to the Internet and runs on the Windows 98 computer that provides the Internet connection for the rest of the computers on the network. You have to connect all the computers using network cards and configure the TCP/IP stacks on the other Windows 98 computers to the gateway computer.

You can download specific instructions on how to configure this type of Internet connection from http://www.windows98.com/connect/lansing.html.

Here are a few other options for Windows 98 TCP/IP routing packages (as ferreted out by John Buchan):

Table 18-1   Windows 98 TCP/IP Routers

Site	Address
Open Sesame	http://www.csm-usa.com
IP Route	http://www.mischler.com/iproute/
Firedoor	http://www.ozemail.com.au/~equival
NAT95	http://willow.canberra.edu.au/~chrisc/nat.html
NetProxy	http://www.grok.co.uk/netproxy/

Microsoft Network (not MSN) over the Internet

The Internet is a TCP/IP network. An Intranet is a TCP/IP local area network. You can treat the Internet as though it were a local area TCP/IP network. It's a really slow local area network if you are connecting to it through anything other than a T1 line.

There are Windows NT and Windows 98 computers connected to the Internet that you can access as though they were connected to a Microsoft Windows network, and there is a Winserver that provides DHCP name resolution so that you can connect to these computers.

To find out more about using the Internet in this semi-strange manner, check out http://www.windows98.com/connect/peercon.html and http://www.winserve.com/.

TCP/IP Utilities

Microsoft ships some low-level TCP/IP utilities with Windows 98. Most of these utilities are DOS-based — which is kinda weird. Well, Unix and DOS are text-based, and TCP/IP is down there below the user interface, so it makes some sense. Microsoft also provides one Windows-based TCP/IP utility.

Table 18-2 lists the TCP/IP utilities you get with Windows 98:

Table 18-2 TCP/IP Utilities

Command	What It Does
DOS Utilities	
Arp	Displays and modifies the IP-to-Physical (Ethernet card) address translation tables used by address resolution protocol (ARP). If you're dialing into the Internet over your own modem, you won't be using this utility.
Ftp	File Transfer Protocol. Allows you to log onto other computers on the Internet (perhaps as anonymous) and download or upload files. We feature much better Windows-based FTP programs on the *Windows 98 Secrets* CD-ROM and suggest that you use them instead.
Nbtstat	Displays protocol statistics and current TCP/IP connections using NBT (NetBIOS over TCP/IP).
Netstat	Displays protocol statistics and current TCP/IP connections.
Ping	Checks for a connection to a remote computer. For example, type **ping ftp.microsoft.com**. We suggest you use FTP Explorer, or Internet Neighborhood, as discussed in "Network file system" instead.
Route	Manually controls network routing tables. Routes added to the table are dynamic and need to be re-established every time your reboot the computer. You can create a batch file with the proper commands and then put a *pif* file that points to it in your StartUp folder.
Tracert	Displays the route taken to a remote computer. For example, type **tracert ftp.microsoft.com**. If you aren't connected, your default DUN connectoid is called. Use Ws_ping instead.
Windows Utility	
Winipcfg	Displays current TCP/IP network configurations. You don't use it to change these configuration; for that you go to the TCP/IP Properties dialog box (accessed through the Network icon in the Control Panel).

To find out how to use the DOS-based TCP/IP applications, open a DOS Windows session and type the command name followed by -?. Winipcfg is stored in the \Windows folder. You can create a shortcut to it and put the shortcut in a folder that you use for Internet utilities. (You can also do this for the DOS-based utilities. You'll find them in the \Windows folder as well.)

Displaying your TCP/IP settings

You can easily use Winipcfg to display your current TCP/IP configuration. Winipcfg.exe is by default stored in your \Windows folder. If you haven't created a shortcut to it, just run it by clicking your Start button, clicking Run, typing **Winipcfg**, and clicking OK. The results are shown in Figure 18-9:

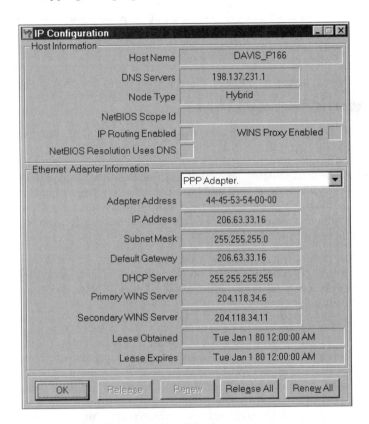

Figure 18-9: The IP Configuration dialog box.

Your adapter address is a number hard coded into a network card if your TCP/IP protocol is bound to a network card. If your TCP/IP protocol is bound to your Dial-Up Adapter (your modem, in other words), the number is meaningless because modems don't have an address hard coded in.

If your IP address is dynamically assigned, this field and the subnet mask field will be filled with zeros. If you have a dynamically assigned IP address from a DHCP server, you can get a new one by clicking the Renew All button.

As soon as you make a DUN connection (even with DCC), you are assigned an IP address. To find out what it is, run Winipcfg and click the Renew All button.

Telnet

Windows 98 comes with a reasonably good Telnet client. Telnet lets you log onto a remote computer (or even your service provider's computer) as a terminal (like HyperTerminal). You can then run the Unix software running on that remote computer.

This might seem like a step backwards, but it is handy at times to be able to get the Internet out of the way of talking to a specific computer. Telnet.exe is stored in the \Windows folder. Create a shortcut to it and place it in an Internet folder.

Network file system

Tip

Windows 98 doesn't include a network file system (NFS) such as the installable file system for Unix. The directories and file systems on Unix computers don't look like the file systems on Windows 98 computers. It's nice to have a translation layer that both makes them look like VFAT, the Windows 98 file system, and adds drag and drop between file systems. That way, you can just drag a file from a remote Unix computer and drop it in your local folder. You can use FTP Explorer found at http://www.windows98.com to provide some of this functionality.

A no-cost program called Samba that runs on a Sun server allows Windows 98 computers to access the files on the Sun server as though they were FAT-type files. You can get information about Samba at http://lake.canberra.edu.au/pub/samba/samba.html.

By default, a Samba server can't work with encrypted passwords. The Windows 98 SMB redirector does not send an unencrypted password unless you add a Registry entry to enable unencrypted passwords. This can cause problems connecting to Windows 98 share-mode servers if the share in question has no password. To enable the Windows 98 client to send an unencrypted user password, use your Registry editor to add a new value to the Registry key HKEY_LOCAL_MACHINE\System\CurrentControlSet\Services\VXD\VNETSUP. Right-click the right pane of the Registry editor after you have navigated to this key, click DWORD, and name the value EnablePlainTextPassword. Double-click this name and give it a value of 1 (default is 0).

You might also try ICE NFS, which provides a virtual drive for Windows 98. It allows Windows 98 to mount drives on other machines. You'll find it at http://www.jriver.com/ice.nfs.html.

If you want an FTP client that is fully integrated into the Explorer, check out Internet Neighborhood. It is a Windows 98 shell extension for browsing remote FTP sites as if they were folders and files on your computer. You'll find it at http://www.knowareinc.com/in32.html.

This shareware program, available in a single-user registered version for $26.50 from KnoWare Inc. of Baltimore, Maryland, integrates itself into the Windows Explorer and makes file transfers intuitive. Unlike other FTP programs that use their own interfaces, Internet Neighborhood uses the Windows Explorer window as a built-in interface. FTP sites show up as folders underneath an Internet Neighborhood icon in your My Computer tree. Since Internet Neighborhood is a 32-bit shell extension to the Explorer, it is loaded into memory by Windows when needed.

Just as Microsoft's Network Neighborhood icon shows subfolders for any computers that reside on a network with your PC, Internet Neighborhood shows folders for FTP sites. You can drag and drop files from an FTP site to your hard drive, and do the same to upload your files to an FTP site (if you have access rights). This process works in exactly the same way as dragging any files in the Explorer.

There's little or nothing to learn. You can also use the Windows Clipboard to upload and download files. Just like files on your hard drive, files on an FTP site can be copied and pasted where you want them. For large files, Internet Neighborhood displays an estimate of the time it will take to complete the transfer, including the percentage completed and number of bytes transferred.

Internet Neighborhood includes an FTP Wizard to make it simple to add FTP sites. For example, if you want to download files from ftp.netscape.com, specifying this site in the FTP Wizard immediately makes it available from within the Explorer window. Internet Neighborhood works with firewalls, if your company has one. The FTP Wizard includes settings to access your company's type of firewall, to establish a connection to the firewall computer, and to run a User without Login command.

In addition to single-user licenses, Internet Neighborhood is also available in a 50-user license for $295, and an unlimited-user site license for $495. In case you happen to need to uninstall Internet Neighborhood, read the uninstall directions at http://www.knowareinc.com/uninstall.html.

Summary

▶ Windows 98 supports three networking protocol stacks, one of which is TCP/IP (the protocol used by the Internet).

▶ Combine TCP/IP support with Dial-Up Networking, and Windows 98 gives you the tools you need to connect to the Internet.

▶ We help you secure the right kind of account with an Internet service provider.

▶ You need to get the right information from your service provider; we tell you what to ask for.

▶ We explain each of the steps for setting up your Windows 98 computer for Dial-Up Networking and TCP/IP support.

▶ We show you how to connect to your service provider and make sure that you've got a good connection.

Chapter 19

Outlook Express

In This Chapter

Outlook Express is a powerful program that combines an Internet e-mail client and a newsgroup reader. It evolved from Microsoft Internet Mail and News, which came with Internet Explorer 3.0. We show you how to:

▶ Immediately reconfigure Outlook Express to make it much easier to use

▶ Avoid giving your e-mail address to a SPAMer

▶ Let Outlook Express manage your Internet dial-up connection

▶ Format your messages using HTML

▶ Access multiple e-mail accounts and configure setups for different users

▶ Transfer your Windows Messaging or Eudora address book to your Windows Address Book

▶ Read the news offline

Outlook Express Is Configurable

Outlook Express has evolved from Microsoft Internet Mail and News into a powerful tool. Like many Microsoft operating system extensions, it provides a level of functionality that will work for most people. With an easy-to-use user interface, it introduces newcomers to the intricacies of newsgroups and Internet mail.

With a few configuration changes, Outlook Express lets you easily peruse and contribute to newsgroups. Outlook Express can connect to multiple news servers. Microsoft included this feature in the precursor to Outlook Express, Internet News, because it wanted you to be able to connect to Microsoft's own news server, which is limited to Microsoft support groups, as well as to the Usenet news server maintained by your own Internet service provider.

Microsoft provides two other e-mail tools in addition to Outlook Express: Windows Messaging, which is included on the Windows 98 CD-ROM, and Outlook, which is bundled with the Office suite. Because Microsoft chose to confuse us by using the name *Outlook* in the names of two different products, it's necessary to provide a bit of explanation.

Outlook grew out of Windows Messaging. It is an e-mail client for numerous propriety mail servers (including those originally installed at MSN and CompuServe) as well as for Internet-standard mail servers (SMTP and POP3). Outlook includes contact-management features beyond those available (or desired) in Outlook Express. It is a full MAPI client (which makes it both big and slow) and, like Windows Messaging, it does faxes. It has its own OLE-structured file system for storing all kinds of documents (unlike the simple one used by Outlook Express).

When first released, Outlook did not have many of the Internet capabilities of Outlook Express, which was designed as an Internet-standard e-mail client and newsgroup reader. It didn't support LDAP, IMAP, S/MIME, or HTML messages, for example. Outlook 98 includes these features.

We discuss Windows Messaging in the next chapter. Windows Messaging is included on the Windows 98 CD-ROM, but is not considered a part of Windows 98. Microsoft has placed it on the CD-ROM for those users who want the fax capability provided by Windows 95, but don't have Microsoft Office. It has not been upgraded since it was released as an upgrade to the Windows 95 Exchange client in 1996.

Windows Messaging lets you connect to your Microsoft postoffice box and Microsoft Mail, as well as to other propriety mail servers. It also can connect to the Internet mail servers and act as a pretty decent Internet e-mail client, but without any HTML formatting, encrypting, digital certificates, or IMAP4 support. Both Outlook and Windows Messaging work well in networked environments and can access shared address books on network servers.

Configuring Outlook Express

If you are connected to the Internet through a dial-up connection, you'll need to properly configure a DUN connectoid as described in Chapters 17 and 18. To use Outlook Express mail, you need to get the names of the SMTP and POP3 servers at your Internet service provider, as well as your e-mail address and e-mail password, your account name (user ID), and your logon password. In the Outlook Express window, choose Tools, Accounts, Add, Mail to start a version of the Internet Connection Wizard that will help you create an entry for your Internet mail account.

By default, the Windows 98 Internet Explorer uses Outlook Express as the mail tool when you click an e-mail address while viewing a web page. If you want to use another e-mail client (such as Outlook or Eudora) you can change this default behavior. Right-click the Internet Explorer icon on your Desktop, click Properties, click the Programs tab, and then display the Mail drop-down list. If you have another e-mail program installed on your computer, you can choose it here.

To read the articles (also called *messages* or *postings*) in newsgroups, you need to connect to a news server. Your Internet service provider probably maintains a Usenet news server. You can also connect to other news servers. The most likely name for your service provider's news server is news.*serviceprovidername*.com. We provide a list of places where you can find news servers near the end of this chapter in the "Access to public news servers" section.

To connect to a news server, choose Tools, Accounts, Add, News to start a version of the Internet Connection Wizard that will help you set up a news server account.

Changing Outlook Express options right away

We don't like the default configurations for Outlook Express — especially for the first time user. We suggest that you make a number of changes along with us.

Choose Tools, Options. Click the Read tab, and mark the Automatically Expand Conversation Threads check box, as shown in Figure 19-1. Click OK. Now you won't have to click the plus symbol repeatedly to follow a discussion thread, at the slight cost of seeing multiple entries in a thread that you might not be particularly interested in.

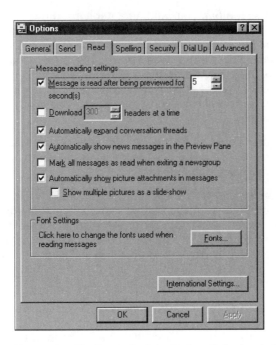

Figure 19-1: The Read tab of the Options dialog box in Outlook Express.

Tip

Choose Tools, Options, and click the General tab. Clear the Check for New Messages Every [   ] Minutes check box if you use a Dial-Up Networking connectoid and are only online for a limited amount of time during any one session.

If you have a dial-up connection, it is a bother to have Outlook Express dial up your Internet service provider every time you invoke it. You can work offline and then force a dial-up connection when you connect to the mail server to send and/or receive mail, or connect to a news server. Choose Tools, Options, click the Dial Up tab, and mark the Do Not Dial a Connection option button. Click OK.

Tip

Choose Tools, Accounts, Add, News to add additional news servers to your list. You'll want to add the msnews.microsoft.com news server. This is Microsoft's support news server. You'll find a basic level of supervision from Microsoft support personnel, peer-to-peer support, and help from Microsoft volunteers. The microsoft.public.inetexplorer.ie40.outlookexpress newsgroup provides the latest information about Outlook Express.

You can choose which news server is the default, or first-accessed server, by choosing Tools, Accounts, News, highlighting your news server account, and clicking the Set As Default button.

If you want people to contact you directly from your postings in newsgroups, type your e-mail address in the E-mail Address field in the General tab of the Properties dialog box for the news server. To do this, choose Tools, Accounts, highlight the news account, and then click the Properties button.

On the Outlook Express toolbar, you will find a Reply to Author button, which lets you send a response directly to the author of a message when you don't feel the need to respond on the newsgroup. You won't be able to send a private message if the author hasn't placed his or her e-mail address in the E-mail Address or Reply Address field. If you leave your Reply Address field blank, the address in your E-mail Address field is used. If you send mail from one address but want replies to go to another, then enter the second address in the Reply Address field.

Undocumented

If you don't want your address picked up by Usenet bots that scan Usenet newsgroups for addresses, then put a fake address in the Reply Address field, such as fakename@fakenet.net.

Choose Tools, Stationery, and click the Signature button. Enter at least a rudimentary "signature"—your name at least—in the Signature dialog box (see Figure 19-2). You can make a more elaborate signature later, but we suggest that you don't get carried away. Mark the Add This Signature to All Outgoing Messages check box. You can choose Insert, Signature in a New Message window to insert your signature when you write a message, but it's easier and more consistent to let the computer do it for you.

These steps add a signature to your e-mail messages. You can also add a signature (perhaps a different one) to your newsgroup messages. Choose Tools, Stationary, click the News tab, and click the Signature button.

A vCard (virtual business card) is a standard format for all your personal contact information. Outlook Express can import the information contained in vCards into its address book. Other software packages can read and write vCards, which allows users to exchange contact information easily.

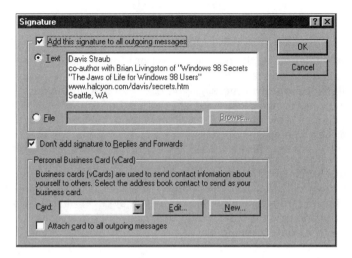

Figure 19-2: Mark the Add This Signature to All Outgoing Messages check box to add a signature to your e-mail messages.

If you want to include a vCard with your signature in e-mail messages, choose Tools, Stationary, and click the Signature button in the Mail tab. Click the New button in the Signature dialog box (see Figure 19-2) and create an entry for yourself in your address book. It's probably not a great idea to send your vCard to a newsgroup. If someone would like your contact information, he or she can send you an e-mail message, and you can respond with your vCard.

Make sure that the Send Messages Immediately check box in the Send tab (Tools, Options) is marked if you work online or want to have messages sent as soon as you finish writing them. If you work offline, clear this check box, and choose Tools, Send when you're ready to send your mail. You can also just click the Send and Receive button in the Outlook Express toolbar to send mail from your Outbox to the mail server.

If you are browsing the Internet online and click an e-mail address on a web page to send a message, you normally want that message to go as soon as you've written it (after all, you are already online). If Outlook Express is your default e-mail client, it will do this for you whether the Send Messages Immediately check box is marked or not. It does this by popping up a dialog box when you click the Send Message button in the toolbar of the New Message window asking if you want to deliver it now.

Tip

If Windows Messaging is your default e-mail client, clicking an e-mail address on a web page can be quite a bother because Windows Messaging takes a long time to load, unlike Outlook Express. Even if you use Windows Messaging as your main e-mail client, it's a good idea to mark the Make Outlook Express My Default E-mail Program check box in the General tab of the Tools, Options dialog box so that you can quickly send messages while browsing the web.

More Outlook Express changes

The Outlook Express window is by default divided into three panes. The message header pane (the one on the left or the top) lists the message headers, and the preview pane (the one on the right or the bottom) displays the contents of whatever message you have selected in the message header pane. You can arrange these two panes either horizontally or vertically. To do this, choose View, Layout, Below Messages or Beside Messages (actually below or beside message headers).

By default, Outlook Express displays its folders in a large pane on the left, called the Folder List. You can turn off this pane by choosing View, Layout and clearing the Folder List check box (see Figure 19-3). You can also easily switch the Folder List pane on and off by placing the Folder List button on your Outlook Express toolbar. To do this, right-click the toolbar and click Buttons in the context menu.

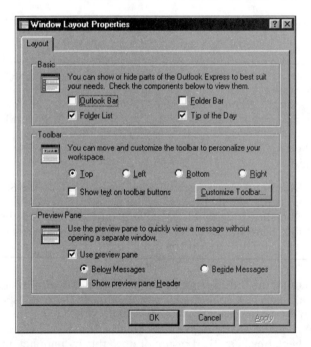

Figure 19-3: Clear the Folder List check box in the Window Layout Properties dialog box to hide the Folder List pane.

When you single-click a message header, you can view its contents in the preview pane. This works just fine most of the time. If you want to view a message in a new (and bigger) window, double-click the message header. If you want to get rid of the preview pane and only view messages in separate message windows, choose View, Layout and clear the Use Preview Pane check box. On low-resolution video cards with small monitors, this may be the way you want to go.

If you want news messages to appear in the preview pane as soon as you select them, choose Tools, Options, click the Read tab, and mark the Automatically Show News Messages in the Preview Pane check box. When this option is turned off, you have to press the spacebar after selecting a message to display its contents in the preview pane.

If you don't like the column order in the message header pane, drag the gray column header buttons to the desired position. You can also change the width of the columns by resting your mouse on the spacer line between column header buttons and dragging to the right or the left. To sort your messages by a particular column (the Subject column, for example), click the column header button. To sort by the same column in reverse order, click the button again.

If you're using the preview pane to view your messages, you can get a little extra room by hiding the header bar at the top of the preview pane. One way to do this is to double-click the bar. If you want it back, double-click the thin line that remains. You can also do this with View, Layout, Show Preview Pane Header.

If you right-click the Outlook Express toolbar, you'll notice that you can align the toolbar on any side of the window. The toolbar gets a lot thinner if you take out the text under the buttons (right-click the toolbar and clear the check mark next to Text Labels), but then it also gets less understandable (although you do get ToolTips to replace the text). If you have a low-resolution video card on a small monitor, you may want to reduce the size of the toolbar. You can also get rid of it altogether by choosing View, and clearing the check mark next to Toolbar.

There are actually three sets of buttons on the Outlook Express toolbar. One set for mail, another for news, and a third for Outlook Express in general. The set that appears changes automatically depending on which part of Outlook Express you have activated, either via the Folder List or the Outlook bar. The mail buttons appear when you click a mail folder (such as the Inbox, Outbox, or Sent Items) the news buttons appear when you click a news folder (either a folder for a news server or a newsgroup), and the general buttons appear when you click Outlook Express at the top of the Folder List or Outlook bar. To customize any set of buttons, activate a folder of the appropriate type, right-click the toolbar, and choose Buttons in the context menu.

We added Mark All As Read and Reply to All to the news buttons. We got rid of Forward Message and Reply to Author. We wish that View All Messages and View Unread Messages Only were available as buttons. To customize the mail buttons, you might want to add the Print button and remove the Delete button (you can simply press Delete to delete messages instead).

If you want to do without the Folder List, you might choose View, Layout, and mark Outlook bar instead. The Outlook bar displays all of the folders as icons. This really cuts down on the amount of space used by the Outlook Express window. If you have subfolders, however, they don't show up in the Outlook bar.

When you're viewing a newsgroup message, if you choose Compose, Reply to Newsgroup and Author (or click the Reply to All button if you have added this button to the toolbar) to reply to a posting in a newsgroup, your message gets sent to the newsgroup and to the author of the message to which you are replying. By default, a copy of the message to the author is stored in the Sent Items folder. If you want to disable (or enable) this feature, click Tools, Options, click the Send tab, and clear (or mark) the Save Copy of Sent Messages in the 'Sent Items' Folder check box. If you clear Save Copy of Sent Messages, your outgoing e-mail messages won't get saved in the Sent Items folder either.

If you need to view mail or news articles in a foreign language, you may need to use other character sets. Turn to "Multilingual e-mail" in Chapter 27 for details.

Shortcuts to Outlook Express

You can start Outlook Express by clicking the Outlook Express icon on your Desktop. You can also start it from a command line, or from a DOS prompt for that matter.

Another flexible and convenient way to start Outlook Express is to create a shortcut for it. If you do this, you can then modify the shortcut to invoke Outlook Express in any number of special ways. (Once you create your own shortcut, you may want to remove the Outlook Express icon from your Desktop by right-clicking it and clicking Delete.)

To create a shortcut, right-click msimn.exe in the \Program Files\Outlook Express\ folder and click Create Shortcut.

To open Outlook Express in mail, right-click the shortcut that you just created (it will be in the same folder), click Properties in the context menu, and modify the contents of the Target field in the Shortcut tab to look like this:

```
"C:\Program Files\Outlook Express\msimn.exe" /mail
```

You can also force Outlook Express to start in mail by choosing Tools, Options in the Outlook Express window, and marking the When Starting, Go Directly to My 'Inbox' Folder check box in the General tab.

To open Outlook Express to your default news server, make sure that the Target field looks like this:

```
"C:\Program Files\Outlook Express\msimn.exe" /news
```

If you want to open Outlook Express from the DOS command prompt, type this:

```
start "C:\Program Files\Outlook Express\msimn.exe"
```

If you want to start an Outlook Express New Message window without starting all of Outlook Express, you can click the Start button, click Run, and type **mailto:*someone@aserviceprovider*.com**. The e-mail address will appear in the To field of the New Message window. If you just type **mailto:**, a

New Message window appears with a blank To field. Outlook Express must be your default e-mail program for this method to work.

POP3, SMTP, and XOVER required

Outlook Express requires that your Internet service provider (or your local area network) have an SMTP server if you want to send mail, and a POP3 server if you want to receive mail. Some service providers use only an SMTP server to send and receive mail. This configuration won't work with Outlook Express.

Undocumented

You can send mail with Outlook Express even if you don't have a POP3 server to receive mail. Just choose Tools, Options, click the Send tab, and mark the Send Messages Immediately check box. This way, Outlook Express won't check for incoming mail.

If you don't have a POP3 server, you can put a bogus entry in the POP3 server field (choose Tools, Accounts, click the account in the Mail tab, click the Properties button, and click the Servers tab). If you set up a bogus POP3 entry and have mail in the Outbox, don't click Tools, Send and Receive. Just click Tools, Send.

You can also choose to skip an account that doesn't have a POP3 server by removing it from the list of accounts that are checked for incoming mail. Choose Tools, Accounts, highlight the account in the Mail tab, click Properties, and clear the Include This Account When Doing a Full Send and Receive check box.

Your Internet service provider's news server must support the XOVER extension of the NNTP protocol (Network News Transfer Protocol). Most likely it does. If not, give your service provider a call or find a new provider.

Where is everything stored?

You'll find your Outlook Express storage files in the Outlook Express subfolders, which are stored in either \Program Files\Outlook Express\ *yourusername* or in \Windows\Application Data\Outlook Express\ *yourusername*. If you have multiple users using user profiles, you'll find these files under \Windows\Profiles\. If you don't have a user name, you won't have a *yourusername* folder but rather a Default User folder.

You won't have a user name if you haven't logged on to your Windows 98 computer. If you don't see the logon box when you first start Windows 98, it is because you entered blank as your password. For more details on how to make sure you have logged on, turn to the "First, Your Password" section of Chapter 6.

In the Mail subfolder, the messages are stored in the *mbx* (mailbox) files. The *idx* files store the indexes of their associated *mbx* files. The *mbx* files are for the most part text files, so you can read them with Notepad or WordPad. In the news account subfolders of the News folder, you'll find *nch* files, which contain the subject headers and messages of the newsgroups to which you are subscribed (or were previously subscribed).

If you like, you can compress (or compact) these mail and news files to get rid of deleted records. To do this, choose File, Clean Up Files if you are focused on a news folder, or File, Folder, Compact (or Compact All Folders) if you are focused on a mail folder.

Secret

You can move your mail and newsgroups files to a new location. You only have to make one simple change to your Registry. After you have copied the *yourusername* folder to its new location, use RegEdit to find HKEY_CURRENT_USER\Software\Microsoft\Outlook Express\Store Root. Double-click Store Root in the right pane and type the new path.

Your Windows Address Book is stored in your *yourusername.wab* file. You'll find it in the \Windows\Application Data\Microsoft\Address Book folder. If you don't have a user name, the file will be called UserMPS.wab.

Undocumented

You'll find this address in your Registry at HKEY_CURRENT_USER\Software\Microsoft\WAB\WAB4\Wab File Name. If you move your Window Address Book, you'll need to change your path in this location of the Registry. You can find out more about this at Eric Miller's "Finding and Moving your WAB" page at http://activeie.com/oe/wab/wab_005.htm.

Transferring Inbox Assistant rules and newsgroup filters to a new computer

Inbox Assistant is a part of Outlook Express designed to help you filter and organize your mail, based on rules you set up in advance. If you first select a mail folder in the Folder List pane, this feature will be under Tools, Inbox Assistant. You can get to the newsgroup filters if you first select a newsgroup in your Folder List pane and then click Tools, Newsgroup Filters.

The rules that you define for your Inbox Assistant and newsgroup filters are stored in your Registry. You can export the rules branches of the Registry into a text file, which you can then import into the Registry of another computer.

You'll find the Inbox Assistant rules at HKEY_CURRENT_USER\Software\Microsoft\Outlook Express\Mail\Inbox Rules. The newsgroup filter rules are stored at HKEY_CURRENT_USER\Software\Microsoft\Outlook Express\News\Group Filters. These Registry entries only appear if you have created some rules.

Notice that each rule is numbered, starting with Rule0000 (if you haven't deleted your first rule previously). You'll want to edit these numbers in the exported text file if they conflict with rule numbers of rules already on the target computer.

First export each of these branches by using RegEdit and choosing Registry, Export Registry File. Then edit the rule numbers, and import the files into the Registry of the target computer.

Connecting with the DUNs

If you connect to the Internet through a dial-up connection, you'll want to customize just how and when that connection is made. Outlook Express lets you connect to your news servers and mail servers in three different ways. To see these options, choose Tools, Accounts, highlight a news or mail server, click Properties, and then click the Connection tab (see Figure 19-4).

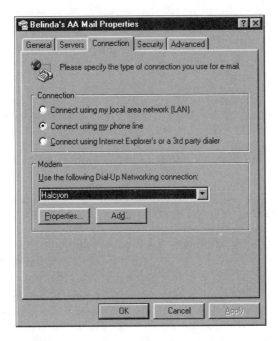

Figure 19-4: The Connection tab of the Properties dialog box for a news or mail account.

If you are connected over a local area network, mark the Connect Using My Local Area Network (LAN) option. You can also use this option if you connect to the Internet first by clicking your Internet service provider's DUN connectoid. Outlook Express won't hang up after sending messages or in any way manage the dial-up connection if you make this choice.

If you want to connect to the mail or news server after you have connected to the Internet by using a DUN connectoid, mark the Connect Using Internet Explorer's Or a 3rd Party Dialer option. You should select this button if you want to use your standard DUN connectoid to connect to the Internet before you invoke Outlook Express, regardless of whether you start the connectoid by clicking the connectoid itself (or a shortcut to it) or by clicking the Internet Explorer icon on the Desktop.

If you want Outlook Express to initiate and manage the dial-up connection with the Internet, choose the Connect Using My Phone Line option button, and then select the DUN connectoid that connects to your local Internet service provider from the drop-down list. Even if you choose Connect Using

My Phone Line, you can still access the Internet first by clicking the appropriate DUN connectoid and then invoking Outlook Express.

Outlook Express will automatically hang up after carrying out the requested task (such as sending and retrieving e-mail). You can change this behavior by choosing Tools, Options, clicking the Dial Up tab, and clearing the Hang Up When Finished Sending, Receiving, or Downloading check box. You can also clear this box by clearing the Hang Up When Finished check box in the message box that appears when you initiate an Outlook Express command that requires a connection to the Internet.

You can modify this hang up behavior by editing your Registry. To see how, check out Eric Miller's "Hangup without Dial" page at http://activeie.com/oe/connect/connect_012.htm.

You can set up Outlook Express to automatically retrieve new mail. Choose Tools, Options, and click the General tab. Mark the Check for New Messages Every [   ] Minute(s) check box. This works, regardless of whether you have chosen Connect Using Internet Explorer's Or a 3rd Party Dialer or Connect Using My Phone Line in the Connection tab of the Properties dialog box for your account.

If you are working offline and want to remain offline until you specifically ask Outlook Express to dial in to your Internet service provider, you'll have to be sure that you've got all the right settings. Choose Tools, Options, Dial Up, and mark Do Not Dial a Connection or Ask Me If I Would Like to Dial a Connection. This keeps Outlook Express from automatically dialing up your Internet service provider when you first start Outlook Express.

Click the General tab in the Options dialog box and clear Check for New Messages Every [   ] Minute(s) so that Outlook Express will not periodically call into your service provider in background mode. For each mail and news server account, make sure that you have chosen Connect Using My Phone Line in the Connection tab of the Properties dialog box for the account (Tools, Accounts, Mail/News tab, Properties). For each news server, make sure that you clear the Automatically Connect to This Server check box in the same tab.

This is still not quite enough. If you open a message (most likely an HTML-formatted one) that contains HTML code referencing a resource of the Internet (in other words, the HREF tag and a URL), Windows will invoke the Internet Explorer. If the Internet Explorer is configured to automatically dial up an Internet service provider and not to stop and ask for user confirmation, you will be forced to click the Cancel button as soon as the Dialing Progress dialog box appears in order to stop the connection.

The only way to stop the Internet Explorer from dialing automatically is by changing its settings. The drastic option is to right-click the Internet Explorer icon on your Desktop, click Properties, click the Connection tab, and mark Connect to the Internet Using a Local Area Network. (You can do this even if you aren't on a local area network.)

You will now be able to work offline and only connect to the Internet when you click the Send and Receive or the Connect button.

If you change this setting, Internet Explorer will no longer automatically invoke the associated DUN connectoid to dial into your Internet service provider when you click the Internet Explorer icon. You'll have to click a DUN connectoid to make the connection before you click the Internet Explorer icon. Therefore, you might want to put up with this little bit of bad behavior in Outlook Express to keep the convenience of automatic dial-up with Internet Explorer.

The friendlier option is to clear the Connect Automatically check box in the Dial-Up Connection dialog box. First right-click the Internet Explorer icon on your Desktop, click Properties, click the Connection tab, mark Connect to the Internet Using a Modem, and click OK. Click the Internet Explorer icon, and click Cancel in the Dialing Progress dialog box. Now you can clear the Connect Automatically check box.

Multiple accounts for the same server

You can name each account that you create, which lets you keep track of different accounts that use the same mail or news server. This is quite handy. For example, during the early beta testing period for Internet Explorer 4.0 and Windows 98, Microsoft included the two beta newsgroups on the same betanews.microsoft.com news server. Each beta required that you log on to the same news server with a different password and beta ID. By setting up two news accounts, we were able to place two different sets of IDs and passwords in the Properties dialog box for each account. (Choose Tools, Accounts, click the News tab, highlight the account, click the Properties button, click the Server tab, mark the This Server Requires Me to Logon check box, and then enter the information under Log On Using.) We could then log on sequentially to the same news server, but under different beta identities.

You can also use this method to make two separate mail accounts that log on to the same mail server, but through different DUNs. In this way, you can use one account to log on to get your e-mail when you are away from home and using a national service provider, and another for when you are at home. If you log on at the office over a LAN and at home over the phone lines, you can set up two mail accounts for the same mail server.

If you are setting up different mail server accounts with different DUNs or LAN connections, you will probably have to have a different SMTP outgoing mail server in each of them, even though the POP3 mail server may be the same. Turn to "Choose which account to send your messages through" later in this chapter for more details.

Corrupted passwords

You may you find that you are repeatedly asked to enter your account name and password when connecting to a news or mail server. Outlook Express doesn't keep its passwords (which are different than your Internet service provider logon password) in the *pwl* file, but rather in your Registry. These passwords are encrypted in RSA RC4 format.

If instead you are having problems with your DUN user name and password when trying to connect to the Internet with Outlook Express, turn to "Saving your DUN connectoid passwords" in Chapter 18.

The first step in fixing the Outlook Express password problem is to create a new news or mail account and then check to see if Outlook Express remembers the password for it.

STEPS

Testing for an Outlook Express Password

Step 1.   Choose Tools, Accounts, Add, News or Mail to invoke the Internet Connection Wizard. Follow the steps in the Wizard to create a new account.

Step 2.   Check to see if the new password was saved correctly by choosing Tools, Accounts, highlighting the account name, clicking the Properties button, and clicking the Server tab. Check if there are asterisks in the Password field. If the field is blank, Outlook Express isn't remembering the password to the server.

Step 3.   If your Password field is blank, open a DOS window. (Click the Start button, point to Programs, and click MS-DOS Prompt.) At the DOS prompt, type **cd \Windows\System** and press Enter to change directories to your \Windows\System folder.

Step 4.   Type **pstores -install** and press Enter. Type **exit** and press Enter to return to Windows.

Step 5.   Enter a new password in one of your mail or news accounts. Click the Connect button in Outlook Express to see if you can successfully connect to that server without being asked about your password.

Different service providers for Internet Explorer and Outlook Express

Outlook Express lets you connect to multiple mail and news servers through different Internet service providers (or LANs) or through one provider. You can have multiple DUN connectoids stored in your Dial-Up Networking folder. If you use a dial-up connection to the Internet, you can set Internet Explorer to call using any one of your DUN connectoids, and it doesn't have to be one that's used by Outlook Express. We've got ourselves a little management job here.

If you have connected to the Internet using Outlook Express and you display a message (most likely an HTML-formatted message) that contains a reference to an Internet resource (using the HREF tag and a URL), Windows will try to connect to that resource using Internet Explorer. If Internet Explorer is configured to call up through a different Internet service provider, it will conflict with your current Internet connection and kick you off of the connection.

One way to fix this is to set the DUN used by Internet Explorer equal to the DUN used by Outlook Express for mail and news. Since Outlook Express can be configured to use multiple DUNs (and multiple Internet service providers), this may not be possible.

You can also configure Internet Explorer to assume that it is on a LAN. If you do, it will use whatever current Internet connection is available to try to connect to the Internet resource. To do this, right-click the Internet Explorer icon on your Desktop, click Properties, click the Connection tab, and mark the Connect to the Internet Using a Local Area Network option button.

Your Windows 98 Explorer won't automatically start dialing a connection to the Internet when you invoke it if you do this. You'll have to click one of your DUNs first to establish the connection.

Sending messages now or later

You have the option of sending messages immediately (as soon as you click the Send or Post button) or storing them in the Outbox to be sent later. Even if they are sent immediately, they do go by way of the Outbox.

If you choose Tools, Options, click the Send tab, and mark the Send Messages Immediately check box, your messages go quickly to your mail or news server, especially if you are already online or connected to a LAN. If you are working offline, Outlook Express calls your Internet service provider and sends your message from your Outbox to the server as soon as it makes the connection. If you have marked Hang Up When Finished Sending, Receiving, or Downloading in the Dial Up tab of the Tools, Options dialog box, the Internet connection is severed after the message is delivered.

If you are working offline, you probably want to store up a few messages before you batch them off to the server, so you'll likely want to clear Send Messages Immediately. However, you can override the Send Messages Immediately setting for individual messages. In the New Message window, choose File, Send Message to send the message now. To place the message in the Outbox, choose File, Send Later.

Outlook Express security

All the Windows 98 Internet applications that come from Microsoft share the same security settings. You can see this if you choose Tools, Options, click the Security tab, and click the Settings button. You can also get to these settings by right-clicking the Internet Explorer icon on your Desktop, clicking Properties, and clicking the Security tab.

It is possible for someone to send you an ActiveX control or a Java applet in an e-mail message or over a newsgroup (one that supports this level of content) that could potentially cause some damage to the files on your computer. To tailor Outlook Express (and all other Windows 98 Internet applications) to check these controls and warn you if they are not from trusted sources, choose Tools, Options, click the Security tab, click the Settings button, click the Custom option button, and then click the Settings button. You can then choose which types of controls to download, which to prompt for before downloading, and which to block.

Spell checking

Outlook Express uses the Microsoft Office for Windows 95 or Office 97 spell checker.

Undocumented

Outlook Express looks in the Registry to find the dictionary and the spelling engine. It goes to HKEY_LOCAL_MACHINE\Software\Microsoft\Shared Tools\Proofing Tools\Spelling*languageID*\Normal. The *languageID* is a 4-digit number. For example, US English is 1033, Australian is 2057, and British English is 3081. You'll find two string values under the Normal key that name the dictionary and the engine.

Tip

The spelling files mssp2_en.lex, mssp232.dll, and custom.dic should be stored in the folder C:\Program Files\Common Files\Microsoft Shared\Proof. If you are having trouble enabling spell checking, use your Windows 98 Explorer to search for these files and make sure that they are stored in this folder.

If you still are having trouble getting spell checking to work, check out http://premium.microsoft.com/support/kb/articles/q154/8/78.asp. You can also look through Eric Miller's "Outlook Express User Tips" at http://www.activeie.com/oe to find explicit help on enabling spell checking.

More than meets the eye

Outlook Express doesn't display much of the message header information in the preview pane or separate message window. Most of this information is really only used by e-mail clients or newsgroup readers to correctly format the message, and it's not all that useful to us. Nonetheless, sometimes you need this information to help troubleshoot a problem or find out an e-mail address.

To see the complete message header, press Ctrl+F3, or right-click the message header in the message header pane, click Properties, and click the Details tab (see Figure 19-5). If you click the Message Source button, a new window opens up and you can cut and paste text from the complete message.

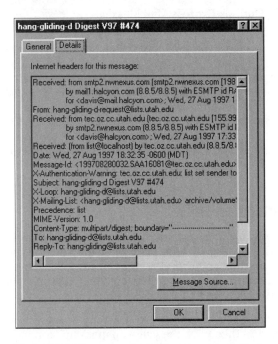

Figure 19-5: The source code for a message is displayed in a separate window.

Adding Outlook Express messages to the New menu

Undocumented

In earlier chapters, we have discussed ways to add items to the New menu. If you like, you can create a New menu item for Outlook Express. Here's how:

STEPS

Placing Outlook Express Mail Messages on Your New Menu

Step 1. Right-click your Desktop, point to New, and click Text Document.

Step 2. Rename the text document **New.eml**. Click Yes.

Step 3. Click the Start button, point to Settings, and click Control Panel. Click your TweakUI icon. Click the New tab.

(continued)

STEPS *(continued)*

Placing Outlook Express Mail Messages on Your New Menu

Step 4. Drag and drop New.eml into the New tab. You'll notice that there is now a new checked entry on the list of new documents in TweakUI: Outlook Express Mail Message.

Undocumented

Do you want to add an item for Outlook Express news postings to the New menu? Follow these same steps, but in step 2, rename the new text document New.nws. Or, instead of following steps 1 and 2, click the Compose Message button while you're using Outlook Express and focused on a newsgroup, click the Save As button in the New Message toolbar, and save the blank news document with the name New.nws on your Desktop. Then continue with steps 3 and 4.

Saving attachments

To save an attachment to a message you have received, double-click the message header in the message header pane to display the message in a separate window. Then drag and drop the attachment icon from the bottom of the window into a folder or onto the Desktop. You can also right-click the attachment icon and click Save As.

To save an attachment without opening a separate message window, click the message header, and then click the yellow paper clip icon in the upper-right corner of the preview pane (the Show Preview Pane Header check box must be marked in the View, Layout dialog box). A menu listing the names of the attachments in the message appears. Click the name of the attachment you want to open or save. You can then choose to open it or save it to a folder. (If, when you click attachments of a particular file type, you find that they open automatically and you'd like the option of saving them instead, you need to edit the file type. See "Confirm open after Download" in Chapter 13 for details.)

You can also just highlight the message header and choose File, Save Attachments.

You can send graphic files in *gif* and *jpeg* format (as well as other formats) as attachments to Outlook Express messages. Outlook Express encodes the graphics in UUENCODE or MIME format. After you receive a message with a *gif* or *jpeg* attachment and it is decoded (Outlook Express does this automatically) you can read the file using the helper application with which it's associated. (To check what applications are associated with *gif* and *jpeg* files, choose View, Folder Options in the Explorer, click File Types, and look through the Registered File Types list for these file types.)

Dragging and dropping messages

You can drag and drop messages from one Outlook Express folder to another, except for the Outbox folder. Outlook Express prepares messages to be sent over the Internet before placing them in the Outbox folder. It does this when you click the Send (or Post) button in the New Message window.

Outlook Express could have been programmed to allow you to drag and drop into the Outbox folder, but the Microsoft developers chose not to add this code to the standard drag and drop function.

If you drag and hold a message icon over a folder in the Folder List pane that contains subfolders, the list expands and the subfolders are displayed. This makes it possible to drag and drop to subfolders. And if you drag a message to the top or bottom of the Folder List pane, the list scrolls up or down to let you drop the message on a folder that was originally hidden.

Sending web addresses

You can include Internet URLs (locations of Internet resources) in your messages. Outlook Express changes the address's font color and makes it clickable. If you click an address in a message, your Internet Explorer displays that web page or other resource.

Your Desktop (and other folders) can also display clickable URLs. Instead of changing the font color, Windows designates these URLs as shortcuts and adds an icon to the URL's name.

Windows 98 makes it easier to send URLs and shortcuts to URLs to your recipients. They can then drag a URL's shortcut to their Desktop for easy access. There are a number of ways to do this.

You'll find a Mail button on the Explorer toolbar when you're viewing a web site. Click this button and choose Send a Link to mail the URL of the current web page along with its shortcut. The URL shortcut is sent as an attachment. If you want to send the whole HTML formatted page instead of just the link to the page, choose Send Page.

If you are viewing a web page in Explorer, you can right-click anywhere in the Address field and click Copy. Then in Outlook Express, click the Compose Message button, right-click in the body of the message, and click Paste to place the URL in the message. The URL is clickable, but there is no URL shortcut added to the message.

If you want to send one of the URLs from your Favorites list, click the Start button, point to Favorites, navigate to the favorite, and drag and drop it into the body of your new message. The shortcut is added as an attachment to the message.

UUENCODE or MIME

A basic e-mail client will let you send messages as plain text—that is, no characters beyond the first 128 (7-bit) US ASCII; no underlining, italics, boldface, fonts, pictures, or attachments. Outlook Express, which is quite a bit more than a basic e-mail client, supports HTML formatting of the text in your message. It also lets you include pictures in your message and add attachments to it.

Because the Internet e-mail standard only supports 7-bit ASCII characters, formatted messages and attachments need to be encoded by the e-mail client into ASCII characters and decoded by the recipient's e-mail client when they arrive. Outlook Express supports the MIME and UUENCODE encoding/decoding standards.

If you are sending e-mail messages to recipients who have powerful e-mail clients, then you'll want to select HTML formatting and MIME encoding. This will allow you to format your messages to your heart's content.

Tip

If you send messages to recipients with Unix e-mail readers, to Unix-based mailing lists, or to news servers that don't support formatted messages (which includes most news servers), then you'll want to ignore MIME altogether and set encoding at UUENCODE. (This will not encode the message text but will encode attachments with UUENCODE.)

To change your encoding scheme, choose Tools, Options, click the Send tab, and then click the Settings button for the selected format, HTML or Plain Text. If you choose MIME in the HTML Settings or Plain Text Settings dialog box (the only option with HTML), you can select None, Quoted Printable, or Base 64 from a drop-down list. These options only apply to the text portion of your message and not to the attachments. The attachments are coded in MIME at Base 64.

Tip

If you choose None, then your message is not encoded at all, although any attachments will be encoded in MIME (Base 64). You message text will be sent as unencoded 8-bit characters. This may cause a problem because your message has a very slight chance of being forwarded through a machine that can't handle 8-bit characters. The advantage of choosing None is that even a recipient who doesn't have a MIME-capable e-mail client can easily read your text.

Undocumented

If you choose Quoted Printable and send your message to a recipient who can't handle MIME, he or she will find equal signs (=) at the end of the lines in your message. This is your clue to stop sending messages formatted with MIME to this recipient.

Outlook Express makes it easy to switch back and forth between sending formatted (HTML) and plain messages. You set the default in the Send tab of the Options dialog box. Then when you're composing a message, you can change the setting for just that message by clicking Format, Rich Text (HTML) or Plain Text in the New Message menu. This lets you set your default for HTML and then switch to plain text when sending to less capable recipients. (For more on HTML-formatted messages, see "Messages Formatted in HTML" later in this chapter.)

Tip

You can also choose to send only plain text to a given recipient by marking the Send E-mail Using Plain Text Only check box in the Personal tab of the recipient's Properties dialog box in your Windows Address Book. This is really the best way to be sure that you don't send badly formatted or unreadable text to a mailing list or to a recipient with an inadequate e-mail client.

Outlook Express automatically encodes and decodes attachments. It can't decode some types of encoded messages and you may find that an attachment isn't decoded properly. If this is the case, you can use another program such as WinZip to decode the attachment.

You'll find WinZip at http://www.winzip.com. To make the attachment available to WinZip or to other decoding programs, you need to save it as a separate file. Use the methods described in "Saving attachments" earlier in this chapter. If you need to decode an e-mail or news message, you can also use File, Save As to save it as a separate file and then decode it with a separate application.

One encoding method that Outlook Express doesn't handle is BinHex, a popular Mac standard. You can see if a message or an attachment is encoded with BinHex by right-clicking it, selecting Properties, and then Details. You'll need to save the message or attachment as a separate file and then decode it with a BinHex decoder. WinZip can handle BinHex.

You can read more about encoding and decoding in Outlook Express at Eric Miller's site at http://www.activeie.com/oe. Be sure to look under "Issues Affecting both Mail and News," "Encoding Information."

You can find encoders and decoders at http://www.windows98.com or ftp:// ftp.andrew.cmu.edu/pub/mpack/ for munpack (MIME decoding), http://www.tucows.com for Wincode (UUdecoding), and http://www.aladdinsys.com/ for StuffIt (BinHex).

Multiple users and user profiles

Outlook Express lets you set up separate e-mail and news server accounts. It is quite possible to poll different e-mail accounts belonging to different people, but have all of the received mail and newsgroup postings arrive in one Inbox. You can even set up separate folders for incoming e-mail and have the Inbox Assistant automatically place each message into the correct box based on the recipient. (See "Multiple e-mail accounts.")

In spite of this capability, you may wish to have completely separate mail and news setups to allow multiple users to access the same computer and keep their messages, newsgroups, and address books separate (and a bit more private). To do this, you'll need to use *user profiles*.

With user profiles, each user logs onto his or her own Windows 98 Desktop. Outlook Express maintains a folder for each user (named with the user name) that contains subfolders for the user's mail and newsgroups. Users set up their own mail servers by logging onto their Windows 98 Desktop, starting Outlook Express, choosing Tools, Accounts, Add, Mail, and entering their SMTP and POP3 mail server information. They set up news servers by starting Outlook Express and following similar steps. To configure Windows 98 to use user profiles, follow the steps in "Setting up Windows 98 for multiple users" in Chapter 12.

Secret

If you set up multiple users after you install Outlook Express, all of your mail and news will go to the original user. You have to edit your Registry to tell Outlook Express that there are now multiple users and that Outlook Express should use multiple user folders when sorting and delivering the mail and news.

You will need to add to the Registry a Mail, News, and address book branch for each new user. Follow the specific instructions at Eric Miller's site at http://www.activeie.com/oe. Go to "Issues Affecting Both Mail and News," and read the instructions under "Multiple Users."

If you don't want to edit the Registry, the other alternative is to reinstall Outlook Express after every time you set up a new user. Click the Start button, choose Log Off, and log on as the new user. Then reinstall Outlook Express.

Where to find more help

You can download the latest version of Outlook Express from Microsoft's web site at http://www.microsoft.com/ie/download/.

Check out Eric Miller's "Outlook Express User Tips" at http://www.activeie. com/oe/. You'll find obscure information about Windows 98 in general, as well as about Outlook Express, at Costas Andriotis' site, http://www-na. biznet.com.gr/sail/isa/tipfrm.html. Microsoft provides its help for Outlook Express at http://www.microsoft.com/ie/ie40/oe.

Messages Formatted in HTML

Outlook Express allows you to format your e-mail messages and newsgroup posts using HTML. Choose Tools, Options, and click the Send tab. You'll find the option to set the default format for messages as HTML.

You can always override the default setting for the current newsgroup post or e-mail message. Just choose Format in the New Message window, and click Rich Text (HTML) or Plain Text. If you're using HTML, you get a formatting toolbar that lets you choose the font, font size, font color, and so on.

Tip

Lots of newsgroup and e-mail clients aren't able to display HTML-formatted text. If they can't, your correspondents will see the HTML tags embedded in the plain text of your messages — something that they might not appreciate.

HTML-formatted messages are always sent as MIME-structured, and by default, Quoted Printable encoded messages. In order for them to be properly displayed, your recipient has to have an e-mail client that can display HTML-formatted messages, and his or her Internet service provider has to have an e-mail server that correctly handles MIME.

If your recipient's e-mail client cannot read HTML, but can read MIME documents, then he or she will receive a text version of your message and an attached HTML version that can be read by a browser.

Outlook Express's default setting is to reply to messages using the same format as the message. If you want to use your own settings instead, clear the Reply to Messages Using the Format in Which They Were Sent check box under Tools, Options, Send.

Undocumented

Outlook Express displays all messages using HTML. This is true even if you create a message in plain text. The reason for this is that Outlook Express uses an HTML display engine, so it has to add HTML tags to non-HTML-formatted messages in order to display them correctly.

You can see this by double-clicking a message header to open a separate message window and then pressing Ctrl+F2. A new window opens to display a plain-text version of the message with its HTML tags.

Outlook Express doesn't include these HTML tags when it sends a message that you have formatted as plain text. It just adds these tags on the fly to allow the message to be displayed correctly. You can see the actual content of the message by pressing Ctrl+F3 or by right-clicking the message header, clicking Properties, clicking the Details tab, and clicking the Message Source button.

The HTML display engine also looks for e-mail addresses and URLs contained within messages. If it finds them, it highlights them to indicate that they are clickable — you can click an e-mail address to send a message to that address, click a URL to view a web site, and so on.

Editing HTML messages

Outlook Express has a simple HTML-capable WYSIWYG editor built in. You can set the font, font style (boldface, italic, underline), font size, font color, and background color. You can format paragraphs as bullets or numbered lists and align them left, right, or center. You can insert a *gif* picture or use one as a background. Microsoft provides a small selection of *gif* files in the \Program Files\Common Files\Microsoft Shared\Stationery folder.

Microsoft also provides a more sophisticated HTML editor/generator with Windows 98 called FrontPage Express. You can edit the body of a message in FrontPage Express and insert the HTML text using the Insert, Text from File command. Because Outlook Express uses the capabilities of the Internet Explorer to display its messages (all of which it formats for display using HTML), you can create and receive all manner of multimedia messages.

Of course, you can send web pages as attachments, but as long as your recipients have Outlook Express or a similar e-mail client, they can view the page as part of (or all of) the message (just paste it in). They won't have any need to open a separate browser window.

Stationery

The HTML tag BACKGROUND lets you create a stationery-like effect for your messages. You can configure Outlook Express to automatically start a new blank message with your background image. You can choose from among the existing stationery files, create new stationery, create stationery that is just a background color, or download new stationery from Microsoft.

You need to format your message with HTML in order to be able to use stationery (click Tools, Options, Send, and mark the HTML option button under Mail Sending Format). To pick a default stationery type, choose Tools, Stationery, click the Mail or News tab, click the This Stationary option button, and click the Select button. You get to view the stationery before you select it. Once you have chosen a stationery type, clicking Compose Message will open a New Message window with that stationery already included in the message.

Undocumented

Press Ctrl+F2 to see that the source code of the *htm* file that Outlook Express uses to create the stationery has been inserted into your new message. In addition, at the top of the HTML view of your message, you'll find a reference pointing to the folder that holds the stationery's *gif* file.

If you want to create a message with something other than the default stationery, click the down arrow to the right of the Compose Message button. You can pick which *htm* file to use as stationery, or choose no stationery at all.

Secret

Outlook Express includes the associated *gif* file as an attachment when it sends out a message with stationery. You can verify this by first creating a new test message with stationery.

In the New Message window, click Format, Plain Text, and then Yes when warned about losing formatting. Click File, Save. Your message will be saved in the Draft folder. (The Draft folder is used to store messages that you save with the File, Save command. The messages remain in this folder until you click Send.) Double-click the message header in your Draft folder in Outlook Express and you'll see the attachment.

We converted the message to plain text in order to make the attached *gif* file apparent. Outlook Express doesn't show this as an attachment as long as you are formatting an HTML-formatted message.

Outlook Express creates stationery by using a very small *gif* file and an *htm* file that contains at least the BACKGROUND tag and maybe more. You can view the source code for the stationery files that Microsoft includes with Outlook Express by opening by the *htm* and *gif* files in the \Program Files\Common Files\Microsoft Shared\Stationery folder. Check out the

Chicken Soup *htm* file as an example of a more complicated stationery file (see Figure 19-6).

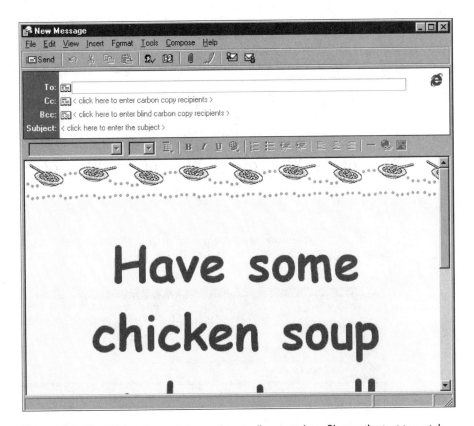

Figure 19-6: The Chicken Soup stationery is actually a template. Change the text to match your needs.

You can create your own stationery using copies of the *htm* files and just editing or replacing the *gif* files. To keep your messages small, make sure that you use very small *gif* files (under 500 bytes) that can be displayed as a repeated pattern on the recipient's computer.

Tip

You can capture stationery from an incoming message. Just double-click the message header and choose File, Save As Stationery. In spite of what *Save As Stationery* sounds like, the whole message is not saved as stationery, just the stationery part of the message.

If you're familiar with HTML, you can make other changes in your new stationery files, including changes to fonts. You can use FrontPage Express to edit these files. If you reference a font in your stationery that isn't widely found on your recipients' computers, your message will be displayed with their default font (found on their computers in Outlook Express under Tools, Options, Read, Fonts).

Tip

When you create an HTML-formatted message that uses stationary, you might want to apply a background color to the message that approximates your stationery color. If you do this, then in the event that your stationery *gif* doesn't get through, the background color will be used instead. This will ensure that your recipients can read your message, since the font color you used over your stationery will also be legible with this background color. To apply a background color, choose Format, Background, Color in the New Message window.

You can easily select a background color for your new messages each time you start one by choosing Format, Background, Color. If you want a default color for message backgrounds, you can set up a stationary file that references a *gif* file that is just a small block of color.

Tip

Another easy way to create stationary that contains a background color is to create a blank HTML-formatted message, choose a background color, and then send the message to yourself. When you receive it, click File, Save As Stationery.

Microsoft makes more stationery available at its web site. Click Tools, Stationery, Select, Get More. Figure 19-7 is an example of what is possible.

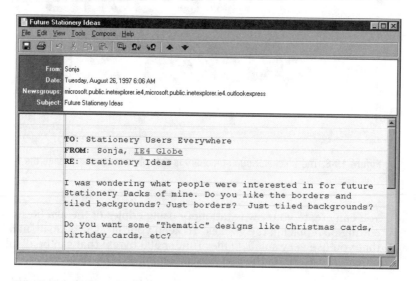

Figure 19-7: This notebook stationery incorporates a margin in its design.

If you want to reply to a message using your own stationery, click Format, Apply Stationery in the reply message window.

Fancy signatures

Most people hate to receive fancy signatures, especially in newsgroups. Such an ego trip. If you must create an HTML-formatted signature with a bouncing name, perhaps you can just use it on messages that you send to your Mom.

You can create a fancy signature using FrontPage Express or any other clever HTML editor and save it as a file. To designate this file as your signature, choose Tools, Stationery, click the Mail or News tab, click the Signature button, mark the File option button, and then click the Browse button.

Of course the easiest way to create a new signature is to rip off someone else's and put your name in there instead—easy to do when these things get shipped around the Internet.

The Signature dialog box also lets you designate your vCard from your entry in your Windows Address Book. There really is no need to send your vCard out every time, so you might refrain from marking the Attach Card to All Outgoing Messages check box. When you want to attach your vCard to an individual message, use the Insert, Business Card command.

Pictures and text

Because Outlook Express implements the MHTML format, it includes any picture files (*bmp*, *gif*, and *jpg*) that you place in HTML-formatted messages (including stationery) as attachments when it sends your message. The default setting is to include pictures, so you'll find the Tools, Send Pictures with Message command marked in the New Message window. To change the default, choose Tools, Options, click the Send tab, and then click the Settings button next to the HTML option button for both news and mail.

If the Tools, Send Pictures with Message command is not marked when you send a message that references a local picture file, this file gets left behind. The recipient will find a reference in his or her message pointing to your hard disk folder where the picture file is stored, but no picture—and, of course, no way to get it.

If you happen to send a reference to a picture file that is stored on your A drive and Send Pictures with Message is turned off, then when your recipient opens your message, his or her computer will try to find the picture on the A drive.

If you receive a message with references to resources located on the Internet—for example, a picture file stored on a web server—your Internet Explorer will try to connect to the resource, download it in background, and display it in your message. If you are connected to the Internet as you read the message, you may not notice this happening, although there may be some delay if the resource is large or the Internet is busy (as always).

If you are not connected to the Internet, Internet Explorer will try to connect to download the resource. This can make offline reading a bit tedious. If you cancel the connection and the resource is in your Internet cache (perhaps you previously viewed that resource or it was referred to in an earlier message from the same source), it will be displayed in your message.

If you are sending a message with stationery that references a picture file stored at an Internet server and not included with your message, you may want to set your background color equal to or close to the color of the stationery. This is especially true if you have set the color of your text to show up against your stationery (for example, white text and black stationery).

If your recipient doesn't get your stationery's picture file and is forced to read white text on a default white background, he or she is not going to know why you sent a message with no text. Since you don't know what the default color of your recipient's background is, it's a good idea to include the background color in any stationery file that includes references to web-based pictures.

Secret

If you communicate often with one person, you can forego sending that person your stationery every time. If you are sending non-standard stationery, you only have to send it once as an attachment. If the recipient stores it in his or her stationery file using the same path as yours, Outlook Express will be able to find it the next time you send a message that just includes the reference to the stationery file (clear the check mark next to Tools, Send Pictures with Message in the New Message window).

This also works for all standard stationery files, as long as your recipient has them stored under the same path as you do. You are just sending the path and filename to your stationery in the message.

Outlook Express Mail

Outlook Express switches to mail mode when you highlight a mail folder in the Folder List pane or the Outlook bar. The toolbar changes to the mail toolbar, and any changes that you make to the toolbar only affect the mail toolbar. The menu items change also. For example, the Inbox Assistant shows up on the Tools menu, and Newsgroups goes away.

Multiple e-mail accounts

Undocumented

Outlook Express allows you to create multiple e-mail accounts that you can contact through one or multiple Internet connections. You can log on to any Internet service provider where you (or an associate) have an account and get your e-mail from any Internet standard e-mail server upon which you have a valid e-mail account.

It is possible to have Outlook Express call up one Internet connection after another and access each e-mail account. You can also access each account through one Internet connection, going one at a time to each e-mail server.

To set up an e-mail account in Outlook Express, choose Tool, Accounts, Add, Mail. Enter the appropriate server, account, and password information. Click Apply. Go through this process again for the next account.

Secret

Many Internet service providers won't let you send e-mail through your e-mail account with them if you are logged onto another service provider. They do this in order to keep SPAMers from using their server to send out their "offerings." This actually doesn't present you with a problem. You can send e-mail out the SMTP outgoing mail server provided by the service you are connected to and receive mail through the POP3 incoming mail server at another provider. Just configure your e-mail accounts to use the SMTP server of your present connection.

If you have multiple e-mail server accounts, you can poll a single account for e-mail manually. Just choose Tools, Send and Receive, and then choose the account from the submenu that appears. You can choose which e-mail accounts are polled when you click the Send and Receive button (which does the same thing as Tools, Send and Receive, All Accounts). Just click Tools, Accounts, highlight a mail account, click the Properties button, and mark or clear the Include This Account When Doing a Full Send and Receive check box. This also works to choose which accounts Outlook Express polls automatically.

Replies to your messages will still go to your stated e-mail address (the reply address you indicate in the General tab of each account's Properties dialog box) even though you don't necessarily send out your e-mail through the SMTP server at your e-mail address location.

Choose which account to send your messages through

If you have multiple e-mail server accounts, the New Message window gives you the choice of sending messages with File, Send Message Using or File, Send Later Using. When you pointing to one of these commands, a submenu appears that lists all your mail server accounts.

You get to choose which account the message will be delivered through. Each account will has a specific SMTP outgoing mail server. This is true even if you are replying to a message that may have been delivered through a different account.

If you just click the Send button, Outlook Express sends the message through your default mail server account. Because each account can have a separate Internet connection, and because you can stack mail in your Outbox, it is quite possible to click the Send and Receive button and have Outlook Express call up multiple Internet service providers and send out mail through each of them.

Duplicate messages downloaded from the mail server

You can set Outlook Express to leave copies of your incoming messages on your mail server. (Choose Tools, Accounts, highlight a mail server account, click the Properties button, click the Advanced tab, and mark the Leave a Copy of Messages on Server check box.) If you have done this, Outlook Express is supposed to know which messages you have already downloaded to your computer and which are new messages. Turn to "Leaving mail on the server" later in this chapter for more details.

If you click Send and Receive and get your already received e-mail messages all over again, you probably have a corrupted pop3uidl.dat file. This can occur if Outlook Express crashes at a crucial moment. You'll find pop3uidl.dat in your \Program Files\Outlook Express*yourusername*\Mail folder. You should delete this file.

After you delete pop3uidl.dat, you need to download all the messages on your mail server once again with the Send and Receive button. After you do this, Outlook Express should remember which messages you've already received, at least until it crashes again.

Outlook Express as the default mail program

When you install Outlook Express, it sets itself up as the default e-mail client. Windows Messaging still works (if you have it installed), but it is no longer used to send e-mail when you click an e-mail address embedded in an HTML document displayed by the Internet Explorer. If you install other e-mail clients or somehow mess up your settings, Outlook Express may not appear when you click e-mail addresses embedded in web pages. To get it back, you'll want to check out your system.

Choose Tools, Options, and click the General tab. Make sure that the Make Outlook Express My Default E-mail Program check box is marked. (To do the same for news, mark the Make Outlook Express My Default News Reader check box.)

You get the same results by right-clicking the Internet Explorer icon on the Desktop, clicking Properties, and clicking the Programs tab. Make sure that Outlook Express is selected in both the Mail and News drop-down lists. This also allows you to click the Mail toolbar button in Internet Explorer to invoke Outlook Express.

Outlook Express is not a full MAPI client. You can't use it to send faxes, for example. It is a simple MAPI client, and if you are willing to disable Windows Messaging or Outlook, you can use it in conjunction with Word, Excel, and PowerPoint. If you click File, Send in any of these programs, the current document is sent to a new message in Outlook Express as an attachment.

To set Outlook Express as the simple MAPI client, click Tools, Options, and mark Make Outlook Express My Default Simple MAPI Client. You can clear this mark if you decide to use Windows Messaging or Outlook instead.

Sending messages to a group

Outlook Express lets you create groups of e-mail recipients from among those listed in your Windows Address Book. It does this to let you send one message to a group of folks.

Undocumented

If you just put the name of the group in the To field, then everyone gets a message starting with a long list of names. That's no fun. To keep this from happening, insert the group name in the BCC field of your message and put your own name in the To field (assuming you have your own name in your address book).

Undeleting deleted messages

If you delete an Outlook Express message, it goes to the Deleted Items folder. It's not exactly deleted—more like moved.

If you delete the message from the Deleted Items folder, you'll no longer be able to find its header in any of your Outlook Express folders. This doesn't mean it's gone though. It's still there, somewhat intact in the Deleted Items folder. Specifically, it's still in the mailbox file called Deleted Items.mbx.

If you compact the Deleted Items folder, it's history. If you have marked the Empty Messages from the 'Deleted Items' Folder on Exit check box in the General tab of the Tools, Options dialog box, Outlook Express compacts this folder and permanently deletes messages when you exit the program. You'll want to clear this check box if you want to be able to undelete deleted messages.

Secret

If you haven't compacted the Deleted Items folder, you can quickly retrieve missing messages. Here's how:

STEPS

Restoring Your Deleted Items Folder

Step 1. Quit Outlook Express. But before you do, be sure to clear the Empty Messages from the 'Deleted Items' Folder on Exit check box in the General tab of the Tools, Options dialog box, if you haven't already.

Step 2. Delete the Deleted Items.idx file in \Program Files\Outlook Express*yourusernname*\Mail or \Windows\Application Data\Outlook Express*yourusername*\Mail.

Step 3. Restart Outlook Express. Click Deleted Items in the Folder List pane. You'll get an error message stating that the folder has been damaged and that it will now be repaired. Click OK. Outlook Express rebuilds the index from the mailbox file.

Your Deleted Items folder has been restored with the missing items back in it. Now you can delete again those messages that you really did want to delete.

Tip

Deleted Items.mbx is for the most part a text file. (This is also true of the other mailbox files.) You can easily read it with Notepad or WordPad. If you want to retrieve a piece of text from any of these files, just open it with either text editor.

You can use a manual method to compact the Deleted Items folder in addition to automatically compacting it with the Empty Messages from the 'Deleted Items' Folder on Exit option. Highlight the Deleted Items folder and choose File, Folder, Compact.

Corrupted folders

Secret

It appears to be quite easy to corrupt one of your Outlook Express folders. If you get error messages complaining about your Outbox, Inbox, Deleted Items, or Sent Items folder, you're going to have to delete at least the folder and its accompanying index. Outlook Express will construct a new, clean, empty folder for you if it is one of the standard folders. (If the corrupted folder is one you created, you'll have to create it again.)

First exit Outlook Express. Use your Explorer to navigate to \Program Files\Outlook Express*your username*\Mail or \Windows\Application Data\Outlook Express*yourusername*\Mail. Delete the index file, which is the *idx* file associated with the corrupted folder—for example, Outbox.idx. Restart Outlook Express.

If that doesn't work, delete the *mbx* file—for example, Outbox.mbx. This will delete all the text of the messages in your Outbox, so you'll have to recreate the messages.

Waving when the mail arrives

You can make your computer play a tune (play a *wav* file) when your mail arrives. To do this, choose Tools, Options, click the General tab, and mark the Play Sound When New Messages Arrive check box. This only makes sense if you have marked Check for New Messages Every [   ] Minute(s) in the same tab.

If you dial up to your Internet service provider, download your mail, and then disconnect, there's no point in doing this. Outlook Express must be running for the tune to play. (And if you receive your mail from the Internet and not an Intranet, you have to be connected to the Internet as well.)

You can, if you like, set your own sound to play when new messages arrive. Use the steps detailed in the "Applying sounds to application events" section in Chapter 16. Find the New Mail Notification event under the Windows events, and choose among the listed *wav* files, or browse for another one.

When Outlook Express is running and you're connected to the Internet (or your Intranet), an envelope appears in your Tray when mail arrives. Be sure to turn on your speakers.

Leaving mail on the server

If you are traveling, you might want to leave mail messages on your mail server until you get back, even though you want to read them now. That way, you can download them to your office computer when you return.

To do this, choose Tools, Accounts, highlight your mail server, click the Properties button, click the Advanced tab, and mark the Leave a Copy of Messages on Server check box.

You can take a copy of your address book with you on your portable just by copying your *username.wab* file from the \Windows\Application Data\ Microsoft\Address Book folder on your desktop computer onto your portable computer. We are assuming that you have already set up Outlook Express on your portable and that the *wab* files have the same name and location on your portable and desktop computer. You are just overwriting your portable's version with your desktop's version.

Undocumented

You need to make sure that both computers use the same location for the Windows Address Book. Open your Registry on both computers and go to HKEY_CURRENT_USER\Software\Microsoft\WAB\WAB4\Wab File Name to find the path.

Converting the mail

You can import Eudora, Netscape, Microsoft Exchange, Windows Messaging, or Outlook e-mail messages into Outlook Express format. In Outlook Express, just choose File, Import. If you have the Microsoft Exchange that came with the early Windows 95, upgrade to Windows Messaging to avoid a conversion bug.

To see how to import Pegasus messages, check out Eric Miller's "Outlook Express User Tips" at http://www.activeie.com/oe/.

You can find out more about Eudora, which uses the same message format as Outlook Express, at http://mango.human.cornell.edu/kens/MoreFAQ.html. Go to Qualcomm's web site at http://www.eudora.com/, where you can also download a freeware version of the program.

Importing and exporting addresses with the Windows Address Book

Wouldn't it be great to have just one universal address book that contained all the information you needed to contact a person and worked with all your other applications? The standalone Windows Address Book, the address book that Outlook Express uses, is Microsoft's latest shot at that moving target.

To encourage you to use the Windows Address Book, Microsoft needs to make it easy to import your contact list from your existing address book. It also has to make it possible to export Outlook Express contacts into Outlook if it hopes to get you to use this more cumbersome e-mail and PIM client.

You can import addresses from your Windows Messaging (or Microsoft Exchange or Outlook) address book into your Outlook Express address book. You can choose which Windows Messaging profile to use when importing, so this lets you choose which personal address book to import.

The problem is that you could quite easily have multiple entries for the same person in your Windows Messaging address book, because Windows Messaging is unable to correctly handle multiple e-mail addresses and fax numbers in one record. As you import the addresses, Outlook Express asks you (by default) whether to overwrite an address that it just imported when it encounters the next record with the same name. You don't know which record is the correct Internet address and which is a CompuServe or MSN address.

You can solve this problem in two ways. Either delete the extra entries in your Windows Address Book or delete them from a copy of your Windows Messaging *pab* file. If you use this second method, create a new Windows Messaging profile that points to this new copy. Open up Windows Messaging using this profile and delete the names with fax numbers or non-Internet addresses. Then use this profile when importing names into your Outlook Express address book.

Outlook Express also allows you to import addresses from Microsoft Internet Mail for Windows 3.1, Netscape Navigator, and Eudora. You can import an address file specified by the LDAP (Lightweight Directory Access Protocol) format or the comma-delimited CSV (Comma Separated Values) format. You can also export addresses in the CSV format, which allows you to import into Outlook.

To import addresses from other databases, you can use a Word macro that first imports them into *pab* files. Go to the Exchange Center at http://www.slipstick.com/exchange to find and download the macro. You'll also find other information on how to convert from other name databases. You should also check the "Interguru e-mail conversion" page at http://www.interguru.com/mailconv.htm.

There is a Registry entry that corresponds to your Outlook Express address book. Each address book uses your user name as its filename and adds the *wab* extension. If you move your Outlook Express address book to a new computer, make sure to update the Registry on the new computer so that it knows where to find the address book and what its name is. Look for an entry at HKEY_CURRENT_USER\Software\Microsoft\WAB\WAB4\Wab File Name. If you don't have this entry, add this key, double-click the Default value in the right pane of your Registry editor, and type the path and filename for your address book.

If you have configured your Windows 98 setup to use user profiles, the current user changes depending on who has logged in, so you can have multiple Outlook Express address books.

Merging Windows Address Books

Because you can import and export data from your Windows Address Book, you can merge data from one or more address books into an existing (or new) address book.

STEPS

Merging a Windows Address Book from Another Computer

Step 1. Open the address book on one computer, choose File, Export, Address Book, select Text File (Comma Separated Values), and click the Export button. In the CSV Export Wizard, set the target file extension as *csv* and mark every field if you want to export everything in the address book. Then click Finish.

Step 2. Copy the file to a folder holding temporary files on the target computer.

Step 3. Open the address book on the target computer. Choose File, Import, Address Book, select Text File (Comma Separated Values), and click the Import button. In the CSV Import Wizard, browse for the exported file name. You can choose which fields to import and where they go. Click Finish.

Step 4. You will be notified of any duplicate names as they are about to be imported, and you will get to choose whether to overwrite the existing names or not. If you choose not to overwrite, you will end up with multiple entries for the same name. You'll need to go back and remove the redundant entries manually.

Tip

You can also create a new blank Windows Address Book and merge names from other address books into it using these steps. To create a new blank Windows Address Book, click the Start button, and then click Run. Type **wab /New**. Enter the path and filename for the new blank address book.

If you want to see what else you can do with the *wab* command, try typing **wab /?**.

Outlook Express News

Highlight a news server account in your Folder List pane or Outlook bar and Outlook Express turns into a newsgroup reader. Notice the various changes on your toolbar and in your Tools menu.

Tip

Even if you use another e-mail client, you can still use Outlook Express as your news reader. To clear out the mail-related clutter, choose Tools, Accounts, and delete any mail accounts. Choose Tools, Options, click the General tab, and clear the Make Outlook Express My Default E-mail Program check box. Finally, you can rename the Outlook Express icon on your Desktop to News (highlight the icon and press F2).

Anti-SPAM

SPAMers build e-mail mailing lists from the addresses they find in postings to newsgroups.

Undocumented

If you don't want your address picked up by Usenet bots that scan Usenet newsgroups for addresses, then put a fake address in the E-mail Address field, such as fakename@fakenet.net. (Choose Tools, Accounts, highlight a news server, and click the Properties button.) Also make sure that you don't have your correct address in the Reply Address field.

Unfortunately, if you put a fake address in the E-mail Address field, newsgroup readers who want to reply to your postings with an e-mail message directly to you will not be able to; they'll have to send their responses only to the newsgroup. If you have different news server accounts, you can have different fake names for each account, and you can use your real e-mail address for your mail account.

Tip

If you want to indicate to other newsgroup subscribers that your indicated e-mail address is a not your actual address, you can change your posted name to something like SPAMers Beware. To do this, choose Tools, Accounts, highlight a news server, click the Properties button, and change the name in the Name field.

You can also use the Inbox Assistant to avoid some of the incoming SPAM. Highlight your Inbox folder, choose Tools, Inbox Assistant, and click the Add button. Click in the Subject field and type one word that you only see in the subject headings of SPAM messages (see Figure 19-8). Mark the Do Not Download from the Server check box and click OK. Repeat for additional such words.

Secret

Ann Tooke, Program Manager for Outlook Express, claims that the Inbox Assistant uses the *contains* criteria (it performs an OR search automatically). If you enter multiple words in the Subject field and separate them with spaces, Outlook Express should reject any SPAM that contains any one of the words in its subject heading.

Another option for avoiding Usenet bots is to add an asterisk to your E-mail Address field. You can then put a note in your signature pointing out the asterisk and asking respondents who want to contact you to remove the asterisk from the To field of their reply message.

If you want to let people respond easily while avoiding the SPAMers, you can also put your e-mail address in your signature. Respondents can just click on your address to create a new message. The disadvantages of this method are that they lose the indented original message (if they have configured their e-mail client to include it in replies), they have to type a subject in the new message, and they can't just click the Reply to All button.

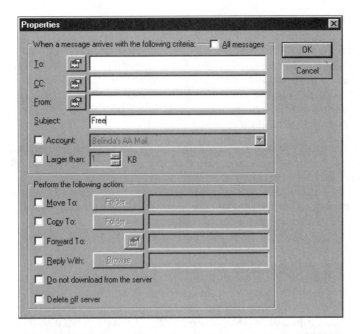

Figure 19-8: Type a word that only appears in the subject of SPAM messages.

Corrupted newsgroups

A number of symptoms have a similar cause: The file that stores the messages and message headers for a given newsgroup is corrupted. These symptoms include losing newsgroups from the list of newsgroups associated with a given news server, finding all new message headers mistakenly marked as read, or having Outlook Express fail to respond when a newsgroup is highlighted (requiring you to abort with Ctrl+Alt+Delete).

If you can carry this out, the first line of defense is to reset the newsgroup. (This may not be possible if Outlook Express crashes when you highlight the newsgroup.) Right-click any newsgroup with a problem, click Properties to display the Properties dialog box for that newsgroup, and click the Local Files tab. Then click the Reset button.

If that doesn't work, click the Delete button in the same Properties dialog box to delete the corrupted newsgroup file. Then resubscribe and download the newsgroup's message header list.

In a case where the new message headers are marked as read when they are updated, you can try to solve the problem by choosing Tools, Options, clicking the Read tab, and clearing the check box labeled Mark All Messages As Read When Exiting a Newsgroup. Also clear the check box labeled Message Is Read After Being Previewed for [ ] Second(s).

If none of these remedies work, you can delete the *nch* files (the files that contain the headers and, if downloaded, the messages) for the offending newsgroup. You'll find them in a folder under your news account's name in the \Program Files\Outlook Express*yourusername*\News or \Windows\ Application Data\Outlook Express*yourusername*\News folder. Unfortunately, the name of each *nch* file is nothing but numbers. Unless you look inside the files (using WordPad, for example), you won't be able to figure out which folder goes with which newsgroup.

If you delete an offending newsgroup file (or all of them), when you reconnect to the news server you'll probably want to download all the message headers currently stored on the news server and start over. If things get so bad that you delete everything in the news account's folder, or even everything under the News folder, you'll have to add your news servers again and resubscribe to your newsgroups.

Beware of cross posters

If you single-click a newsgroup message to view it in the preview pane, you might not notice if it has been posted to multiple newsgroups. You may assume that it has only been posted to the newsgroup that you are currently reading. This might give you the feeling you're part of a little community, and that you're only interacting with the people on this one newsgroup. This can be a false reading.

People can (and do) post messages to many different newsgroups at once. Sometimes this is legitimate; the person who posted the message is simply trying to get help wherever he or she can find it. Sometimes it's just SPAM. If you reply to a message that was posted in multiple newsgroups, your reply will by default get posted in all the newsgroups, not just the one you're currently participating in.

Undocumented

If you want to respond in just one newsgroup, highlight the message header and click the Reply to Group toolbar button. Click the newspaper icon to the left of the Newsgroups field, as shown in Figure 19-9, to display the Pick Newsgroups dialog box. Here, you can remove newsgroups and/or add others.

You can also click the newspaper icon when you're writing new messages if you want to send them off to other newsgroups.

Outlook Express always has a current news server. When you click a newsgroup on a different news server, the current news server changes. When you click the newspaper icon, the Pick Newsgroups dialog box only lists newsgroups available on the current news server.

Secret

If some of the newsgroups to which a message has been posted aren't present on the news server you are currently logged onto, you'll get an error message stating that the newsgroup name can't be resolved. This is particularly true with the Microsoft's news server because it only lists its own newsgroups. If you see this error message, you know without even double-clicking the message header that a cross poster sent the message.

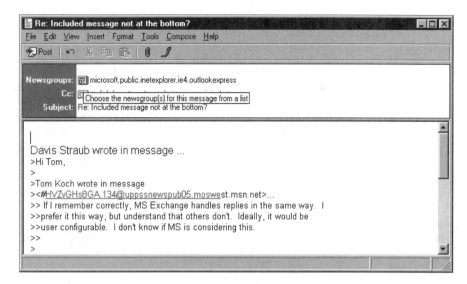

Figure 19-9: Click the newspaper icon on the left side of the Newsgroups field to tailor the list of newsgroups on which your message will be posted.

Reading the news offline

News readers (that is, human ones) who reside outside the United States often have to pay what appear to U.S. residents as exorbitant hourly rates to connect to the Internet. These people, and the few remaining U.S. citizens who don't have nearby Internet service providers with fixed monthly fees, will find it much cheaper to take their reading offline. Outlook Express gives you this option.

Outlook Express keeps on your computer a threaded list of message headers for each subscribed newsgroup. When you go online and browse a newsgroup, Outlook Express updates the threaded list of message headers in that one newsgroup. The message headers are downloaded when you click the newsgroup's name in the Folder List pane.

If you click each of your subscribed newsgroup names in your Folder List pane, you capture all of the message headers currently on the news server. You can then go offline, and by clicking message headers, choose which messages to download later when you go back online.

Alternatively, you can download the message headers in a set of newsgroups (see the next paragraph) and then go offline. You can then browse through the list of headers by highlighting the name of the newsgroup that you want to peruse in the Folder List pane. As you highlight various headers (you can use Shift and Ctrl to choose multiple headers), you can mark the ones whose messages you want to download. To do this, choose Tools, Mark for Retrieval, and then select Mark Message, Mark Thread, Mark All Messages, or Unmark from the submenu that appears. Once you have marked the messages you want to download, choose Tools, Download All. Outlook Express will download the marked messages from the news server.

If you want to download all the message headers from a number of newsgroups at once, it is easiest to specify which newsgroups' headers you want to download while you are offline, then connect and have Outlook Express automatically update the headers for each newsgroup. While you're offline, highlight the desired news server account in the Folder List pane, and then highlight the desired newsgroups in the message header pane. (If you want to download the headers from all the newsgroups on a given news server, highlight that server in your Folder List pane, highlight any newsgroup, and choose Edit, Select All.) Then choose Tools, Mark for Retrieval, New Headers. Finally, choose Tools, Download All.

You can now go through the headers and mark those whose associated messages presumably merit downloading (right-click each message, and choose Mark Message for Download). Choose Tools, Download All to go online and get the marked messages.

Too bad you can't right-click a marked message header and choose Unmark. If you want to unmark a given header, you'll have to highlight it and then click Tools, Mark for Retrieval, Unmark.

If you choose to download both the headers and the messages at the same time, you obviously don't need to go back and download the messages later. Of course, the initial download takes a bit longer than if you just get the headers, and you'll get a lot of messages that aren't of interest to you.

To do this, select the news server account in the Folder List. Select the newsgroups whose messages you wish to download in the message header pane. Right-click the selected newsgroups. Click Mark for Retrieval, All Messages.

If you choose to download New Headers, Outlook Express knows which headers you already have stored on your computer, so it won't download any old ones. Even if you download both the headers and the messages at the same time, you don't have to worry about Outlook Express going out and downloading messages associated with headers you have previously stored.

If you do want to download messages associated with headers that you already have stored on your computer, you can mark those headers for download individually or by using Select All. Or you can right-click the newsgroup name in the Folder List pane and choose Mark for Retrieval, All Messages. Then click Tools, Download This Newsgroup.

Tip

One problem with choosing to download all messages is the chance that there will be some long messages that take an inordinate amount of time to download. You can use Tools, Newsgroup Filters to reject all messages greater than a selected number of lines. Click the Add button in the Newsgroup Filters dialog box, mark the Message Has More Than [   ] Lines check box, and indicate the number of lines.

Keeping newsgroup messages

Only a few of the many newsgroup messages are worth keeping around for any length of time. If you have Tools, Options, Advanced, Delete Messages [   ] Days After Being Downloaded or Don't Keep Read Messages marked, then your newsgroup messages are going to go away after you perform a File, Clean Up Files, Compact command.

There is no way to mark individual messages within the newsgroups as keepers. If you want to preserve them for a while, you are going to have to move them to a folder. Drag and drop works great for this. You can also place the Copy To button on your news toolbar to facilitate moving newsgroup messages.

Catching up with the news

Outlook Express doesn't give you a way to automatically "catch up" on newly subscribed newsgroups — that is, to ignore the past messages and start fresh today. You'll need to download all the previously unread message headers in each of the newsgroups and then set the unread messages counter to zero to start fresh in the newsgroups. This can be quite tedious.

Undocumented

To set your newly subscribed newsgroups to begin today, take the following steps:

STEPS

Catching Up on Your Newsgroups

Step 1. Choose Tools, Options, and click the Read tab.

Step 2. Clear the Download [   ] Headers at a Time check box. Click OK. Outlook Express normally reads all the headers in a newly subscribed newsgroup, so these first two steps may not be necessary.

Step 3. Highlight the news server account in the Folder List pane. Select the newly subscribed newsgroups in the message header pane using the Shift and Ctrl keys.

Step 4. Choose Tools, Mark for Retrieval, New Headers. Then choose Tools, Download This Account. If you have configured other newsgroups under this account to receive new message headers, new messages, or all messages, this will also happen now. If you don't want these other newsgroups updated now, be sure to change their settings before you click Download This Account.

Step 5. When you have received all the message headers from all your newly subscribed newsgroups, keep the newsgroup names highlighted and choose Edit, Mark All As Read.

(continued)

STEPS *(continued)*

Catching Up on Your Newsgroups

Step 6. Click Tools, Options, Advanced, and mark the Don't Keep Read Messages check box. Click the Clean Up Now button.

Step 7. Select the news server from the drop-down list at the top of the Local File Clean Up dialog box, and click the Compact button.

ROT 13 in the news

Some newsgroup messages come in ROT 13 format. If you find a message that looks scrambled, double-click its header to open a separate message window, and then choose Edit, Unscramble (ROT13). This command makes messages formatted with ROT 13 readable by rotating the letters and numbers. It rotates the letters by 13 characters and the numbers by 5. For more information, check out http://premium.microsoft.com/support/kb/articles/q153/9/31.asp.

Multi-part files

In some newsgroups, you might come across postings that are in fact large files, most likely binary files. These files are often broken into several parts that are identified as such. In order to successfully discover the contents of these files, you need to recombine them and decode them. You can use Outlook Express to do just that.

Holding down your Ctrl key, click each message header that indicates it is a part of the larger file. Next, choose Tools, Combine and Decode (or right-click the highlighted headers and choose Combine and Decode from the context menu). You will be asked to select the proper order in which to reassemble the individual messages back into the larger file. Once you have moved the message headers up and down to get the proper order, click OK, and a new window will open with the decoded file.

You can also use this method to combine several postings into one file and print or save it as a separate file.

Connecting to a news server

In previous versions of Outlook Express, the unread message count was updated automatically when you highlighted the news server name (or news account name). The message count is quite useful because it tells you whether there are new messages in a given newsgroup. Now Outlook Express doesn't update the unread message count unless you click the newsgroup.

Secret

To force Outlook Express to go out and check the news server and update the unread message count, choose Tools, Options, click the General tab, and mark Check for New Messages Every [   ] Minutes. Also, choose Tools, Accounts, highlight your news server, click the Properties button, click the General tab, and mark Include This Account When Checking for New Messages. Then click the Connection tab in the same dialog box and mark Automatically Connect to This Server.

Tip

If you are reading news postings online and writing responses, you may at times get disconnected from the news server (but not necessarily from your Internet server provider). Press F5 or click View, Refresh to reconnect.

Some news servers require secure connections through the Secure Socket Layer protocol. If your news server requires this type of connection, choose Tools, Accounts, highlight your news account, click the Properties button, and then click the Advanced tab. Mark the This Server Requires a Secure Connection (SSL) check box. The port number in the field above the check box will change to 563.

Getting rid of old newsgroup files

When you unsubscribe from a newsgroup, Outlook Express doesn't erase the *nch* files that were created when you first subscribed. These files just sit there taking up disk space. Since their names are just numbers, it isn't easy to figure out which files are active and which belong to newsgroups you have dumped.

You can use your Explorer to find out.

STEPS

Removing Outdated Newsgroup Files

Step 1. Open Outlook Express. Highlight a newsgroup, and choose File, Clean Up Files, Compact. This will touch all of your currently subscribed newsgroup files and give them the present date and time.

Step 2. Drill down using Explorer to \Program Files\Outlook Express\ *yourusername*\News or \Windows\Application Data\Outlook Express*yourusername*\News depending on where your Outlook Express news files are stored. Find the *nch* files that have earlier dates. Move them to a temporary folder.

Step 3. Bring Outlook Express to the top of your Desktop. View each of your newsgroups to make sure their messages are still there. If not, copy back *nch* files one at a time to see if your message headers return.

Windows 98 newsgroups

The following is a list of newsgroups pertaining to Windows 98 (and Windows 95). The first newsgroups are hosted on the Microsoft support news server at msnews.microsoft.com. The others are Usenet newsgroups, and you should be able to find them on your Internet service provider's local news server.

You might be able to subscribe to some of the Microsoft newsgroups on your local Internet service provider's news server — your service provider decides which newsgroups it will carry. Microsoft does not officially support sending its newsgroups to other Internet service providers news servers. You can subscribe to the Microsoft newsgroups directly by choosing Tools, Accounts, Add, News and designating msnews.microsoft.com as the news server on the account.

Be sure to configure Outlook Express to access a news server before you try to subscribe to that news server's newsgroups.

This list of newsgroups was developed before Windows 98 was in final release. Undoubtedly new newsgroups are now available. When you subscribe to msnews or any other news server, you will be asked if you want to download the list of newsgroups available on that news server. Click Yes. You can search for Windows 98-specific newsgroups by choosing Tools, Newsgroups, and typing **Win98** in the Display Newsgroups Which Contain field.

http://support.microsoft.com/support/news/default.asp

news:microsoft.public.internet.netmeeting

news:microsoft.public.internet.personwebserv

news:microsoft.public.internetexplorer.ieak

news:microsoft.public.internetexplorer.java.activex

news:microsoft.public.internetexplorer.java.cab

news:microsoft.public.news.server.list

news:microsoft.public.win95.general.discussion

news:microsoft.public.win95.commtelephony

news:microsoft.public.win95.dialupnetwork

news:microsoft.public.win95.exchangefax

news:microsoft.public.win95.filediskmanage

news:microsoft.public.win95.msdosapps

news:microsoft.public.win95.multimedia

news:microsoft.public.win95.networking

news:microsoft.public.win95.printingfontvideo

news:microsoft.public.win95.setup

news:microsoft.public.win95.shellui

news:microsoft.public.win95.win95applets

news:comp.os.ms-windows.networking.win95

news:comp.os.ms-windows.setup.win95

news:comp.os.ms-windows.apps.compatibility.win95

news:comp.os.ms-windows.apps.utilities.win95

news:comp.os.ms-windows.win95.misc

news:comp.os.ms-windows.win95.setup

news:comp.os.ms-windows.networking.windows

news:comp.os.ms-windows.networking.tcp-ip

news:comp.os.ms-windows.apps.misc

news:comp.os.ms-windows.apps.utilities

news:comp.os.ms-windows.apps.winsock.misc

news:comp.os.ms-windows.apps.winsock.news

news:comp.os.ms-windows.apps.winsock.mail

news:comp.os.ms-windows.apps.comm

news:comp.os.ms-windows.networking.ras

news:comp.os.ms-windows.misc

Access to public news servers

If your Internet service provider does not have a news server, check out these web sites for listings of other news servers:

Site	Address
Deja News	http://www.dejanews.com
Public Access Usenet Sites	http://www.yahoo.com/News/Usenet/ Public_Access_Usenet_Sites/
One list	http://www.ts.umu.se/~maxell/Newsgroups/servers.html

Summary

Outlook Express gets you quickly up to speed with Internet e-mail and newsgroups.

▶ We show you how to make Outlook Express a lot easier to use and more powerful by making a few quick changes to its configuration.

▶ You'll find out where to turn to on the web for additional help using these programs.

▶ Make your spell checker work with Outlook Express.

▶ You can create fancy signatures and your own stationery using the built-in HTML capability in Outlook Express.

▶ Fix corrupted Outlook Express folders.

▶ We tell you where Microsoft and others are providing newsgroup support for their products.

Chapter 20

Windows Messaging

In This Chapter

We discuss a left-over Windows 95 product, Windows Messaging (originally called the Microsoft Exchange client), an e-mail and faxing application. If you need help using the strictly Internet/Intranet mail and news tool, Outlook Express, turn back to Chapter 19. In this chapter, we discuss:

▶ Quickly configuring Windows Messaging to send and receive a fax

▶ Sending and receiving e-mail over the Internet, CompuServe, and the Microsoft Network

▶ Using command line parameters to view message headers and begin composition of new messages

▶ Using message stores to manage your documents

▶ Renaming message stores and address books

▶ Composing mail from many different sources

▶ Creating a Microsoft Mail postoffice for your workgroup

▶ Configuring Windows Messaging to continuously monitor your phone line for incoming faxes without requiring that you exit the program to send and receive e-mail messages from your Internet service provider

---

Windows Messaging/Fax Is on the Windows 98 CD-ROM

Windows Messaging (and its predecessor, Microsoft Exchange) is a Windows 95 product. While it is on the Windows 98 CD-ROM, it isn't in the Windows 98 cabinet files, and isn't automatically installed. If your company has Exchange Server, you may have Exchange client, which replaces the version of Microsoft Exchange that came on the original Windows 95 CD-ROM. Outlook, the PIM that is integrated with Microsoft Office, also replaces and greatly enhances it. So why do we devote a chapter to it?

- If you upgrade Windows 95 to Windows 98, Windows Messaging is still there.

- Windows 98 doesn't provide a fax client, so Windows Messaging is very useful if you want to send a fax.

- If you don't have Office, you can use Windows Messaging for e-mail instead. Windows Messaging is a capable e-mail client that works with Microsoft Mail (an older proprietary LAN-based e-mail system), Internet-standard mail servers, as well as other e-mail systems.

- The Exchange client and Windows Messaging are almost identical, so any secrets we provide here will work for Exchange client. Although Outlook is now the client that comes with Exchange Server, you may still have the older Exchange client.

- Windows Messaging, the Microsoft Fax delivery add-ons, the Microsoft Mail delivery services, and the Microsoft Mail workgroup postoffice manager are all available on the Windows 98 CD-ROM.

You'll find the setup file for Windows Messaging in the exchange folder and the fax source file in the fax folder on your Windows 98 CD-ROM.

A little history

The original Windows 95 included the Microsoft Exchange client, version 4.0. The Windows 95 team did not develop this product. Brad Silverberg, Microsoft VP, brought it over from the Exchange team, which was focused on building a corporate e-mail server/client product. It never did fit in well with Windows 95. It was slow, it took much more memory to work well than the amount that was specified for the base Windows 95 configuration, and its hot key assignments were out in left field.

Five months after the release of Windows 95, Microsoft produced the Windows 95 Service Pack 1, which came with a new version of the Microsoft Exchange client. Ten months after Windows 95 was released, Microsoft updated the Microsoft Exchange client version 4.0 with Windows Messaging version 4.0. Microsoft changed the name because you continually had to say all three parts of the name, *Microsoft Exchange client*, to differentiate it from Microsoft Exchange Server. (Exchange Server runs on Windows NT servers and manages e-mail, documents, and discussion forums in corporate settings. It comes with its own clients.)

Windows Messaging is a moderate upgrade of the original Microsoft Exchange client. It loads faster, sends mail four times faster, and gets rid of a bunch of annoying bugs related to the Internet mail delivery services. Windows Messaging was built assuming you are connected to a vast empire of corporate mail (just like at Microsoft). Microsoft felt that what you needed most was a means to control and view this sea of memos and documents. The ability to quickly and easily send and receive a bit of e-mail (or fax) got lost in the design process (requiring one Wizard to bring back some ease of use and another to ease installation).

Microsoft has delivered a number of different and somewhat incompatible e-mail clients (and servers) over the past few years. This incompatibility has also extended to the various address books that accompany these e-mail products. Assuming that you are using the latest versions of these products (if you're not you might want to update them), you could be using:

- Windows Messaging, the updated version of the Microsoft Exchange client that came with the original Windows 95 CD-ROM

- The Microsoft Exchange client that comes with Microsoft Exchange Server

- Outlook Express, the update of Microsoft Internet Mail that comes with Internet Explorer 4.0 and Windows 98

- Outlook, a PIM/e-mail tool that comes with Office 97 or later

The first two clients are similar enough that we can discuss them in this chapter. We cover Outlook Express in the previous chapter. Outlook, which we don't cover because it is neither a Windows 95 nor a Windows 98 product as such, uses much of the Windows Messaging technology for its e-mail delivery and can read and write Windows Messaging files.

You can find the latest information about Windows Messaging, Outlook, and the Exchange Server at the Exchange Center, http://www.slipstick.com/exchange. Be sure to download the Exchange client and Windows Messaging help files (under FAQs). They are incredible. The author of this site, Sue Mosher, has written an excellent book on Exchange Server and Outlook. You can find out more about this and other books at her site.

Quickly Setting Up Windows Messaging to Send a Fax

If you don't have ready access to your Windows 98 CD-ROM, you can download Windows Messaging from the Microsoft web site at http://www.microsoft.com/windows95/info/exupd.htm. After you download the file, Exupdusa.exe, click it to install Windows Messaging. (Exupdusa.exe is the name of the US version; other versions have different names.)

The Inbox Setup Wizard steps you through the process of setting up Windows Messaging (see the steps below). It sets up a default "profile" with the information and mail delivery services that you desire. You'll most likely need to change the properties of your profile and information services after you are finished with the Wizard to correctly configure a profile with a fax delivery service. We'll show you how to do this.

STEPS

Installing, Setting Up, and Running Windows Messaging to Send a Fax

Step 1. Click the Start button, point to Settings, and then click Control Panel. Click the Mail icon in the Control Panel. This starts the Inbox Setup Wizard.

Step 2. The Inbox Setup Wizard will tell you if Windows 98 Setup has correctly detected your fax modem. If it hasn't, this Wizard will run another Wizard to detect your modem. You'll need to step through the modem detection process to be sure that your modem can deliver faxes (for details, turn to "Configuring Your Modem") in Chapter 31.

Step 3. The Inbox Setup Wizard asks you to select from a set of information services. Since you just want to send a fax, go ahead and choose Microsoft Fax (and clear the check marks for other mail delivery services) when given the opportunity. Step through the Inbox Setup Wizard and accept the default values. You will need to type your phone number at one point. Click Finish.

If you have previously installed Windows Messaging, you will be asked for a profile name. FAX would be an appropriate name for a profile that contains only the Microsoft Fax mail delivery service.

If you have previously created a profile, you can add Microsoft Fax to that profile by clicking the Mail icon in the Control Panel, clicking the Add button, and then highlighting Microsoft Fax.

Step 4. Click the Start button, point to Programs, Accessories, Fax, and then click Compose New Fax. This starts the Compose New Fax Wizard.

Step 5. Click Next in the first dialog box of the Compose New Fax Wizard. Enter a known fax number in the third field on the second dialog box (changing the area code if necessary). Click the Add to List button. Click the Next button, and the following Next button as well.

Step 6. Enter a subject and a message. This dialog box isn't much of a fax editor, and in fact, there are much better ways to compose a fax, which we cover later in this chapter in the section entitled "Microsoft Fax." Click Next to display a dialog box that lets you attach a file (document) to your fax. Click the Next button, and click the Finish button.

A fax with your message will now be sent to the number that you typed in step 5.

If you want to receive a fax, carry out steps 1 through 3 and then click the Inbox icon on your Desktop. If your current profile includes the Microsoft Fax, a small icon that looks like a fax/phone combination will appear in the Tray on your Taskbar. You can determine just how the phone is answered by right-clicking this icon. See "Receiving faxes" later in this chapter for more details.

Windows Messaging Features

Here are some of the features included with Windows Messaging:

- Send, receive, view, and store e-mail, faxes, and other documents using a variety of mail delivery services including Microsoft Mail (over your local area network), classic (pre-Internet mail server standards) CompuServe, the Internet or an Intranet, Microsoft Fax, classic Microsoft Network, and any centralized mail system that includes an appropriate MAPI driver

- Include files, documents, and OLE 2 objects in your messages

- A complete workgroup version of the Microsoft Mail Server (the Microsoft Mail postoffice is identical to the one created by WFWG 3.11, so WFWG 3.11 users and Windows 98 users can share the same postoffice)

- The workgroup version of Microsoft Mail Server, which is upgradeable to the enterprise-wide version of Microsoft Mail Server or the Microsoft Exchange Server

- Create and store multiple Windows Messaging configurations (profiles)

- Customizable Windows Messaging toolbar

- Remote access and remote message header preview (call your Microsoft Mail postoffice at work from your computer at home and decide which messages to download)

- Send formatted documents over the Internet transparently using MIME or UUENCODE

- Send editable files through Microsoft Fax with binary file transfer (attach a Word for Windows document to a fax message and ship it to someone with Microsoft Fax running on his or her computer)

- Send e-mail or faxes from Windows applications that enable the Send function (Windows Messaging is a full-featured MAPI client)

- Print (send) faxes from all Windows applications that can print

- Exchange public-key encrypted faxes

- Send faxes over a shared fax modem on your local area network

- Create fax cover pages with a cover page designer/editor

- Send a note on the fax cover page without having to send another fax page

- Use a really cool fax viewer

- Retrieve, without having to use a touch tone phone, faxes (and files) from fax-on-demand systems

- A general OLE 2 data store that can be used to store, organize, find, and view any of your documents — a much more powerful version of a file-management system than FAT or VFAT

- Share an address book with Microsoft Phone, which uses Windows Messaging to send and receive faxes

Or Lack Thereof

So what features are missing from Windows Messaging?

- You can't transparently store messages that come from the Microsoft Network bulletin boards, CompuServe forums, and Internet newsgroups (turn to "Outlook Express News" for a review of Outlook Express News)

- No online conferences, forums, or conference message threading except when used with Exchange Server

- No optical character recognition (Windows Messaging can't turn a Group 3 type fax into an editable document; you need add-on OCR software to accomplish this.)

- No fax annotations (Use the add-on Kodak Imaging for Windows .)

- Only one e-mail or fax address per address-book entry

- No automated distribution of faxes received by a shared fax across a local area network to the intended recipients

- No ">" symbols around quotes in replies (We show you how to add this.)

- No automated signatures (We show you how to add this. You can also use the Exchange client that comes with Exchange Server.)

- No message filtering (except if you use the Exchange client or Outlook with the Exchange Server)

- Limited message organizing

- No spelling checker (If you have installed a 32-bit word processor with a spelling checker, such as the one that comes with Microsoft Office, that spelling checker *will* be used by Windows Messaging. You'll find it in the Tools, Options menu.)

Tip Windows Messaging can eat up resources and swap space. If you experience trouble running it, make sure that you have 20MB of free disk space on the hard disk that includes the Windows 98 dynamic swap file. Also, Microsoft recommends a minimum of 8MB of RAM. We recommend at least 16MB, if not 32MB.

Installing Windows Messaging

Don't use Windows Messaging if you are using the Microsoft Exchange client that comes with Exchange Server. There are some naming and Registry incompatibilities between Windows Messaging and this version of the Microsoft Exchange client.

If you want to use Windows Messaging with the Exchange Server, uninstall the Microsoft Exchange client first. If you have Exchange Server, it is best to update to Outlook and use that as your Exchange client.

If you have previously installed the Microsoft Exchange client under Windows 95 (we are referring to Microsoft Exchange version 4.0, which comes with Windows 95, not with Exchange Server), you can install Windows Messaging without first uninstalling Exchange. Windows Messaging installs into its own folder under the Program Files folder.

If you try to install Windows Messaging after previously installing the Microsoft Exchange client for Exchange Server, you will be notified that you need to uninstall the Microsoft Exchange client. Don't do this. Just abort the install for Windows Messaging.

Secret

Windows Messaging installs itself in the \Program Files\Windows Messaging folder. The Microsoft Exchange client installs in the \Program Files\ Microsoft Exchange folder. The Windows Messaging setup files don't delete this folder when you install Windows Messaging after previously installing Microsoft Exchange. They leave some references to the Microsoft Exchange client in the Registry untouched. To fix this problem, choose View, Folder Options in the Explorer, and click the File Types tab. Select Mail Message, and click the Edit button to change the action that occurs when you click on a file with a *msg* extension. If you feel comfortable editing your Registry, you can change all references to the old location of Exchng32.exe to \Program Files\Windows Messaging.

You won't be able to uninstall Windows Messaging using the Control Panel, Add/Remove Programs, Install/Uninstall tab, Add/Remove Windows Messaging Update 1. This is a bug that Microsoft has chosen not to fix. To uninstall Windows Messaging, you need to run Exupdusa.exe and choose the remove option.

The Inbox Setup Wizard

To invoke the Inbox Setup Wizard, click the Mail icon in your Control Panel. If you have already set up a Windows Messaging profile and want to add a new one, click Show Profiles, and then click Add. If you haven't set up any profiles yet, Click Add.

This Wizard creates a *profile* for you. (We get into profiles in the "Windows Messaging Profiles" section later in this chapter.) You choose which information and mail delivery services will be part of your default profile.

Let the Inbox Setup Wizard configure a profile for you. Don't click Manually Configure Information Services in the Wizard's first dialog box, at least not until you've gone through this process a few times.

Windows Messaging names the default profile with your name (the Registered Owner's name). This name is stored in the Registry at HKEY_CURRENT_USER\Software\Microsoft\Windows Messaging Subsystem\Profiles.

The Inbox Setup Wizard doesn't let you configure all the properties of the services associated with a profile. You'll need to go back later and review and perhaps change the numerous properties associated with each profile and each mail delivery service. The Wizard will prompt you for different properties depending on which mail delivery services you have chosen to include in your profile.

We discuss how to respond to the various Inbox Setup Wizard dialog boxes in, among other sections, "Choosing mail delivery services" and "Message Stores" later in this chapter.

Windows Messaging command line parameters

After you install Windows Messaging, you'll find an Inbox icon on your Desktop. After you have configured Windows Messaging, you'll find that when you click this icon, Windows Messaging displays the contents of the mail folder that you had open when you last quit the program.

You can't change what clicking the Inbox icon does, but you can add a Windows Messaging shortcut to your Desktop that opens Windows Messaging with its focus on something other than the Inbox (see "Creating Shortcuts" in Chapter 10).

Undocumented

You can change the Windows Messaging menu item on the Start menu. To do this, click the Start button, and point to Programs. Right-click Windows Messaging and choose Properties. You can add a command line parameter after Exchng32.exe in the Target field (outside the double quote marks). If you add /n, you will open the New Message window of Windows Messaging when you start the program (see "Creating and Sending Mail" later in this chapter).

The /s command line parameter opens a search window. We discuss the address book command line parameter, /a, in "Opening the address book from the Desktop" later in this chapter.

Other legitimate command line parameters for Exchng32.exe are /f and /p (for opening and printing a file, respectively). However, they only work if the name of a message file (a file with the *msg* extension) is specified in the command line, for example: Exchange32 /f *filename*.msg. Given this restriction, using these command line parameters to modify the Windows Messaging item in the Start menu is probably not a good idea.

You can also invoke Windows Messaging with a shareware application named Exchange Profile Selector. This application feeds Windows Messaging a particular profile name. You can place a shortcut (or multiple shortcuts) to Exchange Profile Selector on your Desktop. We discuss the profile selector in "Opening Windows Messaging with a specific profile" later in this chapter.

Once you place these shortcuts on your Desktop, you can use TweakUI to remove the Inbox icon from the Desktop without losing any Windows Messaging functionality. Click your TweakUI shortcut on the Desktop (or the TweakUI icon in the Control Panel), click the Desktop tab, and clear the Inbox check box. See "Opening Windows Messaging with a specific profile" for more details.

Changing the Windows Messaging User Interface

You can make a few quick changes to the Windows Messaging user interface that can really improve its usability.

First, click the Show/Hide Folder List button on the left end of the Windows Messaging toolbar. This button switches between single- and dual-pane view. Dual-pane view lets you easily display the contents of your message folders. Navigating through your store of messages in single-pane view requires that you click the Up One Level button at the far left end of the toolbar and pay attention to the folder name displayed in the title bar.

Customize your toolbar by clicking Tools, Customize Toolbar. Highlight the Compose - New Message button in the right pane of the Customize Toolbar dialog box and click the Remove button to move it to the Available buttons box.

Next, do the same for the Go to Inbox button. With the highlight on the separator after Tools - Address Book, highlight Compose - New Message in the left pane and click the Add button, and then highlight Tools - Deliver Now and click the Add button again. This puts three commonly used buttons next to each other by moving two buttons from the Available buttons box onto the toolbar.

If you use Windows Messaging to log on remotely (to your office or to your Internet service provider), you may want to use the Tools, Remote Mail command to download file headers and choose which messages to download. Unfortunately, there isn't a toolbar button for this function.

You can reset the toolbar to the default settings by clicking the Reset button in the Customize Toolbar dialog box.

Windows Messaging Profiles

The Inbox Setup Wizard steps you through the configuration of a default Windows Messaging profile. This may be the only profile you ever need. You can edit this profile at any time to reflect the way you want to send and receive e-mail and faxes. You can ignore profiles if you only use this one.

A Windows Messaging profile is just a specific set of information services. These services include:

- Message store(s)
- Your personal address book and perhaps other address books
- E-mail (and fax) delivery service(s)
- The location of your postoffice (which Microsoft insists on spelling as one word) if you are connected to Microsoft Mail

Windows 98 provides hardware profiles (see "Hardware Profiles" in Chapter 25), user profiles, and Windows Messaging profiles. You can set up user profiles for different users on the same computer, and set up different Windows Messaging profiles for each of these users. Logging onto Windows 98 as a given user (using user profiles) connects you to that user's default Windows Messaging profile. To see how to set up multiple users, turn to "Setting up Windows 98 for multiple users" in Chapter 12.

You'll want additional Windows Messaging profiles if:

- More than one person uses the same computer, so each user can have his or her own personal message store
- Your computer is sometimes locally connected to a network, and sometimes calls into a network from a remote location using a modem and connects to a Microsoft Mail postoffice on the network
- You want different profiles in order to keep different information or mail delivery services separate

Tip

You can't change the name of the default profile during the Windows 98 Setup or when you run the Inbox Setup Wizard for the first time (unless you click the Manually Configure Information Services button). Later, you can make a copy of this profile, change its name to something meaningful, and erase the original profile.

If you find Windows Messaging attempting to connect to a second mail delivery service without first closing the connection with the first service, create separate profiles for each mail delivery service you use. Next create a profile containing two mail delivery services and see if they get along, and then try a profile with three, and so on.

There is a major problem with using multiple Windows Messaging profiles with one user. If you open and close Windows Messaging repeatedly (say to switch between profiles) you may find that you are unable to switch to different profiles and that you have to reboot Windows 98 altogether.

This problem is caused by a bug in MAPI (Messaging Application Programming Interface), a Microsoft DLL that runs in the background while you are running Windows Messaging. MAPI isn't swept out of memory when you exit Windows Messaging, but hangs around for a minute or two. If you repeatedly invoke and exit Windows Messaging, MAPI gets confused and Windows Messaging quits working.

Secret

You can get MAPI out of memory after you exit Windows Messaging. Press Ctrl+Alt+Delete, select Mapisp32 in the Close Program dialog box, and click the End Task button.

Windows Messaging has a little trouble with profiles that contain both Internet mail and a fax delivery service. You may get the error message "The port is already open." Sometimes outgoing faxes are never sent. The problem occurs if you invoke Windows Messaging and then click Deliver Now a little too quickly while Windows Messaging is trying to set up Microsoft Fax. If you have Windows Messaging set to poll Internet mail on a schedule, it can also try to dial out while Microsoft Fax is in the process of initializing the modem.

As a partial fix, you can wait to click Deliver Now until you see the Fax icon appear in the Tray. If you are using Microsoft Phone, it is best to combine your fax and other mail delivery services into one profile that is used by Microsoft Phone. If you do this, you can send/receive faxes and send e-mail to your Internet service provider while Microsoft Phone is running.

Undocumented

If you have both the Internet and Microsoft Network mail delivery services in one profile, you should set the Internet mail delivery to happen first. In the Windows Messaging menu bar, choose Tools, Options, and then click the Delivery Tab. Highlight Internet Mail and move it up with the arrow buttons.

The point of putting Internet mail first is that the Microsoft Network mail delivery service tries to deliver Internet mail also (it assumes that it is the Internet service provider). If you want your Internet mail to go by way of your Internet service provider, then its delivery service should go first.

Personal Information Store

A *message store* is a database of messages stored in one file. It includes your message Inbox, Outbox, and Sent Items, as well as other message folders you have created. The default filename for the message store is Mailbox.pst (although you can name it anything you like). By default, Windows Messaging places Mailbox.pst in the \Windows folder (which we consider a very poor place to store this file).

A much better place to keep your message store and your personal address book is the My Documents folder, or a subfolder of that folder. If multiple people use the computer, create subfolders for them under the My Documents folder.

The message store starts with the default name Personal Information Store — although you can rename it if you like — and Windows Messaging refers to it in dialog boxes as Personal Folders (referring to your collection of message folders). You only need one message store, because you can store all your messages from all information services in this single store.

You can, however, create additional special-purpose message stores if you choose. For instance, you might create different message stores for:

- Archival messages
- Messages from different information services
- Messages for different users
- Documents unrelated to messages

Each message store you create is a separate *pst* file, and you can put your various message store files in different Windows 98 folders if you like.

A profile can have multiple message stores, although only one message store can be designated as the active message store. The *active message store* is the one that includes the Inbox, Outbox, and Sent Items folders. If you include multiple message stores in one profile, you can easily copy or move messages from one store to another.

Your message store is compressed automatically after you delete messages. For this to occur, Windows Messaging has to be running, the amount of recoverable space has to be at least 4 percent of the total size of the message store, and the processor must have idle time. If you have heard your hard disk clicking away while you have Windows Messaging running, now you know why.

You can manually start a compression of your message store. In Windows Messaging, choose Tools, Services. Highlight your message store name (Personal Folders is the default), click Properties, and then click Compact Now.

Address books

Your *address book* is a database and, like your message store, it is stored in one file. Your default Windows Messaging address book has the default filename Mailbox.pab. You can name this file anything you like—just use the *pab* extension. Windows Messaging stores your address book in the \Windows folder (poor choice). Its default name is Personal Address Book. You can name your address book anything you like and store it wherever you want.

If you are connected to a local area network, you will find address books tied to the postoffice(s) found on network servers. If you are using Microsoft Mail, you will find a postoffice address list on the computer that houses your workgroup postoffice.

You may want to store the addresses of your regular e-mail correspondents in your personal address book if you are not always connected to the postoffice server. A system or workgroup administrator may maintain the postoffice address list. You can send mail to correspondents on the postoffice list by choosing names from it.

Other information services also maintain mailing lists. For example, the Microsoft Network maintains a list of all the people who have accounts on it.

You can associate your existing CompuServe address book with a profile that contains a personal address book and the CompuServe mail delivery service.

A profile can have only one personal address book attached to it at a time. The CompuServe address book is not considered a personal address book, even though it is your personal CompuServe address book.

If you don't have Microsoft Mail and you want to use a shared address book in addition to your personal address book, you can purchase the Exchange Server. If Exchange Server is a bit much for you, you might want to check out the shared address book feature in OpenSoft's ExpressMail software. You can explore OpenSoft's software at http://www.opensoft.com/products/expressmail. They also provide a POP3/SMTP mail server that works with Windows Messaging.

Mail delivery services

Using Windows Messaging, you can connect to the following e-mail and fax delivery services:

- Microsoft Mail
- The Microsoft Network (MSN)
- CompuServe
- Internet mail
- Microsoft Fax
- Other third-party e-mail delivery services compliant with MAPI

The MAPI drivers that these mail delivery services use to connect to Windows Messaging are considered by Microsoft to be personal gateways — gateways that connect Windows Messaging to another mail system. Microsoft sells other server gateways that link the Microsoft Mail Server and the Exchange Server to other e-mail systems.

Microsoft Mail

A workgroup version of Microsoft Mail is included with Windows Messaging (exupdusa.exe). You can create and administer a workgroup postoffice that can be shared by all the members of a workgroup whether they are running Windows 98, Windows 95, or WFWG 3.11. In most cases, you will want to have only one postoffice for your workgroup.

If you want to exchange mail using the Microsoft Mail connection with postoffices outside your workgroup, you need to upgrade the computer with the postoffice to the Microsoft Mail Server by installing the Microsoft Mail Postoffice upgrade or the Microsoft Exchange Server. Gateways to other mail systems are available and work with Microsoft Mail Server or Microsoft Exchange Server.

The Microsoft Network

The Microsoft Network (MSN) is Microsoft's online information service. You can send and receive e-mail to and from other Microsoft Network subscribers or over MSN's Internet connection to and from anyone with an Internet e-mail address. MSN provides Internet access as well as its own interest areas.

Windows Messaging connects to the Microsoft Network using the MAPI protocol. This was the first e-mail protocol implemented by the Microsoft Network.

Microsoft Network also provides Internet standard POP3 and SMTP e-mail servers. You can't use the Internet mail delivery service with Windows Messaging to log on to these servers because they require Secure Password Authentication, which Windows Messaging doesn't support. If you want to connect to the Internet standard e-mail servers at MSN, you either need to use Outlook or Outlook Express.

CompuServe

If you have a CompuServe account, you can have Windows Messaging call your account (using its TAPI-compatible dialer) and check if you have any mail. Of course, you can also send mail through CompuServe.

You can send and receive mail to and from CompuServe subscribers, or to and from anyone with an Internet e-mail address (using CompuServe as your Internet connection).

Secret

Unfortunately, you can't send and receive messages that are posted on CompuServe forums, even if the messages are addressed to you. You'll still need to use WinCIM or some other CompuServe interface program to manage your forum message traffic.

CompuServe Mail version 1.1 (version 1.0 came with the original Windows 95 CD-ROM) can't handle the Windows Messaging version of Remote Mail. You'll need to download a later version from CompuServe (GO CSMAIL).

CompuServe now provides POP3 and SMTP e-mail servers. You can connect to these servers using the Internet mail delivery service with Windows Messaging, or Outlook Express.

Internet

If you have an account with an Internet service provider, you can use Windows Messaging as your e-mail client. You can send and receive regular ASCII Internet e-mail, and you can send messages in either MIME (Multipurpose Internet Mail Extensions) or UUENCODE format.

The Internet client will connect to SMTP (Simple Mail Transport Protocol) and POP3 (Postoffice Protocol version 3) mail boxes. You'll need to bind

Microsoft's TCP/IP protocol to your Dial-Up Adapter if you call into an Internet service provider, or to your network card if you access the Internet through a server on your local area network. You'll find details about TCP/IP in "Bind TCP/IP to your Dial Up Adapter" and "Dial-Up Networking to the Internet" in Chapter 18.

You'll want to use the Internet Connection Wizard after you have installed Windows Messaging to set up a connection to your Internet service provider. See "The Internet Connection Wizard" in Chapter 18.

Microsoft Fax

You can send and receive faxes if you install the Microsoft Fax delivery service in one of your profiles. Windows 98 can send faxes through the fax/modem card in your computer or over a shared fax modem in your workgroup on a computer running Windows 98.

Third-party MAPI mail delivery systems

Other companies can provide MAPI interfaces to their mail systems. If you have other MAPI drivers, you can configure a Windows Messaging profile to use these mail delivery services just as you would any other delivery service.

Tip

You can't use Windows Messaging to receive e-mail from or deliver e-mail to services that don't have MAPI drivers. This includes almost all the bulletin boards without Internet services.

Windows Messaging works with Netscape Navigator. You can also use Windows Messaging to connect to AT&T mail. WinFax Pro works with Windows Messaging, and it can use the Windows Messaging address book. If you want to use the cc:Mail server with Windows Messaging, you can get a MAPI interface for cc:Mail from Transend Corporation at http://www.transendcorp.com.

You'll find other third-party software that works with Windows Messaging at the Exchange Center, http://www.slipstick.com/exchange.

Creating Windows Messaging Profiles

You don't necessarily have to create Windows Messaging profiles, because you already created one profile when you first configured Windows Messaging. You can edit that profile, if you like, so it matches your needs. See "Editing Windows Messaging profiles" later in this chapter.

If you want to create a new Windows Messaging profile, you have two entry points. To add a new profile when you only have one, take the following steps:

STEPS

Creating a New Windows Messaging Profile

Step 1. Click the Start button, Settings, and then Control Panel.

Step 2. Click the Mail icon.

Step 3. Click the Show Profiles button.

Step 4. Your current profiles are displayed in the list box of the Mail dialog box, as shown in Figure 20-1. Click Add to start the Inbox Setup Wizard or click Copy to make a copy of the highlighted profile. You can edit it later.

Figure 20-1: The Mail dialog box.

Undocumented

If you have more than one Windows Messaging profile and you have chosen the option that lets you pick a profile when you start Windows Messaging, you can start the Inbox Setup Wizard from the Inbox icon on your Desktop. Click the Inbox icon to display the Choose Profile dialog box, and instead of selecting an existing profile, click the New button. To find out how to configure Windows Messaging to prompt you to choose a profile, see "Picking among profiles at Windows Messaging startup" later in this chapter.

Windows Messaging profiles for multiple users

If you have configured your Windows 98 computer for multiple users (using user profiles), you can run the Inbox Setup Wizard while logged onto each user to associate a default Windows Messaging profile for each person. (To see how to set up your computer for multiple users, turn to "Setting up Windows 98 for multiple users" in Chapter 12.) Click the Start button, Log Off, choose a new user name to log in under, and then run the Inbox Setup Wizard. Repeat this process for each user.

Editing Windows Messaging profiles

You can edit your Windows Messaging profile(s), not just to change the properties of a given profile, but also to change the properties of an address book, a message store, or a mail delivery service.

You can start editing a Windows Messaging profile in one of two ways. First, you can click the Mail icon in the Control Panel and click the Show Profiles button (if you have more than one profile). Highlight a particular profile in the Windows Messaging Profiles dialog box, and then click the Properties button.

Second, you can click the Inbox icon on your Desktop, choose a profile (if you're given this option), and then click Tools, Options in the Windows Messaging window.

The first method allows you to pick which profile you are going to edit before you edit it. The second method lets you select a profile to edit, but only if you have previously configured Windows Messaging to give you this choice (see the next section). In addition, the second method gives you access to more properties than the first.

Picking among profiles at Windows Messaging startup

If you want to configure Windows Messaging to let you choose a profile when you start Windows Messaging (assuming you have already created more than one profile), take the following steps:

STEPS

Picking Your Own Startup Profile

Step 1.   Click the Inbox icon on your Desktop.

(continued)

STEPS *(continued)*

Picking Your Own Startup Profile

Step 2.   Click Tools, Options to display the General tab of the Options dialog box, as shown in Figure 20-2. (You won't have the Idioms tab unless you have installed Internet Idioms.)

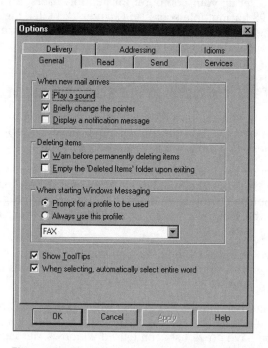

Figure 20-2: The General tab of the Options dialog box. If you want to choose which profile to use when you start Windows Messaging, mark the Prompt for a Profile to Be Used option button.

Step 3.   Mark the Prompt for a Profile to Be Used option button.

Step 4.   Click OK. Choose File, Exit and then restart Windows Messaging to have the changes take effect.

The next time you click the Inbox icon on your Desktop, the Choose Profile dialog box will appear to let you choose among different profiles.

Adding or removing information services

When you originally create a profile, you can choose which mail delivery services you want to include in it. You can later go back and remove or add mail delivery services and message stores, or change to another personal address book.

To add or remove information services, you have two options:

STEPS

Adding or Removing Information Services

Step 1. Click the Start button, point to Settings, and then click Control Panel.

Step 2. Click the Mail icon.

Step 3. If you want to add or remove information services in the profile that normally starts when you click the Inbox icon on your Desktop, click the Add or Remove button. If you want to add or remove services from another profile, click the Show Profiles button first, highlight the desired profile, and then click the Properties button to display the Services tab of the Properties dialog box for the profile, as shown in Figure 20-3.

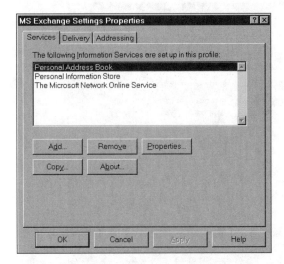

Figure 20-3: The Services properties for profile. Click Add or Remove to add or remove an information service.

Step 4. Click the Add button to add a new information service or the Remove button to remove the highlighted service.

You can also get to the Services properties for a profile by clicking the Inbox icon on your Desktop, choosing Tools, Options in the Windows Messaging window, and then clicking the Services tab.

When adding a mail delivery or other information service, you may be prompted to configure the service. To do this, you'll need to edit the properties associated with that service. We discuss editing the properties of individual mail delivery services in the "Choosing mail delivery services" section later in this chapter.

Editing information services

Each information service—mail delivery services, message stores, and personal address book—has associated properties. To edit these properties, you just highlight the information service in the profile's Services tab and click the Properties button.

Each mail delivery service has its own unique set of properties as determined by the characteristics of the mail delivery system. The first of eight tabs for Microsoft Mail (the Connection tab) is shown in Figure 20-4. We discuss editing the individual properties of the different mail delivery services in the "Choosing mail delivery services" section later in this chapter.

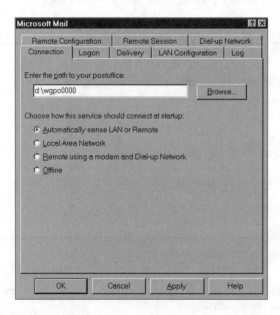

Figure 20-4: The Connection properties for Microsoft Mail. Enter the path for your postoffice in the first field.

You can set the properties for the message store by highlighting the name of the message store in a profile's Services tab, and then clicking the Properties button. We discuss these properties in the "Message Stores" section later in this chapter.

Not only can you change the properties of your address book, you can also change the properties of each address (or individual) in the address book. On the Windows Messaging toolbar, click the Address Book button, then double-click a name in your address book. We discuss address books further in the "Address Book" section later in this chapter.

Opening Windows Messaging with a specific profile

Tip

You can use a shareware program called Exchange Profile Selector to open Windows Messaging with a specific profile, allowing you to bypass the Choose Profile dialog box. Say you have one profile for faxing, another for Internet e-mail, and a third for CompuServe e-mail. You can place three shortcut icons on the Desktop, each of which calls Windows Messaging and uses the appropriate profile.

You'll find the Exchange Profile Selector on our *Windows 98 Secrets* CD-ROM or on the web at http://ourworld.compuserve.com/homepages/jsijm. You'll need version 1.3 or later to work with Windows Messaging. You can use TweakUI to get rid of the Inbox icon from your Desktop. After you place shortcuts to the Exchange Profile Selector on your Desktop, you won't need to keep the Inbox icon around.

Edit each shortcut's Target field to include the profile's name. (To get to the Target field, right-click the shortcut, click Properties, and click the Shortcut tab.) Be sure to include the pathname and Eps.exe in the Target field, and enclose them in double quote marks if there is a space in the pathname. Enclose the profile name in a separate set of double quote marks (if there is a space in its name). Separate the two sets of names with a space.

Using these shortcuts is also a handy way to tell Windows Messaging which folder to open by default when you choose Insert, File in a New Message window. To do this, edit the shortcut (right-click it, click Properties, and click the Shortcut tab) and change the Start In folder to the one you want to use as the default for attachments.

Choosing mail delivery services

The first step in creating a profile is choosing the mail delivery service(s) that will be included in the profile. Each mail delivery service has a specific set of dialog boxes that get included in the Inbox Setup Wizard if you chose that mail delivery service for inclusion in the profile when you created it.

Each mail delivery service will have its own set of properties. Figure 20-4 shows the first of eight tabs for Microsoft Mail delivery service. Most of the values in these tabs are not accessible when you're creating a profile. To change these values, you need to edit them after you've created the profile.

You can have multiple mail delivery services in a single profile. In fact, this is the default when you first install Windows Messaging and run the Inbox Setup Wizard. If you have multiple mail delivery services in one profile, Windows Messaging accesses them one at a time. For example, if you have the MSN, Internet and CompuServe mail delivery services in your profile and you ask Windows Messaging to deliver your e-mail (Tools, Deliver Now), it will call each service in turn and send and receive e-mail from each of them.

If you get an error message stating that no transport was available, it's probably because you are trying to send a message that doesn't have the appropriate mail delivery service in your current profile. For example, you may be trying to send a message to a Microsoft Network user and addressing it with a Microsoft Network name, but there is only an Internet mail delivery service in your current profile.

If you put multiple mail delivery services in one profile, you can avoid or reduce this problem. You can always check the recipient's address (right-click the name in the To field, and click Properties) to see that it is in the correct format for the current mail delivery service.

To edit the properties of a mail delivery service, you need to focus on it. Here's how:

STEPS

Displaying a Mail Delivery Service's Properties

Step 1. Click the Start button, point to Settings, and then click Control Panel.

Step 2. Click the Mail icon.

Step 3. Highlight a profile. Click the Properties button. Highlight a mail delivery service. Click Properties.

Internet mail properties

In the Internet Mail Server field in the General tab of the Internet Mail dialog box (shown in Figure 20-5), you can enter either the IP address or the name of your POP3 mail server. Be sure to get the name of your POP3 and your SMTP mail servers from your Internet service provider when you contact them to establish an account. Typically, the names of these servers are the same and are mail.*yourserviceprovider*.com. Other options include pop3.*yourserviceprovider*.com and smtp.*yourserviceprovider*.com.

Enter the name that you use to log onto your e-mail account in the Account Name field. *Account name* is a synonym for your user ID or host name. The e-mail account name could be different than your logon name (the name you use to log onto your Internet service account), but your ISP will probably set these names to be the same. We describe the differences in "Service provider account information" in Chapter 18.

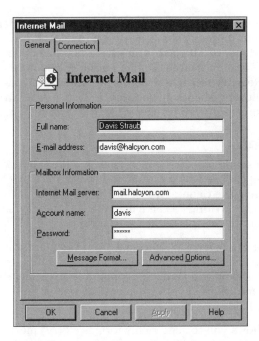

Figure 20-5: The General tab of the Internet Mail dialog box.

Your password is the password for your e-mail account. This is usually the same as your password for logging onto your account with your Internet service provider, but it can be different. You can log onto one Internet service provider, and access your e-mail account on another. See "Multiple e-mail accounts" in Chapter 19.

The SMTP server handles outgoing mail, and the POP3 server handles incoming mail. If your SMTP mail server has a different name than your POP3 server, click the Advanced Options button and type the name of your SMTP mail server. You can type friendly names if your Internet service provider has a DNS (domain name server) server. Otherwise, type IP addresses.

Click the Connection tab in the Internet Mail dialog box to set how Windows Messaging connects to the Internet. If your computer is connected to the Internet (or to an Intranet) through a local area network, choose Connect Using the Network. If you're calling into your Internet service provider, choose Connect Using the Modem, and then choose the Dial-Up Networking connectoid that you'll use to make the connection to your service provider. (See the "Dial-up connection to your service provider" section in Chapter 18.) You'll also want to mark the Work Off-Line and Use Remote Mail options if you are calling in.

If you dial in to log onto your Internet account, click the Login As button in the Connection tab. Type your logon or Internet service provider account name and password. They may be different than your e-mail account name and password.

It is possible, although not likely, that your Internet service provider (or the POP3 mail server on your Intranet) has been set up to use a different port ID than the agreed upon standard 110. If so, you will experience difficulties sending and receiving e-mail messages. To find out more about this problem and how to edit your Registry to change the port address, use your Internet Explorer to find the following Microsoft Knowledge Base article: http:// premium.microsoft.com/support/kb/articles/q133/1/88.asp.

Message format

You have the option of sending outgoing messages in either MIME or UUENCODE format. You choose which format you want to use by clicking the Message Format button in the General tab of the Internet Mail dialog box. If everyone to whom you are writing has an e-mail reader that can handle the MIME format, you'll want to use this higher level format.

The UUENCODE format is a tagged ASCII format. Your recipient will need an UUDECODE program to translate your message into a formatted text message. Windows Messaging and Outlook Express automatically decode MIME or UUENCODED messages. If your recipient has one of these two programs, no worries, mate.

Windows Messaging allows you to send richly formatted (*rtf*) messages to any or all of your recipients. To send such messages, you need to specify this preference for your recipient by marking the Always Send to This Recipient in Microsoft Exchange Rich-Text Format check box in the Address tab of the Properties dialog box for the recipient. (Right-click the recipient in your personal address book and click Properties.)

If your recipient can't read rich formatted text, but you have the rich-text box checked, he or she will receive attachments from you that contain unreadable (but ASCII) characters.

Secret

If your recipients are getting messages from you that contain an = sign at the end of your lines, click the Message Format button in the General tab of the Internet Mail dialog box, and clear the MIME check box. See "UUENCODE or MIME" in Chapter 19 for more details on this issue.

Outlook and Outlook Express both solve the problem of incompatible MIME implementations that give rise to this = sign problem.

Secret

If a recipient is getting e-mail messages from you with lines that are too long, you should turn off rich text formatting for that recipient.

Windows Messaging encodes attachments to your messages using whichever method you have chosen for encoding your messages. Some of your recipients may not be able to read attachments if their e-mail clients do not automatically decode encoded messages. They will have to use separate decoder programs to read your attachments.

Don't encode a file before you attach it to a message. Windows Messaging automatically encodes the attachment, so if you do it, it will be encoded twice. Your recipient will then have to decode it twice.

If you want to know more about MIME, check out: http://www.mathcs. carleton.edu/students/pollatsd/MIME/index.html or gopher://atlas.acpub. duke.edu/00/email/mime or http://www.cis.ohio-state.edu/text/faq/usenet/ mail/mime-faq/.

CompuServe properties

The classic CompuServe mail delivery service comes with its own unique set of properties. You can download the CompuServe MAPI driver from CompuServe at GO CSMAIL.

You'll be asked a number of questions about your CompuServe account after you click Setup.exe. You will be asked to give your CompuServe folder, user name, CompuServe ID number, password, and phone number. If you have been using WinCIM for a while, it's easy to forget your password, and WinCIM just displays it as a bunch of asterisks. Let's hope that you wrote it down someplace.

CompuServe's WinCIM keeps a separate address book. You can use this address book and your personal address book when sending messages through CompuServe (either to people on CompuServe or to Internet addresses through CompuServe). You can also easily move people from your WinCIM address book to your personal address book once you start Windows Messaging with a profile that includes CompuServe.

If you are using CompuServe's POP3 and SMTP mail servers, you can just use the Internet mail delivery service to communicate with them.

Message Stores

Windows Messaging refers to a message store as your Personal Information Store or Personal Folders. Messages that you receive and create are stored in folders in a message store file, which is a database.

You can have multiple message stores, although one is plenty. The default message store (Mailbox.pst) is created for you when you set up Windows Messaging.

A message store comes with a standard set of folders: Inbox, Outbox, Sent Items, and Deleted Items. You can add additional folders to conveniently order your messages.

Undocumented

You can easily move a message store. Just use your Explorer to move the corresponding *pst* file to a new location. When you open Windows Messaging with a profile that uses that message store, you will be asked to provide a new message store. You can simply browse to the new location.

Adding a message store to a profile

A profile can have only one personal address book. It can have only one Internet mail delivery service (although it can have other types of mail delivery services). But any profile can have multiple message stores. You can create a message store that will be an archive for your old messages or one for messages of a certain type.

You can create a profile that doesn't have any mail delivery services or a personal address book, just message stores. You can use this profile to move messages from your regular message store to archive message stores.

Windows Messaging loads faster if you keep your message store small. By using archive message stores and a separate profile to archive messages, you can reduce the size of your regular message store.

A message store is one of the Windows Messaging information services. To add a message store to a profile, first follow the steps detailed in the section earlier in this chapter entitled "Adding or removing information services," and then take the following steps:

STEPS

Adding a Message Store to a Profile

Step 1. When the Add Service to Profile dialog box (shown in Figure 20-6) is displayed on your Desktop, double-click Personal Folders in the Available Information Services list.

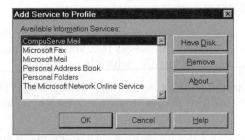

Figure 20-6: The Add Service to Profile dialog box. Double-click the information service you want to add to the profile. In this case, double-click Personal Folders.

Step 2. You'll be asked to provide a name and location for the message store file. You can put a message store file wherever you like. You can name it whatever you want to, but make sure that its extension is *pst*.

Step 3. You now have the option of renaming this particular message store, as shown in Figure 20-7. You can also protect this message store with a password.

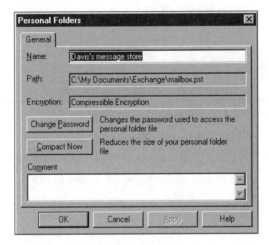

Figure 20-7: The dialog box that appears when you're creating Personal Folders. You can give the message store a password if you like. If the message store file is on a compressed drive and you want to encrypt it, choose Compressible Encryption.

Step 4. Click OK.

Changing a message store's name

You can change the long descriptive name of an existing message store by taking the following steps:

STEPS

Changing a Message Store's Name

Step 1. Click the Inbox icon on your Desktop.

Step 2. Click Tools, Services on the Windows Messaging menu bar. Double-click the name of the message store you want to change.

Step 3. Type a new name in the Name field and click OK.

Which message store?

If you have only one message store, all the messages go there. If you have more than one, you can specify which one you want to store new messages in by taking the following steps:

STEPS

Specifying the Active Message Store

Step 1. Click the Inbox icon on your Desktop.

Step 2. Choose Tools, Options.

Step 3. Click the Delivery tab in the Options dialog box.

Step 4. Choose one of the message stores in the drop-down list at the top of the dialog box.

Step 5. Click OK.

You can switch back and forth between message stores, making first one then another the active store. You can also drag and drop messages between folders in a given message store and between message stores. This works well if one of the message stores is for archival storage.

If you have multiple message stores contained in a profile, they show up in the left pane of your Windows Messaging window. The active message store contains the Inbox and Outbox.

Sorting message headers

Undocumented

Each message in your message store has a header. There are 47 fields — Subject, From (sender), Received (date), Conversation Topic, and so on — in the message header. When you're using the dual-pane view in the Windows Messaging window, the message headers appear in the right pane, and the window looks like an Explorer window in Details view, as shown in Figure 20-8. (Click the Show/Hide Folder List button at the left end of the Windows Messaging toolbar to switch between single- and dual-pane views.)

Tip

A message store doesn't have to store just messages. It is a general document storage, sorting, viewing, and retrieval system. If you store OLE documents in a message store, summary and other information about the documents is available to you as fields that you can use to sort document headers.

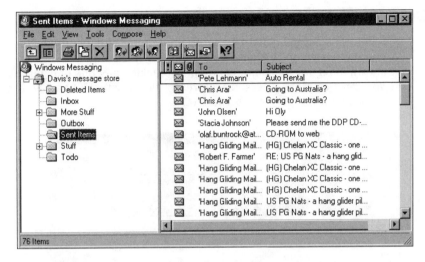

Figure 20-8: Windows Messaging. The message store and its folders are in the left pane. The message headers in a given folder are in the right pane.

Messages outside message stores

You can store messages outside your message stores by saving them as separate files with the *msg* extension. Simply double-click a message header in Windows Messaging, choose File, Save As, select Message Format in the Save As File Type field, and click Save. You can also drag and drop messages from the message store onto the Desktop or into a folder in your regular Windows 98 file system.

If you click the name of a message file that's stored on your hard disk as a separate file and displayed in an Explorer window, the message-composition portion of Windows Messaging will be invoked. Your message will be loaded, ready to be edited or sent.

Importing Other Messages

In the "Upgrading your Microsoft Mail message store" later in the chapter, we show you how to import your existing Microsoft Mail message store into a Windows Messaging message store.

You can import messages from Outlook Express. Turn to "Converting the mail" in Chapter 19 for instructions on how to do this. You'll also find instructions there on how to import mail from other e-mail clients to Outlook Express. Once you convert these messages to the Outlook Express format, you can export them to Outlook or Windows Messaging.

Address Book

Windows Messaging address books are (almost) full featured. For example, you can assign up to eight phone numbers to each person in a book, as shown in Figure 20-9, and dial them by clicking any one of eight Dial buttons. You can also store a person's address, title, assistant's name and number, notes about the person, and so on.

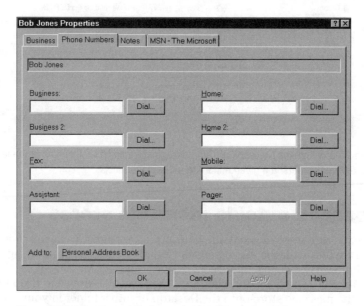

Figure 20-9: The Phone Numbers tab in the Properties dialog box for Bob Jones. Click the Dial button to call any of the numbers.

Funny thing though, there is only one e-mail address or fax number per entry. This causes a lot of problems.

The Windows Address Book that comes with Outlook Express does a better job, but of course, you can't use the fax number stored there to send faxes.

It's not like you can start printing labels from your Windows Messaging address book, but it does provide a name, address, and phone number database upon which third parties can build other applications. You can use Word for Windows to create labels and print envelopes from the address book.

Undocumented

Each profile can only use one personal address book at a time. In addition to the personal address book, you can attach a CompuServe address book to a profile that includes the CompuServe mail delivery service, and you can associate a Microsoft Network address book (maintained in Redmond, not on your computer) with a profile that uses MSN. You can also associate address books stored on various mail servers with Microsoft Mail delivery services. The same personal address book can be used by numerous different profiles.

You must remove a personal address book from a profile before you can add another. Removing an address book does not delete the address book file. If you rename or move an address book file, Windows Messaging will prompt you to create a new connection to an address book. You could have a number of address book files that aren't currently attached to any profile and therefore not able to be viewed, edited, or added to.

Undocumented

You can create personal distribution lists made up of selected members of your address book. You can then send e-mail (or faxes) to any one of these lists.

You can copy names from the MSN, CompuServe, or Microsoft Mail Server address books into your personal address book. You can also create personal distribution lists from names stored in these other address books.

If you use a personal distribution list as the address in a message, you can't edit out a few names on a one-time basis for that message. The address field contains just the personal distribution list name and not the names contained within the list. This makes it a bit difficult to create an ad hoc selection of addresses.

Undocumented

If you right-click an entry in your personal address book, a context menu appears. Choose Properties from the menu to display/edit the properties of the highlighted individual, or choose Delete to remove that entry from the address book.

You can compose a message starting from your address book by highlighting the name of the person to whom you want to send the message, and then clicking the New Message button in the Address Book toolbar. The person's address is automatically loaded into the To field in the new message.

If Windows Messaging is running, you can enter names into your address book. The type of address that you can enter depends on the mail delivery services in your current profile. If you have included all the possible mail delivery services in the profile, Windows Messaging will ask whether you want to enter a fax address, an Internet address, a Microsoft Network address, an Internet address reached through Microsoft Network, a Microsoft Mail address, a CompuServe address, or an Internet address reached through CompuServe. You will only be able to enter addresses that work with the mail delivery services in the current profile.

Changing the name of the address book

Undocumented

While the personal address book will always be named Personal Address Book (unlike the Personal Information Store, whose name you can completely change), you can add another name to identify a particular address book. To do so, take the following steps:

STEPS

Changing the Name of Your Personal Address Book

Step 1.   Click the Inbox icon on the Desktop.

Step 2.   Click Tools, Services, highlight Personal Address Book, and then click the Properties button.

Step 3.   Type a new name in the Name field. This new name will be added to the name Personal Address Book. For example, type in **Brian's Address Book** and the new name becomes Personal Address Book (Brian's Address Book).

The address book's big problem

Each entry (record) in the address book can have only one e-mail address or one fax number (despite the fax and phone number fields displayed in Figure 20-9). This means you must have two records for a given individual if you wish to reach them both by fax and by e-mail using Windows Messaging — two entries that repeat all the same information except for the e-mail or fax number.

This is nuts. It is the fax number or e-mail address and the display name that is the "live" portion of the record, that is, the part of the record that connects to the rest of Windows Messaging. You could easily end up with three or four records for the same person with display names as follows:

Bill Smith - Fax

Bill Smith - Internet

Bill Smith - MSN

Bill Smith - CompuServe

Not only do you need a different record for each e-mail or fax address for a given person, but you need different records for the different methods you use to connect to the Internet to reach that person. For example, assume you have an account with a local Internet service provider and an account with MSN. If you have separate profiles for your service provider and MSN, and you want to send e-mail to a person with an MSN address independently of whether you are logged on to MSN or to your Internet service provider, you need to have one record with the MSN-to-MSN connection and another with the Internet-to-MSN connection.

Opening the address book from the Desktop

Undocumented

You can create a shortcut to Exchng32.exe, the Windows Messaging executable file, and get to your address book with a click. Here's how:

STEPS

Shortcut to the Address Book

Step 1. Open your Explorer to C:\Program Files\Windows Messaging.

Step 2. Drag and drop Exchang32.exe onto your Desktop. Press F2 and rename the new shortcut Address Book. Press Enter.

Step 3. Right-click the new shortcut, and click Properties. Click the Shortcut tab. At the end of the Target field, add a space followed by **/a** . Click OK.

Creating and Sending Mail

You create and send e-mail and faxes from within Windows Messaging using the compose feature. You can also print or send faxes from other Windows applications. Microsoft Fax has the ability to act like a printer driver. If you print to it from a Windows application, it can take whatever it is you are printing and send it out as a fax.

If you have MAPI-enabled applications (such as Word for Windows), you can compose e-mail and faxes from within these applications. To send e-mail or faxes, choose File, Send on the application's menu bar. The current document is sent as an attachment to a message over your active mail delivery service. If Windows Messaging isn't running when you click Send, it will be invoked.

You can use Outlook Express instead of Windows Messaging to send messages composed in Word or other MAPI-enabled applications (but, obviously, you can't use Outlook Express to send faxes). To do this, you must designate Outlook Express as your simple MAPI client. This disables Windows Messaging (or Outlook) as a MAPI client. For more detailed instructions, turn to "Outlook Express as the default mail program" in Chapter 19.

To compose a message while using Windows Messaging, click the New Message button in the toolbar, or choose Compose, New Message. This will bring up what feels like a whole new application, your e-mail message-composition application. The New Message window should remind you a lot of WordPad, as you can see in Figure 20-10.

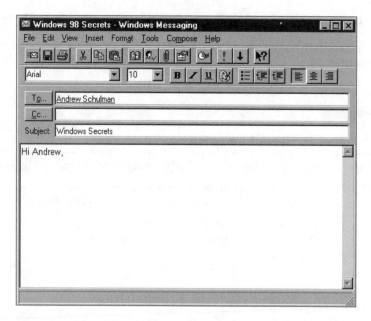

Figure 20-10: The New Message window. Create and send messages from here. Click the Send button (the envelope) on the left end of the toolbar to send a message.

Sending mail

To send a message after you have composed it, click the Send button (the envelope) on the left end of the New Message toolbar. Your message will be placed in the Outbox of your message store. If you are not currently connected to your mail delivery service, your message will sit right there until you do get connected.

You can just drag and drop a message from a Windows Messaging folder to the Outbox. It seems like you should be able to use this method to send your messages, but messages you move to the Outbox with drag and drop aren't actually ready to be delivered. If you look inside the Outbox folder, you'll notice that messages you have placed in the folder via the Send command are displayed in italics. If you use drag and drop to move a message to the Outbox, its name is displayed in a regular font, indicating that it's not ready to be sent. If you want your messages to be delivered when you click the Deliver Now button, you have to move them to the Outbox with the Send command instead of with drag and drop.

You can keep messages in your Outbox and send them later by double-clicking their headers in the Outbox, and then closing the New Message window without clicking the Send button. If you find a message header in your Outbox that isn't italicized and you want to send it, double-click the header and click the Send button on the toolbar. Of course, if you have configured Windows Messaging to send messages immediately (which you would normally do if you work online) then your messages don't spend too much time sitting around in the Outbox.

Undocumented

If you are connected to a LAN, and your active Windows Messaging profile is configured to use Microsoft Mail, and you are sending a message to another person on your Microsoft Mail mailing list, your message will automatically be delivered from your message store's Outbox to your Microsoft Mail postoffice. At the same time, it will be moved to the Sent Items folder of your message store.

Undocumented

If you're using a dial-up connection to an Internet service provider, you should configure your Internet mail delivery service to allow you to compose messages offline. (Choose Off-line instead of Automatic in the Internet portion of the Inbox Setup Wizard.) After you send messages to the Outbox, you can choose Deliver Now to call up your service provider and deliver the messages.

If you have chosen to work offline, your e-mail messages are sent to the Outbox when you click the Send button on the toolbar. They aren't really sent on their way, and your Internet service provider is not called when you click the Send button. This is not particularly intuitive. Not only do you have to send the message, you have to deliver it too.

If you are on an Intranet or you access your service provider through your local area network, you can choose to stay online and your messages will be delivered automatically from your Outbox.

The Internet mail delivery service that came with the original Windows Exchange client placed messages in the Sent Items folder even if it encountered a problem connecting to your service provider and was unable to send the messages. Windows Messaging cleans up this error.

To configure your Internet mail service for one or the other of these connection options, take the following steps:

STEPS

Configuring the Internet Mail Delivery Service

Step 1. Click the Start button, point to Settings, and then click Control Panel. Click the Mail icon in the Control Panel.

Step 2. Click the Show Profiles button first if the Internet mail delivery service is not included in the default profile. Otherwise, highlight Internet Mail and click the Properties button.

Step 3. Click the Connection tab. In the Transferring Internet Mail section, mark the Work Off-Line and Use Remote Mail options if you access your service provider by dial-up modem.

Step 4. Click OK.

If you are sending e-mail via the Microsoft Network, mail will be sent to the Outbox and stay there until you connect to MSN. You can use Tools, Deliver Now on the Windows Messaging menu bar to connect to MSN and send and receive e-mail.

If you are sending a fax and you have configured your fax delivery service to send faxes immediately, Windows Messaging will initialize your fax modem and send the fax as soon as you click the Send button. It will also deliver the fax later (at a time you specify) without further input from you. You can set up faxes for later delivery by choosing Tools, Microsoft Fax Tools, Options.

Undocumented

When you compose a message, you must provide an address to send the message to. This address identifies the mail delivery service that will transport the mail. Even if you have multiple mail delivery services attached to your active Windows Messaging profile, each message will be sent through the correct mail delivery service.

Receiving mail

If you are connected to an Exchange or Microsoft Mail Server over a local area network, messages will be delivered to your Inbox automatically (if Windows Messaging is running on your computer). You have to configure your Microsoft Mail delivery service to notify you of incoming messages by choosing Tools, Services, Microsoft Mail, Properties, Delivery, and Immediate Notification.

If you have dial-up (remote) access, you need to call in and get your messages. The easiest way to do this is to choose Tools, Deliver Now or click the Deliver Now toolbar button.

If you want to see how big your messages are before you download them, or if you want to only download the most important messages, you can choose Tools, Remote Mail, Connect. This automatically downloads the message headers so that you can view the message title, author, date, time, size, and so on. You can then choose which messages you want to download. After downloading a message, you can either delete or keep the original message on the server.

Windows Messaging can't notify you that you have new mail unless it is running. If you don't have enough memory to comfortably run Windows Messaging constantly, there are some shareware products that can do this for you. Check out our *Windows 98 Secrets* CD-ROM.

You can choose the font of incoming non-formatted e-mail if you use WordMail (see the next section) and an add-on applet. Go to http://www.halcyon.com/goetter/.

Using Word to create e-mail messages

You can use Microsoft Word for Windows as your e-mail message composition tool instead of the one that comes built in with Windows Messaging. If you have a recent version of Microsoft Office, you also have Microsoft Outlook, which replaces and enhances Windows Messaging. We suggest that you use Outlook if you have it. If not, continue.

First you have to configure Windows Messaging and Word to work together. If you installed Windows Messaging before you installed Word, choose Compose, Enable Word in the Windows Messaging window.

If you installed Windows Messaging after Word — for example, you may have upgraded from the Microsoft Exchange client after you installed Microsoft Office — then you need to take a different tack. Insert your Microsoft Office CD-ROM, click the Start button, click Run, and type **d:\Setup /y**, where d: is the volume label for your CD-ROM.

This will set up WordMail. After the installation process is complete, start Windows Messaging and choose Compose, Enable Word. You can find out more about this by turning to the Microsoft Knowledge Base, http://premium.microsoft.com/support/kb/articles/q135/2/95.asp.

WordMail makes it easy to create a signature file without using Internet Idioms (see "Signatures and ">" indents" later in this chapter). Format the text that you want to use as signature file, and save it as an AutoText entry with the name *signature*. There are macros available at http://miso.wwa.com/~sam/macro.html that allow you to have multiple signatures as well as set your own the Internet quoted-reply character, ">" for example.

WordMail is a pig; even at 16MB you're going to feel the hit. If you thought Windows Messaging was bad, well this is what "full featured" really adds up to. If you have a fast computer, lots of memory, and you want it all, then give WordMail a try. Of course, WordMail has now been superseded by Microsoft Outlook (which is still a pig).

Internet Explorer and Windows Messaging

Windows Messaging includes a new fast-send capability that invokes a less filling version of Windows Messaging and thereby comes up more quickly. It works well with File, Send menu commands from other Windows applications, and with the Internet Explorer. This fast-send note doesn't invoke the spelling checker, and its window borders are fixed.

You can specify fast-send mode by choosing Tools, Options from the Windows Messaging menu bar, and clicking the Send tab. Mark the check box labeled Use Simplified Note on Internet 'mailto:' and File, Send.

In 1996, Netscape's Navigator came out with an integrated Internet e-mail capability. At first, Microsoft had no response because while the Microsoft

Exchange client could be called from the Internet Explorer (1.0 and 2.0), it took a long time to load into memory, and didn't really deliver the mail. If you had configured your computer to work offline, the e-mail just sat in the Outbox, even if you were online at the time that you created your e-mail message. Only if Windows Messaging was already running could you then click the Deliver Now button and send the mail.

You can choose which e-mail client to use with Internet Explorer by clicking View, Internet Options, in the Internet Explorer menu bar, and clicking the Programs tab. Outlook Express is the default, but you can pick Windows Messaging as well. When you click a mailto: e-mail address in a web page, either Outlook Express or Windows Messaging will start. Outlook Express delivers the mail when you click the Send button (if you have marked Send Messages Immediately in the Send tab of Outlook Express' Tools, Options dialog box). Windows Messaging does not deliver the mail immediately (if you have configured it to work offline); you have to invoke the complete application and then click the Deliver Now toolbar button.

Signatures and ">" indents

As we have pointed out previously, the original Microsoft Exchange client and Windows Messaging are stripped-down versions of the Microsoft Exchange client that comes with Microsoft Exchange Server. There are a couple of add-on utilities you can use to spruce up Windows Messaging by adding signatures and reply quoting. These utilities were written by Ben Goetter, who created them when he was writing a book about programming using Windows Messaging. You can download the latest versions from his web site at http://www.halcyon.com/goetter/.

Ben's Internet Idioms include the Inetxidm.dll and Inetxidm.inf files, which let you add a signature and indent characters (using whatever character you like) to your e-mail. When you reply to someone's e-mail message, you use indent characters to offset the text you're quoting from the original message. The ">" character is the standard method of marking quoted text in Internet e-mail.

Internet Idioms only lets you have one signature, so it is difficult to "wear different hats." If you have installed an older version of it to work with the Microsoft Exchange client, you'll find that it doesn't work with Windows Messaging. When you open a New Message window, you get an error message stating that you are using an older version of Internet Idioms and that it might not work.

You should download the latest version of Internet Idioms if you want it to work with Windows Messaging. Also, make sure that all your references in your Registry refer to Windows Messaging and not to Microsoft Exchange. It is generally a good idea to edit your Registry in this fashion after you have installed Windows Messaging if you previously had Microsoft Exchange installed. Follow these steps to get rid of the old references to Microsoft Exchange in your Registry:

STEPS

Cleaning Up After Microsoft Exchange

Step 1.   Delete the folder C:\Program Files\Microsoft Exchange.

Step 2.   Using your Registry editor, search for *exchng32.exe*.

Step 3.   Change each pathname associated with exchng32.exe that includes Progra~1\Micros~1 to Program Files\Windows Messaging.

Ben has a utility that lets you empty the Deleted Items folder by simply choosing File, Expunge Deleted Items. Another utility of his lets you set the default font for incoming unformatted (plain text) e-mail. His utilities are included on the *Windows 98 Secrets* CD-ROM.

Sending mail without using an address book

Undocumented

You don't have to put someone in your address book before you can send that person mail. You just have to identify the mail delivery service that you are going to use and write a proper address in the To field. Table 20-1 contains examples of what you can type in the To field:

Table 20-1   Sample Addresses

Address	Mail Delivery Service
[FAX:+1 (*nnn*) *nnn-nnnn*]	fax
[MSN:*msn alias*]	Microsoft Network
[MSNINET:*internet address*]	Internet address through MSN
User name from the postoffice	Microsoft Mail (local area network)
[CompuServe: *nnnnn,nnnn*]	CompuServe
[SMTP:*Internet address*]	Internet service provider

If you are sending mail to an Internet address through your Internet service provider, you can just type the Internet address without the SMTP prefix and square brackets.

The New Message window doesn't default to sending a blind courtesy copy or to displaying this field. If you want to send a blind copy to someone, click View and then Bcc Box.

It's more than e-mail

When you think of e-mail, you normally think of ASCII text notes — a short note with little or no formatting. With Windows Messaging and Outlook Express, Microsoft is attempting to change that whole perception. In fact, Outlook Express lets you send HTML-formatted messages that include pictures.

You can use Windows Messaging to create and send fully formatted documents. In addition, you can insert documents into plain or formatted text messages as attachments (either by dragging and dropping or by choosing Insert, File). When your message is received, the recipient can double-click the attachment symbol for the document to open the document using the associated application (if the recipient has an application that is associated with the document type — see "Creating a new file type" in Chapter 13 for details on document types). Windows Messaging is a full OLE 2 application. You can insert OLE 2 objects in a message and mail or fax them.

To see how to edit OLE 2 objects in Windows Messaging, take the following steps:

STEPS

Editing OLE 2 Objects

Step 1. Click the New Message button in the Windows Messaging toolbar.

Step 2. In the New Message window, choose Insert, Object.

Step 3. Scroll through the Object Type list box and highlight the type of object that you want to create. Click OK.

Step 4. The New Message window will be transformed to incorporate the tools needed to edit the new object. Figure 20-11 shows the window created for a bitmapped object.

Step 5. You can send the message with the enclosed object(s).

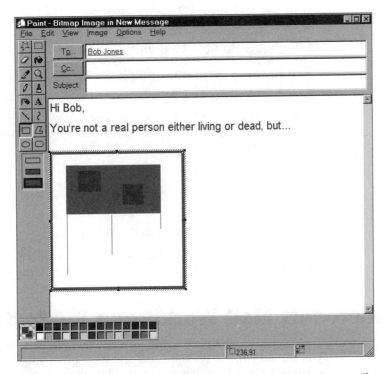

Figure 20-11: The New Message window is now a hybrid of its former self and MS Paint.

Sending pointers to attachments

If you send mail over your LAN using Microsoft Mail, you can send pointers to files instead of the sending the files as attachments themselves. This is just a fancy way of sending someone a file without actually sending it. By sending a pointer to the file (which is itself stored in a shared folder) you cut down on the amount of space used in your postoffice, especially if you are sending a document to a number of people.

STEPS

Sending a Pointer to a File

Step 1.   Click the New Message button in the Windows Messaging toolbar.

(continued)

Sending a Pointer to a File

Step 2.   Click the Insert File button in the New Message toolbar.

Step 3.   Mark the Link Attachment to Original File check box.

Step 4.   Browse to the file (in a shared folder) that you want to link to the message. Click a shared folder (or if the volume is already shared, click the file) and then click the filename.

Step 5.   Click OK.

The pointer is just a shortcut to the document.

You can send shortcuts to web sites. Your recipients can just click the shortcut and it will call up their browser and go to the web site.

Microsoft Mail Workgroup Postoffice

Before you create a profile that includes the Microsoft Mail delivery service, you should either have the name and location of your workgroup's shared Microsoft Mail postoffice, or you need to create such a postoffice. If you included Microsoft Mail as a mail delivery service in the default profile created when you installed Windows 98, you may not have had the opportunity to create a postoffice first. You can go back and do that and then edit your Windows Messaging profile.

If your computer is connected to a LAN and you are using Microsoft Mail, all of the users in your workgroup should use the same postoffice. When you set up Windows Messaging, you need to tell it only the name and location of the shared postoffice.

To create a Microsoft Mail postoffice, click the Microsoft Mail Postoffice icon in your Control Panel. This starts the Microsoft Workgroup Postoffice Administration Wizard, which will guide you through setting up a workgroup postoffice. You'll need to choose the computer on which you want to store the postoffice, and decide who is going to look after it. You should mark the postoffice folder as shared among the members of your workgroup. You'll want only one postoffice for your workgroup so that everyone will be able to send mail to everyone else in the workgroup.

If you want to send mail (using Windows Messaging) to people in other workgroups, you'll need to have Microsoft Mail Server, Microsoft Exchange Server, or some other company's Microsoft Mail-compatible server.

Upgrading your Microsoft Mail message store

Windows Messaging comes with its own form of a message store. If you install Windows 98 over your existing Windows 3.1x directory, your existing message stores (files with the extension *mmf*) will be converted to Personal Information Store format (files with *pst* extension). If you have additional older message stores that weren't converted, you can do it manually.

STEPS

Converting Older Message Stores

Step 1. Click the Inbox icon on your Desktop.

Step 2. If you need to create a message store to store these converted messages, follow the steps detailed in the "Adding a message store to a profile" section earlier in this chapter.

Step 3. If you have more than one message store and you want to store the converted messages in a secondary message store, click Tools, Options, click the Delivery tab, and then choose the appropriate message store. Click OK.

Step 4. Click File, Import on the Windows Messaging menu bar.

Step 5. Browse to find the older message store and then double-click it.

Your older messages will be added to the new message store you chose. Your original *mmf* file is not altered by the conversion process. You cannot convert the *mmf* file if it is located on the postoffice server. To create a new message store from a *mmf* file on your postoffice server, you can log onto your mail account using Microsoft Mail, then click Mail, Options, Server and give the *mmf* file a local name. Exit Microsoft Mail, start Windows Messaging, and use File, Import to create a new message store from the *mmf* file.

Remote access to a Microsoft Mail postoffice

If you use CompuServe, MSN, and/or the Internet as mail delivery services, you are already familiar with remotely accessing your mail delivery service. You need to access them through a modem. This is not the case if your LAN has server access to the Internet.

If you have Microsoft Mail running on your office network, you can also set up your portable computer or computer at home to access your e-mail account at the office over the phone. You can call either your computer at work or your company's network, depending on how these computers are set up.

Any of the remote mail delivery connections give you a number of options. One option is to review just the message headers and decide which messages to download. Outgoing messages are queued in your portable's Outbox until the next time you connect with the office. You can create a schedule that tells your computer (if it is turned on) when to call into the office (or other mail delivery service) and check for e-mail.

If you have a portable computer that you use at the office and on the road, you will most likely want to set up two different profiles, both of which use the Microsoft Mail delivery service, but one that uses it over the phone lines. To configure a new profile for remote access to your Microsoft Mail postoffice, take the following steps:

STEPS

Creating a Profile for Remote Access to a Microsoft Mail Postoffice

Step 1.   Click the Start button, Settings, and then Control Panel.

Step 2.   Click the Mail icon in the Control Panel, and then click the Show Profiles button.

Step 3.   Highlight a profile that contains your Microsoft Mail delivery service. If you don't have such a profile, click the Add button to create a new profile using the Inbox Setup Wizard.

Step 4.   Once you have a profile that uses Microsoft Mail, highlight that profile and click the Properties button. Highlight the Microsoft Mail information service and click the Properties button in the Services tab.

Step 5.   Click the Connection tab and then choose Automatically Sense LAN or Remote, as shown in Figure 20-12. If you want to force a remote connection, click Remote Using a Modem and Dial-Up Network.

Step 6.   Click the Remote Configuration tab and choose the options that you want.

Step 7.   Click the Remote Session tab. If you want to dial up your Microsoft Mail postoffice as soon as you click the Inbox icon, mark the When This Provider Is Started check box, as shown in Figure 20-13.

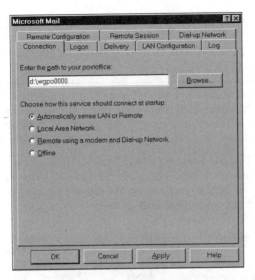

Figure 20-12: The Connection tab in the Microsoft Mail dialog box. Enter the server name and folder name for your Microsoft Mail postoffice. Click one of the two option buttons that allows for a remote connection.

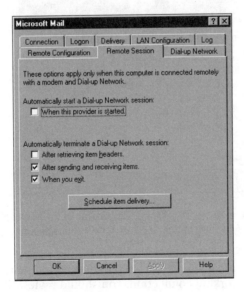

Figure 20-13: The Remote Session tab of the Microsoft Mail dialog box. You determine when the computer at the office will be called up and when it will be terminated.

(continued)

STEPS *(continued)*

Creating a Profile for Remote Access to a Microsoft Mail Postoffice

Step 8.   To create a schedule for regular connections with the office Microsoft Mail postoffice, click the Schedule Item Delivery button. You'll need to already have a Dial-Up Networking (DUN) connection defined, so you might want to do the next step first.

Step 9.   Click the Dial-up Network tab to define how to make a connection with your office. If you don't already have a DUN connection for your office, you can create one by clicking the Add Entry button, as shown in Figure 20-14.

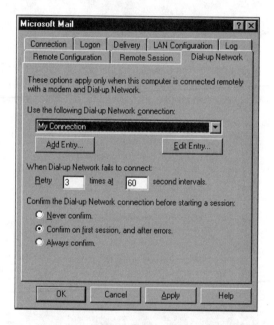

Figure 20-14: The Dial-Up Network tab of the Microsoft Mail dialog box. Click the Add Entry button to create a new connection to your office.

It is not a simple one-step operation to create a new Dial-Up Networking connection. You should review Chapter 17 if you are unfamiliar with how to do it.

Step 10.   Click OK when you are done.

You can create a DUN connection to a computer running Windows 98 or Windows 95 (if you have installed the DUN server on it), a Windows NT server, a Novell NetWare server, Shiva LanRover, an Internet service provider, or other servers. Check Chapter 17 for more details.

Troubleshooting Windows Messaging

Secret

Terri Bronson at Microsoft gives the following advice when you have big general problems with Windows Messaging:

STEPS

Troubleshooting Windows Messaging

Step 1.   Delete the Windows Messaging profile you are having problems with (perhaps your *only* one). Click the Mail icon in the Control Panel, click Show Profiles, highlight the bad profile, and click Delete.

Step 2.   Create a new profile (click Add).

Step 3.   Click the Start button, then Run, type **Awadpr32.exe,** and then press Enter.

Step 4.   Make sure there are no files left in your \Windows\Spool\Fax folder due to prior crashes that are "stuck."

Step 5.   Make sure there are no "stuck" messages in your Outbox.

Step 6.   If you also run Microsoft Mail, make sure it is not the first mail delivery service in your profile.

You may find that Windows Messaging hangs or generates a Mapisp32 error message when you start it. These are symptoms of a damaged Outbox. To see how to removed damaged files from the Windows Messaging Outbox, go to http://premium.microsoft.com/support/kb/articles/q1437/3/64.asp.

If you repeatedly start and exit Windows Messaging, you may also run into Mapisp32 errors. The symptoms include the inability to restart Windows Messaging using anything but the previous profile. The best way of preventing these problems is to have enough memory (16MB or more) to start Windows Messaging and to leave it active throughout the day.

Microsoft Fax

Windows Messaging treats faxes printed from other applications as attachments to messages. The messages are stored in your Windows Messaging message store, and you can view the stored faxes by double-clicking the attachment symbols in their messages. The fax message header contains the pertinent information identifying the fax.

A message store is an OLE 2 container. It can store all sorts of different kinds of files and objects. Faxes printed from other applications just happen to be another kind of document.

With Microsoft Fax, you can send editable documents as faxes to recipients, who can then open them using compatible applications. Microsoft Fax utilizes the Microsoft-developed *binary file transfer* (BFT) capability to fool the fax transport into sending documents instead of dots to Class 1 fax/modems. Of course, you can't send these editable documents as editable documents to a fax machine or Class 2 fax/modems. Microsoft Fax sends documents as faxes to Group 3-compatible fax machines.

Faxing from the Start button

Click the Start button, point to Programs, Accessories, and then Fax. You'll find four options in the Fax menu: Compose New Fax, Cover Page Editor, and Retrieve File.

Compose New Fax

Clicking this menu item starts the Compose New Fax Wizard and Windows Messaging. The Wizard lets you compose a little fax or send a file. Windows Messaging has a much better composition window than the little dialog box that the Wizard gives you. To compose and send a fax from Windows Messaging, take the following steps:

STEPS

Composing and Sending a Fax

Step 1. Click the Inbox icon on your Desktop and choose a profile with a Microsoft Fax mail delivery service if you have more than one profile.

Step 2. Choose Compose, New Message (or click the New Message button on the toolbar).

Step 3. In the New Message window, click the To field to choose someone to send the fax to.

Step 4. Compose the fax, and then click the Send button (the envelope) on the left end of the toolbar to send the fax.

Undocumented

Faxes you compose within Windows Messaging or through the Compose New Fax Wizard are messages and not attachments to messages, as is the case with faxes printed from Windows applications.

Undocumented

Faxes sent by Microsoft Fax will come out as short faxes if you send them to thermal fax machines. These machines cut the paper after the last bit of text. To get around this problem, put footers (date or page number, for example) in the documents that you fax.

Undocumented

You can place a shortcut to the Compose New Fax Wizard on your Desktop. Open your Explorer to \Windows\Start Menu\Accessories\Fax. Copy and paste a copy of the Compose New Fax Wizard onto your Desktop. This is a shortcut to the file Awsnto32.exe. You can drag and drop a document that you want faxed onto this Desktop icon.

Cover Page Editor

The Cover Page Editor is a standalone application that you use to create and edit fax cover pages. Cover pages can be fairly complex and rich documents in and of themselves. The editor allows you to place fax information fields as well as graphics. It is an OLE 2 application, so you can use MS Paint to create graphical items.

You don't need to send cover pages with your faxes or edit any of the existing cover pages before you send your first fax. Cover pages are a frill. The Cover Page Editor is quite a powerful utility that shows off the capability of OLE 2 and reusable code and objects (from WordPad), but it's still just an accessory.

The original Cover Page Editor had a bug. If the Archive bit on a cover page file was cleared (turned off), the cover page was no longer visible. Archive bits are routinely turned off by backup programs. Also, if you had created a cover page in some other format (and the file had a *cpe* extension) the cover pages disappeared. The Windows Messaging source file (exupdusa.exe) includes a new version of the Cover Page Editor.

Kodak Imaging for Windows

Faxes that you have received are stored in your message stores, just like any other messages. Double-click a fax message to invoke Kodak Imaging for Windows and view the fax. Once Kodak Imaging for Windows is invoked, you can save the fax in a file outside of the message store. You can then use the Kodak Imaging for Windows in standalone mode to view the fax file (a file with the *awd* extension). Just click the file. You can also use Kodak Imaging for Windows to annotate faxes.

You can also just drag and drop a fax file onto your Desktop to copy it outside of the message store.

Request a Fax

Do you want to call a fax-on-demand service and download a fax or two? This is what the Request a Fax menu item is for (Start button, Programs, Accessories, Fax, Request a Fax). It invokes a Wizard that makes the call and retrieves the fax (or a document, file, or software update from a fax server that supports BFT).

Click the Retrieve Whatever Is Available option button in the Request a Fax Wizard to get a fax that gives you the names of the other fax/documents that are available on the service. You can then call the fax service again and ask for specific faxes (or files).

Request a Fax is also available from the Windows Messaging menu bar. Click the Inbox icon on your Desktop and choose a profile that includes Microsoft Fax if you have multiple profiles. Click Tools, Microsoft Fax Tools, Request a Fax to start the same Wizard that launches when you choose Request a Fax on the Start menu.

Receiving faxes

You can set your computer to answer the phone when a call comes in and to receive incoming faxes. You first need to click your Inbox icon and then choose a profile (if you have multiple profiles) that includes Microsoft Fax as a mail delivery service.

A little icon that looks like a fax/phone combination will appear in the Tray on the Taskbar. You can click this icon to see the Microsoft fax status. Click Options, Modem Properties in the Microsoft Fax Status menu bar to display the Fax Modem Properties dialog box, as shown in Figure 20-15. You can use this dialog box to change how Windows Messaging answers your phone. If you choose Answer After 2 (Or More) Rings, Windows Messaging will automatically answer the phone and begin to make the fax connection when you don't pick up the phone before two rings. You can't set the automatic answer for fewer than two rings.

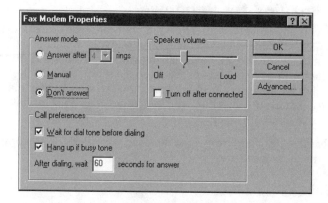

Figure 20-15: The Fax Modem Properties dialog box. Choose how Windows Messaging will answer incoming phone calls.

If you want to use your phone primarily for voice communication, set the answer mode to Manual. The phone status box does appear when a phone call comes in, and you can click Answer Now if you think a fax is coming in.

Tip

You can't use Windows 3.1*x* or DOS communications packages while Windows Messaging is waiting for a fax phone call unless you mark Don't Answer in the Fax Modem Properties dialog box. These other packages will report being unable to use the serial port that is assigned to your modem.

Other Windows 98 TAPI-aware communications packages (including HyperTerminal) can use the modem at the same time Windows Messaging is waiting for a fax phone call. Of course, only one communication can be going on at a time, so you can't use HyperTerminal while you are sending or receiving a fax.

Tip

Fax machines are on all the time. Computers often aren't. If you want your computer to operate as a fax machine and to be always ready to receive faxes, you'll need to run Windows Messaging with a profile that includes Microsoft Fax at all times and leave your computer on.

Microsoft Phone creates a profile for Windows Messaging or Microsoft Exchange the first time that you run it. This profile will include both fax and Internet mail delivery services if they are available. It is best to install Windows Messaging before you install Microsoft Phone, so that Microsoft Phone will configure a profile for Windows Messaging.

You can add an application that will print your faxes as they come in, ship them to another Windows Messaging user, or both. You can download Print Fax at http://home.istar.ca/~anthony/add-ins/printfax.html.

Fax type

You can send faxes as editable files, as regular Group 3 faxes, or as either — depending on the capabilities of the recipient hardware. You can determine how a particular fax is sent by taking these steps:

STEPS

Determining in What Format a Fax Is Sent

Step 1.   Click the Inbox on your Desktop.

Step 2.   Choose a profile that has Microsoft Fax as a mail delivery service if you have more than one profile.

Step 3.   Choose Compose, New Message in the Windows Messaging menu bar.

Step 4.   Choose File, Send Options in the New Message menu bar. The Message Options dialog box, as shown in Figure 20-16, will be displayed on your Desktop.

(continued)

Determining in What Format a Fax Is Sent

Figure 20-16: The Message Options dialog box. Choose the type of fax that you are going to send. Click Paper to set image quality.

Step 5. Choose Editable, If Possible; Editable Only; or Not Editable.

You can set numerous other send options. To set these same properties for all faxes, click Tools, Microsoft Fax Tools, Options in the Windows Messaging menu bar.

Sharing a fax/modem on a network

A fax/modem board in a sufficiently powerful Windows 98 computer at work can be shared with Dial-Up Networking guests, as well as with other computers on a local area network. If you are calling into the Windows 98 computer at work using a modem in your computer at home, the fax/modem that is shared at work must be different than the modem that is answering your call, and must also be on a different phone line.

If the fax-server computer is dedicated to that task, it needs 8MB of RAM; if it's used for other tasks as well, it needs 12MB. In addition, at least a 486 processor is required.

Share the fax/modem on the network by taking the following steps:

STEPS

Sharing a Fax/Modem

Step 1. Click the Inbox icon on the Desktop of a Windows 98 fax-server computer. If you are set up to choose among multiple Windows Messaging profiles, choose a profile that includes Microsoft Fax. If you haven't previously set up a profile that contains Microsoft Fax as a mail delivery service, step back to the "Adding or removing information services" section and do so.

Step 2. Click Tools, Microsoft Fax Tools, Options in the Windows Messaging menu bar. Click the Modem tab (see Figure 20-17).

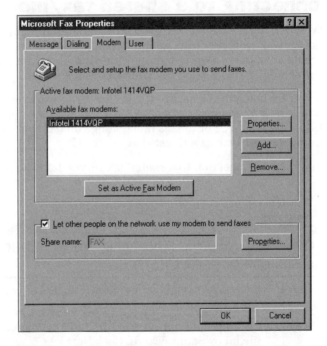

Figure 20-17: The Modem tab of the Microsoft Fax Properties dialog box. Clicking Let Other People on the Network Use My Modem to Send Faxes enables fax/modem sharing.

Step 3. Choose Let Other People on the Network Use My Modem to Send Faxes.

Step 4. Type a shared fax name in the Share Name field, choose a volume on which the NetFax folder will be stored, and click the Properties button.

(continued)

Sharing a Fax/Modem

Step 5.   Define the characteristics of the shared folder (NetFax) that will store the faxes. Enter a password if you want to password-protect this folder and you are using share-level protection.

Step 6.   Click the next two OK buttons.

Connecting to a shared fax/modem server

Whether you are calling in from your computer at home or accessing the networked fax server from another computer on the network, you need to create a Windows Messaging profile on your computer that will let you use the shared fax/modem on the Windows 98 fax server.

If you are going to connect to the fax server at work from a computer at home, be sure to create a Dial-Up Networking connectoid first before you begin these steps. For details on creating connectoids, see "Setting Up Your Computer at Home as a Guest" in Chapter 17.

To create a connection to a shared fax server, take the following steps:

STEPS

Creating a Windows Messaging Profile to Use
a Shared Fax Server

Step 1.   Click the Mail icon in the Control Panel of your computer. Click Show Profiles.

Step 2.   Click the Add button. Choose only the Microsoft Fax Services in the Inbox Setup Wizard. Click Next.

Step 3.   Type a name for this profile, such as **Shared fax.** Click Next.

Step 4.   Click Network Fax Service or Other Type of Device and then Next.

Step 5.   Click the Add button (if necessary). Highlight Network Fax Server and click OK.

Step 6.   Type two back slashes, followed by the name of the shared fax-server computer, another single backslash, and the name of the shared fax/modem (given to the shared fax in step 4 of the Sharing a Fax/Modem steps in the previous section). Click Next.

Если the shared fax is on a remote computer (perhaps your computer at work and you are setting this up on your computer at home) and you enter the name of the computer at work and the name of the shared fax when you are not presently connected to the work computer over the phone lines, you will be asked if you want to connect to the fax server using Dial-Up Networking. Click Yes. Go to step 8.

Step 7. Enter your phone number and click Next. Continue clicking Next until you have completed the Inbox Setup Wizard. You're done.

Step 8. We assume you have previously created a connectoid to connect to the fax server computer. Choose the name of the connectoid after completing step 7.

Step 9. Enter a password for connecting to the shared fax/modem if needed. Click Cancel unless you want to connect to the fax server at work now.

Tip

If you are sending a fax to a Group 3 fax machine, use 14-point Arial (if you have only the basic fonts that come with Windows 98) for the text in your fax. This will significantly improve the readability of your fax, because fax printers are often of poor quality and low resolution (200×100 or 200×200). If you have additional fonts (such as Lucida Fax from the Microsoft TrueType Font Pack), you can use them instead of Arial. The quality of faxes you send from your computer will be significantly better than that of faxes sent from a fax machine, since they don't have to be scanned.

Troubleshooting Microsoft Fax

Secret

Terri Bronson at Microsoft once again provides help. If you have received a fax successfully, but it never appeared in your Inbox, take the following steps:

STEPS

Faxes Don't Appear

Step 1. Exit Windows Messaging.

Step 2. Locate the received files in the fax spool folder. This folder is typically \Windows\Spool\Fax. The files have the following form:

RCV*xxxxx*.MG3

or

RCV*xxxxx*.EFX

where *xxxxx* is a 5-digit hex number. Each of the files contains one fax message.

(continued)

STEPS *(continued)*

Faxes Don't Appear

Step 3. Copy these files to another folder, just as a backup.

Step 4. Open the following key in the Registry:

HKEY_LOCAL_MACHINE\SOFTWARE\Microsoft\At Work\Fax\ LocalModems\Received

This key may have several values, all of type *string* (REG_SZ)), with the format: R*nn* and F*nn,* where *nn* is a two-digit decimal number starting with 00. The F*nn* entries contain filenames (the RCV*xxxxx*.MG3. or RCV*xxxxx*.EFX files referred to in step 2). The R*nn* entry contains the result code for the transmission. A value of 001 indicates a successful receive.

```
Example: F00 = RCV3edd0.MG3
F01 = 001
R00 = 001
R01 = 001
```

Step 5. Add entries for all the files identified in step 2 to this list if they are not already on the list, making sure that each F*nn* has a corresponding R*nn* (you can set all R00 values to 001), and that the *nn* numbers are consecutive, starting from 00 (so we have F00, F01, F02 . . . R00, R01, R02 . . .).

Step 6. Restart Windows Messaging. If all went well, the messages should soon show up in the Inbox, and the Received key will get cleared.

You can also take the steps that Terri provided in the "Troubleshooting Windows Messaging" section earlier in this section, especially if you are having problems rendering faxes. In addition, if you are having trouble sending faxes, click Tools, Deliver Now to force the Outbox to empty. Check the Outbox and if there is anything in it, delete the messages. A message with a non-fax address will cause problems. You can also create a new profile with just the fax delivery service.

Want to see what the faxes that you send out look like? Sue Mosher at Slipstick Systems, http://www.slipstick.com/exchange, came up with a great solution. It won't work to check problems with your modem, but you do get to see your faxes.

STEPS

See What Your Faxes Look Like

Step 1. Click the Inbox icon and choose a profile with a fax delivery service.

Step 2. Choose Compose, New Message. In the To field type **[fax:me]**. Pretty cool, huh!

Step 3. Choose Tools, Microsoft Fax Tools, Options, and in the Message Format area choose Not Editable. (After all, you want to receive it as a regular fax.) Click OK.

Step 4. In a few moments you should have a fax in your Inbox.

If you want to see what faxes look like when you use the Compose New Fax Wizard, click the Start button, Programs, Accessories, Fax, Compose New Fax. In the second dialog box, choose (None - Dial As Entered), which is the first entry in the Country Code list. Enter **me** in the fax number field and click the Add button. Continue on as normal. In a few seconds you will see what your fax cover page and fax look like.

Further help on problems with faxing can be found in the Microsoft Knowledge Base at http://premium.microsoft.com/support/kb/articles/q140/4/32.asp.

Summary

Windows Messaging provides full e-mail and fax connectivity.

▶ You can send and receive e-mail using the Internet, CompuServe, the Microsoft Network, or Microsoft Mail servers.

▶ Windows 98 comes with a complete workgroup version of Microsoft Mail for local e-mail and document exchange.

▶ You can send a fax or e-mail message without putting someone in your address book.

▶ With Windows Messaging, e-mail is not just an ASCII text message, but can include all types of attached files and OLE 2 objects.

▶ You gcan edit OLE 2 objects within Windows Messaging.

▶ If you are sending e-mail over the phone lines, you have to tell Windows Messaging to connect to the remote e-mail service; you can't just send the mail.

Part IV

Connectivity

Chapter 21

Calling the Bulletin Boards

In This Chapter

Windows 98 provides a way to communicate with bulletin boards and other computers over telephone lines. This terminal-to-computer style of communication, while going out of style, is still prevalent among people who use bulletin boards. We discuss:

▶ Setting up different bulletin board connections

▶ Dialing into a bulletin board

▶ Downloading a file

▶ Modifying the parameters of your bulletin board connection

▶ Capturing text to a file

▶ The differences between HyperTerminal in Windows 98 and Terminal in Windows 3.1*x*

A Flash from the Past

This chapter is about using HyperTerminal, a wonderful little application that comes with Windows 98. Communication between computers comes in many different modes. Each type of communication has different applications that are best suited to its mode, and HyperTerminal is an excellent program for occasionally communicating with bulletin boards.

It wasn't too many years ago that using a personal computer to communicate meant working with a program such as HyperTerminal. Now, there are many other options for each communications niche.

HyperTerminal has the word *terminal* in it because it is designed around the metaphor of a terminal calling into a multi-user computer. The *hyper* part of its name means that it can do more than act as a dumb terminal. For example, you can't download files using a binary file transfer protocol such as Zmodem with a dumb terminal, but you can with HyperTerminal.

HyperTerminal 1.2, the version that comes with Windows 98, is TAPI-aware and Unimodem compatible (see Chapters 31 and 32). This means that, unlike the earlier software you may have used, it takes advantage of Windows 98's centralized communications setup capability. This new version also includes Telnet capabilities, Zmodem crash recovery, and redial on busy. Version 1.2

uses the Terminal font for better compatibility with ANSI characters, and it has better support for non-Latin characters.

Terminal-computer communication has been around since the late '60s. It was created because computers then were expensive and needed to be shared to be cost-effective. This type of computer communication is still useful. For example, your hardware vendor may provide certain files on its computer bulletin board that you need to download. Or you might want to call into a community bulletin board hosted on another computer so that you can read messages or post your own.

When you call into a bulletin board, you are typically presented with a screen full of options. You, the user, simply send keystrokes to the remote computer that determine how the bulletin board program presents information to you. The remote computer doesn't care what kind of computer you are using. You might as well be using a terminal—that is, until you want to download or upload a file.

HyperTerminal lets you upload and download files to the bulletin board using one of seven file transfer protocols. This is a handy feature that works well.

Using HyperTerminal's Telnet client, you can call into your local Internet service provider and run programs on the service provider's Unix computer if you have a shell (console or terminal) account. For example, you can use your service provider's Unix e-mail program to send and receive mail on the Internet.

HyperTerminal also lets you communicate with another computer over a Direct Cable Connection (DCC)—a connection through a cable on your serial or parallel port. Depending on what the other computer is, you can send files or use the computer's multiuser operating system.

HyperTerminal is not the most powerful package of its type. The authors of HyperTerminal, Hilgraeve Inc., have more sophisticated communications software they would be happy to sell you. They assume that you will like the ease of use and features in HyperTerminal and hope that once you have gotten used to it you will want more. You can find out more about these products from http://www.hilgraeve.com.

HyperTerminal is easy to use and reliable. It is powerful enough for a significant percentage of the Windows user population. It doesn't have scripting, so you can't automate your sessions or your logon sequences. It won't store your passwords. It doesn't have built-in auto-answer. But it does have the basic features that make it easy to call into a bulletin board and upload or download a file occasionally.

Creating Connections (Connectoids)

Most communications packages for terminal-computer communications store the names and phone numbers of the bulletin boards you call into in a list. To access this list, you have to first start the communications package and then issue a menu command.

One nifty feature of HyperTerminal is that instead of storing this information in a list, it creates an icon (and an associated file) for each bulletin board or connection that you want to call, and then displays these icons in the HyperTerminal folder window — ready for easy access. You can create a shortcut to any of these connections and place it on the Desktop. Just click the icon and you're off and running. (Terminal, the communications package that came with Windows 3.1*x*, created a separate connection file for each bulletin board, but it didn't present them in as straightforward a fashion as HyperTerminal does.)

Because HyperTerminal puts the connection (referred to internally at Microsoft as a *connectoid*) in a separate file, it can store the data specific to that connection within the file. You can create a separate icon to represent each bulletin board in the HyperTerminal folder window, and then customize each connection with the settings appropriate for that bulletin board. HyperTerminal connectoid files have the extension *ht*.

Here's how to create a new connectoid:

STEPS

Creating a New Connection

Step 1. Click the Start button, point to Programs, Accessories, Communications, and then click HyperTerminal.

Step 2. Click Hypertrm.exe in the HyperTerminal folder window. In the Name field of the Connection Description dialog box, type a name for the bulletin board that you want to connect to, and then choose an icon. Unlike almost all other applications in Windows 98, you can only choose icons for HyperTerminal connectoids from the ones shown in this list. Click OK.

Step 3. The Connect To dialog box, as shown in Figure 21-1, appears next. Enter the area code and the phone number (and the country code if necessary) for the bulletin board.

If you are going to create a connection between two nearby computers using a serial cable, don't worry about the phone numbers.

Step 4. The default device for your connection is the modem that you have already installed and configured. You can change to another device, but if you are going to call into a bulletin board over the phone lines, you don't need to change the Connect Using field. Click OK.

If you do want to communicate through one of your serial ports, display the Connect Using drop-down list and choose which serial port to use. You need to have a null modem serial cable to connect the two computers.

Undocumented

(continued)

STEPS *(continued)*

Creating a New Connection

Figure 21-1: The Connect To dialog box.

Step 5. If you are using a modem and not a serial cable, you will see the Connect dialog box shown in Figure 21-2. You can click the Dial button if you want to make a connection immediately. If you just want to save the new connection information, click Cancel, and then choose File, Save.

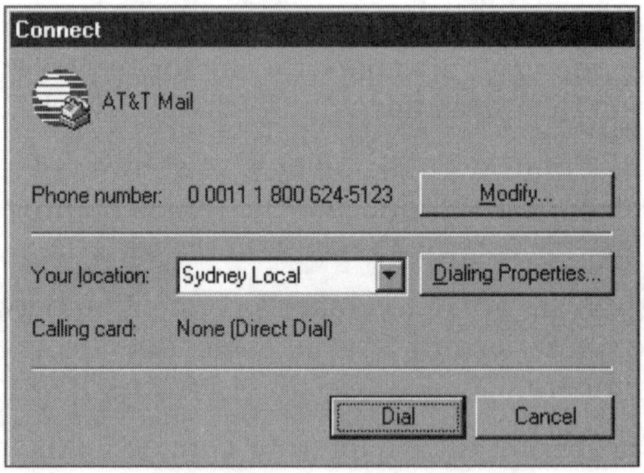

Figure 21-2: The Connect dialog box.

The Modify button in the Connect dialog box lets you change the phone number and settings for the connection, as well as the modem settings. See the section entitled "Changing the Properties of a Connectoid" later in this chapter for information on changing connection settings. Turn to Chapter 25 for information on modem settings.

The Dialing Properties button lets you choose a new originating location or edit the properties associated with the phone system at the location you are dialing from. Turn to Chapter 32 for more details about location settings.

Secret

Occasionally when you create a new HyperTerminal connectoid, you may find that the Country Code list in the Connect To dialog box (Figure 21-1) is empty. This problem can occur if one of the Windows 95 TAPI files or one of the HyperTerminal files has been damaged. If the problem happens only with HyperTerminal connectoids (and not in DUN connectoids, for example), rename the Hypertrm.exe file in your Program Files\Accessories\ HyperTerminal folder and extract a new copy of Hypertrm.exe from your Windows 98 CD-ROM to that folder. (See "Missing files" in Chapter 16 to learn how to extract a file.)

Making a Connection

If you have already created a connectoid, dialing into a bulletin board is pretty easy.

STEPS

Making a Connection

Step 1.   Click the Start button, point to Programs, Accessories, Communications, and then click HyperTerminal.

Step 2.   In the HyperTerminal folder window, click the connectoid icon for the bulletin board that you want to call.

Step 3.   Click the Dial button in the Connect dialog box. If the Connect dialog box isn't showing, click the Connect toolbar button in the HyperTerminal application window (it shows a phone). If the toolbar isn't showing, choose Call, Connect.

Undocumented

If you are connecting two Windows 95 or 98 computers through a serial cable, you don't have to take this step. After you click the connectoids that use the serial ports on both computers, you are connected.

Typing on the Terminal

You communicate with a bulletin board by typing, as if you were typing on a terminal. But typing on a terminal is different than the kind of typing you normally do on your computer. That's because the host computer to which you are connected has control of the characters displayed on your screen.

This means you may not be able to delete characters from the screen once you have typed them. If the Backspace and Delete keys do work, they may only remove half a character per keystroke; it depends on the kind of computer you are connected to.

In addition to the Terminal, Courier, and Fixedsys bitmap fonts, HyperTerminal now gives you access to the Courier New, Lucida Console, MS Line Draw, and OCR A Extended True Type fonts that come with Windows 98. Lucida Console includes several non-Latin character sets (refer to "Windows Character Sets" in Chapter 27 for a more detailed explanation). However, it is still the host computer that determines which character sets actually work.

HyperTerminal sends the host whatever character is generated by your keystroke. What gets displayed on your screen is the character equivalent for the code that is returned from the host (ordinarily, these should match). If characters aren't displaying properly in a particular font, switch to Courier New (the default for all HyperTerminal connectoids).

Hilgraeve offers additional fonts on its web site, including HyperFont, a TrueType font that lets 80 characters fit on one line of display.

Downloading a File

The ability to download files is one of the main reasons people call bulletin boards. Unfortunately, downloading a file from a bulletin board is a two-step process. In contrast, if you use a web browser such as Internet Explorer to download files from FTP (file transfer protocol) servers on the Internet, the process is quite a bit easier. When you use Internet Explorer to connect to an FTP server, you can download a file by simply clicking its name and then giving the file a name and location on your computer.

STEPS

Downloading a File

Step 1. Call into a bulletin board (see the previous section, "Making a Connection").

Step 2. On the bulletin board, use the onscreen menus to choose a file to download and specify a file transfer protocol. If the Zmodem file transfer protocol is available on the bulletin board, it is a good choice. The file transfer protocols supported by HyperTerminal are 1K Xmodem, Xmodem, Ymodem, Ymodem-G, Zmodem,

Zmodem with crash recovery, and Kermit. (These protocols are described after these steps.)

Step 3. Issue whatever command is necessary on the bulletin board to begin sending the file from the bulletin board computer.

Step 4. Click the Receive toolbar button in the HyperTerminal application window (or choose Transfer, Receive File). In the Receive File dialog box, specify the location for the file on your computer, and choose the file transfer protocol that matches the one you told the bulletin board to use in step 2. (If you are using HyperTerminal to download files from CompuServe, you have to use a binary file format such Xmodem, Ymodem, or Kermit instead of CompuServe B, because HyperTerminal doesn't support this protocol.) Click OK.

Step 5. If the file transfer protocol requires a filename on your computer for the downloaded file, you will be prompted for it. The file transfer then completes automatically.

You can also send (upload) a file to a bulletin board using a slight variation on these steps. The Send button is just to the left of the Receive button on the toolbar.

Among HyperTerminal's file transfer protocols, Xmodem is the most basic. This standard and somewhat slow protocol transfers files in 128-byte blocks. 1K Xmodem transfers files in 1024-byte blocks. This protocol is really the same thing as Ymodem. You can use Ymodem-G, a variation on Ymodem, if your modem and modem driver support hardware error correction. Zmodem is the file transfer protocol of choice for most bulletin boards. It is relatively fast and reliable, and it uses a variable block size. Use the Zmodem with crash recovery option if possible. Kermit is used at academic computer centers and on Digital Equipment Corp. VAX systems and some IBM mainframes. It is slow.

Secret

When you're using Zmodem, make sure that the name of the file you are transferring does not begin with a backslash (\) and is not named C. Otherwise, you may find that HyperTerminal seems to stop responding. If for some reason you must use these names, choose a different protocol, such as Xmodem.

You can set the default download and upload folder for each of your HyperTerminal connectoids. If you don't do this, HyperTerminal assumes you want to download files to and upload files from \Program Files\Accessories\HyperTerminal, the folder where your *ht* connectoid files are stored. You can change the default folder for each connectoid simply by specifying a different folder the next time you do an upload or download; HyperTerminal will then use that folder as the default until you specify a new location.

Secret

If you are using Zmodem, you won't have a chance to specify a folder because the protocol starts automatically. Instead, open the connectoid whose folder you want to change (do this by clicking it in the HyperTerminal folder), click Cancel in the Connect dialog box, choose Transfer, Receive, type the path of the folder you would like to use, and click Close. Your downloaded files will be now be stored in this folder, and HyperTerminal will look here for files to upload, until you change the default folder again.

Changing the Properties of a Connectoid

The properties associated with a given connection include the phone number, the type of terminal emulation, how many lines of text are buffered (allowing you to scroll back to display them), and how text files are transferred between your computer and the bulletin board.

You can get at these values in four different ways:

1. Right-click the icon for the connectoid in the HyperTerminal folder window, and choose Properties.

2. Click the connectoid icon, click Cancel in the Connect dialog box, and then choose File, Properties.

3. Click the connectoid icon, click Cancel in the Connect dialog box, click the Call toolbar button (the phone), and then click the Modify button.

4. Click the connectoid icon, click Cancel in the Connect dialog box, and then click the Properties button at the right end of the toolbar.

All of these steps take you to the Properties dialog box for your connectoid. If you use the first method, the Properties box contains a General tab in addition to the Connect To and Settings tabs. The General tab lists the file properties of the connectoid, not the substantive properties of the connectoid itself.

Changing the phone number and modem properties

HyperTerminal stores the properties for a connectoid in the Properties dialog box, as shown in Figure 21-3. The Connect To tab duplicates much of what you see in the Phone Number dialog box, which appears when you are creating a new connection. Two additional options are the Change Icon button, which lets you change the icon for the connectoid, and the Configure button, which brings you to the Properties dialog box for the modem. (See Chapter 31 for a detailed discussion of modem properties.)

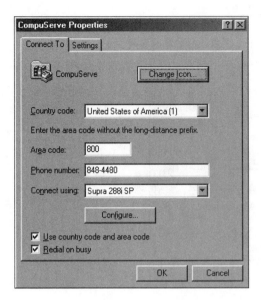

Figure 21-3: The Connect To tab of the Properties dialog box for a connectoid.

Setting terminal emulation and buffer size

The Settings tab of the Properties dialog box for a connectoid, shown in Figure 21-4, lets you change how the function keys are used in terminal emulation, which terminal you are going to emulate, how large a backward scroll buffer to maintain, and the ASCII properties values.

Various terminal emulations can use the Ctrl, arrow, and function keys to control how text is displayed and manipulated on the bulletin board computer. If you want these keys to operate in this fashion, choose Terminal keys.

You can choose from seven terminal emulation types: ANSI, Auto Detect, Minitel (common in France), TTY, Viewdata (common in the UK), VT100, and VT52. You can change some terminal settings in all the terminal emulation modes other than Auto Detect. Click the Terminal Setup button after you choose a terminal emulation to change terminal-specific settings. For most connections, you should set terminal emulation to Auto Detect, VT100, or ANSI.

Secret

To use Minitel emulation, you must use the Arial Alternative True Type font (Arialals.ttf and Arialalt.ttf). This is the only font that contains Minitel's required graphic characters. Minitel operates at 1200 bps. You should not use the XON/XOFF protocol.

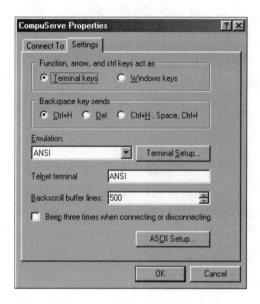

Figure 21-4: The Settings tab of the Properties dialog box for a connectoid. Choose whether the Ctrl, arrow, and function keys are sent to the bulletin board or used by Windows. Pick a terminal to emulate, set how many lines back you can scroll, and choose whether your speaker beeps three times when the bulletin board sends a Ctrl+G.

The Backscroll Buffer Lines field determines how many lines of an ongoing communication you can review in the HyperTerminal application window by scrolling back with the vertical scrollbar or by pressing the up arrow or Page Up key. The maximum (and the default) is 500. To change the size of the backscroll buffer for a connectoid, right-click the connectoid you want to change, click Properties, click the Settings tab, and enter the number of lines you want in the Backscroll Buffer Lines field.

Secret

Since HyperTerminal connectoids save the backscroll buffer from your last session on that host, the connectoid (*ht*) files vary in size depending on the size of the buffer. When you open a HyperTerminal connectoid, you can display your previous session (up to the number of lines you have defined) by dragging the scroll box.

If you want your computer to notify you when it successfully connects or disconnects from a bulletin board, mark the Beep Three Times When Connecting or Disconnecting check box.

ASCII text handling

Click the ASCII Setup button in the Settings tab of the Properties dialog box for a connectoid to set the parameters for sending and displaying text information. The ASCII Setup dialog box is shown in Figure 21-5.

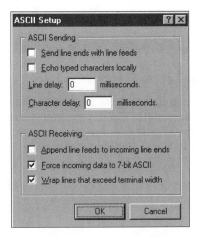

Figure 21-5: The ASCII Setup dialog box. Different bulletin boards send text to you in different ways. Use this dialog box to make up for ASCII miscommunication.

Tip

If the text you are receiving from a bulletin board is writing over itself, mark the Append Line Feeds to Incoming Line Ends check box. If you want to display only ASCII text — just the printable lower 128 characters in the ANSI character set — mark the Force Incoming Data to 7-bit ASCII check box. If the lines of text you're receiving are going off to the right, mark the Wrap Lines That Exceed Terminal Width check box.

If you are not seeing your text when you type it in, mark the Echo Typed Characters Locally check box. If the text that you are sending to the bulletin board is writing over itself, mark the Send Line Ends with Line Feeds check box.

You set the Line Delay and Character Delay values to make sure that the computer you are communicating with can keep up with your input. Some older time-sharing computers assumed that there was a real person typing the text, so they couldn't take rapid input of ASCII data. If the other computer is not receiving all of your text, increase the line delay (if the other computer is line-oriented) and/or the character delay.

Capturing Incoming Text to a File

You might want to keep a record of your communications sessions or just capture text that you're receiving from a bulletin board. To do this, start by choosing Transfer, Capture Text in the HyperTerminal application window. The default capture file is C:\Program Files\Accessories\HyperTerminal\ CAPTURE.TXT. A Notepad icon appears in the HyperTerminal folder window as soon as you click the Start button in the Capture Text dialog box.

You can close the capture file at any time by choosing Transfer, Capture Text, Stop in the HyperTerminal application window.

If the bulletin board computer echoes your keystrokes (that is, sends them back to you), these echoed keystrokes are also captured in the capture file.

Answering Incoming Data Calls

HyperTerminal doesn't really have much of a host mode, but you can tell your modem to answer incoming data calls. You have to tell it directly by typing the commands **ATA** or **ATS0=1** (or higher for a greater number of rings before the modem picks up) in the HyperTerminal application window. Here are the steps:

STEPS

Answering the Phone

Step 1. Click the Start button, point to Programs, Accessories, Communications, and then click HyperTerminal. Click HyperTrm.exe icon in the HyperTerminal folder window. HyperTerminal starts and displays the Connection Description dialog box to ask you for a name for the new connectoid; click Cancel without typing anything.

Step 2. Choose File, Properties. In the Connect Using drop-down list, choose Direct to Com X (where X is the port your modem is connected to).

Step 3. Click the Configure button. Verify the settings in the Port Settings tab, and then click OK.

Step 4. Click the Settings tab, and then click the ASCII Setup button.

Step 5. Mark the Send Line Ends with Line Feeds and Echo Typed Characters Locally check boxes.

Step 6. Click OK, and then click OK again. You can now type AT commands. You can use **AT** or **ATS0**=x to answer the phone.

Step 7. Quit HyperTerminal. When you are prompted "Save session *name*?," click Yes if you want to save the session so that you can use AT commands at another time.

If you create a connectoid instead of clicking Cancel in step 1, you can save all settings for the next time you want to answer the phone manually with HyperTerminal (either version). There are more than 50 articles in the Microsoft Knowledge Base referring to HyperTerminal. You can check them out by going to http://premium.microsoft.com.support.

HyperTerminal vs. Terminal

Microsoft shipped Terminal with Windows 3.1*x*. You would expect that HyperTerminal would be an upgrade of Terminal. It is, but it is also a newly designed product.

Terminal gave you three terminal emulations: TTY (very basic hard-copy terminal), VT100, and VT52 (these last two are Digital Equipment Corp. standards). HyperTerminal gives you six terminal emulations (or seven if you count Auto Detect). Terminal supported three modem types in addition to letting you type your own initialization strings. HyperTerminal supports hundreds of modems directly. Once you set up your modem, these settings can be used by any communications package that knows enough to take advantage of this capability, which is built into the operating system.

Terminal gave you two binary file transfer protocols, Xmodem/CRC and Kermit. HyperTerminal comes with seven: 1K Xmodem, Xmodem, Ymodem, Ymodem-G, Zmodem, Zmodem with crash recovery, and Kermit. Zmodem is the protocol used most widely to transfer files between personal computers and bulletin boards.

The scrollback buffer size can be 500 lines in HyperTerminal. Its maximum size in Terminal was 399 lines.

HyperTerminal creates separate files/icons for each connection. Click the icon for a given bulletin board and you are ready to connect. Terminal created a file for each different connection, but it was difficult to set up a folder of icons that allowed you to quick access to the files. You had to create a program group and then drag and drop the *trm* files that Terminal created for each connection into the group. Windows 98 makes this interface obvious.

In Terminal, you could define function keys (buttons at the bottom of the Terminal window) to carry out a series of commands, such as logging in and sending your name and password. HyperTerminal doesn't let you define function keys. HyperTerminal has a toolbar, which gives you a one-click interface to frequently used menu commands. Terminal only gave you a menu bar.

Terminal allowed you to send commands directly to your modem for troubleshooting. Windows 98 has a help-based modem troubleshooter. You have to create a connectoid in order to be able to send commands to your modem with HyperTerminal.

Summary

Communicating with bulletin boards requires that, for the most part, you turn your computer into a terminal that can upload and download files.

▶ You can use HyperTerminal, a little application that Microsoft bundles with Windows 98, to communicate with bulletin boards.

▶ We show you how to set up HyperTerminal for each bulletin board that you want to dial into.

▶ We show you how to download files from a bulletin board.

▶ We compare HyperTerminal with its previous incarnation — Terminal.

Chapter 22

Laptop to Desktop

In This Chapter

▶ Easily connecting two computers using a serial or parallel cable

▶ LapLink—the software that set the original standard for transferring files

▶ DOS Interlnk—Microsoft's first attempt at serial/parallel cable networking

▶ Direct Cable Connection—Windows 98 serial/parallel cable networking

▶ What to expect in the way of file transfer rates between Windows 98 computers

▶ Using a serial or parallel cable to give your laptop or other computer direct access to your network

▶ Setting up a parallel cable network that gives you much faster communication speeds than you would expect from ordinary parallel ports

▶ Comparing LapLink for Windows 98 with Direct Cable Connection

Connecting Two Computers

You can physically connect two computers using a serial or parallel cable, or even infrared transmitters/receivers. Depending on the software you use to drive the connection, the two computers may be limited to just transferring files. With more powerful software, one computer can use the resources (such as hard disk, files, and printers) of the other as though these resources were directly connected to it.

LapLink for DOS—a history

For years, Traveling Software "owned" the file-transfer franchise with its LapLink program. LapLink was the first popular software that allowed you to connect two computers using an inexpensive serial or parallel cable and easily transfer files back and forth.

All computers have a parallel port built in (some have two or three) and almost all have one or two serial ports. These ports are communication devices. Add a cable and file transfer software that's both quick and simple to use, and you've got yourself a winner.

LapLink's competition in the file-transfer business was the floppy diskette. Traveling Software's first task was to make LapLink quicker and easier to use than a floppy diskette. That was a technical hurdle, but not a high one.

One of LapLink's strengths (in addition to its speed) was its intuitive user interface. You got to see your directories and files in full-screen view. You could simply click a file to copy it from one computer to the other. No typing commands. No searching around with a one-line-high window (such as a DOS command line) to find your file.

Traveling Software did not develop a network based on the serial or parallel port. Perhaps company officials felt that the speeds of these communications devices were too slow. Perhaps they didn't want to dilute their marketing message. But while the DOS version of LapLink competed well against the floppy diskette, competing against Ethernet was a different story.

Interlnk — Microsoft's cable network

Operating systems such as MS-DOS and Windows 95 already have the built-in ability to transfer files between the hard disk and floppy diskette, between directories, between hard disks, and between RAM and the hard disks. You might think an obvious extension of the operating system would be to allow file transfer between two computers — especially when the communications ports are already built into the computers.

Microsoft's first foray in this direction was the Interlnk program. (Interlnk is the DOS eight-character mode spelling for Interlink.)

Interlnk is a DOS program (actually two DOS programs — Interlnk.exe for the guest computer and Intersrv.exe for the host computer) that allows you to connect two computers using a serial or parallel cable and then treat the host computer's hard disks as though they were additional local hard disks belonging to the guest computer. This allows the guest computer to treat the connected computers as if they were one system.

Unlike LapLink, which allows either computer to be in charge, Interlnk defines one computer as a *guest* and one as a *host*. The guest runs the show. The host simply provides the guest with its hard disks to be used as the guest determines. It sits there passively responding to the guest's commands. You type all of the commands on the guest computer.

Treating two computers as one is a much more powerful metaphor than the file-transfer metaphor. You can do anything with two computers that you can with one. The only problem is that the hard disks of the host computer are available only through a relatively slow connection. Microsoft apparently felt this speed penalty was not significant enough to offset the benefit of the networking model.

Unlike LapLink, Interlnk can run programs on the guest that are stored as executable files on the host. You can also transfer files. There isn't a nice user interface built in, just DOS, but you can use any DOS shell, even

DOSSHELL, which comes free with DOS 6.*x*. This gives you a front end for file transfers that is similar to LapLink, and at no additional cost.

Interlnk is a network. Specifically, it's a *zero slot network*, that is, a network without a network card. And because it doesn't have a dedicated network card, it is a relatively slow network.

Here are some of Interlnk's downsides:

- You have to install Interlnk.exe in the guest computer's Config.sys file — where it stays in memory.

- Interlnk doesn't offer any security.

- Interlnk is quite a bit slower than LapLink if you use the serial ports and a serial cable.

- Interlink will not function properly in MS-DOS mode running off of a FAT 32 formatted drive.

Microsoft never heavily promoted Interlnk, and it came out after the company's emphasis had shifted to Windows. Still, it's a useful and very inexpensive product. Too bad you never heard about it. You might call it a DOS 6.*x* secret.

Undocumented

You can use Interlnk to connect a DOS or Windows 3.1*x* computer to a Windows 98 computer. To reconfigure Interlnk to run in a DOS window, right-click it, choose Properties, click the Program tab, click the Advanced button, and clear the MS-DOS Mode check box. You can only use Intersvr in MS-DOS mode (it doesn't run in a DOS window).

Interlnk.exe and Intersvr.exe do not come with Windows 98. You can copy them from the DOS computer to the Windows 98 computer. If you happen to have a Windows 95 CD-ROM, Interlnk is in its \Other\Oldmsdos folder.

You can get help on how to run Interlnk in the DOS help file, which is stored on your Windows 98 CD-ROM in the \tools\oldmsdos folder. You can run the DOS help program from the CD-ROM if you like. Open up a DOS window focused on this folder, and then type **Help** and press Enter. Use your mouse to navigate to the Interlnk help entry.

Interlink will not see the CD-ROM on your Windows 98 computer unless you have the real-mode (DOS) CD-ROM drivers loaded into your Config.sys and Autoexec.bat files. This normally doesn't happen until you start up Windows. See "Running DOS Programs" in Chapter 34 for more on this.

Direct Cable Connection

Windows 98 makes it easy to directly connect two computers using a serial or parallel cable. That's because Windows 98 comes with Direct Cable Connection (DCC), which is a serial and parallel port network. DCC is also part of Windows 95, and you can use it to connect computers running both Windows 95 and Windows 98.

DCC is InterInk taken to the next level. Like InterInk, one computer is the guest (presumably a laptop computer that you've brought into the office) and the other is the host. DCC adds the ability to connect not only to the host but also to the other computers or servers on the network to which the host is attached.

Because DCC is a network, it uses the built-in Windows 98 network protocols to provide the communications link between the guest and both the host and the network connected to the host. You can use NetBEUI (Microsoft's peer-to-peer networking protocol), IPX/SPX (Novell's NetWare protocol), and/or TCP/IP (the protocol used in Unix networks and/or with dial-up Internet connections). Both IPX/SPX and TCP/IP are routeable, so you can communicate across network routing systems to the wider network.

DCC's user interface is a folder window that displays the shared resources (drives, folders, or printers) on the host. You don't have to learn how to use a different set of conventions. The beauty of integrating this kind of capability into the operating system is that you already know how to use it.

When you use DCC, Windows 98 treats other computers and servers networked to your computer like close friends. You can see the files and folders on hard drives that are shared. On your guest computer, you can run programs that reside as executable files on other computers. These programs are loaded into your computer's memory.

Your computer can easily find documents that are stored on other computers. And, of course, you can easily transfer files back and forth, updating older files to the latest versions.

Speed

DCC's speed varies depending on whether you are using serial or parallel port communications. Serial communications can be quite slow, to say the least. If your computer has the older or less expensive serial ports that use the 8250 or 16450 universal asynchronous receiver/transmitter (UART), you are limited to speeds of up to 57,600 bits per second (bps). (A UART is the chip that drives the serial port.) Most new computers come with 16550 UARTs or better. These chips can be driven at up to 115,200 bps.

Unfortunately, DCC can't give you the 14 kilobytes per second (KB/sec) file transfer speed that the 115,200 bps rate would imply (115,200/(1024 × 8)). DCC is slower than LapLink for Windows 98 on a serial cable.

Undocumented

Parallel ports come in a number of varieties. New computers have incorporated enhanced standards for parallel ports, known as EPP or ECP (see the "Parallel ports and cables" section later in this chapter for a full explanation). EPP/ECP ports can facilitate very high-speed communications between computers — approaching the speed that is available from dedicated networking cards. You can reach speeds of 120 KB/sec. with the appropriate cable and automatic data compression that is built into Windows 98 for parallel ports. At these speeds, networking over parallel cables is about a third as fast as dedicated 10 megabit (Mb) Ethernet cards, without the cost of an Ethernet card.

Although they don't have a reputation for speed, the older parallel ports still have better speed performance than serial ports. Windows 98 has enhanced parallel port software drivers that allow computers with standard parallel ports (4-bit unidirectional and 8-bit bidirectional) connected with a standard bidirectional parallel cable to network at speeds that are often quite acceptable — not just for file transfer, but for data and program sharing, too.

Setup

Direct Cable Connection is not installed unless you did a Custom setup when you installed Windows 98 or you installed DCC through the Add/Remove Programs icon in the Control Panel. During a Custom setup, you must choose Communications in the Components dialog box and then specifically mark the Direct Cable Connection check box.

If you didn't install Direct Cable Connection when you set up Windows 98, you can take the following steps to do so now:

STEPS

Installing Direct Cable Connection

Step 1.   Click the Start button, point to Settings, and then click Control Panel.

Step 2.   Click the Add/Remove Programs icon, and then click the Windows Setup tab.

Step 3.   Click Communications, and then click the Details button.

Step 4.   Mark the Direct Cable Connection check box.

Step 5.   Click the OK button in the Communications dialog box and in the Add/Remove Programs Properties dialog box.

If you install Direct Cable Connection, you will also automatically install Dial-Up Networking (DUN) and networking in general. Direct Cable Connection is really just a variant of Dial-Up Networking. It is a dial-up network that doesn't require that you dial up (or have a network card).

DUN is discussed in "Dial-Up Networking" in Chapter 17. Installing DUN during Windows 98 Setup or later from the Add/Remove Programs icon automatically configures the network protocols necessary to run DCC. You can always change these protocols to reconfigure DUN, and thereby also reconfigure DCC.

Secret

The Network Neighborhood icon appears on your Desktop when you install DCC. If you remove it by using TweakUI or the System Policy Editor, or directly by editing the Registry, you can no longer use DCC.

The original version of Windows 95 didn't let you keep a DCC connection and a separate DUN connection open at the same time. However, Microsoft has greatly improved Winsock. Winsock version 1.2 and later (version Winsock 2.2 comes with Windows 98) support multiple connections. Now you don't have to disconnect your modem connection to the Internet in order to open a DCC connection — a big improvement.

Configuration

To access Direct Cable Connection, click your Start button, point to Programs, Accessories, Communications, and finally click Direct Cable Connection.

The first time you use DCC, the Direct Cable Connection Wizard pops up, as shown in Figure 22-1, and helps you configure DCC.

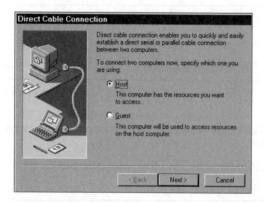

Figure 22-1: Run the Direct Cable Connection Wizard on both computers. Select the Host option button when you run the Wizard on your host computer, and select the Guest option button when you run it on your guest computer. You can later change these settings.

The DCC Wizard identifies the serial and parallel ports that are not already in use and can be used for communication, as shown in Figure 22-2. You can pick from among the available ports. If you add ports later, you can rerun the Wizard and ask it to check for new ports. This dialog box reminds you to plug in your cable. You don't need to do this for the Wizard to complete the configuration, but don't forget to plug it in before you try to connect.

If you are installing the guest computer, click Next, and then click Finish. DCC will begin trying to connect; click Close if you're not ready to connect now.

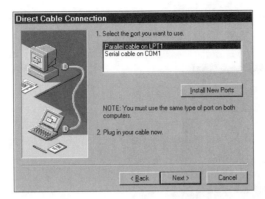

Figure 22-2: Click the Install New Ports button if you have installed new serial or parallel ports since the last time you ran the DCC Wizard.

If you are installing the host, you're not quite done. After you click Next in the dialog box shown in Figure 22-2, the Wizard either brings you to the final Wizard dialog box (shown in Figure 22-3), or, if you haven't yet enabled file and printer sharing, it brings you to a dialog box that contains a File and Print Sharing button. Click this button to configure sharing (see the "Sharing your resources" section of Chapter 24), and then click Next. (If you click Next without enabling sharing, the Wizard warns you that you're setting up DCC without sharing.) In the final Wizard dialog box, you can set a password that is required to connect the guest to the host computer. You can also click Cancel at any time during the process to forget the whole thing.

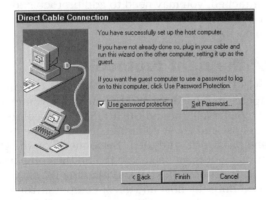

Figure 22-3: Mark the Use Password Protection check box to require a password for access to the host computer.

Network configuration

When DCC is installed, Dial-Up Networking is also installed. The default installation is shown in Figure 22-4. If your host computer isn't connected to a network, you will not need to add other protocols or change this configuration.

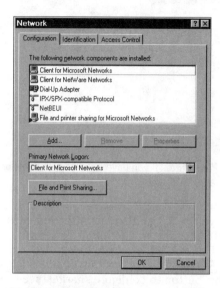

Figure 22-4: The Dial-Up Networking network configuration. All the components of Dial-Up Networking have been installed. The network configuration must be the same on both the guest and the host computer. By default, it will be.

If you want your guest computer to be a full-fledged member of the network to which your host is attached, you may need to add protocols to the Dial-Up Adapter. Turn to the "Network Installation" section of Chapter 24 for instructions on how to do this.

Installing all of the right protocols

If you are trying to use DCC to connect a Windows 98 guest computer to a Windows 98 host computer that is connected to a network, you may experience problems if you haven't bound the IPX/SPX protocol to your Dial-Up Adapter on both the host and guest computer. If you see the messages "Verifying username and password" and then "Disconnect" on the guest computer, the NetBIOS may not have been able to find the computer names on the host. To correct this problem, install and bind the IPX/SPX protocol to the Dial-Up Adapter on both the host and guest computer. You can find further discussion about this and other DCC issues on the "Windows98 Direct Cable Connect Problem Page" at http://www.tecno.demon.co.uk/dcc.htm.

Sharing comes first

If you want a guest computer to see anything on your Windows 98 host computer or on other computers on the network, you have to share their resources. When the guest computer connects to the host, a folder window displaying the shared resources of the host appears on the guest computer's Desktop.

To enable the host to share its resources, file and printer sharing for Microsoft Networks (or file and printer sharing for NetWare Networks) must be installed. File and printer sharing for Microsoft Networks is installed by default when you install DCC.

Furthermore, you must actually share some resources on your host computer. To do this, right-click the folder, drive icon, or printer icon you want to share, choose Sharing from the context menu, choose Shared As in the Sharing tab of the Properties dialog box, and type a name for the shared resource (and an optional comment).

Once you have shared some resources on your host computer, the guest computer will be able to see them.

If the host computer has user-level security (the host computer is connected to a Windows NT or NetWare server that keeps a user database), you need to both share the resources and add to the user list the guest user(s) who will be allowed to access them. To do this, take the following steps:

STEPS

Sharing with User-Level Security

Step 1. On the host computer, open an Explorer or folder window that contains your shared drive, printer, and/or folder.

Step 2. Right-click the resource, and then click Sharing in the context menu.

Step 3. Click the Sharing tab in the Properties dialog box for the resource, mark the Shared As option button, type a name (if different) for the resource, and then click the Add button.

Step 4. In the Add Users dialog box, click the names of the guest(s) who will be allowed to access the resources on the host computer.

Step 5. Choose the desired access type.

Step 6. Click OK buttons until you are out of the Properties dialog box for the resource.

Browsing the host

Secret

By default, the Windows 98 host computer doesn't show up in your Network Neighborhood if you click the Network Neighborhood icon on your Desktop. You also won't be able to see other computers on the network in the Network Neighborhood. If you want to get to them (and their shared resources) you have to type their UNC names in the Find Computer dialog box (Start, Find, Computer).

Microsoft turned off the capability for DCC (and Dial-Up Networking) to see or *browse* the host or the network because they felt this would slow DCC down too much. If you browse, your Windows 98 computer must update lots of information about disks, folders, and files that are on the host computer and on the network connected to the host computer.

You can turn the browsing feature back on and see for yourself if it is too slow for you. To do this, take these steps on your host computer:

STEPS

Forcing Browsing with DCC

Step 1. On your Windows 98 host computer, click the Start button, point to Settings, and then click Control Panel.

Step 2. Click the Network icon. In the Component list on the Configuration tab, highlight File and Printer Sharing for Microsoft Networks, and then click the Properties button. This will bring up the dialog box shown in Figure 22-5.

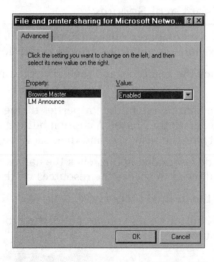

Figure 22-5: The Properties dialog box for file and printer sharing for Microsoft Networks.

Step 3. Highlight Browse Master, choose Enabled in the Value drop-down list, and click OK once.

Step 4. Now click the Identification tab and note the name in the Workgroup field. This name must be the same in both computers. Click OK.

Step 5. Restart your computer for the change to take effect, and start DCC.

Step 6. On the guest, follow step 1 and click the Network icon. Go to the Identification tab and make sure the name in the Workgroup field is the same as on the host. Click OK and start DCC.

Now you will be able to "browse" the Windows 98 host and the network from your guest computer whenever you have DCC running. There is one problem, however. If the Windows 98 host is also configured as a Dial-Up Networking server, you can dial in from a Dial-Up Networking client computer, and the host computer will pick up the phone. When you do this, the Browse Master function will still be enabled to let you browse the host and the network, but it will be enabled for a dial-up connection, which is much slower. A serial DCC connection is also slow, but it isn't slow enough to cause a problem with browsing, at least when the Windows 98 host is not connected to another network.

Secret

Although theoretically you can't browse the guest from the host, Tim Craig showed us a way to do it. Connect the two computers normally using DCC. On the host computer, right-click an empty space on the Desktop and select New, Shortcut. In the Command Line field, type the path with the name of the guest computer and the drive or folder you want to browse—for example:

```
\\Laptop\c
```

Click Next, then type a name for your shortcut, and click Finish. Now click your shortcut icon, and an Explorer window will open showing you the guest computer's shared resources.

Microsoft has prepared a document to help you troubleshoot your connection to your host computer. You can find it in the Knowledge Base at http://support.microsoft.com/support/kb/articles/Q134/3/04.asp.

Connected to what?

The fact that DCC is a network has manifold implications. While you might be interested in just hooking your laptop to your desktop computer, you can actually accomplish much more.

You can use DCC to connect directly to a computer running Windows 98. You can also connect indirectly through the network to a NetWare server computer, to a Windows NT server, to other computers running Windows 95 or Windows 98, or to other computers on the network.

If you want to connect through the network to the NetWare server, be sure to bind the IPX/SPX protocol to the Dial-Up Adapter on your guest computer— your laptop perhaps. IPX/SPX and NetBEUI are the protocols that are initially bound to the Dial-Up Adapter when you install DCC.

You can also connect indirectly to a Windows NT server through a Windows 98 computer if the Windows 98 computer is connected to the Windows NT computer on a network. Just use DCC and whatever protocol your Windows 98 host computer is using to talk to the Windows NT computer — probably NetBEUI, but it could be IPX/SPX.

Running Direct Cable Connection

You run DCC (if you have already set it up) by clicking the Start button, pointing to Programs, Accessories, Communications, and then clicking Direct Cable Connection. (If you use DCC a lot, you can easily put a shortcut to it on your Desktop.) Starting DCC displays the Direct Cable Connection dialog box, as shown in Figure 22-6. You can also configure (or reconfigure) DCC in this dialog box, which really means that you can change it from guest to host (or host to guest) and change which port it is using.

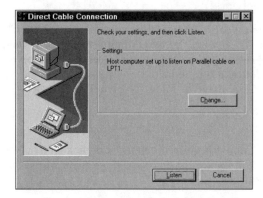

Figure 22-6: The Direct Cable Connection dialog box. On the host computer, the dialog box contains a Listen button. On the guest computer, it contains a Connect button. If you want to invoke the DCC Wizard, click the Change button.

Start DCC on both the guest and the host computer. Click the Listen button on the host computer to begin polling for the guest. Click the Connect button on the guest to begin trying to connect to the host. Once the connection is made, the host's shared drives and folders, as well as the shared resources of whatever other network the host is connected to, are available to the guest in the shared resources window. Furthermore, if you click the Network Neighborhood icon on the guest's Desktop, you will be able to see the resources available to you if you have set the Browse Master to Enabled on the host computer. (See the Forcing Browsing with DCC steps in the "Browsing the host" section earlier in this chapter.)

The options you have set in the Explorer's View, Folder Options dialog box will be operative in the shared resources window and in the Network Neighborhood window. In other words, these two views will behave like your My Computer window. The one difference is that you won't be able to choose View As Web Page until you select a folder, file, or shared printer.

The guest is treated as any other node on the network (except for the fact that the host can't ordinarily browse it). The security provisions of the network are enforced, and the guest may be required to provide a password to connect to the Windows 98 host computer.

Accessing the host

As soon as you make a successful connection with DCC, you will see the host's shared resources in a window on the guest computer. You can click any of the shared folders (or drives) to display the contents of the resource in a folder window.

You won't see drive icons in the shared resource window, even if you have shared the whole disk drive on the host. You'll see folder icons used to represent drives instead. This is true even if you browse the host with the Network Neighborhood.

Undocumented

You can map a networked resource (which may be a complete drive or perhaps just a folder) to a local drive letter. A networked drive icon will then appear in the Network Neighborhood if you enabled Browse Master on the host computer.

If you disconnect from the host, the folders or folder views of the host that are displayed on your guest don't automatically close. They just aren't connected to anything anymore. As soon as you reconnect to the host, these folders become active again.

Undocumented

You can drag a shortcut to a file, folder, or application from the host to the guest's Desktop or to any folder on the guest computer. Click the shortcut icon to open its target. If you click the shortcut icon, but there is no active connection to the host, you won't force DCC to activate and connect to the host. Instead, you will get the message shown in Figure 22-7.

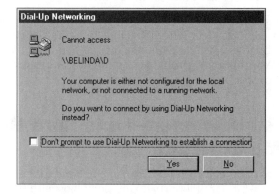

Figure 22-7: The Dial-Up Networking error message. You can see the connection between Dial-Up Networking and DCC. DCC doesn't automatically make the connection.

As soon as you click No, the message shown in Figure 22-8 appears to remind you that you need to make the network resource available.

Figure 22-8: The Problem with Shortcut message box. The shortcut can't find the connection to the host.

You can create a shortcut on the host computer that will automatically start listening for a guest (and skip the DCC dialog box). Right-click an empty part of your Desktop, and select New, Shortcut. In the Command Line field, type **directcc.exe connect**. Click Next, give your shortcut a name, and click Finish. Notice that the shortcut automatically has a DCC icon. When you click the icon, DCC will automatically start up. Thanks to Jerald R. Haggard for this tip.

You can't access the Internet over a DCC connection without special software. Because messages on the Internet are directed to a specific IP address, you need a *proxy server* to interpret the messages and route them correctly. WinGate is a shareware proxy server that can let you do this; you can download an evaluation version from http://www.deerfield.com/wingate/.

Serial ports

You can use DCC with a null modem serial cable or a LapLink serial cable. (See Chapter 31 for a discussion of null modem cables.)

LapLink comes with a blue serial cable and a yellow parallel cable. Both of the LapLink cables are about 8 feet long. Traveling Software sells these cables separately or bundled with its LapLink software. You can use them with DCC and Interlnk without any problem. You might want to get some longer cables, but they will be heavier to carry around.

Parallel ports and cables — one-third the speed of 10Mb Ethernet

There are five types of parallel ports: 4-bit, 8-bit, semi 8-bit, EPP, and ECP. Most PCs have 4-bit or 8-bit parallel ports. Many portables with the Intel 386 SL chipset have EPP ports. Computers that support the full IEEE 1284 parallel port specification (this includes all new computers) have ECP parallel ports.

■ **Standard parallel ports: 4-bit, 8-bit, semi 8-bit.** Almost every PC since the IBM PC-1 has come with an ordinary, 25-pin D-connector parallel port. These low-speed ports are fine for sending output to a printer (which is usually the slowest device in a computer system). But when you're transferring data between two PC parallel ports — using a LapLink cable or something similar — the speed of data transfer varies. While 4-bit ports can output data 8 bits at a time, they can input data only 4 bits at a time, which is about 40 kilobytes per second (KB/sec.). Eight-bit ports can output and input 8 bits (80 KB/sec. or more). Semi 8-bit ports can too, but only with more sophisticated software and peripherals.

■ **EPP ports.** The *enhanced parallel port* (EPP) was developed by Intel, Xircom, Zenith, and other companies that planned to exploit two-way communication with external devices. Some laptops built since mid-1991 have EPP ports. One source estimates that 80 percent of Intel 386SL and 486SL portables support EPP version 1.7, the first widely used version.

■ **ECP ports.** At the same time that Intel and others developed the EPP port, Microsoft and Hewlett-Packard were developing a spec called ECP — the *extended capabilities port.* It has about the same high-speed, two-way throughput as an EPP port, but it can use DMA (direct memory access) and a small buffer to provide smoother performance in a multitasking environment, which is why Microsoft supports ECP over EPP.

Both the EPP and the ECP specs were defined by the IEEE 1284 committee in 1993. Chipsets that support 1284 (and therefore can operate in ECP mode or in EPP 1284 mode) started appearing in PCs in 1994.

Four-bit ports are capable of effective transfer rates of 40–80 KB/sec., while 8-bit ports can handle between 80–150 KB/sec. ECP/EPP ports can sustain rates of 300 KB/sec. Unfortunately, just because a port can sustain this speed doesn't necessarily mean you will get file transfer rates at these speeds.

If your computers have ECP or EPP parallel ports, they can sustain about one-third of Ethernet link speeds when networked together with DCC. (Standard 10Mb Ethernet networks commonly deliver an actual throughput of 350–400 KB/sec.) This means that with a proper cable, you may not need to buy Ethernet cards to link together two computers with ECP or EPP parallel ports.

If you have the LapLink cable package (about $15.95), you already have an 8-foot basic bidirectional parallel cable. This cable is fine for 4-bit ports found on most older computers.

Another type of cable, known as a *universal cable module* (UCM), contains active electronics that speed two-way communications through the ECP/EPP enhanced parallel ports. Because there are several incompatible enhanced parallel ports in the market, the universal cable is key. It detects your port hardware and software and automatically transfers data at the highest available rate.

Microsoft has licensed software code to support the UCM technology from a small firm called Parallel Technologies Inc. and incorporated it into Windows 98 as part of Direct Cable Connection. To purchase Parallel Technologies' UCM cable (called the DirectParallel™ Universal Cable), contact Parallel Technologies Sales at 800-789-4784 or visit their web site, http://www.lpt.com/lpt. You'll also find lots of helpful information here about using DCC.

Parallel Technologies also offers a free program that will help you check out your Direct Cable Connection setup over a parallel cable as well as measure its throughput. You find the Direct Parallel Monitor (DPM) program (DPM171b.zip) at ftp://lpt.com/ftp/parallel.

Computers that use the SMC chip set in their ECP ports (the Hewlett-Packard Vectra, for example) may have trouple printing or making a DCC connection through these ports in ECP mode. The data seems to be transferring correctly, but later it turns out to be damaged. This happens if the ECP port didn't initialize properly when you turned on your computer. If you experience this problem, check with your manufacturer for advice on taking one of these actions: configuring the parallel port so it is not in ECP mode; reconfiguring the ECP port so that it will initialize properly (use the SMC setup disk that came with your computer); or getting a newer version of the SMC chip set.

More on speed

Undocumented

We have made an effort to quantify the file-transfer speeds that you can obtain using the various cables and ports and to compare them with LapLink for Windows 98. The results are shown in Table 22-1. File transfer speeds depend greatly on the compressibility of the files and the speed of the computers to which you connect. We transferred only already zipped files to eliminate compression efficiency as a variable. The file transfer tests used one 486-66 computer with 16MB of RAM and an IDE drive and one Pentium 166 MHz computer with 32MB of RAM and SCSI drives.

Undocumented

We used the Device Manager to set the serial ports at 115,200 bits per second, both in the port settings and in the modem settings. Serial ports default to 9600 bits per second, and you have to change these defaults in order to speed up a serial DCC connection. LapLink defaults to setting the ports to 115,200 bits per second.

Table 22-1   File Transfer Speeds

Port	LapLink for Windows 98	DCC
Serial	22 KB/sec.	11.5 KB/sec.
4-bit parallel	46 KB/sec.	76 KB/sec.
ECP/UCM	N/A	120 KB/sec.

Notice that LapLink for Windows 98 is quite a bit faster than Direct Cable Connection over a serial cable. It is our understanding (from Microsoft support personnel) that Traveling Software has a patent for a particularly fast method of transferring data over a serial cable using more than the normal data lines. Microsoft does not use this technology. No wonder Microsoft strongly encourages you to use the parallel port for DCC.

The ECP ports with the UCM cable are quite a bit faster than the other means of file transfer, but only a third as fast as the potential speed of the ECP ports. This makes file transfer over ECP ports and a UCM cable slower than dedicated Ethernet cards.

Watch the interrupts

Secret

DCC over parallel ports uses the interrupts assigned to those ports. LPT1 most often uses Interrupt 7, and LPT2 most often uses Interrupt 5. Parallel printers don't really use these interrupts, so it usually doesn't matter if something else in your computer grabs them first.

Sound cards and CD-ROMs often use these interrupts. Because the parallel ports don't really use them, Windows 98 doesn't report a conflict between the ports and the sound card or CD-ROM.

If you use DCC over a parallel port and there is a conflict with that port's interrupt, DCC will be slowed down by a factor of three. To prevent this from happening (if you can), you need to be sure that Interrupt 7 is not used by some other card if you are using LPT1 for DCC. The same holds for Interrupt 5 and LPT2.

To find out if there is a conflict, take the following steps:

STEPS

Determining If an Interrupt Conflict Exists

Step 1. Click the Start button, point to Settings, and then click Control Panel.

Step 2. Click the System icon, and then click the Device Manager tab.

Step 3. While Computer is highlighted in the Device Manager, click Properties.

Step 4. From the list of interrupt requests in the Resources tab, you can determine if 7 or 5 is used.

You may be able to change the interrupt used by the card(s) that conflict with DCC. If your card is plug and play compatible, you can do this using the Device Manager (see Chapter 25). If not, you may need to change some jumpers on the card or run a piece of setup software from the card's manufacturer.

Sometimes you may find that after you close a DCC connection using a parallel cable, your mouse pointer is jerky and multimedia sound "stutters." This is a symptom of a conflict over the interrupt — the parallel driver doesn't sense that the remote computer has dropped the connection, so it tries to detect whether the connection is still there. In this situation, and if you are forced to live with interrupt conflicts, just wait for 30 seconds or so. The parallel driver will wise up, and your system will go back to normal.

Using the infrared communications driver

You can install the Infrared (IR) Communications Driver on your Windows 98 computer, and run DCC using wireless infrared communications instead of serial or parallel cables. Many popular notebook computers have built-in IR ports. In addition, it's possible to buy an IR adapter and connect it to a serial port. In either case, the IR link is simulating a serial communications link.

For lists of compatible computers and adapters, and for troubleshooting help, read the Microsoft Knowledge Base articles "Infrared Data Association Release Notes, Parts 1 and 2" (at http://support.microsoft.com/support/kb/ articles/Q139/5/42.asp and http://support.microsoft.com/support/kb/ articles/Q139/5/43.asp), and "IR Communications Driver 2.0 Release Notes, Parts 1 and 2" (at http://support.microsoft.com/support/kb/articles/Q149/4/ 49.asp and http://support.microsoft.com/support/kb/articles/Q149/4/ 50.asp).

Troubleshooting DCC

If you experience problems getting DCC to work, a troubleshooter dialog box appears that gives you some guidance on how to proceed. Answer the questions and carry out the actions it suggests based on your answers.

You can invoke the DCC troubleshooter manually by taking the following steps:

STEPS

Getting to the DCC Troubleshooter

Step 1. Click the Start button, click Help, and then click the Contents tab.

Step 2. Click the Troubleshooting book, then the Windows 98 Troubleshooters book.

Step 3. Click the topic Direct Cable Connection, and then click the "click here" link.

Step 4. The Networking Troubleshooter will start. Answer the questions by clicking the gray buttons next to them.

If you see the following message when you try to connect using DCC:

```
System seems to connect but can't find the host computer.
```

it may be because both computers have the same name. Check the names by opening the Control Panel, clicking the Network icon, and selecting the Identification tab. The Computer Name field will show you the name, and let you change it if necessary.

It's possible that you may receive one of these two error messages when you are trying to make a connection:

```
Status: Connected via parallel cable on LPT1. Looking for shared
folders.
```

or

```
Cannot find the host computer.
```

If you get either of these error messages, try renaming the Vredir.vxd file (if it exists) in the \Windows\System folder, and then extracting a new copy of Vredir.vxd file from your Windows 98 CD-ROM. Vredir.vxd should be located in the Net10.cab file in the \Win98 folder of the CD ROM. To extract it, click the *cab* file to view its contents, then drag Vredir.vxd into the \Windows\ System folder on your hard disk.

If you have trouble with DCC and can't get it to respond, press Ctrl+Alt+Delete, highlight Rnaapp, and click the End Task button. This should allow you to end DCC and start it again.

DCC to Windows NT

Undocumented

You can use DCC to connect a Windows 98 computer to a Windows NT computer. The Windows NT computer will run NT Remote Access Server (RAS) and the Windows 98 computer will run DCC.

On the Windows NT computer, use the Null Modem 19200 driver, because DCC defaults to 19200 speed. Windows NT won't let DCC go any faster than 19,200 bits per second over serial lines. (You can't use a parallel connection between Windows 98 and Windows NT, because Windows NT doesn't have a ParaLnk.VxD driver.) Windows 98 computers can communicate with each other (or with Windows 95 computers) using DCC at 115,200 bits per second over serial lines. Either computer can be the guest or the host (referred to as the *server* in Windows NT-speak).

Windows NT uses user-level security. Your Windows 98 computer needs to log into the NT domain if the Windows NT computer is the host. You can set the NT domain by clicking the Network icon in the Control Panel, highlighting Client for Microsoft Networks, clicking the Properties button, marking the Log on to Windows NT Domain check box, and then typing the domain's name.

To connect the Windows 98 computer to the Windows NT computer, you need to install a null modem driver. For information on this, look at http://www.vt.edu:10021/K/kewells/net/index.html.

DCC to Windows 3.11

It's possible to connect a Windows 98 computer to a computer running Windows for Workgroups 3.11 using a serial connection. The Windows 98 computer uses DCC, and the Windows for Workgroups computer uses the upgraded Remote Access Server (RAS) client. Each computer can be either host or guest.

In many situations you may find it easier to use Interlnk, however, as the setup on the RAS side is somewhat complex. The DCC/RAS method will not work if either computer is connected to a network. However, if the disk on your Windows 98 computer is partitioned using FAT 32, this may be your only option.

For a step-by-step description of how to set up Windows for Workgroups 3.11 for this connection, see http://www.cs.purdue.edu/homes/kim.

Administering the Host Computer's Print Queue

Tip

Let's say you are connecting your laptop to your desktop computer using DCC. Let's assume that the desktop computer (the DCC host) has a printer connected to it. You might want to be able to delete or pause print files that you are printing from your laptop onto the desktop's printer. Unfortunately, the desktop computer's print queue isn't automatically available to you on the laptop; you have to move over to the desktop computer and administer the queue there.

To administer the desktop computer's print queue from the laptop, you need to set your desktop computer to permit remote administration. To do this, click the Passwords icon in the Control Panel of the desktop computer, click the Remote Administration tab, and then mark the Enable Remote Administration on This Server check box. (Note that this tab will not appear unless you have installed either file and printer sharing for Microsoft Networks or file and printer sharing for NetWare.)

So What About LapLink for Windows 98?

LapLink for Windows 98 is not a network on a serial or parallel cable. It doesn't give you full remote access. It does give you easy-to-use file transfer and file synchronization capabilities across a cable, network, modem, or radio modem. It also provides chat and remote control facilities. Remote control lets you run the other computer from your computer. Traveling Software has incorporated a Windows 98 Explorer-like front end to its file transfer software. This cuts down on the cognitive dissonance that you would experience if they had stayed with their old File Manager-like front end. LapLink's serial cable file-transfer speeds are much higher than what is available under DCC on a serial port.

Windows 98 provides file synchronization in the Briefcase applet, which we describe in Chapter 23. LapLink for Windows 98's file synchronization is automatic. When you copy the files back over the originals, LapLink only copies the files that have been modified, updating the originals for you. This is much faster than using the Briefcase.

For more information about Traveling Software and LapLink for Windows 98, call 800-343-8080 or visit http://www.travsoft.com

Summary

▶ Windows 98 comes with a built-in network called Direct Cable Connection, which lets you connect two computers with a serial or parallel cable, or through infrared devices.

▶ We show you how to configure Direct Cable Connection.

▶ We discuss what kinds of network connection speeds you can expect from different serial and parallel ports.

▶ We show how Windows 98 has taken the next step toward making the parallel port connection a true networking connection with close to network-standard speeds.

▶ We compare the file-transfer standard — LapLink for Windows 98 — with the offerings built into Windows 98.

Chapter 23

Synchronized Filing — The Briefcase

In This Chapter

Windows 98 provides the Briefcase to help you keep the same files on two computers up to date on both:

▶ Using the Briefcase to move files between a computer at the office and one at home, between a portable and a desktop computer, or across a network

▶ Creating and moving a Briefcase

▶ Moving files and folders into and out of the Briefcase, and updating files on different computers

---

Why a Briefcase?

Let's take a look at the metaphor of a briefcase before we incorporate its Windows 98 version into our mental framework.

You use a briefcase to take documents with you so that you can work on them outside the office. The documents in a briefcase might be copies, or they might be the originals. All of the changes that you make to these documents are written into the documents as you work on them.

Having two computers with local storage capacity presents a problem. Which document is the most up to date— the one on your computer at the office or the one on your portable? Changes you make to documents stored on computers are not as easily recognizable as those you make to documents on paper. You can quickly lose track.

The Windows 98 Briefcase helps you keep track of files when you are using two computers to work on them. Like a real briefcase, it moves from place to place. Unlike a real one, you carry only copies of your original documents. You can put the Briefcase on a floppy disk, or you can move it from computer to computer over a network. You can use copies in the Briefcase that have been updated to overwrite the originals.

Tip

The Briefcase relies on the date and time stamp of the file to determine whether it is the latest copy, so be sure to match the date and time on both computers.

The following scenarios describe three common ways you might use the Windows 98 Briefcase.

Scenario 1

You have a desktop computer at work and a desktop computer at home. You want to work at home on some documents that you normally work on at work.

You have a Briefcase on the Desktop of your computer at work. You copy files from folders on your work computer into the Briefcase. You move the Briefcase to a floppy disk.

You take the floppy disk with the Briefcase on it home, perhaps in your actual briefcase. At home, you view the floppy disk using the Explorer or My Computer. You copy files from the Briefcase on the floppy disk into folders on your hard disk. You open the documents in their folders on the hard disk and edit them.

Before returning to work, you click Update All in the Briefcase on your floppy disk. This copies the edited files from their folders on the hard disk in your home computer into the Briefcase on your floppy disk.

At work, you put your floppy disk in your computer and open the Briefcase using My Computer or the Explorer. You then click Update All to update the documents in their original folders on your computer at work. The most recent versions of the files in the Briefcase are copied over their original files in the folders on the hard disk of the computer at work.

Both your computer at home and the computer at work now have the latest versions of the documents. Your Briefcase on the floppy disk also has the latest versions.

Scenario 2

You have a laptop and a desktop computer at work. You want to work on documents on your laptop while you are away from the office.

You have a Briefcase on the Desktop of your desktop computer. You copy documents that you are working on into the Briefcase on your desktop computer. You then continue working on these documents in their original folders.

When you are finished working on your documents at the office, you click Update All in the Briefcase to update all the copies of your documents in the Briefcase based on the originals on your desktop computer.

You connect your laptop to your desktop computer with Direct Cable Connection (DCC) or over the office network. You move the Briefcase from the Desktop of your desktop computer to the Desktop of your laptop computer.

The files in the Briefcase remember their relationship with the original files in the folders on the hard disk of the office computer. While you are away from your office, you edit the documents in the Briefcase on your laptop *without copying or moving them out of the Briefcase.*

The next day at work, you connect the two computers with DCC and move the Briefcase from the laptop to the desktop computer. You then click Update All in the Briefcase to update the original documents on the desktop computer.

Scenario 3

You want Janice, whose computer is on your network, to work on your files. She will return the files to you after working on them.

You copy your files into your Briefcase on your Desktop, and then move the Briefcase to Janice's Desktop across the network.

Janice works on your files, *never copying them out of the Briefcase.* Later, when she is done, she moves your Briefcase back to the Desktop of your computer.

You update all your original files by clicking Update All in the Briefcase on your Desktop.

What Does a Briefcase Do?

After you create a Briefcase and copy a file into it, the Briefcase maintains a synchronization relationship, called a *sync link*, between the original file and its copy in the Briefcase. After you have established this sync link, you can edit either the copy in the Briefcase or the original file. If you want to ensure that both the original and the copy are the latest version, choose Update All from inside the Briefcase. Briefcase copies the later version over the earlier version so that both the original and the Briefcase copy are the latest version.

The idea is that you edit either the Briefcase copy or the original copy, but not both, before you perform an update. If you edit both files without an update, you need to manually edit a combination of the files to create a latest version. See the section later in this chapter entitled "Both the original and the Briefcase copy have been modified" for details on how to do this.

The Briefcase can travel. If it couldn't, it wouldn't be of much use. Microsoft assumes you will edit or work on files in different places sequentially — that you will edit files in one place, carry the Briefcase with the files in it to another location, edit the files in this new location, and later return the Briefcase to the original location. Updates and edits happen sequentially.

Creating a Briefcase

If you install the Briefcase during Windows 98 Setup, the Briefcase icon (by default named My Briefcase) will appear on your Desktop. If you do a Portable setup, the Briefcase will be installed automatically. If you do a Custom setup, you need to choose to install the Briefcase when given the option. If you do a Typical setup, the Briefcase will not be installed.

If you install Windows 98 over Windows 95 and have the Briefcase already installed, it will still be installed after Windows 98 is installed. You can also install it later using Add/Remove Programs in the Control Panel.

Once the Briefcase is installed, you cannot use the Add/Remove Programs icon in the Control Panel to remove it from the computer. Briefcase is not listed in the Windows Setup tab of the Add/Remove Programs Properties dialog box. This is because uninstalling Briefcase would make any existing Briefcases (and their contents) become inaccessible. You can, however, delete the Briefcase icon from the Desktop.

In addition, you can use TweakUI to remove Briefcase from the New menu that appears when you right-click the Desktop, a folder window, or the right pane of the Explorer. To do this, go to the New tab of TweakUI, clear the Briefcase check box, and reboot your computer. If you think the Briefcase was installed (remember, it won't appear in the Add/Remove Programs Properties dialog box) but you can't find it in the New menu and want it to be there, you may need to re-add it using TweakUI.

To create a new Briefcase on the Desktop (assuming that Briefcase is installed on your computer), right-click the Desktop, point to New, and then click Briefcase. You can also create Briefcases in any folder. Just right-click in the folder window and issue the same command.

You can create as many Briefcases as you like. You can name the Briefcases anything you like. You can change the names of any of your Briefcases. This can quickly get out of hand because you have to remember which Briefcase contains the copies of which files. We suggest that you stick to one or two Briefcases, or name your Briefcases for projects. You are not allowed to put one Briefcase inside of another.

Putting the Briefcase on the Desktop makes it easy to drag files from the Explorer or other folder windows to the Briefcase, assuming you can see the Briefcase icon on the Desktop. If you can't easily get at the Briefcase on the Desktop, you can also drag files into it in the Explorer. The Briefcase appears in the left pane of the Explorer window, connected by a dotted line to the Desktop at the top of the pane, as shown in Figure 23-1. You can drag files from the right pane of the Explorer into the Briefcase in the left pane.

Figure 23-1: An Explorer view that includes a Briefcase. You can drag and drop files from the right pane into the Briefcase in the left pane.

The first time you create a Briefcase or when you open your Briefcase for the first time during a session, the Welcome to the Windows Briefcase dialog box appears to introduce you to the basic steps of working with the Briefcase (see Figure 23-2). In addition to the quick overview provided in this dialog box, you can find further assistance in the Windows 98 help files.

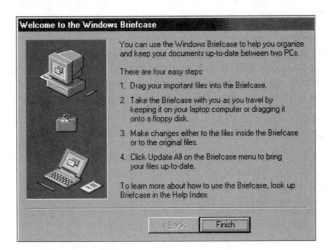

Figure 23-2: The Welcome to the Windows Briefcase dialog box.

Undocumented

You can create a Briefcase on a floppy disk or in a folder other than the Desktop folder. After you create a Briefcase, you can move it into any other folder that you like. For additional information, see the section entitled "Moving a Briefcase" later in this chapter.

If there is more than one user profile on your computer and you switch users, the original My Briefcase icon will not behave properly. After setting up user profiles, you should empty and remove this Briefcase, and have each user create his or her own new Briefcase. Each new Briefcase will only be visible in the user profile to which it belongs.

You can delete a Briefcase to the Recycle Bin and then restore it. The deleted Briefcase loses its icon and appears as a plain folder while it's in the Recycle Bin. Once it's restored, however, the icon comes back, and the contents are restored as well. Folder icons for all deleted Briefcases, regardless of user profile, will appear in the Recycle Bin. If you restore another user's Briefcase, it goes back to that user's Desktop, not yours.

Copying Files or Folders into a Briefcase

You can use the Explorer to copy files and folders to a Briefcase. And if the Briefcase is on the Desktop, you can also drag and drop files or folders from a folder window onto the Briefcase icon.

When you copy files or folders to a Briefcase, they are copied with a *sync link*. The copy in the Briefcase is connected to the original file or folder. If there is a change in the copy or the original, the status of the copy in the Briefcase changes from Up-to-Date to Needs Updating.

You copy every document that you want to work with on another computer into your Briefcase. The originals stay put, and you take the copies in the Briefcase with you. You can delete the copies from the Briefcase without affecting the originals.

Depending on how you installed Windows 98, My Briefcase may already be an option in your Send To menu (displayed when you right-click a file or folder and choose Send To in the context menu). If so, or if you have created a shortcut there, don't forget to update the shortcut if you move or rename the Briefcase. Otherwise, you'll get the following error message:

```
The Briefcase cannot be opened because the disk is inaccessible.
Verify that the disk is accessible.
```

To update the shortcut, go to your \Windows\SendTo folder, right-click My Briefcase, click Properties, click the Shortcut tab, then type your Briefcase's current name and location into the Target field.

You'll also get the above error message if the file you're trying to send to the Briefcase is still open.

Moving a Briefcase

Once you copy all the files and folders that you want into a Briefcase, you can move it to another computer. You don't want to do this until you have finished editing the original documents for the day because you need to move a fully updated Briefcase to the new computer.

Make sure to close the Briefcase before you try to move it. Otherwise, you will get an error message saying that you have to close it first. It may not be obvious that you have the Briefcase open if you are viewing it in the Explorer. The Briefcase is open if you can see its contents in an Explorer or folder window.

Moving a Briefcase to a floppy disk

One option is to move the Briefcase to a floppy disk. You can drag and drop the Briefcase icon from the Desktop to the floppy disk drive icon in your Explorer. If none of the files in the Briefcase is larger than the capacity of the floppy disk, the Briefcase and the files that it contains will be moved to the floppy disk. You won't be able to copy any files that are too big to fit on the floppy disk.

Secret

If there are more files than will fit on one floppy disk, you will be asked to put in additional floppy disks. Unfortunately, the files on the second and later floppy disks will be marked as *orphans*, which means there will be no sync link between these copies and the original files. Because of this feature, a Briefcase that is copied to a floppy disk cannot be any bigger than one floppy disk and still operate as a Briefcase.

The whole point of a Briefcase is to maintain the sync link. While Briefcases can contain orphans, these are no better than regular copies of the original files. This limits Briefcases transported on floppy disks to floppy-disk size, a good reason for creating multiple Briefcases. If you need to have one large Briefcase, you may want to invest in a larger storage medium such as a Zip drive. The Briefcase works on Zip disks the same as it does on floppies. If necessary, you can buy one external Zip drive and transport the drive between computers.

You should not copy the Briefcase onto the floppy disk, only move it. Copying will creat multiple copies of Briefcase, which will only confuse things when you want to synchronize files.

Secret

You should not move the Briefcase off of the floppy disk onto the computer at home. If you want to work on the files in the Briefcase at home, copy the files out of the Briefcase on the floppy disk into folders on your home computer's hard disk. This allows you to edit them more quickly because they are now stored on the hard disk. Just don't copy the Briefcase itself.

When you copy the files from the Briefcase on the floppy disk into folders on the hard disk, an additional sync link is developed between the files in the Briefcase and the new files on the computer at home. The files in the Briefcase now have two sync links: one with the original files on the computer at work and one the copies on your hard disk at home.

If you move the Briefcase from the floppy disk to the Desktop (or to another folder) of the home computer, you will not be able to create the second sync link. If you copy files out of the Briefcase after you move it to the home computer, there will be no connection between these copies and the copies in the Briefcase — although the files in the Briefcase will still maintain a sync link with the original files on the computer at work.

In summary, if you want to maintain two sync links, don't move the Briefcase off of the floppy disk. Copy the files from the Briefcase into folders on your home computer's hard disk and update the Briefcase on the floppy after you have edited the files at home. Then take the Briefcase on the floppy back to work to update the files there.

Moving a Briefcase over a network

You can move the Briefcase from one computer to another across a network. You can do this over a Dial-Up Networking, DCC, or LAN connection. You don't run into the same size limitations when you move the Briefcase over a network that you do when you use a floppy disk.

Say, for example, that you want to send a group of files over the network to a coworker who will work on them and send them back to you.

STEPS

Keeping Files Synchronized on a Network

Step 1. Create a Briefcase on your coworker's Desktop. Over the network, copy the files or folders you want edited from your computer into the Briefcase on his or her Desktop.

In order to copy the files or folders from your computer, you must first share the folders that contain them. (See "Sharing your resources" in Chapter 24.)

Step 2. Your coworker can now edit the files in the Briefcase on his or her computer. The files must stay in the Briefcase to preserve the links. The two computers do not need to be connected while your coworker is editing the files.

Step 3. When you are ready to synchronize the files, connect the two computers. To update all the files in the Briefcase, right-click the Briefcase icon on your coworker's Desktop, and click Update All. To update only certain files, click the Briefcase icon to open it, select the files you want to update, and then click the Update Selection toolbar button.

Occasionally, you may find that after you have moved a Briefcase to another computer on the network, the Briefcase can't update files. You may receive an error message stating that the synchronization copy is unavailable, even though the file is actually available on the network.

Here's what's happening: When you drag a file into the Briefcase, information about the file's path on the network is stored with it in the Briefcase's database. The Briefcase refreshes this information whenever you open it. If a folder above the one that contains the file is not shared when you copy the file into the Briefcase, the path information above that folder will not be available to the Briefcase. If you later share that folder and move the Briefcase without opening it again, the Briefcase will not be refreshed with the new path information.

The solution is to open the Briefcase at least once after the path information for a file or folder inside it has changed, before you move the Briefcase to another computer on the network.

Moving a Briefcase to a portable computer

Secret

When you move the Briefcase from the Desktop of your desktop computer to the Desktop of your portable computer, only one sync link is maintained—that between the files in the Briefcase and the files on the desktop computer. You need to keep the files in the Briefcase on the portable computer and edit them within the Briefcase in order to maintain the sync link.

Moving the Briefcase to the Desktop of the portable is the same as moving the Briefcase from a floppy disk to the Desktop of the home computer. Once you do this, you need to work with the files on the portable or on the home computer only while they are in the Briefcase.

If you have a portable computer connected to a desktop computer at home and to one at the office, you can keep the original files on your portable and create Briefcases on both of your desktop computers. Drag the files from your portable to the Briefcase on each of your desktop computers. Then synchronize the files each time you connect your portable to one of the desktops.

The Briefcase and its Update All command let you copy files back and forth without explicitly copying them or to having to remember which is the latest version. You can still copy files yourself without using the Briefcase if it is easier for you.

Opening a Briefcase

In some ways, the Briefcase is like any other folder. Click its icon on the Desktop and it opens into a folder window. Click its icon in the Explorer, and its contents appear in the right pane. Right-click the Briefcase icon on the Desktop and choose Explore to open an Explorer view of the Briefcase.

Secret

Say you have moved the Briefcase from the Desktop of your desktop computer to the Desktop of your portable computer. When you open the Briefcase on the portable, a message window may appear asking if you want to reconnect with the desktop computer. Just click No. This message window appears because Windows 98 is automatically trying to reestablish the link in the Briefcase with the original files across a network that is no longer connected.

Copying Files or Folders from a Briefcase

Let's say you have copied your Briefcase from your desktop computer to your portable computer. You should leave your documents in the Briefcase on the Desktop of your portable computer. If you copy them out of the

Briefcase, then the copies in the folders on the hard disk of the portable have no relationship to the files in the Briefcase.

On the other hand, you should copy the files from the Briefcase on a floppy disk to the hard disk of your computer at home. The second sync link is created and you can edit your files on the hard disk.

Secret

Update the Briefcase on the floppy disk before you take it back to the office. Update the files on the office computer from the Briefcase on the floppy disk. You can then leave the Briefcase on the floppy disk where it is, or move it back onto the Desktop on the office computer.

Determining the Status of Files or Folders in Your Briefcase

Copying files and folders to the Briefcase establishes a sync link between the original files and the copies in the Briefcase. If you modify any of the files (either the originals or copies), the Briefcase tells you that the files are out of sync and need to be updated.

When you have just finished copying files or folders into a Briefcase, their status is shown as Up-to-Date because the files in the Briefcase haven't yet been modified. If you now edit the original files or the files in the Briefcase, you need to update both the originals and the copies to the latest version, that is, get them in sync.

STEPS

Determining Briefcase File Status

Step 1. Click the Briefcase icon on your Desktop. If the Briefcase isn't showing Details view, choose View, Details.

Step 2. The status of each file and folder is displayed in the Status column. The possible listings in this column are Up-to-Date, Needs Updating, Orphan, or Unavailable.

Step 3. The Sync Copy In column lists the location of the original file or folder. An open Briefcase displaying these columns is shown in Figure 23-3.

Step 4. You can get further details about a particular file or folder by right-clicking it, choosing Properties, and then clicking the Update Status tab, as shown in Figure 23-4.

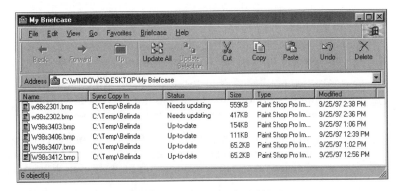

Figure 23-3: An open Briefcase. The Name column lists the filenames, the Sync Copy In column lists the folder where the synched file is stored, and the Status column gives the current status of the link between the two files.

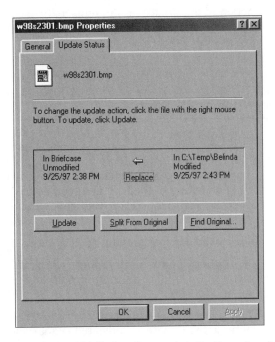

Figure 23-4: The Update Status tab in the Properties dialog box for a file in the Briefcase.

Updating Files and Folders

If you edit your original files after you have placed them in the Briefcase, you need to update them before you move your Briefcase.

When you bring your Briefcase back from home to the computer at work that has the original files, you need to update your original files based on their new modified versions in the Briefcase.

If you have copied your files or folders from the Briefcase on a floppy disk onto your portable or home computer, you need to update the files in the Briefcase on the floppy after you have modified them on the computer.

The files are marked Needs Updating if you have edited or modified either the file/folder outside the Briefcase or the copies inside. Updating the files/folders will ensure that both the originals and the copies in the Briefcase are the latest version.

The default action of the Briefcase is to replace the file that has an earlier date with the file that has a later date. You can override this action if you so desire.

STEPS

Updating Files and Folders

Step 1. Click the Briefcase to open it, and then click the file or folder in the Briefcase that you want to update. Use Ctrl+click or Shift+click to select multiple files and/or folders. If you are going to update all the files and folders in the Briefcase, you don't need to highlight any of them. In fact, you don't even need to open the Briefcase; just right-click it, and choose Update All from the context menu.

Step 2. Display the Briefcase menu.

Step 3. Click either Update All (to update all the files and folders in the Briefcase) or Update Selection (to update only the highlighted files and folders).

Step 4. The Update dialog box, shown in Figure 23-5, appears to let you continue the update as indicated or make some changes.

Step 5. Right-click near the horizontal arrow between filenames to see how you can change the default action. A small context menu appears to let you choose which action to take. You can change the direction of the Replace action to switch which file updates the other, or you can choose Skip to skip this particular update. The context menu may also occasionally contain a Merge command. This command appears if the selected files include any that are associated with an application for which the developer has implemented a merge feature.

Step 6. Click the Update button.

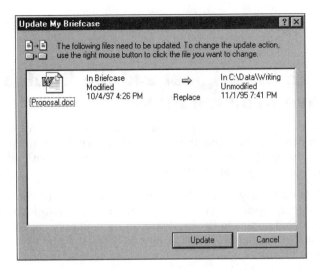

Figure 23-5: The Update dialog box. This dialog box appears when you choose either Update All or Update Selection from the Briefcase menu.

You have now synched the files and their copies in the Briefcase. You may not have synched the files in the Briefcase with the originals or, conversely, with the files on the portable or home computer. You need to move the newly updated Briefcase to the other computer and then update the files once again. The default action is to update the older files on the computer from the newly updated Briefcase.

Multiple syncs

Undocumented

The Briefcase can keep a sync between the original files on the computer at the office and the copies in the Briefcase as well as between the copies on the home computer and the Briefcase. It is this ability to keep multiple sync links for each file, depending on where the Briefcase is stored, that allows you to copy files out of the Briefcase on the floppy disk into other folders on the home computer.

You can see this feature in action when you open the Briefcase. The Sync Copy In column in the Briefcase shows the relationship of the copies inside the Briefcase to the files outside the Briefcase. When you copy files from your desktop computer into a Briefcase and then move the Briefcase onto a floppy, the Sync Copy In column shows the original folders on your desktop computer. If you then copy the files from the Briefcase on the floppy to folders on another computer, the Sync Copy In column changes to the file folders on the second computer. Moving the Briefcase back to the original computer causes the Sync Copy In column to change back to the original folders.

Both the original and the Briefcase copy have been modified

The Briefcase doesn't really solve all the problems of keeping your files up to date. For example, the merge feature has to be implemented by third-party developers so that their applications can, with some action from you, intelligently update their files.

It is quite easy to modify the original files on your computer at work and forget to update their copies in the Briefcase. Later, you modify these non-updated copies in the Briefcase on the computer at home. You now have two files with different modifications to them and no easy way to sort out those modifications.

The Briefcase does give you fair warning. If you modify your file outside the Briefcase, the file is marked as Needs Updating in the Briefcase. If you edit both the copy in the Briefcase and the file outside, then the Briefcase keeps track of the fact that both have changed. When you go to update, you are informed of this sad fact.

If you now try to update your original files you may be wiping out important modifications that you made to them.

STEPS

Dealing with Multiple Modifications

Step 1.   Select the files in the Briefcase that you want to update. Use Ctrl+click or Shift+click if you have more than one file. If you are going to update all the files in the Briefcase, you don't need to highlight any of them.

Step 2.   Display the Briefcase menu.

Step 3.   Choose either Update All (to update all the files and folders in the Briefcase) or Update Selection (to update only the highlighted files and folders).

Step 4.   When you try to update the files, Skip (Both Changed) appears in the Update dialog box.

Step 5.   Right-click the file in the Briefcase that has been updated on both computers. If the application that you used to create these files has the ability to merge files, you'll see the Merge command in the context menu. Click this command.

Step 6. If Merge is not an option on the menu, you can still capture both sets of changes and merge the files manually. To do this, create a third file (using the appropriate application) and copy the original file and the Briefcase file into this third file.

Step 7. Edit or modify this third file to get rid of the redundant information, and manually choose which updates to keep.

Step 8. Copy this third file over the original or over the Briefcase copy, and then perform an update.

Breaking the Sync Link

You can break up the sync relationship between the original file and its Briefcase copy. You might want to do this in order to create a new document and leave the older version as a backup.

STEPS
Orphaning a Briefcase File or Folder

Step 1. Right-click the file in the Briefcase, and choose Properties.

Step 2. Click the Update Status tab.

Step 3. Click the Split From Original button.

If you change the name of the file outside the Briefcase, you will orphan the file inside the Briefcase. To find the copy of the file outside the Briefcase, click Find Original in the Update Status tab.

If you delete the copy in the Briefcase, every time you choose Update All, you will be prompted to delete the original file. To avoid this, orphan the copy by following the steps above before deleting it.

Data Files

One of the potential scenarios for using the Briefcase involves salespeople keeping track of and updating customer files while out in the field. Back at the office, the customer files are also being changed. When the salesperson comes back to the office, the customer files on the office computer have to be updated, but data files on both the salesperson's computer and the office computer have been modified.

The Briefcase doesn't solve this problem, but rather provides a standard method for others to solve the problem. Database developers are encouraged to use the Briefcase facility and combine it with a means of merging data files. This type of merge feature highlights changed records in the data and allows the salesperson (or someone else) to manually decide which modifications to accept. Microsoft Access is a database application that supports this feature, called *replication*, either on its own or using the Briefcase.

The Briefcase doesn't provide any means of copying a file over multiple floppy disks. This means that you need to move large data files in the Briefcase over a network instead—across a DCC, Dial-Up Networking, or LAN connection, for example—or onto large storage media such as Zip disks.

Summary

In this chapter, we describe how to create and use the Briefcase to "carry" files and folders between computers.

▶ If you want to make sure that the files on your desktop computer at the office and your home computer are the same, the Briefcase is for you.

▶ If you use a portable and a desktop computer, the Briefcase can help you make sure that your computers are in sync.

▶ If you have someone else work on your files, you can send that person a Briefcase full of your files.

▶ We describe how to avoid losing the sync relationship between your master files and your copies.

Chapter 24

Networking

In This Chapter

Microsoft has made Windows 98 a very strong networking client as well as a peer server. We discuss:

▶ Connecting to Microsoft and Novell NetWare networks

▶ Working with 16-bit networks

▶ Setting up a $50 network

▶ Dealing with interrupts and I/O addresses in pre-plug and play network adapters

▶ Turning your Windows 98 computer into a NetWare file and print server

▶ Setting up a peer server on a share- or user-level network

▶ Connecting to multiple networks simultaneously

▶ Understanding network security so you can access the resources you need

▶ Connecting to folders and printers with the universal naming convention

▶ Cleaning up network problems with Net Watcher, System Monitor, System Policy Editor, Registry editor, and Password List Editor

▶ Using Windows networking applications

Basic Network Support

Windows 98 comes with all of the necessary networking software required to set up a 32-bit protected-mode Microsoft Windows network of computers running Windows 98 or Windows 95, or to connect to a network with computers running Windows NT, LAN Manager, and Windows for Workgroups 3.11. Additionally, Windows 98 includes a 32-bit protected-mode client for Novell NetWare networks, so your Windows 98 computer can be a compatible client on this type of network as well.

You can configure a Windows 98 computer as a NetWare print and file server on a NetWare network. Windows 98 provides three networking protocols: NetBEUI, IPX/SPX, and TCP/IP. Windows 98 workstations can directly access Windows NT and NetWare servers. Multiple (up to 10) 32-bit network clients can be running on your computer at the same time, allowing your computer to access multiple networks and network services simultaneously. For example, your computer could use TCP/IP to access a Unix server using the Internet Explorer while using Client for NetWare Networks to access a NetWare server. Because these network clients run in protected mode, they don't take up conventional memory.

All the networking components developed by Microsoft are 32-bit protected-mode virtual device drivers (VxDs). Because Windows 98 uses protected-mode network components, it doesn't have to switch your processor from protected mode to real mode (a process that wastes too many processor cycles). Therefore, networking speeds get much faster (50–200 percent) than under Windows 3.1*x*.

Real-mode drivers, especially for NetWare, have a nasty habit of causing some programs to lock up your computer — the dreaded "black screen of death." There isn't any way to completely eliminate this problem without using protected-mode drivers. The real-mode drivers create memory conflicts and have unresolved disputes over control of interrupts.

Real-mode network drivers are loaded in conventional memory, although memory managers allow you to partially load these drivers between the 640K and 1MB memory addresses. Network components are particularly large, and if they run in real mode, they reduce the memory resources available to DOS programs to the point that some DOS programs can't run on networked computers. The new protected-mode network components are loaded above the lower 640K area, leaving this memory available for Doom and other mission-critical DOS programs.

Apart from its 32-bit network drivers, Windows 98 can still be a good client for the 16-bit real-mode versions of all of the major networks that are available for PCs. These include:

- Artisoft LANtastic version 5.0 or later
- Banyan VINES version 5.52 or later
- Beame and Whiteside Network File System 3.0c or later
- DEC Pathworks version 5.0 or later
- IBM Data Link Control protocol
- IBM OS/2 LAN Server
- Microsoft Windows Network version 3.11
- MS-Net compatibles
- Novell NetWare 3.11 or later
- Sunselect PC-NFS version 5.0 or later
- TCS 10Net version 4.1 or later

Of course, many of these 16-bit networks have been upgraded to 32-bit, and you can get new drivers from the network manufacturers or the Windows 98 CD-ROM.

Be sure to read Network.txt in your \Windows folder to learn what Microsoft has to say about networking issues. You can find more extensive coverage of Windows 98 networking in *Windows 98 Networking Secrets* from IDG Books Worldwide.

What Windows 98 Networking Buys You

You network your computers to access resources that are beyond any one computer and to facilitate communication. These resources are shared because they are too expensive to be given exclusively to one user, or because they are a managed resource (for example, a corporate transaction-processing database) that needs to be available to many different users simultaneously.

Windows 98 is designed to be a particularly good networking client (and peer-to-peer server). It supports:

- User profiles and system policies that make it possible (with appropriate network administration) for users to log onto any networked Windows 98 computer and have their own Desktop and applications available to them

- Protected-mode networking clients, protocols, and adapter drivers that don't take any conventional memory

- User-level security that is enforced by either Windows NT or NetWare servers and is centrally administered

- A single logon box that allows users to log onto their Windows 98 computer (and bring up their user-specific Desktop) as well as onto all the network resources and servers available to them

- Backup agents, so backup software running on Windows NT or NetWare servers can back up Windows 98 computers

- Direct Cable Connection (DCC) and Dial-Up Networking (DUN)

- Diskless (or floppy disk-only) workstations connected to shared copies of Windows 98 on Windows NT or NetWare servers (including NetWare 4.*x* servers)

- Browsing of shared network resources or resources on network servers through the Explorer, folder windows, common dialog boxes, or the Network Neighborhood

- Remote printing and printer administration

- NetWare Directory Services running under NetWare 4.*x*

- Network management through Simple Network Management Protocols (SNMP) using third-party software and a supplied agent

- Simultaneous access to multiple networks and multiple networking protocols

- Multiple 32-bit protected-mode networking protocols: NetBEUI, IPX/SPX, and TCP/IP

- 32-bit protected-mode ATM (Asynchronous Transfer Mode) and DLC (Data Link Control) protocols

- Infrared LAN drivers

- Remote administration and network resource monitoring

Quick and Dirty Networking

Given the low cost and ease of installation provided by Windows 98, it makes a lot of sense to connect two or more computers together in a workgroup with inexpensive networking hardware. If you purchase plug and play networking cards (adapters) and install them in computers with plug and play BIOSes, Windows 98 will install its networking software and drivers for you.

Installing a small network requires nothing more than buying a few ISA plug and play NE2000-compatible Ethernet cards, some Class 3 cable with RJ-45 connectors, and a small hub. If you have a portable computer with a Type II PCMCIA slot and card and socket drivers, you can purchase an inexpensive 10Mb (megabit) Ethernet card. Plug everything together, turn on the computers, and the network installs itself.

If you have older equipment, you need to give Windows 98 some help in implementing the network. We provide the details for both types of installations below:

STEPS

Setting Up a Quick and Dirty Network

Step 1. Buy (at about $19 each) two NE2000-compatible plug and play network cards. (There is no need these days to purchase cards that aren't plug and play.) If you are setting up a small network with light networking tasks, you only need 10Mb Ethernet cards that comply with the IEEE 802.3 and 10BASE-T Ethernet standards.

These are very standard cards, and they are widely available. Most come with both BNC and RJ-45 connectors. They'll most likely include BNC T connectors. You can also get Fast Ethernet (100 BASE-TX) cards, which handle both 10 and 100Mb (megabits), although they cost more (about $50).

Cards are available for ISA slots as well as PCI slots. The ISA-slot cards are less expensive and perfectly fine for small networks. In the future, computers will not come with ISA slots, so this option will not be available.

If you need a card that can connect to a portable, you can purchase a PCMCIA 10Mb Ethernet card for about $60. One place to look for this type of card is http://www.zdnet.com. Be sure that the connector cable that goes from the card to the RJ-45 and/or BNC jacks is included. PCMCIA cards that handle both 10 and 100Mb cost about twice as much.

Install the cards in available slots in both of the computers.

Step 2.   Purchase ready-made 25-foot Class 3 cables. They are available for about $4. One place to check out is http://www.computergate. com. Class 5 cables, required for 100Mb Ethernet, cost about $7 for 25-foot lengths with the connectors already installed. Connect the hub and Ethernet cards by plugging in the cables.

Ethernet hubs used to be expensive. If you were just hooking two computers together, it was cheaper to go with a coaxial cable. (The problem with using a coaxial cable is that if one computer connection goes down, the whole network goes down, although with two computers, this doesn't matter.)

Now that you can buy five-port hubs for around $40, it makes sense to just purchase a hub and plug in Class 3 unshielded twisted-pair wire with RJ-45 jacks. This is a star configuration, with each computer plugged into the hub. If one leg goes down, it doesn't effect the other legs.

Hubs that handle 100Mb Ethernet are more expensive.

If you are never going to have more than two computers networked to each other, you can use a *cross over* Class 3 cable.

Step 3.   T-connectors and terminators come with the cards; use them to connect the cable to the T-connectors, the T-connectors to the cards, and the terminators to the other end of the T-connectors.

If you are using a hub, you don't need to worry about this.

Step 4.   If the cards aren't plug and play compatible, run the DOS-based configuration software first to set up their interrupts and I/O addresses. The default values for the cards may be okay, depending on what hardware you have installed in your computers.

To find out which interrupts and I/O addresses are available on your computers, you can boot them, click the System icon in the Control Panel, click the Device Manager tab, and then highlight Computer and click the Properties button. Click the Input/Output (I/O) option button to see what addresses are already used; used interrupts are shown first.

(continued)

Setting Up a Quick and Dirty Network

Reboot your computers and go to the DOS prompt by pressing and holding the Ctrl key during the power-on self test. Run the DOS-based configuration software from the DOS prompt. Otherwise, you can just open a DOS window and run the configuration software in it.

Your PCMCIA card will undoubtedly be plug and play. Be sure that your portable computer supports at least Card and Socket services. You may have a portable that supports CardBus, a 32-bit connection to the PC Card. If so, you can purchase a CardBus-compatible PC Card that allows for a 100Mb Ethernet connection.

To see if your PCMCIA socket has Card and Socket services, right-click My Computer, click Properties, click the Device Manager tab, click Unknown Hardware, and see if you see PCMCIA card services.

If you are stuck with older non-plug and play cards, follow the instructions in steps 5 through 7. If you are using plug and play cards, click the Network icon in the Control Panel, and then skip to step 8.

Step 5. Click the Add New Hardware icon in the Control Panel on both computers. You can have the Add New Hardware Wizard search for your new adapters or you can specify what you have. The Wizard will load and configure the 32-bit protected-mode NDIS 5 driver for your adapters.

Step 6. Click the Network icon in the Control Panel. Highlight your adapter in the list of networking components. To see which networking protocols were bound to the adapter (in step 5), click the Properties button, and then click the Bindings tab. For a small computer network, you'll most likely want to bind either NetBEUI or IPX/SPX. If you need to bind a protocol, click the Add button in the Network dialog box, highlight Protocol, click the next Add button, and select the protocol in the Select Network Protocol dialog box.

You can use the TCP/IP protocol on a small network also. You can then set up the Personal Web Server on one (or all) of your computers and publish web pages.

Step 7. Make sure to allow sharing of your resources so either or both of the computers can be peer servers to the other. Make sure that Client for Microsoft Networks and file and printer sharing for Microsoft Networks are implemented in the Network dialog box. Add them if they aren't. (To add Client for Microsoft Networks, click Add, click Client, and click Add again. In the Select Network Client dialog box, highlight Microsoft on the left, and click Client for Microsoft Networks on the right. To add file and printer sharing for Microsoft Networks, click Add, click Service, and click Add again. In the Select Network Service dialog box, highlight Microsoft on the left, and click File and Printer Sharing for Microsoft Networks on the right.)

Step 8. Click the Identification tab in the Network dialog box. Make sure that the two computers have different names, but the same workgroup name. Click OK.

Step 9. Click the OK button in the Network dialog box, and then reboot your computers for all of this to take effect.

You won't have to reboot if you are using plug and play cards.

Step 10. Open Explorer or folder windows on the Desktops of both computers. Right-click resources (disk drives and/or folders) that you want to share, click Sharing in the context menu, and configure the sharing properties. Do the same in the Printers folder for printers that you are going to share.

Step 11. Click the Network Neighborhood icon on the Desktop of one of the computers. You should see the name of the workgroup in the Network Neighborhood folder window. Click the workgroup name to see the name of the other computer. Click its name to see the shared resources.

Using these steps, you can install the NetBEUI, IPX/SPX, and TCP/IP protocols and bind them to your network cards. If you are running a small network, you don't have to run all three protocols. You can just use NetBEUI if you are just sharing printers, disks, and folders. You can remove the other protocols in the Network dialog box.

If you need further elaboration of these steps, see the next section.

Network Installation

If you are going to install Windows 98 on a computer running Windows 3.1*x*, and you want it to install the Windows 98 client software that will work with 16-bit networks, you should first install the 16-bit real-mode network software from these other vendors. Otherwise, you will have to configure the Windows 98 network components yourself, in addition to installing this third-party software.

Click the Network icon in your Control Panel to display the Network dialog box, as shown in Figure 24-1. This dialog box allows you to choose which network client to install, which network adapter to support, which networking protocol to bind to the adapter, and which networking services (for example, peer file and printer sharing) to offer.

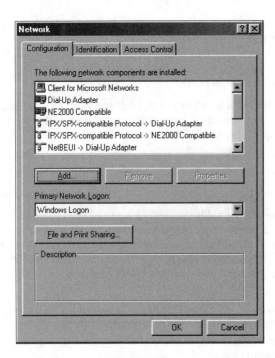

Figure 24-1: The Configuration tab of the Network dialog box. Click the Add button to install additional networking components.

If Windows 98 has successfully detected your existing networking hardware and software network components, you don't need to make any changes in the Network dialog box. This is true even if the only network adapter you have installed is a serial or parallel port. Direct Cable Connection (DCC) will use these ports as though they were network adapters. Your modem will be detected as a network adapter and it can then be used by Dial-Up Networking (DUN) to connect to other computers over the phone lines.

There are cases where you will need to make changes to your network configuration, and we discuss them throughout this chapter.

If you add a network card or install networking software for networks other than Microsoft Networks or NetWare after you have installed Windows 98, you may need to use the Network dialog box to install networking support.

A network configuration consists of networking client software, software drivers for a given network adapter, a networking protocol, and networking services. To install any of these components, click the Add button in the Configuration tab of the Network dialog box to display the Select Network Component Type dialog box, as shown in Figure 24-2.

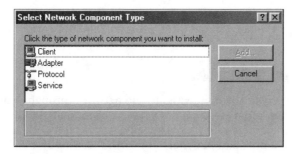

Figure 24-2: The Select Network Component Type dialog box.

Choosing a client

Highlight Client in the list box and click the Add button to display the Select Network Client dialog box, as shown in Figure 24-3. The 32-bit protected-mode clients for Microsoft Networks and NetWare Networks are provided by Microsoft on the Windows 98 CD-ROM.

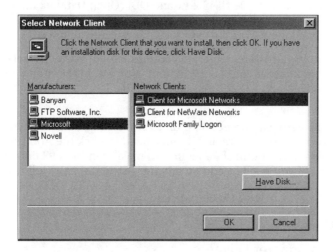

Figure 24-3: The Select Network Client dialog box. You can select a networking client from those provided on the Windows 98 CD-ROM or find a client on another network vendor's diskette.

You can install one 16-bit real-mode networking client and up to 10 protected-mode clients. Only two 32-bit protected-mode clients are available from Microsoft — Client for Microsoft Networks and Client for NetWare Networks.

If you install a 16-bit networking client only, you won't need to deal with the other networking components in this dialog box. Instead, you will use the client software to specify how these items are configured.

If you install the Client for Microsoft Networks or NetWare Networks, you can add or change the network adapter, protocol, and network services.

Choosing an adapter

Your computer is physically connected to the network through your network adapter (card), your serial or parallel port, or your modem. Windows 98 installs adapter driver software that is specific to your network adapter. If you have installed a plug and play network card, the Windows 98 hardware-detection routines should configure it automatically.

Microsoft provides a broad range of adapter drivers that support the Network Device Interface Specification (NDIS) 5 standard. It is this standard that allows for multiple protected-mode networking protocols. Microsoft worked with all the major network adapter manufacturers to include adapter drivers for its cards.

The NDIS 5 specification supports ATM, Ethernet, Token Ring, FDDI, IrDA, and ArcNet networking cards and hot docking with plug and play adapters.

You can also use real-mode NDIS 2.*xx* and ODI (Open Datalink Interface) drivers that come (on diskettes) with pre-plug and play adapters if Microsoft hasn't provided a new NDIS 5 driver for your specific adapter.

The Windows 98 hardware-detection routines should correctly determine which network adapter card is installed in your computer and its range of possible interrupt and I/O address settings. This is true for most cards even if they aren't plug and play.

If Windows 98 hardware detection didn't get it right, you can configure the adapter driver settings yourself. You may need to click the Add New Hardware icon in the Control Panel first to make Windows 98 find your network card. If you need to add an adapter driver, take the following steps:

STEPS

Adding an Adapter Driver

Step 1. Click the Add button in the Network dialog box.

Step 2. In the Select Network Component Type dialog box, highlight Adapter and click Add.

Step 3. In the Select Network Adapter dialog box, select an adapter manufacturer in the left-hand list and an adapter model in the right-hand list. Click OK twice.

If you use Direct Cable Connection (DCC) or Dial-Up Networking (DUN), you should add Microsoft's Dial-Up Adapter driver. The Dial-Up Adapter is the NDIS 5 driver for your serial or parallel port, or modem. DCC and DUN are real networking options and require full network configuration based on the Dial-Up Adapter.

See Chapters 17 and 22 for more details about these networking options.

Your plug and play PC Card isn't found

You plug in a plug and play PCMCIA network card and find that Windows 98 doesn't detect it. This may be true even if you plug in the card before you turn on your computer.

Often the solution is to remove the PCMCIA socket controller driver.

STEPS
Getting Windows 98 to Detect Your PCMCIA Network Card

Step 1. Remove the card from the slot.

Step 2. Click the System icon in your Control Panel, and click the Device Manager tab.

Step 3. Click the plus sign to the left of the PCMCIA Socket icon. Click the PCMCIA controller icon.

Step 4. Click the Remove button. Click OK. Click OK to restart Windows 98.

Step 5. The Windows 98 hardware-detection routines will find the PCMCIA controller chip, notice that it is missing from the hardware list, and automatically reinstall the driver for it.

Step 6. Reinsert the PCMCIA network card. Windows 98 should now detect it. If you have a driver for the card that is separate from the drivers provided by Windows 98 (and more recent), be sure to browse to the diskette that contains the install file when asked.

Step 7. If there are any problems detecting the hardware, click the Add New Hardware icon in the Control Panel, to force a new hardware detection or to allow you to specify the PCMCIA socket.

Configuring resources for the adapter driver

Once Windows 98 knows which network adapter you have physically installed, it loads the correct driver and determines the current hardware settings for your card. This is where it gets sticky, because Windows 98 may not correctly determine your network adapter's interrupt and I/O address settings if it is not a plug and play card. To determine which values Windows 98 has chosen, take the following steps:

STEPS

Determining Network Adapter Resource Values

Step 1. Click the System icon in your Control Panel, click the Device Manager, and click the plus sign next to Network Adapters. Select a network adapter.

Step 2. Click the Properties button to display the Properties dialog box for your network adapter, and then click the Resources tab (see Figure 24-4).

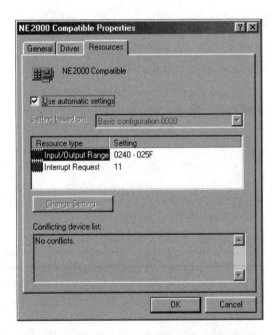

Figure 24-4: The Resources tab in a network adapter's Properties dialog box.

Step 3. Compare the values in the Resources tab with the known values for the adapter card. If you don't know what those values are, you are going to have to accept the values in the dialog box for now.

If you are going to install Windows 98 over Windows for Workgroups 3.11, you can find the previous values for your network card by double-clicking the Network Setup icon in the Windows 3.1x Program Manager. The Windows

98 setup routines will find these values (in the file Protocol.ini) and correctly configure the adapter driver to conform to the current card settings.

If you have a plug and play adapter, Windows 98 will configure it correctly. If you have a pre-plug and play adapter, you can change your adapter's settings either by changing jumpers on the adapter or by running configuration software provided by the manufacturer. The Resources tab for these pre-plug and play adapters (except for the Intel EtherExpress adapters) displays only possible settings for this adapter, not necessarily the actual current settings for the card. It is up to you to get the possible and the actual settings to match.

Windows 98 chooses possible adapter resource settings that don't conflict with other devices — if it can do this given the set of possible settings for the given adapter. If Windows 98 determines that a conflict exists (because all the possible settings of the adapter card conflict with other devices in your computer), it places an asterisk in the appropriate field in the Resources tab.

Secret

You can't change the resource settings during Windows 98 Setup, and this can be a source of some difficulty — especially if you are setting up Windows 98 over a network and through the adapter to which Windows 98 has now assigned the incorrect address or interrupt. For example, the CD-ROM drive that holds your Windows 98 CD-ROM might be connected to another computer on the network. In this case, to complete the setup, Windows 98 will need to copy files over the network after the computer upon which you are installing Windows 98 has been rebooted and is running under Windows 98. But the network will no longer be available to this computer because the network adapter has been incorrectly configured — a little Catch-22.

The source files that may no longer be available include files Windows 98 needs to configure your modem and printer. You will have to go back after you have correctly configured your network adapter and install these items separately, using the Printers folder and the Modems icon in the Control Panel.

To get the adapter's settings to match the settings specified in the Resources tab of the Properties dialog box for your network adapter, you need to first complete as much of the Windows 98 setup process as you can, and then go back and change either the adapter or the settings in the Resources tab.

To change an adapter that uses jumpers: Turn off your computer, pull the card, move the jumpers to match the settings given in the Resources tab, reinstall the card, and restart Windows 98.

To change an adapter using the manufacturer's configuration software: Open a DOS window when Windows 98 restarts after Setup, and run the manufacturer's configuration software for the adapter. You'll need to restart Windows 98 after making these changes.

To change the resource settings to match the adapter's current settings, restart Windows 98, follow the Determining Network Adapter Resource Values steps earlier in this section, and change the values to match your adapter's values. Then restart Windows 98 again.

Choosing a networking protocol

Individual computers have to speak the same language if you want them to talk to each other. The language they speak is the *networking protocol*. Microsoft provides 32-bit protected-mode implementations for three networking protocols: NetBEUI, IPX/SPX, and TCP/IP. You have to bind a networking protocol to the network adapter (or to multiple adapters) for the adapter and the protocol to work together to get the messages across the wire.

- NetBEUI (NetBIOS Extended User Interface) is Microsoft's fast, efficient, workgroup (non-routeable) protocol. It works great between Windows 98 computers and Windows for Workgroup 3.11, LAN Manager, and Windows NT workstations and servers.

- IPX/SPX (Internetwork Packet Exchange) is Novell NetWare's protocol, and therefore a standard for small- to medium-sized businesses and department-level networks. You can use this protocol to access both NetWare and Windows NT servers (as well as Windows 98 computers). You can configure Windows 98 computers as NetWare file and print servers and address them through IPX/SPX. Microsoft's IPX/SPX-compatible protocol is the default for Windows 98.

- TCP/IP (Transmission Control Protocol/Internet Protocol) is the Unix and Internet standard protocol. It provides networking support to a broad range of computer operating systems — indeed, to all computers that can communicate over the Internet. Windows 98 includes a set of TCP/IP utilities, as described in "Microsoft's TCP/IP Stack" in Chapter 18. Internet addresses (which are assigned to each computer on the network) can be dynamically allocated because you can configure this version of TCP/IP to use the Dynamic Host Configuration Protocol (DHCP) or Windows Internet Naming Service (WINS). Microsoft also supplies a Winsock version 2.2 DLL, so Winsock-compliant Internet programs such as FTP Explorer, Netscape Communicator, and Internet mailers can work with TCP/IP.

Windows 98 supports 32-bit protocols from other manufacturers in addition to the three provided by Microsoft.

To choose a protocol, take the following steps:

STEPS

Choosing a Protocol

Step 1. Click the Network icon in the Control Panel, and click the Add button.

Step 2. In the Select Network Component Type dialog box, highlight Protocol and click Add.

Step 3. In the Select Network Protocol dialog box, select a manufacturer in the left-hand list and a protocol in the right-hand list. Click OK.

If you have an ATM card, you'll want to install the ATM network drivers:

STEPS

Installing ATM

Step 1. Click the Add button in the Network dialog box. Select Protocol, and click Add again.

Step 2. Select Microsoft, and then ATM Call Manager. Click OK.

Step 3. Repeat for ATM Emulated LAN and ATM LAN emulation client.

Step 4. You also need to add NetBEUI, IPX/SPX, or TCP/IP (or all three). Click the Add button in the Network dialog box, select Protocol, click the Add button, select Microsoft, and select one of these three network protocols. Click OK.

TPC/IP issues

Windows 98, unlike Windows 95, automatically assigns an IP address to your network card even if your network doesn't have a DHCP server. You can find out more by turning to "Configuring the TCP/IP stack for a network adapter" in Chapter 18. If your IP address isn't assigned (you can check this with Winipcfg.exe), click the Network icon in your Control Panel. Select TCP/IP on your network card, click Properties, mark Specify an IP Address, and enter an address that is unique on your network.

If you have a small network without a DHCP or WINS server, install both NetBEUI and TCP/IP. NetBEUI provides automatic name resolution and browsing through your Explorer. If you want to be able to use basic TCP/IP utilities such as ping and route with computer names, you'll want to create a simple text file called Lmhosts on your client computer in the \Windows folder.

STEPS

Creating an Lmhosts File

Step 1. Click the Start button, Programs, Accessories, Notepad.

(continued)

STEPS *(continued)*

Creating an Lmhosts File

Step 2. On the first line of the new text file, type the IP address of another computer that is on your network. Follow this address by a space, and then the name of that computer (see "Name that computer" later in this chapter).

Step 3. Follow the name with a space and **#PRE**. Continue doing this for all the computers on your network for which you want to associate a friendly name.

Step 4. When you are finished, save the file in the \Windows folder under the name Lmhosts. You'll have to navigate to it in your Explorer after you save it and rename it to get rid of the *txt* extension.

The table in Lmhosts associates the friendly computer name with the IP address for these basic TCP/IP utilities. If you are not using NetBEUI or if you have a larger network and your workgroup is connected to other workgroups through a router, this file will be used to associate computer names with IP addresses. Of course, in larger networks, you would be more likely to have a DHCP or WINS server.

Choosing network services

Most network services — such as the ability to connect to remote computers and browse their disk drives — are available once you've configured your client, adapter, and protocol. Microsoft and other manufacturers provide additional network services. If you use Microsoft's clients for Microsoft or NetWare Networks, you can configure your computer to share its folders, drives, and/or printers with other users on the network. You can use tape-backup software running on a Windows NT or NetWare server to back up your files, and you can administer HP printers running on NetWare networks.

Microsoft also provides Microsoft Service for NetWare Directory Services. If you install this service, you can log onto NetWare 4.*x* servers, use NetWare 4.*x* login scripts, browse the NetWare directory tree using Network Neighborhood, and run 16-bit NDS-aware applications.

To add one or more of these services, take the following steps:

STEPS

Adding Network Services

Step 1. Click the Add button in the Network dialog box.

Step 2. In the Select Network Component Type dialog box, highlight Service and click Add.

Step 3. In the Select Network Service dialog box, select a manufacturer in the left-hand list and the service in the right-hand list. Click OK.

Sharing your resources

You make your hard disk drives, folders, and printers available to others on the network by sharing them. Although sharing isn't always easy, in this case it is.

To share your folders or disk drives and printers using the network services provided on the Windows 98 CD-ROM, you need to install either Client for Microsoft Networks or Client for NetWare Networks. In addition, you need to choose Microsoft as the manufacturer in step 3 of the Adding Network Services steps in the previous section. Choose either file and printer sharing for Microsoft Networks or file and printer sharing for NetWare Networks as the network service. For details on sharing a printer, turn to "Sharing a Printer" in Chapter 29.

You have three options for how you want to share your disk drives (or folders): Read-Only, Full, or Depends on Password (if your computer is set for share-level security). Full access allows users at other computers on the network to create files and folders on your drive. They can also delete or edit new or existing files and folders on your drive (or within a specific folder). If you are using user-level security, you can name the users who have access to your resources. (If you are a network administrator with remote administration privileges, you can determine who has access to which resources on a client computer.) We discuss user-level and share-level security in the "Network Security" section later in this chapter.

Read-Only access allows other users to view, but not change your files or folders. Depends on Password gives them either Full or Read-Only access depending on which of these two privileges you or the network administrator assign to them.

If you share your disk drives or folders with only Read-Only access, other non-administrative users cannot delete your files and folders. If you don't share disk drives and folders at all, other users cannot see what you have on your computer.

Once you have chosen to turn on the ability to share, you still need to specify which resources you are going to share. "Sharing a Printer" in Chapter 29 provides details on making your printer available across your network.

To share a folder or disk drive, take the following steps:

STEPS

Sharing a Folder or Drive

Step 1.   In an Explorer window, right-click the icon for the drive or folder that you want to share.

Step 2.   Click Sharing in the context menu to display the Sharing tab of the Properties dialog box for your drive or folder, as shown in Figure 24-5. (The Sharing option appears in the context menu only if you are on a network, have DCC configured, or have Dial-Up Networking (DUN), which lets you create connectoids to the Internet, MSN, and so on.)

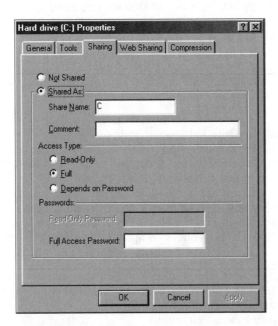

Figure 24-5: The Sharing tab in the Properties dialog box lets you set up share-level security. Choose Not Shared or Shared As. If you have configured your computer for user-level security, you will be able to specify which users can access your computer.

Step 3.   To share your drive or folder, click Shared As.

Step 4.   You can enter a new name for the resource as well as a comment to help other users understand what resource you're sharing.

If you add a dollar sign to the end of the resource's share name, it is hidden from users who are using Network Neighborhood for network browsing. You might want to do this for your Microsoft Mail postoffice, which needs to be shared but not browsed.

Step 5. If your computer is configured for share-level security (most likely on a peer-to-peer network), you can set the access type (Read-Only or Full) and the password required to access your resource.

If your computer is configured for user-level security (you have a Windows NT or NetWare server on your network), you can specify who has access to your resources.

Step 6. Click OK.

Primary Network Logon

If you display the Primary Network Logon drop-down list in the Network dialog box (accessed from the Network icon in the Control Panel), you'll see the following choices (if you have installed all the services):

- Windows Logon
- Client for Microsoft Networks
- Client for NetWare Networks

Choose Windows Logon if you are not logging onto a network or are logging onto a peer-to-peer network. Choose one of the two clients if you are logging onto a network with either a Windows NT server or a NetWare server and have installed one or both of these clients.

File and Print Sharing

You can decide if you are going to share your printer(s), your folders and drives, or both. Click the File and Print Sharing button in the Network dialog box to make this choice.

Name that computer

To network your computer, you need to specify its name and the name of your local workgroup. Click the Network icon on your Control Panel, and then click the Identification tab. The *workgroup name*, as shown in Figure 24-6, is a name that a group of computers will share, and it defines them as an entity. Your computer name must be unique on your LAN.

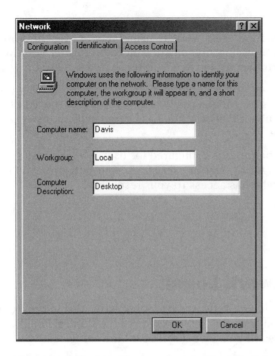

Figure 24-6: The Identification tab of the Network dialog box.

You must give your computer a name and specify a workgroup, no matter which networking software you are using. Your computer name can be as long as 15 characters and can include only alphanumeric characters and these special characters:

! @ # $ % ^ & ( ) - _ ` { } . ~

You can also enter a description of your computer up to 48 characters in length (no commas) to help other users on your network identify your computer.

Microsoft Networks

You can install Client for Microsoft Networks to connect your Windows 98 computer with computers running Windows 98, Windows 95, Windows NT, LAN Manager, Windows for Workgroups 3.11, Workgroup Add-On for MS-DOS, as well as other Microsoft Networks-compatible networks. If you configure it as the primary network logon client, you have the option to:

- Use a Windows NT server as a password server, which lets you configure user-level security (as opposed to share-level security, which is standard on peer-to-peer networks) and control it from the server

- Share your files and printer(s) with other network users

- Create user profiles, which you can use to set up different network connections and configurations for individual users

- Allow remote administration of the Registry on your computer

If you are installing Windows 98 on a computer that is running Windows for Workgroups 3.11 networking, the Windows 98 hardware-detection routines will automatically install Client for Microsoft Networks. Otherwise, you can install Client for Microsoft Networks using the procedure detailed in "Network Installation" earlier in this chapter, choosing Microsoft as the manufacturer in the Select Network Client dialog box.

If you install DCC and/or DUN, Client for Microsoft Networks and the Dial-Up Adapter are automatically installed.

Configuring your computer as Client for Microsoft Networks

If you are connecting your Windows 98 computer to other computers using Windows 98, Windows for Workgroups 3.11, or Workgroup Add-On for MS-DOS, you don't need to worry about logging onto a Windows NT domain for user-level security. This peer-to-peer networking scheme handles all security by assigning passwords to resources (share-level security). You can choose to reconnect to the resources that are shared on your network at startup time, or later when you actually browse the shared folders on another computer or print to a printer connected to another computer.

If you have a Windows NT computer on your Microsoft network, you may need to log onto it if you want to have access to network resources. If the Windows NT server has been configured to provide user-level security, shared resources on other peer servers (Windows 98 computers that are running file and printer sharing for Microsoft Networks) are available to you after you enter your user password.

To configure your Windows 98 computer to Client for Microsoft Networks, take the following steps:

STEPS

Configuring Client for Microsoft Networks

Step 1.   Highlight Client for Microsoft Networks in the Configuration tab of the Network dialog box. Click the Properties button to display the General tab of the Client for Microsoft Networks Properties dialog box, as shown in Figure 24-7.

(continued)

STEPS *(continued)*

Configuring Client for Microsoft Networks

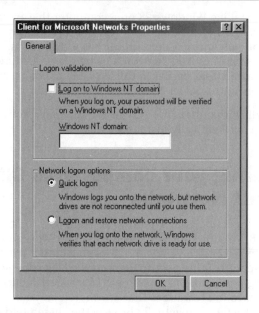

Figure 24-7: The General tab of the Client for Microsoft Networks Properties dialog box.

Step 2. To use a networked Windows NT server for logon validation, mark the Log on to Windows NT Domain check box.

Step 3. To log onto your Microsoft network and delay connecting to network resources until you need them (if you have previously established a persistent network connection), mark the Quick Logon option button.

You can establish a persistent network connection for shared folders and disk drives by checking the Reconnect at Logon check box in the Map Network Drive dialog box (choose Tools, Map Network Drive in the Explorer). For printers, check Reconnect at Logon in the Capture Printer Port dialog box (right-click a printer icon, choose Properties, click Details, and click the Capture Printer Port button).

Step 4. To establish a connection at startup to all the shared network resources with which you have previously specified a persistent connection, mark Logon and Restore Network Connections.

Step 5. Click OK.

Configuring a Microsoft Networking protocol

Client for Microsoft Networks can work with any of the protocols provided by Microsoft. NetBEUI is the default protocol for communication among computers running Windows 98, Windows 95, Windows for Workgroups 3.11, Windows NT, LAN Manager, and Microsoft Workgroup Add-On for MS-DOS. However, you can also use IPX/SPX and TCP/IP to communicate with other Windows 98, Windows 95 and Windows NT computers.

Intranets are based on the TCP/IP protocol. If you are setting up Windows NT and/or Windows 98 web servers, then you should use TCP/IP as your networking protocol. You can use multiple protocols over your network, but it will run faster if you stick to one.

Highlight the protocol (or any of the protocols you've selected to work with your network adapter) in the Network dialog box and then click the Properties button. Click the Bindings tab, and then mark Client for Microsoft Networks to bind it to the chosen protocol, as shown in Figure 24-8.

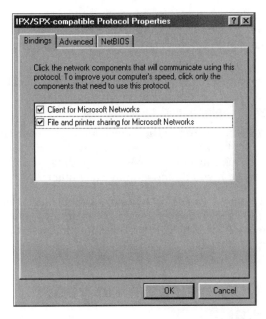

Figure 24-8: The Bindings tab in the Properties dialog box for a protocol. Mark the check boxes for the network components that you want to bind to this protocol.

Diagnosing Microsoft Networking problems

If you are having problems communicating from or to a Windows 98 computer that is attached to a Microsoft network, you might check in a few different areas:

1. Make sure that file and printer sharing for Microsoft Networks is part of your network configuration by clicking the Network icon in the Control Panel. Click the File and Print Sharing button, and make sure that you have enabled sharing by marking one or both of the File and Print Sharing check boxes.

2. Highlight File and Printer Sharing for Microsoft Networks in the Network dialog box, and click the Properties button. Set Browse Master to Enable, and LM Announce to Yes.

3. If you are using the IPX/SPX protocol, highlight that network component in the Network dialog box, click Properties, click the Advanced tab, click Frame, and be sure that the frame type value is set to the frame type that is used on your network. If you are communicating with WFWG 3.11 computers, you may want to set it to 802.3, for example.

4. Click the Identification tab in the Network dialog box, and carefully check your computer name to make sure that it is unique. Also verify that the workgroup name is the same as the workgroup name for the other computers in your workgroup.

5. Make sure that you are actually sharing something. Just because you've enabled the ability to share, doesn't mean you have. Right-click a folder or drive icon in your Explorer, and click Sharing.

6. Check your network card setup in the Device Manager. There may be an unrecognized conflict between your network card and I/O port COM 2. Disable COM 2 to check this out. You can change the resources used by the network card later, if you do indeed have a conflict.

You can troubleshoot your network problems by clicking Start, Help, Troubleshooting, Windows 98 Troubleshooters, Networking. Also check out this Microsoft Knowledge Base article: http://premium.microsoft.com/support/kb/articles/q134/3/04.asp.

Putting your DOS machine on your Windows network

Secret

You don't have to have Windows for Workgroups 3.11 Workgroup Add-On for MS-DOS to connect your DOS computer to your Windows network.

Microsoft charges $55 for this little hummer, but you can download it for free from Microsoft's FTP site. Use FTP Explorer (shareware found at http://www.windows98.com) or Internet Explorer to go to ftp://ftp.microsoft.com/bussys/Clients/MSCLIENT. Download the files DSK3-1.exe and DSK3-2.exe into a temporary folder. Copy them from the temporary folder to your DOS machine. Run them at the DOS prompt to expand them, and then run the setup program that shows up.

Novell NetWare Networks

Microsoft doesn't supply the NetWare network operating system software. That is, it doesn't provide the operating system for the NetWare server. That's Novell's job. Microsoft does provide 32-bit protected-mode versions of NetWare-compatible client software, the IPX/SPX-compatible protocol, and NDIS 5 adapter drivers. These drivers allow your Windows 98 computer to connect to a NetWare server. The server can be running Novell NetWare versions 2.15 or later, 3.x, or 4.x. You won't need to run any of the real-mode software from Novell to turn your computer into a NetWare-compatible client (or NetWare-compatible file and print server).

Novell offers two 16-bit NetWare clients — NETX (for NetWare 3.x) and VLM (for NetWare 4.x). Windows 98 supports these two 16-bit real-mode clients, and you can use them instead of the Microsoft Client for NetWare Networks. There is no benefit to using the NETX client. VLM (Virtual Load Module) provides access to NetWare Directory Services (NDS), an enterprise-wide naming service that makes it simpler for you to manage user access to a wide range of network resources. Microsoft provides NDS access in an updated version of Client for NetWare Networks, which is included in Windows 98.

Novell offers a 32-bit client for IntranetWare and NetWare as well. This client supports DNS. You can download this client directly from Novell at http://www.novell.com/intranetware/products/clients/clientwin95/.

Client for NetWare Networks goes naturally with Microsoft's 32-bit protected-mode IPX/SPX-compatible protocol and NDIS 5 adapter driver. If you choose to install it, these components are automatically configured and installed with it. You can use your existing real-mode ODI adapter drivers and Novell-supplied IPX/SPX protocol stack with Client for NetWare Networks if you want to run TSRs that absolutely require Novell's 16-bit implementation of IPX/SPX.

Because Windows 98 computers can connect to NetWare networks using so many different configurations, you can try different combinations to see what difference the combinations make. It is very easy to go from one to the other, so you don't need to worry about causing problems if you start with something and change it later.

To install Client for NetWare Networks, use the procedure detailed in the "Network Installation" section earlier in this chapter. Choose Microsoft as the manufacturer in the Select Network Client dialog box, and select Client for NetWare Networks in the Network Clients list box.

Configuring your computer as Client for NetWare Networks

Client for NetWare Networks is automatically installed and configured if you install Windows 98 in the \Windows folder of a computer configured correctly as a Novell NetWare client. Log onto a NetWare server before you install Windows 98 to make sure that everything gets configured correctly.

To configure your Windows 98 computer for Client for NetWare Networks, take the following steps:

STEPS

Configuring Client for NetWare Networks

Step 1. Highlight Client for NetWare Networks in the Configuration tab of the Network dialog box. Click the Properties button. The General tab of the Client for NetWare Networks Properties dialog box will be displayed, as shown in Figure 24-9.

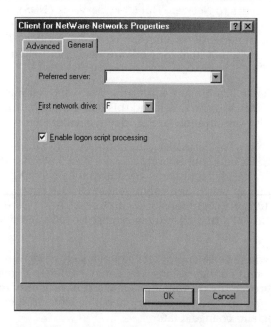

Figure 24-9: The General tab of the Client for NetWare Networks Properties dialog box. Type the UNC name of the NetWare server that you will log onto first.

Step 2. Enter the UNC name of your preferred NetWare server. (See the section "The Universal Naming Convention (UNC)" later in this chapter for information on the UNC.)

Step 3. Enter the volume designation letter for your first network connection.

Step 4. If you want to process a NetWare logon script, mark Enable Logon Script Processing.

Step 5. Click OK.

Using a Windows 98 computer as a NetWare file and print server

The Microsoft file and printer sharing for NetWare Networks software allows your Windows 98 computer to become a NetWare file and print server on a NetWare network. If you use this software, a Windows 98 computer can perform file and print services as if it were a NetWare server, and you can add Windows 98 peer servers to your network without purchasing additional NetWare licenses. For a Windows 98 computer to be a NetWare file and print server, you must have at least one NetWare server on your NetWare network.

Configuring the IPX/SPX-compatible protocol

If you are using Microsoft's 32-bit IPX/SPX-compatible protocol, you can configure it (or any of the Microsoft-supplied networking protocols) using the Network dialog box. Just highlight the protocol and click the Properties button.

Configuring the adapter driver

Highlight your network adapter in the Network dialog box and click the Properties button. You have the choice of three adapter driver types:

- Enhanced mode (32-bit and 16-bit) NDIS driver (NDIS 5)
- Real mode (16-bit) NDIS driver (NDIS 2.*x*)
- Real mode (16-bit) ODI driver

The default adapter driver selected automatically when you choose Client for NetWare Networks or Client for Microsoft Networks is the NDIS 5 driver. The IPX/SPX-compatible networking protocol will be bound to this adapter. Click the Bindings tab to see which protocols are bound to your adapter.

The adapter's interrupt and I/O address are listed in the Resources tab of the network adapter's Properties dialog box (highlight the adapter in the Network dialog box and click the Properties button). For additional information, see the section earlier in this chapter entitled "Configuring resources for the adapter driver."

The properties displayed in the Advanced tab (if available) of the Properties dialog box for the adapter depend on the specific adapter.

Logging onto the Network

If you are connected to a network using a 16-bit real-mode driver, a network logon prompt appears on your screen in text mode before the Windows 98 Desktop is displayed. You need to log on before Windows 98 starts.

If you have installed Client for Microsoft Networks or Client for NetWare Networks, separate logon boxes appear the first time that you restart Windows 98. You will also see a logon box for logging onto your own computer — pretty rude, actually.

If you use the same password in all the logon boxes, the next time you start Windows 98, you will be presented with one "unified" logon box. The only way this is going to work is if you have the same password for your logon to your primary NetWare server, to your Windows NT server, and to your own computer.

If you are logging onto a Microsoft network without a Windows NT server (for example, connecting to other Windows 98, Windows 95 and WFWG 3.11 computers), you won't be faced with a Microsoft Networks logon box. Resources on peer-to-peer networks are protected with passwords that are unique to the resources, not to the users (if the resources are protected at all). You need to configure your logon correctly using the steps outlined earlier in this chapter in the section entitled "Configuring your computer as Client for Microsoft Networks."

Passwords for resources that are protected by share-level (peer-to peer) security are encrypted and remembered in the *password cache*, a file stored on your Windows 98 computer. They are retrieved from the password cache after the first time you successfully log onto a shared network resource, so you don't have to enter the password for a resource again. You (or your network administrator) can configure your computer so passwords aren't cached and you have to enter them anew each time you access a resource or server that requires a password.

If you have configured your Windows 98 computer to enable user profiles, you will always have to (at least) negotiate with the Windows 98 logon box. To enable user profiles, click the Users icon in the Control Panel. Your password can be blank.

You can add the *Windows family logon service*, which allows you to just pick a name from a list of users at logon time. In the Network dialog box, click Add, select Client, and click Add. Select Microsoft, and choose Microsoft Family Logon.

You can log onto the network without seeing a logon box if you disable user profiles, select Windows Logon as the primary network logon in the Network dialog box, use a blank password, and your passwords for logging onto your

NetWare or Windows NT server are also blank. This is also the case if you are logging onto a Microsoft peer-to-peer network under these conditions.

If you want to bypass the logon box, you can also use the TweakUI automated logon feature. Just click the TweakUI shortcut on your Desktop (or click the TweakUI icon in the Control Panel), click the Network tab, mark Log on Automatically at System Startup, and enter your username and password.

Windows 98 caches your various passwords. You only need one logon box to log onto a network (if you do it right), no matter whether it is a peer-to-peer network, a NetWare network, or a Microsoft network with a Windows NT server.

Your passwords are stored in an encrypted file, *username*.pwl, referred to as a *password cache*. If you delete this file, you lose access to password-protected resources and servers.

You can change some passwords by clicking the Passwords icon in the Control Panel. You can also use the Password List Editor, a utility that comes with Windows 98, to manage your passwords. This utility doesn't let you change passwords, but it does let you delete passwords from your password cache. You might use the Password List Editor to get rid of passwords that you aren't using anymore, or, if you are a network administrator, to disallow access to some resources or servers whose passwords were previously cached.

You'll find the Password List Editor on the Windows 98 CD-ROM in the \tools\apptools\pwledit folder. You can use the Add/Remove Programs icon in the Control Panel to install it. Click the Windows Setup tab, click the Have Disk button, and type the pathname in the Install From Disk dialog box.

Secret

If you like, you can also set the minimum length required for a password to be valid. You'll need to edit the Registry to do this.

STEPS

Setting the Minimum Password Length

Step 1.   Click Regedit.exe in the \Windows folder.

Step 2.   Navigate to HKEY_LOCAL_MACHINE\SOFTWARE\Microsoft\ Windows\CurrentVersion\Policies\Network.

Step 3.   With the Network key highlighted, right-click the right pane of the Registry editor, and choose New, Binary Value. Name the binary value **MinPwdLen**.

Step 4.   Double-click MinPwdLen. Give it a value that you want for your minimum password length. Click OK, and exit the Registry editor.

Some network connections will not work if you send an encrypted password to the network server. You can send an unencrypted password if you make a Registry change. For details, turn to "Network file system" in Chapter 18.

The Network Neighborhood

The servers and shared resources on the network are made visible through the Network Neighborhood. You can display the Network Neighborhood folder window by clicking this icon on the Desktop or by clicking it in an Explorer window. You'll also find the Network Neighborhood icon in common dialog boxes (such as the File Open dialog box) used by 32-bit Windows 98-aware applications such as WordPad and MS Paint.

You can click the Map Network Drive button in the Explorer or folder window toolbar (or choose Tools, Map Network Drive in the Explorer) to give a volume drive-letter designation to a server, a shared folder, or a shared drive. You can likewise map a network printer to an LPT port using the Capture Printer Port dialog box, which you access through the Details tab of the Properties dialog box for a network printer. (Right-click a printer icon in the Printers folder, click Properties, click the Details tab, and then click the Capture Printer Port button.)

The Network Neighborhood bridges the chasm between your computer and the network. You browse the network in the same manner that you browse your own computer. There isn't a different interface.

Windows 98 integrates your computer and the network by making files and printers on other computers look and feel the same as local resources.

In Windows 98, unlike in Windows 3.1x, you do not have to map a network drive to be able to see and use the files on that drive. As long as the file is displayed in your Explorer or folder window, it is available to you. You can run programs (you may need to make other adjustments in the program's configuration) and edit documents that reside on another computer without mapping that computer's disk drive to a logical drive letter.

The Universal Naming Convention (UNC)

Every computer and server on your network has a name. You provided a name for your computer when you installed Windows 98 if you installed any network components.

You refer to other computers and resources on the network by their names. For example, \\Billscomputer\Cdrive\Mystuff refers to another computer (Billscomputer) that is sharing a resource, the hard disk drive named Cdrive (most likely the C drive on Bill's computer), and the Mystuff folder on that drive.

This way of referring to servers or computers that are sharing their resources is called the *universal naming convention* (UNC). You use two backslashes before the computer's name, a single backslash between the name of the computer and the name of the shared resource (a hard disk drive, in this example), and a single backslash between the name of the shared resource and the folder.

You can also use this convention to refer to networked printers. (You assign a name to each networked printer.) To see how to assign a name to a printer, turn to the "Installing a Printer Driver" section of Chapter 29.

Resource Sharing

The resources on your computer — printers, folders, drives, CD-ROMs — are accessible to other users over your network if you enable file and printer sharing through the Network dialog box. This peer-to-peer resource sharing requires that you use Client for Microsoft Networks, Client for NetWare Networks, or both. Other users on your network who want to access your resources must be running the matching client as well as the same network protocol.

You don't have to share resources that are connected to individual computers with other computers on the network. You could set up the network so that your network servers are the only computers that have resources available to other users.

If your network is a peer-to-peer network — one without a server — then the only way individual users can access network resources is to share them. Not every computer needs to share its resources, and every computer that does becomes a peer server.

Network Security

Security issues affect all aspects of life on a computer network. As a user, you don't want others — whatever authority they hold over you — messing about with your files and programs. If you are a network administrator, you want to be able to allow people to use resources that are available on the network, no matter whose computer they are connected to. You also want to be able to install software on client computers from your computer. Users and administrators alike want to make sure that someone calling in from outside the network can't download private information from their computers or from the network.

You maintain network security by restricting access to network resources. You can restrict access by assigning passwords to resources or by maintaining lists of authorized users (who are assigned passwords). Your computer is quite secure if you:

- Don't share any resources

- Don't enable remote administration

- Don't enable the Windows 98 Dial-Up Server

- Require a logon password to your computer
- Don't allow others physical access to your computer

If you allow any form of access to your computer, you need to provide some security measures to restrict that access.

Windows 98 computers are not completely (or even very) secure. Even if you require a password to access Windows 98, anyone can press and hold the Ctrl key during the power-on self test to get to your computer's Startup menu. They can then make a choice to go to the DOS prompt.

You can disallow the use of Ctrl key by putting the statement BootKeys=0 in your Msdos.sys file.

Choosing between two kinds of security

Windows 98 provides two different kinds of security. The first is *share-level security*, which is used on peer-to-peer networks, for example, when you network Windows 98 computers together. Share-level security is also available in Windows 95, Windows for Workgroups 3.1*x* and other peer-to-peer Microsoft Networks-compatible networks. The second is *user-level security*, which requires a Windows NT or NetWare server.

You enforce share-level security by attaching passwords to each shared folder, disk drive, and printer. You enforce user-level security by maintaining lists of users on a Windows NT or NetWare server. You can mix both types of security on the same network, as long as you have a Windows NT or NetWare server to maintain user-level security.

Each Windows 98 peer server stores a list of shared resources on that computer, along with the accompanying passwords. The list of users allowed access to shared resources on a particular Windows 98 computer on the network is stored on the Windows NT or NetWare server.

A network administrator with the remote administration password can set up the list of users and passwords for shared resources on any of the client Windows 98 computers on the network, as long as they are configured for remote administration.

Share-level security

Armed with a remote administration password for each computer and for each shared resource, a network administrator in a share-level security system (for example, a peer-to-peer Microsoft Network with no Windows NT server) has some administrative control over the computers on the network. In this type of setup, the network administrator maintains security by managing the peer servers (that is, the Windows 98 computers with shared resources).

In a share-level security system, a remote administration password protects your computer. If someone (an officially designated network administrator or not) has that password, he or she can create, add, or delete shared resources on your computer. If you change the remote administration password, that person loses administrative access until you provide the new password. As a network administrator, you would normally store all the remote administration passwords for the computers that you administer in a cached file on your computer.

If your network does not have a Windows NT or NetWare server, your security options are simple — you use share-level security. Share-level security is not available on computers running file and printer sharing for NetWare Networks.

User-level security

A network administrator who has been given remote administration authority can grant access to the resources on your computer to other users, and administrative access to other system administrators. The names of the users and administrators are kept on the Windows NT or NetWare server.

Administrators who have remote administration authority over your computer can carry out any of the administrative-access actions detailed later in this chapter in the section entitled "Network Administration." They can edit your Registry, customize your computer's configuration and Desktop, edit your password list, and monitor system performance. They can also add or remove other remote administrators.

User-level security is required in order to use the network management tools (other than Net Watcher) that come with Windows 98, and those available from third parties. The tools that come with Windows 98 are described in the "Network Administration" section.

Setting the type of security

It is not a good idea to switch back and forth between share-level and user-level security. Choose one, or follow the guidelines of your network administrator, and stay with it.

STEPS

Setting the Type of Security

Step 1. Click the Network icon in the Control Panel. Click the Access Control tab in the Network dialog box, as shown in Figure 24-10.

(continued)

STEPS *(continued)*

Setting the Type of Security

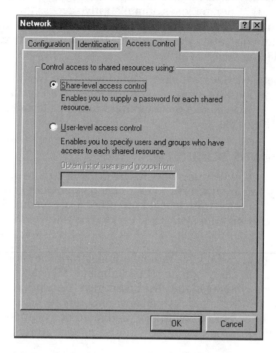

Figure 24-10: The Access Control tab of the Network dialog box.

Step 2.   Mark either Share-Level Access Control or User-Level Access Control.

Step 3.   If you choose User-Level Access Control, enter the name of the server or the domain that stores the list of users who have access to your resources.

Step 4.   Ignore messages about being unable to find the security provider. If you are asked for the authenticator type, enter Server or Domain, depending on which one you are using.

Step 5.   Click OK, and restart your computer.

Network Administration

Windows 98 comes with four network management tools: System Policy Editor, Registry editor, System Monitor, and Net Watcher. Only Net Watcher can be used on a peer-to-peer network to remotely administer shared resources on a peer server. The other tools require a Windows NT or

NetWare server, the designation of user-level security on the computers to be administered, and the installation of Microsoft Remote Registry Service on Windows 98 client computers as well as on the network administrator's computer.

Using Net Watcher, a network administrator can:

- Determine which clients are connected to any peer server on the network
- Disconnect any clients from any peer server
- View which resources any peer server is sharing
- Change the share attributes of any resource on a peer server
- Start/stop sharing any peer server resource
- Determine which files are open on a peer server
- Close open files on a peer server

Because a network administrator can use Net Watcher to create, add, or change the properties of a shared resource, he or she can edit and delete files, as well as create new ones on any disk drive on your computer, even on drives that you have specified as read-only. The network administrator can install new software on your computer while sitting at his or her computer.

You have the ability to determine which disk drives, folders, and printers are shared on your computer; a network administrator with the remote administration password has the same ability.

A network administrator can use System Policy Editor to change many Registry settings and customize the Desktops of remote Windows 98 computers. Of course, you can also use System Policy Editor locally to customize your own Windows 98 computer without having to go through the network.

You can use the Registry editor locally to edit your own Registry, or remotely to edit other people's Registries. This is covered in detail in "Using the Registry editor to edit someone else's Registry" in Chapter 15. If you want to connect to (and possibly edit) a Registry on a remote Windows 98 computer, choose Registry, Connect Network Registry in the Registry editor. Many of the changes you can make to a computer's Registry don't take effect until that computer is rebooted.

You can use the System Monitor both locally and remotely to get information about computer performance.

Enable remote administration

You can enable remote administration on a computer with either user-level or share-level security. If you have implemented user-level security on your Windows 98 computer as described in "Setting the type of security," remote administration is automatically enabled.

To enable remote administration of a Windows 98 computer, take the following steps:

STEPS

Configuring Your Computer for Remote Administration

Step 1. Click the Passwords icon in the Control Panel. Click the Remote Administration tab in the Passwords Properties dialog box, as shown in Figure 24-11.

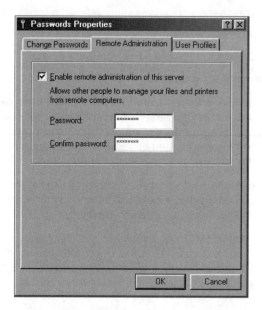

Figure 24-11: The Remote Administration tab of the Passwords Properties dialog box. Mark the Enable Remote Administration of This Server check box and type a password to allow a network administrator to remotely administer your computer.

Step 2. Click Enable Remote Administration of This Server.

Step 3. If the computer is configured for share-level security, enter a password.

If, instead, the computer is configured for user-level security, click the Add button and enter the names of the administrators. (The Add button isn't shown in Figure 24-11. If you have enabled user-level security, it will be displayed.)

Step 4. Click OK.

You can enable remote administration as part of the Windows 98 setup process by editing the MSBatch.inf file. Refer to Bob Cerelli's Windows 98 home page at http://www.halcyon.com/cerelli/admin.htm for more details.

Install Remote Registry services

If you are going to allow a network administrator to edit your Registry using System Policy Editor and/or the Registry editor, or allow him or her to monitor the performance of your computer with System Monitor, you need to install Microsoft Remote Registry Service. Of course, if the administrator has your remote administration password, he or she can take these steps for you. You don't need to install Remote Registry Service unless you have enabled user-level security on your computer, because none of these network management tools work with share-level security. To install Remote Registry Service, take the following steps:

STEPS
Installing Microsoft Remote Registry Service

Step 1. Click the Network icon in the Control Panel. Click the Add button, and in the Select Network Component Type dialog box, click Service, and then click the Add button.

Step 2. Click the Have Disk button.

Step 3. Click the Browse button, and browse to the \tools\nettools\ remotreg folder on the Windows 98 CD-ROM. Regsrv.inf will be highlighted. Click OK.

Step 4. Highlight Microsoft Remote Registry and click OK. Restart your computer.

Install Remote Registry Service on the network administrator's computer also. And keep in mind that the administrator's computer and the client computer must share a common networking protocol.

Net Watcher

If you have multiple peer servers on the network, you can run multiple copies of Net Watcher to continuously keep track of them all. You can use Net Watcher to administer all peer servers that have been configured for remote administration, and you can use it to administer your own computer if it is a peer server (that is, if you are running file and printer sharing for Microsoft or NetWare Networks).

If your computer is using share-level security and file and printer sharing for Microsoft Networks, you can use Net Watcher to administer only other computers of the same configuration. If your computer is configured for user-level security and file and printer sharing for Microsoft Networks, you can use Net Watcher to administer other computers running file and printer sharing for Microsoft Networks irrespective of their security scheme. If you are running file and printer sharing for NetWare Networks, you can only administer peer servers that are also running it.

Net Watcher provides three different views of a peer server. The default view is Connections view, which displays the user connections to the peer server. Shared Folders view displays the resources that are shared on the server, and Open Files view displays the files that are open on the server.

You can install Net Watcher using the Windows Setup tab in the Add/Remove Programs Properties dialog box (click the Add/Remove Programs icon in the Control Panel). Click System Tools, and then mark Net Watcher. You can also find the Net Watcher install files on your Windows 98 CD-ROM in \tools\ nettools\netmon.

To run Net Watcher after it is installed, click Net Watcher in the Programs, Accessories, System Tools menu. When Net Watcher first starts, it is focused on your computer. To administer another peer server, click the Select Server button at the left end of the Net Watcher toolbar (see Figure 24-12).

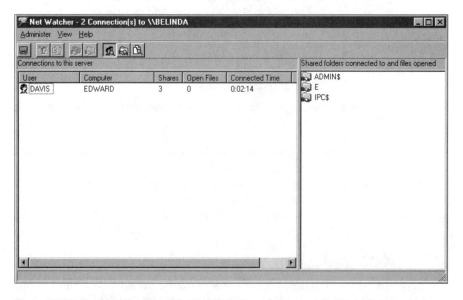

Figure 24-12: The Net Watcher with the default Connections and Details views turned on.

Disconnecting users from a peer server

To disconnect a user from a peer server, highlight the user and click the Disconnect User button (the second button from the left) on the Net Watcher toolbar.

Changing or adding sharing on a peer server

You can share resources that aren't currently being shared on a peer server, change the share properties of an existing shared resource, or quit sharing.

STEPS

Changing Sharing on a Peer Server

Step 1. Click the Show Shared Folders button (the second from the right) in the Net Watcher toolbar to switch to the Shared Folders view. This view displays both shared printers and folders, as shown in Figure 24-13, despite its name.

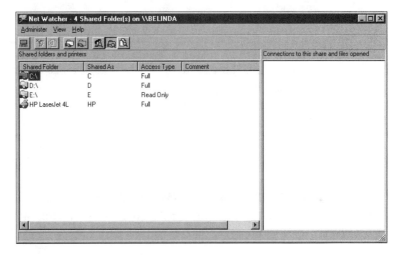

Figure 24-13: Net Watcher in Shared Folders view.

Step 2. Highlight the name of the resource whose sharing properties you want to modify.

Step 3. Press Alt+Enter. The Properties dialog box for this resource appears on your Desktop. You can choose Not Shared to quit sharing the resource, change sharing to Full, Read-Only, or Depends on Password, and change the passwords required to access the resources.

If the peer server uses user-level security, you can change the names of the users who can access that resource.

Step 4. Click OK.

You can also stop sharing a resource by highlighting it in the Shared Folders view, and choosing Administer, Stop Sharing Folder.

To turn the peer server into a shared resource, choose Administer, Add Shared Folder. Click the Browse button in the Enter Path dialog box to display the resources on the peer server.

Dealing with open files

You can determine which files are open and close them if you need to. You might want to do this if a client computer is hung with an open file on the peer server.

STEPS

Closing an Open File on a Peer Server

Step 1. In the Net Watcher window, choose View, By Open Files, or click the Show Files toolbar button (it looks like two pieces of paper and a magnifying glass).

Step 2. Click the file that you want to close.

Step 3. Choose Administrator, Close File.

Watching a particular peer server

You can set up multiple Net Watcher icons, one for each server.

STEPS

Watching Multiple Peer Servers

Step 1. In an Explorer window, click Network Neighborhood.

Step 2. Click the Entire Network icon, one of your workgroups, or the icon for the computer that you want to administer.

Step 3. Right-click the computer icon for the peer server that you want to track with Net Watcher. Click Properties in the context menu. Click the Tools tab (see Figure 24-14).

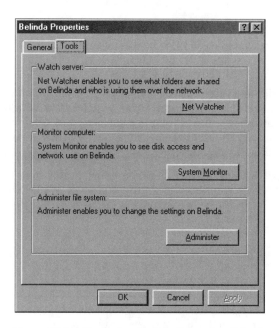

Figure 24-14: The Tools tab of the Properties dialog box for a peer server.

Step 4. Click the Net Watcher button.

Step 5. Continue doing this for as many peer servers as you want to track.

You can also browse for a peer server in Net Watcher by choosing Administer, Select Server.

System Policy Editor

System Policy Editor is a friendly front end to a number of user and computer configuration values stored in the Registry. You can use it to perform these tasks, among others:

- Remove the Shut Down, Settings, and Run commands from user Start menus
- Get the Network Neighborhood icon off of the Desktop
- Remove a number of Control Panel icons, including System, Display, and Network
- Require validation from a network server for access to the local computer

- Disable password caching
- Disable dial-in from Dial-Up Networking
- Disallow print and/or file sharing

You can define system policies for a given user and computer, or for similar groups of users. You can store these policies on a Windows NT or NetWare server, download them at logon time to an individual computer, and use them to modify the Registry settings. Storing the system policies on a server protects them from tampering.

You install System Policy Editor (on your computer or on the network administrator's computer) from the Windows 98 CD-ROM. Take the following steps:

STEPS

Installing System Policy Editor

Step 1. Click the Add/Remove Programs icon in the Control Panel and then click the Windows Setup tab.

Step 2. Click the Have Disk button, and then click Browse. In the Open dialog box, browse to the folder \tools\apptools\poledit on your Windows 98 CD-ROM, and click OK.

Step 3. Click the OK button in the Install From File dialog box, and then click the check boxes next to Group Policies and System Policy Editor in the Have Disk dialog box. Click the Install button.

Step 4. Click OK.

System Policy Editor is installed and its shortcut is now in the System Tools menu (under Start, Programs, Accessories). To use the System Policy Editor to set options for a given user, first log on as that user. In the System Policy Editor menu, click File, New, and open a new policy file. Double-click the User icon to begin choosing policies.

To allow System Policy Editor to create group policies, each client Windows 98 computer needs to have the Grouppol.dll file in its \Windows\System folder. To put this DLL in the System folder, take the steps above on each client computer, but install only Group Policies.

System policies are by default downloaded from your NetWare preferred server or Windows NT PDC when you log onto your network. You can use the System Policy Editor to cancel this download. Simply choose File, Open Registry, double-click Local Computer, and click the plus sign next to Network. Then choose Update, and clear the Remote Update check box.

Registry editor

To edit the Registry resident on another Windows 98 computer, choose Registry, Connect Network Registry in the Registry editor. You can then browse to find the computer whose Registry you wish to edit. The Registry editor is discussed in detail in "The Registry Editor" in Chapter 15.

System Monitor

The source files for the System Monitor are not stuck in some obscure folder on the Windows 98 CD-ROM. You can install it by clicking the Windows Setup tab in the Add/Remove Programs Properties dialog box (click the Add/Remove Programs icon in the Control Panel). Click System Tools, Details, and scroll down to System Monitor.

Once it's installed, you'll find the System Monitor in the Start, Programs, Accessories, System Tools menu. To connect System Monitor to another computer (or to connect multiple copies of System Monitor to monitor multiple computers) choose File, Connect in the System Monitor.

Network Applications

Microsoft still supplies network applications that let you do more than just share resources and administer the network. Windows Messaging (see "Windows Messaging Features" in Chapter 20) lets you send e-mail (and attachments) to anyone on your network. You can also share a fax modem over a network using Windows Messaging (which you'll find on the Windows 98 CD-ROM).

You can install WinPopup — a utility that broadcasts or sends messages and pops up when a job that you have sent to the networked printer is complete. Click Add/Remove Programs in the Control Panel, click the Windows Setup tab, highlight System Tools, click Details, and mark the WinPopup check box.

Windows 95 came with WinChat. Windows 98 provides a similar but more powerful program called NetMeeting. You can use NetMeeting to chat, work on the same application at the same time, and speak to and send video to other people on the network. You must have TCP/IP properly configured. You call a computer using its NetBIOS or NetBEUI name. If your network has a NetMeeting directory server, you can use the directory to contact others on the network.

Summary

We show you how to turn your Windows 98 computer into a networking client or peer server so that it can share resources with other computer users on your network.

▶ You can build a great little two-computer network for $60.

▶ Windows 98 will work with your existing 16-bit real-mode network.

▶ Windows 98 comes with 32-bit protected-mode networking clients, protocols, and adapter drivers, which reduces the load on conventional memory.

▶ It is a lot easier to configure pre-plug and play network adapters using built-in Windows 98 hardware detection and the Device Manager.

▶ You can turn a Windows 98 computer into a full- or part-time (shared) NetWare file and print server.

▶ You can configure Windows 98 as a protected-mode peer server on either a Microsoft network (with or without a Windows NT server) or a NetWare network.

▶ You can use different networking protocols to connect to multiple networks simultaneously.

▶ Windows 98 comes with a raft of network management tools and the ability to interact with third-party network management SNMP tools.

▶ You can configure your computer to allow remote administration.

▶ You don't have to map networked printers or drives to local logical ports or drive letters to access them using the universal naming convention.

Part V

Plug and Play

Chapter 25

Plug and Play: Device Management

In This Chapter

Windows 98 "captures" your PC hardware. Microsoft provides a raft of 32-bit drivers for almost everything under the sun. We discuss:

▶ What's so great about plug and play?

▶ How Windows 98 works with existing hardware and new plug and play devices

▶ Automatic hardware detection during and after Setup

▶ Adding new hardware drivers

▶ Untangling resource conflicts

▶ Setting up multiple hardware configurations (profiles)

▶ Why CD-ROMs and sound cards mess with your parallel ports

Peace Among the Pieces

Microsoft has made a very big deal about plug and play, even adding it to Windows NT 5.0. A consortium of hardware manufacturers and software developers agreed in 1994 to a standard that allows easier installation and tracking of PC hardware independent of the operating system. Windows 95 was the first commercial manifestation of an operating system to completely embrace this standard, and Windows 98 has extended and improved it.

Unlike the Apple Macintosh, nobody (not even the evil empire) owns the PC hardware and software standards. Therefore, companies who would like nothing better than to grind each other into the ground have to cooperate with one another to arrive at standards that offer great benefits to the customer.

Everyone knows it is relatively difficult to set up PC hardware (and accompanying hardware drivers), especially when your computer is filled with cards from different manufacturers. The major difficulties are:

■ Assigning hardware interrupts, of which there are only 16 — and some of these are used by the basic computer hardware

- Assigning non-conflicting I/O addresses so that each add-on card can have its own unique address

- Assigning Direct Memory Access (DMA) channels (in non-PCI bus cards) so there is no conflict

- Installing PC Cards (formerly known as PCMCIA cards) that adhere to different standards

- Setting monitor parameters to automatically work with your video card

- Making sure there are no memory blocks used (especially by video and network cards) that conflict with memory assignments, particularly in upper memory

- Recognizing and highlighting conflicts so they can be resolved

- Gracefully handling multiple hardware configurations for one computer — for example, docking stations with portables

- Recognizing when the hardware configuration changes, so that the operating system and Windows 98-aware application software can take the appropriate action

Microsoft realized that many of its support calls had to do with hardware conflicts of the first three types. Hardware manufacturers realized that it was more difficult to sell add-on devices (in particular multimedia kits) when they were so difficult to install.

The first order of business for plug and play was to make it easier to install hardware and resolve any conflicts with the hardware interrupts, the I/O address, the memory ranges used, and the DMA channel used, if any. Windows 98 solves most of these problems automatically and gives you the tools to solve the rest.

32-bit Drivers

Windows 98 is a 32-bit operating system (for the most part) and one big part of that is its 32-bit drivers. Microsoft has released close to 1400 new 32-bit device drivers in addition to those that initially came with Windows 95. All the 32-bit device drivers get loaded into extended memory so they don't take up conventional or upper memory.

Not only are they 32-bit, but they have lots of new features, features that come about because they have more room to wiggle in extended memory. The Device Manager and the Add New Hardware Wizard install these new drivers for the hardware that they detect. When you run Windows 98 Setup, it casts aside 16-bit drivers for the new 32-bit drivers.

Microsoft has included the most recent version of its Windows Driver Library (WDL) in the \Drivers folder on the Windows 98 CD-ROM. This is a good place to look if you need a driver that is not included in Windows 98. Microsoft also maintains the WDL online at ftp://ftp.microsoft.com/softlib.

New 32-bit drivers are available from the Microsoft Windows Update web site. If you have an Internet connection, click the Start button, point to Settings, and click Windows Update to get the latest drivers for your hardware.

16-bit Drivers

If you need to run 16-bit drivers, you're going to have to use the older installation routines that come from the manufacturers. Only in relatively rare circumstances, however, will you need to run these drivers.

Undocumented

There is a list in your \Windows folder named Ios.ini that contains the names of the hardware driver files that can be (and are) *safely* replaced by 32-bit drivers in Windows 98. *Safe* just means that the 32-bit driver implements at least all of the functionality of the 16-bit driver. If you find that your real-mode driver is on the list but provides functionality missing from the replacement 32-bit driver, you can delete it from the list and reinstall the driver (unremark the call to it in Config.sys).

If you have 16-bit drivers that aren't replaced, you'll find them listed in the Device Manager with a yellow exclamation mark. You can remark out the drivers in Config.sys and Autoexec.bat, install more generic 32-bit drivers using the Add New Hardware Wizard, and reboot your computer. (For details, see "Adding New Hardware Drivers" later in this chapter.)

16-bit drivers come in handy when you are running in MS-DOS mode. If you want access to your CD-ROM, you'll need to load its 16-bit driver. The same goes for your mouse and sound card. See "DOS in MS-DOS mode without a reboot" in Chapter 34.

Plug and Play BIOS and Devices

You may have a computer that doesn't have a plug and play BIOS and has no plug and play cards. That's fine. Windows 98 does its best to search for and identify the hardware you have installed and then install the appropriate drivers.

You may have a computer without a plug and play BIOS, but with some plug and play devices. That's also fine. The plug and play devices give Windows 98 a little more flexibility in configuring the hardware resource usage to avoid conflicts among the devices.

You may have a computer with a plug and play BIOS *and* plug and play cards. Great! Windows 98 can work with the plug and play BIOS to configure your computer automatically so that there are no conflicts among hardware devices.

Windows 98 enumerates all the plug and play devices it recognizes in your computer — including busses such as ISAPNP, PCI, and PCMCIA (PC Card) — each time you start Windows 98. This also happens when a plug and play device sends information that the computer's hardware configuration has changed, and when you click the Refresh button in the Device Manager. This enumeration is different than hardware *detection* (see the next section, "Hardware Detection") because it only applies to plug and play devices.

If Windows 98 does not recognize your computer as being plug and play, there may be an updated system BIOS available for your particular model that is more fully compliant with the Microsoft plug and play standard. Check out your computer manufacturer's web site.

Hardware Detection

Windows 98 Setup detects installed hardware and drivers for a broad range of pre-plug and play hardware as well as the new stuff. Detection happens during Windows 98 Setup, and when you use the Add New Hardware Wizard. Windows doesn't run the hardware-detection program each time you start Windows 98.

Windows 98 creates a hardware-detection log called Detlog.txt in the root directory of your boot drive every time hardware detection runs. You can read this to see what hardware is being detected and in what order.

Undocumented

The installation files contain a database of existing hardware and drivers. This database is stored in specific *inf* files and coordinated by the Msdet.inf file. You will find these files in the \Windows\Inf folder. (If you don't see the Inf folder, choose View, Folder Options in the Explorer, and mark Show All Files in the View tab.) The detection routines are non-invasive and do their best to determine just what you've installed over the years from one of a zillion different manufacturers.

Undocumented

Hardware detection won't be able to determine what monitor you have unless it is plug and play compatible, so you'll need to pick your monitor from a list.

Windows 98 may register your modem as generic, so if you know what modem you have, you should go back later and specify that modem. See "Configuring Your Modem" in Chapter 31 for specifics on how to do this. Knowing the right modem assures you that Windows 98-aware (TAPI compliant) communications software will use the correct initialization string. If you leave the modem in the generic configuration, Windows 98 will use your modem's factory default settings, and you may not be able to adjust some values, such as volume.

Undocumented

Hardware detection most likely will assign your hard drive, diskette drives, and disk controller cards to the generic category, unless you have specific SCSI controllers. You may have manufacturer-specific hard disk driver software, but you shouldn't use it unless it has been updated at least for Windows 95 and is 32-bit. Windows 98 Setup remarks Config.sys lines that call older drivers.

Older IDE drives that are 1GB and larger often came with software that allowed them to be partitioned even in a computer with a BIOS that doesn't understand drives larger than 524MB. Windows 98 works with Ontrack's Disk Manager 6.03 (and later) and other partition software of this nature.

Detecting non-plug and play display adapters is probably the most difficult problem for hardware detection because there are so many. Microsoft has written a series of display drivers, and Windows 98 Setup does its best to install the correct one. If you are upgrading from Windows 3.1x, you may need to install a Windows 98 display driver that doesn't have all the functionality of your previous Windows 3.1x driver. You may be able to download a newer driver for this older hardware from the manufacturer's web site. You can also install the Windows 3.1x driver (and lose some Windows 98 display driver functionality), if you like.

Undocumented

Hardware detection finds only one keyboard, even if you have a portable with an external keyboard plugged into it. Both keyboards will be live. If your external keyboard is an extended keyboard and the one on the portable is not, you should make sure the extended keyboard driver is installed (or install it if it isn't).

Undocumented

Windows 98 Setup checks your BIOS to determine if you have Automated Power Management features compatible with the APM 1.0 and APM 1.1 standards. If you do, a Power Management icon will appear in your Control Panel. You can use this icon to adjust the power control settings of your portable.

Lots of portables have a BIOS that is not really compatible with APM 1.0 or 1.1 (as far as Microsoft is concerned). So even if you have control of your power saving configuration through your BIOS settings, you may not have an APM icon in your Control Panel. You just won't have the convenience of power management through Windows. Look in the Device Manager under System Devices for other APM features, which may or may not work on your portable.

Windows 3.1x didn't do a thorough job of checking for APM features in your BIOS. When it didn't find exactly what it was looking for during setup, it didn't install Windows-based APM at all. Windows 98 does a better job, but it may still find a BIOS that is incompatible and not add an APM icon to the Control Panel.

Undocumented

Windows 98 can support multiple mice simultaneously. If you have a trackball built into your portable as well as a serial mouse attached to a serial port, Windows 98 Setup will recognize and install two mouse drivers. Both mice should work. If only one driver is installed, you can install the other after initial setup. The mice will most likely be on different interrupts, so you won't have to do any interrupt conflict resolution. If not, see the section entitled "The Device Manager" later in this chapter.

Undocumented

If you install Direct Cable Connection (DCC), your serial and parallel ports will also be classified in the Device Manager as modems. They aren't really modems, of course, but storing this definition in the modem device type is a convenient way of keeping track of the fact that DCC will work over these ports. DCC finds all available ports when it uses hardware detection to see what is available. You can remove ports from the modems list using the

Device Manager, if in fact these ports are being used exclusively for mice or other devices.

Undocumented

Windows 98 Setup installs a Dial-Up Adapter if you direct it to install DCC and/or Dial-Up Networking (DUN). No piece of hardware is itself a Dial-Up Adapter, other than your ports or your modem. Again, this is a convenient label to put on a capability. All of the necessary network protocols and services are bound to this pseudo device. The Dial-Up Adapter is referenced as a network adapter device in the Device Manager.

Hardware detection finds your serial and parallel ports. Serial ports are defined as plug and play compatible devices if they have the 16550A UART or better. If hardware detection finds an extended capability parallel (ECP) port, you will have to configure it after Setup. For details, see "Configuring ECP and EPP Ports" in Chapter 31.

During the installation of Windows 98 over Windows 3.1*x*, CD-ROMs and sound cards are detected first through their signature drivers, which are called from Config.sys and Autoexec.bat. The calls to these drivers are remarked out and 32-bit drivers are installed instead, unless there aren't any 32-bit drivers for these devices.

Detection after Setup

Hardware detection takes place during Windows 98 Setup, but you can also force it to happen later, or you can install a driver for a specific device that may or may not be physically installed yet. You use the Add New Hardware icon in your Control Panel, discussed later in this chapter in "Adding New Hardware Drivers," to install new drivers for your devices.

If you physically install new hardware without using the Add New Hardware icon and the device is plug and play compatible, the device will notify Windows 98 that it has been installed, and Windows 98 will install a driver automatically. You will be prompted for the diskette that contains the driver, unless Windows 98 can find the source files on your hard disk or CD-ROM drive.

The Registry of hardware

Windows 98 keeps information about installed hardware and its drivers in the Registry. The original entries are made during Windows 98 Setup. You can use the Registry editor to view the hardware drivers installed on your computer. To see how to invoke the Registry editor, turn to "Starting the Registry editor" in Chapter 15.

Undocumented

You'll find references to your hardware under the HKEY_LOCAL_MACHINE key, specifically under the Enum (enumeration) subkey. It's easy to use the Registry editor to view the values stored there.

When you start Windows 98, a dynamic hardware tree is created based on information in the Registry. This tree is stored in RAM, and you can view it using the Registry editor under the HKEY_DYN_DATA\Config Manager\Enum subkey. Looking at this data is not particularly enlightening, as you will quickly see for yourself. It consists of unique keys that enumerate the installed hardware and its current status.

The hardware tree in RAM is updated every time the hardware configuration changes. Microsoft's favorite example is that the tree updates when you plug your portable into a docking station. We assume they have a lot of these over at Microsoft's Redmond campus.

It is a much better idea to use the Device Manager to manage your hardware configuration. The Device Manager's user interface is a lot more informative and understandable. You should use the Registry editor only if the Device Manager is not working for you and you understand the effect of the changes that you are making.

Adding New Hardware Drivers

In a perfect world, you would physically install your new device, such as a printer, in your computer (or perhaps plug it into a port). The drivers for that device would be automatically installed and the device activated. If you install a plug and play compliant device, this *almost* happens.

You may need to turn off the computer first so you don't inadvertently cause any electrical damage when you install a card in a slot (although you can plug in PC Cards without turning off your computer). After you turn your computer back on, you may be asked for a diskette or CD-ROM from the device manufacturer that contains the drivers needed to use the device. If the drivers for that device were shipped with Windows 98, you may be asked to insert the Windows 98 CD-ROM. After Windows 98 installs the new drivers, you'll be able to use your new device.

If the device is pre-plug and play, you may need to click the Add New Hardware icon in the Control Panel (as shown in Figure 25-1) to inform Windows 98 that it needs to check for the new hardware and add a new driver.

This Wizard will first run through the plug and play enumeration process to make sure that this isn't a plug and play device. You can then have the Wizard attempt to automatically detect your installed hardware (and thereby find the device that you just installed). Alternately (or afterward if your hardware is not detected), you can direct the Wizard to install a specific driver by providing it with a manufacturer and model designation or by pointing it toward an installation diskette from the manufacturer (see Figure 25-2).

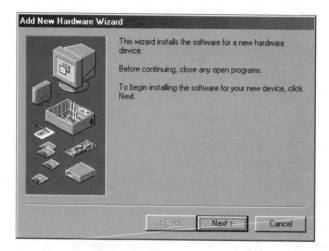

Figure 25-1: The Add New Hardware Wizard. It invokes the hardware-detection routines to find your pre-plug and play device.

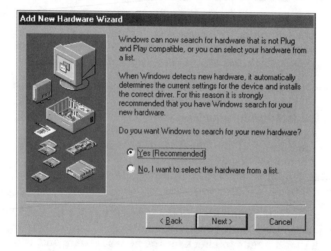

Figure 25-2: You can have the Wizard attempt to automatically detect your hardware. If you know what driver you want installed, you can pick the manufacturer and model yourself.

Getting the Settings Right

Windows 98 can resolve potential conflicts between plug and play devices, setting their IRQ, I/O, memory address, and DMA channel requirements so all these devices can cooperate. It needs your help to do this for pre-plug and play devices (which Microsoft insists on calling *legacy* devices).

We know this is not how plug and play is supposed to work in a plug and play operating system, but Windows 98 has to encompass the past. Pre-plug and play cards and devices can't be configured automatically. You may need to move some jumpers or run a hardware-specific DOS-based configuration program that changes the settings on a given card. You can do this before running the Add New Hardware Wizard or after you determine the conflicts.

Secret

After the Add New Hardware Wizard finds your hardware, or after you direct it to install a driver for a specific device, a dialog box detailing the settings specified for that device appears (see Figure 25-3). The driver settings have been configured by the Wizard not to conflict with any existing settings for other installed hardware. *But these settings may have nothing whatsoever to do with the actual settings or available settings for your device.*

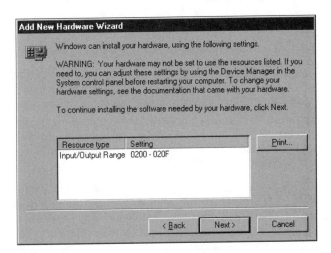

Figure 25-3: The Add New Hardware Wizard's resource settings dialog box. The Wizard has determined the settings that it would like to see you set your device to. You may not be able to do this, given the limitations of your device. These settings will not conflict with any other existing hardware that you have installed. Don't try to change them just yet.

You cannot change these driver settings at this time, even if you know they don't match the actual device settings. The Wizard did not interrogate your device to see what settings you actually have or what settings are possible (unless it's a plug and play device). Understand that the Wizard is not so smart at the moment. You are going to have to provide the smarts to get this process completed.

Secret

Continue with the Add New Hardware Wizard, clicking the Finish button in the last dialog box. The drivers for the new device are now installed. You will find them in the Device Manager, as described later in this chapter, if you care to look for them. *Don't use the Device Manager to change the settings at this time, because it will do no good.* We'll get to that in a minute.

You can now physically reconfigure your device to match the driver settings just assigned to it, change your device to other settings that don't conflict with the driver settings for other hardware, or leave your device settings as they are and change the driver settings for your device in the Device Manager. The actual settings for your device might be determined by jumpers or by device settings stored in ROM on the device. If you need to make changes on your device, you might need to turn off the computer to set jumpers or run a DOS application that allows you to change the device's ROM settings.

You can use the Device Manager, as described in the next section, to make sure that the actual settings for your device do not conflict with existing hardware drivers. If they do, you are going to have to change them. Remember, we are talking about the *actual* device settings, not the driver settings that the Add New Hardware Wizard just assigned to your device, which it *took from those available.*

If you need to change ROM settings on the device, open a DOS window and run the device-specific configuration routines on the manufacturer's diskette now. Change the settings on your device so there is no conflict with existing hardware drivers. When you are done, you are ready to shut down Windows 98.

If you need to change jumpers on a device, shut down Windows 98 and turn off your computer. If you change jumpers, be sure the new device settings don't conflict with existing hardware drivers. For details, see the next section, "The Device Manager." Restart your computer after you have made the changes.

Your device may have a limited range of choices allowed for the various resource settings. Limiting the number of IRQs available to a device is one way that a manufacturer can reduce its price, but this practice causes high user dissatisfaction when conflicts become irresolvable. Do your best to move device resource usage around to avoid conflicts, and keep in mind that you may not be successful. You might have to purchase an improved device, hopefully plug and play enabled.

To get the actual device settings and the driver settings as recorded in the Registry in sync, you need to use the Device Manager. Using the Device Manager now — and not before — you will be able to make changes in the resource settings for your new device driver that match the device's actual settings. After you make these changes, you may need to restart your computer once again to get the new values to take hold.

The Device Manager

The Windows 98 Control Panel is filled with icons that let you manage your computer's hardware and drivers. We outline what some of these icons do in "Control Panel Settings" in Chapter 16, and the rest in the many hardware-specific chapters in this book. If you have a question about a specific piece of hardware, turn to the chapter that focuses on that hardware.

The Device Manager, which you access through the System icon in the Control Panel, provides a general view of all hardware installed on your computer. Sometimes the Device Manager and the hardware-specific icons overlap in functionality, and sometimes you can do something only in one and not the other.

The Device Manager is a powerful tool. Nothing like this was available before Windows 95, even from third-party software developers that created Windows-specific diagnostic tools. The Device Manager supersedes MSD (the Microsoft Diagnostic tool) that came with Windows 3.1*x* but was never documented by Microsoft. It is much easier to use and much more powerful than MSD.

To get to the Device Manager, take the following steps:

STEPS

Starting the Device Manager

Step 1.   Right-click the My Computer icon, and click Properties.

Step 2.   Click the Device Manager tab in the System Properties dialog box. The Device Manager is shown in Figure 25-4.

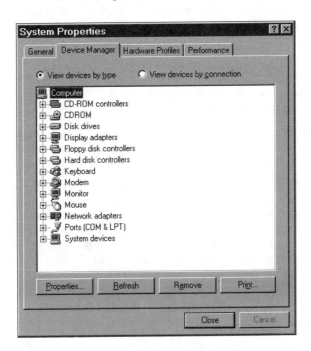

Figure 25-4: The Device Manager. To print your system configuration, highlight Computer and click Print. To view the installed devices of a particular type, click the plus sign next to the type (or double-click the type). To view the properties of a specific device, double-click the device.

Devices are listed in the Device Manager. Click the plus sign to the left of a device type to see the installed devices. Double-click a particular device name to display its Properties dialog box. You can also highlight a device and click the Properties button.

If you mark the View Devices By Connection option button, the devices are displayed hierarchically by their hardware connection to the motherboard.

To get your computer to re-identify the plug and play devices on your computer, click the Refresh button. This button also tells your computer about any SCSI devices that have been newly plugged in.

If there is a yellow exclamation mark over a device name, it means that there is a problem with the device driver. This mostly likely indicates a resource conflict. You may need to set different jumper settings on a non-plug and play device. Use the Device Manager to track down these conflicts.

If you have to hunt for the source of a problem, highlight the Computer icon in the Device Manager, and then click the Properties button. In the View Resources tab of the Computer Properties dialog box, successively click the option buttons to check for interrupt, I/O, memory, and DMA channel conflicts.

The yellow exclamation mark may also indicate a missing device that was previously installed, or a removable device (such as a Zip drive). You can remove the device permanently (until you reinstall it) by highlighting the device and clicking the Remove button.

If there is a red X over your device, the Device Manager is telling you that this device isn't functioning. You may need to install 32-bit drivers, or it may be working with 16-bit drivers and you'll have to just leave it that way.

Click the Print button to generate a report of the devices in the computer. You can specify a summary report, a report on a specific device, or a report for all the devices. The report lists your devices, their properties, and the resources they use. You can print any of these reports to a text file. Be sure to first install the Generic/Text Only printer driver (using the Printers icon in the Control Panel) and then assign it port FILE.

IRQs, I/O, memory addresses, DMA channels

If you double-click Computer in the Device Manager (or highlight it and click the Properties button), you get a wonderfully powerful dialog box that shows all the hardware interrupt request settings for your computer, (see Figure 25-5). You now know just what hardware is using just which interrupt. You'll see which interrupts (between 0 and 15) are available.

You can view other resources by clicking the option buttons at the top of the View Resources tab. These buttons let you view consolidated I/O, memory addresses, and DMA channel usage — very helpful.

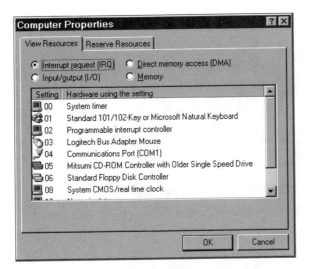

Figure 25-5: The View Resources tab of the Computer Properties dialog box. You can't change anything here, but you do get a consolidated view of interrupt usage.

The Reserve Resources tab lets you set your resources so that Windows 98 won't assign them to a plug and play device.

Specific device drivers

The device drivers installed in your computer are by default displayed by type in the Device Manager. Clicking the plus sign next to a device type displays the device drivers installed. Double-clicking a device driver's name displays its Properties dialog box, as shown in Figure 25-6.

Changing device driver settings

If you have plug and play devices, you should usually let the hardware-detection routines in Windows 98 determine what the resource settings should be. If you set them manually, the settings become fixed and Windows 98 can't adjust them to avoid conflicts. You can, however, change the resource settings for plug and play as well as non-plug and play devices.

To change the resources assigned by Windows 98 to a device in order to match the actual settings for that device and avoid any conflicts with other devices, take the following steps. If your device driver settings don't match the device's settings, the device driver entry in the Device Manager will have a yellow exclamation sign on it.

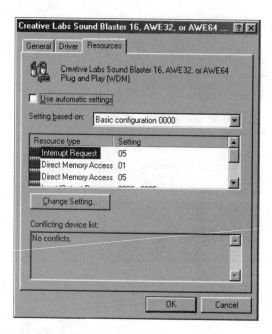

Figure 25-6: The Resources tab of the Properties dialog box for the Creative Labs Sound Blaster. (These values are actually incorrect so don't use them.) You can change them in the Device Manager.

STEPS

Changing a Device's Resource Settings

Step 1. Double-click the specific device in the Device Manager.

Step 2. Click the Resources tab in the Properties dialog box for the device.

Step 3. Double-click a resource type in the Resource Settings field (or highlight a resource and click the Change Setting button). If the Use Automatic Settings box is marked, you'll need to clear it first.

If this resource can be changed, you'll see a dialog box to let you adjust its settings (see Figure 25-7). Use the spin arrows in the Value field to change the values of the resource requested.

Your device driver may allow different basic configurations, which in turn allow for different resource values and the ability to change some resources in one configuration but not in another. In the Resources tab, display the Setting Based On drop-down list to see if there are other configurations. If there are, you can try them to see what difference this makes in allowable resource values.

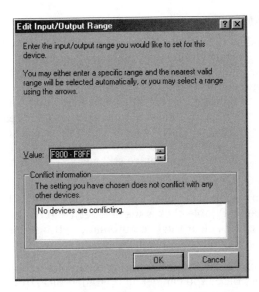

Figure 25-7: The Edit Input/Output Range dialog box. This dialog box is specific to changing an I/O resource. Other resources display different dialog boxes.

Step 4. Click OK in the resource settings dialog box to accept the changes that you have made, and then click OK again in the Properties dialog box.

Step 5. You may be asked to restart your computer to allow the new resource settings to take effect.

Throughout this process, be sure you haven't introduced any new resource use conflicts. If you printed a copy of the system summary, you will have a ready reference on resource use. Also, the Device Manager will track conflicts and warn you when you have created them.

If you have changed settings in the driver for a non-plug and play device, you need to make the same changes to the hardware itself. You may now need to go back and either change the jumpers on the device to match the settings that you just made, or if the hardware device is software configurable, run the manufacturer's software to reconfigure the hardware. This may require opening a DOS window to run the hardware configuration software.

Remember, the process detailed above just changes the device driver settings, and not the actual hardware itself (if it is not plug and play).

IRQ conflicts

Windows 98 lets two physical devices share the same interrupt request line (IRQ) under certain circumstances. Many Peripheral Component Interconnect (PCI) devices are capable of sharing IRQs through the use of IRQ steering (see the next section), and this can be a big help if you have lots of devices fighting for resources. However, it doesn't work for two devices that are used at the same time, such as a modem and a mouse. Devices that are not used at the same time, such as a scanner and a modem, are much better candidates for sharing IRQs. A non-PCI device can't share an IRQ with a PCI device. Each device still keeps a different I/O address.

IRQ sharing should happen automatically when you install new hardware. You can also set the interrupts for a given piece of hardware using the Device Manager. Double-click a specific device in the Device Manager, click the Resources tab, clear the Use Automatic Settings check box, and change settings as described the previous section.

If you have problems with IRQ sharing on an older computer, you may need to upgrade its BIOS. You can get an upgraded BIOS from a third-party supplier, or you can go to your computer manufacturer's web site.

You can also disable a device to eliminate an IRQ conflict. You have to disable it physically first (check the documentation that came with the device to find out how) and then disable it in the Device Manager. If the device is an integrated device that resides on your motherboard (such as a serial port), you also have to disable it in the BIOS. If you don't do this, the next time you power up Windows 98, the plug and play enumeration process will notice the difference, restore the device, and assign resources to it. To completely disable a device and reclaim its resources, follow these steps:

STEPS

Disabling a Device in the Current Configuration

Step 1. Right click the My Computer icon, click Properties, and click the Device Manager tab.

Step 2. Click the plus sign next to the type of device you are looking for, and then double-click the device you want to disable to open its Properties dialog box.

Step 3. Click the General tab, and then click the Disable in This Hardware Profile check box. Click OK. (If you have multiple profiles, this will only apply to the current one.)

Step 4. Restart your computer.

Step 5. If you are disabling a device that is not integrated on your motherboard, you are finished. If this is an integrated device, you must now disable the device in your computer's BIOS settings. The exact steps for doing this vary from one computer to the next. In general terms, you need to press a key during your computer's power-on self test to enter your BIOS's setup program, and then set the value in that program to disable the device.

If your computer has a specialized port—for a PS/2 mouse, for example—you may see that device listed in your Device Manager even if you don't have one connected. Sometimes just having the capability on your motherboard to support such a port is enough to make it show up, even if you don't have a physical port. Disabling the device using the steps above may free up these resources, but not in every case.

IRQ steering

Windows 98 supports a new feature called *IRQ steering* that allows devices to share interrupts. With IRQ steering, Windows can catch messages sent to an interrupt request line (IRQ) and re-route them to the next available IRQ. This is useful for PCI bus devices in laptops with docking stations. As hardware is added and subtracted (when docking occurs), PCI devices can be dynamically re-configured to work together. In addition, if two PCI cards are sharing an interrupt, IRQ steering "steers" the request to the correct card. It can also determine if a PCI card needs an IRQ at all (many don't). If IRQ steering is not enabled, the BIOS handles this routing instead of Windows 98.

IRQ steering is not enabled by default. For this reason, a PCI device may display "Error Code 29" as its status when viewed in the Device Manager. Assuming the device is not physically disabled for some reason, you can correct this error by enabling IRQ steering. To do this, follow these steps:

STEPS

Enabling IRQ Steering

Step 1. Click the Start button, point to Settings, click Control Panel, and click the System icon.

Step 2. Click the Device Manager tab, expand the System Devices branch, and double-click PCI Bus to open its Properties dialog box. Click the IRQ Steering tab.

Step 3. Mark the Use IRQ Steering check box to enable it.

Step 4. You will see a list of four routing tables with check boxes (see Figure 25-8). Windows searches for these tables in the order shown, and uses the first marked table that it finds, ignoring the others.

(continued)

STEPS *(continued)*

Enabling IRQ Steering

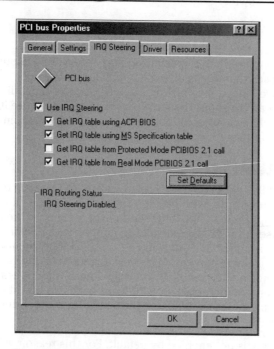

Figure 25-8: IRQ Steering tab of the PCI Bus Properties dialog box. Use this tab to enable IRQ steering.

Ordinarily, the first, second, and fourth tables are marked. Use these default settings unless you have a problem with a PCI device. If you do have a problem, clear the first table and mark the third one. When you have finished, restart your computer.

Forced configurations

You can manually assign IRQs, I/O addresses, and DMA channels, and direct Windows 98 to use the ones you assign. Once you manually assign a specific configuration to a device, Windows 98 is no longer free to change that configuration if new hardware is added later. This is true even if the device that you configure is plug and play compatible.

It is best to allow the Windows 98 hardware enumerator to assign resources to all your plug and play devices. This gives the enumerator maximum flexibility to reconfigure Windows if new devices are added. If you have a plug and play BIOS and you force a configuration, Windows will also change the BIOS to match your forced settings if those settings are available to the BIOS.

PC Cards

PC Cards, previously known as PCMCIA cards, are most popular in laptops. They let you swap devices (such as a modem or floppy drive) "on the fly," without turning off your computer. Windows 98 supports many of these products, including many that are not plug and play compatible.

Plug and play compatible PC Cards won't automatically be detected unless you first run the PC Card Wizard. If you installed Windows 98 over Windows 3.1*x*, the Wizard remarks out the real-mode drivers in the Autoexec.bat and Config.sys files, and enables 32-bit support for your PC Card socket. To run the Wizard, click the PC Card (PCMCIA) icon in the Control Panel. (If clicking the icon displays a Properties dialog box instead of the Wizard, PC Card support has already been enabled.)

You can use the real-mode PCMCIA card drivers instead if you need to, but you won't have plug and play capabilities. Also, you can't mix and match real-mode drivers with plug and play — all of your devices must either use one mode or the other.

After you install your PC Card socket driver using the PC Card Wizard, check the Device Manager for a PC socket listing to verify that the socket is installed properly. If you don't see it, use the Add New Hardware Wizard to indicate the manufacturer and model you are using. (To start the Wizard, click the Add New Hardware icon in the Control Panel.) If your model is not listed, click the Start button, point to Settings, and click Windows Update to download a driver for it (if one is available).

If you have trouble installing or using PC Cards, you can access the Windows 98 PC Card Troubleshooter by clicking Help in the Start menu, clicking Troubleshooting in the Contents tab, clicking Windows 98 Troubleshooting, and clicking PC Card. This document is also maintained online at http://premium.microsoft.com/support/tshoot/w98pcmcia.asp.

Updating device drivers

You can install new device drivers over existing ones for some devices by using the Device Manager. You may want to do this when you get a new driver from your hardware manufacturer, or to see if Microsoft has made new drivers available on its Windows Update web site.

You could, of course, install the new device driver by using the Add New Hardware Wizard. However, this Wizard is primarily designed to search for new hardware and install the corresponding driver. If you haven't installed new hardware and just want to update a driver, the Device Manager provides a semantically friendlier starting point.

STEPS

Installing an Updated Device Driver

Step 1. Double-click the specific device in the Device Manager.

Step 2. Click the Driver tab in the Properties dialog box for the device, if it has one. If there is no Driver tab, you can't update the driver.

Step 3. Click the Upgrade Driver button to launch the Upgrade Device Driver Wizard, and then click Next.

Step 4. The Wizard offers to search for a better driver than the one you have or let you select the driver from a list. If you ask the Wizard to search for the driver and click Next, you can tell the Wizard where to look, including the Microsoft Windows Update location online (see Figure 25-9).

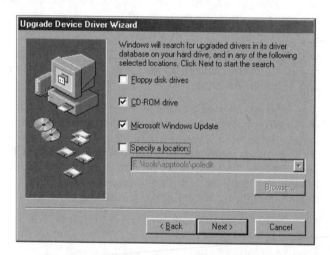

Figure 25-9: The Upgrade Device Driver Wizard offers to search for a better driver, and asks you where to look. If you select Microsoft Windows Update, the search will include Microsoft's driver library on the Internet.

Step 5. If you told the Wizard that you wanted to select the driver in the previous step, it will display a list of the drivers for that device type (modems, for example) that came with Windows 98. By default, the list is set to Show Compatible Hardware; you will see only the drivers that Windows 98 knows are compatible with your device. To see a complete list of available drivers for your device type, select the Show All Hardware option. You can choose one of the drivers on the list, or you can click the Have Disk button if you have a new driver on a diskette, a CD-ROM, or your hard drive.

Step 6. When you've answered all of the questions in the Wizard, click the Finish button, and then click OK in the Driver tab of the Properties dialog box.

Step 7. Restart your computer to allow the new driver to take effect.

Resolving resource conflicts the easy way

There is another way to resolve resource conflicts. Windows 98 help contains a Hardware Conflict Troubleshooter. It gives you a little background on resource conflicts and then promptly leads you to the exact same places that we just covered. It's kind of cute, though.

STEPS

Starting the Hardware Conflict Troubleshooter

Step 1. Click the Start button, and then click Help.

Step 2. Click the Contents tab, and then click Troubleshooting.

Step 3. Click Windows 98 Troubleshooters, and then click Hardware Conflict.

Step 4. Follow the suggestions and shortcuts to the Device Manager.

Hardware Profiles

We have *hardware profiles* for different hardware configurations on one computer, *user profiles* for different users on the same computer, and *Windows Messaging profiles* (if you have Windows Messaging installed) for different mail services. Windows 98 presents us with quite a prolific world.

You don't need hardware profiles if you have a plug and play computer with plug and play devices, except as noted in "TCP/IP conflicts between the LAN card and the Dial-Up Adapter" in Chapter 28. Windows 98 can automatically load the hardware drivers that it needs based on the hardware it detects and stores in the hardware tree in RAM. Change the configuration (by pulling the portable from the docking station, for example), and Windows 98 reconfigures itself dynamically.

The static hardware profiles are a bit of a kludge. A menu comes up in DOS full-screen text mode before the Windows 98 Desktop appears and asks you to choose your current configuration.

Tip

You have to set up the hardware profiles manually. You install all the drivers for all the hardware configurations for all the profiles, and then assign the proper set of drivers to each profile. The hardware doesn't have to be installed at the time that you install the drivers. You can just install the drivers, and then make any necessary changes later if there is a difference between the device settings and the resource settings that you chose.

To create multiple hardware configurations, take the following steps:

STEPS

Creating Multiple Hardware Configurations

Step 1. Use the Add New Hardware Wizard to install all the drivers applicable for all your configurations. Tell the Wizard what to install if you don't have all the hardware physically installed at the moment. You can run the Add New Hardware Wizard in each hardware configuration and have it search for the installed hardware if you like. This will also build up a base of installed hardware.

Step 2. Click the System icon in the Control Panel, and then click the Hardware Profiles tab. Original Configuration (or Undocked if you have a portable) will be highlighted.

Step 3. Click the Copy button and then type a name for the new profile in the Copy Profile dialog box, and click OK. You may want to use the Rename button to give the Original Configuration (or Undocked) a more descriptive name as well.

Step 4. Click OK, close the Control Panel, and restart your computer. Before the Windows 98 Desktop reappears, you will see a text menu showing the profiles you have set up. Select a profile by typing its number (in this case, choose a profile you have just created). Windows 98 will start up in that profile.

Step 5. Open the Control Panel, click the System icon, and click the Device Manager tab. Double-click each applicable device to display its Properties dialog box, and in the Device Usage area of General tab, mark or clear check boxes to disable or remove the device from the profile you are currently in. Figure 25-10 shows the Properties dialog box for a Dial-Up Adapter.

Step 6. After completely defining the hardware available for this hardware profile, repeat steps 4 and 5 for each hardware profile you have created. You must restart your computer each time for the changes in the profile configuration to take effect.

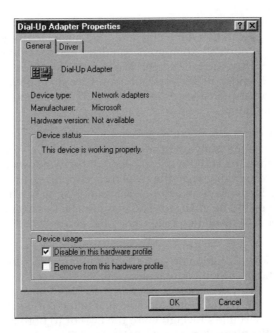

Figure 25-10: The Properties dialog box for a Dial-Up Adapter. Mark the Disable in This Hardware Profile check box to disable the adapter in your current profile. You may have more or fewer check boxes available, depending on the individual device.

For some devices, you will have an additional option in step 5 between the check boxes Remove in This Hardware Profile and Disable in This Hardware Profile. If you remove a device from one of your profiles and then need to restore it later, the Add New Hardware Wizard may not detect it. Instead of removing a device in the Device Manager, you should normally disable it. To restore a device that was accidentally removed from one profile, you'll need to remove it from all the profiles. Then run the Add New Hardware Wizard to reinstall the device, and use steps 4 and 5 above to restore the device to each profile.

LCDs and external monitors

Perhaps you have a portable that uses its built-in LCD screen in one configuration and uses an external monitor in another. You can choose a different monitor for each of the two separate hardware configurations. If the portable is not plug and play compatible, you will probably want to do this. Portable computers that aren't plug and play compatible can have problems with the Windows 98 video drivers supplied by Microsoft (and developed in cooperation with the video chip and card manufacturers). The video chips inside many portable computers can drive external monitors to greater resolutions than the LCD screen can handle. In some cases, the older generic Windows 98 video drivers are not sophisticated enough to be able to handle the switch between a lower resolution LCD screen and a higher resolution external monitor.

Problems occur when you're attempting to view Windows 98 on the LCD display (or after you've set the portable to feed the video signal to both the external monitor and the LCD display). If the Windows 98 video drivers are set for a resolution above the resolution supported by the LCD display, Windows 98 displays an error message indicating that the video driver settings need to be changed. The Windows 98 Desktop is then displayed at the lower LCD resolution (640 × 480) and at a reduced color depth of 16 colors.

The Windows 3.1 video drivers shipped by manufacturers of pre-plug and play portable computers gracefully handle the need for dual-resolution output. These video drivers can switch, without user input, between different video resolutions and still maintain color depth. If the video feed is set in the portable's BIOS to go to the LCD or to both the LCD and external monitor, the video drivers automatically switch to a resolution of 640 × 480 pixels (or display a portion of the 800 × 600 display on the LCD screen). If the video signal is set to only go to the external monitor, you can configure the video drivers to display at a higher resolution.

You can make up for some of the lost functionality of the Windows 98 video drivers for non-plug and play portables, although you can't retain the automatic switching in the previous Windows 3.1 drivers. It takes a bit of doing, but you can configure your computer and Windows 98 to let you manually switch between the LCD screen and the external monitor at bootup time in a manner that will eliminate the Windows 98 video error message, set the proper resolution, and retain 256 color depth.

The first step is to set your portable's BIOS to output to the external monitor. You need to do this because the Windows 98 video drivers determine the maximum video resolution based on the display that's currently set to receive the video signal, and they will drop to the lower resolution if the video signal is set to feed to the LCD screen or (in some cases) to both screens.

How you change your computer's BIOS settings varies among BIOS manufacturers. For example, if your portable has a Phoenix BIOS, press the F2 key when prompted during bootup to display the BIOS setup screen, and use the menus to set the primary display to CRT.

After you've changed your BIOS settings, you need to create two Windows 98 hardware profiles. Unless you have a plug and play external monitor and plug and play video chips in the portable, the Windows 98 hardware-detection routines won't be able to tell that you have two displays, so you're going to have to force the issue.

STEPS

Creating Two Windows 98 Hardware Profiles for Two Monitors

Step 1.   Click the Start button, Settings, and then Control Panel. Click the System icon, and then click the Hardware Profiles tab.

Step 2.   Your original hardware profile should be highlighted. Click the Copy button to make a copy of it.

Step 3.   Enter a new name for the new profile — perhaps "External Monitor (800x600)" if the original profile has the LCD screen as the display. (If the original profile has the external monitor as its display, name the new profile "LCD Screen (640x480).")

Step 4.   Highlight the original profile and click the Rename button to rename the original profile, perhaps to "LCD Screen (640x480)." Click OK.

Step 5.   Shut down Windows 98 normally. Restart Windows 98. You will be given the choice between two hardware profiles, as shown here. Choose the new profile.

```
Windows cannot determine what configuration your computer
is in:
Select one of the following:

    1. External Monitor (800x600)
    2. LCD Screen (640x480)
    3. None of the Above

Enter your choice:
```

Step 6.   Open the Control Panel and click the Device Manager tab. Click the plus sign next to the Monitor icon and double-click the attached icon for your current display. At the bottom of the General tab of the Properties dialog box, clear the Disable in This Hardware Profile check box. Click the OK button, and then click OK again.

Step 7.   Right-click the Desktop and choose Properties. Click the Settings tab. Change the color depth (select it from the Colors drop-down list), and change the resolution (drag the Screen Area slider bar) to match the new display and the new hardware profile.

Step 8.   Click the Advanced button, click the Monitor tab, and click the Change button. The Update Device Driver Wizard will launch. Install a display driver that corresponds to your second configuration in the Select Device dialog box. Click OK, click Close, and then click OK again.

(continued)

STEPS *(continued)*

Creating Two Windows 98 Hardware Profiles for Two Monitors

Step 9. Click the Start button, Settings, then Control Panel. Click the Device Manager tab. Click the plus sign next to the Monitor icon and double-click the attached icon for your other display (the one that doesn't apply to this new profile). Make sure the Disable in This Hardware Profile check box is checked. Click the OK button, and then click OK again.

You have now created two hardware profiles. When you restart your computer, you will be given the choice between them just after the Windows 98 splash screen is displayed and just before Windows 98 starts up.

Just because you have two Windows 98 hardware profiles doesn't mean you've correctly configured your hardware to work with them. Your BIOS has been set to direct the video feed to the external monitor. You need to be able to flexibly override this BIOS setting to direct your internal video hardware to send its signal to the external video port, to the LCD display, or perhaps to both.

Often you can accomplish this with a small DOS utility (or set of utilities) that the portable computer manufacturer supplies. You can run these utilities in a batch file or in the Autoexec.bat file to switch the video hardware output between displays. You still need to use these utilities to correctly set the video feed to correspond with the hardware profile you choose during bootup.

To do this, you can create multiconfiguration Config.sys and Autoexec.bat files. While Microsoft would prefer that you forget about these files, and in particular forget about their ability to support multiple configurations, it didn't provide strong enough video drivers for non-plug and play video chips to make this possible. You still need to use the capability of these files to accomplish your goal of switching somewhat painlessly between displays.

To create multiple configurations for two monitors, take the following steps:

STEPS

Creating Multiple Configurations for Two Monitors

Step 1. Edit your Config.sys file to include the menu items in a configuration menu, as shown here:

```
[menu]
;the two menu items follow
Menuitem=CRT,Display on External Monitor (800x600)
Menuitem=LCD,Display on LCD Screen (640x480)
;next we set which menu item is chosen by default and what
```

```
the time delay is
Menudefault=CRT,5
[global]
;we could put some Config.sys entries here
 [CRT]
;we could put in different items for this configuration
here
include=global
[LCD]
include=global
```

Step 2. You can edit this example file to include other Config.sys elements — in the global area, for example.

Step 3. Edit your Autoexec.bat file as shown here to react differently based on the choice that you make in the multiple configuration menu:

```
@echo off
goto %config%
:CRT
rem portable manufacturer's utility for using the external
monitor
c:\util\crt.com
GOTO END
:LCD
rem utility for directing video output to the LCD screen
c:\util\lcd.com
:END
cls
```

Step 4. The Autoexec.bat and Config.sys file edits that we have made will result in the multiple configuration menu shown here:

```
Microsoft Windows 98 Startup menu
=================================

    1. Display on External Monitor (800x600)
    2. Display on LCD Screen (640x480)

Enter a Choice: 1      Time Remaining: 05

F5=Safe mode   Shift+F5=Command Prompt
Shift+F8=Step-by-Step Confirmation [N]
```

In spite of the heading for this menu, it is not the same as the Windows 98 Startup menu. (You can display that menu before this one appears.) In this menu, Shift+F8 won't work to do a step-by-step startup (even though it's listed), but Shift+F5 will get you to the command prompt.

Step 5. The multiple configuration menu can have a timer. By entering the Menudefault command with a seconds value (as shown in step 1), you can choose which configuration will be chosen by default.

Step 6. After you have created/edited the Autoexec.bat and Config.sys files, restart Windows 98 in the normal fashion.

When Windows 98 restarts, you will first see a menu letting you select your hardware profile, and then you'll see a menu letting you choose between your two configurations. Choosing a hardware profile tells Windows 98 which of the two profiles to use when configuring Windows 98. Choosing between the two configurations tells the hardware which configuration to use. The idea is to choose a profile and a configuration that work together.

You're not done yet. Because you have used a BIOS setting to direct the video output to the external monitor, you may not be able to read the menus when you boot your portable without an external monitor. You can either press a keyboard combination that is particular to your portable (perhaps Ctrl+Alt+.) to switch to the LCD display, or you can enter a choice from the menu without actually seeing the menu (and then press Enter) when your portable stops hitting the hard disk during the bootup process.

Hot swapping and hot docking

A plug and play compatible computer can notify Windows 98 when the connection with a docking station is made or broken. This will trigger a reconfiguration of the hardware tree, which in turn makes Windows 98 aware of the new hardware.

Windows 98-aware applications can respond to messages about hardware changes. Windows 3.1*x* programs have no idea what is going on. If you are using a Windows 3.1*x* application, you have to save any files you are editing to a remote hard disk before you pull your portable out of the docking station.

Undocumented

You can plug a device into your SCSI controller card (if you have one), and then use the SCSI device (for example, a SCSI-based Zip drive) without having to restart Windows 98. Unfortunately Windows 98 doesn't automatically check that you've installed a new device. You need to give it a hint. To do this, open the Device Manager (click the System icon in the Control Panel and click the Device Manager tab), choose the View Devices By Connection option button, highlight Computer, and click the Refresh button.

Look for the new device by opening up the branches in the Device Manager and looking for your SCSI host adapter. Check to see if the new device is connected to it.

Autorun

Windows 98 can automatically start CD-ROMs and audio CDs when you insert them into your CD-ROM player. In order for a CD-ROM to start automatically, it needs to have a file named Autorun.inf in its root directory.

You can turn off Autorun for audio CDs, CD-ROMs, or both, and the easiest way to do so is to use TweakUI, which is located in your Control Panel (see

Chapter 16 for more details). The option to disable Autorun is in the Paranoia tab.

Before this capability was put into TweakUI, the most common way to turn off Autorun was to disable the auto insert notification in the CD-ROM settings. Autorun uses the auto insert notification message to determine whether to run or not. Without the message, Autorun doesn't get to make this decision, so if you want to use the TweakUI method, you'll need to turn on auto insert notification.

As an alternative to TweakUI, you can turn off Autorun in the Device Manager. Highlight your CD-ROM drive, click the Properties button, click the Settings tab, and then clear the Auto Insert Notification check box.

AutoEject

AutoEject, a free utility by Kevin Marty, solves a big problem for users of Jaz, Zip, and CD-ROM drives whose eject mechanisms are under software control. With these drives, you're not really supposed to power down the system with media in the drive. If you forget, on startup Windows 98 may treat a removable drive as a hard drive and assign it a letter. This can make your C drive look like a D drive, and so on, wreaking havoc with programs that expect to find stuff on certain drives.

AutoEject is a good solution to this problem, although it won't work on removable drives with stupid mechanical latches, such as SyQuest drives and floppies. Placed in your StartUp folder, AutoEject will automatically eject any or all removable media when Windows 98 is shut down. You can download AutoEject from http://www.visi.com/~kmarty/software.html.

Sound Cards, CD-ROMs, and LPT Ports

Secret

Windows 98 doesn't flag interrupt conflicts between devices such as sound cards and CD-ROMs and the LPT1 and LPT2 ports. LPT1 and LPT2 use Interrupts 7 and 5 respectively. Many sound cards and CD-ROMs are also set by default to use these very same interrupts. In spite of this conflict, the Device Manager doesn't inform us that it exists.

The Device Manager is silent on this conflict because printers connected to these parallel ports really don't use these interrupts. In some ways the ports are up for grabs.

The problem is that Direct Cable Connection *does* use these interrupts when it is configured to use a parallel cable. DCC is at its fastest when it uses the parallel ports, and it will slow by a factor of three if it finds a sound card or CD-ROM drive using these interrupts. The only way you notice this is by testing the speed of communication across these ports. If you notice a problem, change the resource settings in the Device Manager so that the LPT port is on Interrupt 7 and the sound card or CD-ROM is on Interrupt 5. See "Configuring Serial Ports" in Chapter 31 for more on how to do this.

Detlog.txt, Setuplog.txt, and Ios.log

Undocumented

If you are using any 16-bit drivers, you have three files — the first two are in your root directory and the third is in your Windows 98 folder — that can give you another look at your hardware. Detlog.txt is a record of the hardware-detection process. Setuplog.txt details what files were installed. Ios.log tracks your real-mode drivers.

You can simply read these files with Notepad to get a little added insight into your configuration.

If you inadvertently erase a file that is crucial to the proper running of Windows 98, you can rerun Windows 98 Setup to verify files and install only those that are missing. If you do this, Windows 98 reviews Setuplog.txt during the setup process to see what you originally installed.

Summary

Microsoft has made a concerted effort to bring a new level of standardization to the PC world. By providing an extensive list of 32-bit device drivers and giving manufacturers a new model for creating new ones, it has improved the stability of Windows 98.

▶ Windows 98 deals with both existing and plug and play hardware, providing a way to track it all.

▶ Hardware-detection routines built into Windows 98 do a robust job of matching your hardware to Windows 98 needs.

▶ We show you how to add new hardware drivers to match your devices.

▶ The major benefit of plug and play is the automatic resolution of hardware conflicts. It isn't automatic with non-plug and play hardware, but it is easier.

▶ If you have multiple hardware configurations, you can direct Windows 98 to the current configuration.

▶ You will likely find a conflict between your sound card and CD-ROM driver and your parallel ports.

Chapter 26

Fonts

In This Chapter

We examine how text is displayed on the screen and printed on the printer.
We show:

▶ The differences between screen fonts, printer fonts, TrueType fonts, and
PostScript fonts

▶ How to view, install, and uninstall fonts using the Windows 98 font installer

▶ The essentials of a bitmapped font

▶ The advantages of scaleable fonts such as TrueType

▶ How to set the magnification factor for Windows 98 and what it does to
your fonts

▶ What screen fonts are used for and why

What Are Fonts?

Text is displayed on your screen or printer through the medium of typefaces
or fonts. The characters look different depending on which typeface or font
you use to display the text.

A *font* is a set of character shapes of a given size, weight, style, and design.
For example, Courier 12-point regular or Times New Roman 12-point bold are
different fonts. A *font family* or *typeface* is a family of fonts of a similar design
with different sizes and weights, including italic, bold, condensed, and
expanded versions of the same design. In Windows terminology, *font* is often
used to mean a font file or a typeface. Following the Windows convention,
we use *font* in this book to mean font or typeface, interchangeably.

Most of the fonts available for Windows 98 use the Windows ANSI character
set. Five of the TrueType fonts that come with Windows 98 (Lucida Console,
Lucida Sans Unicode, Symbol, Wingdings, and Webdings) are exceptions. If
you want to use unusual characters, you may need to purchase additional
fonts that include those characters. If you install Multilanguage Support,
your Arial, Courier New, Tahoma, Times New Roman, and Verdana fonts will
use a 652-character set. You can find more details on character sets in
"Windows Character Sets" in Chapter 27.

Using Fonts in an Application

Windows 98 applications have access to a common font dialog box. You can see what the font looks like in the Sample area of the dialog box, as shown in Figure 26-1.

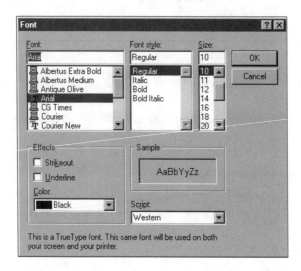

Figure 26-1: The Font dialog box. This dialog box is used by WordPad and can be used by other applications to make it easy to choose a font.

WordPad, a word processing applet that comes with Windows 98, uses the Font dialog box to allow the user to change font style. Choose Format, Font in WordPad to bring it up.

The Script field shown in Figure 26-1 lists the character set used by the font. Western refers to the Windows ANSI character set, DOS/OEM to the IBM PC-8 character set, and Symbol to one of many non-standard character sets. Turkish, Cyrillic, Central European, Greek, Baltic, and so on, refer to other character sets. These designations appear only if you have installed fonts that support these additional characters, which you can do by installing Multilanguage Support. See "Windows Character Sets" in Chapter 27.

You can configure the Fonts folder so that applications do not have access to screen or printer fonts. Turn to the "Freedom from screen fonts and printer fonts" section.

Where Are the Fonts Installed?

To see what fonts you currently have installed, click the Start button on the Taskbar, point to Settings, and then click Control Panel. Click the Fonts folder icon to display the Fonts folder window (shown in Figure 26-2). This folder window displays the extended font names and font file icons of the fonts that come with Windows 98.

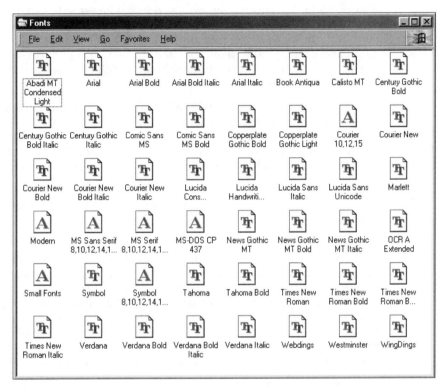

Figure 26-2: The Fonts folder window showing the standard screen (raster) and TrueType fonts that come with Windows 98.

All of the fonts that come with Windows 98 are stored in the \Windows\ Fonts folder. When you view this folder in the Explorer, they are shown with their filenames and font icons in the right pane. The font files stored in the \Windows\Fonts folder are displayed differently than font files that you may have stored in other folders. The Large Icons view of the \Windows\Fonts folder (shown in Figure 26-2) displays the font's long font name. In Details view, the first column shows the long font name, the second the filename, the third the size, and the fourth the date.

It can be a little confusing to see exactly what fonts you have, because there is a separate file for each variation in a font family. For example, the Century Gothic Bold and Century Gothic Italic font files are both part of the Century Gothic font family. To see a display of only the font families (Century Gothic, Times New Roman, and so on), choose View, Hide Variations (Bold, Italic, and so on) while viewing the \Windows\Fonts folder. Note that some variations—Arial Black, for example—will still be visible, because they have been set up by their developers as stand-alone products.

While the font files themselves are in the \Windows\Fonts folder, a listing of all the fonts is stored in the Registry. Under Windows 3.1*x*, this information was stored in the Win.ini file, but when you install Windows 98 over Windows 3.1*x*, the information is moved to the Registry. In fact, if any TrueType font information is later added to the Win.ini file, Windows 98 will move it to the Registry the next time it starts up. PostScript font information, on the other hand, is still installed and kept in the Win.ini file. The old Microsoft TrueType Font Assistant, which looks for font information in the Win.ini file, does not work with Windows 98.

Secret

Not all the font files stored in the \Windows\Fonts folder are displayed in a folder or Explorer window, even if you have set View, Folder Options, View to Show All Files. If you use the Find tool to search for *.fon, you'll see several additional fonts, including 8514sys.fon and Vgasys.fon. Windows 98 defines one of these fonts as the System font, depending on your screen resolution.

Fonts don't have to be physically stored in the \Windows\Fonts folder to be displayed in that folder (and therefore "installed"). You can install fonts stored in other folders by simply placing shortcuts to them in \Windows\Fonts.

For example, you might want to place fonts in your own fonts folder, and place shortcuts to your fonts in the \Windows\Fonts folder. If you have created a folder called \My System (as we suggest in the "Special folders" section of Chapter 8), you can create a subfolder called Fonts and place your additional fonts there. That way, you know what fonts you have installed, and you can protect them from being written over by other applications. Using this method also lets you uninstall your fonts without removing them from your hard disk (see "Uninstalling fonts" later in this chapter).

Secret

If you accidentally move a file that is not a font file into the \Windows\Fonts folder, it will not be displayed in a folder or Explorer window focused on \Windows\Fonts. To check if there are any misplaced files in this folder, use the Tools, Find, Files or Folder command in the Explorer window, or open a DOS window with the DOS prompt at \Windows\Fonts and display the directory using the dir or dir/p command. (It is difficult to inadvertently move a file to the \Windows\Fonts folder, because the Explorer won't allow you to cut and paste or drag and drop a non-font file to this folder.)

Installing Fonts

Windows 3.1*x* stored font files in the \Windows\System folder. This was a terrible place to put them, because it mixed them with the rest of the Windows files. By default, Windows 98 stores fonts in their own folder, \Windows\Fonts.

When an application running under Windows 98 installs a TrueType font, the font is by default copied to the \Windows\Fonts folder. Even though there is only one special \Windows\Fonts folder, you can store font files in any folder on your hard disk.

You can use the Windows 98 font installer to install new fonts (that is, make them visible to Windows applications). The font installer lets you copy the font files you're installing into the \Windows\Fonts folder or leave them where they are and place shortcuts to them in \Windows\Fonts.

To install new fonts, take the following steps:

STEPS

Installing TrueType Fonts

Step 1. Click the Start button, point to Settings, and then click Control Panel. Click the Fonts folder icon in the Control Panel.

Step 2. Choose File, Install New Font in the Fonts folder window to display the Add Fonts dialog box, as shown in Figure 26-3.

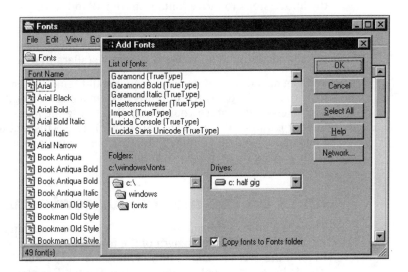

Figure 26-3: The Add Fonts dialog box.

Step 3. The default action is to place a copy of the font file in the \Windows\Fonts folder. The Copy Fonts to Fonts Folder check box is automatically marked every time you display the Add Fonts dialog box. If you copy the font to the \Windows\Fonts folder and it was previously stored in another folder on your hard disk, you might want to delete it from its original location. You probably wouldn't want to do this if it came from a network hard disk or from your original diskettes. Clear the Copy Fonts to Fonts Folder check box if you want to leave the font file where it is (on your hard disk or on a network server's hard disk) and just place a *shortcut* to it in your \Windows\Fonts folder.

(continued)

STEPS *(continued)*

Installing TrueType Fonts

Step 4. Use the Add Fonts dialog box to browse to find the location of the fonts that you want to install. Select the fonts that you will be installing from the list box and click OK.

If you cleared the Copy Fonts to Fonts Folder check box, you will notice that only shortcuts are added to the \Windows\Fonts folder.

TrueType fonts and font packs that worked with Windows 3.1*x* will also work with Windows 98. The font installers that worked with Windows 3.1*x* installed their TrueType fonts in the \Windows\System folder. You can use the above steps to move fonts from the \Windows\System folder to the \Windows\Fonts folder.

Tip

You should install fonts from TrueType font packs using the Windows 98 font installer; ignore the Windows 3.1x font installers that come with these fonts.

You can also drag and drop fonts to install them. Copy a series of fonts from diskettes or CD-ROMs to your \My System\Fonts folder (or another folder you've created to store your fonts). Right-drag the fonts to \Windows\Fonts in your Explorer. Click Create Shortcut(s) Here. This method installs the fonts and makes them immediately visible to applications that use fonts, while leaving them in your own fonts folder.

Limits on the number of fonts installed

There is a limit to the number of TrueType fonts you can install. The total number depends on the length of the font names, but it is about 1,000 fonts — fewer if the average length of the font names is greater than ten characters. This is because all font names are stored in the Registry, and the maximum size of a Registry key is 64K. Fonts that are installed somewhere other than the \Windows\Fonts folder have their full path shown in the Registry, considerably increasing the length of their names.

There is no limit to the number of installed fonts you can use and print at one time.

As you install more fonts, your computer takes longer and longer to boot. Font management becomes a problem, and applications have to access unwieldy Font drop-down lists. If you have a large number of installed fonts, you should consider using more sophisticated font-management tools, such as those we make available as shareware on the *Windows 98 Secrets* CD-ROM. (You should also read the section entitled "Font Cataloging" later in this chapter.)

Where are the missing True Type fonts?

If you upgrade a Windows 3.1*x* computer to Windows 98, you may notice that some of your TrueType fonts are missing from the Fonts folder, and if you install new TrueType fonts, they may not appear in the Fonts folder. (This can happen if you install too many fonts.) To clear the air and reinstall your fonts, take the following steps.

STEPS

Reinstalling TrueType Fonts

Step 1.   Use your Explorer to create a temporary folder, and copy the contents of your Fonts folder to the temporary folder.

Step 2.   Start your Registry editor and navigate to

HKEY_LOCAL_MACHINE\SOFTWARE\Microsoft\Windows\CurrentVersion

Step 3.   You should find a Fonts key in the left pane of the Registry editor. If you do, right-click it and click Delete. Then exit the Registry, and skip to step 5. If you don't find a Fonts key, go to the next step.

Step 4.   Highlight the CurrentVersion key in the left pane of your Registry editor. Right-click the right pane and choose New, Key. Type **Fonts**, and press Enter. Exit the Registry.

Step 5.   Drag the font files for the fonts that you want installed from the temporary font folder to the \Windows\Fonts folder. Make sure you include the bitmapped fonts (the ones with an A in their font icon) or you may not be able to restart Windows 98 in normal mode.

Remember not to install more than 1,000 fonts. If you want to manage a large number of fonts, we suggest that you use a more sophisticated font handler than the one that comes with Windows 98. Check out the tools discussed in "Font Cataloging" later in this chapter.

Uninstalling fonts

If you delete a font file that is stored in the \Windows\Fonts folder, it is both uninstalled (the font is no longer available to Windows 98 applications) and deleted (the font file is moved to the Recycle Bin). If you delete a shortcut in the \Windows\Fonts folder for a font file that is stored in another folder, the font is uninstalled but the font file is not deleted.

To uninstall a font by deleting its font file stored in the \Windows\Fonts folder, click the Start button, point to Settings, and click Control Panel. Click the Fonts folder icon, right-click the font you want to uninstall, and select Delete from the context menu. If you have another copy of the font file stored in another folder, you can later reinstall it using the Installing TrueType Fonts steps in the "Installing Fonts" section earlier in the chapter.

To uninstall a font by deleting its shortcut in the \Windows\Fonts folder, highlight the font's shortcut and press Delete. Answer yes to the message asking if you want to uninstall the font. The original font file is not deleted, but the font is no longer available to be used by Windows 98 applications and is not displayed in the \Windows\Fonts folder.

Viewing fonts

You can see a sample "printout" of a font by double-clicking its icon in any folder window or in the \Windows\Fonts folder. Figure 26-4 shows what Arial Bold looks like.

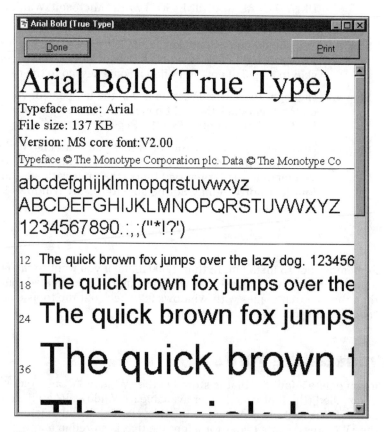

Figure 26-4: Sample "printout" of the Arial Bold TrueType font. Double-click a font icon in a folder window to see what the font looks like at various point sizes.

Undocumented

A font's icon appears in the \Windows\Fonts folder if it is installed. If a font is not installed, you can still view it by opening the folder window where the font is stored and double-clicking its icon. You can produce the same "printout" by double-clicking a font file wherever it is stored.

Most text editing and word processing applications only list TrueType or printer fonts in their font lists. To keep these font lists manageable, you should install only the fonts that you use. You can use Windows 98's built-in font viewing capability to decide whether you want to install a particular font.

Tip

Numerous more sophisticated font viewers and font managers are available from other vendors. The *Windows 98 Secrets* CD-ROM features font utilities that provide additional capabilities for displaying and printing your fonts.

Extended font properties

Windows 98 comes with an expanded Properties dialog box for fonts. To open a font's Properties dialog box, open the Control Panel, click the Fonts icon, right-click a font file, and click Properties in the context menu. There are now a total of nine tabs, instead of the two provided in Windows 95. You can't really change any font properties here; rather, this dialog box gives the font designer or publisher a place to attach information about the font and how you can use it.

The Embedding tab, for example, tells you what kind of embedding, if any, is allowed for the font (see "Send your favorite typeface" later in this chapter for more on embedding). It explains the four levels of embedding and indicates which one applies to this particular font. The Description tab (see Figure 26-5) may give you a little background on the font. For example, it might tell you about the font's special qualities and uses, and provide information about the font designer.

The CharSet/Unicode tab lists all of the Unicode ranges and character sets (code pages) this font supports (see "Windows Character Sets" in Chapter 27 for a discussion of Unicode). If you have installed Multilanguage Support, this is a good place to see what non-Western alphabets may be available in this font. The Statistics tab tells you how many glyphs (unique characters) and kerned pairs are in this font, and what version you are using. The Hinting/Font Smoothing tab shows you at what size characters will be hinted or smoothed (see "Smooth fonts" later in this chapter). Hinting has to do with how much of a character's detail is visible at very small point sizes.

One intriguing tab is Links, where you may find URLs for the font designer and vendor. If you're interested in typography, this can be a great resource for learning more and for finding new fonts. There is also a Names tab to show you the pertinent copyrights and trademarks, and of course the standard General tab to show you the type and location of the font file. The OpenType Layout Tables tab may not contain any data yet, because OpenType is still under development. In the future, however, this tab should let you to determine how an OpenType font is rasterized (see the "OpenType" section later in this chapter).

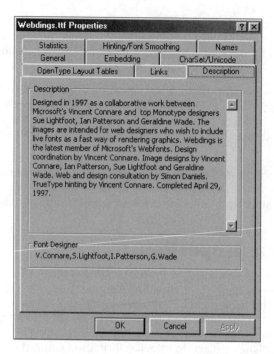

Figure 26-5: The Description tab of the Properties dialog box for the new Webdings font includes information on who designed the font and how it is intended to be used.

You may be surprised to find that even fonts you've had on your computer for a while have data in their Properties dialog boxes. Some fonts will have considerably more than others, however. As your font software is updated, this dialog box should become a rich source of information for learning about your fonts.

The Kinds and Types of Fonts

You can slice and dice the fonts available for Windows into a number of different categories. One cut gives you the bitmapped fonts versus the scaleable fonts. Another gives you screen fonts, printer fonts, and scaleable fonts that work with both the screen and the printer. There are fixed-pitch and proportional fonts. And then there are the DOS fonts. As you shall see, these categories overlap.

Bitmapped fonts

Bitmapped (or *raster*) fonts are fixed-size fonts. The typeface is stored in a *fon* file on your hard disk. Each character is a pattern of a fixed number of dots. Your screen fonts are bitmapped fonts. An example of a bitmapped screen font is MS Sans Serif.

Secret

The MS Sans Serif 10-point font stored in the file Sserife.fon is constructed on a grid that is 16 dots high. The grid varies in width up to 14 dots (with an average of 7), depending on the width of each proportionally spaced character. In Figure 26-6, the lower case letters a, b, c, and d are shown on their dot grids.

Figure 26-6: The lowercase letters a, b, c, and d in MS Sans Serif 10 point. Screen fonts are created on a grid of dots.

Scaleable fonts

Secret

First, a word on terminology. Bitmapped fonts can be enlarged to display larger point sizes by replacing each dot in a font with two, three, or more dots. This results in rather ugly jagged fonts. You might think of this as a crude form of scaling, but this is not what is meant by scaling in the context of Windows 98 scaleable fonts.

Scaleable fonts are stored in files on your hard disk (or in your printer's ROM) as descriptions of each character. This description includes an outline of the font as well as *rules* (known as *hints*) used to display the font. When scaleable fonts are displayed on the screen (or printed on paper) they are rendered by a font-rendering algorithm that takes this description and turns it into dots. In other words, they are *rasterized*. Your TrueType fonts are scaleable fonts. An example of a scaleable font is Times New Roman, a TrueType font created by Monotype, licensed by Microsoft, and included with Windows 98.

Scaleable fonts have a number of advantages over bitmapped fonts:

- Scaleable fonts can be displayed over a wider range of point sizes and magnifications and still look good. Keeping enough fixed-sized bitmapped fonts (in different sizes) to cover such a wide range would require significantly more hard disk space. Enlarging bitmapped fonts on the fly to display larger font sizes produces jagged fonts, and Windows can't shrink bitmapped fonts to display sizes smaller than the smallest size font stored in a font file.

- Scaleable fonts can be used for both your screen and printer. You don't need one set of bitmapped screen fonts (in a limited number of sizes) and another set of bitmapped printer fonts in the same sizes. The rasterizer takes advantage of the highest resolution available on your printer.

- A scaleable font description method provides a standard that font foundries can use for every printer and font size. This considerably reduces the work required to create a font. At the same time, it vastly expands the market because one font can be used on all printers with Windows printer drivers. Fonts become much less expensive. Printer manufacturers can concentrate on producing printers (and printer drivers for Windows) and not on creating fonts (which they aren't very good at anyway).

- The likelihood that a font will look the same when it prints as it does on your screen greatly increases with scaleable fonts. Both the printer rasterizer and the screen font rasterizer are reading from the same book (using the same font description).

Bitmapped fonts have one advantage over scaleable fonts. Each font is created by hand to look its best on a video monitor (or a particular printer) at a certain resolution (dots per inch, or dpi). A team of human beings has taken the time necessary to make each sized font the best it can be. Compare the examples of TrueType and screen fonts shown later in this chapter.

Tip

If you want to check out the difference in rendering speed between bitmapped and scaleable fonts, launch the Character Map applet by clicking Start, Accessories, System Tools, Character Map. Go through each character set, one at a time, and look at bitmapped fonts and TrueType fonts. The first time you view a character set that uses a TrueType font, your computer will take a second to render the characters. In contrast, it can render character sets that use bitmapped screen fonts such as MS Sans Serif instantly. After you view character sets the first time, you won't be able to detect a difference in the time it takes to render characters using a TrueType font versus a screen font.

A crude form of scaleable fonts included with earlier versions of Windows was known as *vector* fonts. The font descriptions for vector fonts are stored as sets of coordinates that make up the letters as stick figures. The only vector font included with Windows 98 is Modern.fon. It has the same *fon* extension as the bitmapped fonts, which makes it difficult to differentiate. Modern.fon is installed by default, but it is only used if you install a plotter.

Screen fonts

Screen fonts are bitmapped fonts used (for the most part) to display icon titles, dialog box text, help files, file and folder names in the Explorer, and so on. Applications assume you won't use these fonts to create text documents. In fact, you can't see them in the font lists in Microsoft Word for Windows.

Unless a printer manufacturer has created matching printer fonts, screen fonts won't print, even if you have created a document using these fonts.

Instead, the printer driver substitutes printer fonts of the same or similar size, and prints your text using those fonts.

When you first install Windows 98, titles in the title bars of folder windows, titles under the icons on the Desktop, menu items, application and document names on Taskbar buttons, file and folder names in the Explorer and folder windows, and text in dialog boxes use either the screen font MS Sans Serif 8 point or MS Sans Serif 10 point, depending on your screen resolution. You can use TrueType fonts or other screen fonts instead, if you like. See "Changing the Size, Color, and Font of Objects on the Desktop" in Chapter 28 to learn which fonts you can use for these screen text entities.

Printer fonts

Printer fonts can be either bitmapped or scaleable fonts. They can be stored in your printer's ROM, in cartridges plugged into your printer, or downloaded from your computer's hard disk to your printer's RAM.

Microsoft does not supply printer fonts with Windows 98, and hasn't done so since Windows 3.0. Printer manufacturers supply these fonts. Many laser printer manufacturers provide built-in (ROM) PostScript or PostScript-compatible fonts. Hewlett-Packard provides built-in scaleable TrueType-compatible fonts in its LaserJet 4, 5, and 6 series. The HP 4L fonts are shown in Figure 26-7.

Albertus Medium	AaBbCcRrXxYyZy
Albertus Extrabold	AaBbCcRrXxYyZz
Antique Olive	AaBbCcRrXxYyZz
CG Times	AaBbCcRrXxYyZz
Coronet	AaBbCcRrXxYyZz
Letter Gothic	AaBbCcRrXxYyZz
Univers	AaBbCcRrXxYyZz
Univers Condensed	AaBbCcRrXxYyZz

Figure 26-7: These printer fonts are stored in ROM in the HP LaserJet 4L printer. You can print with these fonts, and optionally purchase compatible TrueType fonts for display on the screen.

Printer manufacturers may also provide screen fonts that work with their printer fonts. If the printer fonts are bitmapped fonts, most likely the screen fonts are as well.

Undocumented

The printer fonts stored in your printer's ROM don't show up on your hard disk, but they do show up in the font lists in your word processor or text editor. The printer driver passes along the information about the printer fonts to your word processor so you can create a document using these fonts. Unless you have installed the corresponding screen fonts, the text you format with a printer font is displayed on your screen in a screen font of the same size.

Scaleable fonts that work with both the printer and the screen

Adobe introduced the first successful scaleable font technology for personal computers when it brought out PostScript. Later, Microsoft integrated its own TrueType technology into Windows 3.1. (This was a major reason to upgrade from Windows 3.0.)

Microsoft (and Apple) went into competition with Adobe by providing TrueType technology as a no-charge addition to the operating system. It's hard to compete when your competitor gives away its product (or bundles it with something that you are going to have to purchase anyway). Adobe continues to be successful partly because most imagesetting service bureaus are more familiar with PostScript Type 1 fonts than with TrueType fonts.

When PostScript became available, type designers could create computer-based type to one specification and sell it to anyone who used a PostScript device. With the advent of TrueType, a second specification allowed type designers to create fonts in a different popular format. Adobe and Microsoft have now joined together to develop the OpenType format, an extension of TrueType that also supports PostScript (see the "OpenType" section later in this chapter). In essence, OpenType represents the convergence of the TrueType and PostScript formats.

Proportional and fixed-pitch fonts

Almost all the fonts used with Windows are *proportional* fonts; that is, each character has a width that varies with the character's shape. This means that the letter *l* takes up less space than the letter *m* because the width of an *m* is greater than the width of an *l*.

Every character in a *fixed-pitch* font has the same width. Lucida Console, Courier New, Fixedsys, and Terminal are fixed-pitch screen fonts. Lucida Console and Courier New are fixed-pitch TrueType fonts. HyperTerminal uses fixed-pitch fonts to display text coming from computer bulletin boards. DOS applications often use fixed-pitch fonts. You may also want to use fixed-pitch fonts in some of your correspondence. (This will make the person you're corresponding with think that you are using a typewriter!) Check later in this chapter for graphical examples of fixed-pitch and proportional fonts.

DOS fonts

DOS fonts are fixed-pitch fonts used in windowed DOS sessions. The DOS fonts in Windows 98 are stored in four files, Vgaoem.fon (or 8514oem.fon), Dosapp.fon, Courier.ttf, and Lucon.ttf. The default DOS TrueType font is Lucida Console. Vgaoem.fon and 8514oem.fon are hidden files, so you won't see them in the Fonts folder.

Because DOS fonts are also screen fonts, we cover them in more detail later in this chapter.

Font Sizes

Secret

The term *font size* is used in Windows dialog boxes to refer to four quite different ideas. The first use refers to the height of characters when printed on paper. The second is the magnification factor Windows 98 uses to display characters (and other items) on the screen, measured in pixels per "logical" inch. The third refers to the "small" and "large" sets of screen fonts. The fourth is the size in pixels of the fonts used in windowed DOS sessions.

Font sizes, using the first definition, are denoted in *points*, an old printers' term. There are 72 points per inch. As an example, the screen font file Coure.fon contains three fonts: one each of 10, 12, and 15 points. Font height in points is measured from the top of the lower case *f* (the *ascender*) to the bottom of the lower case *g* (the *descender*) plus any invisible space (called a *shoulder*) that the font designer has added to the top or bottom of the letters.

When text is printed on paper, its size is fixed. For example, 24-point text is one-third of an inch high (24 divided by 72 equals ⅓). On paper, an inch is an inch, and, in the United States at least, letter-sized paper is 8½ by 11 inches.

Unlike paper, computer monitors and their associated graphics adapters come in four major nominal sizes and five major screen resolutions. You, the user, can change the size of the display area (the Desktop) just by turning some knobs on the monitor.

Computer screens are usually farther away from our eyes than the distance that we comfortably hold a book or a sheet of paper. To be perceived as being the same size, text on a computer needs to be bigger than its corresponding print on the paper. The "apparent" height of an image decreases as you move back from it.

So, 24-point text on your screen is most likely magnified to display larger than one-third of an inch high.

The logical inch

Undocumented

Enter the logical inch. Twenty-four point text displayed on your Windows Desktop is one-third of a logical inch high, although it will be printed exactly one-third of an inch high on your printer. Text is usually displayed larger than it will be printed, so the logical inch on your monitor is most likely larger than the printed inch.

The logical inch is a magnifier. The size of the logical inch divided by one inch gives the value of the magnification. The actual size of the logical inch depends on the size of your monitor, the resolution of your graphics card, how large you have adjusted your image size, and the value you have chosen for the magnification factor internal to Windows 98. (As you may recall, this is the second meaning of the term *font size*.) The magnification factors available to you are Small Fonts, Large Fonts, and Other. You change the magnification factor by clicking the Advanced button in the Settings tab of the Display Properties dialog box. More details are available in "Setting Windows magnification" in Chapter 28.

So how big is a logical inch? On a 14-inch SVGA monitor, the actual diagonal size of the image of the Windows 98 Desktop on the screen is approximately 13 inches.

Most monitors used with PCs that run Windows are constructed to have greater width than height. They use the ratio of 4 (width) to 3 (height). The height of the Desktop image on our 14-inch monitor is 7⅛ inches, and its width is 10⅜ inches.

The screen resolution on this computer is set to Super VGA, or 800 × 600 pixels (notice the 4-to-3 ratio of width to height). Therefore, our dots per inch (dpi) resolution is approximately 76 pixels per inch.

So, do we know how big a logical inch is yet?

We can set the magnification factor to Small Fonts (96 pixels per logical inch), Large Fonts (120 pixels per logical inch), or Other (allows you to set a custom value). Given these values and our screen resolution of 76 pixels per inch, we can calculate the size of the logical inch.

Secret

For the small font magnification, the size of the logical inch is 96 pixels divided by 76 pixels, or about 1¼ inches. For large font magnification, it is about 1⅝ inches.

We have calculated the size of the logical inch, but to test our calculation, we need to closely examine the characters on our screen to confirm that they display at the correct size.

Windows screen fonts are designed on grids of dots. The screen fonts come in two sets. The large screen font set was designed to be used with a high-resolution display (1024 × 768). The fonts are built on a grid of dots assuming 120 dots per logical inch. The small screen font set was designed for VGA resolution (640 × 480). The fonts assume a grid of 96 dots per logical inch. The small screen font set should not be confused with the font typeface Small Fonts, which is provided in both sets.

Windows 98 uses small screen fonts when the magnification factor is set to Small Fonts (96 pixels per logical inch). Not surprisingly, it uses large screen fonts when the magnification factor is set to Large Fonts (120 pixels per logical inch). You can, of course, also display TrueType fonts (which don't come in sets). TrueType fonts are magnified by the same amount as screen fonts.

Figure 26-8 shows the letters *T, f,* and *g* as designed for the MS Sans Serif 24-point screen font from the small screen font set. Figure 26-9 shows the same letters from the large screen font set.

The height of 24-point type using a font from the large screen font set is 40 dots (for MS Sans Serif — 46 dots minus the 6 dots of internal leading). We are assured by Figure 26-9 that the font designers have correctly named and designed this font because 24 points is one-third of a logical inch and 40 dots is one-third of 120 dots.

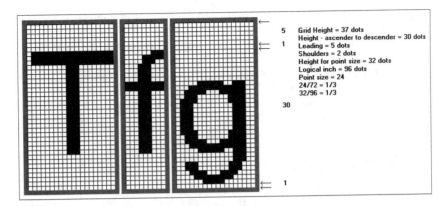

Figure 26-8: Small fonts: MS Sans Serif font at 24 points. You can count the number of dots used to create this font.

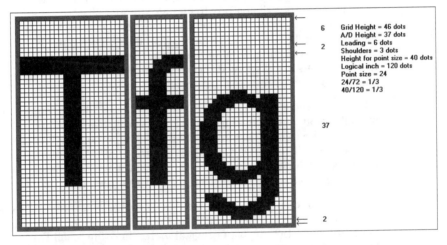

Figure 26-9: Large fonts: MS Sans Serif font at 24 points. More dots were used to create this larger font.

Tip

If each dot on the font design grid corresponds to one pixel on the screen, text displayed in a 24-point font will be 40 pixels high. You can confirm this one-dot-to-one-pixel relationship by using a magnifier utility (we have included Extreme CloseUp and Lens 2.0 on the *Windows 98 Secrets* CD-ROM) that lets you see and count the pixels of displayed text and compare them with the design grid. Our calculation of the size of the logical inch is confirmed.

Undocumented

Text shown on the display when the magnification factor is set to Large Fonts is about 60 percent bigger on the screen than it is when printed. It is about 25 percent bigger when you're using the Small Fonts magnification factor. Again, because you are normally farther away from a screen than you are from a piece of paper, characters may appear to your eyes to be the same size with both.

The logical inch is not restricted to fonts; it is used throughout the internals of Windows. For example, if you were to use the Image, Attributes command in MS Paint to set the size of an image to one inch, you would notice that the displayed square is 96 pixels by 96 pixels if you choose Small Fonts mode. It's 120 pixels by 120 pixels if you choose Large Fonts mode, and 144 pixels by 144 pixels if you choose Other at 150 percent magnification. There is more discussion of this issue in "Changing the System font size" in Chapter 28.

The magnifier

Windows 3.1*x* had only two magnification levels—Small Fonts and Large Fonts. You could change the size of the characters displayed on your screen by using the setup icon to switch between these two font sizes or between different screen resolutions.

In Windows 98, you can use the Advanced button in the Settings tab of the Display Properties dialog box to change the font size to Small Fonts, Large Fonts, or Other. The Other option allows you to specify a custom magnification factor (in pixels per logical inch). The term *font size* in this context refers to the magnifier used to increase (or decrease) the size that the characters are displayed on the screen, while not changing the size at which characters are actually printed.

Microsoft arbitrarily (but neatly) set the value of 100 percent for the magnification factor equal to Small Fonts (or 96 pixels per logical inch). That is, setting the Other (custom) font size to 100 percent is the same thing as choosing Small Fonts. Our example monitor at SVGA resolution displays 76 pixels per inch. On this monitor, 100 percent magnification displays characters that are 25 percent bigger on the screen than on paper.

Magnification of 125 percent corresponds to 120 pixels per logical inch (Large Fonts), 150 percent equals 144 pixels per logical inch, and 200 percent equals 192 pixels per logical inch. Choosing Small Fonts, Large Fonts, or Other just tells Windows how much to magnify the size of the text displayed on the Desktop.

Can you comfortably read the text?

"Man is the measure of all things"—*Protagoras*

You should care about how big the text is displayed on the screen so you can read it in comfort. The size of text you can comfortably read is also often a function of the size of your monitor. The larger the screen size, the more text-size modes you can comfortably use.

Lots of different kinds of text are displayed on your Desktop. These include icon titles, file and folder names in the Explorer, text in menus, text in dialog boxes, and text in WordPad documents. You can change the size, weight, style, and family of fonts used to display all of these text entities. (See "Changing the Size, Color, and Font of Objects on the Desktop" in Chapter 28.)

If you are comfortable reading text on a piece of paper that is 18 inches away from your eyes (a pretty normal distance), then you will be comfortable reading text of the same point size on the computer screen at 2 feet, if it has been magnified by 33 percent. If you are using Small Fonts (which magnifies text by 25 percent), then you will want to be a little closer than 2 feet from your computer monitor (22 to 23 inches).

Can you see enough text?

Tip

The SVGA monitor to which we previously referred displays about 6 vertical inches of text in WordPad if the WordPad toolbar, format bar, ruler, and status bar are turned on and WordPad is at its maximum window size. If your font size is set to Small Fonts, then 25 lines of text in Courier New 12 point are visible on the screen. This is a little less than half a page's worth of text. If your font size is set to Large Fonts, then only 19 lines of text, or a third of a page of printed text, displays.

The size of the font used to display text on the Desktop increases when we use the Advanced button in Settings tab of the Display Properties dialog box to change from Small Fonts to Large Fonts, or go to larger sizes with the Other option. Therefore, we see less text displayed. After all, the Windows 98 Desktop stays the same size. Microsoft Word for Windows has a zoom feature that is equivalent to changing the font size or using custom font sizes. However, it changes only the displayed size of the fonts in the Word for Windows client area and not the size of the fonts used in dialog boxes, and so on. Word users often use this feature to shrink the font size enough that the full width of a line of text is visible on screen.

Screen Fonts in Detail

Microsoft supplies the screen fonts used in Windows, although other manufacturers can, if they wish, supply screen fonts as well—perhaps ones that match their printer fonts.

Secret

Screen fonts are bitmapped fonts. The screen fonts are stored in screen font files that end in the extension *fon*. These files may contain fonts of one or more font sizes. Windows creates, on the fly, the bold, italic and bold italic versions of screen fonts from the regular bitmapped version, which is the only version that is stored in the bitmapped screen font file.

Table 26-1 lists the screen font files that Microsoft ships with Windows 98. Not all of the screen font files are visible in your Fonts folder. If you are using the Small screen fonts, you will not see the files for the Large screen fonts in the Fonts folder, and vice versa. In addition, all of the Fixedsys, Terminal, and System fonts are hidden. You can use the Find tool to see them.

Table 26-1   Windows 98 Screen Fonts by Font Set

Font Filename	Somewhat Esoteric Embedded Typeface Name
Large screen fonts	
8514fix.fon	Fixedsys for the IBM 8514
8514oem.fon	Terminal Font for the IBM 8514
8514sys.fon	System (Set #6)
Courf.fon	Courier 10, 12, 15 (8514/a resolution)
Seriff.fon	MS Serif 8, 10, 12, 14, 18, 24 (8514 resolution)
Smallf.fon	Small Fonts (8514/a resolution)
Sseriff.fon	MS Sans Serif 8, 10, 12, 14, 18, 24 (8514 resolution)
Symbolf.fon	Symbol (8514 resolution)
Small screen fonts	
Vgafix.fon	Fixedsys (Set #6)
Vgaoem.fon	Terminal (US) (Set #6)
Vgasys.fon	System (Set #6)
Coure.fon	Courier 10, 12, 15 (VGA resolution)
Serife.fon	MS Serif 8, 10, 12, 14, 18, 24 (VGA resolution)
Smalle.fon	Small Fonts (VGA resolution)
Sserife.fon	MS Sans Serif 8, 10, 12, 14, 18, 24 (VGA resolution)
Symbole.fon	Symbol (VGA resolution)
DOS fonts	
Dosapp.fon	MS-DOS CP 437

Table 26-2 lists screen fonts by typeface.

Table 26-2   Screen Fonts by Typeface

Typeface	Font Filename	Character Set
Fixed-pitch fonts		
Fixedsys	8514fix.fon	Windows 3.0 ANSI
	Vgafix.fon	Windows 3.0 ANSI
Terminal	8514oem.fon	DOS/OEM
	Vgaoem.fon	DOS/OEM
	Dosapp.fon	DOS/OEM

Typeface	Font Filename	Character Set
Fixed-pitch fonts		
Courier	Coure.fon	Windows 3.0 ANSI
	Courf.fon	Windows 3.0 ANSI
Proportional fonts		
System	8514sys.fon	All Windows 3.0 ANSI
	Vgasys.fon	
Sans Serif	Sserife.fon	
	Sseriff.fon	
Serif	Serife.fon	
	Seriff.fon	
Small Fonts	Smalle.fon	
	Smallf.fon	
Symbol	Symbole.fon	Symbol
	Symbolf.fon	Symbol

Undocumented

Windows 98 stores the references to the screen fonts (other than the DOS fonts) in the Registry files System.dat and User.dat. This is what the Registry entries look like:

```
[HKEY_LOCAL_MACHINE\SOFTWARE\Microsoft\Windows\CurrentVersion\
     fontsize]
[HKEY_LOCAL_MACHINE\SOFTWARE\Microsoft\Windows\CurrentVersion\
     fontsize\96]
"Description"="Small Fonts"
[HKEY_LOCAL_MACHINE\SOFTWARE\Microsoft\Windows\CurrentVersion\
     fontsize\96\System]
"vgasys.fon"="fonts.fon"
"vgafix.fon"="fixedfon.fon"
"vgaoem.fon"="oemfonts.fon"
[HKEY_LOCAL_MACHINE\SOFTWARE\Microsoft\Windows\CurrentVersion\
     fontsize\96\User]
"serife.fon"="MS Serif 8,10,12,14,18,24 (VGA res)"
"sserife.fon"="MS Sans Serif 8,10,12,14,18,24 (VGA res)"
"coure.fon"="Courier 10,12,15 (VGA res)"
"symbole.fon"="Symbol 8,10,12,14,18,24 (VGA res)"
"smalle.fon"="Small Fonts (VGA res)"
[HKEY_LOCAL_MACHINE\SOFTWARE\Microsoft\Windows\CurrentVersion\
     fontsize\120]
"Description"="Large Fonts"
[HKEY_LOCAL_MACHINE\SOFTWARE\Microsoft\Windows\CurrentVersion\
     fontsize\120\System]
"8514sys.fon"="fonts.fon"
"8514fix.fon"="fixedfon.fon"
"8514oem.fon"="oemfonts.fon"
```

```
[HKEY_LOCAL_MACHINE\SOFTWARE\Microsoft\Windows\CurrentVersion\
     fontsize\120\User]
"seriff.fon"="MS Serif 8,10,12,14,18,24 (8514/a res)"
"sseriff.fon"="MS Sans Serif 8,10,12,14,18,24 (8514/a res)"
"courf.fon"="Courier 10,12,15 (8514/a res)"
"symbolf.fon"="Symbol 8,10,12,14,18,24 (8514/a res)"
"smallf.fon"="Small Fonts (8514/a res)"
```

All the screen fonts whose font filenames begin with 8514 or whose names before the *fon* extension end in an *f,* such as Sseriff.fon, are Large Fonts (designed on a dot grid of 120 dots per logical inch). The font files that begin with VGA or whose names end in an *e,* as in Sserfe.fon are the Small Fonts (96 dots per logical inch).

If you are using a different language and a different code page, different font files are installed when you first install Windows 98, so your Registry listings will be different from those shown above. For example, if you are using the Greek code page (known as Code Page 1253), you will see the files serf1253.fon, ssef153.fon, couf1253.fon, and smaf1253.fon in the Registry branch HKEY_LOCAL_MACHINE\SOFTWARE\Microsoft\Windows\CurrentVersion\fontsize\120\User. Because the Symbol font is a non-text font, it does not use a code page.

Font point sizes

Point size is a convenient and consistent method of referring to font size across all kinds of fonts. For example, a 9-point font is $\frac{9}{72}$ of a (logical) inch high. The (small font set) font file Vgafix.fon contains one font of size 9 points. It was created on a grid that is 8 dots wide and 15 dots high. The top 3 dots are line spacing (or internal leading) and are not used to draw the character. The characters are therefore 12 dots high (from the top of the ascender to the bottom of the descender with no shoulder).

A small screen font that's 12 dots high is a 9-point font because 12 dots times the ratio of 72 points per logical inch divided by 96 dots per logical inch equals 9 points: $12(\frac{72}{96}) = 9$. The arithmetic doesn't always produce integers. For example, the MS Serif font file Serife.fon has a 10-point font that is 13 dots high, so it's actually a 9.75-point font.

Fixed-pitch screen fonts

There are three fixed-pitch screen fonts. Each is designed for a different application or purpose. Two are used in communicating with the world of fixed-pitch font computers and operating systems (Fixedsys fonts and Terminal fonts), and one is used to mimic a typewriter (Courier fonts). These fonts let us reach back into the past.

Tip

Figures 26-11, 26-13 and 26-15 show the lower-case *r* for each of the fixed-pitch fonts. You can use these figures (in conjunction with Extreme CloseUp) to identify which font is being used in Windows 98 to display a given text entity. Start Extreme CloseUp and use it to look at an *r* in the icon titles on your Desktop. For an example, refer to Figure 26-10. Compare what Extreme CloseUp shows you with what you see in the figures for each screen and TrueType font to determine which font is in use on your display for that text entity.

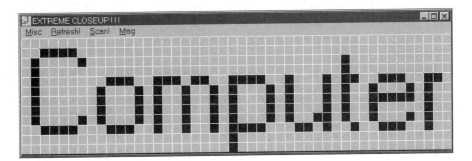

Figure 26-10: Extreme CloseUp view of part of the My Computer icon title in 16x magnification with the grid on. Each grid point represents either a pixel (or dot) on the grid used to create the screen font, or a pixel that is the result of the rasterization of the TrueType font.

Fixedsys fonts

The Fixedsys fonts are fixed-pitch fonts used by Notepad to display ASCII (and Windows ANSI) characters. You can also use them in HyperTerminal to display text coming from the host computer. This font is basically a holdover from the days when Windows 2.*x* and previous versions of Windows used it as the system font to display the text in menus and dialog boxes.

The font file Vgafix.fon contains a 9-point font, and 8514fix.fon contains an 11-point font. The 11-point large Fixedsys font was designed on a grid 10 dots wide and 20 dots high. The height from the ascender to the descender is 16 dots, and the shoulder is 2 dots above the ascender. The point size calculation is as follows: (16+2) times 72 divided by 120 dots per logical inch, which results in 10.8, or 11 points. See Figure 26-11 for a comparison of weights. Throughout this chapter, we use the *r* character to show differences between various fonts.

Terminal fonts

The terminal fonts use the OEM, or the original IBM PC-8 (bit), character set. This is the standard character set used by DOS programs. For more information about character sets, see "The DOS/OEM character set" in Chapter 27.

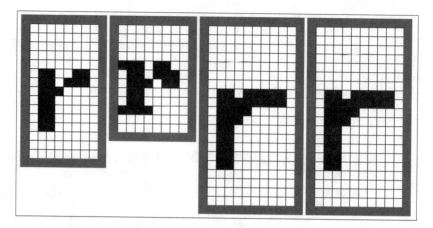

Figure 26-11: Lowercase *r* from Vgafix.fon, Vgaoem.fon, 8514fix.fon, and 8514oem.fon font files, from left to right respectively.

Like Vgafix.fon, the screen font file Vgaoem.fon contains a 9-point font, and 8514oem.fon contains an 11-point font.

These fonts are used by the Clipboard to display DOS text. To open the Clipboard Viewer, click the Start button, Programs, Accessories, System Tools, Clipboard Viewer. If you don't find the Clipboard Viewer here, follow these steps to install it:

STEPS

Installing the Clipboard Viewer

Step 1. Open the Control Panel, click the Add/Remove Programs icon, and go to the Windows Setup tab.

Step 2. Double-click System Tools.

Step 3. Mark the Clipboard Viewer check box.

Step 4. Click OK, and click OK again.

You can copy text from a Windows application into the Clipboard, use the Clipboard Viewer to switch the text to the OEM font (choose Display, OEM Text, as shown in Figure 26-12), and then paste the text into a DOS application. Most of the time, there is no point in switching to the OEM font because the actual characters you are copying back and forth are the same in the Windows application as in the DOS application. Characters with an ASCII number greater than 127, however, differ between Windows and DOS applications. See the character set discussion in "Windows Character Sets" in Chapter 27 for a comparison of the Windows ANSI and the DOS/OEM character sets.

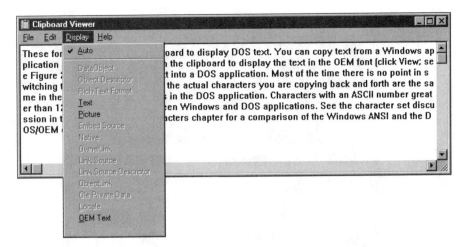

Figure 26-12: You can change from the Windows ANSI to the OEM character set in the Clipboard by using the Display menu in the Clipboard Viewer.

Secret

The Vgaoem.fon file provides one of the DOS fonts, 8 × 12 (which is also found in the Dosapp.fon file) and the 8514oem.fon file provides another DOS font, 10 × 20.

Windows will not boot unless these files are stored in the \Windows\Fonts folder on your computer, and you can't delete them from the Fonts folder.

DOS fonts

The DOS fonts share the typeface name Terminal with the OEM fonts. These fonts are used only in DOS Window sessions. Your DOS window uses eight bitmapped screen fonts from the Dosapp.fon file. The DOS window can also use the TrueType fixed font, as shown by the letter *r* in Figure 26-13.

One line in the System.ini file determines which DOS screen fonts are used by windowed DOS applications. Find the line woafont=dosapp.fon in the [386enh] section.

Secret

The Dosapp.fon file contains eight fonts. They were designed using a grid of 96 dots per logical inch. The DOS fonts don't have separate sets of large and small fonts. They are the same (pixel) size irrespective of what magnification factor, or font size, you set. The windowed DOS session will be the same physical height on your Desktop regardless of which font size you choose in the dialog box that appears when you click the Advanced button in the Settings tab of the Display Properties dialog box.

The DOS font size drop-down list on the toolbar of a windowed DOS session (or on the Font tab of the MS-DOS Prompt Properties dialog box, as shown in Figure 26-14) gives the size of the pixel grid that was used to create each of the DOS screen fonts — first their width and then their height. Dosapp.fon contains the screen fonts created on grids of sizes 4 × 6, 5 × 12, 6 × 8, 8 × 8, 8 × 12, 7 × 12, 10 × 18, and 12 × 16 dots. The additional DOS screen font, 10 × 20, is in the 8514oem.font file.

Figure 26-13: DOS fonts 4 × 6, 5 × 12, 6 × 8, 7 × 12, 8 × 8, 8 × 12, 10 × 18, and 12 × 16.

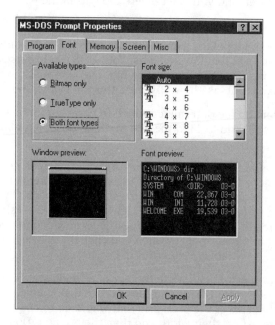

Figure 26-14: The Font tab of the MS-DOS Prompt Properties dialog box.

A DOS window can also use a set of fixed-pitch fonts created from the TrueType fonts Lucida Console and Courier New. These fonts are included in the DOS window font drop-down list when you mark the Both Font Types option button in the Font tab of the MS-DOS Prompt Properties dialog box.

A DOS window using the 8×12 font is 300 pixels high (12 pixels × 25 lines), not including the DOS window title bar and toolbar height. On a 14-inch monitor at SVGA resolution, this DOS window is about 4 inches high, or over half of the screen height (600 pixels). This same DOS window on a monitor with 1280×1024 resolution is less than 30 percent of the height of the screen.

On a 15-inch inch monitor with a resolution of 1024×768, DOS text using the 7×12 DOS screen font is smaller (78 percent of the height) than the same DOS text on the same monitor at SVGA (600×800) resolution (0.131 inches versus 0.168 inches). A large number of DOS text font sizes are required to make sure that everyone can comfortably read text in windowed DOS sessions, given the wide variety of display resolutions and monitor sizes.

Courier fonts

The Courier screen font comes in 10, 12, and 15 points, in both the small and large screen sizes. These Courier font sizes are a subtle joke. Courier is a fixed-pitch font, so you might be tempted to think that these point sizes refer to *pitch*, as in characters per inch. Fifteen characters per inch, a standard size in old-fashioned line printers, requires a small font, while 15-point Courier is bigger than 12-point Courier.

The Windows font developers are having a little fun at our expense. They remember that these three sizes, 10, 12, and 15 pitch, were standards. They encourage us to think in this wrong headed-fashion (by providing Courier in these three sizes, and not, say, 10, 12, and 14 points). Furthermore, in this case the term *fixed pitch* refers to the *width* of the characters, not their height.

The small fonts stored in Coure.fon were created on grids of 8×13, 9×16, and 12×20 dots for the 10-, 12-, and 15-point fonts respectively. For a comparison, see Figure 26-15. The large fonts in Courf.fon were created on grids of 9×16, 12×20, and 15×25 dots. Courier uses the Windows ANSI character set.

You can use Courier to display fixed-pitch text in HyperTerminal (although you may want to use a font that uses the DOS/OEM character set) or in your personal letters. Almost all printers have a corresponding Courier print font—at least 10 and 12 point.

Just because screen fonts are created and stored on a fixed-size grid doesn't mean that you can't display them in a larger size. Windows contains code that enlarges a screen font and displays it at a larger size. The results aren't very pretty because the code doesn't do any filling and smoothing, but it gets the job done quickly.

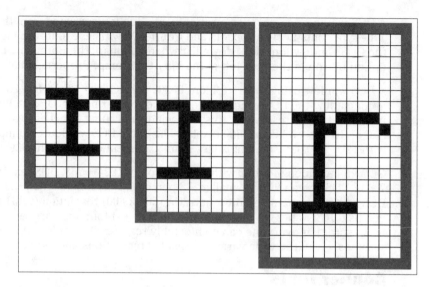

Figure 26-15: Courier screen font in 10, 12, and 15 points. That's 15-point Courier, not Courier at 15 characters per inch.

There is a TrueType font — Courier New — that pretty much replaces Courier. The advantages of using Courier New include better looking fonts at larger than 24 points and perhaps better correspondence between the font size you see on the screen and the font size printed in your letter to Aunt Sally. However, you might prefer to use Lucida Console, another fixed-pitch TrueType font that comes with Windows 98.

Proportional screen fonts

Proportional fonts are used throughout the Windows 98 user interface. You can, if you wish, use a fixed-pitch font such as Courier for your menu items, window titles, and so on, but proportional fonts take up less room. The boxes that the text inhabits adjust to the font size and length of the text within them, so they are smaller and more manageable.

System fonts

The System font comes only in 10-point bold and bold italic. It can be used for text entities such as window titles and menu items. Because it comes only in bold, it can't be used for the finer things in life. While it was once an important font for displaying all sorts of Windows text entities, it has fallen into disuse since the release of Windows 95.

Secret

If all your font files are erased from your hard disk, you cannot boot your computer in Windows and will get a Gdi.exe error message. If, however, the System font files Vgasys.fon and Vgaoem.fon (assuming that you last chose Small Fonts in the dialog box that appears when you click the Advanced button in the Settings tab of the Display Properties dialog box) are still in the \Windows\Fonts folder, you can start and use Windows. These two files (or their equivalent Large Fonts files — 8514sys.fon and 8514oem.fon) are the minimum font files needed to make Windows work. Figure 26-16 shows the lowercase *r* for the two sizes of System fonts.

Figure 26-16: Lowercase *r* from Vgasys.fon and 8514sys.fon screen font files. These are the System font files from the small font and large font screen sets.

The Terminal font in the OEM font files (Vgaoem.fon or 8514oem.fon) is needed to give the DOS window a font. The System font (Vgasys.fon) is used for all the text entities in Windows if there is no other font.

MS Sans Serif fonts

MS Sans Serif is the default font for all Windows 98 screen text entities. Depending on your resolution, either 8 or 10 points is used. The MS Sans Serif font files, Sserife.fon and Sseriff.fon, each contain six fonts in 8, 10, 12, 14, 18, and 24 points, as shown in Figure 26-17. The Windows 98 screen-font rasterizer automatically constructs larger MS Sans Serif fonts if you choose to display bigger screen fonts. They will look a bit crude, though.

This font is Microsoft's replacement for its earlier Helv font, as you can see from the font substitution table in the Win.ini file in your \Windows folder.

Unlike the System font, which MS Sans Serif pretty much replaces, MS Sans Serif comes in regular and italic in addition to bold and bold italic. This broader range of weights accounts for its appeal as a Windows 98 standard font for menu items, icon titles, and so on. For example, MS Sans Serif 10-point bold does well as the window title text. MS Sans Serif 10-point regular does better for menu items (purely a personal opinion).

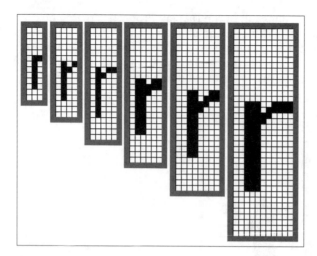

Figure 26-17: MS Sans Serif in six sizes — 8, 10, 12, 14, 18, and 24 points — from the Sserife.fon file.

MS Sans Serif is, of course, a *sans serif* font. Sans serif fonts have less elaboration in their design than serif fonts. An uppercase T in a sans serif font, for example, doesn't have little vertical lines at the ends of the horizontal line.

The System font is a sans serif font, and so are Fixedsys and Lucida Console. These fonts work well for text entities on the screen. Serif fonts are more legible for blocks of text in documents.

MS Serif fonts

Like MS Sans Serif, this replacement for the earlier Tms Rmn font comes in six font sizes: 8, 10, 12, 14, 18, and 24 points. If you like serifs, then this is the font for you. Check out the MS Sans Serif font in Figure 26-18.

Small fonts

These are indeed small fonts — in 2, 3, 4, 5, 6, 7 points. The small font set and large font set each have a file that contains Small fonts — smalle.fon and smallf.fon.

It is not easy to construct a good-looking and meaningful font when the grid size you have to work with is 2 dots wide and 3 dots high. Such is the case for some of the wider characters in the 2-point font in the large font set's Small fonts file, smallf.fon. The larger point sizes of the Small fonts can actually display some useful information. The 7-point size is the smallest that can be clearly read on most popular monitor/adapter combinations. This makes it a reasonable choice for icon titles and the like when space is at a premium.

Figure 26-18: MS Serif in 8, 10, 12, 14, 18, 24 points. These are taken from the Serife.fon file.

Small fonts are used to display TrueType text if it gets too small to be seen legibly, and to display greeked text in Print Preview windows. Small fonts are shown in Figure 26-19.

Figure 26-19: Small fonts in 2, 3, 4, 5, 6, and 7 points, including two sans serif fonts in sizes 6 and 7 point. These are taken from the Smalle.fon file.

Secret

The Small fonts file Smalle.fon also contains two sans serif fonts, one 6 points and one 7 points.

Symbol font

The character set used for the Symbol font has nothing in common with the Windows ANSI or OEM character sets. The Symbol font files contain characters at the same point sizes as MS Sans Serif and MS Serif. Use the Character Map application to display the Symbol character set.

Screen Fonts Turn to Flakes

If you find that some of your screen fonts are displayed incorrectly, this might be due to a damaged TrueType font file. If you have a Monotype Sorts TrueType font installed and the font file is corrupted, then it could be causing this problem. The Monotype Sorts font does not come with Windows 98, but it may have been installed on your computer by another application.

Check in the \Windows\Fonts folder for this font. If it is there, delete it and restart your computer. You can reinstall the original font file later.

TrueType Fonts

One aspect of Windows 3.1 that helped make it a successful product was the addition of TrueType—typeface outlines that Windows smoothly scales to any size on any Windows-supported monitor and printer.

This capability meant that Windows could use the same typefaces to display a document that it used to print the document. It no longer mattered whether a Windows user's printer contained the same typeface as the one used to display the text of a document on the Desktop. Windows prints its TrueType faces to any printer that has the ability to print graphics or download fonts.

TrueType is integrated into Windows 98. When you send a document to another person or company and you use one of the 23 TrueType font families included with Windows 98 that are intended for use in documents (see Table 26-3), the recipients of your document can view it on their monitors and print it on their printers exactly the way you saw it on your monitor and printed it, assuming you both have the same printer.

Table 26-3   Windows 98 TrueType Families for Use in Documents

Abadi MT	Copperplate Gothic	Matisse	Times New Roman
Arial	Courier New	News Gothic	Verdana
Book Antigua	Impact	OCR A Extended	Webdings
Calisto MT	Lucida Handwriting	Symbol	Westminster
Century Gothic	Lucida Sans Italic	Tahoma	Wingdings
Comic Sans	Lucida Sans Unicode MT	Tempus Sans ITC	

If you install Windows 98 over Windows 95 or Windows 3.1x, any additional fonts you had installed will still be there. If you install Windows 98 Multilanguage Support (either during initial setup or later using the Add/Remove Programs icon in the Control Panel), the 652-character versions of Arial, Courier New, Impact, Lucida Console, Lucida Sans Unicode, Tahoma, Times New Roman and Verdana are installed. Other fonts that you have previously installed (Garamond, for example) may also reveal extended character sets. See "Sources of TrueType Fonts" at the end of this chapter for ways to expand your TrueType font collection.

Freedom from screen fonts and printer fonts

Before TrueType, Windows required that a font designer build a set of specific fonts for every point size that you might require on your printer. These printer fonts required several megabytes of disk space for a complete set, especially when you needed larger sizes. Furthermore, the font designer had to build a separate set of screen fonts in a different format to display these printer fonts on screen.

TrueType almost completely eliminates this confusion. If you don't like the typefaces included with Windows 98, you can buy TrueType fonts from a variety of vendors. Once you install these fonts, all sizes of that typeface are immediately supported by all applications, displays, and printers.

You can configure the Fonts folder so that applications do not have access to screen or printer fonts. In the Fonts folder, choose View, Folder Options, and click the TrueType tab. Mark the Show Only TrueType Fonts in the Programs on My Computer check box.

The TrueType fonts that come with Windows 98

As shown in Table 26-4, Windows 98 ships with 26 TrueType font families (compared to six that shipped with Windows 95). These include our old favorites Arial, Courier New, and Times New Roman, plus brand new fonts such as Tahoma and Verdana that were designed especially for web pages.

Four fonts — Comic Sans, Lucida Handwriting, Matisse, and Tempus Sans ITC — imitate hand lettering. Others, such as Impact and Copperplate Gothic, make interesting headlines. Lucida Console is a fixed-pitch font that replaces the Courier screen font. Webdings, a collection of illustrations and icons, has been added to the Symbol, Wingdings and Marlett non-text fonts that came with Windows 95. OCR A Extended and Westminster are special-purpose fonts for optical character recognition (you may find that Westminster is not installed during Windows Setup).

Table 26-4 Windows 98 TrueType Families

Typeface	Font Filename
Fixed-pitch fonts	
Courier New	Cour.ttf
	Courbd.ttf
	Couri.ttf
	Courbi.ttf
Lucida Console	Lucon.ttf
Proportional fonts	
Abadi MT	abalc.ttf
Arial	Arial.ttf
	Arialbd.ttf
	Ariali.ttf
	Arialbi.ttf
Arial Black	Ariblk.ttf
Book Antigua	Bkant.ttf
Calisto MT	Calist.ttf
Century Gothic	Gothic.ttf
	Gothicb.ttf
	Gothicbi.ttf
	Gothici.ttf
Comic Sans	Comic.ttf
	Comicbd.ttf
Copperplate Gothic Bold	Coprgtb.ttf
Copperplate Gothic Light	Coprgtl.ttf
Impact	Impact.ttf
Lucida Handwriting	Lhandw.ttf
Lucida Sans Italic	Lsansi.ttf
Lucida Sans Unicode	Lsansuni.ttf
Matisse	Matisse_.ttf
News Gothic MT	Nwgthc.ttf
	Nwgthcb.ttf
	Nwgthci.ttf
OCR A Extended	Ocraext.ttf

Typeface	Font Filename
Proportional fonts	
Tahoma	Tahoma.ttf
	Tahomabd.ttf
Tempus Sans ITC	Tempsitc.ttf
Times New Roman	Times.ttf
	Timesbd.ttf
	Timesi.ttf
	Timesbi.ttf
Verdana	Verdana.ttf
	Verdanab.ttf
	Verdanai.ttf
	Verdanaz.ttf
Westminster	Westm.ttf
Non-text fonts	
Marlett	Marlett.ttf
Symbol	Symbol.ttf
Webdings	Webdings.ttf
Wingdings	Wingding.ttf

Tahoma, Verdana, and Webdings were designed at Microsoft's request, to be especially readable on the World Wide Web (they work well on paper, too).

When TrueType fonts are installed (or when Windows 98 is first installed), references to them are placed in the Registry. The Registry entries for the installed TrueType fonts look like this:

```
[HKEY_LOCAL_MACHINE\SOFTWARE\Microsoft\Windows\CurrentVersion\Fonts]
Abadi MT Condensed Light (True Type)"="ABALC.TTF"
"Arial (TrueType)"="ARIAL.TTF"
"Arial Bold (TrueType)"="ARIALBD.TTF"
"Arial Bold Italic (TrueType)"="ARIALBI.TTF"
"Arial Italic (TrueType)"="ARIALI.TTF"
"Arial Black (True Type)"="ARIBLK.TTF"
"Book Antiqua (True Type)"="BKANT.TTF"
"Calisto MT (True Type)"="CALIST.TTF"
"Comic Sans MS (True Type)"="COMIC.TTF"
"Comic Sans MS Bold (True Type)"="COMICBD.TTF"
"Copperplate Gothic Bold (True Type)"="COPRGTB.TTF"
"Copperplate Gothic Light (True Type)"="COPRGTL.TTF"
"Courier New (TrueType)"="COUR.TTF"
"Courier New Bold (TrueType)"="COURBD.TTF"
"Courier New Bold Italic (TrueType)"="COURBI.TTF"
```

```
"Courier New Italic (TrueType)"="COURI.TTF"
"Century Gothic (Ture Type)"="GOTHIC.TTF"
"Century Gothic Bold (True Type)"="GOTHICB.TTF"
"Century Gothic Bold Italic (True Type)"="GOTHICBI.TTF"
"Century Gothic Italic (True lype)"="GOTHICI.TTF"
"Impact (True Type)"="IMPACT.TTF"
"Lucida Console Regular (True Type)"="LUCON.TTF"
"Lucida Handwriting Italic (True Type)"="LHANDW.TTF"
"Lucida Sans Italic (True Type)"="LSANSI.TTF"
"Lucida Sans Unicode (True Type)"="LSANSUNI.TTF"
"Marlett (TrueType)"="MARLETT.TTF"
"Matisse ITC (True Type)"="MATISSE_.TTF"
"News Gothic MT (True Type)"="NWGTHC.TTF"
"News Gothic MT Bold (True Type)"="NWGTHCB.TTF"
"News Gothic MT Italic (True Type)"="NWGTHCI.TTF"
"OCR A Extended (True Type)"="OCRAEXT.TTF"
"Symbol (True Type)"="SYMBOL.TTF"
"Tahoma (True Type)"="TAHOMA.TTF"
"Tahoma Bold (True Type)"="TAHOMABD.TTF"
"Tempus Sans ITC (True Type)"="TEMPSITC.TTF"
"Times New Roman (TrueType)"="TIMES.TTF"
"Times New Roman Bold (TrueType)"="TIMESBD.TTF"
"Times New Roman Bold Italic (TrueType)"="TIMESBI.TTF"
"Times New Roman Italic (TrueType)"="TIMESI.TTF"
"Verdana (True Type)"="VERDANA.TTF"
"Verdana Bold (True Type)"="VERDANAB.TTF"
"Verdana Bold Italic (True Type)"="VERDANAZ.TTF"
"Verdana Italic (True Type)"="VERDANAI.TTF"
"Webdings (True Type)"="WEBDINGS.TTF"
"Westminster (True Type)"="WESTM.TTF"
"WingDings (TrueType)"="WINGDING.TTF"
```

Secret

A helpful reader (Hellmut Golde, Professor Emeritus, Department of Computer Science and Engineering at the University of Washington) pointed out that you can edit the Registry (at the above location) and place your fonts where you want them to go. For example:

```
"Arial (TrueType)"="F:\Fonts\ARIAL.TTF"
```

This creates a shortcut in the \Windows\Fonts folder to the Arial font in the Fonts folder on drive F, which you can easily see when you open the \Windows\Fonts folder. Of course, it is easier just to move all the fonts to a convenient folder and then install them in the \Windows\Fonts folder without moving them. The steps are detailed in the "Installing Fonts" section earlier in this chapter.

Tip

TrueType fonts are stored as font descriptions in files with the file extension ttf. Windows 3.1x required an accompanying file with the same filename as the TrueType font file, but with a different extension — *fot*. The *fot* files merely provided Windows with the location of the *ttf* file. These files are no longer needed, and you can erase them from your hard disk.

Unlike screen font files, the font descriptions are not patterns of dots on a grid, but consist of a font outline and rules (hints) for rendering the font.

The description is used by one of the TrueType font rasterizers in Windows to render the fonts as a pattern on dots (pixels on the screen, ink dots on the paper).

We have constructed pseudo-grid patterns for a small sample of TrueType fonts based on the closest screen font. For Arial we used the grid from MS Sans Serif, for Times New Roman we used the grid from MS Serif, and for Courier New we used the Courier screen font grid. We had to widen only the middle grid for Times New Roman by one pixel — this is for the 14-point font.

Using these grids taken from bitmapped screen fonts allows you to more closely compare the quality of hand-tuned screen fonts and those generated by the TrueType rasterizers. You can compare the results of the TrueType font rasterization with the dot patterns for screen fonts. You might review the three TrueType font renderings in Figures 26-20, 26-21, and 26-22, and compare them with their corresponding screen fonts in Figures 26-17, 26-18, and 26-15. Screen fonts are better than TrueType fonts at their fixed sizes, and TrueType fonts are less jagged for all other sizes.

Smooth fonts

The smooth fonts feature that was part of Microsoft's Plus! for Windows 95 is now an integrated part of Windows 98. Font smoothing makes TrueType fonts easier to read on your screen by means of an optical illusion. You are probably familiar with the jagged appearance that the curved and diagonal strokes of characters often have, especially in larger sizes or zoom settings. Font smoothing uses a technique called *anti-aliasing* to soften the edges with intermediate colors. For example, with black text on a white background, it adds shades of gray to fill in the "jaggies."

Figure 26-20: The lowercase *r* in Arial at 8, 10, 12, 14, 18, and 24 points. Compare these r's with those MS Sans Serif r's in Figure 26-17.

Figure 26-21: The lowercase *r* in Times New Roman at 8, 10, 12, 14, 18, and 24 points. Compare these r's with those MS Serif r's in Figure 26-18.

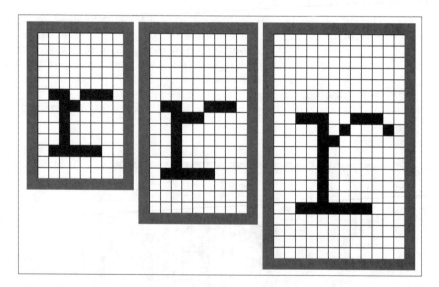

Figure 26-22: The lowercase *r* in Courier New Roman at 10, 12, and 15 points. Compare these r's with those Courier r's in Figure 26-15.

To enable font smoothing, right-click an empty spot on your Desktop and click Properties. Click the Effects tab, and mark the Smooth Edges of Screen Fonts check box. You must be using at least High Color (16 bit) on your display for the font smoothing to work (see "Changing the Size, Color, and Font of Objects on the Desktop" in Chapter 28 for more on setting the colors in your display).

Marlett

The Marlett font provides some of the "furniture" for the Windows 98 Desktop. You don't want to delete this font. The Minimize, Maximize, and Close buttons on the right end of any Windows title bar are constructed using this font.

Send your favorite typeface

TrueType gives you the ability to send TrueType faces to anyone, including typesetting service bureaus, without violating the copyright of the owner of the typeface. This is made possible by a TrueType feature called *font embedding*—you simply include the typefaces required by the document in an encoded form within the document itself.

Font embedding is a response to a serious problem within the PostScript service industry. A PostScript typesetter, such as a Linotronic 300, will not print a PostScript job unless the typesetter contains *exactly* the same typefaces that were used in the preparation of a document. If a document calls for a typeface with a name unknown to the device, it will often substitute a Courier font or not print at all. In either case, expensive service bureau time is wasted.

Many PostScript users, therefore, copy their special PostScript typefaces — Helvetica Black for headlines, say — onto a disk and send them along with their print job to the service bureau. This is a copyright violation (which is widely ignored), it wastes service bureau time in downloading the fonts, and it doesn't always work.

TrueType solves this problem by allowing you to embed typefaces into a document in an encrypted form. This encryption, which is easily supported by any application, prevents the recipient of a document from removing the typeface file and using it without paying for it. But the document can be viewed on any monitor and printed to any device supported by Windows — complete with the exact fonts used by the document's originator.

Microsoft has built four levels of usability into TrueType font embedding.

- At the most restrictive level, a vendor of TrueType faces can choose *not* to allow them to be embedded into documents for transmission. In this case, applications that support font embedding simply refrain from embedding those typefaces. The recipient of the document must purchase the required typefaces or substitute a generic typeface such as Times or Helvetica.

- At the second level, a TrueType vendor can choose to allow *print and preview* (also called *read-only*) *embedding*. A document embedded with print and preview typefaces can be viewed and printed, but not edited. (If the document could be edited, the original contents could be deleted and the file used over and over again to produce other documents, with no payment to the owner of the typeface.) This kind of document can be edited if the embedded typefaces are deleted first.

- The third level of font embedding is *editable* (also called *read-write*) *embedding*. When editable TrueType faces are embedded in a document, the document can be freely viewed, printed, and saved by the recipient, as well as edited. However, the fonts (and therefore the document) can only reside on that computer temporarily.

- The fourth and most useful level of embedding is *installable* embedding. The user of a document that contains fonts embedded this way has the option of permanently installing the embedded typefaces into Windows so that other applications and documents can also use the faces. This type of embedding is most appropriate for free and public-domain TrueType faces.

All of the TrueType faces included in Windows 98 are editable. This allows you to embed these faces into documents you send to people who, for whatever reason, have Windows but deleted the TrueType faces from their system. Some of the fonts, such as Verdana and Webdings, which were both designed for use on web pages, have installable embedding.

As technology that lets web site designers specify fonts becomes more prevalent, font embedding takes on an even greater significance. Since a web page is downloaded onto your computer every time you view it, you need a means of legally using the fonts in that page on your computer. Embedding lets web site designers use fonts without worrying about breaking copyright laws. Microsoft's Web Embedding Fonts Tool (WEFT) is one way to embed a specific font in a web site. In late 1997, a free preview version could be downloaded from http://www.microsoft.com/typography/web/embedding/weft/weft0.htm.

PostScript

The best-known type rasterizing program for Windows is probably Adobe Type Manager (ATM). After you install ATM, you have 13 scaleable outlines on your hard disk: Times, Helvetica, and Courier (in four weights: roman, italic, bold, and bold italic), and Symbol (in a single weight). Purchasing the Adobe Plus Pack gives you the additional 22 typefaces normally found in PostScript printers: Avant Garde, Bookman, Century, Helvetica Compressed (useful for spreadsheets), Palatino, Zapf Chancery, and Zapf Dingbats.

One of the advantages of ATM is that you can configure it to scale type on the screen at a certain point size and above. This is useful because of the horrible truth about VGA—a VGA screen simply doesn't have enough pixels to accurately represent the shape of letters below 15 points in size.

Below that size, the hand-tuned screen fonts look better than fonts scaled on the fly by a type rasterizer. The TrueType rasterizer quits drawing fonts on the screen below 6 points (smaller sizes are represented by the Small Fonts screen font).

For a comparison of the look of fully-formed characters and the onscreen representation of these characters created by Windows screen fonts, TrueType, and ATM, see Figure 26-23.

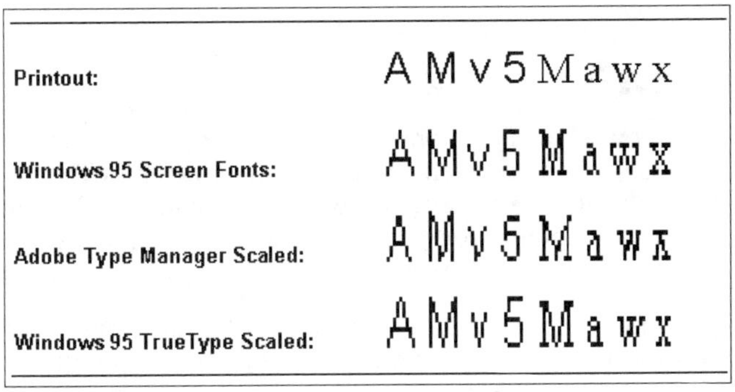

Figure 26-23: The differences between the look of typefaces when printed and the look of the same typefaces on a Windows screen.

The first line in Figure 26-23 is printed on an HP LaserJet. The second line shows the 10-point screen font (MS Serif and MS Sans Serif). The third and fourth lines show the same 10-point type scaled for a VGA screen by Adobe Type Manager and the TrueType rasterizer built into Windows 98, respectively. (Each font has been enlarged to show detail.) At this size, none of the screen fonts has enough pixels to show anything like the true shape of the characters. But the hand-tuned screen fonts are easier to read and closer to the desired shape of these characters than those scaled by ATM and TrueType.

One of the disadvantages of ATM is that it scales only typeface outlines that are in Adobe's own Type 1 format. While this is a popular standard, it is by no means the only format in which scaleable typefaces are sold.

OpenType

In May 1997, Adobe and Microsoft jointly announced an initiative to develop a new font format called OpenType. OpenType has been described as a superset of both TrueType and Adobe Type 1 — it supports both formats and allows them to work interchangeably in the same environment. Both formats will appear together in the Registry. An OpenType font can contain data for either or both of the supported formats, and it can be rasterized using either technology, depending on user preference.

The purpose of the new format is to make fonts easier to use and manage, and to give web designers more flexibility in specifying fonts on web sites. New font compression technology is expected to make fonts used in web pages faster to download. Microsoft and Adobe say that they plan to produce OpenType format fonts in the future and cross-license font technologies.

By late 1997, the OpenType initiative was well underway, although no specific OpenType products had been announced. Since OpenType is to be backward compatible by definition, its impact on the average user should be small. The potential benefits, on the other hand, could be significant.

Font Cataloging

If you use Windows TrueType fonts (and who among us doesn't), the time eventually comes when you want to use a font other than Times Roman and Arial. And when that time comes, you want to look at your potential typefaces with something more powerful than the plain-text drop-down list of font names that you can display in most Windows applications.

There are dozens of freeware and shareware programs that will merely catalog and print the TrueType fonts that are installed in your Windows\Fonts folder. The tricky part is to find programs that will do the same thing for fonts that you haven't installed into Windows yet.

A good program should be able to catalog fonts that are located anywhere on your hard drive, a network drive, or a CD-ROM. It's much more convenient to keep collections of fonts in a separate location and install them into Windows only as needed. For one thing, scrolling through a drop-down list containing the names of hundreds of typefaces is our least favorite way to choose a specific one for use in a document.

We have evaluated four shareware font-management packages for this task:

- FontFinder by Maverick Land & Cattle Co., http://radio.wustl.edu/~alan/fntfnd/fntfnd10.zip.

- FontFinder32 (no relation to FontFinder) by Sunshine Software, http://www.alliance.net/~fasttrax/sunshine/fontfinder.html.

- Printer's Apprentice by Lose Your Mind Development, http://www.igi.net/~btkinkel. (This program also requires Visual Basic 4.0 runtime files, available from http://www.igi.net/~btkinkel/zipfiles/vbrun4.zip.)

- TTFPlus by Watermark Software, http://www.wmsoftware.com.

The winner, in our opinion, is a venerable standard: Printer's Apprentice. It's easily worth the $25 registration fee requested, and you get a 15-day free trial period during which it's fully functional.

An additional source of font-management utilities is QualiType Corp. Their FontHandler lets you view, preview, print, and manage both TrueType and Adobe Type 1 fonts, installing and uninstalling them individually or by special font groups. QualiType's Font Sentry utility can install fonts for you on-the-fly, as they are needed by programs or documents. It also gives you control over the font list in your application programs, and lets you access uninstalled fonts from within your applications.

While FontHandler and Font Sentry are not shareware, they are reasonably priced at $79 and $89 each, or bundled together with 150 TrueType fonts for $99. Free demos of these and other font utilities are available from QualiType's web site at http://www.qualitype.com. (The QualiType web site is worth visiting anyway, for its informative "Fonts 101" primer.)

Sources of TrueType Fonts

When you're ready to move beyond the fonts that come with Windows 98, one of the best bargains in truly professional fonts is the Bitstream 500 Font CD-ROM for Windows. This collection is exactly what it sounds like: 500 different typefaces, most of them useful for normal business correspondence (as opposed to novelty, headline typefaces), in both TrueType and PostScript formats. The CD-ROM lists for $49.95. Contact Bitstream at 800-522-FONT or 617-497-6222, or online at http://www.bitstream.com/.

There are great font resources online. Check out Fonts Unlimited at http://fonts.eyecandy.com/ main.html. Or visit http://www.fonthead.com/, and be sure to download GoodDogCool.ttf.

One of the slickest places to download many good freeware and shareware fonts is a web site managed by the Freedom High Tech Fonts Centre. You can preview and download fonts by many experienced and avant-garde designers here. The Fonts Centre site is at http://members.tripod.com/~FreedomHigh/fonts.htm. If you really want to go nuts with free fonts, you can keep yourself busy for a long, long while by perusing the sites listed at http://www.yahoo.com/Arts/Design_Arts/Graphic_Design/Typography/Typefaces. This is Yahoo's index of web sites with downloadable fonts or links to fonts.

An extensive source of information about fonts and typography is Norman Walsh's Frequently Asked Questions About Fonts (http://www.rzg.mpg.de/rzg/text/comp.fonts/cf_toc.htm#SEC69). This comprehensive site includes lots of links to font publishers, discussions of font terminology, a history of typography, online sources for font software, and much, much more. If you find fonts at all interesting or puzzling, you should not miss this site.

Microsoft itself has put together a very useful resource on the subject of typography, with an emphasis on developing font technology and electronic publication. This is a good place to keep up with developments in the OpenType initiative and font embedding, for example. You can also download free fonts designed for use on the web, all with editable embedding (and some with installable embedding). You'll find the Microsoft Typography site at http://www.microsoft.com/typography/web/embedding/weft/weft0.htm.

Summary

▶ We show you how to use the font installer that is built into Windows 98 to view both installed and uninstalled fonts, as well as to install and uninstall them.

▶ We examine the construction of both bitmapped and TrueType fonts and look closely at each of the fonts that comes with Windows 98.

▶ We detail the differences between screen fonts, printer fonts, TrueType fonts, and PostScript fonts.

▶ We show how to adjust the magnification that Windows 98 uses to size the text displayed on your screen.

Chapter 27

Keyboards and Characters

In This Chapter

We show you how to type the characters available to you in Windows 98, how to pick a keyboard layout for easier access, and how to use shortcuts to run Windows 98 from the keyboard. We reveal:

▶ The relationship between fonts and characters

▶ What characters and character sets come with Windows 98

▶ The five ways to type (or insert) little-used characters into your documents

▶ Modifying your keyboard layout to more easily enter these little-used characters

▶ Creating multilingual documents

▶ Using multilingual e-mail and web sites

▶ Windows shortcut keys that can speed up your work

▶ Speeding up your keyboard

▶ Changing your keyboard driver if you get a new and different keyboard

Fonts and Characters

There is a relationship (although it is a complex one) between the characters you see on your keyboard's keys and the characters that appear on your screen when you press those keys. For one thing, the appearance of the characters you type depends on which font you are using. For another, you can type characters that may not appear on your keyboard, such as ©, ™, ®, ¼, ½, ¾, é, ō, ä, ¢, £, and ¥.

The characters that are displayed on your screen are stored on your computer's hard disk in font files. Each font file has at least 224 character definitions (known collectively as a *character set*) stored in it. Most of the basic Windows 98 fonts come with 652 character definitions. A *font* is a visual expression of a character set. When you purchase a packet of fonts, the characters come with it at no additional charge (this is a typographer's little joke).

As explained in Chapter 26, TrueType and bitmapped screen fonts ship with Windows 98. The TrueType fonts consist of font descriptions for each character and the ability to scale the font across a wide variety of sizes. TrueType fonts work with both the screen and the printer. The bitmapped fonts are for display on the screen, and consist of dots on a grid.

For a more complete understanding of fonts, you should read this chapter in conjunction with "The Kinds and Types of Fonts" in Chapter 26 and "Fonts on the Desktop" in Chapter 28.

Windows Character Sets

The fonts that ship with Windows 98 are based on these ten character sets:

- Extended Windows ANSI (652 characters—also called Windows Glyph List 4, or WGL4)

- Windows ANSI, Windows 3.1 version (224 characters—also called ISO-8859-1 or Latin 1)

- Windows ANSI, Windows 3.0 version

- DOS/OEM (also called IBM PC-8 or Code Page 437)

- Symbol

- Wingdings

- Webdings

- Marlett

- Lucida Sans Unicode

- Lucida Console

Five of the TrueType fonts (Arial, Courier New, Tahoma, Times New Roman, and Verdana) use the Extended Windows ANSI character set. This character set, also referred to as *Windows Glyph List 4* (WGL4), consists of 652 characters, including the basic 224 ANSI characters plus support for Baltic, Central European, Cyrillic, Greek, and Turkish alphabets. The extra characters are accessible only when you use the appropriate keyboard driver (see "Using Multiple Languages" later in this chapter).

Abadi MT, Calisto MT, Comic Sans, Copperplate Gothic, Century Gothic, Impact, Lucida Handwriting Italic, News Gothic, and OCRA Extended use the 224-character Windows ANSI character set, defined when Windows 3.1 and TrueType fonts were developed, and known more esoterically as the *ISO 8859-1* or *Latin-1* character set. These fonts were formerly part of Microsoft Plus! for Windows 95, but are now included with Windows 98. Most commercially available English fonts also use this standard.

Five of the bitmapped screen fonts (Courier, Fixedsys, MS Sans Serif, MS Serif, and System) use the earlier Windows 3.0 version of the Windows ANSI character set, which defined fewer characters between positions 128 and 160.

The bitmapped screen font Terminal and the bitmapped DOS fonts used in windowed DOS sessions all use the DOS/OEM character set. This is also referred to as the *IBM PC-8* (which stands for 8-bit) or *Code Page 437* character set. IBM developed this character set when it created the first IBM PC. This same character set is stored in ROM in U.S.-made PCs and used by full-screen DOS programs.

Four additional TrueType character sets ship with Windows 98 — Symbol, Wingdings, Webdings and Marlett. They have their own particular characters and don't relate to the previously mentioned "standards." Figure 27-1 shows characters from the TrueType fonts Times New Roman, Symbol, and Wingdings with their corresponding character numbers. The Times New Roman characters display the first 255 characters of the Extended Windows ANSI character set.

The Marlett font contains the Windows 98 "furniture." The symbols on the Minimize, Maximize, and Close buttons at the right end of Windows title bars are in this font. Because the symbols in the buttons are fonts, it is easy to resize the buttons. Make sure not to delete this font from your \Windows\Fonts folder.

Lucida Sans Unicode and Lucida Console use subsets of the Unicode character set, and have 660 and 1738 characters, respectively. They include letters (Latin, Greek, Hebrew, Cyrillic, and so on), symbols, and characters for drawing boxes on a non-graphic terminal. Lucida Console replaces the TrueType DOS fonts that were used with earlier versions of Windows.

Tip

Unicode is a 16-bit character set intended to accommodate all commonly used data-processing characters of all the earth's languages in its 64,000 data points. While adoption of Unicode is in its early stages — currently, the data points are only two-thirds full — Microsoft has indicated this is the direction it will be going. Typically, a font only contains one or more *ranges* of Unicode, because the entire set is so big.

The Windows ANSI character set

The Windows ANSI characters numbered 0 through 127 are identical to their counterparts in the DOS/OEM (IBM PC-8) character set. (These characters are also called the *ASCII* or *lower ASCII* character set, after the American Standards Committee for Information Interchange, which codified them decades ago.) The next 32 characters, 128 through 159, are mostly punctuation marks, although some character numbers are left unused. Of special interest are the curly single and double quotes. Following these are 32 characters of legal and currency symbols, then 32 characters of uppercase accented letters, and, finally, 32 characters of lowercase accented letters.

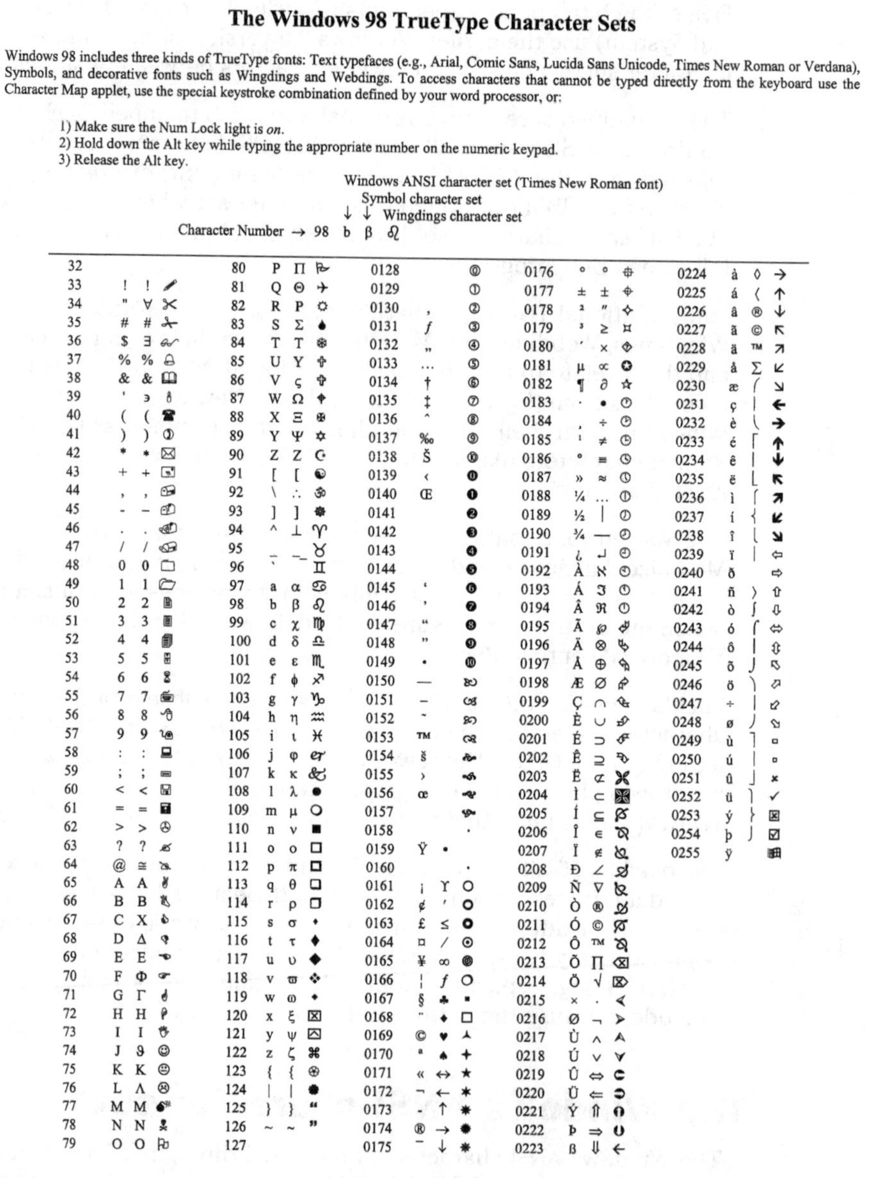

The Windows 98 TrueType Character Sets

Windows 98 includes three kinds of TrueType fonts: Text typefaces (e.g., Arial, Comic Sans, Lucida Sans Unicode, Times New Roman or Verdana), Symbols, and decorative fonts such as Wingdings and Webdings. To access characters that cannot be typed directly from the keyboard use the Character Map applet, use the special keystroke combination defined by your word processor, or:

1) Make sure the Num Lock light is *on*.
2) Hold down the Alt key while typing the appropriate number on the numeric keypad.
3) Release the Alt key.

Windows ANSI character set (Times New Roman font)
↓ Symbol character set
↓ ↓ Wingdings character set
Character Number → 98 b β Ω

No.	ANSI	Sym	Wing	No.	ANSI	Sym	Wing	No.	ANSI	Sym	Wing	No.	ANSI	Sym	Wing	No.	ANSI	Sym	Wing
32				80	P	Π		0128			◎	0176	°	°	⊕	0224	à	◊	→
33	!	!		81	Q	Θ		0129			①	0177	±	±	⊕	0225	á	⟨	↑
34	"	∀	✂	82	R	P		0130	,		②	0178	²	″	◆	0226	â	®	↓
35	#	#		83	S	Σ	♠	0131	ƒ		③	0179	³	≥	¤	0227	ã	©	↖
36	$	∃		84	T	T	❀	0132	„		④	0180	´	×	◆	0228	ä	™	↗
37	%	%		85	U	Y	❦	0133	…		⑤	0181	µ	∝	❂	0229	å	Σ	↙
38	&	&		86	V	ς	❧	0134	†		⑥	0182	¶	∂	☆	0230	æ	⎛	↘
39	'	∋		87	W	Ω	✦	0135	‡		⑦	0183	·	•	☉	0231	ç	⎜	
40	(	(	☎	88	X	Ξ	✧	0136	^		⑧	0184	¸	÷	☺	0232	è	⎝	→
41	)	)	①	89	Y	Ψ	✩	0137	‰		⑨	0185	¹	≠	☻	0233	é	⎛	↑
42	*	∗	✉	90	Z	Z	☿	0138	Š		⑩	0186	º	≡	☺	0234	ê	⎜	↓
43	+	+		91	[	[	●	0139	‹		❶	0187	»	≈	☀	0235	ë	⎝	↖
44	,	,		92	\	∴		0140	Œ		❷	0188	¼	…	①	0236	ì	⎛	↗
45	-	−		93	]	]	❋	0141			❸	0189	½		②	0237	í	⟨	↙
46	.	.		94	^	⊥	♈	0142			❹	0190	¾	—	③	0238	î	⎜	↘
47	/	/		95	_	_	♉	0143			❺	0191	¿	↵	④	0239	ï	⎟	⇦
48	0	0		96	`	‾	♊	0144			❻	0192	À	ℵ	⑤	0240	ð		
49	1	1		97	a	α	♋	0145	'		❼	0193	Á	ℑ	⑥	0241	ñ	⟩	⇧
50	2	2		98	b	β	♌	0146	'		❽	0194	Â	ℜ	⑦	0242	ò	⎞	⇩
51	3	3		99	c	χ	♍	0147	"		❾	0195	Ã	℘	⑧	0243	ó	⎟	
52	4	4		100	d	δ	♎	0148	"		❿	0196	Ä	⊗	⑨	0244	ô		⇳
53	5	5		101	e	ε	♏	0149	•		⓫	0197	Å	⊕	⑩	0245	õ	⎠	
54	6	6		102	f	φ	♐	0150	—			0198	Æ	∅		0246	ö	⟩	
55	7	7		103	g	γ	♑	0151	–			0199	Ç	∩		0247	÷		
56	8	8		104	h	η	♒	0152	˜			0200	È	∪		0248	ø	⎞	
57	9	9		105	i	ι	♓	0153	™	™		0201	É	⊃		0249	ù	⟩	
58	:	:		106	j	φ		0154	š			0202	Ê	⊇		0250	ú		□
59	;	;		107	k	κ		0155	›	›		0203	Ë	⊄	✂	0251	û		×
60	<	<		108	l	λ	●	0156	œ			0204	Ì	⊂		0252	ü	⟩	✓
61	=	=		109	m	μ	○	0157				0205	Í	⊆		0253	ý	⎟	☒
62	>	>		110	n	ν	■	0158				0206	Î	∈		0254	þ	⎠	☑
63	?	?		111	o	o	□	0159	Ÿ	•		0207	Ï	∉		0255	ÿ		
64	@	≅		112	p	π	□	0160			·	0208	Ð	∠					
65	A	A		113	q	θ	○	0161	¡	Υ	○	0209	Ñ	∇					
66	B	B		114	r	ρ	□	0162	¢	′	○	0210	Ò	®					
67	C	X		115	s	σ	◆	0163	£	≤	●	0211	Ó	©					
68	D	Δ		116	t	τ	◆	0164	¤	⁄	◉	0212	Ô	™					
69	E	E		117	u	υ	◆	0165	¥	∞	◉	0213	Õ	∏					
70	F	Φ		118	v	ϖ	✦	0166	¦	ƒ	○	0214	Ö	√					
71	G	Γ		119	w	ω	✦	0167	§	♣	■	0215	×	·	◁				
72	H	H		120	x	ξ	☒	0168	¨	♦	□	0216	Ø	¬	▷				
73	I	I		121	y	ψ	☑	0169	©	♥	▲	0217	Ù	∧	▲				
74	J	ϑ		122	z	ζ	⌘	0170	ª	♠	✚	0218	Ú	∨	▼				
75	K	K		123	{	{	⊕	0171	«	↔	✶	0219	Û	⇔	⊂				
76	L	Λ		124					●	0172	¬	←	✷	0220	Ü	⇐	⊃				
77	M	M		125	}	}	"	0173		↑	✳	0221	Ý	⇑	∩				
78	N	N		126	~	~	"	0174	®	→	●	0222	Þ	⇒	∪				
79	O	O		127				0175	¯	↓	✳	0223	ß	⇓	←				

Figure 27-1: The Windows 98 TrueType character sets (ISO-8859-1).

One way to access the characters numbered above 127 is to hold down the Alt key, type a zero (0) on the numeric keypad, and then type the three digits of the character's number — 0189, for example. This extra zero is already included in the character numbers shown in Figure 27-1. This is the most basic method of accessing these additional characters. Better methods are detailed later in this chapter.

You must add a leading zero when using this method to insert characters numbered 128 through 255 in the Windows ANSI character set because Windows is downward compatible with the IBM PC-8 character set, which is used by DOS applications. The IBM PC-8 character set already uses the Alt+*number* method for its own characters, and Windows allows you to enter characters from this set using the same method.

For example, regardless of whether you're typing in DOS or Windows, Alt+171 inserts character number 171 from the IBM PC-8 character set, the one-half symbol (½). If you type Alt+0171 in Windows, you get character number 171 from the Windows ANSI character set, which is a chevron bracket («). (Windows ignores characters in the IBM PC-8 character set that do not exist in Windows, such as line-draw characters, or converts them into other keyboard characters.)

The difference between the Windows 3.0 ANSI character set and the Windows 3.1 version is that fewer characters between character numbers 128 and 160 are defined in the older version. Because this character set is not used for TrueType fonts, you don't need to be concerned about it when you're creating documents. In Figure 27-2, the Windows 3.0 ANSI character set is shown in MS Sans Serif.

	!	"	#	$	%	&	'	(	)	*	+	,	-	.	/	0	1	2	3	4	5	6	7	8	9	:	;	<	=	>	?
@	A	B	C	D	E	F	G	H	I	J	K	L	M	N	O	P	Q	R	S	T	U	V	W	X	Y	Z	[	\	]	^	_
`	a	b	c	d	e	f	g	h	i	j	k	l	m	n	o	p	q	r	s	t	u	v	w	x	y	z	{			}	~	.
.	.	.	.	.	.	.	.	.	.	.	.	.	.	.	'	'	.	.	.	.	.	.	.	.	.	.	.	.	.	.	.
	¡	¢	£	¤	¥	¦	§	¨	©	ª	«	¬	-	®	¯	°	±	²	³	´	µ	¶	·	¸	¹	º	»	¼	½	¾	¿
À	Á	Â	Ã	Ä	Å	Æ	Ç	È	É	Ê	Ë	Ì	Í	Î	Ï	Ð	Ñ	Ò	Ó	Ô	Õ	Ö	×	Ø	Ù	Ú	Û	Ü	Ý	Þ	ß
à	á	â	ã	ä	å	æ	ç	è	é	ê	ë	ì	í	î	ï	ð	ñ	ò	ó	ô	õ	ö	÷	ø	ù	ú	û	ü	ý	þ	ÿ

Figure 27-2: The Windows 3.0 version of the Windows ANSI character set, used by the current bitmapped screen fonts. It is shown in MS Sans Serif.

Font designers are supposed to base their TrueType fonts on the Windows ANSI (Windows 3.1) character set or on the Extended Windows ANSI 652-character set, which includes the previous 224 Windows 3.1 ANSI characters. That is, their fonts are supposed to be an expression of the same characters as those defined by the Windows ANSI character set. Font designers generally stick to this standard unless they are designing a special-purpose font such as Wingdings.

It is important that font designers use the Windows ANSI character set. As computer users, we are interested in easily accessing the ANSI characters no matter what text font we are using. If the copyright symbol is displayed when we use Times New Roman, we would like that to also be the case if we are using Coronet. This will be true only if the copyright symbol is present in the Coronet font, and if it has the same character number as it has in Times New Roman.

The five ANSI accents

One reason that many English-speaking computer users aren't more familiar with the accented letters in the ANSI set is that these letters seem to be a jumble of random, unrelated symbols. Actually, all of the accented letters in the ANSI character set fall into one of five types:

1. **Characters with an acute accent**

   Á É Í Ó Ú Ý á é í ó ú ý

2. **Characters with a grave accent (*grave* rhymes with "Slav" or "slave")**

   À È Ì Ò Ù à è ì ò ù

3. **Characters with an umlaut (also called a *dieresis*)**

   Ä Ë Ï Ö Ü ä ë ï ö ü ÿ

4. **Characters with a circumflex (also informally called a *hat*)**

   Â Ê Î Ô Û â ê î ô û

5. **Characters with a tilde, or an Iberian or Nordic form**

   Ã Æ Ç Ð Ñ Õ Ø ¡ ¿ ã æ ª ç ñ õ ø º ß

These accented characters largely occupy the positions numbered 192 through 224 — the uppercase letters start at 192, while the lowercase versions are exactly 32 positions higher. On non-U.S. keyboards, the accented characters that are common in the national language are assigned to keys, so that pressing, say, the ñ key on a Spanish keyboard automatically inserts ANSI character 241 into the document.

When you use accented characters in your documents, they still sort correctly in alphabetical order. Windows applications use the "sort value" of each letter, not the numerical ANSI value, so characters are sorted *a, á, b, c,* not *a, b, c, á,* as their numerical value might suggest. The actual sort order is determined by the sort rules associated with the locale that you set in the Regional Settings Properties dialog box (which you access by clicking the Regional Settings icon in the Control Panel).

The DOS/OEM character set

The number of total characters possible under the Windows 3.1 ANSI standard is the same as under DOS — 224. (You can form 256 characters by using all possible combinations of an 8-bit byte, which is used in both character sets. The first 32 characters are nonprinting "control" characters, which leaves 224 that can be used for printing characters.) However, more international characters and symbols are available in Windows because the ANSI set eliminates the line-drawing and math characters that are part of the IBM PC-8 set.

Because it moved IBM's math characters into a new Symbol font and deleted the line-draw characters entirely, Windows has room to add several accented letters needed in various languages, as well as copyright and trademark symbols, and the like. (Most Windows word processing applications can draw lines without having to use text characters.)

The IBM PC-8 character set is shown in Figure 27-3. In the U.S. keyboard layout, the main keyboard provides keys for each of the alphabetic characters and punctuation marks, numbered 32 through 127. You access the other characters (number 128 and up) by holding down the Alt key, typing the appropriate character number on the numeric keypad (with the Num Lock light on), and then releasing the Alt key. Alt+157, for example, produces ¥, the Japanese yen symbol. Notice that if you use this method with the DOS/OEM character set, you don't need to type the additional zero for the characters above character number 127, as you would for the Windows ANSI characters.

CTRL & PUNC:		ALPHABETIC:		ACCENTS & LINE DRAW:			MATH:
0 ■	32	64 @	96 `	128 Ç	160 á	192 └	224 α
1 ■	33 !	65 A	97 a	129 ü	161 í	193 ┴	225 β
2 ■	34 "	66 B	98 b	130 é	162 ó	194 ┬	226 Γ
3 ■	35 #	67 C	99 c	131 â	163 ú	195 ├	227 π
4 ■	36 $	68 D	100 d	132 ä	164 ñ	196 ─	228 Σ
5 ■	37 %	69 E	101 e	133 à	165 Ñ	197 ┼	229 σ
6 ■	38 &	70 F	102 f	134 å	166 ª	198 ╞	230 µ
7 ■	39 '	71 G	103 g	135 ç	167 º	199 ╟	231 τ
8 ■	40 (	72 H	104 h	136 ê	168 ¿	200 ╚	232 Φ
9 ■	41)	73 I	105 i	137 ë	169 ⌐	201 ╔	233 Θ
10 ■	42 *	74 J	106 j	138 è	170 ¬	202 ╩	234 Ω
11 ■	43 +	75 K	107 k	139 ï	171 ½	203 ╦	235 δ
12 ■	44 ,	76 L	108 l	140 î	172 ¼	204 ╠	236 ∞
13 ■	45 -	77 M	109 m	141 ì	173 ¡	205 ═	237 ø
14 ■	46 .	78 N	110 n	142 Ä	174 «	206 ╬	238 ε
15 ■	47 /	79 O	111 o	143 Å	175 »	207 ╧	239 ∩
16 ■	48 0	80 P	112 p	144 É	176 ▒	208 ╨	240 ≡
17 ■	49 1	81 Q	113 q	145 æ	177 ▓	209 ╤	241 ±
18 ■	50 2	82 R	114 r	146 Æ	178 ▓	210 ╥	242 ≥
19 ■	51 3	83 S	115 s	147 ô	179 │	211 ╙	243 ≤
20 ■	52 4	84 T	116 t	148 ö	180 ┤	212 ╘	244 ⌠
21 ■	53 5	85 U	117 u	149 ò	181 ╡	213 ╒	245 ⌡
22 ■	54 6	86 V	118 v	150 û	182 ╢	214 ╓	246 ÷
23 ■	55 7	87 W	119 w	151 ù	183 ╖	215 ╫	247 ≈
24 ■	56 8	88 X	120 x	152 ÿ	184 ╕	216 ╪	248 °
25 ■	57 9	89 Y	121 y	153 Ö	185 ╣	217 ┘	249 ∙
26 ■	58 :	90 Z	122 z	154 Ü	186 ║	218 ┌	250 ·
27 ■	59 ;	91 [	123 {	155 ¢	187 ╗	219 █	251 √
28 ■	60 <	92 \	124		156 £	188 ╝	220 ▄	252 ⁿ
29 ■	61 =	93]	125 }	157 ¥	189 ╜	221 ▌	253 ²
30 ■	62 >	94 ^	126 ~	158 ₧	190 ╛	222 ▐	254 ■
31 ■	63 ?	95 _	127	159 ƒ	191 ┐	223 ▀	255

Figure 27-3: The IBM PC-8 character set. In addition to nonprintable control codes, punctuation, and alphabetic characters, the PC-8 character set includes accented characters, line-draw characters, and math symbols. You access these last three types of characters using the Alt key and the numeric keypad.

Although the IBM PC-8 character set seems to be a chaotic jumble of letters and signs, there is a natural order of sorts (no pun intended). For instance, the first 32 characters are control codes (including tab and carriage return characters), the next 32 are punctuation and numerals, the next 32 are uppercase letters, and exactly 32 places above that are the lowercase letters.

Easily Typing the Less-Used Characters

As you can see in Figure 27-1, Windows 98 provides a broad array of characters that do not appear on your keyboard. These characters include fractions, footnote superscripts, copyright and trademark symbols, and many others. Even if you are using a French, German, or other European-style keyboard, you only get a few different characters defined on your keyboard, mostly for the accented letters.

One standard (but awkward) method of inserting characters that don't appear on the keyboard is to use the Alt+*number* method. You turn Num Lock on, hold down the Alt key, type a number on the numeric keypad, then release the Alt key. For example, typing Alt+0169 inserts the © symbol.

Another (somewhat awkward) method is to use the Character Map applet that comes with Windows 98 (Start, Programs, Accessories, System Tools). In the Character Map window, you select a symbol (or several symbols), copy it, and then switch to your word processing program and paste it into your document. Note that if you are using multiple languages, you must use the Character Map's Select and Copy buttons, not the keyboard shortcuts or context-menu versions of these commands.

This method is cumbersome because it requires that you switch between applications, but you might find it useful at times because it lets you preview all of the 224 available characters in a font before you actually insert them in your document. They do look pretty small on high-resolution monitors, but clicking a character lets you see a magnified view of it.

If you're using the Character Map to view a font that uses the Extended Windows ANSI character set, you will still see only 224 characters at one time. Display the Font drop-down list, and you'll see that Windows 98 divides up the font into language groups, such as Arial, Arial Baltic, and Arial Greek. If you switch among fonts for different languages, the first 96 characters stay the same, while the other characters change with the language group. You must have installed Multilanguage Support in order to see these additional characters; see "Using Multiple Languages" later in this chapter to find out how.

In addition to using the Alt+*number* method and the Character Map, Windows provides four other more efficient ways of inserting characters that don't appear on the keyboard. If you install the U.S.-International keyboard layout (see the "U.S.-International keyboard layout" section), you can type characters such as © into text in any Windows application by pressing a simple two-key combination.

In the "Switching between keyboard layouts in one language" section, you learn how to type non-standard characters using only one or two keystrokes. You can switch this ability on and off at any time (by switching between keyboard layouts), and you can use it in conjunction with the Character Map applet or the Alt+*number* method whenever you wish.

If you have a full-featured word processing program such as Word for Windows or WordPerfect for Windows, you can also insert many special characters using keyboard shortcuts defined in those programs. See the section entitled "Accessing unusual characters in Word for Windows 95 and 97" for details about typing these characters in Word.

Finally, the "Accessing more hidden characters" section introduces you to a typeface that comes with Windows 98 that contains hundreds of symbols. You also learn about the typefaces from Microsoft and third-party vendors that contain literally thousands of other special characters you can use in your documents.

The U.S.-International keyboard layout

One way of inserting additional characters is to use the U.S.-International keyboard layout. Most Windows users, in the U.S. at least, use the plain United States 101 keyboard layout with the English (United States) language. This layout corresponds with the keys on typical U.S. keyboards. Each key inserts a lowercase letter and an uppercase letter, and that is it. There are no keys for extra symbols or accented letters, such as the *é* in *café*.

There are five keyboard layouts associated with the U.S.: 101, Dvorak, LH Dvorak, RH Dvorak, and International. The LH (left hand) and RH (right hand) Dvorak layouts are new with Windows 98.

When you switch to the U.S.-International keyboard layout, most of the keys on a regular U.S. keyboard gain a third or a fourth meaning. The *C* key, for example, lets you insert the copyright symbol (©) and cent sign (¢), as well as the normal uppercase *C* and lowercase *c*.

You don't need to have a U.S. keyboard to use the U.S.-International keyboard layout. Any of the keyboard layouts provided by Windows work with any of the U.S. or European keyboards. The only problem with using a keyboard layout for one language with a keyboard designed for another is that the character that you see on the keyboard may not be the character that appears on screen when you press a key.

Undocumented

There are two problems with the U.S.-International keyboard layout: Shift+Tab doesn't do a back tab, and you have to resolve conflicts with your word processor regarding Alt+Ctrl key redefinitions.

Installing the U.S.-International keyboard

To switch to the U.S.-International keyboard layout, take the following steps:

STEPS

Installing the U.S.-International Keyboard Layout

Step 1. Open the Control Panel by clicking the Start button, pointing to Settings, and then clicking Control Panel.

Step 2. Click the Keyboard icon.

(continued)

STEPS *(continued)*

Installing the U.S.-International Keyboard Layout

Step 3.   Click the Language tab.

Step 4.   Double-click the first (and most likely only) entry in the Language and Layout box (or highlight it and click the Properties button) to display the Language Properties dialog box (see Figure 27-4).

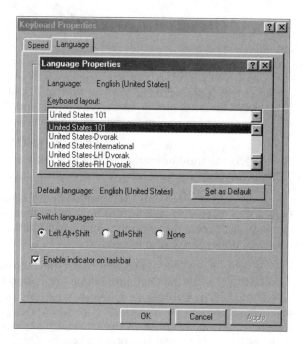

Figure 27-4: The Keyboard Properties dialog box somewhat covered over by the Language Properties dialog box.

Step 5.   Display the Keyboard Layout drop-down list, and choose United States-International.

Step 6.   Click OK to close the Language Properties dialog box.

Step 7.   Click OK to close the Keyboard Properties dialog box. You will be asked to insert your Windows 98 CD-ROM.

The change is available immediately in all applications.

While the U.S.-International keyboard layout is in effect, the *right* Alt key on your keyboard turns into an "Alternate Character" key. When you hold down this key (alone or with the Shift key), most of the keys on your normal U.S. keyboard gain new meanings.

We refer to this Alternate Character key as AltChar. The location of this key on extended 101-key keyboards and the meaning of each of the keys in the U.S.- International keyboard layout are shown in Figure 27-5. When you're using the U.S.-International keyboard, the AltChar key is the same as Ctrl+Alt. This can cause conflicts if any Ctrl+Alt key combinations are redefined in your word processor.

Figure 27-5: The U.S.-International keyboard layout.

The normal character is shown on the left of each key, and the character inserted when you hold down AltChar or Shift+AltChar is shown on the right.

Unusual characters on the keyboard

You gain access to many characters by switching to the U.S.-International keyboard. For clarity's sake, we break them into the following categories:

- Legal characters, such as the copyright symbol (©), the registered trademark symbol (®), the section mark (§), and the paragraph mark (¶) used by lawyers

- Currency symbols, such as the British pound (£), the Japanese yen (¥), the cent sign (¢), and the international generic currency symbol (¤)

- The fractions one-fourth (¼), one-half (½), and three-fourths (¾), and the degree symbol (°), useful when typing addresses such as 120½ Main St. or recipes (300°)

- Superscripts from one to three (^{123}), useful for inserting footnotes into a page of text, or for expressions such as x^2. Windows 98 doesn't offer superscript numbers higher than three, but Windows NT provides a full set of superscript and subscript numbers, from 0 to 9

- True multiplication and division symbols (÷), so you don't have to use a lowercase *x* and a forward slash (/) in your documents

- Open and closed quote marks (' '), also called "smart quotes," which look like the quote marks used in professionally typeset magazines and newspapers

- Accented characters, so you can correctly spell words such as *résumé* and *mañana*

The U.S.-International keyboard actually provides two different ways to insert accented letters into your documents. This ability is becoming more important as more Americans have names that include accented letters, such as Frederico Peña, Secretary of the Department of Transportation.

The first way to insert accented letters is to hold down the AltChar key and press one of the letters on your keyboard that has an accented alternate character. For example, AltChar+E produces the accented *é,* while AltChar+N produces the accented *ñ.*

The second way is to use what are called *dead keys.* These are keys that do nothing until you press another key on the keyboard.

On the U.S.-International keyboard, five keys are converted into dead keys. These are:

- The circumflex or "hat" over the 6 key (^) — used in words such as *crêpes Suzette*

- The back quote (`) — produces a *grave accent* in words such as *à la carte*

- The tilde (~) — used in words such as *jalapeño*

- The apostrophe (') — produces an *acute accent* in words such as *exposé*

- The double quote (") — produces an *umlaut* (or *dieresis*) in words such as *naïve*

When you press one of these dead keys, Windows shows nothing on your screen until you press another key. If the second key you press is a letter that has an accented form, such as most vowels, the appropriate accented letter is inserted into your document. If a letter doesn't have an accented form, the letter *t* for example, both the accent and the *t* are inserted, one after the other. If you want to insert just the accent itself, press the corresponding dead key followed by the spacebar.

This behavior produces a small irritation when you're using the apostrophe and double-quote key on your keyboard. When you press the apostrophe, which is common in contractions such as *don't* and possessives such as *Brian's,* you don't see the apostrophe until the second letter is typed. But you don't get an apostrophe at all if you type an unusual contraction, such as Hallowe'en. With the U.S.-International keyboard, pressing the apostrophe and then *e* produces the letter *é,* unless you remember to press the spacebar after the apostrophe.

This is a very minor problem, because most English contractions end in *s* or *t,* not in vowels. But it is a more serious problem with the double-quote key, which you use to begin sentences that are quotations, such as "Are you there?" Sentences often begin with *A, E,* and other vowels, and you must remember to press the spacebar after the double-quote key when typing any such sentence.

If you often use symbols or accented characters, the advantages of using the U.S.-International keyboard far outweigh the slight disadvantage of remembering how to use the apostrophe and double-quote key. But because it *is* irritating, we wish Microsoft hadn't used the apostrophe and double-quote key as a dead key. Instead, they should have used the colon (:) and the semicolon (;). The colon looks like an umlaut, and the bottom of the semicolon resembles an acute accent mark. Because colons and semicolons are always followed by spaces or carriage returns in normal English usage, you wouldn't need to remember to press the spacebar before pressing a vowel after these keys. If a letter immediately followed a colon or semicolon, you could be sure that it was meant to be an accented letter.

In any case, using the U.S.-International keyboard is usually better for users of U.S. keyboards than switching to an entirely different keyboard layout to type in another language, such as French. You can, of course, use the Keyboard Properties dialog box in the Control Panel to add keyboard layouts in addition to (or instead of) U.S. layout. There are now 67 available keyboard layouts (up from 26 with Windows 95). They range from Afrikaans to Ukrainian. But the non-U.S. keyboard layouts almost always move some alphabetical keys to new positions that are customary in those locales. For example, the top row of alphabetical keys on keyboards sold in France starts out with the letters AZERTY, not QWERTY, as on U.S. keyboards. Unless you're a touch typist who learned to type on keyboards in a different country, it's better to stick with the U.S.-International keyboard.

What if you don't have an extended keyboard?

For users with older 84-key keyboards (the ones on the original IBM AT, with 10 function keys on the left side), the U.S.-International keyboard provides another way to access alternate characters. This is necessary, of course, because 84-key keyboards do not have two Alt keys and therefore cannot convert one into an AltChar key.

While the U.S.-International keyboard is in effect, you can hold down Ctrl+Alt while pressing a letter as a substitute for holding down the right Alt key (the AltChar key). Shift+Ctrl+Alt does the same thing as Shift+AltChar.

Unfortunately, these parallel methods are in force even if you are using a 101-key extended keyboard. This means that you must take care when using a macro language in your word processor to redefine Ctrl+Alt keys or Shift+Ctrl+Alt keys to run macros. These macro definitions overrule the meaning of letters that have an alternate form when used with the AltChar key. In other words, a macro that you have defined to run when you press Ctrl+Alt+A takes precedence over AltChar+A. Instead of AltChar+A inserting *á* into your document, the macro will execute.

Switching between keyboard layouts in one language

You can set up two (or more) keyboard layouts and easily switch between them. You can switch back and forth between the U.S. and the U.S.-International keyboard if you like. This can help you avoid the irritation of dealing with poorly defined dead keys (see the "Unusual characters on the keyboard" section earlier in this chapter).

Undocumented

To set up both the U.S. and U.S.-International keyboard layouts, follow the steps in the section entitled "Setting up and using multilingual identifiers" later in this chapter. Choose the language English (United States) and associate the U.S.-International keyboard layout with it; then choose English (Australian) and associate the U.S.-101 keyboard layout with it. You now have two language identifiers on your Taskbar that are in fact the same language (almost) but refer to two different keyboard layouts. You switch between layouts by choosing one or the other language identifier.

The only problem this can cause occurs if you have two spelling dictionaries in your word processor, perhaps one for the U.S. and one for Australia. The text that you type while you are typing Australian English (using the plain U.S. keyboard layout) will be proofed by the Australian spelling dictionary.

Accessing unusual characters in Word for Windows 95 and 97

For an example of how a full-featured word processor handles non-standard characters, see Table 27-2. The elements in this chart were taken directly from the Word for Windows help files (and edited to improve clarity).

Table 27-2	Shortcut Keys for Inserting Accented Letter in Word for Windows 95 and 97
Character	**Keystrokes**
à, è, ì, ò, ù, À, È, Ì, Ò, Ù	Ctrl+` (accent-grave), the letter
á, é, í, ó, ú, ý, Á, É, Í, Ó, Ú, Ý	Ctrl+' (apostrophe), the letter
â, ê, î, ô, û, Â, Ê, Î, Ô, Û	Ctrl+Shift+ ^ (caret), the letter
ã, ñ, õ, Ã, Ñ, Õ	Ctrl+Shift+~ (tilde), the letter
ä, ë, ï, ö, ü, ÿ, Ä, Ë, Ï, Ö, Ü, Ÿ	Ctrl+Shift+: (colon), the letter
å, Å	Ctrl+Shift+@, a or A
æ, Æ	Ctrl+Shift+&, a or A
œ, Œ	Ctrl+Shift+&, o or O

Character	Keystrokes
ß	Ctrl+Shift+&, s
ç, Ç	Ctrl+, (comma), c or C
ð, Ð	Ctrl+' (apostrophe), d or D
ø, Ø	Ctrl+/, o or O
¿	Ctrl+Alt+Shift+?
¡	Ctrl+Alt+Shift+!
©	Ctrl+Alt+C
®	Ctrl+Alt+R
™	Ctrl+Alt+T
… (ellipsis)	Ctrl+Alt+. (period)
' (single opening quotation mark)	Ctrl+` (accent-grave), `
' (single closing quotation mark)	Ctrl+'(apostrophe),'
" (double opening quotation mark)	Ctrl+`(accent-grave)," (double quote)
" (double closing quotation mark)	Ctrl+'(apostrophe)," (double quote)

Word for Windows (6.0 and later) is by default set to replace straight quote marks with the typesetter's quote marks. You won't have to use the last four keystroke combinations in the table if you leave this setting at its default.

Undocumented

There are some conflicts between the U.S.-International keyboard layout and Word for Windows. The Word team at Microsoft has chosen to redefine a number of the Ctrl+Alt shortcut keys, so many of the AltChar+*letter* shortcuts don't work as indicated. Fortunately, you have a number of options if you want to use the convenient U.S.-International keyboard layout with Word.

First, many of the keys on the U.S.-International keyboard that conflict with a Word shortcut key have a different shortcut key in Word (refer to Table 27-2). You can just use these shortcut keys instead of AltChar+*letter*. For example, on the U.S.-International keyboard layout, you type AltChar+N to get the letter ñ, but Word defines Ctrl+Alt+N as a shortcut for choosing View, Normal. If you're typing in Word, you can use Word's keyboard shortcut **Ctrl+Shift+~ (tilde), n** to get the letter ñ instead.

Second, you can remove 13 of the 16 keyboard shortcuts in Word that conflict with the U.S.-International keyboard layout. Fortunately, these shortcut definitions are stored in the Normal.dot template. You can easily change or eliminate these shortcut key combinations in Normal.dot or whatever template you use with Word.

STEPS

Easing Use of the U.S.-International Keyboard with Word

Step 1. Click your Microsoft Word icon to open Word. Choose File, New from the menu.

You can make the changes to the Normal.dot template or to a new template. If you create a new template and then decide you want your new template to be the default template, you can use the Explorer to rename Normal.dot to Normal.old, and then rename your new template to Normal.dot.

Step 2. If you want to make changes to Normal.dot, click the OK button in the New dialog box. If you want to make a new template based on Normal.dot, click the Template option button, and then click OK.

Step 3. Choose Tools, Customize, and click the Keyboard tab (or click the Keyboard button in Word 97).

Step 4. Select the template that you want to change from the Save Changes In drop-down list in the lower-right corner window of the Customize (or Customize Keyboard) dialog box.

Step 5. Choose the categories shown in Table 27-3 in the Categories list, and scroll through the Commands list until you find the ones listed in the table.

Step 6. In the Current Keys field of the Customize (or Customize Keyboard) dialog box, highlight the shortcut key that you want to remove. Click the Remove button.

Step 7. Repeat steps 5 and 6 until you have removed all the shortcut key definitions that you want. The changes are made immediately to your new template or to Normal.dot.

Step 8. If you are creating a new template, choose File, Save when you are done.

Table 27-3 Word for Windows Shortcut Keys That Can Be Removed

Category	Command	Predefined Shortcut	Alternate
File	FilePrintPreview	Ctrl+Alt+I	Ctrl+F2
Edit	GoBack	Ctrl+Alt+Z	Shift+F5
Edit	RepeatFind	Ctrl+Alt+Y	Shift+F4
View	ViewNormal	Ctrl+Alt+N	
View	ViewOutline	Ctrl+Alt+O	
View	ViewPage	Ctrl+Alt+P	

Category	Command	Predefined Shortcut	Alternate
Insert	InsertAnnotation	Ctrl+Alt+A (Word 6.0 and 7.0)	
Insert	InsertComment	Ctrl+Alt+M (Word 97)	
Insert	InsertEndnoteNow	Ctrl+Alt+E	
Format	ApplyHeading1	Ctrl+Alt+1	
Format	ApplyHeading2	Ctrl+Alt+2	
Format	ApplyHeading3	Ctrl+Alt+3	
Table	TableUpdate AutoFormat	Ctrl+Alt+U	
Window and Help	DocSplit	Ctrl+Alt+S	

The third conflict involves the fact that you can't easily redefine two Word shortcut keys that conflict with the U.S.-International keyboard layout. They are:

Add a command to a menu   Ctrl+Alt+ = (equals sign)

Remove a command from a menu   Ctrl+Alt+ - (minus sign)

Word has defined another keyboard combination, Ctrl+Alt+T, to insert the trademark symbol. You can remove this keyboard shortcut if you so desire. (Choose Insert, Symbol, choose Normal Text in the Font drop-down list, click the ™ symbol, click the Shortcut Key button, click Alt+Ctrl+T in the Current Keys field, and click the Remove button.) In Word 95 and Word 97, you can very easily insert a trademark symbol without using Ctrl+Alt+T. Simply type **(tm)** in your text. As soon as you continue to type, Word's AutoCorrect feature automatically replaces (tm) with ™.

You can, of course, choose to ignore these three conflicts and choose Insert, Symbol to pick the × and ¥ characters from Word's built-in character map. (By the way, this character map is the only place we've found that shows all 1726 characters of the Lucida Sans Unicode character set. Unfortunately, it only works with fonts that Word considers to be symbol fonts.) Another alternative is to define a new AltChar+*letter* shortcut for the three orphan symbols by choosing Insert, Symbol, highlighting them one at a time, and clicking the Shortcut Key button.

Accessing more hidden characters

A little-known benefit of Windows 98 is that it includes two bundled fonts containing numerous clipart-like characters. These fonts are called Wingdings and Webdings, and they can definitely add interest to your documents — once you know what characters they contain. Wingdings has been around for a while and is similar to the Zapf Dingbats font. (*Dingbat* is a traditional printer's term for a piece of decorative type.) Webdings is brand new with Windows 98, and it is intended as an aid for web site designers (though it looks just fine in print).

Every Windows 98 user has access to hundreds of characters that are not visible on any keyboard. And users who previously purchased the Microsoft TrueType Font Pack have access to more than 1000 additional math symbols, bullets, arrows, and dingbats. (Unfortunately, the Font Pack is no longer available.) All this, and there is almost no way for the average person to find out what characters are available.

To be fair, we must mention that Microsoft does provide the Character Map applet with Windows 98 to try to help people access these symbols. When you start this map, it displays 224 characters that belong to a Windows font: the first 96 characters in the font, plus 128 characters that pertain to the language you are using. Unfortunately, the Character Map window is small (and it can't be resized, although you can click on one character at a time to see an enlarged view of each character), so it's difficult to use it to browse through your type collection.

To give you a place to see many of these characters and symbols, we've collected all the characters (other than the extended multilingual fonts) available to Windows 98 users into two charts. Figure 27-1, which is at the beginning of this chapter, is for all Windows 98 users, while Figure 27-6 is for users who have the TrueType Font Pack. You might want to photocopy these charts and tack them on the nearest bulletin board for the next time you need just the right symbol.

You can insert about half of the characters in these figures into a document by pressing a key on your keyboard. Pressing the *w* key, for example, inserts character number 119 into your document. (Refer to Figure 27-1.) If you're using a text typeface such as Arial, the inserted character is, in fact, a *w*. But if you're using Wingdings, the same keystroke inserts a diamond-shaped bullet (◆), and if you're using Webdings, that keystroke inserts a little golf flag (⛳).

We use many of the higher-numbered special characters in the standard Windows ANSI character set all the time. Windows makes it easy for us to use a long dash for emphasis — like this — by typing Alt+0151. A bullet that you can use to set off paragraphs is at Alt+0149.

The Wingdings and Webdings character sets take these special symbols much, much farther. Many of their characters are pictorial. This includes keyboard and mouse symbols (Alt+55 and Alt+56), and electronic mail symbols (Alt+42 through Alt+47) in the Wingdings font.

Using Multiple Languages

Many North American companies routinely use different languages in their documents. Companies in the southern U.S. often produce documents containing both English and Spanish text, while Canadian documents often include both English and French.

The Windows 95 TrueType Font Pack Character Sets

The True Type Font Pack included four TrueType special character fonts: Lucida Bright Math Extension, Math Italic, Math Symbol, and Monotype Sorts. To access characters that cannot be typed directly from the keyboard:

1) Make sure the Num Lock light is *on*.
2) Hold down the Alt key while typing the appropriate number on the numeric keypad.
3) Release the Alt key.

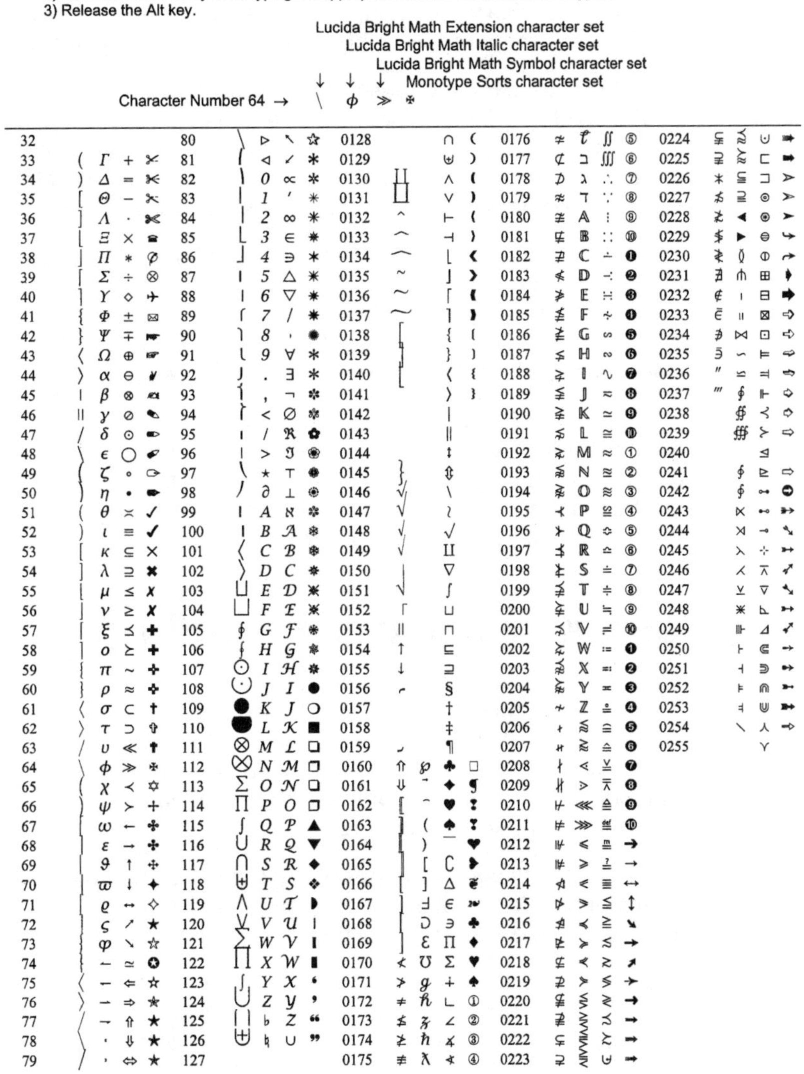

```
                            Lucida Bright Math Extension character set
                              Lucida Bright Math Italic character set
                                Lucida Bright Math Symbol character set
                                  Monotype Sorts character set
                            ↓    ↓    ↓
        Character Number 64 →    \    φ    ≫    ✽
```

The table below lists character numbers 32–127 and 0128–0255, each followed by its corresponding symbol in the four character sets (Lucida Bright Math Extension, Lucida Bright Math Italic, Lucida Bright Math Symbol, and Monotype Sorts). The individual special-font glyphs cannot be faithfully reproduced here.

Number					Number					Number					Number			
32					80					0128					0176				
33					81					0129					0177				
34					82					0130					0178				
35					83					0131					0179				
36					84					0132					0180				
37					85					0133					0181				
38					86					0134					0182				
39					87					0135					0183				
40					88					0136					0184				
41					89					0137					0185				
42					90					0138					0186				
43					91					0139					0187				
44					92					0140					0188				
45					93					0141					0189				
46					94					0142					0190				
47					95					0143					0191				
48					96					0144					0192				
49					97					0145					0193				
50					98					0146					0194				
51					99					0147					0195				
52					100					0148					0196				
53					101					0149					0197				
54					102					0150					0198				
55					103					0151					0199				
56					104					0152					0200				
57					105					0153					0201				
58					106					0154					0202				
59					107					0155					0203				
60					108					0156					0204				
61					109					0157					0205				
62					110					0158					0206				
63					111					0159					0207				
64					112					0160					0208				
65					113					0161					0209				
66					114					0162					0210				
67					115					0163					0211				
68					116					0164					0212				
69					117					0165					0213				
70					118					0166					0214				
71					119					0167					0215				
72					120					0168					0216				
73					121					0169					0217				
74					122					0170					0218				
75					123					0171					0219				
76					124					0172					0220				
77					125					0173					0221				
78					126					0174					0222				
79					127					0175					0223				
															0224				
															0225				
															0226				
															0227				
															0228				
															0229				
															0230				
															0231				
															0232				
															0233				
															0234				
															0235				
															0236				
															0237				
															0238				
															0239				
															0240				
															0241				
															0242				
															0243				
															0244				
															0245				
															0246				
															0247				
															0248				
															0249				
															0250				
															0251				
															0252				
															0253				
															0254				
															0255				

Figure 27-6: Many users are unaware of the non-text character sets in the Microsoft TrueType Font Pack. This product is no longer available, but it still works with Windows 98 if you already have it.

In WordPad, Word for Windows, and other word processors, you can mark text as belonging to a particular language. By default, text in Word documents is marked as the language you have selected using the Keyboard icon in the Control Panel. But you could use the Tools, Language command to mark one section as English (United States), and mark another section as French (Canadian), for example. You can mark text blocks as small as a single word or character as belonging to a particular language.

The ability to mark sections of text for different languages is helpful when you're spell-checking, hyphenating, and using a thesaurus in a document with text in multiple languages. If you have installed proofing utilities in another language, Word for Windows automatically uses those utilities when operating on any section of text marked as that language.

This ability to keep track of what text is in what language is part of the operating system in Windows 98, so many applications can take advantage of this capability. In fact, Windows 98 has added support for many new languages, including Albanian, Belarusian, Estonian, Latvian, Lithuanian, Romanian, Serbian, Slovak, Ukrainian, and Turkish.

In addition, Windows 98 makes it easy to switch among different languages and, if you like, among different keyboard layouts. You can set up a number of different language identifiers and choose among them as you write a multilingual document. You just pick the appropriate identifier to tell Windows 98 which language you're going to use for the next section.

Setting up and using multilingual identifiers

If you have installed Multilanguage Support, you can write documents using Baltic, Greek, Turkish, Cyrillic, or Central European character sets (and Hebrew in Lucida Unicode). Installing Multilanguage Support installs the Arial, Times New Roman, Tahoma, Verdana, Lucida Console, Lucida Sans Unicode, and Courier New fonts with the Extended Windows ANSI character set, which contains 652 characters.

To install Multilanguage Support, click the Add/Remove Programs icon in your Control Panel, click the Windows Setup tab, and mark the Multilanguage Support check box.

You use the Keyboard Properties dialog box in the Control Panel (under the Keyboard icon) to set up multilingual identifiers. Once you've created the identifiers, they appear in the Tray on your Taskbar, as shown in Figure 27-7.

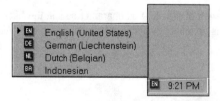

Figure 27-7: Language identifiers in the Tray on the Taskbar.

To create these identifiers, follow these steps:

STEPS

Adding Multilingual Identifiers

Step 1. Open the Control Panel by clicking the Start button, pointing to Settings, and then clicking Control Panel.

Step 2. Click the Keyboard icon.

Step 3. Click the Language tab.

Step 4. Click the Add button to display the Add Language dialog box.

Step 5. Display the Language drop-down list.

Step 6. Pick the language that you want, and click OK. The default keyboard layout for that language or location is now displayed next to the language in the Keyboard Properties dialog box.

Step 7. If you want a different keyboard layout, click the Properties button, and choose a new layout.

Step 8. Repeat steps 4 through 7 until you have added all the language identifiers that you will be using regularly, and then close the Keyboard Properties dialog box.

Once you have set up a list of language identifiers, you can choose among them by picking them from the Taskbar. Click the language identifier in the Tray (the identifier for the currently selected language). When the list of identifiers pops up, click the one that you want to use.

You can also use the Left Alt+Shift key combination to rotate through the list. You have to release the Alt key before you press the next Shift key.

If you prefer, you can change the Left Alt+Shift shortcut key to Ctrl+Shift, or to no shortcut key at all. To do this, select the desired option button in the Language tab of the Keyboard Properties dialog box.

One language/keyboard layout combination is always set as the default. To designate the default combination, highlight it in the Language tab of the Keyboard Properties dialog box, and click the Set As Default button.

Multilingual documents

Once you have set up multilingual identifiers, as described in the previous section, you are ready to start typing in a foreign language. Of course, your keyboard keys often won't have the correct characters engraved upon them (check out Greek in Figure 27-8, for example), so you'll need to make up a chart that tells you which characters show up in your document when you type specific keys.

Figure 27-8: The Greek keyboard layouts for unshifted (bottom) and shifted (top) characters.

The standard version of Windows 98 does not yet support Arabic, Japanese, Korean, or Chinese. However, the versions of Windows 98 that are localized for these countries do. In addition, these localized versions of Windows 98 include Pan-European Multilanguage Support — so if you need to write in Arabic or an Asian language, buy the localized version and you'll get Baltic, Central European, Cyrillic, Greek, Turkish and Western thrown in.

All you need to do to switch among languages and keyboard layouts is press Left Alt+Shift. To test this, start WordPad. Type text and then press Left Alt+Shift to switch your language/keyboard layout to Greek (assuming you set up a Greek identifier). The font list box in the WordPad format bar switches from a font identified as Western to one identified as Greek, and Greek letters now appear in your document as you type. If you're using a font that doesn't have the expanded character set, Windows 98 will substitute another font that does, so your readers can still read your text.

You may want to write in a language for which Windows 98 does not provide a keyboard identifier — Hawaiian, for instance, or Hebrew. Fonts are available (often as shareware from universities) for a number of languages not specifically supported by Microsoft — but they're pretty cumbersome to use if you have to remember and type a special code for each letter. Fortunately, Janko's Keyboard Generator makes it easy to set up a native Windows 98 keyboard layout for just about any written language with an alphabet (recent examples include Thai and Mongolian). Using a graphical representation of a keyboard, you assign a character to a key simply by dragging it. Janko's Keyboard Generator is shareware; the license fee is $15, and there is no license fee if you use it only on your home computer. You can download the latest version from http://solair.eunet.yu/~janko/engdload.htm. Janko also includes a number of links to sites that offer ready-to-use keyboard files built with his generator (as well as fonts), so you may be able to save yourself some work.

Multilingual proofing tools

If you find yourself using different languages frequently, you would probably benefit from one or more proofing tools specific to your languages. A web search reveals a number of proofing tools for single languages; there are a few companies that make a business of offering tools for a variety of languages.

Alki Software Corp.'s Proofing Tools packages are designed specifically to work with Microsoft Word, including Word 97. A significant number of languages supported by Windows 98 are represented in their catalog. The manual alone is valuable for its extensive charts showing the location of Windows characters and the layout of every different keyboard language supported by Windows. More importantly, each package provides a spelling checker, thesaurus, and hyphenation utility for the language. You can visit Alki Software Corp. at http://www.proofing.com.

World Language Resources (http://www.worldlanguage.com) offers browsers, word processors, spelling checkers and Office 97 proofing tools for over 400 languages. They also sell translation tools and offer an online translation service.

Microsoft Foreign Proofing Tools from Language Partners International Inc. allows you to check spelling, find synonyms, and hyphenate in over thirty languages, from Basque to Turkish. The company says it uses the same spelling dictionary, hyphenation file, and thesaurus that Microsoft incorporates in its foreign versions of Word. Each package (one language) is $99.95. Call Language Partners International at 800-222-9242, send e-mail to info@languagepartners.com, or visit http://www.languagepartners.com.

Fingertip Software makes keyboards, keycaps, fonts, and utilities for over twenty Slavic and European languages (Cyrillic and Latin characters). Their Cyrillic Starter Kit includes support for KOI8-R, a Cyrillic character set used on the Internet but not supported by Microsoft. Fingertip's 3-D Keyboards are software applications designed to make it easier to type in more than one language. Contact Fingertip Software at 800-209-4063, or visit http://www.fingertipsoft.com.

The web is multilingual

Even a small amount of time spent browsing the web makes it clear that English is no longer the only language spoken there. Windows 98's Multilanguage Support extends to Internet Explorer, making it easy to read web pages written in other languages. However, you implement it separately from the Windows 98 Multilanguage Support detailed in "Setting up and using multilingual identifiers" earlier in this chapter. Here's how:

STEPS

Viewing Web Pages in Different Languages

Step 1. Click the Internet Explorer icon on your Desktop to open it.

Step 2. Go to the Internet Explorer Components Download page on the Microsoft web site, http://www.microsoft.com/ie/ie40/download/b2/x86/en/download/addon95.htm.

Step 3. Scroll down to the Multi-Language Support section, and mark the language groups that you want to download. Pan-European Support includes support for Central European, Cyrillic, Greek, Turkish and Baltic characters. When you click Next, the web site prompts you to choose a download site and then downloads and *automatically* installs the software on your computer (without asking you whether to open or save the file).

Step 4. Restart your computer when you are prompted, and reopen Internet Explorer.

Step 5. Choose View, Internet Options, click the General tab, and click the Languages button to display the Language Preference dialog box.

Step 6. Click the Add button. In the Add Language dialog box, select the languages that you want to be able to view with your browser. (You can Ctrl+click to select multiple languages.) Click OK.

Step 7. If you have several languages listed in the Language Preference dialog box, you can arrange them in order of priority; many multilanguage web sites are set up to deliver content in the highest priority language available. Click OK twice.

You should now be able to see web pages in multiple languages, even on the same page.

Note that many Russian speakers on the Internet use an older Cyrillic character set called KOI8-R. This standard came out of the Unix computing environment (as did the Internet) and is still widespread, especially among academics, who tend to be Unix users. KOI8-R is not compatible with Unicode, and is not supported by Office 97 — but it is supported by Internet Explorer and Outlook Express.

If you find web sites or e-mail messages that should appear in Cyrillic but do not, choose View, Fonts in Internet Explorer or View, Language in Outlook Express and select the KOI8-R character set. KOI8-R fonts are available from some third parties; if you need to communicate in Russian, it's worth a visit to Janko's web site (see "Multilingual documents" earlier in this chapter), or to the KOI8-R Russian Net Character Set site at http://www.nagual.pp.ru/~ache/koi8.html.

Multilingual e-mail

The Internet and many other e-mail systems handle only the lower ASCII character set (unless you are using MIME or UUENCODE). Windows Messaging takes that a step further by letting you send and receive e-mail with the full Windows ANSI character set (224 characters).

Outlook Express supports the full range of both ANSI and Extended ANSI characters, giving you access to the non-Latin character sets. To read messages containing these characters, you must have first installed Multilanguage Support for Windows 98 by clicking the Add/Remove Programs icon in your Control Panel, clicking the Windows Setup tab, and marking the Multilanguage Support check box.

When you receive an e-mail message, Outlook Express looks in its header to see what character set it should use (you can't ordinarily see the header information). If the message header sufficiently identifies the language of the contents, Outlook Express will display the message in that language. If it doesn't, choose View, Language (either in the Outlook Express menu bar or in your message's menu bar), and select the correct language for viewing the message.

When you do this, you may see an error message asking if you want to use the character set you have just selected to view all messages whose headers contain the same character set as this e-mail message. You should click Yes. This will affect all messages you receive in the future whose headers contain that character set. If you find you have made this substitution in error (maybe you substituted Greek for English and now *everything* appears in Greek), you can go back. Choose Tools, Options, click the Read tab, and click the International Settings button. You'll see all the substitutions you've set up — highlight the one you want to remove, and click Remove (see Figure 27-9).

To send e-mail messages in other languages, you must not only have Multilanguage Support installed, but you must also set up one or more multilingual identifiers for your keyboard, as described in "Setting up and using multilingual identifiers" earlier in this chapter. In the menu bar of the New Message window, choose Format, Language, and select the language you want to put in the header of your message. You can still change languages as you type in the body of the message, simply by picking the identifiers from the Tray or using the Left Alt+Shift key combination.

When you send a message whose header information is in the Western alphabet, but that contains characters from a different language (Greek, for example), you will see a Message Character Set Conflict dialog box (shown in Figure 27-10). It offers you a choice between sending your e-mail message in Unicode, or sending it As Is. For the best results, choose Cancel to go back to your New Message window, click Format, Language, and choose Greek. The Western characters you have already typed for the address and subject will not change.

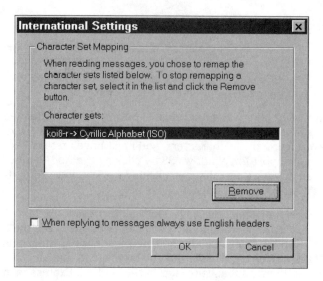

Figure 27-9: The International Settings dialog box. You can see what character set substitutions you have set up, and remove them if necessary.

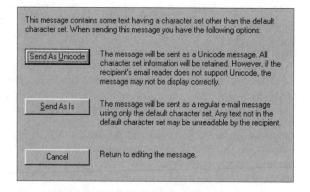

Figure 27-10: The Message Character Set Conflict dialog box.

If you prefer to use an English header (perhaps you only quoted one line of Homer and the rest is in English), it's best to format your message using Rich Text (HTML)—you can then send it As Is. You can also send As Is by using the UUENCODE and MIME formats; see "UUENCODE or MIME" in Chapter 19 for details on how to set the format for your outgoing mail. If you send a plain text message in Unicode, your recipient must view the message using the Unicode (not the Greek or Western) character set. Unicode is called Universal Alphabet (UTF-8) in the Outlook Express pull-down menus. If you send your message As Is in plain text, the Greek letters will probably not be readable.

When you reply to a message, Outlook Express attempts to use the same language by default (within the limitations of the character sets you have available). To use a different character set, you must use the Rich Text (HTML) format. Keep in mind that your correspondent must be able to receive whatever format you send. It may take some experimentation to find the combination of formats and characters that your pen pal finds the most palatable.

Using Keyboard Shortcuts

In this section, we examine the many shortcuts Windows and Windows applications assign to key combinations, such as Ctrl+Insert and Ctrl+A. Additionally, we teach you how to redefine key combinations that aren't used by *any* Windows applications in order to support your own macros.

You can specify that you have to press and release the Shift, Ctrl, or Alt keys *before* pressing the letter key of the combination by marking the Use StickyKeys check box in the Keyboard tab of the Accessibility Properties dialog box. You'll find this dialog box under the Accessibility Options icon in the Control Panel.

The most important (and poorly documented) shortcuts

Despite the ease-of-use publicity about Windows, a novice Windows user is confronted with a bewildering array of new objects to click and shortcut keys to learn. These shortcut keys are difficult to memorize, and some shortcuts are not documented at all. Furthermore, once you've learned these shortcuts, they are hard to remember because many of the key combinations are confusingly similar and do not follow any logical pattern.

Pressing Alt+Esc, for example, switches you from your current application to other applications running under Windows, while Alt+F4 exits the application that is running. Quick — do you remember which is which? Why is the act of exiting assigned to an F4 key combination instead of one based on the "Escape" key?

As another example, most Windows applications that support multiple, smaller windows (*child windows*) inside their main application window allow you to jump quickly from child window to child window by pressing Ctrl+Tab. But not Word for Windows — Ctrl+Tab actually inserts a tab character inside a document table. To cycle through child windows in Word, you have to press Ctrl+F6.

Despite these inconsistencies, there *are* many shortcut keys that work the same way in all or most Windows applications. We have gathered many of these in Table 27-4. You'll find other shortcut keys in "Startup Keys" in Chapter 5, "Hot keys" in Chapter 10, and "Windows shortcut keys" in Chapter 34.

Table 27-4   Windows 98 Shortcut Keys

Key or Combination	Effect
Alt or F10	If you press and release either of these keys without any other keys, it activates an application's menu bar. You can then choose a command from the menu system with the keyboard. Press the underlined letter in the menu name, and then press the underlined letter in the desired command. (You can also press the right and left arrow keys to highlight a menu name, press the down arrow key to highlight the desired command, and then press Enter.)
Alt+*letter*	Activates the menu on an application's menu bar that has an underlined letter corresponding to the letter you pressed. Works the same way if you press and release Alt, and then press the underlined letter.
Alt+Down Arrow	Displays the contents of a drop-down list. This combination is a toggle.
End	Moves to the end of a line (in a word processor).
Ctrl+End	Moves to the end of a document (in a word processor).
Enter	Selects a choice that is highlighted on a menu or in a dialog box.
Alt+Enter	Switches a DOS application that is running full-screen to running in a window (and back). This doesn't work to toggle a Windows application from a maximized to a restored window and back. If you have highlighted an icon, pressing Alt+Enter is the same as right-clicking and then clicking Properties.
Esc	Closes a dialog box or drop-down menu without taking any action.
Alt+Esc	Each time you press this combination, you switch (in a round-robin fashion) to another application running under Windows.
Ctrl+Esc	Displays the Start menu and the Taskbar. The Taskbar buttons are covered up by the Start menu if the Taskbar is docked on the right or left edge of your Desktop.
Ctrl+Esc, Esc, Tab	After you've pressed these keys, you can use the arrow keys to navigate between Taskbar buttons, or use the Tab key to navigate between the Start button, the Taskbar, and the Desktop.
Tab or F6	Switches the focus between the Start button, the Taskbar, and the Desktop. Focus must first be on one of these items before pressing the key. If the Taskbar is set to Auto hide mode, pressing either key brings up the Taskbar.
Alt+F4	Closes the current application. If the current application is the Taskbar, this also exits Windows after you give confirmation.
Ctrl+F4	Closes a child window in multidocument Windows applications (File Manager, Word for Windows, and so on).

Key or Combination	Effect
Home	Moves to the beginning of a line (in a word processor).
Ctrl+Home	Moves to the beginning of a document (in a word processor).
Alt+Hyphen	Pulls down an application's multidocument control menu from the multidocument control menu icon at the far left end of the menu bar. This menu controls the size and other aspects of the child window. Do not confuse this icon with the system menu icon, which controls the application itself (see Alt+Spacebar) and is located directly above the multidocument control menu icon.
Print Screen	Copies the entire Windows display to the Clipboard. You can then paste the image into MS Paint or another graphics application and print it if you like.
Alt+Print Screen	Copies only the currently active window to the Clipboard. This could be the current application or a dialog box that has the keyboard focus within that application. This may not work on 84-key keyboards and computers with old BIOS chips. If it doesn't, try Shift+Print Screen instead.
Spacebar	Marks or clears a check box.
Alt+Spacebar	Pulls down the system control menu, the icon in the upper-left corner of an application window that controls that application's size and position, among other things.
Tab	Moves the selection box (the dotted rectangular box) to the next choice in a dialog box.
Shift+Tab	Moves the selection box in reverse order.
Alt+Tab	Switches to the application that was the current application before the application you are presently in. Switches back when pressed again. This may not work on 84-key keyboards and computers with old keyboard BIOS chips.
Alt+Shift+Tab	Switches between applications in the opposite direction as Alt+Tab.
Alt+Tab+Tab	Switches to every application currently running under Windows. Hold down Alt and press Tab repeatedly until the icon of the application you want to switch to is highlighted. Then release the Alt key. This is like Alt+Esc, but it displays only the icon and application names until you release the Alt key. (See the "Alt+Tab+Tab — the task switcher" section below.) This may not work on 84-key keyboards and computers with old keyboard BIOS chips.
Ctrl+Tab or Ctrl+F6	Jumps to the next child window in a multidocument application such as File Manager. (Use Ctrl+F6 in Word for Windows.)
Ctrl+X	Cuts highlighted item.
Ctrl+C	Copies highlighted item.

(continued)

Table 27-4 *(Continued)*

Key or Combination	Effect
Ctrl+V	Pastes a copied or cut item.
Ctrl+Z	Undoes a previous action.

The following keyboard shortcuts work with the Microsoft Natural Keyboard. The Win key is the key with the Windows flag.

Key or Combination	Effect
Win	Displays the Start menu.
Win+E	Starts the Explorer.
Win+F	Opens the Find Files dialog box, similar to F3.
Ctrl+Win+F	Opens the Find Computer dialog box.
Win+M	Minimize All Windows.
Shift+Win+M	Undo Minimize All.
Win+R	Opens the Run dialog box .
Win+Tab	Switches between Taskbar buttons.
Win+Break	Opens the System Properties dialog box.

The following keyboard shortcuts let you modify how Windows 98 starts up. You press them before the Windows 98 graphic appears on your screen, while the Starting Windows 98 message is displayed.

Key or Combination	Effect
F4	Start the previous operating system. Boot MS-DOS. If Windows 98 has been installed in its own directory on the computer that has the MS-DOS 6.*x* or previous DOS operating system, then this key will start DOS instead of Windows. This also works for OS/2 and Windows NT.
F5	Safe mode startup of Windows 98. This allows Windows 98 to start with its most basic configuration, bypassing your Autoexec.bat and Config.sys files, using the VGA driver for video, and not loading any networking software. Use this if you have any problems starting Windows 98.
Shift+F5	Command line start. Boots into real-mode version of DOS 7.1. MS-DOS, Command.com and Dblspace are loaded low, taking up valuable conventional memory. Bypasses Config.sys and Autoexec.bat.
Ctrl+F5	Command line start without compressed drives. The Dblspace.bin and Drvspace.bin files are ignored, and double-spaced and drive-spaced drives are not mounted.
F6	Safe mode startup (like F5) but with the addition of the network.

Key or Combination	Effect
F8 (or Ctrl)	Starts the Windows 98 Startup menu. You need to hold down the Ctrl key before the DOS bootup process begins. If you have quick fingers, you can press the F8 key in between the end of the power-on self test and the beginning of the DOS bootup phase.
Shift+F8	Interactive start that goes through Config.sys and Autoexec.bat one line at a time and lets you decide if you want that line read and acted upon. Also goes through each command that Io.sys initiates before it carries out the commands in Config.sys. (This is interesting to watch in itself.) Same as menu item 5 on the Windows 98 Startup menu.

Alt+Tab+Tab — the task switcher

You probably already know two shortcut key combinations that allow you to switch among running applications. Alt+Esc opens a different application every time you press it, and Alt+Tab switches from your current application to the application you previously used, and back.

But the best way to switch among your running applications isn't documented at all. Just *hold down* the Alt key while you press the Tab key several times, pausing slightly between each press. Unlike Alt+Esc, which switches applications and redraws the window for every application in turn, Alt+Tab+Tab switches applications but shows only the application's icon and name. Alt+Tab+Tab is a much faster method than Alt+Esc, because it lets you cycle quickly through all your running applications until you find the one you want. Simply release the Alt key when the desired application's icon is highlighted. The application's window is fully drawn and shifts to the foreground.

Alt+Esc and Alt+Tab+Tab work with both Windows applications and DOS applications running under Windows, whether they are running maximized, restored, or minimized as icons on the Taskbar.

84-key keyboards and computers with older keyboard BIOS chips may not recognize the Alt+Tab key combination. IBM's BIOS for its enhanced-AT 101-key keyboard was one of the first to accept the Alt key as a way to modify the meaning of the Tab key. Test your keyboard to see which combinations of keys you can take advantage of. If you have a 101-key keyboard, you shouldn't have a problem with Alt+Tab+Tab or any of the other possible combinations.

Using the humble Shift key

Behold the lowly Shift key. You hold it down while you type, and all you get is an uppercase letter, right? Not quite. Beneath the Shift key's humble reputation lies a world of undocumented functionality.

Many Windows users know the most basic ways the Shift key has been redefined. One of the first lessons for a new Windows user, for example, is that holding down the Shift key in a word processor while pressing an arrow key actually highlights text, instead of just moving the insertion point. And holding down Shift while clicking in text highlights everything between the insertion point and the place you clicked (in most word processors).

In the Explorer and on the Desktop, holding down the Shift key while hovering over an icon with your mouse pointer selects all the icons between (and including) the previously highlighted one and the one you hover over. (If you want to select multiple icons that aren't adjacent to one another, hold down the Ctrl key while you hover over each one.)

Other functions of the Shift key are much less well known. When you use the straight-line tool in MS Paint and many other drawing programs, for example, holding down Shift forces the line you draw to be perfectly horizontal or vertical. Similarly, when you use the box or oval tools, Shift forces these shapes into perfect squares or circles, respectively.

If you have redefined any application menu items — by writing a Word for Windows macro to modify the File Print routine, say — you can often force the application to revert to the original, built-in procedure by holding down Shift while clicking that menu choice. (To defeat Word's AutoExec macro, however, you must start the application with the command Winword /m.)

Another great use of the Shift key involves the \Windows\Start Menu\ Programs\StartUp folder. If you put shortcuts to applications in this folder, Windows automatically loads the applications every time it starts. But if you hold down Shift when you see the Windows 98 logo — and keep it held down until the Taskbar is displayed on your Desktop — the StartUp folder is completely ignored! This is *very* handy if something in the StartUp folder is hanging Windows. You might also use this just to get Windows up and running quickly for some short task.

If you hold down Shift as soon as you see the "Starting Windows 98" message, your Config.sys and Autoexec.bat files are ignored. (If you don't see the "Starting Windows 98" message on your computer, hold down the Shift key during the Windows phase of the bootup process.)

If you are using the File Manager, you can use the Shift key to display subdirectories only when you *care* to see them. For example, clicking the drive C icon (or pressing Ctrl+C) displays the top-level directories of the C drive. If you instead hold down the Shift key when you click the drive C icon, you force the File Manager to display all of the subdirectories on that drive. The Shift key works as a keyboard shortcut, too. When you press Ctrl+Shift+C, File Manager changes to drive C and displays all subdirectories, and so forth. This (undocumented) feature does not work in the Windows 98 Explorer.

Undocumented

If you mark the Restart option button in the Shut Down Windows dialog box and then hold down the Shift key as you click the Yes button, Windows 98 restarts without a warm reboot.

Undocumented

If you want to open a file using an application that is different than the application associated with its file type, you can hold down the Shift key as you right-click the file, and then choose Open With in the context menu.

Do you want to really delete a file instead of sending it to the Recycle Bin? Highlight the file in a folder or Explorer window, and hold down the Shift key as you press Delete.

If you don't want a CD-ROM to start up automatically when you insert it in your CD-ROM drive, hold down the Shift key for a few seconds after you insert the CD-ROM.

Caps Lock Notification

Tip

If you find yourself accidentally hitting Caps Lock, you can provide yourself with a little notification so you won't end up typing something LIKE THIS. You'll need to install the Accessibility options when you install Windows 98 or later using the Add/Remove Programs icon in the Control Panel.

STEPS

Turning on Caps Lock Notification

Step 1. Click the Start button, point to Settings, and then click Control Panel.

Step 2. Click the Accessibility Options icon.

Step 3. Mark the Use ToggleKeys check box. Click OK.

You will now hear a tone every time you press the Caps Lock, Num Lock, or Scroll Lock keys. The tone for enabling the key function is different from the tone for disabling it.

Keyboard Remap

Download Microsoft's Kernel Toys from http://www.microsoft.com/windows/software/krnltoy.htm and try out the keyboard remapper.

Keyboard Remap lets you swap your Caps Lock and Ctrl keys through a Control Panel applet. You can also turn your Right Alt and Right Ctrl keys into Menu and Windows keys, just like the keys on the Microsoft Natural Keyboard.

Turning Num Lock On or Off at Boot Time

If you have an enhanced keyboard with two sets of arrow keys, you may want the default state of the Num Lock key to be on when you start up Windows 98. Microsoft didn't see the need to build a switch into Windows 98 that allowed you to set the state of the Num Lock key, so you'll have to use lower level methods.

You first option is to edit your BIOS settings to turn the Num Lock key on or off. When you first boot up your computer, you are usually given a prompt that allows you to go to the BIOS by pressing a key such as Escape or F2 (the actual key depends on your computer). Once you're there, you can hunt around for a Num Lock setting.

Another option is to edit your Config.sys file, if you have one. Include a line that says:

```
NUMLOCK = OFF
```

or

```
NUMLOCK = ON
```

DOS National Language Support

When you install Windows 98, Setup reads your existing Autoexec.bat and Config.sys files to determine if you are using something other than a standard U.S. keyboard layout and require a character set other than the standard IBM PC-8 to display characters on your computer screen. If it finds the National Language Support calls in these files (lines that refer to the code pages specific to the keyboard layouts used in your country), it keeps them in the new Autoexec.bat and Config.sys files and chooses the appropriate keyboard layout for Windows 98.

The Change Code Page tool (changecp.exe) on the Windows 98 CD-ROM lets you choose a different code page (character set) for DOS programs when you set up Windows 98. You'll find it in the \tools\changecp folder. If you run Change Code Page after you've been using Windows 98 for a while, it can make some of your filenames unreadable—so use it with caution if at all.

It is quite easy to change your keyboard layout or use another language in Windows 98, but not in DOS applications. You need to reconfigure your Autoexec.bat and Config.sys files to reflect the changes you make to your keyboard layout and language settings in Windows 98 if you want your DOS programs to display the correct characters.

You'll need your DOS documentation for all the numerous details regarding National Language Support (keyboard layout and character sets) for DOS.

Making the Keys Repeat Faster

If you use your arrow keys a lot (and who doesn't), you'll want your insertion point to rip around your documents at the fastest speed possible. You can set the key repeat rate and the delay time before the key repeats itself in the Speed tab of the Keyboard Properties dialog box.

To change the keyboard speed:

STEPS

Changing Key Repeat Rate and Delay Time

Step 1. Open the Control Panel by clicking the Start button, pointing to Settings, and then clicking Control Panel.

Step 2. Click the Keyboard icon.

Step 3. Move the sliders, as shown in Figure 27-11.

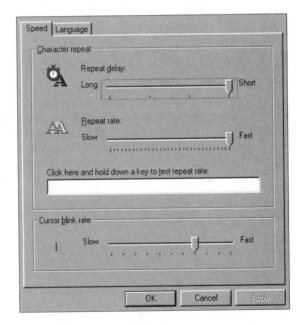

Figure 27-11: The Speed tab of the Keyboard Properties dialog box.

Step 4. Test your settings by clicking in the test field and holding down a key.

Step 5. Click OK.

The Speed tab of the Keyboard Properties dialog box is part of the user interface to the Registry. The actual Registry information about the keyboard is stored in the User.dat file in the \Windows folder. It is part of the information that is particular to a given user. This is what the exported ASCII file version of it looks like:

```
[HKEY_USERS\.Default\Control Panel\Keyboard]
"KeyboardSpeed"="31"
"KeyboardDelay"="0"
```

This Registry entry states that the repeat delay time is as short as possible, and that the key repeat rate is as fast as possible. We tried entering a number of values greater than 31, and it made no difference. If you set the sliders in the Speed tab of the Keyboard Properties dialog box all the way to the left, the values stored in the Registry are 0 and 3, respectively.

Secret

If you have a portable computer and an external keyboard, the speed and repeat rate settings may not be applied to them when you first start Windows 98. You'll have to open the Keyboard Properties dialog box every time you start Windows 98 and change these settings. You can put a shortcut to the Keyboard Properties dialog box on your Desktop to help with this process. For details, turn to "Creating Shortcuts" in Chapter 10.

If You Get a New and Different Keyboard

Almost all keyboards sold now are based on and compatible with the PC/AT Enhanced Keyboard (101/102-Key) standard. If you have a different keyboard attached to your computer, when you install Windows 98, it should detect the keyboard and install the correct keyboard driver. If you change your keyboard or if the hardware-detection procedures in Windows 98 Setup didn't install the correct driver, then you can manually identify the keyboard to Windows 98 and get the correct keyboard driver installed.

Follow these steps to change the keyboard driver:

STEPS

Changing the Keyboard Driver

Step 1. Open the Control Panel by clicking the Start button, pointing to Settings, and then clicking Control Panel.

Step 2. Click the System icon, click the Device Manager tab, click the plus sign next to the Keyboard icon, and double-click the icon for your keyboard.

Step 3. Click the Driver tab.

Step 4. Click the Upgrade Driver button, click Next, and then mark the option button to display a list of all drivers in a specific location and click Next again.

Step 5. Mark the Show All Hardware option button and choose a new keyboard driver from the list, as shown in Figure 27-12.

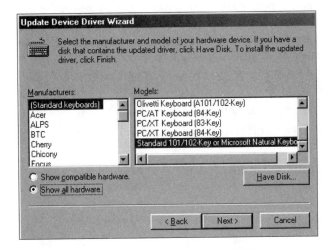

Figure 27-12: The Upgrade Device Driver Wizard. Choose a new keyboard driver here.

Behind the Keyboard Properties

Information about your keyboard type, layout, and language is stored in the Registry in the System.dat and User.dat files in the \Windows folder. You can start the Registry editor and search on *keyboard* to see how it is stored.

You can find other hardware and driver properties of the keyboard by clicking the System icon in the Control Panel, clicking the Device Manager tab, clicking the plus sign next to the Keyboard icon, highlighting your keyboard description, and then clicking the Properties button. There is not much you can change (unless you want to change the keyboard driver, as described in the "If You Get a New and Different Keyboard" section).

Summary

We detail the characters that you can use in Windows 98 and show you how to type characters that are not shown on your keyboard. We also discuss keyboard shortcuts and hot keys. Finally, we tell you how to modify properties of your keyboard driver to, for example, increase the key repeat rate. We provide:

▶ Lists of the character sets that come with Windows 98 and the fonts they are associated with.

▶ Tables of characters so you can find just the ones you want to spice up your documents.

▶ Four methods of typing characters that don't show up on your keyboard.

▶ Steps for creating multiple keyboard layouts, as well as multilingual documents.

▶ A table of all Windows 98 hot keys.

▶ Instructions on how to fix the Shift key so that it works the way a touch typist would expect it to.

▶ Steps for modifying your keyboard speed.

Chapter 28

Displays

In This Chapter

Windows 98 gives you the option to size your Desktop items to fit your screen size and resolution. We discuss:

▶ Installing new video drivers

▶ Choosing the correct video performance level

▶ Setting the magnification level to change the size of Desktop items

▶ Making the Desktop and all the elements on it look the way you want them to by changing their color, size, font, and font color

▶ Creating a fancy Desktop background and picking a screen saver

Getting the Picture

The image you see on your screen is sent to the monitor by your *graphics adapter*—also called a *display card, display adapter, video card, video adapter, graphics board, or graphics card.* Computers that can run Windows 98 have video cards (graphics chip sets on their motherboards) that are capable of displaying graphical images. We may use any of the preceding terms to refer to the graphics adapter that sends to the display (and often creates much of) the Windows 98 images.

Ordinarily, you won't have to tell Windows 98 about your graphics adapter or your monitor. During Windows 98 Setup, the hardware-detection process will most likely determine what card and monitor you have and install drivers for them (see "Hardware Detection" in Chapter 25). Even if you change your monitor or adapter, Windows 98 will normally learn of this during the hardware enumeration that occurs every time you start up. It will then either install the necessary driver automatically (if the Windows 98 cabinet files are stored on your hard disk), or lead you through the installation process. See "Plug and Play BIOS and Devices" in Chapter 25 for more on enumeration.

Installing a New Video Driver

If Windows 98 hasn't correctly detected your video card, you can install another video driver. If you are installing a non-plug and play video card, first change your video driver to the Standard Display Adapter (VGA) driver. Next, shut down Windows 98, power down your computer, install the new video card, reboot Windows 98, and install the new video driver.

If you install the new video card before installing the new driver, Windows may boot up in Safe mode, which is VGA, and then you can install the new video driver.

You can also upgrade or update your existing driver if a new one is available.

STEPS

Changing the Video Driver

Step 1. Right-click the Desktop. Click Properties, and then click the Settings tab. Click the Advanced button, the Adapter tab, and then the Change button to invoke the Upgrade Device Driver Wizard, as shown in Figure 28-1. Click Next.

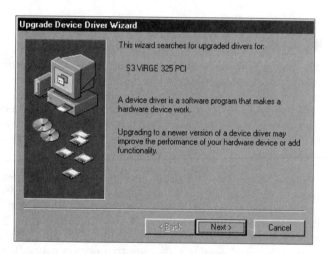

Figure 28-1: The Upgrade Device Driver Wizard.

Step 2. If you are installing a non-plug and play adapter and want to force the display to VGA, mark Display a List of All the Drivers in a Specific Location, So You Can Select the Driver You Want, as shown in Figure 28-2. Click Next, and then skip to step 7.

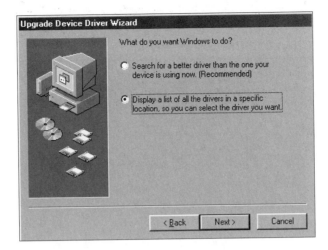

Figure 28-2: Display a list of all the video drivers.

Step 3. If you want to install a better driver for your existing video card, mark Search for a Better Driver Than the One Your Device Is Using Now. Click Next.

Step 4. You can specify where the Wizard will look for a new driver. Microsoft Windows Update is a Microsoft web site that has the latest drivers. Go there (mark the Microsoft Windows Update check box) if you think that the driver on your CD-ROM is out of date. Click Next.

If you know where the install file for the new driver for your video card is, mark the Floppy Disk Drive check box if it is on the root directory of a floppy disk. Mark Specify a Location if it is in a folder on your CD-ROM, hard disk, or floppy. Click the Browse button and navigate to the folder, as shown in Figure 28-3. Once you have chosen a folder, click OK, and then Next.

Step 5. Windows 98 will tell you if it finds a better driver. You can also choose to install a different driver, as shown in Figure 28-4. Click Next.

Step 6. Click Next and then Finish. You will have to restart Windows to have the new driver take effect.

Step 7. If you chose in step 2 to display a list of drivers, the Wizard displays the dialog box shown in Figure 28-5. The Show Compatible Hardware option is marked by default. Click the Show All Hardware option button to get the complete list of video drivers for Windows 98.

(continued)

STEPS *(continued)*

Changing the Video Driver

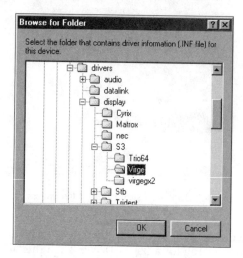

Figure 28-3: The Browse for Folder dialog box.

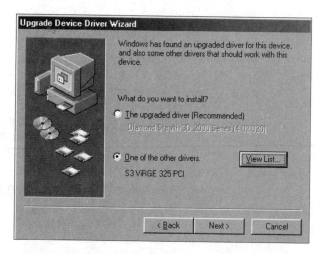

Figure 28-4: Choose to install a new driver — either the one Windows 98 recommends, or the one you prefer.

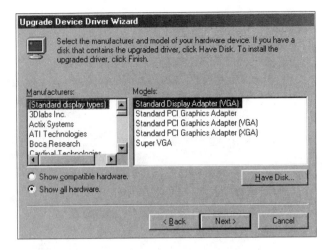

Figure 28-5: You see a list of all the video drivers that are available from the manufacturers for all video cards.

Step 8. Scroll up the Manufacturers list and select (Standard display types). Choose any model in the Models list on the right that is appropriate, say Standard Display Adapter (VGA). Click Next. If you receive the warning shown in Figure 28-6, click Yes.

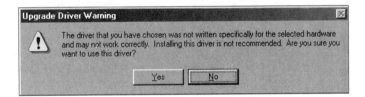

Figure 28-6: You are loading a standard VGA driver that is not optimal for your card.

Step 9. Click Next to accept the VGA driver. Then click Finish, as shown in Figure 28-7.

Step 10. A message box appears asking you to restart Windows 98. If you want the new video driver to take effect now, you should do so.

(continued)

STEPS *(continued)*

Changing the Video Driver

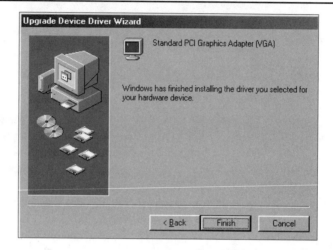

Figure 28-7: The VGA driver is installed.

Windows 98 may start in Safe mode or display an error message stating that it can't use the video driver choices you have implemented. If this happens, you can easily go back to the Settings tab of the Display Properties dialog box and install a new video driver. Windows 98 will start in VGA mode if it can't start in any other video mode.

Installing Windows 3.1 drivers

If you an older computer and are having problems with the Windows 98 drivers, you can install a video driver that worked with Windows 3.1, and use it with Windows 98.

STEPS

Installing a Windows 3.1 Video Driver

Step 1. Right-click the Desktop. Click Properties, and click the Settings tab. Click the Advanced button, the Adapter tab, and then the Change button to invoke the Upgrade Device Driver Wizard.

Step 2. Click Next. Mark Display a List of All The Drivers in a Specific Location, So You Can Select the Driver You Want. Click Next.

Step 3. Click the Have Disk button. Insert the manufacturer's Windows 3.1 driver diskette in your floppy drive. Alternatively, browse to the folder that contains the Oemsetup.inf file for that video driver.

Step 4. Choose the configuration from the alternatives presented.

Step 5. Click OK. Your video card driver is now installed. Click Finish.

Step 6. A message box appears asking you to restart Windows 98. If you want the new video driver to take effect now, you should do so.

Performance Graphics

Microsoft makes an effort to get the best performance out of video cards, but this may cause problems with your card. If you experience problems with your mouse pointer or unexplained crashes, you might want to back off from the default setting for hardware acceleration of your video card. Here's how:

STEPS

Changing Video Hardware Acceleration

Step 1. Right-click the Desktop. Click Properties, and click the Settings tab. Click the Advanced button, and then the Performance tab.

Step 2. Move the slider shown in Figure 28-8 to reduce hardware acceleration.

Step 3. Click OK, and then click Close to close the Display Properties dialog box.

Step 4. Click Yes when prompted to restart Windows.

(continued)

STEPS *(continued)*

Changing Video Hardware Acceleration

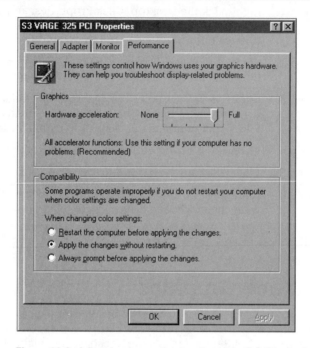

Figure 28-8: Adjust hardware acceleration with the slider in the Performance tab of the Properties dialog box for your video card.

The Performance tab of the Properties dialog box for your video card lets you see the settings in force for your hardware. Assuming that your video hardware is compatible with acceleration, you can use the slider to select one of four levels of acceleration: None, Basic, Most, or Full.

The Full setting lets Windows send display information to your video adapter in the most accelerated form. Some video hardware (described in more detail in the next section) may not be able to receive information this quickly in all cases, leading to unexplained crashes in applications. Unfortunately, when this happens you don't get error messages such as, "Change from Full acceleration to a lower setting." Instead, you get error messages such as, "Explorer.exe caused a General Protection Fault in Kernel32.dll." If you've been seeing this type of message, changing to a lower setting may help (and may not even hurt) your system's video performance.

The Most setting enables most acceleration functions, but disables some video functions related to displaying the mouse pointer. Specifically, this setting disables the *hardware cursor*, which is a way to make your video adapter display the position of the mouse pointer, thus taking a processing load off your CPU.

Changing to the Most setting inserts the line SWCursor=1 into the [Display] section of your System.ini file. This is one of many cases in which Windows 98 uses settings in System.ini to set the proper mode for various devices. Setting SWCursor=1 in System.ini has the same effect as loading the real-mode Microsoft Mouse driver in Autoexec.bat with the /Y switch. When Autoexec.bat includes /Y (for Yes) on the Mouse.exe line, the hardware cursor is disabled for the real-mode driver. (If you never use your mouse outside of Windows, you have no need for the real-mode Microsoft Mouse driver.)

The Most setting is often useful with Western Digital and S3-based video adapters.

The Basic setting adds two more lines to your System.ini and Win.ini files (in addition to the SWCursor line in System.ini). The line SafeMode=1 is added to the [Windows] section of your Win.ini file. This enables a fairly safe type of acceleration involving small screen patterns (*bit-block transfers*). And the line MMIO=0 is added to the [Display] section of your System.ini file, thus disabling memory-mapped input/output on S3-compatible video adapters. The Basic setting is useful primarily for some models of video hardware based on S3 chip sets.

The None setting eliminates all of the acceleration "tricks" Windows uses. Setting acceleration to None writes into your System.ini and Win.ini files all the lines that are added if you use the Basic setting. The only difference is that a setting of None writes the line SafeMode=2 instead of SafeMode=1 into Win.ini. SafeMode=2 forces Windows to draw to the screen using its own functions, rather than relying on your video display driver. If you are experiencing intermittent crashes that are related to the fact that your video hardware can't handle information as fast as Windows pushes it out, a setting of None will almost certainly solve the problem.

In summary, here are the effects of the four hardware acceleration settings:

- Full allows Windows 98 to accelerate all video commands.

- Most disables the hardware cursor for video adapters that have difficulty with mouse pointers.

- Basic disables the hardware cursor and memory-mapped input/output for some video adapters.

- None disables all video acceleration for maximum compatibility with all video adapters.

Specific video adapters with problems

If you are experiencing some of the symptoms discussed in the previous section, you should know about some specific hardware that might be responsible.

S3 Video Adapters. As mentioned earlier, some adapters based on the S3 video chip set may need a lower acceleration rate than Full. Some S3-based adapters may also conflict with modems attached to a COM4 serial port. A symptom of this is that the lights on an external modem will flash when you move your mouse or initiate any hard disk or network activity. According to Microsoft, this particular kind of problem affects older S3-based adapters such as Diamond Stealth 32 and 64, and Orchid Technology Fahrenheit 1280.

The cure for problems with S3-based adapters is to use less than Full acceleration and move your modem from COM4 to a lower number serial port, such as COM1, COM2, or COM3. You may also resolve the modem problem by changing your display properties to a video mode of 256 colors or fewer. (Right-click the Desktop, click Properties, click the Settings tab, and choose the desired setting from the Colors drop-down list.)

Microsoft also recommends that S3 users add the line HighColor=15 to the [Windows] section of the Win.ini file. This corrects a problem with incorrect color display in modes that support 16 colors per pixel (High Color).

Diamond Viper. If you installed Windows 98 over Windows 3.1 while running Setup from within Windows 3.1, the Windows 3.1 drivers for this video adapter are correctly preserved. If you happened to run Setup for Windows 98 from a DOS prompt, however, Windows 98 incorrectly uses its own Standard VGA driver. If you have done this, go to the \drivers\display\ diamond folder of the Windows 98 CD-ROM and run the setup.exe program located there to install the correct Viper driver.

Diamond Stealth 64. Microsoft recommends that you insert the line TrueColor=24 into the [Display] section of System.ini to obtain true 16.7-million-color support for the Diamond Stealth 64 video adapter.

ATI Mach 8/32/64. Microsoft states that you have to use the ATI Install.exe program to correctly configure both your adapter and your monitor before Windows 98 can properly handle high-resolution modes with the ATI Mach 8, 32, and 64 adapters. Otherwise, Windows may not be able to switch to a high-resolution mode, or your PC may crash when you attempt to do so.

Setting Windows Magnification

Windows 98 allows you to set the magnification of the font size used by the Desktop. This is a lot like the zoom capability built into full-featured word processors. Zoom lets you increase the displayed size of the text in a document window, without actually switching to a font of a larger point size. This makes it easier to see what you are writing on screen, but it doesn't change the size of the text when it prints.

Changing the magnification factor for the Desktop changes more than just the displayed size of text in a document. It changes the size of most things on the Desktop, including icons, icon titles, and the spacing between icons. It also changes the text in window titles and in menus, including the Start menu. Dialog boxes get bigger when you increase the magnification factor as well.

The magnification factor is arbitrarily set to equal 100 percent at 96 dots per inch—Windows refers to this as the Small Fonts size. In "The magnifier" in Chapter 26, we demonstrate that the actual magnification of the text display on 14-inch screens, compared to the same text printed on paper, is 125 percent. On a 17-inch display with the same video resolution, you see the same amount of text, but now the text is 44 percent larger than its printed size. The actual magnification you experience depends on the size of your display, the resolution you have set for your video card, and the font size you have chosen. We discuss font sizes further in "The logical inch" in Chapter 26.

To set the font size (or magnification), carry out the following steps:

STEPS

Changing the Windows Magnification Factor

Step 1.   Right-click the Desktop. Click Properties to bring up the Display Properties dialog box, and click the Settings tab, as shown in Figure 28-9. (If you have multiple monitors, you won't have a Settings tab. Click the Monitors tab instead.)

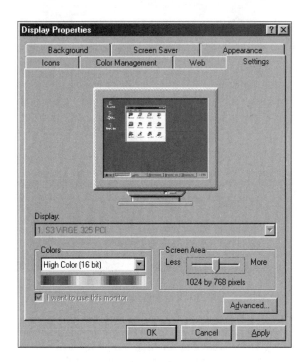

Figure 28-9: The Display Properties dialog box.

(continued)

STEPS *(continued)*

Changing the Windows Magnification Factor

Windows 98 integrates an improved version of the QuickRes utility that was first released right after Windows 95. It lets you quickly change your screen's color depth and resolution. You'll find it in your Tray on the Taskbar — it looks like a monitor icon. As an alternate route to the Settings tab of the Display Properties dialog box, you can click the QuickRes icon, and then click Adjust Display Properties. (If you don't have the QuickRes icon in your Tray, see the next step.)

Step 2. Click the Advanced button to display the Properties dialog box for your video card, as shown in Figure 28-10. Display the Font Size list, and choose Small Fonts, Large Fonts, or Other. Small Fonts gives you 100-percent magnification (96 dots per inch) and Large Fonts gives you 125-percent magnification (120 dots per inch).

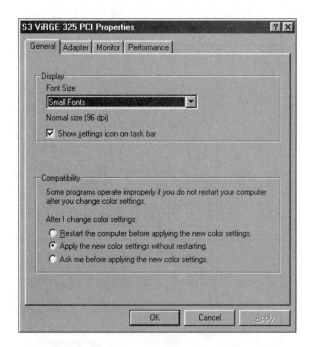

Figure 28-10: The Properties dialog box for your video card.

You can also decide whether to display the QuickRes icon your Tray. Clear the Show Settings Icon on Task Bar check box if you don't want QuickRes on your Taskbar.

Step 3. If you choose Other, use the Custom Font Size dialog box that appears to choose a magnification factor (see Figure 28-11). You can type an amount, use the drop-down list to choose an amount (150% is the next step up after Large Fonts), or drag the ruler.

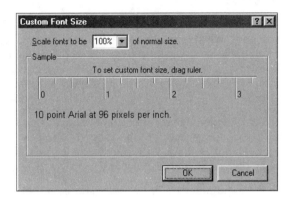

Figure 28-11: The Custom Font Size dialog box.

Step 4. Click OK in the Custom Font Size dialog box when you have chosen a magnification factor. Click OK in the Change System Font message box, click OK in the Properties dialog box for your video card, and click OK again in the Display Properties dialog box. You will be asked to restart Windows so that the changes can take effect.

You have to restart Windows every time you change font size. You can change the resolution and color depth without restarting.

The displayed inch

The ruler in the Custom Font Size dialog box, as shown in Figure 28-11, measures the *logical inch* or, more descriptively, the *displayed inch*.

If you have Windows 98 set at the Small Fonts magnification factor, your screen displays text at 96 pixels per displayed inch. If your monitor displays fewer than 96 pixels per actual inch (as measured by placing a ruler on your screen), then the displayed inch will be bigger than an actual inch.

The displayed inch is equal to the magnification factor (or font size) that you choose times the resolution (or dots per inch) that your screen displays, divided by 96 dots per inch.

Place a physical ruler over the ruler displayed on the screen and see how much bigger (or smaller) the displayed inch is compared to an actual inch. The ratio of the size of the displayed inch to the actual inch is the magnification of the text on your screen. An inch of text is displayed at the size of the displayed inch.

Changing the Size, Color, and Font of Objects on the Desktop

You can make a number of changes to the appearance of your Desktop and the objects on it. We strongly recommend that you make as many changes as necessary to make your Desktop pleasing to the eye and easy to read. The default Windows scheme for colors and fonts is okay, but it represents the lowest common denominator. It assumes the worst hardware. You can do much better.

Your video card, video driver, and monitor have their limitations and their strengths. These are reflected in the range of choices that are available in the Settings tab of the Display Properties dialog box. Within these limits, you can make further refinements.

You make these refinements in the Appearance tab of the Display Properties dialog box, which is shown in Figure 28-12. (Right-click the Desktop, choose Properties, and then click the Appearance tab.)

Figure 28-12: The Appearance tab of the Display Properties dialog box.

The top half of this tab is a mock display of typical Desktop objects. When you click an object, the value in the Item field changes to the name of that object. The name that appears may not be the one you'd expect to see, so it can be a bit frustrating. For example, you may click the word Disabled in the menu bar of the mock display thinking that you'll be able to change the color of disabled menu items, but what you get in the Item field is Menu.

Well, there is no accounting for taste.

The bottom half of the Appearance tab has eight attribute fields. These allow you to make changes in the color, size, font, font size, font color, and font style associated with the Desktop object listed in the Item field. The complete collection of all the attributes of all the Desktop objects is referred to as a *scheme*.

The schemes

Tip

All of the properties of Desktop objects that you can change can be stored in a scheme. If you change the attributes of a number of Desktop objects, it's a good idea to store these changes, plus the values that you didn't change, in a named scheme.

Windows 98 comes with 33 predefined schemes, and you can add your own. While you can modify the predefined schemes, it's best to save your modifications under a new name.

To see how schemes work, pull down the Schemes drop-down list and select various schemes. Once you've selected the first scheme, you can move to other schemes with the keyboard, by pressing the key for the first letter in the scheme's name.

The Windows 98 schemes are more powerful than those that came with Windows 3.1. They not only include color schemes (the origin of the use of the word *schemes*) but also sizes, fonts, font styles, font sizes, and font colors.

Check out the Windows Standard (large) and Windows Standard (extra large) schemes to see how enlargement works. Notice that some of the schemes are set up for High Color displays. These will only work if you have your color palette set to High Color in the Settings tab of the Display Properties dialog box.

Secret

Unless you use the Save As button to save your changes to a new scheme, Windows 98 saves the changes you make to attributes of the Desktop objects in the unnamed "current" scheme. These changes are lost if you switch to a named scheme and then try to go back.

The schematic values are stored in the Registry. You don't save any real space by deleting any of the existing schemes, although you might want to delete some of your test schemes.

Once you have designed a scheme, you'll probably stick with that one for a while. If you have enabled user profiles, different users can have different schemes on the same computer because the schemes are stored in the user portion (User.dat) of the Registry (see "Whose Desktop Is This Anyway?" in Chapter 12).

The items

There are 18 Desktop objects in the Item drop-down list (in the Appearance tab of the Display Properties dialog box). Twelve are displayed in the mock Desktop window at the top of the dialog box. Some, such as Icon Spacing (Horizontal) and Icon Spacing (Vertical), would be difficult to show on the mock Desktop.

If you click an object on the mock Desktop, its name appears in the Item field, and its attribute values are shown in the other fields. You can also pick a Desktop object from the Item drop-down list.

Lots of objects on your Desktop aren't listed in the Item drop-down list. Some names in the list refer to something other than what you would expect. And it isn't always obvious which attributes you're affecting when you make changes to a Desktop object. To make certain changes to Desktop objects, you have to edit the Registry.

Table 28-1 lists the attributes associated with every Desktop object in the Item drop-down list. This table not only lists most of the Desktop objects, it also tells you what attributes you can change for each object.

Table 28-1   Attributes of Desktop Objects

Item	Color	Font	Size	Font Color	Font Size
3D Objects	x			x	
Active Title Bar	x	x	x	x	x
Active Window Border	x	x			
Application Background		x			
Caption Buttons	x				
Desktop		x			
Icon	x		x	x	
Icon Spacing (Horizontal)	x				
Icon Spacing (Vertical)	x				
Inactive Title Bar	x	x	x	x	x
Inactive Window Border	x	x			
Menu	x	x	x	x	x
Message Box			x	x	x
Palette Title	x		x	x	
Scrollbar				x	
Selected Items	x	x	x	x	x
ToolTip		x	x	x	x
Window		x			x

In addition, the Active Title Bar and Inactive Title Bar can have a second color, Color 2. Title bars can display a color gradient. Color 2 is the color on the right end of the title bar, and Color is the color on the left end. The color gradient is only visible if you have your color palette set to High Color or True Color in the Settings tab of the Display Properties dialog box.

Table 28-2 lists the Desktop objects in the Item drop-down list and describes what they mean.

Table 28-2 What the Names of Desktop Objects Mean

Name of Item	What Is It?
3D Objects	Setting the color for 3D Objects sets the colors for message boxes, title bars, scroll bars, caption buttons, the Taskbar, window borders, and dialog boxes. You can reset the colors associated with some of these items directly by choosing the items from the Item drop-down list.
Active Title Bar	The horizontal strip at the top of an active window. Setting the font style and size here also sets the font style and size used by the Taskbar.
Active Window Border	The thin (sizable) line around the window that has the focus. It is two pixels in from the actual border. Dialog boxes that are active don't get one. As you make it thicker, you also increase the thickness of the inactive window border.
Application Background	The background color of the application window. You see this color in multidocument applications when there are no documents open or they are all minimized.
Caption Buttons	The buttons in the upper-right corner of the window title bar. You can't change their color independently of 3D Objects.
Desktop	The color of the Desktop itself and the background color of the icon titles. If your Desktop is completely wallpapered, you won't see this color except behind the icon titles.
Icon	The size of icons and the font style and size used by the icon titles. You can only change the color to black or white, depending on the Desktop color. The font style and size attributes you set for this object are also used by the Explorer and folder windows.
Icon Spacing (Horizontal)	The space between large icons on the Desktop and in folder windows (measured in pixels). This value changes with the font size setting in the Settings tab of the Display Properties dialog box.
Icon Spacing (Vertical)	The same as horizontal icon spacing, except vertical.
Inactive Title Bar	The horizontal strip at the top of an inactive window. Contains the caption buttons.

(continued)

Table 28-2 *(Continued)*

Name of Item	What Is It?
Inactive Window Border	The thin (sizable) line around windows that don't have the focus. See Active Window Border.
Menu	The menu area below the window title bar. You can change all five attributes. The font changes are also reflected in the Start menu and in all other menus.
Message Box	The little messages, often error messages, that pop up on your Desktop. This is not the same as a dialog box.
Palette Title	Unknown, no visible effect.
Scrollbar	You can't set the color of scroll bars through this item.
Selected Items	The block of color around the menu item that you have clicked or pointed to, often a bright color and a contrasting font color to let you quickly see where you are.
ToolTip	Little boxes with text that appear when you leave your mouse pointer over items such as Taskbar buttons. The ToolTip font size also sets the size of the text in status bars.
Window	A major item. The background color of the client window. In your word processor, this sets the background color of your document windows.

Changing the color of Explorer items

Secret

You can change the color of the squares around the plus signs in the Explorer and the color of the dotted lines connecting Explorer items in the left pane.

STEPS

Changing the Color of Explorer Items

Step 1. Click Regedit.exe in your \Windows folder.

Step 2. Navigate to HKEY_CURRENT_USER\Control Panel\Colors in the Registry editor window.

Step 3. Click GrayText in the right pane as shown in Figure 28-13.

Colors will not exist as an item in the Registry unless you have previously changed one of your Desktop colors and saved it. (If you don't see the Colors item, exit the Registry, change the color of an item in the Appearance tab of the Display Properties dialog box, save the change as a new scheme, and then come back to these steps.)

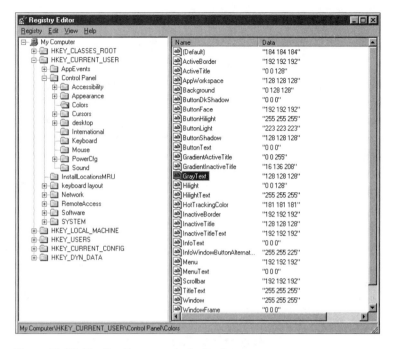

Figure 28-13: The GrayText entry in the Registry.

Step 4. Double-click GrayText.

Step 5. Type an RGB value for the color you want to use. You can check out the RGB values for various colors in the Color dialog box. When you click a color, its RGB value is displayed in the Red, Green, and Blue fields. See "The Color dialog box" later in the chapter.

Step 6. Click OK, and exit the Registry. The next time you start Windows, the new colors will be used.

Color

Most of what we say about colors here assumes you have configured your video card driver to display at least 256 colors. We mention differences related to using 16-color drivers throughout the text.

You can change the color and/or font color of many Desktop objects. For example, you can change the color and font color of the menu bar. In general, you want the font color of an object to contrast with the color of the object itself so that you can read the text.

Changing the color of 3D Objects changes the color of everything but ToolTip, Desktop, Application Background, and Window. The 3D Objects color is also the color used for the Taskbar, status bars, toolbars, dialog boxes, and so on.

If you have wallpaper covering your Desktop, the color of the Desktop won't show up except as a background to the icon title text.

The major color that you see on your Desktop when you open an application or a document is the one labeled Window. It is the background color for your text. The default color is bright white. This can be quite hard on the eyes, especially if the contrast and brightness on your monitor are turned up, you are in a highly lit room with fluorescent lights, and your monitor's refresh rate is less than 70 Hz. You should try out other Window colors to see how your eyes feel.

The Window color is also dithered with the 3D Objects color to create the Scrollbar color. The Application Background color is different from the Window color. For example, in Microsoft Word, the Application Background color is the color behind your document windows. You see it when you don't have any documents open, or when they are all minimized. In contrast, the Window color is the background color of the document itself.

The Color pick box

When a Desktop object whose color you can modify is selected in the Item drop-down list and you click the Color (or Color 2) button, a Color pick box appears, as shown in Figure 28-14. The pick box contains 20 solid colors. The top 16 are always the same colors. The bottom four can change. If you are using 16-color mode, the bottom colors just repeat four of the other colors. Pick the color that you want for the currently selected Desktop object by clicking it.

Figure 28-14: The Color pick box.

Windows reserves the 20 colors in the Color pick box for use with the Desktop objects. If your video card and video driver supports at least 256 colors, your applications can use the additional 236 colors. For example, the producers of a Video for Windows file can use whatever colors they desire out of these 236 in the palette for the video.

The Color dialog box

The Color pick box has an Other button that opens the Color dialog box, which in some cases allows you to choose from a larger number of colors. This dialog box is shown in Figure 28-15.

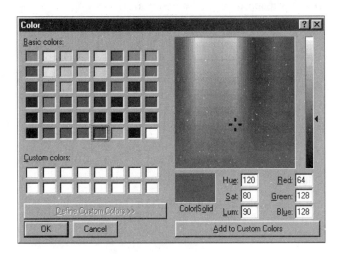

Figure 28-15: The Color dialog box.

If you have set your color depth at 256 colors, the increased colors are created by *dithering*, or combining, the first 16 colors displayed in the Color pick box. The Basic Colors grid in the Color dialog box contains 48 colors. Thirty-two of them are dithered colors, and the other 16 are the same 16 solid colors shown in the Color pick box. The last four colors in the Color pick box are not shown in the Basic Colors grid.

Undocumented

The Color dialog box includes dithered colors when the selected Desktop object can use a dithered color. These objects include 3D Objects (some items whose colors are set by 3D Objects can also use dithered colors), Active Window Border, Desktop, Application Background, and Inactive Window Border.

If a Desktop object can't use a dithered color, then the Basic Colors grid displays only the 16 colors from the Color pick box. The colors are just repeated to fill the 48 slots.

Defining and using custom dithered colors

You can define custom dithered colors for Desktop objects that can use dithered colors. You can't define custom solid colors if you are only displaying 256 colors or less. The only solid colors that are available in this case are the 20 from the Color pick box.

STEPS

Defining Custom Dithered Colors

Step 1.   In the Appearance tab of the Display Properties dialog box, select the Desktop object for which you want to define a custom dithered color in the Item list, click the Color (or Color 2) button, and then click Other to display the Color dialog box.

Step 2.   Create the new color by clicking to place the crosshair on the desired spot in the color matrix, typing the RGB values in the Red, Green, and Blue fields, or typing the Hue, Saturation, and Luminosity values.

Step 3.   Click the Add to Custom Colors button to add your color to the Custom Colors grid.

Step 4.   Click the color you just defined in the Custom Colors grid.

Step 5.   Click OK.

Step 6.   Your new color is now applied to the currently selected Desktop object.

Undocumented

You can't define dithered custom colors for Desktop objects that can't use dithered colors. If the currently selected Desktop object can't use dithered colors, the label just below the color matrix in the Color dialog box changes from Color I Solid to Color, and the matrix shows only solid colors when you drag the crosshair pointer around it.

If you are displaying 256 colors or less, the solid colors you see in the Basic Colors grid in the Color dialog box come from the Color pick box. You'll find only the first 16 colors from the Color pick box. The bottom four colors of the Color pick box appear in the Color I Solid box when you click the cross hair within a very small area of the matrix around the particular color's position in the matrix. This is not the case for the first 16 colors, which show up when you click the color matrix anywhere near their position.

The color of the cursor and the text select pointer

Secret

If there is one problem with choosing colors for the Desktop objects, it is the cursor color.

The *cursor* (or *insertion point*) is the vertical line in your word processor that shows you where your text will be inserted. The mouse pointer becomes a *text select pointer* (or *I-beam*) when it is inside the client window of your word processor.

Undocumented

Windows 98 includes a variety of custom pointer files that let you change the appearance and color of the text select pointer (see the "Using different mouse pointers" section in Chapter 30), but not the color or appearance of the cursor.

The color of the cursor is determined by which *palette slot* is used by the Window color (see Table 28-2). If you have set your video card to display 256 colors, the palette consists of 256 slots, each with a color. The first and last ten slots are reserved for basic colors that Windows 98 controls.

The color of the cursor is the color in the slot that is the "inverse" of the slot where the Window color is stored. If you have your display card set to 256 colors, the 20 Windows colors that you see in the Color pick box are stored in the slots 0 through 9 (the dark colors) and 246 through 255 (the bright colors). If the Window color is the color in slot 8, then the cursor color is the color in the "inverse" slot, 247 (255 minus 8).

This "inverse" color may not be the best choice for a cursor color that contrasts sharply with the Window color (and therefore makes your cursor more visible). Microsoft does not give you any way to change this color or the slot chosen as the inverse of the Window color slot.

Check all the schemes that Microsoft provides. You will notice that the Window color is either white, black, or light gray. This is no coincidence. The color in the inverse slots for each of these Window colors contrasts with them (by design). To change the color stored in the palette slot used for the cursor, you need to use software that can change the hardware palette of your video card.

We have fortunately found a shareware application that allows you to change your hardware palette so that you can change the cursor colors if you have your display set to 256 colors. (This won't work at 16 colors, and above 256 you don't need it). You'll find the shareware program Better Colors on the *Windows 98 Secrets* CD-ROM.

If you have set your display to 256 colors and you merge the file Color.reg (also on the CD-ROM) into your Registry, you'll notice that in any of your text-editing or word-processing packages, the cursor is a medium gray, and the Window color — the background color for the document — is a light green. (Read the section "Registry values" later in this chapter to learn more about Color.reg and the steps for merging it into your Registry.) You can use the Better Colors program to change the cursor color to something like dark blue, which shows up very nicely over light green.

To see which palette slot stores the Window color and which stores the cursor color, you can use Palette.exe, a reworking of an earlier Microsoft Windows utility. You'll find it on the *Windows 98 Secrets* CD-ROM. While this sort of works for display settings greater than 256 colors, it is most useful at 256 colors.

Tip

A much better solution is to use a video card that supports High Color or True Color at your preferred resolution. If you use Color.reg, your cursor color will be quite visible.

The button colors

Buttons are actually made up of six colors, two of which you can control in the Appearance tab of the Display Properties dialog box. You can change the color of the text on the button and the color of the button face (by setting the color of 3D Objects). The other four colors are the colors that surround an actual button and make it look like a button. There are two lines of colored pixels on the right and bottom of the button and two lines that use other colors on the top and left sides.

These four additional button colors are referred to in the Registry as ButtonShadow, ButtonDkShadow, ButtonLight, and ButtonHilight. ButtonDkShadow refers to the outside lines of pixels on the bottom and right sides of the button. ButtonShadow refers to the lines of pixels just above and to the left of the ButtonDkShadow lines. The outside lines on the top and left sides of the button are ButtonHilight. The lines just inside the ButtonHilight lines are ButtonLight.

Two of the four colors, ButtonShadow and ButtonHilight, are also used to display text in disabled buttons.

If you are familiar with the Color applet in the Control Panel of Windows 3.1, you will remember that you could change the ButtonShadow color and the ButtonHilight color in addition to the button face color and the button font color. Not so in Windows 98.

Secret

Changing the button face color (3D Objects) changes the color of many Desktop objects, including status bars, toolbars, scroll bar buttons, caption buttons, and dialog boxes. It doesn't change the other five colors associated with buttons. You can, however, change all six colors in the Registry.

STEPS

Changing the Button Colors

Step 1. Click Regedit.exe in the \Windows folder.

Step 2. Navigate to HKEY_CURRENT_USER\Control Panel\Colors.

Step 3. Click ButtonDkShadow or any of the six button color names in the right pane.

If you haven't changed the colors of a Desktop object previously, there won't be a Colors item in the Registry. (If you don't see the Colors item, exit the Registry, change the color of an item in the Appearance tab of the Display Properties dialog box, save the change as a new scheme, and then come back to these steps.)

Step 4. Choose Edit, Modify.

Step 5. Type an RGB value for that button color, and click OK. Yes, you have to be familiar with RGB values to make sense of this step. To determine the RGB values for various colors, display the Color dialog box (see "The Color dialog box" section earlier in the chapter), and click various colors. The RGB value for the color you click is displayed in the Red, Green, and Blue fields.

Step 6. Optionally repeat steps 3 through 5 for other button colors.

Step 7.   Exit the Registry. The next time you start Windows 98, the new colors will be used.

Undocumented

Windows 98 can easily wipe out the changes you make to the button colors. If you change to another scheme and then go back to your current scheme, your changes will be gone, unless you first save your scheme under a new name.

STEPS

Updating the Button Colors

Step 1.   Right-click the Desktop. Choose Properties, and then click the Appearance tab. Display the Item drop-down list, and choose 3D Objects. Then choose the color that you want from the Color pick box.

Step 2.   Click Apply to apply this button color to your Desktop objects.

Step 3.   Click the Save As button, type a name for this scheme, and click OK.

Step 4.   Pull down the Scheme drop-down list and choose another scheme. Click Apply.

Step 5.   Pull down the Scheme drop-down list and choose the scheme that you just saved. Click Apply.

Step 6.   The six button colors are automatically updated to the colors you set in the Registry.

This is not a particularly great way to get these colors to update. Microsoft should have written Windows 98 so that it updated these button colors when you chose the button face color. Unfortunately, it didn't.

Fonts on the Desktop

Windows 3.1 gave you the power to change the colors of the Desktop objects and the sizes of the borders. Windows 98 also lets you change the size of the objects and their fonts. You can choose among screen fonts and TrueType fonts, and you can specify the font point size, font style (regular, bold, or italic), and font color.

These are excellent improvements over Windows 3.1. Given the fact that more people are now using large monitors and high-resolution video cards, it is important for end users to be able to adjust the size of their Desktop objects. We encourage you to make adjustments until you find the right combination.

The font point size multiplied by the ratio of the displayed inch to an actual inch determines the displayed size of text entities on the Desktop. Increasing the font size (magnification) in the Properties dialog box for your video card (click the Advanced button in the Settings tab of the Display Properties dialog box) increases the size of the displayed fonts, although their "point size" remains the same.

The default font and font point size on the Desktop and in dialog boxes is 8-point MS Sans Serif (10 points for screen resolutions higher than 800 × 600). MS Sans Serif is a screen font that is specifically designed for VGA-resolution screens. It looks fine on Super VGA screens. MS Sans Serif looks good at 10, 12, 14, 18, and 24 points. It doesn't look so good at other point sizes.

Arial, a TrueType font, looks almost as good on the screen as MS Sans Serif at these point sizes, and it looks better at other point sizes.

Some combinations of font, font point size, and magnification will not work. For example, MS Sans Serif at 8 points and 75-percent magnification does not result in smaller displayed fonts on the Desktop because MS Sans Serif is a screen font, and it isn't displayed below 8 points. In contrast, if you select Arial as the icon font, 8 point and 75 percent *would* reduce the size of the displayed text.

You cannot change the font in the item labeled 3D Objects, which also means that you don't have control over the dialog box font. (The font used for the text on the Taskbar buttons is controlled through the Active Title Bar font settings.) Because dialog boxes are automatically sized based on the font size, you don't have independent control of dialog box size. Dialog box size is determined by the setting in the Font Size drop-down list in the Properties dialog box for your video card.

Changing the System font size

You can change the font size used by dialog boxes and the Contents and Index tabs of the Windows 98 help files. Right-click the Desktop, choose Properties, click the Settings tab, click the Advanced button, select Other from the Font Size drop-down list, and choose a large custom font size. Setting a large custom font size increases the size of the dialog boxes and help pages, as well as the size of the font.

When you choose a large custom font size, the displayed size of all the text on your screen is changed, no matter what the point size of its font. If you have a small monitor with a video adapter set to a low or moderate resolution, the dialog boxes may no longer fit on your screen.

Changing the magnification by setting a large custom font size works well as a way to enlarge text entities whose font point sizes you can't directly control in the Appearance tab. You can use this method in combination with "manually" adjusting font point size settings in the Appearance tab for text entities whose values you can change.

Be sure to read the discussion in "The Kinds and Types of Fonts" in Chapter 26 regarding fonts.

Size

Review Table 28-1 earlier in this chapter to see which items can be resized. The vertical and horizontal icon spacing values don't change the size of the icons, just the distance that separates them. You can change the size of the title bars, the menu bar height, the width of vertical scroll bars, the height of horizontal scroll bars, and the thickness of window borders.

Many of the size properties interact with each other, and often with font sizes. For example, if you increase the size of the caption buttons, this in turn increases the height of the title bar. If you choose a bigger font point size for the menu bar, the menu bar height increases so that it can fit the larger menu bar text.

Icons on the Desktop are normally 32 × 32 pixels. You can increase (or decrease) their size in the Appearance tab of the Display Properties dialog box. Because these icons were originally created by hand on a 32 × 32 pixel grid, multiplying them by some factor will produce icons that don't look as sharp as the originals.

When you change video resolution, icon size is automatically changed (in some cases). You can change it back to the original 32 × 32 size easily enough in the Appearance tab.

Changing icon size, icon spacing, and icon font sizes is easy, so you can play with these settings a bit to see what you like. If only it were as easy to change all the text objects on your Desktop!

Registry values

The values you set in the Appearance tab of the Display Properties dialog box are stored in the Registry. To view these values, follow the steps in the section earlier in this chapter entitled "Changing the color of Explorer items." The values are stored in the following areas:

```
HKEY_CURRENT_USER\Control Panel\Appearance\Schemes
HKEY_CURRENT_USER\Control Panel\Colors
HKEY_CURRENT_USER\Control Panel\Desktop\WindowMetrics
```

We have included an exported Registry branch that you can import to change the colors of your Desktop. Its name is Color.reg, and it is stored in the Registry folder on the *Windows 98 Secrets* CD-ROM. If you are using a standard color scheme, or if you have previously saved your existing color scheme, you can easily revert back to your previous colors. To import Color.reg into your Registry, take the following steps:

STEPS

Importing Color.reg into Your Registry

Step 1. Save your current color scheme if you are not using one of the schemes that comes with Windows 98.

Step 2. Open an Explorer window focused on the Registry folder on the *Windows 98 Secrets* CD-ROM.

Step 3. Right-click Color.reg. Click Merge.

Step 4. Restart Windows 98.

Step 5. Right-click your Desktop. Choose Properties, and click the Appearance tab.

Step 6. Click the Save As button, enter a name for this color scheme, and click OK.

Themes

Themes are expanded schemes. They include not only Desktop colors, sizes, and fonts, but also mouse pointers, wallpaper art, screen savers, icons, and sounds. You can mix and match themes to create your own theme by clearing check boxes for various parts of a theme, applying the theme, and then bringing up another theme and clearing the parts of it that you previously chose. You can use portions of your current settings, if you like, by clearing parts of themes before you apply them.

The themes that came on the Microsoft Plus! CD-ROM now come on the Windows 98 CD-ROM. If you don't see a Desktop Themes icon in your Control Panel, click the Add/Remove Programs icon there, go to the Windows Setup tab, and mark the Desktop Themes checkbox, then click OK. You can also create your own themes, and you can download themes (mostly consisting of pirated copyrighted material) from various sites on the Internet. Theme files are just text files, and you can edit them directly if you choose. If you previously installed Microsoft Plus! you'll find those themes stored in \Program Files\Plus!\Themes and have the extension of *theme*.

Check out the *Windows 98 Secrets* CD-ROM or http://www.windows98.com for theme editors. You'll also find lots of themes at http://www.monash.edu.au/ftp/pub/win95.themes/.

One very cool theme editor is Theme.Create. You can download it from http://web.idirect.com/~lizard/.

You can take any *gif* or *bmp* picture (*gif* files are frequently used in web pages) and transform it into your Desktop background by right-clicking it while viewing it with the Internet Explorer and choosing Save As Wallpaper from the context menu.

Smoothing edges in bitmap files

If you work with bitmap graphics files frequently, you've probably run into a common problem: bitmap scaling. This difficulty especially affects people who design Windows help files or web pages. How do you display, for example, a screen shot of a 640×480 screen, when the users viewing your page must subtract menus, scroll bars, and so on from their own 640×480 displays, leaving more like 600×440 at best?

Bitmaps that are reduced become jagged. The text and shapes in a reduced bitmap lose their original form and take on an unpleasant stair-step appearance. Even if you reduce a bitmap to 50 percent of the original size, whole pixels in the image will be dropped, leaving type almost unreadable.

A simple utility called Smooth Scaling can smooth over those rough edges. It uses a proprietary algorithm to reduce bitmaps while retaining their readability. Instead of dropping pixels to make a bitmap smaller, Smooth Scaling inserts shades of gray or muted colors where two pixels would ordinarily have been reduced to one. This technique, related to a graphics concept called *anti-aliasing,* has previously been available only in more expensive drawing and image-manipulation packages.

Smooth Scaling is available for $49 from WexTech Systems Inc. at http://www.wextech.com or 800-939-8324, 212-949-9595.

The Desktop Wallpaper

Talk about a mixed metaphor — when was the last time you put wallpaper on a real Desktop? Not likely.

You choose the color of your Desktop in the Appearance tab of the Display Properties dialog box. The Desktop is one of the items in the Item drop-down list. If you don't put up any wallpaper, this is the color you get as the background color on your screen. If you do put up some wallpaper, this is the background color of the titles of the icons on the Desktop.

Whatever graphic image you choose as your wallpaper functions as background to your Desktop on your screen. Your Desktop feels like a clear piece of glass on top of this graphical background. The Taskbar and folders appear to lie on the glass.

Right-click the Desktop and choose Properties in the context menu to display the Background tab of the Display Properties dialog box. As shown in Figure 28-16, you can choose a wallpaper or a pattern. (See the next section for more information about patterns.)

If you have activated your Active Desktop, you can use a web page as your background graphic (although you can still use wallpaper if you like). For more details, turn back to "The Active Desktop" in Chapter 6.

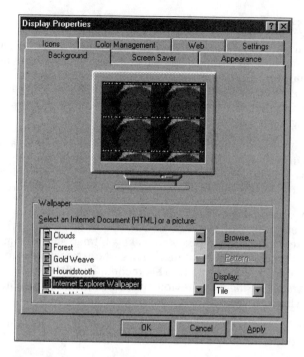

Figure 28-16: The Background tab of the Display Properties dialog box.

Two-color patterned wallpaper

Wallpaper is something of a misnomer. We normally think of wallpaper as patterned paper. There can be all kinds of wallpaper in Windows 98.

Windows 98 comes with lots of graphical patterns that, when repeated across your screen, create a two-color patterned wallpaper. To create this type of wallpaper, choose None in the Wallpaper list, click the Pattern button, and choose a pattern in the Pattern dialog box. One color in the pattern is your Desktop color, and the other is black.

Repeated picture element wallpaper

You can create another type of wallpaper by choosing a wallpaper in the Wallpaper list and selecting Tile in the Display drop-down list. Windows 98 repeats the picture (a small *bmp* file) across your screen. The wallpaper can contain more than two colors, and it completely covers the Desktop color.

Right-click the satellite image at http://www.intellicast.com/weather/sea/sat. Click Set As Wallpaper to tile it on your Desktop. You'll find the satellite image under the name Internet Explorer Wallpaper in the wallpaper list, as shown in Figure 28-16.

Big-picture wallpaper

If you want to have one non-repeating graphic element as your wallpaper, then choose a *bmp* file in the Wallpaper list and select Center in the Display drop-down list. You can also use the Browse button to find a *bmp* file of your own. If your *bmp* file is the same size as your current display resolution (the same number of horizontal and vertical pixels), then the picture from the *bmp* file will cover the whole Desktop. If it is smaller than the display resolution, you will see a border around the picture made up of your Desktop color.

You can tile a large *bmp* file, but it will be cut off on one or more sides if your screen resolution is not an exact multiple of the *bmp* dimensions. In other words, the *bmp* must be exactly ½, ⅓, ¼ (and so on) the size of the screen resolution.

It is great fun to have a splashy photo up on your Desktop. Using Paint Shop Pro from the shareware on the *Windows 98 Secrets* CD-ROM, you can size your bitmapped graphics to the resolution of your screen.

Using RLE files as graphic backgrounds

The Wallpaper list box neglects to display Run Length Encoded *(rle)* files, although you can use them as graphical backdrops.

An *rle* file is just an ordinary bitmap file—like the bitmap wallpaper files included with Windows that are provided as wallpaper, such as Leaves.bmp or Winlogo.bmp—after it has been compressed into *rle* format.

Before compression, monochrome bitmap files contain one bit of data for every pixel displayed on the screen—the first bit is black, the second bit is black, the third bit is white, and so on. 16-color bitmaps require *four* bits of data to represent every pixel, because each pixel could be one of 16 (or 24) possible colors.

If you convert a *bmp* file to an *rle* file, it takes up less space on disk. The *rle* file contains such information as "2 pixels of black, 12 pixels of white, 20 pixels of blue," and so on. The file stores the number of pixels (the *run length*) of each color instead of storing the meaning of each individual pixel.

You can convert any *bmp* file that's in the Windows proprietary *bmp* format to an *rle* file by using a graphics program that can read and write both formats. Paint Shop Pro, a program featured on the *Windows 98 Secrets* CD-ROM, is perfectly suited to do just that.

To use an *rle* file as a background graphic, do the following:

STEPS

Using RLE Files as Background

Step 1. Right-click the Desktop, choose Properties, and then click the Background tab.

Step 2. Click the Browse button, type ***.rle** in the File Name field of the Browse dialog box, and press Enter.

Step 3. Double-click various folder names in the dialog box to navigate to the folder that stores the *rle* file you want to use as a background.

Step 4. Double-click the *rle* file, and then click OK in the Desktop Properties dialog box.

Choosing a Screen Saver

Windows 98 comes with a number of different screen savers. You can buy additional ones from third-party software developers.

STEPS

Choosing a Screen Saver

Step 1. Right-click the Desktop, and select Properties.

Step 2. Click the Screen Saver tab, and then select a screen saver in the Screen Saver list box, as shown in Figure 28-17.

Step 3. You can view the screen saver in full-screen mode by clicking the Preview button. To stop the preview, just move your mouse.

To browse through Microsoft's list of available channels, select Channel Screen Saver in the Screen Saver list, click Preview, and then click the Microsoft Channel Guide link at the bottom of the screen. Your Internet Explorer window will open, and if you connect to the Internet through Dial-Up Networking, your dialer will connect you to Microsoft's Active Channel Guide web page. For more on channels, turn back to "Tune in the Channels" in Chapter 3.

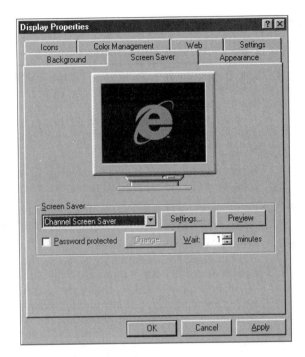

Figure 28-17: The Screen Saver tab of the Display Properties dialog box.

Step 4.   Optionally change settings specific to the selected screen saver by clicking the Settings button. When you're done, click OK.

A hot key and Desktop shortcut for screen savers

Tip

You can, of course, start your screen saver by right-clicking the Desktop, choosing Properties, clicking the Screen Saver tab, and clicking Preview — the saver will then begin. But there is a much faster method, which isn't in the Windows manual. If you've obtained any compatible screen savers from companies other than Microsoft, the following steps should work with them, too.

STEPS

Creating a Hot Key to Your Screen Saver

Step 1. Use the Explorer to view your \Windows\System folder. Click the Details toolbar button (or choose View, Details), and then click the Type column header button in the right pane to arrange the filenames by type. Scroll down to the screen saver files. You should see Flying Windows.scr, Flying Through Space.scr, and any other screen savers that you have.

Step 2. Right-drag the desired screen saver from the right pane of the Explorer to your Desktop. Choose Create Shortcut(s) Here.

Step 3. Right-click the shortcut to your screen saver and click Properties. Click the Shortcut tab and click in the Shortcut Key field.

Step 4. Press a key that you'll combine with Ctrl+Alt to form your hot key combination. For example, if you press the letter *s*, the hot key combination Ctrl+Alt+S appears in the Shortcut Key field. (In Word for Windows, this is the keyboard shortcut for the Window, Split command. The hot key you are creating will override keyboard shortcuts for applications like Word; so be careful what letter you choose here.) Click the OK button.

Now you can instantly invoke your screen saver by clicking the screen saver shortcut on your Desktop, or by holding down the Ctrl and Alt keys and pressing the associated letter key.

Non-Plug and Play Monitors and Cards

When you install Windows 98, it won't figure out what kind of monitor you have if your monitor isn't plug and play compatible. If you have a non-plug and play monitor, you need to choose the appropriate monitor model during the setup process.

If you want to install a new monitor at a later date, right-click the Desktop, click Properties, click the Settings tab, the Advanced button, and the Monitor tab. Click the Change button to invoke the Upgrade Device Driver Wizard.

It is important to tell Windows 98 which monitor you have so that it can use the proper values for the maximum display resolution in the Settings tab of the Display Properties dialog box. Some older monitors require their scan rates to be set by a program called from Autoexec.bat. If yours requires such a program, choose your display resolution to match your scan rate.

To set the monitor refresh rate in the Registry, take the following steps:

STEPS

Setting the Monitor Refresh Rate

Step 1. Click Regedit.exe in your \Windows folder. Navigate to the following key:

HKEY_LOCAL_MACHINE\System\CurrentControlSet\Services\ Class\Display\0000\DEFAULT

Step 2. Right-click the right pane of the Registry editor, and choose New, String Value. Enter the name **RefreshRate**.

Step 3. Double-click RefreshRate and enter the value **-1** for automatic rate setting, or a number for a specific value for the refresh rate.

Step 4. Click OK, exit the Registry, and then restart Windows.

Windows detects video cards whether they are plug and play compatible or not. Plug and play video cards also implement the VESA DPMS specification, which allows them to control the monitor.

LCD Displays and External Monitors

Some Windows 3.1 video drivers that came with portable computers could switch resolutions automatically to the lower 640 × 480 if the external monitor wasn't plugged in. Windows 98 video drivers for pre-plug and play video chip sets can sort of do this. Sort of, because they don't do it elegantly. They drop back to a basic VGA with 16 colors.

Unfortunately, for older portables with non-plug and play video chips, there are no settings in the Display Properties dialog box for multiple monitors. You have to change your BIOS setting, run a small program in Autoexec.bat, or use a keyboard switch (for example, Ctrl+Alt+Comma). The keyboard switch usually only works when you are in full-screen DOS mode.

If you configure your display settings to 800 × 600 × 256, for example, and then unplug your external monitor on a portable with a 640 × 480 LCD screen, you will be informed that your display settings are incorrect and then given the opportunity to change them and restart Windows. This takes place on the Desktop, so Windows has already switched video modes to VGA, but it hasn't found it necessary (or helpful) to go into Safe mode. You can ignore the requests to change video modes, and continue in VGA mode on your LCD screen, or switch to 640 × 480 × 256 if your video chip set/memory can handle this mode. Later, when you plug your external monitor back in and restart Windows 98, it will maintain your desired 800 × 600 × 256 video mode if you haven't changed modes.

In "LCDs and external monitors" in Chapter 25, we show you a way to configure pre-plug and play portable computers to work with Windows 95 and external monitors. If you have a plug and play portable, hopefully you have a Windows 98 video driver that can handle the transition between an external monitor and an LCD screen.

Summary

- ▶ We show you how to change the size of all the elements on your Desktop.
- ▶ We teach you how to change all the button colors.
- ▶ You learn how to change the color of the cursor.
- ▶ You find out how to change monitor refresh rates in the Registry.
- ▶ We tell you where you can find new themes.

Chapter 29

Printer Drivers

In This Chapter

We look at the Windows 98 print subsystem, the software that drives physical printers. We go over the significant features and discuss:

▶ Using the Printers folder to install, configure, and manage your printers

▶ Putting a shortcut to each of your printers on your Desktop

▶ Dragging and dropping documents to any of your printers

▶ Making the drag and drop to a printer icon do anything you want it to

▶ Turning off DOS print spooling or printing Windows files directly to the printer

▶ Printing TrueType fonts correctly on PostScript printers

▶ Printing to a printer that isn't physically connected to your computer

▶ Troubleshooting printing problems

▶ Automatically installing network printer drivers

Printing Features

The Windows printing subsystem has not changed radically since Windows 3.1*x*. Windows printer drivers continue to be based on a universal driver that gives printer manufacturers a big head start toward producing specific drivers for their printers.

But many incremental improvements in both Windows 95 and Windows 98 have increased configuration flexibility and provided faster and more stable printing. And Windows 98 includes drivers for approximately 600 new printers, in addition to over 800 drivers made available after the release Windows 95.

32-bit printer driver

Like all the other drivers that come with Windows 98, the printer driver has entered the 32-bit world. This means that it spools the print jobs as threads, which Windows 98 can preemptively multitask. The 32-bit driver gives the print subsystem more control over the printing process, including bidirectional communication with the printer.

Each printer has its own print queue. You can have multiple printers connected to different ports, all printing at the same time and all managed by a different print-queue manager.

The print-queue managers do a better job of spooling print jobs to the printers than the Windows 3.1 Print Manager did. They are aware of when the printer is ready for more data and don't send it until it is.

Image Color Management

Windows 98 includes Image Color Management (ICM) 2.0, a utility designed to produce more consistent color among displays, and between your display and your printer. The latter has been a big challenge in desktop publishing, because the way your eye perceives color emitted from a monitor is very different from the way it perceives color reflected from a printed page. Programmers of individual applications, such as Adobe's PhotoShop, must include calls in their programs to implement ICM, and Microsoft has made this easier with ICM 2.0.

The initial ICM version that shipped with Windows 95 only supported RGB color, and it was designed to be transparent to you as a user. The new version has more powerful features and supports more color models, including CMYK (the standard for printing on a commercial press). It also lets you set the *rendering intent* — the way you ultimately want the image or document to be seen — from within the application you use to create the document or image.

To set the rendering intent, select Color Management from the program's File menu. Windows 98 offers a choice of four rendering intents:

- Perceptual matching — best for photographic images
- Saturation matching — best for graphs and pie charts
- Relative Colorimetric matching — best for logos and artwork in which a few colors must be matched exactly
- Absolute Colorimetric matching — best for creating idealized, device-independent images, such those on web sites

Universal print driver

The universal print driver communicates between printer-specific mini drivers and the rest of the operating system. It supports 600-dpi laser printers, and it can download TrueType outlines to printers that support the PCL language (the HP LaserJet printer control language). This lets the printer rasterize fonts without using the resources of the computer.

The universal print driver also supports Hewlett-Packard's HPGL/2 plotter language, so CAD and similar applications can send their HPGL output to a printer instead of to a plotter.

Unified printer control interface

In Windows 98, printer configuration, installation, and the print-queue management functions are combined and associated with the individual printer icons in the Printers folder. Each printer has an icon representing its own print-queue manager and printer driver properties. You set the configuration information for each printer individually, and manage each print queue separately and simultaneously.

Spooling EMF, not RAW printer codes

When you print a document, the document file has to be translated into the printer's codes that instruct the printer on how to print each character. Microsoft refers to these printer codes as the RAW data. (We capitalize RAW here because Microsoft does in order to contrast it with EMF, or *Enhanced Metafile Format*.)

In Windows 98, both translation to RAW data and print spooling are done in the background. You don't have to wait for the lengthy translation to RAW data to finish before you can continue working with your application. Your document is instead translated to EMF, which is a much higher-level and more-compact format than the RAW data. This reduces the initial translation time and returns you to your application more quickly.

The temporary EMF file is spooled and translated as it is sent to the printer. EMF is built into the Graphic Device Interface (GDI) module of Windows 98. If you run into problems spooling EMF files, you can switch to the old way of spooling RAW data files instead. We show you how later in this chapter in the section entitled "Details."

PostScript printer drivers spool PostScript files to the PostScript printer. There is no EMF translation available for PostScript printers. PostScript is already a high-level page description language like the Enhanced Metafile Format, so there is little or no benefit in translating first to EMF and then from EMF to PostScript. The PostScript printer driver translates your document to a temporary PostScript file, spools this file, and starts sending it to the printer as the driver creates the temporary file.

DOS and Windows printing work together

The Windows 98 print subsystem spools DOS print files, so you can print from any application and let the operating system handle the printer. The printer ports are virtualized, which makes the DOS application think it is printing to a real port, when in fact it is printing to the Windows 98 print subsystem. You can turn off DOS print spooling.

DOS print files are not translated into EMF print files. Rather, the translation occurs as the files (as RAW data files) are spooled. This still releases the DOS application faster than it would be without a spooler. The spooler is not available in MS-DOS mode.

Offline printing

If you don't have a printer currently hooked up to your computer, you can still create print files. They will be printed automatically the next time you get connected to a printer and use the queue manager to put the printer back online. To do this, you must first install on your computer a printer driver that references a printer connected to a network server or to another computer over a peer-to-peer network. This network can be as simple as the Direct Cable Connection (DCC) program, which lets your laptop computer connect to your Desktop computer.

Undocumented

Offline (or *deferred*) printing is useful whenever your computer is not connected to a network printer. Unfortunately, offline printing works only for printing to non-local (network) printers. You can't use it with a local printer that, for whatever reason, is not currently connected to your computer. You can pause printing while you reconnect your local printer, if for some reason it was offline when you started printing, but pausing does not save the print jobs for later printing.

Bidirectional communications

For years, users couldn't have cared less what a printer had to say to them. Now we all realize that things are a lot easier when the printer can talk back.

Plug and play printers can give the Windows 98 printer installation routines all the information they need to set up the printer, without requiring you to answer any questions about manufacturer, model, and so on. Many plug and play printers can send status reports to the printer driver reporting such things as "paper jam" or "out of paper." This helps if the printer is down the hall. And some sophisticated plug and play printers can supply even more detailed status reports.

Support for enhanced parallel port

The EPP and ECP specifications for parallel ports permit higher speeds and improved bidirectional communication. This is most evident when you use devices that can deal with these higher speeds. See the section in Chapter 31 entitled "Configuring ECP and EPP Ports."

PostScript

Adobe and Microsoft jointly developed the Windows 95 and 98 PostScript printer driver. The fact that Microsoft is willing to credit Adobe with joint development speaks volumes about Adobe's power and prestige, and Microsoft's desire to have a well-respected printer driver.

The PostScript printer driver is used for all PostScript printers. Windows 98 uses a separate *spd* (Simplified PostScript printer description) or *ppd*

(PostScript printer description) file to modify the driver to reflect the features of each PostScript printer. These files are stored in the \Windows\ System folder. The filenames are shortened versions of the printer name.

The Windows 98 PostScript driver includes PostScript Level 2 support as well as numerous incremental upgrades to better handle more complex PostScript documents.

If you have a PostScript printer and are using Adobe Type Manager (ATM), you'll want to make sure you have a fairly recent version of the ATM software. ATM versions 3.01 and earlier do not support Windows 98's Image Color Management, and this incompatibility can cause your system to crash when you try to print.

Printer shortcuts

Because each printer has its own associated icon in the Printers folder, you can place shortcuts to each printer driver on your Desktop (or in any other folder). When you want to print to the printer, drag and drop your document file onto the shortcut.

If you drag a printer icon from the Printers folder, Windows assumes you want to create a shortcut when you drop the icon. You don't need to hold down the Ctrl+Shift keys.

Print without installing printer drivers first

You may have installed a local printer by installing its driver on your computer. You can always print to that printer. If you want to print to another printer on your network, you don't necessarily have to install the driver beforehand. You do need to have a driver for that printer installed on your computer, but the installation process can be automatic. This comes in handy, because there could be all sorts of printers on an extensive network, and it would be a bit of a pain to manually install drivers for all of the 1500 printers that Windows 98 supports.

If you print to a shared printer on your network that's on a computer running Windows 98, Windows NT, or Novell NetWare, Windows 98 automatically installs the printer driver for that printer on your computer. Microsoft calls this *point and print.*

If the network printer is connected to a Windows 98 computer, all the information about the printer and the location of the files associated with it is stored in the Registry of that computer. Point and print uses this information to change your Registry, copy the appropriate files from the other Windows 98 computer, and install the printer driver on your computer.

See the section later in this chapter entitled "Point and Print" for details on how to set up your computer to use and share this capability.

Network printer management

Both Digital Equipment Corporation and Hewlett Packard provide printer server software that eases the job of managing printers that are connected directly to NetWare, Microsoft, and Digital networks. A Windows 98 computer using this software becomes a network print-management station.

NetWare print services

A computer running Windows 98 can serve as a single-printer, NetWare-compatible print services provider when it's connected to a Novell NetWare print server. A NetWare print server can send print jobs to a printer connected to a Windows 98 computer as long as that computer is also running Microsoft Client for NetWare and Microsoft Print Server for NetWare. The Windows 98 computer providing print services does not need to be running Microsoft's file and printer sharing for NetWare. All of these programs come with Windows 98.

The Windows 98 computer does not need to be a dedicated print services provider, and you can use it to carry out other tasks. It can manage only one local printer for the NetWare server. Microsoft Print Server for NetWare runs in the background and has minimal effect on foreground tasks.

No need for logical port redirection

Windows 3.1*x* required that you assign a network printer to a specific logical port if you wanted to print to it. This is not necessary in Windows 98, as long as your network supports the universal naming convention (UNC) for naming its server, folders and printers. When you install a network printer, Windows 98 retains its UNC name and uses it to direct the output to the correct printer, for example, \\Billserver\HP5.

If your network doesn't support UNC (the 16-bit networks that worked with Windows 3.1*x* do not), you can still redirect printer output to logical ports LPT1 through LPT9 through the Capture Printer Port button (in the Details tab of the Properties dialog box for your printer). Some DOS programs may require that you print to a logical port and not to a printer through a UNC port name.

The Printers Folder

You'll find that most printing functions in Windows 98 are consolidated in the Printers folder. You can get to the Printers folder in four ways:

1. Click the Start button, point to Settings, and then click Printers.

2. Click My Computer, and click the Printers folder icon.

3. Right-click My Computer, click Explore, and click the Printers folder icon in the left pane of the Explorer.

4. Use any of the above methods, but click the Control Panel folder instead of the Printers folder, and then click the Printers folder in the Control Panel.

Your Printers folder window will look something like the one shown in Figure 29-1. You won't have any icons other than the Add Printer icon in this folder until you install some printers (or have them installed for you). Each installed printer driver has its own printer icon in the Printers folder.

Figure 29-1: The Printers folder window. This folder contains the Add Printer icon and icons for each of your installed printers.

You can use the Printers folder and the icons in it for a variety of purposes. Click the Add Printer icon to install a new printer. Click a printer icon to view its print queue. Right-click a printer icon and click Properties to view a printer driver's properties, or click Set As Default to change the default printer. Right-click the client area of the Printers folder window and click Capture Printer Port to redirect a logical printer port to a network printer.

You'll find most everything to do with printers in the Printers folder. You can:

- Install new printer drivers
- Delete printer drivers you are no longer using
- Change the characteristics of your printer driver
- View and manage the print queues (pause and purge print jobs)
- Set the default printer
- Give LPTx names to printers connected to networked servers (redirect logical printer ports to network printers)

Printer driver installation and configuration and print-queue management are combined in Windows 98 to make it easier to get at the important printer functions. So what is outside of the Printers folder that relates to printing?

- The Fonts folder, where you'll find the fonts that are installed on your computer (See "Where Are the Fonts Installed?" in Chapter 26 for details on fonts.)

- Printer and communication port configurations, including the new enhanced parallel port, which you will find in the Device Manager under the System icon in the Control Panel

- The Add New Hardware icon in the Control Panel, which you can use to run the Add Printer Wizard (You can also run this Wizard from the Printers folder by clicking the Add Printer icon.)

- The Network icon in the Control Panel, which lets you enable printer sharing.

- Shortcuts to printer icons (You can't drag a printer icon out of the Printers folder, but you can drag to create a shortcut to the printer icon on the Desktop.)

- The Print Preview capability, a system wide dynamic link library (DLL) that developers can incorporate into their applications (An example of Print Preview is found in WordPad.)

- The common print dialog box, which developers can use in their applications (An example of this dialog box is found in WordPad.)

- Shared printers attached to servers on your network. You can view shared printers by clicking the servers' icons in the Explorer; they also appear in your Printers folder if you print to them, drag and drop them to the Printers folder, or click them.

- Network printer management tools from DEC and HP

Tip   The Device Manager tracks most of the hardware attached to your computer, but it doesn't track your printers. The Properties dialog box associated with a particular printer is the only place that displays the parameters of that printer driver stored in the Registry. The Device Manager does track the printer port parameters.

Drag and Drop to a Printer Icon

You can drag and drop a file icon from a folder window, the Explorer, or the Desktop, to a printer's icon or its queue window. The printer's icon could be a shortcut on your Desktop, or it could be an icon in the Printers folder. With this action, you are telling Windows 98 to invoke the application associated with the print command for this file type and then execute the application's print command.

If you want to quickly print a file or a group of files, this is an easy way to do it. The associated application starts, and you may see the document in the application window on the Desktop while the document is spooled to the printer. The application is closed as soon as the document is completely spooled.

This is the same thing that would happen if you right-clicked a document file and chose Print from the context menu. The actions listed at the top of the context menu are the ones defined for the file type in the Registry and listed in the File Types tab of the Folder Options dialog box. We discuss file types in detail in "Associating Actions with File Extensions" in Chapter 13.

If you drag and drop a file to a network printer icon in a shared folder, and your computer doesn't have that printer's driver installed, you are instructing Windows 98 to start installing the driver on your computer.

You can define an action named Print for a given file type, and then associate that action with a specific application's print command. This connects the user action of dragging and dropping a file of that type onto the printer icon with the specified application's print command. You define the Print action using the method for "Creating and Editing File Types and Actions" detailed in Chapter 13.

Undocumented

You can define the "Print" action to be something other than Print, if you like. This will let you drag and drop a file to a printer icon to invoke a different action. For example, you can define the Print action to invoke a file translator that converts the specified file type into another file type. If you do this, you can convert files of the specified type by simply dragging and dropping them onto any printer icon.

The Print action is defined by default for many file types. This happens when you install the Windows application associated with the file type (after you've installed Windows 98).

Installing a Printer Driver

Windows 98 documentation often refers to *installing a printer*. That really means *installing a printer driver*, in other words, installing software. This is confusing, because the intuitive meaning of installing a printer is to physically place a printer next to a computer and connect them with a printer cable. You'll have to do a little translation in your head when you see the words *install a printer*.

If you have a new computer running Windows 98, or if you get a new plug and play printer, chances are you won't have to install a printer driver at all. After you physically connect the printer to the computer, turn on the printer and start Windows 98, your system will detect the new printer, and will attempt to identify and install it. Especially with newer equipment, that should be all there is to it.

On the other hand, you may want to install drivers for printers you don't own. Perhaps your work will be printed at a service bureau, for example, or on a specialized printer at your office. You can use the Add Printer Wizard to easily install drivers for printers that are not connected to your computer.

If you install Windows 98 into an existing Windows 3.1*x* directory, Windows 98 Setup automatically installs the printer drivers for the printers that you previously installed. On the other hand, if you install Windows 98 into a new folder on a computer running Windows 3.1*x*, you will be asked during Setup to install a new printer. You'll see the Add Printer Wizard, and you just need to answer the questions. If you install Windows 98 as an update to Windows 95, all your previous printer drivers will remain intact.

After Windows 98 is installed, if it does not detect your new printer on startup, you can invoke the Add Printer Wizard (to add a new printer driver) by opening the Printers folder and clicking the Add Printer icon. If your printer is plug and play compatible, the Add Printer Wizard can communicate with it, find the correct printer driver, and install the correctly configured printer driver itself.

Otherwise, the Add Printer Wizard asks you for the manufacturer's name and printer model before it proceeds to find the correct files from the Windows 98 CD-ROM. To do this, it uses the *inf* files Msprint.inf and Msprint2.inf in the \Windows\Inf folder. (This folder is only visible if the Show All Files option button is selected in the View tab of the Folder Options dialog box, which you display by choosing View, Folder Options in any Explorer or folder window.)

If you have a printer that isn't covered in these two *inf* files and you have a printer setup diskette from your printer manufacturer, you can click the Have Disk button in the Add Printer Wizard. This diskette has to include an *inf* file for the new printer.

The Add Printer Wizard will ask you to choose a port if it can't detect a connection (see Figure 29-2). If this driver is for a printer you can't physically connect to a port, choose FILE. If the printer is connected to a serial port and is not plug and play compliant, indicate the correct serial port. The Wizard will let you change the port's baud rate, and so on. The Wizard also lets you choose a meaningful name for your printer, so if you share it on a network, others will know where to find their output.

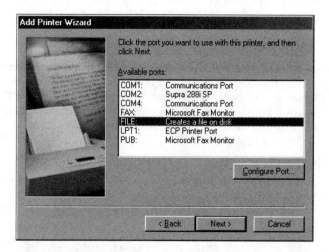

Figure 29-2: The Add Printer Wizard will ask you to choose a port for a printer if it's not currently connected to your computer. It might be across town at a service bureau, for example.

When the Add Printer Wizard has finished installing the driver, it asks if you want to print a test page. You should do this if you're setting up the printer for the first time. Printing a test page lets Windows 98 check out the printer, and if Windows 98 finds a problem, it leads you to a Windows 98 help-based print troubleshooter. The troubleshooter asks you questions to help you track down glitches in your printer driver configuration.

You can also invoke the print troubleshooter from the Contents tab of the Windows Help window. Click the Start button, click Help, click the Contents tab, click Troubleshooting, click Windows 98 Troubleshooters, and then click Print.

You can install a printer driver for a network printer in the same manner that you install a driver for a local printer. The only difference is that you will be asked for the server and printer name. Type the name using the UNC. Your network must support this convention if you install a network printer this way.

You can install a printer driver on your computer for a printer on a network in a few other ways, a couple of which are a little more automated. See the section entitled "Point and Print" later in this chapter for details.

It goes without saying that new printers are constantly coming onto the market. If a driver for your printer is not included with Windows 98, you may want to check Microsoft's Hardware Compatibility List (HCL). This list is constantly updated with the latest available drivers, as well as other information. You can search the HCL for your printer: Go to http://www. microsoft.com/hwtest/hcl/, select Printer in the Category list, choose your manufacturer, and click the Search button. The search will tell you the compatibility level of your printer, and whether a driver is available for download.

To get the latest update, you can click the Start button, point to Settings, and click Windows Update. This connects to Microsoft Windows Update site, which will interrogate your computer to see if you have the latest drivers.

Printer Driver Properties

Each printer driver has its own icon in the Printers folder. Attached to each printer icon is a Properties dialog box containing numerous properties that you can customize for that printer.

Properties that were previously global for all printer drivers have been moved to each printer driver's Properties dialog box. For example, you can determine for each printer whether to print directly to the printer or through a print queue.

Getting to a printer's properties

You get to a printer driver's properties by right-clicking its icon in the Printers folder and clicking Properties in the context menu. You can also highlight a printer icon in the Printers folder and choose File, Properties. If a printer's print-queue window is open, you can choose Printer, Properties in that window.

You can't get to a printer's properties by right-clicking a shortcut icon for the printer on your Desktop and clicking Properties (unless you have installed Target, a utility in Microsoft PowerToys). This will just get you to the properties of the shortcut. You need to click the shortcut icon and then choose Printer, Properties in the print-queue window.

You can also get to some of a printer's properties through the printer setup options in your application, usually through the Print or Print Setup command in the File menu. 32-bit applications can use the common print dialog box *dll* to get to the printer properties. The properties you access through your applications will not exactly match the ones connected to the printer's icon in the Printers folder. Settings that you make in the application — the number of copies, for example — will override any settings you make in the printer's Properties dialog box, or physically on the printer itself.

Basic printer properties

There are too many printer properties to go through all of them in this book. Besides, we want to focus on the undocumented aspects of printer drivers, not those features that are obvious.

You can find out what the various option buttons and fields in the Properties dialog box do by right-clicking them and then clicking the What's This? button that appears. You can also click the question mark in the upper-right corner of the dialog box and then click an area of interest.

Here, we'll go over a few of the options in the Properties dialog box to give you an idea of the range of things you can set. After that, we give you some guidance on how to deal with some of the less well-explained printer driver properties.

The Graphics tabs of the Properties dialog box for a LaserJet compatible printer and a PostScript compatible printer are shown in Figures 29-3 and 29-4. The specific graphics properties depend on the features available in the printer and the printer driver.

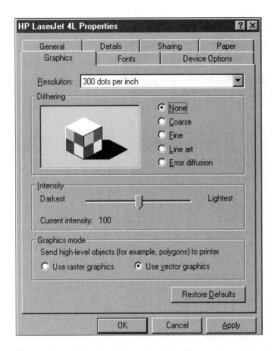

Figure 29-3: The Graphics tab of the Properties dialog box for a Hewlett Packard 4L printer. You get to determine the quality of the graphics output (traded against time to produce the output and per-sheet costs). Resolution doesn't affect text unless you print the text as a graphic (a setting on another tab).

Separator page

The General tab of the Properties dialog box is the same for all printers. One of the options on it lets you print a separator page between print jobs so that you can easily separate them. Separator pages are useful if many different people print to one printer.

The separator page can be blank, or it can contain a graphic that more easily identifies it. The graphic needs to be in the Windows Metafile format. Files of this type have the extension *wmf*.

Undocumented

Microsoft doesn't ship any applications with Windows 98 that can produce Windows Metafile files. You have to purchase an application that creates such files if you want to be able to create a separator page with a graphic on it. We include Paint Shop Pro on the *Windows 98 Secrets* CD-ROM, which allows you to create *wmf* files or convert them from *bmp* files.

Figure 29-4: The Graphics tab of the Properties dialog box for a Linotronic 300. The Linotronic is often used at service bureaus to produce film and other high-end output. You send PostScript from your application to a file using this driver, and then send the file to the service bureau. If you're printing to film, you can use the two check boxes in the Special area to flip or reverse the image.

After you turn off separator pages, you may still get them when you print from MS-DOS-based programs. This happens when the program is printing to a UNC printer name instead of to a port. To stop the extra pages, capture a specific port for this printer (see "Logical printer port redirection" later in this chapter).

Details

All Windows 98 printer drivers have the same Details tab, which is shown in Figure 29-5. Use the Print to the Following Port drop-down list to change the port to which you are printing (after you physically reconnect your local printer) or to print to a file.

Click the Capture Printer Port button if you want to redirect output from a named LPT port to a network printer. Use the Port Settings button if you need to turn off the spooling of DOS print jobs. You can even switch to the properties of one of the other printer drivers by using the Print Using the Following Driver drop-down list (this overwrites your existing driver). You can also update your printer driver from a diskette using the New Driver button.

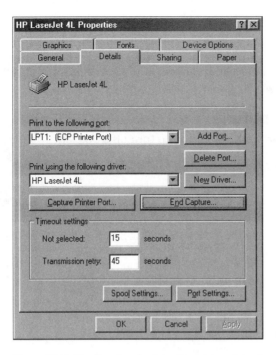

Figure 29-5: The Details tab of the Properties dialog box.

Undocumented

If you change the Print to the Following Port field to a network printer path, and that printer is of the same type as the printer whose properties you are currently viewing and editing, you will switch the current printer to the network printer as soon as you click Apply or OK. This is probably not what you want to do, as you lose your driver to your current printer. It's better to add a separate driver for the network printer than to switch connections in this field.

If you move the network or local printer, you can use the Add Port button to specify the new path to the printer.

You can adjust the time interval that your applications wait before Windows 98 reports a printer time-out error. Change the number of seconds in the Not Selected field to a higher value if you find that you continually get the "Windows will retry in 5 seconds" message box when you try to print.

Logical printer port redirection

The Capture Printer Port button lets you redirect output from a named LPT port to a network printer. You can set up nine redirections (LPT1 through LPT9) and specify if they will be valid the next time you reboot your computer. If you do, Windows 98 connects to the servers where these printers are located every time you restart your computer while connected to your network.

Add a port

If you want to connect to a different printer, or if your network printer has moved, click the Add Port button. The network path to your already installed network printer will be shown in the list of ports. You can type the path to a network printer for later use.

DOS print spooling

You can use the Port Settings button to turn off DOS print spooling. Most of the actual port settings (including the I/O address and IRQ setting) are found in the Device Manager.

Printing directly to the printer with no spooling

If you want to turn off spooling and print directly to the printer (with no intermediate temporary file), click the Spool Settings button to display the Spool Settings dialog box, and mark the Print Directly to the Printer option button. You can also use the Spool Data Format drop-down list to choose the RAW or EMF format. If you turn off spooling, the format has to be RAW.

If you are printing to a file, the bottom third of the Details tab will be grayed out. These properties are not used when you're printing to a file instead of to a physical printer.

Spooling and speed

Print speed is measured in two ways in Windows 98. One is the length of time it takes to regain control of the system after you issue the Print command (called the *return to application* or RTA speed). The other is the time from when you issue the Print command to when your finished page drops into the printer's paper catch (called *page drop speed*). Both of these speeds are affected by the spool settings in Windows 98.

You can affect each of these times by setting options in the Spool Settings dialog box (click the Spool Settings button in the Details tab of the Properties dialog box).

For faster RTA speed, mark the Click Start Printing After First Page Is Spooled option button. If this is not a PostScript printer, choose EMF as the spool data format.

For faster page drop speed, mark either the Print Directly to the Printer option button or the Start Printing After Last Page Is Spooled option button.

Fonts

Almost all of the printer drivers have a Fonts tab in the Properties dialog box. Unlike the Details tab, each type of printer has different options on the Fonts tab.

If you are printing to an inkjet printer at a lower resolution (75–150 dpi), or if you are using the Generic/Text Only printer driver, you will probably find that TrueType fonts are not available.

HP font installer

Tip

The HP printer driver lets you install HP Intellifonts using the Install Printer Fonts button on the Fonts tab. This brings up HP's font installer, which has the old Windows 3.1x look to it. Newer HP printers have a number of built-in TrueType printer fonts that correspond to TrueType fonts in the font packs from Microsoft and HP. You install these fonts using the Fonts folder, not HP's font installer. Even if you don't have a newer HP-compatible printer with built-in fonts, it's better to install TrueType fonts than HP Intellifonts. See "Installing Fonts" in Chapter 26 for more about fonts.

TrueType fonts on PostScript printers

Tip

It's easy to use TrueType fonts and print to a PostScript printer or a PostScript file that you will take to a service bureau. In almost all cases, unless you are doing a quick draft document, you should mark the Always Use TrueType Fonts option button on the Fonts tab, as shown in Figure 29-6. (This is not the default setting.)

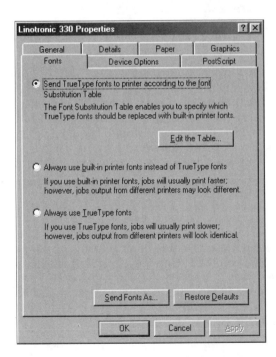

Figure 29-6: The Fonts tab of the Properties dialog box for the Linotronic 300. Mark the Always Use TrueType Fonts option button, and then click the Send Fonts As button.

You should also click the Send Fonts As button and choose Outlines in the Send TrueType Fonts As drop-down list, shown in Figure 29-7. If you don't do this, the output you see on your screen may not match the output from the printer.

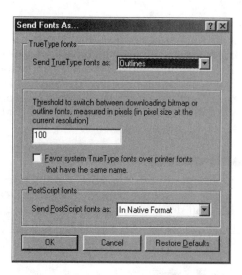

Figure 29-7: The Send Fonts As dialog box. Choose Outlines from the Send TrueType Fonts As drop-down list.

If you treat TrueType fonts in this manner, the printed version of your document should match the one you see on screen. The spacing and line breaks won't shift because the PostScript printer won't substitute the TrueType fonts with PostScript fonts, as it would if you did not mark the Always Use TrueType fonts option. However, if you are using a fancy font or a font designed for use in headlines, you may want to test it before printing your final output.

Sharing

Tip

You can use drivers for printers that you don't actually have — no problem with that. For example, if you want to create a PostScript file for a Linotronic 300 that is many miles away in a service bureau, you install a printer driver for it on your computer and then print to a file. You can then ship the file through your modem to the bulletin board at the service bureau for printing later that day or overnight.

One thing that you can't do with a printer driver that is configured to print to a file is share the printer (because there isn't any printer there to share). If you have an actual printer connected locally and you've enabled print sharing (using the Network icon in your Control Panel), you have a Sharing tab in the printer driver's Properties dialog box that lets you specify whether or not to share the printer.

You can also get to the Sharing tab by right-clicking a local printer's icon in the Printers folder and clicking Sharing in the context menu. For more details, see the section later in this chapter entitled "Sharing a Printer."

PostScript properties

The PostScript driver has its own PostScript-specific tab, as shown in Figure 29-8. The Advanced options let you do such wonderful things as getting rid of the Ctrl+D at the beginning or end of your PostScript output so you don't have to manually edit them out if you run over a Unix network to a PostScript printer.

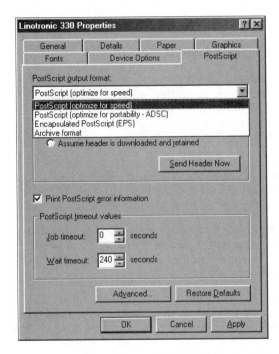

Figure 29-8: The PostScript tab of the Properties dialog box. Use the PostScript Output Format drop-down list to specify an output format, and click the Advanced button for more options.

You can choose among several PostScript output formats. The default format, Optimize for Speed, is fine for local printers. If you're printing to a file for off-site printing, you might want to try Optimize for Portability - ADSC. (ADSC stands for Adobe Document Structuring Conventions.) Choose Encapsulated PostScript (EPS) if you're printing to a file that will be incorporated into another file.

Defining your own printer

If you have installed the Generic/Text Only printer driver, you can define escape sequences (printer commands) that control your specific printer and set the various font sizes and types. In most cases, you don't have to do this, because Microsoft has included printer drivers for 1,500 different printers with Windows 98. But the capability is there if you run into printer number 1,501.

Use the Device Options and Fonts tabs associated with the Generic/Text only printer driver to define the printer codes for your particular printer.

Tip Installing the Generic/Text Only printer is a great way to produce text-only output from applications that don't have an option to save unformatted text-only files.

Managing Print Queues

You can change the order in which documents will be printed by changing their order in the print queue. To do this, open the Printers folder, click the printer icon to open the print-queue window, and simply drag the documents into the order you want. You can only do this for documents that haven't started printing yet.

Windows 98 doesn't let you move documents from one printer's queue to that of another. This is because the documents have already been translated into RAW format for that specific printer. Instead, you must remove the document from the old queue and print it again to the other printer.

You can use the Purge Print Documents command in the Printer menu of a queue to remove all documents from the queue (and not print any of them). However, you cannot use your computer to remove documents from the print queue of a network printer.

The print spool folder is \Windows\Spool\Printers. This is where the translated documents are held while they wait to be printed. You can't move this folder without reinstalling Windows 98, and there's no good reason to do so.

Deferred Printing

You can print documents using a printer driver for a network printer that isn't currently connected through the network to your computer. The print jobs will be spooled, and you can print them later when you reconnect to the printer through the network. The print jobs are tracked in the print queue for that printer, and when you put the printer online, they are automatically printed. Deferred printing will not work if you have turned off spooling in your printer properties (as described in "Printing directly to the printer with no spooling" earlier in this chapter).

One way you can use deferred printing is to create documents on a portable, print them to the print queue, and then print them later when you connect your portable to a computer with a printer (perhaps your desktop computer). The portable has to have a printer driver for the desktop's printer installed as a network printer, and the two computers need to be connected with Direct Cable Connection (DCC) or through another network connection. If you use a docking station, the files you send to the queue while undocked will be printed automatically when you re-dock. See "Connecting Two Computers" in Chapter 22 for more on connecting laptops and desktops.

You can also use Dial-Up Networking (DUN) to phone in from the portable to the desktop computer and print your documents at the office while you are on the road or at home. You need to have the desktop computer configured as a DUN server. (See "Setting Up Your Windows 98 Computer at Work as a Host" in Chapter 17.)

If you are on a network and printing to a network printer and you lose the connection to that printer, your print jobs will be spooled until the connection is reestablished and you place the printer online. The printer driver for the network printer will display itself as offline as soon as the network connection is broken.

Even if you are presently connected to the network printer, you can take it offline (for you) by right-clicking its icon in your Printers folder and clicking Use Printer Offline.

Undocumented

If you take a network printer offline by right-clicking its icon in the Printers folder and clicking Use Printer Offline, the icon in the Printers folder is ghosted. If you have a shortcut to that icon on your Desktop, however, it is not ghosted when the printer is offline. If you click the shortcut icon on the Desktop, you will see a message stating that the printer is offline in the title bar of the print-queue window. To turn the printer back online, click the Use Printer Offline command again.

Printing with the Task Scheduler

One approach to deferred printing that works on a local printer is to use the Windows 98 Task Scheduler (previously called System Agent) to schedule your print job. You can set it up to print on an as-needed basis, or on a regular schedule—to print your modem log every night, for example. Follow these steps to set up a print job in the Task Scheduler:

STEPS

Scheduling Unattended Printing

Step 1. If you have the Task Scheduler icon in your Tray, double-click it to open the Scheduled Tasks window. You can also open the window by clicking the Scheduled Tasks icon in the My Computer window, or by clicking Start, Programs, Accessories, System Tools, Scheduled Tasks.

Step 2. In the Scheduled Tasks window, click the Add Scheduled Task icon to start the Scheduled Task Wizard, and then click Next.

Step 3. From the Wizard's list, select the program you used to create the document you want to print — or click Browse if you don't see the one you want. Click Next.

Step 4. Give your task a name, such as *Print Weekly Status Report*, and indicate when you want the task to run, as shown in Figure 29-9. If this is the only time you want to print this file, mark the One Time Only option button. Click Next. If you choose one of the last two options (When My Computer Starts or When I Log On), skip to step 6.

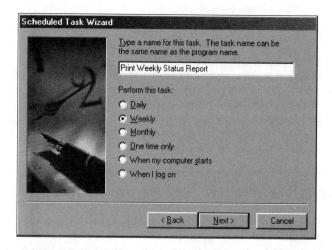

Figure 29-9: The Scheduled Task Wizard lets you name your task and indicate how often it will run.

Step 5. Enter the time and date when the task should run, and click Next.

Step 6. Mark the Open Advanced Properties for This Task When I Click Finish check box. Click Finish.

Step 7. The Task tab of the Properties dialog box for this task will open. In the Run field, add a space after the path for the program you have chosen, and then type the command to print a document, using this syntax:

```
/p "drive:\foldername\filename"
```

You must use the quote marks if any of your files or folders have spaces in their names. As the example in Figure 29-10 shows, the command to print a report you wrote in WordPad might look like this:

```
C:\Program Files\Accessories\Wordpad.exe /p "C:\My
Documents\Report.txt"
```

Step 8.   Click OK, and then close Task Scheduler.

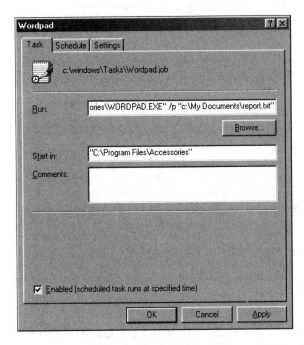

Figure 29-10: Type /p after the program's filename in the task's Properties dialog box, followed by the path and name of the file you want to print.

Although the /p switch for printing is quite common, it is by no means universal. Microsoft Word and Excel are two noteworthy exceptions. (Word uses /x and Excel uses /e.) The switch is defined for an application by the developers. If you have trouble getting the Task Scheduler to work for your document, you can check the application's syntax for printing. In the Explorer, choose View, Folder Options, and click the File Types tab. In the list there, highlight the file type that you want to use and click Edit. Highlight Print in the Actions list, and click Edit. Look at the contents of the Application Used to Perform Action field. After the filename of the application (probably ending in *exe*), you'll see the appropriate characters needed to carry out the Print action. Use these characters instead of /p in the steps above. For a more complete discussion of actions associated with file types, see "General actions on any file type" in Chapter 13.

If you want to get back to the Properties dialog box for a task, simply right-click the task in the Scheduled Tasks window and click Properties in the context menu. You can temporarily disable a task without deleting it by clearing the Enabled checkbox on the Task tab. To change your task's schedule, go to the Scheduled tab and change the contents of the fields there. On the Settings tab, you'll find additional ways to constrain your task—for example, the Power Management settings let you avoid running a task if you're on battery power, or let you tell your computer to "wake up" for tasks that run late at night.

The Task Scheduler also keeps a log, which can be handy if you're troubleshooting. To see the log, click Advanced, View Log in the Scheduled Tasks window.

Printing to a file

Tip

You can always create a print file for a specific printer and manually send this file to the printer later. To do this, change the Print to the Following Port field in the Details tab for that printer's driver from a specific port to FILE. When you print your document, you can use all the settings available for that printer, including the paper tray and the number of copies to print. A new file will be created that contains the document formatted with the printer codes for that specific printer. You will be prompted by your application to choose a name and location for the file. The default extension for a print file is usually *ps* or *prn*, depending on whether the printer driver you're using is PostScript or not.

Printing to a file can be a very effective way to work with a service bureau, since they don't have to have your application or your fonts to print your file. Printing to a file also lets you design a document at home, and then print it on a specialized PostScript printer at the office or a copy center. Keep in mind that the file you produce will often be considerably larger than your original document, especially if you include imported images or print color separations. Perhaps the biggest drawback is that you cannot edit the print file after you create it. If your service bureau finds a mistake, or you don't want that paper tray after all, you must go back to your original document and print to a new file.

When you later have access to the printer whose driver you chose, you can copy the file to the printer port. You actually need to use the DOS Copy command. You can't drag and drop the print file to the printer icon. This method would make the most sense (visually), but it doesn't work.

Undocumented

You can run the DOS Copy command from the Run dialog box if you like (click the Start button, and click Run). Assuming that the name of your print file is File1.hp, you would type the following command in the Run dialog box:

```
command /c copy /b file1.hp lpt2:
```

This copies the file of print commands to the second parallel port (which could also be redirected to a network printer). The /c parameter tells Command to execute the following command and then return to the DOS prompt. The /b parameter tells Copy to copy the file in binary mode. For some trickier approaches to printing files, turn to the "Printing to an offline Postscript printer" section coming up next.

Note that if you use this method for a network printer, you'll need to capture a printer port to make it work.

Some people print to a file to generate ASCII text reports—from a database application, for example—which they can read on their computers as well as print. To do this in Windows 98, make sure to set Spool Data Format to RAW before you print. (Click the Spool Settings button in the Details tab of the printer's Properties dialog box to check this setting.) For the most readable results, install the driver for a generic printer (by choosing Generic/Text Only in the manufacturer list of the Add Printer Wizard) with FILE as its port. Then target that printer in your application when you print the report.

The whole point of deferred printing is to get around this tiresome technique of manually copying print files to the printer port. Unfortunately, deferred printing works only for network printers and not for local printers that are presently offline.

Printing to an offline PostScript printer

You can also use the technique described in the previous section to print to an offline (off-premises) PostScript printer. First install a PostScript driver on your computer for your target PostScript printer. Then use the PostScript driver to print the document to a file. Transfer this file via diskette or over the phone lines to the location with the PostScript printer. Finally, use the DOS Copy command to print the PostScript file on the target printer.

Printing PostScript files

You can create a print file of PostScript output on a computer that doesn't have a PostScript printer connected to it (or to the network that the computer is connected to). You then take this PostScript output file, which usually has a *ps* extension, to a computer with a PostScript printer and copy the file to the printer. (The PostScript output file is just a series of ASCII commands and parameters.)

Copying a file to the printer is a DOS-based function, but we can configure Windows 98 to carry out this function without using the Start, Run dialog box or opening a DOS window and issuing the DOS Copy command.

Undocumented

There are two ways to do this. First, you can create an association between the *ps* file extension and a command that copies the file to the printer. Second, you can create a batch file (and a shortcut to it) that consists of the DOS commands to send the file to the printer. Then you can place the shortcut to the PostScript printing batch file in the SendTo folder. Because the batch file is generic, it will send any file to the printer, not just PostScript files.

To create an association to the *ps* file type, take the following steps:

STEPS

Create a Print Command Associated with a PostScript Print File

Step 1.   Open your Explorer, choose View, Folder Options, and click the File Types tab.

Step 2.   Click the New Type button.

Step 3.   Type **PostScript Print Output File** in the Description of Type field, **ps** in the Associated Extension field, and **PostScript Commands** in the Content Type (MIME) field.

Step 4.   Click the New button, and then type **Copy to Printer** in the Action field and **C:\Windows\Command.com /c Copy /b %1 Lpt1:** in the Application Used to Perform Action field. Click OK.

You can replace *Lpt1:* in this command line with another printer port designator, or with the UNC name of a network printer.

Step 5.   Click the Choose Icon button, and browse to find an appropriate printer-type icon. Click OK.

Step 6.   Click OK, and then click Close.

You can now click any file with a *ps* extension to print it on your PostScript printer. Unfortunately, the DOS window will flash briefly when you use this method.

To create a batch file and an accompanying shortcut that will print any file (and not flash a DOS window), take the following steps:

STEPS

Create a Print Batch File

Step 1.   Click Edit.com in your \Windows\Command folder (if you haven't already made a shortcut to this nifty DOS editor).

Step 2.   Type **C:\Windows\Command.com /c Copy /b %1 Lpt1:**

Step 3.   Choose File, Save As, and save the file as Ps.bat.

Step 4. Right-drag and drop Ps.bat to your Desktop to create a shortcut to it. (You could also try another method to create a shortcut on your Desktop. Right-click Ps.bat, and click Create Shortcut. Right-click the shortcut, which appears in the same folder as Ps.bat, and click Cut. Then right-click the Desktop and click Paste.)

Step 5. With the new shortcut on the Desktop highlighted, press F2, rename the shortcut something like Print Files, and press Enter.

Step 6. Right-click the shortcut, choose Properties, and then click the Program tab.

Step 7. Choose Minimized in the Run drop-down list, and mark the Close on Exit check box. Click the Change Icon button and find an appropriate icon for this shortcut that prints files. Click OK.

Step 8. Right-click a PostScript print output file in a folder or Explorer window, and click Copy in the context menu.

Step 9. Right-click the new shortcut on the Desktop and click Paste. The PostScript file will be copied to the PostScript printer. A button will appear briefly on the Taskbar as the file is copied.

The file is treated as a DOS file, and it will be spooled to the printer if you haven't turned off DOS print spooling.

You can place this shortcut in the \Windows\SendTo folder. If you do this, you can right-click the PostScript (or text) file, point to Send To in the context menu, and then click the shortcut in the Send To submenu to copy the file to the printer.

Troubleshooting with Windows 98 Help

If you are having trouble printing, you can use the Print Troubleshooter section of the help system to track down the problem. Windows 98 help is not just a semi-meaningless collection of statements of the obvious; it is actually useful in the real world. The print troubleshooter can pinpoint a problem for you, as long as you answer the questions correctly.

To get to the print troubleshooter, click the Start button, click Help, click the Contents tab, click Troubleshooting, click Windows 98 Troubleshooters, and then click Print.

Undocumented

The CD-ROM version of Windows 98 contains an enhanced print troubleshooter. You'll find it in the \tools\misc\epts folder. Just click Epts.exe to start it.

You may also want to check a file called Printers.txt, located in your \Windows folder and in the \readme folder of the Windows 98 CD-ROM. It contains information about problems and workarounds for specific printers.

There is an online troubleshooter in the Microsoft Knowledge Base called "Solving problems with Printing in Windows 98," which is located at http://premium.microsoft.com/support/tshoot/w98print.asp. You can also search the Microsoft Knowledge Base for articles related to your particular printer or problem; the address is http://premium.microsoft.com/support/.

Other troubleshooting strategies

If you are having trouble printing, and have established that the printer is connected properly and that its properties are set correctly, try these strategies to isolate your problem:

- **Make sure you have enough disk space for spooling.** You should have at least 3MB free on the logical disk drive that contains your \Windows\Temp folder. Although the temporary files are supposed to be automatically deleted when you shut your computer down, sometimes (after a crash, for example) they remain on your disk and cause problems.

  To delete these files, restart your computer in MS-DOS mode by clicking the Start button, clicking Shut Down, and choosing the Restart in MS-DOS Mode option. At the DOS prompt, type **cd \windows\temp** and press Enter. Type **del *.tmp** and press Enter to delete all temporary files in this folder. Type **cd \windows\spool\printers** and press Enter to change to the spool folder, and then type **del *.spl** and press Enter to delete any leftover spool files. When you're finished with DOS, type **exit**. The reason for using MS-DOS mode is that if Windows 98 is running, it may be using some of the files in these folders.

- **Try printing from a DOS prompt.** Restart your computer in Safe mode, and then try printing a test file to LPT1 (or whichever port you've assigned your printer). To do this, type **copy c:\autoexec.bat lpt1** (or **copy c:\Windows\System\testps.txt lpt1** if you have a PostScript printer) and press Enter.

  If autoexec.bat (or testps.txt) does not print, the problem may be with the port, the cable, or the printer. If it does print, the problem may relate to the spool settings or bidirectional communication. Click the Spool Settings button in the Details tab of your printer's Properties dialog box, and mark the Print Directly to the Printer option button. If your printer supports bidirectional communication, mark the Disable Bi-Directional Support for This Printer option button.

- **Try printing from Notepad or WordPad.** If you can't, check to make sure the port is set up correctly, and that there are no resource conflicts. To do this, open the Control Panel, click the System icon, and click the Device Manager tab. Click the plus sign next to Ports (COM & LPT), Double-click the port you have assigned to this printer, and click the Resources tab. Look at the Conflicting Device List box. If there is a resource conflict, Windows 98 will tell you what the conflicting device is, and which resource the two devices are fighting over. You can change the port's resource setting in this tab; see "Configuring Serial Ports" or "Configuring Parallel Ports" in Chapter 31.

If you can print from Notepad or WordPad, click the Spool Settings button in the Details tab of the printer's Properties dialog box, and try different combinations of spool settings and bidirectional support until you find a combination that works in your other applications.

■ **Try disabling the Enhanced Capabilities Port (ECP port) if you have one.** Open the Device Manager, find the ECP port, and double-click it. On the General tab in the Properties dialog box for the port, mark Disable in This Hardware Profile.

■ **Try reinstalling the printer port.** Using the Device Manager, select the port assigned to your printer and click the Remove button. Restart your computer. In the Control Panel, click the Add New Hardware icon and let Windows 98 detect your hardware and walk you through reinstalling the port.

■ **Try a different printer driver.** In the Printers folder, click the Add Printer icon and use the Add Printer Wizard to install the Generic/Text Only driver (to determine whether the problem is your driver). If the generic driver works, you may be able to solve the problem by deleting your printer from the Printers folder and reinstalling the driver for your printer's manufacturer and model. If that doesn't work, try installing a driver for a printer that your printer emulates. For example, if you have a PostScript printer, try using the Apple LaserWriter II NTX driver. If you have a Windows 3.1*x* driver for your printer, try installing it as a last resort.

Windows Printing System

Microsoft introduced the Windows Printing System (WPS) in December 1992 as a way for printer manufacturers to speed up printing and reduce the cost of printers. WPS is a combination of software and hardware that comes with your printer and lets the translation to the printer's codes take place on the computer, instead of on the printer. There are also several printers on the market that use third-party software to offer similar features but without the hardware component of WPS. You will need to have the setup disks for this software when you install the printer in Windows 98.

Windows 98 supports WPS. If you are already running WPS when you install Windows 98, Setup will automatically update several key WPS files. If you install WPS later, Windows 98 will detect this and prompt you to load the Windows 98 CD-ROM to update these files.

Windows 98 changes some of the ways WPS works. For example, separator pages are now handled in the printer's Properties dialog box. If you're on a network, you need to capture a logical port for the printer, rather than using a UNC name. And you should enable bidirectional communication even if the port you are using is not bidirectional. (To do this, click the Spool Settings button in the Details tab of the Properties dialog box for your printer and mark Enable Bi-Directional Support for This Printer.)

Sharing a Printer

You can share your printer over your network so that others can use it to print their documents. There are two basic ways to do this. The first is to configure your computer as a server (either a file server, a print server, or both), as described in the next section. Your computer can become a file and print server on a peer-to-peer network such as Microsoft Network, or on a server-based network such as a Novell NetWare or Windows NT network.

Unlike Windows NT or Novell servers, the Windows 98 file and print server doesn't have a database that can track users and maintain user-level security. If you want the kind of security that allows users to use your resources by group or user name instead of by password, you'll need to use these other servers.

The second way to share your printer is only possible if you are on a NetWare network. If you are, you can to set up Microsoft Print Server for NetWare on your Windows 98 computer and use your computer to service the NetWare print queue on the NetWare server. Microsoft Print Server for NetWare cooperates with the NetWare print server to print the jobs that are queued by the NetWare server. We discuss this second method in the "Microsoft Print Server for NetWare" section later in the chapter.

Enabling print sharing

If you want share your local printer with others on a network, you must first enable print sharing. To do so, take the following steps:

STEPS

Enabling Print Sharing

Step 1. Click the Start button, point to Settings, and then click Control Panel.

Step 2. Click the Network icon. Click the Add button.

Step 3. Highlight Service in the Select Network Component Type dialog box, and click the Add button.

Step 4. Highlight Microsoft in the Select Network Service dialog box. Then highlight either File and Printer Sharing for Microsoft Networks or File and Printer Sharing for NetWare Networks. If you are installing print sharing for another network and you have a diskette from the manufacturer, click the Have Disk button instead, select the correct diskette drive and choose the appropriate service. Click OK.

Step 5.   Click the File and Print Sharing button.

Step 6.   In the File and Print Sharing dialog box, shown in Figure 29-11, mark I Want to Be Able to Allow Others to Print to My Printer(s).

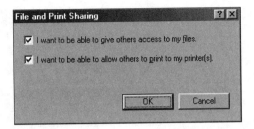

Figure 29-11: The File and Print Sharing dialog box. Mark the check boxes next to the resources that you want to share.

Step 7.   Click both OK buttons.

You have to restart your computer so that the changes you made can take effect.

Actually sharing your printer

To share a printer, take the following steps:

STEPS

Sharing a Printer

Step 1.   Click the Start button, point to Settings, and then click Printers.

Step 2.   Right-click the icon of the printer that you want to share, and then click Sharing in the context menu.

Step 3.   You'll see the Sharing tab of the Properties dialog box for the printer, as shown in Figure 29-12. Mark the Shared As option button.

Step 4.   Fill out the three Shared As fields.

Step 5.   Click OK.

(continued)

Sharing a Printer

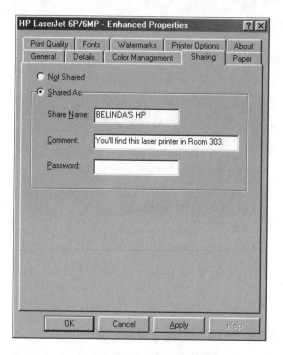

Figure 29-12: The Sharing tab. Click Shared As to allow your printer to be used by others. You can give a useful comment and name to help others decide if they want to use your printer and determine where to find the output.

Your computer is now a full-fledged print server. If you are using a NetWare network, you can use the Windows 98 computer as a complete print server and off-load the extra resource use from your NetWare server.

If you are using a Windows NT or NetWare server to provide user-level security, you won't see the Password field that appears in Figure 29-12. The users who can access your printer will be determined by the database of users to whom you have granted access to your resources. This list of groups and users is kept on the Windows NT or NetWare server.

To specify which server the list of users is kept on, take the following steps:

STEPS

Specifying User-Access Control

Step 1. Click the Start button, point to Settings, and then click Control Panel.

Step 2. Click the Network icon. Click the Access Control tab.

Step 3. Click the User-Level Access Control option button.

Step 4. Type the name of the server that has the list.

A shortcut to a shared printer

If you create a shortcut from your printer icon in the Printers folder, that shortcut will only work on your computer. You cannot e-mail it to someone else on your network and have it work for them. Here's how to make a shortcut that you can send to your co-workers:

STEPS

Creating a Shortcut to a Shared Printer

Step 1. Click Network Neighborhood on your Desktop and locate the print server.

Step 2. Click the print server to view its resources.

Step 3. Right-click the shared printer icon, and click Create Shortcut in the context menu.

Monitoring shared printer use

If you have a shared printer or other resource on your computer, you may want to see who is using it. If you have installed Client for Microsoft Networks, you can use the Net Watcher utility to perform this and other network housekeeping functions.

To start Net Watcher, click Start, Programs, Accessories, System Tools, Net Watcher. If you don't find Net Watcher, use Add/Remove Programs to install it. (Click the Add/Remove Programs icon in the Control Panel, click the Windows Setup tab, highlight System Tools, click the Details button, and mark the Net Watcher check box.)

Slow network printing with MS-DOS programs

If you print a document from a DOS program or press the Print Screen key while in a DOS window and it takes from 60 to 90 seconds for the printing to begin, the DOS program might not have closed the printer port. The Windows 98 default setting is to wait 45 seconds after the DOS program stops sending information to begin printing if the printer port isn't closed by the DOS program, so this can mean some rather long waits.

To solve this problem, add the following lines to your System.ini file:

```
[Network]
    PrintBufTime=10
[IFSMGR]
    PrintBufTime=10
```

If these lines aren't already in your System.ini file, create them after the [386Enh] section. They set the print buffer time at 10 seconds (instead of the default 45 seconds). If you experience problems, you should try increasing the values.

Microsoft Print Server for NetWare

If you are on a NetWare network, you can configure your Windows 98 computer as a print services provider for a NetWare server. Instead of setting up your computer to be an independent print server, you use Microsoft Print Server for NetWare to have your computer log on to the NetWare print server, de-spool the print jobs, and then print them on its local printer.

To configure your printer as an independent print server, you run file and printer sharing for NetWare Networks. You won't need to do this if you are configuring your computer as a print services provider for a NetWare print server.

Your computer will log onto the NetWare print server and then poll the print queue on the server for print jobs. To install Microsoft Print Server for NetWare, take the following steps:

STEPS

Installing Microsoft Print Server for NetWare

Step 1. Click the Start button, point to Settings, and then click Control Panel.

Step 2. Click the Network, and click the Add button.

Step 3.   In the Select Network Component Type dialog box, highlight Service, click the Add button, and insert your Windows 98 CD-ROM.

Step 4.   In the Select Network Service dialog box, click the Have Disk button.

Step 5.   In the Install From Disk dialog box, type the drive letter for your CD-ROM and the path **\Admin\Nettools\Prtagent**, and press Enter. Microsoft Print Agent for NetWare Networks appears highlighted in the Select Network Service dialog box.

Step 6.   Click OK twice.

Now that Microsoft Print Server for NetWare is installed, you need to enable it. First check your NetWare print server and make sure that it is operating correctly, and then take these steps:

STEPS

Enabling Microsoft Print Server for NetWare

Step 1.   Click the Start button, point to Settings, and then click Printers.

Step 2.   Right-click the icon for the local printer that you will use to print jobs coming from the NetWare print queue. Click Properties in the context menu.

Step 3.   Click the Print Server tab. Click the Enable Microsoft Print Server for NetWare option button.

Step 4.   Choose the NetWare server in the NetWare Server drop-down list. In the Print Server field, choose the NetWare print server names whose queues your Windows 98 computer will service.

Step 5.   Adjust the print queue polling time interval.

Step 6.   Click OK.

Point and Print

You can, of course, install a printer driver on your computer for a network printer in the normal (non-point and print) fashion by using the Add Printer Wizard. Just click the Add Printer icon in the Printers folder.

When you do this, the Wizard finds the printer driver files necessary to install that printer driver. You need to know exactly what kind of printer you are installing so you can tell this to the Add Printer Wizard, and you need to have the printer driver source diskettes or CD-ROM handy.

You can install printers that are shared on networked Windows 98, Windows NT, and NetWare servers with point and print. If you are printing to a Windows 98 print server, all the information about the printer drivers and the drivers themselves are stored there. You don't have to do anything to allow the drivers to be transferred to the client Windows 98 computer. The Windows 98 printer server must be running file and printer sharing for NetWare Networks or file and printer sharing for Microsoft Networks.

Automated printer driver installation

A better way to install a printer driver for a network printer is to have Windows 98 install the driver automatically. You can do this in three ways: Drag and drop a document icon to the network printer's icon in its shared folder window, drag and drop the network printer's icon to your Desktop or your Printers folder, or click the network printer's icon in the shared resources folder window of the server.

Drag and drop a document to a network printer icon

When you print a document by dragging and dropping it to the icon of a network printer that you haven't yet installed, you invoke a version of the Add Printer Wizard.

STEPS

Installing a Network Printer By Drag and Drop Printing

Step 1. Open a folder window containing a document file or a shortcut to a document file.

Step 2. Make sure you have the shared resources folder window open for the server whose printer you are going to install.

Step 3. Drag and drop the document icon to the printer icon in the shared resources folder window. The message box shown in Figure 29-13 will appear.

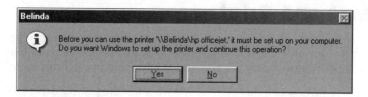

Figure 29-13: A message box telling you that you have to set up the printer driver on your computer.

Step 4. Click the Yes button. The Add Printer Wizard (network printer installation version) appears, as shown in Figure 29-14. If you want to assign a logical printer port to your network printer, click the Yes option button to indicate that you want to print from MS-DOS programs, and then click the Next button. (MS-DOS programs often require that you print to an LPT port.)

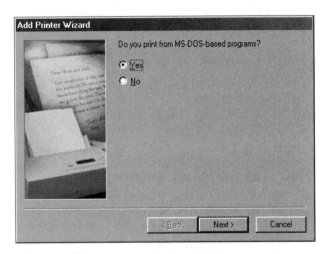

Figure 29-14: The network printer installation version of the Add Printer Wizard. If you don't want to capture a printer port, click Next. Otherwise, click the Yes option button, and then click Next.

Step 5. Finish answering the Wizard's questions. Give the printer a name that reminds you which one it is when you print to it. When you click Finish, the Wizard will copy the printer drivers from the network server and install them on your computer. While the Wizard is running, you may see a message that a *dll* file needed for this printer is in use by another program. If so, exit any other applications you may be running (Microsoft Word, for example), and click the Retry button.

If the printer has trouble printing your file, the Print Troubleshooter will automatically start and lead you through a troubleshooting process.

The printer driver for the network printer is now installed. When you open your Printers folder window, you'll see an icon for the network printer.

Undocumented Now that you have installed the network printer, you can drag and drop documents to either of its icons to print documents. The network printer's icons in the shared resources folder and in your local Printers folder behave in the same way. Click either and you will see the same print-queue window. One minor difference is that only the icon in the Printers folder is ghosted if the network printer is offline.

Drag and drop a network printer icon

The network printer icon should be visible to you in the Explorer or in a shared resources folder window that is focused on the network server computer. You can drag and drop the network printer's icon from the Explorer or folder window to your Desktop or to your Printers folder window or folder icon, creating a shortcut to the network printer.

Now follow steps 4 through 5 in the Installing a Network Printer By Drag and Drop Printing steps in the previous section. After the Wizard is finished, the network printer's icon will appear in your Printers folder as well as in the place where you made the shortcut.

Undocumented

You have created a shortcut to the network printer, but the network connection must be there for the printer to work. If your network connection is DCC, you can't invoke the connection by clicking the network printer's icon if it isn't already set up. You have to make the connection first before the network printer can be seen.

Click the network printer icon

If you can see the icon that represents the shared printer on the network computer, just click it. The Wizard will start, as described in "Drag and drop a document to a network printer icon," and install the network printer. It copies the shared printer's driver over to your computer and puts the printer icon in your Printers folder. As an alternative, you can also right-click the network printer's icon and click Install.

Point and print to a NetWare server

If you want to be able to have Windows 98 client computers point and print to your printers managed by a NetWare printer server, you're going to need to do a little more work. You have to copy the driver files that are used for each of the printers managed by that server to a directory on the server. It turns out that this is more akin to the Add Printer Wizard than to point and print.

Set up a NetWare print server for point and print

If you have administrative privileges on the NetWare server that you are logged onto, you can configure the server to store the needed printer drivers and auxiliary files. Take the following steps to do so:

STEPS
Configuring a NetWare Server to Store Point and Print Files

Step 1. Right-click a NetWare print queue icon displayed in the NetWare shared resources window. Click Point and Print Setup in the context menu.

Step 2. Click Set Printer Model. In the Select dialog box, highlight the manufacturer and model of the printer associated with the print queue on the NetWare server. Click OK.

Step 3. Right-click the same NetWare print queue again, and then click Set Driver Path.

Step 4. Type a path and folder name that is valid for the NetWare server and in which you will store the printer driver files for this printer.

Step 5. Open Msprint.inf or Msprint2.inf in your Inf folder with Notepad. See which files are going to be copied when you install this printer. Extract these files from your Windows 98 CD-ROM cabinet files and copy them into the directory you just created on your NetWare server.

You now have the printer driver source files on your NetWare server. This makes it somewhat easier to point and print to a NetWare printer from a Windows 98 client computer.

Point and print to a NetWare printer

Now that you have set up your NetWare server to allow point and print (after a fashion), you can use it to install printer drivers on a Windows 98 client computer. To do this, take the following steps:

STEPS

Installing a Printer Driver from a NetWare Server

Step 1. Log onto a NetWare server from a client Windows 98 computer.

Step 2. In the Network Neighborhood on the client computer, click the NetWare server's icon to display a folder window listing the resources of the NetWare server.

Step 3. Drag and drop a printer icon from the NetWare window to your local Printers folder window. This activates the Add Printer Wizard.

Step 4. Type the name of the new printer.

Your NetWare network printer driver is now installed on your local Windows 98 computer.

Summary

Windows 98 arrives with a significant number of improvements in printing capabilities. We describe them for you.

▶ We discuss how the new Printers folder unites almost all of the print functions in Windows, making it easier for you to manage your printers.

▶ Because each printer has its own icon, you can put a shortcut to each printer on your Desktop. You can drag and drop documents to the particular printer that you want without having to change the default printer.

▶ You can define drag and drop to a printer to be any possible action, not just printing.

▶ DOS files are, by default, spooled to the printer through the Windows 98 print spooler. This alleviates printer device contention.

▶ We show you how to print TrueType fonts correctly on PostScript printers.

▶ You can print to a print queue and have your files printed later when you actually connect to your printer.

▶ You can have the appropriate printer drivers automatically installed when you print to network printers.

Chapter 30

The Mighty Mouse
(Other Pointing Devices, Too)

In This Chapter

Windows 98 builds on the big mouse support improvements that came with Windows 95. With the new ability to open by single-clicking, your mouse is friendlier and more useful than ever. We describe:

▶ Taking advantage of the new single-clicking capabilities

▶ The power of the right mouse button and why you'll want to use it often

▶ When you still need to use double-click

▶ What's so great about the 32-bit protected-mode mouse driver

▶ Improving your mouse's responsiveness

▶ Turning your mouse pointer into a nifty animated pointer

▶ Turning your middle button into a double-click button

Mouse Basics

In this chapter, we don't mean *mouse* exactly, but whatever pointing device you use that acts like a mouse, be it a trackball, BallPoint, InPort, pen and tablet, or one of the other devices that are variants on these themes. The purpose of all these devices is to move the mouse pointer about the screen.

The Windows user interface is a point-and-click interface. The mouse is the instrument you use to point and click. Windows 95 made the mouse more important than it was in Windows 3.1*x* by making it more powerful — and Windows 98 has made it easier to use by letting you single-click in a lot more situations.

Windows 98 supports, right out of the box, a broad variety of mice from different manufacturers. All Microsoft Mouse-compatible mice, of course, are supported as though they were, in fact, manufactured by Microsoft. Windows 98 specifically names mice manufactured by many companies, including Logitech, Kensington, Compaq, and Texas Instruments (TI). Windows 98 also offers generic support for various "standard" mice.

Among the mouse models that Windows 98 supports are serial mice, bus mice, PS/2 mice, the TI QuickPort BallPoint mouse, the Compaq LTE trackball, and the Kensington Serial Expert mouse, as well as all models compatible with these models.

Windows 3.1*x* mouse drivers work as before. When you set up Windows 98, it remarks out calls to the older mouse drivers in your Autoexec.bat and Config.sys files if the new Windows 98 mouse drivers support your mouse. If you have a Windows 3.1*x* mouse driver that provides features not found in the Windows 98 mouse driver, you can continue to use it or upgrade to a new Windows 98 version if one is available from your mouse manufacturer.

Double-Clicking Versus Single-Clicking

A *click* means a press and release of the left mouse button. A *double-click* is two clicks within a set time interval. A *right-click* is a click of the right mouse button.

Windows 98 lets you cut down significantly on double-clicking. When the beta version of Windows 98 first came out, single-clicking was the new default for actions such as opening files. Later, Microsoft went back to double-clicking as the default, with single-clicking as an option. We highly recommend that you enable single-clicking; although it may take a little getting used to, it will be a lot easier on your mouse hand in the long run.

Tip

What is the keyboard equivalent of a double-click (or, if single-clicking is enabled, a single click)? Use the arrow keys to move the highlight to the icon. When the item that you want to open is highlighted, press Enter.

Clicking to open

An important new feature of Windows 98 is the ability to simply click to perform many actions that used to require double-clicking. This is a part of Microsoft's effort to make Windows 98 more "web-like" in its behavior; Microsoft also found that many people have trouble getting the hang of double-clicking.

To set single-clicking as the default, if you haven't already, open the Explorer and choose View, Folder Options. In the General tab, mark the Custom option button, and then click the Settings button and mark Single-Click to Open an Item (Point to Select). Underneath this option, you're given a choice of when to underline items in the Explorer; choose the one you prefer. Click OK, and then click OK again.

You can now complete many, but not all, actions using a single-click. Double-clicks are still required to initiate actions in some places. For example, you need to double-click in the common File Open dialog box and within many applications. You also need to double-click to open keys in the Registry editor, and to select devices in the Device Manager. However, on your Desktop and within the Explorer, a single-click will suffice.

Of course, you can continue to double-click as you have in the past. However, we feel strongly enough about the advantages of Web style that this book assumes you are using it. If you are using what Microsoft refers to as Classic style (AKA The Old Way), you'll need to mentally adjust the directions you find in these pages.

You can open all icons on the Desktop by clicking them. *Open* has multiple meanings. If the icon is a folder, it means open a folder in a window to display its contents. If the icon represents an application, it means start the application. If the icon represents a document, it means start the application associated with the document and open the document within the application.

Open is often the default action associated with a click, but you can choose or define other actions that will take place instead. For example, you could choose the Explore action, a variation on Open that opens the item in an Explorer window. If you set this action as the default action, then clicking an icon on the Desktop initiates the Explore action. See "Associating Actions with File Extensions" in Chapter 13 for more details.

Clicking a filename or icon in a folder window often opens it. You still need to double-click filenames and folder names in common file dialog boxes (dialog boxes associated with File Open). This opens them within the associated application.

If a folder icon appears in the left pane of the Explorer, you only have to single-click it to open it and display the folder's contents in the right pane.

Hovering to select

In Windows 3.1*x* and Windows 95, you used to single-click a file, application, or folder icon when you wanted to select (highlight) it without performing an action on it. For example, you might want to select multiple file icons in preparation for moving them to another folder. But if you have single-clicking enabled in Windows 98, clicking will actually open the file — in this case, not what you had in mind.

When single-clicking is turned on, you can select an icon simply by "hovering" your mouse over it for a moment (no clicking needed). The icon becomes highlighted to indicate that it's selected. To select a consecutive group of icons, highlight the first icon by hovering over it, and then hold down the Shift key and hover over the last. To select non-consecutive multiple icons, highlight the first icon, and then hold down the Ctrl key as you hover over each additional one you want to select.

In the common file dialog boxes (associated with File Open in many applications) you'll still need to click to select. This is also true for applications, including RegEdit and the Device Manager.

Other places where single-clicking works

Even if you're using the Classic style, you don't have to double-click to open a file because Windows 98 provides an alternative — you can right-click the file and choose an action from the context menu. The first action listed in the menu is often Open.

If an application is active but minimized, you only have to single-click its Taskbar button to restore the application to a window. With Windows 3.1*x*, you had to double-click a minimized icon for a running application to restore it.

You can single-click items in the Start menu to open their associated applications. In Windows 3.1*x*, you had to double-click application icons in program groups to start them.

In the Explorer, you can single-click the plus symbol next to a folder icon in the folder tree to open the branch. In the File Manager, you had to double-click the folder icon.

To display the Task Manager in Windows 3.1*x*, you had to double-click the Desktop. In Windows 98, you can right-click the Taskbar to display a context menu that lets you perform similar functions.

In all cases where a double-click was required under Windows 3.1*x* for an action, Windows 98 lets you instead right-click and then click a command in a context menu.

The Right Mouse Button Stuff

Windows 98 makes extensive use of the right mouse button. This represents a fantastic improvement in functionality and ease of use over the Windows 3.1*x* user interface.

The right-click is not implemented consistently. Programs written for Windows 3.1*x* don't use the right mouse button in the same manner as programs written for Windows 98. However, it never hurts to just right-click and see what happens. You can't get into any trouble. In other words, you can't start something that you didn't want to with a right-click.

Tip

You can right-click nearly everything that you see on the Desktop, including the Desktop itself. You can right-click anything in a folder window or in the Explorer. Our advice is to right-click anything and everything just to see what happens.

Tip

What is the keyboard equivalent of the right mouse button? Shift+F10.

You can set the speed with which menus cascade from context menus. See "Changing mouse menu speed" later in this chapter.

Right-clicking My Computer

If you right-click the My Computer icon on the Desktop, you can use commands in the context menu to open a My Computer folder window, open the Explorer, map or disconnect network drives, find files or computers, and bring up the System properties, including the Device Manager (click Properties in the My Computer context menu).

Right-clicking the Start button

Right-clicking the Start button lets you:

- Open the Start Menu folder window, which contains the Programs folder icon (and possibly other icons as well)
- Open the Explorer focused on the Start Menu
- Find a file in the Start Menu folder or one of its subfolders

Tip

Right-clicking the Start button and choosing commands from the context menu can be quite useful if you want to make changes in the folders and shortcut icons associated with the Start menu. For example, if you right-click and choose Explore, you can use the Explorer to move folders and shortcut icons in the Start Menu folder or the Programs subfolder. Changes you make in the Explorer will be reflected in the Start menu and the Programs submenu. You may find additional commands in this context menu; they are added automatically when you install some applications, such as WinZip. With Windows 98, you can also right-click menu items and shortcuts in some of the Start menus (including Programs and Favorites) to display appropriate context menus.

Right-clicking the Taskbar

The Taskbar displays buttons for running applications or folders; you single-click a Taskbar button to bring the associated application or folder to the top of the Desktop. Right-clicking the Taskbar lets you:

- Open or close toolbars
- Cascade the open windows on the Desktop
- Tile the open windows horizontally or vertically
- Minimize all open windows (or undo the previous minimization)
- Edit the properties of the Taskbar

Turn to "The Taskbar and its Toolbars" in Chapter 6 for more details on using the Taskbar.

Right-clicking the time

Right-clicking the time at the right end of the Taskbar gives you the same options as right-clicking the Taskbar itself, and it also lets you adjust the settings for the date and time.

Right-clicking a file icon

Right-clicking a file icon lets you open the file with its associated application, and if a document has an associated Quick Viewer, you can quickly view the document's contents by choosing Quick View (assuming you have installed the Quick View component of Windows 98).

When you right-click a file icon, you can also access all the standard file-management commands, including Cut, Copy, Delete, and Rename.

Shift+right-clicking a file icon

If the file is of a registered file type, Shift+right-click adds the Open With command to the context menu. Open With lets you open the file with an application other than the one associated with that file type.

Right-clicking a folder icon

The context menu for a folder is similar to that of a file. Choosing the Open command in a folder's context menu displays the contents of that folder in a folder window (if the icon is in a folder window) or in the Explorer (if the icon is in the Explorer). You can also use the context menu to move, share, create a shortcut to, rename, or delete a folder, and to bring up its properties.

Right-clicking a shortcut

Right-clicking a shortcut brings up a similar context menu to that which appears when you right-click the target of the shortcut. The difference is that the Properties command in the context menu for a shortcut brings up the Properties dialog box for the shortcut itself, not for the target.

However, if you have installed Target.dll, the context menu for a shortcut includes an important additional command, Target, that lets you get to the application or document to which the shortcut points. When you point to Target, a submenu appears that includes, among other things, an Open Container command and a Properties command. Open Container opens a folder window with the focus on the target. Properties displays the Properties dialog box for the target.

Target is a component of Microsoft Windows PowerToys. Download PowerToys from http://www.microsoft.com/windows/software powertoy.htm.

Right-clicking the Desktop

If you right-click the Desktop itself (staying clear of icons and the Taskbar) you display the Desktop's context menu. This context menu lets you:

- View, update, and customize the Active Desktop
- Arrange (line up) the icons on the Desktop
- Create a new folder, file, or shortcut on the Desktop
- Open the Display Properties dialog box

The last item is the same as clicking the Display icon in the Control Panel.

Right-clicking the client area of a folder window

The options you get when you right-click the client area of a folder window are similar to those you get when you right-click the Desktop, with a few differences.

You don't get a Properties command for bringing up the Display Properties dialog box, and you do get commands for changing how the icons are displayed in the folder window: Large Icons, Small Icons, List, and Details. You also get options that let you toggle in and out of web page view for the folder and customize the web page view. For example, you could add a background photo for the folder.

Right-clicking the title bar of the active application

If you right-click the title bar of the application window with the focus, you display the system menu for that window. (The title bar of a window with the focus is blue if you are using standard Windows colors.)

The system menu is programmable, so it can change from application to application. The standard functions that are available in this menu include moving, sizing, and closing the window.

You can also right-click the title bar of a folder window to display its system menu, or right-click a Taskbar button to display the system menu for the associated folder or application.

Right-clicking in a dialog box

Dialog boxes are a little different than most windows that show up on your Desktop. You may see common resource dialog boxes used by 16-bit Windows 3.1x applications or common dialog boxes used by 32-bit Windows 98 applications. Many Windows applications also have their own unique dialog boxes.

Many Windows 98-compliant dialog boxes have a question-mark button in the upper-right corner. If you click that button and then click an item in the dialog box, you get an explanation of the item. As an alternative to using the question-mark button, you can right-click an item, and then click the What's This? button that appears.

Right-clicking in a 16-bit File Open dialog box

Common resource dialog boxes for 16-bit Windows 3.1x applications include the File Open and Fonts dialog boxes. If you right-click within one of these dialog boxes, a What's This? button appears.

Right-clicking in a 32-bit File Open dialog box

Right-clicking a filename in a 32-bit Windows 98 common File Open dialog box highlights the filename and displays a context menu with options to open the file and perform other file-management tasks. Right-clicking in other places gives you other context menus appropriate to the item you clicked. In some areas, you get the What's This? button.

Figure 30-1 shows the 32-bit File Open dialog box with the context menu for the first filename displayed.

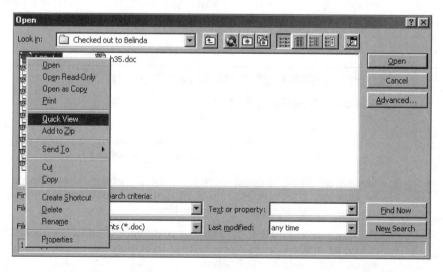

Figure 30-1: The File Open dialog box. Right-click a filename to display its context menu.

Right-clicking in the client area of an active application

You can right-click within an application. If the application is Windows 98-aware, a context menu appears with frequently used commands that are appropriate to the place you clicked. When you right-click a document in your word processor, for example, the context menu might give you commands for copying, cutting, and pasting text.

Disabling the right mouse button

If for some reason you want to disable the right mouse button in Windows 98, you might try IKIOSK from Hyper Technologies Inc. IKIOSK is designed to let system administrators disable or gray out various features and menus of Windows 98. You can download a 60-day trial copy from http://www.hypertec.com. Disabling features can be somewhat unpredictable, so make sure you have a good system backup, and start slowly.

Driving Your Mouse

The Windows 98 mouse drivers are 32-bit protected-mode drivers. They take up zero conventional memory, leaving more room for your DOS programs. You can remove any references to your old mouse drivers, such as Mouse.com or Mouse.sys, in your Autoexec.bat or Config.sys files if Windows 98 Setup has not already done so.

The mouse driver supports MS-DOS programs in Windows DOS sessions, in either full-screen or windowed mode. As long as Windows 98 is running and you're running your DOS program in a DOS virtual machine, the mouse works with your DOS program.

This is a big plus because it eliminates the need to remember to load Mouse.com or Mouse.sys before starting a DOS program. It also saves precious real-mode memory below 640K RAM. In Windows 3.1*x,* you had to load a separate MS-DOS mouse driver to support a mouse in DOS sessions. In Windows 98, you only need to load a real-mode mouse driver if you run DOS programs that use a mouse in *MS-DOS mode* — a mode that unloads Windows 98 and all its 32-bit protected mode-drivers and reloads real-mode DOS. You can configure a shortcut to load your real-mode mouse driver into memory at the time you switch to MS-DOS mode.

You can connect a serial mouse to serial ports COM1 through COM4. Under Windows 3.1*x* you could only connect a serial mouse to COM1 or COM2.

The Windows 98 mouse driver supports plug and play mice. Windows 98 automatically recognizes and installs these mice during Setup. Windows 98 hardware-detection routines can detect pre-plug and play mice.

Windows 98 includes an easy-to-use Mouse Properties dialog box with lots of functionality. Mouse manufacturers can still substitute their own Properties dialog box for this one, or add to it.

You can define the middle button of your Logitech three-button mouse to substitute for a double-click.

All along, the mice used with PCs and compatible computers have had at least two buttons, but the right one didn't do anything in Windows 3.1*x* itself. Some Windows 3.1*x* programs took advantage of the right button. The Borland C++ compiler, for example, used it extensively. Starting with Windows 95, Microsoft decided to define the behavior of the right mouse button. In Windows 95 and Windows 98 and in applications designed for them, clicking the right mouse button brings up a *context menu*, a menu of options available for the item you clicked, as we saw in the section entitled "The Right Mouse Button Stuff" earlier in this chapter.

Setting Up Your Mouse Driver

The Windows 98 installation and setup procedures include automatic hardware detection. Make sure your mouse is plugged in when you run Windows 98 Setup, so that the hardware-detection routines can identify your mouse and install the correct driver.

If your mouse isn't detected properly, you can easily add it using the steps detailed later in this chapter in the section entitled "Adding a driver for a new mouse."

If your mouse isn't supported by the mouse drivers that come with Windows 98, you can still use your existing mouse driver. If you have installed Windows 98 in your existing Windows directory without first deleting Windows 3.1*x,* your mouse driver will still be functioning. The calls to this mouse driver will still be in your Autoexec.bat and/or Config.sys files.

Changing the driver for an existing mouse

You can change to a different mouse driver if you find that the one you have installed is incorrect for the mouse you're using, or if an updated driver becomes available. Follow these steps to change your mouse driver:

STEPS

Changing the Driver for an Existing Mouse

Step 1. Click the Start button, point to Settings, click Control Panel, and click the System icon. Next, click the Device Manager tab in the System Properties dialog box, and click the View Devices By Type option button. Click the plus sign next to Mouse, highlight your mouse, and then click the Properties button. Click the Driver tab, and then click the Upgrade Driver button to launch the Upgrade Device Driver Wizard.

Step 2. Click the Next button to progress to the second Wizard dialog box. Here you can have the Wizard search for a better driver for you, or you can tell it to use a specific driver file. If you want to use a specific driver file, skip to step 5.

Step 3. To have the Wizard search for you, click Search for a Better Driver Than the One Your Device Is Using Now (Recommended), and click Next. You will be given a list of places you want the Wizard to look for new drivers (see Figure 30-2). Click all the check boxes that are appropriate. If you select Microsoft Windows Update, your computer will connect to the Microsoft web site and download the Update Agent to search that site.

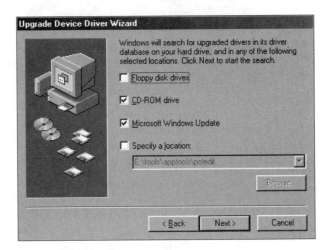

Figure 30-2: The Upgrade Device Driver Wizard asks you where to look for a better driver. If you select Microsoft Windows Update, your computer will connect to the Microsoft web site and download the Update Agent to search that site.

(continued)

STEPS *(continued)*

Changing the Driver for an Existing Mouse

Step 4. Click Next, and the Wizard will carry out its search (this may take a couple of minutes). At the end, the Wizard will tell you whether it found another driver for your mouse (see Figures 30-3 and 30-4). If there is more than one driver that would work for your mouse, the Wizard will advise you which one is the best (it may be the one you already have). If another driver would be an improvement, you'll have the option of downloading it (if necessary) and installing it. Follow the Wizard's prompts to complete the installation.

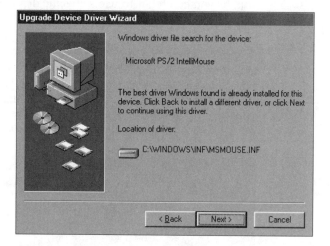

Figure 30-3: The Wizard will notify you if it found a better driver. In this case, it only found the current driver.

Step 5. If you have a specific driver you want to use, click Display a List of All the Drivers in a Specific Location, So You Can Select the Driver You Want, in the Wizard's second dialog box. Then click Next, and mark Show All Hardware.

Step 6. Choose a mouse manufacturer and model from the list, as shown in Figure 30-5. (If the mouse you have isn't listed, if you know it is not compatible with the models listed, and if you have a mouse driver diskette, click the Have Disk button. Put your mouse driver diskette in the disk drive and click the OK button if the correct path to your diskette drive is shown. Otherwise, type the correct path or browse to find it before clicking OK.) Click Next to install the driver you have selected, and then click Finish.

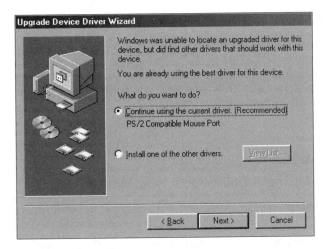

Figure 30-4: If there are other drivers that would work with your mouse, the Wizard will tell you whether one might be an improvement. It will let you choose whether to keep the driver you have or install a new one.

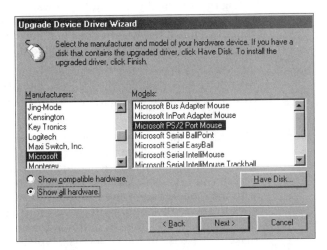

Figure 30-5: Highlight a manufacturer and then a mouse model, and then click Next. You will have to restart Windows after you install a new mouse driver.

Step 7. Click OK until you have exited all the dialog boxes, and then restart Windows 98 to have the new mouse driver take effect.

Adding a driver for a new mouse

If you get a new mouse after you have installed Windows 98, you probably won't need to do anything but plug it in and restart the computer. Windows 98 should recognize that you have added new hardware, and install it automatically. However, if this doesn't happen, it's easy to install a new mouse driver by following the steps below:

STEPS

Adding a Driver for a New Mouse

Step 1.   Click the Start button, point to Settings, and then click Control Panel. Click the Add New Hardware icon. Click Next.

Step 2.   Windows 98 tells you it will now search for new hardware. Click Next, and be prepared to wait for a few minutes, while the Wizard searches for any new plug and play devices.

Step 3.   If it doesn't find any new plug and play devices, it displays a dialog box asking if you want Windows to search for hardware that is not plug and play compatible. If you see this dialog box, skip to step 5. If the Wizard does find new plug and play devices, it asks you if the one(s) it found include the one you want.

Step 4.   If the answer is yes, click the mouse you want to install, click Yes the Device Is in the List, click Next to install the driver, and skip to step 6. If your mouse is not on the list, mark No, the Device Isn't in the List, and click Next.

Step 5.   Click No, I Want to Select the Hardware from a List, and click Next. Select Mouse from the list of hardware types, and click Next. Then choose a mouse manufacturer and model. (If the mouse you have isn't listed, if you know that it is not compatible with the models listed, and if you have a mouse driver diskette, click the Have Disk button. Put your mouse driver diskette in the disk drive and click the OK button if the correct path to your diskette drive is shown. Otherwise, type the correct path or browse to find it before clicking OK.) Click Next to install the driver you have selected.

Step 6.   Click Finish.

Step 7.   Restart Windows 98 to have the mouse driver take effect.

You can install mouse drivers that were written for Windows 3.1*x* if you don't find one that works with your mouse. Try to install one of the new ones first before you install an older driver. Just because your mouse and the mouse driver don't have the same names doesn't mean one of the new drivers won't work—try a few first.

Undocumented

To install a Windows 3.1*x* mouse driver or a mouse driver that didn't come with Windows 98, click the Have Disk button in step 5 above. You need to have a diskette with the mouse driver on it. The diskette needs to include a mouse setup file. This file has an *inf* extension and defines how to install the mouse drivers.

Many mice, including newer Microsoft Mice that use Mouse Driver 9.0, will not support what Microsoft refers to as "nonstandard" IRQs and I/O addresses. This means you may only be able to assign this type of mouse to the serial ports COM1 or COM2 .

Configuring Your Mouse Driver Properties

Use the Mouse Properties dialog box to set the properties of the mouse driver. You can use this dialog box to change the responsiveness or speed of the mouse pointer relative to your movements of the mouse. You can switch the function of the right and left mouse buttons for left-handed operation. You can also change the double-click time interval. A longer interval counts two separate mouse clicks that are separated by a longer period of time as a single double-click.

You get to pick from a collection of mouse pointer icons, including animated pointers that correspond to a range of mouse functions. You can turn the hourglass pointer into a spinning world, for example. Since Windows 98 uses the same *ani* file format as Windows NT, you can select from a wide variety of shareware and freeware animated icons available on online services and the Internet, as well as on the *Windows 98 Secrets* CD-ROM. And if you're using an LCD screen, you can add mouse pointer trails by setting the number of ghost images that get left behind (briefly) at the mouse pointer's former location.

Follow these steps to change the properties of your mouse:

STEPS

Configuring the Mouse Driver

Step 1.   Click the Start button, point to Settings, and then click Control Panel. Click the Mouse icon (it looks like a white right-handed bar of soap).

Step 2.   The Buttons tab of the Mouse Properties dialog box, as shown in Figure 30-6, lets you switch the "handedness" of the mouse buttons and set the speed at which you have to click the mouse twice in order to get the two clicks to count as a single double-click.

(continued)

STEPS *(continued)*

Configuring the Mouse Driver

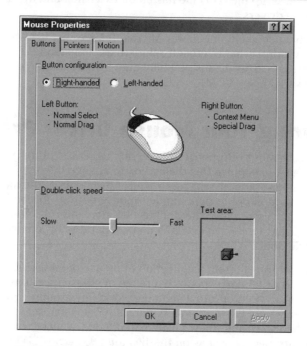

Figure 30-6: The Buttons tab of the standard Mouse Properties dialog box. You can swap the left and right mouse buttons and adjust the time interval between mouse clicks that will count as a double-click. The Properties dialog box for your particular pointing device may look different, depending on your driver.

Changing the handedness of the mouse buttons

Click the Left-Handed option button to switch the left and right mouse buttons. On a three-button mouse, these are the two outside buttons. If you are left-handed, swapping the function of the left and right mouse buttons lets you use your index finger to single- and double-click when you're controlling the mouse with your left hand.

Changing the double-click speed

Although Windows 98 let you use a single-click for many actions that used to require a double-click, there are still some times when a double-click is required (selecting a word in text, for example). And if you prefer the old way, you can still revert to double-clicking. To do this, choose View, Folder Options in the Explorer, and mark the Classic Style option button.

To adjust how fast you need to double-click, do the following:

STEPS

Changing Double-Click Speed

Step 1.   Move the Double-Click Speed slider to the left to increase the time interval allowed between two mouse clicks that are counted as one double-click. Move the slider to the right to increase the speed with which you must twice click the left mouse button (assuming a right-handed configuration) in order for it to count as a double-click.

Step 2.   To test your double-click agility, click twice in the test area. If your two clicks count as one double-click, the jack-in-the-box goes up or down.

Secret

The range of the slider is between 900 milliseconds (⁹⁄₁₀ of a second) at the left end and 100 milliseconds (¹⁄₁₀ of a second) on the right end. This makes the middle of the slider equal to half a second.

Changing the double-click height and width

Secret

Windows 3.1x allowed you to determine the size in pixels of an invisible box around the location of the mouse pointer where the first click of a double-click takes place. The mouse pointer must be located within this box for a second click to count as part of the double-click. You could insert the variables DoubleClickWidth and DoubleClickHeight in the [Windows] section of the Win.ini file to do this. If you didn't add these variables to Win.ini, the default size of the box was four pixels on a side.

The size of the double-click box is now set in the Registry, and the default is two pixels. You might want to enlarge the box if you find that Windows 98 is missing a lot of your double-clicks (because you are moving the mouse a bit between clicks). The easiest way to do this is by using TweakUI. Just open TweakUI in your Control Panel, click the Mouse tab, and increase the number in the Double-Click field. (TweakUI assumes you want a square box.) You can test the sensitivity by double-clicking the gear icon.

Desensitizing dragging

If you find that you are often inadvertently moving folder icons around in your Explorer, you can widen the area that you have to drag an icon before it begins moving. Signs that accidental dragging is a problem for you include folders disappearing when you click on them and error messages stating that you can't move a folder when you weren't trying to move one to begin with.

The default Windows 98 setting for initiating a drag is two pixels. That is, if you highlight an icon, press and hold down the left mouse button, and move the mouse pointer just two pixels, then the icon begins to move. The hand movement required to do this is comparable to a slow left click with a slight movement of your wrist.

You can increase the distance that you have to move an icon before dragging starts by using TweakUI. Open TweakUI in your Control Panel, click the Mouse tab, and increase the number in the Drag field to something like five or ten pixels (see Figure 30-7). Test the setting using the gear icon. If you're still having problems, increase the size again.

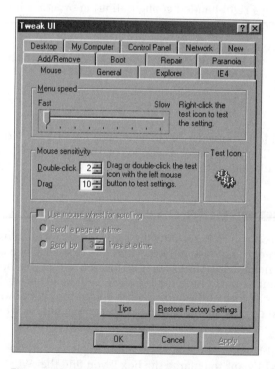

Figure 30-7: The Mouse tab of TweakUI lets you set double-click and drag sensitivity, as well as the speed of some menus.

High-resolution displays with high-density mice are the source of this problem. Microsoft's defaults are for VGA resolution screens. Two pixels is much too small a distance for high-resolution displays, and high-density mice take only the slightest movement to move this far.

Changing mouse menu speed

The context menus that appear when you right-click often contain submenus. You can change the speed at which these submenus appear. At the slowest setting, you must right-click again to see the submenu.

You adjust the menu speed using TweakUI. Click the TweakUI icon in the Control Panel, click the Mouse tab, and drag the Menu Speed slider bar in the desired direction. Click Apply, and then test the setting by right-clicking the gear icon in the Mouse tab and hovering over a command to display its submenu. When you have the speed adjusted the way you want it, click OK.

Using different mouse pointers

You can (and we feel should) use some of the newer static and animated mouse pointers created for Windows 98. They are a lot of fun and are often better designed than the Windows standard ones. Only a few animated pointers come with Windows 95; these pointers are stored in the \Windows\Cursors folder.

You must have your display card driver set to at least 256 colors in order for animated cursors to work. See "Installing a New Video Driver" in Chapter 28 for details about display cards.

Secret

Some cards that can display 256 colors have video drivers that don't work with animated pointers. The Diamond Viper is one such video card. You'll need to test your card and driver with one animated pointer to make sure that it works.

Secret

Animated pointers don't work if you use 16-bit real-mode hard disk drivers instead of the 32-bit protected-mode drivers that come with Windows 98. Your Config.sys file references these drivers if you are using them. You can also check to see if you are using 32-bit hard disk drivers by double-clicking the System icon in your Control Panel, and then clicking the Performance tab. If File System and Virtual Memory are marked as 32-bit, you are not using 16-bit hard disk drivers.

If you did a custom Windows 98 installation, as is our recommendation, or installed over Windows 95, you must have installed the mouse pointers initially (as an accessory) in order to have them available now. If you didn't install them during Setup, you can click the Add/Remove Programs icon in the Control Panel, click the Windows Setup tab, click Accessories, and mark the Mouse Pointers check box to install them.

Tip

The *Windows 98 Secrets* CD-ROM that accompanies this book contains a number of interesting animated and static pointers you can use to replace some of your existing pointers. We suggest you create a folder called Ani as a subfolder of your \Windows folder and move your animated cursors into this folder, even the ones currently stored in \Windows\Cursors. This way, you can easily get at the animated pointers with the Browse button in the steps below.

STEPS

Changing Mouse Pointers

Step 1. Click the Mouse icon in the Control Panel, and click the Pointers tab, as shown in Figure 30-8. Starting with Normal Select, scroll down the list of pointer functions and their associated pointers. Try clicking different pointers as you go down the list. When you click a pointer, it appears in the gray box in the upper-right corner of the dialog box, and if the pointer is animated, you see what the animation looks like.

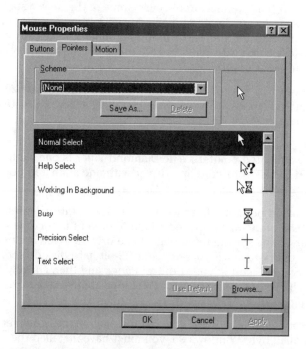

Figure 30-8: The Pointers tab of the Mouse Properties dialog box. Each mouse function has an associated mouse pointer.

Step 2.   Click the Schemes pull-down menu in this tab, and you will see various pointer schemes designed by Microsoft. If you have installed any Themes (see "Themes" in Chapter 22), you will see pointer schemes that relate to those themes. In these pointer schemes supplied by Microsoft, only the Busy and Working in Background pointers are animated. You can use this Schemes menu to choose a new pointer scheme, or mix and match.

Step 3.   To use a different mouse pointer for a particular mouse function, click that mouse function, and then click the Browse button. In the Browse dialog box, you will see the animated pointers stored in the \Windows\Ani folder (if you have created this folder) or other pointers in the \Windows\Cursors folder. Animated pointer files have the *ani* extension, and static pointers have the *cur* extension. When you highlight a pointer file, it appears in the preview box in the lower-left corner of the dialog box.

Step 4.   Double-click the pointer that you want to replace the existing pointer.

Tip

We suggest you do not replace the mouse pointers associated with Normal Select, Precision Select, or Text Select with animated pointers. They will be too distracting. Go ahead and replace the mouse pointers associated with Working In Background and Busy with two animated icons that express waiting.

Table 30-1 describes the mouse pointers associated with the different mouse functions.

A very important cursor not included in this list shows the insertion point in text editors and word processors. This cursor, aptly called the *insertion point*, tells you where your text will get inserted if you start typing.

If you use the Display Properties dialog box to change the background color of your windows to something other than the default stark white, you'll need to set the color of the insertion point so that it shows up well on top of the background color. For more details, see "The color of the cursor and the text select pointer" in Chapter 28.

View the Animated Cursor Schemes web site at http://www.islandnet.com/~wwseb/cursors.htm to see more animated pointer themes.

Table 30-1   Windows 98 Mouse Pointers

Pointer	Function
Normal Select	This is the normal mouse pointer for selecting items.
Help Select	When you click the ? button in the upper-right corner of a dialog box, you get this mouse pointer. When you see this pointer, you can click any option in the dialog box to get a brief explanation of what the option is for.
Working In Background	Windows 98 or a 32-bit multithreaded application is busy but using a background thread, so you can proceed with something else if you want.
Busy	Windows 98 or an application is busy trying to accomplish some task before it can proceed.
Precision Select	This pointer guides your eye to its center to help you select with precision.
Text Select	This pointer is also called the *I-beam*. You use it in word processors to select text.
Handwriting	This pointer appears when you have switched to a mode that is expecting handwritten or ink input from you (in an application that supports handwriting).
Unavailable	When you drag a file icon over an area or application that won't accept the file if you drop it there, this pointer appears to remind you of that fact.
Vertical, Horizontal, Diagonal Resize	The double-headed arrow pointers appear when you position your mouse pointer along the edges of a sizable window.
Move	When you click the Move command in the system menu of a window, this pointer appears. When you see it, you can move the window with your arrow keys.
Alternate Select	The only place we have seen this pointer is in the FreeCell solitaire card game.
Link Select	This pointer appears when you hover over a clickable link, whether in the Explorer, in a Help file, or when viewing a web page.

Changing mouse pointer speed

Undocumented

Speed is a bit of a misnomer. What you are determining is how much faster the mouse pointer moves as you move the mouse faster. This is a semi-complicated multiplier of the already-set ratio of mouse-pointer movement to mouse movement.

The ratio of mouse-pointer movement to mouse movement has already been set by your mouse and video driver. The pointer speed values multiply this ratio so that the mouse pointer moves even faster if you move the mouse faster. Each one of the tick marks in the Pointer Speed slider, shown in Figure 30-9, corresponds to a different set of values for Mouse Speed, MouseThreshold1, and MouseThreshold2. These values are shown in Table 30-2.

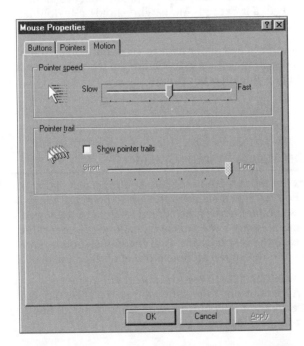

Figure 30-9: The Motion tab of the Mouse Properties dialog box. Change the responsiveness of the mouse pointer to movements of the mouse. Add trails to the mouse pointer on LCD screens. The units for MouseThreshold1 and 2 are pixels.

If you move your mouse slowly, the mouse pointer moves slowly. If you move the mouse quickly, the mouse pointer moves even more quickly if the MouseSpeed is greater than zero.

Windows compares the number of pixels the mouse pointer has moved during the time interval between mouse interrupts against the mouse thresholds. The mouse sends out interrupts periodically. If you move the mouse quickly, the mouse-pointer movement exceeds the number of pixels of one or both of the mouse thresholds.

Table 30-2 The Pointer Speed Values

Slider Position	1	2	3	4	5	6	7
MouseSpeed	0	1	1	1	2	2	2
MouseThreshold1	0	10	7	4	4	4	4
MouseThreshold2	0	0	0	0	12	9	6

If the MouseSpeed is set to 1 and the mouse-pointer movement exceeds the number of pixels given by the value of MouseThreshold1, the mouse-pointer speed is double the normal rate. If the MouseSpeed is set to 2 and the mouse-pointer movement exceeds MouseThreshold2, the mouse-pointer speed is quadrupled. If it exceeds MouseThreshold1 it is doubled, the same as if MouseSpeed is set to 1.

Play with this Pointer Speed slider a bit to see what you are comfortable with. The optimal setting will vary depending on whether you have a trackball or a mouse, among other things.

STEPS

Changing the Mouse Pointer Speed

Step 1.   Click the Motion tab in the Mouse Properties dialog box. Move the Pointer Speed slider to the left to decrease the travel of the mouse pointer across the screen relative to the speed of travel of the mouse across the mouse pad. Move the slider to the right to increase the responsiveness of the mouse pointer movement on screen to the speed of mouse travel on the mouse pad.

Step 2.   You won't be able to test the speed difference unless you click the Apply button. You might want to try a few different speeds and click the Apply button after each change. When you've found a setting you like, click OK.

Changing mouse speed values in the Registry

Secret

You may wonder how we figured out what values are set by the Pointer Speed slider. They turn out to be the same values as those set by the mouse driver in Windows 3.1x. But to determine the actual values, we looked in the Registry. The way we did it is generally quite useful and bears detailing:

STEPS

Seeing Your Registry Values Change

Step 1.   Display the Motion tab of the Mouse Properties dialog box. (Click the Mouse icon in the Control Panel and click the Motion tab.)

Step 2.   Also display the Registry editor by opening Explorer and clicking Regedit.exe in your \Windows folder.

Step 3.   Open the Registry editor to HKEY_CURRENT_USER\Control Panel\Mouse. Highlight Mouse, as shown in Figure 30-10. If you don't see this Mouse branch in the Registry, check the undocumented feature at the end of this section.

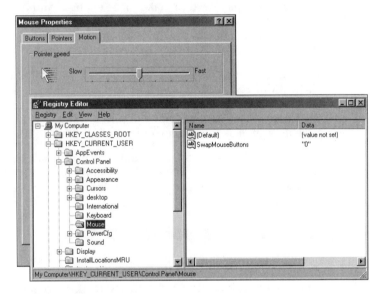

Figure 30-10: The Motion tab of the Mouse Properties dialog box and the Registry editor working together.

Step 4.   Click the Motion tab of the Mouse Properties dialog box. Move the Pointer Speed slider. Click Apply.

Step 5.   Click the Registry editor and press the F5 key. You will see the values of MouseSpeed, MouseThreshold1, and MouseThreshold2 change.

Step 6.   Repeat steps 4 and 5 to check all the values assigned by the Pointer Speed slider. You can do the same thing with the Double-Click Speed slider (in the Buttons tab).

Step 7.   Exit the Registry editor.

Secret

The values set in a user interface to the Registry (in this case the Mouse Properties dialog box) are immediately reflected in the Registry, and used by the applications that rely on them.

Undocumented

You can also edit the values directly in the Registry. If you use this method, the mouse doesn't use these new values until you restart Windows. Until you do, the mouse uses 0, 0, 0 instead, meaning no acceleration.

If you have user profiles enabled for your computer, there is a separate mouse setting for each user. If you edit these values in the Registry, you need to change them in the branch that applies to the particular user.

Undocumented

You have to make some changes in your mouse speed values (through the Mouse Properties dialog box) before the Mouse branch will show up in the Registry. You may need to make these changes and quit Windows 98 before you see the branch, because it takes Windows a while to write these changes back out of memory to the disk files that contain the permanent copy of the Registry.

If you have made changes to mouse speed, you will find the Mouse branch in HKEY_CURRENT_USER, as well as in HKEY_USERS. If you have disabled user profiles in the Passwords Properties dialog box (under the Passwords icon in the Control Panel), these branches are the same. The HKEY_CURRENT_USER branch is an alias for the current user found in the HKEY_USERS branch.

Numerous values are not stored in the Registry unless they are different than the default values. For example, if you don't make any changes in the mouse double-click speed, you won't find an entry for it in the Registry.

Changing the pointer trails

Pointer trails, which leave "ghosts" of the mouse pointer in the mouse pointer's former position, are really useful only on LCD screens where the mouse pointer is hard to find. Otherwise, they are just a distraction. (The default is no pointer trails at all.) Here's how to modify them:

STEPS

Changing the Number of Pointer Ghosts

Step 1. On the Motion tab of the Mouse Properties dialog box, click the Show Pointer Trails check box and then move the Pointer Trail slider to the left and right. You will see the effect immediately.

Step 2. To apply the change that you have made to the mouse pointer trails, click OK.

Creating Your Own Mouse Pointers

Windows 98 comes with a number of static and animated mouse pointers that you can assign to different mouse pointer functions. More are available online, and the *Windows 98 Secrets* CD-ROM has more still.

You can edit these mouse pointers to create your own pointers, or you can create your own static and animated pointers, if you still have your Windows 95 CD-ROM (or can borrow one). It contains two programs, Imagedit.exe and Aniedit.exe, that help you create pointers and string pointers together to create animated pointers. Unfortunately, they are not included on the Windows 98 CD-ROM. Use both programs to look at existing animated and static pointers to get an idea of how they are created.

These programs are stored in the \Admin\Reskit\Apptools\Aniedit folder on the Windows 95 CD-ROM. You can copy them to your \Program Files\ Accessories folder (or any folder you like) on your hard disk. They have an accompanying setup (*inf*) file, so you can use the Add/Remove Programs icon in your Control Panel to "install" them if you like. Use the Windows Setup tab, click the Have Disk button, and then browse to the folder on the hard disk that holds these applications. (Installing sets up an association of Aniedit.exe with the file type *cur.*)

You can have even more fun tracking the distance that your mouse has traveled with Odometer for Windows. You'll find it at http://www. windows98.com.

What Is Missing in Mouse Configuration?

You can't set the mouse pointer to *snap to* the active button or item in a dialog box, as you can with some other mouse drivers, including the ones that come with the Windows 3.1*x* Microsoft Mouse. *Snap to* can substantially cut down on mouse movement — although it can also be annoying because the mouse moves to unexpected places.

The mouse doesn't wrap around the edge of the screen. When it goes off the left edge, you can't make it come in the right edge.

Undocumented

Microsoft doesn't give you a straightforward way to define the middle mouse button to function as a keystroke of your choice. (We discuss the only definition that you can make later in this chapter.)

All of these missing features and more are available in software provided by mouse manufacturers, and by Microsoft for Microsoft Mice.

Built-in Trackballs and Mice

Undocumented

If you have a built-in trackball in your portable, you can use a plug-in serial mouse along with it without having to disable the trackball. Both devices are detected by Windows 98 and both are functional at the same time.

If you add a serial mouse later or enable the internal trackball (using your BIOS setup) after Windows 98 is installed, you have to force Windows 98 to detect the "new" hardware (unless these are plug and play devices). Use the Add New Hardware icon in the Control Panel, and follow the steps in the section earlier in this chapter entitled "Adding a driver for a new mouse."

A generic built-in trackball is most likely supported by the Microsoft PS/2 Port Mouse or Standard PS/2 Port Mouse drivers in Windows 98.

The Mouse in a DOS Box

If you have a DOS program that is mouse-aware — that is, it can accept and use mouse movements and mouse button presses — Windows 98 automatically allows you to use your mouse with the DOS program in a DOS Windows session. You don't have to do anything special to let it know that you are using a mouse; Windows 98 passes along mouse movements and button presses to the DOS program.

In Windows 3.1*x*, if you wanted to have your mouse available for your DOS programs, you had to load a DOS real-mode mouse driver with calls in your Autoexec.bat or Config.sys files. The mouse drivers that ship with Windows 98 are clever enough to handle both Windows and DOS (in DOS Windows sessions), so you don't need to load your old mouse driver.

On the other hand, if you run DOS programs that use a mouse in MS-DOS mode, you do need to load a real-mode mouse driver when you enter that mode. You are able to do this because MS-DOS mode gives you the option of creating specific Autoexec.bat and Config.sys files for that mode. See "Creating private Autoexec.bat and Config.sys data" in Chapter 34 for details.

You have two options for modifying how the mouse works with your DOS programs while running in a Windows DOS session. You specify both options in the Misc tab of the Properties dialog box for a given DOS application or for your general DOS Windows sessions. (To display the Properties dialog box, right-click the shortcut icon for a specific DOS program or, if you want to change these options for all DOS Windows sessions, right-click the Dosprmpt shortcut in the \Windows folder. Then click Properties.)

First, you can select the QuickEdit option, which disables the mouse functions of the DOS program (if it has any) and dedicates the mouse to marking, copying, and pasting between the DOS program and Windows programs or other windowed DOS programs. This is particularly useful if the DOS program is not mouse-aware. Second, you can choose the Exclusive Mode option to force the mouse to work only within the DOS client window area and only under control of the DOS program. Turn to "Misc properties" in Chapter 34 for more details on how to set these options.

Double-Clicking with the Middle Mouse Button

Logitech builds and sells more mice than Microsoft (although not more at retail) and most of its mice (and trackballs, for that matter) have three buttons. If the mouse that came with your computer has three buttons, it is very likely a Logitech mouse. Look on the underside of the mouse for a label.

Logitech sells a piece of software — the Mouse Control Center — that lets you define, among other things, the function of the middle button as well as the right button. The default setting for the Logitech middle button is double-click, and we prefer to use this button rather than double-clicking the left mouse button. Even though there's a lot less double-clicking in Windows 98, it hasn't been eliminated entirely.

Secret

You can set the middle button of the Logitech mouse to double-click even if you don't have Logitech's Mouse Control Center. By editing the Registry, you can define this mouse behavior using only the Logitech mouse driver that Microsoft ships with Windows 98:

STEPS

Making the Middle Mouse Button Double-Click

Step 1. Install the Logitech mouse driver that comes with Windows 98 first. See the steps in the earlier section entitled "Setting Up Your Mouse Driver."

Step 2. Use the Explorer to find Regedit.exe in the \Windows folder. Click it to start the Registry editor.

Step 3. Click the plus signs to navigate to

HKEY_LOCAL_MACHINE\SOFTWARE\Logitech\MouseWare\ Current Version

Figure 30-11 shows the Registry editor at this location for a particular mouse (in this case, the Logitech MouseMan).

(continued)

STEPS *(continued)*

Making the Middle Mouse Button Double-Click

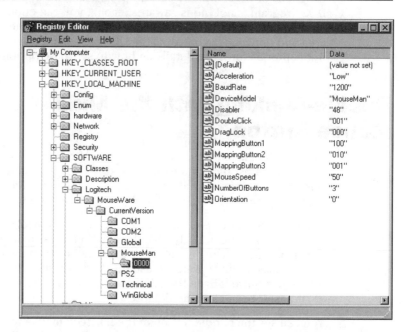

Figure 30-11: The Registry editor. Edit the DoubleClick value in the right pane by double-clicking it. To get the middle key to be a double-click, change this value to 001.

Step 4. Click the plus sign next to your Logitech mouse type. Click the 0000 key in the left pane.

Step 5. Double-click the DoubleClick key in the right pane. Change the value from 000 to 001.

Step 6. Exit the Registry, and restart Windows 98 to have this change take effect.

Tip

This double-click definition doesn't work with Microsoft Edit. We use Edit all the time to edit Autoexec.bat, Config.sys, and other text files.

Secret

This double-click definition also doesn't work if you have configured the mouse to be a left-handed mouse.

Placing the Mouse Icon on the Desktop

Tip

You can have ready access to the properties controlling the way your mouse behaves if you place a shortcut to the Mouse Properties dialog box on your Desktop:

STEPS

Putting the Mouse Icon on the Desktop

Step 1. Click the Start button, point to Settings, and then click Control Panel.

Step 2. Right-drag the Mouse icon to the Desktop.

Step 3. Drop the Mouse icon on the Desktop and click Create Shortcut(s) Here.

Step 4. Press F2, type a new name for the shortcut to the Mouse Properties dialog box, and press Enter.

If you have a Logitech mouse and want to have Logitech's purple mouse icon on your Desktop (Microsoft provides only the soap-bar-like icon in the Control Panel with its Logitech driver), you can change the shortcut icon you just created. Here's how:

STEPS

Putting the Logitech Purple Mouse Icon on the Desktop

Step 1. Right-click the Mouse shortcut on the Desktop. Click Properties, and click the Shortcut tab.

Step 2. Click the Change Icon button. Click the Browse button and search for the folder for your old Logitech driver (Lmouse, perhaps?).

Step 3. Look for a Logitech executable file in this folder, such as Wmousecc.exe. When you find it, double-click it.

Step 4. Choose the mouse icon you want, click OK, and then click OK again.

Your Mouse in the Device Manager

If you click the System icon in your Control Panel and then click the Device Manager tab, you'll see an entry for Mouse, and one for Ports. These two entries list the driver files for the mouse and serial ports, and they display the characteristics of the serial ports.

The Ports section of the Device Manager stores the address and interrupt of the serial port to which your mouse may be attached. If there are conflicts between these assignments and other port hardware in your computer, they will be highlighted. For details on dealing with ports, turn to "Changing serial port settings" in Chapter 31.

Whipping Your Mouse Clicks into Shape

Microsoft sells a special $80 mouse called IntelliMouse with a wheel between the left and right mouse buttons, designed to let you scroll up and down web pages without using the vertical scroll bar. However, an inexpensive utility called Scroll from Pointix Corp. lets any mouse do the same thing by adding a "drag" function to your right mouse button. You can drag the entire contents of your browser window (or any other window for that matter).

This is a lot more fun to do than it is to describe. With Scroll installed, right-clicking works as expected: a context menu pops up. If you hold down the right mouse button and move your mouse a little bit, though, you start scrolling the contents of the window in the direction of your move. It's very easy to control the action. Sliding up and down in long web pages and navigating long documents and spreadsheets is a breeze. When you reach the point in the window you want, just let up on the mouse button and the movement stops. (If your mouse has a middle button, you can use that for the scrolling action instead of the right button, if you prefer.)

Scroll adds four other powers to your mouse that bring up various Windows functions or utilities. These functions appear when you slide your mouse rapidly in one of these directions: side-to-side, up-and-down, clockwise, or counter-clockwise. The four unique motions, which Pointix calls *glicks* (for *slide clicks*, or actions that are executed by a certain kind of glide), are patented technology known as *Ergopoint*. Pointix also makes Engine 2.6, a set of utilities that work with Scroll to enhance these four functions.

Pointix's Scroll and Engine are available in a 15-day free trial version from the company's web site, http://www.pointix.com. Scroll 1.0 sells for $9.95 by itself, or for $24.95 packaged with Engine. When installed, Engine takes up about 3MB of hard disk space. Contact Pointix Corp. at 888-POINTIX.

If you already have an IntelliMouse, you'll want to try Flywheel, a $10 shareware utility available from Plannet Crafters Inc. (http://www.plannetarium.com). Flywheel lets the mouse's tracking wheel work with all software applications, not just those that offer IntelliMouse support, and it offers two new ways of using the wheel. Contact Plannet Crafters at 770-667-1278, or e-mail info@plannetarium.com.

Summary

In Windows 98, using the mouse is a lot less work. You need to know how to customize your mouse, and how to take advantage of its power.

▶ A Mouse Properties dialog box lets you easily change the responsiveness of the mouse pointer to mouse movements.

▶ You can do a lot more with a single click.

▶ You can use animated pointers in place of some of the duller mouse pointers.

▶ You can turn the middle button on your Logitech mouse into a double-click button.

▶ The right mouse button is a powerful tool.

Chapter 31

Modems, Serial Ports, and Parallel Ports

In This Chapter

Modems and ports (serial and parallel) are communications devices. Windows 98 automatically detects them and helps you set them up. We discuss:

▶ Configuring your modem driver

▶ Getting behind the configuration routines and changing modem driver parameters

▶ Manually controlling which ports can be used by Direct Cable Connection (DCC) and adding ports that were inadvertently removed

▶ Configuring your modem settings to work with DOS communication programs

▶ Configuring your serial and parallel ports

▶ Testing for the presence of an advanced serial port chip

Hello, World

When the personal computer was envisioned and designed, the focus of its communication facilities was the monitor, the keyboard, and the printer — the electronic typewriter model. Serial ports and modem communications were peripheral considerations, so to speak. This legacy has hung on.

Computer-mediated communication is now the major reason to own a personal computer. The widespread use of laptop and portable computers in business has increased the demand for reliable, easy to use, fast communications links. Inexpensive high-speed fax/modems, the advent of commercial Internet service providers, and the adoption of graphical user interfaces for online services all speak to a popular interest in electronic communications.

Windows 3.1x was not up to the task of effectively handling these communications demands. High-speed communications (over 9,600 bits per second, or *bps*) required third-party replacements to the Windows 3.1x serial port driver (Comm.drv). Personal computers required a new chip, the

16550A Universal Asynchronous Receiver/Transmitter (UART), to keep up with the data flow through the serial port or modem.

When Microsoft began designing Windows 95, it was already clear that the operating system's communications capabilities had to be much stronger than they were in Windows 3.1*x*. At the minimum, a new communications driver was required. Ideally, communications would be seamlessly integrated into the basic functionality of the operating system. Windows 98 has taken this integration even further, into the user interface.

Windows 98 Communications

Microsoft had to make changes to the basic operating system to reduce the frequency and duration of time intervals during which the CPU can't deal with data coming into the serial and parallel ports. The CPU can't handle incoming data when it is switching between 16- and 32-bit mode. The 32-bit protected-mode drivers that come with Windows 95 and 98 have reduced the amount of mode switching required of the processor.

The designers of Windows 98 have provided a way for applications to determine which one gets to use the modem or port without having to unload one of the applications. By defining a common modem interface, all communications packages can communicate with the modem at a high level.

Windows 98 uses a virtual communications driver, VxD, in combination with Unimodem, the universal modem driver, to provide high-level services that developers can employ to make their communications packages easier to use and more cooperative.

In addition, some modems, called *Windows modems* (also referred to as *WinModems* or *controller-less modems*), now rely on VxD for many functions that used to be handled by the hardware. Because WinModems require VxD in order to operate, they will not work in DOS mode. These modems are usually bundled with new computer systems; they are rarely sold separately.

With the release of Windows 98, a variety of new data/fax/voice modems (also called *VoiceView* modems) is now supported by Unimodem. These modems are designed to support new telephony applications such as Microsoft Phone.

One modem for all communications software

You have to configure your modem only once, and communications packages that are supported by Windows 98 don't have to know how to configure the modem themselves. Modem configuration was not provided in Windows 3.1*x*. Every communications package had to know about a large number of different modems in order to properly initialize them and utilize their capabilities.

Communications packages built for Windows 98 don't have to know which command strings to send to get the modem moving. They can send higher level, more general, and more abstract commands that work on any modem Windows 98 recognizes. Communications software providers can turn their resources to other more fruitful areas of product design.

Windows 98 ships with many modem-mediated communications facilities built in. These include Phone Dialer, Dial-Up Networking (DUN), HyperTerminal, Internet Explorer, Outlook Express, NetMeeting, Personal Web Server, Web Publisher, NetShow, MS Chat, remote network administration (Net Watcher), online registration, CompuServe e-mail, MSN, System Monitor, and others. All of them operate through the interface that defines the capabilities your particular modem.

Windows 3.1x communications support

Your existing Windows 3.1x communications applications will still work with Windows 98 because the old communications driver (Comm.drv) hasn't changed and is still used by these applications. Although Comm.drv thinks that it's talking directly to the hardware, it now talks to the new communications driver.

Only one Windows 3.1x-style communications application can have access to the modem at a time. Windows 95- and 98-style communications applications can share the modem. For example, Microsoft Fax can be active and set to wait for a fax while you use Internet Explorer to connect to a web site. While the phone line is off-hook, Microsoft Fax can't answer an incoming call, but you don't have to unload the fax software while you connect to the Internet.

Some applications replaced Comm.drv with their own communications port drivers. These applications will still work with Windows 98. The replacement communications drivers work with the virtual communication VxD instead of directly with the communications hardware.

DOS communications support

You can still run DOS-based communications software in a DOS window (see "Running DOS Programs" in Chapter 34 for more on DOS). When an MS-DOS-based or Windows-based communications program requests the use of a serial port, Windows 98 checks to see if the port is in use. If the port is available, Windows 98 gives the program access to the port.

However, after you are finished running the DOS program, Windows 98 by default does not give the serial port back to your Windows-based programs until the DOS window is closed. If a Windows-based program attempts to use the serial port before the DOS window is closed, you receive an error message such as, "Another program is using the selected Telephony device" or "Cannot initialize port."

This is different from Windows 3.1*x*, which by default released the port after two seconds of inactivity. Microsoft changed this for compatibility with some of the Windows 95 and 98 tools that have an automatic answering capability, such as Microsoft Fax and Dial-Up Networking Server.

If you need "hot-swapping capability" between an MS-DOS-based communications program and a Windows-based communication program, you can change the default behavior by editing the System.ini file.

STEPS

Enabling "Hot Swapping" Between DOS- and Windows-Based Communications Programs

Step 1. You'll find System.ini in your \Windows folder. Make a backup copy before you start editing.

Step 2. Click the Sysedit.exe icon in \Windows\System.

Step 3. Add this line to the [386Enh] section of System.ini:

```
COM<n>AutoAssign=0
```

where <n> is the number of the serial port.

Step 4. Save System.ini, shut down, and restart Windows.

The default COM<n>AutoAssign setting in Windows 98 is -1. This setting causes Windows 98 to not release a serial port previously used by a non-Windows-based program running in a DOS window until that program's DOS window is closed.

The default value for this setting in Windows 3.1*x* was 2, causing Windows to grant access to the port after two seconds of port inactivity. However, if you set this value to 2 on a Windows 98 computer, you should not run a 32-bit communications program (such as HyperTerminal) and then attempt to run an MS-DOS-based communications program. Because of the way the 32-bit program controls the port, the MS-DOS-based program will be unable to access it and may cause your system to hang (stop responding).

Setting the value to 0 allows an MS-DOS-based application to hand off a "hot port" to a Windows-based program with no delay. This might be necessary in bulletin board administration, for example. Keep in mind that this configuration can cause problems or instabilities because two programs will be able to send commands to the modem at the same time. Unless you have a pressing need and are willing to live with some instability, we recommend that you keep the default setting of -1.

Configuring Your Modem

If you are installing Windows 98 and its hardware-detection program identifies an internal or external modem, you'll be automatically prompted to configure it. If you install a modem later, Windows 98 should detect it automatically and start the Install New Modem Wizard. If this doesn't happen, or if you declined to configure your modem during initial setup, you can engage the Install New Modem Wizard from the Control Panel.

Before installing a pre-plug and play modem in your computer, you may need to physically configure it by setting the jumper switches; read the modem's documentation to see what to do. If your computer has a plug and play BIOS, the modem may not require any configuration on your part; Windows 98's hardware-detection modules may be able to configure your modem for you automatically. For a plug and play modem, this should all be set in the modem itself, so all you have to do is insert it according to the manufacturer's guidelines.

If you are not sure whether Windows 98 has configured your modem, click the Start button, point to Settings, click Control Panel, and click the Modems icon. If your modem has already been configured, you'll see it listed in the General tab of the Modems Properties dialog box. If your modem has not been configured, you can do it now by following these steps:

STEPS

Configuring a Modem

Step 1. Click the Start button, point to Settings, and then click Control Panel. Click the Modems icon. If you have already installed a modem, you'll see the General tab of the Modems Properties dialog box, as shown in Figure 31-1. Click the Add button to start the Wizard, and skip to step 3. (If a modem is already listed, you can optionally remove it before installing another modem by highlighting it and clicking the Remove button.)

Step 2. If you haven't yet configured a modem, the Install New Modem Wizard automatically starts. You can have the Windows 98 hardware-detection routines look for your modem or, if you do not have a plug and play BIOS, you can select it from the list of explicitly supported modems. You can change the selection during this configuration process, so it doesn't hurt to let Windows 98 try to detect your modem. Make sure you are not running any communications programs, because they won't allow the detection routines to access the modem. If you do not have a plug and play BIOS and want to specify the modem yourself, mark the check box labeled Don't Detect My Modem; I Will Select It from a List (see Figure 31-2); if you have a plug and play BIOS, you do not have this option at this point (you will later). Click Next.

(continued)

STEPS *(continued)*

Configuring a Modem

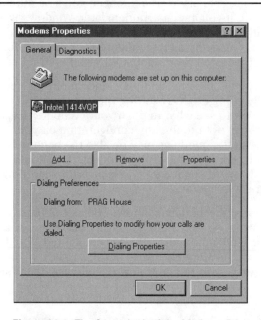

Figure 31-1: The General tab of the Modems Properties dialog box.

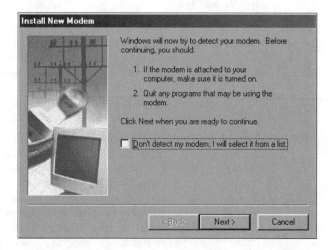

Figure 31-2: Choose whether to have Windows 98 detect your modem.

Step 3.   If you choose to have Windows 98 detect the modem, it will take a few seconds to query the modem to determine its type and which communications port it is using. Windows 98 can't detect all modems. The fallback position for the detection routines is Standard modem at a certain speed, such as 14,400 bps. Click Change if you don't think the modem that has been detected is correct or you think you can do a better job.

Step 4. If you are choosing your own modem, or if you clicked Change, you will see a list of modem manufacturers in the next Wizard dialog box, as shown in Figure 31-3. Select your modem's manufacturer in the list on the left, and select the model of your modem on the right. Click Next.

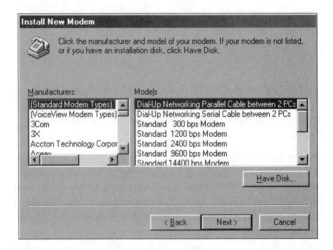

Figure 31-3: The modem selection dialog box in the Install New Modem Wizard.

If you have a diskette from a modem manufacturer that includes a Windows 95 or Windows 98 setup routine for the modem, click Have Disk instead. Modems manufactured after the release of Windows 95 may have these diskettes. Microsoft also publishes setup files for new modems on its web site.

Step 5. If your modem is not listed, select Standard Modem Types (but only for the time being — you'll change it later) and specify your modem's speed, if you know that value. Click Next.

Step 6. If you choose the modem from the list yourself, and it's not plug and play, you need to tell Windows 98 which port it is connected to. Most modems are serial modems, so you have a choice of COM ports. Choose the port based on how you have physically configured the modem, or the manufacturer's recommendations. If you have a parallel modem, you should choose an LPT port. After highlighting your port, click Next.

(continued)

STEPS *(continued)*

Configuring a Modem

Step 7.   The first time you set up a modem, you will be asked for your area code, the number required to get an outside line (if any), whether you are using tone or pulse dialing, and your country code. This information defines the location you are calling from and how the modem should make the call. See "Where Am I Calling From?" in Chapter 32 for more on telephony issues.

Step 8.   Click Finish. The modem name now appears in the General tab of the Modems Properties dialog box.

As mentioned in step 3, if Windows identifies your modem as Standard and you have a better idea of what your modem is, go ahead and set the driver to your best guess. You can always replace the driver if it doesn't work correctly.

Undocumented

If your modem doesn't show up on the list of supported models, try selecting a model similar to yours from the same manufacturer. You don't want to use the Standard modem setting if you can help it because this setting doesn't support data compression and correction, so you won't be able to run your modem at its highest speed. It is much better to choose a modem model similar to yours, even if you can't find one from the same manufacturer. (This may take some guesswork on your part.)

Tip

If your modem is unnamed—generic as far as you can tell—try setting it as a Hayes, U.S. Robotics, Practical Peripherals, or Microcom modem. If you have a generic 28.8 Kbps modem, try the Boca Research Bocamodem 28.8 Kbps V.34bis Data-Fax modem.

When you select a particular modem model, you're telling Windows 98 about the initialization string and the various other strings that control basic modem functions. These strings do vary from one modem to the next, but they often have enough in common that strings for one modem will work with another.

Testing your modem configuration

Tip

You can test whether your modem configuration is the right one by calling the Microsoft Network. Simply click the MSN icon on your Desktop. You can also test your modem with HyperTerminal. Click the Start button, select Programs, Accessories, Communications, and click HyperTerminal. HyperTerminal comes already set up for connecting to several bulletin boards. Click one of the icons and click the Dial button when the Connect dialog box appears. If your connection is successful, you will see a message in the HyperTerminal window from the computer you called. Choose Call, Disconnect to end your call.

Tip

If you have an external modem and the hardware-detection routines did not find it, you may have an incorrect cable connecting your serial (or parallel) port to your modem. Either that or your port may be incorrectly set up.

Whenever you have an active modem connection, the Modem Status icon, which looks like two connected computers, appears in your Tray. When data is being transferred, the two computer screens in the icon blink. Right-click this icon and click Status to see the current status of your modem connection.

Changing basic global modem settings

You can adjust some of the properties associated with your modem by highlighting your modem driver and clicking the Properties button in the General tab of the Modems Properties dialog box:

STEPS

Changing Modem Driver Settings

Step 1.   Click the Start button, point to Settings, and then click Control Panel. Click the Modems icon. Highlight your modem in the list.

Step 2.   Click Properties to display the General tab of the Properties dialog box for your modem, as shown in Figure 31-4 (note that some modem manufacturers may add tabs that let you access your modem's special features).

Step 3.   An alternate and equivalent way of carrying out steps 1 and 2 is to click the System icon in the Control Panel. Then click the Device Manager tab, click the plus sign next to the Modem icon, click the icon associated with your modem, click Properties, and click the Modem tab.

Step 4.   If necessary, change one or more values in your modem's General tab. The maximum speed at which your modem can receive data from your computer depends on what kind of error correction protocol it has and the speed of your CPU. For instance, if you have a 14.4 Kbps modem (it talks to other modems at a rate of 14.4 Kbps) and it implements the V.32bis standard when combined with a 486 processor, it may be able to sustain 57.6 Kbps with compression. If you find your communications applications are reporting high error rates, reduce this maximum value.

(continued)

STEPS *(continued)*
Changing Modem Driver Settings

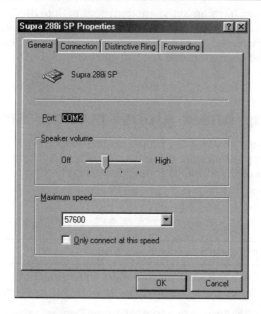

Figure 31-4: The General tab of the Properties dialog box for a modem. You have already selected the port, so unless you move the modem, you shouldn't change that. You can set a global volume for the speaker and the maximum speed your computer/modem combination can handle.

Changing the basic modem connection properties

Each connection—each bulletin board, Internet service provider, friend with a computer and a modem, or server at work that you connect to using your modem—requires unique connection settings. You can follow these steps to set the default choices that your modem will use until you modify them for a given connection:

STEPS

Setting Modem Connection Properties

Step 1. Carry out steps 1-3 in Changing Modem Driver Settings in the preceding section. Click the Connection tab to display the connection properties for the specific modem, as shown in Figure 31-5.

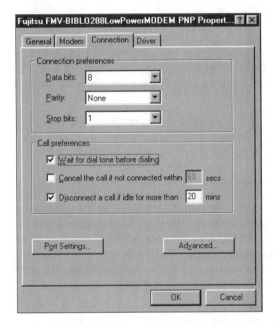

Figure 31-5: The Connection tab of the Properties dialog box for a modem. You can set global default values for the data bits, parity, and stop bits.

Step 2. The values of 8, None, and 1 for data bits, parity, and stop bits are probably just fine. Change them only if you are attaching to a new service that regularly calls for other values.

Step 3. By default, Windows 98 waits for the dial tone before dialing. If you are calling outside the U.S., you should clear the check box labeled Wait for Dial Tone Before Dialing to turn off this U.S.-specific behavior. You may also need to clear this check box if you purchased a modem in a country other than the one you are presently calling from.

Step 4. You can adjust how long you're willing to wait for the connection to be made by marking the check box labeled Cancel the Call If Not Connected within [   ] Secs and entering a number of seconds.

(continued)

STEPS *(continued)*

Setting Modem Connection Properties

Step 5. To disconnect the phone after a set time of idleness, mark the check box labeled Disconnect a Call If Idle for More Than [   ] Mins, and enter a number of minutes.

Step 6. Click OK.

You can customize these values for each connection, so you should only change the default settings if you are creating new connectoids that regularly use values different from the defaults created by your Windows 98 Setup.

Tip

In addition to the global modem settings, each Dial-Up Networking connectoid has its own Modem Properties dialog box. To find it, click the Start button, choose Programs, Accessories, Communications, and click Dial-Up Networking. Right-click the icon for the connectoid whose properties you want to change, and choose Properties. Then click the Configure button on the General tab, next to the Connect Using field. The settings you make here will be in effect for all applications (such as Internet Explorer, Outlook Express, and Microsoft Fax) that use this particular DUN connectoid. HyperTerminal has its own connectoids, which are displayed when you open the HyperTerminal folder. To display the modem settings for the connectoid, right-click the connectoid icon, choose Properties, click the Connect To tab, and then click the Configure button.

When you create a new DUN connectoid, the defaults are set to whatever the global settings were when you started the application the first time. But once you have created a connectoid, you must change the settings within the connectoid itself, because the connectoid no longer uses the global settings. See "Setting Up Your Computer at Home As a Guest" in Chapter 17 for more about setting up connectoids.

If you can't open the Modems Properties dialog box, or if the Configure button is not available in a DUN connectoid's Properties dialog box, the Modemui.dll file may be missing or damaged. This file should be in your \Windows\System folder. If it's there, rename it to something like Modemui.xxx and extract a new copy from the *cab* files in the \win98 folder of your Windows 98 CD-ROM. (To learn how to locate the correct cab file, see "Missing files" in Chapter 16.) Once you've found the correct *cab* file, just click it in the Explorer window, locate Modemui.dll, and drag a copy of it into your \Windows\System folder.

Your particular modem may offer additional tabs besides General and Connection in the Modems Properties box. For example, you may be able to take advantage of distinctive ringing on your phone line, and designate a different ring pattern for fax, voice, and data. Or you may be able to enable call forwarding — a handy feature if you use telephony software such as Microsoft Phone. These tabs are put there by the manufacturer of your modem at the time you install it, and are not part of Windows 98.

Changing more advanced connection settings

Your communications software can set specific connection settings (referred to as *connectoids*) that override the default connection settings. The Windows 98 modem driver sends the command strings that are associated with the default settings to the modem when it is first initialized. A communications package can ask the modem driver to send to the modem other command strings that override these values.

Tip

The Extra Settings field in the Advanced Connection Settings dialog box (available through the Advanced button in the Connection tab of the Modems Properties dialog box) lets you enter a specific command string that you want the driver to send to the modem along with the initialization string. You normally use this field to put the modem into a debug mode in order to track communications errors. Don't use it unless you are familiar with your modem's commands.

STEPS

Setting Advanced Connection Properties

Step 1. Carry out the Changing Modem Driver Settings or Setting Modem Connection Properties steps in the two previous sections to change driver settings or connection properties as appropriate.

Step 2. Click the Connection tab in the Modems Properties dialog box for your modem, and then click the Advanced button to display the Advanced Connection Settings dialog box, as shown in Figure 31-6.

Step 3. The Advanced Connection Settings dialog box lets you add to the string that Windows 98 normally sends when initializing your modem (preparing it for communication) by typing additional strings in the Extra Settings field. Do not type the attention (AT) command. It is sent automatically by the modem initialization string.

(continued)

STEPS *(continued)*

Setting Advanced Connection Properties

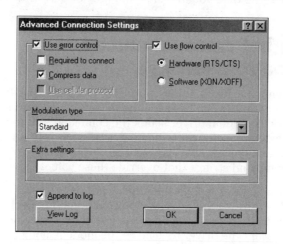

Figure 31-6: The Advanced Connection Settings dialog box.

Step 4. Mark the Use Error Control and Compress Data check boxes if you are sending data to modems or services that support these functions. Some, such as CompuServe, do not. If you are using software compression (for example, compressed SLIP with your Internet service provider), enabling hardware compression here (by marking the Compress Data check box) might cause conflict. One sign that you have conflict between two types of compression is if your communications are very slow. You can turn off either software or hardware compression. (You should only mark the Compress Data check box if you are using an external modem and the serial port is faster than the modem port.)

Don't mark the Required to Connect check box if you have a SLIP or PPP account. If the modems can't negotiate error control, TCP/IP will handle it.

Step 5. Choose Use Flow Control (*handshaking*) if you are running at 9600 bps or better, and if you have an external modem and the modem cable has the RTS and the CTS lines. You have to use hardware flow control if you have a SLIP account because SLIP requires it, and hardware flow control also works with PPP. You'll most likely never need to use software flow control. (One situation where it might be useful is described just after these steps.)

Step 6. If you are using a cellular modem, mark the Use Cellular Protocol check box to reduce errors over multiple cellular connections. This box is only enabled if you're using a CDPD (Cellular Digital Packet Data) modem and the TCP/IP protocol.

Step 7.   The default setting in the Modulation Type drop-down list is Standard. This is the fallback low-speed communications standard if two modems can't communicate at a higher speed. If you experience trouble while trying to communicate with a given site at 300 and 1200 bps, switch from Standard to Non-standard (Bell, HST).

Step 8.   Mark the Append to Log check box if you want to keep a log file to help with debugging a connection. The file, Modemlog.txt, will be in your \Windows folder.

If you enable the log file, Windows 98 adds to it whenever a TAPI-enabled communications programs (such as DUN, HyperTerminal, or Phone Dialer) connects through your modem. The entries are in sequential order, stamped with the date and time of the connection. The Modemlog.txt file will continue to grow as long as you have this option turned on, so you'll need to delete it periodically, or use this feature only when you are troubleshooting.

Step 9.   Click OK.

Windows 3.1*x* used software flow control (XON/XOFF) by default. Starting with Windows 95, Microsoft turned on hardware flow control (RTS/CTS) by default because it results in better modem performance. If you have installed Windows 98 over Windows 3.1*x* and are using an external modem, however, you may find that your serial cable or switch box will not work with hardware flow control. While your modem can send data just fine, it can't receive anything. Ideally you should replace the connecting device (not the modem itself, just the cable or switch). But you may be able to get around this by configuring your modem for software flow control. If you are using a 16-bit communications program, you have to do this in the application itself.

Secret

You may notice that the Modemlog.txt file masks out the phone numbers you dialed (so they look like ATDT#######, for example). This is an intentional security measure, designed to protect calling card numbers. But you can disable it (for troubleshooting purposes only) by typing **E1** in the Extra Settings field of the Advanced Connection Settings dialog box. Be sure to change it back when you're done troubleshooting.

Changing 16550A UART settings

If your serial port uses a 16550A UART, you have the option of adjusting the size of its receive and transmit buffers. You might want to do this if you are dropping characters during transmissions or if you want to increase your throughput. To change these settings, click the Port Settings button in the Connection tab of the Properties dialog box for your modem.

The same Port Settings button is associated with each DUN connectoid. To verify this, right-click a connectoid in the Dial-Up Networking folder. Then click Properties, click the Configure button, click the Connection tab, and there it is. Each connectoid can have its own Advanced and Port Setting values. You can also do this for HyperTerminal connectoids. However, to find the Configure button in a HyperTerminal connectoid, you must go to the Connect To tab after you right-click the connectoid and click Properties.

Changing any modem settings

The file Modems.inf and the files starting with Mdm in the \Windows\Inf folder contain the modem manufacturer and model information displayed when you click the Have Disk button in the Install New Modem Wizard. (The Inf folder is only visible if you have chosen View, Folder Options in an Explorer or folder window and marked Show All Files in the View tab.) Modem manufacturers can ship a file on a diskette with their modem that provides equivalent information about their new modem. Plug and play modems contain the pertinent information on a ROM chip.

Secret

Each modem model has an associated initialization string or set of initialization strings that are defined in the modem setup files. Additional strings for hanging up the modem, setting it in auto-answer mode, turning on or off the speaker and setting its volume, data compression, tone or pulse dial, and so on, are provided in the modem's setup, or *inf*, file.

You can edit the information in these files if you want to change the values Windows 98 uses when you configure a modem. You do this by changing the *inf* file before you add the particular modem driver. From the Explorer, click the *inf* file that has a name resembling the manufacturer of your modem. You can then edit it with Notepad. Be sure to make a backup file first.

After you have added a modem driver to your Windows 98 configuration (using the associated *inf* file), you can change any of the settings associated with the modem by using the Registry editor. This is a bit easier than editing the esoteric *inf* file directly. Turn to "The Registry Editor" in Chapter 15 if you are not familiar with how to edit the Registry.

Go to this branch of the Registry:

HKEY_LOCAL_MACHINE\System\CurrentControlSet\Services\Class\Modem

There may be a number of modems specified on this branch, each designated as a branch and starting with the branch key numbered 0000. This area of the Registry is shown in Figure 31-7.

Find the branch that corresponds to your modem driver by checking the DriverDesc field (in the right pane of the Registry editor) for its familiar name as you highlight each key, starting with 0000. If you have set up DCC, you will see modems in the DriverDesc field labeled Serial Cable Between 2 PCs. Expand the branch for your modem by clicking the plus sign in front of its designated number to see the keys that you can edit.

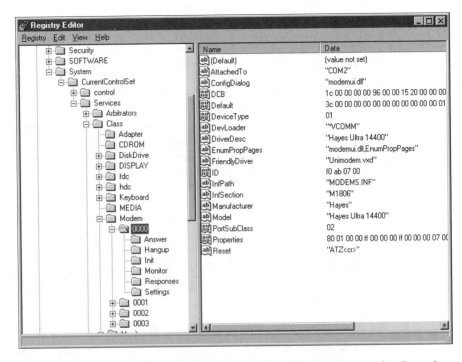

Figure 31-7: The Registry editor displaying the area of the Registry that contains the modem configuration information. Click the plus signs next to the names in the branch to get to this area. (The names on the branch now have minus signs in front of them.)

If you want to change the initialization string for your modem in the Registry, click the Init folder for your modem in the left pane of the Registry editor. The initialization string is displayed in the right pane. Double-click the 2 in the right pane and edit the string. You might want to edit the Answer, Hangup, Fax, and Settings values. (You may see other values and variables as well, depending on what items your modem manufacturer chose to place in the Registry.)

It's a good idea to make a copy of System.dat and User.dat in your \Windows folder before you make any changes to your modem configuration in the Registry.

Test and Interrogate Your Modem

You can find out if your modem is working and what values are stored in its registers. To do this, you can use Terminal, the Windows 3.1x communications package, because it makes it easy to talk directly to your modem. Alternatively, you can configure HyperTerminal.

If you upgraded over Windows 3.1x, you'll find Terminal.exe still in your \Windows folder. Otherwise, you may need to retrieve it from your Windows 3.1x diskettes.

Click Terminal.exe in a folder window or in the Explorer. To check if the modem is working, type the command string **atz** or **ath** or **ate1m1v1**. (Check your modem manual to see which one you should use.) If the modem returns *OK*, then it is there and listening to you.

Next, send the ati? command, replacing the ? with the numbers 2 through 9, one at a time. This should tell you what kind of modem you have.

You can send AT commands to your modem using HyperTerminal. Just follow the steps detailed in the "Answering Incoming Data Calls" section of Chapter 21. You can also send AT commands from a terminal window associated with a particular connection. If you have created a connectoid for HyperTerminal, take the following steps:

STEPS

Sending AT Commands in HyperTerminal

Step 1. Right-click a HyperTerminal connectoid. Click Properties, and choose the Connect To tab.

Step 2. Click the Configure button, and then click the Options tab.

Step 3. Mark the Bring Up Terminal Window Before Dialing check box.

Step 4. Click OK. Click OK again.

Step 5. Click this connectoid. Click the Dial button in the Connect dialog box.

Step 6. The Pre-Dial Terminal Screen appears on your Desktop. Type the AT commands and see what response you get.

Step 7. Press F3 to cancel the attempted connection when you are done.

Step 8. Click Cancel in the Connect dialog box, and then close the HyperTerminal window.

You can invoke a modem diagnostic dialog box by clicking the Modems icon in the Control Panel, clicking the Diagnostics tab, highlighting the port to which your modem is attached, and then clicking the More Info button. Windows 98 sends various AT commands to your modem and reports the responses in the dialog box, as shown in Figure 31-8. It's not too interesting unless you know from looking in your modem's manual what the correct responses are supposed to be.

Bruce Pennypacker shared this tip for testing the COM port and modem configuration. Because this test doesn't use any TAPI applications, it helps you make sure that your hardware is set up properly. In a DOS window, type the following at the command prompt:

```
echo ATDTnnnnnnn > COMx
```

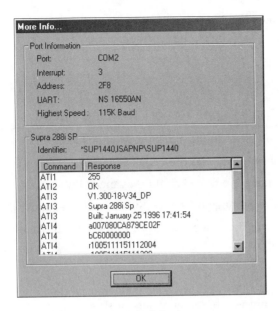

Figure 31-8: The More Info dialog box.

Where *nnnnnnn* is a number to dial and *x* is the number of the COM port. This should cause the modem to go off-hook and dial the number. To disconnect, type:

```
echo ATH > COMx
```

When you're finished, type **exit** to close the DOS window.

Modem speed

After you have made a modem connection, right-click the Modem Status icon in your tray and click Status. If you are using a 32-bit communications program designed for Windows 98, you'll see a box that displays the status of the current connection, including the *line* speed (also known as the *data link* speed or *data circuit-terminating equipment (DCE)* speed). This is the speed between your modem and the modem you are connected to. In other words, it's the speed at which data is transmitted over the telephone line.

Most 16-bit communications programs that are designed for Windows 3.1*x* report the *port* speed (also known as the *serial port connection* speed or *data terminal equipment (DTE)* speed) in the status box. The port speed is the speed between your modem and your computer. More precisely, it's the speed between the serial port that your modem is connected to and your computer. The port speed is typically faster than the line speed, causing 16-bit programs to report a faster speed than 32-bit programs (for example, 57,600 bps instead of 28,800 bps or less). Most people are interested in knowing the line speed, which changes depending on the connection.

Here is a way to make your 16-bit applications report the line speed instead of the port speed:

STEPS

Making 16-bit Applications Report the Line Speed

Step 1.   In Control Panel, double-click the Modems icon.

Step 2.   Click your modem, and then click Properties.

Step 3.   In the Connection tab, click the Advanced button.

Step 4.   In the Extra Settings field, type **S95=0**, and then click OK.

Step 5.   Click OK and then Close to return to the Control Panel.

If the S95=0 setting doesn't work for you, check your modem documentation to see if it specifies another character string for this.

Tracking a dial-up connection with System Monitor

While the modem status box (which you display by right-clicking the Modem Status icon in the Tray when you are connected and choosing Status) shows you the line speed at which the modem is connected, the line speed is not necessarily a true indicator of the rate of data transfer. A modem can be running at its full capacity of 28.8 Kbps, but the online service to which it's connected might be sending out information at a fraction of that rate. Whether the server is overloaded with too many users, or you have a bad telephone connection that's slowing down the signal, a utility called System Monitor (Sysmon.exe) can tell you whether you're getting the throughput you expect.

In order to view modem performance statistics in System Monitor, you must be using a 32-bit communications program, and you must have marked the Append to Log check box in the Advanced Connection Settings dialog box (see "Changing more advanced connection settings" earlier in this chapter).

You may have installed System Monitor when you installed Windows 98; if so, it should be in your \Windows folder. If not, you can retrieve it from the Windows 98 CD-ROM. Click Add/Remove Programs in the Control Panel, click the Windows Setup tab, highlight System Tools, click the Details button, and mark the System Monitor check box.

Start System Monitor, either by clicking its icon in the Explorer or by clicking Start, Programs, Accessories, System Tools, System Monitor. In the System Monitor, choose Edit, Add Item. The Dial-Up Adapter should appear in the Categories list. Highlight it, click Bytes Received/Second and Shift+click

Bytes Transmitted/Second (to select them both), and click OK. Then log on to a web site with lots of graphics and see what happens (as in Figure 31-9).

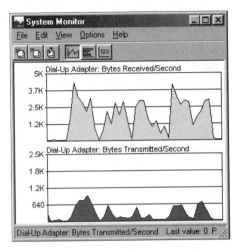

Figure 31-9: System Monitor is set up to show the data transfer rates through the Dial-Up Adapter. In this case, the update interval is every three seconds.

When you add Bytes Received or Bytes Transmitted to your System Monitor window, you'll want to configure the applet to show a meaningful period of time. A rapid update interval of 1 second or 3 seconds should give you an accurate indication of the real throughput you're getting from your online connection. To set this parameter, choose Options, Chart and move the slider bar to the interval you prefer.

If you check your throughput from various servers at various times of the day, you may find that your online provider is the cause of slowdowns in your data throughput. If you get close to the rated speed of your modem when connected at midnight, but a much lower number during the business day, you've just found some peak hours to avoid—unless your service provider can be shamed into upgrading his or her lines and modems.

If you have a 56K modem, you'll notice that the charts for Bytes Received and Bytes Transmitted show quite different transfer rates. The rate for bytes received is probably much higher than for bytes transmitted. There's nothing wrong with your modem; this is normal. These modems take advantage of digital technology to push more information over the phone lines than they theoretically should handle. They count on the fact that your service provider's server can generate a digital signal directly, without using a modem at all. This data can travel faster over the phone lines. Data sent from your modem, however, regardless of the modem's quality or speed, cannot be sent faster than 33.6 KB/sec. Too much "noise" is created when the modem converts your digital data to analog for transmission on your local phone loop (the telephone system then reconverts it to digital for further transmission). Of course, your actual speed will vary, depending on the quality of your connection to the phone company and other factors.

Using a modem with DOS programs

Some people still want to be able to run their modems with DOS programs. This might be especially important if you like to play DOS games online. However, it may be difficult to get the application to even see that your modem is there.

Because DOS programs do not support the newer TAPI standard, they cannot "share" a modem with any other programs — even if they aren't connected at the moment. So make sure that any other communications programs (such as Microsoft Fax or HyperTerminal) are completely shut down.

If the DOS program still fails to locate the modem, you may have one of the newer WinModems. These modems depend on the Windows VxD driver, and probably won't work with your DOS software at all. If you have a WinModem, you're stuck with a decision between giving up the DOS applications and replacing your modem.

If you don't have a WinModem and you can't get DOS to locate your modem, you probably have a plug and play modem that has been configured to a setting that older DOS programs have problems with. The easiest way around this is to manually configure your modem port to settings familiar for DOS programs. In the Control Panel, click the System icon, click the Device Manager tab, click the plus sign next to Modem, and double-click your modem. Look in the Modem tab of the Properties dialog box to see which COM port your modem is configured to use. Click OK, click the plus sign next to Ports, and then double-click the port assigned to your modem. In the Resources tab of the port's Properties dialog box, clear the Use Automatic Settings box. Depending on the resources available on your computer, change the setting for this port to one of the settings listed in Table 31-1 in the "Serial port address and interrupt values" section later in this chapter. Try to stick to COM1 or COM2.

Two modems

Some people need to use two modems — one for a fax line and one for Dial-Up Networking, for example. It is entirely possible to set this up, as long as each modem has its own COM port and its own interrupt (IRQ). This might be easier said than done, however, since COM ports share interrupts. (See "Serial port address and interrupt values" later in this chapter.) You should look for modems that allow you flexibility in setting the IRQ value and COM port. If you can't find this type of modem, you can try freeing up an IRQ by switching to a non-serial mouse.

A different problem can occur if the two modems are the same model. When you install them, Windows 98 will give them the same "friendly" name, which is the name you see in the Modems Properties dialog box (accessed through the Modems icon in the Control Panel). Especially if the friendly name is long, Windows 98 may not use the right modem for a given communications program. If the modems are identical and are installed as the same model, both modems will appear in the Modems Properties dialog box. The solution is to remove the second modem and then reinstall it as a different model. To do so, follow these steps:

STEPS

Re-Installing a Second Modem

Step 1. In the Control Panel, click the Modems icon.

Step 2. Click the second modem, and then click Remove.

Step 3. Click the Add button to launch the Install New Modem Wizard, mark the Don't Detect My Modem; I Will Select It from a List check box, and then click Next.

Step 4. In the Manufacturers and Models lists, choose a manufacturer and a model that is compatible with your modem. If your modem is not compatible with another modem, choose Standard Modem Types at the top of the Manufacturers list and select the model that matches the speed of your modem in the Models list.

Note that if you choose one of the standard modems, you may not be able to use some of the advanced features of your modem. For example, the option to use data compression may not be available.

Step 5. Click Next. Click the appropriate port for the modem, and then click Next again.

Step 6. Click Finish.

Serial and Parallel Ports as Modems

In Chapter 22, we discuss DCC, which lets you hook two computers together using a serial or parallel cable.

DCC keeps track of your serial and parallel ports as though they were modems. When you first click DCC, hardware-detection routines determine which serial and parallel ports are available. They create modem designations for each of these ports and allow you to choose between Serial Cable on COM*x* and Parallel Cable on LPT*x*. The modem descriptions and properties of each port are stored in the Registry in the area referred to in the "Changing any modem settings" section of this chapter.

These are not real modems, but the Modems area of the Registry is a convenient place to keep track of the fact that these ports are available to be used by DCC. These port connections do not show up on the list of modems when you click the Modems icon in the Control Panel.

There are two ways to see which ports the hardware-detection routines have found. You can click the Start button, point to Programs, Accessories, Communications, and then click Direct Cable Connection. If you click the Change button and then click Next, you'll see a list of ports available for DCC.

The other way to see the list of ports is to click the Start button, point to Settings, and then click Control Panel. Click the System icon, and then click the plus sign next to the Modem icon. A list of all "modems" will appear, including your serial and parallel cables on ports if you have previously run DCC.

If you use this second method, you can remove certain ports that you won't be using with DCC — perhaps ports that are being used only by your mouse, for instance. If you remove a port/cable that you decide later to use with DCC, you must restore it manually.

To add back a removed port, take the following steps:

STEPS

Adding a Removed Port

Step 1. Click the Start button, point to Programs, Accessories, Communications, and finally click Direct Cable Connection.

Step 2. Click the Change button, and then click Next.

Step 3. Click the Install New Ports button.

Cable Modems

Modems that connect to your television cable instead of the phone line are becoming available, and cable companies in some parts of the country have begun to offer this service. The cable modem connects to your computer through an Ethernet card, so it doesn't use a COM port at all. Instead, you select the Network option from within your application. There's no need for dial-up, because you're always connected. Early users have reported much faster performance than telephone lines can provide.

Configuring Serial Ports

You can change a serial port's settings as well its address and interrupt values. You make all changes to serial and parallel ports through the Device Manager, found under the System icon in the Control Panel.

Changing serial port settings

Windows 3.1*x* included a Ports icon in the Control Panel. The functions of this Ports icon are now included in the Device Manager. You can use the Device Manager to change a serial port's speed, data bits, stop bits, parity, and flow control (handshaking). If you are using this serial port for a connection, the settings for that particular connection override these settings.

STEPS
Changing Serial Port Settings

Step 1. Click the Start button, point to Settings, and then click Control Panel. Click the System icon to display the System Properties dialog box, and click the Device Manager tab.

Step 2. Click the plus sign to the left of the Ports icon in the Device Manager. You will see a listing of all the serial and parallel ports connected to your computer.

Step 3. Highlight the serial port you want to change and click the Properties button. Click the Port Settings tab.

Step 4. Using the options in this tab, shown in Figure 31-10, you can change the values for speed, data bits, stop bits, parity, and flow control (handshaking).

(continued)

STEPS *(continued)*
Changing Serial Port Settings

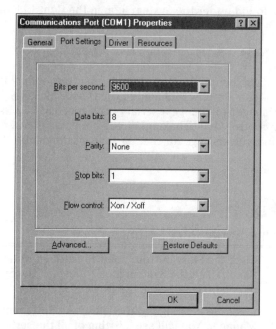

Figure 31-10: The Port Settings tab in the Communications Port (COM*x*) Properties dialog box.

These port settings are similar to the basic global connection settings for a modem. You should set these settings only when you use the port with a device, such as a scanner, a printer, or even a mouse. The specific software that uses the port — a communications package or a connectoid (whether HyperTerminal or DUN) — can have different settings, and these settings override the serial port settings.

In Windows 98, after you install a modem, the serial port that the modem is configured to use may not be listed in Device Manager. To determine which serial port the modem is configured to use, click the plus sign next to Modem in Device Manager, highlight your modem, click Properties, and go to the Modem tab.

Serial port address and interrupt values

During Setup, Windows 98 recognizes the serial ports that are already installed in your computer. Serial ports in personal computers with ISA buses (not MCA or EISA) have default values for addresses and interrupts. Table 31-1 lists these values.

Table 31-1 Default Address and Interrupt Values

Port	Address	Interrupt
COM1	03F8h	4
COM2	02F8h	3
COM3	03E8h	4
COM4	02E8h	3

You can remove any special utilities or debug scripts you had in Autoexec.bat to handle problems with Windows recognizing your modems. Previously, some Windows 3.1x users had problems with internal modems set to COM4, which failed to operate if there was no COM3. Other users had trouble with serial mice on COM2 if COM4 was present but COM3 wasn't. These problems have been fixed starting with Windows 95.

You'll notice in Table 31-1 that COM1 and COM3 share the same interrupt. The same is true for COM2 and COM4. If you have devices on the higher numbered COM ports, they will conflict with devices on the port they share the interrupt with. You can't use both devices at the same time if they share an interrupt and you are using a computer with an ISA bus.

If one device is, say, a scanner and the other is a modem, then it is unlikely that you will use them both at the same time, so sharing an interrupt is okay. If one is a mouse and another is a printer, your mouse will go haywire when you are printing. You can change the interrupts so there is no conflict.

You can determine a serial port's I/O address with Debug, a DOS program used for troubleshooting problems with your system setup. See "Finding a Serial Port I/O Address Using Debug" in the Microsoft Knowledge Base at http://premium.microsoft.com/support/kb/articles/q78/6/04.asp.

Changing serial port addresses and interrupts

You can configure your serial port addresses and interrupts to avoid conflicts between devices that can't share the same interrupt. You can have a modem on COM3 and a mouse on COM1 and use different interrupts for each device. Your serial port hardware must support the new interrupt number and you must change the configuration switches on the (pre-plug and play) hardware to match the interrupts that you choose in Windows 98.

Secret

The address and interrupt information for each port is stored as a *basic configuration* (which is just a grouping of resource settings). Only one basic configuration is active at any one time for a given port. Depending on your BIOS, you can set each serial port to use one of either four or nine basic configurations, as we show in the steps in this section. A computer with a plug and play BIOS will only show four basic configurations, and they will not be editable (since the BIOS should take care of the configuration for you). The default basic configuration of the COM1 serial port is basic configuration 0 (shown as 0000 if you have a plug and play BIOS). For the COM2 serial port, it is basic configuration 2 (or 0001 for a plug and play BIOS).

If you have a non-plug and play BIOS, serial port basic configurations 0, 2, and 4 are non-editable. You can change the interrupt in basic configurations 1, 3, 5, 6, 7. You can change either the serial port address or the interrupt in basic configuration 8.

Basic configurations 0 and 1 are designed for COM1; 2 and 3 for COM2; 4 and 5 for COM3; and 6 and 7 for COM4.

Use the Resources tab of the Communications Port (COM*x*) Properties dialog box to choose which basic configuration to use for each port.

STEPS

Changing Serial Port Addresses and Interrupts

Step 1. Click the Start button, point to Settings, and then click Control Panel. Click the System icon. Click the Device Manager tab.

Step 2. Click the plus sign next to the Ports icon in the Device Manager. You will see a listing of all the serial and parallel ports connected to your computer.

Step 3. Highlight the communications port that you want to change and click the Properties button. Click the Resources tab to display the resource properties for the communications port (see Figure 31-11).

Step 4. If you have a plug and play BIOS, you can only change the basic configuration. Clear the Use Automatic Settings check box so that you can change the default settings. Display the Setting Based On drop-down list, and highlight a basic configuration. You are warned if there is a conflict with another hardware device driver. Once you have selected a new basic configuration, go on to step 9.

Step 5. If you have a non-plug and play BIOS, you can change the Input/Output Range or the Interrupt Request settings. Highlight either Input/Output Range (the address of the serial port) or Interrupt Request. Click the Change Setting button. If you get a message stating that this setting can't be changed, try another configuration. Basic configurations 0, 2, and 4 are not editable. Basic configurations 1, 3, 5, 6, and 7 have editable interrupts. Basic configuration 8 has editable address and interrupt values.

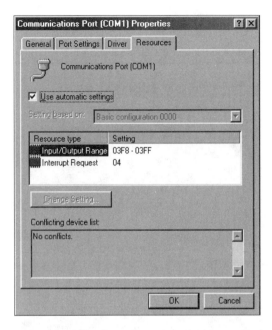

Figure 31-11: The Resources tab in the Communications Port (COM*x*) Properties dialog box.

Step 6. If the address in the currently selected basic configuration can be changed, when you highlight Input/Output Range and click the Change Setting button, you'll see the Edit Input/Output Range dialog box, as shown in Figure 31-12. You can give the port a new address if the documentation for the port hardware indicates support for the new address.

Step 7. Scroll through the various available addresses to set a new address for this port. You are warned if there is a conflict with another hardware device driver.

Step 8. If the interrupt in the currently selected basic configuration can be changed, you can highlight Interrupt Request in the Resources tab, click the Change Setting button, and then change the interrupt value in the Edit Interrupt Request dialog box. You will be warned if there is a conflict.

Step 9. Click OK. Click OK again.

Step 10. Restart Windows 98.

(continued)

STEPS *(continued)*

Changing Serial Port Addresses and Interrupts

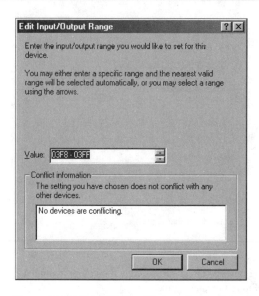

Figure 31-12: The Edit Input/Output Range dialog box for a computer without a plug and play BIOS. Change the value of the port address by scrolling through the available addresses. The lower field reports whether a hardware device driver is already using this address.

If you disable a COM port for any reason, you should also make sure you also remove it in the Device Manager. Otherwise, you'll see a yellow warning symbol in the Device Manager, indicating that the port is not working or not configured in the way Windows expects.

Infrared communications

Using infrared (IR) devices and the Microsoft Infrared Communications Driver, you can use wireless infrared links instead of serial and parallel cables. For example, instead of using a serial or parallel cable to exchange files using DCC, you can use an infrared link. You can also print to infrared-capable printers without the need for cable.

While some computers (mostly notebooks) have built-in IR ports, you can also buy IR adapters that connect to serial ports. The IR devices simulate serial connections, and require that you assign them a COM port on installation. Make sure you find out in advance what the correct COM port is for your device; if you assign an incorrect COM port, the device will not be able to recognize other IR devices.

Better Serial Ports

Over the lifetime of PC-compatible architecture, the UART chip that controls serial ports has evolved. It began in the IBM PC as the 8250. In the AT class machines, it was upgraded to a 16540. The current chip of choice in Intel 486 and Pentium-based PCs is the 16550A.

Undocumented

The 16550A has two advantages over its predecessors. First, it incorporates a 16-byte buffer. By buffering incoming and outgoing data, the 16550A UART can accumulate characters without losing them while waiting for its interrupt request to be serviced by the CPU. Second, the 8250 and the 16540 UARTs send an interrupt to the CPU whenever they receive a character. The 16550A can send one interrupt to service all the characters in the buffer.

By accumulating characters while waiting for the CPU to be available, the 16550A greatly enhances the reliability of high-speed communications, which is a very important feature, given our increased usage of the serial port as a networking device.

Undocumented

Windows 3.1*x* didn't take much advantage of this buffering capability of the 16550A UART. It didn't use it to transmit data and used only a single byte of the buffer in the receive mode. This allowed third-party software developers to find a niche in the market by creating additional COM port drivers to replace Comm.drv.

Windows 98 takes full advantage of the 16650A UART, enabling the full 16 bytes of the receive and transmit buffers.

Testing Your Internal Modem for a 16550A UART

You can test whether your internal modem includes a 16550A UART:

STEPS

Testing an Internal Modem

Step 1.   Set up your modem driver, as described in the steps in the "Configuring Your Modem" section earlier in this chapter.

Step 2.   Click the Start button, point to Settings, and click Control Panel. Click the Modems icon.

(continued)

STEPS *(continued)*

Testing an Internal Modem

Step 3. Click the Diagnostics tab. Highlight the port with your modem attached. Click More Info. The More Info dialog box will tell you which UART you have.

Configuring Parallel Ports

The Windows 98 user interface for configuring parallel ports is almost the same as that used for serial ports. As with the serial port settings, the number of basic configurations available for a parallel port depends on your BIOS. However, for parallel ports there are fewer configurations: two if you have a plug and play BIOS, and four if you do not. Both of the plug and play basic configurations have interrupts; for non-plug and play, basic configurations 0 and 2 do not.

Tip

Windows 98 by default does not assign an interrupt to a parallel port. The interrupt is rarely needed for printing. The previous standard was to assign Interrupt 7 to LPT1 and LPT3, and Interrupt 5 to LPT2. Here's how to change addresses and interrupts:

STEPS

Changing Parallel Port Addresses and Interrupts

Step 1. Click Start, point to Settings, and click Control Panel. Click the System icon to display the System Properties dialog box. Click the Device Manager tab.

Step 2. Click the plus sign next to the Ports icon in the Device Manager tab to see a listing of all serial and parallel ports connected to your computer.

Step 3. Highlight the parallel port that you want to change, and click Properties. Click the Resources tab.

Step 4. If you have a plug and play BIOS, you can change the basic configuration. Clear the Use Automatic Settings check box, and display the Setting Based On drop-down list to see the possible basic configurations (0000 or 0001 in this case). Highlight a basic configuration and go on to step 8.

Step 5. If you do not have a plug and play BIOS, you can change the Input/Output Range or the Interrupt Request settings. Highlight either Input/Output Range (the address of the parallel port) or Interrupt Request. Clear the Use Automatic Settings check box to allow settings other than the default ones. Display the Setting

Based On drop-down list to see the possible basic configurations (0, 1, 2, or 3). Highlight a basic configuration and click the Change Setting button.

Step 6.   If you highlighted Input/Output Range in step 5, you can change the port address setting with the arrow buttons.

Step 7.   If you highlighted Interrupt Request in step 5, you can change the interrupt value. You will be warned if there is a conflict. There isn't an interrupt displayed with every basic configuration.

Step 8.   Click OK. Click OK again.

Step 9.   Restart Windows 98.

Configuring ECP and EPP Ports

Windows 98 Setup detects whether you have an *extended capabilities port* (ECP) or an *enhanced parallel port* (EPP), but it won't set up the port for you. Both of these port types provide you with high-speed and bidirectional communication capabilities. If you want high-speed communication, you have to enable ECP or EPP support yourself. Here's how:

STEPS
Configuring ECP or EPP Support

Step 1.   First make sure that the ECP or EPP port is implemented in your computer's BIOS (usually it won't be if it's coming right from the manufacturer). Restart your computer, and during power-on self test, press the key indicated on your display to get to the BIOS setup screen (this may happen fast, so be ready). Once you are in the setup screen for your particular BIOS, look for the place where you change the parallel port (this will be different for every BIOS manufacturer). Most likely the BIOS will assign a configuration for your port. Once the port is configured, save your changes and continue with the Windows boot up process.

Step 2.   When Windows 98 starts it will do a hardware search. Windows 98 should find your ECP or EPP port and configure it.

Step 3.   If Windows 98 doesn't find your port, click the Start button, point to Settings, and then click Control Panel. Click the Add New Hardware icon to start the Add New Hardware Wizard. The Wizard will first search for new plug and play compatible hardware. If the Wizard doesn't find your port, click the No, I Want to Select the Hardware from a List option, and click Next.

(continued)

Step 4. Double-click Ports in the list that appears. Double-click ECP Printer Port in the next list, click Next to accept the configuration settings, and click Finish.

Step 5. If you need to change the configuration your port has been assigned, follow the Changing Parallel Port Addresses and Interrupts steps in the previous section.

How Many Serial and Parallel Ports?

Windows 3.1*x* could handle up to four serial ports and nine parallel ports. The four serial ports shared two interrupts.

Windows 98 can logically address up to 128 serial and 128 parallel ports—the same as previous versions of MS-DOS. Most computers come with far fewer actual serial and parallel ports. Some manufacturers sell add-in cards that give you additional ports. These are useful for handling such tasks as answering multiple modems or collecting data from laboratories.

Port Values Stored in Win.ini

To maintain compatibility with existing Windows 3.1*x* applications, Windows 98 stores port information in the Win.ini file. If you make changes to the serial port settings, they are reflected in changes to the settings in Win.ini as well as the Registry. Therefore, you shouldn't edit Win.ini directly. Use the Device Manager (double-click the System icon in the Control Panel) and make changes in the Port Settings tab of the Communications Port (COM*x*) Properties dialog box for the desired serial port. The changes will show up in both places.

Printer port information—what printer drivers have been set up and which ports they are connected to—comes from the Printers folder. It is stored both in the Registry and Win.ini.

Table 31-2 shows a typical set of entries for port information in your Windows 98 Win.ini file.

The [Devices] section, which lists the available printers, is useless and is necessary only for compatibility with Windows 2.*x* applications.

The [PrinterPorts] section lists again the available printers, the ports they are attached to, and their time-out settings in seconds. The first time-out is how long to wait for the printer to report that it is alive. The second is how long to wait for the printer to respond to an attempt to communicate with it before reporting an error. See "Printer Driver Properties" in Chapter 29 for further discussion of printer issues.

Table 31-2 Port Information in Win.ini

Entry	Explanation
[Ports]	Ports section heading
LPT1:= LPT2:= LPT3:=	Possible parallel ports
COM1:=9600,n,8,1,x COM2:=9600,n,8,1,x COM3:=9600,n,8,1,x COM4:=9600,n,8,1,x	Serial port settings. 9600 bits per second, no parity, 8 data bits, 1 stop bit, xon/xoff
FILE:=	Print to a file
FAX:=	Print to a fax
PUB:=	Fax rendering
\\OurServer\hp=	Network printer

[Devices]
Linotronic 300 v47.1=PSCRIPT,FILE:
HP LaserJet 4L=HPPCL5MS,LPT1:
Microsoft Fax=WPSUNI,FAX:
Rendering Subsystem=WPSUNI,PUB:
Server's HP=HPPCL5MS,\\OurServer\hp

[PrinterPorts]
Linotronic 300 v47.1=PSCRIPT,FILE:,15,45
HP LaserJet 4L=HPPCL5MS,LPT1:,15,45
Microsoft Fax=WPSUNI,FAX:,15,45
Rendering Subsystem=WPSUNI,PUB:,15,45
Server's HP=HPPCL5MS,\\OurServer\hp,15,45

Previously, the base I/O port address and the IRQ values were stored on the COMxBASE and COMxIRQ lines (where x is a number between 1 and 4) in the [386Enh] section of the System.ini file in the \Windows folder. These lines are no longer operative. If you want to edit your System.ini with Notepad, you can remove these lines.

Null Modem Cables

If you are going to use Direct Cable Connection across serial ports, you should use null modem cables to connect two Windows 98 computers. When you ask for a *null modem*, sometimes the sales people at the computer store will know what you're talking about, and sometimes they won't. This is not exactly a brand name. It's easier to pick these items out of a mail order catalog. If you need to be specific, Tables 31-3 and 31-4 describe the connections for null modem cables.

Table 31-3   Serial 9-Pin to 9-Pin Null Modem Cable

Signal	*Host serial port pins*	*Guest serial port pins*
Transmit Data	3	2
Receive Data	2	3
Request to Send	7	8
Clear to Send	8	7
Data Set Ready and Data Carrier Detect	6, 1	4
Signal Ground	5	5
Data Terminal Ready	4	6, 1

Table 31-4 Serial 25-Pin to 25-Pin Null Modem Cable

Signal	Host serial port pins	Guest serial port pins
Transmit Data	2	3
Receive Data	3	2
Request to Send	4	5
Clear to Send	5	4
Data Set Ready and Data Carrier Detect	6, 8	20
Signal Ground	7	7
Data Terminal Ready	20	6, 8

Summary

Windows 98 gives you a great deal of control over your ports and modems:

▶ You can change the address and interrupt values for serial or parallel ports to avoid conflicts with other hardware devices.

▶ You can configure your modem once, and this configuration will be used by all Windows 98-aware communications software.

▶ You can determine whether your internal modem has an advanced serial port (UART) chip.

Chapter 32

Telephony

In This Chapter

Windows 98 provides a powerful resource to aid in telephone communications. Among other features, TAPI 2.1 (Telephone Application Programming Interface) indicates to TAPI-compliant communications applications the characteristics of the location you are dialing from. We show you how to use the Dialing Properties dialog box for:

▶ Entering the numbers that you have to dial to get an outside line or a long-distance line

▶ Automatically using calling cards to bill calls correctly from out-of-town locations

▶ Defining alternative dialing methods for unusual situations

▶ Formatting phone numbers so you can dial them from anywhere

▶ Designating the first three digits of a phone number in your area code as requiring long-distance dialing

▶ Setting up speed dialing with Phone Dialer

Where Am I Calling From?

Microsoft provides a resource in Windows 98 for keeping track of where you are. What problem are they trying to solve?

Consider for a moment your garden-variety communications package. You know that it keeps track of the phone numbers of the computer services that you use. That is, it keeps track of the area codes and local numbers. It also knows that if you place an area code in a phone number, it has to dial a 1 to make a long-distance call.

If you stay in one place (say, your office) and have your calls billed to one number (most likely the number you are calling from), your communications software only needs to know the number that you are dialing. It knows how to complete the call because the billing and other information required are implicit.

If, on the other hand, you and your computer travel around at all, your computer needs to know not only where you are calling *to,* but also the special features of the phone system you are dialing *from.* In addition, you need to be able to easily choose the long-distance carriers that handle your calls and determine how they will bill you.

Different locations have different means of accessing outside lines or long-distance carriers. For example, calling from the office may require that you preface your phone numbers with a 9, while calling from home does not. If you call from a hotel, you might have to use a credit card and dial into a specific long-distance carrier. A phone number may be local when you call from home and long-distance when you call from the office. Some phones have only pulse dialing services. Some locations require special calling methods.

You can handle all these situations with the Dialing Properties dialog box.

Preliminary Location Information

The first time you set up your modem (see "Configuring Your Modem" in Chapter 31 for details) you encounter the Location Information dialog box as part of the Install New Modem Wizard (shown in Figure 32-1). At this point, all you need to do is type your area code.

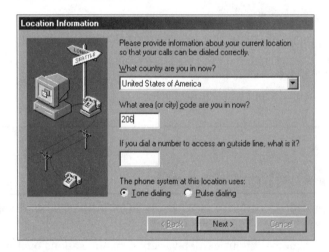

Figure 32-1: The Location Information dialog box.

You have the option of changing the country code, typing a number required to get an outside line, and choosing whether or not to use pulse dialing. You can change all these values later in the Dialing Properties dialog box.

Dialing Properties

The Dialing Properties dialog box (shown in Figure 32-2) lets you define the characteristics of the (perhaps numerous) locations you will be calling from. You will most likely define your office and/or home location right away. Define others as you need them.

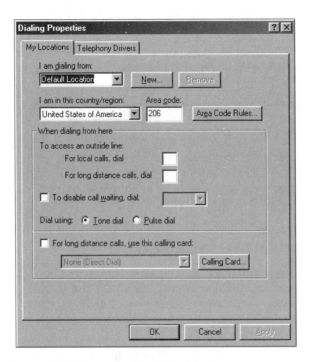

Figure 32-2: The Dialing Properties dialog box.

One fast way to display the Dialing Properties dialog box is to click the Telephony icon in the Control Panel. If you access this dialog box frequently and want to create a shortcut to it, just drag and drop the Telephony icon from the Control Panel onto the Desktop.

Perhaps an even easier way to get to Dialing Properties is through the Telephony Location Manager (\Windows\System\Tlocmgr.exe), now an integrated part of Windows 98. Put a shortcut to this applet on your Desktop, or better yet in your \Windows\Start Menu\Programs\StartUp folder, and you'll have immediate access to the Dialing Properties box, your list of location names, and the Phone Dialer. We talk more about this in the "Telephony Location Manager" section later in this chapter.

You can also access the Dialing Properties dialog box through the Modems icon in the Control Panel or in these Windows 98-aware communications programs: Phone Dialer, Dial-Up Networking, HyperTerminal, and Microsoft Fax. Here are the specific methods for each program:

■ Phone Dialer (Start, Programs, Accessories, Communications, Phone Dialer) — Choose Tools, Dialing Properties.

■ Dial-Up Networking (Start, Programs, Accessories, Communications, Dial-Up Networking) — Click a connectoid and click the Dial Properties button in the Connect To dialog box. (Make sure the Prompt for Information Before Dialing option is enabled under Connections, Settings.)

■ HyperTerminal (Start, Programs, Accessories, Communications, HyperTerminal) — Click a connectoid and click the Dial Properties button in the Connect To dialog box. (Make sure the Prompt for Information Before Dialing option is enabled under Connections, Settings.)

■ Microsoft Fax — Open Windows Messaging, click Tools, Services, select Microsoft Fax, click Properties, click the Dialing tab, and click the Dialing Properties button.

The Dialing Properties dialog box is independent of the application that you use to call it up. It works the same for all Windows 98 TAPI applications. All of the features discussed in this chapter are applicable to any TAPI-compliant communications software.

Setting up a new location

The particular characteristics of each location are stored by location name. Location names can be anything: Grandma's house, Home Office, HO with ATT, Michigan - direct, Timbuktu - pulse. When you set up a new location, choose a name that is unique and meaningful to you.

A location name stands for a location and for the unique dialing sequence used to make a phone call from there. This includes whether you use a calling card, have to dial a number to get an outside line, and so on. If the number you're dialing is in the international format (see the section later in this chapter entitled "Format for the Numbers That You Dial Out"), the information stored in the location is used to create the sequence of numbers needed to place the call correctly.

Click the New button to define a new location, and click OK when you are informed that a new location was created. Then in the I Am Dialing From field, type over the default name (New Location) with the location name you want to use.

Each location should have an area code. The area code field can accommodate a number up to 29 digits in length, but your entry will most likely be no more than 5 digits in length. A location should also have a country code, since each country has its own set of rules for dialing local, long distance, and international calls. The drop-down list contains 242 country codes, so you will probably be able to find yours. However, if your country code or dialing rules have changed recently or your country is not on the list, you may need to edit your Telephon.ini file to correct this. See "Changes in international dialing access codes and Telephon.ini" below.

You can set up rules for how to use the area code in dialing. Click the Area Code Rules button. In the Area Code Rules dialog box, mark the Always Dial the Area Code (10-Digit Dialing) check box if your location always requires you to dial the area code first.

You'll also see a box under When Calling within My Area Code for entering prefixes (the first three digits after the area code) that are in the area code for your location but are long distance and therefore require you to dial 1 first. Click New to the right of this box to enter these prefixes. You may also need to dial other area codes from your location that are not long distance, and therefore don't require you to dial 1 first. Click the New button next to the box under When Calling to Other Area Codes to enter these area codes.

Defining how to dial out

Your location may require that you enter a number to get an outside line. You might also have to enter a long-distance access number to get a line that is used for special billing purposes. You may have multiple such billing numbers at work. If this is the case, you could set up separate locations for each billing number.

Tip

Call waiting can interfere with modem access. If the line you are using at a given location has the call waiting feature, you need to turn it off for the duration of your call when you are using a modem. In the U.S., you normally disable call waiting by dialing *70, 70#, or 1170. These three choices are displayed in the drop-down list to the right of the call waiting check box.

You have the choice of pulse or tone dialing with your modem. If the local telephone office can handle only pulse dialing, you need to mark that option button.

Credit card calls

The procedures for making credit cards calls (or for using a specific long-distance carrier) are uniform enough in most cases for you to automate them. Windows 98 includes specific phone numbers for some long-distance carriers (AT&T, British Telecom, MCI, U.S. Sprint, and others), and you can add more to the basic list. Information on long-distance carriers and calling card numbers is a part of the location definition, so you can have different location names for the same physical location but with different calling cards.

To specify a specific long-distance carrier, or to bill calls from the location that you are defining to a calling card, mark the For Long Distance Calls, Use This Calling Card check box, and then click the Calling Card button. The Calling Card dialog box appears, as shown in Figure 32-3. Click this same button if you need to change the settings for a calling card.

The drop-down list at the top of the dialog box by default contains 23 calling card numbers from numerous long-distance vendors, including AT&T, British Telecom, Carte France Telecom, MCI, Telecom Australia, U.S. Sprint, and others. If the list includes the long-distance carrier that you want to use, select it, and enter your PIN number. Then check to make sure that the access numbers shown for your card are correct, and change them if necessary. Your card number will be encrypted when it is stored on your hard disk in the Telephon.ini file and the Registry. If you want to add a calling card that's not on this list, see the next section.

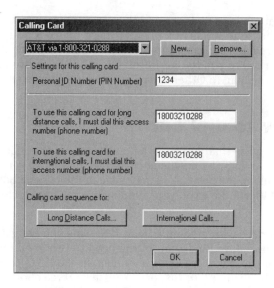

Figure 32-3: The Calling Card dialog box.

Adding a long-distance carrier/ method to your list

If your long-distance carrier is not on the list in the Calling Card dialog box, or if you want to access your carrier through another method, you can use the steps below to create a new carrier listing. You can also use these steps to define another dialing method to match your situation. The Calling Card Sequence dialog box is not only useful for entering information about calling cards and accessing long-distance carriers, you can also use it to dial a string of numbers that you need for other purposes.

STEPS

Adding a New Long-Distance Carrier

Step 1. Click the New button in the Calling Card dialog box to display the Create New Calling Card dialog box. Type a name to identify a carrier or a method. Click OK. Click OK again when you see a message box informing you that you must enter dialing rules in order to use this calling card.

Step 2. In the Calling Card dialog box, enter your PIN and the access numbers (phone numbers to dial) for long distance and international calls.

Step 3. Now click the Long Distance Calls button at the bottom of this box. The Calling Card Sequence dialog box appears, as shown in Figure 32-4.

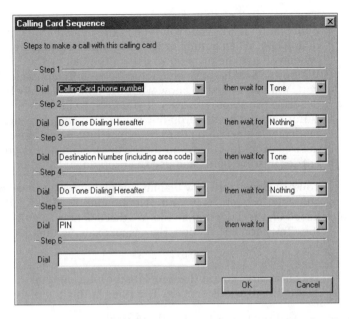

Figure 32-4: The Calling Card Sequence dialog box. When you first display this dialog box, the fields contain a suggested sequence of steps, which you can change using the drop-down arrows.

Step 4. You use the Calling Card Sequence dialog box to enter the steps you must go through to make a long distance call. Windows 98 starts you out with some suggestions in the first three fields. You can click the drop-down arrow for each field to select from a list of choices for that step, or you can type a number if necessary.

Step 5. When you have finished entering the dialing sequence for long distance calls, click OK. Now click the International Calls button in the Calling Card dialog box and enter the dialing sequence for international calls as you did in step 4. Click OK.

Step 6. Click OK in the Calling Card dialog box, and then click OK again to exit the Dialing Properties box. You have defined the properties of a given location as well as a new long-distance carrier.

The dialing rules

Each of the long-distance carriers/methods has a set of three templates of dialing rules: local, long-distance, and international. You can add a long-distance carrier to your list and edit the dialing rules to match those required by that carrier. The templates are not associated with particular long-distance carriers; you can use them to define any dialing method.

The templates of dialing rules are a series of numbers, letters, and punctuation marks that you type in the fields in the Calling Card Sequence dialog box. When a number is dialed, these rules are read and carried out. When you use the drop-down lists in the Calling Card Sequence dialog box, Windows 98 adds these characters to your Telephon.ini file and Registry for you. You don't need to know what the template really looks like, you just describe the steps. However, if you need to indicate a sequence of steps that is not covered by the drop-down lists, you can also enter the template manually in the Calling Card Sequence box. Select Specified Digits in the desired drop-down list, and then type the characters you need. You can type entries in some fields and use the drop-down list in others.

You can also create new dialing rules by entering these number and character sequences in your Telephon.ini file. The Registry will update itself based on the Telephon.ini file. We discuss how to edit Telephon.ini later in the "Telephon.ini" section. Here is an example template of dialing rules:

```
1 - (800) 674-7000 $TH$T01EFG
```

This is a variation on the template for international dialing shown in Figure 32-4 in the previous section. The rules in this template are as follows:

1. Dial the number 1 - (800) 674-7000.

2. Wait for the "bong" tone ($).

3. Using touch tone, send the calling card number (TH).

4. Wait again for the "bong" tone ($).

5. Using touch tone, send 01 (T01).

6. Send the country code, area code, and local number (EFG).

Spaces, hyphens, periods, and parentheses are ignored.

The dialing rules shown in Table 32-1 let you complete a phone call throughout much of the world.

Table 32-1   Dialing Rules

Code	Represents
0-9	Number to be dialed
#	Touch tone pound sign
*	Touch tone star
!	Hook flash
,	Pause for two seconds
@	Wait for a ringing tone followed by five seconds of silence
$	Wait for the calling card tone — the "bong" tone
?	Prompt user for input

Code	Represents
E	Country code
F	Area code
G	Local phone number
T	Dial the following number using touch tone
P	Dial the following number using pulse dialing
W	Wait for a second dial tone
H	Your calling card number

Waiting for the "bong"

Undocumented

Your modem may not support the option of waiting for the "bong" tone. If it doesn't, it will ignore the $ and dial your calling card number before the phone company is ready to receive it.

If this happens, try substituting the @ symbol for the $ in your version of the dialing rules. Your modem may respond to this. If not, you can also substitute commas (,,,, instead of $) to force an eight-second wait until the calling card number is sent.

Suppressing the 1 prefix

Your company's phone system may dial the prefix 1 for you when you dial long-distance numbers. You can use the Calling Card dialog box to create a set of dialing rules that suppresses the prefix 1 for all of the calls you make from work:

STEPS

Creating Dialing Rules to Suppress the 1 Prefix

Step 1. Click the Start button, point to Settings, and click Control Panel. Click the Telephony icon to open the Dialing Properties dialog box.

Step 2. Click the New button, click OK, and then type a name that describes your office location and phone system.

Step 3. Mark the For Long Distance Calls, Use This Calling Card check box. Click the Calling Card button. Click the New button, type a description for the dialing method used at your office (perhaps a name that describes the dialing rules), and click OK.

Step 4. Click the Long Distance Calls button. In the Step 1 Dial field, select Destination Number (Including Area Code) from the drop-down list, and click OK.

(continued)

STEPS *(continued)*

Creating Dialing Rules to Suppress the 1 Prefix

Step 5.   Click the International Calls button. In the Step 1 Dial field, select Specified Digits from the drop-down list, type **011**, and click OK. Then fill in the four fields listed here, choosing the indicated options from the drop-down lists:

Field	Option
Step 1 Then Wait For	Nothing
Step 2 Dial	Destination Country/Region.
Step 2 Then Wait For	Nothing
Step 3 Dial	Destination Number (Including Area Code)

Step 6.   Click OK three times.

Format for the Numbers That You Dial Out

Windows 98-aware communications applications use certain styles to designate numbers that can be dialed out. The most flexible style is the international style:

```
+CC (AC) LocalNumber
```

The plus sign, spaces, and parentheses are all required elements of this format. CC is the country code, which in the U.S. is 1. AC is the area code. There is a space between the country code and the area code and a space between the area code and the local number. The local number can have hyphens in it.

If you enter a number in this format, you can call it from anywhere. If you are calling it from the same area code in the same country, TAPI-compliant software won't use the area code and country code (unless you specify to dial this number as a long-distance number — see the next section).

If you want to dial a number such as 911 or an extension number within your company, you shouldn't put the number in the international format. Just type it as is.

You can type phone numbers in Phone Dialer, as shown in the section entitled "Setting up speed-dial numbers" later in this chapter.

Undocumented

Dial-Up Networking and HyperTerminal connectoids automatically format phone numbers in the international format. You can change this by clearing the Use Area Code and Dialing Properties check box in any connection's Properties dialog box. To get to this check box, right-click the appropriate connectoid in the Dial-Up Networking or HyperTerminal folder window and click Properties.

If you clear the Use Area Code and Dialing Properties check box, the software sends only the phone number as you have entered it. It doesn't use any of the location properties from the Dialing Properties dialog box to format the sequence of numbers sent when you make this call.

Which local prefixes require long-distance dialing

Undocumented

Windows 98-aware communication applications assume that all phone numbers with the same local area code as your location's area code are local numbers; that is, they can be reached without dialing a 1 followed by the area code. This may not be the case, however, so you need a way of telling applications which numbers are not really local to a given location.

Windows 98 allows you to indicate which prefixes (the first three numbers of a local phone number) are long-distance numbers with respect to a given location. It assumes that any local number you enter with one of these prefixes requires the long-distance dialing rules.

To tell Windows 98 which prefixes in the area code of a given location require long-distance dialing, click the Area Code Rules button in the Dialing Properties box to display the Area Code Rules dialog box, as shown in Figure 32-5. Click the New button under When Calling within My Area Code. Enter a prefix that requires long-distance dialing, and click OK. Repeat this process for each of the prefixes you need to dial that require long-distance dialing. You can indicate whether the area code is required in addition to a 1, by marking the Always Dial the Area Code (10-Digit Dialing) check box.

Now whenever you call from that location, TAPI-compliant applications will automatically dial phone numbers with these prefixes as long-distance calls. The list of prefixes that require long-distance calls is stored in the [Locations] section of the Telephon.ini file. See the section entitled "Telephon.ini" later in this chapter to find out how to read this file.

10-digit phone numbers

You may live in an area that requires you to dial the area code and the phone number even to make a local call. In these areas, the prefix 1 is not used, and local calls may have different area codes. Go to the Dialing Properties box and click the Area Code Rules button to get to the Area Code Rules dialog box. At the top of the box, mark the Always Dial the Area Code (10-Digit Dialing) check box to enable this option.

If there are some area codes that do not require you to dial 1 first, you can enter them in the When Calling to Other Area Codes section in the lower half of the Area Code Rules dialog box. Click New to add an area code, and then click OK.

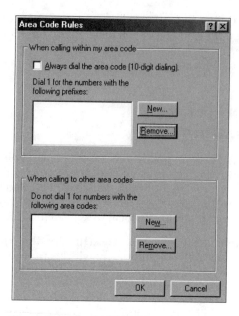

Figure 32-5: The Area Code Rules dialog box. Use it to specify prefixes that require long-distance dialing.

Using a prefix other than 1 to dial long distance

Perhaps in your location you use a number other than 1 to begin a long distance call. To configure Windows 98 for this situation, follow these steps:

STEPS

Using a Number Other Than 1 to Begin a Long Distance Call

Step 1. Click the Start button, point to Settings, and then click Control Panel. Click the Telephony icon to open the Dialing Properties dialog box.

Step 2. Click the Calling Card button. Click the New button. Type a description for the dialing method that describes these dialing rules. Click OK.

Step 3. Click the Long Distance Calls button. In the Step 1 Dial field, choose Specific Digits from the drop-down list. Type the long distance prefix for your phone system (this could be a whole string of digits if necessary—your office security code, for example) and click OK. In the Step 1 Wait For field, choose Nothing from the drop-down list.

Step 4. In the Step 2 Dial field, choose Destination Number (Including Area Code).

Step 5. Click the OK button three times.

Phone Dialer

If ever there was an application that is in fact an applet, it is Phone Dialer. This program uses your modem to dial your phone for you. You then pick up the phone and speak with the person whose number your modem dialed. Of course, the phone and the modem must be on the same phone line for this to work.

Microsoft didn't intend Phone Dialer to be a serious application. It is just an example to developers of how they can use the facilities provided by Windows 98 to create full-fledged communications applications. Unless you have a shortcut to Phone Dialer on your Desktop so that you can get at it quickly, or you have to dial a long string of numbers to place a call (as you might if you're using a calling card), you won't use Phone Dialer, because it is more work than just dialing the number on your phone.

Phone Dialer uses the information in the Dialing Properties dialog box to make phone calls. It can store up to eight phone numbers on its speed-dial buttons, and it keeps a record of the last 20 numbers you called. It can prompt you to keep a record of the phone numbers of calls coming in and/or going out. Phone Dialer is shown in Figure 32-6.

Figure 32-6: Phone Dialer. Click a speed-dial button, and Phone Dialer will dial the number for you if your modem is hooked up to your phone line.

Setting up speed-dial numbers

You can define the eight blank speed-dial buttons to dial a number when you click the button, just like on a real phone. This is the productivity benefit of Phone Dialer.

STEPS

Setting Up the Speed Dialer

Step 1.   Click the Start button, point to Programs, Accessories, Communications, and then click Phone Dialer.

Step 2.   Choose Edit, Speed Dial.

Step 3.   Click the button that you want to define in the Edit Speed Dial dialog box. Type the person's name and phone number. Repeat this step for all the buttons that you want to define.

Step 4.   Click the Save button when you are done.

Step 5.   If you want to quickly define a single blank button in Phone Dialer, just click the button, enter the person's name and phone number in the Program Speed Dial dialog box, and click Save or Save and Dial.

When you're entering numbers for the speed-dial buttons, use the international style if you want the numbers to be dialed correctly from any location.

Undocumented   The speed-dial phone numbers and the last 20 phone numbers you have dialed with Phone Dialer are stored in the Dialer.ini file in the \Windows folder. You can edit this file with Notepad if you like. Dialer.ini also stores the position of Phone Dialer on the Desktop and log book information.

One click speed dialing

Toby Nixon, a program manager in Microsoft's Internet Platform and Tools Division, replied to a question on the Windows 95 beta testing forum about whether you could use command line parameters with Phone Dialer by stating that Phone Dialer doesn't take command line parameters. However, he went on to say that you could write a little program that does take command line parameters, and then pass the parameters to Phone Dialer. He attached a little program that he wrote to do just that. We have included his program, Dial.exe, on the *Windows 98 Secrets* CD-ROM. Put it in your \Windows folder. Because it takes a phone number as a command line parameter, you can use it to dial a phone number from the Start, Run dialog box by typing a command such as **62792** or **+1 (206) 882-8080**. The number doesn't need to use the International format; it could even be an internal extension.

Tip

Better yet, you can put Dial.exe shortcuts for phone numbers you dial frequently on your Desktop or in your Start menu to make single-click dialing a reality. Find the Dial.exe icon where you put it in the \Windows folder and drag it onto the Desktop or into the \Windows\Start Menu folder to create a shortcut. Rename the shortcut with the name of the person or company you want to dial. Right-click the shortcut, click Properties, click at the end of the path in the Target field, and type a space followed by the command (phone number) you want to execute (dial). Then click OK. When you want to dial the number, just click the shortcut icon. You will be prompted to choose Talk or Hang Up.

Telephony Location Manager

A handy applet for changing dialing locations as well as getting to Phone Dialer and the Dialing Properties dialog box is the Telephony Location Manager (\Windows\System\Tlocmgr.exe). When you click Tlocmgr.exe, it puts itself in your Tray until you shut down your computer. If you would like it to always be in your Tray, put a shortcut to Tlocmgr.exe in your \Windows\Start Menu\Programs\StartUp folder.

When you click the Telephony Location Manager icon in the Tray, a list of your dialing locations appears to let you change your location without opening the Dialing Properties dialog box. When you right-click the icon, a context menu appears with options to start Phone Dialer or open the Dialing Properties box. If you are using a laptop with a docking station, this context menu may also include a HOTDOCK Properties command for changing locations automatically when you dock or undock.

Telephon.ini

The Telephon.ini file is stored in the \Windows folder. It stores data about your locations and calling cards, as well as pointers to applications that use the telephony services provided by Windows 98. Windows 98 updates the Registry based on what it finds in Telephon.ini.

In Windows 95 there were no telephony keys in the Registry; all telephony was managed by Telephon.ini. We think Telephon.ini is still probably easier to edit. However, if you prefer to edit the Registry directly, the relevant keys are HKEY_CURRENT_USER\Software\Microsoft\Windows\CurrentVersion\Telephony and HKEY_LOCAL_MACHINE\SOFTWARE\Microsoft\Windows\CurrentVersion\Telephony.

If you don't have any stored locations or calling card data, you may have a damaged or missing Telephon.ini file. You can create a new one (which will be missing your special edits) by clicking the file Tapiini.exe in the \Windows\System folder.

The sections in Telephon.ini of interest to us are [Locations] and [Cards].

Locations section

Here is an example of a line in the [Locations] section:

```
Location1=1, "Home," "9","","206",1,0,0,1,"357,847",0," "
```

Here is how to interpret the line:

Location*x*=ID, "location name", "# (number) for outside line", "# (number) for long-distance line", "area code", countrycode, card ID, previous card ID, use area codes, "LD prefixes"

These and other variables are listed in Table 32-2.

Table 32-2   Location Variables

Variable	Stands For
x	Ordered sequence of location numbers
ID	The location's identification number
location name	Your name for the location
# for outside line	The prefix you have to dial to get an outside line
# for LD line	The number you have to dial to get a long-distance line
area code	Area code
countrycode	Country code
card ID	If a calling card is used, this is its ID, otherwise it is 0 for direct dialing.
previous card ID	The previous calling card ID before its last modification
use area codes	If 1, then dial local phone numbers with prefixes listed in the LD prefixes (next variable) using the area code. This is true only in North America, only if the country code and the area code for the number being dialed are the same as the current location, and only if the prefix of the number being dialed is listed in LD prefixes. If 0, then don't include the area code before the local call number.
LD prefixes	List of prefixes that are long-distance calls from Locationx

Cards section

The [Cards] section stores the data about the calling card methods. These methods don't have to be calling cards exactly, but they can include any alternative dialing methods that can use a special phone number and/or a user code number. You can define these calling methods yourself using the methods detailed in the "Adding a long-distance carrier/method to your list" section. Here's an example:

```
Card12=1, "AT&T Direct Dial via 10ATT1","55041111938112","102881FG",
"102881FG","10288011EFG",1
```

The format of this line is as follows.

Card*x*=ID, "card name", "encrypted card", "local call", "long-distance", "international", hidden

These and other variables are shown in Table 32-3.

Table 32-3	Card Variables
Variable	**Stands For**
x	Ordered sequence of card numbers
ID	Card ID
card name	Your dialing method name
encrypted card	Your card number encrypted
local call	The dialing rules for making a local call
long-distance	The dialing rules for making a long-distance call
international	The dialing rules for making an international call
hidden 0,1,2,3	Whether or not this calling card method is displayed as an available dialing method
0	Not hidden
1	Not hidden — values can only be set up by an application
2	Hidden
3	Hidden — values can only be set up by an application

Changes in international dialing access codes

Since the original version of Windows 95 was released, the international dialing access codes (codes you dial to access international long distance) have changed for forty countries. Although these have been updated in Windows 98, it seems reasonable to expect that more country codes will change in the future. You can revise them by editing your Telephon.ini file or your Registry.

The rules for how to dial local, long distance, and international calls from any given country are also constantly changing. Windows 98 comes with updated sets of rules for the countries that have changed recently. When you install Windows 98, the updates are automatically written into the

[CountryOverrides] section of your Telephon.ini file, and consequently into your Registry. If the dialing rules change for the country you are dialing from, you will need to edit them in Telephon.ini.

Microsoft maintains a Knowledge Base article that lets you easily update your Telephon.ini file to incorporate changes in the country codes and country dialing rules. You can find it at http://premium.microsoft.com/ support/kb/articles/Q142/3/28.asp. Check the date on the Knowledge Base document to make sure it is more recent than what you already have, then copy the last part of the article into your Telephon.ini file, which is stored in the \Windows folder. You can't just add one country, since the number sequence is important; paste in the whole section instead.

Summary

We focus on how to work with the Dialing Properties dialog box to define the properties of each location you dial out from. The Dialing Properties dialog box is used by all Windows 98-aware communications applications.

▶ We show you how to define each of your dialing locations.

▶ We describe how to use calling cards or alternative dialing methods with your modem or voice calls.

▶ We show you how to tell communications applications just which local phone prefixes require long-distance dialing.

▶ We show you how to use Phone Dialer as a speed dialer.

Chapter 33

Disk Tools and File Systems

In This Chapter

Windows 98 provides powerful tools to give you lots of hard disk space while keeping your files safe and your disk fast. We discuss:

▶ Navigating through Windows to find all the tools

▶ Repairing your disks when trouble comes knocking

▶ Speeding up your disk drives

▶ Doubling the size of your hard disk and floppy drives

▶ Letting weird programs have direct disk access

▶ Setting your disk cache parameters for optimum performance

▶ Choosing from new characters in long filenames

▶ Repartitioning your drives

▶ Creating super-high-density diskettes

The Real Changes

If you want to look at the changes that have been made to the fundamentals of an operating system, look at how it works with files that are stored on disk drives. They don't call it the Disk Operating System (DOS) for nothing.

Moving from Windows 3.1x to Windows 98

If you are moving from Windows 3.1x to Windows 98, you'll notice that most of the changes Microsoft has made to the "disk operating system" affect what is under the hood — speeding up access to your hard disk, diskettes, and CD-ROM drive. Microsoft also reduced the amount of user interaction required to set obscure performance parameters — such as permanent swap files and disk cache size — while at the same time improving the performance that tuning these parameters is supposed to provide.

These advances have vastly increased the amount of available conventional memory and improved the responsiveness of your computer to multiple tasks. Compression drivers let you double (more or less) your hard disk (and diskette) space. In this section, we look at the major changes and additions since Windows 3.1x.

VFAT

In Windows for Workgroups 3.11, the Virtual File Allocation Table (VFAT) was called *32-bit file access*. You access it through the Enhanced icon in the Windows for Workgroups Control Panel. Starting with Windows 95, it's called the *32-bit protected-mode* VFAT file system. Microsoft released the prebeta version of this code when it produced Windows for Workgroups 3.11. It worked, except for numerous software and hardware incompatibilities. And it sped up read and write operations, at least when you didn't have to turn it off because of these incompatibilities.

Microsoft much improved the code in Windows 95 and 98, and it actually works reliably. It provides fast access to files. It improves multitasking by reducing the amount of time that it blocks other tasks. It is compatible with existing DOS partitions — the original FAT — on your disks as well as FAT-32 partitions. Because your processor doesn't have to switch to real-mode to read and write to the disk, everything gets faster.

In addition to providing 32-bit hard disk access, Windows 95 and 98 use VFAT to implement long filenames.

Vcache

Windows 98 comes with a 32-bit protected-mode dynamic cache. It replaces 16-bit, real-mode SmartDrive (Smartdrv.exe). Vcache doesn't take up conventional or upper memory space. It does a much better job than SmartDrive does of caching disk reads and writes. It also caches CD-ROMs and networked drives.

You don't have to specify how much memory should be set aside for Vcache (unlike SmartDrive). It sizes itself based on available free memory and disk read/write activity. (That's the dynamic part of Vcache.)

Direct CD-ROM support

No more messy ducks (Mscdex.exe) in your Autoexec.bat file or CD-ROM driver in your Config.sys file. Windows 98 provides another one of its 32-bit protected-mode drivers, CDFS (CD-ROM file system), to support CD-ROM drives. This driver replaces 16-bit real-mode Mscdex.exe that comes with Windows 3.1*x* and MS-DOS as well as the CD-ROM manufacturer's 16-bit CD-ROM driver.

You get a dynamic CD-ROM cache that works with Vcache. The driver uses no conventional or upper memory. It isn't an add-on afterthought called by a line in Config.sys. (Consequently, there is even less need for Config.sys.) CDFS is also quite a bit faster than Mscdex.exe.

Long filenames

You can type filenames up to 255 characters long. The names can include spaces. Windows 98 can read and write long filenames supported by other operating systems, such as Windows NT, NetWare, Unix, and OS/2.

Files with long filenames also have short filenames that are recognized by applications that can't handle long filenames (including DOS). Windows 98 manages these short names to ensure that only unique names are created.

The unique short filenames consist of the first six characters of the long filename, plus ~1 or additional ordinals. See the section entitled "Long Filenames" later in this chapter for details.

Windows 98-based disk tools

Windows 3.1x required that you quit Windows and go to DOS if you needed to work directly with your disk drive at a low level. While you can still do this, it's a lot harder to "get out of" Windows 98.

Windows 98 comes with very powerful Windows-based disk tools that help you manage and protect your files. ScanDisk finds and repairs problems with your disks. Defrag makes your files contiguous. These are both Windows 98 programs, although you can also run ScanDisk from DOS and in batch files.

Compression disk drivers

Windows 98 comes with a 32-bit protected-mode compression disk driver that works with both DoubleSpace and DriveSpace disks. Instead of taking 50K of conventional memory, it is loaded into extended memory (except in MS-DOS mode).

You can approximately double your disk space with, in many cases, minimal or no loss of file-access speed. You can also approximately double the room available on your diskettes.

Built-in SCSI hard disk support

Earlier versions of DOS and Windows didn't support SCSI drives without special drivers from hardware manufacturers that you loaded in Config.sys. Windows 98 has built-in support for SCSI devices.

Installable File System Manager

Both the VFAT and the CDFS are installable file systems managed by the Windows 98 Installable File System Manager. You can add other file systems, and you will if you connect your computer to network servers. Windows 98 can manage multiple file systems, which makes it much easier to connect to many different networks at once.

Windows 98 doesn't support HPFS (high performance file system), which is native to OS/2, or NTFS (the Windows NT file system) on local hard disks, but it does over a network.

Dynamically sized swap file

Virtual memory no longer requires a permanent swap file for the fastest operation. Windows 98 can dynamically size the required swap file. This cuts down on the user decisions required to optimize Windows. The swap file can even be on a compressed drive without incurring a performance hit.

Support for enhanced IDE devices

Windows 98 supports the enhanced IDE (EIDE) specification, so it can handle drives larger than 1GB directly. In fact, Windows 98 supports EIDE hard disks as large as 137GB.

Windows 98 also supports IDE-based CD-ROMs. You can hook these drives to the existing IDE card used by your hard disk without buying a separate SCSI card to support the CD-ROM.

Multitasked floppy drive formatting

No longer does everything grind to a halt while you format a diskette. A Windows 98 32-bit driver handles multitasked access to your floppy drives.

Moving from Windows 95 to Windows 98

While the file system tools new with Windows 98 are less fundamental than those introduced with Windows 95, they are significant, especially for users with larger disks.

FAT 32

Windows 98's 32-bit File Allocation Table (FAT 32) allows a single hard drive letter (partition) to be larger than 2 gigabytes in size. (This was a limitation of FAT 16, the 16-bit file system used in previous versions of Windows and DOS.) FAT 32 also stores files without the 30 percent or so of wasted space typical of older 2GB FAT-16 drives, because it supports cluster sizes of 4K (instead of 32K for 2GB drives) and up to 8GB partitions.

The fixed cluster size of 4K for FAT-32 volumes up to 8GB in size results in an average of 4 percent slack. The much higher slack percentages for large FAT-16 volumes of different sizes are provided in Table 33-1.

As you can see from the table, FAT-32 greatly reduces the amount of wasted space on large hard disk drives relative to FAT-16. Now that standard hard disk drives are greater than 2GB, Microsoft had to come out with a FAT that could handle the large drives without excessive wasted space.

Table 33-1   FAT 16 Partition Size Versus Slack

Cluster Size	Maximum Partition Size (FAT 16)	Slack
2K	128MB	2%
4K	256MB	4%
8K	512MB	8%
16K	1024MB (1GB)	16%
32K	2048MB (2GB)	32%

DriveSpace 3

Windows 98 adds a higher level of disk compression with its DriveSpace 3 utility for computers with 486 or faster processors. DriveSpace 3, which previously was available on the Microsoft Plus! CD-ROM, compresses files (quite often at a ratio greater than 2.5-to-1) to free up more room on your hard disk. The file volumes can be up to 2GB in size. DriveSpace 3 does not work with FAT-32 volumes. It can recognize the drives, but will not compress them.

The real-mode DriveSpace 3 driver that loads in MS-DOS mode is too large to fit in UMBs. This does make it difficult to run many DOS programs that require significant amounts of conventional memory in MS-DOS mode. We discuss how to get around this in "Handling the DriveSpace 3 driver in memory" in Chapter 35.

You can use a Windows 98 utility called Compression Agent to schedule compression, error scanning, and defragging to take place during idle times. Compression Agent is a part of the Windows 98 Task Scheduler.

Disk Defragmenter Optimization Wizard

The new Disk Defragmenter Optimization Wizard automatically tracks the programs that you use most often. The Wizard arranges program files in the order that they are accessed when a program starts, allowing the program to start more quickly.

Direct memory access to drives

Direct Memory Access (DMA) for hard drives and CD-ROM drives enables your PC to directly access data on an IDE drive or CD-ROM drive without using CPU time. IDE controllers that support *bus-mastering*, the ability to take over traffic control on the hardware bus, have their own processors that can handle most of the work. This makes access times faster and saves CPU time for other multitasking purposes.

Hiding drives with TweakUI

You can use TweakUI to modify the list of drives that show up in your Explorer or My Computer window. Click your TweakUI shortcut on your Desktop (or the TweakUI icon in the Control Panel), click the My Computer tab, and mark or clear your drive letters. Hidden host drives (see "Disk Compression" later in this chapter) won't show up whether they are marked here or not.

This is a per-user setting, so if you have multiple users, you'll either have to use TweakUI for every user, or use the System Policy Editor to globally restrict access to some drives. (See the "System Policy Editor" section in Chapter 24.)

Finding Your Disks and the Disk Tools

You've got to be able to find the disk tools if you're going to use them. Fortunately, you can easily reach this collection of programs through several different routes.

The Start button

The easiest way to find the disk tools is to click the Start button, point to Programs, then Accessories, and finally click System Tools. If you haven't edited your Start menu, the System Tools submenu will contain Disk Defragmenter, ScanDisk, Scheduled Tasks, System Information, and DriveSpace, as well as Backup, System Monitor, and Net Watcher, if you installed them.

A drive icon

Another way to display the disk tools that is almost as easy, is to click My Computer, right-click one of the hard drive icons, click Properties, and then click the Tools tab. Windows 98 displays the dialog box shown in Figure 33-1. You have access to ScanDisk, Backup, Disk Defragmenter, and Compression. You can right-click any drive icon in any folder or Explorer window and click Properties to get to this Tools tab.

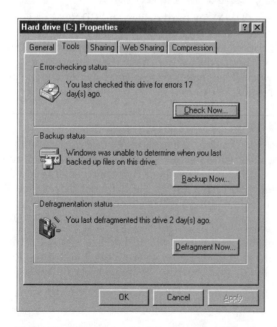

Figure 33-1: The Tools tab of the Properties dialog box for a hard drive. Click Check Now to launch ScanDisk, Backup Now to launch Backup, or Defragment Now to launch the Disk Defragmenter. Click the Compression tab to check or start disk compression.

Using help

There are many ways you can access the disk tools through shortcuts in the help system. Click the Start button, click Help, and then try any of the following:

- Click the Using Windows Accessories book in the Contents tab of the Windows Help dialog box, and then click System Tools. You now have numerous options for reaching various disk tools. Backup, Compression Agent, Disk Defragmenter, DriveSpace, FAT32 Converter, and ScanDisk are among the options. All of these help pages have shortcuts to the utilities.

- Click Troubleshooting in the Contents tab. Then click Windows 98 Troubleshooters, and click DriveSpace. This starts a series of questions that will help you troubleshoot DriveSpace problems.

- Click the Index tab in the Windows Help dialog box. Type **disk**. You again have access to the disk tools under disk compression, Disk Defragmenter, disk errors, and disk space.

In a DOS window

You can type **Scandisk**, **Defrag**, or **Drvspace** in a DOS window. Each of these commands invokes the Windows 98 graphical version of these programs. You can run Windows programs from your DOS window.

Tip

If you type **Scandisk /?** in a DOS window and press Enter, you'll see the following instructions for finding the section of the Windows 98 help system that tells you how to use command line parameters with ScanDisk:

```
For information about the command-line parameters supported by
ScanDisk for Windows, look up 'checking for errors, in disks' in the
Windows Help index. Then view the topic 'Checking your disk for errors
every time your computer starts.'
```

The instructions that are printed in the DOS window are a bit out of date. You should look for "checking for disk errors," instead. Then click "To check for disk errors when your computer starts."

You can run a DOS 7.1 version of ScanDisk from MS-DOS mode or from the DOS command prompt before Windows 98 starts. You can't run Disk Defragmenter or DriveSpace in MS-DOS mode.

Device Manager

The Device Manager lets you look at the basic resources used by your devices, including your disk drives and controller card(s). You can get to the Device Manager (a tab in the System Properties dialog box) in at least two ways:

- Right-click My Computer, click Properties, and then click the Device Manager tab.

- Click the Start button, point to Settings, and then click Control Panel. Click the System icon and choose the Device Manager tab.

Once you're in the Device Manager, click the plus signs next to the icons labeled Disk Drives, Floppy Disk Controllers, or Hard Disk Controllers. Highlight the controller or drive name that is displayed, click the Properties button, and then click the Resources tab. The resources used by an IDE hard disk controller are shown in Figure 33-2.

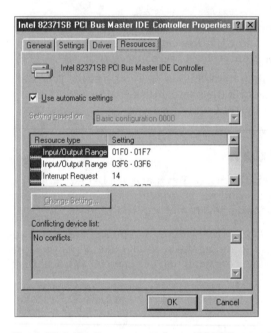

Figure 33-2: The Resources tab for an IDE/ESDI controller.

File system performance

The Performance tab of the System Properties dialog box lets you disable all sorts of 32-bit file access settings as well as optimize your disk caching scheme.

Use the same steps to get to the System Properties dialog box as described in the preceding section, but click the Performance tab instead of the Device Manager tab. Click the File System button to display the File System Properties dialog box, as shown in Figure 33-3.

To see how to optimize file system performance, turn to the "Setting disk cache parameters" section of this chapter.

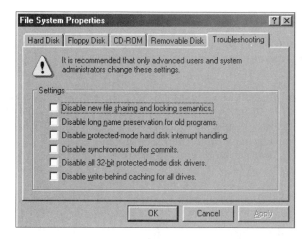

Figure 33-3: The Troubleshooting tab of the File System Properties dialog box.

Virtual memory performance

Windows 98 can manage your swap file without any input from you. If you want to change its location and set a minimum or maximum size, you can do so.

Use the same steps to get to the System Properties dialog box as described in the earlier section entitled "Device Manager," but click the Performance tab instead of the Device Manager tab. Click the Virtual Memory button to display the Virtual Memory dialog box, as shown in Figure 33-4. See the "Managing Your Swap Space" section of this chapter to learn about changing your swap file size.

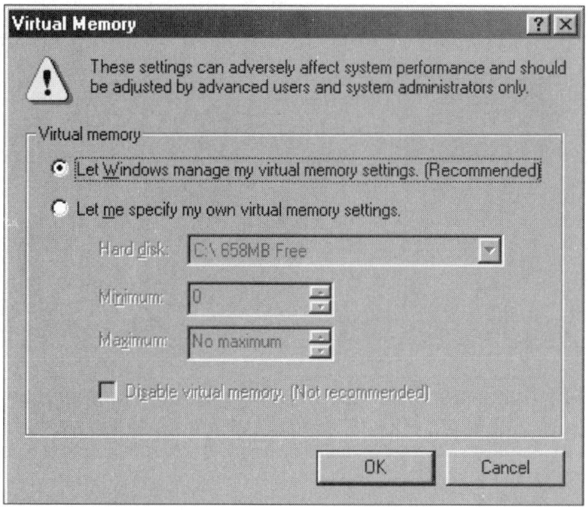

Figure 33-4: The Virtual Memory dialog box.

System Monitor

You can use System Monitor to track how your hard disks (or hard disks on other computers on your network) are being used to supply virtual memory to your operating system. You'll find System Monitor in the Start menu.

Click the Start button, point to Programs, Accessories, System Tools, and then click System Monitor. It won't be there unless you did a custom installation of Windows 98 and specifically chose to install it. You can use the Add/Remove Programs icon in the Control Panel to add it. Click the Windows Setup tab, and look under System Tools.

STEPS

Using System Monitor to Evaluate Virtual Memory Performance

Step 1.   Configure System Monitor to display graphs for Allocated Memory, Disk Cache Size, Swapfile in Use, Swapfile Size, Swappable Memory, and Unused Physical Memory, as shown in Figure 33-5. To do this, choose Edit, Add Item, highlight Memory Manager, select the six items in the list on the right, and click OK. (To select all of the items at once, click the first one, and then Ctrl+click the remaining ones.) Use Edit, Remove Item to take out any other graphs. Once you've got System Monitor's six graphs sized the way you want, choose View, mark Always on Top, and then close System Monitor.

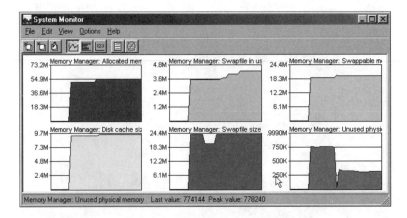

Figure 33-5: The System Monitor showing Allocated Memory, Disk Cache Size, Swapfile in Use, Swapfile Size, Swappable Memory, and Unused Physical Memory.

Step 2.   Temporarily stop unnecessary programs in your StartUp folder from loading at startup. Click your Start button, Programs,

Accessories, System Tools, System Information. Choose Tools, System Configuration Utility. Click the Startup tab and clear all the check boxes of the startup applications. If you really need a certain program to run, don't clear its check box. Click OK.

You can also click the Win.ini tab, click the plus sign next to [windows], and see if there are any programs called on the load= or run= lines. You can clear these check boxes. The same is true for any load= or run= lines in the Autoexec.bat and Config.sys tabs.

Step 3. Once you've lightened up your StartUp group and other files, click OK, close the Microsoft System Information window, and restart Windows.

Step 4. Immediately after Window 98 has finished loading, click Start, Programs, Accessories, System Tools, System Monitor.

Step 5. After System Monitor loads, start your favorite large application, perhaps your word processor or spreadsheet program, and open a data file within it. Then start another program, and then another. Write down the number of minutes and seconds that elapse while loading these applications and data files. If you have a certain long routine you often run, such as sorting a database or recalculating a spreadsheet, do that as soon as you have the necessary application running.

Step 6. Close all of the applications you opened in step 5, and then reopen the same programs and documents again, writing down the elapsed time now that your system's disk cache (usually Windows 98's own disk cache) contains some of the applications and files.

Armed with these times and the graphs in System Monitor, you're ready do a little interpretation. Here's how to read what each of the graphs means to your system:

- **Allocated Memory** is a combination of Free Memory, Swapfile Size, and Disk Cache Size, among other uses of memory by applications and DLLs. When this chart rises above the amount of physical memory (RAM) you have installed, you know that Windows 98 is swapping some code or data out of main memory and onto disk storage, which is much slower.

- **Disk Cache Size** is a visual indication of Windows 98's dynamic disk cache. Windows 98 tries to determine the optimum size for the cache. (Sometimes a smaller cache can be just as effective as a larger one, because more RAM is available to the operating system for its needs when the cache is smaller.)

- **Swapfile in Use** refers to the amount of the Windows swap file that contains parts of programs that have been moved from memory into hard disk space. When Swapfile in Use starts going up, it means that Windows can't hold everything in its faster RAM space. When this happens, your performance will start to go down.

- **Swapfile Size** reports on the physical size of the Windows 98 swap file. Not all of this is still being used.

- **Swappable Memory** is the amount of memory Windows *can* swap from disk to memory, or vice versa, if it needs to. You should see Swappable Memory rising as each new application is loaded.

- **Unused Physical Memory** is memory that isn't currently occupied by a program or data. As you load each program you should see Unused Physical Memory reduced, until it approaches zero.

SuperMonitor

Gary Tessler of TNT (Tessler's Nifty Tools) has developed a replacement for System Monitor. It's called SuperMonitor, and it displays different resources in separate windows. You can use it to determine usage by individual applications.

To determine an application's memory usage with SuperMonitor, you start a window on memory and then stop that window's monitoring. (This "freezes" the figures.) Then start your application and open another SuperMonitor window. The difference between the two readings is the amount of memory used by the application or any combination of applications you choose.

SuperMonitor can display continuous, average, or maximum values in different windows. You can set the timing interval SuperMonitor uses, and you can log the figures to a disk file.

You'll find the latest version of SuperMonitor at http://ourworld.compuserve. com/homepages/nifty_tools/tnt.htm.

WinTop

One of Windows' endearing little habits is to periodically take over your system for no apparent reason. Seemingly out of the blue, Windows will spin your hard disk, make an odd sound, or generally do something that you're sure you didn't actually command it to do.

You can use a free little tool called WinTop to help track down the cause. Microsoft gives away this handy utility with its downloadable Kernel Toys package. Point your browser at http://www.microsoft.com/windows/ windows95/info/kerneltoys.htm.

WinTop reveals the percentage of your CPU time that is being used by various programs, threads, and processes. It displays the name of each task and updates its usage figures every two seconds. WinTop is modeled after a Unix utility named Top (hence the name WinTop). WinTop is also very similar to the Processes tab in Windows NT 4.0.

You can put WinTop on top of other applications by clicking View, Always On Top in the WinTop window. After doing this, run a few of your applications. You may be surprised at the amount of CPU time some of them consume when they are "doing nothing." To use WinTop to kill a process, select a program in WinTop's display, and then choose Process, Properties. Select the Priority tab, and then click the Terminate Process Now button.

Monitoring WinTop while you *aren't* running any of your application programs may be even more enlightening. Processes you didn't even know you were running may "wake up" and take over most or all of your CPU time—causing those lock-ups that mystify so many Windows users.

Disk Tools

You use ScanDisk and Disk Defragmenter to fix your hard disks, diskettes, and other removable media (not CD-ROMs) when your files get corrupted or are stored in too many pieces. If parts of the surface of your hard disk are bad, ScanDisk marks them so files won't be stored there. ScanDisk also moves the data off of these spots if it can.

ScanDisk

ScanDisk does an excellent job of analyzing your hard disk and repairing errors. Microsoft has taken great pains to make sure it works under all circumstances.

ScanDisk reviews and repairs errors on compressed drives as well as on physical drives. It repairs problems with long filenames, the FAT and FAT 32, the directory and file structure, the drive surface, and the internal structure of compressed volume files (CVFs). It can find and fix errors on diskettes and hard drives, and, as if you really cared, RAM drives and memory cards that are treated as drives.

ScanDisk can find and repair problems on both DriveSpace and DoubleSpace drives (but not on Stacker or SuperStor drives). The CVFs don't have to be mounted (have a drive letter associated with them) for ScanDisk to work with them, although in most cases they will be.

ScanDisk can't find or fix errors on CD-ROMs, networked drives, or pseudo drives created by using Assign, Subst, Join, or Interlnk (all of these are DOS commands).

If one of your applications reports disk problems when reading a file, run ScanDisk immediately to repair the file. If Windows 98 crashes while you are editing a file and the file is damaged, it is very likely that ScanDisk can fix it.

ScanDisk options

As stated earlier in this chapter, you can start ScanDisk by right-clicking a drive icon in a folder or Explorer window, choosing Properties, clicking the Tools tab, and then clicking the Check Now button. If you do this, you are presented with a ScanDisk dialog box containing buttons labeled Options and Advanced, as shown in Figure 33-6.

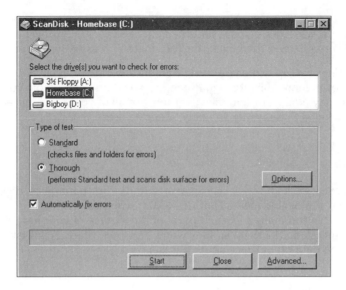

Figure 33-6: The ScanDisk dialog box.

To find out what all these buttons do, take the following steps:

STEPS

Exploring ScanDisk Options

Step 1.   Start ScanDisk and mark the Thorough option button (see Figure 33-6), and then click the Options button.

Step 2.   Right-click any item in the Surface Scan Options dialog box. Click the What's This? button to see what the option really does.

Step 3.   Click the Cancel button in the Surface Scan Options dialog box, and then click the Advanced button.

Step 4.   Right-click any item in the ScanDisk Advanced Options dialog box, and click What's This? to learn more about what it does. Click the Cancel button when you're done.

One advanced option that doesn't respond to a right-click is Report MS-DOS Mode Name Length Errors. Windows 98 allows paths of more than 66 characters. MS-DOS does not. If you have paths that exceed 66 characters, you will experience error messages when you run any of the other disk utilities discussed in this chapter and they call ScanDisk. The error messages occur frequently if you have set up user profiles, because user profiles automatically create long paths.

Clearing this field allows ScanDisk to automatically correct any problems in any folder, no matter how long the path. In Windows 95, you had to manually move the folders in the paths to allow ScanDisk to work automatically without stopping.

ScanDisk command line parameters

You can run ScanDisk from a Windows DOS prompt. You may want to add some command line parameters to the command line of the shortcut. (Right-click the shortcut, choose Properties, click the Shortcut tab, and type the command line in the Target field.)

ScanDisk can take the following parameters:

```
Scandisk {x:} {options}
```

or

```
Scandisk x:\drvspace.nnn
```

or

```
Scandisk x:\dblspace.nnn
```

x: is the drive letter for the drive you want to check. It can be the drive letter assigned to a compressed volume file.

ScanDisk can take the following options:

/all or /a	Checks all your local, nonremovable hard disks
/noninteractive or /n	Starts and finishes ScanDisk without user input
/preview or /p	Prevents ScanDisk from correcting errors that it finds
dblspace.nnn	Name of compressed volume file (CVF) to check
drvspace.nnn	Name of compressed volume file (CVF) to check

Hidden CVFs reside on host drives and are named by their type of compression (DoubleSpace or DriveSpace) and a number (*nnn*) as the file extension. If you want to scan an unmounted compressed drive, include dblspace.*nnn* or drvspace.*nnn* on the command line. The drive letter in this case would be the host drive letter.

Running ScanDisk from DOS

Undocumented

There are really two ScanDisk programs, Scandskw.exe and Scandisk.exe. The Windows 98 version is Scandskw.exe, an executable stub, which calls code located in the dynamic link libraries Shell.dll and Dskmaint.dll.

Scandskw.exe is called when you click the Check Now button in the Tools tab of the Properties dialog box for a hard drive, or ScanDisk in the System Tools submenu of the Start menu. It is also called when you type **Scandisk** at a DOS prompt in a Windows DOS session. You can also type **Scandskw** at the command prompt in a Windows DOS session, although there is one exception to this. If you type a command of the form **Scandisk C:/dblspace.000** in a Windows DOS session, the DOS version of ScanDisk is executed because the Windows version works only with mounted drives.

If you boot your computer to the DOS command prompt, exit Windows to MS-DOS mode, or start an MS-DOS mode session, type **Scandisk** at the DOS command prompt to run the DOS version of ScanDisk. If you dual boot into your previous version of DOS, you can still run the DOS 7.1 (Windows 98) version of ScanDisk, as long is it isn't stored on a FAT-32 partition. This comes in handy when you are setting up Windows 98.

The command line parameters available for the DOS real-mode version of ScanDisk are much different than those for the Windows version. To see what they are, click Start, Shut Down, Restart in MS-DOS mode, OK, and then type **scandisk /?**.

Scandisk.ini

Undocumented

Scandisk.ini, the ScanDisk configuration file, is stored in your \Windows\ Command folder. This file works only with the DOS version of ScanDisk and is not used if you run ScanDisk from Windows or from a Windows DOS session.

Scandisk.ini is internally well documented, and you can edit it to change the way the DOS version of ScanDisk operates. In Windows, just click it to open it. In MS-DOS mode, open it with Edit.com, and you will find plenty of documentation explaining how to change ScanDisk's parameters.

ScanDisk and your file allocation tables

Undocumented

The DOS version of ScanDisk always uses the primary copy of your File Allocation Table (unless it finds a physical disk error). The primary File Allocation Table replaces the backup File Allocation Table when ScanDisk repairs errors.

The Windows 98 version of ScanDisk checks both of your file allocation tables, and, if they are out of sync, determines which File Allocation Table is "better" and uses that one.

ScanDisk and Setup

The DOS version of ScanDisk is run automatically when you run Windows 98 Setup. If you start Setup from the DOS prompt, you can see ScanDisk; otherwise, it is hidden behind a Windows face. If ScanDisk finds problems with your hard disk, you can fix them before you continue with the setup process.

If you run Setup from Windows 3.1x and there are problems, exit Setup and run the DOS 7.1 version of ScanDisk from the DOS prompt.

Setup runs ScanDisk to put everything in order and to cut down on the number of variables before you install this very complex operating system. ScanDisk is discussed in more detail in "Running ScanDisk" in Chapter 2.

Defrag, the disk defragmenter

As you probably know, DOS and Windows (all versions) don't necessarily keep the contents of your files stored in contiguous sectors of your hard disk. Your files become more fragmented as they are rewritten, and fragmented files take longer to read and write. You can speed up disk access by occasionally defragmenting the files on your hard disk.

Defrag is a Windows program. You can run it from the DOS prompt in a Windows DOS session, but unlike ScanDisk, you can't run it in an MS-DOS mode session.

You can run Defrag while you are running other programs. Disk reads and writes interrupt the defragmentation process, but Defrag is always operating and continues to defragment where it left off, after the read or write is complete.

Tip

If you find that Defrag is restarting often, you may be running another program that is making frequent writes to the disk. Try quitting other programs while Defrag is running. If you are running the Microsoft Office Find Fast utility (which indexes files in the background), you may need to pause Find Fast while Defrag runs. To do this, click Start, Settings, Control Panel, and click the Find Fast icon. From the Index menu, select Pause Indexing.

Defrag in Details view

Defrag is a fun program to watch if you put it into Details view. Here's how:

STEPS

Running Defrag in Details View

Step 1.   Click the Start button, point to Programs, Accessories, System Tools, and then click Disk Defragmenter.

Step 2.   In the Select Drive dialog box, display the drop-down list to show the available drives. You can defrag your floppies if you want to (but why?). Highlight the hard drive that you want to defragment (or select All Hard Drives to defragment all of them), and click OK.

Step 3.   Click the Start button in the Disk Defragmenter dialog box, click the Show Details button, and then click the Legend button. The Defrag Legend dialog box appears on top of the Defragmenting window, which contains rows and rows of little colored squares that represent disk clusters (see Figure 33-7).

(continued)

STEPS *(continued)*

Running Defrag in Details View

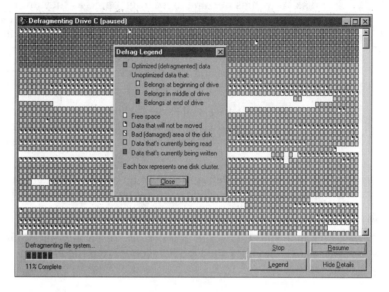

Figure 33-7: The disk defragmenter in Details view with the Defrag Legend showing.

Showing details slows down the defragmentation process a little, but what you lose in speed you make up for in visual interest.

Before you click the Start button in the Disk Defragmenter dialog box, you can choose how extensive you want the defragmentation process to be. To see these options, click the Advanced button. To find out what each option does, right-click the text next to each option and click the What's This? button.

Disk Defragmenter Optimization Wizard settings

A feature that's new with Windows 98 is the Disk Defragmenter Optimization Wizard. Task Monitor is automatically loaded when you start Windows. Task Monitor checks which programs you are running and directs Disk Defragmenter when it defragments your disk to place the most used programs in the spot on your hard disk where they will get loaded the fastest.

To access the few settings available for this Wizard, click the Settings button in the Select Drive dialog box.

Data that will not be moved

Secret

You may notice that some or many sectors on your hard disk are marked "Data that will not be moved" in the Details view of the Defragmenting window. Defrag doesn't move files that are marked *both* hidden and system. Some copy protection schemes put a file or two in certain locations and mark them as both system and hidden. If they are moved, the copy protection scheme fails.

Defrag takes the conservative approach. In reality, almost all files that are marked both system and hidden are, in fact, not related to any copy protection schemes. Windows 98 marks many of its files as both system and hidden. Of course, they are easy enough to see in a folder or Explorer window, so they are not really all that hidden.

If you have a CVF on a host drive, it will probably appear as a large block of contiguous sectors and will be marked as "Data that will not be moved." If you view the compressed drive itself, you'll see that data in these clusters can indeed be moved. Both views are right.

The CVF shouldn't be moved, and you can defragment the files within it by defragmenting the compressed drive directly.

Secret

Your dynamically sized swap file is also marked as unable to be moved, but it doesn't have the hidden or system attribute.

You can have Defrag move the files marked both system and hidden by changing their attributes. You (not Defrag) are taking the responsibility for the consequences.

To remove the system and hidden attributes from a file, type the following command at any DOS prompt:

```
attrib -s -h {drive:\pathname\filename}
```

Unfortunately, the Windows 98 Find dialog box doesn't let you collect all the files that have a certain attribute turned on (or off). If it did, you could search for all the files with the attributes system and hidden, and decide for yourself whether to turn these attributes off for each file displayed in the Find dialog box.

If you want to find out more about the attrib command, type **attrib/?** at the DOS prompt.

It's very important to reset any CVFs back to hidden and system so that they are not moved by Defrag. To do this, type the following command at the DOS prompt:

```
attrib +s +h c:\Drvspace.nnn
```

or

```
attrib +s +h c:\Dblspace.nnn
```

In the preceding command line, *nnn* is the number of the CVF volume.

DOS 6.*x* versions of Defrag would not move files if they were marked either hidden or system or both. The Windows 98 Defrag is a little less reluctant to move files.

Never use earlier versions of Defrag from MS-DOS 6.*x* because they will destroy long filenames.

Tip

The disk defragmenter will not work with Stacker or SuperStor compressed drives. If you have these types of compressed drives, get a third-party disk defragmenter program, such as the one included in Symantec's Norton Utilities for Windows 98. You also can't use Defrag over a network. It has real trouble with CD-ROMs, which are read-only. Don't try it on drives that are created by Assign, Subst, or Join.

You can run Defrag on the host drive and/or on the compressed drive if you have DoubleSpace or DriveSpace drives.

Defrag command line parameters

If you run Defrag from a DOS prompt, from the Run dialog box (Start, Run), from a batch file, or from a shortcut, you can change the way it runs by adding command line parameters.

```
Defrag {x: or /all} {options} {/noprompt} {/concise or /detailed}
```

The command line parameters are as follows:

`x:`	Drive letter designator for drive to be defragmented
`/all`	Defragment all local, nonremovable drives
`{options}`	
`/f`	Defragment files and free space
`/u`	Defragment files only
`/q`	Defragment free space only
`/noprompt`	Do not display confirmation message boxes
`/concise`	Don't show the Details view (this is the default)
`/detailed`	Show the Details view

Disk-Related Functions

Numerous commands and functions affect the drive performance and file-access speed.

Disk space

When you select a folder in the left pane of the Explorer, the status bar displays the total size of the files stored in the folder. It also lists the amount of free space available on the drive partition that contains the highlighted folder.

Another way to find the size and available disk space on a particular drive is to take the following steps:

STEPS

Displaying Disk Size

Step 1. Click My Computer.

Step 2. Right-click a drive icon, and then click Properties.

These steps display the General tab of the Properties dialog box for the selected drive, as shown in Figure 33-8.

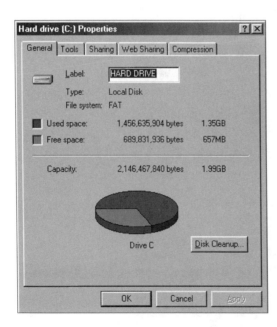

Figure 33-8: The General tab of the Properties dialog box for a hard drive. You can type a new name for the disk in the Label field.

If you are viewing your folder or Explorer window as a web page (right-click the client area, and click View, As Web Page), you can place your mouse pointer over a hard disk icon to display the disk size and amount of used and free space.

Click the Disk Cleanup button to access a few utilities that identify files you can delete from your hard disk.

Disk Cleanup

Disk Cleanup adds up the space that you could reclaim by deleting some temporary files. After it searches your disk for these files, it displays the Disk Cleanup tab of the Disk Cleanup dialog box. Just mark the check boxes for the categories that you want to remove.

Click the More Options tab to find other ways to access the Drive Converter (FAT32) and the Add/Remove Programs utility.

File size and attributes

The status bar of the Explorer (or any folder window) tells you the size of the files you have highlighted or, if you have highlighted a folder in the left pane, the number and total size of all the files in the folder.

Right-click a file in an Explorer or folder window and click Properties to display the General tab of the file's Properties dialog box, as shown in Figure 33-9. This tab tells you the size of the file as well as its attributes (Read-Only, Archive, Hidden, System).

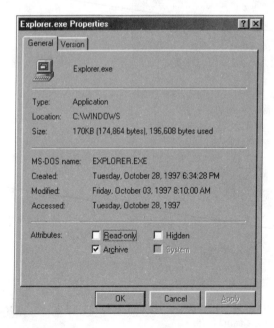

Figure 33-9: The General tab of a file's Properties dialog box. You can change a file's attributes by marking or clearing the Attributes check boxes.

If you select a folder, or a group of files and then right-click the group (or the folder icon) and choose Properties, the General tab shows the total size of all the files. This is handy if you are dragging these files to your floppy disk drive. The total size of the selected files is also displayed in the status bar of the Explorer or folder window.

Undocumented

Do you want to know the total size of all the files on a hard disk? Take the following steps:

STEPS

Finding the Total Size of All Files on a Disk

Step 1.   Highlight a drive icon in the left pane of an Explorer window.

Step 2.   Highlight the top entry in the right pane.

Step 3.   Scroll down the right pane, and Shift+right-click the last entry.

Step 4.   Click Properties.

The total number of files and their accumulated size will be displayed. It may take a few seconds to count all the files.

Format

You can format a hard disk, diskette, or other removable media by right-clicking the icon representing the drive in either a folder or Explorer window and choosing Format from the context menu.

Undocumented

You can't format a compressed diskette in this manner. If you try to format the compressed volume or the host drive, you'll receive error messages. If you want to format such a diskette, you'll need to uncompress it first (which may require that you erase the files on it).

You can format a compressed drive using DriveSpace. See the "Other DriveSpace options" section later in this chapter for details.

Thankfully, clicking Format in the context menu does not immediately begin the formatting process. You're given the opportunity to determine some format parameters. If you accidentally click Format after you right-click your boot drive, you will have a chance to back out.

Diskcopy

Tip

Do you want to make a copy of a diskette? Put the diskette in the diskette drive, click My Computer, right-click the diskette drive icon, and then click Copy Disk.

Sharing

If you are on a network (even if you just have Direct Cable Connection installed), you can give other computers access to files on your disk drives. To share access to all the files on a drive, right-click the drive icon in a folder or Explorer window, and click Sharing in the context menu to display the Sharing tab shown in Figure 33-10.

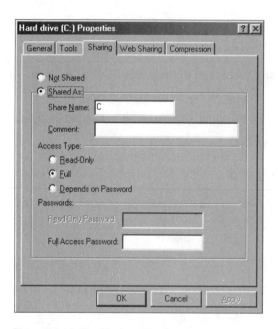

Figure 33-10: The Sharing tab of the Properties dialog box for a hard disk drive. Choose the Shared As option button to share your drive with other computers on the network.

Secret

If you place a $ as the last character in a folder's share name, you create a hidden share. The remote user must know the full UNC name for the hidden folder in order to access it.

Recycle Bin size

Just because you delete a file doesn't mean it is gone. The files sit in your Recycle Bin, taking up disk space until you empty it. The free space on your disk doesn't increase until you empty the trash. (An exception to this is if you right-click the Recycle Bin on the Desktop, choose Properties, and mark the check box labeled Do Not Move Files to the Recycle Bin. Remove Files Immediately When Deleted.)

If you like, you can adjust the maximum amount of space the Recycle Bin can occupy on your drive(s). By default, the maximum size is set to 10 percent of each drive. To change this setting, right-click the Recycle Bin on the Desktop and choose Properties. If you want to use the same size setting on each drive, mark the Use One Setting for All Drives option button, and drag the slider on the Global tab. If you prefer to set different maximum sizes for each of your drives, mark the Configure Drives Independently option button, and then use the tabs for each drive to configure the maximum Recycle Bin size on each drive individually.

Testing direct memory access to drives

In order to take advantage of direct memory access (DMA), your computer must have a bus-mastering IDE drive. However, not all IDE drives are compliant with bus mastering. To see if yours is, set your browser to a Microsoft document at http://premium.microsoft.com/support/kb/articles/ q159/5/60. Run the test recommended in this article to see if your IDE components support bus mastering. You must have the Windows 98 drivers for IDE controllers installed.

Once you've determined that your hardware supports DMA, you must turn this feature on with a little-known switch in the Control Panel. Click the System icon, click the Device Manager tab, and then click the plus sign next to Disk Drives. Select the drive for which you want to enable DMA, click Properties, and then click the Settings tab and mark the DMA check box. You must restart Windows for the change to take effect.

If your system doesn't support DMA or you aren't using the bus-mastering drivers that are included with Windows 98, the DMA check box won't appear. Some third-party drivers that enable bus mastering also don't display a DMA check box, because DMA is always on and can't be disabled.

Chkdsk /f

Chkdsk (Check disk) is an outdated DOS command that deletes bad files when you specify the /f parameter. It doesn't work anymore in a Windows DOS session, and you should instead use ScanDisk to fix files or the DOS command Mem to give you a memory usage breakdown. You can use it in MS-DOS mode.

Troubleshooting disk access

Even though the 32-bit disk and file access provided by Windows 98 is much better than what came with Windows for Workgroups 3.11, there may still be incompatibilities. You can turn off various portions of the disk driver to track down problems with disk access. To get to these troubleshooting options, take the following steps:

Troubleshooting Disk Access

Step 1.   Right-click My Computer. Choose Properties, and click the
Performance tab.

Step 2.   Click the File System button.

Step 3.   Click the Troubleshooting tab.

Disk Compression

Windows 98 supports two versions of disk compression: DriveSpace and
DoubleSpace. They are slightly different because of a legal settlement with
Stac Electronics, the manufacturer of Stacker disk compression software.
Windows 98 creates DriveSpace compressed drives.

Windows 98 includes DriveSpace 3, an upgrade to DriveSpace compression,
and the Compression Agent, which gives you even higher levels of
compression, as well as control over which files are compressed to what
levels when. Unlike the compression schemes that came with Windows 95,
DriveSpace 3 lets you create compressed volume files as large as 2GB.
DriveSpace 3 cannot compress FAT-32 formatted drives or partitions.

Starting with Windows 95, Microsoft has provided a unified driver that
handles both DoubleSpace and DriveSpace. The files Dblspace.bin and
Drvspace.bin, the disk compression drivers in the root directory of your
host drive, are exactly the same.

Undocumented

You shouldn't erase either Drvspace.bin or Dblspace.bin. Only Drvspace.bin
is needed for drives you compressed while running Windows 98.
Dblspace.bin (which is the same as Drvspace.bin but with a different name)
is used when you mount old volume files compressed with DoubleSpace,
such as when you place a DoubleSpace diskette in your diskette drive.

When you start your computer, either Dblspace.bin or Drvspace.bin is
loaded in conventional memory if you have a mounted compressed drive.
Once Windows 98 starts, the real-mode D??space.bin driver is unloaded, the
conventional memory is reclaimed, and the 32-bit driver takes over.

Windows 98 can work with five disk compression schemes: DoubleSpace,
DriveSpace, Stacker, SuperStor, and AddStor. Microsoft provides 32-bit
drivers for DoubleSpace and DriveSpace compressed drives. You can use the
existing Stacker or SuperStor real-mode drivers in conventional or upper
memory to access drives compressed with these products. 32-bit drivers are
available for these disk compression schemes (but not from Microsoft). The
discussion in this chapter refers to DriveSpace 3, the disk compression
scheme supplied by Microsoft.

A *compressed drive* is not a physical drive or a volume (a DOS FAT partition), but rather a file stored on a disk drive. Windows refers to a compressed drive as a *compressed volume file* (CVF) and gives it a disk drive letter designator just as though it were a volume. Application software (and most of the operating system, including Defrag and ScanDisk) treats it as though it were a volume.

The CVF is stored in the root directory of an uncompressed drive, which is referred to as the *host drive*. The CVF has the attributes Read-Only, Hidden, and System. Defrag doesn't move it. If it is a Microsoft CVF, its name will be something like Drvspace.000 or Dblspace.002. CVFs created by Windows 98 use the Drvspace name.

Because the compressed drive is actually a file on a host drive, you can cause all sorts of mischief if you erase the file or in other ways fool with it. You might consider refraining from messing with this file.

You can compress an existing uncompressed volume or create a compressed drive from the free space on an existing FAT-16 partition. If you compress an existing volume, DriveSpace creates a CVF and stores the existing files and free space in the CVF. If you are creating a compressed drive from free disk space, DriveSpace creates an empty CVF.

Compressed disk size

You can divide a disk partition or volume into at least two logical drives, one for the host drive and one for the compressed drive. Compressed drives can't be larger than 512MB with earlier Windows 95 compression schemes, and 2GB with DriveSpace 3. The size of the CVF will depend on how compressible the files in the CVF are. If you create a compressed drive from free disk space, the CVF will be half the reported size of the compressed drive.

The Explorer displays the uncompressed size of files stored on a compressed drive. Their actual file size can be (and most often is) less than the size that's reported. If you compress a file on a physical drive, using WinZip, for example, the file size reported by the Explorer is the compressed size. Because DriveSpace can't compress a WinZip file any further than it already is, its actual size when stored on a compressed drive is about the same as its reported size. You don't get any benefit from storing zipped files on a compressed drive.

A compressed drive isn't actually compressed, of course; it is the *files* on the drive (in the CVF) that are compressed. VFAT and FAT report the uncompressed size of the files, so it appears as though you have a bigger drive when you actually have smaller files.

When you create a new compressed drive from free disk space, VFAT doubles the amount of reported free disk space so that the reported drive size is twice the size of its CVF on the physical disk. The size of the compressed drive decreases if you start filling it with files that can't be compressed at a 2-to-1 ratio.

Secret

If you create a compressed drive from free disk space, the CVF won't be any larger than 1GB because the estimated compression ratio is 2 to 1, and the maximum size of a compressed drive is 2GB. If you fill the compressed drive with 2GB of highly compressible files, there will be unused (and unusable) space in your CVF. You can go back and reduce the size of the CVF, which will give you more space on your host drive to create another CVF.

Secret

If you have an existing physical disk with more than 2GB of files (in one partition) you won't be able to compress it.

So why does a compressed drive that reports, for example, 100MB free before you copy 40MB of files to it report only 40MB free afterward? Because 100MB free is an estimate based on the anticipated compression ratio of the files yet to be copied to the compressed disk (defaulted at a 2-to-1 ratio). It turns out, in this example, that the files could be compressed only at a 1.5-to-1 ratio. They therefore took up 30MB of the CVF, or 60MB of the estimated space.

Creating a compressed drive

It is quite easy to experiment with disk compression, so there is no reason not to create a compressed drive out of some of the free space on your existing drive and play with it a bit. You can always uncompress the drive as long as the total file size isn't greater than what will fit on your drive uncompressed.

You can compress an existing uncompressed volume or create a compressed drive from the free space on an existing partition. Compressing an existing volume creates a CVF and stores the existing files and free space in the CVF. Creating a compressed drive from free disk space creates an empty CVF.

Remember that compression doesn't work with FAT-32 volumes.

Compressing existing files and free space

You have to have at least 2MB of free disk space on a boot hard drive to compress it. Non-bootable hard drive partitions (and diskettes) require at least 768K of free space.

To create a compressed drive with existing files, take the following steps:

STEPS

Compressing a Drive

Step 1. Click the Start button, point to Programs, Accessories, System Tools, and then click DriveSpace to display the DriveSpace window, as shown in Figure 33-11.

Step 2. Highlight an existing physical drive.

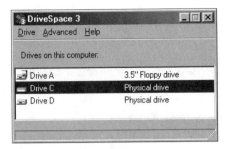

Figure 33-11: The DriveSpace window. Highlight a drive you are going to examine. You can compress, uncompress, mount, or unmount a drive from here.

Step 3. To compress both the files and the free disk space on an existing drive, choose Drive, Compress. The Compress a Drive dialog box appears, as shown in Figure 33-12.

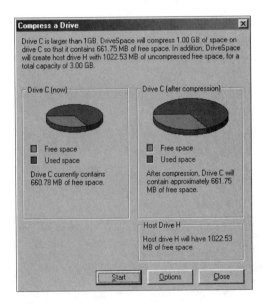

Figure 33-12: The Compress a Drive dialog box. Your only option is the letter designator for the host drive.

Step 4. Click the Start button to begin the compression process.

DriveSpace will figure out how to compress your drive based on its size and the total size of the files on your drive. If the drive is too big to compress into one CVF, it leaves the extra space on the host drive, which you can then compress into a new CVF.

While a host drive is a physical drive, you can always change the host drive's letter designator. Your physical drive may start out as C, but after you put on a bunch of compressed drives, it will be set by DriveSpace to H (or a letter greater than the last drive on your computer). You can change the host and compressed drive volume letter designators, although you can't change the letter designator for the drive that contains the \Windows folder.

Compressing free space

To create a compressed drive out of free disk space, follow these steps:

STEPS

Creating a Compressed Drive out of Free Disk Space

Step 1.   Click the Start button, point to Programs, Accessories, System Tools, and then click DriveSpace.

Step 2.   Highlight an existing physical drive.

Step 3.   Choose Advanced, Create Empty to display the Create New Compressed Drive dialog box, as shown in Figure 33-13.

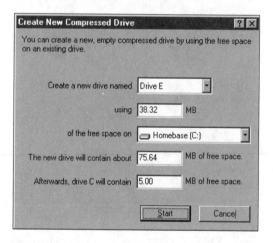

Figure 33-13: The Create New Compressed Drive dialog box.

Step 4.   You can type a new size in the any of the size fields, change the new drive name, or choose a different drive from which to take the free space. Click the Start button to begin the compression process.

The new compressed drive will be as large as it can be (up to 2GB) taking all the free space that is available (up to 1GB). A CVF will be created on the physical drive that contains the free space, and you can choose the letter designator for the new compressed drive.

Later, you can adjust the size of the compressed drive and the amount of free space left on the host drive (see the next section for details).

Changing the size of the compressed drive

You can increase the size of a compressed drive if there is free space available on the host drive. You are just increasing the size of the CVF that is stored on the host drive, and thereby taking up more free space. You can't increase the size of the compressed drive beyond 2GB.

If there is free space on your compressed drive, you can increase the amount of free space on the host drive by decreasing the size of the compressed drive (CVF).

To change the size of the compressed drive, take the following steps:

STEPS

Changing the Size of the Compressed Drive

Step 1. Click the Start button, point to Programs, Accessories, System Tools, and then click DriveSpace.

Step 2. Highlight an existing drive.

Step 3. Choose Drive, Adjust Free Space to display the Adjust Free Space dialog box, as shown in Figure 33-14.

Step 4. Drag the slider to move the free space from the host to the compressed drive, and vice versa. If you move the slider into the red area, Disk Defragmenter will be called to defragment the drive.

(continued)

Changing the Size of the Compressed Drive

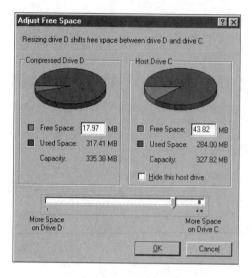

Figure 33-14: The Adjust Free Space dialog box.

When you adjust the free space, the amount of used space on the compressed drive and the capacity of the host drive does not change.

The amount of space you can adjust on the compressed drive is determined by the sum of the free disk space on the compressed drive and the host drive. If you need to make larger changes, you must first delete files.

Estimated compression ratio

The size of the compressed drive is determined by the size of the CVF and the actual compression ratio of the files in the CVF. When DriveSpace creates a CVF, it automatically sets the estimated compression ratio to 2 to 1. This is before any file is compressed and put in the CVF.

After DriveSpace copies files to the compressed drive, it reports the actual compression ratio, as well as the estimated compression ratio for the remaining free space on the compressed drive. The estimated compression ratio is, by default, set to 2 to 1.

Some files compress to a greater extent than others. Just because the files that you have copied to your compressed drive have a certain average compression ratio doesn't mean that the next group of files will have a similar compression ratio.

DriveSpace uses the estimated compression ratio to report the size of the free space available on the compressed drive. If this ratio is higher than the average for files that you subsequently copy to the compressed drive, the actual amount of free space available will be less than what was reported.

If you believe your actual compression ratio is a better estimate of the compression ratio of the files you will be adding to your compressed drive, you can change the estimated ratio to match your actual ratio (as long as it doesn't make the compressed drive greater than 2GB). This will give you a more realistic idea of the free space available on your compressed drive.

To change the estimated compression ratio, take the following steps:

STEPS

Changing the Estimated Compression Ratio

Step 1. Click the Start button, point to Programs, Accessories, System Tools, and then click DriveSpace.

Step 2. Highlight a compressed drive.

Step 3. Choose Advanced, Change Ratio to display the Compression Ratio dialog box, as shown in Figure 33-15.

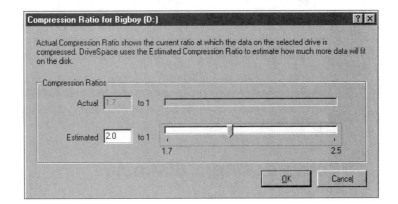

Figure 33-15: The Compression Ratio dialog box.

Step 4. Move the slider to change the estimated compression ratio.

Other DriveSpace options

DriveSpace gives you numerous other ways to manage your compressed drives.

You can use the Drive, Format command in the DriveSpace window to format a compressed drive, thereby erasing all the files within the CVF.

You can hide the host drive. You can do this regardless of how much free space it has, although you'll most likely want to hide the host drive if the CVF takes up almost all of it. You don't need to see an extraneous letter designator for the host drive if there isn't any space to store files on it. To hide the host drive, highlight it in the DriveSpace window, choose Drive, Properties, and mark the Hide This Host Drive check box.

Compressed drives, like physical drives, volumes, and drive partitions, are automatically mounted when you start your computer. You don't even think about the process because the drives are always there. With compressed drives that weren't there when you booted your computer (a compressed diskette, for example), you can choose whether you want to mount them automatically. One example of when you should turn off auto-mounting is if a removable drive doesn't always have a cartridge in it.

You can turn off auto-mounting for new compressed drives by choosing Advanced, Settings in the DriveSpace window, and then clearing the Automatically Mount New Compressed Devices check box in the Disk Compression Settings dialog box. If you want to subsequently mount a compressed drive (or unmount one) choose Advanced, Mount or Advanced, Unmount.

You can change the letter designator of a host drive and/or a compressed drive by choosing Advanced, Change Letter. You can't change the letter designator for the drive that contains the \Windows folder.

Tip

Your application configuration files and/or the Registry quite probably contain references to the drive letters that you are contemplating changing. You have to make changes to these files and to the Registry if you want your applications to track the "new" location of their files.

Compressing a diskette

One of the great things about disk compression is that you can increase the capacity of your diskettes by compressing files as they are copied to them. Of course, DriveSpace must be on the computer that is going to read the diskettes you create on your computer.

Tip

Windows 98 computers can read diskettes with DoubleSpace and DriveSpace compression. Computers with DOS 6.x and Dblspace.bin in their root directories can read DoubleSpace diskettes. Computers with Drvspace.bin in their root directories can read DriveSpace diskettes.

Compressing a diskette is the same as compressing a hard disk. The diskette will contain the compressed drive and the host drive. The host drive will start off with zero free space. The letter designator for the compressed drive will be either A or B. The host drive letter designator will be a letter greater than the last drive on your computer.

You can't hide the letter designator of a host drive for removable media. The host drive shows up in your Explorer or My Computer window as soon as you click on the diskette drive icon (if the drive is automatically mounted).

If you haven't mounted a compressed diskette (auto-mounting is turned off), you will find a file on the diskette named Readthis.txt. Use the command dir /a in a Windows DOS session to find this file. This file explains how to mount the diskette. You will also see a CVF, Dblspace.000, when you use the dir /a command.

Secret

You cannot compress a diskette unless it has at least 512K of free space. Also, it cannot contain a single file that is greater than half the uncompressed size of the diskette.

The amount of file compression

You can see how much an individual file is compressed by using the Dir command in a Windows DOS session. At the DOS command prompt type:

```
dir /c
```

This command reports the actual file compression ratio for each file in the current directory. It assumes a cluster size of 8 kilobytes. You can also use the command dir /ch, which will give the same answer as dir /c unless your cluster size is different.

Compression safety

You can turn off your computer in the middle of compressing a physical drive. When you turn it on again, compression will continue where it left off without any problems with the files being compressed. Microsoft made safety its number one design priority when developing disk compression.

Dblspace.ini

Undocumented

The parameters that define your DriveSpace or DoubleSpace drives are kept in a hidden, system, read-only file called Dblspace.ini, which is stored in the root directory of your host drive(s). If you change these file attributes (by right-clicking the file in the Explorer, choosing Properties, and then clearing these Attributes check boxes), you can edit this file. Here are some sample parameters:

```
AutoMount=1
FirstDrive=D
LastDrive=E
MaxRemovableDrives=1
```

```
MaxFileFragments=241
ActivateDrive=D,C1
```

For example, to change the drive letter designator for the compressed drive from D to E, make the following changes:

```
ActivateDrive=E,C1
LastDrive=F
```

DriveSpace speed

This file compression is all fine and good, but doesn't it take longer to access your files from a CVF?

Secret

Small files should load more quickly because they are being loaded from a sector instead of from a cluster. (Files on compressed drives are allotted space one sector, or 512 bytes, at a time.) Large files, such as Windows 98 files or big applications, should load slightly more slowly because of the DriveSpace overhead as DriveSpace sorts out sectors and reports them as clusters.

If you are running a system with only 8MB of RAM, you'll see some slowdown because you have less disk cache space. But then, on an 8MB system, everything is slow.

DriveSpace command line parameters

DriveSpace is not a DOS program. You put the command line parameters in the Target field in a shortcut to DriveSpace (right-click the shortcut, choose Properties, and click the Shortcut tab). You can also use them in batch files. You can't run DriveSpace in MS-DOS mode. All of the parameters you can add to the Drvspace command have equivalent commands in the more friendly DriveSpace menus, so you may opt to start the program and then use the menu commands instead of adding command line parameters.

```
Drvspace {options}

{options}

/compress e: {/reserve=n} {/new=f:}
    Compress an existing physical drive e:, reserve a certain amount
    of space (n) uncompressed, and give the host drive the letter
    designator f:.

/create e: {/size=n or /reserve=n} {/new=f:} {/cvf=nnn}
    Create a new compressed drive (CVF) from the free space on
    physical drive e:. Set the amount of uncompressed space on the
    host drive for the CVF, reserve an amount of uncompressed space on
    the host drive, give the compressed drive the letter designator
    f:, and report the CVF extension.

/delete e:\d??space.nnn
    Delete the named CVF.
```

```
/format e:\d??space.nnn
    Format the named CVF.

{/info} e:
    Report the amount of free and used space on the compressed drive
    e: and other information.

/interactive
    Coupled with an operation switch (/ratio, /mount, and so on),
    tells DriveSpace to display the interactive path for the
    particular operation switch. If you don't specify a drive letter
    or volume file, DriveSpace prompts you for additional input.

/mount {=nnn e: or e:\d??space.nnn} {/new=f:}
    Mount the named or extension numbered CVF.

/move e: /new=f:
    Change the letter designator of the e: compressed drive to f:.

/ratio{=n} e:
    Change the estimated compression ratio of the e: drive.

/noprompt
    Prevent the display of confirmation dialog boxes. You can add this
    to any command but /info and /settings.

/size{=n or /reserve=n} e:
    Change the size of the compressed drive e:.

/uncompress e:
    Uncompress the compressed drive e:.

/unmount e:
    Unmount the compressed drive e:.

d??space.nnn
    The CVF filename, either Drvspace.nnn or Dblspace.nnn.
```

Upgrading to DriveSpace 3

If you are installing Windows 98 over Windows 95, you can upgrade your existing DriveSpace or DoubleSpace CVFs to DriveSpace 3 drives. DriveSpace 3 will read your drives that were compressed under the earlier schemes. You can upgrade the drives after installing Windows 98 by clicking DriveSpace in the System Tools menu (Start, Programs, Accessories), and then choosing Drive, Upgrade in the DriveSpace window.

By default, DriveSpace 3 uses Standard compression, which is the same compression method as the one used by the previous version of DriveSpace. You can also set DriveSpace 3 to use HiPack compression, which compresses your files an additional 10 to 20 percent. To do this, choose Advanced, Settings in the DriveSpace 3 window to display the Disk Compression Settings dialog box, and then click the HiPack Compression option button (see Figure 33-16).

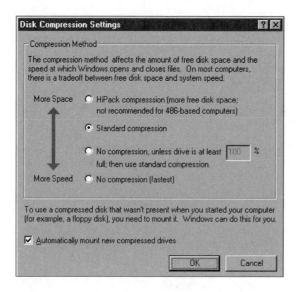

Figure 33-16: The Disk Compression Settings dialog box.

Compression Agent

If you want to compress files on a compressed drive even further, you can run Compression Agent, a part of the Windows 98 Task Scheduler. You will find this agent on the System Tools menu. Note that Compression Agent does not work with versions of DriveSpace prior to DriveSpace 3.

Compression Agent gives you two levels of compression higher than Standard compression, called HiPack and UltraPack. (Choosing HiPack in Compression Agent is the same as choosing it in DriveSpace 3.) The trade-off for using one of these higher compression levels is that it takes somewhat longer to read and write compressed files, and it takes a lot longer to compress them in the first place.

You can reach Task Scheduler through Start, Programs, Accessories, System Tools, Scheduled Tasks. By default, Task Scheduler runs Compression Agent every day after 8 p.m., assuming that your computer is idle. (It checks to see if your computer is idle every 20 minutes after 8 p.m.) You can set Task Scheduler to run Compression Agent whenever it is convenient for you. If you leave your computer on, you might want to run Compression Agent while you're sleeping or away from work.

Once you have created a CVF, DriveSpace continually compresses files as you write them to the compressed drive. The DriveSpace window is just a front end for the behind-the-scenes, on-the-fly file compression that is always going on if you have a CVF.

You can turn off this on-the-fly file compression and just write the uncompressed file to your compressed drive, of course. While this speeds up file writes, it also eats up disk space more quickly. To turn off compression, choose the No Compression option button in DriveSpace 3's Disk Compression Settings dialog box (Advanced, Settings), as shown in Figure 33-16.

Tip

If you set DriveSpace 3 to no compression in the Disk Compression Settings dialog box, set the Compression Agent to use HiPack, and set Task Scheduler both to warn you when you're low on disk space (the default setting) and to run Compression Agent at night, you can speed up your disk access to compressed drives (by not compressing files on-the-fly), and still compress your newly written files at night.

You can choose the option button labeled No Compression, Unless Drive Is at Least [ ]% Full; Then Use Standard Compression in the Disk Compression Settings dialog box to turn off on-the-fly file compression until the drive starts to fill up. If you do this, you can still set Compression Agent to compress files at night, which will give you more room by morning.

Even if you have set Compression Agent to compress files in UltraPack format, DriveSpace doesn't store your files in this format during the day. Instead, it writes your files back to the compressed drive using the compression format you specified in the Disk Compression Settings dialog box (Standard Compression, HiPack Compression, or No Compression). At night, Compression Agent gets to work recompressing the files to HiPack or UltraPack (or a combination of the two), depending on the compression settings you choose in Compression Agent (shown in Figure 33-17).

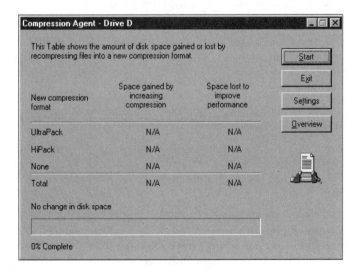

Figure 33-17: The Compression Agent.

To specify the compression format in Compression Agent, click the Settings button, and select the desired option buttons in the Compression Agent Settings dialog box, as shown in Figure 33-18. You can configure Compression Agent to UltraPack all of your files (not recommended if you have a 486), not to UltraPack any files at all, or to only UltraPack files that you haven't used in a specified number of days. For all of the files you've chosen not to UltraPack (which may be all of them) you can tell Compression Agent to HiPack them or to store them uncompressed.

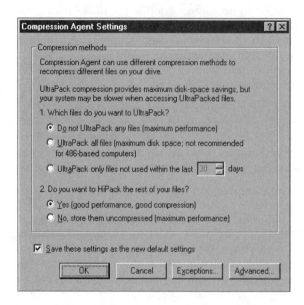

Figure 33-18: The Compression Agent Settings dialog box.

To view the results of all these different levels of compression on a CVF, right-click the drive icon of a compressed drive in an Explorer or folder window, choose Properties, and click the Compression tab. You will see something similar to Figure 33-19.

Why would you create a CVF (a compressed drive) and then not compress any of the files that you store in it?

Secret

If you have a 1GB disk partition, then the minimum cluster (and therefore file) size is 32K under FAT 16. Even a small file with only a letter to your aunt in it will be stored as though it contained 32,768 characters—a lot of slack space here.

If you store these small files in a CVF, they don't take up a cluster apiece. Space for files on compressed drives is doled out one sector (512 bytes) at a time. The letter to your aunt may now take up only 1024 bytes—a 32-to-1 "compression" ratio without any compressing at all!

Why is there a 2GB limit to a DriveSpace 3 CVF? Let's not get greedy here. Windows 98 quadruples the size of any one compressed drive.

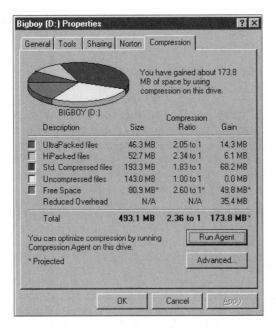

Figure 33-19: The Compression tab of a Properties dialog box for a compressed drive.

Secret

Chad Petersen at Microsoft tells us that the 2GB limit is imposed by the maximum number of clusters and the largest cluster size supported by the FAT 16 (and therefore VFAT 16) file system. The FAT file system is limited to 65,525 clusters. The size of a cluster must be a power of 2 and less than 65,536 bytes — this results in a maximum cluster size of 32,768 bytes (32K). Multiplying the maximum number of clusters (65,525) by the maximum cluster size (32,768) equals 2GB.

Windows NT allows a volume size of up to 4GB and 4K clusters. FAT 32 also supports 4GB drives and cluster sizes of 4K.

You might want to see just how much space you are currently wasting on your hard disk. You can download a little $5 shareware package that measures this for you. Waste for Windows 95 reports how much space is wasted due to the disk's cluster size, and how much more or less would be wasted with other cluster sizes. You'll find Waste for Windows 95 at http://www.windows98.com.

Moving to FAT 32

The Windows 98 disk utilities, including Fdisk, Format, ScanDisk, Defrag and DriveSpace, have been revised to work with FAT 32. However, FAT 32 is not compatible with earlier programs that directly access the hard disk, including all disk utilities. DriveSpace 3 can read but will not compress FAT-32 drives. File Manager (and many applications) will not display more than 2GB of free space.

Because MS-DOS 7.1 (the version of included with Windows 98) fully supports FAT 32, you should be able to run most MS-DOS mode games and applications from FAT-32 drives.

The new FAT-32 file system theoretically supports drive partitions much larger than 2GB in size, but 8GB is currently the optimum size. This is because the FAT-32 file system stores files less efficiently (with more cluster waste) on partitions larger than 8GB. The 8GB size is also the absolute limit for IDE and SCSI hard disk controllers that do not support Interrupt 13 extensions. Without support for these extensions, which implement a feature called *logical block addressing* (LBA) that FAT 32 needs, you cannot create a partition larger than the default LBA limit of 7.9GB. A disk controller needs a BIOS chip upgrade if it doesn't support Interrupt 13 extensions.

Speaking of LBA, there are reports that FAT 32 won't work at all on some laptops and 486-class systems with BIOS chips that don't support LBA. You should check with your hardware manufacturer to make sure you can run FAT 32 before reformatting your hard disk.

Most computer manufacturers have ignored FAT 32 and instead continue to configure their hard drives as FAT-16 volumes. Of course, as computer disks continue to increase in size, this will become a less tenable solution. To find out how your hard disk is configured, click My Computer, right-click the drive, and select Properties. The File System field indicates whether a drive is FAT or FAT 32.

Windows 98 comes with the Drive Converter (FAT 32), which lets you convert your hard disk for Drive without losing all your data and programs. You can access the FAT32 Converter by clicking Start, Programs, Accessories, System Tools, Drive Converter (FAT 32), or by clicking Cvt1.exe in your \Windows folder. After the conversion, you will need to run Defrag; be prepared for that part of the operation to take up to several hours.

You can also convert to FAT 32 by running Fdisk on any drive over 512MB. It will ask you whether to enable *large disk support*. If you answer yes, any partitions you create that are over 512MB in size will be marked as FAT-32 partitions and will be formatted as such. Fdisk will destroy any programs or data on that drive, so back them up first.

Do not use FAT 32 on any drives that you need to access from other operating systems, including Windows 95, all versions of Windows NT, and earlier versions of Windows or MS-DOS. If you need to dual boot another operating system, you can do this only if drive C is FAT 16, even if the other operating system is installed on a different drive. If you have other partitions that are FAT 32, they will not be visible to the other operating systems. You *can* share your FAT-32 drives across a network, just like any other FAT drives.

If you have anti-virus software enabled when you convert to FAT 32, it may intercept the request to update the partition table and/or the boot record and ask whether to allow them to be updated. You should answer yes. After you've finished the conversion and rebooted your computer, your anti-virus software may detect that the partition table and/or boot record has changed and offer to "repair" it for you. *Do not* allow the anti-virus software to restore the boot record or partition table, or your drive and all of the data on it will become inaccessible.

Windows 98 does not give you a way to go back to FAT 16 after you have made the conversion to FAT 32. However, a third-party utility called Partition Magic (http://www.powerquest.com) does let you go back and forth between FAT 16 and FAT 32 without destroying your setup.

Disk Caching

You don't need SmartDrive for disk caching. The Windows 98 Vcache dynamically adjusts the size in memory of your disk cache.

Vcache caches on a per-file basis, unlike SmartDrive, which caches on a per-contiguous-sector basis. If your hard disk is fragmented, SmartDrive won't store your files together (in contiguous sectors), so it isn't as smart as Vcache when it comes to caching a complete file.

Vcache can read-cache removable media, although it can't cache their disk writes.

Setting disk cache parameters

You can give Vcache a few suggestions about how to optimize caching the file system on your hard disk and, separately, on your CD-ROM.

Secret

You have three options that affect how fast Windows 98 displays filenames and folders: Desktop Computer, Mobile or Docking System, and Network Server. If you choose Network Server, Vcache caches 64 directory paths and 2729 filenames in memory. If you choose Desktop Computer, it caches 32 paths and 677 files. The Desktop Computer setting uses 10K of memory as cache and the Network Server setting uses 40K. You can mostly likely spare the additional 30K to speed up access to your files and folders.

To modify your file system cache, take the following steps:

STEPS
Modifying Your Hard Disk File System Cache

Step 1. Right-click My Computer. Choose Properties to display the System Properties dialog box, and click the Performance tab.

Step 2. Click the File System button to display the File System Properties dialog box.

Step 3. In the Hard Disk tab, choose from among the options in the Typical Role of This Computer field.

The Windows 95 Registry stored the wrong values of the cache sizes for the mobile and network servers in the Registry at HKEY_LOCAL_MACHINE\ SOFTWARE\Microsoft\Windows\CurrentVersion\FS Templates. Microsoft fixed these values in Windows 98.

To optimize caching the CD-ROM, click the CD-ROM tab in the File System Properties dialog box, and specify both a cache memory size and the CD-ROM drive's speed. This cache should be sized like this:

Your Computer's RAM	CD-ROM Speed	Cache Size
8MB	Single	64K
8-12MB	Double	626K
12MB or more	Quad or more	1238K

The Windows 98 memory manager wants to page your loaded applications to the hard disk and manage your RAM for caching the latest applications and data. You can restrict its ability to assign your RAM to cache by fixing the size of the cache. If you want to do this, take these steps:

STEPS

Fixing the Size of Your Cache

Step 1. Click System.ini in your \Windows folder.

Step 2. Add the following two lines to the [vcache] section (add the section if it's not there):

```
MinFileCache=4096
MaxFileCache=4096
```

Step 3. If you have more than 16MB of RAM, set the above values to about 25 percent of your installed RAM.

Step 4. Save the edited System.ini file, and restart Windows 98.

You are restricting the amount of RAM that Windows 98 is allowed to use for disk caching.

Managing Your Swap Space

You don't need a permanent swap file because Windows 98 dynamically sizes your swap file space.

Windows 98 manages your dynamically sized swap space for you, so you don't have to assign the volume or minimum and maximum size parameters. If you want to change these parameters, take the following steps:

STEPS

Managing Your Swap Space

Step 1. Right-click My Computer. Choose Properties, and click the Performance tab.

Step 2. Click the Virtual Memory button to display the Virtual Memory dialog box (shown in Figure 33-20).

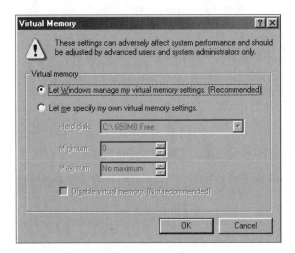

Figure 33-20: The Virtual Memory dialog box. You decide where to place your swap file, and its minimum and maximum size.

Step 3. Choose Let Me Specify My Own Virtual Memory Settings.

Step 4. Choose volume and size parameters.

If you go back to the Virtual Memory dialog box after restarting Windows, you'll see that the option is set back to Let Windows Manage My Virtual Memory Settings. This is normal. It's managing using the settings you specified earlier.

When you let Windows 98 manage your swap space and your memory, it will take every opportunity to page your loaded applications to the swap space on your hard disk. It uses the freed-up RAM to cache your data and most recently used application code. You might find your hard disk chattering away as this paging occurs in the background.

You can reduce this paging and caching by fixing the size of your swap space. To do this, first defragment your drive to set up a contiguous area on your hard disk big enough for your fixed-size swap space. See the "Defrag, the disk defragmenter" section of this chapter for instructions on how to do this.

Next, set the swap space at 2.5 times the size of your total RAM. To do this, set the minimum and maximum size to the same value in step 4 above, choosing a value in megabytes that is 2.5 times the size of your RAM in megabytes.

Swap space on a compressed drive

Your swap drive can be on a compressed drive (CVF). It is stored in an uncompressed form on the compressed drive to ensure that writing to the swap space will never fail.

A swap file is not particularly compressible, so it doesn't hurt to write it out in an uncompressed form. There is an advantage to putting the swap space on a compressed drive. You don't have to set aside enough unused uncompressed disk space for the maximum amount of space that the swap space might occupy, because much of the time this space will never be used.

Windows 3.1x permanent swap file

Windows 98 and Windows 3.1x can share the permanent swap file space. If you have both Windows 3.1x and Windows 98 on your computer and Windows 3.1x has a permanent swap file, you may get an error message stating that the swap file has been corrupted when you start Windows 3.1x.

To fix this problem, add MinPagingFileSize= to the [386enh] section of your System.ini file in your Windows 98 folder. Set the value to the size of your Windows 3.1x swap file.

Undocumented

If this doesn't help, do the following:

- Allow Windows 98 to manage virtual memory settings. (Right-click My Computer, choose Properties, click the Performance tab, click the Virtual Memory button, and choose Let Windows Manage My Virtual Memory Settings.)

- While running Windows 98, delete the files 386spart.par (in the root directory), and Spart.par and/or Win386.swp from the Windows 3.1x directory.

- Open the System.ini file in the Windows 3.1x directory, and comment out these lines in the [386enh] section:

```
PermSwapDOSDrive= {a drive letter}
PermSwapSizeK= {size in K}
```

- Add these lines to the [386enh] section of System.ini in the Windows 3.1x directory:

```
MaxPagingFileSize={max swapfile size in K}
PagingFile={drive letter}:\{Windows 98 directory}\Win386.swp
```

Virtual File System

Starting with Windows for Workgroups 3.11, Windows significantly reduced its use of DOS for disk/file access. In WFWG 3.11, the file access subsystem was called *32-bit file access*. In Windows 98 it is called the Virtual File Allocation Table (VFAT).

VFAT is compatible with the existing DOS file allocation system. All DOS disks that were partitioned and formatted as FAT partitions can be read and written to by VFAT. This includes hard disks and removable media, including diskettes.

Both VFAT and CDFS (CD-ROM file system) are installable file systems that are automatically loaded by Windows 98. When the DOS portion of Windows 98 (Io.sys) loads, it calls a real-mode installable file system helper file (Ifshlp.sys) that gets the whole virtual file system going.

VFAT was implemented to handle the new long filenames introduced in Windows 95.

Lock and unlock

All disk access is directed through VFAT, so you don't normally access the disk directly or through DOS or your BIOS. If you have programs, usually pre-Windows 95 disk utilities, that access the hard disk directly (using Interrupts 25 and 26), Windows 98 prevents them from accessing the disks.

You can use the Lock command to allow direct disk access. After you are done, you use the Unlock command to prevent direct disk access again. You can do this in batch files or at the DOS prompt. You can't access the disk directly even in MS-DOS mode unless you use Lock and Unlock. No access by other programs is allowed when a drive is locked.

If you have a DOS program that requires direct disk access (see "Undelete and Unerase" in Chapter 14), create a batch file that runs Lock and Unlock around the program. It is not a good idea to run pre-Windows 95 disk utilities because they can destroy long filenames. You should update your disk utilities to ones that are compatible with Windows 98.

Disk utilities provided with Windows 98 (including Defrag and ScanDisk) use the Microsoft-developed *volume locking* API. The commands in this application programming interface lock and unlock the disk drive. All third-party disk utilities should use this API.

Real-mode disk drivers

You may have a hard disk drive that requires a 16-bit driver. Microsoft has made a special effort to provide 32-bit protected-mode drivers for almost all disk drives available, but it didn't cover all of them.

You may be tempted to keep your 16-bit driver because some disk manufacturers boast that they shipped "fast" 16-bit drivers. These drivers are not as fast as the 32-bit drivers from Microsoft. Comment them out of your Config.sys file.

You can check if your hard disk is running in MS-DOS compatibility mode (16-bit) by clicking the System icon in your Control Panel, and then clicking the Performance tab. If File System is listed as 16-bit, you may be able to upgrade to 32-bit mode.

Microsoft provides a troubleshooting guide to determine how to fix this problem. You'll find it in the Knowledge Base at http://premium.microsoft. com/support/kb/articles/q130/1/79.

Long Filenames

The VFAT file system can handle long filenames — up to 255 characters. Every file has two names, the new long filename and a short filename that is compatible with the FAT file system. The backward-compatible short filename complies with the 8.3 filename rules.

You see the long filename in Explorer and folder windows. If you open a DOS window, you see both names. VFAT creates a short filename using the long filename as a template, and it makes sure that all of the short filenames in a folder are unique.

Valid filenames

A filename that obeys the 8.3 filename rules can contain any alphanumeric character, any ASCII character greater than 127, and these special characters:

$ % ' - @ ~ ` ! { } ( ) ^ # & _

In addition to these characters, a long filename can contain spaces, and it can also contain the following characters:

+ , ; = [ ] .

A null (one of the ASCII control characters) is included at the end of the long filename, so the total length of the filename, including the null, can be 256 characters. With DOS 6.22 and previous versions, the maximum length of a path and filename combined was 80 characters. It is now 260 characters, including the null. Filenames and folder names obey the same rules.

You can mix case throughout the filename. Filenames are not case sensitive, but the case you choose is preserved and displayed on screen. However, if you type a filename of eight letters or less in all capitals *and* you type its extension in all capitals, Windows 98 "corrects" your typing to sentence case (for example, JUNK.TXT becomes Junk.txt). Windows 95 used to always correct names with all capitals, but Windows 98 only does this if the extension is that way too. Long filenames are not changed.

You can't have two files in the same folder with the same name except for the case of the letters. For example, ToDo.txt and TODO.txt are seen by VFAT as the same filename.

The double quote mark is not a valid character to use in a filename. You use double quote marks to demarcate long path and/or filenames that contain spaces. For example, if you want to copy a file that has spaces in the filename from the DOS prompt, use this format:

```
Copy "File with a long name" "A new name for the long name file"
```

DOS commands and long filenames

Undocumented

The DOS commands that come with Windows 98 have been updated to handle long filenames (and the short filenames that must go with them). If you use versions of these commands from DOS 6.22 or earlier, you lose the long filenames. If the long filename and the short filename are the same, it doesn't matter.

If you copy files from a Windows 98 computer to a diskette, take that diskette to a computer running DOS 6.*x* or Windows 3.1*x*, and then edit those files on the diskette, the long filenames are preserved when you copy those files back to the Windows 98 computer. If, on the other hand, you copy the files off the diskette onto the hard disk of the DOS computer, edit those files, and then copy them back onto the diskette, you will lose the long filenames. Only the short 8.3 filenames will be preserved.

Long filenames across the network

Windows 95 and 98 32-bit network clients give you long filenames over the network if the server supports them. Earlier 16-bit real-mode network clients can only provide short filenames. This includes NetWare NETX and VLM drivers. You'll need to use Microsoft's Client for NetWare Networks or a 32-bit client provided by Novell instead if you want to support long filenames.

Other file systems on the servers create different short filenames from the long filenames. No big deal. They are still compatible with Windows 98.

You have to configure NetWare servers to use the OS/2 namespace (which emulates the native OS/2 HPFS file system) in order for Windows 98 to see long filenames on them. Doesn't it seem a little weird that Windows 98 would rely on an OS/2 standard? Well, the OS/2 standard is the past, after all.

To configure the NetWare server to use the OS/2 namespace, take the following steps:

STEPS

Enabling Long Filenames to Be Seen on a NetWare Server

Step 1. On the NetWare server, type these commands at the prompt:

```
load OS/2
add name space os2 to volume sys
```

Step 2. Add this line to the file Startup.cnf:

```
load os2
```

Step 3. Shut down the NetWare server. Copy the file Os2.nam from your NetWare diskettes or CD-ROM to the disk and directory on the NetWare server that contains the file Server.exe.

Step 4. Reboot the NetWare server.

Turning off long filename support

Undocumented

You can turn off long filename support completely. You shouldn't do this unless you have applications that don't work when long filenames are enabled. If you need to disable long filenames, first remove all the long filenames from your hard disk. The utility Lfnbk.exe lets you do this. (You'll find it in the \tools\apptools\lfnback folder on the Windows 98 CD-ROM.) Then follow these steps:

STEPS

Turning Off Long Filename Support

Step 1. Using the Explorer, click Regedit.exe in your \Windows folder to invoke the Registry editor.

Step 2. Click the plus signs to navigate to this branch:

HKEY_LOCAL_MACHINE\System\CurrentControlSet\control

Step 3. Highlight FileSystem.

Step 4. Double-click Win31FileSystem in the right pane.

Step 5. Press the Delete key, and then replace the 00 binary value with **01**. Click OK.

Step 6. Close the Registry editor, and reboot your computer.

Changing Drive Letters for Removable Media

Unlike your floppy and hard drives, you can set the drive letter designator for your CD-ROM, Zip, Jaz, or Syquest drive. You must be using the native Windows 98 32-bit drivers for this to work. Older CD-ROM drives may still be using 16-bit Windows 3.1 drivers, even under Windows 98. (If you're using a 16-bit driver for your CD-ROM drive, you'll see a reference to Mscdex.exe in your Autoexec.bat.) Here's how to change your drive letter if you are using a 32-bit driver:

STEPS

Designating Your Drive Letter

Step 1. Right-click My Computer, choose Properties, and click the Device Manager tab.

Step 2. For your CD-ROM, click the plus sign next to CDROM, highlight your CD-ROM drive, and click the Properties button. For Syquest and Zip drives, click the plus sign next to Disk Drives, highlight your Zip or Syquest drive, and then click the Properties button.

Step 3. Click the Settings tab.

Step 4. Select the letter you want for this drive in the Start Drive Letter and End Drive Letter fields (choose the same letter in both fields).

Step 5. Click both OK buttons. You will be prompted to reboot your computer.

Disk Drive Partitioning

You have to partition physical drives before you can format them into FAT-16 or FAT-32 volumes. A physical drive can have just one partition, in which case the partition must be bootable, or it can have multiple partitions, including one bootable partition. You assign a drive letter to each partition, and refer to each one as a *drive*.

Windows 98 works with third-party disk partitioning schemes, including Disk Manager, SuperStor, and Golden Bow. These schemes were created to let you partition hard drives that were larger than what earlier versions of Fdisk, which Microsoft supplies, could handle. Windows 98 also works with Fdisk-partitioned drives on removable media.

Windows 98 comes with an updated Fdisk, which you can use to partition your drives. In most cases, the computer manufacturer will have already set up disk partitions on your hard drive when you get a new computer. You can use Fdisk.exe to change these partitions, but you will lose any files stored on them unless you back them up first.

You shouldn't use Fdisk if your hard disk is already partitioned with a third-party scheme. Use the third party's tools instead. You can determine if your hard disk was partitioned with a third-party product by examining Config.sys. You are using a third-party disk partitioner if you find references to the following files: Dmdrvr.bin, Sstor.sys, HarDrive.sys, or Evdisk.sys.

If you want to change the partition structure on your hard disk and you'd rather not go through the pain of redoing your Windows 98 and software installation, you'll need to get Partition Magic. You'll find it at http://www.powerquest.com.

DMF Diskettes

If you purchased Windows 98 on diskettes, you have diskettes that contain 1.7MB of compressed data. Since the data was already compressed before the files were copied to the diskette, it wouldn't have done any good to make these diskettes into compressed drives. Microsoft found a way to store more data (in whatever form) on 3½-inch diskettes.

These 1.7MB formatted diskettes are referred to as Distribution Media Format (DMF) diskettes.

If you want to copy files from the DMF diskettes onto your hard disk, use the Extract command as follows:

```
extract /c a:filename.cab d:\filename.cab
```

You can find out more about the Extract command in the Microsoft Knowledge Base. Turn your Internet Explorer to http://premium.microsoft.com/support/kb/articles/q129/6/05.

If you want to format DMF diskettes and write files to them, you'll need to use the WinImage package featured on the *Windows 98 Secrets* CD-ROM. You can also find it at http://ourworld.compuserve.com/homepages/gvollant/winimage.html.

To format a DMF diskette with WinImage, take the following steps:

STEPS

Running WinImage to Format a DMF Diskette

Step 1.   Click Winmaint.exe in a folder or Explorer window.

Step 2.   Choose Option, Preference. Clear the Use Only Standard Formats check box. Click OK.

Step 3.   Choose File, New. Drag and drop some files into the new image file.

Step 4.   Choose File, Save, and give the image file a name.

Step 5.   Choose Disk, Format, and then choose Write Disk. Select the 1.7MB format when prompted, and click OK.

The diskette in your diskette drive is now formatted to store 1.7MB of data. You can write more data to it later using WinImage.

Booting from a Zip Drive

Zip drives from the Iomega Corp. are an increasingly popular removable storage medium. With $15 disks that are only slightly larger and thicker than a 1.44MB floppy disk, Zip drives let you store about 100MB in a convenient package.

Not only can you use Zip drives for large data files, but you can also install on them whole programs that are bulky and infrequently used. A Zip drive installed on an IDE or SCSI controller is comparable to a hard drive in access time. People who can't spare an IDE or SCSI connection can use a version of the Zip drive that operates off of a parallel port (these drives are quite a bit slower).

With all its similarities to a floppy drive, however, a Zip drive (no relation to PKZIP compression software) doesn't work well as an A or B floppy drive. That's too bad, because many people have vacant B drives and could use a removable disk drive there. And if a Zip drive could be configured as drive A, you could boot from a 100MB removable drive, making it easy to switch between different configurations or entire operating systems. (Your data files could reside on a hard drive and continue to be accessible from whichever configuration you were currently using.)

Now there is a shareware utility that allows you to boot from a Zip disk in the same way many people boot from different floppy diskettes. Benedict Chong has developed two related programs: Z-pA works with IDE/ATA Zip drives, while ZppA works with parallel-port Zip drives. There is no version at present for SCSI Zip drives. (Some SCSI adapters already allow devices 5 and/or 6 to be configured as bootable devices. Check your documentation.)

You have an IDE/ATA Zip drive if it is mounted internally (like a floppy drive) and has a 40-pin connector at the back of the drive. A Zip drive that requires an external AC adapter is not an IDE/ATA drive. A SCSI Zip drive, of course, has a cable that plugs into a SCSI controller.

Both versions of Chong's program will reside in the master boot record (MBR) of your C drive. They run before the operating system is loaded, and detect a Zip drive whether or not a disk is present in the drive.

When Z-pA detects a Zip drive, it configures it as the letter A or B. A Zip drive configured as drive A can boot up just like a floppy drive configured as drive A. And if you designate your Zip drive as drive A, you can right-click files in the Explorer and use the Send To menu to copy files to the drive. The command to Send To drive A appears automatically when you install Windows 98.

Windows 98 is a particularly hospitable environment for Zip drives. It supports floppy drives over 100MB, while previous versions of DOS and Windows only supported floppies up to 32MB.

Z-pA and ZppA are available for download in 30-day trial versions from a Chong's web site. Z-pA is at http://www.blueskyinnovations.com/zpa.html. Use the same URL for ZppA, but change the filename at the end to zppa.html. You should also read the FAQ at zpafaq.html.

Summary

The people staffing the Microsoft support lines want to quit hearing from you about problems with your disk drives. Windows 98 provides you with a set of tools to keep everything in working order.

▶ We show you how to find all the disk tools in all the little corners of Windows 98.

▶ We explain how to take advantage of the new Windows 98 FAT 32 file system, and what to watch out for in converting to FAT 32.

▶ We show you how to repair your disks when you experience a problem, and how to keep an eye on your disks to prevent trouble.

▶ Microsoft includes a great little disk defragmenter that can speed up disk access. We show you how to get the most from it.

▶ Do you want to double your hard disk space at little or no cost in disk access speed? Try DriveSpace 3.

▶ We show you how to create super-high-density diskettes.

Part VI

DOS Secrets

Chapter 34

Meet the New DOS . . . Same As the Old DOS

In This Chapter

Who says DOS is dead? Sure, it doesn't have that much to do anymore, but lots of DOS programs could use a friendly C:\> prompt. We discuss:

▶ The relationship between Windows 98 and DOS

▶ The real concerns of Windows 98 users regarding DOS

▶ Designing the DOS *screen* in a DOS *window*

▶ Editing shortcuts to DOS programs to make them work better with Windows

▶ Private DOS in MS-DOS mode — letting DOS programs work even when they're cranky

▶ Writing Windows/DOS batch files

▶ Finding the Windows folder

DOS Lives On

DOS lives on as a vestige — still useful, but only a small part of Windows 95 and 98. In this chapter, we first look at DOS as that thing that starts up before Windows 98 takes command. Second, we examine the part of DOS you get with Windows 98. Third, we cover how to best run DOS programs.

DOS, the former operating system, now but a shell of its former self, will not be our main emphasis in this chapter. After all, our object in writing *Windows 98 Secrets* is to make your life easier as a user, not to debate the finer points of operating system philosophy.

DOS and Windows, Together

Andrew Schulman argued in his book, *Unauthorized Windows 95*, that with the advent of Windows/386 2.*x* in 1988, Windows became a real operating system. Windows is an operating system because it handles the requests that programs make of the computer. When necessary, it hands those requests to DOS to let it do some of the work. Since the advent of Windows for Workgroups 3.11, and especially the 32-bit file access that came with it, DOS has had even less of the grunt work to do.

According to Schulman, 32-bit file access, which was introduced with Windows for Workgroups 3.11, was "pre-beta" code for the disk/file access subsystem of Windows 95. In Windows for Workgroups, 32-bit file access really did not work well, and it failed under some conditions. For example, certain legitimate DOS-read functions caused Windows for Workgroups with 32-bit file access to halt with a "system integrity" error. In Windows 95, it is hard to turn off 32-bit file access, and we have not seen few reports of difficulties with it.

It is the fact that Windows is first in line to deal with disk-access requests that makes it an operating system. Windows makes the decision about how to handle these requests and uses some of the DOS code routines if they are useful. Windows 98 treats DOS as a real-mode driver.

Schulman states early in his book:

> "If I had to explain how Windows 95 relates to DOS in 25 words or less, I'd say this: *Windows 95 relates to DOS in the same way that WfW 3.11 does.* Windows provides 32BFA [32-bit file access]. For non-file calls, it calls (in V86 mode) the real-mode DOS code in WINBOOT.SYS [*called Io.sys since the released version of Windows 95*]. Windows 95 is a genuine operating system; so were WfW 3.11, Windows 3.1 Enhanced mode, and Windows 3.0 Enhanced mode."

It Sure Looks Like DOS

Of course, it sure looks like DOS when you start your computer. The first thing you see is a text screen with familiar messages, undoubtedly output from your computer's BIOS. These messages are generated by your BIOS's power-on self test, and because they are text messages, they remind us of DOS's textual flavor.

The Basic Input/Output System (BIOS) chip(s) used to play a much more important role. In the days before 386 systems, the BIOS chips contained the only code that told DOS enough about the hardware to allow DOS to talk to said hardware. Some DOS programs bypassed the BIOS to get directly at the hardware and speed their screen display. Later versions of DOS bypassed the BIOS to use their own descriptions of the hard disk to provide quicker access. Now, Windows—especially Windows 95 and 98—keeps its own account of the hardware and provides all the hardware drivers it needs.

This doesn't mean the BIOS is ignored by Windows 98. Instead, once the hardware description is read from the BIOS and DOS loads whatever real-mode drivers may still be called by Config.sys, Windows then uses its own routines to interact with the hardware.

After its power-on self test, your computer's BIOS hands over the bootup process to the file that occupies the boot tracks of your hard disk. If you have Windows 98 installed as the only operating system, the BIOS will find the Windows 98 version of Io.sys. Io.sys is real-mode DOS.

Many of you may think of Command.com as DOS. However, Command.com is only the user interface (the *shell*) for DOS. It can easily be replaced by another user interface, such as 4DOS.

Io.sys does the work of reading Config.sys. If you have an Autoexec.bat file, Io.sys loads Command.com to execute the statements in Autoexec.bat. Even if these two files don't exist, Io.sys does much of the work that they would have done, such as loading Ifshlp.sys. The last thing Io.sys does is start Windows by sending out the instruction Win.com as if there was a call to it in your Autoexec.bat.

This Windows startup process is discussed in much more detail in "What Gets Loaded When" in Chapter 5.

The data structures and routines created in conventional memory by Io.sys are still there after Windows 98 starts up, and Windows 98 calls upon them (in V86 mode) as it needs them. As developers rewrite more Windows components using 32-bit equivalents, Windows needs less and less of Io.sys.

A Thing on a Thing

The fact that your computer first boots into real-mode DOS, that you have DOS-looking text on your screen, and that DOS is necessary for Windows to run, creates the perception that Windows is "a thing on a thing." IBM, in its marketing of OS/2, made much of this fact as it struggled to compete in the marketplace against Windows 95.

Microsoft wants us to see Windows 95 and 98 as "real" operating systems, which they are. In order to enhance that perception, Microsoft constructed Io.sys so that it calls Windows 98 automatically without your having to put a line in your Autoexec.bat file to call Win.com. Microsoft also made it somewhat difficult to get to DOS other than through a Windows DOS box.

Microsoft couldn't go all the way, because so many people still relied on DOS programs and continually whined about their problems with Windows DOS boxes. Users were unable to get all their DOS programs to run in Windows DOS sessions, so Microsoft had to provide "MS-DOS mode." Early in the Windows 95 beta test cycle, Microsoft tried to get this mode to work with all DOS programs with a stub of Windows 95 still loaded in memory, but couldn't. Some DOS programs required that the processor be reset with a warm boot before they would work.

Therefore, Windows 95 and 98 provide two "MS-DOS modes." One maintains a Windows stub in memory that allows you to return to Windows 98 without rebooting the computer by typing **exit** at the DOS prompt. The other forces a warm boot before starting real-mode DOS. Real-mode DOS is running your computer in both cases.

A second copy of Command.com is loaded in both cases if you exit Windows to go to MS-DOS mode. This allows you to "exit" this second instance of the command line interface (exit MS-DOS mode) and carry out the next line of Autoexec.bat, which is a call to reload Windows 98 (and return to Windows 98). If you warmed booted to DOS, your computer will be rebooted to return to Windows 98.

Windows has difficulty running DOS programs that use memory managers not in compliance with the Windows memory manager specification. This affects DOS games especially. DOS games really eat up computer resources and often don't want to cooperate with Windows at all. It is this issue of DOS games that forced Microsoft to include MS-DOS mode.

By making DOS harder to get to, and by automatically starting Windows 98, Microsoft is trying to change our perception about whether Windows is a "real" operating system. Of course, the fact that you see text messages during the power-on self test and just before the Windows 98 logo screen dilutes that message.

Windows 98 is not "a thing on a thing." Ignore the man behind the curtain. Windows 98 is the *real* thing.

The Real DOS Concerns of Windows 98 Users

There is an issue beyond perceptions. Aren't there some problems with DOS that make Windows 98 unstable, that "crash the system?"

Windows 98, like any other operating system, makes compromises. It compromises "un-crashability" in exchange for performance, given minimum resources. Minimum resources, in this case, means 8MB of memory and a 486/66 processor. These compromises are not really related to DOS as a real-mode driver for Windows. They would be there anyway, however Windows 98 was designed, as long as Windows 98 had to fit within these computer resources.

Some older Windows programs use conventional memory resources, and this can be seen as a DOS problem. Windows 98 does a good job of reducing the consequences of this bad behavior, but it still allows these programs to put parts of themselves into conventional memory. Turn to "Piggy Windows programs" in Chapter 35 for more discussion of this issue.

Both Windows 95 and 98 make most DOS 16-bit drivers unnecessary. This is a great benefit. Not only are Windows 95 and 98 more stable than earlier versions of Windows because their 32-bit drivers are more stable, but this also lessens the demands on conventional memory and the upper memory blocks (UMBs). DOS and some Windows programs benefit from this reduced demand. This increased stability is particularly noticeable in video card drivers.

Microsoft provides a unified Windows NT and Windows 98 driver model for the development of new drivers that can be used with both operating systems. The next version of Windows will be built around the Windows NT kernel, and drivers written to this unified specification will work on all versions of Windows.

What's Left of DOS?

What does it mean that DOS comes in the same package as Windows 98? DOS itself means a lot of different things. It is Io.sys, which sits in the boot tracks and boots up DOS 7.1 when the BIOS is finished. Io.sys definitely comes with Windows 98.

The DOS routines perform some of the low-level tasks of controlling the hardware and providing pointers to active applications. This is the part of DOS that is called by the VxDs that make up Windows 98. This DOS is running in V86 mode in the system virtual machine. It definitely comes with Windows 98.

On top of DOS is Command.com: the DOS user interface and the DOS prompt. A new and bigger version of Command.com comes with Windows 98.

DOS also includes DOS commands (both internal to Command.com and external) and the files that were previously stored in the DOS directory. Windows 98 doesn't create a DOS directory but puts most of its "DOS" files in the C:\Windows\Command folder.

Internal DOS commands (DIR, Copy, CD, and so on) are resident in Command.com. External DOS commands (XCopy, Find, Mem) are DOS files —separate executable programs.

All the internal DOS commands found in DOS 6.x are still there in the DOS that comes with Windows 98. However, only some of the DOS external commands (executable files) that came with DOS 6.x come with Windows 98.

Secret

When you write DOS commands, you need to put double quote marks around long folder and filenames that contain spaces (for example, CD \"Another folder").

Windows 98 doesn't come with a virus checker, an undelete program, or DOS-based backup. These were big new functions that came with DOS 6.2x. Microsoft decided to drop virus checking with Windows 95, and to let others provide that functionality.

Windows 98 comes with a Recycle Bin, but files deleted from the DOS prompt (or over the network or on diskettes) don't go to the Recycle Bin. If you want to undelete files deleted at the DOS prompt, you have to use the DOS 6.2x Undelete command (see "Undelete and Unerase" in Chapter 14) or a package from another developer.

Do you want the files you delete in a DOS window to go to the Recycle Bin? You can if you use a little freeware application called Delete.exe. You'll find it at http://www.easytools.com.

Windows 98 does come with a Windows-based backup program that works with SCSI and floppy-based tape backup hardware. Other developers provide more extensive backup software.

The remaining DOS commands

Microsoft claims that DOS commands are native Windows 98 commands. They certainly are in the sense that they have been changed to work with long filenames and the VFAT (Virtual Fat Allocation Table), and with FAT 32. All of the previous internal DOS commands are available and have been updated.

Table 34-1 lists the DOS external commands that come with Windows 98.

Table 34-1   DOS External Commands in Windows 98

Filename	Definition
Attrib.exe	Show or change file attributes
Chkdsk.exe	Check disk and provide status report (use ScanDisk instead)
Choice.com	Accept user input in a batch file
Cvt.exe	Convert Fat 16 to Fat 32
Deltree.exe	Delete tree (directory and subdirectories)
Diskcopy.com	Full copy of diskettes
Doskey.com	Edit command lines, recall them, create macros
Edit.com	File editing application
Extract.exe	Extract files from a cabinet file
Fc.exe	Compare two files
Fdisk.exe	Low-level disk partitioning and configuration
Find.exe	Find text in a file
Format.com	Format a disk
Lextract.exe	Extract a file from a backup file
Keyb.com	Configure a keyboard for a specific language
Label.exe	Label a disk
Mem.exe	Display memory use
Mode.com	Mode of port or display, or code page (character set)
More.com	Pause for output one screen at a time
Move.exe	Move files (copy and delete original)
Mscdex.exe	Real-mode CD-ROM extensions
Nlsfunc.exe	Load country-specific information for DOS programs

Filename	Definition
Scandisk.exe	Fix disks. Parameters to control it are found in Scandisk.ini
Scanreg.exe	Registry backup, restore, and scanner
Share.exe	File locking
Sort.exe	Sort the contents of a file
Start.exe	Run a Windows program
Subst.exe	Substitute a drive letter for a directory
Sys.com	Create a system disk
Xcopy.exe	Extended file and directories copy
Xcopy32.exe	Improved version of Xcopy.exe, called by Xcopy.exe

You can't copy long file or folder names with Xcopy.exe (or Xcopy32.exe) in MS-DOS mode (even when you use double quote marks around the filenames), but you can in a Windows DOS session.

You can learn how to use almost all of these commands, and the internal ones as well, by typing the command and adding /? before pressing Enter.

If you use Xcopy in real-mode DOS, it is a much different animal than if you use it in a Windows DOS session. Typing a space and /? after the Xcopy command in both modes shows you a much different set of switches.

DOS 6.2*x* came with an external DOS help program. You could get extensive information about DOS commands by just typing **help** at the DOS prompt. This help program (Help.hlp) hasn't been updated for the Windows 95 or 98 version of DOS commands, but it is still quite useful. You'll find it on the Windows 98 CD-ROM in the \other\oldmsdos folder. You can run it in a DOS window.

You can copy all the files in the \other\oldmsdos folder on the Windows 98 CD-ROM into your \Windows\Command folder. Because this folder is on the path, you will then be able to get to the help program by typing **help** *command* at any DOS prompt.

DOS Edit

Windows 98 ships with DOS Edit. Written by a contractor to Microsoft, Emory Horvath, it is a nifty little editor, and it's quite useful for dealing with text and batch files. For example, it can do find and replace, while Notepad can't.

You can easily create a shortcut to it and put it on your Start menu or your Desktop (see "Create Shortcuts to DOS Programs") in Chapter 10. You'll find Edit.com in your \Windows\Command folder.

Undocumented

Edit can load up to nine files and can have two windows open at any one time. It can use up to 5.5MB of virtual memory to load and manage files, handling files of up to 64,000 lines. The maximum line length is 1024 characters. It doesn't require Windows 98 to run, and it should run on any processor equal to or greater than a 286. It requires only 160K of conventional memory.

Edit is great for looking for text in binary files, and it has a switch in its File Open dialog box to give you that option. The Edit command's File Open dialog box defaults to opening files with any extension — a big improvement over the Windows 3.1x version if you use it to edit batch files.

Secret

The Edit command doesn't recognize a mouse double-click setting in the Registry. If you have set your middle mouse button on a Logitech mouse to double-click (as described in "Double-Clicking with the Middle Mouse Button" in Chapter 24), it won't work with Edit. You'll have to remember to double-click with the left mouse button.

Config.sys commands

A number of commands are used only in your Config.sys file. They include:

Break	Files	Rem
Buffers	Include	Set
Country	Install	Shell
Device	Lastdrive	Stacks
Devicehigh	Menucolor	Submenu
Dos	Menuitem	Switches
Drivparm	Numlock	Verify
Fcbs		

DOS commands that are no longer around

The following external DOS commands do not come with Windows 98:

Append	Interlnk	Recover
Assign	Intersvr	Replace
Backup	Join	Restore
Comp	Memcard	Ramdrive.sys
Dosshell	Memmaker	Romdrive.sys
Edlin	Mirror	Smartmon
ega.sys	Msav	Tree
Fasthelp	Msbackup	Undelete
Fastopen	Power	Unformat
Graftabl	Print	Vsafe
Graphics	print.sys	
help	Qbasic	

Some of these external DOS command files are stored in the \Other\ Oldmsdos folder on the Windows 95 CD-ROM, but not on the Windows 98 CD-ROM. They are the MS-DOS 6.22 versions, and they haven't been updated.

Cautions about some DOS commands

Chkdsk has been superseded in functionality by Mem.exe and Scandisk.exe. ScanDisk is now both a Windows program and a DOS program that checks for problems with your disk (hard or floppy). Mem gives you a great deal more information than Chkdsk about your available conventional memory. Chkdsk /f is rejected in a Windows DOS session.

Share.exe is not needed in Windows DOS sessions. A virtual device driver takes care of file locking. Windows 98 doesn't support Share.exe in real-mode MD-DOS. However, some programs check for the existence of a file named Share.exe. To work around this problem, create a dummy file named Share.exe in the \Windows\Command folder.

Subst.exe hasn't fully worked for quite a while. It doesn't work with networked drives, and it fails with Fdisk, Format, and Sys. It will work just fine in a Windows DOS session or in MS-DOS mode to substitute a drive letter for a path or folder name. This makes it easier to use really old DOS programs that weren't designed to use pathnames.

Do not use the earlier DOS Append utility. It prevents Windows 98 and Windows-based applications from creating valid pathnames for the files they are using.

Wonderful DOS commands

If you want to rename a set of files, you have to use either the File Manager or the DOS Ren command. To compare files, you need to use either Fc.exe or the file-matching shareware that we feature on the *Windows 98 Secrets* CD-ROM accompanying this book.

Using DOS 7.1, you can navigate up the folder tree using just dots as names for grandparent and great grandparent folders. The dots are stand-ins for the various folders as follows:

.	The current folder
..	The parent folder
...	The grandparent folder
....	The great grandparent folder

You can use these stand-in dot names in place of the actual names in DOS commands. For example:

| `Copy thisfile.ext ...` | Copies *thisfile.ext* to the grandparent folder |
| `CD ....` | Changes the current folder to the great grandparent folder |

Modifying DOS commands

You can modify the default behavior of some DOS commands so that they do just what you want them to. You do this by setting the value of certain environmental variables. For example, if you want to change the default behavior of the DIR command, you can add the following line to your Autoexec.bat file (or to a batch file that runs when you start a Windows DOS session):

```
set dircmd=/p /l /o:-d
```

This line modifies the DIR command to pause after each screen-full of listed files, display the filenames in lowercase, and order the filenames in descending date order.

You can modify the Copy command by setting the value of *copycmd*.

How do you know which modifiers to use when changing these commands? They are the same ones you could type in manually when you enter the command. Type **copy /?** or **dir /?** at the command prompt and press Enter to see the available modifiers.

Doskey lets you define macros, so you can redefine any of the DOS internal or external commands. You run the commands after loading Doskey and the macro definitions (most likely in your Autoexec.bat file or in a batch file that is run when you start a Windows DOS session). For example, if you want to redefine the Mem command to pause after each page of information, add the following to your batch file:

```
c:\Windows\Command\Doskey
Doskey mem=mem.exe $* /p
```

The Mem command is now changed to mean "Mem with the page pause modifier." The symbol $* means "include whatever is typed after Mem on the command line." For more information on Doskey, type **doskey/?** at the command prompt.

Shortcuts to DOS commands

You can make further modifications to DOS commands by using shortcuts to MS-DOS programs (also known as *pif*s) to call the commands. Some of these are carried out automatically. To see what we mean, take the following steps:

STEPS

Creating a Shortcut to Mem.exe

Step 1. Using your Explorer, navigate to the C:\Windows\Command folder. Right-click Mem.exe. Click Properties.

Step 2. Click the Program tab. Notice that the Cmd Line field has the following entry:

```
C:\WINDOWS\COMMAND\MEM.EXE /c /p
```

This entry modifies the Mem command to display greater details about memory allocation, and to pause after displaying one page of information. These commands were automatically added to the command line.

Step 3.   Click OK (or Cancel).

Step 4.   Press the F5 key to refresh the Explorer window. Scroll through the Command folder until you find the MS-DOS icon labeled Mem. It will be right below the Mem.exe file (if you are using details view and name order) and its type is listed as Shortcut to MS-DOS Program.

Step 5.   Click the shortcut to Mem icon. Pretty cool, huh?

Clicking the shortcut to Mem icon opens a Windows DOS session, displays the memory details, and then pauses, waiting for you to press another key. You will want to edit this shortcut so that it doesn't close on exit (right-click the shortcut icon, click Properties, click the Program tab, and clear the Close on Exit check box).

You can create a Windows shortcut for any of the DOS commands. You can put these shortcuts anywhere that makes sense to you — on your Desktop, in the Start menus, in a DOS folder that has a shortcut on your Desktop. In this way, the DOS commands become Windows programs.

Undocumented

If you create a shortcut that can't be added to the same folder, Windows will put it in the \Windows\Pif folder. You'll notice this if you create a shortcut to a DOS command in the \other\oldmsdos folder on your Windows 98 CD-ROM.

If you have DOS parameters or filenames that change, add a space and a question mark after the DOS command name in the command line, as in **Edit ?**.

DOS commands you shouldn't run

We want to be sure to cover a few DOS commands and applications that you must *never* run while in a Windows DOS session or in MS-DOS mode.

Don't ever run any disk utilities that haven't been updated to work with long filenames, unless you have saved your long filenames. You can run earlier versions of Norton Disk Editor, but do so after pressing F8 at the Windows 98 startup message (or pressing Ctrl during the power-on self test) and getting to a command prompt. Note that the earlier disk utilities will not work on any FAT 32 drives or partitions.

Don't ever run backup programs that are unaware of long filenames unless you have saved your long filenames with Lfnbk.exe (Long filename backup). This program saves the long filenames and restores them after you run an older DOS-based backup program. You can read more about this program in the file lfnbk.txt, which you'll find the in the \tools\apptools\lfnback folder on your Windows 98 CD-ROM.

You won't be able to run Chkdsk /f, Fdisk, Format C: (but Format A: and Format B: are fine), or Sys C: while in a Windows DOS session.

Don't ever run a disk optimization package other than Defrag (which comes with Windows 98) if it hasn't been updated for long filenames. Don't run programs that change your hard disk interleave from a Windows DOS session.

Windows has a built-in disk cache. Don't run third-party disk cache programs that aren't specifically designed for Windows 98.

Don't ever run utilities that undelete files unless they have been specifically designed for Windows 98. You can use the DOS 6.*x* version of Undelete using the steps provided in "Undelete and Unerase" in Chapter 14.

The path and Windows 98 applications

The default path that is set if you don't have an Autoexec.bat file is

```
C:\Windows;C:\Windows\Command
```

This assumes, of course, that your Windows 98 folder is called Windows and that it is on the C drive. If not, then the path statement will be automatically changed to the correct values.

You can add more folders to the path if you have an Autoexec.bat file. You can also change the path in a batch file that you run when you open a DOS window.

Undocumented

Windows 98 applications can set a pointer to the folder that contains their executable files. The reference is stored in the Registry at HKEY_LOCAL_MACHINE\Software\Microsoft\Windows\CurrentVersion\ AppPaths.

When a Windows 98 application starts, the shell looks at the entry at this location and appends the referenced folder(s) to the path.

You can set up references at this location in the Registry so you don't have to type the full pathname in front of an executable file's name when you use the Run menu item to run a program. This also works with the Start command in DOS batch files.

Use the Registry editor to add folder references, patterned after the ones already in the Registry at the above location, for your own Windows applications that don't know about this Windows 98 feature. You can then reference the applications in Start commands without using their full pathname.

Running DOS Programs

Our major concern in this chapter is providing you with the tools to make it easier to run DOS programs, both in Windows DOS sessions and in MS-DOS mode (that is, real-mode DOS). You'll find significant improvements relative to Windows 3.1*x* in Windows 98's ability to run DOS programs, and we want you to be able to take advantage of these improvements.

You can run DOS programs:

- Before Windows 98 starts by booting to a command prompt
- After Windows 98 starts in a Windows DOS session
- By quitting Windows to get to MS-DOS mode without a reboot
- By warm booting to MS-DOS mode, with a call to send you back to Windows at an exit command

DOS before Windows

To get to the DOS prompt before Windows 98 starts, press and hold the Ctrl key during the BIOS power-on self test. Choose the menu item 6, Command Prompt Only. You can edit your Msdos.sys file to have your computer automatically start at the DOS prompt or give you a menu of choices before Windows 98 starts. (For more information, see "BootMenu" in Chapter 5.)

Undocumented

Windows 98 hasn't loaded yet, but the commands in your Config.sys and Autoexec.bat files (if you have such files) are executed. You won't have access to some hardware devices such as your mouse, CD-ROM, or sound card unless you have loaded their 16-bit drivers. Windows 98 loads the 32-bit drivers for these devices only when Windows 98 is loaded.

Unless you have configured your Autoexec.bat and Config.sys files to work with DOS programs that you would normally start before you start Windows 98, it is unlikely you will have these 16-bit drivers loaded. Windows 98 doesn't need them and can, by itself, provide these services to DOS programs that run in Windows DOS sessions.

To increase conventional memory, you may want to load your 16-bit drivers and DOS TSRs in the upper memory blocks. If your DOS program requires expanded memory, you should put a line in your Config.sys file to load an expanded memory manager. Turn to "Emm386.exe" in Chapter 35 for more details.

Secret

At this point, because Windows 98 hasn't loaded, you are in DOS 7.1. You have real-mode direct disk access, not 32-bit file/disk access. If you want disk caching, you are going to need to run SmartDrive (Smartdrv.exe).

While you certainly can run your DOS programs by booting up DOS instead of Windows 98, this may not be the best method. You will probably want to optimize Autoexec.bat and Config.sys to run Windows 98, not DOS programs.

You can run DOS programs in MS-DOS mode with their own individually optimized Autoexec.bat and Config.sys files, so that is a better way to run them. You can also run DOS programs in Windows DOS sessions, which provide 32-bit drivers, thereby reducing demands for conventional memory.

Tip

DOS 7.1 can access FAT-32 formatted hard drives, but it's real slow. You'll probably want to load Smartdrv.exe in MS-DOS mode to speed up access to these drives.

DOS in Windows

If your DOS programs run in Windows DOS sessions, by all means run them there. Windows 98 creates a "virtual machine" for each Windows DOS session. As far as your DOS program is concerned, it is running in its own computer.

Each Windows DOS session is its own virtual machine. Each virtual machine can be different. You can run a number of them at once. Each is preemptively multitasked. This means no one session can hog all of your computer's resources.

You can set a number of virtual machine operational parameters. You determine what the computer looks like to the DOS program by editing the Windows DOS session properties found in Program Information Files (*pif*s).

The easiest way to run a DOS program in Windows 98 is to click its icon in a folder window or the Explorer. In many cases, the DOS program will just run and that's all there is to it. You can create shortcuts to DOS programs (*pif*s) and documents, and treat them just as you would shortcuts to Windows programs and documents. (*Pif*s have been enhanced since their first use in Windows 3.1*x* to take on the function of shortcuts to DOS programs.)

You can also run a DOS program from the Run command in the Start menu. Click the Start button, and then click Run. Type the full name of the program, including its path. Type any command line parameters after the program's name.

Undocumented

If you want to run the DOS internal commands such as Copy from the Run command, you need to use something like the following syntax:

```
command /c copy filename lpt1
```

The /c switch loads another copy of the DOS command processor and allows you to run internal DOS commands.

Tip

If you have an application that writes a PostScript file to disk, and later you want to send that PostScript file to the printer, there is no "Windows" way to do this. You have to copy the file to the printer port, as shown in the example above—one good reason to keep DOS around. (Note that the previous example will not eject the last page of text files from laser printers; you must do this manually.)

Windows 98 provides Windows DOS sessions with 32-bit file access to the hard drive as well as disk caching. This significantly speeds hard disk access by DOS programs. DOS programs have full mouse functionality (if they are designed to use a mouse) without having to load a 16-bit mouse driver. You don't need 16-bit sound card drivers, CD-ROM drivers, or network drivers, because these services are provided by Windows 98 32-bit drivers.

You can run DOS programs in a window or full screen. To switch a DOS session between windowed and full-screen modes, press Alt+Enter. To switch between DOS sessions, press Alt+Tab. You can copy data in a DOS window and paste it into a Windows 98 window.

Your Start menu contains an MS-DOS Prompt menu item. Click the Start button, point to Programs, and click MS-DOS Prompt. This starts a generic Windows DOS Session. You can run a DOS program in the Windows DOS session from the DOS prompt. You can open multiple Windows DOS sessions by choosing this Start menu item. You can edit its parameters by right-clicking the MS-DOS Prompt icon on the Start menu and clicking Properties.

Given all the features you get when you run your DOS programs in a Windows DOS session, you might conclude that Windows 98 provides a better DOS than DOS. If all DOS programs were able to take advantage of the DOS box, this would surely be the case.

DOS in MS-DOS mode without a reboot

If your DOS program won't run in a Windows DOS session, no matter how you set the properties of its virtual machine, you'll need to run it in MS-DOS mode. You don't have to click the Start button and then click Shut Down to use this version of MS-DOS mode, but you are given the option to restart in MS-DOS mode when you do shut down Windows.

To shut down Windows to MS-DOS mode without rebooting, take the following steps:

STEPS

Quitting Windows to MS-DOS Mode

Step 1.   Click the Start button.

Step 2.   Click Shut Down.

Step 3.   Click Restart in MS-DOS Mode.

Step 4.   Click Yes.

Undocumented

All but a 4K stub of Windows is unloaded from memory, and the file Dosstart.bat is run. This file is in your \Windows folder. It was created when you first installed Windows 98, and it consists of the calls to DOS TSRs that were remarked out of your previous DOS/Windows 3.1*x* Autoexec.bat file (if you installed Windows 95 or 98 on a computer with Windows 3.1*x* or DOS 6.*x*).

You can edit the Dosstart.bat file so it calls the TSRs that are appropriate for when you start MS-DOS mode (such as Smartdrv.exe, Mscdex.exe, a 16-bit sound card driver, and/or a 16-bit mouse driver). Because you are not doing a warm boot when you start non-rebooted MS-DOS mode, you will be unable to start any 16-bit drivers you would have normally called from a Config.sys file that you configured for DOS. If you need to load these drivers to run DOS programs in MS-DOS mode, either load them in the Windows 98 Config.sys file or use the warm-boot version of MS-DOS mode.

Secret

If you want to access your CD-ROM while in MS-DOS mode, you'll need to load your real-mode CD-ROM driver in your Config.sys file or load it in a private Config.sys if you use the reboot version of MS-DOS mode. In addition, Mscdex.exe, which is normally loaded by your Autoexec.bat, must be loaded. When Windows 98 is installed over Windows 3.1*x*, Mscdex.exe is remarked out (because Windows 98 has its own 32-bit protected-mode version of Mscdex.exe) and the unremarked call from your previous Autoexec.bat file is moved to Dosstart.bat. The real-mode CD-ROM driver in your Config.sys file is not remarked out.

When you go to MS-DOS mode, Mscdex.exe is called by Dosstart.bat, and because the real-mode CD-ROM driver has been previously loaded, you will now be able to access your CD-ROM drive in MS-DOS mode. If you have removed the real-mode CD-ROM driver from your Config.sys (perhaps to reclaim the conventional memory it uses), you won't be able to access your CD-ROM in MS-DOS mode without a reboot. In addition, you will get a series of error messages about Mscdex.exe unless you also remove it from Dosstart.bat.

If you have plenty of conventional memory even when you load the real-mode CD-ROM driver, you will be able to play your CD-ROM-based DOS games without having to go to rebooted MS-DOS mode. If this is not the case, you should load your real-mode CD-ROM drivers in private Config.sys files, and load Mscdex.exe in private Autoexec.bat files.

Undocumented

A shortcut to a DOS program, Exit to Dos.pif. is automatically created the first time you exit to MS-DOS mode in this manner. You'll find it in the Windows 98 folder.

You can edit Exit to Dos.pif. If you right-click this file in your Explorer and click Properties in the context menu, you can set whatever properties you like, including creating your own private Autoexec.bat and Config.sys. Of course, if you go that far, you are rebooting into DOS when you restart the computer in MS-DOS mode, which we discuss next.

Undocumented

You can also get to the non-reboot version of MS-DOS mode by creating a shortcut to MS-DOS (a *pif*) that doesn't create its own Autoexec.bat and Config.sys files. This is an option in the Advanced Program Settings dialog box, which we discuss later in this chapter in the section entitled "Advanced button."

When you exit this non-reboot version MS-DOS mode, your computer restarts Windows 98 without rebooting.

DOS in MS-DOS mode with a reboot

Windows 98 restarts (warm boots) your computer when it goes into rebooted MS-DOS mode. You exit this mode back into Windows 98 by typing **exit** at the command prompt and pressing Enter. Your computer is again restarted (warm booted) and Windows 98 reloads.

Undocumented

A restart is a warm boot. Io.sys runs again and reads Msdos.sys, Config.sys, and Autoexec.bat. Be careful: If you have edited your Msdos.sys file so that BootMulti=1 and the default boot is to DOS 6.2 (BootWin=0), you will restart to your previous version of DOS instead of MS-DOS mode. A way around this is to press F4 at reboot time to boot to Windows 98. You'll also need to do this when you exit MS-DOS mode.

To get to rebooted MS-DOS mode, you first need to create a DOS shortcut with the proper properties. We show you how to do this in the "MS-DOS Mode" section of this chapter. Each DOS program that uses MS-DOS mode can have its own shortcut with these properties.

If you want to reboot to DOS when you click the Start button, Shut Down, and Restart in MS-DOS Mode, you need to edit the Exit to Dos.pif file to specify the contents of the Autoexec.bat and Config.sys files that are used upon rebooting. Refer to the "Advanced button" section later in this chapter.

DOS in a Box

You can either display a DOS program that's running in a Windows DOS session in a window on the Windows 98 Desktop, or full screen. A DOS window can have a toolbar just like any respectable Windows program (see Figure 34-1). If your DOS window doesn't have a toolbar, click the system menu icon on the left end of the DOS window's title bar, and choose Toolbar.

Figure 34-1: A Windows DOS session. Notice the toolbar. The title bar is at the top of the window. The system menu icon is at the left end of the title bar.

You can use the DOS window toolbar to:

■ Change the DOS font size and thereby the DOS window size

■ Mark, copy, and paste text to and from the DOS window and the Clipboard

■ Expand the DOS window to full screen

■ Change the properties of the shortcut to the DOS application

■ Choose to not suspend the DOS program when it is in the background (doesn't have the focus)

DOS window vs. DOS screen

There is a difference between a DOS *screen* and a DOS *window*. In full-screen mode, there is no DOS window, and the DOS screen is the same as your computer's screen. A DOS screen on the Desktop is contained in a DOS window. In Figure 34-1 in the previous section, the DOS screen is the area underneath the toolbar and inside the edges of the DOS window.

You will frequently want to see the whole DOS screen inside the DOS window, because DOS programs are designed with the assumption that you can see the entire screen. If you can't see the complete DOS screen in the DOS window, it may be more difficult to run the program effectively.

The DOS window is smaller than the DOS screen if you can see a horizontal and/or vertical scroll bar in the DOS window. In this case, the DOS window only shows you a part of the DOS screen at any one time.

Sizing and locating the DOS window

You can change the size of a DOS window and/or a DOS screen in three ways:

- Set the DOS font size to Auto and drag the edge or corner of the DOS window
- Change the DOS font size
- Set the DOS font size to a fixed size and drag the edge or corner of the DOS window

Drag a DOS window with font set to Auto

First, set the font size to Auto in the font size box at the left end of the DOS toolbar. You should be able to see the whole DOS screen. If you can't, click one of the corners of the DOS window. The DOS window and screen will shrink to fit.

Now, stretch or shrink the DOS window by dragging one of its corners. The whole DOS screen stretches and shrinks along with the DOS window. The DOS font changes size to match the changing DOS screen size (after you release the mouse button).

Dragging the DOS window will not smoothly resize it. The DOS window resizes in increments that correspond to multiples of the available font sizes.

Tip

You can drag a side of the DOS window, but it is quite a bit easier to drag from a corner. Because the DOS window's width and height jumps in increments that are multiples of the fixed ratios of font pixel width to height, the window may get a lot shorter all of a sudden or not expand at all in another direction. Dragging by the corner opens up possible moves along both axes, making dragging somewhat smoother.

If you have clicked the maximize button in the DOS window title bar, you won't be able to resize the DOS window. In fact, the resize arrows won't appear if the DOS window has been maximized. The DOS window is already maximized anyway if the whole DOS screen is visible and the font size is fixed. That is the meaning of the "maximum" DOS window size (with fixed font size) — the whole DOS screen is visible.

If the font is set on Auto, maximizing the DOS window enlarges the font size, and consequently, the DOS screen. The DOS window will be the largest it can be and still be within the boundaries of the Desktop.

As you adjust the DOS window size, you are adjusting the size of a full DOS screen. Everything on the DOS screen is displayed in the window. Nothing is scrolled. There is no window on a DOS screen that allows you to see only part of the DOS screen at a time.

Size the DOS window by changing the font size

The DOS window and the DOS screen will automatically resize themselves if you change the font size. Just pick a new font (other than Auto) in the font size box on the left end of the DOS window's toolbar.

The DOS screen must be completely visible—no scroll bars. If there are scroll bars and you make the screen smaller, the DOS screen and window will shrink to the new size, and the scroll bar may disappear if you shrink it enough.

If you call for a larger font and the DOS window is smaller than the DOS screen, the DOS screen and the font will increase in size, but the DOS window will not. The scroll bars will stay right where they are.

Drag the DOS window edges or corner

Set the DOS fonts to a fixed size. You can shrink the DOS window so that only part of the DOS screen shows. The resize arrows move the DOS window edges smoothly. When you release the mouse button, the scroll bars appear. You now have a window on your DOS screen.

If the DOS window is maximized, the resize arrows do not appear.

Relocate the DOS window

To relocate the DOS window, drag its title bar. The DOS window remembers its new size and location. This information is stored in its *pif*. The next time you start this DOS application, the window will be located in the same place with the same font at the same size.

Choosing the DOS display fonts

Windows 98 provides 25 different fonts for displaying text in a DOS window. Sixteen of the fonts are fixed-pitch TrueType fonts (Lucida Console), and nine are bitmapped Terminal fonts. More details about fonts are available in "DOS fonts" in Chapter 26.

Windows 98 makes Lucida Console the default DOS font instead of Courier New. You can see the differences between these two fonts if you move Lucida Console out of the Fonts folder. Your DOS windows will automatically use the Courier font if Lucida is not found. In fact, the only way you can use Courier New is by moving Lucida Console.

Secret

You won't be able to move Lucida Console unless you restart Windows 98, press the Ctrl key during the power-on self test, and boot to the command prompt. You can then use the DOS Move command to move Lucida Console to another folder.

These fonts aren't used when DOS is displayed at full-screen size. The font built into your computer's ROM is used instead.

You can choose the font size and type (True Type or bitmap) for displaying DOS commands and programs in a window in two ways. The first is as follows:

STEPS

Choosing a DOS Font, First Method

Step 1. If your DOS application is displayed at full-screen size, press Alt+Enter to get DOS into a window.

Step 2. If the DOS window does not have a toolbar, click the system menu icon in the upper-left corner of the DOS window, and select Toolbar.

Step 3. Click the arrow on the font size combo box at the left end of the toolbar.

Step 4. Use the scroll bar on the font list box to review the choices.

Step 5. Choose a font size and type.

The second method is as follows:

STEPS

Choosing a DOS Font, Second Method

Step 1. Click the Font button (the button with an *A* on its face) at the right end of the DOS window toolbar.

Step 2. Choose a font from the Font size list, as shown in Figure 34-2. A preview of the DOS window size appears along with a preview of the font itself.

Step 3. Click OK.

(continued)

STEPS *(continued)*

Choosing a DOS Font, Second Method

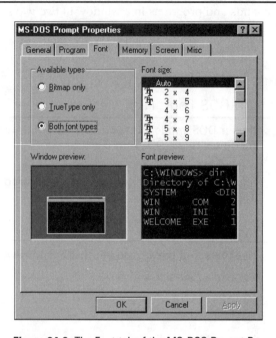

Figure 34-2: The Font tab of the MS-DOS Prompt Properties dialog box. When you choose a font from the list in the upper-right corner, the result is displayed in the two preview boxes.

Secret

If the Both Font Types option is marked in the Available Types area, only 23 fonts are shown, in addition to Auto. This is in spite of the fact that 25 fonts are available (sixteen TrueType and nine bitmapped). There is an overlap of the 4×6 and 7×12 TrueType and bitmapped fonts. Only the bitmapped fonts for these sizes are shown when this box is checked.

To choose the TrueType font for these two font sizes, mark the TrueType Only option button. These fonts of the same size look quite a bit different.

Auto font

If you want the font to change based on the size of the DOS window, set the font size to Auto. As you drag the window, Auto will choose the font size that best fits your DOS window size from among 23, 18, 16, or 9 fonts (depending on your choice of available fonts).

Mark, copy, and paste text or graphics to and from the DOS window and the Clipboard

The toolbar in a DOS window makes it easy to mark and copy data and text to and from the Clipboard. You can copy data and text into DOS documents from Windows documents and vice versa.

STEPS

Copying DOS Data to the Clipboard

Step 1. To start marking data (graphics or text), click the Mark button (it shows a dotted square) on the left side of the toolbar.

Step 2. Move your mouse pointer to anywhere just outside the area that contains the data or text that you want to copy to the Clipboard.

Step 3. Press and hold the left mouse button.

Step 4. Drag until the rectangle you are dragging with your mouse pointer completely covers the desired data or text.

Step 5. Release the mouse button.

Step 6. Click the Copy toolbar button (it shows two pieces of paper), or press Enter.

To paste text or graphics from the Clipboard into your DOS (or Windows) document, position your cursor in the document, and click the Paste toolbar button (it shows a clipboard), located to the right of the Copy button.

Changing directories in a DOS window

Here's a cool trick from Kaleb Axon, a Windows beta tester. It is an interesting way to change directories in a DOS window.

Undocumented

STEPS

Changing Directories in DOS

Step 1. Open a DOS window by clicking the Start button, Programs, MS-DOS Prompt.

Step 2. Open an Explorer window by right-clicking My Computer, and then clicking Explore. Navigate in the Explorer to any folder or subfolder.

(continued)

STEPS *(continued)*

Changing Directories in DOS

Step 3.   Type **cd** at the DOS prompt in the DOS window. Press the spacebar.

Step 4.   Drag and drop a folder icon from the Explorer window to the DOS window.

Step 5.   The folder name now appears on the DOS command line.

This is an example of a general class of behaviors. Drag and drop works with DOS, sort of. While you can't drag and drop text from a Windows 98 application into a DOS application, you can drag and drop filenames to the command line of a DOS application. (If you do need to drag and drop text from a Windows application, you can copy it to the Clipboard, and then paste it into a DOS text-editing application.)

Connecting a DOS window to the Explorer

Undocumented

Want to quickly open a DOS window into the current directory while you are navigating about your hard disk in the Explorer? This makes it easy to use DIR to look more closely at the files in that folder.

STEPS

DOS Windows and Folder Together

Step 1.   Open an Explorer window.

Step 2.   Choose View, Folder Options, and click the File Types tab.

Step 3.   Click File Folder in the Registered File Types list, and then click the Edit button.

Step 4.   Click the New button.

Step 5.   In the Action field, type **MS-DOS Prompt**.

Step 6.   In the Application Used to Perform Action field, type **C:\Command.com /k cd**.

Step 7.   Click OK, click Close, and then click Close again.

Step 8.   Right-click any folder icon in the Explorer window, and click MS-DOS Prompt in the context menu.

You now have a new context menu command, MS-DOS Prompt, associated with any folder. This always works, regardless of whether you right-click a folder icon in the right or left pane of the Explorer, a folder icon in a folder window, or a shortcut to a folder on the Desktop (or in any other folder). The DOS window opens up with its current directory equal to the folder that you right-clicked. This gives you a quick way to open a DOS window on any current folder in the Explorer.

You can use Doshere.inf, a file in Microsoft PowerToys, to do this automatically. Doshere.inf edits your Registry to insert the command shown in step 6 above. It puts the words *Command Prompt Here* in your context menu. If you'd rather have Doshere.inf add the words *MS-DOS Prompt*, you can edit it by opening it in Notepad. Download PowerToys from http://www. microsoft.com/windows/software/powertoy.htm.

Expand the DOS window to full screen

You can run DOS in a DOS window or you can run it at the full-screen size. It's easy to switch back and forth. Press Alt+Enter to switch between the two modes. If you have the toolbar displayed, you can switch to full screen by clicking the Full Screen toolbar button (the button with four arrowheads).

Change the properties of the shortcut to the DOS application

Click the Properties button in the DOS window toolbar. It is the fourth button from the right, and it shows a hand holding a sheet of paper. We discuss the effect of changing these properties in the "Editing Shortcut Properties" section later in this chapter.

Background button

Click the Background button on the DOS window toolbar to *not* suspend the DOS application while it is in the background; that is, when the DOS application doesn't have the focus. (This button is turned on by default.) See the "Background" section later in this chapter.

Closing a DOS application

Under normal circumstances, you exit your DOS application by whatever means the developer of your DOS program provided. If you mark the Close on Exit check box in your DOS application's *pif*, the DOS window will also close when you exit your application.

If you are unable to exit normally, you can exit by clicking the Close button (the X) at the right end of the DOS window's title bar. You will get a warning message if the Warn If Still Active check box is marked in the DOS application's *pif*.

Using Windows 3.1*x*, you exited from the DOS command prompt in a Windows DOS session by typing **exit** and pressing Enter. You can now just click the Close button. Placing an X.bat file on your path that contains the single line *exit* also gives you an easy way to end a DOS session. If you do this, you can simply press the letter *X*, and then press Enter to exit.

Creating a Virtual Machine for DOS Programs

Windows creates a "virtual machine" for every DOS program you start from Windows (every Windows DOS session). You have the option of designing this "virtual machine." Instead of interacting with your computer hardware (the real machine), the DOS program interacts with something that it "sees" as a real machine: the virtual machine.

Undocumented

If you start your DOS programs from MS-DOS Prompt in the Start menu, they will run in the virtual computer associated with that MS-DOS prompt. This virtual machine is defined by properties stored in the MS-DOS Prompt shortcut in the \Windows\Start Menu folder. You can edit these properties to redefine the virtual machine associated with the Start menu's MS-DOS Prompt.

Undocumented

When you click an icon that represents a DOS program in a folder window, or the Explorer, you automatically create a shortcut. This is also true if you choose Run from the Start menu. This shortcut to a DOS program is stored in the same folder the DOS program is stored in. If a shortcut is already there, a new one isn't created.

Undocumented

If you delete or move the shortcut, clicking the DOS application's icon in the Explorer creates a new shortcut in the folder that contains the DOS application, unless you moved the shortcut to the \Windows\Pif folder. If the DOS program doesn't execute, the shortcut won't be created.

These shortcuts to DOS programs are like shortcuts to Windows programs. However, the properties of a shortcut to a DOS program, a *pif*, are different from those of a shortcut to a Windows program because the properties of a shortcut to a DOS program define a virtual machine.

Click a shortcut to a DOS program and the program starts. You can move and copy these shortcuts. You can place them on your Desktop or on your Start menus. You can have multiple shortcuts for one DOS program, just as you can have multiple, and different, shortcuts for Windows programs or documents.

Shortcuts to DOS can be associated with documents instead of programs, just like Windows shortcuts. You can associate the DOS applications that open these documents with the documents' extension. See "Creating and Editing File Types and Actions" in Chapter 13 for details on how to associate applications with document extensions.

Undocumented

While the task of identifying the needs of each and every DOS program is too daunting for Microsoft to attempt, Windows 98 comes with Apps.inf, which is stored in the \Windows\Inf folder. Apps.inf provides the basic virtual machine configuration for over 300 DOS applications. You don't have to do anything to access this file; Windows 98 automatically uses it to help create shortcuts for the DOS programs referenced in it.

In many cases, the default shortcut that is created when you click a DOS application icon works just fine.

Undocumented

Many DOS software developers include *pif*s with their DOS applications. *Pif*s created for Windows 3.1*x* are compatible with shortcuts to DOS programs for Windows 98. You can place them wherever they are appropriate for your work.

Secret

When a shortcut is created automatically, it has the same name as the DOS program, but a different extension: *pif*. You won't see this extension even if you have chosen View, Folder Options, View in the Explorer and cleared the Hide File Extensions for Known File Types check box. (Likewise, you won't see the *lnk* extension used for shortcuts to Windows programs.) You will see the file type Shortcut to MS-DOS Program.

Secret

There is a difference between starting a DOS program at the MS-DOS prompt within a Windows DOS session and clicking the DOS program icon in a folder window.

- If you start the DOS program from the MS-DOS prompt in a Windows DOS session, no shortcut is created.

- If you click the DOS program icon (or run the DOS program by choosing Run from the Start menu), a shortcut is created.

You can also create a shortcut by right-clicking a DOS program icon and clicking Create Shortcut.

Creating multiple shortcuts

You can create multiple shortcuts that are all associated with the same DOS program. By setting different properties in each shortcut, you can start the DOS program in different configurations by clicking the different shortcuts. Here's how:

STEPS

Creating Multiple Shortcuts

Step 1.   Click a DOS program's executable icon in the Explorer (or in a folder window).

Step 2.   Exit the DOS program.

(continued)

STEPS *(continued)*

Creating Multiple Shortcuts

Step 3.   Use the Explorer to display the folder that contains the DOS program.

Step 4.   Highlight the shortcut associated with your DOS program. Press F2.

Step 5.   Type a new filename for the shortcut and press Enter.

Step 6.   Right-click the shortcut, choose Copy. Right-click the right pane of the Explorer and choose Paste.

Step 7.   Click the new shortcut and press F2. Type a new name for this shortcut and press Enter.

Step 8.   Repeat steps 6 and 7 to create new shortcuts associated with the same DOS program.

Step 9.   Edit each of these shortcuts for different properties, as detailed in the following sections. You can move these shortcuts to different folders or onto the Desktop or Start menus.

Opening Program Information Files (*pif*s)

If you are familiar with editing *pif*s using Windows 3.1*x*, you'll notice the Pif Editor is gone. Good riddance.

In its place, you can easily change the properties that are stored in a DOS program's shortcut. The shortcut stores these changes. We show two ways to display these properties. Our sample DOS application is Command.com. Here's the first method:

STEPS

Displaying a DOS Application's Properties

Step 1.   Use the Explorer to view the \Windows folder.

Step 2.   Right-click the Command.com icon, and then select Properties. A shortcut to Command.com is created.

If a shortcut has already been created for a DOS application, you can use the Explorer, perhaps in conjunction with the Find tool, to find the shortcut. Once you have found it, right-click it and choose Properties. You can open the shortcut associated with any DOS program in this same manner.

The following steps describe another method:

Getting to a DOS Shortcut

Step 1.   Using the Explorer, find Command.com in the \Windows folder. Click Command.com.

Step 2.   Click the system menu icon at the left end of the DOS window's title bar, or right-click the title bar. (If you are using a full-screen Windows DOS session, press Alt+Enter to switch to a windowed DOS session.)

Step 3.   Choose Properties from the menu.

Step 4.   You can now change the properties of the virtual machine. The properties will be stored in the shortcut.

You can use this method whenever you are running a DOS program in a window. If the toolbar is displayed, you can also click the Properties toolbar button.

Editing Shortcut Properties

There are seven tabs associated with a DOS program. The first one, the General tab, is for any DOS or Windows file or folder. You won't see this tab if you have the DOS window open and you click the Properties toolbar button, or click the system menu icon (or right-click the title bar) and choose Properties.

Program properties

The Program tab is the meat of the matter. Take a look at Figure 34-3 to see what we mean. The Program tab contains the command line for the DOS program, its working directory, an optional startup batch file that runs before the DOS application, a hot key definition, a window configuration, and buttons to change the associated shortcut's icon and define MS-DOS mode. You'll find a big chunk of DOS program functionality here.

The Program tab for a shortcut to a DOS program is a lot like the Shortcut tab associated with Windows programs. Figure 34-4 shows the similarities. Where there are differences, we point them out.

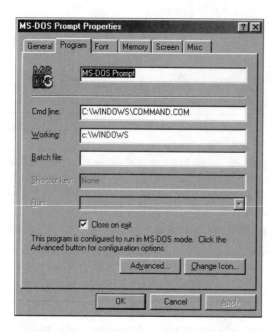

Figure 34-3: The Program tab. Define the title of the application, its command line, working directory, startup batch file, shortcut key combination, state of the DOS window, and icon. Also specify whether the application needs to run in MS-DOS mode or not.

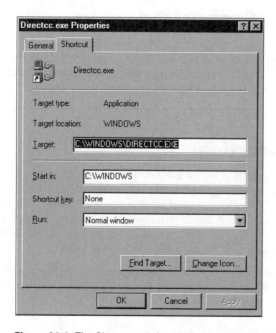

Figure 34-4: The Shortcut tab for a Windows shortcut. The Target field is like the Cmd line field in the Program tab. The Start In field is similar to the Working field. Both tabs have Run and Shortcut Key fields, and both have Change Icon buttons.

Notice that the Program and Shortcut properties have titles, command lines (Cmd Line and Target), working directories (Working and Start In), Shortcut Key and Run fields, and Change Icon buttons. For more on shortcuts, see "DOS shortcut properties" in Chapter 10.

Title

The title is displayed on the left side of a DOS application's title bar, which appears when the application is running in a window (not in full-screen mode). The title is also displayed on the Taskbar button for the window. By default, Windows uses the name of the shortcut for the title, but you can change it by typing a new title in the field at the top of the Program tab.

Command line

When you start a DOS program for the first time by clicking its icon in a folder window, you automatically create a shortcut that contains the complete pathname of the DOS application in the Cmd Line field. The command line can contain the driver letter, folder name, filename, extension, and any command line parameters.

You can set the values for what are referred to as *environmental variables* in your Autoexec.bat file and other DOS batch files. You do this with a Set command. You can use these variables in the Cmd Line field in the Program tab to insert their associated values in the command line. You use the following form:

%variablename%

For example, if you entered the command Set location = ABC in your Autoexec.bat, you could then enter the command line c:\%location%\ Myprog.exe in the Cmd Line field to run the program Myprog in the ABC directory.

Secret

If you move the DOS program, or if you want the shortcut to refer to another program, you can edit this command line. Unlike shortcuts to Windows applications or documents, a shortcut to a DOS program or document will not go looking for the associated DOS program or document if you move it. You have to edit the command line to give it a new location.

The Shortcut tab has a Find Target button. There is no such button in a shortcut to a DOS program. You have to navigate to the DOS application's folder by yourself, using the Explorer or a folder window.

If your DOS program can accept different command line parameters and you want to be able to type them whenever you start the DOS program, you need to add a space and a question mark at the end of the command line string. You only need to type one question mark, no matter how many parameters your DOS program can accept. If you make this modification to your command line, the MS-DOS Prompt dialog box, shown in Figure 34-5, will appear each time you start the DOS program to let you enter your parameters.

Figure 34-5: If you enter a question mark after the program name in the command line of a DOS shortcut, you get to specify the command line parameters every time you start this DOS application.

If you use the same command line parameters every time you start a DOS application, just type them in the Cmd Line field after the program's pathname. You can create multiple shortcuts associated with one DOS program, each with different command line parameters, and perhaps one with a question mark.

When you run a shortcut from the Run command on the Start menu, any parameters you type after the shortcut name *override* the parameters that you specified in the Cmd Line field on the shortcut's Program tab. For example, doing a command such as Run Myapp.lnk /abc forces your app to use the parameter /abc instead of whatever command line you defined in the shortcut. This is one way to use one set of switches to start the application most of the time, and use a different set occasionally.

The command line can contain a DOS application name and a filename, something like C:\Windows\Command\Edit.com C:\Windows\Temp\ New.txt, for example. The shortcut will be a shortcut to the document, just like a Windows shortcut to a document.

If the DOS application is associated with a file extension, you can easily create a *lnk* shortcut to a DOS document. Right-click a document with that extension and click Create Shortcut. This creates a Windows shortcut, a file with the *lnk* extension, not a *pif*. You have to create the association between the file extension and the DOS program first. Turn to "Associating Actions with File Extensions" in Chapter 13 for details.

You can change a *lnk* file to a *pif* just by adding the DOS application name in front of the document filename in the Target field of the Shortcut tab. For example, assume you have a shortcut to a text file that is normally associated with Notepad. You can edit the command line in the Shortcut tab for this document to use Edit.com instead. When you do, the *lnk* file turns into a *pif*.

You can't create a *lnk* shortcut from a *pif*. If you right-click a *pif* and choose Create Shortcut, you'll create another *pif*.

Working directory

The working directory is the folder meant to contain files that work in conjunction with your DOS application or the data or text files you edit with the DOS application. The DOS program will search the directory you enter in the Working field for any files it needs. Whether an entry is needed here or not depends on the DOS program.

Tip

For example, one of the authors runs the DOS program Doom (don't so many misguided souls?). The Doom shortcut is stored in \Windows\Desktop. The command line for Doom is d:\games\doom\doom.exe. The working directory for Doom is d:\games\doom. If the Working field is blank, Doom 1.2 won't run when you click the Doom shortcut icon. Heretic, another product from id Software, the developers of Doom, doesn't require an entry in the Working field.

Batch file

You can run a DOS batch file before your application starts up.

This is one way to set certain environmental variables for a DOS application before you run it. For example, put the following line in this batch file:

```
Set Mydir=C:\thisone
```

Alternatively, you can load TSR programs in the batch file before your primary DOS application starts. You then can access the TSR from within that DOS application — without using memory in every DOS session by loading that TSR prior to starting Windows.

Hot key(s)

You can type an entry in the hot key field (it's labeled Shortcut Key) to define a set of keys that you press at the same time to start a DOS application. Hot keys work for shortcuts that are in the Start menus or on the Desktop.

Hot keys let you start an application from the keyboard without mousing around. People who use DOS applications in full-screen mode and want to quickly start and switch between applications are particularly fond of them.

While the name of the field, Shortcut Key, is singular, it is best to assign a *set* of keys to be pressed together as one hot key. That way, you can define three keys that probably won't be used for something in another application that might be open at the time you press these three keys. For example, you could define Ctrl+Alt+D to start the MS-DOS Prompt window.

If you use the Ctrl, Alt, and/or Shift key, it is easy to press and hold down one or two of these keys while you press the last key, most likely a letter key. These keys are modifier keys, and usually your applications won't react to them until you press another key. This makes it easier to press three keys at once.

Even if another application has the focus and you are in full-screen DOS mode, the hot key will work. The hot key takes precedence. If you define a hot key combination that was originally used in another application, that application loses the ability to use that combination, even if it has the focus. The keyboard combination opens the application for which you defined the hot key instead.

Tip

For example, if you define a hot key as Shift+D without Ctrl or Alt, you will be unable to type a *D* (uppercase *d*) in your word processor. Or if you define a hot key as Ctrl+Shift+D and that combination is used in your spreadsheet for some function, the spreadsheet will not be able to see that combination, because Windows will grab it before the spreadsheet can get a hold of it — even if the spreadsheet has the focus.

Undocumented

Your hot key should (by convention) include either an Alt or Ctrl key, plus a function key or printable key. The Windows 98 help files say it has to, but it doesn't. You can include the Shift key in the combination, but not the keys Backspace, Enter, Esc, Print Screen, Spacebar, or Tab. Ctrl+Shift or Ctrl+Alt plus a letter key is often a good combination. Windows applications often leave combinations with these keys undefined so you can define macros with them.

Something else to try is Ctrl or Alt in combination with the punctuation keys (period, comma, and so on). Windows applications rarely use these combinations.

If you just want to switch to running applications, an easier way to do this is to press Alt+Tab. This allows you to switch to any running application, DOS *or* Windows. You can also use Ctrl+Esc to get to the Start menu.

Tip

If you set a hot key for a shortcut and later want to get rid of it, you can't just delete the key combination from the Shortcut Key field, and then save the shortcut. The previous key assignment isn't actually deleted unless you succeed in entering None in the box. And you can't just type the word *none* — you must place your insertion point in the field and press Backspace to specify None.

Undocumented

The Shortcut tab of a *lnk* file also has a hot key definition field. While hot keys work the same way with both types of shortcuts (*pif* and *lnk*), entering keystrokes into the hot key field works differently. If you type the *d* key in the Shortcut Key field of the Program tab for a *pif* file, it gets entered as a *d*. In contrast, if you type a *d* in the same field of the Shortcut tab for a *lnk* file, Windows automatically adds Ctrl+Alt+ before the *d*.

It is not a good idea to redefine function keys, such as F1 (help), as hot keys. This reduces the functionality of Windows 98. Many applications also use the combinations Ctrl+F1, Ctrl+Shift+F1, and so on.

Run — normal, minimized, maximized

In what size window do you want to start your DOS application?

If your font size is set to Auto, you can maximize the DOS window so that it fills up the Desktop as much as possible. DOS windows are sized based on the height-to-width ratio of the DOS font you're using, and their size is limited by the size of the Desktop. If you choose Maximized with Auto font sizing, you'll get a large DOS window.

If you have a fixed DOS font size, the Maximized setting will display a DOS *window* that encompasses a whole DOS *screen* at the set DOS font.

If you choose Normal, you will get a DOS window that is the restored size. If the maximized and restored size are the same because you are using a fixed DOS font size, and the DOS window is big enough to display the whole DOS screen, the only difference between Normal and Maximized may be the location of the window.

If you choose Minimized, the DOS application opens as a button on the Taskbar. This is great for running DOS programs that don't require any interaction with the user (as is true of many batch files).

Close on exit

The Close on Exit check box is a very nice feature. If you want to run a quick DOS batch file, you can have it show up only as a button on your Taskbar and make it go away as soon as it carries out its work.

In many cases, you will want the DOS window to close after you have completed working with the DOS application or document. This is the way all Windows programs work; nothing is left open after you quit them. The only reason you would want to leave the DOS window open is if you wanted to run another DOS program after you finished working on the one that you are currently running.

You can open a DOS window with just the DOS prompt, as you do when you click the MS-DOS Prompt item in the Start menu. Even with Close on Exit checked, the DOS prompt is there ready for you to run the next DOS program. You don't exit the command prompt DOS window until you type **exit** at the prompt or click the Close button (the X) in the upper-right corner of the DOS window.

Tip

If your DOS program does some work, writes some output to the DOS screen, and then quits, you won't be able to see what the output was if you mark Close on Exit. Lots of DOS programs do this, so clear this check box if you want to see their output.

If you quit a DOS application and the DOS window is still on the Desktop, the title bar of the DOS window states that the application is inactive. To get rid of the DOS window, click its Close button.

Change Icon button

The Change Icon button is pretty straightforward. You are given a choice of icons contained in C:\Windows\System\Pifmgr.dll, as shown in Figure 34-6. If your current icon is contained in another file, the icons in that file are displayed. You can choose a new icon from among those displayed, or browse through other files for other icons.

The Browse button brings up the common File Open dialog box. You use this dialog box to find the file that contains the icons you want to use.

Figure 34-6: Choose an icon. Use the scroll bar to move to the right or left and then double-click the icon you want. If you want to get an icon from another file, click Browse.

Advanced button

Clicking the Advanced button in the Program tab displays the Advanced Program Settings dialog box shown in Figure 34-7.

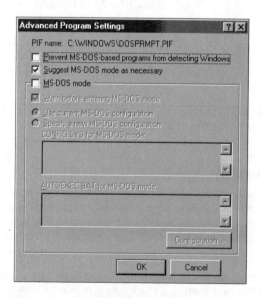

Figure 34-7: The Advanced Program Settings dialog box.

Mark the Prevent MS-DOS-Based Programs from Detecting Windows check box if you want the DOS box to try to fool any program that checks to see if it is running under Windows by telling the program that it isn't. If you mark the Suggest MS-DOS Mode As Necessary check box, Windows will see if the DOS program you're running could better use MS-DOS mode. The third check box turns on MS-DOS mode. If you click a DOS program icon that has this check box marked, your computer is switched to MS-DOS mode.

Many DOS programs that didn't run well under Windows 3.1x will run fine in a Windows DOS session under Windows 98. Some of these Windows-unfriendly DOS programs check to make sure they aren't running under Windows so that they can warn you to quit Windows before running them.

Tip

If you have a Windows-unfriendly program that can, in fact, run in the Windows 98 DOS session, you can send a message to it when it asks if it is running under Windows telling it that it is not (when, of course, it is). This allows it to run in a Windows 98 DOS session (hopefully) successfully. You send this message by marking the Prevent MS-DOS-Based Programs from Detecting Windows check box.

By default, you can run Windows programs from the DOS prompt of a Windows DOS session. If you mark the first check box in the Advanced Program Settings dialog box, Windows 98 will no longer be able to recognize that you typed the name of the Windows program at the DOS prompt, and Windows programs will not run from a Windows DOS session.

Windows checks to see if there are incompatibilities in a DOS program that will most likely prevent it from running successfully in a Windows DOS session. If you leave the Suggest MS-DOS Mode As Necessary check box marked (the default), Windows tells you if it finds such incompatibilities. If you clear this check box, you run the risk of running a badly behaved DOS program in your Windows DOS session.

If you mark the MS-DOS Mode check box and mark the Specify a New MS-DOS Configuration option button, the lower portion of the Advanced Program Settings dialog box becomes active, and you can edit the CONFIG.SYS for MS-DOS Mode and AUTOEXEC.BAT for MS-DOS Mode fields.

If you clear the MS-DOS Mode check box, the rest of the dialog box doesn't apply and is dimmed. We discuss MS-DOS mode in the "MS-DOS Mode" section later in this chapter, so we'll quit talking about it here.

Font properties

For details on the Font tab, see the section earlier in this chapter entitled "Choosing the DOS display fonts."

Memory properties

The amount of memory available to a DOS program running in a Windows DOS session depends on the configuration of the Autoexec.bat and Config.sys files (if you have them), and whether DOS TSRs and 16-bit drivers are loaded in conventional memory or in the upper memory blocks (UMBs).

You can find further details in "Getting the best of conventional and upper memory" in Chapter 35.

Windows 98 can provide DOS programs with expanded, extended, and/or DOS protected-mode memory (DPMI, for DOS Protected Mode Interface). The DOS programs must comply with Windows expanded, extended, and/or DPMI memory specifications in order to be able to use this memory.

Because Windows 98 makes extensive use of 32-bit protected-mode drivers that do not use conventional memory or UMBs, it can provide up to 612K of conventional memory for DOS programs that run in Windows DOS sessions.

The Memory tab in the Properties dialog box, as shown in Figure 34-8, is divided into four sections, one for each type of memory available to DOS programs. You can use these sections to set the amount of each type of memory that's available to your DOS program.

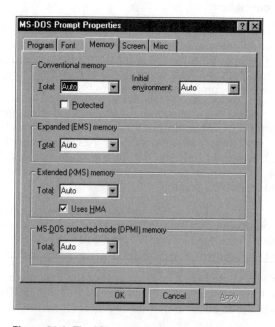

Figure 34-8: The Memory tab. You can set the amount of available conventional, expanded, extended, and/or DPMI memory.

The default setting is Auto, which means, "let the DOS programs determine how much they need or want." Some DOS programs don't do a good job of restraining themselves and need to be limited in their memory acquisition.

Conventional memory

The maximum amount of conventional memory available is about 612K under the best of circumstances. DOS games and other large programs will likely take all they can get. The only reason to limit the amount of conventional memory available to a DOS program is to let the program load slightly faster. This may help on slower computers, but won't be noticeable on faster ones.

Tip

You could create a separate shortcut, for example, for "small" DOS sessions in which you plan to run only DOS commands such as DIR, Del, and so on. Setting conventional memory at 160K would be adequate for these tasks. This would conserve physical memory for other applications while a "small" DOS session is running.

Protected

Does your DOS program contain a bug? Does it write to memory in areas that it shouldn't? If so, click the Protected check box to help protect Windows from crashing because of bugs caused by your DOS application.

When the Protected check box is marked, the MS-DOS system memory area is write-protected so your DOS application can't write into this area and corrupt it.

Environment

If you are running a batch file to set environment variables before your DOS application runs, you might want to expand the size of the environment that stores these variables. You may have a smaller environment size in your common Config.sys file. Use the Initial Environment drop-down list to set aside a larger environment for environment variables that are particular to your DOS application.

Expanded (EMS) memory

If a DOS program makes use of expanded memory that meets the LIM 4.0 specification, Windows itself can provide it with expanded memory. Windows includes its own expanded memory manager separate from Emm386.exe. DOS games such as Xwing use expanded memory for handling sound effects and music. Some DOS spreadsheets also use expanded memory.

You can set the value for expanded memory to Auto if you want the DOS program to determine how much it needs, or you can limit its appetite. Some DOS programs don't know when they have had enough, so you'll have to tell them.

If you have a Config.sys file with a line calling the MS-DOS expanded memory manager (Emm386.exe), and if the parameter *noems* is on that line, expanded memory will not be available to DOS programs running in Windows DOS sessions. The Memory tab will be altered to show this state of affairs, as shown in Figure 34-9.

For most DOS programs, you can set expanded memory equal to zero. If you have any DOS programs that use expanded or extended memory, you should give these programs their own shortcuts.

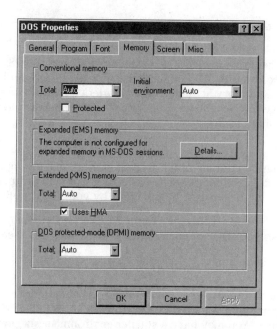

Figure 34-9: The Memory tab with no expanded memory available. If you have a line such as Device=Emm386.exe noems in your Config.sys file, there will be no expanded memory available to your DOS programs.

Extended (XMS) memory

If your DOS application makes use of extended memory in a way that is compatible with running under Windows, the XMS memory settings allow you to specify the amount of available extended memory.

Applications that use DPMI (DOS Protected Mode Interface) — which Microsoft prescribes as the correct way to access extended memory under a multitasking environment — can use this extended memory. (DPMI applications obtain extended memory through Himem.sys or other "XMS managers.")

HMA

If DOS or other 16-bit drivers are loaded high in your Config.sys file, marking the Uses HMA check box doesn't do anything. Otherwise, you can use this memory like extended memory.

The High Memory Area (HMA) is the first 64K of extended memory. It is the only part of extended memory that an application running under DOS can access while still in real mode. Very few DOS applications currently use this memory area. This is unfortunate, because if they did, they would be able to add almost 64K to the amount of conventional memory available to them (unless the line DOS=High is in your Config.sys file). The Windows memory manager, Himem.sys, and all other compatible memory managers make this 64K area available to Windows or any other program that requests it.

The rule for the Uses HMA check box is: If you start two shortcuts under Windows — both using the HMA — Windows will switch this memory between them in turn, so they can both benefit from using it.

If you turn *off* the Uses HMA check box, an application started from that shortcut cannot access any HMA from within Windows, even if it would otherwise be capable of doing so.

If, however, DOS or a DOS application claims the HMA *before* you start Windows, then no Windows application or shortcut to a DOS program can ever use it.

DOS applications that can use the HMA generally make this fact very well known in their publicity and documentation. You can leave this check box marked, unless you know that two particular applications using it at once would conflict. In that case, turn it off for the application that requires less memory.

DOS protected-mode (DPMI) memory

Some DOS programs use this specification for turning extended memory into something that DOS programs can use.

Screen properties

The default setting for a new shortcut is to run your DOS application windowed on the Windows 98 Desktop. This makes DOS programs look and feel more like Windows programs, which is a nice touch.

Tip

MS-DOS programs that run in VGA graphics mode can run in a window on the Desktop. This wasn't the case in Windows 3.1*x*. DOS games that rely on hand-eye coordination will probably run too slowly in a window. You'll want to run them at full-screen size.

You can always switch between full-screen and windowed views with Alt+Enter.

Starting a Windows DOS session in a small window takes slightly more memory than starting it full-screen. So if your application won't start in a window, mark the Full-Screen option button in the tab of the Properties dialog box (see Figure 34-10).

Initial size — number of lines displayed

If your video display driver can provide support for more than 25 lines of DOS text in a DOS window or full-screen display (and most VGA or higher-resolution systems can) the Initial Size drop-down list will be active. You can change the number of lines displayed in the first box.

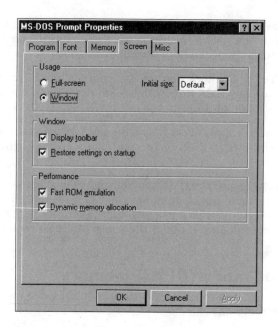

Figure 34-10: The Screen tab. Choose how your DOS program will be windowed.

This works great for a windowed DOS session, even one that merely displays the good old DOS C:\> prompt. When you configure Windows for a number of screen lines greater than 25 — let's say 50 — DOS commands *know* that the screen now contains that many lines. For example, the command dir /p, which halts a directory listing at the end of each screen page, now stops scrolling the display after showing 50 lines instead of 25.

DOS applications themselves vary in their support for higher-than-25-line screens. Some applications automatically adjust to the number of lines in effect when they start up. Other applications, presuming that no one would ever have a display with more than 25 lines, are hard-coded to force themselves into that mode every time.

No matter how many DOS screen lines you configure Windows for, Windows won't open a windowed DOS session any taller than your screen will allow. If you specify a number of lines that would make a windowed DOS session extend beyond the top and bottom of your screen (with the DOS screen font you're using), Windows creates a window only the height of your physical screen — with scroll bars so you can see the rest.

Most VGA adapters support 25-, 43-, and 50-line modes, although if yours doesn't, this setting won't change anything. A 43-line display takes up less room on your display than a 50-line display, while still giving you a lot more information than the bad old 25-line display.

Restore settings on start-up

You can change your font, window size, and position while running your DOS application. If your want your original values to be used the next time you start the application, mark the Restore Settings on Start-Up check box.

If this check box is cleared, Windows retains the values you used in your last session. For example, if you exit your DOS application and close the DOS window while you are in full-screen mode, the next time you start this application, it will come up in full-screen mode.

Fast ROM emulation

Applications that display text run faster if you mark the Fast ROM Emulation check box. This allows Windows to use faster routines in RAM if the application normally uses standard ROM BIOS calls to write text to the screen. You must turn off this setting if garbage appears on the application's screen or if you lose control of its mouse when you run it under Windows.

Dynamic memory allocation

If your DOS application switches back and forth between text and graphics modes or starts in text mode and switches later to graphics mode, you need to be sure always to have enough memory for the graphics mode. In these cases, you'll want to clear the Dynamic Memory Allocation check box. Otherwise you can release this memory for other programs if they start in graphics mode and then switch to text mode. This switch appears to be written in the most part for Microsoft Word for MS-DOS.

Check this box if you want to let other programs use the small amount of extra available memory when the DOS application goes into text mode.

Misc properties

Microsoft had no other place to put these properties of the DOS virtual machine, so it created a Misc tab, as shown in Figure 34-11. Not too original, but what the heck.

Allow screen saver

Screen savers can be pretty unruly. If you want to allow your screen saver to start up even though you are in full-screen DOS mode, mark the Allow Screen Saver check box.

Screen savers can interfere with DOS communications or terminal emulation programs, which is the biggest reason to clear this check box.

Background

Background refers to the time when an application doesn't have the focus. If the DOS application is running in full-screen mode and you can see it, it has the focus. If it is running in a window and its title bar is highlighted, it has the focus.

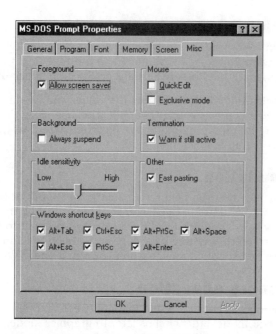

Figure 34-11: The Misc tab. This is the grab bag of the DOS properties. Whatever didn't fit elsewhere is here.

If your program is a DOS communications application that runs in the background, clear the Always Suspend check box so that it can download files and do other tasks for you as you're working in another application in the foreground. You don't want to suspend communications programs when they are in the background, because they are productive even when they don't have the focus.

Other DOS applications don't do anything if they don't have the focus, so for these programs, you might as well mark the Always Suspend check box to give all the computer's resources to the foreground task.

Idle sensitivity

When you turn the idle sensitivity to high, Windows can stop giving DOS applications any time slices if it determines that the application is doing nothing but waiting for you to press a key. This cutoff can make foreground Windows applications run faster when a DOS session that needs no time slices is running in the background.

Whether Windows *correctly* determines that a DOS application is idle, however, varies from application to application.

Newer DOS applications can detect when they are running under Windows and send it a message whenever they are merely waiting for a keystroke. This makes your whole system run faster, since Windows doesn't have to give time slices to that application until you start using it again.

The Idle Sensitivity option is intended for older kinds of DOS applications. The rules for using it with the newer DOS programs are not intuitive. You should set this option according to one of the following three rules:

1. If the application is an older one and does not do *anything* in the background that is important, turn idle sensitivity to high.

2. If the application does something once a second, or intermittently when a certain event occurs (such as midnight), turn idle sensitivity to low.

3. If the application is a newer, Windows-aware type, turn idle sensitivity to low. Your applications will all run a little faster if Windows gets the "idle" message directly from these applications and does not have to test for it.

Unfortunately, it is difficult to determine whether a particular DOS application does or does not send this "idle" message to Windows. If the documentation doesn't mention this feature, you have to assume that it hasn't been added to the program.

Mouse

Don't mark the QuickEdit check box if your DOS application uses a mouse. Marking this check box makes it easier to use your mouse to mark, copy, and paste selections to the Clipboard, but it does this at the cost of disabling the mouse for other actions.

Normally, if you want to mark a selection to copy to the Clipboard from a DOS window, you have to click the Mark toolbar button before you start dragging to select the text (or graphics). If you mark the QuickEdit check box, you don't have to do this. As soon as you begin to drag, Windows turns on the Mark button for you.

This setting is useful if you are copying and pasting a great deal of data from your DOS application to Windows or to other DOS applications.

If you check Exclusive Mode, you lose your Windows mouse pointer while this DOS application is in the foreground. The only reason to do this is if your DOS program won't use the mouse correctly unless it exclusively controls it.

To get your Windows mouse pointer back while this DOS application is in the foreground, press Alt+Spacebar, P. This is the keyboard shortcut to display the Properties dialog box. You can then use the mouse to click the Misc tab and clear this check box.

Termination

You can exit your DOS application in a number of ways. If your DOS application is Command.com (the DOS prompt), you can type **exit** and press Enter. If you are in some other DOS application, you exit that application in the fashion determined by the application. If you have chosen Close on Exit in the Program tab, the DOS window closes.

You can also close a DOS window just by clicking the Close button (the X) in the upper-right corner of the window. If you are at the DOS prompt, the DOS window closes without further ado. If you are in a DOS program, you may want to close this DOS program first before you close the DOS window. This way, you can be sure you have saved any unsaved data to your disk.

If you want Windows to remind you to close your DOS application before you close its DOS window, mark the Warn If Still Active check box.

Other

Some old DOS programs can take input only so fast. They expect you to be typing, not piping stuff over from some Windows file. If you paste data into your DOS application and it has trouble with it, clear the Fast Pasting check box.

Windows shortcut keys

Windows has a defined set of what we call *hot keys*, which it refers to as *shortcut keys*. It grabs them first whenever you press them. If your DOS program wants these keys for its own uses, you have to configure a shortcut for that application that tells Windows to back off and let the keystrokes go to the DOS application.

Table 34-2 lists these hot keys and their definitions.

Table 34-2 Windows Hot Keys

Hot Key	Definition
Alt+Tab	Tab from one active application to another. Switch to graphics mode if DOS is in full-screen text mode. This is the "cool switch." Windows 3.1x has a text-mode version of the cool switch that doesn't switch to graphics mode when you switch between full-screen DOS applications.
Alt+Tab+Click	If your DOS application is in full-screen mode and you press and hold the Alt+Tab key combination, clicking any mouse button brings up the Desktop.
Ctrl+Esc	Switch to graphics mode, if necessary, from full-screen DOS, display the Desktop and the Taskbar, and click the Start button.
Alt+Print Screen	Copy the active window to the Clipboard. If the DOS application is in a DOS window, copy it as a graphic; if the DOS application is in full-screen text mode, copy it as text.
Alt+Spacebar	Click the system menu icon.
Alt+Esc	Switch to the next active application.
Print Screen	Copy the complete Desktop, including all windows, to the Clipboard. In full-screen DOS text mode, copy all the text to the Clipboard.
Alt+Enter	Switch between full-screen and DOS window.

To let the DOS application use any of these keystrokes while it has the focus or is in full-screen mode, clear the check box associated with the appropriate keystrokes.

If you clear the PrtSc check box and the Windows DOS session is in full-screen mode, the Print Screen key sends the current DOS screen to the printer in the same way it would under the DOS operating system.

Undocumented

Pressing Alt+Enter toggles between the Window and Full-Screen option buttons in the shortcut's Screen tab. You may want your DOS application to come up the same way you set it the first time and not the way you left it the last time. To preserve the settings in a shortcut's properties, you can set the shortcut's file attribute to Read-Only. Right-click the shortcut icon, click Properties, and then mark the Read-Only check box in the General tab.

MS-DOS Mode

If your DOS program doesn't work in a Windows DOS session, you can run it in MS-DOS mode (real-mode DOS). Rebooted MS-DOS mode works by shutting down Windows 98, performing a warm reboot, and booting into MS-DOS after calling a second copy of Command.com. When you exit MS-DOS mode, Windows 98 restarts.

Non-rebooted MS-DOS mode doesn't require a reboot before DOS starts. It runs the Dosstart.bat file right after it switches to DOS mode. You can exit back to Windows 98 by typing **exit** at the DOS prompt.

To get to a command prompt (the DOS prompt) in rebooted MS-DOS mode, you need to create a shortcut for Command.com with the proper properties (see the next section). You can put the icon associated with this shortcut on your Desktop, in one of your Start menus, or wherever is convenient. You can create properly configured shortcuts for every DOS application that requires MS-DOS mode.

Creating an MS-DOS mode shortcut

To create an MS-DOS mode shortcut for your Desktop, carry out the following steps:

STEPS

Creating a Shortcut for MS-DOS Mode

Step 1. Open the Explorer and navigate to your Windows 98 folder. Find Command.com.

Step 2. Right-click Command.com, and click Properties.

(continued)

STEPS *(continued)*

Creating a Shortcut for MS-DOS Mode

Step 3.   Click the Program tab and then the Advanced button.

Step 4.   Mark the MS-DOS Mode check box. If you don't want a warning before you switch to MS-DOS mode, clear the Warn Before Entering MS-DOS Mode check box.

Step 5.   The default is to use the current MS-DOS configuration. This means that you won't need to reboot to get to MS-DOS mode. If you want private Autoexec.bat and Config.sys files for this DOS application, you should mark the Specify a New MS-DOS Configuration option button. See the next section.

Step 6.   Click OK in the Advanced Program Settings dialog box, and click OK again in the Properties dialog box.

Step 7.   Click F5 to refresh your Explorer. If you order your Explorer window in details view by name, a new MS-DOS shortcut icon labeled Command will be right below Command.com. If not, check in the \Windows\Pif folder. Right-drag the shortcut to the Desktop. Click Move Here in the context menu.

Step 8.   The name of your new shortcut icon, Command, will be highlighted. Press F2, type **MS-DOS mode**, and press Enter.

You now have an icon on the Desktop that will get you to the non-rebooted MS-DOS mode (real-mode DOS) and give you a DOS prompt. The MS-DOS mode created in this fashion will use versions of the same Autoexec.bat and Config.sys files (if you have them) that are read when Windows 98 starts, as well as the Dosstart.bat file.

Private Autoexec.bat and Config.sys files

Each MS-DOS mode shortcut can have its own private Autoexec.bat and Config.sys files. The information used to create these files is stored in the shortcut. The files will be created when you switch from Windows 98 to rebooted MS-DOS mode; that is, when you click the icon associated with the shortcut.

Having private Autoexec.bat and Config.sys files is a great idea. Each DOS program that runs in rebooted MS-DOS mode can have its own special configuration or drivers and DOS TSRs that work just right for it. You can also create an MS-DOS mode shortcut just for the command prompt, but with Autoexec.bat and Config.sys files that are completely independent of those used to start Windows 98.

Previously, the only way to have different startup configurations was to create a multiconfiguration Config.sys file by creating different sections of your Config.sys file as documented in your MS-DOS manual.

At startup, you then chose which set of drivers and DOS TSRs you wanted to load from a menu. You often had to create a multiconfiguration Config.sys file to have enough conventional memory for some DOS programs, or to allow for expanded or extended memory for other DOS programs.

Allowing completely different Autoexec.bat and Config.sys files is a much cleaner and easier-to-understand solution to the problem of multiple configurations. (Of course, the best solution is to have one configuration that works for all programs.) You create and save in the shortcut the information necessary to create the Autoexec.bat and Config.sys files that work with your DOS application.

Creating private Autoexec.bat and Config.sys data

To see how to create private Autoexec.bat and Config.sys files, you will use the shortcut that you just created for Command.com. You already configured it to start in MS-DOS mode.

STEPS

Creating Private Autoexec.bat and Config.sys Files

Step 1. Right-click the MS-DOS mode icon on the Desktop (assuming you created it using the steps for Creating a Shortcut for MS-DOS Mode in the "Creating an MS-DOS mode shortcut" section earlier in the chapter).

Step 2. Click Properties, click the Program tab, and then click the Advanced button. The Advanced Program Settings dialog box will appear, as shown in Figure 34-12.

Step 3. Make sure that the MS-DOS Mode check box is marked.

Step 4. Mark the Specify a New MS-DOS Configuration option button. The bottom half of this dialog box becomes active.

Step 5. Type what you want in the CONFIG.SYS for MS-DOS Mode and AUTOEXEC.BAT for MS-DOS Mode fields. You can get a head start by clicking the Configuration button to display the Select MS-DOS Configuration Options dialog box, shown in Figure 34-13.

Step 6. Choose the options you want in this dialog box. If you highlight an option, its description appears at the bottom of the dialog box. You can highlight it before you click its check box.

(continued)

STEPS *(continued)*

Creating Private Autoexec.bat and Config.sys Files

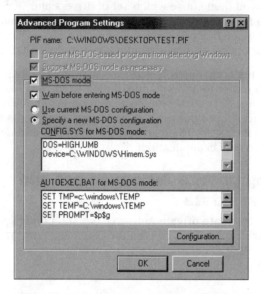

Figure 34-12: The Advanced Program Settings dialog box. You can create your own private Autoexec.bat and Config.sys files by typing what you want in these files in the two fields at the bottom of this dialog box, or by clicking the Configuration button.

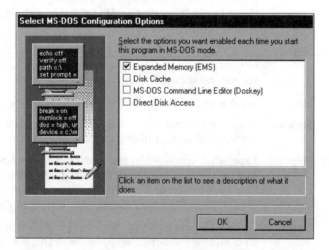

Figure 34-13: The Select MS-DOS Configuration Options dialog box. As you highlight each option, its description appears at the bottom of the dialog box.

Step 7. Click the OK button in the Select MS-DOS Configuration Options dialog box. The options you chose will be used to fill the CONFIG.SYS for MS-DOS Mode and AUTOEXEC.BAT for MS-DOS Mode fields. You can further edit these fields now.

Step 8. Click OK in the Advanced Program Settings dialog box, and then click OK again in the Properties dialog box.

Editing private Autoexec.bat and Config.sys data

Secret

You should carefully edit the CONFIG.SYS for MS-DOS Mode and AUTOEXEC.BAT for MS-DOS Mode fields. They will include lines from your Autoexec.bat and Config.sys files that are read before Windows 98 starts. You may not want some of these lines in the private Autoexec.bat and Config.sys files for MS-DOS mode.

These fields may also include some instructions that are (by default) carried out by Io.sys. For example:

```
SET TMP=C:\Windows\Temp
SET TEMP=C:\Windows\Temp
```

You may want to delete these lines or edit them.

Tip

If you choose to install the expanded memory manager (Emm386.exe), you can load 16-bit drivers and DOS TSRs in UMBs. They will then be loaded in UMBs by default if you choose them from the Select MS-DOS Configuration Options dialog box. You need to add the *noems* or *ram* parameter to the line with the Emm386.exe driver (after Emm386.exe).

Disk caching in MS-DOS mode is handled by the 16-bit driver Smartdrv.exe. It will be loaded high if you use Emm386.exe.

If you want to have an easily accessible history of your previous DOS commands while in MS-DOS mode, load Doskey. It is also loaded high if you load Emm386.exe with the *noems* or *ram* parameter.

If your DOS program requires direct disk access, choose this option from the Select MS-DOS Configuration Options dialog box. This option adds the Lock command as the last line in your private Autoexec.bat file.

Tip

You'll need to add a 16-bit mouse driver to your private Autoexec.bat or Config.sys file if you want to have a mouse in rebooted MS-DOS mode.

Where are the private files?

Secret

The lines that you add to the CONFIG.SYS for MS-DOS Mode and AUTOEXEC.BAT for MS-DOS Mode fields are stored in the MS-DOS mode shortcut you created for your DOS application or for Command.com. You can use Edit.com to see this for yourself. To do so, take the following steps:

Seeing the Internals of the MS-DOS Mode Shortcut

Step 1. Click the Start button, point to Programs, and then click MS-DOS Prompt.

Step 2. Type **Edit** and press Enter.

Step 3. Choose File, Open. In the Directories field, navigate to C:\Windows\Desktop.

Step 4. In the Files field, scroll to **MS-DOS mode.pif** and double-click it.

You'll see the lines from your CONFIG.SYS for MS-DOS Mode and AUTOEXEC.BAT for MS-DOS Mode fields at the bottom of the file. Be sure *not* to save this file when you are finished looking at it.

The private files exposed

Secret

When you switch to rebooted MS-DOS mode, new private Autoexec.bat and Config.sys files are created just for that session. The text designated for use in these files is found in the shortcut used to start this MS-DOS session. The existing Autoexec.bat and Config.sys files used to start Windows 98 are stored in temporary files with the extension *wos* (Windows Operating System).

When you exit MS-DOS mode (by typing **exit** at the DOS prompt, or by quitting your DOS application if the Close on Exit check box is marked), the copies of the private Autoexec.bat and Config.sys files are deleted from the root directory. In addition, the temporary Autoexec.wos and Config.wos files are renamed back to their original names.

Secret

If you make changes to the copies of your private Autoexec.bat and Config.sys files in the root directory while in MS-DOS mode, these changes are copied back to the MS-DOS shortcut that you used.

This is an example of what a copy of a private Autoexec.bat looks like:

```
@ECHO OFF
SET TMP=C:\Windows\Temp
SET TEMP=C:\Windows\Temp
SET WINPMT=$p$g
SET Path=C:\Windows;C:\Windows\Command
LoadHigh C:\WINDOWS\SmartDrv
LoadHigh C:\WINDOWS\Command\DOSKey
Lock
REM
REM The following lines have been created by Windows. Do not modify
    them.
REM
CALL C:\WINDOWS\COMMAND.COM
C:\WINDOWS\WIN.COM /WX
```

Notice that Command.com is called to create the DOS prompt in the MS-DOS mode session. Command.com was already loaded before this Autoexec.bat was read, so this is a second copy of Command.com. You exit from MS-DOS mode by typing **exit** at the DOS prompt and pressing Enter.

Exiting from this call allows the next line of the Autoexec.bat file to be carried out. The next line is the call to restart Windows with the /WX switch. When MS-DOS mode starts, it displays a text-mode message that Windows 98 is starting the MS-DOS based program.

This is an example of what a temporary private Config.sys file looks like:

```
DOS=SINGLE
Device=C:\Windows\Himem.sys
DeviceHigh=C:\Windows\Emm386.exe noems
DOS=HIGH,UMB
```

You don't need to load the memory manager, Himem.sys, unless you want to load Emm386.exe and thereby provide access to the UMBs and expanded memory.

Tip

You must add the *noems* parameter manually. This parameter allows upper memory to be used as UMBs. There is no reason for DeviceHigh= in the third line. This line is automatically written when you choose to load the expanded memory manager option from the Select MS-DOS Configuration Options dialog box. Emm386.exe is loaded in conventional memory, so it might as well read Device=.

MS-DOS Wizard, part of Microsoft's Kernel Toys, gives you a new level of control over drivers and commands in your system. You load separate Config.sys and Autoexec.bat files for the various 16-bit programs that need them. Download Kernel Toys from http://www.microsoft.com/windows/software/krnltoy.htm.

Problems in MS-DOS mode

If you have trouble getting out of MS-DOS mode, you may have multiple copies of Command.com in memory. If Windows continually restarts, you may have a bad call to Win in your Autoexec.bat file. These and other problems are addressed in the Microsoft Knowledge Base. Here are a few of the articles and their URLs:

Article	*Address*
Cannot Access CD-ROM Drive from MS-DOS Mode or Command Prompt	http://premium.microsoft.com/support/kb/articles/Q135/1/74.asp
Cannot Exit MS-DOS Mode	http://premium.microsoft.com/support/kb/articles/Q151/7/17.asp
Cannot Quit MS-DOS Mode	http://premium.microsoft.com/support/kb/articles/Q130/4/48.asp

(continued)

(Continued)

Article	Address
Computer Appears to Stop Responding Restarting in MS-DOS	http://premium.microsoft.com/support/kb/articles/Q150/3/23.asp
Computer Restarts When Exiting MS-DOS Mode	http://premium.microsoft.com/support/kb/articles/Q148/7/95.asp
Description of Restarting Computer in MS-DOS Mode	http://premium.microsoft.com/support/kb/articles/Q138/9/96.asp
General Tips for Using MS-DOS Mode	http://premium.microsoft.com/support/kb/articles/Q134/4/00.asp
How to Disable MS-DOS Mode in Windows 95	http://premium.microsoft.com/support/kb/articles/Q120/3/89.asp
How to Run Automatic Commands When Starting in MS-DOS Mode	http://premium.microsoft.com/support/kb/articles/Q141/3/08.asp
Multiple Copies of Command.com in Memory in MS-DOS Mode	http://premium.microsoft.com/support/kb/articles/Q149/5/48.asp
Problems Running MS-DOS-Based Programs with Windows 3.x PIF	http://premium.microsoft.com/support/kb/articles/Q138/4/10.asp
Problems Using the XCOPY Command and Long Filenames	http://premium.microsoft.com/support/kb/articles/Q134/7/68.asp
Using the UNDELETE Command in Windows 95	http://premium.microsoft.com/support/kb/articles/Q142/1/89.asp
Windows Restarts Continuously	http://premium.microsoft.com/support/kb/articles/Q148/9/19.asp

Creating a Distinct Prompt for DOS

You can create a prompt for Windows DOS sessions that is different than the DOS prompt you see in MS-DOS mode (or before Windows 98 starts up). You can also create a different prompt for each MS-DOS mode shortcut.

Windows 98 prevents you from starting another instance of itself if you type **win** at a DOS prompt while in a Windows DOS session or in MS-DOS mode. (If you try, it just displays a warning message.) But you still might find it desirable to remind yourself — in full-screen DOS sessions — whether you are running a Windows DOS session or an MS-DOS mode session.

There is a good reason to have a reminder that you are in a DOS session under Windows 98. While it is safe to turn off your PC while in DOS before Windows starts (or MS-DOS mode), it is not such a good idea when you're at a DOS prompt in a full-screen Windows DOS session. Even in rebooted MS-DOS mode, you should return to Windows so your Autoexec.bat and Config.sys files get renamed correctly.

DOS prompt for Windows DOS sessions

Tip

You can alert yourself to the fact that you are in a Windows DOS session by adding a line to your Autoexec.bat file. This line might look like the following:

```
Set Winpmt=Press ALT+ENTER or type EXIT to return to Windows
    98.$_$_$P$G
```

The $_ symbols insert blank lines between your message and the normal path and greater-than signs used in the default prompt. (PG means path and greater-than sign). Be sure to make this all one line in Autoexec.bat.

After you shut down and restart Windows 98 so this Autoexec.bat file is executed, you should see your new prompt inside a Windows DOS session.

If you type **set** by itself in a Windows DOS session, you can see what's happening. The Set command displays the contents of the DOS environment. In Windows DOS sessions, Windows reverses the meaning of Set Prompt and Set Winpmt. Set Winpmt is either equal to PG (which is the default) or to whatever your normal prompt setting is in your Autoexec.bat file. Set Prompt is equal to your longer message.

DOS prompt for MS-DOS mode sessions

Just as you can create a distinctive DOS prompt for your Windows DOS sessions, you can also create unique DOS prompts for every different MS-DOS session type. Each shortcut you use to start a DOS program in MS-DOS mode can have its own Autoexec.bat file. Edit the Winpmt settings in these Autoexec.bat files, and you can have unique prompts.

You can create and edit the CONFIG.SYS for MS-DOS Mode and AUTOEXEC.BAT for MS-DOS Mode fields for a given MS-DOS mode shortcut using the Select MS-DOS Configuration Options dialog box. If you do, the Winpmt setting from your Windows 98 Autoexec.bat is placed by default in your AUTOEXEC.BAT for MS-DOS Mode field. You can edit it or replace it with a more appropriate choice.

You can create a distinct DOS prompt for your shortcut that just opens with Command.com. You might want to set a prompt by adding the following line to your AUTOEXEC.BAT for MS-DOS mode field:

```
Set Winpmt=Type EXIT and press Enter to return to Windows 98.$_$_$P$G
```

A Way Cool DOS Banner Instead

A distinctive DOS prompt is nice, but a DOS banner is way cool. It sits at the top of your DOS window (as well as in full screen) and quietly informs you that you are indeed in DOS.

The wording, "Press ALT+ENTER or type EXIT to return to Windows 98," certainly reminds you that you are in a Windows DOS session, but this black-and-white prompt is tiresome, especially as you watch it repeated over and over again, every time you type a command.

You can replace boring DOS prompts with a colorful prompt. To create a prompt like this, you need to have the DOS screen and keyboard driver Ansi.sys loaded in your Config.sys file. Add this line anywhere in Config.sys:

```
Device=C:\Windows\Command\Ansi.sys
```

If you want to load this driver in the UMBs, make it DeviceHigh= (but be sure to include a call to the real-mode expanded memory manager, Emm386.exe, first, as well as the line DOS=High,UMB).

If you have a third-party replacement for Ansi.sys with a slightly different name (such as Fansi.sys), change the Device= line to reflect the name and location of your version of this driver. If you've just added this line to Config.sys, you must shut down Windows and restart to make the change take effect (but don't do that just yet).

Next, you have to add a new line to your Autoexec.bat file. Put this line (and only this line) in the file Winpmt.txt. You'll find this file in the DOS folder on the *Windows 98 Secrets* CD-ROM. You can copy and paste this line from this file into your Autoexec.bat or you can type it out as shown below.

The Windows prompt is one long line in Ansi.sys's terse jargon, which we explain in the "Making your own prompt using Ansi.sys" section later in this chapter:

```
SET WINPMT=$e[s$e[f$e[0;30;46m$e[K DOS Session In Windows 98
$e[16CAlt+Tab to switch; type Exit to
close$_$e[0;40;37;1m$e[K$e[u$P$G
```

(Again, this should be one long line in your Autoexec.bat file; it should not be split over multiple lines, as it is shown here.)

Now that you have edited both your Autoexec.bat and Config.sys files, you can shut down Windows and restart so these changes take effect.

Open a Windows DOS session (click the Start button, point to Programs, and click MS-DOS Prompt). You should see something like Figure 34-14.

This prompt is an improvement over the plain C:\> prompt in many ways. First of all, it's all on the top line, so it isn't repeated on every line down the side of the screen as you type commands. And instead of listing Exit as the only command to return to Windows, it also displays Alt+Tab, which reminds you that you can Alt+Tab to another active application. You can, in fact, *hold down* the Alt key and press Tab repeatedly to see a listing, one after another, of all other running applications. Release the Alt key, and that application comes to the foreground. (In case you have a BIOS that doesn't support Alt+Tab, use Alt+Esc instead.)

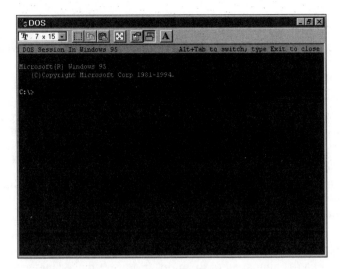

Figure 34-14: A Windows DOS session with our new banner prompt. Notice that the banner hangs out at the top of the window and doesn't bother the C:\> prompt.

Of course, this banner prompt is most useful in full-screen mode. Press Alt+Enter to switch to full-screen mode, as shown in Figure 34-15:

```
DOS Session In Windows 98    Alt+Tab to switch; type Exit to close

Microsoftú Windows 98

÷Copyright Microsoft Corp 1981-1998.
```

Figure 34-15: A Windows DOS session in full-screen mode.

The banner line is re-drawn every time the C:\> prompt appears. But if you're in the midst of a long DOS command, such as a DIR /P command that lists a directory longer then one screen page, the banner conveniently disappears until another C:\> prompt is available.

If your system has a fast video ROM BIOS, or if this ROM is copied into fast "shadow RAM" by your PC, this re-drawing of the banner shouldn't noticeably affect the performance of your DOS session.

A banner for MS-DOS mode

You can create a similar banner for your shortcut that switches Windows to MS-DOS mode. You want a different message because you can't switch to another application with Alt+Tab while you are in MS-DOS mode.

You need to make the same types of editing changes to your CONFIG.SYS for MS-DOS Mode and AUTOEXEC.BAT for MS-DOS Mode fields that you made to Autoexec.bat and Config.sys in the previous section. We have included a prompt you can use for your MS-DOS mode shortcut in the file Msmdpmt.txt, which is stored in the DOS folder on the *Windows 98 Secrets* CD-ROM.

Be sure to edit the MS-DOS mode shortcut's CONFIG.SYS for MS-DOS Mode field to include the reference to Ansi.sys. You have to load this 16-bit driver when you enter MS-DOS mode.

You can create unique banners for each of your different MS-DOS mode shortcuts. But if the DOS application associated with a given shortcut uses the full screen (as almost all of them do) it doesn't make any sense to do this, because you'll never see the banner.

Making your own prompt using Ansi.sys

If you want to design your *own* banner prompt (or a prompt that shows up in any location you like), you'll need to know how to change the Set Winpmt= statement that creates this type of banner. First, we'll explain what each element of the Ansi.sys statement that creates the banner does. In the following three tables, the characters *$e* are interpreted by Ansi.sys as an escape character ASCII number 27, and these prompt strings are known as *escape commands*.

In Table 34-3, which takes apart the Prompt= statement item by item, each element is listed on the left, and what it does is explained on the right.

Table 34-3 Ansi.sys Commands

Command	Action
Set Winpmt=	Set the DOS prompt in a Windows DOS session or in a MS-DOS mode session equal to the following.
$e[s	Save the present cursor location.
$e[f	Move the cursor to row 1, column 1; the setting $e[2;3f would move it to row 2, column 3.
$e[0;30;46m	Reset colors to 0, then set them to cyan and black; the number for each color is explained below.
$e[K	Erase line from the current cursor position to end.
DOS Session ...	Write this text string to the screen.
$e[16C	Move cursor 1 space to the right.

Command	Action
Alt+Tab to switch; ...	Write this text string to the screen.
$_	Set the prompt command to start a new line.
$e[0;37;40;1m	Set colors to black and white, intensified.
$e[K	Erase the line immediately beneath the banner.
$e[u	Restore the cursor to its original location.
PG	Set the prompt command to display path and > sign.

The preceding explains almost all the Ansi.sys commands available. However, if you are designing your own prompt, you might also need the commands in Table 34-4:

Table 34-4	Commands for Designing Your Own Prompt
Command	**Action**
$e[B	Move cursor 1 line down (for a new C:\> prompt).
$e[nA	Move the cursor up n rows.
$e[nB	Move the cursor down n rows.
$e[nC	Move the cursor right n columns.
$e[nD	Move the cursor left n columns.
$e[2J	Clear the screen with current colors and move the cursor to the Home position: row 1, column 1.

And if you want to design your own colors, you need to refer to Table 34-5, which lists the numbers that stand for each available color:

Table 34-5	Commands for Choosing Colors
Command	**Action**
0	Reset all attributes to light gray on black.
1	Intensify the foreground (text) color.
4	Underline text (on monochrome systems).
5	Make the foreground text blink.
7	Turn on reverse video.
8	Make canceled (invisible) text; black on black.
30	Black foreground

(continued)

Table 34-5	*(Continued)*
Command	**Action**
31	Red foreground
32	Green foreground
33	Yellow foreground
34	Blue foreground (underlined on mono)
35	Magenta foreground
36	Cyan foreground
37	White foreground
40	Black background
41	Red background
42	Green background
43	Yellow background
44	Blue background
45	Magenta background
46	Cyan background
47	White background

You set the colors in the table by using the command

`$e[color1;color2;...;colorNm`

where *color1* is one of the numbers in the list of color attributes. You can have as many of these attributes in the same command as you need. They must be separated by semicolons (;) and the command must end with a lowercase *m*.

You usually begin a color command with a zero (0) to reset everything — turn blinking off, for example — and then continue with the numbers for foreground color (the text color) and background color. If you use the number 1 as one of the attributes, the text color is made brighter (intensified). Intensified colors are not always what you would expect. Intensified yellow is yellow, but "unintensified" yellow is actually brown.

You could set all of your DOS sessions to black text on a light gray background (similar to Windows' own black-on-white color scheme) by using the following in your Winpmt= statement:

`$e[0;30;47m`

If you set your Winpmt to this color, don't forget to then clear the entire screen to this color scheme. This requires the DOS command Cls in batch files you start from Windows. Using white on black in DOS sessions is easier.

Windows/DOS Batch Files

DOS batch files are no longer just DOS batch files. They can now contain the Start command, which allows them to start Windows programs. You can run Windows programs and use their internal macro languages to carry out further commands. Batch files can pause until the Windows program has completed its work.

The Start command has the following format:

```
START {options} program
START {options} document.ext
```

The options are as follows:

/m   Run the new program minimized (in the background).

/max   Run the new program maximized (in the foreground).

/r   Run the new program restored (in the foreground). The default.

/w   Wait. Do not return until the other program exits.

A batch file can run Windows programs, it can run in a minimized window so it doesn't open a window that looks like DOS, it can start from a shortcut icon, and it can run Windows application macros. DOS batch files are now Windows batch files.

Commands you can use in batch files

A number of DOS commands work only in batch files. These mostly control the flow of the execution of the commands in the batch file. They are as follows:

Call

Choice

Echo

For

Goto

If

Pause

Rem

Shift

These commands are documented in the DOS 6.2x help file. If you have DOS 6.2x still on your computer, you can change to the DOS 6.2 directory in a DOS window, and type **help batch**.

Launching batch files from macro languages

In other cases, you might want to start a DOS batch file from within a Windows application. For example, you could command a Windows application to start a batch file in order to send a listing of the current directory to your printer — a common task that almost no Windows application can perform.

To do this, you would create a macro within your Windows application, assuming it has something like Visual Basic or its own macro language. For example, in versions of Excel prior to Excel 97, a macro to start a batch file named Mybatch.bat (from a shortcut) would look like the following:

```
RunMyBatch
=EXEC("mybatch.bat")
=RETURN()
```

In Visual Basic for Applications (used for macros in Excel 97 and Word 97), this same action would appear something like this:

```
SUB MAIN
SHELL "mybatch.bat", 3
END SUB
```

These examples illustrate a good reason why you should define shortcut files to run all your batch files (or define a single, master shortcut file that you rename over and over for each of your batch files). Make sure that the shortcut for a batch file you run from a Windows macro language has the Always Suspend check box (in the Misc tab of the Properties dialog box) cleared, or Windows may switch away from the batch file before it is finished carrying out its tasks. This would return control to the Windows application that launched the batch file *prior to the batch file's completion*. This could lead to errors that might be hard to diagnose.

Finding the Windows folder

A full-blown Windows program can always find the folder that contains Win.com (C:\Windows) by asking Windows through a published Application Programming Interface (API) call. But what about a batch file?

The developers of Windows created an environmental variable specifically to meet this need in batch files. If you open a Windows DOS session and type **set** by itself (no parameters), you'll see the current DOS environment strings. One of them should be something like windir=c:\windows. This variable's value is the directory that contains Win.com — the directory C:\Windows, in this case. Of course, if the Windows folder was always C:\Windows, there would be little point in having this environmental variable.

Unfortunately, this variable is of little use in its original form. This is because batch files always treat the names of environmental variables as ALL CAPS. You might try to use the *windir* variable in a batch file, as in this line:

```
COPY A:\MY.DLL %WINDIR%\MY.DLL
```

DOS looks for a variable named *windir*, which should have the value c:\windows. But Windows names its *windir* variable in all *lowercase*. Therefore, there is no match. A DOS batch file can't *see* the variable at all.

There are two fixes.

First, the brute-force method: You can use the shareware hexadecimal editor we feature on the *Windows 98 Secrets* CD-ROM to change the string *windir* to WINDIR in Win.com. If this string is in all caps, DOS batch files can test for it.

But if you'd rather not perform this surgery, you *can* write a batch file that uses the value of *windir* correctly.

The following batch file (Wintest.bat) tests for the existence of the string windir= in the environment, and jumps to the label *nowin* if it isn't found:

```
@Echo off
SET|FIND "windir=">C:\TEMP_1.BAT
COPY C:\TEMP_1.BAT C:\TEMP_2.BAT
IF NOT EXIST C:\TEMP_2.BAT GOTO :NOWIN
C:\TEMP_2.BAT
:NOWIN
DEL C:\TEMP_1.BAT
ECHO Windows 98, where are you?
```

The first line pipes the output of the Set command into Find, which is case-sensitive. Find writes the line it finds into a temporary file. If no line contains *windir=*, this will be a 0-byte file. This will be the case if you booted Windows 98 to the command prompt. It will also be true if you are in MS-DOS mode. It will not be true if you are in a Windows DOS session.

The second line copies the temporary file to a new name. Due to a feature of Copy (which thousands of batch files now rely upon), if the first file is a 0-byte file, the second file will not be created.

The third line, therefore, tests for the existence of the second file. If there is none, no *windir=* was in the environment.

If the batch file was run in a Windows DOS session, however, temp_2.bat will contain a single line:

```
windir=C:\WINDOWS
```

Running temp_2.bat executes this line, which runs a file (which you must create) called windir.bat and feeds it a single parameter: the directory name. (DOS considers a single equals sign to be a blank, so this line looks like windir c:\windows to DOS.)

windir.bat does your *real* work starting with the line as follows:

```
@echo off
SET WIN-DIR=%1
DEL C:\TEMP_2.BAT
```

The replaceable parameter %1 has the value c:\windows. This is just what you want. This batch file leaves an environmental variable, %win-dir%, available for future use (until this DOS session is terminated or the PC is rebooted).

You can then create and use any batch file that uses the environmental variable %win-dir%. Both of these batch files are in the DOS folder on the *Windows 98 Secrets* CD-ROM. You might want to copy both of these files to your C:\Windows\Command folder (or wherever you have stored your Windows 98 DOS files).

Using the Clipboard in DOS Sessions

The Windows Clipboard is an extremely useful area of memory for Windows applications. You'll find it in the \other folder on the Windows 98 CD-ROM.

DOS applications recognize the Clipboard/Clipbook

In Windows applications, highlighting some text and then pressing Ctrl+Insert copies the text into the Clipboard. Pressing Shift+Delete has the effect of *deleting* the text from the application while moving it to the Clipboard. In either case, moving the insertion point to another location or another application and then pressing Shift+Insert pastes the text into the new location. You can perform the same operations with a mouse by choosing Edit, Copy; Edit, Cut; and Edit, Paste — choices that appear in the menu bar of almost all Windows applications. After performing any of these actions, you can view the contents of the Clipboard memory area by running the Clipbrd.exe program that is included with Windows. This program is actually a *viewer* of the Clipboard, not the Clipboard itself. The Clipboard memory area can contain many types of data other than text — bitmapped graphics, Windows metafile graphics, and so on.

DOS applications vary widely in their support for the Windows Clipboard. Many DOS apps (such as Edit.com) can't use it directly. But other programs, such as Microsoft Word for DOS, have choices right on their menus for copying to and pasting from the Clipboard. (This assumes that Windows is running and, therefore, a Clipboard exists.)

You can copy text *from* a DOS application *into* the Clipboard; simply use the Mark and Copy toolbar buttons in the DOS window. If you are in full-screen text mode in a Windows DOS session, press the Print Screen key to copy text to the Clipboard. If you are in a window, Alt+PrtSc prints your DOS window in graphics mode to the Clipboard.

To paste text *from* the Clipboard *into* a DOS application, run the DOS application in a window, and click the Paste toolbar button. The text is pasted at the location of the cursor in the DOS application.

If the text that appears in your DOS application is missing a few characters, the program may not be able to receive keystrokes as fast as the Clipboard is capable of sending them. In this case, you need to change the DOS application's shortcut to clear the Fast Pasting option (click the Misc tab in the Properties dialog box).

End runs around the Clipboard

If you have major problems making a DOS application accept material from the Windows Clipboard (and you've tried the method explained above), there may be a formatting conflict. All three applications involved in a copy-and-paste—the source of the material, the Clipboard, and the recipient of the material—must have *some* format in common in order for the transfer to work.

To get around this, you may have to first save the material into a file on your hard disk. You can then merge this file into your DOS application to transfer the material. You can save text into a plain-text file on disk using the Windows Notepad. If you want to save textual material that has *formatting* you don't want to lose, such as boldface and italic type or different type sizes, try saving it with Windows Write as a Microsoft Word format file. Many DOS programs can import Microsoft Word files, complete with formatting.

A possibility for getting graphics into your DOS application is to save the graphic in a *pcx* format on disk using MS Paint or another format using Paint Shop Pro. Then try to open this file in your DOS application.

Can't start a DOS app? Delete stuff in the Clipboard

If you can't start a DOS session because of low memory, the Clipboard may, surprisingly, be the cause. The Clipboard can handle almost anything, and any large objects that you copy stay in memory until you cut or copy something else.

You might think that the solution to this problem would be to start the Clipboard application (Start, Programs, Accessories, System Tools, Clipboard Viewer), and then choose Edit, Delete. This displays a dialog box asking you to confirm (by clicking OK) that you want to clear whatever is taking up memory in the Clipboard. But there's a better way.

Secret

If you are in a low-memory situation, simply copy *a single character* into the Clipboard from any application. This erases whatever was previously in the Clipboard and releases the corresponding amount of memory, except what's needed for the one character. You needn't leave your current application or answer any dialog boxes.

Now try to run whatever program would not start earlier due to lack of memory.

Using the Print Screen Key in DOS Sessions

We want to emphasize that you can Print Screen to the printer when you're running a DOS application (or Command.com). If you clear the PrtSc check box in the shortcut associated with the DOS application (located in the Misc tab of the Properties dialog box), your text (or graphics) goes to the printer instead of to the Clipboard.

Getting a Directory Listing

It's hard to print out a directory (folder) listing from Windows. You can focus on a folder using your Explorer or a folder window. You can send this view of your folder to the Clipboard by pressing Alt+PrtSc. You can then print this view by pasting it into a new empty MS Paint file and printing from MS Paint.

This will work only if your whole folder view is visible in one screen (unless you wish to do this multiple times).

DOS gives you a better way.

STEPS

Printing a Directory Listing from DOS

Step 1. Click the Start button, point to Programs, and then click MS-DOS Prompt.

Step 2. Use the CD, or *change directory*, command to move to the folder or directory whose file listing you are interested in printing.

Step 3. Type in the command **dir > dir.txt** and press Enter. If you have redefined your DIR command to pause for each page, type this instead: **dir /-p > dir.txt**. This transfers the directory listing to a file that can then be printed.

While you can print the directory listing directly to the printer with dir > lpt1:, this method will fail to eject the last page from a laser printer.

Step 4. Navigate using your Explorer to the directory whose listing you have just printed. Right-click dir.txt to select this file in the Explorer. (If you can't find dir.txt, press F5 to refresh your file listing in your Explorer.)

Step 5. Click Print on the context menu.

If you have created a quick way to the DOS prompt using the methods detailed in the "Connecting a DOS window to the Explorer" section of this chapter, you'll be able to skip the first two steps above.

Undocumented

While the above method is a good ad-hoc way of printing a directory of a given folder, you might want to create a permanent method that will always reside in the context menu. You can do this by creating a directory-printing batch file and editing your Registry to connect this file to your folders. Here's how:

STEPS
Printing a Directory Listing from the Context Menu

Step 1.   Using Notepad, create a file with the following two lines:

```
cd %1
dir>lpt1
```

Step 2.   If you have modified your DIR command, you should change the second line as described in step 3 of the Printing a Directory Listing from DOS steps above. If you print to a port other than LPT1, you need to substitute the name of that printer port in step 1.

Step 3.   Save the file in the folder My System (which we suggested you create in Chapter 3) as Printdir.bat.

Step 4.   Using the Explorer, right-click Printdir.bat, click Properties, and then click the Program tab. Mark the Close on Exit check box, and choose Minimized in the Run drop-down list. Click OK.

Step 5.   Start your Registry editor (Regedit.exe in the \Windows folder). Navigate to HKEY_CLASSES_ROOT\Directory\shell, highlighting *shell* in the left pane.

Step 6.   Right-click the right pane, and choose New, Key. Type **Print** as the name of the new key, and then press Enter.

Step 7.   Highlight Print in the left pane, right-click the right pane, and choose New, Key. Type **Command** as the new key name and press Enter.

Step 8.   Double-click Default in the right pane, and type **C:\My System\ Printdir.bat**.

Step 9.   Close the Registry editor. The changes take place immediately.

These steps add a new Print command to the context menu. When you right-click a folder, you can choose this command to print the contents to your printer.

Increasing Files in Config.sys vs. System.ini

All applications open files when they run. DOS provides a method to set aside enough memory to keep track of the various files that applications may need to read and leave open. This memory area is set aside by a statement in the Config.sys file such as Files=30. This allows DOS to reserve memory for the names that applications use to manipulate files; these names are called *file handles*.

When you start a DOS application in a Windows DOS session that uses a lot of open files, you may see the following error message:

```
Insufficient File Handles, Increase Files in Config.sys
```

This message is in error, and changing the Files= statement in your Config.sys will not cause it to go away. Instead, the message should advise as follows:

```
Add "PerVMFiles=15" to the [386Enh] section of SYSTEM.INI.
If 15 is not enough file handles, increase the number to 20.
```

The number of file handles specified in the Config.sys file relates to the number of file handles that are available to applications. The Pervmfiles= statement in System.ini refers to the number of file handles that can be open per virtual machine under Windows. Without any Pervmfiles= statement in System.ini, Windows defaults to only 10 file handles allowed within a DOS session. This may not be enough for some DOS applications.

Windows recommends 30 file handles in Config.sys. You should change the file handles per virtual machine in System.ini only if you receive an error message. Each file handle requires a very small amount of memory—only a few bytes under DOS.

The number of handles specified by the Files= line in Config.sys and Pervmfiles= in System.ini combined cannot be greater than 255 (although it is unlikely anyone would need to approach this limit).

Summary

Windows 98 provides a better virtual machine for DOS programs. Lots of DOS programs can run in Windows DOS sessions.

▶ Windows 98 takes over even more of the functions formerly provided by DOS. We discuss which is the real operating system.

▶ Windows programs can use conventional memory, which is always in short supply. We discuss the impact of this design flaw.

▶ Windows 98 provides a DOS window for the DOS screen. The DOS screen has access to 20 different fonts and can be extensively manipulated by the DOS window.

▶ DOS programs can have shortcuts to them just like Windows programs. These shortcuts also define the virtual machine that surrounds the DOS program.

▶ If you can't run the DOS program in a Windows DOS session, you should be able to run it in MS-DOS mode (real-mode DOS). Each program can have its own Autoexec.bat and Config.sys files.

▶ Batch files now work with both DOS and Windows programs, so you can use DOS batch files for Windows programming.

Chapter 35

Configuring Windows 98 Memory

In This Chapter

Memory is an issue of our common DOS heritage. If you use DOS programs that demand large amounts of conventional memory or expanded memory (DOS games perhaps?) you will do well to study this chapter. We discuss:

▶ Determining whether you need to be concerned about memory

▶ The six most important memory issues

▶ Getting more conventional memory for your DOS programs

▶ Using MS-DOS mode to provide just the memory that you need tailored for each DOS application

▶ Cleaning up your Autoexec.bat and Config.sys files — or eliminating them altogether

▶ Using Mem to see your memory use

Why Worry About Memory?

Why should end users have to be concerned about the issue of how memory is configured or used on their computer? After all, you should be able to just buy enough memory to run your programs and leave it at that. The fact that it hasn't been that way has made Windows just that much more difficult to use.

Windows 98 does a significantly better job of dealing with memory issues than Windows 3.1*x* and even a better job than Windows 95. Most of the fixes are under the surface, and you won't have to worry about them. It may be that you if you install Windows 98 over your old Windows 3.1*x* setup, you can eliminate (or greatly pare down) your Autoexec.bat and Config.sys files, and go on your merry way. This should be your starting point.

If you have done this and things are working well for you, you don't need to be concerned about memory optimization. Go on to another chapter.

If you are still losing memory and performance because of obsolete items in Config.sys and Autoexec.bat, read on.

No More Real-Mode Drivers

The major memory improvement in Windows 95 was the introduction of a broad list of 32-bit protected-mode drivers. These drivers replaced 16-bit DOS drivers that had to be loaded in conventional memory (the first 640K of RAM in your system) or upper memory blocks (UMBs, the memory between 640K and 1MB in your system). This reduced the amount of memory available for DOS programs running either stand-alone or in Windows DOS virtual machines. (DOS programs depend in large part on the first 640K of RAM on your PC. To the extent that you have video, SCSI, sound, and network drivers in that memory area, less memory is left to run DOS programs. This partially explains why owners of PCs with multimedia upgrade kits and multiple add-on boards often have trouble running DOS programs under Windows 3.1. (To find out more about DOS virtual machines, turn to "Creating a Virtual Machine for DOS Programs" in Chapter 34.)

These 32-bit drivers are loaded when Windows 98 is loaded. For example, a properly configured Windows 98 computer with a DoubleSpace/DriveSpace hard disk will first load a 16-bit version of the DriveSpace driver in conventional memory. When Windows 98 is loaded, the 16-bit driver is removed from memory and the 32-bit driver takes over.

Tip

You no longer have to load mouse drivers in Config.sys or Autoexec.bat (unless you are going to run DOS programs that use the mouse in MS-DOS mode). The Windows 98 mouse drivers are 32-bit and support the mouse both for Windows programs and for DOS programs running in Windows DOS sessions. But 16-bit mouse drivers are not automatically removed from memory, so you need to remove instructions to load them from your Autoexec.bat or Config.sys files.

CD-ROM and sound card drivers, which were previously loaded in conventional memory or in UMBs, have been replaced by protected-mode drivers. Your sound card and CD-ROM will work with Windows programs and DOS programs running in Windows DOS sessions.

Network drivers that could eat up lots of conventional memory as well as UMBs have been replaced with protected-mode drivers. This is true for Microsoft Networks, NetWare, and TCP/IP networks. Other network providers have been encouraged by Microsoft to provide protected-mode drivers for their networks.

In addition, you no longer have to use Smartdrv.exe to provide a RAM cache for your hard disk reads and writes. Smartdrv.exe is a 16-bit driver that takes up conventional memory or UMBs. Disk caching is built into Windows 98 and works for all Windows programs and DOS programs running in Windows DOS sessions.

Starting with Windows for Workgroups 3.11 (WFWG), you no longer had to load Share.exe for those programs that needed it (such as Word 6.0). WFWG 3.11 came with a VxD, a protected-mode version of Share called Vshare.386. Vshare is now part of Vmm32.exe, and it is automatically loaded when Windows 98 starts. Sharing works for all Windows programs and DOS programs running in Windows DOS sessions.

Windows 98 does not provide the benefits of 32-bit protected-mode drivers to DOS programs that need to run in MS-DOS mode. If you run DOS programs that need a mouse or access to a CD-ROM in MS-DOS mode, you need to load those 16-bit drivers in the Autoexec.bat or Config.sys files. You can also just load them in Autoexec.bat and Config.sys files that are created on the fly when you run specific DOS programs, as discussed in "DOS in MS-DOS mode with a reboot" in Chapter 34.

If you do not run DOS programs in MS-DOS mode (except with a reboot), and all your computer hardware is supported by 32-bit drivers, you can eliminate all calls to 16-bit drivers from your Autoexec.bat and Config.sys files. In fact, you can rid yourself of these files.

Keep Autoexec.bat and Config.sys if you wish to get a little more memory for DOS programs running in a Windows DOS session. You can also use them to run a DOS utility such as Doskey, which will then be active in all Windows DOS sessions.

When to Worry About Memory

There are six major memory issues with Windows:

- Configuring your memory so you can run DOS programs that require large amounts of conventional memory and/or expanded memory

- Having enough hard disk space so the Windows swap area for virtual memory is large enough to handle all your active applications as well as the Windows 98 components

- Running out of Windows resources when you have a number of Windows applications open

- Windows applications that can (and often do) spring memory leaks, eating up resources until they are all gone

- Windows programs that use significant amounts of conventional memory, which is always limited

- Unrecognized memory address conflicts between video and network cards in upper memory

In this chapter, we concentrate on the first issue, configuring memory for running DOS programs. So let's look at the other issues first.

Hard disk space for virtual memory

To get the full story on virtual memory, turn to "Managing Your Swap Space" in Chapter 33. Windows 98, like Windows 3.1x, uses your hard disk to "swap" programs and data out of RAM when it needs this memory to accomplish your more pressing tasks. Unlike Windows 3.1x, Windows 98 doesn't ask you to create a permanent swap file for maximum performance. It handles swapping automatically.

It is a very good idea to let Windows 98 have plenty of room on your fastest hard disk for swap space. Depending on the amount of RAM that you have (more RAM calls for more hard disk swap space—see "Setting Disk Cache Parameters" in Chapter 33), it is best to have at least 20MB of unused hard disk space available.

If you don't have enough hard disk space and the swap file takes up every bit of it, you will get an error message about not being able to write User.dat, a file that is part of the Registry. Windows 98 produces information about the state of the machine dynamically and every so often writes it out to User.dat in the background. If you don't have enough hard disk space, it can't write the information to disk.

Again, turn to "Managing Your Swap Space" in Chapter 33 for more information on swap space.

Windows 98 resources

Windows 3.1*x* often ran out of resources and displayed error messages that blamed limited memory as the problem. This was very frustrating to users who had just purchased 16MB of memory and were quite willing to yell back at their machines that they had plenty of "memory."

If you received such a message when using Windows 3.1*x*, what was really happening was that one of your applications asked for more system resources and Windows 3.1*x* ran out of them. You may have had plenty of unused memory (RAM) and plenty of swap space left, but you just couldn't use them because of a limitation in the ability of Windows 3.1*x* to assign system resources.

Resources are essentially lists (referred to as *heaps*) of memory. The lengths of the lists under Windows 3.1*x* were quite small. The lists can be much longer with Windows 98. The lists point to areas of memory where user interface elements (and other items) are stored—things like dialog boxes, windows, and so on.

System resources under Windows 3.1*x* employed four 16-bit heaps. Three of the heaps were part of the User resource, which managed the user interface portion of Windows. One was the Graphic Device Interface (GDI) resource, which managed drawing objects to the screen. Because these lists were 16-bit heaps, they could address only 64K of memory each—a total of 256K of memory to store the objects used in the user interface and displayed on your screen.

If one of your applications asked Windows 3.1*x* for more objects and one of the heaps had already allocated all the memory on its list, Windows generated the out-of-memory message.

Windows 95 greatly expanded the lists for the GDI and User resource areas. George Moore from Microsoft has reported that, "In addition to all of the things in User and GDI that were moved to the 32-bit heap, Device Contexts and Logical Font structures in GDI are moved to the 32-bit heap. This means that the old system-wide limit on the number of Device Contexts has been raised from around 150–200 to over 10,000. In addition, you can now also easily load many, many more TrueType fonts than you ever could under Windows 3.1."

In Windows 95 and 98, the three heaps in User have been replaced by one 32-bit heap with the ability to address 2 gigabytes of memory — probably enough for the next couple of years. Microsoft maintained the 16-bit heap for the GDI for compatibility reasons. Essentially, some programs managed this heap directly without going through the Windows application program interfaces (APIs), and changing it to a 32-bit heap would break these programs. Some of the elements that were in the GDI heap have been moved to the 32-bit User heap, as George Moore points out.

Table 35-1 shows how system-wide resources have increased in Windows 98.

Table 35-1   System-Wide Resources Then and Now

Resource	Windows 3.1	Windows 98
Window/menu handles	About 299	32K (each)
Timers	32	Unlimited
Listbox items (per listbox)	8K	32K
Listbox data (per listbox)	64K	Unlimited
Edit control data (per control)	64K	Unlimited
Regions	All in 64K	Unlimited
Physical pens, brushes, and so on	All in 64K	Unlimited
Logical fonts	All in 64K	750–800
Installed fonts	250–300	1000
Device contexts	200 (best case)	16K

Windows 3.1*x* programs spring memory leaks

Many applications written for Windows 3.1*x* had the unfortunate habit of asking for system resources and then not giving them back after they quit. The longer you ran Windows 3.1*x,* the fewer resources you had until you finally ran out of resources and were forced to start Windows again.

These same programs will have the same problems running under Windows 98, but Windows 98 has two defenses. First, with greater system resources, the problems will show up less frequently. Second, Windows 98 cleans up after Win-16 applications (those written for Windows 3.1*x*), making sure that the resources they were allocated get back in the common pool.

It can do this only after all Win-16 applications (excluding those that have been specifically tagged as Windows 98-aware) have quit. Windows 98 must wait because Win-16 applications can share the same resources. Therefore, you have to be sure that you quit all your old Win-16 applications every now and then to get the resources back.

Windows 98 cleans up the resources used by 32-bit applications if they don't do it properly themselves.

Piggy Windows programs

Some Windows programs, 16-bit drivers, and even 32-bit protected-mode video drivers use up lots of conventional memory. If you tried to run a couple of these oinkers, you would soon see the error message saying you were out of memory when, again, you had plenty of memory. In this case you ran out of conventional memory.

The problem here is poor programming. The writers most likely included fixed memory segments in their programs, which under Windows 3.1x, have to be allocated out of the limited pool of 640K of conventional memory. Microsoft has fixed most of this problem in Windows 98 by loading these structures in extended memory instead of conventional memory. Windows 98 automatically provides a good deal more DOS memory than Windows 3.1x because it substitutes 32-bit protected-mode drivers for the 16-bit drivers that work with Windows 3.1x. These 32-bit drivers reside in extended memory. In many cases, you have to check your Config.sys and Autoexec.bat files, and if you haven't done so yet, remark out the 16-bit drivers.

Under Windows 98, these piggy programs will have more conventional memory available to them. Given that portions of the programs that were previously loaded in conventional memory are now loaded in extended memory, they should be less of a problem than under Windows 3.1x. You should upgrade your applications if this continues to be a problem for you. Just because the program is a newer version doesn't mean its authors have fixed the problem.

In this chapter, we concentrate on increasing conventional memory for DOS programs that require much more than even these piggy Windows programs, although any increases in conventional memory will also help these Windows programs work better.

Conventional Memory Tracker, a component of Microsoft's Kernel Toys, lets you find out which programs and drivers are using a portion the lower 640K of your memory. Download Kernel Toys from http://www.microsoft.com/windows/windows95/info/kerneltoys.htm.

You'll find additional memory tracking tools at http://www.windows98.com/apps/system-analyze.html. Also see "Using Mem to Determine Available Memory" later in this chapter.

Memory conflicts

Windows 98 should be able to identify most, if not all, potential memory conflicts. These occur when a video, network, or some other card uses a memory address between A000 and FFFF without revealing that address to Windows. This used to cause serious configuration difficulties for Windows 3.1x. Windows 98 is much better at spotting these cards and not using the forbidden memory addresses.

The Device Manager will highlight any detected memory-use conflicts. You can also use the Device Manager to reserve memory address ranges for use by hardware devices.

Memory conflicts are discussed in detail in the "Troubleshooting Memory Conflicts" section near the end of this chapter. The Device Manager is revealed in all its glory in "The Device Manager" in Chapter 25.

Fatal exception errors

If you receive error messages in the form of "Fatal Exception Error 0x:xxxxxxxx" it probably means that you have a bad physical memory chip in your computer. The first thing you can do to try to get rid of these errors is to turn off your external (L2) cache. You can often do this by restarting your computer and pressing a key when prompted to bring up your BIOS setup screen. You then need to follow the instructions on your screen to see how to disable this cache.

If this is not the problem, you can also try increasing the number of memory wait states in BIOS.

If neither of these methods work, you are in the position of replacing SIMMs. You can test RAM using a RAM drive configuration. To see how, check out the following article in Microsoft's Knowledge Base: http://www.microsoft. com/kb/articles/q142/5/46.htm.

The Short of It—More Conventional Memory

Before we go into all the gory details, we want to give you some quick tips on how to get the most conventional memory possible if you need it to run your DOS programs or if your Windows programs are running out of conventional memory.

DOS programs in Windows DOS sessions

Tip

If you want to have the largest amount of conventional memory for Windows programs and DOS programs that can run in Windows DOS sessions, you'll need to have a Config.sys file that starts off looking like this:

```
Device=C:\Windows\Himem.sys
Device=C:\Windows\Emm386.exe noems
DOS=High,UMB
```

Pull from your Config.sys and Autoexec.bat files any references to 16-bit drivers that have 32-bit replacements with Windows 98. Load high any DOS TSRs that you want easily available to all DOS virtual machines in your Autoexec.bat, as in this example:

```
LoadHigh C:\Windows\Command\Doskey.exe
```

If you need expanded memory for your DOS programs running in Windows DOS sessions, change the *noems* parameter after Emm386.exe to *ram*.

If you still need more free UMBs in order to get drivers or whatever out of conventional memory, and there isn't a memory conflict with your video or network card, change the second line in your Config.sys to:

```
Device=Emm386.exe i=b000-b7FF noems
```

or

```
Device=Emm386.exe i=b000-b7FF ram
```

You can see if this area of memory is available by using the Device Manager as detailed in the "Troubleshooting Memory Conflicts" section later in this chapter.

Pull all unneeded references to Files, Stacks, and so on in Config.sys and go with the default values (described in the section entitled "Cleaning up Config.sys and Autoexec.bat").

If you have compressed a hard disk, don't load the DoubleSpace or DriveSpace compression drivers in UMBs. That is, don't include a line like the following in Config.sys:

```
Devicehigh=C:\Windows\Command\Drvspace.sys /move
```

If you have a drive that was compressed with DriveSpace 3, the standard Windows 98 compression, the previous line won't actually load Drvspace.sys in the UMBs as it is too big to fit there. Therefore, in this case, it doesn't matter whether you include this line or not.

DOS programs in MS-DOS mode

If you need to run DOS programs in MS-DOS mode (that is, you have really tried to run them in a Windows DOS session and they won't work), you have the option of exiting Windows to DOS mode with or without a reboot. If you don't reboot (the default when you click the Start button, Shut Down, Restart in MS-DOS Mode), a stub of Windows stays in memory and the drivers loaded in Config.sys and Autoexec.bat are in memory.

If the other drivers are needed to run your DOS programs, modify your MS-DOS mode *pif*s to create private Config.sys and Autoexec.bat files. You can associate these private files with each program that runs in MS-DOS mode or with MS-DOS mode in general. They are stored in a *pif* file for that program or in the *pif* for the shortcut icon associated with MS-DOS mode in general. See "Creating an MS-DOS mode shortcut" in Chapter 34 for more details.

You don't have to change the values in the Config.sys or Autoexec.bat files associated with Windows (or even have such files) because you can configure the *pif* file to go into MS-DOS mode with a reboot. After your computer reboots, it reads the Autoexec.bat and Config.sys files created by the *pif* file. On the other hand, if you start your computer, and then press and hold the Ctrl key and go to the DOS prompt, the Autoexec.bat and Config.sys files associated with Windows are used.

Modify the private files using the tips given in the preceding section. Include your 16-bit drivers and DOS TSRs in your private Config.sys and Autoexec.bat files. Otherwise, the DOS programs can't use your mouse, CD-ROM, and so on.

Load all the 16-bit drivers high. You may need to fiddle with the order of these drivers to get them all to load in UMBs. You may not have room to put them all there and might have to put some of them in conventional memory. In the "Windows Memory Management" section later in this chapter, we discuss fiddling in more detail.

Handling the DriveSpace 3 driver in memory

If you have a compressed drive, in order to access it you need to include a call to your DoubleSpace or DriveSpace driver in your private Config.sys. If the drive is compressed using DriveSpace 2 or earlier, you can load the driver in UMBs and thereby gain more DOS conventional memory for your program by including the following line in your private Config.sys:

```
Devicehigh=C:\Windows\Command\Drvspace.sys /move
```

If you have a hard drive compressed with DriveSpace 3, the standard that comes with Windows 98, you will not be able to load Drvspace.bin in the UMBs and it will load in conventional memory. Because this driver is quite large, over 100K, your DOS programs will most likely not be able to run.

The only way around this is to create a boot diskette that doesn't load the DriveSpace 3 driver. You won't be able to access your compressed hard drive. You can configure the Msdos.sys file on the boot diskette so that the DriveSpace driver isn't called. You will have access to non-compressed drives and your CD-ROM, if you've included a 16-bit CD-ROM driver on your boot diskette and added calls to it in the Config.sys and Autoexec.bat files.

STEPS

Creating a Boot Diskette That Doesn't Load Drvspace.bin

Step 1. Click the Start button, Settings, Control Panel, Add/Remove Programs.

Step 2. Insert a diskette in drive A. Click the Startup Disk tab, click the Create Disk button, and click OK.

Step3. After the new Startup diskette is created, right-click the Mydos.sys file on the diskette. Click Properties. Clear the Read-Only check box. Click OK.

Step 4. Right-click Msdos.sys, click Send To, click Notepad (assuming that you have placed a shortcut to Notepad.exe in the \Windows\SendTo folder).

Step 5. Add the following lines to the Msdos.sys file on the Startup diskette:

[Options]

Drvspace=0

Dblspace=0

Step 6. Choose File, Save, and then File, Exit.

The PC Memory Map

Before we continue with the issue of configuring memory to run DOS programs, here's an overview of how memory is structured on personal computers. If you already understand this structure, then go right to the next section.

Figure 35-1 shows a memory map that applies to most 386, 486, and Pentium computers with 16MB of memory. 16MB equals 16384K of RAM. The first 640K of the first megabyte of RAM is addressed from 0–640K (0000h–9FFFh), and the next 384K is addressed starting at 1024K (10000h). The rest of RAM starts at 1408K (16000h) and continues through 16768K (106000h).

The Windows 98 Device Manager uses a slightly different memory address notation than is standard for DOS and Windows 3.1x. For example, the address A000 (the notation used in DOS) is shorthand for 000A0000 (the notation used by the Device Manager).

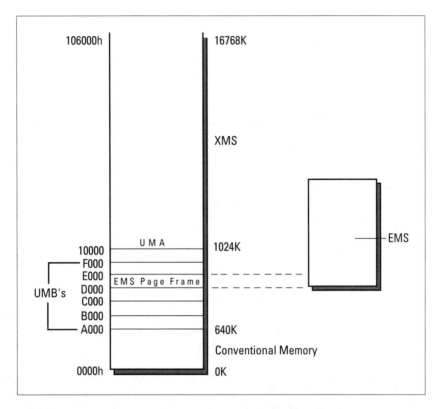

Figure 35-1: This diagram shows a PC with 16MB of RAM (640K of conventional memory plus 15744K of extended memory =16384K plus 384K of UMBs, for a total of 16768K). EMS memory is taken from the extended memory by using EMM386.exe or another third-party memory manager, or is given to DOS programs running in Windows DOS sessions by Windows 98 itself.

The first notation recognizes the fact that we were concentrating our attention on a small range of memory below 1MB, so it ignores anything smaller than a paragraph (16 bytes). Therefore, it drops the three higher digits and ignores the first digit.

The second notation points out the fact that Windows can address FFFFFFFF (4,294,967,295) bytes of memory using its flat-memory, protected-mode model. All eight places are used, as in 000A0000. We use the notations interchangeably.

You should be concerned with six types of memory: *conventional memory, UMBs,* and *extended memory* are the first three. You can load portions of DOS into the *high memory area,* the fourth type. DOS applications also use a fifth type of memory, *expanded memory. Virtual memory,* the sixth, is a combination of RAM and swap space on your hard disk.

■ *Conventional memory* is the first 640K of memory in your PC. DOS applications run in this memory. Real-mode drivers that start before Windows 98 starts use this memory unless they are loaded into UMBs. DOS TSRs that are loaded before Windows 98 starts use this memory. Windows also uses this memory when it switches to V86 mode in order to access some DOS device drivers and PC hardware. Some Windows programs use significant amounts of conventional memory. Windows can put some (or all) of its translation buffers in conventional memory.

■ *UMBs* (upper memory blocks) are memory addresses where hardware devices and software drivers may be accessed by DOS and Windows. Exactly 384K of memory addresses are reserved for UMBs, and it is always located just above the first 640K of conventional memory. Much of this memory can't be used to relocate 16-bit drivers and DOS TSRs from conventional memory, because it is used by the ROM on your video card and/or network card and the system ROM. The 64K EMS page frame, if any, is located here. 16-bit drivers and DOS TSRs can use UMBs if the parameter *ram* or *noems* is present after EMM386.exe in your Config.sys file.

■ *Extended memory* (also called XMS, for eXtended Memory Specification) is the memory above conventional memory and the UMBs. It begins at the 1MB line, which is the same as 1024K (640K plus 384K). If you have 16MB of RAM in your system, the first 640K is conventional memory, and the rest begins at the 1024K line and is counted upward from there.

■ The *high memory area* (HMA) is the first 64K of extended memory (minus 16 bytes), and it is used by DOS, Windows, and a few other programs. No more than one program can be loaded into HMA, which is typically a part of DOS. Loading DOS in HMA saves about 46K in conventional memory. The DOS buffers also get loaded here.

■ *Expanded memory* (also called EMS, for Expanded Memory Specification) is a special type of memory that requires at least 64K of address space in the UMBs. On a 386 and higher, expanded memory is usually provided by an expanded memory manager, a program that converts extended to expanded memory as required. Expanded memory requires a 64K page frame somewhere below the 1MB line in order to function. The Emm386.exe file provided by Windows 98 is an expanded memory manager. Additionally, QEMM, 386Max, NetRoom, and other products available from other software vendors provide somewhat more functionality than the Microsoft utility.

■ *Virtual memory* is the combination of RAM that can be addressed by Windows 98 and the dynamic swap file space on your hard disk. Windows 98 manages this combined memory to allow you to load a significant number of applications at once without running out of physical (RAM) memory. The programs that are actually doing something are in RAM, while those sitting idly are swapped to the hard disk.

We discuss the UMBs a lot in this chapter. This is because you can increase the amount of conventional memory available under Windows 98 by moving device drivers and DOS itself from conventional memory into UMBs and into HMA.

UMBs from A to F

You can think of the 384K of UMBs as six separate areas, each of which is 64K in size. These six blocks are known as A, B, C, D, E, and F. This is because the address of the first byte of memory in the A block is A000 (pronounced "A thousand") in hexadecimal numbering.

The A block is used for the addresses of the RAM on your VGA or higher video board. When the board is in graphics mode (as opposed to text mode), the 64K of address space at A000 is used by Windows to write information into the RAM on the board. No matter how much RAM is physically installed on the board, the same 64K block is used to write to all video memory.

The B block is used for two purposes. The first 32K, which begins at B000, is used when a VGA or higher resolution video board is in monochrome graphics mode. These memory addresses would be used, for example, if you were using a monochrome monitor and the Windows VGA monochrome driver. The second 32K, from B800 to C000, is used for VGA or higher text mode. A portion of this address space is used when you are at a DOS prompt and type a command. The DOS output is written to B800, where it appears on your screen as text characters.

The C block is used for the read-only memory (ROM) chip that is present on all VGA and higher video adapters. This chip always begins using address spaces at C000. From that point, the chip may claim 16K, 24K, or more, depending on the complexity of the adapter and how many video modes it supports.

The D block has no reserved function, but it is often claimed by memory managers for the 64K page frame required to use expanded memory.

The E block is often unused on AT- and EISA-bus machines, but it is usually claimed by machines with a Micro Channel Architecture (MCA) bus. MCA machines include a unique set of ROM chips that reside at addresses starting at E000 and continue toward F000. These chips contain instructions in ROM that are used when OS/2 is running. For those people who are not using OS/2, many memory managers can claim these addresses for other purposes.

Finally, the F000 block is reserved on all PCs for the ROM chips that hold the basic input-output system (BIOS)—instructions that run low-level functions, such as writing to disk drives.

Knowing the purpose of each UMB can help you claim more conventional memory for both Windows and DOS applications running under Windows 98.

Windows Memory Management

Windows 98, in concert with two real-mode memory managers, manages all the memory on your computer, both real and virtual. One of the memory managers, Himem.sys, must be loaded before Windows 98 can start. Io.sys loads it automatically if you don't have a Config.sys file or don't refer to Himem.sys in Config.sys.

You don't need the other memory manager, Emm386.exe, unless you want to load 16-bit drivers or DOS TSRs in UMBs or provide expanded memory for DOS programs not running in Windows DOS sessions. You have to reference Emm386.exe explicitly in a Config.sys file to use it.

Windows has its own expanded memory manager that provides expanded memory for DOS programs running in Windows DOS sessions. It can also place Windows translation buffers and a 64K page frame in upper memory.

Himem.sys

Io.sys is the first thing loaded after your computer's BIOS goes through its power-on self test. Io.sys automatically loads Himem.sys with the /testmem:on switch unless your computer has a Config.sys file with a line in it such as:

```
Device=Himem.sys /testmem:off
```

Even without this line in your Config.sys file, Io.sys issues an instruction to load Himem.sys. Himem.sys is a real-mode driver that takes about 1K of conventional memory.

Himem.sys must be loaded for Windows 98 to load. Warning: If you erase this file from your computer, you will not be able to start Windows.

Because Io.sys loads Himem.sys by default, you don't need to put the above sample line in your Config.sys file unless you are going to add parameters to this line (not too likely) or load Emm386.exe. Himem.sys has to be loaded before Emm386.exe is loaded.

Io.sys will read the Config.sys file before it tries to load Himem.sys. Io.sys chokes if it finds a call to load Emm386.exe in Config.sys without a preceding call in Config.sys to load Himem.sys.

Io.sys loads Himem.sys with the test for extended memory on (/testmem:on) but with *verbose* off. It doesn't appear as though the test for memory is really turned on in spite of this reference in the Io.sys because it doesn't make any difference in the load time for Windows 98 to turn the test off. You can turn on the *testmem* switch in the Config.sys file or, if you would like to see the reports of any errors that Himem.sys encounters, you can use the command line parameter /v to turn on *verbose*. You don't have to do anything to invoke memory management when you start your Windows 98 computer. You had to add a line to your DOS 3 through DOS 6.2 Config.sys to load Himem.sys if you wanted to run Windows 3.1*x*. Windows 98 will run because Himem.sys is loaded automatically. You don't even have to have a Config.sys file.

Himem.sys is a memory manager that allows Windows programs to use extended memory. Windows can provide expanded or extended memory to DOS programs that run in Windows DOS sessions.

Emm386.exe

Himem.sys does not provide expanded memory to DOS programs that run in MS-DOS mode. It also doesn't manage UMBs. If you want to take real-mode drivers (and portions of DOS) out of conventional memory and place them into upper memory, you must load Emm386.exe (and Himem.sys) in Config.sys.

If you are not running DOS programs that require expanded memory in MS-DOS mode, and if your DOS programs do not need additional conventional memory, and you are not having problems with some Windows programs that are caused by low available conventional memory, don't do any of this. Relax. Go to another chapter.

Emm386.exe is stored in the \Windows folder. It is a real-mode driver that takes up about 3K of conventional memory. It also takes up about 150K of extended memory to provide mappable memory. If you don't need it, don't use it.

To make the UMBs available for loading 16-bit drivers and portions of DOS, you should to create a Config.sys file that starts off as follows:

```
Device=C:\Windows\Himem.sys
Device=C:\Windows\Emm386.exe noems
DOS=High,UMB
```

The second line loads Emm386, the real-mode manger for expanded and upper memory, with a parameter (*noems*) that tells it not to set aside a 64K page frame for handling expanded memory and thereby not provide any expanded memory. All upper memory that Emm386.exe marks as available can be used for loading 16-bit drivers, TSRs, and portions of DOS.

The *noems* parameter means that no expanded memory will be available for DOS programs whether they are running in Windows DOS sessions or in MS-DOS mode (unless your computer is rebooted). It doesn't matter where you set the EMS value in the DOS *pif*, if *noems* has been specified in Config.sys, no EMS will be available to DOS programs.

If you want to set aside a page frame in upper memory so that you can provide expanded memory for DOS programs, then instead of the parameter *noems*, use the parameter *ram*. This allows both EMS memory and the use of UMBs for 16-bit drivers and TSRs.

Using the parameter *ram* decreases by 64K the amount of UMBs that can be used to store 16-bit drivers and DOS TSRs. If they can't fit in UMBs, they will be loaded in conventional memory.

If you don't include the second line in your Config.sys (or you don't have a Config.sys file), Windows is free to allow EMS memory in Windows DOS sessions to be configured as you see fit. You can set the limit of the EMS memory for each Windows DOS session in its *pif*. See "Expanded EMS memory" in Chapter 34 for further details.

The third line loads a portion of DOS into HMA — a 64K area just above the 1024K boundary — instead of in conventional memory. It also directs DOS to manage the UMBs so that 16-bit drivers and TSRs can be loaded there and still retain their connection to conventional memory and DOS. If UMB is not included in this line (or in a separate line of the form DOS=UMB), no drivers are loaded into UMBs.

You can use a number of specific and esoteric parameters with Himem.sys and Emm386.exe. If you have copied the contents of the \tools\oldmsdos folder from your Windows 98 CD-ROM to your \Windows\Command folder, you can find out more about them by opening up a Windows DOS session, and typing **help Emm386.exe** or **help Himem.sys.**

Loading drivers in UMBs

If you are going to load your 16-bit drivers into the UMBs, you need to use Devicehigh= in Config.sys and/or Loadhigh in Autoexec.bat. Here's an example Config.sys that loads a real-mode CD-ROM driver in upper memory:

```
Device=C:\Windows\Himem.sys /testmem:off /v
Device=C:\Windows\Emm386.exe noems /v
DOS=High,UMB
Devicehigh=C:\Kmeatapi.sys /D:OEMCD001 /P:S /O:M
```

An Autoexec.bat that loads Doskey.exe (a DOS TSR) in a UMB would look like this:

```
LoadHigh C:\Windows\Command\Doskey.exe
```

Stack pages

In Brian's Windows Manager column for InfoWorld Magazine, he has dealt thoroughly with the setting MaxBPs=768. This setting, added to the [386Enh] section of a Windows 3.1 system, reduces crashes by setting aside an extra 4K of extended memory for Windows "break points."

Windows 98, by contrast, dynamically allocates break points, which are 10-byte chunks of memory used to track virtual device drivers (VxDs). As VxDs use more memory, Windows 98 simply assigns more memory to break points as needed. This is why the MaxBPs line is no longer necessary in Windows 98.

The MaxBPs=768 setting does still work in Windows 3.11 and Windows for Workgroups 3.11, but it is not needed in Windows 98.

Windows 98 has its own setting to deal with a similar but different kind of program crash. This setting deals exclusively with 32-bit software.

The problem that afflicts 32-bit software affects stack pages. *Stack pages* are 4K blocks of memory that Windows 98 sets aside for 32-bit device drivers to use as a stack. (A *stack*, in this case, refers to a scratch area of memory used by programs. This entire discussion of stack pages, by the way, is unrelated to the Stacks= command found in Config.sys, which is used by 16-bit DOS drivers.)

If a 32-bit device driver exceeds 4K of memory for its stack, the program causes an error, but Windows 98 can recover. This is because Windows 98, by default, maintains two extra memory pages known as *spare stack pages*.

If you have a bug-ridden device driver, you may get the following error message:

```
There are no spare stack pages. It may be necessary to increase the
setting of "MinSPs" in System.ini to prevent possible stack faults.
There are currently 2 SPs allocated.
```

The typical user, facing this message, could be forgiven for having a blank look. What's a "MinSPs" and what should it be increased to? Looking in Windows 98's System.ini file doesn't reveal anything that looks like "MinSPs."

The solution is to add a MinSPs (minimum stack pages) line to the [386Enh] section of your System.ini. Start with a value of 4, which doubles the spare stack pages, and restart Windows. If that value doesn't resolve the problem, try 6 and then 8. Each spare stack page consumes 4K of extended memory.

Add the setting to your System.ini file like this:

```
[386Enh]
; Increases stack pages from 2 to 4.
MinSPs=4
```

You can make this change using the System Configuration Utility.

STEPS

Editing Your System.ini File

Step 1. Click the Start button, Programs, Accessories, System Tools, System Information.

Step 2. Click Tools, System Configuration Utility.

Step 3. Click the System.ini tab, highlight [386Enh], and click the New button.

Step 4. Type **MinSPs=4**. Click OK.

Step 5. Click the Start button, Shut Down, Restart, OK to have the changes take effect.

How Windows uses upper memory

Windows looks for space in UMBs for two different purposes:

- ■ It places an expanded memory page frame, 64K in size, in an unused area above 640K. If an expanded memory manager was loaded in Config.sys, Windows "inherits" the settings for that EMS page frame.

- ■ Windows claims another area, approximately 16K in size, for DOS translation buffers. These buffers are used by Windows to transfer data to and from real-mode devices such as disk drives. If there is not enough space left in UMBs, Windows takes the equivalent amount of space out of conventional memory.

Windows doesn't need EMM386.exe to accomplish these tasks. It has its own built-in expanded and UMB memory manager.

Memory for DOS Programs

You can run DOS programs in a Windows DOS session or in MS-DOS mode either before or after Windows 98 starts. Each method provides a different amount of conventional memory for DOS programs. Restarting in MS-DOS mode (without a reboot) makes available about 3K less conventional memory than starting a DOS program at the DOS command prompt before Windows 98 starts (if they both use the same Autoexec.bat and Config.sys files). See "Running DOS Programs" in Chapter 34 for more details.

Windows provides each DOS program in a Windows DOS session with a "virtual machine." The memory available to the virtual machine is determined by what was loaded by Io.sys, Autoexec.bat, Config.sys, and Windows. Windows 98 provides protected-mode drivers that are used by DOS programs running in Windows DOS sessions. These protected-mode drivers aren't available to DOS programs that are running in MS-DOS mode.

You may need to run DOS programs that can't run in Windows DOS sessions (for whatever reasons) and need resources that require 16-bit drivers. You either have to load these drivers before Windows 98 starts or load them in each MS-DOS mode session. Each DOS program that has to run in MS-DOS mode can have its own private Autoexec.bat and Config.sys files. Again, "Creating private Autoexec.bat and Config.sys data" in Chapter 34 provides more details.

If Autoexec.bat and Config.sys load these 16-bit drivers, you can have them load the drivers into the UMBs. This increases the amount of conventional memory available to DOS programs you do run in Windows DOS sessions and provides more conventional memory for DOS programs you run in MS-DOS mode.

You can load the DoubleSpace/DriveSpace driver into conventional memory and it won't take up any conventional memory in a virtual machine because it is replaced by the 32-bit driver. DOS programs that run outside Windows DOS sessions have less available conventional memory because the real-mode DoubleSpace/DriveSpace is taking up conventional memory.

If you run a DOS program that requires expanded or extended memory in a Windows DOS session, you can configure the *pif* associated with that DOS program to tell Windows to provide the required expanded or extended memory. Windows won't be able to allocate expanded memory to DOS programs if the line

```
Device=C:\Windows\Emm386.exe noems
```

or

```
Device=C:\Windows\Emm386.exe frame=none
```

is in Config.sys. You don't need a line in your Config.sys file (or even a Config.sys file, for that matter) for Windows 98 to be able to provide expanded memory to DOS programs running in Windows DOS sessions.

Examples of available memory for DOS programs

You can configure Config.sys and Autoexec.bat in different ways to load different drivers and make them available to DOS programs. Here are the consequences of these configurations.

No Config.sys or Autoexec.bat

If you don't have Config.sys or Autoexec.bat and don't have any real-mode drivers or DOS TSRs, and if you used the default values for variables such as Files and Stacks (more about this "Cleaning up Config.sys and Autoexcec.bat" later in the chapter), you will find that on a representative computer, a Windows DOS session has about 604K of conventional memory available. In MS-DOS mode (without a reboot), 606K is available.

If the computer has a hard drive compressed with DriveSpace 3, the respective values would be 604K and 513K of conventional memory. Because Windows 98 replaces the real-mode compressed disk driver that was automatically loaded in conventional memory with a protected-mode driver, the Windows DOS session's conventional memory is not reduced at all.

Minimum real-mode drivers in Config.sys

Assume you used a Config.sys to allow access into the UMBs to load the real-mode CD-ROM driver, as shown in the Config.sys file in the "Loading drivers in UMBs" section. The respective values for conventional memory would be 612K for a Windows DOS session, and 623K in MS-DOS mode.

Some real-mode drivers that would have been loaded in conventional memory by Io.sys if there was no Config.sys file are now loaded into UMBs.

These include Ifshlp.sys and Command.com. This accounts for the increased conventional memory across the board.

While the DOS programs have more memory outside of Windows 98, they are without the services of the protected-mode drivers for a mouse, sound card, network, and so on. If your DOS programs need these services, you can have their 16-bit drivers loaded into the UMBs or conventional memory.

You should be able to load all the real-mode equivalents of the protected-mode drivers mentioned in the previous paragraph (minus the network drivers) into the UMBs, as long as you don't have to provide expanded memory for any of the DOS programs.

More Memory for DOS Programs

There are numerous ways that you can claim additional UMBs to provide more conventional memory for DOS programs.

Claiming the space used by the page frame

If you have large DOS programs that need lots of conventional memory but don't require expanded memory, you can get more memory for these programs by disabling the creation of a 64K page frame in upper memory when you load EMM386.exe in your Config.sys file.

If you are using Emm386.exe, do this by adding *frame=none* to the command line in Config.sys, as in:

```
Device=C:\windows\emm386.exe frame=none
```

This parameter also works with Qemm386, but varies with other memory managers. The parameter *frame=none* does not work in some configurations. It usually frees a little more memory than putting *noems* on the Emm386 command line. But if *frame=none* does not work in your system (Windows 98 won't start, for example), go back to using the *noems* parameter.

If you eliminate the page frame in your memory manager in Config.sys, you should also keep Windows 98 from creating one. To do this, place a line in the [386Enh] section of your System.ini file with Notepad or Sysedit, as follows:

```
[386Enh]
NoEMMDriver=TRUE
```

By preventing the creation of the 64K page frame in Emm386 and in Windows, you open up this much space to load additional device drivers and memory-resident programs into UMBs. Drivers that wouldn't load high before you reconfigured your memory managers may now fit just fine.

Claiming the space used by translation buffers

Windows 98 tries to load approximately 16K of translation buffers in the UMBs. Only if it is prevented from doing so will it take up 16K of conventional memory.

You can see Windows move its translation buffers to conventional memory by taking the following steps.

STEPS

Showing the Memory Used by Translation Buffers

Step 1.   Rename Config.sys and Autoexec.bat to filenames that won't be used by Windows 98.

Step 2.   Reboot Windows 98 and open a Windows DOS session.

Step 3.   Type **mem /c/p** at the DOS command prompt, press Enter, and write down how much conventional memory is available.

Step 4.   Exit the Windows DOS session and then restart Windows 98. Hold down the Ctrl key before the Starting Windows 98 message appears, and then choose to go to the command prompt.

Step 5.   Type **Win /d:x** to start Windows 98 in the debug mode and exclude it from using the UMBs.

Step 6.   Open a Windows DOS session. Type **mem /c/p** and press Enter. Write down the amount of conventional memory available.

Step 7.   Rename the files that you created in step 1 back to Config.sys and Autoexec.bat.

The difference in the two measurements of conventional memory is the size of your translation buffers. If Windows finds room for these buffers in the UMBs, it will place them there. If there is not enough room, they go into conventional memory.

If you fill up your UMBs with 16-bit drivers, you might be able to get more conventional memory for DOS applications under Windows by loading one of the smaller drivers into conventional memory instead of UMB. Even a 1K device driver might be taking up a 16K address space that could be used for Windows translation buffers.

There is one other thing that might be preventing Windows from finding a free 16K space in UMB. If an expanded memory manager claims all UMBs, Windows may find there are none for it to use. Emm386.exe doesn't do this.

Tip

If Windows is forcing its translation buffers into conventional memory, try setting aside a 16K area of UMBs from your expanded memory manager. Emm386.exe allows you to do this by adding the switch /win to the command line in Config.sys, followed by an equals sign and the exact addresses to exclude. For example, if you want to exclude the last 16K of the D000 block, you would put the following line in Config.sys:

```
Device=C:\Windows\Emm386.exe /win=dc00-dfff
```

Getting the best of conventional and upper memory

If you have fit the translation buffers and page frame into upper memory as well as you can and your DOS programs are still not getting enough conventional memory to run, you can add another trick to your arsenal: claiming the monochrome UMB area.

If you run Windows with a VGA or super VGA color driver, it's likely that no program is using the memory area that starts at B000. Additionally, DOS text-mode programs rarely use all of the text-mode memory that starts at B800 and continues to C000. (IBM XGA adapters, however, do use the B000 area to store information, so don't use the following technique with them.)

Even if you have a monochrome monitor or a laptop with a monochrome display, you may be able to use this technique. Instead of using the VGA with Monochrome Display driver that comes with Windows, try switching to the color VGA driver. Many monochrome displays simply use shades of gray when color information is output and will work fine with color VGA drivers.

To find out if your display driver uses this area of upper memory, take the following steps:

STEPS

Determining Memory Usage

Step 1.   Click the Start button, point to Settings, and then click Control Panel.

Step 2.   Click the System icon in the Control Panel. Click the Device Manager tab in the System Properties dialog box.

Step 3.   At the top of the tree, Computer should be highlighted. If not, highlight it.

Step 4.   Click the Properties button. Click the Memory option button on the View Resources tab of the Computer Properties dialog box, as shown in Figure 35-2.

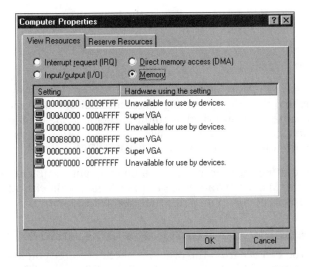

Figure 35-2: The View Resources tab of the Computer Properties dialog box. You can view the memory addresses used by the display adapter and system BIOS.

The memory addresses used by your video card and video driver as well as the system ROM are shown in this dialog box. As you can see in Figure 35-2, the memory between 000B0000 and 000B7FFFF is marked "Unavailable for use by devices." This memory is marked to be used by the monochrome portion of your video driver.

You can use this memory range if it is marked "Unavailable for use by devices." To give your expanded memory manager access to the monochrome B000 area, use an *include* parameter in Config.sys similar to the following:

```
Device=C:\Windows\Emm386.exe i=b000-b7ff ram
```

This statement instructs your memory manager to use the entire block between B000 and B800 (the address B7FF is one byte lower than B800 in hexadecimal numbering). Memory managers often avoid this block because VGA adapters can be switched into monochrome mode by programs at any time. But if you don't use such programs, your 386 memory manager can safely manage this area.

If you give access to this area to your memory manager in Config.sys, you should also specify this to the Windows 386 memory manager. This is not absolutely necessary, since Windows inherits Emm386.exe settings, but it makes this memory available if you ever disable Emm386.exe for any reason.

To do so, add an *include* line to the [386Enh] section of System.ini with Notepad or Sysedit, as follows:

```
[386Enh]
EMMInclude=B000-B7FF
```

When you restart Windows and run Mem in a Windows DOS session, you may find that a substantially larger amount of conventional memory is now available (if 16-bit drivers couldn't previously be loaded in the UMBs). There is now more room to locate Windows translation buffers, a page frame (if you use one), 16-bit drivers, and DOS TSRs.

You can find further information on managing UMBs in the Knowledge Base article "Managing Your Use of Upper Memory Blocks" at http://premium. microsoft.com/support/kb/articles/q77/0/83.

Cleaning up Config.sys and Autoexec.bat

As you can see from the previous sections, after you install Windows 98 on a computer that already has DOS 5.0 or DOS 6.*x* and Windows 3.1*x* installed, you will benefit from examining Config.sys and Autoexec.bat files. These files may contain references to 16-bit drivers that you no longer need. You may be able to get rid of these files entirely.

The major functions of Config.sys were to set a series of system values and to load 16-bit drivers. Io.sys now sets most of these values. If it can, Windows will replace 16-bit drivers with 32-bit drivers when it loads.

Io.sys sets the following values for parameters that were normally set in Config.sys in Windows 3.1*x*:

```
Files=30
Fcbs=4
Buffers=12
Lastdrive=Z
Stacks=9,256
```

It also sets the path equal to C:\Windows;C:\Windows\Command; the prompt equal to pg; TMP=C:\Windows\Temp; and TEMP=C:\Windows\Temp.

If these values work for you, you don't need to repeat them in Config.sys or Autoexec.bat. The Windows 98 Setup program may have already modified these files, changing your path statement and remarking out redundant lines. You can take out the 16-bit drivers that you don't need anymore if you can run your DOS programs without them.

The DOS buffers get loaded into the HMA, so you may be able to increase their number if needed without affecting conventional memory.

Troubleshooting Memory Conflicts

Windows 98 relocates some extended memory from addresses above 1MB to UMB addresses between 640K and 1MB. Problems occur when Windows relocates memory into a block that is also used by a device such as a video board or a network adapter. Boards such as these require some address space between 640K and 1MB to operate. Windows attempts to identify all UMBs in use, but this attempt may not always be successful.

Conflicts can also occur if the real-mode expanded memory manager loads 16-bit drivers or DOS TSRs into upper memory areas used by other devices. Before you continue troubleshooting, remark out the line in Config.sys that loads Emm386.exe to force all the drivers and DOS TSRs to load in conventional memory.

You can check for memory conflicts between different devices by using the Device Manager. Windows highlights known conflicts in the Device Manager.

STEPS

Checking for Memory Conflicts

Step 1. Click the Start button, point to Settings, and then click Control Panel.

Step 2. Click the System icon in the Control Panel. Click the Device Manager tab in the System Properties dialog box.

Step 3. At the top of the tree, Computer should be highlighted. If not, highlight it.

Step 4. Click the Properties button to display the View Resources tab of the Computer Properties dialog box.

Any memory conflicts that Windows 98 detects are displayed in this dialog box.

The addresses between 640K and 1MB that Windows relocates memory into are referred to in the Device Manager in hexadecimal numbering as 000A0000 to 000FFFFF.

Using Mem to Determine Available Memory

If you type **Mem /c/p** within a Windows DOS session, you see something like Table 35-2:

Table 35-2   Results Produced By Mem

Modules Using Memory Below 1MB:

Name	Total		Conventional		Upper Memory	
SYSTEM	18,736	(18K)	11,056	(11K)	7,600	(8K)
HIMEM	1,168	(1K)	1,168	(1K)	0	(0K)
EMM386	4,320	(4K)	4,320	(4K)	0	(0K)
DBLBUFF	2,976	(3K)	2,976	(3K)	0	(0K)
WIN	3,712	(4K)	3,712	(4K)	0	(0K)
vmm32	75,408	74K)	1,392	(1K)	74,016	(72K)
COMMAND	7,456	(7K)	7,456	(7K)	0	(0K)
IFSHLP	2,864	(3K)	0	(0K)	2,864	(3K)
Free	623,024	(608K)	623,024	(608K)	0	(0K)

Memory Summary:

Type of Memory	Total	Used	Free
Conventional	655,360	32,336	623,024
Upper	84,560	84,560	0
Reserved	393,216	393,216	0
Extended (XMS)	32,421,296	140,720	32,280,576
Total memory	33,554,432	650,832	32,903,600
Total under 1MB	739,920	116,896	623,024
Largest executable program size	623,008 (608K)		
Largest free upper memory block	0 (0K)		
MS-DOS is resident in the high memory area.			

Mem tells you which DOS programs, 16-bit drivers, and TSRs are loaded in memory, how big they are, and where in memory they are loaded (conventional or UMBs). You can see how much conventional memory is available, the size set aside for UMBs, and how much is used. Reserved memory is the memory between 640K and 1024K (384 * 1024 bytes).

You can also run Mem in MS-DOS mode. Mem has a number of command line parameters that alter its behavior as follows:

```
MEM {/CLASSIFY /DEBUG /FREE /MODULE modulename} {/PAGE}
```

```
/CLASSIFY or /C  Classifies programs by memory usage. Lists the size
                 of programs, provides a summary of memory in use,
                 and lists largest memory block available.
```

/DEBUG or /D	Displays status of all modules in memory, internal drivers, and other information.
/FREE or /F	Displays information about the amount of free memory left in both conventional and upper memory.
/MODULE or /M	Displays a detailed listing of a module's memory use. This option must be followed by the name of a module, optionally separated from /M by a colon.
/PAGE or /P	Pauses after each screenful of information.

Mem is invaluable for determining how well you are doing in placing 16-bit drivers and DOS TSRs into UMBs.

Windows 98 and DOS Games

So let's finally get to the real point of this chapter. How can your get your games to work under Windows 98?

Many games written for PCs are written for DOS. This is because doing so gives the game's author access to the hardware and therefore the best chance at getting the best performance. Since the games market is highly competitive and very technically sophisticated (compared to the business market), game authors really have to know how to deal with the hardware.

Until Microsoft introduced DirectX, games that relied on Windows suffered. Game makers didn't care if their programs even worked with Windows in Windows DOS sessions. They figured that their clients would just exit Windows (or not even start it) to run the game. DOS games often have memory managers that conflict with the Windows memory-management specification.

Microsoft is of course very interested in having games work in Windows and with Windows. It is embarrassed that this "technical" part of the market considers Microsoft and Windows a stumbling block to performance.

Consequently, Microsoft programmers have worked hard to make sure that Windows 98 can run DOS games in Windows DOS sessions. That doesn't mean they have always succeeded. Of course, the fact that it is more difficult to get to DOS in Windows 98 than it was in Windows 3.1*x* makes Microsoft committed to getting DOS games to work in Windows DOS sessions.

Try your DOS games first in a Windows DOS session. You may need to provide expanded memory for some games or make other changes to the Windows DOS session properties. If they don't work, try the DOS games in MS-DOS mode with their own Config.sys and Autoexec.bat files.

Three lists of DOS games that require MS-DOS mode are provided in the Microsoft Knowledge Base. You'll find them at:

http://premium.microsoft.com/support/kb/articles/q132/9/94

http://premium.microsoft.com/support/kb/articles/q132/9/95

http://premium.microsoft.com/support/kb/articles/q132/9/96

Summary

When we combined previous versions of Windows with existing DOS programs, we learned to be very careful about how we configure memory. In a lot of cases it was way too difficult.

▶ Windows 98 makes memory management a lot easier by reducing the drain on conventional memory.

▶ We show you how to see if you are suffering from afflictions that could be caused by memory problems.

▶ We give you a lot of ways (and show you the quick and dirty ways) to give your DOS programs more conventional memory.

▶ We also show you how to get more upper memory so you can get more conventional memory.

Part VII

Shareware

Chapter 36

The Best in Windows Shareware

The *Windows 98 Secrets* CD-ROM contains hundreds of freeware and shareware programs. We are pleased to offer you this huge sampling of the best Windows shareware programs.

What Is Shareware?

Shareware refers to "try before you buy" software that is distributed electronically or on disks by software authors. You get a trial period to use the software—usually 30 days. After this period, you are required to register with the software author if you continue to use the software. Each program has its own accompanying file that explains how to register. Note that you do not receive a license to the software when you buy the *Windows 98 Secrets* CD-ROM. In this regard, the *Windows 98 Secrets* CD-ROM is like a trail shareware diskette from a shareware catalog. If you plan to use a shareware program after the trial period, you must register it with the author.

Shareware is copyrighted software that is owned by the software author. We, the authors of *Windows 98 Secrets*, are authorized vendors of the *Association of Shareware Professionals* (ASP), and have permission from the ASP and from individual shareware authors to distribute their shareware to the public.

The two of us, as coauthors, have registered scores of shareware programs over the years, paying whatever registration fees were required. The benefits of registration have far outweighed the small registration fees. The upgraded versions, free additional software, and other offers continue to amaze us. Shareware programs are truly the biggest bargain in the software industry today.

What Is Freeware?

Freeware refers to programs that require no registration fee. Some freeware programs are also called *public domain* software. This means the software author has released the copyright to the program, and anyone may use the software for any purpose. Most freeware, however, is not in the public domain, and you should not assume you can use a freeware program for a commercial purpose (bundling it with retail software, for example) without contacting the software author for permission.

Freeware programs come with no technical support. If certain programs do not work on your system, try other similar programs on the CD-ROM.

The CD-ROM and Software are Copyrighted

The software on the *Windows 98 Secrets* CD-ROM is copyrighted by the various shareware authors, and the CD-ROM and its installation routines are copyrighted by the coauthors of *Windows 98 Secrets*. You may copy the contents of the CD-ROM to your personal computer system, but you may not distribute or sell the contents of the CD-ROM or bundle it with any product that is for sale without permission from the copyright holders.

How Do I Get Technical Support?

All Windows programs have bugs. This includes all retail Windows software and all shareware featured on the *Windows 98 Secrets* CD-ROM. Every program, no matter how simple, has some unexpected behavior. This is the nature of software, and bugs are usually fixed with the release of a newer version.

Most shareware authors, but not all, provide technical support to users after they register. Some shareware authors provide limited technical support to unregistered users if they have problems installing the software. In either case, the best way to get technical support is to look in the text file or help file that accompanies each program and send electronic mail to the e-mail address listed there. Some shareware authors also provide technical support by fax or by U.S. mail. Shareware authors do not usually have a technical support telephone line, although some do for registered users.

Many shareware authors maintain web sites for registration and technical support purposes. The best way to contact shareware authors is through their web site, if they have one. A shareware developer's web site my contain updated versions of a program, entirely new programs, and information about accessory or related products. You may also be able to leave e-mail at the site for the author. Most shareware authors check and respond to their electronic message once or more each business day.

If a program is freeware, it probably has no technical support. In this case, if a program does not work on your particular PC configuration, you probably will not be able to obtain technical support for it.

The coauthors of this book, and IDG Books Worldwide, Inc., are not familiar with the details of every program and do not provide any technical support for the programs on the *Windows 98 Secrets* CD-ROM. The programs are supplied as is. Brian Livingston, Davis Straub, and IDG Books Worldwide individually and together disclaim all warranties, expressed or implied, including, without limitation, the warranties of merchantability and of fitness for any particular purpose; and assume no liability for damages, direct or consequential, which may result from the use of the programs or reliance on the documentation.

See the *IDG Books Worldwide End-User License Agreement* at the back of the book for a complete description of the uses and limitations of the CD-ROM and the programs it contains.

What Do I Get if I Register?

We strongly encourage you to register any shareware you use past the initial "try before you buy" free evaluation period. Registration brings you a variety of benefits. Each program has its own set of registration benefits which are described in the accompanying text or help files. Depending on the specific program, you may receive one or more of the following:

- At the very least, you receive a permanent license to use the program on your PC.

- In most cases, you receive the capability to upgrade to a future version of the program with features that may significantly enhance the version you have.

- In most cases, you are entitled to receive technical support to configure the software for optimum performance on your particular type of PC. This technical support is usually provided by electronic mail, in which case you receive a response directly from the software authors in a matter of hours. In other cases, technical support is also provided by fax, by mail, or by telephone.

- Sometimes you receive a printed manual with more detail or better illustrations than can be provided in the shareware version. If you register multiple copies for a company installation, you may be able to receive a copy of the printed materials for each of the users in your company.

- In a few cases, you may receive a diskette that contains "bonus" shareware programs along with the registered version of the program you licensed. Some shareware authors include a whole mini-library of shareware programs along with your registered diskette.

- In *all* cases, when you register shareware, you help finance the development of new Windows shareware programs. This helps to bring new "killer apps" to the shareware marketplace — which you can, again, try out in advance, like all shareware.

Shareware Registration from Outside the U.S.

Most of the shareware authors in the U.S. require payment "in U.S. funds, drawn on a U.S. bank." The reason for this requirement is that U.S. banks charge large fees — sometimes more than the entire registration fee for a shareware package — to accept non-U.S. checks.

If you want to register a shareware package with a shareware author who lives in a different country, you can send payment in the form of a Postal International Money Order with a U.S. dollar amount. These money orders are available at most post offices around the world and are accepted without a fee by all U.S. post offices and by many U.S. banks. If you are in Europe, do not send Eurochecks to U.S. shareware authors because Eurochecks are not accepted by U.S. banks.

Why Have Shareware Registration Notices?

All shareware programs have some kind of popup window that lets you know how to contact the author and register the program. Some programs display this window after you click Help About or another menu choice, while others display it automatically when you start or exit the program.

The ASP specifically allows this type of reminder notice. It does not cripple a program in any way, but provides the user with the address of the shareware author and an incentive to register.

We view these incentives like the membership appeals you sometimes hear on listener-supported radio stations. The appeals are slightly annoying, but the stations could not continue to broadcast without the memberships they receive. Similarly, the shareware authors cannot continue to distribute their programs without the registrations they receive. Reminder notices—which disappear totally after you register a package—are a slight irritation but are well justified by the full functionality (no crippling) you get in a true shareware package.

What is the Association of Shareware Professionals?

Shareware has become an accepted means of distributing serious software. In the mid-1980s shareware authors began to feel a need for a nonprofit organization to promote this new form of distribution. As a result, they formed the ASP in 1987 to "strengthen the future of 'shareware' (user-supported software) as an alternative to software distributed under normal retail marketing methods."

The ASP certifies programs as meeting its criteria for shareware and also sponsors events at computer industry shows. If you are a software author, the ASP my help you find distribution channels for your programs. For more information, visit the ASP web site at http://www.asp-shareware.org.

The ASP Ombudsman program

To resolve any questions about the role of shareware—registrations, licenses, and so on—the ASP established an ombudsman program to hear all parties. Not every shareware author represented on the *Windows 98 Secrets* CD-ROM is a member of the ASP, but a good number of shareware authors *are* members. ASP members usually list this fact in the text or help files that accompany their programs.

If you have a problem with a software author who is an ASP member, and you have tried unsuccessfully to resolve the problem directly with that author, the ASP ombudsman may find a remedy. Remember that you cannot expect technical support from the author of a program unless you are a registered user of that program.

As the ASP's literature describes it, "The ASP wants to make sure that the shareware concept works for you. If you are unable to resolve a shareware-related problem with an ASP member by contacting the member directly, the ASP may be able to help. The ASP Ombudsman can help you resolve a dispute or problem with an ASP member, but does not provide technical support for members' products."

You can write to the ASP Ombudsman at 545 Grover Road, Muskegon, MI, 49442, or send e-mail to `70007.3536@compuserve.com`.

General ASP license agreement

Each of the shareware programs on the accompanying disk has its own license agreement and terms. These may be found in a text or help file accompanying each program. In general, you should assume that any shareware program adheres to at least the following license terms suggested by the ASP, where *Program* is the specific shareware program, and *Company* is the program's author or publisher:

The Program is supplied as is. The author disclaims all warranties, expressed or implied, including, without limitation, the warranties of merchantability and of fitness for any purpose. The author assumes no liability for damages, direct or consequential, which may result from the use of the Program.

The Program is a "shareware program," and is provided at no charge to the user for evaluation. Feel free to share it with your friends, but please do not give it away altered or as part of another system. The essence of "user-supported" software is to provide personal computer users with quality software without high prices, and yet to provide incentives for programmers to continue to develop new products. If you find this Program useful, and find that you continue to use the Program after a reasonable trial period, you must make a registration payment to the Company. The registration fee will license one copy for one use on any one computer at any one time. You must treat this software just like a copyrighted book. An example is that this software may be used by any number of people and may be freely moved from one computer location to another as long as there is no possibility of it being used at one location while it's being used at another — just as a book cannot be read by two different persons at the same time.

Commercial users of the Program must register and pay for their copies of the Program within 30 days after first use or their license is withdrawn. Site-license arrangements may be made by contacting the Company.

Anyone distributing the Program for any kind of remuneration must first contact the Company at the address provided for authorization. This authorization will be automatically granted to distributors recognized by the ASP as adhering to its guidelines for shareware distributors, and such distributors may begin offering the Program immediately. (However, the Company must still be advised so that the distributor can be kept up-to-date with the latest version of the Program.)

You are encouraged to pass a copy of the Program along to your friends for evaluation. Please encourage them to register their copy if they find that they can use it. All registered users will receive a copy of the latest version of the Program.

Tips for New Windows Users

If you are a relatively new user of Windows, or PCs in general, the following tips can help you get the most out of your system.

How to add a program to a new directory or folder

Always install a new program into its own directory (or *folder*). Do not install a program into your Windows folder (such as C:\Windows) unless you are specifically instructed to do so by a program's documentation or installation instructions. Also, do not install a program into the root directory of your C drive (C:\) or into a folder that already contains another program. It would be a bad idea, for example, to create a folder called C:\Games and then install all game programs into that folder. Some files may have the same name, which would cause problems with other programs and would also make it hard to remove a particular program at a later date.

When you run a setup program and you are given a choice of which folder to install the program into, use a new folder name, such as **C:\Program Files\ Blue** for a program named Blue, or **C:\Program Files\Red** for a program named Red.

How to add an application to your path

A path is a list of folders that Windows will search for applications. Windows programs do not need to be on the path as much as they used to in the early days of Windows. However, if the documentation for a program asks that you "place it on the path," here's how to do it.

In Windows 98, click the Start button on the Taskbar, and then click Run. In the Run dialog box, type the command **Notepad C:\Autoexec.bat** and click OK. In the Auotexec.bat file, you should see a line that reads like the following:

```
path=c:\windows;c:\windows\command;c:\bat
```

This line indicates that three folders are on the path: the Windows 98 folder (Windows), the DOS 7.1 folder (called Windows\Command), and a folder containing batch files.

To add a folder, add a semicolon (;) to the end of the line, and then type the full name of the folder. If you added the folder C:\Calendar, for example, your path statement would look like this:

```
path=c:\windows;c:\windows\command;c:\bat;c:\calendar
```

You must save the file, exit Windows 98, and restart your PC for the change to take effect.

If you are at a plain DOS prompt, you can type Edit C:\Autoexec.bat to run a character-based editor to make changes in your Autoexec.bat file.

You must make sure that your path statement does not exceed 127 characters (including the word *path* and the equals sign). The characters after the 127th are ignored as part of the path, but they can cause strange behavior. If your path gets too long, you must take some folders out of the path or change their names to shorter alternatives.

How to make an application run when you start Windows 98

To make an application load automatically every time you run Windows 98, you must place a shortcut for that program in the Startup folder. One way to do this is with the Windows 98 Explorer. Find a copy of the program you want to start up every time, such as C:\Windows\Notepad.exe. Use your *right* mouse button to drag the program's icon to the C:\Windows\Start Menu\Programs\StartUp folder. Drop the icon on this folder, and then click Create Shortcut(s) Here in the context menu that appears. (Do *not* click Copy Here or Move Here, which can create problems running your application.) The shortcut in your Startup folder will load Notepad every time you start Windows.

The Best Is Yet to Come

On the *Windows 98 Secrets* CD-ROM, we have featured some of the best and most popular Windows shareware and freeware available today. Some of the software is specific for Windows 95 or 98 (with support for long filenames or Internet Explorer, for example), while some of the software will run under Windows NT. Check each program's documentation for the operating system it supports. Some Windows shareware is still available only in a Windows 3.1

version (has support only for 8-character filenames, for example) but still performs well under Windows 98. To the best of our knowledge, we have not included any programs that are not appropriate for Windows 98, such as utilities and shells that work poorly or not at all in the Windows 98 environment.

We hope you enjoy using the programs on the *Windows 98 Secrets* CD-ROM.

Index

* (asterisk) wildcard character, in Find, 316, 318
= (equal) sign, in e-mail messages, 586
\> indents, in e-mail, 600–601
& (ampersand), for keyboard shortcuts, 354–355
? (question mark) wildcard character, in Find, 316, 318
[ ] (square brackets), in commands, 6
3D objects, 849, 852
4-bit ports, 651
8-bit ports, 651
16-bit color, 138
16-bit drivers, 105, 723
16-bit File Open dialog box
  right-clicking, 916
24-bit color, 138
25-pin D-connector parallel port, 651
32-bit drivers, 105, 722–723
  for printer, 869–870
  protected mode, 1124–1125
32-bit file access, 998
32-bit File Allocation Table, 1000
32-bit File Open dialog box
  right-clicking, *916*, 916
128-bit encryption, 231
386 file extension
  missing files, 433
8514fix.fon file, 773
8514sys.fon file, 754
16550 UART chip
  for modem, 503
16550A UART chip, 944, 973
  settings, 957–958

A

acceleration, for video hardware, 839–841
accelerator keys. *See* keyboard shortcuts
accented letters, 800, 802, 806
Accessibility Properties dialog box, 821
Accessories, installing, 45, *46*
active applications
  right-clicking client area, 917
  right-clicking title bar, 915
  on Taskbar, 140
Active Channel Guide web site (Microsoft), 75
Active Desktop, 71–72, *72*, 131–134, 308, 325, 339–340
  adding active item to, 71
  changing to, 81
  updating content, 72
  web page as background, 861
  Windows 98 Secrets, *133*

Active Desktop Gallery, 131
active message store, 574, 590
active title bar, 849
active Window border, 849
active windows, 122, 325
  copying to Clipboard, 823, 1098
ActiveIE, 132
ActiveX controls
  in Internet Explorer, 357
  risk from, 532
  warnings for, 248
ActiveX documents, 228–229
acute accent, 800, 806
Add Fonts dialog box, *755*, 755–756
Add New File Type dialog box, *353*, 353–354
  Always Show Extension check box, 357
  Confirm Open after Download, 357
Add New Hardware Wizard, 722, 724, 727, *728*, 742
  to install driver, 739
  for mouse, 922
  for network cards, 680
  resource settings dialog box, *729*
Add Printer Wizard, 877–878, *878*, 903–904
Add/Remove Programs Properties dialog box,
    428–437
  Install/Uninstall, *428*, 428–430
  missing Windows Setup and Startup Disk tabs, 427
  Network Install tab, 434–435
  Startup Disk tab, 50, 220, 437
  Windows Setup tab, 435–437, *436*
Add Service to Profile dialog box, *588*, 588
address books
  changing name for, 593–594
  for CompuServe WinCIM, 587
  context menu for entry, 593
  copying, 549
  limitations, 594
  opening from Desktop, 595
  properties for, 582
  sending mail without using, 601–602
  for Windows Messaging, 574–575, *592*, 592–595
    command line parameters to open, 570
Address toolbar, 147, 169, 170
  function key (F4) to display list, 212
AddStor, 1022
Adjust Free Space dialog box, 1027, *1028*
Adobe, 764
Adobe Plus Pack, 790–791
Adobe Type Manager (ATM), 790–791
  and PostScript, 873

Advanced Connection Settings dialog box, 955–957, *956*
Advanced Program Settings dialog box, *1088*, 1088–1089, 1101–1102, *1102*
Advantis, Passport, 438
Air Mosaic, 503
Alignment Errors, monitoring, 476
Alki Software Corp., Proofing Tools, 817
All file types, displaying in Folder Options dialog box, 366–367
allocated memory, 1007
Alt key, 7
   right, on U.S.-international keyboard layout, 804–805, *805*
Alt key+numeric keypad
   for ASCII characters, 798–799
   for IBM PC-8 character set, 801
Alta Vista, 257
Alta Vista Personal Search 97, 319
Always on Top option
   for Taskbar, 142–143
America Online, 481
ampersand (&), for keyboard shortcuts, 354–355
ani file extension, 923, 929
Aniedit.exe, 935
Animated Cursor Schemes, 258
animated cursors, 927
animated icons, 923
animated logos, 112
Anonymous Cookie, 250
"Another program is using the selected Telephony device" message, 945
Ansi.sys, 1110–1112
answering phone
   with modem, 634
   by Windows Messaging, 612
anti-aliasing, 787, 861
anti-virus software, 1038–1039
apostrophe, as dead key, 806–807
Append utility (DOS), 1061
AppHacks, 440
application background, 849
Application Background color, 852
applications
   active on Taskbar, 140
   adding to path, 1158–1159
   applying sounds to events, 443–444
   associating single with two file extensions, 358
   closing, 822
   command line parameters in shortcuts, 267
   CPU time used by, 1008–1009
   deleting icon for, 263
   determining parent folder for, 431
   drag and drop files, 176
   fonts in, 752
   installing, 428, 1158
   keyboard shortcuts to switch between, 1098
   memory use by, 1128

   printing files in other, 367–368
   reinstalling after changing Windows directory, 38
   running when starting Windows 98, 1159
   setup warning about open, 35
   shareware, 1153–1160
   shortcuts on Desktop for, 263–264
   switching between, 822, 823, 825, 1086
   uninstalling, 429
Apps.inf file, 1079
Apps.ini file, 434–435
Arabic, 816
Archive bit, 611
area code, for dialing location, 982
Area Code Rules dialog box, 989, *990*
Arial Alternative True Type font, 631
Arp utility (DOS), 512
arrow keys, for Start menu, 314
ascender in font, 765
ascending sort order, in Explorer, 221
ASCII character set, 797. *See also* Windows ANSI character set
   Alt key+numeric keypad to type, 798–799
ASCII Setup dialog box
   for HyperTerminal, *633*
ASCII text
   exporting Registry as, 409, *410*
   handling in HyperTerminal, 632–633
   importing or merging into Registry, 411
   printing file to generate reports, 893
associating actions with file extensions, 350–351
   creating and editing, 351–363
   File Manager vs. Explorer for, 218
   overriding when opening file, 827
Association of Shareware Professionals, 1153, 1156–1158
   general license agreement, 1157–1158
asterisk (*) wildcard character
   in Find, 316, 318
AT commands, sending in HyperTerminal, 960
ATI Mach 8/32/64 adapters, 842
ATM card, installing drivers, 689
AT&T mail, 577
attachments
   faxes as, 609–610
   in Outlook Express, saving, 534
   sending pointers to, 603–604
   Windows Messaging encoding of, 586
Attrib command (DOS), 57, 1015
attributes
   for Desktop objects, 848
   in File Manager vs. Explorer, 223–224
   viewing for Msdos.sys, 92
Attributes column, in folder window, 167
audio CDs, 276–278
   automatically starting, 748
audio, missing components, 445
Auto font, 1071, 1074, 1086
Auto Hide, for Taskbar, 142–143

AutoEject utility, 749
Autoexec.bat file, 19, 106, 1055
    and available memory for DOS programs, 1141
    CD-ROM device drivers in, 17
    cleaning up, 1146
    editing for dual boot, 55
    editing to increase memory, 32
    individualized for DOS programs, 1066
    Io.sys file and, 91
    multiconfiguration version of, 30, 108
    multiple for laptop, 746
    private, 1100–1105
        location for, 1103–1104
    real-mode drivers in, 30
    references to old mouse drivers, 917
    removing calls to TSRs in, 29
AutoFit columns, in Details view, 169
Automated Power Management (APM) facility, 296, 725
Autorun, 748–749
AutoScan option, in Msdos.sys file, 100
avi file extension, 445
awd file extension, 611

B

background
    DOS program running in, 1077, 1095
    RLE files as, 863–864
background color, and eye strain, 852
BACKGROUND tag (HTML), 540
backquote, as dead key, 806–807
Backscroll Buffer Lines, for HyperTerminal, 632
/backup switch, for Scanreg, 401
backups
    automatic, for System.dat and User.dat, 399
    location for, 400
    and long file names, 1063–1064
    of Registry, 406
    before Windows 98 setup, 29
bank web sites, encryption for, 231
banner
    for DOS, 1107–1112
    for MS-DOS mode, 1110
basic configuration, for ports, 970
batch files, 1113–1116
    to automate setup process, 31
    changing edit application for, 360
    commands for, 1113
    to control program startup, 264
    DOS commands for, 1113
    for DOS shortcut, 1085
    dragging to Desktop, 272
    to edit Msdos.sys, 92–93
    launching from macro languages, 1114
    for printing, 894–895
    shortcuts to, 267
beginning of document, moving to, 823
beginning of line, moving to, 823

Ben's Internet Idioms, 600
Better Colors (shareware), 855
binary file transfer (BFT), 610
binary files, Edit for viewing text in, 1060
binding protocols, 470
    to network adapter, 680, 681
BinHex, 537
BIOS
    changing settings, 744
    in laptop, and external monitor, 746
    power-on self test, 1054
    upgrading, 736
    virus checking option, 29
    web sites for information, 90
bitmap files. *See* bmp files
bitmapped fonts, 760–761, *761*
    vs. scaleable fonts, 761–762
    screen fonts as, 769
Bitstream 500 Font CD-ROM for Windows, 793
blank documents, creating, 373
bmp files
    as Desktop background, 860
    for shut down screens, 297
    smoothing edges, 861
    thumbnail view of, 200
    as wallpaper, 134
BMP icons, changing to show thumbnail, 368–369
boilerplate text, on Taskbar tray, 139
"bong" tone, modem wait for, 987
Bookmark Importer, 242
Bookmark Manager, 242
Bookmark.htm file, 242
bookmarks, converting Netscape bookmarks to
        Favorites, 242
boot disk
    creating, 402
    that doesn't load Drvspace.bin, 1132
boot drive
    disk space requirements for, 19
    as FAT-32 volume, 94
    files required on, 112
    vs. slave drive, 60
    Zip drive as, 1049–1050
Boot Manager for OS/2, 95
boot process, 1054–1055. *See also* startup
    failure from missing fonts, 775
    using Emergency Startup disk, 51
    warm reboot, 297, 1055, 1069
BootFailSafe option, in Msdos.sys file, 100
BootGUI option, in Msdos.sys file, 96–97, 98
BootKeys option, in Msdos.sys file, 98, 102, 706
Bootlog.txt file, 101, 103
BootMenu, in Msdos.sys file, 97–98
BootMenuDefault option, in Msdos.sys file, 98
BootMenuDelay option, in Msdos.sys file, 98
BootMulti option, in Msdos.sys file, 94–96
BootWarn option, in Msdos.sys file, 100
BootWin option, in Msdos.sys file, 96

break points, 1138
Brian's InfoWorld Column, 258
Briefcase, 657, 659–661, *669*
  copying files or folders from, 667–668
  copying files or folders into, 664
  creating, 662–664
  creating orphan, 673
  data files, 673–674
  deleting, 664
  on Desktop, 662
  modifications to original and copy, 672–673
  moving, 664–667
  multiple syncs, 671
  opening, 667
  scenarios on use, 660–661
  status of files or folders on, 668
  troubleshooting updating files, 666–667
  updating files and folders, 670–673
  what it does, 661–662
Browser Master, 473–474
browsers. *See also* Internet Explorer; Netscape
     Navigator
  integration in Windows, 225
  Netscape vs. Microsoft, 255–256
browsing
  guest from Direct Cable Connection host, 647
  host in Direct Cable Connection, 645–647
buffer size, for HyperTerminal, 631–632
buffers= variable
  in Config.sys file, 105
bugs, 1154
bulletin boards, 623–624
  creating connectoids, 624–627
  downloading from, 628–630
buttons, color for, 855–857

C

cab (cabinet) files, 27
  displaying contents, 427
Cabinet Viewer, 27
cable
  for Direct Cable Connection, 651
  for network, 679
  null modem, 977–978
cable modems, 966
cached web site, 244
call waiting, and modem access, 983
Calling Card dialog box, *984*
Calling Card Sequence dialog box, 984–985, *985*
canceling
  drag and drop, 177, 188
  Windows 98 setup, 32
"Cannot find a device file that may be needed to
     run Windows or a Windows application"
     message, 432
"Cannot find the host computer" message, 655
"Cannot initialize port" message, 945

Caps Lock notification, 827
caption buttons, on Desktop, 849
Capture Printer Port dialog box, 696, 704
capturing incoming text to file, in HyperTerminal,
     633–634
Card and Socket services, for PCMCIA socket, 680
case sensitivity
  of commands, 7
  and file names, 1044–1045
  in shortcuts to news account, 270
cataloging, fonts, 792–793
cc:Mail server, MAPI interface, 577
CD Player, 276
CD-ROM
  copying cabinet files from, 27
  driver on Emergency Startup disk, 51
  installing Windows 98 from, 28–29
  technical support for, 11–12
CD-ROM drivers, 17
  and memory, 1124
CD-ROM drives
  access in MS-DOS mode, 1068
  AutoEject utility for, 749
  automatically starting, 748
  Direct Memory Access (DMA) for, 1001
  direct support for, 998
  IDE-based, 1000
  Interlnk and, 639
  interrupt conflicts, 749
  letter designator for, 1047
  optimizing caching, 1040
  preventing automatic startup, 827
  Windows detection of, 726
cda extension, 277
CDFS (CD-ROM file system), 998
cellular modem, 956
Cfback.exe, 400
Change Code Page tool (changecp.exe), 828
Change File Type application, 181
Channel Bar, 75–76, 227, 228
Channel Definition Format (CDF), 227
Channel Screen Saver, 864
channels, 325, 339, *340*
  in Internet Explorer, 227–228
CHAP (Challenge-Handshake Authentication
     Protocol), 484
Character Map applet, 762, 802, 812
character map, in Word, 811
character sets, 795
  font support of, 759
  for HyperTerminal, 628
  for Microsoft TrueType Font Pack, *813*
  for Windows 98 fonts, 796–801
characters
  accessing hidden, 811–812
  fonts and, 795–796
  typing the less-used, 802–812
child window, closing, 822

Chinese, 816
Chkdsk command, 1021, 1061
circumflex
    characters with, 800
    as dead key, 806–807
Clasp97, 333
Class ID, for Desktop items, 136–137
Classic style, 71, 79, 158, 201, 911
    setting, 204
    switching to single window view on the fly, 165–166
    switching with Web style, 80
    for viewing folders, 164
clearing, Documents menu, 302–303
clicking, 158, 910–911. *See also* double-clicking; right-clicking; single-clicking
client
    for Dial-Up Networking, 453
    running multiple, 675–676
    selecting for network, 683
    Windows 98 install and software for, 20
client area of active application, right-clicking, 917
client area of folder window, right-clicking, 915
Client for Microsoft Networks, 333, 683
    configuring, 695–696
    protocols for, 697
    to share resources, 691
Client for Microsoft Networks Properties dialog box
    General tab, 700–701, *701*
Client for NetWare Networks, 683, 699
    configuring, 700–701
    to share resources, 691
Clipboard, 25
    copying display to, 823
    Desktop as, 338
    in DOS sessions, 1116–1117
    and DOS window, 1075, 1097
    files or folders on, 181
    and problems starting DOS applications, 1117
    Scraps as alternative, 139
Clipboard Viewer, installing, 774
Clipbook, 25
clock on Taskbar, 150–153, 304
ClockMan98, 297
Close on exit, for DOS programs, 1087
Close Program dialog box, to close MAPI, 573
closing
    applications, 822
    dialog boxes, 822
    DOS programs, 1077–1078
    Explorer, 82
    folder windows, 166
    open file on peer server, 714
cluster size, 1000
CMYK model, 870
Code Page 437 character set, 797
codecs, 445

color
    for animated cursors, 927
    ANSI commands for, 1111–1112
    for buttons, 855–857
    of cursor, 854–855
    of Explorer items, 850–851
    of HTML-formatted message background, 542
    of insertion point, 929
    in Registry, 850–851, *851*
color depth
    for icons, 138
    for logo.sys file, 112
    when switching monitors, 744
Color dialog box, *853*, 853
Color pick box, 852, *852*
Color.reg, 855, 859–860
columns
    changing in Details view, 168–169
    in Outlook Express message header pane, 523
com extension, 176
COM ports. *See also* serial ports
COM4 serial port, conflict with graphics adapter, 842
command line, for DOS program shortcut, 1083–1084
command line parameters, 6
    in action for associated file, 355
    in application shortcuts, 267
    for Defrag, 1016
    for DriveSpace, 1032–1033
    for Phone Dialer, 992–993
    for ScanDisk, 1011
    and Send To shortcut, 367
    in shortcut Properties dialog box, 287
    for Windows 98 setup, 30, 31
    for Windows Messaging, 570–571
command line startup, function keys for, 102–103
command prompt, as startup option, 102
Command.com, 19, 1055, 1056, 1057
    on bootable disk, 402
    loading at top of conventional memory, 101
commands, 6–7
    suppressing those loaded by Io.sys, 104
common file dialog boxes
    clicking to select in, 911
    deleting files from, *381*, 381–382
communications, 943–944
    hotswapping between applications, 946
    infrared, 654, 972–973
    installing components, 45–46, *46*
    log file for, 957
    terminal-computer, 624
    Windows 3.1x support for, 945
    in Windows 98, 944–946
    and Windows Messaging setup for fax, 613
Communications Port (COMx) Properties dialog box
    Port Settings tab, 968
    Resources tab, 970–971, *971*
Compact install option, 41, *42*
compacting Deleted Items folder, 547

comparing files, 1061
Compatibility Hacks, 440
Compatible with Windows 98 logo, 429
components, selecting for install, *43*, 43–47, *44*
Compose New Fax Wizard, 566, 610–611, 619
Compress a Drive dialog box, 1025, *1025*
compressed drives, 19, 163, 1022–1037. *See also*
     DriveSpace
   changing size, 1027–1028
   creating, 1024
   and disk space requirements, 18
   DoubleSpace, 22, 66, 999, 1022, 1030
   drivers, 999
   estimated compression ratio, 1028–1029
   formatting, 1019, 1030
   safety of, 1031
   size of, 1023
   swap space on, 1042
   and Windows folder, 19
compressed volume file (CVF), 1023
   benefits with no compression, 1036
   hiding host drive, 1030
compression
   data for connections, 956
   of diskettes, 1030–1031
   of message store, 574
   of software for Internet connections, 494
Compression Agent, 1001, 1022, 1034–1037, *1035*
Compression Ratio dialog box, 1029, *1029*
CompuServe, 9, 481
   address book, 575
   connecting to, 503–505
   for mail, 576
   mail delivery service properties, 587
   sample address for, 601
   technical support on, 10–11
computer at home, 452
computer at work, 452
computer name
   associating with IP address, 690
   for network, 693–694, *694*
Computer Properties dialog box
   View Resources tab, 732, *733*, 1144–1145, *1145*
computers. *See also* portable computers
   connections between, 637–639
   requirements for Dial-Up Networking, 453
   searching network for, 316
   setup as Dial-Up Networking guest, 460–468
   shortcuts to, 278–279
   standalone, 15
Config.sys file, 19, 104–105
   and available memory for DOS programs, 1141
   CD-ROM device drivers in, 17
   cleaning up, 1146
   commands for, 1060
   editing for dual boot, 55
   editing to increase memory, 32
   on Emergency Startup disk, 51

   increasing Files= in, 1120
   individualized for DOS programs, 1066
   Io.sys file and, 91
   multiconfiguration version of, 30
   for multiple configuration menu, 107–108, *109*
   multiple for laptop, 746
   option to run, 103
   private, 1100–1105
   real-mode drivers in, 30
   references to old mouse drivers, 917
   removing calls to TSRs in, 29
   and third-party disk partitioning, 1048
Confirm File Delete message box, 380
conflicts, with network adapter, 687
Connect To dialog box, 461, *462*, 470, *498*
   eliminating need for Connect button, 464
   for HyperTerminal, 625–627, *626*
connecting computers, 637–639. *See also* Internet
     connections
   for HyperTerminal, 627
Connections view (Net Watcher), 712, *712*
connectoids, 955–957. *See also* Dial-Up Networking
     connectoids
   for bulletin boards, 624–627
Content Advisor rating system, 253
context menu, 339, 918
   clicking in, 912
   printing directory listing from, 1119
   Send To, 282
   Sharing, 645
   Shift+F10 to display, 212
context menu for Desktop, 125, *125*
   Active Desktop, 131
   Arrange Icons, 126, 159
   Auto Arrange, 126
   Create Shortcut, 241
   New, 373
     Folder, 274
     Shortcut, 130
   Paste, 130–131
   Properties, 133, 138, 420
   Undo, 131
context menu for drive window
   Cut, 84
   New, 83
   Paste, 85
context menu for Explorer, 217
   Format, 402
   New, Folder, 209
   Open With, 364
   Send To command, 371, *371*
   Sharing, 223
context menu for file or folder
   Copy, 179
   MS-DOS prompt, 1076–1077
   Print, 876
   for registered file type, 351
   Rename, 181

Sent to, 178
context menu for folder window
    Cut, 174
    New, 84
    New, Folder, 173
context menu for lassoed items, 186
context menu for Modem Status icon
    Disconnect, 461
context menu for My Computer, 162, *163*
    adding Open command, 195
    Properties, 420
context menu for Recycle Bin
    Undo Delete, 386
context menu for Registry Editor
    New, 407, *407*, 408, *408*
context menu for shortcut
    Rename, 272
context menu for Start button, 310–311
context menu for Taskbar
    Cascade, 211
    Tile Windows, 211, 344, 344
    Toolbars, 147
context menus for submenus in Start menu, 298
Control Panel, *420*, 420–421. *See also* Add/Remove
    Programs dialog box; System Properties
    dialog box
    file and applet names, 423–424
    folder in Explorer, 199
    folder location, 162
    HTML template file to view, 192
    inability to delete, 384
    Internet Icon configuration for, 230
    missing files, 426–427
    for multimedia, 440–441
    regional settings in, 441
    and Registry, 393
    in Settings menu, 303, 304
    setup, 54
    shortcuts to, 279–280, 421–425
        fine-tuning, 422–423
    Sounds, 441–446
    on Start menu, 313–314
    Telephony icon, 981
Control.exe, 422–423
controller-less modems, 944
Controlp.htt file, 192
conventional memory, 1129–1132, 1134
    application use of, 1128
    for DOS programs, 1090–1091
Conventional Memory Tracker, 1128
Cookie Pal, 250
cookies, 249–250
copy and paste, 823–824
    to Desktop, 130–131
    for files or folders, 179
    keyboard shortcuts for, 213
Copy command (DOS), for print file, 892–893

copy of Windows 3.1x, installing Windows 98 over,
    54–57
copying
    cabinet files from CD-ROM, 27
    Dial-Up Networking connectoids to other
        computers, 466
    DOS data to Clipboard, 1075
    executable files vs. shortcut creation, 59
    with Explorer, 190, 209–210
    File Manager vs. Explorer, 217
    files, 85
    files during setup, 53, *53*
    files or folders, 178–181
        from Briefcase, 667–668
        into Briefcase, 664
    vs. moving with drag and drop, 175–176
    Windows 98 files to new hard disk, 58–60
copyright, on shareware, 1153
copyright symbol, 802
corrupted files, in Internet cache folder, 250–255
country codes
    for phone numbers, 982, 988
Courier screen fonts, 777–778, *778*
Cover Page Editor, 611
cpl file extension, 162, 280, 421, 423–424
    corrupted file, 426–427
    on Windows 98 CD-ROM, 427
CRC Errors, monitoring, 475
Create New Compressed Drive dialog box, 1026, *1026*
Create Shortcut Wizard, 273, *274*, 305, *305*
credit card calls, 983
credits for Internet Explorer
    displaying, 259
cross-linked files, 31
cross posters, in newsgroups, 554
CSLIP (SLIP with IP header compression), 454
CSV (Comma Separated Values) format, 550
Ctrl key, 7
    to bypass logon box, 706
    to copy with drag and drop, 180
    for interactive startup, 103
    to select multiple items, 183
Ctrl+Esc to display Start menu, 147, 154, 314
cur file extension, 929
currency symbols, 805
cursor. *See also* mouse pointers
    color of, 854–855
Custom Font Size dialog box, 845
Custom install option, 41, *42*
Custom style, for viewing folders, 164–165
customization. *See also* shortcuts; startup
    customization
Customize This Folder Wizard, 160
    and Icon Wizard, 172
cutting and pasting, 823–824
    keyboard shortcuts for, 213
    to move files or folders, 174
    shortcuts, 273

CVF (compressed volume file), 1023
   benefits with no compression, 1036
   and Defrag.exe, 1015
   hiding host drive, 1030
cyclical redundancy check (CRC), 475
Cyrillic, web sites in, 818

D

D-connector parallel port, 651
data circuit-terminating equipment (DCE) speed, 961
data/fax/voice modems, 944
data link speed, 961
data telephone calls, vs. fax or voice, 458
data terminal equipment (DTE) speed, 961
data transfer rates, monitoring, 474–476, *475*
date
   and Briefcase files, 660
   in clock ToolTip, 150
   regional settings for, 441
Date/Time control panel, 420
Date/Time Properties dialog box, 151
daylight savings time, 152
Dblspace option, in Msdos.sys file, 99
Dblspace.ini file, 1031–1032
dead keys, for accented letters, 806–807
debug switch, starting Windows 98 with, 115
default settings
   for browser, 255
   DOS prompt, 106
   HTML background for Active Desktop, 133
   for icon title text font, 128
   for Internet Explorer, 234
   language/keyboard layout, 815
   for news server, 520
   program for opening unregistered file types, 365–366
deferred printing, 872, 888–895
   to PostScript printer, 893
Defrag.exe, 33, 999, 1013–1016
   command line parameters for, 1016
   data that will not be moved, 1015–1016
   in DOS window, 1003
   and fixed-size swap space, 1041
   hang by, 252
   problems from, 23
Deja News, 561
delete confirmation message, turning off, 383
Deleted Items folder, emptying, 601
Deleted Items.mbx file, 547
Delete.exe (freeware), 382
deleting. *See also* Recycle Bin
   all files on hard drive, 384
   application icon, 263
   Briefcase, 664
   documents from \Windows\Recent folder, 373
   DOS files during Windows 98 install, 23
   with Explorer, 190

   in File Manager vs. Explorer, 217, 222–223
   files and/or folders, 86–87, 182
      from common file dialog boxes, *381*, 381–382
      from root directory, 65
      impact on shortcut, 291–292
   font files, 757–758
   Internet cache files, 251
   items from New menu, 375
   items on Desktop, 338
   meaning of, 382
   outdated newsgroup files, 559
   Shift key and, 827
   shortcuts, 86, 262, 383
      from Documents menu, 301–302
   URL in Internet Explorer Address field, 242
   without sending to Recycle Bin, 384
Depends on Password access, to shared resources, 691
descender in font, 765
descending sort order, in Explorer, 221
Deskmenu icon in Tray, 312
Desktop, 69–71, *70*, 122, *124*, 124–131. *See also* Active Desktop; Taskbar; windows
   adding new items to, 130
   appearance, 846–861
   Briefcase on, 662
   changing icons, 135–137
   Channel Bar, 75–76
   clearing Recycle Bin from, 378
   color of, 849
   contents, 74
   Control Panel shortcuts on, 425
   copying, 1098
   display of HTML documents, 350
   document segment shortcuts on, 268
   folder icons on, 161
   grid size adjustments, 126–128
   HTML document on, 133, 340
   hyperlink appearance on, 235–236
   icons and items on, 126, 134–139, 848–850
   Internet Explorer settings and, 235
   invisible grid for, 125–128, *127*
   logon box, 326–327, *327*
   magnification factor for, 842
   Marlett font for, 789
   opening address book from, 595
   placing Explorer on, 194
   placing mouse icon on, 939
   placing Quick Viewer on, 371
   removing all icons, 134–135
   returning to from full-screen DOS Windows session, 154
   right-clicking, 915. *See also* context menu for Desktop
   schemes, 847
   scraps, 139, 268
   security for, 333
   in Send To menu, 283, 285

setup to resemble Program Manager, 341–342, *343*
shortcut to DOS on, 266
shortcuts on, 274, 337–338
shortcuts to recent documents folder on, 303
single-click icons, 72–73
size of items, 859
sizing and moving windows on, 146
sliding windows, 153–154
Start button, 73. *See also* Start button
on Start menu, 312
strategy for setup, 326
as subfolder in \Windows folder, 197, 264
Task Manager, 155, *155*
Taskbar position on, 144–145
toolbars, 336–337
as top, 215
TweakUI to clear Inbox from, 583
URL shortcut on, 241
user options to customize, 330
viewing in Explorer, *198*
wallpaper, 861–864
Desktop Properties dialog box
    Background tab, 133
    Effects tab, 135
    Settings tab, 138
desktop themes, 442–443
Desktop.ini file, 172, 199, 392
    in History folder, 252
destination folder window, and focus during move, *178*
Details view, 166, *168*, 343
    column changes in, 168–169
    Defrag.exe in, 1013–1014, *1014*
    of Fonts folder, 753
    sort order for, 167
Detlog.txt file, 724, 750
Device Contexts, 1127
device drivers. *See* drivers
Device Manager, 727, 729, 730–741, *731*, 1003–1004
    disabled COM port and, 972
    and driver installation, 722
    exclamation mark in, 732, 733
    to indicate hardware inclusion in profile, 742
    keyboard information, 831
    memory address notation, 1132
    mouse in, 940
    nonfunctioning devices in, 732
    and printers, 876
    serial port settings, 967–968
    shortcut to, 279
    starting, 731
    to turn off Autorun, 749
    to update drivers, 739–741, *740*
DHCP server, 506, 509
dial-in access, disallowing, 459
dial tone, Windows 98 pause for, 953
Dial-Up Adapter, 468–470
    binding TCP/IP stack to, 482, 489
    conflicts with LAN card, 509

Windows 98 setup and, 726
Dial-Up Adapter Properties dialog box, *469*
dial-up connection
    and mail delivery, 597
    System Monitor to track, 962–963, *963*
Dial-Up Magic, 466
Dial-Up Networking
    automating logon, 500–501
    capabilities, 452
    checking connection quality, 501–503
    client, 453
    command line parameters, 472
    computer setup as host, 455–460
    connection for Outlook Express, 527–529
    Dial-Up Adapter driver for, 685
    dialing office from home, 470–471
    for dialing other operating system, 465–466
    and Direct Cable Connection, 641
    ending connection, 461
    folder in Explorer, 199
    installing, 45–46, 488–489
    for Internet connections, 488–489
    manual dial, 471
    modem setup for host, 456
    networking over modem, 472–474
    printing on printer at work from home, 476
    protocols for, 454
    security for, 460
    server dial-back preparation, 464–465
    shared resources access, 472–473
    shortcuts for files accessed by, 280
    troubleshooting problems, 479–480
    version 1.2, 453
"Dial-Up Networking cannot negotiate a compatible
        set of protocols" message, 479–480, 502–503
Dial-Up Networking connectoids
    copying to other computer, 466
    general settings, *463*, 463–464
    from Internet Connection Wizard, 230
    for Internet service provider, 492–496
    Modems Properties dialog box for, 954
    for Netcom account, 505
    and password problems, 334
    phone numbers in, 988
    preventing automatic startup, 237–238
    properties, Server Types tab, 455
    saving passwords, 497
    server type for, 462
    for SLIP connection, 467
Dial-Up Networking dialog box
    General tab, *463*, 463–464
    Make New Connection, 493
Dial-Up Networking folder, inability to delete, 384
Dial-Up Networking guest, computer setup as,
        460–468
Dial-Up Networking Server, 455, 456
    dial-back preparation, 464–465
    fax software and, 458–459

                                                continued

Dial-Up Networking Server *(continued)*
RunServe to start and stop, 458
setup, 459
SLIP to connect to, 467–468
TCP/IP and, 506
Dial-Up Server dialog box, 456, *457*
Dialer.ini file, 992
dialing
preventing automatic by Internet Explorer, 528–529
dialing properties
10-digit phone numbers, 989
credit card calls, 983
defining dial-out process, 983
format for numbers, 988–991
long-distance carrier, *984*, 984–985
long-distance dialing, for local prefixes, 989
long distance prefix other than 1, 990–991
new location setup, 982
rules, 985–987
suppressing 1 prefix, 987–988
Dialing Properties dialog box, 468, 980–988, *981*
accessing, 981–982
and Phone Dialer, 991
dialog boxes
clicking to select in, 911
closing, 822
font size used, 858
right-clicking, 916
Diamond Stealth adapter, 842
Diamond Viper adapters, 842, 927
dingbat, 811
DIR command, 1062
Direct Cable Connection, 464, 639–655
accessing host, 649–650
browsing host, 645–647
cable for, 651
configuring, 642–643
connection possibilities, 647–648
Dial-Up Adapter driver for, 685
host computer print queue administration, 656
and HyperTerminal, 624
installing, 45–46, 641
installing protocols, 644
interrupts for, 749
and mapping networked resource, 473
network configuration for, 643–647, *644*
null modem cable for, 977–978
and ports as modems, 725, 965–966
and ports as network adapter, 682
running, 648–649
serial ports for, 650
setup, 641–642
shortcuts for, 280
and simultaneous modem connection, 642
speed, 640–641, 652–653
troubleshooting problems, 654–655
to Windows 3.11, 656
to Windows NT, 655–656

Direct Cable Connection dialog box, *648*
Direct Cable Connection Wizard, 642, *642*
Direct Memory Access (DMA), 1001
testing, 1021
Direct Parallel Monitor, 652
directories. *See* folders
DirectX, 1149
disconnecting users from peer servers, 712
disk caching, 1039–1040, 1124
size, 1007
Disk Compression Settings dialog box, *1034*
disk copies, 219
Disk Defragmenter, 1027
Disk Defragmenter Optimization Wizard, 1001, 1014
disk drives. *See* hard drives
Disk Manager, 1047
Disk Manager (Ontrack), 725
disk space
displaying, 1016–1017, *1017*
displaying, File Manager vs. Explorer, 223
for installing Windows 98, 17–18
for Internet cache folder, 244, 250
Recycle Bin and, 382
requirements displayed in Add/Remove Programs dialog box, 435
requirements for upgrade from Windows 3.1x, 22
for spooling, 896
for virtual memory, 1125–1126
when installing over Windows 3.1 copy, 55
Windows 98 requirements for, 16
for Windows Messaging, 568
disk tools
Defrag.exe, 1013–1016. *See also* Defrag.exe
finding, 1002–1009
moving from Windows 3.1x to Windows 98, 997–1000
moving from Windows 95 to Windows 98, 1000–1001
ScanDisk, 1009–1012. *See also* ScanDisk
Diskcopy command, 1019
diskette drive icons, in My Computer, 160
diskettes
compressing, 1030–1031
copying, 1019
formatting for 1.7 MB, 1048–1049
display adapters. *See* graphics adapters
display card. *See* graphics adapters
Display Properties dialog box
Appearance tab, 127, *129*, 220, *846*, 859
for button color, 855–857
Background tab, 861, *862*
displaying from Settings menu, 303
Screen Saver tab, 864, *865*
Settings tab, *843*, 866
shortcut for, 279–280
displayed inch, 845
distinctive ring service, modem support for, 459
Distribution Media Format (DMF) diskettes, 1048

dithering, 853–854
division symbol, 806
dll files, on Windows 98 CD-ROM, 427
DLLs (dynamical link libraries), 20, 21
DMA controller, and DoubleBuffer setting, 99
DMF (Distribution Media Format) diskettes, 1048
docking station, plug and play connection with, 748
document-centrism, 349–350
documentation. *See also* help
    for Extract command, 27
    for Windows 98, 13
documents
    blank on Desktop, 130
    changing program in shortcut opening, 267
    creating blank, 373
    multilingual, 815–817
    names on Taskbar button, 140
    pasting shortcut in, 281
    shortcuts for segments on Desktop, 268
    viewing non-HTML in Internet Explorer, 228–229
Documents menu (Start menu), 301–302, 372–373
    clearing, 302–303
domain name server
    disabling connection to, 230–231
    search for common root, 234
domain name, of service provider, 486
DOS. *See also* MS-DOS mode
    after uninstalling Windows 98, 64–66
    BootGUI and startup, 97
    BootWin option to start, 96
    communications support, 945–946
    default prompt, 106
    loading previous version, 102
    multiuser games played over network, 477
    national language support, 828
    Registry Editor for, 417–418
    remaining components, 1057–1064
    running ScanDisk from, 1011–1012
    running Windows 98 setup from, 30
    shortcut on Desktop for, 266
    at startup, 90–91
    upgrading to Windows 98, 19–20
    version 7.1
        after uninstalling Windows 98, 62–64
        and FAT 32, 1038
    and Windows, 1053–1054
DOS banner, 1107–1112, *1109*
DOS commands. *See also* batch files
    for batch files, 1113
    cautions about, 1061
    and long file names, 1045
    modifying, 1062
    no longer available, 1060–1061
    shortcuts to, 1062–1063
    that shouldn't be run, 1063–1064
DOS Edit, 1059–1060
DOS files
    deletion by Windows 98, 95

protecting during Windows 98 install, 22–23
DOS fonts, 764, 770, 775, *776*, 777, 1072–1074
DOS machine, including in Windows network, 698–699
DOS/OEM character set, 797, 800–801, *801*
DOS partition, creating primary, 58
DOS print spooling, 871, 882, 884
DOS programs, 1055
    Close on exit, 1087
    closing, 1077–1078
    conventional memory for, 1130
    displaying properties, 1080
    exiting, 1097–1098
    gaining memory for, 1142–1146
    games, 477, 1056, 1149
    keyboard shortcuts for, 289
    memory for, 1140–1146
    modem use with, 964
    multiple shortcuts for, 1079–1080
    restoring settings on startup, 1095
    running, 1065–1069
    virtual machine for, 1078–1081
DOS prompt
    accessing before Windows 98 starts, 1065–1066
    Ansi.sys to create, 1110–1112
    creating distinct, 1106–1107
    exiting at, 1055
    opening Outlook Express from, 524
    printing from, 896
DOS Protected Mode Interface (DPMI), 1092, 1093
DOS sessions
    Clipboard in, 1116–1117
    directory listing from, 1118–1119
    files deleted in, 382
    Print Screen key in, 1118
DOS shortcuts, 262, 285–286
    icon changed for, 1087, *1088*
    properties for, 290–291, 1077
DOS utilities, location for dual boot, 56
DOS window, 1069–1078
    Auto font, 1071, 1074
    Clipboard and, 1075, 1097
    connecting to Explorer, 1076–1077
    directories in, 1075–1076
    disk tools in, 1003
    vs. DOS screen, *1070*
    Interlnk configuration to run in, 639
    moving, 1072
    properties for, *1094*
    size for, 1086–1087
    sizing and locating, 1071–1072
    Terminal font for, 779
DOS Windows session, full-screen
    returning to Desktop, 154
Dosapp.fon file, 775
Doskey, 1062
Dosstart.bat file, 30, 1068

double-clicking, 73, 204
  height and width, 925
  with middle mouse button, 937–938, 937–938
  vs. single-clicking, 158, 910–912
  speed, 925
double quote, as dead key, 806–807
DoubleBuffer option, in Msdos.sys file, 99–100
DoubleSpace, 23, 66, 999, 1022
  for compressed diskettes, 1030
downloading
  with HyperTerminal, 628–630
  managing, 233
  newsgroup messages, 556
  only message headers, 598
  speed, 474–476, 475
  Windows Messaging, 565
DPMI (DOS Protected Mode Interface), 1092, 1093
DR DOS
  installing Windows 98 with, 60
drag and drop
  canceling, 177
  to copy, 180
  to create shortcut, 272
  documents into Internet Explorer Address bar, 228
  documents to network printer, 904–906
  DUN connectoids between computers, 466
  Escape key to cancel, 188
  for file in Explorer, 283
  files to printer, 279
  for icon group, 187
  to install fonts, 756
  Internet Explorer links, 244–245
  to move Favorites folder, 238
  to move files or folders, 85, 174–177
  multiple icons, 187–188, 188
  to Outbox, 596
  to printer icon, 876–877
  for Programs, Favorites and Documents menu
    items, 307
  to Quick Viewer shortcut, 369
  shortcuts in Start button, 335–336
  shortcuts in Start menu, 311, 311
  web graphics, 245
drive icons, 1002
drive letters, changing for removable media, 1047
Driver Converter, 1038
drivers
  16-bit, 105, 723
  adding, 727, 728
  changing settings, 733–738
  for DOS, 1065
  installing video, 834–838
  loading in UMBs, 1138
  missing, 432
  for network adapter, 684, 1124
  properties dialog box for, 733, 734
  updating, 308, 739–741
  for Windows 98, 17

drives. See CD-ROM drives; hard drives
DriveSpace, 23, 66, 999, 1001, 1022, 1025
  on bootable disk, 402
  command line parameters, 1032–1033
  for compressed diskettes, 1030
  in DOS window, 1003
  loading at top of conventional memory, 101
  memory for, 1131
  option in Msdos.sys file, 99
  speed of, 1032
  upgrading to version 3, 1033
drop-down lists, displaying contents, 822
dual-booting, 25–26
  Windows 3.1x or Windows 98, 21, 54
dual-pane windows, 157
  for Windows Messaging, 571
DUN. See Dial-Up Networking
Dvorak keyboard layouts, 803
DWORD values, in exported Registry file, 410
dynamic cache, 998
Dynamic Data Exchange (DDE), 355, 356
dynamic IP address, 484
dynamic memory allocation, 1095
dynamic swap files, 22

E

e-mail. See also Outlook Express
  > indents in, 600–601
  adding signature to, 520, 521
  from Internet Explorer, 232
  leaving on server, 549
  manually polling account for, 545
  multilingual, 819–821
  passwords for, 585
  pasting shortcut in, 281
  POP3 server for incoming, 585
  sending pointers to attachments, 603–63–604
  sending without using address book, 601–602
  shortcuts in, 268–269
  signatures for, 600–601
  SMTP server for outgoing, 585
  Windows Messaging access when away, 476
  Word to create, 599
e-mail client
  from Microsoft, 565
  Outlook Express as default, 546
  Windows Messaging as, 521, 576
e-mail recipients, shortcuts to, 269–271
ECP (Extended Capabilities Port), 651, 653, 974
  disabling, 897
Edit File Type dialog box, 358
Edit Input/Output Range dialog box, 735, 972
editable font embedding, 790
editing
  batch files, application for, 360
  exported Registry file, 411
  HTML in Outlook Express, 539–540

Msdos.sys, 92–93
  OLE objects in Windows Messaging, 602
  Windows Messaging profiles, 579
embedding fonts, 759, 789–790
Emergency Recovery utility (Eru.exe), 400, 401
  adding to bootable disk, 402
  custom dialog box, *403*
  rebooting with, 403–404
Emergency Startup disk, 401
  command line parameter for, 31
  creating, 220, 437
  creating in setup, 49–53, *50*
  files on, 51–53
EMF (Enhanced Metafile Format), 871
eml extension, 244
Emm386.exe, 63, 1136, 1137–1138
emptying Recycle Bin, 380, 386
EMS (expanded) memory, 1091, 1134
encryption, 128-bit, 231
end of document, moving to, 822
end of line, moving to, 822
enhanced IDE devices, 1000
enhanced meta files, 439
enhanced parallel port (EPP), 651, 974
environment variables, 1083, 1091, 1114
  Tmp, 106
EPP (enhanced parallel port), 651, 974
equal (=) sign, in e-mail messages, 586
Erd.e_e file, 403, 404
Ergopoint, 940
"Error Code 29" message, 737
Error Control, for connections, 956
errors, checking drive for, 163
Eru.inf file, sample, *404*, 404–405
Eru.txt file, 403
escape commands, 1110
Escape key, to cancel drag and drop, 177
estimated compression ratio, 1028–1029
Ethernet cards, 678
Ethernet hubs, 679
Ethernet link, 651
Eudora, importing messages into Outlook Express, 549
Exchange Center, 565
Exchange client, 564
  and Windows Messaging, 569
Exchange Profile Selector, 571, 583
Excite, 257
exclamation mark, in Device Manager, 732, 733
exe extension, 176
executable code, in Registry, 392
executable files
  copying vs. shortcut creation, 59
  drag and drop file to icon for, 180
  problems from drag and drop, 188
  saving or opening after download, 254
Exit to Dos.pif file, 298, 1068
exiting DOS programs, 1097–1098

exiting Windows
  graphic displayed at, 112
expanded (EMS) memory, 1091, 1134
expanded memory manager, 105
  in private Autoexec.bat and Config.sys files, 1103
expanding, Registry branches, 393
Explorer, 81–82, 157, *214*
  advantages over File Manager, 224
  background graphics, 171
  basics, 189–190, *190*
  closing, 82
  color of items, 850–851
  command line parameter for, 213–215
  compressed file size in, 1023
  for computer overview, 196–199, *197*
  connecting DOS window to, 1076–1077
  to copy and move files and folders, 209–210
  creating two windows, 210–211
  display of HTML documents, 350
  drives displayed in, 1001
  as File Manager, 343–344, *344*
  file thumbnails in, 200–201, *201*
  finding, 193
  folder icons in, 206
  folder options, 201–204
  forcing new window display, 215
  full-screen, 206–207, *207*
  going from File Manager to, 216–224
  highlighting folder icon in, 205
  hyperlink appearance on, 235–236
  including Briefcase, *663*
  keyboard shortcuts for, 211–213
  keyboard use with folder tree, 208
  navigating with, 204–206, 339
  opening window in, 166
  options for display, 82
  panes in, 200
  to rearrange menu folders, 335
  from right-clicking Start button, 310
  running Windows 98 setup from, 30
  shut down and open windows in, 211
  single-pane windows from, 205
  sizing panes in, 206
  toolbars, 169–170
  vs. My Computer, 82
  web page viewed in, *191*, 191–193
Explorer bar, 171, *172*, 192, 200, 204–205
"Explorer Caused a Divide error in Module
    Shell32.dll" error message, 128
Explorer.exe
  editing to change Start button name, 295
"Explorer.exe caused a General Protection Fault in
    Kernel32.dll" message, 840
Export Registry File dialog box, 409, *409*
exported Registry file, 362, 410–412, 418
exporting, from Windows Address Book, 549–550
ExpressMail (OpenSoft), 575
Extended Capabilities Port (ECP), 651, 653, 974

extended keyboard, typing characters without, 807
extended memory, 32-bit drivers loaded in, 722
Extended Windows ANSI character set, 796
extended (XMS) memory, 1092–1093, 1134
extensions. *See* file extensions
external DOS commands, 1057
Extract command (DOS), 27, 427, 1048
Extreme CloseUp utility, 767
Exupdusa.exe, 565, 569

F

Fast Ethernet, 678
Fast Paste, 1098
Fast ROM Emulation, 1095
FAT-16 hard disk volumes, 95
FAT 32 file system, 1037–1039
FAT-32 volume
    boot drive as, 94
    DOS 7.1 programs' handling of, 23
    and dual-booting, 113
FAT (File Allocation Table), 61
    report on compressed file, 1023
    ScanDisk and, 1012
FAT partition, 1043
    Windows 98 requirements for, 16
    for Windows folder, 19
"Fatal Exception Error" message, 1129
"Fatal exception OE has occurred..." message, 426
\Favorites folder, 238, 239–240, 242
fax/modem
    connecting to shared server, 616–617
    sharing on network, 614–616
Fax Modem Properties dialog box, 612, *612*
fax-on-demand service, 611–612
fax software, and Dial-Up Networking server, 458–459
fax spool folder, 617
faxes
    cover pages for, 611
    format, 613–614
    receiving, 567, 612–613
    requesting, 611–612
    sample address for, 601
    from Start button, 610–612
    viewing appearance of those sent, 618–619
    vs. voice or data call, 458
    Windows Messaging for, 564, 598
    Windows Messaging setup to send, 565–567
    from work while away from office, 477
fcbs= variable
    in Config.sys file, 105
Fdisk, 1038, 1048
file and print server for NetWare
    Windows 98 computer as, 701
File and Print Sharing dialog box, *899*
file associations
    creating, 351–363
    File Manager vs. Explorer, 218

multiple programs with single type, 363
    overriding when opening file, 817
file contents, viewing in File Manager vs. Explorer, 222
File Download dialog box, 254–255
file extensions. *See also* file types
    changing, 181
    displaying, 182, 203, 357, 361
    Microsoft attitudes on, 202
    multiple, for one application, 360–361
    one application associated with two, 358
    recognized by Windows 98, 370
    sorting by in Explorer, 221–222
    viewing, 84
File Find, File Manager vs. Explorer, 219
file handles, 1120
file icons, right-clicking, 914
File Manager, Explorer as, 343–344, *344*
File Manager Long File Name Support for
        Windows 95, 217
File Manager (Windows 3.1x), 161, 340, 345–346
    advantages, 224
    going to Explorer from, 216–224
    multiple child windows, 210
    running Windows 98 setup from, 30
    Shift key to display subdirectories, 826
    vs. Explorer, 190
File menu (File Manager), 217
File menu, focus on, 212
File menu (Internet Explorer)
    Send, Link By E-mail, 269
    Send, Page By E-mail, 244
    Send, Shortcut to Desktop, 241, 269
file names
    changing, 181–182
    function key (F2) to change, 212
    on Taskbar button, 140
File Open dialog box, right-clicking, 916, *916*
File System Properties dialog box, 1004, *1004*
file transfer protocol (ftp), 512
    for bulletin board downloads, 628–629
    HyperTerminal vs. Terminal, 635
file transfer speed, over Internet, 490–492
file types
    creating, 352–357
    displaying registered, *352*, 352
    editing, 357–358
    general actions on any, 366–367
    opening registered in other application, 364–365
    opening unregistered, 363–364
        default program, 365–366
FileHound, 233
filenames. *See also* long file names
    changing with File Manager, 345
files
    comparing, 1061
    compressing existing, 1024–1026
    copying, 85, 178–181
        from Briefcase, 667–668

into Briefcase, 664
creating, 83–84
    in File Manager vs. Explorer, 219
creating shortcut to, 85–86
defragmenting. *See* Defrag.exe
deleting, 86–87, 182
deleting from root directory, 65
in disk drive window, 77
displaying size, 224
dragging to Taskbar button, 141–142
DriveSpace and loading speed, 1032
on Emergency Startup disk, 51–53
finding, 316–318
moving, 84–85, 173–178
moving and copying with Explorer, 209–210
opening in different application from
        association, 827
printing in other applications, 367–368
printing to, 892–893
selecting multiple, 183
sharing in Microsoft Network, 645
shortcuts on Desktop for, 263–264
shortcuts to manage, 266
size and attributes, 1018–1019
sorting in File Manager vs. Explorer, 221–222
updating in Briefcase, 670–673
viewing all on computer, 202–203, *203*
viewing amount of compression, 1031
viewing/opening unregistered, 371–372
files= variable
    in Config.sys file, 105
filters, for file view, File Manager vs. Explorer, 219
Find command, in Start menu, 308
Find Computer dialog box, 646
Find dialog box
    Advanced tab, *320*
    Date tab, *319*
    function key (F3) to open, 212
    Name & Location tab, *317*
Find Fast (Microsoft Office), 319, 1013
Find feature
    for computers on network, 316
    dates to limit search, 319
    file type and size, 320
    for files or folders, 316–318
    for Internet, 322–323
    for network computer, 322
    results pane, 320, *321*
    saving search, 320–321
    in Start menu, 315–323
    starting, 320
    text strings in, 319
    ways of using, 321–322
finding web sites, 233
Fingertip Software, 817
Firedoor, 511
firewall, 506, 510
/fix switch, for Scanreg, 400

fixed-pitch fonts, 764
    for screen, 772–773
    in Windows 98, 784
FlexiCD (PowerToys), 278
floppy disks
    compressing, 1030–1031
    copying, 1019
    deleting files on, 384–385
    moving Briefcase to, 665
    multitasked formatting, 1000
Flow Control, for connections, 956
Flywheel, 940
focus
    drag and drop and, 177
    function key (F6) to move, 212
    for Start menu, 314
    switching, 314–315, 822
folder icons, 77
    right-clicking, 914
Folder List, in Outlook Express, 522
Folder Options dialog box, 80, 158, 308
    Direct Cable Connection options, 648
    displaying from Settings menu, 303
    displaying Unknown or All file types, 366–367
    File Types tab, 24, 136, 222, 236, 352, *352*
        to edit video clip, 446
    General tab, 164, *165*
        Web style or Classic style, 204
    View tab, 84, 202, *203*
        and file display after Find, 318
        to add toolbar buttons, 208
folder tree
    in Explorer
        Alt+* to expand branches, 212
        expanding or collapsing with keyboard, 208
        navigating using dots, 1061
folder view, in Explorer, 190
folder windows
    background graphics, 171
    changing to Windows 95 appearance, *170*
    inverting selection, 186
    parameter to display when opening Explorer, 215
    right-clicking client area, 915
    selecting all, 186
    setting maintenance, 202
    updating display, 169
folder.htt file, 171, 192
folders, 161
    Attributes column in window, 167
    closing windows, 166
    containing shortcuts, 275–276
    copying, 178–181
        from Briefcase, 667–668
        into Briefcase, 664
    corrupted, in Outlook Express, 548
    creating, 83, 173, 208–209
        in File Manager vs. Explorer, 218
    default for Mailbox.pst, 573

continued

folders *(continued)*
    deleted, in Recycle Bin, 380–381
    deleting, 182
    on Desktop, shortcuts in, 274
    determining parent for application, 431
    displaying listings side-by-side, File Manager vs.
        Explorer, 221
    displaying properties, 213
    in DOS window, 1075–1076
    expanding and collapsing Explorer display, 204, 212
    finding, 316–318
    function key (F2) to change name, 212
    highlight icon in Explorer, 205
    for HyperTerminal download file, 629
    icons
        custom, 172–173
        in Explorer, 206
    installing Windows 98 in new, 21
    listing from DOS session, 1118–1119
    moving, 173–178, 212
    moving and copying with Explorer, 209–210
    names as security feature, 246
    new on Desktop, 130
    printing listing, 220
    renaming, 181–182
    selecting multiple, 183
    sharing, 692–693
    shortcuts to, 276, 338
    specifying for cached web pages, 251
    in Start menu folder, 312–313
    toolbar for contents, 147–148
    updating in Briefcase, 670–673
    web page view for, 160
    window for, 77
    for Windows 98, 36–39, *37, 38*
fon file extension, 769
Font dialog box, 752
font family, 751
Font Sentry, 792–793
FontFinder, 792
FontHandler, 792–793
fonts
    boot failure from missing, 775
    cataloging, 792–793
    and characters, 795–796
    deleting before upgrade, 21
    on Desktop, 857–858
    for DOS window, 1072–1074
    embedding, 789–790
    extended properties, 759–760, *760*
    for faxes, 617
    in File Manager vs. Explorer, 220
    hidden, 754
    in HTML messages, 541
    for HyperTerminal, 628
    for icon title text, 128–129
    for incoming non-formatted e-mail, 598
    installing, 754–756
    kinds and types, 760–764

    for languages not supported by Microsoft, 816
    limits to number installed, 756
    location for, 752–754
    magnification on Desktop, 842
    point to measure, 772
    screen vs. printer, *791*
    size, 765–769
        and amount of text displayed, 769
        and reading from screen, 768–769
        and DOS window size, 1072
    uninstalling, 757–758
    using in applications, 752
    viewing, *758,* 758–759
    what they are, 751
    Windows minimum requirement for, 778–779
Fonts folder, 753
    accessing, 420
    inability to delete, 384
    non-font files in, 754
    window for, 752–753, *753*
footnote superscripts, 802
Format dialog box, *220*
formatting, 219
    compressed drives, 1030
    hard drive, 1019
    multitasked for floppy drives, 1000
forums on CompuServe, 10
fot file extension, 786
fractions, 802, 805
frame=none parameter, 1142
frames in web page, capturing URLs in, 241
Frames Received/Second, 475
Frames Transmitted/Second, 475
Framing Errors, 475
Freedom High Tech Fonts Centre, 793
freeware, 1153
FrontPage, 236
FrontPage Express, 539
FTP Explorer, 514
ftp (file transfer protocol), 512
    for bulletin board downloads, 628–629
    HyperTerminal vs. Terminal, 635
FTP sites, log in to, 232
FTP Wizard, 515
Full access, to shared resources, 691
full-screen mode
    expanding DOS window to, 1077
    for Explorer, 206–207, *207*
    for Internet Explorer, 75, 325
    and Start menu display, 314
    switching between window and, 822
function keys
    enabling during boot process, 98
    in Explorer and My Computer, 211–213
    F3 for Find, 316
    F4 and BootMulti, 95
    F4, BootWin and, 96
    F5 to refresh folder window, 169
    startup options, 102

G

games, 1056
  multiuser, played over network, 477
  in Windows 98 and DOS, 1149
gateway address, associating resource address
    with, 510
Gdi.exe error message, 778–779
Generic DUN Password Saving Advice, 497
Generic/Text Only printer driver, 888
Getright, 233
gif files
  as Desktop background, 860
  as Outlook Express attachments, 534
  for stationery background, 540
  thumbnail view of, 200
  as wallpaper, 134
G.L. Liadis Software, WinTray, 150
glicks from Scroll utility, 940
globe icon, changing in Internet Explorer, 234
glyphs, 759
Go To Folder dialog box, 213
Golden Bow, 1047
Graphic Device Interface (GDI) resource, 1126–1127
graphic files. *See also* bmp files; gif files; jpg files
  as Outlook Express attachments, 534
  thumbnail view of, 200
graphics
  displaying when exiting Windows, 112
  saving off Internet, 245
  on Web pages, 243
graphics adapters, 833
  detecting non-plug and play, 725
  non-plug and play, 834, 866–867
  performance graphics, 839–842
  sizes and resolution, 765
  specific problems, 841–842
graphics board. *See* graphics adapters
graphics display
  color, 851–857
  fonts for, 857–858. *See also* screen fonts
  LCD screen and external monitors, 867–868
  magnification setting, 842–845
  non-plug and play, 866–867
  screen saver, 864, *865*
  themes for, 860
graphics mode
  switching to, 1098
grave accent, 800, 806
grids, for folder windows, 167
Group 3 fax machine, 617
group policies, for System Policy Editor, 716
group, sending messages to, 546–547
Grouppol.dll file, 716
groups of files, selecting, *184,* 184–185, *185*
guest
  browsing from Direct Cable Connection host, 647
  for Interlnk, 638

H

handshaking, 956
hard drive icons, in My Computer, 160
Hard drive Properties dialog box
  General tab, *163*
  Tools tab, *1002*
hard drives. *See also* disk space
  cleaning up, 1018
  copying Windows 98 files to new, 58–60
  creating compressed drive out of free space,
    1026–1027
  deleting all files on, 384
  Direct Memory Access (DMA) for, 1001
  file system cache, 1039
  Find search of multiple, 318
  formatting, 1019
  installing Windows 98 from, 27
  labels for, 219
  maximum size, 1000
  MS-DOS compatibility mode, 1044
  opening new window for contents, 164
  optimization and long file names, 1064
  partition for Windows folder, 19
  partitions, 1047–1048
  Recycled folders in, 378
  saving web pages on, 243–245
  ScanDisk to correct problems, 34
  setup check for space, 39, 41, *42*
  sharing, 692–693
  shortcuts to, 276
  space requirements for components, 44–45
  System Monitor to track, 1006–1008
  total size of all files, 1019
  troubleshooting access, 1021–1022
  wasted space, 1000
  window for, 77
  Windows 98 requirements for, 16
  Windows detection of, 724
  Windows DOS sessions access to, 1067
hardware
  compatibility issues, 721–722
  creating multple configurations, 742
  detection after setup, 726
  disabling to eliminate IRQ conflict, 736–737
  forced configurations, 738–739
  interrupt conflicts, 736–737
  jumpers on, 729, 730, 735
  multiple configurations, 108–111
  Registry key for, 394–395
  settings adjustment, 728–730
  unsupported by Windows 98, 17
  Windows 98 requirements for, 16
  Windows 98 setup detection, 724–727
Hardware Compatibility List (HCL), 879
Hardware Conflict Troubleshooter, 740
hardware cursor, disabling, 841
hardware profiles, 741–748
  creating 2 for monitors, 745

heaps, 1126

height of font, 765

help, 73

    to access disk tools, 1003

    for DOS, 23, 1059

    function key (F1) for, 212

    for importing and exporting Registry, 418

    for printer properties, 880

    for printing, 895–897

    shortcuts in files for, 292–293

hex:, in exported Registry file, 410

hidden applications, 140

hidden characters, accessing, 811–812

hidden files

    Defrag.exe and, 1015

    displaying in DOS, 63

    in File Manager vs. Explorer, 223

hidden folders

    Recycled folders as, 379

    viewing, 203

hidden programs, viewing and creating for
        startup, 114

hidden share, 1020

hiding

    columns in Details view, 168

    host drive for CVF, 1030

    Taskbar, 142–144

High Color color palette, 847

high color icons, 138

High Memory Area (HMA), 1092–1093, 1134

Hilgraeve Inc., 624

Himem.sys file, 104, 1136–1137

hinting, 759

HiPack compression, 1033, 1034

History Explorer bar, *171*

History folder

    adding to Links toolbar, 237

    corrupted, 251–252

hk, 393

HKEY, 407

HKEY_CLASSES_ROOT, 254, 359–360, 365, 393

    \CLSID, 136, 195, 380

HKEY_CURRENT_CONFIGURATION, 395

HKEY_CURRENT_USER, 153, 394, 1039

    \AppEvents\EventLabels, 444

    \AppEvents\Schemes\Apps, 443, 444

    \Control Panel, 859

    \Control Panel\Colors, 850, 856

    \Control Panel\Mouse, 933

    \InstallLocations MRU, 415–416

    \RemoteAccess, 466

    \Software\Microsoft\Internet Explorer, 233

    \Software\Microsoft\Internet Explorer\
        Toolbar, 234

    \Software\Microsoft\Internet
        Explorer\TypedURLs, 242

    \Software\Microsoft\Outlook Express\Mail\Inbox
        Rules, 526

    \Software\Microsoft\Outlook Express\News\
        Group Filters, 526

    \Software\Microsoft\Outlook Express\Store
        Root, 526

    \Software\Microsoft\WAB\WAB4\Wab File Name,
        526, 549, 550

    \Software\Microsoft\Windows Messaging
        Subsystem\Profiles, 570

    \Software\Microsoft\Windows\
        CurrentVersion, 414

    \Software\Microsoft\Windows\CurrentVersion\
        Explorer\Shell folders, 113, 238, 302

    \Software\Microsoft\Windows\CurrentVersion\
        Explorer\Tips, 414

    \Software\Microsoft\Windows\CurrentVersion\
        Explorer\User Shell folders, 238

    \Software\Microsoft\Windows\CurrentVersion\
        Telephony, 993

HKEY_DYN_DATA, 395

    \Config Manager\Enum, 727

HKEY_LOCAL_MACHINE, 394–395, 726

    \Enum\NetWork\MSTCP, 491

    \Enum\Root\Net, 491

    \SOFTWARE\Logitech\MouseWare\Current
        Version, 937, *938*

    \SOFTWARE\Microsoft\At Work\Fax\
        LocalModems\Received, 618

    \Software\Microsoft\CurrentVersion\
        AppPaths, 1064

    \SOFTWARE\Microsoft\Internet Explorer\Main, 257

    \Software\Microsoft\Shared Tools\Proofing
        Tools\Spelling\languageID\Normal, 532

    \SOFTWARE\Microsoft\Windows\
        CurrentVersion, 757

    \SOFTWARE\Microsoft\Windows\CurrentVersion\
        App Paths, 293

    \SOFTWARE\Microsoft\Windows\CurrentVersion\
        Explorer\shellfolders, 199

    \SOFTWARE\Microsoft\Windows\CurrentVersion\
        FS Templates, 1040

    \SOFTWARE\Microsoft\Windows\CurrentVersion\
        Policies\Network, 703

    \SOFTWARE\Microsoft\Windows\CurrentVersion\
        Run, 114

    \SOFTWARE\Microsoft\Windows\CurrentVersion\
        RunOnce, 114

    \SOFTWARE\Microsoft\Windows\CurrentVersion\
        SETUP, 28–29

    \SOFTWARE\Microsoft\Windows\CurrentVersion\
        Telephony, 993

    \SOFTWARE\Microsoft\Windows\CurrentVersion\
        Uninstall, 432

    \System\CurrentControlSet\control, 1046

    \System\CurrentControlSet\Services\Class\
        Display\0000\DEFAULT, 867

    \System\CurrentControlSet\Services\Class\
        Modem, 958

\System\CurrentControlSet\Services\Class\ NetTrans, 491
\System\CurrentControlSet\Services\VXD, 433, 433–434
\System\CurrentControlSet\Services\VXD\ MSTCP, 492
\System\CurrentControlSet\Services\VXD\ VNETSUP, 514
HKEY_USERS, 394
HMA (High Memory Area), 1092–1093, 1134
host
 for Dial-Up Networking, 453
 for Direct Cable Connection
  accessing, 649–650
  browsing, 645–647
 for Dial-Up Networking, 455–460
 for Interlnk, 638
 print queue administration, 656
 shortcuts, to start listening automatically, 650
host drives, 1023
host name, 485–486
hot swapping, 946
hovering, 158, 183, 235, 911
HP font installer, 885
HP Intellifonts, 885
HPFS file system, 61
HPFS (high performance file system), 999
htm extension, 243
htm files
 opening, 227
 viewing source code, 540
HTML documents, 243. See also web pages
 adding to Desktop, 133
 on Desktop, 131, 340
 Explorer and Desktop display of, 191, 350
 Notepad to edit, 236
 opening, 227
 thumbnail view of, 200
HTML (Hypertext Markup Language), 243, 601
 Outlook Express support for, 536
HTML in Outlook Express, 538–544, 602
 background color, 542
 editing, 539–540
 fonts for, 541
 stationery, 540–542, 541
HTML template file
 customizing, 171
 editing, 192
 and My Computer web page view, 160
 to view folders, 192
HyperFont, 628
hyperlinks, 124–125
 underlining, 235–236
 on web pages to Word documents, 229
HyperTerminal, 46, 484
 accessing dialing properties from, 982
 answering incoming data calls, 634
 basic functions, 623–624

capturing incoming text to file, 633–634
connectoids for, 954
 phone numbers in, 988
 properties, 630–633
 troubleshooting, 627
downloading file, 624, 628–630
making connection, 627
protocols supported, 628–629
sending AT commands in, 960
shortcuts for, 280
vs. Terminal, 635
to test modem, 950
typing on Terminal, 628
uploading files, 624
Hypertrm.exe, 625
hyphenation utility, multilingual, 817

I

IBM PC-8 character set, 797, 800
 Alt key+numeric keypad for, 801
ICE NFS, 514
Icon Corral, 150
Icon Wizard, 172–173
icons. See also shortcuts
 animated, 923
 in book, 8
 changing to show BMP thumbnail, 368–369
 creating, 137–138
 custom for folders, 172–173
 for DOS shortcut, 1087, 1088
 dragging multiple, 187–188, 188
 editing spacing, 127–128
 files containing, 290
 for folders, 77
 font and size of title text, 128–129
 high color, 138
 locating files containing, 135
 from Pifmgr.dll file, 93
 plus sign when copying file, 176
 for Recycle items, 379–380
 selecting by hovering, 911
 for shortcuts, 86, 262, 289–290
 size of, 859
 on Taskbar buttons, 140
 TweakUI to rebuild, 139
icons on Desktop, 122, 134–139, 849
 arranging, 126
 changing, 135–137
 corrupted, 139
 and grid size, 126–128
 removing all, 134–135
IDE/ATA Zip drive, 1049
IDE drives, testing for DMA, 1021
identification, setup, 47–49, 48
IDG Books, web site, 258
idle sensitivity, 1096–1097
idx file extension, 525

IE Gallery, 132
IKIOSK, 917
Image Color Management, 870
image maps, 256
Image Toggler (PowerToys), 229–230
Imagedit.exe, 935
importing
    Outlook Express messages to Windows
        Messaging, 591
    Registry, 409–411
        help for, 418
    to Windows Address Book, 549–550
inactive applications, 140
inactive title bar, on Desktop, 849
inactive window border, on Desktop, 850
Inbox
    in active message store, 590
    troubleshooting fax not in, 617–619
    TweakUI to clear from Desktop, 583
Inbox Assistant, 526
    to reject SPAM, 552, *553*
Inbox icon, 567
Inbox Setup Wizard, 565, 569–570
    starting, 578
incoming mail, POP3 server for, 585
Incomplete Frames, 475
Inetxidm.dll file, 600
Inetxidm.inf file, 600
inf files, 57, 435, 724
InfoSeek, 257
infrared communications, 654, 972–973
ini files, 21, 391–392
    editing for dual boot, 55
initialization string, for modem, 958
inserting keys into Register, *407*
insertion point, 929
    color of, 854–855
Inso Corporation, 357, 371
    Outside In program for Windows, 222
Install New Modem Wizard, 460, 468, 947–950, *948, 949*
    file for, 958
Install Shield software, 428
installable font embedding, 790
installing
    Accessories, 45, *46*
    ATM network drivers, 689
    Briefcase, 662
    Clipboard Viewer, 774
    communications components, 45–46, *46*
    Dial-Up Networking, 488–489
    Direct Cable Connection, 641
    fonts, 754–756
    Internet dial-up connection, 483
    Make Compatible for troubleshooting application
        install, 437–440
    Microsoft Print Server for NetWare, 902–903
    modem, 483

    monitor, 866
    multimedia components, 47, *48*
    Net Watcher, 712
    network. *See also* network installation
    PCMCIA network card, 680
    Personal Web Server, 478
    printer drivers, 877–879, 904–906
    programs, 1158
    protocols for Direct Cable Connection, 644
    Remote Registry services, 711
    second modem, 965
    software, 428
    sound schemes in Windows 98, 442
    System Policy Editor, 716
    system tools, *47*, 47
    TweakUI, 446–447
    U.S.-international keyboard layout, 803–805
    video driver, 834–838
    Windows Messaging, 569–571
installing Windows 98
    advantages of using Windows 3.1x directory, 20
    with DR DOS, 60
    hard disk space for, 17–18
    with OS/2, 61–62
    over network or from CD-ROM, 28–29
    over Windows 3.1x, 20–26
        copy, 54–57
        Start menu after, 334
    upgrading from DOS, 19–20
    with Windows NT, 61
"Insufficient File Handles" message, 1120
IntelliMouse, 940
intensified colors, 1112
interactive startup, Ctrl key for, 103
Interlnk (Microsoft), 638–639, 656
    disadvantages, 639
internal DOS commands, 1057
    from Run command, 1066
international dialing rules, changes in access codes,
        995–996
International Settings dialog box, 819, *820*
Internet
    Dial-Up Networking to connect to, 466
    Find feature for, 322–323
    saving graphics off, 245
Internet cache folder
    corrupted files in, 250–255
    disk space for, 244
Internet Connection Wizard, 487–488
    for mail account, 518
Internet connections
    basic options, 481–482
    binding TCP/IP to Dial-Up Adapter, 489
    commands for, 232
    to CompuServe, 503–505
    configuring TCP/IP stack for, 490
    Dial-Up Networking for, 488–489

file transfer speed, 490–492
installing dial-up connection, 483
with Internet Explorer, 230–232
Microsoft Network over, 511
to news servers, 558–559
TCP/IP stack, 482
through LAN, 506–511
for Windows 98 network, 510–511
Internet Explorer, 122, 125, 225–260
128-bit encryption, 231
and Active Desktop, 71
ActiveX applications in, 357
capturing URLS in frames, 241
Channel Bar, 75
channels, 227–228
for CompuServe connection, 504–505
configuring for automatic connection, 500
cookies, 249–250
corrupt History folder, 251–252
creating custom versions, 234
customizing Address field, 233–234
deleting URLs in Address field, 242
different service providers for, 530–531
displaying credits, 259
drag and drop links, 244–245
e-mail client for, 518
error from forms, 253
Explore option for, 193
Favorites and URL shortcuts, 238–242
File Download dialog box, 254–255
in full-screen mode, 75, 325
icon in Explorer, 191, 199
Internet connections with, 230–232
keyboard shortcuts for, 256
Multilanguage support, 817–818
opening memory space, 255
opening new window to display web site, 227
PowerToys, 229–230
preventing automatic dialing, 528–529
redial settings in Registry, 464
security levels, 245–250
starting, 226–227
TweakUI to remove from Desktop, 264
version 4.0 release, 226
web searches in, 233
and Windows Messaging, 599–600
Internet Explorer Administration Kit, 234
Internet Explorer Components Download pge, 818
Internet Explorer for Mac, 233
Internet Idioms, 600
Internet Mail Delivery Service, 597
Internet Mail dialog box
Connection tab, 585
General tab, 584, *585*, 586
Internet Neighborhood, 514–515
Internet Options dialog box, 227
Advanced tab, 248, *249*, 255
General tab, 250, 251

Internet Properties dialog box, 230
Connection tab, 500
Internet Referral Server, 488
Internet service provider, 481–482
account information, 484–487
account with, 483–484
calling, 497–500
database, 485
dial-up connection to, 492–496
different for Internet Explorer and Outlook
Express, 530–531
e-mail restrictions, 544
log file for connection, 501–502
multiple TCP/IP settings for different, 492
preventing dial-up to, 237–238
sample address for, 601
software from, 487
Windows Messaging as e-mail client, 576
Internet toolbar, 169, 206, 226
Search button, 257
Internet Zone, 247
Interrupt 13 extensions, 1038
interrupts
conflicts, 736–737
displaying settings, 732–733
for multiple modems, 964
for parallel port, 974
for serial port, 968–969
sharing with IRQ steering, 737–738
Intersvr.exe, 638, 639
intranet, 482
TCP/IP for, 697
IntranetWare, client for, 699
invalid characters, Scandisk check for, 65
Ios.log file, 750
Io.sys file, 90–91, 103–104, 1055
on bootable disk, 402
and Himem.sys file, 1136
location for, 19
suppressing commands loaded by, 104
IP address
assignment to network card, 689
and Domain Name System server, 486
entry for SLIP account, 499, *500*
static or dynamic, 484
IP Configuration dialog box, 513
IP header, disabling compression, 502
IP Route, 511
IPX/SPX network protocol, 455, 461, 688, 698
binding to Dial-Up Adapter, 644
configuring, 701
for Direct Cable Connection, 640
IRQ steering, 737–738
ISA slots, for network cards, 678
ISDN, 482
ISDN version 1.1, and Dial-Up Networking, 453
ISO 8859–1 character set, 796

J

jaggies, 787
Janko's Keyboard Generator, 816–817
Japanese, 816
Java applets, risk from, 532
Jaz drives
   AutoEject utility for, 749
   letter designator for, 1047
jpg files
   as Outlook Express attachments, 534
   thumbnail view of, 200
jumpers
   on hardware, 729, 730, 735
   to set network adapter, 687

K

Kermit file transfer protocol, 629
kerned pairs, 759
Kernel Toys, 153
   Conventional Memory Tracker, 1128
   Keyboard Remap, 827
   MS-DOS Wizard, 1105
keyboard
   Caps Lock notification, 827
   to control Start menu, 314–315
   driver changes, 830–831
   hardware detection of, 725
   Registry information, 830, 831
   remapping, 827
   repeat speed, 829–830
   right-clicking equivalent, 912
   setting Num Lock at boot time, 828
   switching between layouts, 808
   task switching with, 154
   typing characters without extended, 807
   U.S.-international layout, 803–807
   use with Explorer folder tree, 208
Keyboard Properties dialog box, 807, 814, 815
   Speed tab, *829*, 829–830
keyboard shortcuts, 262, 821–827
   Alt+Tab to display active application window, 154
   ampersand (&) to indicate, 354–355
   for Control Panel shortcuts, 425
   Ctrl+A to select all, 186
   Ctrl+Esc to display Start menu, 147, 154, 314
   Ctrl+Z for undo, 183
   for DOS shortcut, 1085–1086
   for Explorer, 211–213
   for Internet Explorer, 256
   for My Computer, 211–213
   for screen saver, 865–866
   Shift key in, 825–827
   for shortcuts, 278, 288–289
   for shortcuts on Start menu, 315
   in Windows and DOS, 1098–1099
keys in Registry, 392
Kodak Imaging for Windows, 611

KOI8-R character set, 818
Korean, 816

L

labels
   for disk drives, 219
   for toolbar buttons, 337
language/keyboard layout
   default, 815
   Greek, *816*
Language Partners International, 817
Language Properties dialog box, *804*
languages
   DOS support, 828
   using multiple, 812, 814–821
LapLink, 650
LapLink for DOS, 637–638
LapLink for Windows 98, 653, 657
laptops. *See* portable computers
large disk support, enabling, 1038
Large Fonts, 770, 772
   magnification factor and, 766, *767*
   selecting, 844
Large Icons view, 166, 340
   of Fonts folder, 753, *753*
   icon placement in, 167
   selecting multiple files in, *184*
lasso, for selecting objects, 185–186, *186*
lastdrive= variable, in Config.sys file, 105
Latin-1 character set, 796
LCD screen
   and external monitor, 743–748, 867–868
   mouse pointer trails for, 923
LDAP (Lightweight Directory Access Protocol), 550
left drag and drop
   to copy, 180
   for icon group, 187
   to Recycle bin, 383
left-handed operation, of mouse, 923, *924*
legacy devices, 728
legal characters, 805
Lens 2.0 utility, 767
Lfnbk.exe, 1063–1064
license agreement, 36, *37*
licensing screen, setup switch to bypass, 31
line speed, 961
linked objects, and Active Desktop, 73
Links folder, 234
links on web page, right-dragging to Desktop, 72
Links toolbar, 148, 169, 236–237
List view, 166
   selecting multiple files in, 185, *185*
Lmhosts file, creating, 478, 689–690
lnk extension, 287
LoadTop option, in Msdos.sys file, 101
local area networks, 452
   connection, and sending mail, 597

default TCP/IP properties for, 507–508
Internet connections through, 506–511
for Outlook Express connection, 527
postoffice for mail, 604
local dialing rules, 985
Local Intranet Zone, 247
Location Information dialog box, *980*
Lock command, for direct disk access, 1043
log file
   for communications, 957
   of HyperTerminal session, 633–634
   for service provider connection, 501–502
   from setup process, 36
Log Off, from Start menu, 310
Logged (Startup menu), 101
logical block addressing (LBA), 1038
logical drives, Recycled folders in, 378
logical inch, 845
   and font size, 765–768
logical printer port redirection, 883
Logo option, in Msdos.sys file, 99, 112
logon
   automatic for Dial-Up Networking, 500–501
   to network, 702–704
   setting network option, 331–333
logon box
   for Desktop, 326–327, *327*
   terminal window for, 498, *499*
Logos.sys file, 297
Logo.sys file, 111, 112
Logow.sys file, 112, 297
long-distance access number, 983
long distance carrier, *984*, 984–985
long-distance dialing rules, 985
long file names, 202, 998–999, 1044–1046
   across network, 1045–1046
   Defrag.exe and, 1016
   DOS commands and, 1045, 1063
   File Manager and, 217
   pre-Windows 95 disk utilities and, 1043
   turning off support, 1046
lower ASCII character set, 797
LPT ports. *See* parallel ports
Lucida Sans Unicode character set, 811
Lycos, 257

M

macro language
   and associated file, 355
   vs. special characters, 807
macro recorder, 24
macros, 1062
   launching batch files from, 1114
Magellan, 257
magnification factor, 765
   customizing, 768
   setting for display, 842–845

mail. *See* e-mail; Outlook Express
mail delivery services
   choosing, 583–584
   properties for CompuServe, 587
   for Windows Messaging, 575–577
Mail dialog box, 578, *578*
Mailbox.pab file, 574
Mailbox.pst (message store), 587
   folder for, 573
Make Compatible utility (Mkcompat.exe), 437–440
   advanced options for, 439–440, *440*
Make New Connection Wizard, 460–461, 467, 493
manual answer mode, by Windows Messaging, 612
manual dialing, for network connection, 471
MAPI (Messaging Application Programming
      Interface), 572
   third-party delivery systems, 577
Mapisp32 error, for Windows Messaging, 609
mapping
   networked resource, 473, 649, 704
   shared folder, 208
markup language, 243
Marlett font, 789, 797
math characters, 801
MaxBPs= setting, 1138
maximized view
   for DOS window, 1071
   and Explorer window, 207
MaxMTU value, 491
mbx (mailbox) file extension, 525
Mem.exe, 1061
   to determine available memory, 1147–1149
   shortcut to, 1062–1063
memory, 1123. *See also* conventional memory
   32-bit protected mode drivers and, 1124–1125
   available, 1147–1149
   concerns, 1125–1129
   conflicts, 1129, 1147
   determining usage, 1144
   for DOS programs, 1089–1093, *1090, 1092,*
      1140–1146
   for drivers, 105
   dynamic allocation, 1095
   hardware tree in, 727
   loading Command.com and Drvspace at top, 101
   managing, 105–106
   for mouse drivers, 917
   opening space for Internet Explorer, 255
   restricting amount for disk caching, 1040
   ScanDisk report of lack, 32–33
   skipping check in setup, 31
   translation buffers and, 1143–1144
   types of, 1133
   ways of increasing, 1142–1146
   Windows 98 requirements for, 16
   Windows management, 1136–1140
   for Windows Messaging, 568

memory leaks, Windows 3.1x programs with, 1127–1128

memory manager, DOS use of, 1056

memory map, 1132–1135, *1133*

menu bar, keyboard shortcuts to access, 822

Menudefault command, 747

menus, on Desktop, 850

merging, text file into Registry, 411

message boxes, on Desktop, 850

Message Character Set Conflict dialog box, 819, *820*

message header information
downloading only, 598
in Outlook Express, *532*, 532–533

message headers
pane in Outlook Express, 522
sorting, 590

Message Options dialog box, *614*

message stores, 573, 587–591
active, 574, 590
adding to profile, 588–589
name changes, 589
password for, 589
properties for, 582
storing messages outside, 591
upgrading, 605

messages
"Another program is using the selected Telephony device", 945
"Cannot find a device file that may be needed to run Windows or a Windows application", 432
"Cannot find the host computer", 655
"Cannot initialize port", 945
"Dial-Up Networking cannot negotiate a compatible set of protocols", 479–480, 502–503
dll file needed is in use by another program, 905
"Error Code 29", 737
"Explorer.exe caused a General Protection Fault in Kernel32.dll", 840
"Fatal Exception Error", 1129
"Fatal exception OE has occurred...", 426
Gdi.exe error, 778–779
"Insufficient File Handles", 1120
"Mmsystem296: The file cannot be played on the specified MCI device", 445
"Mmsystem326; No wave device that can play files in the current format is installed", 445
"MPREXE caused an invalid page fault in module Kernel32.dll", 253, 334
newsgroup name can't be resolved, 554
in newsgroups, 518
out-of-memory, 1126
Outlook Express timing of sending, 531
"The port is already open", 573
"Status: Connected via parallel cable on LPT1", 655
"System seems to connect but can't find the host computer", 655
"There are no spare stack pages", 1139

"This program requires Windows 3.1 or higher", 437, 438
"Windows will retry in 5 seconds", 883
"Your audio hardware cannot play files like the current file", 445

mht extension, 245

MHTML, 244

mice. *See also* mouse drivers; right-clicking
adding driver for new, 922–923
basics, 909–910
and built-in trackball, 936
changing driver for existing, 918–921
desensitizing dragging, 926–927
disabling right button, 917
for DOS programs, 1097
double-clicking, 73, 204
height and width, 925
speed, 925
vs. single-clicking, 910–912
left-handed operation, 923, *924*
middle button, 918
missing configuration options, 935
submenus speed of appearance, 927
support for multiple, 725

microprocessor, Windows 98 requirements for, 16

Microsoft
vs. Netscape, 255–256
web sites, 258–259

Microsoft Access, and Briefcase, 674

Microsoft Active Desktop gallery, 71

Microsoft advertising graphics, setup switch to bypass, 31

Microsoft Audio Compression Manager (MSACM), 445

Microsoft Dial-Up Adapter, 456

Microsoft Exchange. *See also* Windows Messaging
importing messages into Outlook Express, 549

Microsoft Exchange Server, 564

Microsoft Fax, 577, 609–617, *611*
accessing dialing properties from, 982
as printer driver, 595
status, 612
troubleshooting problems, 617–619

Microsoft Fax Properties dialog box
Modem tab, 615

Microsoft Foreign Proofing Tools, 817

Microsoft Knowledge Base, 10, 13
on connections to remote server, 463
on Direct Cable Connection, 647
on DOS games, 1149
on Extract, 27, 427
on Extract command, 1048
on faxing, 619
on HyperTerminal, 634
on infrared data, 654
on mail server port address, 586
on MS-DOS mode, 1105–1106
on networks, 698
on password issues, 334

printing, 896
on shut down problems, 297
and system setup, 969
Telephon.ini file updates, 996
on testing memory, 1129
for troubleshooting guidelines, 115
on unsupported CD-ROM drives, 17
on upgrading file system, 1044
on Word for mail, 599
Microsoft Mail, 575
sample address for, 601
schedule for connections to postoffice, 608
Microsoft Mail delivery service
laptop computer profile for, 606
Microsoft Mail dialog box
Connection tab, *582, 607*
Dial-Up Network tab, *608*
Remote Session tab, *607*
Microsoft Mail Workgroup Postoffice, 604–609
Microsoft Natural Keyboard
Win key, 824
Microsoft Network, 694–699
for mail, 576
over Internet, 511
sample address for, 601
troubleshooting problems, 698
Microsoft Network address book, associating with
profile, 592
Microsoft newsgroups, subscribing to, 560
Microsoft Office Find Fast utility, 319, 1013
Microsoft Outlook, 599
Microsoft Phone, 458
and profiles, 573, 613
setup, 459
Microsoft Plus! CD-ROM, 135, 1001
Microsoft Print Server for NetWare, 874, 902–903
Microsoft Service for NetWare Directory Services, 690
Microsoft TrueType Font Assistant, 754
Microsoft TrueType Font Pack, 812
character sets, *813*
Microsoft Windows Update, 835
Microsoft's Plus! for Windows 95, 787
middle button, 918
double-clicking with, 937–938
MIME format, 534, 536–537, 586–587
Minimize All Windows function, 146
minimized application, restoring, 912
Minitel emulation, 631
MinSPs, 1139
Missing Shortcut dialog box, 291, *292*
mmf extension, 605
"Mmsystem296: The file cannot be played on the
specified MCI device" message, 445
"Mmsystem326; No wave device that can play files in
the current format is installed" message, 445
modem, 468. *See also* Properties dialog box for
modem
16550 UART chip for, 503

16550A UART chip settings, 957–958
access to properties, 421
cable, 966
cellular, 956
changing basic connection properties, 952–955
changing basic global settings, 951, *952*
configuring, 483, 947–959
for dialing phone numbers, *991*, 991–993
driver options for generic, 950
forcing delay in dial process, 987
installing, 483
location information for, 980
maximum speed, 951
as network adapter, 463, 469, 682
networking over, 472–474
one for all communications software, 944–945
properties for HyperTerminal, 630
setting to answer phone, 634
setup, 54
setup for Dial-Up Networking host, 456
speed of, 961–964
support for distinctive ring service, 459
testing and interrogating, 959–965
testing configuration, 950–951
testing internal for 16550A UART chip, 973–974
use with DOS programs, 964
using multiple, 964–965
web sites about, 491
Windows detection of, 724
Modemlog.txt file, 957
Modems Properties dialog box, 947, *948*
additional tabs, 954–955
Diagnostics tab, 960
for DUN connectoids, 954
General tab, 951
Modems.inf file, 958–959
Modemui.dll file, 954
money, regional settings for, 441
monitors. *See also* graphics display
creating hardware profiles for two, 745
external and LCD for laptop, 743–748, 867–868
refresh rate, 866–867
Windows detection of, 724
Most Recently Used list, editing, 414–416
mounted compressed drives, 1030, 1031
mouse. *See* mice
Mouse Control Center, 937
mouse drivers, 917–918, 1124
adding for new mouse, 922–923
setup, 918–923
mouse pointers, 927–930
changing, 928–929
creating, 935
pointer trails, 923, 934
speed of, 931–932
in Windows 98, 930
Mouse Properties dialog box, 918, 923–934
Motion tab, 931
Pointers tab, *928*

moving
    Briefcase, 664–667
    DOS window, 1072
    with Explorer, 190
    File Manager vs. Explorer, 217
    Taskbar, 70–71, 144–145
    toolbars, 147
    windows on Desktop, 146
moving files or folders, 84–85, 173–178
    with cut and paste, 174
    with Explorer, 209–210
    impact on shortcut, 291–292
    left drag and drop for, 175–177
    right drag and drop, 174–175
"MPREXE caused an invalid page fault in module
        Kernel32.dll message, 253, 334
MS Chat, 46
MS-DOS. *See* DOS
MS-DOS mode, 1055, 1099–1106
    16-bit CD-ROM drivers in, 17
    16-bit drivers for, 105
    banner for, 1110
    to delete temporary files, 896
    DOS programs and memory, 1130–1131
    extracting file from CD-ROM, 427
    mouse drivers for, 917, 936
    network printing speed with, 902
    restart in, 297–298
    for Undelete, 388
    warm boot to, 1069
    without reboot, 1067–1069
MS-DOS mode shortcuts, 1099–1100
    private Autoexec.bat and Config.sys for, 1100–1105
    viewing internals, 1104
MS-DOS Prompt Properties dialog box. *See also*
        Shortcut properties
    Font tab, *776*, *1074*
MS-DOS prompt, in Start menu, 1067
MS-DOS Wizard, 1105
MS Sans Serif font, 128, 779–780, *780*
MSBatch.ini file, 711
Mscdex.exe, 998, 1047, 1068
Msconfig.exe utility, 116
MSD (Microsoft Diagnostic tool), 731
Msdet.inf file, 724
Msdos.sys file, 56–57, 91–101, 1065
    on bootable disk, 402
    BootKeys option, 706
    editing, 92–93
    editing for DOS 7.1, 63
    file contents, 93–94
    Io.sys file and, 91
    for multiboot with Windows NT, 61
    options, 94–101
Msdossys.bat, 92
msg file extension, 591
MSN, 482
MSNEWS Weather Map, 131, *132*

msnews.microsoft.com news server, 10
MTU-Speed, 492
multi-part files, in newsgroups, 558
Multi-User Wizard, 328–329, *329*
multidocument interface, 210, 344, *344*
Multilanguage support
    for Character Map with Extended Windows ANSI
        character set, 802
    for e-mail, 819
    fonts for, 751
    installing, 814
multilingual documents, 815–817
    e-mail as, 819–821
    proofing tools, 817
multilingual identifiers, 814–815
multimedia components, installing, 47, 48
Multimedia control panel, 440–441
multiplication symbol, 806
multitasking, 141
My Briefcase icon, 77. *See also* Briefcase
My Computer, 158–159
    changing icon name, 159
    changing to Explorer, 194–196
    changing window name, 192
    displaying contents as web page, 160, *161*, 162
    drive icons in, 163
    drives displayed in, 1001
    Explorer to open, 196
    Favorites option, 226
    folders, 161
    HTML template file to view, 192
    hyperlink appearance on, 235–236
    inability to delete, 384
    keyboard shortcuts for, 211–213
    move operation and icons in, 177
    navigating with, 339
    options for display, 82
    right-clicking, 913
    special folders, 162
    toolbars, 169–170
    TweakUI to remove from Desktop, 264
    vs. Explorer, 82
    window, *159*, 159–160
    window contents, 76
    window properties, 162
My Computer icon, 74
\My Documents folder, 198, 199
\My Documents folder
    shortcut to Favorites in, 239
\My System folder, 200
Mycomp.htt file, 192

N

name changes
    with Explorer, 190
    in File Manager vs. Explorer, 217
    for files or folders, 181–182

and multiple selected files, 183
names, for shortcuts, 272
NAT95, 511
national language support, by DOS, 828
navigating
    with Explorer, 204–206
    folder tree using dots, 1061
Nbtstat utility (DOS), 512
nch file extension, 525–526, 554
    unsubscribing newsgroups and, 559
NDIS (Network Driver Interface Specification) 5 level
        driver, 469, 701
Net Watcher, 709, 711–715, 901
    installing, 712
NetBEUI (NetBIOS Extended User Interface), 455,
        461, 688
    for Client for Microsoft Networks, 697
    for Direct Cable Connection, 640
Netcom account, Dial-Up Networking connectoid
        for, 505
NetDDE.exe, 25
Netinst.reg file, 434
NetMeeting, 46, 500, 717
NetProxy, 511
Netscape Communicator, 236
Netscape Navigator, 225–226
    configuring for automatic connection, 500
    converting bookmarks to Favorites, 242
    e-mail in, 599
    and form problems, 253
    importing messages into Outlook Express, 549
    vs. Microsoft, 255–256
    Windows Messaging and, 577
NetWare file and print server, 701
NetWare print services, 874
NetWare printer, 907
NetWare server
    configuring to use OS/2 namespace, 1045–1046
    point and print to, 906–907
network, 451–452. See also client; shared resources
    applications for, 717
    basic setup, 678–681
    basic support, 675–677
    components of, 682
    configuring for Direct Cable connection,
        643–647, 644
    editing other computers' Registry, 417
    finding computer on, 322
    including DOS machine in, 698–699
    installing Windows 98 over, 28–29
    logging onto, 702–704
    moving Briefcase over, 666–667
    multiuser games played over, 477
    Novell NetWare, 699–702
    persistent connections, 696
    Send To menu on, 284–285
    setting logon option, 331–333
    TCP/IP, Dial-Up Adapter, 231

Windows 98 as client, 676
Windows 98 features, 677–678
network administration, 708–717. See a. See also
        Registry Editor (Regedit.exe); System
        Monitor; System Policy Editor
    authority for, 707
    enabling remote, 709–711
    installing Remote Registry services, 711
    Net Watcher, 711–715
    NetWatcher, 709
    System Policy Editor, 715–716
Network control panel, 421
Network Device Interface Specification (NDIS) 5
        standard, 684
Network dialog box, 681, 697
    Access Control tab, 708
    Configuration tab, 332, 682
network drivers, 684
    and memory, 1124
network file system (NFS), 514–515
network information required, for setup, 49, 49
network installation, 681–694
    adapter, 684–685
    choosing services, 690–691
    client selection, 683
    computer name, 693–694, 694
    Primary Network Logon, 693
    protocol selection, 688–690
    resource configuration for adapter driver, 685–687
    shared resources, 691–693
network interface card
    configuring, 54
    configuring driver, 701–702
    configuring driver resources, 685–687
    configuring TCP/IP stack for, 482, 506–510
    conflicts with Dial-Up Adapter, 509
    installing PCMCIA, 680
    jumpers on, 687
    manufacturer's software to change, 687
    modem as, 463, 469, 682
    pre-plug and play, 687
    selecting, 684–685
Network Neighborhood, 198, 207–208, 452, 704
    and Direct Cable Connection, 642
    Explore option for, 193
    hiding shared resources, 693
    inability to delete, 384
    networked drive icon in, 649
    shortcuts for computers in, 279
Network option, in Msdos.sys file, 100
network printers, 873, 874
    drag and drop document to, 904–906
    driver for, 883
    installing driver for, 879
    printing to one not currently connected, 888–895
network protocols
    for Dial-Up Networking, 454
    for service provider connection, 503

networks
long file names across, 1045–1046
Recycle Bin and, 387
security for, 705–708
NETX client, 699
New Action dialog box, 354, *354*
New Active Desktop Item Wizard, 132–133
New menu (context menu)
adding items to, 373–374
adding Outlook Express message to, 533–534
removing Briefcase from, 662
removing items from, 375
New Message window, 595, *596*
for OLE objects, 602, *603*
shortcut to display, 270
for Windows Messaging, 570
New Messages toolbar, creating, 270–271
New Toolbar dialog box, 148
news reader. *See* Outlook Express, news reader
news servers
adding additional to Outlook Express, 520
connecting to, 519, 558–559
from Microsoft, 9
opening Outlook Express to open to, 524
newsgroup files, removing outdated, 559
newsgroup name can't be resolved message, 554
newsgroups, 10. *See also* Outlook Express, news
reader
corrupted, 553–554
filters, 526
New Message window for, 271
shortcuts to, 269–271
storing replies to, 524
unsubscribing, 559
Windows 98, 560–561
noems parameter, 1105, 1137
non-text fonts, in Windows 98, 785
nonprinting control characters, *801*
Normal (Startup menu), 101
Norton Disk Editor, 1063
Norton Utilities for Windows 98 (Symantec), 388
notebook computers. *See* portable computers
Notepad, 84
to edit HTML documents, 236
fonts used by, 773
printing from, 896–897
sending file to, 372
Novell NetWare networks, 699–702
client, 675
NRN (Novell NetWare Connect), 454
NTFS (Windows NT file system), 999
partitions, 61
Ntldr file, 20
null modem cable, 977–978
null modem driver, 656
Num Lock, setting at boot time, 828
numbers, regional settings for, 441

O

ODI (Open Datalink Interface), 684
Odometer for Windows, 935
OEM font, switching text to, 774, *775*
offline printing, 872, 888–895
to PostScript printer, 893
offline reading from newsgroups, 555–556
OLE objects, editing in Windows Messaging, 602
One-list, 561
online news, 9
Online Services folder, 197, 487
Ontrack, Disk Manager, 725
Open command, adding to context menu of My
Computer, 195
Open Datalink Interface (ODI), 684
Open dialog box, deleting files from, 381–382
Open Files view (Net Watcher), 712
open programs, setup warning about, 35
Open Sesame, 511
Open With command, 914
Open With dialog box
to associate file type, 361
for unregistered file types, 363, *364*
openas key, 365
opening
address books from Desktop, 595
Briefcase, 667
File Manager vs. Explorer, 217
folder window from Explorer, 205
meaning of, 911
memory space for Internet Explorer, 255
Outlook Express, 524
pifs, 1080–1081
registered file types in other application, 364–365
unregistered file types, 363–364, 371–372
default program for, 365–366
in File Manager vs. Explorer, 218
windows, 160
windows in Explorer, 166
OpenSoft, ExpressMail, 575
OpenType fonts, 759, 764, *791*
operating systems, Dial-Up Networking to dial other,
465–466
Operator Agent, 458
setup, 459
/opt switch, for Scanreg, 401
optical character recognition, fonts for, 783
Options dialog box (Inbox)
General tab, *580*
Options dialog box (Outlook Express)
Read tab, *519*
Orchid Technology Fahrenheit adapter, 842
Organize Favorites window, 239
orphans
from Briefcase, 665
creating for Briefcase file, 673
OS/2
and boot options, 96

installing Windows 98 with, 61–62
OS/2 Boot Manager, 62
OS/2 namespace, 1045
out-of-memory message, 1126
Outbox
    in active message store, 590
    damaged, 609
    messages in, 596
outgoing mail, SMTP server for, 585
Outlook Express, 545. *See also* HTML in Outlook
        Express
    adding message to New menu, 533–534
    automatic hang up, 528
    automatic mail retrieval, 519, 528
    configuring, 518–524
    configuring for automatic connection, 500
    corrupted passwords, 530
    Dial-Up Networking connectoids for, 527–529
    different service providers for, 530–531
    drag and drop in, 535
    Extended ANSI character support, 819
    features, 517
    importing messages to Windows Messaging, 591
    location of files, 525
    mail mode, 544–551
        corrupted folders in, 548
        as default e-mail client, 546
        duplicate messages downloaded, 545–546
        forcing start in, 524
        importing messages into, 549
        leaving mail on server, 549
        multiple accounts, 544–545
        sending messages to group, 546–547
        undeleting deleted messages, 547–548
        wav files for mail retrieval indicator, 548
    multiple accounts for the same server, 529
    multiple users and user profiles, 537–538
    news reader, 551–561
        anti-SPAM, 552
        connecting to news server, 558–559
        cross posters, 554
        keeping messages, 557
        multi-part files, 558
        reading offline, 555–556
        setting subscriptions to begin today, 557–558
    opening, 524
    pictures and text, 543–544
    reply to author vs. reply to group, 520
    to save web pages, 244
    saving attachments, 534
    security, 532
    to send messages, 595
    sending web addresses, 535
    shortcuts to, 269, 524–525
    signatures, 542–543
    spelling check in, 532
    timing of sending messages, 531
    UUENCODE or MIME format, 536–537

window panes in, 522–523
Outpost (Sierra On-line), 438
Outside In program for Windows (Inso Corp), 222
owner, changing registered, 413–414

P

padlock, on Internet Explorer status bar, 246
page drop speed, 884
page frames, memory use by, 1142
Paint, to create icons, 137–138
Paint Shop Pro, 863, 881
palette slot, and cursor color, 855
palette title, on Desktop, 850
Palette.exe, 855
Pan-European Multilanguage Support, 816
PAP (Password Authentication Protocol), 484
parallel cable, for connecting computers, 637
parallel ports, 650–652
    configuring, 974–975
    Device Manager and, 725
    and Direct Cable Connection speed, 640–641
    enhanced, 872
    interrupts, 653–654, 749
    maximum supported by Windows 98, 976
    as modems, 965
Parallel Technologies Inc., 652
parent folder, 431
parent windows, closing all for folder window, 166
Partition Magic, 60, 1039, 1048
partitions. *See also* FAT partition
    for hard drive, 1047–1048
Passport (Advantis), 438
password cache, 702, 703
Password List Editor, 703
passwords, 122–123
    to access computer through Dial-Up
            connection, 457
    for CompuServe connection, 587
    corrupted, 333–334
        in Outlook Express, 530
    for Direct Cable Connection, 643
    for e-mail account, 585
    for Internet connections, 494
    for message store, 589
    for network logon, 702
    for remote administration, 656
    for Samba, 514
    saving for Dial-Up Networking connectoid, 497
    setting minimum length, 703
    for Windows 98 logon, 328
Passwords Properties dialog box, 331, 436
    Remote Administration tab, 710, *710*
    User Profiles tab, 330, *330*
paste command (Desktop context menu), 130–131
paths
    adding application to, 1158–1159

                                        continued

paths *(continued)*
    application-specific for shortcuts, 293–294
    default for Windows 98, 106
    and erased DOS files, 95
    old Windows and System directories in, 21
    and Windows 98 applications, 1064
pause, for dial tone, 953
PC Card Wizard, 739
PC cards, 739
PCI Bus Properties dialog box
    IRQ Steering tab, 737, *738*
PCI (Peripheral Component Interconnect) devices, 736
PCI slots, for network cards, 678
PCMCIA cards, 739
    installing, 680
    problems detecting, 685
PCT (Private Communications Technology), 249
peer servers
    closing open file on, 714
    disconnecting users from, 712
    Net Watcher to track, 711–715
    shared resources on, 713–714
peer-to-peer network
    connecting to Internet, 510–511
    security for, 695
Pegasus, 549
Peripheral Component Interconnect (PCI) devices, 736
persistent network connection, 696
Personal Address Book, 574
Personal Information Store, 573–574
    format, 605
Personal Web Server (Microsoft), 455, 487
    connecting to, 477–479
    installing, 478
Personalized Items Settings dialog box, 328, *329*
Pervmfiles= statement, 1120
phone answering, by Windows Messaging, 612
Phone Dialer, 46, 981, *991*, 991–993
phone number, for HyperTerminal, 630
pictures, in Outlook Express, 543–544
Pifmgr.dll file
    icons from, 93
pifs (Program Information Files), 272, 290–291,
        1062–1063, 1066, 1078, 1079
    opening, 1080–1081
ping command, 501
Ping utility (DOS), 512
/play switch for CD Player, 278
plug and play
    assigning resources to devices, 738–739
    BIOS, 723–724
    and docking station connection, 748
    hotswapping and hot docking, 748
    mice, 917
    for network, 678
    PC cards as, 739
point and print, 873, 903–907
    to NetWare printer, 907

    to NetWare server, 906–907
points, 765
pol extension, 397
policy files, 397
POP3 server, 525, 584, 585
pop3uidl.dat file, corrupted, 546
"The port is already open" message, 573
port speed, 961
portable computers
    built-in trackball and plug-in mouse, 936
    deferred printing for, 889
    with external keyboard, 830
    IR ports, 972
    LCDs and external monitors, 743–748, 867–868
    moving Briefcase to, 667
    network card for, 679
    PC cards in, 739
    profiles for Microsoft Mail delivery service, 606
Portable install option, 41, *42*
ports. *See also* parallel ports; serial ports
    DCC Wizard identification of, 642, *643*
    maximum supported by Windows 98, 976
    for printers, 884
    for serial mouse, 917
posting messages
    on CompuServe forums, 11
    in newsgroups, 518
postoffice address list, 574
PostScript fonts, 754, 764, 790–791
    and copyright, 789
PostScript printer drivers, 872–873
    spooling by, 871
PostScript printers, TrueType fonts on, 885–886
PostScript printing, 893–895
    deferred, 893
    properties for, 887
power-on self test, 115, 1054
PowerPoint files, thumbnail view of, 200
PowerToys, 229–230
    Cabinet Viewer, 27
    Deskmenu icon in Tray, 149
    FlexiCD, 278
    Image Toggler, 229–230
    Send To Any Folder, 210
    SendToX, 178, 282–283
    Target.dll, 276
    X Mouse, 177
ppd files, 872–873
PPP (Point-to-Point Protocol), 454, 463, 484
Preparing Directory dialog box, *40*
preview pane, in Outlook Express, 522
Primary Network Logon, 693
print and preview font embedding, 789–790
Print Fax, 613
print jobs, separator page between, 881
print queue, 870, 888
    administration on host, 656
Print Screen key, in DOS sessions, 1118

Print Troubleshooter, 905
printer device mode size, 439
printer drivers
    32-bit, 869–870
    automated installation, 904–906
    installing, 877–879
    Microsoft Fax as, 595
    printing without installing first, 873
    properties for, 875, 879–888
        help with, 880
    universal, 870
printer fonts, 763, *763*, 884–886, *885*
    scaleable, 764
    vs. screen, *791*
    vs. TrueType fonts, 783
printer icons
    drag and drop to, 876–877
printers. *See also* network printers
    defining, 888
    logical port redirection, 883
    Send To, 283
    setup, 54
    shared, 886–887, 898–902
        connection to, 208
        in Microsoft Network, 645
        monitoring use, 901
        shortcut to, 901
    shortcuts to, 264, 279, 873
    time-out error report, 883
    user-access control, 901
Printer's Apprentice, 792
Printers folder, 160, 871, 874–876, *875*
    accessing, 420
    in Explorer, 199
    inability to delete, 384
    in Settings menu, 303, 304
    sharing, 681
Printers.txt file, 895
printing, 869–874. *See also* spooling
    bidirectional communications, 872
    deferred, 872, 888–895
    from Device Manager, 732
    directory listing from DOS, 1118–1119
    to file, 892–893
    files in other applications, 367–368
    folder listing, 220
    Image Color Management, 870
    to offline PostScript printer, 893
    system configuration, 731
    with Task Scheduler, 889–892
    unattended, 890
Private Communications Technology (PCT), 249
processor, Windows 98 requirements for, 16
Prodigy, 481
profiles. *See also* hardware profiles
    configuring, 328–329, *329*
    log on with different, 310

from Microsoft Phone, 613
    in Windows 98, 572
    for Windows Messaging, 569–570, 571–577
        creating, 577–587
Progman.exe, 345–346
\Program Files folder, 199
Program Information File (PIF), 290–291. *See also* pifs
Program Manager (Windows 3.1x), 134, 340, *345*,
    345–346
    Desktop setup to resemble, 341–342, *343*
    group conversion to Start button menus, 20
    network card values in, 686
programs. *See* applications
Programs folder
    naming new folder as, 299
Programs folder, naming new folder as, 300
Programs (Start menu), 299–301
    submenus, 336
proofing tools, for multilingual documents, 817
properties, 447–448
    for DOS programs, 1080
    for DOS shortcut, 290–291
    for HyperTerminal connectoid, 630–633
    of printer drivers, 875, 879–888
    of shortcuts, 267, *268*, 286–291. *See also* Shortcut
        properties dialog box
Properties dialog box
    for shortcuts, 914
    for URL shortcut, *240*
Properties dialog box for Briefcase file
    Update Status tab, *669*
Properties dialog box for Client for Microsoft
    Networks
    General tab, *696*
Properties dialog box for compressed drive
    Compression tab, 1037
Properties dialog box for connectoid
    Connect To tab, *631*
    Settings tab, *632*
Properties dialog box for Desktop
    Web tab, 75
Properties dialog box for Dial-Up Adapter, *743*
Properties dialog box for drive or folder
    General tab, *1017*
    Sharing tab, *692*, 692–693, 1020
Properties dialog box for drivers, 733, *734*
Properties dialog box for DUN connectoid
    Server Types tab, 455
Properties dialog box for file
    General tab, 1018
Properties dialog box for file and printer sharing, *646*
Properties dialog box for fonts, 759
Properties dialog box for IDE/ESDI controller
    Resources tab, 1004, *1004*
Properties dialog box for Internet Explorer
    General tab, 244
    Security tab, 246

Properties dialog box for modem
  Connection tab, *953*
  Options tab, 495–496, *496*
Properties dialog box for network adapter
  Resources tab, *686,* 686–687
Properties dialog box for news or mail account
  Connection tab, *527*
Properties dialog box for peer server
  Tools tab, *715*
Properties dialog box for printer
  Details tab, 882–884, *883*
  Fonts tab, *885*
  General tab, 881–882
  Graphics tab, *881, 882*
  PostScript tab, 887
  Sharing tab, 886–887, 899, *900*
Properties dialog box for protocol
  Bindings tab, *697*
Properties dialog box for service provider
      connection
  Server Types tab, *493,* 493–494
Properties dialog box for video card, *840, 844,* 844
Properties dialog box for Windows Messaging profile
  Services tab, 581, *581*
proportional fonts, 764
  for screen, 778–782
  in Windows 98, 784–785
protected memory, for DOS programs, 1091
protected-mode drivers, 105
Protocol.ini file (Windows 3.1x), 392
  and Windows 98 install, 20
protocols
  for Client for Microsoft Networks, 697
  for Dial-Up Networking, 454
  installing for Direct Cable Connection, 644
  for Internet connections, 494
  selecting network, 688–690
proxy server, to access Internet over DCC
      connection, 650
pst files, 574, 588, 605
Public Access Usenet Sites, 561
public domain software, 1153
pulse dialing, for modem, 983
purged files, 388
pwl extension, 253, 334, 497

Q

Qbik Software
  WinGate, 511
QualiType Corp., 792
question mark (?) wildcard character
  in Find, 316, 318
Quick Launch toolbar, 148, 149, 266
  Show Desktop button, 146
Quick Links, 236–237
  setting default for Internet Explorer, 234
Quick View Plus, 371

Quick Viewers, 222, 357, 369–371
  placing on Desktop, 371
  shortcuts to, 264
QuickRes utility, 844
QuickSearch, for Internet search engine, 230
quitting Windows 98, 77–78
quote marks, 806

R

RAM. *See* memory
RAS (Remote Access Server), 454
raster fonts, 760, 761
RAW data, printer codes as, 871
Read-Only access, to shared resources, 691
read-only font embedding, 789–790
read-write font embedding, 790
real-mode drivers, 105
  for disk drives, 1043–1044
  minimum in Config.sys, 1141–1142
  for network, 676
  for PCMCIA cards, 739
  and Windows 98 install, 30
reboot, warm, 297, 1055, 1069
receiving faxes, 567, 612–613
Recorder, 24
Recycle Bin, 182, 198, 222, 377–378, *385*
  deleted Briefcase in, 664
  DOS and, 1057
  emptying, 386
  Explore option for, 193
  function of, 380–384
  icons, 77, 137
  and networks, 387
  property to remove files immediately, 386–387
  restoring files from, 385–386
  size of, 1020–1021
  turning off, 302
  TweakUI to remove from Desktop, 264
Recycle Bin Properties dialog box
  Global tab, *387*
\Recycled folder, 199, 378–379
Recycled icon, 77
refreshing windows, 212
reg file extension, 362, 409
Regedit.exe, 358, *359*
regional settings, in Control Panel, 441
Regional Settings Properties dialog box, and sort
      rules, 800
registered owner, changing, 413–414
Registry, 726–727. *See also* HKEY *entries*
  associated actions defined in, 351, 358–359
  autoinsertion at startup, 412–413
  branches, 392–393, *393*
  button colors in, 856
  to change My Computer to Explorer, 195
  colors in, 850–851, *851*
  command line parameter for consistency check, 31

computer setup to permit editing, 416–417
double-click box size setting, 925
editing file type entry, 374
editing to access New Active Desktop Item dialog box, 132
editing to replace Desktop icons, 136–137
exporting and importing, 362, 409–411
file corruption and, 398
files for, 397–405
fonts list in, 754, 756, 785–786
hidden startup programs in, 114
importing or merging text file into, 411
Internet Explorer redial settings, 464
key, 397
keyboard information in, 830, 831
keys and structure, 392–397
monitor refresh rate, 866–867
mouse speed values in, 932–934
option to process, 103
for Outlook Express address book, 550
putting changes in effect, 405
recovery, 400–401
screen font information in, 771–772
SmoothScroll setting in, 396
source file path, 28–29
special folders for information in, 162
to specify paths to applications, 293–294
startup folder specified, 113
telephony keys, 993
to track folders, 199
to track Most Recently Used list, 414–416
updating from Windows 3.1x files, 20
in Windows 3.1, 392
Registry Editor (Regedit.exe), *393*, 405–409, 708, 709, 717
    DOS version, 417–418
    to edit Registry on other computer, 416–417
    editing with, 406–408
    for modem settings, 958–959, *959*
    starting, 406
Registry Monitor (Regmon.exe), 395–397, *396*
Registry server, computer configuration as, 417
Regrecov.bat, 399
RegSrch.exe utility, 411
Regsvr32, 252
remapping keyboard, 827
remote access, 452
Remote Access Server, 655
remote administration, enabling, 656
remote control, 452
Remote Network Access Application (Rnaapp.exe), 479
remote network administration, 709–711
Remote Registry services, installing, 711
removable media
    AutoEject utility for, 749
    deleting files on, 384–385

drive letters for, 1047
Remove Shortcuts/Folders dialog box, *306*, 306
Ren command (DOS), 1061
rendering intent, 870
replication, 674
requesting fax, 611–612
resource address, associating with gateway address, 510
resource ID, for Printers window, 284
Resource Meter (Rsrcmtr.exe), 150
resources, 1126–1127
    configuring for adapter driver, 685–687
    for passwords, 702
    resolving conflicts, 740
responding, to cross postings, 554
restart options
    MS-DOS mode as, 297–298
    for Windows 98, 297
/restore switch, for Scanreg, 400
restored view, and Explorer window, 207
restoring files
    from Recycle Bin, 380, 385–386, 385–386
Restricted Sites Zone, 247
returning to application (RTA) speed, 884
RGB value, 856
right-clicking, 910, 912–917. *See also* context menu
    keyboard equivalent, 912
    to select, 183
    Start button (Windows 98), 310–311
right drag and drop
    to copy, 179
    for icon group, 187
    to Recycle bin, 383
RLE files, as background, 863–864
Rnaapp.exe (Remote Network Access Application), 479
root directory for Windows 98, deleting files from, 65
root, for Explorer, 215, *216*
ROT 13 format, 558
route add command, 510
Route utility (DOS), 512
routes, for TCP/IP network, 510
Rsrcmtr.exe (Resource meter), 150
RTA speed (returning to application), 884
RTF (Rich Text Format), 586
    for foreign language in e-mail, 820–821
    reassociating files with WordPad, 362
RtvReco utility, 412
rules, for font display, 761
Run command
    File Manager vs. Explorer, 217–218
    from Start menu, 309–310, *310*
Run dialog box, typing URL in, 232
Run Length Encoded (rle) files, 863–864
RunServe, 458
RWIN, and file transfer rates, 491–492

S

/s switch, for RegEdit, 413
S3 video adapters, 842
Safe mode
    function keys for, 102
    as startup option, 101, 824
Safe Mode with Network Support
    enabling, 100
    function keys for, 103
    as startup option, 101
Safe Recovery dialog box, 35–36, *36*
Samba, 514
sans serif font, 780
Save As dialog box, deleting files from, 381–382
saving
    Outlook Express attachments, 534
    web pages on hard disk, 243–245
    Windows 3.1x applets, 24
scaleable fonts, 761–762
    for printer and screen, 764
ScanDisk, 999, 1009–1012, *1010*, 1061
    command line parameters for, 1011
    DOS 6.2x version, 33
    DOS 7.1 version of, 30, 32–33
    in DOS window, 1003
    problems from, 23
    setting prompt to run at startup, 100
    setup switch for, 31
    in Windows 98 setup, 32–35
Scandisk.ini file, 65, 1012
ScanReg, 399–400
Scanreg.exe, real-mode DOS to run, 400–401
Scanregw.exe, 400
schedule, for connections with office Microsoft Mail
        postoffice, 608
Scheduled Tasks folder, 162, 199
Scheduled Tasks Wizard, 890
schemes, 847
scp file extension, 501
scr extension, 363
scraps on Desktop, 139, 268
screen fonts, 128, 762–763, 769–782
    Courier fonts, 777–778, *778*
    fixed-pitch, 772–773
    Fixedsys, 773
    point sizes, 772
    vs. printer, *791*
    proportional, 778–782
    scaleable, 764
    Terminal fonts, 773–777
    vs. TrueType fonts, 783
screen resolution, 766
screen saver, 864, *865*
    and DOS programs, 1095
script file, for Dial-Up Networking connectoid, 501
Scroll and Engine, 940
scroll bars
    on Desktop, 850

    for long Start menus, 315
Scroll utility (Pointix Corp.), 940
scrollback buffer size, HyperTerminal vs.
        Terminal, 635
SCSI controller card
    and DoubleBuffer setting, 99
    Windows 98 awareness of attachments, 748
SCSI hard disk support, 999
search page, setting default for Internet Explorer, 234
search window, for Windows Messaging, 570
searches
    on Internet, 257
searching
    exported Registry file, 410–411
    File Manager vs. Explorer, 219
Secret icon, 8
Secure Sockets Layer (SSL), 249, 559
security
    for Desktop, 333
    for Dial-Up Networking, 460
    in Internet Explorer, 245–250
    for network, 705–708
    in Outlook Express, 532
    passwords and, 123
    for peer-to-peer networking, 695
    server dial-back for, 464–465
    setting type, 707–708
    share-level, 706–707
    user-level, 417, 707
Security Settings dialog box, in Internet Explorer,
        246, *246*
Select Components dialog box, 39, *44*, 44
Select Directory dialog box, *37*
Select MS-DOS Configuration Options dialog box, *1102*
Select Network Client dialog box, *683*
Select Network Component Type dialog box, 682, *683*
selected items, on Desktop, 850
selecting, 80, 183–188
    bunches of icons, 187
    deselecting within, 186–187
    hovering for, 911
    inverting choices, 186
    lasso for, 185–186, *186*
    Shift key for, 826
Send Fonts As dialog box, 886
Send To Any Folder (PowerToys), 210
Send To command, for printer, 283
Send To menu
    cascading printer menu in, 284
    My Briefcase, 664
    on network, 284–285
sending faxes
    Windows Messaging setup for, 565–567
sending file to Notepad, 372
sending mail, 596–598
    with pointers to attachments, 603–604
SendTo folder
    shortcut to SendTo folder in, 285

shortcuts in, 266, 282–283
SendToX (PowerToys), 178, 282–283
Sent Items folders, 597
separator page, between print jobs, 881
serial cable between computers, 637
serial ports
    address and interrupts, 968–972
    configuring, 967–973
    connection speed, 961
        for Direct Cable Connection, 640
    default settings and speed, 652
    Device Manager and, 725
    for Direct Cable Connection, 650
    hardware detection of, 726
    maximum supported by Windows 98, 976
    as modems, 965
    testing, 960–961
serif fonts, 780
server
    dial-up, 453–454
    leaving mail on, 549
    Outlook Express multiple accounts for, 529
    type for Dial-Up Networking connectoid, 462
    universal naming convention (unc) for, 322
service bureaus
    printer drivers for, 877
    printing file for, 892
Set command, 1083, 1114
Set Winpmt= statement, 1110
Setup Options dialog box, 39
Setuplog.txt file, 36, 750
setup.txt file, 29
Setupx.dll file, missing or damaged, 427
share configuration, for drive, 163
share-level security, 706–707
shared drives, File Manager vs. Explorer, 223
Shared Folders view (Net Watcher), 712
shared resources, 691–693, 705
    Dial-Up Networking access, 472–473
    in Direct Cable Connection, 644–645
    fax/modem as, 477, 614–616
    files, 1020
    hiding, 693
    mapping folders to drive letter, 208
    for network access, 681
    peer servers on, 713–714
    postoffice folder, 604
    printers as, 476, 886–887, 898–902
    shortcuts to, 473
    troubleshooting problems, 698
    uninstall and files shared, 429
    viewing, 473
Share.exe, 1061
shareware
    registration benefits, 1155
    registration notices, 1156
    registration outside U.S., 1155
    technical support, 1154
    what it is, 1153
    on *Windows 98 Secrets* CD-ROM, 1153–1160
shareware for Windows 98
    technical support for, 10
    technical support for CD-ROM, 11–12
shell account, 484
Shell32.dll, 379
ShellIconCache file, 139
ShellNew key, 374
Shift key, 7
    to delete without recycle, 182
    to force move, 176
    in keyboard shortcuts, 825–827
    to select groups of files, 184
Shiva LanRova, 455
Short Date style, for clock, 152
shortcut icons, 85
shortcut keys. *See* keyboard shortcuts
Shortcut properties dialog box, 267, *268*, 286–291
    for DOS programs, 1081–1099
        General tab, 1081
        memory, 1089–1093
        Miscellaneous tab, 1095–1099, *1096*
        Program tab, 1081–1089, *1082*
        screen properties, 1093–1095
    Start in field in, 288
    Target field in, 287–288
shortcuts
    adding to Start Menu, *311*, 311–314
    application-specific paths for, 293–294
    for applications with command line parameters, 267
    to Compose New Fax Wizard, 611
    to Control Panel, 421–425
        keyboard shortcuts for, 425
    creating, 85–86, 272–274
        vs. copying executable files, 59
        for applications, 176
        then linking, 273, *274*
    cutting and pasting, 273
    deleting, 86, 262, 301–302, 383
    on Desktop, 263–264, 274, 337–338
    disabling link-tracking feature, 294
    to disk drive, 276
    to documents, changing program for, 267
    to DOS batch files, 267
    to DOS commands, 1062–1063
    to DOS programs, 285–286
        properties for, 1077
    drag and drop on Start button, 335–336
    in e-mail, 232, 281
    to e-mail recipients and newsgroups, 269–271
    to Explorer, 194
    to favorite Internet sites, 232
    for files accessed by Dial-Up Networking, 280
    finding target for, 290
    to folders, 276
        in Start menu, vs. folder, 312–313

continued

shortcuts *(continued)*
of shortcuts, 275–276
on Desktop, 338
to fonts, 754, 755
in help files, 292–293
to host file on guest, 649
for HyperTerminal, 280
icons for, 289–290
for icons in Control Panel, 279–280
keyboard shortcuts for, 278
to Mouse Properties dialog box, 939
and moving or deleting linked file, 291–292
for MS-DOS mode, 1099–1100
for My Briefcase, 664
names for, 272
to network printer, 905
new on Desktop, 130
to Outlook Express, 524–525
to printers, 279, 873
properties for, 267, *268*, 286–291
to Quick Viewer, drag and drop to, 369
to recent documents folder, 303
right-clicking, 914–915
for screen saver, 865–866
to SendTo folder in SendTo folder, 285
to shared printer, 901
to shared resources on computer at work, 473
to shortcuts, 291
in Start menu, 265
in Startup folder, 264–265
to System Policy Editor, 716
for toolbars, 148
in toolbars, 266
types of, 262
to URL, 240–241
sending in e-mail, 535
viewing in Explorer, 199
to web pages, 268–269
what it is, 262–263
shoulder in font, 765
 Shovelt, 144, 146
shut down
and open Explorer windows, 211
Shut Down
for Windows 98, 77–78, 147, 296–298
Shut Down Windows dialog box, *296*, 826
Shutdown 95 and Task Scheduler, 297
Sierra On-line, Outpost, 438
signatures, 599
for e-mail, 600–601
in Outlook Express, 520, *521*, 542–543
single-click icons, 72–73
single-clicking, 204
vs. double-clicking, 158, 910–912
enabling, 80
single-pane windows, 157
in Explorer, 192, 205
for Windows Messaging, 571

Site Builder Network, 132
site map, 227
sizing
DOS window, 1071–1072
Taskbar, 144
windows for shortcut display of application, 289
windows on Desktop, 146
slave drive, vs. bootable drive, 60
sliding windows, 153–154
SLIP (Serial Line Internet Protocol), 454, 484
to connect to server, 467–468
hardware flow control for, 956
IP address entry for, 499, *500*
Small Fonts, 770, 772, 780–781, *781*, 843
magnification factor and, 766, *767*
selecting, 844
Small Icons view, 166
icon placement in, 167
selecting files in, 184
smart quotes, 806
SmartDrive (Smartdrv.exe), 17, 63, 998, 1124
setup switch for, 31
smooth fonts, 787–788
Smooth Scaling utility, 861
SmoothScroll setting
in Registry, 396
SMTP server
for outgoing mail, 585
Outlook Express requirements for, 525
snap-to mosue action, 935
software. *See also* applications
from Internet service provider, 487
shareware, 1153–1160
software compression
for Internet connections, 494
Software for the Internet, 259
sorting
accented letters and order, 800
files
File Manager vs. Explorer, 221–222
in folder and Explorer windows, 354
message headers, 590
results of Find, 320
sound card drivers, 1124
sound cards
interrupt conflicts, 749
Windows detection of, 726
sound schemes, 442
Sounds control panel, 441–446, 442
source code for HTML, viewing, 131
source files
changing location and type, 28–29
loading for upgrade from Windows 95, 26–27
source folder windows, and focus during move, *178*
spaces, Scandisk check for, 65
SPAM, 544
rejecting, 552, 553
spare stack pages, 1139

spd files, 872–873
special folders, 160, 199–200
    in My Computer, 162
    windows for, 77
speed
    of Direct Cable Connection, 652–653
    of Internet file transfer, 490–492
    maximum for modem, 951
    of modem, 961–964
    of mouse pointers, 931–932
    of printing, spooling and, 884
    of uploads and downloads, 474–476, *475*
speed-dial, in Phone Dialer, 992
spelling check
    multilingual, 817
    in Outlook Express, 532
spin control, on Taskbar, 144
spooling
    disk space for, 896
    of DOS print jobs, 871, 882
    faxes, 617
square brackets ([ ]), in commands, 6
Sserife.fon file, 779
Sseriff.fon file, 779
SSL (Secure Sockets Layer), 249
stack pages, 1138–1139
stack space, for application, 439
Stacker, 1022
    disk defragmenter and, 1016
    version 3.1, 66
stacks= variable
    in Config.sys file, 105
Stand by, in Start menu, 298
standalone computer, 15
Standard Buttons toolbar, 169, 206
    adding buttons, 208
Standard Display Adapter (VGA) driver, 834
Start button (Windows 98), 73, 122, 147, 295, 298–310,
        299, 325–326
    to access disk tools, 1002
    adding shortcut, 311–314
    changing name, 295
    cleaning up, 334–337
    Control Panel on, 313–314
    Control Panel shortcuts on, 421
    Desktop on, 312
    displaying, 822
    Documents menu, 301–302, 350, 372–373
    drag and drop shortcuts on, 335–336
    Explorer view of, 306–307, *307*
    Favorites, 226
        removing, 303
    faxes from, 610–612
    Find, 308, 315–323
    Help, 308–309, *309*
    keyboard shortcuts for shortcuts on, 315
    keyboard to control, 314–315
    Log Off, 310

Programs, 299–301
    Accessories, Fax, Request a Fax, 611
    Explorer, 193, 194
    submenus, 334
    removing Favorites and Documents from, 303
    removing items from, 306, *306*
    right-clicking, 310–311, 913
    Run, 7, 309–310, *310*
    scroll bars for long, 315
    in Send To menu, 283
    Settings, 303–307
        Active Desktop, 71
        Control Panel, 420
        Control Panel, Add/Remove Programs, Startup
            Disk, 50
        Folder Options, 158
        Folders & Icons, 73, 80
        Taskbar & Start Menu, 143
    shortcuts in, 265
    Shut Down, 77–78
    Stand by, 298
    Startup menu, 301
    user options to customize, 330
Start command, 1113
Start Copying Files dialog box, 53, *53*
Start in field
    in shortcut Properties dialog box, 288
Start menu folder, 310
    folders in, 312–313
    TweakUI to name folder as, 299
start page, setting default for Internet Explorer, 234
startup. *See also* boot process
    process for Windows 98, 90–91
    restoring DOS program settings on, 1095
    temporarily turning off programs, 114, *115*
    viewing and creating hidden programs, 114
    Windows 98, autoinsertion into Registry at,
        412–413
startup customization, 89–117. *See also*
        Autoexec.bat file
    clearing Document History at logon, 373
    Config.sys file, 104–105
    dual-boot configuration, 112–113
    Io.sys file and, 103–104
    Msdos.sys, 91–101
    multiple configurations, 107–108
    multiple hardware configurations, 108–111
Startup diskette
    creating, 402
Startup folder, 113–114, *115*
    cleaning up, 26
    in Send To menu, 283
    Shift key to ignore, 826
    shortcut to Explorer.exe in, 343–344
    shortcuts in, 264–265
    TweakUI to name folder as, 299
startup graphic, changing, 111–112
startup keys, 102–103

Startup menu, *97*, 101–102, 301
  Command Prompt Only, 417
  function keys for, 103
  length of display time, 98
  setting option to display, 97
Startup menu (Start menu), 301–302
static IP address, 484
  benefits of, 486
StaticVXD value, troubleshooting missing, 433–434
stationery
  background color, 544
  in Outlook Express, 540–542, *541*
  repeated use, 544
"Status: Connected via parallel cable on LPT1"
    message, 655
step-by-step confirmation, 101
StickyKeys, 821
StopLight 95 ELS, 333
stopping Windows 98, 296–298
subfolders
  displaying in Explorer while dragging, 206
  including in search for file, 317
submenus
  in Programs menu, 300
  speed of appearance, 927
subscribing
  to channels, 75, 228
  to Microsoft newsgroups, 560
  to multiple news servers, 10
Subst.exe, 1061
Sun server, 514
SuperMonitor, 1008
superscript characters, 805
SuperStor, 1022, 1047
  disk defragmenter and, 1016
swap files
  and compression, 19
  disk space for, 18
  dynamically sized, 999
  hard disk space and, 1126
  managing, 1040–1042
  for Windows 3.1x, getting rid of, 22
Swapfile in use, 1007
Swapfile Size, 1008
Swappable Memory, 1008
switching views, in windows, 79–81
Symantec, Norton Utilities for Windows 98, 388
Symbol character set, 797, *798*, 801
Symbol font, 782
sync link, 661, 664
  breaking, 673
  multiple in Briefcase, 671
  and orphans, 665
Syquest drives, letter designator for, 1047
sys extension, for shut down screen graphics, 297
Sys.com, 64
Sysmon.exe. *See* System Monitor
sysops, 11

System Agent, 889. *See also* Task Scheduler
System applet, 422–423
System attribute, of folder, 172
System Commander, 96
system configuration, printing, 731
system configuration utility (Msconfig.exe), 116
system control menu, opening, 823
System control panel, accessing, 420
system disk, creating, 219–220
system files
  Defrag.exe and, 1015
  saving, 39–41, *40, 41*
System font, 754, 858
system menu
  keyboard shortcut for, 1098
  opening, 213
System Monitor, 708, 717, 1006–1008
  Dial-Up Networking and, 474
  to track dial-up connection, 962–963, *963*
System Policy Editor, 708, 709, 715–716
  and Remote Registry services, 711
  to remove icon from Desktop, 134
System Properties dialog box, 162
  Device Manager tab, *731. See also* Device Manager
  Hardware Profiles tab, 109–110, *110*, 742
  Performance tab, 1004
system resources, 1126
  Recycled folders as, 379
"System seems to connect but can't find the host
    computer" message, 655
system tools, installing, 47, *47*
System.dat file, 397–398
  automatic backups of, 399
System.ini file (Windows 3.1x), 391
  automatic backups of, 399–400
  DOS screen fonts included in, 775
  editing, 21, 1139
  increasing Files= in, 1120
  MinPagingFileSize setting, 1042
  MMIO setting, 841
  and network port speed, 902
  shell setting in, 346
  SWCursor setting, 841
  and Windows 98 install, 20
  and Windows 98 settings, 54

T

T-connectors, 679
Tab key
  to switch Desktop focus, 314
Tab2Desk shareware application, 312
tags (HTML), 243
TAPI-aware, HyperTerminal as, 623
Target field, in shortcut Properties dialog box,
    287–288
target object
  finding for shortcut, 290

Target.dll (PowerToys), 276, 914–915
Task Manager, *155*, 155
    hotkey for, 289
Task Monitor, 1014
Task Scheduler
    for Compression Agent, 1034
    printing with, 889–892
task switcher
    Alt+Tab+Tab for, 825
    keyboard for, 154
    Taskbar as, 141
Taskbar, 69–70, 122, 140–154
    Auto Hide, 70
    boilerplate text on, 139
    buttons on, 140–141
    clock on, 150–153
    displaying, 822
    drag and wait to button, 141–142
    focus on, 315
    hiding, 142–144
    keyboard access to, 154
    moving, 70–71, 144–145
    QuickRes utility on, 844
    recommended placement, 145–146
    right-clicking, 913
    sizing, 144
    Start button, 147
    toolbars, 147–149, 336–337
    Tray on, 149–150
    for window manipulation, 146
Taskbar Properties dialog box, 304–307, 373
    Start Menu Programs tab, *305*, 305–306
        Advanced, 306–307
    Taskbar Options tab, 143, *143*
Taskman.exe, 155
TCP/IP, 455, 461, 688, 689–690
    for Dial-Up Adapters, 478
    for Direct Cable Connection, 640
    multiple settings for multiple connections, 492
    for SLIP connection, 467
    utilities, 511–515
    Winipcfg to display settings, 513
TCP/IP Properties dialog box
    DNS Configuration tab, 507, *507*
    Gateway tab, 508
    IP Address tab, 508, *508*
    WINS Configuration tab, 508
TCP/IP Settings dialog box, *495*
TCP/IP stack, 482
    binding to Dial-Up Adapter, 489
    configuring for Internet connection, 490
    configuring for network adapter, 506–510
    conflicts between LAN card and Dial-Up
        adapter, 509
    information from service provider to configure,
        485–487
technical support, 8–12
    for CD-ROM, 11–12

    on CompuServe, 10–11
    Microsoft telephone numbers, 9
    newsgroups, 10
    online news, 9
    for shareware, 1154
telephone. *See also* phone *entries*
    modem support for distinctive ring service, 459
    setting basic information, 468
Telephon.ini file, 392, 982, 986, 993–996
    cards section, 994–995
    CountryOverrides section, 996
    locations section, 994
    updates, 996
Telephony Location Manager (Tlocmgr.exe), 981, 993
Telnet, 514
    in HyperTerminal, 624
Temp environment variable, 106
temporary files
    command line parameters to name directory, 31
    deleting, 896
    folder for, 106
    space claimed by, 1018
    for Windows 98 install, 17–18
Temporary Internet Files folder, 246
temporary storage, Desktop as, 338
terminal, 623
    emulation for HyperTerminal, 631–632
terminal-computer communication, 624
Terminal fonts, 773–777
terminal window
    for logon, 498, *499*
    typing on, 628
Terminal (Windows 3.1x), 625
    HyperTerminal vs., 635
    to test modem, 959–960
termination, of DOS program, 1097–1098
Tessler's Nifty Tools batch file creator, 55–56
test page, printing after installing printer driver, 879
testing
    COM ports, 960–961
    direct memory access, 1021
    modem, 959–965
text files. *See* ASCII text
text select pointer, color of, 854–855
themes, 860
    pointers related to, 929
"There are no spare stack pages" message, 1139
thesaurus, multilingual, 817
"This program requires Windows 3.1 or higher"
        message, 437, 438
threads
    print jobs as, 869
thumbnails
    changing BMP icons to show, 368–369
    of files in Explorer, 200–201, *201*
    and web pages, 245
TIA (The Internet Adapter) account, 484
tif files, thumbnail view of, 200

tilde (~)
  characters with, 800
  as dead key, 806–807
tiling, wallpaper, 862
time
  format for clock, 151
  regional settings for, 441
  right-clicking, 914
time interval, for printer time-out error report, 883
time slices, for idle DOS session, 1096–1097
time zones, 54, 152
Timeout Errors, 475
timer
  for multiple configuration menu, 747
Tip icon, 8
title
  of DOS program shortcut, 1083
  of web page, as file name, 243
title bar
  color gradient for, 849
  of active application, right-clicking, 915
  setting default for Internet Explorer, 234
Tmp environment variable, 106
tone dialing, for modem, 983
toolbars, 122, 140, 147–149, 169–170
  browser-friendly, 226
  customizing for Windows Messaging, 571
  customizing in File Manager vs. Explorer, 223
  for Desktop access, 149
  displaying for Desktop, 312
  for DOS window, 1069–1070, *1070*
  hiding and displaying, 337
  multiple for Desktop, 336–337
  for Outlook Express, 523
  shortcuts in, 266
Tools menu (Explorer)
  Find, Files or Folders, 219
  Map Network Drive, 208
ToolTips
  on Desktop, 850
  for Taskbar buttons, 144
Tracert utility (DOS), 512
trackball. *See also* mice
  built-in and mice, 936
trademark symbol, 802
  in Word, 811
translation buffers, and memory, 1143–1144
trash can. *See* Recycle Bin
Traveling Software, 657
Tray on Taskbar, 149–150
  language identifiers on, 815
Tray Shortcuts, 150
TrayDay, 153
TrayText, 139
tree view, in Explorer, 190, *190*
troubleshooting problems
  after uninstall, 432
  ASCII text problems in HyperTerminal, 633

boot failure from missing fonts, 775
Control Panel missing files, 426–427
corrupted files in Internet cache folder, 250–255
corrupted folders in Outlook Express, 548
corrupted newsgroups, 553–554
corrupted password file, 333–334
corrupted pop3uidl.dat file, 546
crash from video hardware settings, 840
Defrag.exe hangs, 252
Dial-Up Networking, 479–480
Direct Cable Connection, 654–655
disappearing cover page, 611
disk problems, 1009
downloading 128-bit version of Internet
    Explorer, 232
drive access, 1021–1022
failure to open Modems Properties dialog box, 954
HyperTerminal connectoid, 627
and install process, 439
installing applications, Make Compatible for,
    437–440
memory conflicts, 1147
Microsoft Fax, 617–619
Microsoft Network, 698
non-functioning programs after drag and drop, 188
parallel port interrupts, 653–654
PC Cards, 739
PCMCIA network card detection, 685
printing, 879, 895–897
starting DOS application, 1117
switching Windows Messaging profiles, 572
system resources, 1126
TCP/IP conflicts between LAN card and Dial-Up
    adapter, 509
from TSRs, 29
updating Briefcase files, 666–667
video driver in laptop, 744
from web sites, 253
Windows 98, 115–116
with Windows 98 shut down, 297
Windows Messaging, 609
True Color, 138
TrueType fonts, 764, 782–790
  Arial Alternative, 631
  installing, 755–756
  magnification on screen, 766
  missing, 757
  on PostScript printers, 885–886
  reinstalling, 757
  sources of, 793
  in Windows 98, 751, 783–787
Trusted Sites Zone, 247
TSRs
  Dosstart.bat file call to, 1068
  troubleshooting problems from, 29
ttf file extension, 786
TTFPlus, 792
TweakUI, 393

to add items to New menu, 373–374
Add/Remove tab, 431
automated logon, 703
Boot tab, 112
to bypass logon box, 123
to change folder location, 199
to change shortcut icon, 262
to clear Documents menu, 302
to clear Inbox from Desktop, 583
to clear Recycle Bin from Desktop, 378
to display hard drives, 164
to display tips, 414
Explorer tab, *447*
and Favorites folder, 238–239
General tab, 113
    to set default search site, 233
to hide drives, 1001
installing, 446–447
Mouse tab, 926, *926*
to name folders as Start, Programs, and
    StartUp, 299
New menu management by, 375
Paranoia tab, Clear Document History at Logon, 373
to rebuild icons, 139, 173
to remove Briefcase from New menu, 662
to remove Favorites and Documents from Start
    menu, 303
to remove icons from Desktop, 264
to select icons for Desktop, 135
to send name & password to logon, 327–328
to set BootGUI, 97
to set BootMenu, 98
and Shortcut name, 273
to size double-click field, 925
to turn off Autorun, 748–749
to turn off "Shortcut to", 237
for zooming windows effect, 154
typefaces, 751
Typical install option, 41, *42*

U

UART chip, 640
    improvements to, 973
UCM (universal cable module), 651–652
UltraPack compression, 1034
UMBs (upper memory blocks), 1134
    Emm386.exe and, 1137
    loading drivers in, 1137
    monochrome, 1144–1146
    purpose of, 1135
    Windows use of, 1140
umlaut, 800, 806
unattended printing, 890
undeleting, 388, 1064
    in Outlook Express, 547–548
underlining, hyperlinks, 235–236
undo feature, 182–183

Ctrl+Z for, 213, 824
    in File Manager vs. Explorer, 222–223
Undocumented icon, 8
Unerase, 388
Unicode character set, 797, 820
Unimodem, 623, 944
Unimodem V driver, 458
uninstall programs, before Windows 98 install, 21
uninstalling
    commercial packages for, 429–430
    fonts, 757–758
    information for, 395
    manual, 430–432
    programs, 429
    Windows 98, 21, 62–67
    Windows Messaging, 569
Universal Alphabet (UTF-8), 820
universal cable module (UCM), 651
universal naming convention (unc), 224, 472, 704–705
    and network printing, 874
    for server, 322
universal print driver, 870
Unix computer server, 466
Unknown file types, displaying in Folder Options
    dialog box, 366–367
Unlock command, for direct disk access, 1043
Unused Physical Memory, 1008
Up-to-Date status, for Briefcase contents, 668
Update dialog box, for Briefcase, *671*
updating, Active Desktop content, 72
Upgrade Device Driver Wizard, *740*, 740
    for graphic display, 866
    for keyboard, *831*
    for mouse, 919–921, *919–921*
    for video, 834–838, *834–838*
upgrading to Windows 98
    from Windows 95, 26–29
uploads, speed of, 474–476, *475*
upper memory blocks (UMBs), 1065, 1134
    Emm386.exe and, 1137
    loading drivers in, 1137
    monochrome, 1144–1146
    purpose of, 1135
    Windows use of, 1140
URL (Uniform Resource Locator), 238. *See also*
    web sites
    capturing in frames, 241
    deleting in Internet Explorer Address field, 242
    for font designers, 759
    sending in Outlook Express, 535
    shortcuts to, 240–241, 262
        e-mailing, 281
        errors from missing, 292
    specifying for Internet searches, 257
Url.dll file, corrupted, 254
U.S.-international keyboard layout, 803–807
    AltChar key, 804–805, *805*
    unusual characters on, 805–807
    use with Word, 810

Usenet bots, 520
Usenet news server, 518
user-access control, 901
user interface, 121–122, *124*, 225–226. *See also*
    Desktop
    changing, 346
    multidocument, 210
    as point and click, 909
    for Windows Messaging, 571
user-level security, 417, 707
    sharing with, 645
user logon box, *122*
user policies, 328
user profiles, 436
    for Outlook Express, 537–538
    problems from long paths, 1010
    schemes in, 847
    and Windows 98 logon box, 702
User Settings dialog box, 330, *331*
user tips, displaying, 414
User.dat file, 397–398
    automatic backups of, 399
UserMPS.wab file, 526
username.pwl file, 703
users
    disconnecting from peer servers, 712
    options to customize Desktop & Start menu, 330
    Windows 98 setup for multiple, 328–331
UUENCODE format, 534, 536–537, 586–587
UUNET, 482

V

Vcache, 998
vCard (virtual business card), 520–521, 543
vector fonts, 762
vendors, CompuServe forums for, 11
VFAT (Virtual File Allocation Table) file system,
    104, 998
    report on compressed file, 1023
VGA resolution, fonts for, 766
Vgafix.fon file, 773, *774*
Vgasys.fon file, 754
video adapters. *See* graphics adapters
video cards. *See* graphics adapters
video chip, in portable computers, 744
video clips, preventing disappearance, 445–446
video driver
    installing, 834–838
    number of lines displayed in DOS, 1093–1094
video resolution
    and icon size, 859
video, Windows 98 requirements for, 16
View menu, 166
    Refresh, 169
    As Web Page, 74, 131
View menu (Explorer)
    Folder Options, 201

Internet Options, 201
View menu (Internet Explorer)
    Internet options, 246
    Refresh, 250
View menu (My Computer)
    Customize This Folder, 171–172
    Explorer Bar, 171, *172*
    Folder Options, 136, 164, 236
    Toolbars, 170
viewing. *See also* Quick Viewers
    all files on computer, 202–203, *203*
    attributes for Msdos.sys, 92
    cabinet file contents, 27
    file contents in File Manager vs. Explorer, 222
    file extensions, 84
    hidden folders, 203
    HTML source code, 243
    source code for HTML, 131
    unregistered file types, 371–372
views
    setting for folder windows, 202
    switching in windows, 79–81
virtual device driver (vxd) file, 429, 944
    memory to track, 1138
    missing, 432, 433–434
    for networking components, 676
Virtual File Allocation Table (VFAT) file system, 104,
    998, 1043–1044
virtual machine, 1066, 1140
    creating for DOS programs, 1078–1081
    file handles per, 1120
virtual memory, 1134
    disk space for, 1125–1126
    performance, 1005
    swap file for, 999
    System Monitor to evaluate performance,
        1006–1007
    turning off, 59
Virtual Memory dialog box, 1041, *1041*
virus checking, 1057
    in BIOS, 29
VLM client, 699
voice telephone calls, vs. fax or data, 458
VoiceView modems, 944
volume label, for drive, 163
volume locking API, 1043
vxd. *See* virtual device driver (vxd) file

W

wab file extension, 526, 550
wallpaper, 121, 852, 861–864
    big picture as, 863
    files for, 134
    tiling, 862
    web graphics as, 245
warm boot, 297, 1055, 1069
warning, about incoming cookies, 249–250

Waste for Windows 95, 1037
wav files, 442
   to indicate received mail, 548
Wavemapper, 445
Web Embedding Fonts Tool (WEFT), 790
web graphics
   drag and drop, 245
   turning on or off, 229–230
web pages
   displaying My Computer contents as, 160, *161*, 162
   folders for cached, 251
   fonts for, 783, 785
   hyperlink appearance on, 235–236
   mailto: option, 600
   multilingual, 817–818
   My Computer window as, 74
   Outlook Express to save, 244
   saving on hard disk, 243–245
   shortcuts to, 268–269
   viewing in Explorer, *191*, 191–193
web server, computer setup as, 455
web sites. *See also* Microsoft Knowledge Base
   for 128-bit encryption, 231
   for Active Desktop, 132
   Alta Vista Personal Search 97, 319
   Animated Cursor Schemes, 929
   for animated Logo.sys replacements, 112
   applet to convert Netscape Navigator
      bookmarks, 242
   Association of Shareware Professionals, 1156
   AutoEject utility, 749
   for BIOS information, 90
   Change File Type application, 181
   on Channel Definition Format, 228
   on cookie control, 250
   for Desktop themes, 135
   Dial-Up Magic, 466
   on Direct Cable Connection, 644
   on DMA testing, 1021
   for DOS machine on network, 698
   for download manager, 233
   for drivers, 722
   on editing other Registries, 417
   on encoding and decoding, 537
   Exchange Center, 565
   Exchange Profile Selector, 583
   for ExpressMail, 575
   File Manager Long File Name Support for Windows
      95, 217
   on file transfer speed, 492
   finding, 233
   folder to track URLs, 199
   for fonts, 793
   Generic DUN Password Saving Advice, 497
   Hardware Compatibility List (HCL), 879
   Hilgraeve Inc., 624
   for Icon Corral, 150
   Icon Wizard, 172

IKIOSK, 917
Inso Corporation, 371
   for Internet Explorer, 226
Internet service providers database, 485
Janko's Keyboard Generator, 817
Kernel Toys, 153, 827
on mail import to Outlook Express, 549
MAPI interface for cc:Mail server, 577
Microsoft Typography site, 793
on MIME, 587
on modems, 491
for multilingual proofing tools, 817
for network file systems, 514
for network hardware, 679
for Nifty Tools, 56
for Novell clients, 699
null modem driver, 656
Odometer for Windows, 935
opening new window to display, 227
for Outlook Express, 528, 538
Parallel Technologies Inc., 652
Partition Magic, 1039
on PC cards, 739
PowerToys, 149, 230, 276
Print Fax, 613
problems locating, 253–254
public news servers, 561
Qbik Software's WinGate, 511
QualiType Corp., 793
Registry Editor Extensions, 406
for RegMon for Windows 98, 397
on remote administration, 711
on ROT 13 format, 558
Scroll and Engine, 940
search and replace program, 322
for searching, 257
on security, 246
security shareware, 333
on service provider connections, 503
for shareware, 1154
shortcuts to favorite, 232
Smooth Scaling utility, 861
software for copying Windows 98, 60
on spell checking, 532
SuperMonitor, 1008
TCP/IP routers, 511
for technical support, 9
for theme editors, 860
Traveling Software, 657
for Tray Shortcuts, 150
TrayDay, 153
for TrayText, 139
troubleshooting problems from, 253
for Undelete, 388
Web Embedding Fonts Tool (WEFT), 790
for web page view with thumbnails, 201, *201*
on Windows 98, 257–259

continued

web sites *(continued)*
   on Windows for Workgroups DCC, 656
   for Windows Messaging troubleshooting, 609
   for Windows Messaging utilities, 600
   WinGate, 650
   WinHacker, 296
   WinTop, 1008–1009
   for WinTray, 150
   WinZip, 537
   for Word macro to import addresses, 550
   Z-pA and ZppA, 1050
Web style, 71, 73, 79, 125, 201, 911
   setting, 204
   for viewing folders, 164
Webdings font, 783, 797, 811–812
Welcome to the Windows Briefcase dialog box,
     663, 663
width of column, in Details view, 168
wildcard characters
   in Find, 219, 316, 318
Win 3.1-style controls, 439
Win key, on Microsoft Natural Keyboard, 824
Win32s directory, 57
WIN386.swp file, 59
WinChat, 717
Window color, 852
windows, 74
   background color, 850
   changing view for, 166–167
   to Desktop, 312
   function key (F5) to refresh, 212
   icon order in, 167
   opening, 160
      in Explorer, 166
      new for drive contents, 164
      new for new web sites, 227
   resizing and moving on Desktop, 146
   selecting items in, 183–188
   single- or dual-pane, 157
   size for DOS program, 1086–1087
   sizing for shortcut display of application, 289
   sliding, 153–154
   for special folders, 77
   switching between full-screen mode and, 822
   switching to single view on the fly, 165–166
   switching views, 79–81
   viewing as web page, 80–81
Windows 3.1x. *See also* File Manager (Windows 3.1x)
   communications support, 945
   and docking station connection, 748
   emptying Startup group, 26
   font location in, 754
   installing video drivers from, 838–839
   installing Windows 98 over copy, 54–57
   moving to Windows 98, and disk tools, 997–1000
   permanent swap file, 1042

Program Manager, 134
   programs with memory leaks, 1127–1128
   running Windows 98 setup from, 30
   saving applets, 24
   upgrading to Windows 98, 20–26
   and Windows 98 install, 20
   Working Directory, 288
Windows 95
   Exchange client in, 564
   startup, 90
   upgrading to Windows 98, 26–29
Windows 95 CD-ROM, Interlnk, 639
Windows 95 Service Pack 1
   Exchange client in, 564
Windows 98
   automatic backups of Registry files, 399
   components related to printing, 875–876
   copying files to new hard disk, 58–60
   file extensions recognized by, 370
   fonts included in, *753*, 753
   games in, 1149
   keyboard shortcuts during startup, 824
   maximum ports supported, 976
   modem detection, 947–948
   mouse pointers in, 930
   network access during install, 28
   as operating system, 346–347, 1053–1054
   quitting, 77–78
   requirements, 16
   restart options, 297
   restart without warm reboot, 826
   returning to after DOS mode, 297
   running application when starting, 1159
   screen font files included with, 769–771
   shut down, 296–298
   at startup, 91
   troubleshooting problems, 115–116
   TrueType fonts in, 782, 783–787
   uninstalling, 62–67
   updating software and drivers, 308
   web sites on, 257–259
Windows 98 CD-ROM
   Change Code Page tool (changecp.exe), 828
   drivers on, 722
   OEM version, 20
   shortcut.exe program, 294
   themes, 135, 860
   Windows Messaging on, 563–565
Windows 98 logo screen, 99
Windows 98 network, connecting to Internet, 510–511
Windows 98 newsgroups, 560–561
Windows 98 Secrets CD-ROM
   animated and static mouse pointers, 928
   Better Colors, 855
   Color.reg, 855, 859–860
   copyright, 1154

Dial.exe, 992–993
Exchange Profile Selector, 583
font management tools, 756, 759
magnifier utility, 767
Paint Shop Pro, 863, 881
Palette.exe, 855
Registry editors and extensions, 406
RegSrch.exe utility, 411
security shareware, 333
shareware, 347, 1153–1160
shareware for icons, 290
Shovelt, 146
themes, 860
WinImage, 1048
Windows 98 setup, 32–54
    adding and removing parts, 57–58
    canceling, 32
    components, *43*, 43–44
    copying files, 53, *53*
    directory for, 36–39, *37*, *38*
    Emergency Startup disk, 49–53, *50*
    finishing, 54
    hard drive space check, 39
    hardware detection, 724–727
    identification, 47–49, *48*
    license agreement, 36, *37*
    for multiple users, 328–331
    network features, 677–678
    network information required, 49, *49*
    options for, 41, *42*
    preparing to start, 29–31
    Safe Recovery dialog box, 35–36, *36*
    ScanDisk and, 1012
    starting, 32, *33*
    system files, 39–41, *40*, *41*
    user information, 42–43, *43*
    warning about open programs, 35
Windows 98 Setup dialog box, disk space display in, 18
Windows 98 Setup Wizard, 35
Windows 98 Time Zone Editor, 152–153
Windows Address Books, 526
    creating new blank, 551
    importing and exporting addresses, 549–550
    merging, 551
    in Outlook Express, 592
Windows ANSI character set, 751, 796, 797–799, *798*
    accented letters, 800
    Alt key+numeric keypad to type, 798–799
    Windows 3.0 version, 799
Windows DOS sessions, 1066–1067
    DOS prompt for, 1107
Windows Driver Library (WDL), 722
Windows events, assigning sound to, 441–446
Windows family logon service, 702
\Windows folder
    batch file locating, 1114

hidden folders in, 203
location for install, 19
Windows for Workgroups 3.11, 998
    32-bit file access, 1054
    Clipbook, 25
    Direct Cable Connection to, 656
    networking, 695
Windows Glyph List 4 (WGL4), 796
Windows Layout Properties dialog box, 522
Windows Messaging, *591*
    address books, 574–575, *592*, 592–595
    answering phone by, 612
    command line parameters, 570–571
    composing and sending fax from, 610–611
    as default e-mail client, 521
    downloading, 565
    for e-mail access, 476
    editing OLE objects in, 602
    to fax, 477
    faxes as attachments, 609–610
    features, 567–568
    features missing from, 568
    importing addresses from, 550
    importing messages into Outlook Express, 549
    importing Outlook Express messages to, 591
    installing, 569–571
    Internet Explorer and, 599–600
    mail creation and sending, 595–604
        sending mail, 596–598
    mail delivery services for, 575–577
    message stores, 573, 587–591
    and Outlook Express, 518
    Personal Information Store, 573–574
    profiles, 571–577
        adding message store to, 588–589
        adding or removing information services,
            580–582
        associating address book with, 592
        creating, 577–587
        editing, 579
        editing information services, 582–583
        mail delivery services selection, 583–584
        for multiple users, 579
        opening with specific, 583
        selecting at startup, 579–580
        for shared fax server, 616–617
    receiving mail, 598
    setup to send fax, 565–567
    sorting message headers, 590
    troubleshooting problems, 609
    troubleshooting profile switching, 572
    user interface, 571
    on Windows 98 CD-ROM, 563–565
    Windows ANSI character set for, 819
Windows modems, 944

Windows NT
after uninstalling Windows 98, 66–67
and boot options, 96
Direct Cable Connection to, 655–656
installing Windows 98 with, 61
volume size limits, 1037
Windows NT Boot Loader, 95
Windows Printing System, 897–898
Windows shortcuts Properties dialog box
General tab, *286*
Shortcut tab, *287, 1082*
Windows Standard scheme, 847
Windows Startup Logos, 259
"Windows will retry in 5 second" message, 883
Windows Write
retaining, 24
vs. WordPad, 24
\Windows\Cookies folder, 249
\Windows\Cursors folder, 927
\Windows\Explorer.exe
icons in, 290
\Windows\Fonts folder, 199, 753. *See also* Fonts
folder
\Windows\History folder, 199
\Windows\Moricons.dll
icons in, 290
\Windows\Pif folder, 290
\Windows\Recent folder, 199
\Windows\Recent folder
deleting documents from, 373
\Windows\SendTo folder, 199, 282
\Windows\System\Shell32.dll
icons in, 290
\Windows\System\Viewers folder, 369
WinFax Pro, 577
Winfile.exe, 345–346
WinGate (Qbik Software), 511, 650
Wingdings font, 797, *798*, 811–812
WinHacker, 296
WinImage, 1048
Win.ini file (Windows 3.1x), 391
automatic backups of, 399–400
[Compatibility] section, 440, *441*
DoubleClickHeight setting, 925
DoubleClickWidth setting, 925
editing, 21
font information in, 754
port values stored in, 976–977
SafeMode setting, 841
updating Registry based on [Extensions]
section, 362
and Windows 98 install, 20
and Windows 98 setttings, 54
Winipcfg utility, 509, 512, 513
WinModems, 944, 964

WinNews forum, 10
WinPopup, 717
Winsock 2.2, 453
Winsock.dll, incompatibilities, 503
Winstart.bat, 91
WinTop, 1008–1009
WinTray (G.L. Liadis Software), 150
WinZip, 537
wireless infrared communications, 654, 972
wmf file extension, 881
Word
accessing unusual characters, 808–811
to create e-mail messages, 599
including documents as e-mail attachments, 232
macro to import addresses, 550
shortcut keys and keyboard layout conflicts,
810–811
word processing, special characters in, 802
WordMail, 598, 599
Wordpad, 24
WordPad
Font dialog box, *752*
including documents as e-mail attachments, 232
to open unassigned file, 366
printing from, 367–368, 896–897
to read Registry, 397, 409–410, *410*
reassociating RTF files with, 362
vs. Write, 24
workgroups
name for, 48, 693, *694*
shared postoffice, 604–609
working directory, for DOS program shortcut,
1084–1085
Working Directory (Windows 3.1x), 288
World Language Resources, 817
World Wide Web server, 506
wos file extension, 1104–1105
wri file extension, changing association, 24
write-protection, Windows 98 setup and, 24

X
X Mouse, 177
Xcopy command (DOS), 55, 59
Xmodem file transfer protocol, 629
XMS (extended) memory, 1092–1093, 1134
XrX Animated Logo Utility, 112

Y
Yahoo, 233, 257
downloadable fonts link list, 793
Ymodem file transfer protocol, 629
"Your audio hardware cannot play files like the
current file" message, 445

Z

Z-pA, 1049–1050
Zapf Dingbats font, 811–812
zero slot network, 639
Zip disks, Briefcase for, 665
Zip drives
   AutoEject utility for, 749

   booting from, 1049–1050
   letter designator for, 1047
Zmodem file transfer protocol, 629
   and folder for download, 630
zones, in Microsoft security model, 247
zooming windows, 153–154
ZppA, 1049–1050

IDG BOOKS WORLDWIDE, INC.
END-USER LICENSE AGREEMENT

Read This. You should carefully read these terms and conditions before opening the software packet(s) included with this book ("Book"). This is a license agreement ("Agreement") between you and IDG Books Worldwide, Inc. ("IDGB"). By opening the accompanying software packet(s), you acknowledge that you have read and accept the following terms and conditions. If you do not agree and do not want to be bound by such terms and conditions, promptly return the Book and the unopened software packet(s) to the place you obtained them for a full refund.

1. **License Grant.** IDGB grants to you (either an individual or entity) a nonexclusive license to use one copy of the enclosed software program(s) (collectively, the "Software") solely for your own personal or business purposes on a single computer (whether a standard computer or a workstation component of a multiuser network). The Software is in use on a computer when it is loaded into temporary memory (i.e., RAM) or installed into permanent memory (e.g., hard disk, CD-ROM, or other storage device). IDGB reserves all rights not expressly granted herein.

2. **Ownership.** IDGB is the owner of all right, title, and interest, including copyright, in and to the compilation of the Software recorded on the disk(s)/CD-ROM. Copyright to the individual programs on the disk(s)/ CD-ROM is owned by the author or other authorized copyright owner of each program. Ownership of the Software and all proprietary rights relating thereto remain with IDGB and its licensors.

3. **Restrictions on Use and Transfer.**

(a) You may only (i) make one copy of the Software for backup or archival purposes, or (ii) transfer the Software to a single hard disk, provided that you keep the original for backup or archival purposes. You may not (i) rent or lease the Software, (ii) copy or reproduce the Software through a LAN or other network system or through any computer subscriber system or bulletin-board system, or (iii) modify, adapt, or create derivative works based on the Software.

(b) You may not reverse engineer, decompile, or disassemble the Software. You may transfer the Software and user documentation on a permanent basis, provided that the transferee agrees to accept the terms and conditions of this Agreement and you retain no copies. If the Software is an update or has been updated, any transfer must include the most recent update and all prior versions.

4. **Restrictions on Use of Individual Programs.** You must follow the individual requirements and restrictions detailed for each individual program in Chapter 36, "Shareware" of this Book. These limitations are contained in the individual license agreements recorded on the disk(s)/ CD-ROM. These restrictions may include a requirement that after using the program for the period of time specified in its text, the user must pay a registration fee or discontinue use. By opening the Software packet(s), you

will be agreeing to abide by the licenses and restrictions for these individual programs. None of the material on this disk(s) or listed in this Book may ever be distributed, in original or modified form, for commercial purposes.

5. Limited Warranty.

(a) IDGB warrants that the Software and disk(s)/CD-ROM are free from defects in materials and workmanship under normal use for a period of sixty (60) days from the date of purchase of this Book. If IDGB receives notification within the warranty period of defects in materials or workmanship, IDGB will replace the defective disk(s)/CD-ROM.

(b) IDGB AND THE AUTHORS OF THE BOOK DISCLAIM ALL OTHER WARRANTIES, EXPRESS OR IMPLIED, INCLUDING WITHOUT LIMITATION IMPLIED WARRANTIES OF MERCHANTABILITY AND FITNESS FOR A PARTICULAR PURPOSE, WITH RESPECT TO THE SOFTWARE, THE PROGRAMS, THE SOURCE CODE CONTAINED THEREIN, AND/OR THE TECHNIQUES DESCRIBED IN THIS BOOK. IDGB DOES NOT WARRANT THAT THE FUNCTIONS CONTAINED IN THE SOFTWARE WILL MEET YOUR REQUIREMENTS OR THAT THE OPERATION OF THE SOFTWARE WILL BE ERROR FREE.

(c) This limited warranty gives you specific legal rights, and you may have other rights which vary from jurisdiction to jurisdiction.

6. Remedies.

(a) IDGB's entire liability and your exclusive remedy for defects in materials and workmanship shall be limited to replacement of the Software, which may be returned to IDGB with a copy of your receipt at the following address: Disk Fulfillment Department, Attn: Windows® 98 SECRETS®, IDG Books Worldwide, Inc., 7260 Shadeland Station, Ste. 100, Indianapolis, IN 46256, or call 1-800-762-2974. Please allow 3-4 weeks for delivery. This Limited Warranty is void if failure of the Software has resulted from accident, abuse, or misapplication. Any replacement Software will be warranted for the remainder of the original warranty period or thirty (30) days, whichever is longer.

(b) In no event shall IDGB or the author be liable for any damages whatsoever (including without limitation damages for loss of business profits, business interruption, loss of business information, or any other pecuniary loss) arising from the use of or inability to use the Book or the Software, even if IDGB has been advised of the possibility of such damages.

(c) Because some jurisdictions do not allow the exclusion or limitation of liability for consequential or incidental damages, the above limitation or exclusion may not apply to you.

7. U.S. Government Restricted Rights.
Use, duplication, or disclosure of the Software by the U.S. Government is subject to restrictions stated in paragraph (c) (1) (ii) of the Rights in Technical Data and Computer Software clause of DFARS 252.227-7013, and in subparagraphs (a) through (d) of the Commercial Computer — Restricted Rights clause at FAR 52.227-19, and in similar clauses in the NASA FAR supplement, when applicable.

8. General. This Agreement constitutes the entire understanding of the parties and revokes and supersedes all prior agreements, oral or written, between them and may not be modified or amended except in a writing signed by both parties hereto which specifically refers to this Agreement. This Agreement shall take precedence over any other documents that may be in conflict herewith. If any one or more provisions contained in this Agreement are held by any court or tribunal to be invalid, illegal, or otherwise unenforceable, each and every other provision shall remain in full force and effect.

my2cents.idgbooks.com

Register This Book — And Win!

Visit **http://my2cents.idgbooks.com** to register this book and we'll automatically enter you in our fantastic monthly prize giveaway. It's also your opportunity to give us feedback: let us know what you thought of this book and how you would like to see other topics covered.

Discover IDG Books Online!

The IDG Books Online Web site is your online resource for tackling technology — at home and at the office. Frequently updated, the IDG Books Online Web site features exclusive software, insider information, online books, and live events!

10 Productive & Career-Enhancing Things You Can Do at www.idgbooks.com

- Nab source code for your own programming projects.

- Download software.

- Read Web exclusives: special articles and book excerpts by IDG Books Worldwide authors.

- Take advantage of resources to help you advance your career as a Novell or Microsoft professional.

- Buy IDG Books Worldwide titles or find a convenient bookstore that carries them.

- Register your book and win a prize.

- Chat live online with authors.

- Sign up for regular e-mail updates about our latest books.

- Suggest a book you'd like to read or write.

- Give us your 2¢ about our books and about our Web site.

You say you're not on the Web yet? It's easy to get started with IDG Books' *Discover the Internet,* available at local retailers everywhere.

CD-ROM Installation Instructions

The *Windows 98 Secrets* CD-ROM presents over 250MB of software you can try. We've made it easy for you with a push-button interface that organizes and installs the *Windows 98 Secrets* CD-ROM software. The CD-ROM interface is designed to start automatically after you insert the disc into your CD-ROM drive.

The left-hand column of buttons on the interface accesses major program groups, such as Applications. Program groups offer you sets of program categories, such as "Calendars and Time Management Programs." Click the program category to see a list of program descriptions. To try a program, double-click its name.

Buttons at the top of the *Windows 98 Secrets* CD-ROM interface find product categories and print descriptions of the software on the CD-ROM.

If your system doesn't start the CD-ROM automatically, follow these steps to start the interface:

STEPS

Step 1. In Windows 98, click the Start button, then select Programs and start Windows Explorer.

Step 2. In the left-hand pane of Windows Explorer, click your CD-ROM drive to select it. Then click Setup (or Setup.exe) in the right pane. (If you have not enabled single-clicking, double-click Setup instead.)

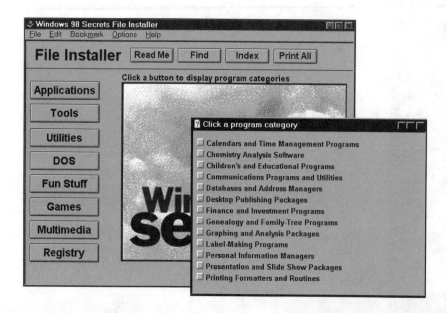